THE
WORLD BOOK
ENCYCLOPEDIA

Ci *to* Cz

Volume 4

FIELD ENTERPRISES EDUCATIONAL CORPORATION

CHICAGO LONDON ROME SYDNEY TORONTO

THE WORLD BOOK ENCYCLOPEDIA

COPYRIGHT © 1970, U.S.A.

by FIELD ENTERPRISES EDUCATIONAL CORPORATION

"WORLD BOOK" Reg. U.S. Pat. Off.   Marca Registrada

Printed in the United States of America

LIBRARY OF CONGRESS CATALOG CARD NUMBER 70-79247

CIARDI, *chee AHR dee,* **JOHN** (1916-   ), is an American poet. Unlike the work of many modern poets, Ciardi's poetry usually is not difficult or surprising. Critics have praised his verse for its musical grace and ease. According to Ciardi, style should serve the purposes of the subject rather than express the individuality of the writer. Critics sometimes accused him of sentimentality, but he achieved the highest excellence in many of his poems and in his translations of Dante's *Divine Comedy* (*Inferno,* 1954; *Purgatory,* 1961). A representative collection of Ciardi's poetry appears in *As If: Poems New and Selected* (1955).

Ciardi was born in Boston. He taught at Rutgers University from 1953 to 1961, and became poetry editor for *The Saturday Review* in 1956. Ciardi has written several children's books. He also wrote *How Does a Poem Mean?* (1959), a critical introduction to the study of poetry at the college level.   MONA VAN DUYN

CIBBER, COLLEY. See POET LAUREATE; POPE, ALEXANDER.

CIBOLA, *SEE boh lah,* **SEVEN CITIES OF.** The Spanish conquerors of Mexico came to believe in a sort of fairy tale concerning seven wonderful cities in what is now the Southwest United States. These cities were said to have great riches. One expedition set forth for the cities, guided by a black Moorish slave named Estevanico, also called Estéban. The Moor, with Cabeza de Vaca and two others, had survived a shipwreck on the Texas coast, and wandered for several years before being rescued. Estevanico led the conquerors to the seven Zuñi Indian villages in the area where Gallup, N.M., now stands. In 1540, the explorer Francisco Coronado started with his army for the fabulous cities. He, too, found only the simple Indian settlements. The only jewels the Zuñis had were turquoises, not the emeralds Coronado had hoped to find.   RICHARD A. BARTLETT

See also CORONADO, FRANCISCO VÁSQUEZ DE.

CICADA, *sih KAY dah,* or *sih KAD ah,* or HARVEST FLY, is a heavy-bodied insect with four thin wings that it folds over its body like a roof. The cicada is a darkly colored insect from 1 to 2 inches long. Its head is short and wide and its *antennae* (feelers) are short and bristle-like. Most cicadas live in tropical and subtropical countries, but many types live in North America.

Cicadas are commonly known for the buzzing song the male makes. The male makes a drum-like *membrane* (thin sheath of skin) on the abdomen vibrate rapidly to produce the sound. The sound attracts females or calls large numbers of males together. Each *species* (kind) of cicada has its own song. Many types of male cicadas often assemble in large groups and produce a loud chorus of sounds. Most cicadas produce a short "protest" sound if they are disturbed.

Types of Cicadas. Two common groups of cicadas are the *dog-day* cicadas and the *periodical* cicadas. *Dog-day cicadas* are large, very dark, and often have greenish markings. They appear each year in July and August. It takes from two to five years for a dog-day cicada to develop from an egg into an adult. But some adults are seen each year, because different *broods* (groups of young) develop at different times. *Periodical cicadas* are dark, and have red eyes and wing veins. They appear in late May and early June. Periodical cicadas take either 13 years or 17 years to develop, depending on their species. Cicadas that take 17 years to develop

Cicada Nymphs burrow into the ground after they hatch and do not emerge, *above,* until 13 or 17 years later in the spring.

Cornelia Clarke; John E. Spangler

The Insect immediately climbs a tree trunk, sheds its skin, and emerges with pale wings that quickly grow strong and colorful.

Several Hours After the Cicada Leaves Its Shell, *above,* it takes on brilliant red, white, green, or brown markings. The adult cicada, *below,* mates and then dies before winter.

Cornelia Clarke; Black Star

are also called *17-year locusts*. Adult periodical cicadas appear in a region only once every 13 or 17 years. But so many broods exist that they appear somewhere in the United States nearly every year.

Development. A female cicada lays her eggs in the twigs of trees and shrubs. She places the eggs in small holes that she makes with a saw-like organ near the tip of her abdomen. The twigs usually are so badly injured by the process that the tips of the twigs die. In a few weeks, the eggs hatch and young cicadas called *nymphs* appear. The nymphs fall to the ground, enter the soil, and feed on roots. The nymph remains in the ground until it is full-grown, which in some types takes 17 years. Then it comes out of the ground, climbs a tree or some other object, sheds its skin, and emerges as an adult. The adult cicada lives only a few weeks.

Scientific Classification. Cicadas belong to order *Homoptera*, the cicada family, *Cicadidae*. The most common dog-day cicadas belong to the genus *Tibicen*. The periodical cicadas belong to the genus *Magicicada*. DONALD J. BORROR

See also HOMOPTERA.

CICELY, *SIS uh lih*, or **CHERVIL**, is a perennial European herb of the parsley family. It is sometimes called *sweet cicely*, or *sweet chervil*, because of its fragrant leaves which smell much like anise. Cicely grows about 3 feet high and has downy gray leaves and small white flowers. The Scottish people call it *myrrh*. The roots and seeds are used for flavoring. Europeans use the leaves in soups and salads. In the United States, the name sweet cicely is given to members of a closely related group of herbs used for seasoning.

Scientific Classification. Cicely is a member of the parsley family, *Umbelliferae*. It is classified as genus *Myrrhis*, species *M. odorata*. American sweet cicely is classified as *Osmorhiza longistylis*. HAROLD NORMAN MOLDENKE

CICERO, *SIHS er oh*, Ill. (pop. 69,130; alt. 606 ft.), is a residential and industrial suburb just west of Chicago (see ILLINOIS [political map]). It has over 100 factories. Cicero attracted settlers before the Civil War, and was incorporated as a town in 1867. The city has a mayor-council form of government. PAUL M. ANGLE

CICERO, *SISS uh roh*, **MARCUS TULLIUS** (106-43 B.C.), was a distinguished Roman orator and statesman. He believed sincerely in the republican form of government, and fought hard to save the dying Roman Republic.

Cicero was born in Arpinum of a well-to-do family. He studied law, oratory, Greek literature, and philosophy in Rome and in Greece. He won his first fame and riches as a defense lawyer. His chief role as prosecutor was in representing the people of Sicily against Gaius Verres, robber-governor of the island. Cicero's attack was so effective that Verres went into exile without awaiting a verdict.

Marcus Tullius Cicero
Bettmann Archive

Political Career. Cicero gained the office of praetor in 66 B.C. and consul in 63 B.C. As consul, he crushed the conspiracy of Catiline against the republic; his greatest speech at this time was his "First Oration Against Catiline" (see CATILINE).

Cicero was not well-liked by the conservative nobles, but he refused to join Julius Caesar, Pompey, and Crassus in the First Triumvirate in 60 B.C. (see TRIUMVIRATE). As a result, he was banished from Rome during 58-57 B.C., and played only a small role in the struggle between Caesar and Pompey. He turned to writing essays on philosophy, oratory, political theory, and theology. These have had great influence on later writers. His letters, of which almost 1,000 survive, give an excellent picture of the times, and reflect his feelings and cultured outlook.

Caesar and Cicero were reconciled after Pompey's defeat at Pharsalus in 48 B.C. But Cicero approved of Caesar's murder, and for a short time in 44 B.C., he was real, though unofficial, leader of the Senate. He launched a great attack on Mark Antony in a series of 14 speeches, known as the *Philippics*, which drove Antony out of Rome. But Cicero's triumph was short-lived, and this attack caused his downfall.

In 43 B.C., Octavian (later the Emperor Augustus), Antony, and Marcus Aemilius Lepidus formed the Second Triumvirate. Cicero was one of many they condemned to death. While trying to escape from his home in Tusculum, he was slain.

His Place in Literature. Cicero ranks among the greatest of ancient writers, and his eloquent orations are unsurpassed in Roman literature. He was responsible for developing a style in Latin prose that has become the basis of literary expression in the languages of Europe. His orations have been among the most commonly studied Latin works. CHESTER G. STARR

See also CAESAR, GAIUS JULIUS; ORATORS AND ORATORY (Classical Orators); POMPEY THE GREAT; ROSCIUS, QUINTUS.

CID, *sihd*, **THE** (1040?-1099), or **EL CID**, is one of Spain's national heroes. His real name was RODRIGO DÍAZ. *The Cid* comes from the Arabic *El Sayyid*, meaning *the lord*. The Cid served in the army of Sancho II of Castile. When Sancho was murdered, his hated brother Alfonso became king and banished The Cid. The Cid then gathered a small army and fought for anyone who hired him, whether Christian or Moor. In those times, the Moors held a large part of Spain. Soon The Cid gained great power and wealth. In 1094, he conquered Valencia from the Moors.

The Cid's story became a legend in *The Poem of the Cid*, written about 1140, and in many later ballads. His story also inspired a drama by Pierre Corneille and an opera by Jules Massenet. The Cid was born near Burgos, and is buried there (see BURGOS). ARTHUR M. SELVI

See also SPANISH LITERATURE (Early Medieval Literature).

CIDER is the fermented, or partially fermented, juice of apples. Fully fermented apple juice is called *hard cider* or *extra dry cider*, and contains 2 to 7 per cent of alcohol. Late apples or winter varieties make the best cider, because they have higher fruit-sugar content and superior flavor. The apples are first crushed to a pulp, then subjected to pressure in a cider press to obtain the juice. The unfermented juice of apples is apple juice, frequently miscalled *sweet cider*. WALTER H. HILDICK

See also VINEGAR.

CIENFUEGOS, *syen FWAY gohs* (pop. 78,700), is the principal sugar-shipping port on Cuba's southern coast. It lies 230 miles southeast of Havana (see CUBA [color map]).   OTIS P. STARKEY

CIERVA, JUAN DE LA. See AUTOGIRO.

CIGAR, *sih GAHR*, is a small, tight roll of cured tobacco leaves. The word *cigar* comes from the Spanish *cigarro*. In 1492, Christopher Columbus and his men found the people of the West Indies islands smoking crude cigars. They used these early cigars in tribal ceremonies. Cigars are made by binding tobacco leaves together. The *filler* (inner leaves) is covered with the *wrapper* (outer leaf). See also TOBACCO.   ROY FLANNAGAN

CIGARETTE, *SIHG uh REHT*, is a roll of shredded tobacco wrapped in paper. Virtually all cigarettes smoked in the United States are "domestic blends." They are made of flue-cured Bright tobacco (grown in Virginia, North Carolina, South Carolina, Georgia, and Florida), and burley tobacco (grown in Kentucky and Tennessee). They also have small amounts of Maryland and Turkish leaf. The blend is usually sprayed with flavoring and a moisture-retaining agent.

Cigarette smoking became common among Europeans after French and British soldiers adopted the habit from Turkish officers during the Crimean War of 1853-1856. Hand-rolled cigarettes achieved limited popularity in the United States between 1855 and 1885. They contained either straight Turkish tobacco, straight Bright tobacco, or a blend of the two. The automatic cigarette-making machine was perfected in Durham, N.C., in 1883. Cigarette companies introduced domestic blends about 30 years later.

In the early 1960's, scientists appointed by the U.S. Public Health Service studied the effect of cigarette smoking on health. They reported that the risk of developing lung cancer is greater for smokers than for nonsmokers. They also reported that smoking contributed to other kinds of cancer, heart diseases, bronchitis, and emphysema. The major tobacco companies donated $10 million to the American Medical Association for further study on smoking and disease. They also set up a code that, in part, prohibits cigarette advertising directed toward young persons. Canadian cigarette makers adopted a similar code. In 1965, the U.S. Congress passed a law requiring manufacturers to label all cigarette packages—"Caution: cigarette smoking may be hazardous to your health."

See also CANCER (What Causes Cancer); FILTER; NICOTINE; TOBACCO.

CILIA, *SIHL ee uh*, are tiny, hairlike bits of protoplasm that project from certain kinds of cells. Cilia are slender and long, and move constantly. They can be seen only under a microscope. The motion of some cilia is wavy, much like that of a field of wheat swaying in the wind. Other cilia bend into the shape of a hook, then straighten out forcefully.

Cilia are found in cells of the membranes of the nose, ear, windpipe, and lungs. The wavy motion of the cilia in these organs pushes out dust, bacteria, and mucus, and keeps the passages clean. Cilia in the mouth cells of a clam fan currents of water and food into the animal. Almost all one-celled animals and many bacteria have cilia that serve as sense organs and provide a means of locomotion.   TERENCE A. ROGERS

See also PROTOZOAN (The Ciliates).

National Gallery of Art, Washington, D.C., Mellon Collection

A Painting of Christ by Cimabue. This is the center panel of his *Christ Between Saint Peter and Saint James.*

CILIARY MUSCLE. See EYE (The Eyeball).

CILIATE. See PROTOZOAN (The Ciliates).

CIMABUE, *CHEE mah BOO eh*, **GIOVANNI** (1240?-1302?), an Italian painter, was the first famous painter of the city of Florence. He began an era of famous Florentine painters that included Leonardo da Vinci.

Cimabue's art does not show obvious originality. He painted in a traditional style based on the medieval art of the Byzantine Empire, and used little of the realism of the later Florentine painters. His faces and figures are the formalized types of the Byzantine period. But his works have great personal force and effect, even though the forms are traditional. See PAINTING (The Renaissance in Southern Europe).

Five or six of Cimabue's works exist today. The most famous include the altarpiece of the Madonna and Child with Angels in the Uffizi Gallery in Florence, and frescoes of a similar subject and of the Crucifixion in the church of Saint Francis at Assisi. These works show great power and grandeur, and the Crucifixion combines those qualities with dramatic impact.   CREIGHTON GILBERT

CIMBRI, *SIM bry*, was a tribe that threatened Roman control of Italy in the 100's B.C. The Cimbri and the Teutones were driven from northern Germany by tidal invasions of the sea. The tribes roamed through central Germany to the Danube River. In 113 B.C., they defeated a Roman army that barred their entrance to Italy. The Cimbri then moved into Gaul (France).

The Cimbri destroyed two Roman armies at Arausio (now Orange, France) in 105 B.C. This was Rome's worst defeat in more than 100 years. The Cimbri still did not enter Italy, but went to Spain, where they were stopped by fierce Celtiberians.

The Cimbri, Teutones, and Tigurini finally invaded Italy in 102 and 101 B.C. The tribesmen were killed or enslaved by Roman forces under Marius. HENRY C. BOREN

CIMMERIAN is the name of a large group of nomads who invaded Asia Minor in the 700's B.C. The Greek historian Herodotus says they were chased from Russia across the Caucasus Mountains and into Asia Minor by other nomads, called the Scythians. The Cimmerians swept through Asia Minor, destroying the kingdom of Phrygia about 700 B.C. They raided Lydia in the mid-600's B.C., and terrorized western and southern Asia Minor for about 150 years, until the Lydians scattered them. The Cimmerians are called *Gomer* in the Bible.

Until the A.D. mid-1800's, scholars knew about the Cimmerians only through the writings of Herodotus and other ancient historians. Assyrian inscriptions discovered since then also mention the Cimmerians as invaders, but little else is known about them. LOUIS L. ORLIN

CIMON, *SY mun* (507?-449 B.C.) was a military and political leader in ancient Athens. He commanded the fleet that drove the Persians from Europe in 479 B.C., during the Persian wars. Cimon helped form the Delian league, which tried unsuccessfully to unite all Greeks. Cimon was the leader of the powerful aristocrats in Athens. The aristocrats opposed reforms that Pericles, leader of the democrats, wished to make. When the democrats came to power in 461 B.C., Pericles forced Cimon into exile. Cimon returned in 451 B.C., however, and arranged a truce in a struggle between Athens and Sparta.   RICHARD N. FRYE

CINCHONA, *sin KO nuh*, or CHINCHONA, is a group of valuable South American trees and shrubs. Cinchona bark is used to make the drugs quinine and cinchona, with which doctors treat malaria. The cinchona is an evergreen. Cinchona plants were first found in Peru and Ecuador. They are now grown in India and Ceylon, eastern Asia, tropical America, and parts of Africa. The flowers are usually fragrant. They vary from rose purple to greenish-white and look like lilac blossoms.

Scientific Classification. Cinchona belongs to the madder family, *Rubiaceae*. Cinchona makes up the genus *Cinchona*.   HAROLD NORMAN MOLDENKE

See also BITTERS; QUININE.

CINCHOPHEN. See ATOPHAN.

CINCINNATI, Ohio (pop. 502,550; met. area 1,268,-479; alt. 550 ft.), is one of the industrial and commercial centers of the Middle West. It was named for the Society of the Cincinnati, a group of officers who served in the Continental Army during the Revolutionary War. General Arthur St. Clair, a member of this organization, gave the village its name when he took command of nearby Fort Washington in 1790.

Early in its history Cincinnati became known as the *Queen City of the West*, because it was enthroned on beautiful hills and terraces which rise high above the north bank of the Ohio River. It is also sometimes called *The Gateway to the South*. Many river steamboat and railroad lines lead to southern markets.

Location, Size, and Description. Cincinnati lies midway between the source of the Ohio River at Pittsburgh and the mouth of the river at Cairo, Ill. The Big Miami and the Little Miami rivers flow into the Ohio on either side of Cincinnati. The northernmost part of Kentucky lies across the Ohio River from Cincinnati. For location, see OHIO (political map). For information about the monthly rainfall and temperature in Cincinnati, see OHIO (Climate).

Cincinnati is second only to Cleveland in population

in the state. Cincinnati covers an area of about 75 square miles.

The streets of Cincinnati rise up from the river front by way of a series of *terraces* (steps). The wholesale and manufacturing sections cover the lower terrace, which ranges from 50 to 65 feet above the low water mark of the Ohio River. The business district occupies most of the second terrace, which rises from 50 to 100 feet. The business district centers around Fountain and Government squares. The residential sections lie mainly on steep hills which rise to about 460 feet.

The Cincinnati metropolitan area includes Hamilton County in Ohio, to which Cincinnati belongs, and Campbell and Kenton counties in Kentucky, across the Ohio River. The Ohio suburbs include Norwood, Saint Bernard, College Hill, Mount Healthy, Mariemount, Reading, Lockland, Wyoming, Glendale, and Cheviot. Kentucky cities, connected to Cincinnati by bridges across the Ohio, include Dayton, Bellevue, Ludlow, Covington, Newport, and Fort Thomas.

The People. The first settlers on the site of Cincinnati were persons from New Jersey and other eastern states who joined the westward movement of settlement in 1788. Some also came from Kentucky. In the 1830's, Cincinnati acquired its reputation as a German city. Thousands of Germans fled political persecution in Europe and settled in the city. In the 1840's, many Irish immigrants, forced to leave their homeland because of the potato famine, came to Cincinnati. More than 95 per cent of the present population is made up of native-born Americans. Negroes represent slightly more than 15 per cent of the population.

Education and Cultural Life. The Cincinnati-Hamilton County school system includes over 150 public schools, several colleges and technical schools, and two universities. The University of Cincinnati was the first city-owned and operated university in the U.S. Other institutions of higher learning include Edgecliff College and Xavier University.

The Cincinnati Public Library with its 37 branches circulates about 4 million volumes every year. The Taft Museum, formerly the home of Charles Phelps Taft, houses displays of paintings and art objects. The Cincinnati Art Museum, in Eden Park, has more than 50 rooms of famous works of art, ranging from ancient Egyptian sculptures to American Indian pottery. The

Fairchild Aerial Surveys

Cincinnati's Business District is built on a plateau that rises above the city's wholesale and manufacturing sections.

museum's academy offers classes in the arts. Cincinnati also has a Museum of Natural History.

The Cincinnati Symphony Orchestra is famous throughout the world of music. It performs at Music Hall. Cincinnati offers summer opera at the Zoological Garden. The city also has a conservatory of music.

Recreation. Many excursion boats operate on the Ohio River during the summer. The Zoological Garden has one of the largest collections of wild-animal life in the United States. The Cincinnati Reds, the nation's first professional baseball team, play in the National League. The Cincinnati Royals play in the National Basketball Association. The Cincinnati Bengals play in the National Football League.

Parks and playgrounds cover about 4,000 acres. Eden Park has 185 acres of rolling hills, a small lake, and a large conservatory with unusual displays of flowers and plants. Ault Park features open-air dancing. The city also maintains about 70 neighborhood playfields.

Interesting Places to Visit in the city include: *Carew Tower*, at Vine and Fifth streets. It is one of the three tallest buildings in Ohio, with 48 stories. It also ranks as the tallest building in the city.

Coney Island, a 148-acre park on the Ohio River and Lake Como. The park has an amusement park for children and adults, one of the world's largest swimming pools, restaurants, sports fields, and a ballroom.

Industry and Commerce. Cincinnati is one of the world's leading producers of machine tools, playing cards, and soap. In addition, Cincinnati makes aircraft engines and parts; athletic goods; automobiles; automobile, bus and truck bodies; automatic transmissions for automobiles; chemicals and chemical products; fans; and generators. Cincinnati factories make industrial machinery, leather goods, metal cans, metal office furniture, pianos, plastic products, radios, television sets, textiles and clothing, valves and pipe fittings, electrotypes, and watches. The meat-packing industry and printing and publishing are also important.

Cincinnati is one of the world's largest inland coal ports. It handles about $2\frac{1}{2}$ million tons of bituminous coal each year. The coal is shipped by railroad and also by barge on the Ohio River.

Transportation. Most heavy traffic between the north-central states and the South passes through Cincinnati. Cincinnati Union Terminal serves eight major railroad lines. The city owns the Cincinnati Southern Railway, which runs from Cincinnati to Chattanooga, Tenn. Six scheduled airlines serve the Greater Cincinnati Airport which lies in Boone County, Kentucky, 10 miles away.

In early days, Cincinnati was a busy river port, with many huge side-wheel and stern-wheel steamers bringing cargoes from the South. The Ohio River is still used for heavy freight such as coal, lumber, and iron. The *Delta Queen* steamer provides excursion service between Cincinnati and Louisville and other river ports.

Communication. Cincinnati has two daily newspapers, the *Enquirer* and the *Post and Times-Star*. Over 30 suburban papers are published. The city has eight radio stations and four television stations. In 1955, it became the first city in the United States to have a licensed educational television station (WCET).

Government. Cincinnati adopted the city-manager form of government in 1926. The city manager is selected by the nine members of the city council, which also elects one councilman as mayor. Cincinnati is the seat of Hamilton County.

History. A party of pioneers who came down the Ohio River in 1788 established the first permanent settlement on the site of Cincinnati. The settlement grew rapidly after Fort Washington was built nearby. In 1802, Cincinnati was chartered as a town. It received its city charter in 1819. By 1850, Cincinnati was the greatest pork-packing center in the country. Hogs were herded from Ohio and Indiana to the Cincinnati slaughterhouses. The meat was shipped on the Ohio River.

During the Civil War, Cincinnati became a refuge for runaway slaves. Harriet Beecher Stowe gathered much material for her famous story *Uncle Tom's Cabin* in Cincinnati. The completion of the first part of the Miami and Erie Canal in 1827 had much to do with the city's growth. It helped local commerce and provided power for industry.   JAMES H. RODABAUGH

See also FIRE FIGHTING (History of Fire Fighting).

CINCINNATI, SOCIETY OF THE, is the oldest military organization in the United States. Officers of the Continental Army founded it in 1783. George Washington was its first president. The name *Cincinnati* comes from the Roman hero Lucius Quinctius Cincinnatus. The city of Cincinnati, Ohio, was named for the society. The organization restricts membership to the oldest male descendants of commissioned officers in the regular forces of the Continental Army or Navy. It has about 2,400 members. Headquarters are at 2218 Massachusetts Avenue NW, Washington, D.C. 20008.

Critically reviewed by the SOCIETY OF THE CINCINNATI

CINCINNATI, UNIVERSITY OF, is a coeducational university in Cincinnati, Ohio. In 1870, it became the first municipal university in the United States. But some of its older units, such as the liberal arts college and the college of medicine, were founded in 1819. The cooperative plan of education, which combines periods of study with on-the-job experience, was introduced there in 1906. For enrollment, see UNIVERSITIES AND COLLEGES (table).   WALTER C. LANGSAM

431

CINCINNATUS, *SIN sih NAY tus,* **LUCIUS QUINCTIUS** (519?-439? B.C.), a Roman statesman and general, was a legendary model of patriotism. In 458 B.C., Rome was threatened by the Aequi, a tribe of central Italy. The Senate sent messengers to tell Cincinnatus that he had been named commander in chief. The messengers found him plowing his fields. He joined the army at once, and marched to rescue a *consul* (chief government official) who was in great danger. Cincinnatus surrounded and defeated the enemy, marched his army back to Rome, and resigned. He returned to his farm 16 days after he took office.

George Washington was sometimes called the "American Cincinnatus" because he also held his office only as long as necessary. After the American Revolution, a group of former officers formed the patriotic Society of the Cincinnati. The city of Cincinnati, Ohio, is named after this organization. HERBERT M. HOWE

CINDERELLA is the beautiful but mistreated heroine of a fairy tale. Her stepmother and jealous stepsisters leave Cinderella at home when they go to the prince's ball. But Cinderella's fairy godmother turns a pumpkin into a coach and mice into horses, and dresses Cinderella in a beautiful gown and dainty glass slippers. She warns Cinderella to leave the ball by midnight.

The prince falls in love with Cinderella, and she forgets the time. Fleeing from the ball as the clock is striking 12, she loses one slipper. The prince finds her by trying the tiny slipper on every girl in the kingdom.

A similar story is told from China to Peru. Our version is adapted from Perrault's *Cendrillon* (see PERRAULT, CHARLES). GEORGE ROBERT CARLSEN

CINEMA. See MOTION PICTURE.

CINEMASCOPE. See MOTION PICTURE (Wide-Screen Processes; Competition with Television).

CINERAMA. See MOTION PICTURE (Wide-Screen Processes).

CINERARIA, *SIN uh RAY ree uh,* is a group of small herbs that belong to the composite family. They grow wild in the Canary Islands, but are cultivated in gardens throughout the world. The flowers are usually purple, red, or purple and white, with dark centers.

Cineraria Blossoms. The name, from the Latin word for *ashes,* was given because the lower leaves have the color of ashes. W. Atlee Burpee

Cinerarias are easily grown from seed. They make fine window plants, but must be grown at a temperature of less than 65° F.

Scientific Classification. Cinerarias belong to the composite family, *Compositae.* The florist's cineraria is genus *Senecio,* species *S. cruentus.* DONALD WYMAN

See also COMPOSITE FAMILY.

CINNABAR, *SIN uh bahr* (chemical formula, HgS), is the most important ore of mercury. It is a heavy compound of mercury and sulfur. Cinnabar is usually found in bright-red earthy masses, and sometimes in crystals. It is abundant in Spain, California, and China. Artificial cinnabar may be formed by purifying a mixture of sulfur and mercury. It is brighter red than the native cinnabar, and when used in paint is called *vermilion.* See also MERCURY (element); MINERAL (color picture); VERMILION. A. PABST

American Spice Trade Assoc.

Bark of the Cinnamon Tree must be carefully peeled off in long strips, *left.* It curls into rolls when it dries, *right.*

CINNAMON is a spice used in cooking and in flavoring candies. It has a pleasant taste and odor. Cinnamon is made from the inner bark of branches of the cinnamon laurel tree, which grows in Ceylon, Malabar, and other tropical regions. It grows as high as 20 to 30 feet, and has oval leaves and tiny pale-yellow flowers. The fruit of the cinnamon laurel is shaped like an acorn.

Cinnamon trees grown for their bark are usually kept small, or dwarfed. This is done by cutting the tree close to the lower buds. The bark of the lower branches is peeled for use as cinnamon. In Ceylon, the bark is usually peeled in April and November. As the bark dries, it curls up and turns light brown. The bark is divided according to quality by people who taste samples. Then it is packed into 90-pound bundles for sale.

An oil is also prepared from the leaves, fruit, and the root of the cinnamon plant. The thick, fragrant oil from the fruit was once used to make candles for the king of Ceylon. The oil of the cassia plant is often used in place of cinnamon oil. Cassia bark sometimes replaces cinnamon bark.

Scientific Classification. The cinnamon tree belongs to the laurel family, *Lauraceae.* It is genus *Cinnamomum,* species *C. zeylanicum.* HAROLD NORMAN MOLDENKE

See also CASSIA; LAUREL.

CINQUEFOIL, *SINK foil,* is any one of a group of plants that belong to the rose family. About 250 kinds of cinquefoils grow in most cool and cold regions throughout the world. These herblike plants may grow erect, or close to the ground in creeping fashion. The leaves have three, five, or more leaflets. Because of the shape of their leaves, the plants are sometimes called *five-finger* or *false strawberry*. The bright yellow or white blossoms of the cinquefoil grow in loose clusters. Some of the American kinds of cinquefoil are troublesome weeds to gardeners and farmers.

Scientific Classification. The cinquefoils are members of the rose family, *Rosaceae*. They make up the genus *Potentilla*.　　　　　　　　　　　　　　EARL L. CORE

CIO. See CONGRESS OF INDUSTRIAL ORGANIZATIONS.

CION. See GRAFTING.

CIPANGO. See JAPAN (Foreign Relations).

CIPHER. See CODES AND CIPHERS.

CIRCADIAN RHYTHM. See BIOLOGICAL CLOCK.

CIRCASSIAN, *sir KASH un*, is the name of a people living on the northeast shores of the Black Sea. They are called *Cherkesses* by the Russians and Turks, but their word for themselves is *Adighe*. The Circassians are less round-headed than other Caucasians, and are the tallest and darkest of the peoples of Caucasia. They are related to the Bulgarians, Romanians, and Ukrainians. The Circassians have always been noted for the fierceness of their warriors and the beauty of their women, who are often called "Circassian belles." Circassian women were once sold into Turkish and Persian harems by their fathers. Upper-class Circassians are Moslems. The lower classes practice a mixture of paganism and Christianity.　　　　　WILTON MARION KROGMAN

See also CAUCASIA.

CIRCE, *SIR see*, a beautiful enchantress in Greek mythology, had the power to turn men into beasts. She lived on an island in the Mediterranean Sea. When Ulysses landed on her island, Circe turned most of his men into pigs and drove them into a pigsty. But the god Mercury had given Ulysses a magic herb which protected him from Circe's power (see MERCURY; ULYSSES). Ulysses forced Circe to give his men their human form again.

After that, Circe became friendly. She loved Ulysses, and persuaded him to stay with her on the island for a year. When he prepared to leave, she warned him about the dangers that awaited him, and told him how to overcome them. For example, Circe told Ulysses how to pass the island where the Sirens lived by stopping his sailors' ears with wax.　　　　JOSEPH FONTENROSE

See also ODYSSEY; SCYLLA.

Circe, a Character in Greek Mythology, is said to have had magic powers which enabled her to change men into animals.
Painting by Burne-Jones, Art Institute of Chicago

CIRCLE is a closed curve on a plane. All points of the curve are the same distance from a point within called the *center*. There are 360 degrees in a circle.

Many common objects have a circular shape, including rings, hoops, and wheels. You can easily draw a circle with an instrument called a *compass*. A compass looks like a pair of scissors with a pencil where one point should be. To draw a circle, place one point of the compass at the point chosen as the center, and rotate the pencil around it.

Parts of a Circle. Sometimes people use the word *circle* to mean the area inside the curve. They call the

PARTS OF A CIRCLE

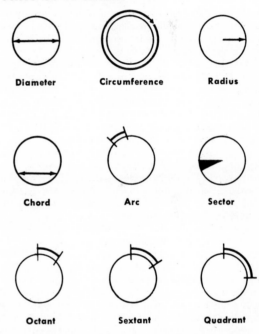

Diameter	Circumference	Radius
Chord	Arc	Sector
Octant	Sextant	Quadrant

curve itself the *circumference*. The length of the curve is also called the circumference. An *arc* forms part of the circumference. It may be of any size.

A *chord* is a straight line between two points on the circumference of a circle. If a chord goes through the center, it forms a *diameter*. A diameter is the longest chord of a circle, and divides the circle into two equal parts called *semicircles*.

The *radius* is the distance from the center to the circumference. It equals half the length of a diameter. The word *radius* is also used to mean any line that joins the center to the circumference.

A *secant* is a straight line that intersects a circle at two points. A line that just touches the circle, or meets the circle at just one point, is called a *tangent*. If you move a secant away from the center of the circle so that it always lies parallel to its previous position, the two points at which it touches the circle will get closer to each other. When the points come together, the secant has reached the position of a tangent. The point where the tangent touches the circle is the *point of tangency*. The radius at the point of tangency makes a right angle with the tangent.

The Use of Pi. The Greek letter *pi* (written π) stands for the number by which the diameter of a circle (*d*) must be multiplied to obtain the circumference (*c*). That is, $c = \pi d$ or $2\pi r$, where *r* is the radius. The area of a circle (*A*) is given by the formula $A = \pi r^2$.

You cannot write π exactly as a decimal. But by increasing the number of digits, you can get a number as near to it as you want. Common values used for π include $\frac{22}{7}$, 3.14, 3.1416, and 3.14159.

History. The ancient Chinese used 3 as the value of π. About 1650 B.C., the Egyptians improved on the approximation. The Greek mathematician Ptolemy calculated a value for π that was the equivalent of 3.1416. After decimals came into use in the 1600's, men labored to find an exact value in decimals for π. Mathematicians now know that this is impossible.   ROTHWELL STEPHENS

See also DEGREE.

CIRCUIT, ELECTRIC. See ELECTRIC CURRENT.

CIRCUIT BREAKER is an automatic switch. It protects electric motors, household wiring, long-distance power lines, and other electric circuits against damage caused by too much electric current. Too much current may flow in a circuit as a result either of a fault in the circuit or of an outside event, such as lightning.

Every circuit breaker is designed to allow a specific maximum amount of electric current to pass. If the current exceeds this limit, an automatic mechanism inside the circuit breaker throws open a *set of contacts* (switch) and stops the current. Mechanisms used to open the switch include electromagnets and temperature-sensitive devices similar to a thermostat.

As the switch opens, an electric arc leaps across the open contacts. Electricity continues to flow through this arc until it is extinguished. In an *oil circuit breaker*, the switch is immersed in an oil that extinguishes the arc. In an *air-blast circuit breaker*, a blast of compressed air blows out the arc. In a *magnetic arc-suppression circuit breaker*, a magnetic field deflects and breaks the arc.

Some circuit breakers are only a few inches on a side. But some are as large as a small two-story house. A large circuit breaker can interrupt currents up to 40,000 amperes at 345,000 volts. It can open a circuit in less than $\frac{1}{30}$ of a second, and reclose it in less than $\frac{1}{3}$ of a second.   WILLIAM W. SEIFERT

See also SAINT LAWRENCE SEAWAY (picture).

CIRCUIT COURT OF APPEALS. See COURT OF APPEALS.

CIRCUIT RIDER was an important figure in pioneer times in America. There were two kinds of circuit riders. One was a religious man who rode a *circuit* (regular route) conducting services. The other was a judge who rode a circuit hearing cases. Either kind of circuit might cover several hundred miles.

Preachers, often called *backwoods preachers*, began riding circuits in what is now the United States during the 1760's. John Wesley, founder of the Methodist movement in Great Britain, sent several *lay preachers* (persons not ordained as ministers) to preach the gospel in America. Famous early circuit riders included Francis Asbury, the first Methodist bishop in the United States, and Peter Cartwright, a pioneer preacher in Kentucky and Illinois.

Judges began riding circuits in 1790. Congress divided the 13 states into three circuits, with two Supreme Court justices appointed to hear cases in each circuit. This system was changed when more states joined the Union and the Supreme Court had more work to do. Many state judges also rode circuits. Lawyers usually traveled with the judges and would argue cases brought to the court. Abraham Lincoln spent several years riding circuits as a lawyer in Illinois.   CHARLTON G. LAIRD

Related Articles in WORLD BOOK include:

Asbury, Francis	Pioneer Life in America
Cartwright, Peter	(Religion)
Lincoln, Abraham	Wesley (John)
(Riding the Circuit)	Western Frontier Life
	(Religion)

CIRCULAR MEASURE. See WEIGHTS AND MEASURES (Circular and Angular Measure).

CIRCULATION is the means by which food is carried to the tissues of animals, and wastes are carried away. Even the simplest animals have some sort of a circulatory system.

In man, the circulatory system consists of the heart, which pumps the blood through the body, and the arteries, veins, and tinier blood vessels called *capillaries*, through which the blood travels. The human circulatory system has two main parts. One part, called *pulmonary circulation*, carries the blood from the heart to the lungs and back again. When the blood passes to the lungs, it gives off the waste gas, carbon dioxide, and takes in oxygen which it carries to the other parts of the body. The system that carries the blood from the heart to the other parts of the body is called *systemic circulation*.

The *portal circulation* is a part of the systemic circulation. It carries blood from the stomach, pancreas, small intestine, and spleen to the liver. The blood obtains the food it carries from the digestive system. Many wastes obtained from the body tissues are carried to the kidneys or to the lungs to be given off as wastes.

The human body also has another system called the *lymph system*. The fluid called *lymph* circulates between the tissues and cells that make up the body. It carries food to the cells, and carries wastes away from them. The lymph receives its food from the blood, and carries the body wastes into the blood. It also picks up fats from the small intestine.

The human heart has four chambers, two on each side. The blood enters the heart at the upper right-hand chamber, called the *right atrium* (auricle), and flows into the lower right-hand chamber, called the *right ventricle*. From here it flows to the lungs, and returns to the left atrium. It then passes into the left ventricle and out into the rest of the body through a large artery called the *aorta*.   JOHN B. MIALE

Related Articles in WORLD BOOK include:

Artery	Human Body	Lung
Blood (color picture)	(Trans-Vision	Lymph
Capillary	three-dimensional	Respiration
Harvey, William	color picture)	Vein
Heart		

CIRCUMFERENCE. See CIRCLE.

CIRCUMNAVIGATION. See EXPLORATION AND DISCOVERY (Ferdinand Magellan); DRAKE, SIR FRANCIS.

CIRCUMSTANTIAL EVIDENCE. See EVIDENCE.

Circus Posters from the Circus World Museum,
Baraboo, Wis.—William R. Wilson

CIRCUS

CIRCUS is a huge show where people see mischief-making clowns, daring trapeze artists, fearless lion tamers, and many other thrilling acts. Children in the audience nibble fluffy cotton candy and munch popcorn and peanuts. The circus band and circus stars in bright costumes add color and excitement to the show.

The circus goes back thousands of years. The ancient Romans held circuses that featured chariot races and battles between warriors. Roman circuses were held outdoors in large arenas. The largest Roman arena, the Circus Maximus, seated more than 180,000 persons.

The modern circus developed in England during the 1700's, and soon spread to America. The early circuses were small shows with riding acts, jugglers, and clowns. Rickett's circus, established in Philadelphia in 1792, may have been the first real American circus.

The golden age of the American circus began in the late 1800's. About 10 large circuses toured the country. Each circus boasted that it was the biggest or the best. And each tried to outdo the others with new acts and new kinds of animals. One of these circuses, established in 1871, belonged to Phineas T. Barnum. Barnum

called it the "Greatest Show on Earth." In 1881, Barnum combined his show with James A. Bailey's circus. The combined show was called the Barnum, Bailey, and Hutchinson Circus. After 1886, this circus operated under the name of Barnum and Bailey's Greatest Show on Earth. In 1884, the five Ringling brothers started a rival show in Baraboo, Wis. The Ringlings bought the Barnum and Bailey show in 1907. They joined the two circuses in 1919 to form the Ringling Brothers and Barnum & Bailey Circus. This circus became the largest and most famous in history. The Ringling family sold it in 1967, but the name of the circus did not change.

Circuses used to travel from town to town in colorful wagons pulled by horses. In each town, many young boys earned tickets to the circus by watering the elephants or doing other chores. The shows were held in large canvas tents called *tops*. The main circus acts appeared in the *big top*, the largest tent. The Ringling circus had a big top that measured 500 feet long and 200 feet wide, and seated more than 12,000 persons.

Today, circuses travel by train or truck. They often perform in stadiums and auditoriums to avoid the high cost of transporting the heavy tents and setting them up. In 1956, the Ringling circus gave up its tent entirely and began to hold all its performances indoors. But circus fans still refer to the main showroom as the big top. And the show is as exciting as ever.

Henry Ringling North, the contributor of this article, is vice-president of the Ringling Brothers and Barnum & Bailey Circus. Mel Miller, the critical reviewer, is curator of the Ringling Museum of the Circus in Sarasota, Fla. The WORLD BOOK *illustrations are by Fred Steffen.*

435

Fierce Lions in the Wild Animal Act Snarl at Their Trainer But Obey Him.

THE GREATEST SHOW ON EARTH

The Parade. Circuses used to parade through the streets before a performance. The red and gold wagons, saddle horses, and elephants made a colorful sight. The circus band played spirited music. But the parades had to be discontinued in most places because city streets became crowded with traffic.

Today, the circus performance itself may begin with a parade called a *spectacle*. As the band plays a lively tune, circus performers and animals march around the arena. The elephants wear bright velvet or satin ornaments. Each elephant may have a pretty girl perched on its head, or riding in a large saddle called a *howdah*.

Beautiful horses with shiny coats prance by proudly. Sometimes dozens of dancers in colorful costumes take part in the spectacle.

As the circus performers pass in review, the clowns make the audience laugh with their funny tricks. A dozen of them may pile out of a tiny car. Others may set a toy house on fire, then put out the flames with water from a miniature fire truck.

Under the Big Top. Most circus acts take place in round areas called *rings*. A small circus may have only one or two rings. Large circuses have three rings where three acts go on at the same time. There is so much to

Bareback Riders form a pyramid while their horses gallop around the circus ring.

Robert Bradley

Ike Vern, Photo Researchers

Clowns such as Lou Jacobs amuse the audience with funny tricks.

Sue McCarntney, Photo Researchers

Performing Elephants put on an exciting act under the big top. The elephants do tricks in all three circus rings. A group of dancers carrying feathery fans adds color to the act.

Henry Genn, Pictorial Parade

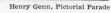

Trapeze Artists Perform Leaps and Somersaults in the Air.

see that no one can follow everything that happens in all the rings.

In one ring, elephants stand on their hind legs and dance. In another ring, trained seals balance big rubber balls on their noses. Trained horses gallop in a circle while riders jump from horse to horse. A family of riders stand on each other's shoulders on the backs of horses trotting side by side around the ring. A lion tamer enters a cage and cracks his whip. The big cats leap onto platforms at his command.

Performers called *aerialists* climb high overhead on ropes or rope ladders. Some aerialists hang by their teeth from a rope and twirl around and around. Others, called *flyers*, leap through the air from one trapeze to another. They perform daring somersaults in the air before being caught by other members of the act. Other acts feature performers on the high wire, riding bicycles or doing acrobatics.

The circus band plays throughout the show. The band helps keep the different acts running on time. By playing faster or slower, or by changing songs, it signals the performers when to finish the various parts of their acts. The music keeps up the feeling of excitement and pride in showmanship that is as old as the circus itself.

437

The Daring Wallendas walk slowly along a cable during practice. The family became famous for a dangerous high wire act that included a seven-man pyramid.

Beauty and Beast balance on balls. Circus bears do many tricks.

Tightrope Walker perches on a slanting cable.

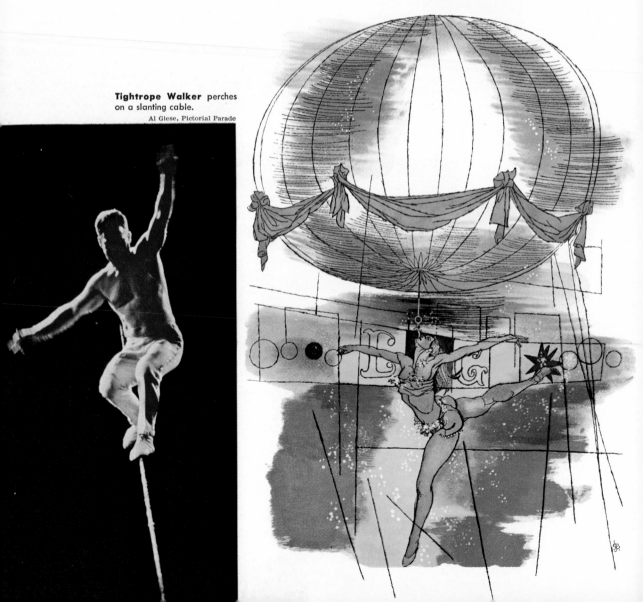

Unus, a Famous Acrobat, balances on top of a hoop. He became the first circus star to do a handstand on only one finger.
Grunzweig, Photo Researchers

Many circus stars have become world famous. Poodles Hanneford and his family combined clowning with skillful bareback riding. Arthur Concello and his wife Antoinette won fame on the flying trapeze. Antoinette Concello became the first woman to perform a triple somersault, the most difficult trapeze stunt. Clyde Beatty and Mabel Stark became known for their acts with wild jungle animals. Famous circus clowns include Felix Adler, Otto Griebling, Lou Jacobs, and Emmett Kelly.

Franz Furstner, known as "Unus," stands on top of a pole on one finger. His daughter, Vicki, does one-armed swings while hanging from a rope high in the air. Chrys Holt performs a juggling act while hanging by her hair at the top of the tent.

Some circus acts are dangerous, and the performers risk their lives at each show. Lillian Leitzel became world famous for her breathtaking aerial act. She hung by one wrist from a rope and swung her body around and around. She fell to her death during a performance in 1931. The Wallendas, a famous circus family, developed the most spectacular high wire act in circus history. Seven of them stand on each other's shoulders, then walk along the wire. Three members of the Wallenda act were killed and one was paralyzed in two accidents during the early 1960's.

The Side Shows are smaller, separate shows near the main entrance to the big top. The side shows offer such exhibits as a snake charmer, a sword swallower, a fire eater, and a tattooed man. Also on display are human and animal freaks, including midgets, giants, a bearded lady, a fat lady, and a five-legged calf. Men called *talkers* tell the crowd about the wonders to be seen in the side shows.

Many persons visit the *menagerie* to see the circus animals up close. Fierce lions and tigers pace back and forth in cages. Elephants stick out their trunks for peanuts. Monkeys jump and climb around their cages, chattering at the crowds.

Joseph Janney Steinmetz
Between Acts, Circus Performers Rest and Talk Together.

Monkmeyer
At Winter Quarters, Riders Rehearse.

Black Star
After the Show, Roustabouts Take Down the Circus Tents.

BEHIND THE SCENES

On Tour. A circus travels most of the year, giving performances in many cities and towns. A circus that travels by train usually owns its own railroad cars. The locomotive belongs to the railroad company. The circus performers and workers ride in sleeping cars, and the animals ride in boxcars. A circus may take along its own blacksmith shop, barbershop, post office, and doctor and first-aid unit. Every day, circus cooks prepare meals for hundreds of circus people.

Before the circus comes to town, publicity men put up gaily colored posters advertising the show. As soon as the circus arrives, workmen called *roustabouts* begin to unload the equipment and set it up. If the circus uses tents, machines help unload great sections of canvas and drive the tent stakes into the ground. The roustabouts have plenty of work even if the show is given in a building, rather than "under canvas." After the last performance on the final day, the roustabouts quickly take everything down so it can be moved on to the next city.

Circus people work together like members of a huge family. Sometimes even the stars of the show perform in acts besides their own, or help with the everyday circus chores. For example, a trapeze artist may ride an elephant in the elephant act. A clown may spend some time every day brushing the circus horses.

Circus stars often teach their acts to their children. When the children grow up, they carry on the traditional family acts, such as the Wallendas' high wire act. Sometimes aunts, uncles, cousins, and other relatives become members of a family act.

Winter Quarters. Late in the fall, the circus gives its last performance of the season and heads for its winter quarters. But the busy life of the circus people does not slow down for long. Soon they are hard at work preparing for the next season. Wild animal trainers begin to train new jungle beasts. The flyers, acrobats, and other circus stars practice for several hours every day. The clowns plan new stunts. Hundreds of other circus workers design and sew costumes, buy and mend equipment, and care for the circus animals.

The circus winter quarters look like a small city. They have streets and shops, large storehouses, barns for the animals, and a ring where the circus stars practice their acts. Many circus people live nearby in houses and trailers. The Ringling Brothers and Barnum & Bailey Circus has winter quarters at Venice, Fla. Thousands of tourists go there each year to watch the circus rehearse and to see how circus people live.

Many tourists also visit the Circus Hall of Fame and the Ringling Museum of the Circus in Sarasota, Fla. This museum has displays of historic circus posters, documents, wagons, and equipment.

In spring, the circus goes on tour again. A crowd gathers at the railroad station to watch it leave. People and animals board the circus train, and a priest blesses the entire show. Then the circus starts on its yearly tour that brings delight to millions of circus fans of all ages. HENRY RINGLING NORTH

Critically reviewed by MEL MILLER

Related Articles in WORLD BOOK include:

Barnum, Phineas Taylor
Buffalo Bill
Clown
Elephant (picture: Circus Elephants)
Florida (Places to Visit)
Giant (picture: The Long and Short of It)
Hagenbeck, Karl

Painting (color picture: *In the Circus Fernando*)
Ringling Brothers
Roman Empire (Recreation)
Stratton, Charles S.
Wisconsin (Places to Visit)

Outline

I. **The Greatest Show on Earth**
    A. The Parade
    B. Under the Big Top
    C. The Side Shows
II. **Behind the Scenes**
    A. On Tour
    B. Winter Quarters

Questions

Where were the first circuses held?
What does a *roustabout* do?
How many rings does a large circus have?
What is a *top* in a circus?
What act made Antoinette Concello famous?
How does the band keep the circus running on time?
What animals perform in circuses?
Why is Phineas T. Barnum famous in circus history?
What do circus people do in winter?
What exhibits appear in side shows?

CIRCUS MAXIMUS. See ROMAN EMPIRE (Family Life).
CIRE-PERDUE. See SCULPTURE (Greek Sculptors).
CIRQUE. See GLACIER (Erosion).
CIRRHOSIS, *sih RO sis,* is a disorder and inflammation of the liver, kidney, or other organ. It causes the organ cells to shrink and the organ itself to become smaller.

A hard, fibrous tissue grows over the affected organ.

In cirrhosis of the liver, the organ becomes small and hard. Fluid collects in the abdomen. Cirrhosis of the liver is aggravated by the use of liquor, but doctors are not sure that alcohol causes it. Cirrhosis of the kidney is chronic Bright's Disease. HYMAN S. RUBINSTEIN

CIRRUS. See CLOUD.
CISLUNAR SPACE. See SPACE TRAVEL (What is Space?).
CISTERCIAN, *sis TUR shun,* is a monk of the Order of Cîteaux (Cistertium). The brotherhood was founded at Cîteaux, France, in 1098 by Saint Robert of Molesme, and later developed by Saint Alberic and Saint Stephen Harding. The Cistercian monks observe the Rule of Saint Benedict, which emphasizes moderation. They maintain silence except in cases of absolute necessity. They do not eat flesh, fish, or eggs, and they participate in much outdoor work, especially farming. There are about a hundred Cistercian monasteries. The Cistercian nuns observe the same regulations as the monks, and live contemplative lives. The Trappists, who have monasteries in the United States, are a branch of the Cistercian order (see TRAPPIST). FULTON J. SHEEN
CISTERN. See RESERVOIR.
CITADEL, *SIT uh dell,* is a high, walled fortress built to defend a city. A citadel usually stands on a high hill overlooking a city. In early days, its walls surrounded and protected the palace of the ruler. The citadels of Mycenae and Tiryns in Greece were important ancient fortresses. The citadel known as Acrocorinth, on a hill more than 1,800 feet high, guarded the Greek city of Corinth. The French citadel of Carcassonne was an important stronghold in the Middle Ages.

The best known citadel in North America stands atop Cape Diamond in Quebec, Canada. The French built it about 1665, and the British rebuilt it from 1823 to 1832. La Citadelle in Haiti is another famous citadel of the Western Hemisphere. CARL K. HERSEY

See also ACROPOLIS; CARCASSONNE; HAITI (picture); QUEBEC (The Citadel; picture).
CITADEL, THE, is the Military College of South Carolina in Charleston. It was established in 1842 and is controlled and supported by the state. It offers courses in the arts, sciences, engineering, and business administration. The Citadel has army and air force ROTC units. General Mark W. Clark became president of The Citadel in 1954. For enrollment, see UNIVERSITIES AND COLLEGES (table). MARK W. CLARK
CITIES. See CITY.
CITIES OF REFUGE were six cities of ancient Palestine. They were set apart as places of refuge for people who had killed other persons either accidentally or in self-defense. They included Bezer, Ramoth-Gilead, and Golan, on the east side of the Jordan (Deut. 4:41-43), and Kedesh, Shechem, and Hebron (now Al Khalîl), on the west side (Josh. 20). A person who fled to one of these cities received a fair trial. If found not guilty of willful murder, he might continue living in the city. If declared guilty, he was returned for punishment to the place from which he had fled. LOUIS L. MANN
CITIZEN KING. See LOUIS PHILIPPE.
CITIZENS RADIO SERVICE. See RADIO (In Business and Industry).

WORLD BOOK photo by Henry Gill

Training for Citizenship is a basic goal of the educational systems of democratic countries. In this mock legislative session, students learn about the art of government. Student councils and other school organizations also provide opportunities to practice good citizenship.

CITIZENSHIP

CITIZENSHIP means full membership in a country. The word *citizenship* comes from the Latin word *civitas*, meaning *citizens united in a community*. Citizenship is still sometimes used to mean membership in some smaller unit of government, such as a state, province, or city. A person who holds the legal position of citizenship is called a *citizen*. A country grants certain rights to its citizens, and demands certain duties from them.

A country offers its citizens protection when they are away from it and privileges when they are at home. A country and its citizens are not really separate. A country exists only when the people of a certain area are organized politically.

Not all persons living under the same flag are citizens. Persons who are not citizens may be either aliens or noncitizen nationals. *Aliens* are persons from other countries who have not become citizens of their new country. *Noncitizen nationals* are persons who are not citizens of a country, but owe allegiance to it. The government protects them, but they do not have the full privileges of citizens. For example, the people of American Samoa are noncitizen nationals.

What Is Good Citizenship?

The citizens of a country guide the destiny of the nation. The freedoms that persons in the United States receive from the Bill of Rights belong to all, citizens and aliens alike. But it is the faith and the beliefs of the citizens that keep the spirit of this liberty alive and let aliens and themselves benefit from it.

Rights and Duties. Citizenship involves both civic and political rights, as well as civic and political duties. Bills of rights in the United States Constitution and in state constitutions guarantee *civic rights* to all Americans. These bills of rights offer protection and give privileges (see BILL OF RIGHTS). A child possesses civic rights, such as the right to worship as he pleases, from the day he is born. In turn, each citizen owes allegiance to his country. It is his *civic duty* to support his government, obey its laws, and defend his country.

Only citizens have full *political rights* (the rights to take part in the government). These rights have some limitations. In the United States, for example, all the states require a citizen to reach a certain age before he can vote. The age is 21 in most states. He must be even older before he can seek election to certain public offices. Every state requires its citizens to establish a permanent residence in order to vote. These restrictions in no way lessen the citizen's civic and political duty to help elect officers of his government when he becomes eligible to vote.

A citizen can do much to improve his community,

In the Community, all citizens have civic duties. Adult citizens may be called to serve as members of juries in trials.

In the Classroom, students practice good citizenship when they give the pledge of allegiance to the flag. They also learn how citizens can take an active part in their government.

In Everyday Life, good citizens obey laws. One way boys learn responsibility is by acting as junior safety patrolmen.

even if he cannot vote. He can help shape public opinion by using his freedom of speech. He can contribute to the general welfare by sacrificing personal advantages to the common good. For example, he may be called on to serve in the armed forces even before he is old enough to vote.

Later, he may serve on juries, give his time to the state militia or reserve forces, become a school-board member, work on a community drive, appear at hearings of his state legislature, or help a political party. By such acts, a good citizen carries out his civic responsibilities.

Education for Citizenship. Democratic government fails unless citizens show the same eagerness to serve their country that they expect the country to show in serving them. Schools seek to train young citizens to accept their responsibilities. Most schools have civic-education programs that emphasize citizenship activities both in and out of the classroom. Students study current affairs and American history and government as part of their classroom activities. They often have opportunities to elect class officers, make plans and decisions, and discuss matters that concern them as a group.

Outside their classes but still in school, students take part in bands, clubs, teams, and student govern-

ment. They learn how to work together in a friendly, democratic, and cooperative manner. Outside the school, they help on community drives, encourage adults to vote, and assist in making civic improvements.

Many private and public organizations promote citizenship education. Groups that train young men and women to become good citizens include agricultural, business, civic, fraternal, government, labor, patriotic, professional, religious, service, and youth organizations. They help citizens get information about their government and encourage them to take part in the government. Many groups sponsor conferences, exhibits, and discussions. Others distribute pamphlets and send representatives to government hearings on proposed bills. Some groups hold *mock conventions* or *mock legislatures* that train young men and young women on how a government operates.

Governmental and private organizations work with aliens in the Americanization program. The Americanization program helps qualified aliens prepare for American citizenship.

How Citizenship Is Acquired

A person becomes a citizen of a country by *birth* or by *naturalization*. Every country has its own citizenship laws. The United Nations, recognizing the conflicts in

443

CITIZENSHIP

citizenship laws throughout the world, tries to promote a uniform arrangement.

Birth. Nations generally follow one or both of two rules regarding citizenship by birth. The rule of *jus soli* (place of birth) provides that any person born within a country's boundaries is a citizen of that country, regardless of the nationality of his parents. The rule of *jus sanguinis* (blood relationship) provides that a child's citizenship is determined by his parents' nationality, regardless of his place of birth.

Some countries use both rules. They may do so in order to increase the number of their citizens, or to prevent hardships resulting from conflicting rules. The United States and Canada emphasize *jus soli*, but also follow a modified version of *jus sanguinis*.

Some countries, such as Great Britain, follow primarily the rule of place of birth. The British consider that anyone born "under the British flag" is a subject of the Crown, regardless of the nationality of his parents. Many other European countries, such as France, follow the rule of blood relationship. The French regard anyone born of French parents anywhere in the world as a French citizen. France also uses the rule of *jus soli*.

Naturalization. Many countries grant citizenship to aliens who meet certain requirements that guarantee their loyalty. This procedure is called *naturalization*. An alien who qualifies for naturalization must renounce all allegiance to the country of his birth. He takes an oath of loyalty to his new country in a formal ceremony. In the United States, naturalization ceremonies are often performed on Citizenship Day (September 17), at the start of Constitution Week. See NATURALIZATION.

Special Legislation that *waives* (excuses) one of the regular requirements for naturalization may be passed by Congress. Each year, congressmen propose about 500 special acts to allow designated aliens to become naturalized citizens without meeting one of the usual requirements.

Boys' Club members learn an important lesson in citizenship as they take part in a campaign urging adults to register to vote.

The New York *Times*

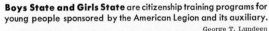

Boys State and Girls State are citizenship training programs for young people sponsored by the American Legion and its auxiliary.

George T. Lundeen

Cession of Territory may result in another form of naturalization. An act of Congress or a treaty can confer citizenship on an entire group of people. When the United States bought the Louisiana territory from France in 1803, the treaty provided that all the people in the area become American citizens.

United States Citizenship

Under the Constitution. Amendment 14 to the United States Constitution established the principle of *jus soli* in the United States. It states that "All persons born or naturalized in the United States, and subject to the jurisdiction thereof, are citizens of the United States and of the State wherein they reside."

This amendment makes clear that, in the United States, state citizenship is a by-product of national citizenship. Every citizen of the United States is also a citizen of the state in which he lives. He is entitled to all the rights, and is bound by all the obligations, granted or imposed by either the federal or state government. For example, he may be required to serve in the state militia as well as in the national armed forces. But this double citizenship creates no problems, because in any conflict between state and national law, national law comes first.

Military Service is a citizenship duty for young men in most countries. The recruits at the left are being sworn in for service as members of the United States Air Force.

Under the terms of Amendment 14, children who are born in the United States while their parents are serving as diplomats of other countries do not automatically become citizens of the United States. This is because diplomats are not "subject to the jurisdiction" of the United States.

Under Legislative Acts. Congress has passed laws that state how citizenship will be granted according to *jus sanguinis*. The Immigration and Nationality Act of 1952 combined all laws on American citizenship, nationality, and immigration. This law provides that a person born outside the United States is an American citizen if both his parents are American citizens and if either one of them has established residence in the United States. He is also a citizen if one of his parents is a citizen who has lived in the United States for a certain length of time. The length of time depends on the nationality of his other parent. For example, if one parent is a citizen and the other parent is an American noncitizen national, the child is a citizen if his citizen parent has lived in the United States for at least one year before the child's birth. But if one parent is a citizen and the other parent is an alien, the citizen parent must have lived in the United States at least 10 years before the child's birth. Of the 10 years, 5 must have been after the parent reached the age of 14. A child who acquires citizenship at birth abroad in this

THE OATH OF ALLEGIANCE

Every alien applying for American citizenship must, as the final step, take the following oath of allegiance to the United States:

"I hereby declare, on oath, that I absolutely and entirely renounce and abjure all allegiance and fidelity to any foreign prince, potentate, state, or sovereignty, of whom or which I have heretofore been a subject or citizen; that I will support and defend the Constitution and laws of the United States against all enemies, foreign and domestic; that I will bear true faith and allegiance to the same; that I will bear arms on behalf of the United States when required by the law; or that I will perform noncombatant service in the armed forces of the United States when required by the law; or that I will perform work of national importance under civilian direction when required by the law; and that I take this obligation freely without any mental reservation or purpose of evasion; so help me God."

last manner must live in the United States for a continuous period of five years between his 14th and 28th birthdays in order to keep his citizenship.

Court cases have determined that a person born of alien parents aboard an American vessel on the high seas is not entitled to American citizenship. But there is some question as to whether a child born on a ship of another country in American territorial waters acquires American citizenship by the rule of place of birth. Considerable evidence exists to show that an American citizen born in another country is considered "natural born" and eligible to be elected U.S. President. But an official ruling on this point has not yet been made.

Dual Citizenship

A person sometimes finds himself with two nationalities, because every country has its own citizenship laws. This situation is called *dual citizenship* or *dual nationality*. A person may have one nationality because of his place of birth, and another because of his parents' citizenship. For example, a child born in the United States of Italian parents may claim citizenship in both countries. At the same time, both countries can demand that the citizen fulfill his civic duties. In some cases, agreements between countries ban this kind of dual citizenship. A person might also gain dual citizenship as the result of naturalization. This situation may occur if the country he leaves does not recognize his change of allegiance, and still claims him as a citizen.

Persons who have dual citizenship are usually not aware of their unusual situations. Under international law, every nation is supreme within its own boundaries. For example, a child of Italian parents born in the United States is considered an American citizen within the borders of the United States. He is also considered an American while he travels with an American passport anywhere in the world except Italy. Italy has agreed not to claim such a dual citizen if he visits the country in time of peace. But it becomes difficult to determine his status if he remains in Italy for a long time, or if Italy becomes involved in a war while he is there. In the same way, it is difficult to decide the nationality of a naturalized citizen if the United States withdraws its protection from him because he returns to the land of his birth for an extended stay.

445

CITIZENSHIP

A person with dual citizenship faces another danger in time of war. If he fulfills his obligations of allegiance to one country, he may find that he is committing treason against the other.

Loss of Citizenship

Expatriation. Most countries recognize the right of any citizen to *expatriate* himself, or give up his allegiance to one country for allegiance to another. A person gives up his citizenship in one country when he is naturalized in another, if the country he leaves recognizes his right of expatriation.

The Immigration and Nationality Act of 1952 lists specific actions that may cause a person to lose his United States citizenship. Some of its provisions were designed to reduce the number of American citizens having dual citizenship. Other provisions were designed to expatriate American citizens for conduct that Congress considered improper for American citizens. However, the Supreme Court of the United States has declared some of these provisions unconstitutional.

A person can lose his U.S. citizenship if he voluntarily becomes naturalized in another country, voluntarily takes an oath of allegiance to another country, or serves in another country's military forces or its government. A person can also lose his citizenship by committing treason, or by formally renouncing his citizenship.

Statelessness. When a person is not the citizen or national of any country, he is *stateless*. If his homeland withdraws his citizenship as a punishment, he is not a citizen of any country. The same thing happens if he renounces his citizenship in one country, but does not acquire another nationality. A child could be born without being a citizen of any country if his alien parents come from a country that does not recognize the right of blood relationship, and if he is born in a country that does not recognize the right of place of birth. Under the laws of some countries, a person can become stateless as a result of marriage. A person whose homeland has been destroyed by another country may find himself in a similar situation. In the United States, a person who is not a citizen of any country is considered an alien. His legal position is worse than that of an alien, because he has no government to which he can appeal for protection. Many persons became stateless during World War II (see DISPLACED PERSON).

History

Ancient Times. The idea of citizenship goes back thousands of years. The city-states of ancient Greece had citizens, slaves or serfs, and aliens or noncitizens. Greek laws and traditions gave citizens many privileges, but also imposed heavy responsibilities. Citizens were expected to vote, to attend the assembly, to serve on juries, and to give military service. Slaves had few rights, and aliens had almost none, but they did have personal freedom and the protection of the law. See GREECE, ANCIENT (The People).

Some philosophers of ancient Greece, called *Stoics*, regarded all men as brothers (see STOIC PHILOSOPHY). They did much to promote the expansion of citizenship from the few to the many. Christianity, with its idea of the equality of man, also influenced the growth of the idea of citizenship. For years, Roman citizenship was a privilege highly regarded and eagerly sought. The Romans extended citizenship as their empire grew. In A.D. 212, Emperor Caracalla granted citizenship to all free men in the empire. He did this to force more people to pay heavy inheritance taxes. But his selfish act promoted liberty by extending the idea of citizenship (see ROMAN EMPIRE [The People]).

The Middle Ages. Citizenship declined with the fall of the Roman Empire and the rise of feudalism in Europe (see FEUDALISM; MIDDLE AGES). Millions of persons became serfs who owed service to the lords of the land. Each lord owed allegiance to a feudal lord above him, who in turn owed loyalty to the king. Under this system, there was little thought of citizenship.

Modern Times. As national governments grew in power, the people of each country began to owe allegiance to only one person, the king. With the spread of democracy, people usually transferred their allegiance from the king to the state. Citizens of kingdoms were usually called *subjects*. But as allegiance to a country began to replace allegiance to a king, the terms *citizen* and

Citizenship Classes help people prepare to become citizens. Most adults seeking U.S. citizenship must pass a literacy test and show that they know something about the nation's history and government.

national gradually replaced the term *subject*.

In the United States, the Constitution did not define American citizenship precisely. The authors of the Constitution assumed that a citizen of one of the 13 original states would become a citizen of the United States without losing his state citizenship. Later, the United States followed British common law in accepting the rule of place of birth. In 1790, Congress adopted laws that also recognized the rule of blood relationship. These laws provided that children born of American citizens abroad were citizens of the United States, unless the father had never lived in the United States.

The rule of place of birth became a part of the Constitution when Amendment 14 was adopted in 1868. The Supreme Court fully established the legality of this rule in a case decided in 1898. It held that Congress could not deny citizenship to any person born within the borders of the United States, regardless of the citizenship of his parents.

Most nations began to accept the idea of expatriation in the 1800's. Before that time, a person remained a citizen of the land of his birth, no matter where he lived. The United States has always tried to protect naturalized Americans against their nation of origin. It insists on a person's right to give up his former nationality in favor of a new one. But, at the same time, American courts declared that American citizens owed permanent allegiance to the United States.

Congress in 1868 gave Americans the right of voluntary expatriation. This action followed a storm of protest against the British who punished American citizens of Irish descent for taking part in the Fenian rebellion. After the act of 1868, the federal government had to be consistent in its actions. It had to protect persons who sought naturalization in the United States. But it also had to allow American citizens the right to renounce their citizenship.

In 1907, Congress defined the acts that automatically lead to voluntary expatriation. The 1907 law was succeeded by the Nationality Act of 1940 which, in turn, was replaced by the present Immigration and Nationality Act of 1952. The last two acts list in detail the grounds on which a United States citizen may lose his citizenship.

In 1963, Congress awarded an honorary citizenship for the first time. It was given to British statesman Sir Winston Churchill. ROBERT RIENOW

Related Articles in WORLD BOOK include:

Alien	Democracy	Immigration
Bill of Rights	Freedom	and Emigration
Boys State	Girls State	Nationality
Citizenship Day	Government	Naturalization
Civics	Human	Patriotism
Civil Rights	Relations	Pledge to the Flag
Community		Voting

Outline

I. What Is Good Citizenship?
  A. Rights and Duties B. Education for Citizenship
II. How Citizenship Is Acquired
  A. Birth   B. Naturalization
III. United States Citizenship
  A. Under the Constitution   C. The Oath of
  B. Under Legislative Acts   Allegiance
IV. Dual Citizenship
V. Loss of Citizenship
VI. History

Questions

What is a good citizen? What are his duties?
What acts could cause an American to lose his citizenship?
How do *civic rights* differ from *political rights*?
How is it possible for a citizen to be loyal and commit treason at the same time?
What are the two general methods by which a person acquires citizenship?
What status does a stateless person have in the U.S.?
What is the rule of *jus soli*? *Jus sanguinis*?
What is the origin of the word *citizenship*?
What is *citizenship education*?
What is a *noncitizen national*?

Books for Young Readers

LIFE INTERNATIONAL. *Nine Who Chose America*. Dutton, 1959.
RICHARDS, W. MARVIN, and ISELY, B. *We the People*. 2nd ed. Beckley-Cardy, 1964.
SCHOLASTIC MAGAZINES. *What You Should Know About Democracy, and Why*. Four Winds, 1965.
STARRATT, EDITH E., and others. *Our American Government Today*. Prentice-Hall, 1958.
WAGNER, RUTH H., and GREEN, I. E. *Put Democracy to Work*. Rev. ed. Abelard-Schuman, 1961. This book traces citizenship from ancient Greece to the present.
WEAVER, WARREN. *Making Our Government Work: The Challenge of American Citizenship*. Coward-McCann, 1964.

Books for Older Readers

AMERICAN COUNCIL FOR NATIONALITIES SERVICE. *How to Become a Citizen of the United States*. 20th ed. Oceana, 1963.
APPLEBY, PAUL H. *Citizens as Sovereigns*. Syracuse Univ. Press, 1962.
BARD, HARRY, and others. *Citizenship and Government in Modern America*. Holt, Rinehart & Winston, 1966.
HUGHES, RAY O. *Today's Problems: Social, Political, Economic Issues Facing America*. Rev. ed. Allyn and Bacon, 1962.
JOHNSON, GERALD W. *This American People*. Harper, 1951. The rights and duties of citizenship in the United States described in their historical context.
RIENOW, ROBERT. *The Citizen and His Government: Rights and Responsibilities*. Houghton, 1963.
UNITED STATES IMMIGRATION AND NATURALIZATION SERVICE, JUSTICE DEPARTMENT. *Gateway to Citizenship*. Rev. ed. U.S. Govt. Ptg. Office, 1962.

CITIZENSHIP DAY is celebrated in the United States each year on September 17. The day honors native-born citizens who have reached voting age and naturalized foreign-born citizens. Citizenship Day ceremonies and celebrations include pageantry, music, and speeches to impress Americans with the privileges and responsibilities of citizenship.

A movement to recognize new citizens began in 1939. William Randolph Hearst gave it national prominence through his chain of daily newspapers. In 1940, Congress passed a resolution designating the third Sunday in May as *I Am an American Day*. It authorized the President to issue an annual proclamation urging its celebration. On February 29, 1952, President Harry S. Truman signed a bill establishing September 17 as Citizenship Day. This act of Congress replaced I Am an American Day and moved the celebration to the date on which the United States Constitution was signed in 1787. Many cities continue to observe I Am an American Day in May. RAYMOND HOYT JAHN

CITLALTÉPETL. See ORIZABA (mountain).

CITRANGE

CITRANGE, *SIT rehnj,* is a hybrid plant derived from the sweet orange and the trifoliate orange. Although the fruit of the trifoliate orange is not eaten, the plants are hardier than ordinary oranges. Plant breeders developed the citrange to be raised in Georgia and in other regions of the South where the climate and soil do not allow oranges to grow. Commercial citrus plants have been grafted to the *rootstocks* (underground stems) of some types of citranges. The rootstocks provide a hardy, disease-resistant system for citrus plants. The citrange orange may grow to 2 or 3 inches in diameter. It has an acid, orangelike taste. It is used in cooking and to flavor various kinds of beverages.   WILLIAM GRIERSON

See also BREEDING (Plant).

CITRATE. See CITRIC ACID.

CITRIC ACID, *SIHT rik,* is a common organic acid that gives lemons, oranges, and other citrus fruits their sour taste. Lemon juice contains 6 to 7 per cent of the acid. The name *citric* comes from the Latin word *citrus,* which means *citron tree* (similar to lemon and lime trees). Carl Wilhelm Scheele, a Swedish chemist, first isolated citric acid from lemon juice in 1784.

Citric acid is used as a flavoring for soft drinks and pharmaceuticals. Industry uses it in chemicals, alkyd resins, and as a *mordant* (dye-fixative). It is also used to clean and polish steel, and to preserve color and flavor in canned and frozen fruits and fish. Citric acid is prepared commercially from fermentation of sugar, and by extraction from lemon juice, lime juice, and pineapple canning residues.

Pure citric acid forms colorless, odorless crystals that have a pleasant, sour taste. It is very soluble in water. Its chemical formula is $C_3H_4(OH)(COOH)_3$, and it melts at 153° C. (307° F.). Citric acid combines with metals to form salts called *citrates.*   JOHN E. LEFFLER

See also ACID; SCHEELE, CARL WILHELM.

CITRIC ACID CYCLE. See KREBS CYCLE.

CITRIN is a chemical substance that belongs to a group of chemicals called *flavonoids.* Scientists do not know exactly what citrin is, or if it is essential to man's health. But they have found that flavonoid substances help to control bleeding from the *capillaries* (the tiny blood vessels) in the body. Citrin, also called *vitamin P,* affects the capillary walls, making them less likely to hemorrhage. Citrin used in medicine is usually prepared from paprika and lemon peel.   JOHN R. KOCH

CITRON is a large, usually sour fruit much like the lemon. It ranks among the largest of all citrus fruits. The citron tree grows wild in northeastern India. It is also grown commercially in Italy and the fruit is exported to other countries. The thorny, unattractive citron tree has leaves that range from 4 to 7 inches in length, and have slightly toothed edges.

The fruit is 6 to 10 or more inches long and shaped like an egg. It has a thick, firm *rind* (peel) that is preserved and candied for use in cakes, puddings, and candies. The rind also furnishes fragrant oils. The *etrog,* a variety of citron with small fruits, is grown for use in a Jewish ceremony called the Feast of the Tabernacles.

Scientific Classification. The citron belongs to the rue family, *Rutaceae.* It is classified as genus *Citrus,* species *C. medica.*   WILLIAM GRIERSON

448

CITRONELLA is a pale yellow oil made from citronella grass. Citronella grass grows in Ceylon, Communist China, Formosa, Guatemala, Indonesia, Malaysia, and other countries. Its oil contains citronellal and geraniol. These two substances have different boiling points, and separate from citronella as the oil is distilled. Citronellal is used to make synthetic perfume ingredients. Geraniol smells like roses, and is used in many perfumes.   PAUL Z. BEDOUKIAN

CITRUS is the name of a group of trees and shrubs which belong to the rue family. Some citrus fruits are the orange, grapefruit, lemon, mandarin, kumquat, tangerine, bitter orange, lime, citron, shaddock, and bergamot. Citrus trees grow wild in parts of India and southeastern Asia. The Chinese were the first to cultivate citrus trees, about 1000 B.C. These trees and shrubs have been grown in other parts of the world for their fruits for many years.

Citrus trees are thorny, but usually attractive. They are evergreen, with long, shiny, pointed leaves. The flowers are fragrant. Ripe citrus fruits are yellow to orange-red in color. All citrus fruits are a type of berry that scientists call a *hesperidium.*

Citrus fruits all grow in rather warm climates. They grow best where there is almost no frost or wind. All grow in tropical regions, but produce better fruit in a slightly cooler climate. Citrus plants grow best in Florida, Texas, California, and Arizona in the United States. Citrus fruits are grown in greater quantity than any other fruit in the United States. Citrus fruits are valuable foods. They contain large amounts of vitamins and minerals. Citrus fruits are usually high in vitamin C.

Scientific Classification. All citrus plants belong to the rue family, *Rutaceae.* These plants as a group make up the genus *Citrus.*   WILLIAM GRIERSON

Related Articles in WORLD BOOK include:

Bergamot	Lemon	Tangelo
Citron	Lime	Tangerine
Grapefruit	Orange	Tangor
Kumquat		

The Citron Tree bears large sour fruit with a thick rind, *right,* that is often preserved and candied. The tree's thorny branches have long, slightly tooth-edged leaves, *below.*

Dr. W. P. Bitters, Citrus Research Center, University of California

CITY

J. Clarence Davies Collection, Museum of the City of New York; U.S. Coast & Geodetic Survey

Cities thrive because they provide good places to do business. An excellent harbor made New Amsterdam a trading outpost in 1626, *top*. Today, the harbor helps maintain New York City as one of the largest cities in the world, *bottom*.

CITY is a community in which thousands of persons live and work. They make their homes in tall apartment buildings, in rows of attached houses, or in single homes on small lots. City people can easily walk or ride to work, to shop, or to play. They need travel only short distances to nearby factories, offices, stores, schools, theaters, and parks.

A city may be the headquarters of many companies, large and small, that serve an entire region. It may be the location of large factories, each employing thousands of workers. Or a city may be a transportation center from which cargoes travel to all parts of the world by airplanes, railroads, trucks, or ships. Some great cities combine all these activities with many more in such fields as government, education, and creative arts. But almost all cities exist because they are convenient and efficient places in which to do business.

The people of a city come from many different places. Some are born in the city. Others move to the city from small towns or farms. Still others come from foreign countries. City people live close together, sometimes with hundreds of families in a single large apartment building. This gives city people a chance to learn a great deal about people with different backgrounds.

City people retain their sense of privacy even though they live and work close together. One way they do this is by simply ignoring many of the strangers they see. Visitors from small towns sometimes think this means city people are unfriendly. But this is not so. It simply demonstrates one of the differences between city life and country life. In the country, people live far apart but they usually "feel" near each other. In the city, people live near each other, but often "feel" far apart.

A City Seen from the Air

Flying over the city is an excellent way to get a picture of the entire area. The central business district in the middle of the city is filled with tall office buildings, hotels, and large department stores. The streets look narrow. The only open spaces are parking lots.

Industrial Areas. Near the business district is the harbor, with big piers jutting out into the water. Freighters are unloading their cargoes into boxcars and heavy trucks. Near the harbor lies a railroad yard with many freight cars waiting to be loaded.

The railroad tracks run from the central business district through a factory district with many large, low, buildings; tall chimneys; and large storage yards. Even-

449

tually the tracks lead to a new factory district near the edge of the city. The new, one-story factories in this district are surrounded by green lawns and large parking lots for the workers' cars.

Residential Areas. Crowded residential districts lie between the downtown factory area and the central business district. Here are street after street of small houses and apartments. Some of them are row houses, and others are small, detached houses only a few feet apart. In some of these sections, the houses are neatly painted and the small, green back yards are carefully kept. Window boxes with flowers add color and beauty.

Other sections of this older residential district are run down. There are few window boxes, and the back yards are bare of grass. Rickety shacks, and piles of old lumber and other rubbish line the alleys. These are *slum* areas. People here live crowded together, sometimes an entire family in one room. Nearby, workmen are tearing down some of these slums to make way for an urban renewal project (see URBAN RENEWAL). The government and private businessmen are cooperating to build this project, which will put modern apartment buildings and playgrounds in the old slum district.

The residential areas become less crowded farther from the center of the city. Houses are a little larger and farther apart. Trees shade the front and rear lawns. Along a broad avenue stand rows of apartment houses, some 2 or 3 stories high, others perhaps 15 to 20 stories. Each neighborhood has a school and a park or playground. One street is lined with stores and shops. It leads on through a park with woods and ball fields.

Beyond this lie the suburbs. The people in some of the suburban areas live in large homes with broad, well-kept lawns. Others live in new developments of smaller homes. Trees that line the streets in these new developments are still small, but someday will shade the houses.

Life in a City

Life in a city differs greatly from life in a small town or on a farm. It also differs within itself. An apartment dweller, for example, lives quite differently from his friend who lives in a house on the next block. Different backgrounds also create differences in the lives of city people. A person who has recently come to the city from another country may still follow some of his old customs. He may continue to eat the traditional foods of his former land, attend festivals and dances sponsored by his nationality group, and pattern his family relationships after the customs of his homeland.

At Home. Many city families live in apartment houses. Most of these are *"walk-ups"* of only two or three stories. Others are *elevator* apartment buildings, sometimes more than 20 stories tall. Most apartment buildings have small, if any, front yards or back yards. Children go to the neighborhood playground or to the park to play. Or they play in the streets or alleys.

A central laundry room may serve all the families of an apartment building. Many landlords maintain automatic washing machines and clothes dryers in this room for the tenants' use. Rubbish and garbage may be burned in the building's own incinerator, or it may be picked up by collectors once or twice a week.

Shopping is simple for a city person. There may be a small store or delicatessen on the next corner. A grocery supermarket is probably only an easy walk from home. And a short bus ride will take the shopper into the central business district, where stores sell almost anything a person could want to buy.

People who live close to others must be careful not to interfere with their neighbors' lives. Landlords often establish rules to prevent this. These involve playing in the hallways, making unnecessary noise late at night, keeping pets, and the use of laundry facilities.

A city person has many neighbors, but he may not even know the names of some of them. Other neighbors may be his good friends. City women borrow flour back and forth, just as women in small towns do. They visit over a morning cup of coffee, and take turns watching each other's children. In the evening, neighboring families may get together for a game of cards or a trip to a nearby bowling alley.

At School. A city boy or girl may go to a school with hundreds or even thousands of other children. On the way to school, he must perhaps cross a street crowded with cars, buses, and trucks. This traffic is headed for the central business area during the *morning rush hour*. Friendly policemen or policewomen stand watch at the busiest corners to help the children across safely.

A large city school may have five or more homerooms for a single grade, but each class is about the same size as a class in a small town. The class may take several field trips during the year, perhaps to a museum, a zoo, an art gallery, or a factory. Four or five buses may be needed to carry all the children going on one of these field trips.

At Work. During the morning rush hour, thousands of persons hurry to their jobs. Some of them work in offices high in downtown skyscrapers. Others go to giant factories, or sell merchandise behind the counters of large department stores. Most of these people work until 4:30 or 5 P.M., except for a short lunch hour and perhaps one or two "breaks" for coffee and relaxation. Then they head back to their homes, creating another period of heavy traffic, the *evening rush hour*.

When night comes and most people are thinking about going to bed, still other city dwellers are just going to work. Buildings must be cleaned to be ready for use early the next morning. Many factories operate around the clock. Hospitals, newspapers, power stations, and police and fire departments never close. Restaurants, drugstores, radio stations, and other establishments remain open to serve the people who work at night. A big city never sleeps.

Recreation in a city is as varied as the city itself. On a warm summer day, many families pack picnic baskets and head for the park or the beach. In the evenings, a family may walk to the neighborhood motion-picture theater. Or the city family may board a downtown-bound bus to see a play or to attend a musical concert. Art galleries and museums attract millions of city people every year. City parks offer many recreational programs, including handicraft, dramatics, and art. The many athletic fields in city parks are alive with people on pleasant days. See AMUSEMENTS.

How Cities Grow and Change

Increases in population and wealth, new inventions, and new fashions all contribute to the growth of cities.

COMPARING THE SIZES OF CITIES

A city determines its population by counting the people that live within its political boundaries. But cities of the world define their city limits differently, making population comparisons difficult. United States cities fix their limits so that they do not overlap or include other cities and towns. But some foreign cities include other urban and heavily populated areas.

Countries also determine metropolitan areas in various ways. In the United States, metropolitan area boundaries follow county lines. Each metropolitan area includes a county with a large city and perhaps nearby counties. But in most countries, a metropolitan area does not have definite political boundaries. Such areas include the major city and a variety of urban and rural areas that are socially or economically identified with the city.

Tokyo has the largest population of any city in the world. The New York City metropolitan area has the largest population of any metropolitan area. It includes five counties in New York City itself, four other counties in New York State, and eight counties in New Jersey.

The city and metropolitan populations in the tables below are census figures or estimates from governments or from *Demographic Yearbooks* of the United Nations Statistical Office. If these sources do not report a metropolitan population, the same city proper figure appears in both the cities and the metropolitan areas tables to show the existence of a metropolitan area.

——— 50 LARGEST CITIES IN THE WORLD ———

1. Tokyo.......	9,018,633	26. Santiago	
2. London.....	7,881,000	(Chile).....	2,447,741
3. New York....	7,781,984	27. Madrid.....	2,443,152
4. Shanghai....	6,900,000	28. Mukden.....	2,411,000
5. Moscow.....	6,427,000	29. Wuhan......	2,146,000
6. São Paulo....	5,383,000	30. Chungking...	2,121,000
7. Bombay.....	4,902,651	31. Philadelphia .	2,002,512
8. Rio de Janeiro......	4,031,000	32. Nagoya......	1,990,277
9. Peking......	4,010,000	33. Yokohama....	1,976,111
10. Chicago.....	3,550,404	34. Madras......	1,927,431
11. Cairo.......	3,518,200	35. Budapest.....	1,919,700
12. Seoul.......	3,470,880	36. Karāchi.....	1,912,598
13. Berlin (East and West)..	3,280,000	37. Hamburg.....	1,856,953
14. Mexico City .	3,269,335	38. Canton (China)....	1,840,000
15. Tientsin.....	3,220,000	39. Singapore....	1,820,000
16. Leningrad....	3,218,000	40. Istanbul......	1,750,642
17. Osaka.......	3,084,092	41. Detroit.......	1,670,144
18. Calcutta....	3,072,196	42. Milan.......	1,666,300
19. Buenos Aires......	2,966,816	43. Bogotá......	1,661,935
20. Djakarta....	2,906,533	44. Vienna......	1,640,106
21. Paris........	2,790,091	45. Barcelona....	1,633,921
22. Teheran.....	2,719,730	46. Bangkok.....	1,608,305
23. Delhi.......	2,511,482	47. Alexandria...	1,587,700
24. Los Angeles .	2,479,015	48. Harbin......	1,552,000
25. Rome........	2,455,302	49. Port Arthur-Dairen.....	1,508,000
		50. Lima........	1,436,231

—— 50 LARGEST METROPOLITAN AREAS IN THE WORLD ——

1. New York ...	14,759,429	27. San Francisco-Oakland.....	2,648,762
2. Tokyo......	11,319,841	28. Boston......	2,595,481
3. London.....	7,881,000	29. Rome.......	2,455,302
4. Paris.......	7,735,342	30. Manchester..	2,451,660
5. Buenos Aires.....	7,000,000	31. Santiago (Chile)....	2,447,741
6. Shanghai ...	6,900,000	32. Birmingham (England).	2,446,400
7. Chicago....	6,794,461	33. Sydney.....	2,444,735
8. Moscow	6,427,000	34. Madrid....	2,443,152
9. Los Angeles-Long Beach	6,038,771	35. Montreal....	2,436,817
10. São Paulo...	5,383,000	36. Mukden....	2,411,000
11. Bombay	4,902,651	37. Pittsburgh...	2,405,435
12. Calcutta....	4,764,979	38. Toronto....	2,158,496
13. Philadelphia	4,342,897	39. Wuhan.....	2,146,000
14. Rio de Janeiro	4,031,000	40. Chungking..	2,121,000
15. Peking.....	4,010,000	41. Melbourne..	2,108,499
16. Detroit.....	3,762,360	42. St. Louis....	2,104,669
17. Leningrad...	3,607,000	43. Washington, D.C.......	2,076,610
18. Cairo......	3,518,200	44. Istanbul....	2,052,368
19. Seoul......	3,470,880	45. Nagoya....	1,990,277
20. Berlin (East and West)	3,280,000	46. Yokohama..	1,976,111
21. Mexico City .	3,269,335	47. Caracas....	1,958,977
22. Tientsin....	3,220,000	48. Madras.....	1,927,431
23. Osaka......	3,084,092	49. Budapest....	1,919,700
24. Djakarta....	2,906,533	50. Karāchi.....	1,912,598
25. Delhi......	2,874,454		
26. Teheran.....	2,719,730		

——— 50 LARGEST CITIES IN THE UNITED STATES ———

1. New York City .	7,781,984	25. Indianapolis....	491,360
2. Chicago......	3,550,404	26. Atlanta........	487,455
3. Los Angeles ..	2,479,015	27. Minneapolis....	482,872
4. Philadelphia ..	2,002,512	28. Buffalo........	481,453
5. Detroit.......	1,670,144	29. Columbus.....	471,316
6. Baltimore.....	939,024	30. Jacksonville....	436,097
7. Houston......	938,219	31. Newark.......	405,220
8. Cleveland....	810,858	32. Louisville.....	389,044
9. Washington, D.C.........	763,956	33. Portland.......	372,676
10. St. Louis......	750,026	34. Oakland.......	367,548
11. Milwaukee....	741,324	35. Fort Worth.....	356,268
12. San Francisco..	740,316	36. Long Beach....	344,168
13. Boston........	697,197	37. Birmingham....	340,887
14. Dallas.......	679,684	38. Oklahoma City..	324,253
15. New Orleans...	627,525	39. Toledo........	318,003
16. Pittsburgh....	604,332	40. St. Paul.......	313,411
17. San Antonio...	587,718	41. Rochester, N.Y...	305,849
18. San Diego.....	573,224	42. Norfolk.......	304,869
19. Seattle........	557,087	43. Omaha.......	301,598
20. Memphis.....	536,585	44. Honolulu.....	294,179
21. Kansas City, Mo.......	518,525	45. Miami........	291,688
22. Phoenix......	505,666	46. Akron........	290,351
23. Cincinnati....	502,550	47. El Paso........	276,687
24. Denver.......	493,887	48. Jersey City....	276,101
		49. Tampa........	274,970
		50. Dayton........	262,332

——— 50 LARGEST CITIES AND TOWNS IN CANADA ———

1. Montreal......	1,222,255	25. Burlington.......	65,941
2. Toronto.......	664,584	26. Hull...........	60,176
3. Vancouver....	410,375	27. Brantford.......	59,854
4. Edmonton....	376,925	28. St. Laurent.....	59,479
5. Calgary.....	330,575	29. Kingston.......	59,004
6. Hamilton.....	298,121	30. Dartmouth.......	58,745
7. Ottawa......	290,741	31. Trois-Rivières....	57,540
8. Winnipeg....	257,005	32. Victoria.......	57,453
9. Laval (Ville de)	196,088	33. Niagara Falls....	56,891
10. London.......	194,416	34. Peterborough....	56,177
11. Windsor......	192,544	35. Sarnia.........	54,552
12. Quebec......	166,984	36. Oakville.......	52,793
13. Regina......	131,127	37. Jacques-Cartier...	52,527
14. Saskatoon.....	115,892	38. Saint John.....	51,567
15. Saint Catharines.......	97,101	39. Guelph.........	51,377
16. Kitchener....	93,255	40. Port Arthur.....	48,340
17. Halifax.......	86,792	41. La Salle.......	48,322
18. Sudbury......	84,888	42. Ste. Foy.......	48,298
19. St. John's.....	79,884	43. Fort William.....	48,208
20. Oshawa......	78,082	44. Moncton.......	45,847
21. Verdun......	76,832	45. Cornwall......	45,766
22. Sherbrooke....	75,690	46. St. Boniface.....	43,214
23. Sault Sainte Marie......	74,594	47. Lachine.........	43,155
24. Montreal-Nord	67,806	48. Welland.......	39,960
		49. New Westminster.	38,013
		50. Lethbridge......	37,186

As long as goods and services can be produced and exchanged easily and inexpensively in a city, the city will grow. But this growth cannot always be measured in terms of population. Some flourishing cities, such as Chicago, decrease in population because more and more people move from the city to the suburbs. But these people continue to work or shop in the city.

But all cities do not prosper. New trade routes may bypass them. Some cities do not have room to expand. Others do not have an adequate water supply. Cities that are dependent on nearby natural resources lose their importance when these resources are used up or are no longer in demand.

Population Changes. All city neighborhoods undergo steady population changes. Young couples often live in apartment districts. When they begin to rear children, they may move to a neighborhood of small homes so the youngsters will have yards to play in. As the parents grow older and earn more, they may move to a neighborhood of larger homes. After the children have grown up, the parents may move back into an apartment. But the population within the city limits of the largest cities in the United States is declining, and suburban areas are rapidly gaining population.

Slums. Some slum buildings were built as cheap tenements for immigrants. Other slum areas were once fine neighborhoods that have become run down. Many forces can cause *blight* (neighborhood deterioration). One of the major causes is the conversion of homes into rooming houses or into many small apartments. Buildings deteriorate rapidly from overcrowding and lack of repairs. Poor community services can also cause a neighborhood to become run down. Among these are poor schools, police and fire protection, garbage collection, and parks. Heavy traffic on residential streets can damage a neighborhood. Still another cause of blight is the construction in a residential area of nonresidential buildings such as stores, offices, and factories.

As a neighborhood begins to decline, many of its residents move to other neighborhoods, often in the suburbs. Their homes may be taken over by people moving into the city from other countries or from poor rural areas. Often these people are unskilled and can obtain only the lowest-paid jobs. They crowd together in small rooms or apartments in order to save rent. And the neighborhood declines even faster.

As slum dwellers become better educated and more highly skilled, they are able to hold better jobs. They can afford to move to better neighborhoods, vacating the slums for newer migrants.

History

Cities develop where they do because of the advantages specific locations offer that people wish to use. Some cities are established near natural resources, such as water power, coal, or valuable ores. Other cities are located along major trading routes at points where goods are changed from one type of carrier, such as ships or trains, to another. These points may be ports on seas, lakes, and rivers, or places where overland routes meet. All important cities throughout history have had a combination of advantages that have been developed to meet the varied demands of people.

City Flags of the United States

Many cities throughout the world have their own flags. The 18 flags of cities in the United States, *right*, have colors and designs that symbolize historical events, important industries, or ideals. The Washington, D.C., flag is shown in the FLAG article under District of Columbia. Canadian cities do not have official flags, but each usually has a coat of arms.

The First Cities developed around a temple and fortress, which shared prominence in each city. These cities were usually built on easily defended sites, such as hilltops, islands in streams, and peninsulas. The cities that stood above neighboring settlements were most common. Cities developed in heavily populated rural areas that could provide enough food for the city dwellers. All food had to be grown on nearby farms and transported on foot or by small boats. A thousand farmers could produce enough surplus food to support only a hundred city dwellers. Farmers and city dwellers became increasingly dependent on each other. The city needed the farmers' food, and the farmers turned to the city for protection.

Ancient Cities grew in size with the development of better methods of agriculture and transportation. Improved tools and weapons enabled armies to conquer large areas, and the surplus food of whole countries could be appropriated for one large city. During the 5000's and 4000's B.C., large cities developed in Mesopotamia, India, and China. Only a few ancient cities, such as Rome, Peking, and Nanking, reached populations of 1 million. Athens at its peak had a population of only 150,000. These cities dominated empires which held power for a few hundred years. When their military power declined, they dwindled in wealth and population. Rome, for example, declined from a city of over 1 million to fewer than 20,000. See CITY-STATE.

Medieval Cities. During the Middle Ages, wars ravaged Europe and made trade difficult. Cities survived by building walls which could be defended against roving warriors. Their sizes were again limited to populations that could be supported by nearby farms. The gradual establishment of peace during the A.D. 1100's and 1200's brought a revival of trade and the slow growth of medieval cities. Venice, Paris, London, Amsterdam, and the Hanseatic cities grew as trading or port cities (see HANSEATIC LEAGUE). Few cities had populations as large as 100,000, and 90 per cent of the world's people lived on farms at the start of the Industrial Revolution. See MIDDLE AGES (Medieval Towns).

Growing Cities. The Industrial Revolution, beginning in the 1700's, urbanized the Western countries. Better implements and knowledge raised agricultural productivity so that only 10 or 20 per cent of a country's population could raise all the food needed. New methods of transportation—boats, canals, roads, and railroads—made it possible for huge cities to have food and raw materials from all parts of the world. New manufacturing methods enabled the cities to produce goods which they could trade for raw materials. Fairly peaceful and stable world conditions made trade and investment possible. Surplus resources let society spend

Baltimore

Boston

Buffalo

Chicago

Cleveland

Dallas

Detroit

Houston

Los Angeles

Milwaukee

New Orleans

New York

Philadelphia

Pittsburgh

Saint Louis

San Antonio

San Diego

San Francisco

New Cities That Follow an Overall Central Plan make efficient, orderly use of land. Most homes in the new community of Reston, Va., above, near Washington, D.C., are within walking distance of shopping, dining, and recreational facilities.

larger and larger amounts on research and training, thus speeding technological development. All these changes occurred in cities. Today, there are more cities in the United States with populations of over 100,000 than there were in the entire world before 1700. See INDUSTRIAL REVOLUTION.

City Problems Today

In the United States, the population has been constantly increasing, and more and more people are moving from rural areas to the cities. About 70 of every 100 Americans now live in cities. As cities have grown, the political, social, and economic problems of city dwellers have increased enormously.

The rapid growth of cities causes serious problems for their governments. Many are hard pressed to provide such necessary services as sanitary water, sewers, streets, and police protection. Many suburbs and cities have grown together and some of these services overlap. Some services can best be provided for a whole *metropolitan area*, which includes a central city and its surrounding suburbs. In some places, special agencies have been established to administer these services. For example, the Port of New York Authority manages several bridges, tunnels, airports, and port activities in the New York City metropolitan area. Toronto and Miami have established metropolitan governments to handle many services for the entire area.

Transportation problems also increase as more people use automobiles. Old streets are overcrowded and new freeways cannot be built fast enough to keep up with demand. As more people drive cars, bus, railroad, and other public transportation systems lose money and reduce services. But large cities need rapid-transit service. If all workers drove to their jobs, streets and parking lots would be even more crowded. Public funds are often used to keep public transportation systems operating.

School financing is a problem in most cities, especially in large cities. Some communities cannot afford the costs of good education. Their school buildings are old and run-down, teachers are underpaid, and classes are too large. The federal and state governments give funds to needy local districts to improve their facilities and provide better education.

Removing slums and providing decent housing are major problems. Run-down buildings must be fixed up, or torn down so new apartments and homes can be built in their place. Sometimes, neighborhoods are cleared to provide space for new highways, factories, hospitals, offices, or shopping districts. The residents and shopkeepers displaced there must be relocated in other areas. Most cities have housing or renewal agencies to deal with these problems. Such agencies receive financial aid from the federal government to clear slum areas and to help provide adequate housing for low-income families.

Poverty and unemployment plague aging inner city areas and some suburbs. New industries are often established in suburban areas, while the poorer families who need jobs the most are concentrated in older parts of the inner city. New jobs often require skilled workers. Many persons living in central cities are unskilled and poorly educated. As a result, a large number of them are unemployed. Many unemployed persons are Negroes or members of other minority groups that are discriminated against in jobs, housing, and education. Local governments receive federal funds to help improve the living and working conditions of underprivileged city families. Federally-financed projects include poverty, renewal, and model cities programs.   WILLIAM L. C. WHEATON

Related Articles in WORLD BOOK include:

Outline

I. A City Seen from the Air
II. Life in a City
III. How Cities Grow and Change
    A. Population Changes   B. Slums
IV. History
V. City Problems Today

Questions

What are the three major districts that are included in most cities?

When were the first cities established?

What factors cause cities to be built in certain places?

What are some factors that cause cities to grow and change?

Why have some fine neighborhoods become slums?

Why do more persons today live in cities than on farms?

What development beginning in the 1700's caused cities to expand greatly?

What are two ways that cities have met the need for services involving both cities and suburbs?

CITY AND LOCAL GOVERNMENTS manage the affairs and provide the services for a city or other local area. People in a city demand more services, need stricter regulation, and require the helping hand of government more often than do their country neighbors, because they are crowded closer together. They come into contact with their city government almost daily. A policeman directs traffic at a busy corner. A fire engine roars down a crowded street. Rumbling trucks collect household garbage and refuse. At night bright street lights chase the shadows. Motor-driven sprinklers and street sweepers clean the city streets. A new playground is opened to boys and girls. These are some of the services and facilities that city governments offer.

The American system of government operates on three levels: local, state, and national. Local government includes governments in counties, cities, boroughs, villages, townships, and towns. It also includes school districts and special districts. The state creates and has legal control over all local governments. It determines what kinds of units there shall be. Some states require that a community have a certain population before it may become a city, borough, village, or town. Other states do not. State laws group communities into classes according to their populations. Each class has its own kind of organization, and has the right to provide for the needs of the community.

After the state has approved the boundaries of a local unit, the people set up its government. The state allows each city or town to govern itself in certain matters. Each state has a slightly different pattern.

Forms of government vary from city to city. Many cities have a council and a mayor. Others have a commission or a city manager, or elements of both.

The same person usually lives under and pays taxes to more than one local government. Local governments are usually completely independent of each other. But they often cooperate on mutual problems.

Units of Local Government

State legislatures set up local units of government to provide the people with certain services. To be a true government, a local unit must have (1) territory, (2) population, (3) legal standing, (4) power to carry out governmental functions, (5) independence from other local units, and (6) the right to raise revenue.

Units of local government include municipalities, townships, school districts, and special districts. Municipalities include cities, boroughs, villages, and incorporated towns.

The United States has about 90,000 local units of government. Illinois leads the states with about 6,500 units. Hawaii has the fewest, about 20.

Municipalities serve urban areas. They have the power to provide police and fire protection, street and traffic control, health and welfare services, and other services necessary to maintain community life. Illinois has more than 1,100 municipalities, the largest number of any state. Some states, including Nevada, New Hampshire, Hawaii, and Rhode Island, have fewer than 25 municipalities each.

Townships usually serve rural areas, providing only a few governmental services. Only 16 Midwestern and Middle Atlantic states have townships. In New York, Wisconsin, and the six New England states, township

governments are called *town* governments. They have wide authority. When a township government includes urban areas, it performs many functions and services that are normally handled by a municipality. In some New England states, the towns direct local schools.

School Districts. About half the local governmental units in the United States are school districts. More than half the states have independent school districts. Most of them are small, rural units that furnish only elementary education. Other districts provide high schools as well, and a few have facilities for junior colleges. Some districts do not maintain schools. Instead, they furnish transportation and pay tuition for boys and girls to attend schools in other districts.

Eight Middle Western states have 3,000 or more school districts each. The number of school districts has dropped since 1940, because many small districts have been consolidated to form larger units.

Special Districts carry out particular government functions. These districts are also called *authorities, commissions,* or *boards.* Most special districts were set up to perform a single function. But some provide several services. About two of every three special districts in the United States deal with fire protection, soil conservation, drainage, regulation of cemeteries, or housing. Other special districts handle water irrigation and conservation, sewage disposal, parking, sanitation, and management of highways, hospitals, libraries, parks, and playgrounds. Special districts, often called *authorities,* build and operate bridges, toll roads, seaports, airports, and public buildings.

Special-district types of local government may be found in every state. Illinois has the largest number, with more than 1,800.

Forms of Local Government

Local government in the United States has roots that reach into the past. Much of the American government system came from England. But many local government offices go back even farther than English history. In late Roman times, the *constable* directed mounted troops. The *city* dates from the Latin *civitas,* or a body of citizens. The *borough* comes from the Teutonic *burg,* or walled settlement. The *village* comes from the Latin *vicus,* or Roman settlement without walls. *Township* had its origin in the Germanic *tun scipe,* or a group of families that governed themselves in northern Europe during the Middle Ages.

Mayor-Council. Most large cities in the United States have a *strong-mayor* form of government. In this government, the mayor has broad powers. He can appoint subordinate city officials, veto acts of the council, prepare a budget, plan a program, and direct the operation of all city departments. The council acts as the agency that determines basic policy and raises revenue for the city. But the mayor acts as the leader in city government, and voters consider him the chief executive of the city. Many municipalities retain the council as the most powerful agency. More than half the cities in the United States with populations over 5,000 have a mayor-council form of government.

Before the Revolutionary War, the first city governments in the colonies were patterned after those in

CITY AND LOCAL GOVERNMENTS

England. A council was the chief organ of government. The mayor was a member of the council, and presided over it. The council held all executive, legislative, and judicial powers. Throughout American history, a popularly elected council has remained the chief authority in city government. All present forms of local government are based on this principle.

In the early 1800's, many cities changed their forms of government. They copied the system of *separation of powers* used in the national and state governments (see UNITED STATES, GOVERNMENT OF [Separation of Powers]). Under this system, the mayor operated from a separate office and was not a member of the council. During the 1800's, most cities had *weak-mayor* governments, with little executive authority. The mayors had to share their powers with councils and with other elected officials. But, as towns began to grow in size, many large cities adopted the strong-mayor form.

Commission governments have several elected executives, called *commissioners*, who supervise operations. About 300 cities in the United States with populations of 5,000 or more have commission governments.

The first commission government was set up after a tidal wave and hurricane struck Galveston, Tex., in 1900 and destroyed a large part of the city. The disaster caused so much devastation that the weak mayor-council government could not function properly. The state legislature provided for a city government by a popularly elected commission of five persons. The commission had powers to pass ordinances, impose taxes, distribute funds for city needs, and appoint officials. A commissioner headed each of four departments: (1) finance and revenue, (2) waterworks and sewage, (3) streets and public property, and (4) police and fire protection. A fifth commissioner, who acted as mayor-president, coordinated the work of the others.

The commission achieved such success that it began to gain wide acceptance as a new form of local government throughout the United States. Des Moines, Iowa, adopted the commission form in 1907. Within eight years, more than 400 cities had copied it. Most of these cities were fairly small, but they also included Oakland, Calif.; New Orleans, La.; and St. Paul, Minn. After 1914, the commission form became less popular. Some cities went back to the mayor-council form, or tried the new city-manager type of government.

The chief weakness of the commission form is its lack of unity in operations. Each commissioner has charge of one department, and may administer it without regard to the government as a whole. The commissioners are elected to represent the people, but there is no guarantee that they will be good administrators.

Many persons regard the commission form as a good method for eliminating political bosses and machines, graft, and waste. With only five persons to direct city government, administration is simplified.

Council-Manager plan developed from the commission form of local government. A city council hires a professional administrator as manager to supervise all municipal affairs. The council then has the same kinds of functions as the board of directors in a large corporation. The city manager has the same kinds of duties that the chief executive officer would have in the corporation.

The city council retains full legislative authority, and passes ordinances. It may dismiss the city manager, but generally it does not interfere with his work. In most communities, the council determines how long the manager will serve. In a few cities, the manager has a specific term of office. Most managers are nonpolitical appointees, experienced in public administration.

The purpose of the council-manager plan is to improve administration and to gain efficiency and economy. The short ballot is another feature of the plan. Voters elect only a few officials directly. They can examine the candidates more carefully than can voters who elect many officials listed on a long ballot (see VOTING).

The National Short Ballot Organization devised the original council-manager plan in the early 1900's. In 1908, the city of Staunton, Va., hired a general manager to handle its administrative affairs. It kept its council and mayor. In 1912, the city of Sumter, S.C., became the first to adopt the commission-manager form of government by direct vote. The voters elected a three-man commission that in turn appointed a city manager. The plan gained national attention in 1914, after a disastrous flood almost engulfed Dayton, Ohio. In January of that year, Dayton became the first large city to use the city-manager plan.

More than 2,100 cities in the United States and Canada have city managers. Almost half the cities in the United States with populations of 25,000 or more use the council-manager plan. It ranks second to the mayor-council plan in use in the United States. Other countries, including West Germany, Norway, and Finland, also have the council-manager form of government.

District Government. Most other forms of local government—townships, school districts, and special districts—have elected governing bodies. But many, notably the school district with a school superintendent, have appointed executives who function in somewhat the same manner as city managers.

City Governments in Other Countries

There are three basic systems of city government in widespread use in all parts of the world outside the United States. They are known as English, French, and Russian.

The English System provides that the national government grant specific powers and duties to the local units. Popularly elected local governing bodies exercise these powers without much supervision from the national government. In Great Britain, the city government is called the *borough*. The mayor, the aldermen, and the councilors act as one body. No separation of powers exists between the mayor and the council. Committees conduct much of the city's administration. The English system has been adopted in Australia, Canada, New Zealand, and South Africa.

The French System gives the national government strict and detailed control over local governmental units. It does this through *prefects* (officials) who direct the departments into which France is divided. City governments in France are called *communes*. An elected council and mayor meet four times a year. They adopt an annual budget, and have authority to regulate such local matters as water supply, streets, parks, and fire protection. But the prefect and the minister of the interior in the national government control finance, edu-

THE VOTERS

Voters form the basis for all city governments. They elect the mayor and other officials in the mayor-council form, *left*. Citizens of the various wards elect members of the council, and mayor and council together run the city. Voters directly elect members of the commission, *below*. Or they directly elect a small council, *right*. It hires a professional city manager to run the government.

MAYOR-COUNCIL

7
1
4
6
2
3
5

Council

Mayor

Treasurer

Other Officials

COMMISSION

Five-Man Commission

COUNCIL-MANAGER

Council

Manager

GOVERNMENT SERVICES

Each of the three forms of city government must provide the people with basic protection and services. Under some mayor-council systems, the people elect officials to supervise some of these services. Under the commission form, each member of the commission may be responsible for a particular government function.

Police and Fire Protection

Health and Welfare

Water and Sewerage

Streets and Public Property

Finance and Revenue

cation, police, and other functions that would be handled by the cities in the United States. The French system dates from the time of Napoleon I, in the early 1800's. With slight changes, it has been adopted in most countries in the Middle East, Far East, Africa, and Latin America. For example, cities in Mexico fall under the strict control of state governments and laws.

The Russian System. The *soviet* (council) forms the structure of local government in Russian-dominated countries. An all-powerful national government dominates the various levels of soviets. The local district or city soviet serves as the representative of the national government. An executive and several committees handle such municipal affairs as housing, fuel use, education, and transportation.

The local government in Russia has some power. But the next higher level of government maintains strict control over it. The Communist party organization keeps a watchful eye on local officials. Local governments do not debate issues freely and do not use elections to decide local policies.

Services of Local Government

Local governments provide a wide variety of services for their people. In rural areas, these services are not so numerous or expensive as they are in large cities. State and national governments have taken over many functions once performed by local governments. They have found that local government could not finance these services, or did not have the organization to administer them efficiently. This has been particularly true of functions relating to streets, highways, health, and welfare.

Safety and Protection. The police force of every city usually has a full-time job protecting people and property from lawbreakers. It must guard them from violence in the streets, in public places, and in their homes. It must arrest criminals and bring them to trial. It must curb juvenile delinquents and keep them from a criminal career. City police must keep traffic flowing and streets safe for travel. They cooperate with state policemen to help find criminals who escape over city boundary lines. The county government usually tries persons accused of a crime. Its district attorney, grand jury, judge, sheriff, and coroner handle such cases. See COUNTY.

The city fire department fights fires, and tries to prevent them by enforcing building regulations and making regular safety inspections. All large cities have trained professional firemen with the most modern fire-fighting equipment. In many smaller cities, villages, and towns, volunteer fire companies composed of citizens of the community provide fire protection.

Public Utilities and public works include government-owned or government-supplied facilities and services. They may be bridges, streets, street-lighting systems, public-transportation systems, airports, waterworks, refuse- and sewage-disposal systems, parks, and playgrounds. They may also include public housing and public buildings such as auditoriums, schools, libraries, museums, hospitals, and health centers.

The city may own an enterprise and finance it through taxation or rates collected for services. The city may regulate privately owned enterprises, such as transpor-

tation systems, in the public interest and convenience. Or the city may own an enterprise, but lease it to a private firm to operate and maintain. Municipal ownership has been more widely accepted in European countries than in the United States. Many European cities own their own theaters. But private firms often produce the plays or operas. In such cities as London and Paris, housing units have been built on city land and public authorities organized to operate them. In Canada, water power may be developed by municipalities, provinces, or private firms.

Cities in the United States tend to own certain kinds of services, including water-supply and distribution systems, sewage-treatment plants, airports, electric-power and light systems, incinerators, and auditoriums. Some public utilities are natural monopolies, or services of the kind in which competition would be wasteful. For example, no city would allow two companies to build their own streetcar tracks along the same streets, or to lay water pipes beneath the streets. People could not depend upon competition to regulate the prices charged for such services. But authorities do not agree on whether it is wiser for government to own and operate such facilities, or to regulate them by law under private ownership.

Health and Welfare rank among the major responsibilities of city government. City health departments strive to control communicable diseases, eliminate unsanitary conditions that breed diseases, and supervise public eating places. They may set up laboratories and clinics. City governments build hospitals and provide care for the sick, the unemployed and those unable to work, orphans, and widowed mothers. Other city departments work to demolish slums and blighted areas, and to provide housing for low-income groups. Local taxation finances most of these services, but other governments may lend financial and technical help.

Planning. Local government must gather and examine facts of city life and relate them to the present and future needs of the community. City planners seek answers to such questions as these: Will the population increase? Where will it be concentrated? Will there be adequate public facilities? Shall the city be divided into business, industrial, and residential zones? These problems can be solved only by a continuous program of city planning. See CITY PLANNING.

Relations with Other Governments

Each state creates its units of local government. It decides what kind of local government it must have. It also outlines the pattern of cities, towns, townships, villages, and school districts. State laws describe the powers that local governmental units may exercise, and how these units shall raise revenue. Often a state constitution has provisions relating to local government. The state may give its own departments the power to supervise local government in such activities as education. This is called *state administrative control*.

Local governments are independent of each other. The county does not supervise the city. The city does not govern the village outside its borders. Some authorities believe that one defect of local government is the vast number of local units in one economic area. They believe that a plan must be devised to solve governmental problems that affect more than one unit.

The federal government has no direct control over

city governments. But it has greatly increased its interest in local problems. It has made large grants of money to local governments for such purposes as highways, hospitals, welfare, health, housing, and slum clearance.

Problems of Local Government

Local government in the United States has always adjusted to changing conditions of American life. Popular demands for improvements have usually led to changes in the form and structure of local governments. These governments face two major changes in the character of the American people: urbanization, and a rapidly growing population, particularly in the suburbs.

The United States has become an urban nation. In 1790, only 5 of every 100 persons lived in urban areas. By 1960, the number had risen to 70 of every 100. City governments must be chiefly concerned with problems of urban life and providing for urban services.

Population growth in the suburbs also causes problems. From 1950 to 1960, nearly two-thirds of the population increase in the United States occurred in the suburbs. These areas are often called the *urban fringe*. City governments face the problem of supplying services to these newly developed communities.

Duplications of Government. Many towns and villages cluster around a central city. Together they comprise a *metropolitan area* that forms a single economic unit (see METROPOLITAN AREA). But political authority is divided among the many local governmental units in an area. Many authorities believe that the smaller, ineffective local units should be consolidated into larger, more efficient ones. They believe that local government in urban areas is too divided to adequately serve the more than 125 million persons in these areas.

Finances are a major problem for many local governments. State constitutions and laws restrict and limit the amount of taxes and other revenues that local governments can raise. They also limit the amount of debt that local units may incur. Most states provide that local units may raise money, but require that it come almost entirely from property taxes. Urban areas may have adequate wealth, but they cannot always be taxed sufficiently to furnish modern local services for all the people. As a result, state and national governments must help city governments. They make grants for such services as highways and education. Or they may simply take over an increasing number of local functions.

Representation in Government. Many urban areas lack adequate representation in state legislatures. In about half the states, each county, no matter how small its population, must have one representative in the lower house of the legislature. In many other states, laws restrict the number of legislative representatives from cities. In 1962, the Supreme Court of the United States ruled that questions of unfair representation in state legislatures can be brought to federal courts.

Authorities believe that many local governments can improve by modernizing their organizations and practices. Local government officials themselves have often stood in the way of progress, because they do not want any changes. Local governments must use more efficient methods, hire trained personnel, and cooperate with each other to achieve unity within neighboring areas that have similar problems.　　　　　H. F. ALDERFER

Related Articles in WORLD BOOK include:

SERVICES OF LOCAL GOVERNMENT

Airport	Health, Board of	Safety
Bridge	Hospital	Sanitation
City Planning	Housing	School
Civil Defense	Law Enforcement	Sheriff
Conservation	Library	Smoke
Constable	Park	Prevention
Court	Playground	Social Work
Fire Fighting	Police	Street
Fire Prevention	Public Health	Traffic
Franchise	Public Utility	Transportation
Garbage Disposal	Roads and Highways	Water

OTHER RELATED ARTICLES

Alderman	Community	Taxation
Assessor	County	Town
Borough	Democracy	Town Meeting
Burgomaster	Government	Township
Canada,	Legislature	United States,
Government of	Mayor	Government of
City	Metropolitan Area	Village
City-State	Soviet	Voting
Commune	State Government	

Outline

I. Units of Local Government
  A. Municipalities　　　　　C. School Districts
  B. Townships　　　　　　　D. Special Districts
II. Forms of Local Government
  A. Mayor-Council　　　　　C. Council-Manager
  B. Commission　　　　　　D. District Government
III. City Governments in Other Countries
  A. The English System　　　C. The Russian System
  B. The French System
IV. Services of Local Government
  A. Safety and Protection　　C. Health and Welfare
  B. Public Utilities　　　　　D. Planning
V. Relations with Other Governments
VI. Problems of Local Government

Questions

What are three forms of city government?

How does the French system of local government differ from the English system? From the Russian system?

What services do city governments usually provide?

What controls does a state government have over local governments?

What is a local unit of government?

Why have many local government functions been taken over by state or federal governments?

What authority does the national government have over local governments?

What state has the most local units of government?

What state has the largest number of municipalities?

What disaster led to the development of the commission form of government?

CITY COLLEGE is a coeducational, municipal, nonresident college in New York City. It is part of The City University of New York. City College offers courses which lead to bachelor's and master's degrees. It was founded in 1847. For the college's enrollment, see UNIVERSITIES AND COLLEGES (table [New York, The City University of]).

CITY MANAGER. See CITY AND LOCAL GOVERNMENTS (Council-Manager).

CITY OF BROTHERLY LOVE. See PHILADELPHIA.

CITY OF ORANGES. See SALTO.

CITY OF REFUGE NATIONAL HISTORICAL PARK. See NATIONAL PARK (Historical Parks).

CITY OF ROSES. See MONTEVIDEO (Location and Description); PORTLAND (Ore.).

Chicago Department of City Planning

City Planners build scale model development plans for a given area. This model of a central business area for Chicago covers the district outlined on the map, *left*. It contains office buildings, stores, theaters, a transportation terminal, and open park spaces.

N

SCALE IN THOUSAND FEET

DEPARTMENT OF CITY PLANNING

CITY OF CHICAGO

CITY PLANNING determines a city's future needs for land, buildings, highways, and other facilities, through an analysis of current and future urban growth. Communities plan and rebuild old areas and develop new areas to meet present and future needs.

Agencies. Most major cities of the world have city planning offices. For example, Paris has an inspector-general of town planning. In Rio de Janeiro, the mayor is responsible for city planning. In Tokyo, the Capital Area Readjustment Committee develops city planning. A city planning board in Toronto directs activities in that city.

In the United States, city planning usually is handled by a city planning commission. The mayor appoints the members of the commission. Larger cities, counties, and towns employ full-time planning staffs. Small towns may retain a professional consultant. Most state governments have state planning commissions. The Tennessee Valley Authority is the outstanding example of regional planning by the United States government, which now assists local and metropolitan planning.

The General Plan, or master plan, sets forth the future needs and character of the city. It consists of a series of maps, reports, and studies that undergo continuous revision. Planners base their work on studies of current and future employment in commerce and industry. They use these estimates to forecast future population growth resulting from migration and births. Estimates of future employment and population permit planners to determine the areas required for future residences, industrial districts, shopping centers, and other land uses.

The general plan divides the city into communities or neighborhoods. It shows all the community facilities required for the city as a whole, and for each neighborhood. Each neighborhood needs an elementary school, shopping center, playground, church, and other facilities. Several adjoining neighborhoods make up a larger community that will require a high school, library, health center, park, and a larger shopping center. Planners provide districts for industry, offices, and trade.

The transportation plan links together the various land uses in the city, and provides for the movement of both people and goods. Major highways can create boundaries between different communities and channel heavy traffic around them. The transportation plan also provides for railroads, port and harbor facilities, airports, buses, subway or elevated lines, and passenger, truck, and railway terminals.

The general plan provides for new residential neighborhoods and the renewal of older districts that have become blighted or are deteriorating. The plan includes proposals for future industry and commerce in new planned industrial parks or rebuilt areas.

Zoning. City governments have many powers to guide urban growth according to development plans. Under city laws, cities can adopt zoning ordinances that control the use, height, area, and set-back of new buildings. A zoning map controls the use of land in each area. The city may reserve some areas for single homes on large lots, and others for apartment houses and higher density residential uses. It may reserve other areas for heavy or light industry, for office buildings, or for stores and shops. Municipal subdivision control ordinances regulate the size of lots; the coverage and set-back of

A Fully Landscaped Shoppers' Mall replaced a traffic-packed street in the downtown business district of Kalamazoo, Mich., in 1959. It was the first of its type in the United States.

Wide World

buildings; the width, grade, and alignment of streets, curbs, and sidewalks; sewage, and water facilities. Building, sanitary, and housing codes protect public health, safety, and welfare by regulating building structure, plumbing, wiring, fire exits, use, and occupancy.

Cities also have the power of *eminent domain*, or compulsory purchase of private property needed for some public purpose, such as streets or parks. They may use this authority to condemn and acquire for a fair price slum and blighted areas that need rebuilding. After a city has acquired such an area, it can demolish deteriorated buildings and replan the area for rebuilding. The city's capital budget lists all foreseeable needs for public works, buildings, streets, and open spaces. It schedules those most urgently needed.

Regional, State, and National Planning. Many communities have citizens' planning or housing associations. People can express their desires and work for a better planned community through these groups. National organizations devoted to city planning include the American Planning and Civic Association and the American Institute of Planners, Washington, D.C.; American Society of Planning Officials, Chicago; and the American Council to Improve Our Neighborhoods, New York City.

Professional training programs for city planners have been established in about 30 colleges and universities in the United States.

History. Most major cities of the world developed without being planned in the modern sense of the word. But as cities grew in size and complexity, the need for orderly planning of new sections arose. In the American colonies, several towns were planned cities. Philadelphia, planned in 1682 by William Penn, and Savannah, Ga., are examples. In 1791, George Washington hired Major Pierre Charles L'Enfant to prepare a plan for Washington, D.C. Planners developed the major street system of Detroit and of Manhattan in New York shortly after 1800. Little planning occurred during the 1800's, when industrial expansion attracted millions of peoples to cities. Communities grew increasingly dirty, ugly, crowded, and unhealthy.

A revival of interest in city planning developed after 1893. A commission revised L'Enfant's master plan for Washington, D.C. Daniel H. Burnham prepared a city plan for Chicago. Many cities prepared similar "city beautiful" plans. Charles Eliot developed the first metropolitan park plan for Boston. Jane Addams and others began settlement houses to help immigrants in slum areas. Jacob Riis worked for reform in housing and for the adoption of tenement house laws. Gifford Pinchot led a movement to preserve natural resources. In 1913, New York City adopted the first zoning ordinance. In the 1930's, cities prepared plans to encourage industry and provide jobs. In the late 1950's, gleaming new buildings and recreational areas began appearing according to development plans in many major American cities.   WILLIAM L. C. WHEATON

Related Articles in WORLD BOOK include:

Architecture
Burnham, Daniel H.
City and Local Governments
Housing

L'Enfant, Pierre C.
State Government
Traffic

CITY-STATE

CITY-STATE is a state in which political life and political control center in a single city. The city-state had its fullest development in ancient times. The most famous examples were Athens and Rome. The Athenian state consisted of Athens itself and also the outlying villages of Attica. The free inhabitants of this territory owed allegiance not to Attica but to the city of Athens, and were Athenian citizens. The ancient city-state was like a modern city in territory and a nation in powers.

In the Middle Ages, the Italian cities of Milan, Florence, Genoa, Venice, and Naples rose to power as independent states. The free cities of Germany, including Hamburg, Bremen, and Lübeck, were examples of the city-state in a modified form.   PAYSON S. WILD, JR.

See also FREE CITY; GREECE, ANCIENT (The City-State); ITALY (Rise of the City-States).

CIUDAD BOLÍVAR, *syoo THAHTH voh LEE vahr* (pop. 98,007; alt. 187 ft.), is the commercial outlet for more than half of Venezuela—the southern Orinoco plains and Guiana highlands. It is on the Orinoco River, about 270 miles inland from the Atlantic Ocean. For location, see VENEZUELA (color map). Ocean-going cargo ships carry rubber, gold, diamonds, hides, chicle, and tonka beans (used in tobaccos and perfumes) from Ciudad Bolívar. A steel mill and a hydroelectric plant are located nearby. The city was founded in 1764 as Angostura. It was the original home of angostura bitters, used in drinks (see BITTERS).   W. DONALD BEATTY

CIUDAD JUÁREZ. See JUÁREZ.

N.Y. Zoological Society

The Civet is valued because it produces a fatty substance with a musky odor. This substance is taken from pouches close to the animal's tail, and is used in making several kinds of perfumes.

CIUDAD TRUJILLO. See SANTO DOMINGO.

CIVET, *SIV et*, is a flesh-eating mammal found in warm regions of Africa and southern Asia. This slender animal grows 2 or 3 feet long and 10 inches high. It has gray fur above and white below, with a tinge of yellow and rows of dark spots. Civets eat crocodile eggs, birds, and other small animals. They produce a musky substance used in perfumes. Only a few drops a week are taken from a civet, but the perfume industry uses thousands of ounces every year.

Scientific Classification. Civets belong to the family *Viverridae*. The common African civet is genus *Civettictis*, species *C. civetta.*   HAROLD E. ANTHONY

See also PERFUME.

CIVIC CENTER is a group of public buildings and landscaped spaces in a city. The center may include an auditorium, a library, a band shell, shops, hotels, and government and office buildings.

The idea of such a community gathering place developed in ancient Greece. The Forum in Rome was a center of politics, business, and religion. Medieval towns had public squares for religious and other activities. Today, the great size of cities increases the need for civic centers.   BERNARD LEMANN

The Detroit Civic Center began with a planned architectural model, *left.* The completed Center, *below,* includes a circular convention area next to a 9-acre exhibit hall with roof parking.

City of Detroit

CIVICS is a course of study that teaches the duties and rights of citizenship. It considers the functions, structures, and some of the problems of political, social, and economic institutions on local, state, national, and international levels.

In addition to formal studies in civics, some teachers encourage student participation in such activities as student councils and clubs, and school newspapers. Here, students learn to cooperate with others in deciding what needs to be done and how to do it. Some schools encourage direct student participation in community projects. PAUL R. HANNA

Related Articles. See the Government section in the state and province articles, such as CALIFORNIA (Government); BRITISH COLUMBIA (Government). See also the following articles:

Canada, Government of
Citizenship
City and Local Governments
Community
Democracy (Making Democracy Work)
Government

Human Relations
International Relations
State Government
United States, Government of
World

CIVIL AERONAUTICS ADMINISTRATION. See FEDERAL AVIATION ADMINISTRATION.

CIVIL AERONAUTICS BOARD (CAB), is an independent agency of the federal government of the United States. The President appoints its five members with the approval of the Senate. The CAB regulates the economic phases of United States domestic and international airline activities. The board issues certificates to American airlines for domestic and international service and issues permits to foreign airplanes entering the United States. It determines air rates and mail rate payments. It works to establish and maintain reasonable and adequate public service in civil aviation.

The Civil Aeronautics Board aids in establishing and developing international air transportation in cooperation with the Department of State. It cooperates in forming international standards for air operations. Congress established the Civil Aeronautics Authority in 1938. In 1940, the agency was renamed the Civil Aeronautics Board. Critically reviewed by the CIVIL AERONAUTICS BOARD

CIVIL AIR PATROL (CAP) is a civilian auxiliary of the United States Air Force. It operates under the Air Force Continental Air Command, but it is not a federal government agency. It has about 85,000 adult and teen-age members who serve without pay.

The CAP has about 48,000 cadets who are from 13 to 21 years old. It has about 37,000 senior members over 21 years old. Members are organized into 52 wings and about 2,300 local groups, squadrons, and flights. Members wear uniforms similar to U.S. Air Force uniforms, but they wear different insignia and badges. The CAP has more than 11,000 FAA-licensed pilots and almost 5,000 aircraft. It operates a radio network that includes more than 21,000 fixed, mobile, and airborne stations.

The CAP participates in search and rescue missions that are authorized by the air force. In the 1960's, the CAP annually accounted for over half the search and rescue missions flown in the United States. CAP pilots fly thousands of hours each year, searching for lost airplanes and doing relief work during local and national disasters.

More than 600 high schools offer CAP aerospace education courses. The CAP also conducts many work-

Civil Air Patrol—USAF

Civil Air Patrol Cadets get training in subjects ranging from weather to rocketry. They get training at such sites as the USAF Technical Training Center at Chanute (Ill.) AFB.

shops and institutes for teachers. It publishes a complete series of aerospace education and training textbooks. The CAP awards scholarships and educational grants to selected members annually. It participates in an International Air Cadet Exchange program with 22 other countries, and offers cadets training in aerospace developments through courses conducted at air force bases.

The Civil Air Patrol was established in 1941 in the Office of Civilian Defense. It organized and directed the activities of volunteer civilian airmen using their own aircraft and equipment for wartime tasks. The CAP was transferred to the War Department in 1943 as an auxiliary of the Army Air Forces. In 1946, Congress chartered it as a nonprofit private corporation. The CAP became a civilian auxiliary of the U.S. Air Force in 1948. CAP headquarters is at Maxwell Air Force Base, Ala. 36112. Critically reviewed by the CIVIL AIR PATROL

CIVIL AND DEFENSE MOBILIZATION, OFFICE OF (OCDM). See NATIONAL DEFENSE (History).

CIVIL CODE, or CODE CIVIL, contains the civil, as distinguished from the criminal, law of France. In 1800, Napoleon Bonaparte appointed a commission to consolidate all French civil laws into one code. The new code went into effect in 1804. After Napoleon became Emperor of France that same year, the code became known as the *Code Napoléon*. It is sometimes called that today, but its official name is *Code Civil*.

The Civil Code represented a compromise between the customary law of northern France and the Roman law of the south. It also compromised between the ideas of the French Revolution and older ideas. It gave new liberty to the people, but kept such ideas as the system of inheritance. The Civil Code influenced law in Europe, South America, the state of Louisiana, and the province of Quebec. But its influence has declined. Even in France, it has been changed by new laws and court decisions. EDWARD W. CLEARY

CIVIL DEATH. See DEATH, CIVIL.

463

Chicago Civil Defense Corps

Air-Raid Sirens attract attention to indicate when persons should take shelter or evacuate. Local radio and television stations broadcast civil defense instructions in case of an enemy attack.

CIVIL DEFENSE is a program of nonmilitary plans and actions for saving lives and property if an enemy attacks a country. Civil defense may also deal with such emergencies as fires, floods, hurricanes, tornadoes, and other natural disasters. Trained civilian auxiliary groups help the regular emergency services—policemen, firemen, health officials, and others—in providing civil defense.

Civil-defense preparations range from building huge underground public shelters to training families in first aid. Canada, Denmark, Great Britain, Norway, Russia, Sweden, the United States, and other countries have nationwide civil defense programs.

Civil defense in the United States began in a small way in pioneer days. While colonial soldiers fought the enemy, civilians repaired and restored community life at home.

The problems of civil defense are far greater than ever before in this present-day age of modern warfare. Any country may be attacked with atomic, biological, and chemical weapons from land, sea, or air. A missile carrying an atomic warhead can speed 6,000 miles in 25 minutes, giving little opportunity for advance warning. A country must have all its civilian and military strength prepared in advance, if it is to survive and recover from an attack.

People can do one of two things when an enemy strikes or a natural disaster occurs. If they have enough time, they may evacuate or leave the endangered area and go to a safe place. Or they must seek shelter or get under cover if there is not enough time for evacuation. Every person should be prepared by knowing (1) the civil-defense warning signals and what they mean, (2) his community's plan for emergency action, (3) the methods of protecting himself from fallout, (4) first aid

CIVIL-DEFENSE WARNING SIGNALS

Every person in the United States and Canada should know what to do when a warning signal sounds. In the United States, a long, steady siren blast means "attack alert." A person should follow the instructions of local civil-defense authorities. As part of the *Emergency Broadcast System (EBS)*, AM radio stations on several frequencies will give information. A warbling tone, or short blasts, of a siren means "attack." Everyone should dash immediately for the nearest available shelter. In Canada, a steady siren or long blast of a horn means that a person should listen for instructions on his radio or television set. If he is a civil-defense official, he should phone for orders. Either an *undulating* (wavering) siren or short blasts of a horn mean "take cover."

and home emergency preparedness, and (5) the proper means of obtaining official civil-defense instructions.

Defense at Home

The heart of civil defense in the United States is individual and family preparedness. Families should be prepared to care for themselves for two weeks after a national disaster. Communities and states would be prepared to help after the first two weeks. Full aid from the federal government would be available as soon as possible, but probably no later than the fifth week. Family defense includes (1) building a shelter for protection against fallout, and (2) learning and practicing home emergency measures.

Building a Shelter. A fallout shelter serves as a shield that protects the family from dangerous radiation that could result from an atomic attack. The thicker and heavier the shield, the better the protection. Radioactive fallout produces highly penetrating rays that can sicken and even kill people and animals (see FALLOUT).

CIVIL DEFENSE IN THE HOME

A First-Aid Kit should be kept ready for emergencies.

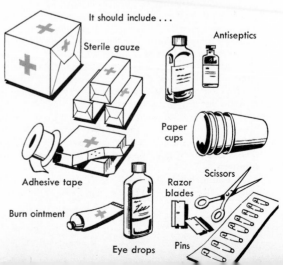

It should include . . .

Sterile gauze

Antiseptics

Paper cups

Adhesive tape

Razor blades

Scissors

Burn ointment

Eye drops

Pins

One of the best fallout shelters is an underground structure covered by at least three feet of earth. An emergency shelter can be built in the corner of a basement by piling sandbags above and around a wooden frame. The main purpose of the shelter is protection, not comfort. Construction of the shelter starts with the wooden framework. Bags or boxes filled with sand or earth are added to the framework. All such shelters could save lives, because it might take one or two hours for the wind to carry radioactive fallout to the area, and many people would have time to reach safety.

Families must strengthen their fallout shelters at all weak points, such as basement windows, by adding sandbags or other thick objects. If the family cannot build an underground or basement home shelter, it should select an inside room with the fewest windows and doorways, or an inside hallway, as a shelter.

Local governments have set up public shelters in suitable areas of large office and public buildings. They may arrange for food, water, and medical supplies to be provided on short notice.

Equipping a Shelter. Each shelter area should have (1) a battery-operated radio for receiving instructions, (2) equipment to dispose of wastes, (3) bedding, (4) a

CIVIL DEFENSE TERMS

ABC Warfare is atomic, biological, and chemical warfare.

Aerosol Cloud is a man-made spray or mist in which disease-producing or chemical agents are suspended.

Air Burst is the explosion of a bomb in the air.

Air-Defense Control Center is a land-based air-operations post that provides aircraft control and warning, and directs the air defenses of an area.

Assembly Point is a meeting place for mobile support groups.

Attack Warning Devices include horns, sirens, bells, and alarms that warn of enemy attack.

Biological Warfare is the use of living organisms or their products to kill or injure people, animals, or plants.

CBR Warfare is chemical, biological, and radiological warfare.

Chemical Warfare is the use of chemicals in solids, liquids, or gases to kill or injure.

Control Center is civil defense headquarters or the alternate seat of government for directing forces and activities during emergencies.

Emergency Broadcast System (EBS) is an emergency AM radio communication system. Before and during an enemy attack, the President would have first priority to broadcast on local stations. He would be followed by local, state, regional, and national reports.

Evacuation means the organized and supervised removal of civilians from dangerous areas, and their care in safer areas.

Fallout is material contaminated by radioactivity, which falls to the earth or water after an atomic bomb explodes above, on, or below the ground.

Film Badge is a small piece of photographic film that a person carries in a badge to record the amount of radiation to which he has been exposed.

Flash Burn is a burn caused by exposure to intense light or heat.

Geiger Counter is an instrument used to detect and measure radioactivity.

Ground Zero is the point on the earth's surface directly beneath the point where an atomic bomb explodes.

Kiloton is the explosive power of 1,000 tons of TNT.

Megaton is the explosive force of 1,000,000 tons of TNT.

Mobile Support means the self-contained civil defense services or teams organized by local or state civil defense agencies.

Nominal Atomic Bomb is an atomic bomb similar to those used in World War II, with the destructive force of 20,000 tons of TNT.

Radiological Warfare means the use of weapons that produce radioactivity, such as thermonuclear bombs in surface or near-surface bursts.

Reconnaissance is the search for casualties, survivors, radioactive areas, damage, and unexploded bombs after an enemy attack.

Support Area is an area designated to provide aid and assistance to a disaster area.

Surface Burst is a bomb explosion on or near the ground or water, with the fireball touching the surface.

Tactical Dispersal means the movement of people outward from the center of a target area, in anticipation of an imminent enemy attack.

Target Areas have major concentrations of people and industries, such as cities of more than 50,000 population, state capitals, and the District of Columbia.

Emergency Equipment should be stored in a safe area.

It should include . . .

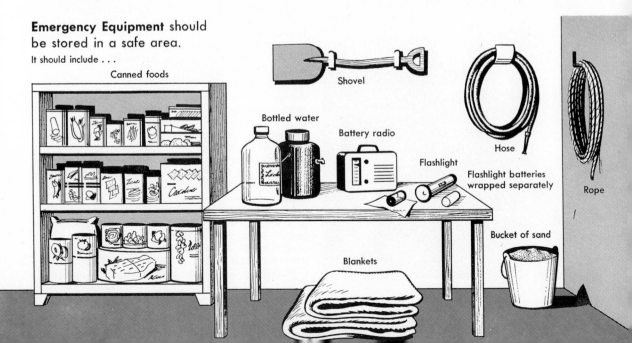

Canned foods

Shovel

Bottled water

Battery radio

Flashlight

Flashlight batteries wrapped separately

Hose

Rope

Bucket of sand

Blankets

CIVIL DEFENSE

flashlight, (5) a first-aid kit, and (6) a two-week supply of food and water.

Families should know how to fight fires, take sanitary precautions, and administer first aid. At least one adult in each family should take a course in first aid and home nursing. A home fire extinguisher, garden hose, and hand water-pump should be kept ready, and all members of the family should be trained to use them.

Defense in Industry

Businesses and industries provide shelter areas within factories or office buildings, or nearby. They also develop and practice plans for evacuation. Industrial civil defense includes a self-help organization and plan. Most factories already have fire-fighting, safety, and rescue equipment, and trained personnel are available for immediate action in case of emergencies.

The company enlarges these services for civil defense. It sets up plans to combat sabotage and espionage within the plant. It marks off safe areas in existing buildings, and plans for protective features when it designs new structures. The firm plans how to evacuate and care for employees in safer areas, and how to return them to their communities and jobs after an enemy attack. It provides for the continuity of management by organizing alternate company headquarters, setting up personnel-succession lists, developing emergency financial arrangements, and duplicating and storing vital records in areas comparatively safe from attack.

Industries also plan for emergency repair and restoration. They set up systems to assess damage quickly and to restore production. They establish industrial mutual-aid associations for civil defense. They join with other neighborhood industrial plants to provide mutual aid in the form of equipment, materials, and personnel. They make sure that essential items are manufactured

Highway Signs warn motorists to stay off certain roads in the event of an enemy attack. Highways must be kept open in an emergency so that mobile support groups can speed to the assistance of communities hit by bombs or other disasters.

Ohio State Highway Patrol

466

in more than one place. They disperse new industrial plants over wide areas.

Survival Suggestions

Civil defense officials urge six steps to help increase your chances of survival in an enemy atomic attack.

1. Take Cover. When this signal sounds, hurry to the nearest shelter, such as a basement, subway, culvert, or gulley. If you cannot reach a shelter, or are in an automobile, lie face down on the ground or crouch on the car floor.

2. Drop to the Floor immediately if you see a flash and have not been warned. The best place in your home is close to a wall or under a bed or table. Stay away from windows.

3. Cover Your Face. The flash of an atomic explosion will cause blindness for several minutes if you face it. If you know an attack is about to occur, hide your eyes in the crook of your elbow to prevent flash burns and eye injury.

4. Do Not Rush Outside after an atomic attack. Civil defense and other authorities will survey the area, and let you know by loudspeakers or radio when it is safe to leave your shelter. Radio broadcasts will be heard on AM stations until the danger of attack is over.

5. Avoid Using Food and Water in Open Containers. Use only canned, boxed, or bottled foods. Destroy all other unpackaged foods, because they may be contaminated by radiation.

6. Do Not Spread Rumors. Atomic weapons are the most destructive known. But they cannot blow the earth apart or kill everyone by radiation. Blast and heat are the chief causes of damage in an atomic explosion. Radioactive fallout could be as great a cause of casualties. Proper civil defense preparations can lessen damage and injury from these causes. It is better to be prepared than to die needlessly.

Civil Defense in the United States

National Planning. The Office of Emergency Planning (OEP) is a federal agency that advises the President on defense policy. A part of the Executive Office of the President, it coordinates all defense operations. It determines the civil defense role of each federal agency and of state and local governments. It also acts to protect the operation of the federal government and of the national economy during wartime. The director of the OEP is a member of the National Security Council (see NATIONAL SECURITY COUNCIL).

The Office of Civil Defense (OCD), established under the Department of the Army, develops specific civil defense programs. These include a fallout shelter program, programs for emergency aid to state and local governments, and warning and communications systems. The Civil Defense Warning System can transmit an attack warning to more than 700 locations throughout the United States at the same time. Persons at these locations would then warn local officials, who would sound sirens and other warning devices.

Many other federal agencies share in the country's civil defense effort. The Department of Agriculture and the Department of Health, Education, and Welfare have programs for stockpiling and distributing emergency food and medical supplies. The Department of Commerce would take control of the nation's transportation facilities. The Interstate Commerce Commission is prepared to direct the use of railroads, motor carriers, and inland waterways. The Federal Aviation Administration would control civil airports. In emergencies, the Department of the Interior is responsible for electric power and certain strategic materials. The Department of Labor must mobilize civilian manpower, stabilize wages and salaries, and supervise labor-management relations. The Post Office and other agencies also have emergency functions.

Local Planning. State and local governments share responsibility with the federal government for civil defense. A civil defense director, appointed by the governor, coordinates state defense planning. The actual backbone of civil defense is government itself. Government at every level must keep control and give direction in any emergency. The basic organization is formed around government officials who have the same kinds of responsibilities in peacetime. State civil defense officials prepare emergency disaster plans, set up training programs, and test their plans.

Most local communities have similar emergency disaster plans, with authority given to the mayor or city manager. Usually a city civil defense director works out plans to conform with those on the state level.

Some counties have civil defense offices under their boards of supervisors or their county commissioners. These offices prepare plans to provide rural civil defense, to care for persons evacuated from endangered cities, and to teach how to protect farms and livestock from radioactive fallout.

Federal, state, and local officials cooperate in the *Continuity of Government* program to prepare governments to carry on during extreme emergencies. It has four main objectives: (1) to establish by law successors for all key government officials, (2) to provide emergency relocation sites for governments outside likely damage areas, (3) to arrange for the safe storage of vital public records, and (4) to use all government personnel and resources in an emergency.

Local governments decide whether their people should evacuate the area or take shelter. The choice of evacuation or shelter, or both, depends on the amount of warning time, the local plans, available shelters, and the area's location, resources, and nearby safe areas.

Civil defense planning calls for a threatened city to be able to care for itself to the limits of its people and resources. It would then turn for help, if available, to neighboring local governments, then to the state, and then to the federal government.

Civil Defense in Other Countries

Canada. The prime minister, through the Emergency Measures Organization of the Privy Council Office, coordinates civil defense planning of other federal agencies. He also assists provincial and local governments in civil defense. Other major responsibilities are divided among the Department of National Defence (Army), the Department of National Health and Welfare, and the Royal Canadian Mounted Police. The Canadian Civil Defence College at Arnprior, Ont., trains civil defense instructors. It provides training in fire fighting, rescue, radiation monitoring, and health and welfare services. It serves as the federal control center in nationwide civil defense tests.

Denmark has an active civil defense program based on mobile columns, or units, of trained, full-time workers. Mobile columns include communications, fire, rescue, antichemical warfare, debris-clearance, water, and transportation units. Public shelters have been built. A civil defense academy trains officers.

Great Britain. Some homes have a *refuge room*, similar to a *shelter area* in the United States. Each year thousands of persons receive training in special civil defense schools and colleges. About 1 of every 4 persons is trained in rescue, first aid, and fire fighting. A women's voluntary service manages emergency welfare, feeding, lodging, and care of evacuees.

Norway. Private and public shelters have been built in homes and garages. Civilians receive extensive civil defense training. Mobile columns of trained personnel support the regular emergency services, such as police and fire departments and rescue workers. The government has stockpiled survival supplies, and conducts practice evacuation of large cities.

Russia has a tightly organized civil defense program with a career corps of full-time trained personnel and a voluntary organization for civilian training. It probably has about 22 million men and women trained in civil defense. The government has set up defense units in many factories, collective farms, schools, universities, and institutions. Every citizen is required to take a 22-hour training course. Some cities have public shelters.

Sweden. Underground public shelters, factories, industries, and stockpiles of survival goods have been built. In the major cities, 14 shelters carved from solid rock can protect up to 20,000 persons each. These shelters are normally used as garages. Civil defense training is compulsory, with nearly a million persons involved. Every new home must have a fallout shelter for personal protection.   LEO A. HOEGH

Related Articles in WORLD BOOK include:

Atomic Bomb	Guided Missile
Chemical-Biological-	Hydrogen Bomb
Radiological Warfare	National Defense
Fallout	Radiation
Fallout Shelter	Radio (National Defense)
Geiger Counter	Radioactivity

Outline

I. Defense at Home
 A. Building a Shelter   B. Equipping a Shelter
II. Defense in Industry
III. Survival Suggestions
IV. Civil Defense in the United States
 A. National Planning   B. Local Planning
V. Civil Defense in Other Countries
 A. Canada   C. Great Britain   E. Russia
 B. Denmark   D. Norway   F. Sweden

Questions

What are six ways to increase your chances for survival in an atomic attack?

Why is civil defense necessary to a nation?

What is the Office of Emergency Planning?

What is the responsibility of the family in civil defense?

What should a person do if an enemy attacks suddenly?

What is fallout? A megaton?

How does civil defense in industry differ from civil defense in the home?

When did civil defense begin in the United States?

What country requires every citizen to take a 22-hour civil defense training course?

What essentials should every shelter area have?

CIVIL DISOBEDIENCE

CIVIL DISOBEDIENCE is the deliberate and public refusal to obey a law. Some persons use civil disobedience as a form of protest to attract attention to what they consider unjust or unconstitutional laws or policies. They hope their actions will move other people to correct the injustices. Other persons regard civil disobedience as a matter of individual religious or moral conviction. They refuse to obey laws that they believe violate their personal principles.

Most lawbreakers try to escape punishment. On the other hand—at least in theory—a person who practices civil disobedience accepts willingly his punishment for breaking the law. He thus demonstrates his deep concern about the situation he is protesting.

Many lawbreakers do not hesitate to use violence. But most acts of civil disobedience are nonviolent. Civil disobedience is usually distinguished from riot, rebellion, revolution, and other types of violent opposition to law and authority.

Is Civil Disobedience Ever Justified? Throughout history, there has been widespread disagreement concerning the use of civil disobedience in a society based on law and order. Some persons claim that every citizen has the obligation to disobey laws he considers basically unjust. They point out that such law-breaking may be the best way to test the constitutionality of a law. Some defend civil disobedience by pointing to Nazi Germany's laws calling for extermination of Jews and certain other groups.

Other persons claim that it is never right to break a law deliberately. They argue that defiance of any law leads to contempt for other laws. Any act of civil disobedience, they believe, weakens society and leads to possible violence and *anarchy* (no government or law).

Many persons approve civil disobedience only in extreme circumstances, and then only if it is nonviolent. But they point out that injustices can usually be corrected legally through democratic processes. For example, free elections give people a chance to choose their leaders and express their views on various issues. Various constitutional provisions also protect the right of dissent.

History of Civil Disobedience. Men have practiced civil disobedience for hundreds of years. When the disciples of Jesus Christ were ordered by the state to stop their teachings, they replied that they would obey God rather than men. In the A.D. 1200's, the Christian theologian Saint Thomas Aquinas argued that men must disobey earthly rulers when the laws of the state disagree with the laws of nature, or God.

During the 1600's and 1700's, certain religious sects became known for civil disobedience. For example, the Quakers in colonial America refused to pay taxes for military purposes because they disapproved of war. In the 1850's, abolitionists refused to obey the Fugitive Slave Law, which provided for the return of runaway slaves to the South.

The American writer Henry David Thoreau was one of the most influential spokesmen for civil disobedience. In 1845, he spent a night in jail for refusing to pay taxes. He argued that he did not owe allegiance to a government that captured runaway slaves and waged war on Mexico to expand its area of slavery. In his essay "On the Duty of Civil Disobedience" (1849), Thoreau declared that men should refuse to obey any law they believe is unjust.

Thoreau's essay strongly influenced Mohandas K. Gandhi of India. Led by Gandhi, the Indian people used such nonviolent acts as strikes and protest marches to free themselves of British rule. They gained independence in 1946.

In the United States, during the 1950's and 1960's, Martin Luther King, Jr., and other civil rights workers deliberately violated Southern segregation laws as a means of fighting racial injustice. In the North, black people used civil disobedience to press their demands for open-housing laws and equal employment opportunities. In the 1960's, many opponents of the Vietnam War committed various illegal acts in attempts to change U.S. policy. Some refused to pay their taxes. Others refused to register for the draft.   LEON F. LITWACK

See also THOREAU, HENRY DAVID.

CIVIL ENGINEERING. See ENGINEERING (Main Branches); SURVEYING (Careers).

CIVIL LAW is a term with several meanings. The term is often used to describe the rules of private law and to set them apart from the rules of criminal law. When used in this way, civil law covers such matters as contracts, ownership of property, and payment for personal injury. Criminal law deals with actions that are harmful to society.

The term *civil law* can also mean the law of most European countries, as opposed to the *common law* of Great Britain and every state of the United States except Louisiana. Under this type of civil law, *codes* (sets of rules) approved by legislatures are the primary sources used by judges to decide cases. Under common law, judges base their decisions chiefly on previous court decisions in similar cases. See COMMON LAW; LOUISIANA (Courts).

Originally, civil law referred to the code of laws collected by the Roman emperor Justinian in the A.D. 500's. These laws were used to govern the Roman Empire. A new civil law became popular in most of Europe after it took effect in France in 1804. This law combined the Roman law and the law of northern France. This civil law is the basis of the present law in Quebec, Mexico, and some South American nations. In the United States, there has been much interest in arranging some existing laws into codes. Examples include the law of business and the law of crimes.   ROBERT E. SULLIVAN

Related Articles in WORLD BOOK include:

Civil Code	Damages	Justinian Code	Suit
Code Napoléon	Equity	Law	Tort
Contract	Fraud	Negligence	

CIVIL LIBERTIES. See CIVIL RIGHTS.

CIVIL LIBERTIES UNION, AMERICAN (ACLU), is a nonpartisan organization devoted to the defense of civil liberties in the United States. It has about 125,000 members. The ACLU supplies counsel and files legal briefs in important cases involving violations of civil liberties. Its officials discuss problems of civil liberties with officials of the U.S. government and testify before legislative committees. The ACLU also conducts an active educational program. The organization has headquarters at 156 Fifth Avenue, New York, N.Y. 10010.   Critically reviewed by the AMERICAN CIVIL LIBERTIES UNION

CIVIL RIGHTS are the freedoms and rights that a person may have as a member of a community, state, or nation. Civil rights include freedom of speech, of the press, and of religion. Among others are a person's right to own property, and to receive fair and equal treatment from government, other persons, and private groups.

In democratic countries, a person's civil rights are protected by law and custom. The constitutions of many democracies have *bills of rights* that describe the people's basic liberties and rights. Courts of law decide whether a person's civil rights have been violated. The courts also determine the limits of civil rights, so that people do not use their freedoms to violate the rights of other persons.

In many nondemocratic countries, the government claims to respect and guarantee civil rights. But in most of these countries, such claims differ greatly from the actual conditions. In most Communist countries, for example, the people are denied such basic rights as freedom of speech and of the press. Yet their constitutions guarantee these rights.

Some people draw sharp distinctions between *civil liberties* and *civil rights*. They regard civil liberties as guarantees to a person against government interference. They think of civil rights as guarantees of equal treatment for all persons. For example, civil liberties would include freedom from government interference with a person's right to free speech. Civil rights would include the right of all people to receive equal protection of the law. Civil rights often refers particularly to the condition and treatment of minority groups. This is especially true in the United States. In this article, the term *civil rights* refers to both civil liberties and civil rights.

Limits of Civil Rights

All civil rights have limits, even in democratic countries. For example, a person may be denied freedom of speech in a democracy if it can clearly be shown that his speech might lead to the overthrow of the government. A person may not use civil rights to justify actions that might seriously harm the health, welfare, safety, or morals of others. In 1919, U.S. Supreme Court Justice Oliver Wendell Holmes, Jr., wrote: "The most stringent protection of free speech would not protect a man in falsely shouting fire in a theatre and causing a panic."

A person may be denied a civil right if he uses that right to violate other people's rights. Freedom of expression, for example, does not permit a man to tell lies that ruin another person's reputation. A person's right to do what he chooses with his property may not allow him legally to refuse to sell it to a person of a certain race or religion. The property owner would be denying the other person equal freedom of choice.

The specific limits of civil rights vary with the times. In time of war, a government may restrict personal freedoms to safeguard the country. Changing social and economic conditions also cause changes in the importance that people give certain rights. During the late

William C. Havard, the contributor of this article, is Chairman of the Department of Government at the University of Massachusetts.

1800's, most people in the United States considered property rights more important than personal freedoms. But during the 1900's, most Americans have shown greater concern for personal freedoms and equality of opportunity.

Civil Rights in the United States

The United States Constitution describes the basic civil rights of American citizens. The first 10 amendments to the Constitution are usually regarded as the U.S. Bill of Rights. However, civil rights are also mentioned in the main body of the Constitution and in later amendments. Each state constitution also has a bill or declaration of rights. Since the mid-1950's, the federal, state, and local governments have passed several civil rights laws. But it has been the courts—especially the Supreme Court—that have probably done the most to define the civil rights of all Americans. When Americans raise questions about the extent and limits of civil rights, they turn to the Supreme Court's decisions for the answers.

For a detailed description of the constitutional rights of Americans, see UNITED STATES CONSTITUTION. For information on the Supreme Court's part in protecting civil rights, see SUPREME COURT OF THE UNITED STATES (Civil Rights and Liberties).

The First Amendment is the basis of the democratic process in the United States. The First Amendment forbids Congress to pass laws restricting freedom of speech, of the press, of peaceful assembly, or of petition. Many people consider freedom of speech the most important freedom and the foundation of all other freedoms. The First Amendment also forbids Congress to pass laws establishing a state religion or prohibiting religious freedom. The Supreme Court has ruled that the 14th Amendment makes the guarantees of the 1st Amendment apply to the state governments as well as to the federal government.

Due Process. Many parts of the Constitution, congressional and state laws, and court decisions protect the rights of persons accused of crime. These protections reflect a basic principle in the American legal system. This principle, called *due process of law*, requires the government to treat people fairly. The 5th and 14th amendments forbid the government from depriving a person of life, liberty, or property "without due process of law."

Various statements in the Constitution guarantee due process. For example, the Constitution forbids the government from suspending the *writ of habeas corpus*. This right protects citizens against arrest and detention without good reason. Neither Congress nor the states may pass *bills of attainder*. Such bills declare a person guilty of a crime and take away his property and civil rights without a trial. The Constitution also prohibits *ex post facto laws*. Such laws make a particular act a crime, and punish even those persons who committed the act before it was a crime.

Due process of law also includes court procedures that protect persons accused of wrongdoing. For example, a person may not be brought to trial for a major federal crime unless a grand jury has first decided that enough evidence exists against him. Persons may not be tried twice for the same crime, and they may not be forced to testify against themselves. A person accused of a crime must be informed of his constitutional rights. He also must be informed of the charges against him. He may demand a jury trial, which must be held soon after the charges are filed. If he cannot afford a lawyer and wants one, the government must provide one.

The person on trial may cross-examine his accusers and may force witnesses to testify. Persons accused of crimes must not be required to pay excessive bail. Those convicted of crimes must not be fined excessively nor made to suffer cruel or unusual punishment.

Other Constitutional Guarantees. The Constitution provides for the security of people and their property. The government may not conduct "unreasonable searches and seizures" of persons or property. It may not take a person's property without due process of law. If the government takes private property for public use, it must pay the owner a fair price.

The Constitution forbids the states to pass laws interfering with contracts made between persons or groups. Each state must recognize the legislative acts, public records, and court decisions of other states. A state must extend its legal protections to the citizen of any other state while he is within its jurisdiction.

Protecting the Rights of Minorities. The United States has many minority groups. These minorities include Negroes, Jews, Orientals, European immigrants, Spanish-speaking Americans, and American Indians. Members of these groups often have not had an equal chance for economic, political, or social advancement. Members of some minority groups have been denied the right to vote. Many persons have been discriminated against in housing, education, and employment, and have been denied equal access to restaurants, hotels, and other public accommodations and facilities. A main civil rights goal has been to eliminate such discrimination and to guarantee equal rights and opportunities for all people.

The Struggle for Negroes' Rights. Negroes, who make up the largest minority group in the United States, have been denied their full civil rights more than any other minority group.

Negro Americans made significant gains in their struggle for equal rights during *Reconstruction*, the 12-year period after the Civil War. The 13th Amendment, adopted in 1865, abolished slavery in the United States. In 1868, the 14th Amendment made the former slaves citizens. The 15th Amendment, which became law in 1870, prohibited the states from denying people the right to vote because of their race. It also provided that the states must grant all persons within their jurisdiction "equal protection of the laws." During Reconstruction, Congress passed several laws to protect Negroes' civil rights. See RECONSTRUCTION.

During the late 1870's, white Americans increasingly disregarded the newly won rights of Negroes. The government itself contributed greatly to denying Negroes their rights. In 1883, the Supreme Court ruled that congressional acts to prevent racial discrimination by private persons were unconstitutional. In 1896, in the case of *Plessy v. Ferguson*, the Supreme Court upheld a Louisiana law requiring separate but equal accommodations for Negroes and whites in railroad cars. For more than 50 years, many Southern states used the "separate but equal" rule established in this case to segregate the races in public schools, and in transportation, recreation, and dining facilities. Many states also used literacy tests, poll taxes, and other means to deprive Negroes of their voting rights.

Since the 1930's, Negroes have had fairer hearings on civil rights cases in the federal courts. The high point came in 1954 in *Brown v. Board of Education of Topeka*. In this case, the Supreme Court ruled that segregation in public schools is unconstitutional. In time, this decision broke down the "separate but equal" principle in all the fields in which it had been used.

In 1957, Congress passed the first federal civil rights law since Reconstruction. The Civil Rights Act of 1957 set up the Commission on Civil Rights to investigate charges of denial of civil rights. It also created the Civil Rights Division in the Department of Justice to enforce federal civil rights laws and regulations.

During the 1960's, Negroes' voting rights received increased protection. The Civil Rights Act of 1960 provided for the appointment of referees to help Negroes register to vote. The 24th Amendment, adopted in 1964, barred poll taxes in federal elections. The Voting Rights Act of 1965 outlawed literacy tests in many Southern states. In 1966, the Supreme Court prohibited poll taxes in state and local elections.

The Civil Rights Act of 1964 was the strongest civil rights bill in U.S. history. It ordered restaurants, hotels, and other businesses that serve the general public to serve all persons without regard to race, color, religion, or national origin. It also barred discrimination by employers and unions, and established the Equal Employment Opportunity Commission to enforce fair employment practices. In addition, the act provided for a cutoff of federal funds from any program or activity that allowed racial discrimination.

The Civil Rights Act of 1968 aimed chiefly at ending discrimination in the sale or rental of housing. Also in 1968, the Supreme Court ruled that a federal law passed in 1866 prohibits racial discrimination in the sale or rental of all housing.

Civil Rights in Canada

The governments of Canada and of the United States apply the same broad principles in dealing with civil rights problems. Generally, Canadian courts have protected individual liberties, and most of the provinces have civil rights laws similar to those in the United States. In 1960, Canada's Parliament passed an act establishing the Canadian Bill of Rights. The bill is similar to the United States Bill of Rights. It guarantees the same basic freedoms and most of the same protections of judicial processes.

As in the United States, the main civil rights problems in Canada involve assuring equal rights for members of minority groups. In the past, Canadian Eskimos and Indians were sometimes denied their full civil rights. French Canadians of the province of Quebec have long struggled against what they consider discrimination by Canada's English-speaking majority. Many French Canadians claim they have been denied jobs in government and industry because they speak French rather than English. The French Canadians fear that if they give up the French language, they will lose their national identity, culture, and customs.

Development of Civil Rights

Natural Law. The idea that people have certain rights that cannot be taken away probably began thousands of years ago with the theory of natural law. This theory states that a natural order exists in the universe because all things are created by nature, or God. Everything has its own qualities and is subject to the rules of nature to achieve its full potential. According to this theory, anything that detracts from man's human qualities, or prevents their full achievement, violates the laws of nature.

The ancient Greek philosophers and the writers of the Old Testament stressed that there is a higher law than man's law. In the first century B.C., the Roman philosopher Cicero insisted that this higher (natural) law is universal and can be discovered through human reason. This idea led to the belief that governmental power has limits, and that men and governments everywhere are bound by natural law.

Some of the most historic English legal documents are based on the principles of natural law. The earliest and most famous was Magna Carta, which the king approved against his will in 1215. The document placed the king himself under the law. In 1628, Parliament drew up a Petition of Right. The petition claimed that certain actions of the king, such as levying taxes without the consent of Parliament, were unconstitutional.

Natural Rights. Natural law had always stressed the duties more than the rights of government and individuals. But during the late 1600's, the natural law tradition began to emphasize natural rights. The change was brought about largely by the writings of the English philosopher John Locke.

Locke argued that governmental authority depends on the people's consent. According to Locke, men originally lived in a state of nature with no restrictions on their freedom. Then they came to realize that confusion would result if each person enforced his own rights. Men agreed to live under a common government, but not to surrender their "rights of nature" to the government. Instead, they expected the government to protect these rights, especially the rights of life, liberty, and property. Locke's ideas of limited government and natural rights became part of the English Bill of Rights (1689), the French Declaration of the Rights of Man (1789), and the United States Bill of Rights (1791).

Today, many scholars reject the natural law and natural rights theories. They believe that all laws—including those guaranteeing civil rights—are simply devices that men find convenient or useful at a particular time. Nevertheless, much of the Western tradition of freedom—and nearly all civil rights laws—have resulted from the theories of natural law and natural rights.

Civil Rights Today. Civil rights have long been protected in the constitutional democracies of Western Europe. These nations include France, Great Britain, Switzerland, and the Scandinavian countries. Personal liberties are also secure in such newer democracies as Australia, New Zealand, Canada, and the United States. Many new nations of Africa and Asia have adopted constitutions that guarantee basic civil rights. But in many of these countries, unstable governments and inexperi-

ence with self-rule have often led to political arrests, censorship, and other denials of civil rights.

Most nondemocratic governments claim to protect civil rights. But in practice, they grant civil rights only when they find it politically convenient to do so. The civil rights tradition is weak in Spain, Portugal, and many Latin-American countries. Most Communist nations have constitutions that guarantee the people basic rights and liberties. However, the governments seldom enforce these rights. The Soviet Constitution, for example, guarantees the people the right to vote and assures them freedom of speech, of the press, and of assembly. But the Communist Party is the only political party allowed in Russia, and the people may be punished if they publicly criticize the party or its leaders. The government controls newspapers, magazines, and other forms of communication.

The United Nations General Assembly adopted a Universal Declaration of Human Rights in 1948. The declaration states that all persons are born free and are equal in dignity and rights. The declaration has been described as an international Magna Carta. Although many experts in international law believe the declaration lacks legal authority, most agree it has high moral authority. WILLIAM C. HAVARD

Related Articles in WORLD BOOK include:

Attainder	Habeas Corpus
Bill of Rights	Human Rights, Universal
Censorship	Declaration of
Citizenship	Jury and Trial by Jury
Constitution	Magna Carta
Declaration of Inde-	Minority Group
pendence	Negro (The Civil Rights
Democracy	Movement)
Due Process of Law	Petition of Right
Ex Post Facto	Privacy, Right of
Fifth Amendment	Rights of Man, Declaration
Freedom	of the
Freedom of Religion	Search Warrant
Freedom of Speech	Segregation
Freedom of the Press	United States Constitution
Government (Individual	Wiretapping
Rights)	

CIVIL SERVICE includes all civilian government employees who are appointed rather than elected. It usually covers only those workers who were hired under the *merit system*. This system provides a means of selecting the best qualified person for each job. It guarantees that he will keep his job on the basis of good performance, and not on allegiance to a political party.

Civil Service in the United States

Federal Employment. The United States government hires and assigns workers in all parts of the country, in the territories and possessions, and in many other lands. Less than 10 of every 100 such employees work in the nation's capital, Washington, D.C.

The federal government is the largest single employer in the country. It has more than 2,680,000 employees working for about 80 different agencies. Nearly half of them work for the Department of Defense, and about one-fourth work for the Post Office Department.

Skilled government artists and engravers design and print maps, books, and currency. Plant and animal experts help improve the quality and nutritional value of foods. Engineers, administrators, and technicians conduct research on road materials, missiles, ceramics, and aeronautical safety devices. Air traffic controllers guide aircraft at all airports. Government agents block counterfeiters and smugglers. Chemists insure the purity of foods and drugs. Practically any occupation may be found in government, and few are unique to it.

Services. Positions not subject to civil-service laws are considered *excepted service*. A few agencies are entirely excepted. For example, the Foreign Service of the Department of State and the Atomic Energy Commission have their own merit-system career programs. All agencies have some excepted positions, including the politically appointed heads of departments and agencies, policy-determining officials, persons hired as temporary or occasional consultants, laborers hired in out-of-the-way places, and seasonal workers. Positions not included in excepted service are in *competitive service*. About 85 of every 100 civil-service workers are included in competitive service.

Examinations. Applicants for federal jobs in the competitive service must take civil-service examinations. Many post offices have information about examinations. Newspapers, radio, and television stations often publicize such information. Government recruiting representatives often visit colleges and universities.

Different kinds of examinations apply to various types of jobs. Some examinations are written. Some are oral. Some include performance tests, such as operating a machine or writing a report. For many occupations, the examiner simply grades applications on education, training, and experience in that occupation.

Appointments. The names of persons who pass, by scoring 70 or better, are placed on a list of eligibles in the order of their grades, plus any points given for veterans' preferences. The government grants extra points to veterans, disabled veterans or their wives, widows of veterans, and dependent mothers of deceased or disabled veterans. When a vacancy occurs, the hiring officer of an agency has the choice of appointing one of the three available persons with the highest grades on the appropriate eligible list.

The government conducts background investigations of the applicant. It inquires into his past record, achievements, reputation, and conduct to determine the person's honesty, integrity, loyalty, and dependability. For example, it checks former employers, and schools.

Civil-Service Jobs. Federal employees belong to a modern, progressive career system. They have promotion and transfer privileges without loss of any civil-service rights. Many workers have career-development and training programs, including opportunities for special job-related courses outside the service. Workers receive generous vacations, and sick-leave allowance that can be accumulated without limit until needed. They have a liberal retirement plan and may buy low-cost life insurance. Retirement may come as early as age 55 with 30 years of service, or as late as age 70.

Federal employment has one important restriction in the matter of political activity. The worker may vote as he chooses, and he is encouraged to exercise his political rights. But he may not be active in party politics. The penalty involves the suspension or dismissal

of the worker (see HATCH POLITICAL ACTIVITY ACTS).

Compensation. The government pays federal workers according to their duties and responsibilities under several different pay plans. Mechanics and laborers have their pay set on the basis of rates prevailing in the locality where they work. Congress sets the pay of postal employees and office and administrative workers. Pay rates established by law cannot be changed except by the amendment of the law. But most statutory pay scales have a number of grades with a series of pay steps or a range for each grade. While remaining in the same grade, a satisfactory employee's pay progresses up the range at intervals until he reaches the maximum rate. He may also be promoted to a job in a higher grade at increased pay if vacancies occur, and if he is among the best who demonstrate their readiness for additional responsibility. Federal employees receive extra pay for overtime work, and allowances if they must travel or buy uniforms for their job.

Evaluation is usually made of the work of the civil-service employee at least once a year. If his performance is not satisfactory, he is dismissed or is assigned to a job that he can learn to do satisfactorily. Superior performance may be rewarded by cash awards or other recognition. Suggestions that benefit the government also receive rewards. But employees whose work or conduct is not satisfactory may be dismissed. The government must take certain procedural steps before such action can be taken against career employees. It also provides the right of appeal for workers.

Management of the federal civil-service rests with the United States Civil Service Commission (see CIVIL SERVICE COMMISSION).

From time to time, Congress passes laws that change or modify the civil-service system. The President of the United States issues rules for carrying out civil-service laws. The commission publishes rules and regulations within this framework that agencies must follow in hiring their employees and operating their personnel programs.

State and Local Civil Service. Many states and cities, and a few counties, have civil-service systems similar to that of the federal government. Since Jan. 1, 1940, employees administering certain federal funds have been placed under a merit system. These funds include federal grants under the Social Security Act and grants for public health, child welfare, public employment, and vocational rehabilitation. As a result, a state may have a limited merit system at the same time its agencies operate under the patronage system. City merit systems have increased in number steadily since the first ones were established in New York state in 1884.

History. The earliest Presidents generally gave first consideration to an individual's qualifications for a job, although they tended to favor their own political supporters. By 1820, it had become fairly common to use government jobs as political rewards. An incoming President would dismiss a large number of government workers and replace them with members of his own party, regardless of their qualifications.

This turnover was based on the idea that "to the victor belong the spoils." The system became known as the *spoils system* (see SPOILS SYSTEM). By 1841, when William Henry Harrison became President, the spoils system had reached great proportions. Into Washington, D.C. swarmed 30,000 to 40,000 office-seekers to claim the 23,700 jobs that then composed the federal service.

Many persons hired through the spoils system had no training for their work and no interest in it. Many were dishonest. In the early days, government work was quite simple. But as the government grew, a serious need for qualified workers developed. The government passed laws in 1853 and 1855 requiring clerk examinations to make sure that new employees would be qualified to do the work. In 1871, Congress gave the President the authority to establish tests for people seeking government jobs. But this merit-system trial ended in 1875, because Congress failed to provide funds to carry it out. The experiment proved the merit system to be both workable and helpful.

Many thoughtful leaders were pressing for a more thorough merit system in the federal, state, and local governments. In 1881, a disappointed office-seeker shot and killed President James A. Garfield (see GARFIELD, JAMES ABRAM). His death brought public demands for civil-service reforms and led to the passage of a bill introduced by Senator George H. Pendleton of Ohio. The bill became the Civil Service Act of 1883. About the same time, New York state and Massachusetts began merit programs.

The new federal law called for examinations open to all citizens. It provided for selection of new workers from among those making the highest grades in these examinations. It made unlawful the firing or demoting of workers for political reasons. It relieved government workers from any obligation to give political service or payments. It established the United States Civil Service Commission to enforce the law.

At first the Civil Service Act covered only about 1 of every 10 federal positions. Later laws and executive orders have placed more jobs under civil service. They have sought to make civil service a true career service, with opportunity for advancement on merit, and with benefits in line with those offered by progressive private employers. For example, the Retirement Act of 1920 set up a pension system for civil service workers. The Classification Act of 1923 provided that all government jobs in the Washington departments be analyzed and classified so that workers would be paid according to the requirements of their jobs. A law passed in 1940 extended the provisions of that act to many positions outside Washington. By the late 1950's, the merit system covered about 90 of every 100 federal workers.

Civil Service in Other Lands

Civil service systems have been established in many other countries. For example, Germany has one of the oldest. It dates from the Prussian system of the late 1700's. The merit system occupies a strong position in the French government. Each local government unit must have its own merit system, or accept the system developed for local administration by the national government. The British Civil Service Commission, established in 1855, administers the government's merit system. Government workers are grouped in four classes: subclerk, clerk, executive, and administrative.

Canada set up its first examining system for government employees in the Civil Service Act of 1908. This law covered most government positions in Ottawa. The

act of 1918 established the competitive examination system and extended the number of positions covered to include most jobs in government service. The Canadian Civil Service has about 150,000 competitive positions, not including mechanics and laborers paid prevailing rates, and those positions in crown corporations. The Canadian Civil Service Commission consists of three members. It classifies all positions so that the same pay is provided for the same level of work throughout the government service. It also determines what positions should be set up in government departments. It examines applicants, and provides an advisory service to departments on operations and methods, and counseling of employees. It administers a system of efficiency ratings and training activities for government executives and other personnel. Its retirement system provides an allowance for government workers who reach age 65 or who serve 35 years. Canada grants preference to veterans with overseas service.   O. GLENN STAHL

See also EMPLOYEES' COMPENSATION, BUREAU OF.

CIVIL SERVICE COMMISSION (CSC) is an independent agency of the federal government of the United States. Congress created this agency in 1883 by passing the Pendleton Act. The main purposes of this law are to have persons selected for nonmilitary governmental jobs on the basis of merit and to give them job security during good behavior. The CSC is made up of three members, appointed by the President with the approval of the Senate. No more than two of the members may belong to the same political party.

Activities. The Civil Service Commission carries on many activities. It provides for tests and examinations of people wanting positions in the competitive service of the federal government. It helps government agencies find the best qualified persons to fill vacancies. The CSC also establishes standards that reinstate, transfer, and promote federal workers. It carries out the provisions of the congressional act of 1944, which grants preference in government service to persons who have had military service.

The Commission groups positions on the basis of duties. It studies, and approves or disapproves, the plans of government agencies for rating the work performance of their employees. It also keeps records of the service of government employees, and enforces restrictions on their political activity.

The CSC manages the retirement program for government workers. It investigates persons entering or employed in the federal service in the interests of national security. Regional offices which have their headquarters in major cities throughout the United States carry out much of the Commission's work.

Publications. The CSC issues many publications. One of the most important for persons interested in federal employment is the announcement of current federal examinations. It lists tests to be given and the titles, salaries, and locations of positions. A copy of this announcement can be obtained from the Commission's main office in Washington. These announcements can also be seen on the bulletin board of any first- or second-class postoffice or at regional offices of the Civil Service Commission.   JOHN C. BOLLENS

CIVIL SUIT. See LAW (Kinds).

CIVIL WAR

United States. It ended the Southern way of life that depended on slave labor in the cotton and tobacco fields. It settled the question of whether a state could secede. And it finally cemented the Union of the states.

More persons are interested in the Civil War than in any other period in United States history. It fascinates people for many reasons. It took place within the United States, and Americans can easily visit the main battlefields. The Civil War was bigger than any American war before it, but it was not too big for the student to follow. But perhaps the most appealing thing is the "human side" of the war—the men who wore the gray uniforms of the Confederacy and the blue uniforms of the Union. They fought and died for what they were sure was right. Historians have written more about the Civil War than about any other period in the American past. The American people have probably read more books about these four years than about all the rest of their history put together.

The Civil War produced many colorful personalities. By far the most outstanding figures were Abraham Lincoln and Robert E. Lee. Lincoln, the 16th President of the United States, supplied the firm but patient leadership that preserved the Union. Lee, a great general, stood off superior numbers for four years and came to stand for the gallantry and devotion of the lost cause. These two men will always rank among the most beloved national heroes. The Union Army had harddriving, cigar-chewing Ulysses S. Grant; Philip H. "Little Phil" Sheridan, the fighting cavalryman; and nervous, excitable William T. Sherman, who summed it all up when he said that "war is hell." The Confederate Army had such leaders as the Bible-quoting, lemonsucking infantry genius, Thomas J. "Stonewall" Jackson; Nathan Bedford Forrest, perhaps the greatest cavalryman of the war; and Pierre Gustave Toutant Beauregard, the romantic Creole general who commanded the Confederate forces that attacked Fort Sumter.

The Civil War was the first modern war because, in a sense, it was the first *total war*. The North used its superior strength to destroy the economic and industrial basis of the Confederacy. In some ways, especially at the beginning, strategy and weapons followed old patterns. But the Civil War introduced methods of warfare seldom used before, such as mines and rifled weapons. It also brought such new techniques as telegraphy, photography, balloon observation, breech-loading and repeating rifles, and trenches and wire entanglements. Railroads played an important part for the first time in a large-scale war. New types of ships proved the value of armored vessels. Volunteer forces no longer furnished

CIVIL WAR took more American lives than any other war in history. It divided the people of the United States, so that in many families brother fought against brother. The four years of bloodshed left a heritage of grief and bitterness that remains in part even today. The Civil War started on Apr. 12, 1861, when Southern artillery shelled Fort Sumter in the harbor of Charleston, S.C. It ended four years later. On Apr. 9, 1865, Confederate General Robert E. Lee surrendered his ragged, exhausted army to General Ulysses S. Grant at Appomattox Court House in Virginia. The other Confederate armies surrendered shortly afterward.

Many persons call this tragic conflict the War Between the States, the War of the Rebellion, the War of the Secession, or the War for Southern Independence. But whatever it is called, the war was a great turning point in American history. It destroyed slavery in the

One of the Greatest Battles in History took place at Gettysburg, Pa., in July, 1863. This section of a cyclorama shows the "high-water mark" of General George E. Pickett's charge. Confederates broke through Union lines at "bloody angle" on the crest of Cemetery Ridge. Strong Union resistance forced the Confederates to retreat after three days of fighting.

Photograph for *Time* by George Strock from the cyclorama painting by Henry Phillippoteaux

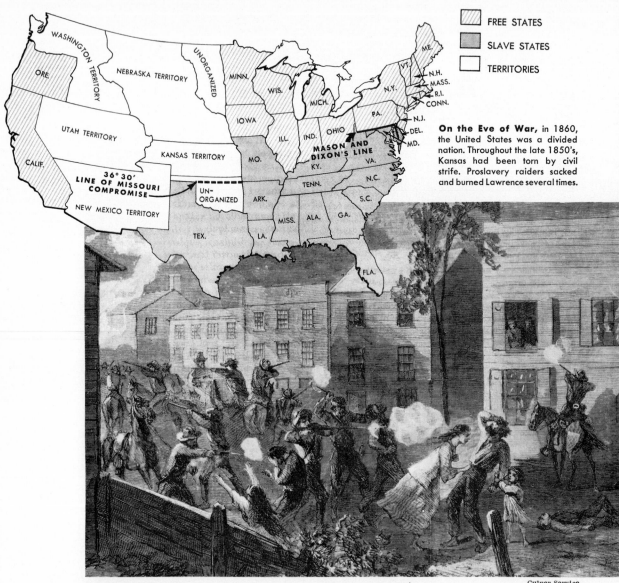

On the Eve of War, in 1860, the United States was a divided nation. Throughout the late 1850's, Kansas had been torn by civil strife. Proslavery raiders sacked and burned Lawrence several times.

Culver Service

enough manpower. The Union and Confederate governments both had to draft men into the armies. The Civil War also showed the importance of warfare that aims at the heart of a country, rather than at its army.

It was a war of total objectives. The North had to force the South back into the Union. The South wanted to force the North to recognize its independence. Neither side could accept a compromise.

Causes of the War

Historians have never reached any general agreement about the causes of the Civil War. Some believe that the slavery issue was the basic cause. Others think that the war resulted from economic rivalry between the industrial North and the agricultural South. Most agree that many factors, not just one, contributed to the situation that finally developed into the Civil War. Certainly slavery was basic to the issue.

"A House Divided"

In 1860 the United States was composed of 18 free states and 15 slave states. Abraham Lincoln called the nation "A house divided . . . half slave and half free." Actually, the United States had three great sections: the Northeast, the South, and the West. The Northeast included the New England states and New York, Pennsylvania, and New Jersey. Beyond lay the growing West (now called the Middle West). The South stretched from Maryland to Texas.

Each section had a different type of economy. Industry and finance dominated the Northeast. The South relied on farming, and produced such crops as cotton, tobacco, and sugar, mainly for export to Europe. The West also had an agricultural economy. But it grew a greater variety of crops than the South did, and sold most of its products to the Northeast.

The class that controlled the main economic activity in each section tended to direct its politics, too. The businessmen of the Northeast and the planters of the South, both powerful minorities, provided leadership for the other classes. In the West, the farmers made up the majority group and dominated politics.

The Northeast and the West had many common interests. They had a natural trade relationship, because the West supplied the Northeast with food, and the Northeast furnished the West with manufactured goods. They also had what could be called a common set of ideals. Broadly speaking, both believed in an expanding economy and in the progressive, democratic ideas of the 1800's. These beliefs set them apart from the more conservative, aristocratic South. The agricultural West came to feel that it had more in common with the industrial Northeast than with the agricultural South.

The South had few cities or towns. Most of its people owned small farms. Some operated large plantations (see PLANTATION). But the feature of the Southern way of life that made it different from the rest of the nation was Negro slavery (see NEGRO [Slavery]). Fewer than 10 of every 100 Southern white men owned slaves. In 1850, when the white population of the slave states stood at 6,000,000, only 347,000 families owned slaves. About half of these families owned fewer than five slaves, although some men owned as many as 500. But even Southerners who did not own slaves favored the system. Southerners defended slavery as a positive good, rather than as a necessary evil. They felt it should be the permanent basis of their society.

"An Irrepressible Conflict"

During the 1850's, there was almost continuous quarreling between sections of the country. Senator William H. Seward of New York, who later became Lincoln's Secretary of State, called the controversy "an irrepressible conflict between opposing and enduring forces."

Each section demanded special national legislation. The Northeast wanted a protective tariff for its industries (see TARIFF [Types]). The West sought free farms for settlers, and federal aid for roads and other improvements. Southerners resisted measures that they felt would strengthen the national government, and opposed many demands of the other sections. The South wanted mainly to be let alone.

All the various sectional demands were mixed up with the slavery issue. Antislavery forces demanded that Congress should keep slavery out of the expanding country's new territories. The Wilmot Proviso, first introduced in Congress in 1846, represented continuous attempts to limit slavery (see WILMOT PROVISO). Southerners replied that slavery could not legally be barred from land that belonged to the whole nation.

Some leaders tried to settle the issue by compromise. Two important measures were the Missouri Compromise and the Compromise of 1850 (see MISSOURI COMPROMISE; COMPROMISE OF 1850). But the organization of new territories usually brought the problem up again.

In 1854, Senator Stephen A. Douglas of Illinois pushed through Congress the Kansas-Nebraska Act, which established two new territories. This measure proposed to settle the slavery question by "popular sovereignty"—that is, by letting the territorial legislatures decide whether the areas should have slavery. The Kansas-Nebraska Act made slavery legally possible in two territories from which it had been barred. See KANSAS-NEBRASKA ACT.

Public opinion in the North ran strongly against the bill. The Whig party broke up over the slavery question. In its place appeared the new Republican party, dedicated to preventing slavery from expanding to the territories. Abraham Lincoln soon joined the new party. In 1858, he and Douglas aroused national interest in a series of famous debates on the slavery question.

In Kansas, meanwhile, opponents and supporters of slavery poured into the new territory and clashed in armed conflict. Much of the violence resulted from the rough frontier spirit. But many Northerners believed that the South wanted to force slavery on "bleeding Kansas."

The Supreme Court entered the situation in 1857 with the Dred Scott decision, a case involving a slave who claimed freedom because he had been taken into territory where slavery was illegal. The court ruled that Congress could not exclude slavery from the territories (see DRED SCOTT DECISION). Southerners rejoiced, but became angry when Republican leaders refused to accept the decision as legally binding.

Several Northern states passed "personal-liberty laws." These acts encouraged people to disobey federal laws providing for the return of fugitive slaves. *Abolitionists*, or persons who wanted to destroy slavery, had attacked the Southern system since 1830. They formed only a small minority, but Southerners felt they were a real danger to the South. Abolitionists organized the "underground railroad," which helped runaway slaves escape (see UNDERGROUND RAILROAD). The most effective abolitionist attack on slavery was the book *Uncle Tom's Cabin*, which appeared in 1852. This novel by Harriet Beecher Stowe sold 300,000 copies within a year. Then, in 1859, a fanatical abolitionist named John Brown led a raid on Harpers Ferry, Va. He planned to seize the federal arsenal and start a slave uprising. Government troops under Col. Robert E. Lee captured Brown, and he was later hanged. But Southerners thought that Northern leaders had encouraged Brown's scheme.

In the presidential election of 1860, the Democratic

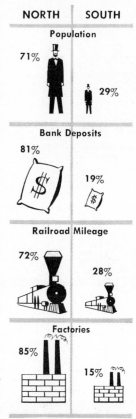

	NORTH	SOUTH
Population	71%	29%
Bank Deposits	81%	19%
Railroad Mileage	72%	28%
Factories	85%	15%

Resources in 1860 favored the North. But the South had the advantage of fighting on its own soil and, in the beginning, better commanders.

HIGHLIGHTS OF THE CIVIL WAR

1861

Apr. 12	Confederate troops attacked Fort Sumter.
Apr. 15	Lincoln issued a call for troops.
Apr. 19	Lincoln proclaimed a blockade of the South.
May 21	Richmond, Va. was chosen as the Confederate capital.
July 21	Northern troops retreated in disorder after the first Battle of Bull Run (Manassas).

1862

Feb. 6	Grant's Northern troops captured Ft. Henry.
Feb. 16	Fort Donelson fell to Union forces.
Mar. 9	The ironclad ships *Monitor* and *Merrimack* battled to a draw.
Apr. 6-7	Both sides suffered heavy losses in the Battle of Shiloh, won by the Union.
Apr. 16	The Confederacy began to draft soldiers.
Apr. 18-29	A Union fleet under Farragut captured New Orleans.
May 4	McClellan's Union troops occupied Yorktown, Va., and advanced on Richmond.
May 30	Northern forces occupied Corinth, Miss.
June 6	Memphis fell to Union armies.
June 25-July 1	Confederate forces under Lee saved Richmond in the Battles of the Seven Days.
Aug. 29-30	Lee and Jackson led Southern troops to victory in the second Battle of Bull Run.
Sept. 17	Confederate forces retreated in defeat after the bloody Battle of Antietam (Sharpsburg).
Sept. 22	Lincoln issued a preliminary Emancipation Proclamation.
Oct. 8	Buell's forces ended Bragg's invasion of Kentucky in the Battle of Perryville.
Dec. 13	Burnside's Union forces received a crushing blow in the Battle of Fredericksburg.
Dec. 31-Jan. 2, 1863	Union troops under Rosecrans forced the Confederates to retreat after the Battle of Murfreesboro (Stones River).

1863

Jan. 1	Lincoln issued the Emancipation Proclamation.
Mar. 3	The North passed a draft law.
May 1-4	Northern troops under Hooker were defeated in the Battle of Chancellorsville.
May 1-19	Grant's army defeated Confederates in Mississippi and began to besiege Vicksburg.
July 1-3	The Battle of Gettysburg ended in a Southern defeat and marked a turning point in the war.
July 4	Vicksburg fell to Northern troops.
July 8	Northern forces occupied Port Hudson, La.
Sept. 19-20	Southern troops under Bragg won the Battle of Chickamauga.
Nov. 19	Lincoln delivered the Gettysburg Address.
Nov. 23-25	Grant and Thomas led Union armies to victory in the Battle of Chattanooga.

1864

Mar. 9	Grant became general in chief of the North.
Apr. 8-9	Federal troops under Banks met defeat in the Red River expedition.
May 5-6	Union and Confederate troops clashed in the Battle of the Wilderness.
May 8-12	Grant and Lee held their positions in the Battle of Spotsylvania Court House.
June 3	The Union suffered heavy losses in the Battle of Cold Harbor.
June 20	Grant's troops laid siege to Petersburg, Va.
July 11-12	Early's Confederate forces almost reached Washington, but retreated after brief fighting.
Aug. 5	Farragut won the Battle of Mobile Bay.
Sept. 2	Northern troops under Sherman entered Atlanta.
Nov. 8	Lincoln was re-elected President.
Nov. 15	Sherman began his march to the sea.
Nov. 16	Hood invaded Tennessee.
Nov. 30	Schofield's Union forces inflicted heavy losses on Hood in the Battle of Franklin.
Dec. 15-16	The Battle of Nashville smashed Hood's army.
Dec. 21	Sherman's troops occupied Savannah, Ga.

1865

Feb. 3	The Hampton Roads Peace Conference failed to end the war.
Feb. 6	Lee became general in chief of the South.
Apr. 2	Confederate troops gave up Petersburg and Richmond.
Apr. 9	Lee surrendered to Grant at Appomattox.
Apr. 14	Lincoln was assassinated.
Apr. 26	Johnston surrendered to Sherman.
May 4	Confederate forces in Alabama and Mississippi surrendered.
May 26	The last Confederate troops surrendered.

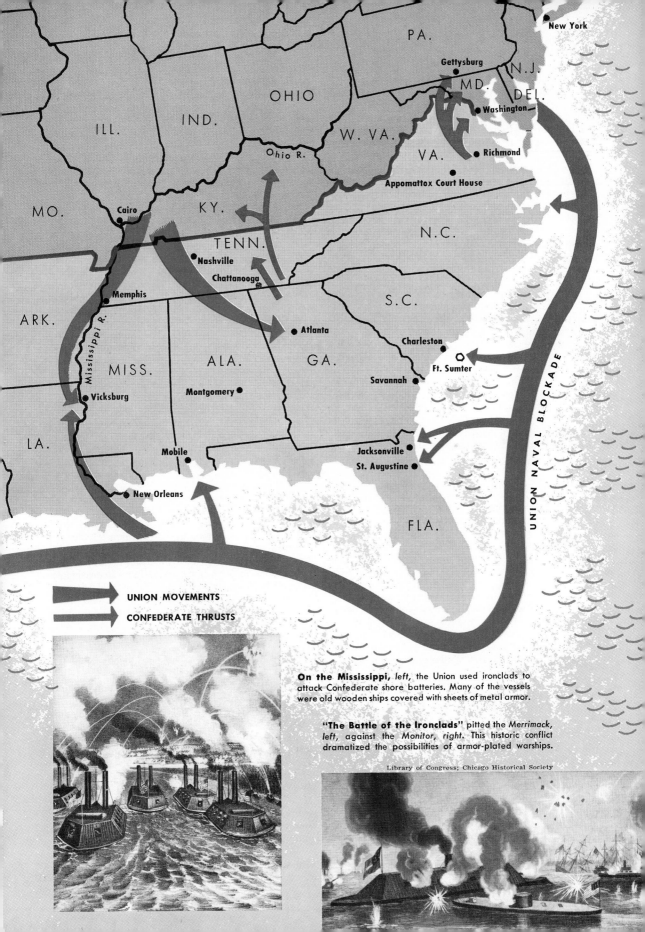

New York

PA.

Gettysburg

MD.

N.J.

DEL.

OHIO

Washington

ILL.

IND.

W. VA.

Ohio R.

VA.

Richmond

MO.

Cairo

KY.

Appomattox Court House

TENN.

N.C.

Nashville

Chattanooga

Memphis

ARK.

S.C.

Mississippi R.

MISS.

ALA.

GA.

Atlanta

Charleston

Ft. Sumter

Savannah

Vicksburg

Montgomery

LA.

Mobile

Jacksonville

St. Augustine

New Orleans

FLA.

UNION NAVAL BLOCKADE

UNION MOVEMENTS

CONFEDERATE THRUSTS

On the Mississippi, *left,* the Union used ironclads to attack Confederate shore batteries. Many of the vessels were old wooden ships covered with sheets of metal armor.

"The Battle of the Ironclads" pitted the *Merrimack, left,* against the *Monitor, right.* This historic conflict dramatized the possibilities of armor-plated warships.

Library of Congress; Chicago Historical Society

party split into Northern and Southern branches. Stephen A. Douglas ran on the Northern ticket, and John C. Breckinridge on the Southern one. Former Whigs formed the Constitutional Union party to urge national unity, and nominated John Bell. The Republicans nominated Abraham Lincoln of Illinois. Their platform went beyond mere opposition to the spread of slavery. They wanted to unite the major economic groups in the North with a program favoring tariffs for manufacturers, free homesteads for farmers and workers, central banking for merchants and financiers, and government-subsidized railways for everyone. Lincoln received only about 40 per cent of the popular vote. But this was more than any of his opponents received. He had a majority of electoral votes, and he became President.

Secession

Before the election, many Southern leaders had urged *secession*, or withdrawal from the Union, if Lincoln should win. Many Southerners favored secession as part of the doctrine of states' rights (see STATES' RIGHTS). Secessionists held that the national government was a league of sovereign states, and that any state had a legal right to withdraw from the Union.

South Carolina had always firmly supported states' rights. It had threatened to secede in 1832 in a crisis involving the national tariff (see NULLIFICATION). In December, 1860, South Carolina adopted the Ordinance of Secession, and became the first state to secede from the Union. By the time Lincoln was inaugurated

in March, 1861, six other states had followed. They were, in order of their withdrawal, Mississippi, Florida, Alabama, Georgia, Louisiana, and Texas. In February, representatives from six of these states met in Montgomery, Ala., and established a Southern nation, the Confederate States of America. They elected Jefferson Davis as President and Alexander Stephens as Vice-President.

Secession led to the proposal of a number of compromise measures. But only the Crittenden Compromise received serious consideration, and it did not have much support from either Republicans or secessionists. See CRITTENDEN COMPROMISE.

In Lincoln's inaugural address, he avoided any threat of immediate force against the South. But he stated that secession was illegal, and that he would hold federal possessions in the South. One of these possessions, Fort Sumter, lay in the harbor of Charleston, S.C. Lincoln sent supplies to Sumter in April, 1861. The Confederates fired on the fort on April 12, and forced the garrison to surrender on April 14 (see FORT SUMTER). On April 15, Lincoln called for troops to enforce the nation's laws. The South regarded this move as the equivalent of a declaration of war. Virginia, Arkansas, North Carolina, and Tennessee promptly joined the Confederacy.

Virginia had long been undecided about which side to join. Its decision to join the Confederacy boosted Southern morale, and Richmond became the capital of the Confederacy in May. The federal government offered Robert E. Lee of Virginia the field command of the United States Army, but he refused. "How can I draw my sword upon Virginia, my native state?" Lee asked when he resigned from the federal army.

Mobilizing for War

How the States Lined Up

Eleven states fought for the Confederacy. From east to west, they were: Virginia, North Carolina, South Carolina, Georgia, Florida, Tennessee, Alabama, Mississippi, Arkansas, Louisiana, and Texas. The 23 Union states stretched from coast to coast. They were, from east to west: Maine, New Hampshire, Vermont, Massachusetts, Rhode Island, Connecticut, New York, New Jersey, Delaware, Maryland, Pennsylvania, Ohio, Michigan, Indiana, Kentucky, Illinois, Wisconsin, Minnesota, Iowa, Missouri, Kansas, Oregon, and California. The territories of Colorado, Dakota, Nebraska, Nevada, New Mexico, Utah, and Washington also fought on the Union side.

Both the Union and the Confederacy included *border states*, or slave states that lay between the North and the Deep South. Some people in these states supported the North, but others believed in the Southern cause. Ironically, the heaviest fighting of the war took place in the border states. Border states on the Southern side were Virginia, North Carolina, Tennessee, and Arkansas. However, Virginians in the western part of the state remained loyal to the Union, and in 1863 formed the new state of West Virginia. Border states that remained in the Union were Delaware, Maryland, Kentucky, and Missouri. But secessionist groups from Kentucky and Missouri set up their own state governments, and even sent representatives to the Confederate Congress.

The terms "the North" and "the South" do not

mean that all the people in these sections agreed among themselves. Many families were torn by divided loyalties, and close relatives often fought each other. Men from every state fought in both armies. George H. Thomas, one of the best Union generals, was born in Virginia. General John C. Pemberton, the Confederate commander at Vicksburg, came from Pennsylvania. One of the most successful Union financial agents in Europe, Robert J. Walker, had once represented Mississippi in the United States Senate. Caleb Huse, a Confederate purchasing agent in Europe, came from Massachusetts. Three of Mrs. Mary Todd Lincoln's brothers died in the service of the Confederacy.

Rallying Round the Flags

About 22,000,000 persons lived in the North, of whom 4,000,000 were men between the ages of 15 and 40. The Confederacy had a population of more than 9,000,000, but this included about 3,500,000 slaves. The South had only about 1,140,000 white men between 15 and 40 to fight under the Stars and Bars, the Confederate flag.

At the beginning of the war, neither government had a plan of mobilization. The Regular Army of the United States at that time consisted of only about 16,000 men, most of whom fought for the North. Both sides tried to raise their armies by appealing to volunteers. This system worked at first. The states, rather than the Union or Confederate governments, recruited most volunteers, and often supplied them. Any man who wanted to organize a company or a regiment could do so. Some units of both sides marched into battle wearing the colorful uniforms of French zouaves. In the North, especially late in the war, volunteers often received a *bounty*, or payment for enlisting. The bounty system encouraged thousands of *bounty jumpers*, who deserted after being paid. Many of these men enlisted several times, often using a different name each time.

The Draft. As the war went on, volunteer enlistments decreased. Both sides then tried drafting soldiers. Southern draft laws, first passed in April, 1862, made all able-bodied men between 18 and 35 (later 17 to 50) liable for three years' service. The Northern program, begun in March, 1863, drafted men between 20 and 45 for three years. Both sides allowed a draftee to pay a substitute to serve for him. In the North, a draftee could pay the government $300 to avoid military service. Many soldiers grumbled that this made it "a rich man's war and a poor man's fight."

The draft proved extremely unpopular in many areas of the North. In New York City in July, 1863, armed mobs set fire to buildings and took over parts of the city before police restored order.

No one knows exactly how many men served in the Civil War. The totals on both sides included many short-term enlistments and "repeaters." According to the best estimates, 1,500,000 men served three-year terms in the Union Army, and 900,000 men served in the Confederate Army for the same period. The Southern army reached peak strength in 1863, then declined sharply. But the Northern armies grew steadily. In the last year of the war, the North had more than 800,000 men in arms. The South probably had no more than 200,000.

Military Leadership. Abraham Lincoln and Jefferson Davis had to choose their commanders on the basis of what they knew about them or what their advisers told them. Sometimes they selected a man because of his reputation, and sometimes for political, rather than military, reasons.

Davis fortunately had Robert E. Lee to take command of the eastern Confederate army, the Army of Northern Virginia. Lee's able officers included Stonewall Jackson and James Longstreet. The Confederate commanders in the West—Albert Sidney Johnston, Pierre G. T. Beauregard, Braxton Bragg, and Joseph E. Johnston—had less ability.

Lincoln tried several commanders for the eastern Union army, the Army of the Potomac: George B. McClellan, Ambrose E. Burnside, Joseph Hooker, and George G. Meade. All had serious weaknesses. Lincoln's western generals—Henry W. Halleck, Don Carlos Buell, and William S. Rosecrans—also failed to meet his expectations. None of his commanders seemed aggressive enough. But, as the war progressed, four great generals emerged from the battlefields to lead the Union armies to victory: Ulysses S. Grant, William T. Sherman, Philip H. Sheridan, and George H. Thomas.

Johnny Reb and Billy Yank

Civil War "G.I.'s" were much like American enlisted men of earlier and later wars. Northern troops called the gray-uniformed Southern soldier *Johnny Reb* (for "rebel"). The Southerners called the blue-uniformed enemy *Billy Yank*, or simply *Yank*. Johnny and Billy

fought well, but they remained civilians, with the civilian's dislike of military rules and regulations. In most regiments, the men all came from the same area. Many units elected their own officers. One soldier wrote: "We . . . had no patience with the red-tape tomfoolery of the regular service . . . a private was ready at the drop of a hat to thrash his commander—a thing that occurred more than once."

"A Soldier Has a Hard Life, and but little consideration," Lee wrote to his wife. Civil War soldiers received more leaves and furloughs than soldiers of previous wars, and had better food and clothing. But, compared to modern standards, Johnny and Billy suffered many hardships. Like all soldiers, they griped about their lot. The pay was poor. Both sides paid their soldiers only $11 a month at first. The pay was later raised to $16 in the North and $18 in the South. Food supplies included flour, corn, pork, and beans. But most army cooks had never cooked before, and many soldiers preferred to prepare their own food. Armies on the march ate salt pork and hard biscuits called *hardtack*, and drank coffee. Poorly made clothing of *shoddy*, or rewoven wool, often fell apart in the first storm. Southern soldiers frequently lacked shoes and had to march and fight barefoot.

Most soldiers on both sides carried Springfield rifles. These muzzle-loading, one-shot guns seem primitive compared with today's weapons. But they had an effective range of 250 yards, twice as long as earlier muskets. However, Civil War infantry still often marched in close-order formation, as in earlier days, and presented an easy target. A determined force in a strong position could withstand almost any frontal assault. The brass muzzle-loading, smoothbore "Napoleon" provided the basic artillery weapon. It could fire a mile, but was most effective at half a mile, and at shorter ranges was murderous on attacking troops. Many Civil War battles proved extremely costly. An army often lost 25 of every 100 men in a major battle. Some regiments at Gettysburg and other battles lost 80 of every 100. Because of heavy casualties, Civil War soldiers devised the first "dog tags." A soldier often lettered his name and address on his handkerchief or a piece of paper and pinned it to his uniform before going into battle.

Hospitals and Prisons. Sanitary conditions during the Civil War were shocking by modern standards. Medical science had not yet discovered the importance of antiseptics in preventing infection, and many thousands of men died from wounds and disease. The government maintained some medical facilities. Dorothea Dix, famous for her earlier work in mental institutions, served as superintendent of women nurses. Private organizations also helped care for ill and wounded soldiers. The United States Sanitary Commission, created in June, 1861, operated hospitals and distributed supplies. It cared for Southern, as well as Northern, men. A similar organization, the Christian Commission, provided welfare assistance. The thousands of volunteer nurses included Clara Barton, who later founded the American Red Cross.

As the war went on, both North and South became burdened with large numbers of prisoners. Earlier systems of exchange broke down because of bad feeling and confusion as to the legal status of the Confederacy.

Civilian Hardships were greater during the Civil War than in any other American war. "The Mother's Sacrifice," above, typifies the sentimentality of the period, and shows a little child leaving his home to be a drummer boy. The people of Charleston, *left*, watched the bombardment of Fort Sumter from their roofs. Many cheered. Others wept at the thought of the coming conflict.

The South especially had difficulty in taking adequate care of prisoners when many of its own civilians and soldiers lacked food and clothing. At Andersonville, in southwestern Georgia, as many as 30,000 Northern prisoners at a time were crowded into a log stockade that enclosed only 16½ acres. More than 12,000 graves bear witness to the frightful conditions there. Other Confederate prisons included Libby and Belle Isle in Richmond. Overcrowding and shortages also existed in Northern prisons, such as those at Rock Island, Ill., Johnson's Island in Lake Erie near Sandusky, Ohio, and Fort Lafayette in New York harbor.

Negroes in the Civil War

Throughout the war, the problem of the Negro perplexed both North and South. Lincoln delayed taking a firm stand on slavery, for fear of antagonizing the slave-owning border states. After the Emancipation Proclamation, a Northern song took note of the new situation. Southern Negroes no longer had to flee to find freedom. Now it was their masters who left to escape from the "Linkum gunboats."

"De massa run? ha, ha!
De darkey stay? ho, ho!
It mus' be now de kingdom comin',
An' de year ob Jubilo!"

But many Negroes found that the war brought suffering and hardship, as well as freedom.

As Union armies drove into Southern territory, large numbers of former slaves flocked to Union camps. Early in the war, General Benjamin F. Butler declared that such slaves were "contraband of war" and should not be given back to their owners. But Northern armies did return many "contrabands," because of difficulties in providing for them.

Others enlisted in the Union Army, which, by the end of the war, had a total of 186,000 Negroes, 93,000 from Confederate states. At first the army discriminated against Negroes, giving them less pay and smaller bounties than white men, and delegating them to labor details. But several Negro regiments, under white commanders, saw action. Southern troops regarded these Negro soldiers as escaped slaves. When Confederates took Negro prisoners, they often executed them to set an example. After a battle at Fort Pillow, Tenn., on Apr. 12, 1864, Confederate forces under General Nathan Bedford Forrest reportedly massacred more than 300 surrendering Negroes.

In the South, the government hired slaves from their masters for war work, or simply *impressed* (seized) them. Many slaves also served the army as cooks and construction workers. Late in the war, the Confederate Congress passed a bill authorizing the enlistment of 200,000 Negroes, who were to receive their freedom at the end of the war. But the war ended before this program could be carried out by the South.

The Home Fronts

In the North

Abraham Lincoln conducted the war with unceasing vigor. He dominated his Cabinet, but one group in his own party, the Radical Republicans, opposed him in Congress. The Radicals wanted to use the war to destroy slavery. Lincoln favored a gradual form of freeing the slaves. The pressures of war helped the Radicals. Northerners grew more bitter against the South and

more hostile to slavery. Lincoln noted the shift in feeling. On Sept. 22, 1862, he announced that, unless the Southern States returned to the Union by Jan. 1, 1863, he would issue an Emancipation Proclamation freeing their slaves (see EMANCIPATION PROCLAMATION). From then on, the North fought to free the slaves as well as to preserve the Union.

Lincoln was the first President to use the vast war powers of his office. He boldly summoned troops to

L. Berman Collection

Brady, Library of Congress

War Correspondents traveled with the armies to report events for those at home. Mathew Brady, the famous photographer, showed the artist A. R. Waud sketching for *Harper's Weekly*.

Recruiting Volunteers was no easy task. Posters advertised the merits of individual companies. This one praises a New York cavalry regiment, which "allowed" men to bring their own horses.

suppress the "rebellion," increased the size of the army, and proclaimed a naval blockade of the South. He was widely criticized for suspending the right of habeas corpus in many areas where people opposed the war. Most of these persons belonged to a group in the Democratic party known as "Peace Democrats." Unionists called them "Copperheads," after a poisonous snake. The Copperheads wanted an immediate armistice and a peaceful settlement of the war. Lincoln had many of them arrested as Southern sympathizers and imprisoned without trial. But freedom of the press continued, and many newspapers and individual citizens still denounced the Lincoln administration.

Expansion. The war plunged the North into a period of booming prosperity. Government purchases for military needs stimulated industry and farming. Expanding industries included iron and steel, woolen clothing, shoes, munitions, railroads, and coal. Farmers vastly increased wheat and wool production. Factories and farms made the first widespread use of laborsaving machines such as the sewing machine and the reaper. The war forced the economy into an early form of mass production. And the nation itself expanded as settlers moved westward.

Popular Feeling. Leading newspapers sent their best correspondents to the field. The Civil War became the first conflict to be completely and immediately reported, even though poor communications systems usually delayed publication of the news for several days. Winslow Homer drew and painted war scenes for *Harper's Weekly* magazine. Photography came into its own through the work of Mathew Brady and others. A flood of popular songs and ballads included "John Brown's Body" (the melody was later used for Julia Ward Howe's "Battle Hymn of the Republic"), "The Battle Cry of Freedom," and "Marching Through Georgia." Some Northern songs, such as "Tenting on the Old Camp Ground" and "When Johnny Comes Marching Home," also became popular in the South.

In the South

Jefferson Davis, President of the Confederacy, did not have Lincoln's vigor and certainty. Lincoln assumed that he had the power to suspend civil law, and did so. Davis asked the Confederate Congress for this power, and received only limited permission. Davis also lacked Lincoln's skill in managing men. For years, Southerners had resisted a powerful central government. Some found it difficult to cooperate with officials of their own government, states, and cities. States' rights supporters backed the war, but opposed conscription and other measures needed to carry it out.

How People Lived. The demands of total war strained the economy of the South almost to the breaking point. The Confederacy lacked the industries to supply its armies and civilians. Imports dwindled as the Northern blockade tightened. Southern troops were never so well equipped as their Northern foes. Northern factories could produce about 5,000 rifles a day, but Southern factories could turn out only 300. The war gradually used up Southern resources. People made clothes out of carpets and curtains, and printed newspapers on the back of wallpaper. Wild inflation set in. Flour sometimes cost $300 a barrel, and shoes $200 a pair.

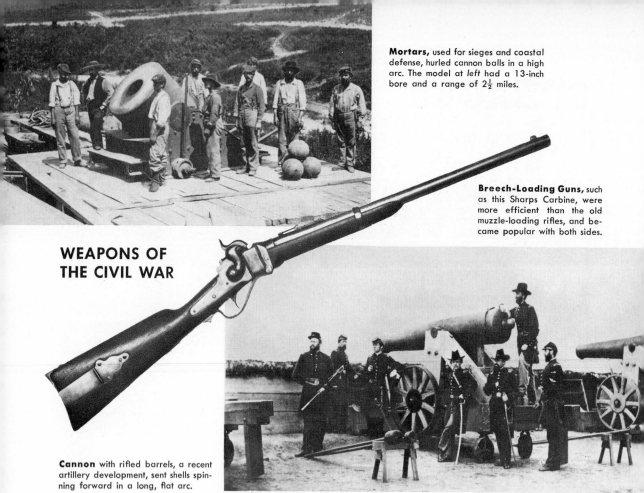

Mortars, used for sieges and coastal defense, hurled cannon balls in a high arc. The model at *left* had a 13-inch bore and a range of $2\frac{1}{2}$ miles.

Breech-Loading Guns, such as this Sharps Carbine, were more efficient than the old muzzle-loading rifles, and became popular with both sides.

WEAPONS OF THE CIVIL WAR

Cannon with rifled barrels, a recent artillery development, sent shells spinning forward in a long, flat arc.

Chicago Historical Society

Shortages of necessities weakened the people's will to fight, but most Southerners vigorously supported the war effort. As in the North, songs showed the spirit of the people. Men marched to war to the stirring music of "Dixie" and "The Bonnie Blue Flag." The mournful notes of "Lorena" and "All Quiet Along the Potomac Tonight" were popular in the North as well.

Cotton Diplomacy. At the beginning of the war, Confederate leaders felt sure that Europe would come to the aid of the South. Southerners believed that, because Great Britain and France depended on Southern cotton for their textile industries, a shortage of cotton would force them to intervene on the Southern side. In 1861, the Confederacy sent two diplomats, James Mason and John Slidell, to Europe to persuade Britain and France

to take up the Southern cause. Mason and Slidell sailed from Havana, Cuba, on a British ship, the *Trent*. The captain of a Northern warship rashly stopped the *Trent* and seized the diplomats. Great Britain threatened war, and the North gave in. See TRENT AFFAIR.

But the South failed to obtain European recognition or any substantial help through its "cotton diplomacy." Britain and France did allow the Confederacy to have six raiders built in their shipyards. The most famous ship, the *Alabama*, caused millions of dollars worth of damage to Northern shipping before the Union ship *Kearsarge* sank it in 1864 (see ALABAMA [ship]). But Britain and France would not intervene in the war unless the South could show that it might win a final victory on the battlefield. And that never happened.

The War in the East, 1861-1864

The Appalachian Mountains divided the Civil War into two main areas of operations. The Eastern front stretched east of the mountains to the Atlantic Coast. The Western theater lay between the mountains and the Mississippi River. A third area, west of the Mississippi, had little strategic importance.

At the beginning of the war, neither North nor South had a prepared plan of strategy. The North had to defeat the South in order to restore the Union, and so its commanders had to plan military offensives. Southern

commanders designed strategy to hurl back Northern thrusts, and seldom launched great offensive campaigns. The Confederacy did not have to conquer the North. It needed only to defend its own territory until the North became weary of the war.

Opening Battles

Fort Sumter. The Civil War began on Apr. 12, 1861, when Confederate forces under General Pierre G. T. Beauregard successfully attacked Fort Sumter in Charles-

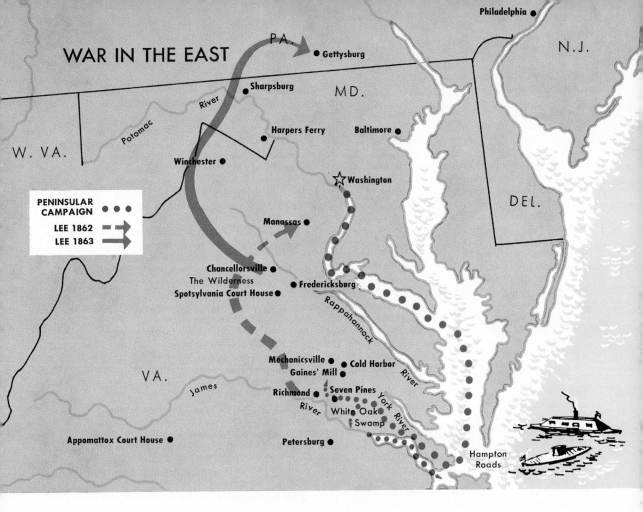

WAR IN THE EAST

PENINSULAR
CAMPAIGN ● ● ●
LEE 1862 ➤ ➤ ➤
LEE 1863 ➤

ton harbor (see FORT SUMTER). The federal government collected an army of more than 30,000 men near Washington, D.C., under General Irvin McDowell. Another Union force of 14,000 under General Robert Patterson held the northern end of the Shenandoah River Valley, a secondary route between the rival capitals of Washington and Richmond. A Confederate force of more than 20,000 under Beauregard faced McDowell at Manassas, Va. General Joseph E. Johnston commanded 11,000 more Confederates in the Shenandoah Valley.

First Bull Run, or Manassas. In July, McDowell approached Manassas, on a creek called Bull Run. (Many Civil War battles have two names because the Confederates named them after the nearest settlement, and Northerners often named them after the nearest body of water.) McDowell thought his troops could destroy Beauregard's forces while the Union Army in the Shenandoah Valley kept Johnston occupied. But Johnston slipped away and joined Beauregard just before the battle. The opposing forces, both composed mainly of poorly trained volunteers, clashed on July 21. The North launched several assaults. During one attack, General Thomas J. Jackson stood his ground so firmly that he received the nickname "Stonewall." After halting several assaults, Beauregard counterattacked. The tired Union forces broke and fled to Washington in wild retreat.

The North realized for the first time that it faced a

long fight. The war would not be over in three months, as many Northerners had confidently predicted. The Southern cause had gained great prestige, and Confederate optimism and confidence ran high.

On to Richmond!

After Bull Run, Lincoln made General George B. McClellan commander of the eastern army, soon to be known as the Army of the Potomac. During the winter of 1861-1862, McClellan assembled a force of 150,000 men. He proved to be a superb trainer of troops. "Little Mac" planned to capture Richmond from the southeast. He wanted to land his forces on the peninsula between the York and James rivers, and advance along one of the rivers toward the Southern capital. Lincoln feared that this scheme would leave Washington open to a Confederate raid, but he let McClellan try it. However, before McClellan could move, a naval action changed his plans.

The Monitor and the Merrimack. The Confederates had raised a sunken federal ship, the Merrimack, at Norfolk, Va., and covered it with iron plates. On Mar. 8, 1862, this ship (renamed the Virginia) attacked Northern ships at Hampton Roads and destroyed two of them. When the ship returned the next day, it found a newly arrived Northern ironclad, the Monitor, waiting. Neither ship won the battle that followed. But the Virginia (Merrimack) did prevent McClellan from using the

483

James River, the best route to Richmond. See MONITOR AND MERRIMACK.

The Peninsular Campaign. In March, 1862, McClellan landed on the Virginia Peninsula with more than 100,000 men. He occupied Yorktown and advanced along the York River. By late May, the Union army had marched to within 6 miles of Richmond. Johnston led an attack against McClellan on May 31. The Confederates failed to follow up their initial success in the two-day Battle of Fair Oaks (or Seven Pines), and fell back toward Richmond. Johnston was wounded, and President Davis chose General Robert E. Lee to replace him.

Jackson's Valley Campaign. The Confederate high command feared that McClellan would receive reinforcements from the numerous troops that had stayed behind to protect Washington. To prevent this, Stonewall Jackson launched his famous Valley Campaign along the Shenandoah Valley. He planned to make the Northerners think he was going to attack Washington. In a series of brilliant moves between May 4 and June 9, Jackson advanced up the Shenandoah Valley. His 17,000 men received the name "foot cavalry" because they marched so fast. They defeated several federal forces and drove to the Potomac River. Jackson soon had to retreat, but he had forced the Union government to withhold powerful reinforcements which McClellan had counted on.

Stuart's Raid. While Lee planned his strategy as the new commander of the Army of Northern Virginia, General J. E. B. Stuart led a remarkable cavalry raid. Jeb Stuart and his men galloped completely around the Union army in three days, losing only one man. Stuart's raid not only gained valuable information about Union troop movements but also boosted Southern morale.

The Seven Days. Lee planned a daring move to destroy McClellan's army, which lay straddled over the Chickahominy River. With his army reinforced by Jackson's men to 85,000, Lee fell on McClellan in a series of attacks called the Battles of the Seven Days. Several battles and skirmishes took place between June 25 and July 1. They included Mechanicsville, or Beaver Dam Creek (June 26), Gaines' Mill (June 27), Savage's Station (June 29), White Oak Swamp and Frayser's Farm, or Glendale (June 30), and Malvern Hill (July 1). The advantage shifted from side to side, but McClellan believed his forces were hopelessly outnumbered and finally retreated to the James River. The Northern high command soon ordered McClellan's army to northern Virginia, to be united with a force under General John Pope. McClellan was to command the combined army.

The South Strikes Back

Second Bull Run. Lee moved rapidly northward to attack Pope, stationed at Manassas, before McClellan's men could join him. Lee sent Jackson ahead to swing around behind Pope's army and force a battle. On August 29, Pope unsuccessfully attacked Jackson, sending in McClellan's troops as fast as they arrived by boat from the south. Meanwhile, Lee and General James Longstreet had arrived and joined Jackson. On August 30, Pope rashly attacked Lee's army, but a Confederate counterattack swept the Union forces from the field. The beaten federal army plodded back to Washington in a heavy rain.

Antietam, or Sharpsburg. The South hoped to gain foreign recognition for the Confederacy by winning a victory in Union territory. Lee invaded Maryland in September, 1862, with about 50,000 troops. This march served as the background for the legend recorded in John Greenleaf Whittier's poem "Barbara Frietchie" (see FRIETCHIE, BARBARA). The Southern commander divided his army and sent Jackson with 25,000 troops to capture Harpers Ferry. McClellan moved to meet Lee with about 90,000 men. On September 13, a Union soldier found a copy of Lee's orders to his commanders wrapped around three cigars at an abandoned Confederate campsite. Lee learned of this loss and took up a position at Sharpsburg, on Antietam Creek. But McClellan did not attack until September 17, giving the Confederate forces time to reunite after Jackson's success at Harpers Ferry. A series of powerful Union attacks almost cracked the Southern lines. But, at a crucial moment, the last of Lee's absent troops, headed by General A. P. Hill, arrived to save the day. Lee suffered heavy losses and had to retreat to Virginia. The Battle of Antietam, one of the bloodiest of the war, killed or wounded about 12,500 Northerners and almost 11,000 Southerners. The Confederate retreat gave the North the victory that Lincoln had waited for. The President announced the preliminary Emancipation Proclamation on September 22.

Fredericksburg. Lincoln lost patience with McClellan because he did not follow up the Union victory at Antietam. The President replaced him with General Ambrose E. Burnside, who decided to attack Lee at Fredericksburg, Va., on the Rappahannock River. The Confederates defended the town from a line of fortified hills called Marye's Heights. On December 13, Burnside's men tried to storm the hills in a brave but hopeless attack. More than 12,000 Union soldiers were killed or wounded, and the Northern army retreated. Burnside was relieved of command at his own request.

Chancellorsville. General Joseph "Fighting Joe" Hooker replaced Burnside as commander of the Army of the Potomac. By the spring of 1863, the army numbered 120,000. Lee, with 60,000 men, still held the Rappahannock line. Hooker planned to keep Lee's attention at Fredericksburg while he sent another force around the town to attack the Confederate flank. The movement began on April 27 and seemed about to succeed. But Hooker hesitated, and on April 30 withdrew his flanking troops to a defensive position at Chancellorsville. The next day, Lee left a small force at Fredericksburg and boldly moved to attack Hooker. He sent Stonewall Jackson to attack Hooker's right while he struck in front. The attack, on May 2, cut the Northern army almost in two, but Union troops managed to set up a defensive line. Hooker retreated four days later. But the Confederate victory cost the life of Jackson, Lee's ablest general, who was shot accidentally by one of his own men. His left arm had to be amputated, and Lee told Jackson's chaplain: " . . . He has lost his left arm, but I have lost my right arm." Jackson, wounded on May 2, died eight days later from pneumonia and the effects of the amputation.

Gettysburg. Lee, confident because of the victory, decided to invade the North again. In June, the Confederate army swung up the Shenandoah Valley route into Pennsylvania. The Army of the Potomac, now commanded by General George G. Meade, followed it northward. Both the enemy armies moved toward the little town of Gettysburg, although neither planned to fight there. Lee did not know exactly where the Union army lay, because his "eyes," Stuart's cavalry, had set out on a raid. The shooting began when a Confederate brigade, searching for badly needed shoes, ran into Union cavalry in Gettysburg on July 1. For the first three days of July, a Northern army of 90,000 men met a Southern army of 75,000 in the greatest battle ever fought in the Western Hemisphere.

On the first day, the two armies maneuvered for position. By the end of the day, Northern troops had settled south of the town in a strong defensive location that resembled an upside-down fishhook. Culp's Hill and Cemetery Hill, at the right, formed the barb of the hook. The front ran for three miles along Cemetery Ridge, and ended at two hills called Little Round Top and Round Top. Confederate forces occupied Seminary Ridge, to the west. On the second day, July 2, Lee tried to crack the Union left and roll up Cemetery Ridge. The attack crushed a Northern corps, but failed to occupy the ridge.

On July 3, Lee decided to aim directly at the Union center. After a fierce artillery duel, he ordered 15,000 men under General George E. Pickett to charge the Union lines. The men, marching in perfect parade formation, swept across an open field and up the slopes of Cemetery Ridge, ignoring the murderous enemy fire. Only a fraction of the troops reached the crest of the ridge. For 20 dreadful minutes they held their ground. Then they yielded to superior strength and fell back. One Confederate soldier summed up the situation: "It ain't so hard to get to that ridge. The hell of it is to stay there." Pickett's charge, often called "the high-water mark of the Confederacy," showed the hopelessness of frontal assaults over open ground against a strong enemy.

Lee withdrew his battered army to Virginia after the battle. Much to Lincoln's disgust, Meade made little effort to follow him, and the Confederate army escaped. Gettysburg proved to be a turning point in the war. Lee had lost more than 20,000 men dead and wounded. Never again would he have the strength to undertake a major offensive.

The War in the West, 1862-1864

In the Western theater of the war, the North struck early and hard in order to seize and control the Mississippi River. Success would split the Confederacy into two parts. The Northern forces totaled 100,000. General Henry W. Halleck commanded in Missouri and western Kentucky. General Don Carlos Buell led Union forces in eastern Kentucky. General Albert Sidney Johnston commanded Confederate forces in Kentucky. His command included an army in Arkansas under General Earl Van Dorn. The Southern forces in this Western region numbered about 70,000.

In the Mississippi Valley

Fort Henry and Fort Donelson. The center of the Confederate line rested on two forts, Henry on the Tennessee River and Donelson on the Cumberland River. If Union forces could capture these forts, the whole Confederate position in Kentucky and western Tennessee would collapse. General Ulysses S. Grant, commanding officer under Halleck in western Kentucky, grasped this fact. He easily captured Fort Henry in February, 1862, with the support of a fleet of ironclad ships. Grant then moved against Fort Donelson. The Confederate commander, General Simon Bolivar Buckner, asked for "the best terms of capitulation." Grant replied: "No terms except an unconditional and immediate surrender can be accepted." Fort Donelson was captured, with nearly 15,000 Confederate troops. The stumpy, silent general gained the nickname of "Unconditional Surrender" Grant, and became a national hero.

Grant's force lay between the two flanks of the Confederate army. To escape destruction, Johnston pulled back all the way to Corinth, Miss., an important railroad center. The Confederacy had now lost Kentucky and half of Tennessee. West of the Mississippi River, on March 6-8, a Union army under General Samuel R. Curtis defeated Van Dorn at Pea Ridge, Ark. This defeat put Missouri solidly in Northern hands.

Shiloh, or Pittsburg Landing. Halleck, now commander of all western Union forces, ordered Grant to move down the Tennessee River, and told Buell to join Grant. Grant and about 42,000 men moved to Pittsburg Landing, Tenn., 30 miles north of Corinth. Johnston and Beauregard decided that they had to strike Grant before Buell arrived. They planned to destroy Grant's forces with an army of 40,000. The Battle of Shiloh (named after a church on the battlefield) took place on April 6 and 7. On the first day, Confederate troops almost smashed Grant, but he managed to hold his lines. Johnston, the Confederate commander, was killed in the battle. The next day, with about 20,000 reinforcements from Buell, Grant forced the Southerners to retreat to Corinth. Many persons urged Lincoln to replace Grant after Shiloh, because of the heavy Union losses, which totaled more than 10,000. But Lincoln refused: "I can't spare this man—he fights!"

After Shiloh, Halleck took command of Grant's and Buell's forces, moved cautiously southward, and forced Beauregard to evacuate Corinth. By early June, the Union held the Mississippi River as far south as Memphis.

New Orleans. In the meantime, Northern forces were moving up the Mississippi from the South. In April, a naval squadron under Captain David G. Farragut appeared at the mouth of the river. Farragut steamed through the weak Confederate defenses, and forced New Orleans to surrender on May 1. Behind him came an army force under General Benjamin F. Butler, to occupy the South's largest city. Northerners held New Orleans and southern Louisiana for the rest of the war.

Raids. Some of the most daring exploits of the Civil War occurred behind the front lines. In April, 1862, a Union spy named James J. Andrews led 21 men

Winter Camp for Union soldiers provided few comforts. The men lived in crude huts and lined up outdoors for their food. Covered wagons, shown in the distance, carried food and supplies to the armies.

AT THE FRONT

Bomb Shelters protected picket posts near Atlanta. This one, built by Confederates, was later occupied by Union forces. The Civil War was the first to make wide use of dugouts and trench systems.

Library of Congress

through the Confederate lines to Marietta, Ga., where they captured a railroad engine, the *General*. They ran it northward toward Chattanooga, Tenn., destroying telegraph communications as they went. But Confederate troops in another engine, the *Texas*, pursued the *General* and caught it after an exciting chase. The Confederacy hanged Andrews and seven of his men.

Two famous Confederate generals, Nathan Bedford Forrest and John Hunt Morgan, led many cavalry raids into Tennessee, Kentucky, Ohio, and neighboring states. Forrest's men galloped as far north as Paducah, Ky., destroying Union supplies and communication lines. "Morgan's Raiders" made an even more spectacular dash into Ohio in July, 1863. They destroyed property worth $500,000 before they were captured at Buffington Island. Morgan escaped in November, but was killed a year later in Tennessee.

Perryville. After Corinth fell to Union forces, Halleck went to Washington to act as Lincoln's military adviser. Before he left, he assigned to Grant, the best Union general yet to appear, the inactive job of guarding communications along the Mississippi River. Halleck ordered Buell, who had yet to prove himself, to capture Chattanooga. Before Buell could advance, General Braxton Bragg, the Confederate commander in Tennessee, suddenly invaded Kentucky. He wanted to draw the Northerners out of Tennessee. Buell raced to meet him, and the two armies met on October 8 in the Battle of Perryville. The result was indecisive, but Bragg retreated to Murfreesboro, Tenn.

Murfreesboro, or Stones River. Lincoln felt that Buell was too cautious, and replaced him with General William S. Rosecrans. Rosecrans advanced south from Nashville toward Bragg's army at Murfreesboro. A hard-fought battle dragged on from Dec. 31, 1862, to Jan. 2, 1863. Bragg retreated after losing 9,000 men. The battle brought into prominence a Union leader who later gained fame—General Philip H. Sheridan.

Vicksburg. In the winter of 1862-1863, Grant proposed to capture Vicksburg, the key city that guarded the Mississippi River between Memphis and New Orleans. At first, Grant tried to take Vicksburg from above, with naval support from Captain David D. Porter. But the ground north of Vicksburg was low and marshy, and the army bogged down. Grant's army tried several times to approach the city. Engineers even tried to dig a canal to divert the waters of the Mississippi so that troops moving down the river could bypass the city.

In April, 1863, Grant launched a new plan. Union gunboats and supply ships slipped past the Confederate batteries in the dead of night, and established a base on the river below the city. The army then marched

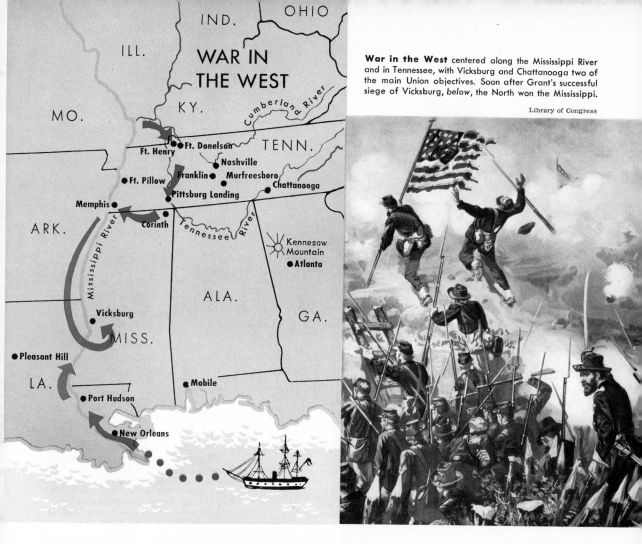

WAR IN THE WEST

War in the West centered along the Mississippi River and in Tennessee, with Vicksburg and Chattanooga two of the main Union objectives. Soon after Grant's successful siege of Vicksburg, *below*, the North won the Mississippi.

down the west side of the river and crossed over by ship to the eastern side. Grant had now reached dry ground below the city. In a brilliant campaign, he scattered Confederate forces in the field and drove toward Vicksburg. After direct attacks failed, Grant started to besiege the city in mid-May. The Confederate garrison held out for six weeks. People hid in caves during the constant bombardment, and ate mule meat. Vicksburg finally surrendered on July 4, the day after the Southern defeat at Gettysburg.

Five days later, Port Hudson, La., fell to Union forces under General Nathaniel P. Banks. The Confederacy had been split into two parts, and the North controlled the Mississippi. As Lincoln put it, "The Father of Waters again goes unvexed to the sea."

The Tennessee Campaign

Chickamauga. In the fall of 1863, Rosecrans advanced on Chattanooga with an army of 55,000 men. Bragg, seeking to keep his army free for action, evacuated the city and withdrew southward into Georgia. Rosecrans pursued him rashly. Bragg had received reinforcements from Virginia, and his forces numbered close to 70,000. He fell on Rosecrans savagely in the Battle of Chickamauga on September 19 and 20. The Northern right flank crumbled and broke completely.

Only the left flank fought on under General George H. Thomas, who earned the nickname of "The Rock of Chickamauga." Rosecrans' entire Union army, badly mauled, eventually had to retreat into Chattanooga.

Chattanooga. Bragg did not follow up his victory immediately. He had lost 17,000 men. He finally advanced and occupied Lookout Mountain, Missionary Ridge, and other heights south of Chattanooga. From these points, Confederate artillery commanded the roads and the Tennessee River, which supplied the city. Starvation threatened the Northern army. But the North had enough manpower available in the West to meet any threat. Grant, now commander of all western forces, replaced Rosecrans with Thomas. Grant then advanced to Chattanooga with part of his own Army of the Tennessee. On November 23-25, the Northerners dealt Bragg a staggering blow in the Battle of Chattanooga. Lookout Mountain and other heights fell on the first two days. On November 25, Thomas' Army of the Cumberland, anxious to redeem its defeat at Chickamauga, swept up Missionary Ridge without orders. The successful charge ended the battle in an hour.

The Union had now won Chattanooga, the second objective of the western army. From this base, Northern armies could move into Georgia and Alabama and split the eastern Confederacy in two.

The Two Great Antagonists of the Civil War have come to symbolize differing concepts of warfare. Lee, *above*, shown after the surrender at Appomattox, conducted superb defensive campaigns that represented the best in conventional tactics. Grant, *left*, fought with the slogging determination, extremely costly in men and materials, that has become characteristic of modern war.

Martin Schmidt; Sketch by A. R. Waud, Library of Congress

Grant and Lee, 1864-1865

All signs pointed to victory for the Union in early 1864. Northern resources seemed endless, while those of the South were fast giving out. Southern armies had dwindled in size because of battle losses, war weariness, and Northern occupation of large areas of the Confederacy. Southern railroads had almost stopped running, and supplies were desperately short. But the South, still capable of tough resistance, battled the North for more than a year before finally surrendering.

This last phase of the Civil War brought Grant into supreme command, and pitted him directly against Lee. In some ways, the final campaigns resembled a duel between the short, stocky Northerner in the shabby blue uniform and the tall, dignified, aristocratic Southerner in the perfectly tailored gray.

"If It Takes All Summer"

Early in 1864, Lincoln promoted Grant to the rank of lieutenant general and gave him command of all Northern armies. This appointment gave the North the advantage of coordinated strategy. Northern armies could now move, as Grant said, "like a team pulling together." Grant planned three main offensives. The Army of the Potomac, commanded by Meade, would try to defeat Lee in northern Virginia and occupy

Richmond. Grant intended to accompany this army and largely direct its movements. An army under General William T. Sherman would advance from Chattanooga into Georgia and seize Atlanta. Banks would move from New Orleans to Montgomery, Ala., and later join Sherman. This third offensive never developed. Banks tried to fight his way up the Red River to capture Shreveport, La. But the Confederates under General Richard Taylor defeated him so badly in the Battle of Pleasant Hill on April 9 that he played no important part in the rest of the war.

The Wilderness. In May, the Army of the Potomac plunged into a desolate area of northern Virginia known as the Wilderness. This vast region of tangled forest and underbrush lay west of Chancellorsville. Grant, with 115,000 men, planned to march through the Wilderness, turn Lee's right flank, and force the Confederates into a decisive battle. Lee, with only 75,000 troops, marched to meet Grant on May 5, and the Battle of the Wilderness raged for two days. Troops stumbled blindly through the forest, where cavalry proved useless and artillery did little better. The underbrush caught fire, and wounded men died screaming in the flames. Both sides lost heavily, but Lee prevented Grant from turning the Confederate flank.

488

Spotsylvania Court House. In spite of heavy losses, Grant refused to turn back. He moved off to his left toward Richmond. Lee marched to meet him, and the great antagonists clashed again at Spotsylvania Court House on May 8-12. Spotsylvania, like the Wilderness, brought bloody losses but no victory for either army. Grant showed a dogged determination to achieve his purpose. He telegraphed to Halleck in Washington: "I propose to fight it out on this line if it takes all summer."

Cold Harbor. Again Grant moved off to his left toward Richmond, and again Lee followed. By June 1, Grant had reached Cold Harbor, a few miles north of the Confederate capital. There, on June 3, he made another attempt to smash Lee. Northern troops charged in a direct frontal assault. Murderous fire cut down 6,000 men in one hour, and stopped the attack.

Cold Harbor forced Grant to change his strategy. Lee had demonstrated superb defensive skill, and Northern losses had reached staggering totals. In a month of fighting, Grant had lost almost 55,000 men. He felt that if he repeated his previous moves, Lee would fall back into the Richmond defenses where the Confederates could withstand a siege. So Grant made one more attempt to force a quick showdown battle.

Petersburg. Concealing his movement temporarily from Lee, Grant marched south and crossed the James River. His men built a pontoon bridge more than 2,000 feet long, one of the longest continuous pontoon bridges ever used in warfare. Then Grant advanced on Petersburg, a railroad center south of Richmond. All the railroads supplying the capital ran through Petersburg. If Grant could seize these roads, he could force Lee to come out and fight in the open. Grant almost succeeded. But a small Confederate force under Beauregard held him off until Lee arrived. Grant then realized that he could not destroy Lee's army without a siege. His men dug miles of trenches around the city. Lee's weary troops did the same. The deadly siege of Petersburg began on June 20 and dragged on for nine long months.

Union troops tried several times to break through the Confederate line. The most unusual attempt, the Battle of the Crater, took place on July 30. Northern engineers had dug a 511-foot tunnel under the Confederate lines, and set off a 4-ton powder charge at the end. The explosion blew a huge crater more than 170 feet long. Northern soldiers poured forward, but milled about helplessly in the deep crater, at the mercy of Southern fire. The Confederates soon beat back the attack, which Grant called a "stupendous failure."

Cavalry Maneuvers. As Grant moved south toward Richmond, he sent his cavalry under Sheridan to attack the city's communications. The Confederate cavalryman Jeb Stuart opposed Sheridan. The forces met in the Battle of Yellow Tavern on May 11, and Stuart was killed.

In June, Lee sent an infantry force under General Jubal A. Early through the Shenandoah Valley to raid Washington. He hoped that Grant would send some of his troops to guard the capital. Early attacked one of the forts on the outskirts of Washington. During the fighting, Lincoln stood on a parapet as bullets spattered around him, the only President ever to be under enemy fire while in office. Early retreated to Virginia, but he remained a threat in the Valley.

Grant put all the Union forces in the Valley under Sheridan's command, and ordered "Little Phil" to follow Early to the death. Sheridan drove the Confederates from the region in a series of smashing victories. His greatest success came at Cedar Creek on October 19, when Early made a surprise attack while Sheridan was returning from a quick conference in Washington. Riding to the field from nearby Winchester, Sheridan rallied his men and won the battle. His exploit became famous in Thomas Read's poem "Sheridan's Ride." But he did not really ride 20 miles, as the poem says, and the Confederate attack had been partly stopped before his arrival.

Mobile Bay. The blockade of Southern ports grew more and more effective. Union forces worked steadily to seize the main ports still open to blockade runners that slipped through the ring of Northern ships. In August, 1864, a naval squadron under Admiral David G. Farragut sailed into the harbor of Mobile, Ala. Farragut was warned that the harbor bristled with mines, which were called torpedoes in those days. "Damn the torpedoes! Full steam ahead!" Farragut bellowed, and drove on. The Northerners did not occupy Mobile, but completely blockaded it. In January, 1865, Wilmington, N.C., fell to Northern ships. But Charleston, S.C., still held out.

Closing In

The Atlanta Campaign. In May, while Grant drove into the Wilderness, Sherman's army of 90,000 advanced on Atlanta, Ga., from Chattanooga. General Joseph E. Johnston opposed him with a force of 60,000. Johnston planned to delay Sherman and draw him away from his base. He did not intend to fight unless his chances for victory were good. The summer of 1864 found the North discouraged and war-weary. The Confederacy hoped to stall for time until the November elections in the North, praying that Lincoln would lose. The Atlanta campaign developed into a gigantic chess game. Sherman moved forward, trying to trap Johnston. Each time, Johnston slipped away. The two armies clashed frequently in small battles. The largest battle occurred at Kennesaw Mountain, on June 27, and resulted in a Union setback.

As Sherman reached the outskirts of Atlanta, President Davis decided that Johnston fought too cautiously, and replaced him with General John B. Hood. The new commander attacked the Union columns as Sherman approached Atlanta. But his attacks failed, and he took up a position in the city. Sherman at first tried siege operations. But he did not want to be delayed too long. So he wheeled part of his army south of the city and seized its only railroad, to cut Hood's supply line. Hood evacuated Atlanta on September 1, and Sherman occupied the city the next day. His victory helped Lincoln win re-election.

North to Nashville. Sherman's victory was not quite so complete as it seemed. His forces had captured Atlanta, an important industrial center and a possible base for another push into the South. But Hood's army began hit-and-run raids on Sherman's railroad communications with Chattanooga. Sherman thought it would be useless to chase Hood along the railroad.

MAJOR BATTLES OF THE CIVIL WAR

This table lists the most important Civil War battles. Accurate casualty figures are almost impossible to obtain, and must usually represent a compromise between several conflicting estimates. Those given below are approximate totals of dead and wounded.

Battle	State	Date	Commanders North	South	Casualties North	South	Results
Antietam (Sharpsburg)	Md.	Sept. 17, 1862	McClellan	Lee	12,500	10,750	Confederate retreat gave Lincoln the occasion to announce the Emancipation Proclamation.
Bull Run (Manassas) First	Va.	July 21, 1861	McDowell	Beauregard	1,500	2,000	The North first realized the seriousness of the war ahead.
Second		Aug. 29-30, 1862	Pope	Lee	10,000	9,000	The South regained almost all of Virginia.
Chancellorsville	Va.	May 1-4, 1863	Hooker	Lee	11,000	10,000	Outnumbered Confederate forces defeated the Union, but Stonewall Jackson was killed.
Chattanooga	Tenn.	Nov. 23-25, 1863	Grant	Bragg	5,500	2,500	Union victory brought most of Tennessee into Northern hands.
Chickamauga	Ga.	Sept. 19-20, 1863	Rosecrans	Bragg	11,500	17,000	Southern victory trapped Rosecrans in Chattanooga.
Cold Harbor	Va.	June 3, 1864	Grant	Lee	6,500	1,500	Heavy losses forced Grant to change his tactics.
Fair Oaks (Seven Pines)	Va.	May 31—June 1, 1862	McClellan	Johnston	4,500	5,500	Confederate forces were driven back toward Richmond.
Fort Donelson	Tenn.	Feb. 16, 1862	Grant	Buckner	2,500	2,000	The North won its first important victory.
Fort Henry	Tenn.	Feb. 6, 1862	Grant	Tilghman	34	16	Initial success encouraged Grant's western campaign.
Franklin	Tenn.	Nov. 30, 1864	Schofield	Hood	1,000	5,500	Hood's Tennessee campaign failed to draw Sherman from Georgia.
Fredericksburg	Va.	Dec. 13, 1862	Burnside	Lee	12,000	5,500	A terrible defeat left the North dispirited.
Gettysburg	Pa.	July 1-3, 1863	Meade	Lee	17,500	22,500	Northern victory marked a turning point in the war.
Kennesaw Mountain	Ga.	June 27, 1864	Sherman	Johnston	2,000	270	In spite of Confederate success, Davis replaced Johnston with Hood.
Mobile Bay	Ala.	Aug. 5, 1864	Farragut	Buchanan	315	32	The North blockaded Mobile.
Murfreesboro (Stones River)	Tenn.	Dec. 31, 1862—Jan. 2, 1863	Rosecrans	Bragg	9,000	9,000	Southern forces failed to follow up an initial victory.
Nashville	Tenn.	Dec. 15-16, 1864	Thomas	Hood	3,000	3,000	Northern victory practically ended Southern resistance in the West.
Perryville	Ky.	Oct. 8, 1862	Buell	Bragg	3,500	3,000	Confederate troops abandoned Kentucky.
Petersburg, Siege of	Va.	June 20, 1864—Apr. 2, 1865	Grant	Lee	17,000	13,000	Months of trench warfare pinned Lee to a static defensive and depleted his forces.
Seven Days	Va.	June 25—July 1, 1862	McClellan	Lee	16,000	20,000	Richmond was saved from capture, and Northern forces retreated.
Shiloh (Pittsburg Landing)	Tenn.	Apr. 6-7, 1862	Grant	Johnston, Beauregard	13,000	10,500	A surprise attack spoiled Grant's plans for quick victory in the West.
Spotsylvania Court House	Va.	May 8-12, 1864	Grant	Lee	10,000	9,000	Southern resistance stiffened Grant's determination to win.
Vicksburg, Siege of	Miss.	May 19—July 4, 1863	Grant	Pemberton	9,000	10,000	Northern victory proved decisive in winning the Mississippi and the West.
The Wilderness	Va.	May 5-6, 1864	Grant	Lee	17,000	11,000	Heavy losses failed to halt Grant's progress southward.

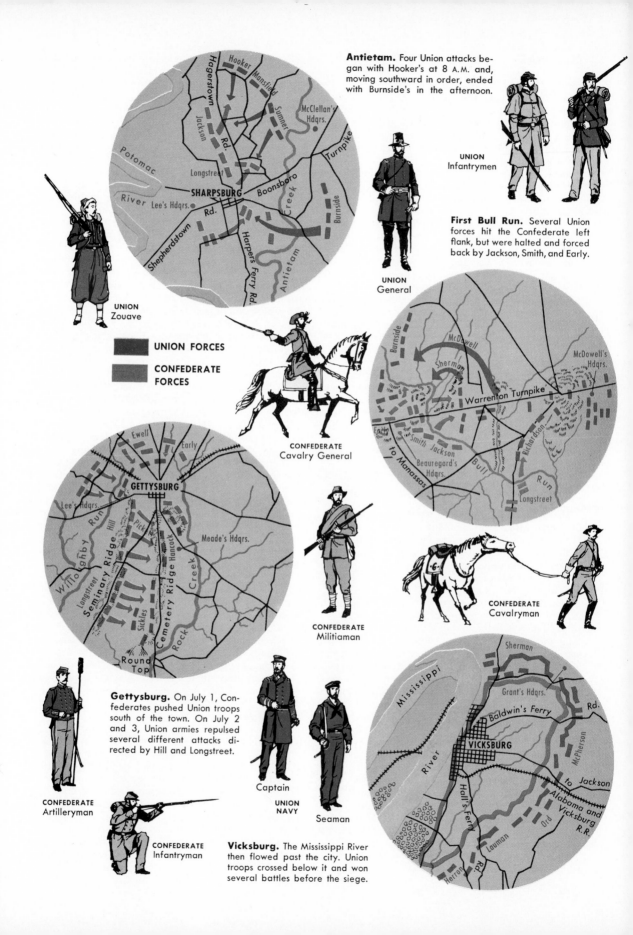

Antietam. Four Union attacks began with Hooker's at 8 A.M. and, moving southward in order, ended with Burnside's in the afternoon.

UNION
Infantrymen

First Bull Run. Several Union forces hit the Confederate left flank, but were halted and forced back by Jackson, Smith, and Early.

UNION
Zouave

UNION
General

UNION FORCES

CONFEDERATE
FORCES

CONFEDERATE
Cavalry General

CONFEDERATE
Militiaman

CONFEDERATE
Cavalryman

Gettysburg. On July 1, Confederates pushed Union troops south of the town. On July 2 and 3, Union armies repulsed several different attacks directed by Hill and Longstreet.

CONFEDERATE
Artilleryman

Captain

UNION
NAVY

Seaman

CONFEDERATE
Infantryman

Vicksburg. The Mississippi River then flowed past the city. Union troops crossed below it and won several battles before the siege.

Instead, he sent Thomas back to Tennessee to take command, and gave him 30,000 men under General John M. Schofield. He ordered Thomas, at Nashville, to assemble more troops in Tennessee and keep Hood out of the state. With his remaining men, Sherman planned to march across Georgia to Savannah, near the Atlantic Coast.

Hood boldly decided to invade Tennessee in the hope that Sherman would follow him. He felt sure that he could beat Sherman in the mountains. Then he would either invade Kentucky or cross into Virginia and join Lee. But Hood's plan was too big for his army.

Franklin. Hood might have scored a partial success if he had moved into Tennessee immediately. But he delayed his advance, and met Schofield's force at Franklin, Tenn., on November 30. Hood, an aggressive commander, had complained that his army had retreated so much under Johnston's command that it had forgotten how to attack. His generals now seemed determined to show him he was wrong. In six headlong charges, the Confederates lost more than 6,000 men, including 11 generals killed or wounded.

Nashville. Hood had no chance of success after his defeat at Franklin. But he took a position south of Nashville and waited. In the city, Thomas had time to gather an army of 60,000. He attacked Hood in the Battle of Nashville on December 15 and 16, and won one of the most smashing victories of the war. On their long retreat to Mississippi, Confederate soldiers sang a bitter song to the tune of "The Yellow Rose of Texas."

> "You may talk about your Beauregard
> And sing of General Lee,
> But the gallant Hood of Texas
> Played hell in Tennessee."

Sherman's March began on November 15, when his troops left Atlanta in flames and set out for Savannah. His 60,000 men brought a new kind of war to the heart of the South as they marched almost unopposed across Georgia. They destroyed civilian property and laid waste to everything that might help the South continue fighting.

Sherman's army swept forward on a 60-mile front. Advance troops scouted an area. The men who followed stripped houses, barns, and fields, and destroyed everything they could not use. Stragglers, known as *bummers*, caused much destruction. They tore up railroad tracks and made fires with the ties. Then they heated the rails until they were red-hot and wound them around trees to make "Sherman hairpins" or "Sherman neckties."

Sherman estimated that his men destroyed $100,000,000 worth of property in Georgia. He hoped this horrible destruction would break the South's will to continue the war.

Sherman occupied Savannah on December 21, and sent a message to Lincoln: ". . . General Sherman makes the American people a Christmas present of the city of Savannah with 150 heavy guns and 25,000 bales of cotton." From Savannah, the army swung into South Carolina, burning and plundering, and then into North Carolina. A small Confederate army under Johnston tried vainly to halt Sherman in his drive northward to Virginia and a link with Grant.

The South Surrenders. In Virginia, Grant at last achieved his goal. In April, 1865, he turned Lee's right flank and seized the railroads supplying Richmond. The Confederate troops had to evacuate Petersburg and Richmond. Lee retreated westward, hoping to join forces with Johnston in North Carolina. But Grant overtook him and barred his way. Representatives of the Union and Confederate governments had tried unsuccessfully to arrange for peace on February 3 (see HAMPTON ROADS CONFERENCE). Lee now realized that continued fighting would mean useless sacrifice of life. He wrote Grant asking for an interview to arrange surrender terms.

On Sunday, April 9, the two great generals met in a farmhouse at the little country settlement of Appomattox Court House, Va. The house belonged to Wilmer McLean, whose former home had been Beauregard's headquarters during the first Battle of Bull Run. McLean had moved south to avoid the fighting.

The meeting of Grant and Lee was one of the most dramatic scenes of American history. Grant wore a mud-spattered private's coat, with only his shoulder straps revealing his rank. Lee had put on a spotless uniform, complete with sword. Grant offered generous terms, and Lee accepted them with deep appreciation. The Confederate soldiers received a full day's rations, and were released on parole. They were allowed to keep their horses, and officers retained their side arms.

When the news of Appomattox reached North Carolina, Johnston surrendered to Sherman on April 26 near Durham. Jefferson Davis fled southward, and was captured in Georgia. News of the collapse of the government spread slowly through the South. General Richard Taylor surrendered the Confederate forces in Alabama and Mississippi on May 4. On May 26, at Shreveport, La., General Edmund Kirby-Smith surrendered the last Confederate army still in the field. The war to preserve the American Union was over.

Results of the War

In terms of human casualties, the Civil War cost more than any other American war. About 1,000,000 men were killed or wounded. Deaths, including those from disease, totaled 622,511. By comparison, about 126,000 Americans died in World War I and 407,000 in World War II. The North lost 364,511 men, the South, 258,000. Disease killed far more men than bullets did. Only 110,000 Union soldiers and 94,000 Confederate troops died on the battlefield.

It is difficult to estimate the financial cost of the Civil War. Direct costs for the four years of fighting totaled more than $3,000,000,000 for the North and over $2,000,000,000 for the South. Indirect costs, such as pensions and interest on the national debt, burdened the nation for years after the war. Other expenses included those borne by state and local governments, the property damages caused by the war, and the value of freed slaves. The total cost for both sides probably exceeded $15,000,000,000.

Some of the costs of the Civil War cannot be reckoned in terms of money. The South suffered the worst damage, because most of the fighting occurred there.

The war destroyed many Southern cities and towns. Farmlands and fine old homes lay in ruins. Railroads were shattered, and industry and trade had almost stopped. The economy of the South had almost completely collapsed. By comparison, the North suffered little physical damage.

Perhaps the most important result of the war was the heritage of hate that it left on both sides. Southerners were the only Americans to be defeated in war and to undergo military occupation. Some Southerners grew bitter in defeat, and some Northerners revengeful.

On Dec. 19, 1959, the last surviving veteran of the Civil War died. He was 117-year-old Walter Williams of Houston, Tex., who had fought in the Confederate Army. The last Union veteran of the war, 109-year-old Albert Woolson of Duluth, Minn., died on Aug. 2, 1956.   T. HARRY WILLIAMS. Critically reviewed by BRUCE CATTON

Related Articles. See the Places to Visit and History sections of the articles for those states which fought in the Civil War, such as VIRGINIA (Places to Visit; History). See also the following articles:

BIOGRAPHIES

NORTHERN MILITARY LEADERS

Burnside, Ambrose E.	Meade, George G.
Butler, Benjamin F.	Porter (David D.)
Dahlgren, John A. B.	Porter, Fitz-John
Farragut, David G.	Rosecrans, William S.
Foote, Andrew H.	Schofield, John M.
Grant, Ulysses S.	Sheridan, Philip H.
Halleck, Henry W.	Sherman (William T.)
Hancock, Winfield S.	Shields, James
Hooker, Joseph	Thomas, George H.
Kearny, Philip	Wallace,"Lew," Lewis
Logan, John A.	Wilkes, Charles
McClellan, George B.	

SOUTHERN MILITARY LEADERS

Beauregard, Pierre G. T.	Johnston, Albert S.
Bragg, Braxton	Johnston, Joseph E.
Breckinridge, John C.	Kirby-Smith, Edmund
Buckner (Simon Bolivar)	Lee, Robert E.
Early, Jubal A.	Longstreet, James
Ewell, Richard S.	Morgan, John H.
Forrest, Nathan B.	Mosby, John S.
Gordon, John Brown	Pickett, George E.
Hampton, Wade	Polk, Leonidas
Hood, John B.	Semmes, Raphael
Jackson, "Stonewall,"	Stuart, James E. B.
Thomas J.	Wheeler, Joseph

OTHER BIOGRAPHIES

Barton, Clara	Mallory, Stephen R.
Beecher (Henry Ward)	Mason and Slidell
Benjamin, Judah P.	Memminger, Christopher G.
Bickerdyke, Mary A. B.	Randolph (George W.)
Boyd, Belle	Reagan, John H.
Brady, Mathew B.	Seddon, James A.
Brown, John	Seward, William H.
Buchanan, James	Stanton, Edwin M.
Chase, Salmon P.	Stephens, Alexander H.
Crane, Stephen	Walker, Leroy P.
Davis, Jefferson	Welles, Gideon
Douglas, Stephen A.	Whitman, Walt
Lincoln, Abraham	

CAUSES AND BACKGROUND

Abolitionist	Kansas-Nebraska Act
Border State	Missouri Compromise
Compromise of 1850	Negro (Changing Status)
Crittenden Compromise	Nullification
Dred Scott Decision	Slavery
Fugitive Slave Law	

Squatter Sovereignty	Underground Railroad
States' Rights	Wilmot Proviso
Uncle Tom's Cabin	

EVENTS

Alabama (ship)	Hampton Roads Conference
Emancipation Proclamation	Harpers Ferry
Fort Sumter	Monitor and Merrimack
Gettysburg, Battle of	Trent Affair
Gettysburg Address	

OTHER RELATED ARTICLES

Balloon (Balloons in War)	Frietchie, Barbara
Battleground National Cemetery	Grand Army of the
Confederate Memorial Day	Republic
Confederate States of America	National Park
Dixie (song)	Petersburg
Flag (Changes in the	(pictures)
United States Flag;	Reconstruction
color pictures)	Sons of Liberty

Outline

I. Causes of the War
 A. "A House Divided"   C. Secession
 B. "An Irrepressible Conflict"
II. Mobilizing for War
 A. How the States   C. Johnny Reb and
  Lined Up   Billy Yank
 B. Rallying Round the Flags D. Negroes in the
           Civil War
III. The Home Fronts
 A. In the North   B. In the South
IV. The War in the East, 1861-1864
 A. Opening Battles   C. The South Strikes Back
 B. On to Richmond!
V. The War in the West, 1862-1864
 A. In the Mississippi B. The Tennessee Campaign
  Valley
VI. Grant and Lee, 1864-1865
 A. "If It Takes All Summer"   B. Closing In
VII. Results of the War

Questions

Why is the Civil War often called the first modern war?

How did the Emancipation Proclamation change the war aims of the North?

Why do many Civil War battles have two names?

How did the North and South compare in population at the beginning of the war?

What were (1) *Bounty jumpers?* (2) *Bummers?* (3) *Copperheads?*

What two important victories did the North win within a day of each other?

Why did the South usually wage defensive, rather than offensive, warfare?

What were the political consequences of the Battle of Antietam? The capture of Atlanta?

Who were by far the outstanding figures of the Civil War?

CIVIL WAR, ENGLISH. See ENGLAND (The Civil War); CHARLES (I) of England; CROMWELL, OLIVER.

CIVIL WAR, SPANISH. See SPAIN (History).

CIVILIAN CONSERVATION CORPS was an agency authorized by the government to hire unemployed young men for public conservation work. The corps was set up as part of the New Deal program in 1933, and formally organized by an act of Congress in 1937. It provided training and employment. The CCC conserved and developed natural resources by such activities as planting trees, building dams, and fighting forest fires. More than 2 million men served in the CCC before Congress abolished it in 1942.   MARGARET WILLIS

CIVILIZATION

CIVILIZATION means a way of life that is advanced enough to include living in cities. The word comes from the Latin *civis*, meaning *citizen of a city*. Primitive people who are not considered *civilized* have camps and villages as their largest communities. People who are civilized usually have a knowledge of writing. Their way of life also usually provides for a division of labor. This means that farmers, herdsmen, and fishermen produce food, while merchants, craftsmen, clerks, soldiers, and others furnish manufactured goods and services. Government, religion, and education are in the hands of kings, priests, judges, teachers, and officials. Most scholars consider that history begins with writing, and thus with civilization. The long period before history began to be recorded is called the *prehistoric* era.

We often refer to individual civilizations, such as Chinese civilization or Western civilization. In this sense, a civilization means the *culture* (way of life) of a certain people (see CULTURE). Any way of life, whether simple or complicated, can be called a culture. But only a complex culture is a civilization.

The Rise of Civilizations

People had much to learn before they became civilized. For about a million years, they got their food by hunting animals and collecting roots, berries, and other products of nature. Such food was often scarce. People had to move about constantly to find enough to eat. Rarely could more than a dozen people live together for more than a few days at a time. Usually they had no extra food to support specialists, and no time to develop skills and trades.

The first advance toward civilization came with the discovery that man could tame animals and grow plants. This discovery made it possible for groups of people to settle in villages as farmers and herdsmen. They began to weave cloth and make pottery in their spare time. They could afford to support a few specialists, because they had extra food. Priests helped reduce the villagers' fears and quarrels by uniting them in the worship of gods. Chiefs learned to keep peace between neighboring villages, and to protect travelers and merchants. Peace and order helped trade develop and encouraged the spread of new ideas.

The second advance came with the discovery of metals (see BRONZE AGE; IRON AGE). Metals gave craftsmen better tools, warriors better weapons, and merchants a useful medium of exchange. As trade and production grew, chiefs became kings. Priests, craftsmen, merchants, tax collectors, and soldiers settled around the royal court. Wealth and trade led to a need for accounting. People invented systems of mathematics and writing. Scribes and teachers became necessary. The courts grew into cities, where groups of specialists, stimulating each other, produced works of art. Science came into being as priests studied the movements of planets and the positions of stars in order to arrange calendars for planting crops.

Some persons have believed that civilizations grow up only in certain climates, or among certain races. Most of the world's great civilizations have risen in temperate climates. But some cultures, such as those of the Khmers in Cambodia and the Maya Indians in Yucatán, developed in wet, tropical regions. Several different races of men have created civilizations.

Cradlelands

The world's oldest civilizations arose independently. Later civilizations grew up mainly because of the spread of earlier civilizations to new areas. Historians generally consider four areas of the Eastern Hemisphere to be *cradlelands*, where the oldest civilizations arose. These regions had distinct advantages over other territories in food supply and in ease of transportation. The four cradlelands were (1) Egypt, (2) the Middle East, (3) the Indus Valley of India, and (4) the Hwang Ho Valley of China.

Egypt. The ancient Egyptians lived on the banks of the Nile River, which had many fishes and waterfowl. They could travel and carry goods up and down the river in boats. They grew wheat and other crops in the rich silt deposited regularly each year by the flooding of the Nile, so they had no fear of variations in rainfall. Villages grouped together in independent districts called *nomes* dotted the riverbanks. In prehistoric times, the nomes were united into two kingdoms, Upper Egypt and Lower Egypt. By the dawn of Egyptian history, about 3000 B.C., they had joined in a single kingdom. Egyptian civilization soon took on individual characteristics, and remained essentially the same for 2,500 years. Great stone temples and pyramids still stand to remind us of the Egyptians' concern with death. The alphabetic part of their hieroglyphic writing helped shape our own alphabet.

The Middle East includes a sickle-shaped area, curving from the Mediterranean seacoast to the Persian Gulf, which used to be extremely fertile (see FERTILE CRESCENT). In the eastern part of this crescent lay Mesopotamia, the land between the Tigris and Euphrates rivers. Here the early Sumerians built up a civilization at about the time that Egyptian civilization arose. They too grew wheat, raised cattle and sheep, and worked metals brought from distant mines. They were organized into separate city-states. The Sumerians built palaces and towering temples of sun-dried brick, because their country had no stone. They developed cuneiform writing, written on clay with pointed sticks. A series of later peoples, including the Akkadians and Babylonians, took over Sumerian civilization and carried it throughout Mesopotamia. It spread more widely than Egyptian civilization, and influenced many others, including Western civilization. From it come our seven-day week and 360-degree circle.

Other Middle Eastern peoples learned much from the Sumerians, and added their own contributions. In the western part of the Fertile Crescent lived the Phoenicians, Aramaeans, and Hebrews. The Hittites established a kingdom in Asia Minor. In later years, the Assyrians and then the Persians united huge areas of the Middle East to form great empires.

Indus Valley. Around 2500 B.C., a people whose name we do not know established a civilization in the valley of the Indus River in what is now West Pakistan. They built cities of fired brick with straight streets and good drains and sewers. They worked bronze and wrote in an alphabet that has not yet been deciphered. Sumerian seals found in the ruins of such cities as Harappa and Mohenjo Daro show that the Indus Val-

Control of fire

Use of metals

Planting of crops

Domestication of animals

SOME IMPORTANT EVENTS IN THE DEVELOPMENT OF CIVILIZATION

Invention of the wheel

Art of writing

Building of fixed dwellings

Organization of government

ley people traded with Mesopotamia. Their civilization came to an end about 1500 B.C., with the invasion of the Aryans, ancestors of the present-day Hindus.

Hwang Ho Valley. Around 1500 B.C., a civilization arose on the banks of the Hwang Ho, a river in north-central China. Archaeologists have excavated a large city of the so-called Shang dynasty near Anyang. The people built palaces of wood, and cast the finest bronze vessels ever made. They also left the oldest Chinese writing yet found. This writing was engraved on scraps of bone used for telling fortunes. The early Hwang Ho culture is the only one of the several cradleland civilizations that has continued to the present day.

Mediterranean Civilizations

The Mediterranean Sea is the world's largest inland body of water. The people living along its shores and on its islands enjoy a mild climate and easy sailing conditions. Their civilization developed from cultural contributions that came from Egypt and Mesopotamia, as well as from the north.

Aegean. The earliest civilization along the Mediterranean, the Aegean, arose about 3000 B.C. The Minoans of Crete built beautiful cities, such as Knossos, with good plumbing and fine wall paintings. Scholars have deciphered some of their writing. The Minoans were good sailors and traders, and spread their goods and civilization throughout the eastern Mediterranean. Aegean civilization on the Greek mainland is often called *Mycenean*, after its capital, Mycenae. Troy, in Asia Minor, had a related culture.

Greek civilization arose from a combination of Aegean civilization and the culture of invaders from the north. It reached its height by the 400's B.C. The Greeks wrote with a true alphabet derived from the Egyptians through the Phoenicians, and produced the world's first works of history and science. Their architecture and sculpture remain unsurpassed. Greek concepts of democracy and justice helped form those of Western civilization.

Roman. The citizens of Rome rose to power in central Italy during the 400's B.C., and gradually extended their empire until they controlled the region from Britain to Syria. The Romans absorbed elements of civilization from the Etruscans, Greeks, Egyptians, and other civilized peoples of antiquity. They blended these elements into a culture of their own. Roman achievements included the construction of paved roads and aqueducts, and the codification of a system of laws still used by many nations. Latin survived for hundreds of years as the speech of learned men, and formed the basis for today's Romance languages. The final collapse of the Roman Empire in A.D. 476 ended the period of ancient civilizations.

An offshoot of Greek and Roman civilization, the Byzantine Empire, preserved classical learning for a thousand years, and spread it to new areas in central and eastern Europe (see BYZANTINE EMPIRE).

Early American Indian Civilizations

Several groups of Indians in North and South America attained a relatively high degree of civilization. They lacked most beasts of burden, and did not use wheels. Neither their cities nor their writing systems developed to a great degree. But they had made much progress before the coming of the white man in the A.D. 1500's ended their civilizations.

Andean. Indians of the Andes Mountains area in South America began developing advanced ways of living about A.D. 400. They grew potatoes, beans, maize, and a local pigweed called *quinoa*. They domesticated the llama and the guinea pig. These peoples also invented bronze without contact with the Eastern Hemisphere, and cast beautiful objects of gold and silver. They wove intricate textiles of cotton, and of llama and alpaca wool. In the 1400's, the Inca united a large region into a single empire. Their stone walls remain among the wonders of the world, because they used single stones weighing many tons that fit closely together without mortar. The Inca also built paved roads and spanned mountain gorges with suspension bridges.

Mayan. Meanwhile, Indians in Guatemala and the lowlands of Yucatán and Honduras developed another American civilization. Maya culture reached its peak in the A.D. 700's. The people built beautiful limestone temples and produced fine paintings, sculpture, and pottery. They invented a calendar system based on the movements of the sun, moon, and planet Venus. The Maya also developed a hieroglyphic writing, and invented the mathematical concepts of zero and the place system.

Mexican. The Valley of Mexico, where Mexico City now stands, was the scene of another great cultural movement. Early peoples, among them the Toltec Indians, grew crops and built stone pyramids. The later Aztec Indians controlled much of central Mexico by the time Hernando Cortes and his men arrived in the early 1500's. The Aztec worked in metal, but also used stone tools. They had an elaborate priesthood, and sacrificed thousands of victims to their gods.

Later Civilizations in Asia and Africa

European invasions brought American Indian civilizations to a sudden end. But such contact did not halt the development of civilizations in Asia and Africa. These cultures had grown too big and had advanced too far in technology to be overthrown.

Chinese civilization has had an uninterrupted growth for more than 4,000 years. The Chinese live by intensive farming, with rice as their main food. They have their own system of ideographic writing. It is hard to learn, because it consists of thousands of characters. But it is easy to write, because each character represents a whole word. The Chinese developed movable type and gunpowder long before Europeans did. Chinese art has given the world beautiful porcelain, silks, jade, and architecture. The civilizations of Japan and Korea drew much of their inspiration from China.

Hindu civilization in India arose from a union of Aryan culture with the earlier Indus Valley civilization. India has often contained many different tribes and nations. Hindu civilization arose to accommodate many of them in a complex structure known as the caste system (see CASTE). Hinduism has a rich religious lore,

and ornate temples devoted to many gods and goddesses. Our numerals and the decimal system come to us from India by way of the Arabs. The Khmer Empire of Cambodia developed a related civilization in the A.D. 800's, and left magnificent temples at Angkor Wat and other sites.

Islamic. About A.D. 570, a prophet named Mohammed was born in Mecca, a city in southwestern Arabia. He combined certain beliefs and teachings of the Jewish and Christian religions with old local beliefs and rites into a new faith called Islam, which recognized a single god, Allah. This strict faith spread quickly. Mohammed's followers moved north to Syria, Egypt, and Iraq, and then westward to Morocco and Spain and eastward to India, eventually reaching Indonesia and the Philippines. They developed a characteristic art by blending elements from many of these cultures (see ISLAMIC ART). Moslems took over the learning of classical Greece and translated into Arabic many works that might otherwise have been lost. The Moslems respected learning, and founded the first universities.

Western Civilization

Our own Western civilization arose in Europe out of many sources. It had its roots in Greek and Roman culture. It also received contributions from Celtic and Germanic peoples. Its religion, Christianity, came from Palestine.

Western civilization falls into several periods. The medieval period, or Middle Ages, followed the breakup of the Roman Empire. During this era, Greco-Roman civilization blended with Celtic and Germanic elements. The Crusades of the 1100's and 1200's introduced Islamic skills and learning. As the way of life grew more complex, a new period, the Renaissance, began in the 1200's. Europeans invented firearms, deepwater ships, and printing. They sailed to all parts of the world in the so-called Age of Exploration. In the 1700's, Europeans and Americans made great progress in science and industry, and introduced the Industrial Revolution. Western civilization in one form or another has since spread throughout most of the world, and has had a strong influence on almost all other cultures.

Theories About Civilization

Philosophers and historians have speculated for hundreds of years about the principles that underlie the rise and fall of civilizations. The philosopher G. W. F. Hegel said that states are individuals that pass the torch of civilization from one to another. During this process, civilization goes through three stages: the rule of a single despot, who alone is free; the rule of a single class, which alone is free; and the rule of all the people, who are all free. Karl Marx held that the transition from the second stage to the third comes about when working people learn discipline and regimentation, and organize themselves for political action.

Oswald Spengler, author of *The Decline of the West*, believed that civilizations are born, ripen, and die like living things. Spengler thought that modern Western civilization is dying, and will be replaced by a new civilization from Asia. Arnold Toynbee stated his challenge-and-response theory in *A Study of History*. He said that civilizations can arise only where the environment is just right to issue a challenge to a people, and when they are just ready to respond to it. According to Toynbee, civilizations collapse when the genius of the creative minority has gone.

Few historians try to measure civilizations on any definite scale to determine which is higher or lower. But we may measure certain aspects, such as the amount of energy used for various projects. If we compare the manpower needed to haul stones for pyramids with the windpower captured by a ship's sails, and in turn with the energy released by atomic fission, we can see that people have progressed steadily from early times to the present. Despite local setbacks, civilization as a whole has grown continuously. CARLETON S. COON

Related Articles. For the story of man before civilization, see PREHISTORIC MAN. For a discussion of how we learn about early civilizations, see ARCHAEOLOGY. For the story of man's civilized progress, see WORLD, HISTORY OF. See also the History section in the articles on the various continents and countries, such as INDIA (History). See also the following articles in WORLD BOOK:

ANCIENT CIVILIZATIONS

See the article on ANCIENT CIVILIZATION. See also:

Aegean Civilization	Egypt, Ancient	Phoenicia
Assyria	Greece, Ancient	Roman Empire
Babylonia	Hittite	Sumer
	Persia, Ancient	

EARLY AMERICAN INDIAN CIVILIZATIONS

Aztec	Maya	Toltec Indians
Inca	Olmec Indians	Zapotec Indians

PERIODS OF WESTERN CIVILIZATION

Exploration and Discovery	Middle Ages
Industrial Revolution	Renaissance

CIVITAN INTERNATIONAL, *SIHV ih tan,* is an association of civic service clubs throughout the United States and Canada that are dedicated to the task of developing better citizenship. Civitan strives to encourage fellowship, increase knowledge, and to render patriotic service to community, state, and nation. The motto of the organization is "Builders of Good Citizenship." Its program includes the care of orphaned and crippled children, aid to mentally retarded children, city improvements, aid to veterans, support of the "Get Out the Vote" campaign, and the control of crime. Civitan has about 35,000 members in more than 1,100 clubs. It also sponsors Civitan clubs at about 400 high schools and 50 colleges. It sponsors about 500 Boy Scout and Girl Scout troops. Chartered in 1920, Civitan has headquarters at 115 N. 21st Street, Birmingham, Ala. 35203. Critically reviewed by CIVITAN INTERNATIONAL

CLAFLIN COLLEGE. See UNIVERSITIES AND COLLEGES (table).

CLAIBORNE, WILLIAM CHARLES COLE. See LOUISIANA (Territorial Days).

CLAIBORNE'S REBELLION was a series of conflicts in the 1630's and 1640's in which William Claiborne, a Virginia fur trader, refused to accept the authority of Leonard Calvert, the governor of Maryland. Claiborne came to Virginia from England in 1621. He explored Chesapeake Bay and became interested in the Indian fur trade. Claiborne went to England and obtained a trading license in 1631. When he returned, he set up a trading post on Kent Island in Chesapeake Bay.

Under a charter issued to the Calvert family in 1632, Kent Island lay within the boundaries of Maryland. Claiborne refused to acknowledge the authority of the Calverts, and war broke out. Claiborne was forced out.

But in 1644, with some Puritan settlers, he drove Calvert out and seized control of the colony. Oliver Cromwell ordered the restoration of the Calvert government in 1657, and Claiborne returned to Virginia. He played a prominent role in the affairs of the Virginia colony until he died in 1677. MARSHALL SMELSER

See also MARYLAND (Colonial Days).

CLAIM, in its general meaning, is a legal demand. It may be one that a person asserts without basis. Or it may be one that he is actually entitled to have satisfied. A claim may involve property, money damages, or any other legal right. In mining law, a claim is a piece of public land that a miner takes up for the purpose of extracting minerals. In patent law, the claim is the part of the patent application in which the applicant points out the improvement that he claims as his invention. See also COURT OF CLAIMS. EDWARD W. CLEARY

CLAIMS, COURT OF. See COURT OF CLAIMS.

CLAIR, RENÉ (1898-   ), is a French motion-picture director. In his early films, he used fantasy to poke fun at everyday life. He gained his first popular acclaim with the comedy *The Italian Straw Hat* (1927). When sound films arrived, Clair began directing musical comedies. His most successful ones include *Under the Roofs of Paris* (1929), *The Million* (1931), and *Give Us Liberty* (1931). Clair won praise for his creative use of sound in these films.

Clair was born in Paris. His real name was RENÉ-LUCIEN CHOMETTE. During World War II, he worked in the United States where he directed the comedy *It Happened Tomorrow* (1944). He returned to France in 1946. His other comic films include *The Ghost Goes West* (1935), *Man About Town* (1947), and *The Grand Maneuver* (1955). In 1960, Clair became the first moviemaker to be elected to the French Academy. HARVEY R. DENEROFF

CLAIRVOYANCE, *klair VOY uns,* is sometimes called *second sight.* It is the power to see or perceive things by methods not known or understood. Clairvoyance has never been scientifically proved, but some scientists have reported evidence of it. See also EXTRASENSORY PERCEPTION; FORTUNETELLING. WILSON D. WALLIS

CLAM is an animal whose soft body is covered with a protective shell. Clams live on the bottoms of oceans, lakes, and streams in many parts of the world. They feed on tiny water plants and animals called *plankton.* Clams have a large organ called a *foot,* which they use

Soft-Shell Clams burrow deeply into the sand. When disturbed, they send out spurts of water and pull in their siphons.

L. W. Brownell

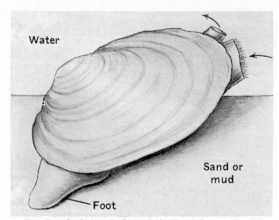

From *Everyday Biology*, by Curtis, Caldwell, and Sherman (Ginn & Co.)

The Clam Gets Its Food from the Water. Food enters by way of a siphon (see arrow). The food particles are taken into the stomach, and the water leaves the clam as shown.

to burrow in mud or sand. Their shell is made up of two parts that are called *valves*. A *ligament* fastens the valves together. The growth lines on the valves show how the shell has enlarged from time to time. The *mantle*, a fleshy part of the body just inside the shell, secretes the shell material. The space between the main body of the clam and the mantle with its shell is called the *mantle cavity*. The clam has gills that hang into the mantle cavity.

Two openings at the back end called *siphons* allow water filled with food and oxygen to pass into the mantle cavity through the *ventral* (lower) siphon, and out again through the *dorsal* (upper) siphon. The clam's blood circulates through the gills, takes oxygen from the water, and gives off carbon dioxide. Tiny hairs on the gills fan the food particles to a small mouth and into the stomach. The food is digested in the stomach and passes into the intestine where most of it is absorbed. The clam has a heart and blood vessels. Other spaces in the clam's body in which the blood circulates are called *sinuses*.

Clams are valuable as food. The Indian name *quahog* is sometimes given to the hard-shell clam. This clam was used as *wampum* (money) by the Indians. It is a salt-water clam and is found in the mud and sand of the waters south of Cape Cod. The meaty Pacific razor clam lives from California to the Aleutian Islands.

Soft-shell clams have a smooth, thin shell. They are found on tidal flats from South Carolina to Greenland. These clams burrow into the sand and have long siphons that extend above the sand into the water. Fishermen take great numbers of these popular food clams from the mud flats of New England.

Giant clams live on the coral reefs in the East Indies and off Australia. Their shells may weigh over 500 pounds and may be up to 4 feet long. They feed on microscopic seaweeds.

Scientific Classification. The hard-shell clam belongs to the family *Veneridae*. The soft-shell clam is in the family *Myacidae*. The giant clam is a member of the family *Tridacnidae*.   R. TUCKER ABBOTT

See also GOEDUCK; MOLLUSK; WAMPUM.

CLAN is a group of persons who are related through one line of descent from a common ancestor. Some clans

are *matrilineal* (related through the female line). Others are *patrilineal* (related through the male line). Members of a clan feel a close relationship to each other, and usually have a strong spirit of unity. They often share property or special privileges. Most clans are *exogamous*. That is, the members must marry outside of the clan (see INDIAN, AMERICAN [Tribal Life]). Clans are often named after a *totem* (a symbolic animal or plant). American Indian tribes had clans such as the Bear clan or Tobacco clan.

The word *clan* also refers to groups of people in early Scotland and Ireland who had common ancestors and a common name, and were organized under the rule of a chief. These clans were *bilateral* (related through both men and women), and marriage within the clan was customary. The Scottish clans began about A.D. 1000. They carried on feuds in the Highlands, and clan members were expected to defend one another. Most clans lost power after the rebellion of 1745, but a spirit of clan loyalty remains among Scotsmen. They are distinguished by their names—such as the MacDonalds, the Campbells, and the MacGregors—and by their *tartans*, the plaids which clansmen wear as emblems of membership (see TARTAN).   FRED EGGAN

CLAREMONT MEN'S COLLEGE. See UNIVERSITIES AND COLLEGES (table).

CLAREMONT UNIVERSITY CENTER. See UNIVERSITIES AND COLLEGES (table).

CLARENDON, EARL OF (1609-1674), played a leading part in restoring the monarchy in England in 1660. Clarendon originally sided with Parliament in its dispute with King Charles I, who tried to keep all political power for himself. But when civil war broke out in 1642, Clarendon joined the *Royalists* (supporters of the king). He insisted that the king represented the entire kingdom, not just a royal group.

Named lord chancellor in 1660, he tried to restore England to, in his words, "its old good manners, its old good humor, and its old good nature." But he was forced into exile in 1667. In exile he wrote the 10-volume *History of the Rebellion*, which defends the Royalist activities during the civil war. Clarendon was born EDWARD HYDE in Dinton, England. He studied at Oxford University.   LACEY BALDWIN SMITH

CLARET. See WINE (Types).

CLARINET, *KLAR uh NET*, is a single-reed wood-wind instrument, usually made of wood but sometimes of metals or other materials. It serves as the leading instru-

The Clarinet can produce full, rich tones over a range of about three octaves.

Bowmar Educational Records

Mouthpiece

Tone Holes

Keys

Bell

ment in military bands, corresponding to the violin in the orchestra. It is also important in the orchestra, and is sometimes used as a solo instrument. It consists of a cylindrical tube with a bell-shaped opening at one end and a mouthpiece at the other. A flat cane reed attached to the mouthpiece vibrates when the player blows on it. This vibration produces a full, rich tone. The tube contains open holes and holes covered by keys. The fingers open and close the holes and operate the keys to produce notes within a range of over three octaves. The Boehm system of fingering is used for modern clarinets. Clarinets are made in six or more sizes. Those most frequently used are the B-flat, A, E-flat alto, and B-flat bass clarinets.   CHARLES B. RIGHTER

CLARION STATE COLLEGE. See UNIVERSITIES AND COLLEGES (table).

CLARK is the family name of two Americans—father and son—who held important government positions.

Tom Campbell Clark (1899-   ), the father, served as an associate justice of the Supreme Court of the United States from 1949 to 1967. He generally voted with the conservative group on the court. Clark became known for the clearness and preciseness of his written opinions on court decisions. He also took an active part in movements to improve the judicial system.

Clark was born in Dallas, Tex. He received A.B. and LL.B. degrees from the University of Texas. He joined the Department of Justice in 1937, and became assistant attorney general of the United States in 1943. President Harry S. Truman appointed Clark attorney general in 1945. He served in that position until 1949, when Truman named him to the Supreme Court.

Ramsey Clark (1927-   ), the son, served as attorney general of the United States from 1967 to 1969, under President Lyndon B. Johnson. He had been assistant attorney general from 1961 to 1965 and deputy attorney general from 1965 to 1967.

Clark was born in Dallas, Tex. His full name is WILLIAM RAMSEY CLARK. Clark received a B.A. degree from the University of Texas, and A.M. and J.D. degrees from the University of Chicago.   H. G. REUSCHLEIN

CLARK, ABRAHAM (1726-1794), was an American political leader during the Revolutionary War, and a New Jersey signer of the Declaration of Independence. He served in the Second Continental Congress, in the Congress of the Confederation, and in the United States Congress. Clark was born in Elizabethtown, N.J. He won the title of *The Poor Man's Counselor* for his defense of poor farmers in land cases.   CLARENCE L. VER STEEG

CLARK, ANN NOLAN (1898-   ), an author of children's books, received the Newbery medal in 1953 for *Secret of the Andes*. She won the Regina medal in 1963. In her work, Mrs. Clark shows an understanding of American Indians. She has taught Indian children and has written texts for them. Her books include *In My Mother's House* (1941), *Looking-for-Something* (1952), and *Santiago* (1955). Mrs. Clark was born in Las Vegas, N.Mex. She was an education specialist for the U.S. Bureau of Indian Affairs from 1930 to 1962.   ELOISE RUE

CLARK, "CHAMP," JAMES BEAUCHAMP (1850-1921), an American politician, became one of the best-known Democratic party leaders of his time. He served 26 years in the U.S. House of Representatives between 1893 and 1921, and was Speaker of the House from 1911 to 1919. Woodrow Wilson narrowly defeated Clark

in 1912 for the Democratic presidential nomination.

Clark was born near Lawrenceburg, Ky. He was graduated from Bethany (W.Va.) College in 1873, and from the Cincinnati Law School in 1875.   NELSON M. BLAKE

CLARK, FRANCIS E. See CHRISTIAN ENDEAVOR.

CLARK, GEORGE ROGERS (1752-1818), an American soldier, won important victories in the Northwest Territory during the Revolutionary War. His victories gave the United States its chief claim to boundaries west to the Mississippi River and north to the Great Lakes in peace negotiations with England.

Clark was born on Nov. 19, 1752, near Charlottesville, Va. When the Revolutionary War started, he was living in Kentucky, then a frontier district of Virginia. He served as a delegate in negotiations that resulted in the organization of Kentucky as a separate Virginia county. When denied military aid, he said that "if a country is not worth protecting, it is not worth claiming." This statement influenced the Virginia Council to send powder to Kentucky before the British and Indians attacked the settlers there.

England hoped to destroy the Kentucky forts and control all the region west of the Allegheny Mountains. The English supplied the Indians with arms to make war on the pioneers. Clark decided to carry the fight into the enemy's territory. With a small band of men, he captured Kaskaskia, Cahokia, and Vincennes, three British supply bases in the Illinois region. Clark could not get financial help to feed and pay his soldiers, so he used his own money. This left him penniless, but his action saved the Northwest Territory. When the peace treaty was signed in 1783, the British surrendered the

Lieutenant Colonel George Rogers Clark led his men on the march toward Vincennes during the Revolutionary War.

Reprinted from a drawing by F. C. Yohn in *The Hero of Vincennes* by Lowell Thomas, through the courtesy of the publisher Houghton Mifflin Co.

region to the United States because it was under Clark's control (see NORTHWEST TERRITORY).

Thomas Jefferson once asked Clark to explore the land beyond the Mississippi River, but Clark refused. In 1803, his younger brother, William, accepted a similar request and became a leader of the Lewis and Clark Expedition (see CLARK, WILLIAM). WILLIAM O. STEELE

CLARK, GEORGIA NEESE (1900-   ), was the first woman to serve as treasurer of the United States. Appointed by President Harry S. Truman in 1949, she served until 1953. She was born in Richland, Kans., and became president of the Richland State Bank (now Capital City State Bank in Topeka) in 1937. She served for many years as a Democratic national committeewoman from Kansas. She was married to Andrew J. Gray in 1953. HOMER E. SOCOLOFSKY

CLARK, JIM (1936-1968), became one of the world's greatest automobile racing drivers. Clark won 25 Grand Prix races. Grand Prix races are road races held in many countries in which points are awarded to the top drivers. Clark won world racing titles in 1963 and 1965 by earning the most points in Grand Prix races. In 1963, he became the youngest driver ever to win the world title. He won seven Grand Prix races that year, and six Grand Prix races in 1965. He won the 1965 Indianapolis 500-mile Memorial Day race.

Clark was born in Fife County, Scotland. He began racing in 1957. He was killed in a race in Hockenheim, West Germany, in April, 1968. HERMAN WEISKOPF

CLARK, JOSEPH SILL (1901-   ), a Pennsylvania Democrat, served in the United States Senate from 1957 to 1969. As mayor of Philadelphia from 1952 to 1956, Clark started an urban renewal program there (see PHILADELPHIA [A New Philadelphia]). In the Senate, Clark became a leader of the liberals. He favored eliminating the filibuster and procedures that slow congressional debate. His book, *Congress: The Sapless Branch* (1964), urged congressional reforms. Clark was born in Philadelphia. SYLVESTER K. STEVENS

CLARK, MARK WAYNE (1896-   ), was one of the top U.S. generals of World War II. Later, during the Korean War, he became United Nations commander in Korea. In 1953, he signed the military armistice agreement that ended the Korean fighting.

Clark was born in Madison Barracks, N.Y. He graduated from the United States Military Academy (West Point) in 1917, and served in Europe during World War I.

In 1942, during World War II, Clark secretly went ashore in North Africa to obtain the aid of the French for the Allied invasion. From 1943 to 1944, Clark commanded the U.S. Fifth Army in Italy. As commander of all Allied forces in Italy, he freed the final third of that country. In 1945, Clark became commander in chief of the U.S. forces stationed in Austria, and U.S. High Commissioner for Austria. Clark later served as commander of the Sixth Army. In 1952, he succeeded General Matthew B. Ridgway as United Nations commander in Korea and as commander of U.S. Armed Forces in the Far East.

Clark retired from the army in 1953. He wrote two accounts of his war experiences, *Calculated Risk* (1950) and *From the Danube to the Yalu* (1954). In 1954, he became president of The Citadel, a South Carolina military college. MAURICE MATLOFF

CLARK, WILLIAM (1770-1838), was an American soldier and explorer. He and Meriwether Lewis led an expedition that explored from the Louisiana Territory to the Pacific Coast from 1804 to 1806. The group started up the Missouri River in May, 1804. By boat, on horseback, and on foot, the men pushed north and west until they reached the Pacific Ocean. On the return trip Clark explored the Yellowstone River to its mouth.

Before this expedition, Clark served in several campaigns against the Indians. In 1792, he became a lieutenant in the regular army and served under General Anthony Wayne. Clark resigned from the army in 1796, but joined it again in 1803 to go west with Lewis. His military experience and his enthusiasm were of great value to the expedition. He recruited and trained men for the hazardous trip. He mapped routes covered by the expedition and made sketches of the animal life along the way. Clark also assembled records of the journey and helped prepare them for publication.

Clark was born in Caroline County, Virginia. His brother was George Rogers Clark, a Revolutionary War hero. In 1807, William Clark became superintendent of Indian affairs at St. Louis, and in 1813 he became governor of the Missouri Territory. WILLIAM P. BRANDON

See also CLARK, GEORGE ROGERS; LEWIS, MERIWETHER; LEWIS AND CLARK EXPEDITION; SACAGAWEA.

CLARK, WILLIAM A. See MONTANA (Statehood).

CLARK COLLEGE. See UNIVERSITIES AND COLLEGES (table).

CLARK SCHOOL FOR THE DEAF. See BANCROFT, GEORGE.

CLARK UNIVERSITY. See UNIVERSITIES AND COLLEGES (table).

CLARKE, JAMES PAUL (1854-1916), served as a United States senator from Arkansas from 1903 to 1916. He won recognition as an independent Democrat, and served as president *pro tempore* of the Senate in 1913. Clarke advocated strict railroad regulation, and independence for the Philippines.

Clarke was born in Yazoo City, Miss., and was graduated from the University of Virginia. He held several state offices, and served as governor of Arkansas from 1895 to 1897. A statue of Clarke represents Arkansas in the U.S. Capitol in Washington, D.C. NELSON M. BLAKE

CLARKE COLLEGE. See UNIVERSITIES AND COLLEGES (table).

CLARKSBURG, W.Va. (pop. 28,112; alt. 1,035 ft.), is an industrial city, and a shipping center for a region of coal mines and oil and gas fields. The city lies at the meeting point of the West Fork of the Monongahela River and Elk Creek, in north-central West Virginia. For location, see WEST VIRGINIA (political map).

Factories and mills in Clarksburg manufacture glass and clay products, chemicals, precision instruments, clothing, and lumber, paper, metal, and food products. Clarksburg was settled in 1773, and is the seat of Harrison County. The city has a council-manager form of government. F. P. SUMMERS

CLARKSON COLLEGE OF TECHNOLOGY. See UNIVERSITIES AND COLLEGES (table).

CLASS, in biology. See CLASSIFICATION.

CLASSIC CAR. See AUTOMOBILE (The Classic Car [with pictures]).

CLASSICAL POETRY. See POETRY (The Three Traditions).

CLASSICISM is a philosophy of art and life that emphasizes order, balance, and simplicity. The ancient Greeks were the first great classicists. Later, the Romans, French, English, and others produced classical movements. Each group developed its own unique characteristics, but all reflected certain common ideals of art, man, and the world.

The Qualities of Classicism

Classicism contrasts with the philosophy of art and life called *romanticism*. Classicism stresses reason and analysis, while romanticism stresses the use of the imagination and the emotions. Classicism seeks what is universally true, good, and beautiful. Romanticism seeks the exceptional and the unconventional. Classical art reflects the artist's attempt to live in harmony with society. Many romantics are rebels. Classical artists follow formal rules of composition more closely than romantic artists. See ROMANTICISM.

Classicists know that reality is complex. However, they try to approach it through simple structures. For example, the classical playwright concentrates on essentials by following the formal unities of time, place, and action. This means he restricts his play to a single line of action that could happen within one day, in one place or in nearby places.

In the 1600's, the French artists Nicolas Poussin and Claude painted pictures illustrating the finest qualities of classical art. Both painters carefully balanced their compositions. Many of their pictures have a poetic mood, but the organization of the subject matter is always restrained and orderly. These qualities can be seen in Claude's *Seaport: The Embarkation of the Queen of Sheba* and Poussin's *St. John on Patmos*. Both are reproduced in color in the PAINTING article. The works of the Italian composer Giovanni Palestrina in the 1500's show the classical qualities of balance and clarity.

Great Classical Movements

A classical movement develops when a spirit of order and refinement joins with a previously developed spirit of intense thought, action, and passion. The most important classical movements in western culture developed in Greece and Rome during ancient times, and in Western Europe during the 1600's and 1700's.

Greece. The first classical period in the West arose in ancient Greece, and reached its height in the 400's and 300's B.C. The Greeks praised reason and denounced emotionalism, excess, and exaggeration. They tried to see all reality within a unified system that gave it meaning and direction. Greek artists showed beauty on a human rather than a supernatural scale. The sculptures of Phidias and Praxiteles are magnificent examples of proportioned human figures. Aeschylus, Sophocles, and Euripides wrote tragedies that show the value of moderation and the danger of excessive pride. See GREEK LITERATURE; GREECE, ANCIENT (The Arts).

Rome. Roman classicism developed in two stages—the age of Cicero from 80 B.C. to 27 B.C., and the age of Augustus from 27 B.C. to A.D. 14. The Romans adopted the Greek classical values, and added a unique emphasis on civilization as an organized, cooperative undertaking. Under the influence of the statesman and orator Cicero, civic responsibility gained a new importance. There was a new concern for the family, the role of

Ewing Galloway

The Influence of Classicism is reflected in the design of the Church of the Madeleine in Paris. Built in the style of a Roman temple, the Church of the Madeleine was begun about 1806 and was completed about 35 years later.

women, and the well-being of the state. Rome's literature reached its highest achievement during the reign of Augustus Caesar. Almost all writers were classicists. The classical poet Virgil wrote works intended in part to reform public morality and thinking. During the Augustan age, the romantic poet Catullus was the only important artist deeply concerned with the feelings of the individual. See LATIN LITERATURE.

France. The French classical movement of the 1600's developed the most diverse expression of classical values ever seen in the western world. French classicists placed especially strong emphasis on reason and the intellect in analyzing ideas and human actions. The most important persons in the intellectual and literary history of the period include the mathematician-philosophers Blaise Pascal and René Descartes, the moralist writer Duc de La Rochefoucauld; the writer of fables Jean de La Fontaine; and the dramatists Pierre Corneille and Jean Racine. See FRENCH LITERATURE (The 1600's—The Classical Age).

England. The English classical period followed French classicism. It arose in the late 1600's and reached its height during the first half of the 1700's. The English called their movement *neoclassicism*, modeling it on the classicism of France, Greece, and Rome. For a more detailed discussion of English classicism, see ENGLISH LITERATURE (The Classical Age [1660-1798]).

Germany. In Germany and in German-speaking Austria, music rather than literature best expressed classical ideals. Ludwig van Beethoven, Joseph Haydn, and Wolfgang Amadeus Mozart rank among the great classical composers (see MUSIC [The Later 1700's]). In the late 1700's in Germany, a classical literature flourished side by side with romantic literature. Gotthold Lessing was the outstanding classical writer. HOWARD LEE NOSTRAND

CLASSIFICATION

CLASSIFICATION is the arrangement of objects, ideas, or information into groups. The members of each group have one or more characteristics in common. They may be the same size, shape, or color. They may come from the same place, have the same ancestors, or be classified according to their use. Classification makes things easy to find, and helps in the study of objects or information.

Most of the things we use daily are grouped in some kind of classification. We separate garden tools from work tools, and glassware from pots and pans. Supermarkets keep dairy products in one place, canned goods in another, and fresh meats in still another. Telephone directories list businesses in classified sections.

Scientific Classification is a method scientists have developed to arrange all animals and plants in related groups. It is the orderly arrangement of all living things. It indicates certain relationships among animal groups and among plant groups. Detailed classifications also show how ancient and extinct animals and plants fit into this arrangement. The classification of animals

and plants is a science called *taxonomy* or *systematics*.

Scientific classification is an interpretation of facts. It is based on the opinion and judgment a biologist forms after studying specimens of animals and plants. Most biologists use the same basic framework for classification, but not all biologists agree on how

---

Richard G. Van Gelder, the contributor of this article, is Associate Curator and Chairman of the Mammalogy Department of the American Museum of Natural History.

---

individual animals and plants fit into this scheme. Because biologists differ, classifications often differ in details.

The Language of Classification. Latin and Greek words are used in scientific classification, because early scholars used these languages. Every known animal and plant has a Latin or Greek name that has two parts. We call this the *binomial system of nomenclature*, or *binomial nomenclature*. These are Latin terms that mean *two-name naming*. The two names identify an animal or

HOW ANIMALS AND PLANTS ARE CLASSIFIED

The illustrated tables, *below*, are simplified examples of classification. They show how an Eastern red squirrel (*Tamiasciurus hudsonicus*) and a common buttercup (*Ranunculus acris*) can be separated from any other species of animal or plant. As you go down the tables, from kingdom to species, the animals and plants in each group have more and more features in common. The captions at each level enumerate these features. Individuals in a species have so many similar features that they look alike.

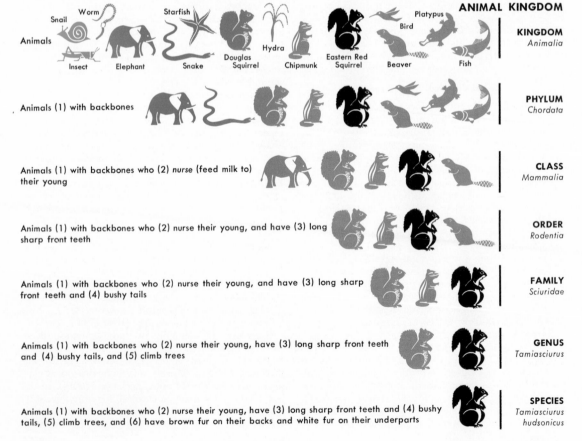

a plant in much the same way that your first and last names identify you.

Animals or plants are known by different common names in different regions. But each has only one correct scientific name, and scientists anywhere in the world can recognize an animal or plant by its scientific name. For example, the same large member of the cat family may be known in various parts of North and South America as a puma, cougar, mountain lion, panther, or león. The cat's scientific name is *Felis concolor*. A scientist can identify the animal by that name no matter what language he speaks.

An international commission of scientists establishes the rules for adopting scientific names. Some scientific names are descriptive. The scientific name of the spotted skunk, for example, is *Spilogale putorius*, which means *smelly, spotted weasel*. But many scientific names have no descriptive meaning.

Groups in Classification. Seven chief groups make up a system in scientific classification. The groups are: (1) kingdom, (2) phylum, (3) class, (4) order, (5) family, (6) genus, and (7) species. The kingdom is the largest group, and the species is the smallest. Every known animal and plant has a particular place in each group.

Kingdom contains the most kinds of animals or plants. All animals belong to the animal kingdom, *Animalia*.

All plants are members of the plant kingdom, *Plantae*.

However, some living things so small that they can be seen only under a microscope seem to have some of the characteristics of animals and some of plants. So some scientists classify them in a special kingdom called *Protista*. Other scientists separate them into two kingdoms: the *Protista* or protists, and the *Monera* or monerans. In this classification, the monerans include bacteria and blue-green algae, which are sometimes considered plants. The protists are one-celled creatures, some of which are other kinds of algae, and others are protozoans, which are sometimes considered animals.

Phylum is the second largest group. The animal kingdom may be divided into 20 or more phyla. All animals with backbones belong to the phylum *Chordata*. In the plant kingdom, the phyla are sometimes called *divisions*. All plants that bear seeds belong to the phylum *Spermatophyta*.

Class members have more characteristics in common than do members of a phylum. For example, mammals, reptiles, and birds all belong to the phylum *Chordata*. But each belongs to a different class. Apes, bears, and mice are in the class *Mammalia*. Mammals have hair on their bodies and feed milk to their young. Reptiles, including lizards, snakes, and turtles, make up the class *Reptilia*. Scales cover the bodies of all reptiles, and none of them feed milk to their young. Birds make up the

PLANT KINGDOM

KINGDOM
Plantae

Fern   Mushroom   Plants

Cattail   Larkspur   Sunflower   Buttercup   Pine   Alga   Crowfoot   Magnolia   Cedar   Moss

PHYLUM
Spermatophyta

Plants (1) that reproduce from *ovules*, which develop into seeds when fertilized

CLASS
Angiospermae

Plants (1) that reproduce from ovules that are (2) enclosed in an ovary, a structure that protects the fertilized ovules as they develop into seeds

ORDER
Ranales

Plants (1) that reproduce from ovules that are (2) enclosed in an ovary, and with (3) *floral parts* (petals, sepals, stamens) that grow from beneath the ovary

FAMILY
Ranunculaceae

Plants (1) that reproduce from ovules that are (2) enclosed in an ovary, with (3) floral parts growing from beneath the ovary, and with (4) many spirally arranged stamens

GENUS
Ranunculus

Plants (1) that reproduce from ovules that are (2) enclosed in an ovary, and that have (3) floral parts growing from beneath the ovary, (4) many spirally arranged stamens, and (5) all petals exactly alike

SPECIES
Ranunculus acris

Plants (1) that reproduce from ovules that are (2) enclosed in an ovary, and that have (3) floral parts growing from beneath the ovary, (4) many spirally arranged stamens, (5) petals alike, and (6) yellow flowers

502a

class *Aves*. Feathers grow on their bodies, and they do not feed milk to their young.

Order consists of groups that are more alike than those in a class. In the class *Mammalia*, all the animals produce milk for their young. Dogs, moles, raccoons, and shrews are all mammals. But dogs and raccoons eat flesh, and are grouped together in the order *Carnivora*, with other flesh-eating animals. Moles and shrews eat insects, and are classified in the order *Insectivora*, with other insect-eating animals.

Family is made up of groups that are even more alike than those in the order. For example, wolves and cats are both in the order *Carnivora*. But wolves are in the family *Canidae*. All members of this family have long snouts and bushy tails. Cats belong in the family *Felidae*. Members of this family have short snouts and short-haired tails.

Genus members are very similar, but they usually cannot breed with one another. Both the coyote and timber wolf are in the genus *Canis*. But coyotes breed only with other coyotes, and timber wolves breed only with other timber wolves.

Species is the basic unit of scientific classification. Members of a species have many common characteristics, but they differ from all other forms of life in one or more ways. Members of a species can breed with one another and the young look like the parents. No two species in a genus have the same scientific name. The coyote is *Canis latrans*, and the timber wolf is *Canis lupus*. Sometimes groups within a species differ enough from other groups in the species that they are called *subspecies* or *varieties*.

Development of Classification. For thousands of years man has tried to classify animals and plants. Early man divided all living things into two groups: (1) useful, and (2) harmful. As man began to recognize more kinds of living things, he developed new ways to classify them. One of the most useful was suggested by the Greek philosopher and naturalist Aristotle (384-322 B.C.). Only about a thousand animals and plants were known in his time. He classified the animals as those with red blood (animals with backbones) and those with no red blood (animals without backbones). He divided the plants by size and appearance as herbs, shrubs, or trees. Aristotle's scheme served as the basis for classification for almost 2,000 years.

The English biologist John Ray (1627-1705) first suggested the idea of species in classification. But the basic design for modern classification began with the work of the Swedish naturalist Carolus Linnaeus (1707-1778). Linnaeus separated animals and plants according to their *structure* (arrangement of parts), and gave distinctive names to each species. Biologists still rearrange classification, but today, our classification method is based on the principles that Linnaeus established.   RICHARD G. VAN GELDER

Related Articles in WORLD BOOK include:

CLAUDE (1600-1682), a French painter, became a founder of the European landscape tradition. His paintings of the Roman countryside, with golden light slanting across fields, captured the visual imagination of European landscape painters for almost 150 years.

Claude often sketched outdoors from sunrise to sunset, watching the effects of changing light on the landscape. But he painted his canvases in his studio, organizing trees, streams, mountains, and fields into carefully planned artificial scenes. The human figures appearing in the foregrounds were probably painted by others. Claude confined himself to a rather narrow range of greens, blues, and golden browns. But he used these colors so skillfully that the effect of late afternoon light is instantly suggested. His painting, *Seaport: The Embarkation of the Queen of Sheba*, appears in color in the PAINTING article.

Claude was born at Chamagne, France, in the province of Lorraine. His real name was CLAUDE GELLÉE, but he took the name of his province and is sometimes called CLAUDE LORRAIN. Claude was orphaned as a child and wandered through Europe for several years. In 1627, he settled in Rome. He lived and painted there until his death.   JOSEPH C. SLOANE

CLAUDEL, PAUL (1868-1955), became one of the foremost French poets and playwrights in the 1900's. His writings are examples of the Catholic revival in French art and literature. He expressed his deep religious faith in such poems as *Cinq Grandes Odes* (1910) and in his plays, of which the most famous is *Tidings Brought to Mary* (1912). Claudel also had a long diplomatic career as a consul and ambassador in China, Japan, Germany, Italy, and the United States. Claudel was born in France.   WALLACE FOWLIE

CLAUDIUS (10 B.C.-A.D. 54) was the emperor of Rome from A.D. 41 to 54. Claudius was an excellent ruler. He formed a civil service system that placed specialized bureaus, headed by secretaries, in charge of the various branches of government. He built aqueducts, drained marshes, and made a harbor at Ostia, a town near Rome. Claudius conquered parts of England, and the Balkan Peninsula (then called Thrace). He also granted citizenship to certain persons in Rome's provinces.

Claudius was born in Lugdunum (now Lyon), France. His full name was TIBERIUS CLAUDIUS NERO. Lame and a stutterer, Claudius was kept from public view in his youth. He spent his time studying and writing histories of Etruria and Carthage. Claudius married several times. When he married his niece Agrippina the Younger, he adopted her son Nero. Some historians believe Agrippina murdered Claudius so that Nero could become emperor (see NERO).   MARY FRANCIS GYLES

CLAUSE is a group of words with a subject and a predicate. A clause may or may not be a sentence. A clause that is a sentence is called a *main clause*, or *independent clause*. A clause that forms part of a sentence is called a *dependent*, or *subordinate*, *clause*. In linguistic science, *clause* is sometimes defined as an utterance occurring with certain intonation patterns.   PAUL ROBERTS

See also SENTENCE (Forms of Sentences).

CLAUSEWITZ, *KLOW zuh vits*, **KARL VON** (1780-1831), a Prussian military author, wrote *On War*, one of the most important books on military matters. He was the first to make a complete study of all aspects of warfare. He stressed the importance of political, social, and personal factors, as well as strategy, tactics, and training. His military ideal was total destruction of the enemy. Clausewitz was born in Burg, Prussia, the son of a Prussian military officer. He began his military career when he was 12. In 1818, he became director of the General War Academy.   ROBERT G. L. WAITE

CLAUSIUS, *KLOW zih oos,* **RUDOLF JULIUS EMMANUEL** (1822-1888), a German physicist, helped establish thermodynamics as a science. In 1850, he stated the second law of thermodynamics: "Heat cannot of itself pass from a colder to a hotter body" (see THERMODYNAMICS). He derived an equation that relates the saturated vapor pressure of a liquid to the temperature. He also developed a theory to explain electrolysis (see ELECTROLYSIS). Clausius was born in Köslin, Germany (now Koszalin, Poland).   R. T. ELLICKSON

CLAUSTROPHOBIA. See PHOBIA.

CLAVICHORD, *KLAV ih cord,* was a keyboard instrument which was an ancestor of the piano. The soft metallic tone of the clavichord was produced by means of metal pins which struck the strings when the keys were pressed. It was popular from about the 1500's to the 1700's. See also HARPSICHORD; PIANO; DULCIMER.

CLAVICLE. See COLLARBONE.

CLAVILUX, *KLAV ih lucks,* is an instrument used to project patterns of light and color in rhythmic order on a screen. The motion and combination of forms are supposed to resemble the phrases and themes of music. Thomas Wilfrid invented the clavilux, also called *color organ,* in 1922. The composer Alexander Scriabin had used a *lightclavier,* a similar instrument, to accompany the music in his *Prometheus, the Poem of Fire* (1909-1910). See also WILFRID, THOMAS.   KARL GEIRINGER

CLAW. See ANIMAL (Ways of Life).

CLAY is the kind of earth made up of extremely fine particles. Typical clay feels smooth and a little oily. When wet it becomes a sticky, yet slippery, mud. Dry clay does not hold together well and is easy to turn to powder or dust. The minerals that make up ordinary clay are mostly hydrous silicates of aluminum. A few clays contain little aluminous material or none at all. The purest clay, called kaolin, is white. Most clay is colored by other materials. Iron oxide may color it red; carbonaceous matter may color it different shades of gray; and other materials may give it still other colors. A large amount of calcium carbonate is present in the clay called *marl,* while much silica is present in *fire clay.*

Kinds of Clay. Clays are of two sorts—residual and sedimentary. *Residual clays* result when rocks wear down and crumble in a process called weathering. The best rock for this clay is the kind with considerable aluminous minerals. Residual clay is found in layers if the rock from which it was formed was that way. Clay that comes in *strata* (layers) is called *stratified. Sedimentary clays,* the second kind, may originally have been formed the same way as the residual clays. Then the wind or water carried the clay particles to another place.

Uses for Clay. The clay in the soil is important for agriculture. It absorbs ammonia and other gases necessary for the growth of plants. It also holds in the soil the fertilizing substances supplied by manures. Without a certain amount of clay, soil will not keep its fertility from season to season. Too much clay makes the soil stiff and cold, holds too much water on the surface, and hardens it too much in time of drought.

Moist clay can be molded into any form, rolled into thin sheets, or drawn into rods and twisted into ornamental shapes. When clay is heated to the proper temperature, it shrinks and hardens. It no longer turns to mud when wet, or crumbles when exposed to the weather. In this form it finds a great many uses, such as building brick for houses and other durable structures.

Different clays have different names and uses depending on their composition. Pure *kaolin* is used to make the finest porcelain. *Potter's clay* and *pipe clay* are less pure than kaolin. They are used for inexpensive pottery and pipes. *Fire clay,* which can stand high temperatures, serves for stove and furnace linings, firebrick, gas retorts, and crucibles. *Paper clay* is a fine variety which is used to give paper a smooth shiny surface.   A. PABST

Related Articles in WORLD BOOK include:

Adobe	Fuller's Earth	Pottery
Alumina	Kaolin	Silica
Bentonite	Loam	Soil
Brick and Bricklaying	Marl	Terra Cotta
Feldspar	Porcelain	Tile

SOME USES OF CLAY

Structural Clay Products Institute
Hollow Clay Tile weighs less than brick. In building construction, it may be used by itself or with brick.

Clay Bricks form attractive building walls. Bricklayers arrange the bricks in designs called *bonds* for strength.

Kaolin Clay is used in fine china porcelain. Called *china clay,* it is pure white. Thin china dishes allow light to shine through without being transparent.

Pickard, Inc.

CLAY, CASSIUS (1942-   ), or MUHAMMAD ALI, became world heavyweight boxing champion in 1964. He was stripped of the title by boxing groups in 1967 after he refused to report for U.S. Army service. Clay won the title from Sonny Liston on a technical knockout in Miami Beach, Fla. Clay won all of his 28 professional fights, including nine title defenses. Clay frequently bragged about his speedy footwork and fast punches and made fun of his opponents.

CASSIUS MARCELLUS CLAY was born in Louisville, Ky. He became a professional boxer after winning the light-heavyweight title at the 1960 Olympic Games. In 1964, Clay joined the Black Muslims, a group that urges creation of a separate all-Negro state in America, and changed his name to Muhammad Ali. He refused to serve in the Army on grounds that he was a conscientious objector.   HERMAN WEISKOPF

CLAY, CASSIUS MARCELLUS (1810-1903), was an American politician and abolitionist. He was the son of a slaveholder, but he learned to despise slavery and preached against it. In 1845, he founded an antislavery newspaper, *True American*, in Lexington, Ky. After moving to Louisville, he called it the *Examiner*. His views on slavery and his fiery nature earned him a reputation as a rebel and a brawler. He carried two loaded pistols and a bowie knife because of threats on his life, and he guarded his newspaper office and his home with a cannon.

Clay was born in Madison County, Kentucky, and studied at Yale. He served in the Kentucky legislature in 1835, 1837, and 1840. He worked for Abraham Lincoln's election in 1860 and was minister to Russia in 1861 and 1862 and from 1863 to 1869.   FRANK L. KLEMENT

CLAY, HENRY (1777-1852), was a leading American statesman for nearly 40 years. He repeatedly helped hold the Union together through compromises between the North and the South. Clay became known as "the Great Pacificator." With John C. Calhoun and Daniel Webster, he formed a "great triumvirate" of United States senators. Their opinions largely controlled Congress during the second quarter of the 1800's (see CALHOUN, JOHN C.; WEBSTER, DANIEL). Clay was the best loved of the three. His generous nature, charming manner, ready wit, and moving eloquence made him one of the most idolized figures of his time. Clay's famous remark, "I had rather be right than President," is often quoted to show his devotion to principle. In 1957, he was elected to the U.S. Senate Hall of Fame. A statue of Clay represents Kentucky in Statuary Hall in the U.S. Capitol in Washington, D.C.

Early Career. Clay, the son of a Baptist minister, was born on April 12, 1777, in Hanover County, Virginia. He had little education, but had a keen mind and liked to read. He studied law, was admitted to the Virginia bar in 1797, and began to practice in Lexington, Ky. Success came to him almost at once.

Clay began his long political career in 1801 as a member of the Kentucky constitutional convention. From 1806 to 1807, and from 1809 to 1811, he filled unexpired terms in the United States Senate. When first chosen senator, he was not quite 30 years old, the legal age required by the Constitution. But his fellow senators made no official investigation of his age.

Clay entered the U.S. House of Representatives in 1811, and was elected speaker on the first day of the session. He was re-elected to the House and to the speakership five more times. As chief of "the War Hawks," he argued in favor of the War of 1812 so strongly that some people called it "Mr. Clay's War." He was one of the commissioners chosen to make peace, and signed the Treaty of Ghent (see WAR OF 1812).

After the war, Clay advocated a kind of national planning that he called "the American System." It included a protective tariff, a national bank, and government support of internal improvements for better transportation. Clay hoped that these measures would encourage prosperity and tie together the different sections of the country. He became a leader of the National Republican Party, later called the Whig Party.

Advocate of Compromise. In 1820, Clay used his influence in getting the Missouri Compromise passed (see MISSOURI COMPROMISE). Missouri was admitted to the Union as a slave state and Maine as a free state. In this way, Clay helped to settle a dispute between proslavery and antislavery groups.

In 1832, South Carolina nullified a tariff law and refused to obey it. The next year, Clay arranged a compromise tariff that ended this threat to peace. Clay also sponsored the Compromise of 1850, which delayed the Civil War for over 10 years (see COMPROMISE OF 1850).

Candidate for President. No man was ever more eager than Clay to be President of the United States. He ran for President three times, but never won. In 1824, no candidate had a majority of the electoral votes, and the election was decided by the House of Representatives. Its members voted on the three candidates who had received the most votes. Clay had come out fourth in the election, and so could not be chosen. He gave his support to John Quincy Adams, who was elected. Adams then appointed Clay secretary of state. The two men were accused of a "corrupt bargain" because of this ap-

Henry Clay

U&U

Henry Clay displayed charm and wit in his speeches. He became one of the most noted statesmen of his time.

Brown Bros.

pointment. The charge was not true, but it was used against Clay throughout his career. As secretary of state, Clay worked for friendly relations with the countries of Latin America.

In 1832, the Whigs nominated Clay for the presidency. But he had supported high tariffs and the United States Bank, which were unpopular. He lost overwhelmingly to Andrew Jackson. In 1844, Clay ran for President against James K. Polk. Clay refused to take sides on the question of annexing Texas, and lost the votes of both the antislavery men of the North and the slave owners of the South. Again he was defeated.

Life at Ashland. Clay made a good income during the years that he devoted himself to his law practice. Ashland, his beautiful country estate at Lexington, was one of the show places of Kentucky. Clay was interested in stock breeding, and became the first to import pedigreed sheep and cattle to the West. He also owned prize-winning race horses.

Clay suffered several tragedies in his home life. His oldest son, Theodore, was confined to a mental institution. His six daughters died when they were young, and his brilliant son, Henry, was killed in the Mexican War.

On a placard at Clay's grave at Lexington appears a quotation from one of his speeches: "I know no North—no South—no East—no West."   RICHARD N. CURRENT

CLAY, LUCIUS DUBIGNON (1897-   ), served as commander in chief of the United States armed forces in Europe and as military governor of the U.S. zone in Germany from 1947 to 1949. In 1948, Russia blockaded all supply routes to the Western section of Berlin. The Russians hoped to drive the forces of the United States, Great Britain, and France out of Berlin. But the Berlin Airlift, directed by Clay, flew tons of food and other supplies into the city (see BERLIN AIRLIFT).

Clay was born in Marietta, Ga., and graduated from the United States Military Academy in 1918. He served as an Army engineer. During World War II, Clay directed the delivery of supplies to invasion fronts. He retired from the Army in 1949, and became associated with several civilian firms. Clay served as an adviser to the Office of Defense Mobilization in 1951, and as the representative of President John F. Kennedy in 1961. He later headed a presidential commission that studied U.S. foreign aid programs. Clay wrote a book, *Decision in Germany* (1950), based on his experiences in military government.   MAURICE MATLOFF

CLAY MODELING. See SCULPTURE (The Sculptor at Work).

CLAYMORE. See SWORD.

CLAYTON, JOHN MIDDLETON (1796-1856), an American statesman, served three terms as U.S. senator from Delaware. His greatest achievement was the Clayton-Bulwer Treaty of 1850 (see CLAYTON-BULWER TREATY). He entered the Senate in 1829, but resigned in 1836 to become chief justice of Delaware. From 1845 until his death, he served as senator, except for one year as secretary of state under President Zachary Taylor. Clayton was born in Dagsboro, Del. A statue of him represents Delaware in the Statuary Hall Collection in the U.S. Capitol.   ARTHUR A. EKIRCH, JR.

CLAYTON ANTITRUST ACT. See TRUST (Trust Legislation); WILSON, WOODROW (Legislative Program).

CLAYTON-BULWER TREATY, signed by the United States and Great Britain in 1850, gave both countries

an equal share in the protection of a canal to be built through Central America. Both countries agreed to maintain the neutrality of the canal and the land on either side of it. The treaty was named for John M. Clayton, American secretary of state, and Sir Henry Bulwer (1801-1872), British minister to the United States. This treaty became unpopular in the United States. In 1901, the Hay-Pauncefote Treaty replaced the Clayton-Bulwer Treaty. It granted the U.S. the right to build and manage the canal.   JOHN D. HICKS

See also CLAYTON, JOHN MIDDLETON; HAY-PAUNCE-FOTE TREATY; NICARAGUA CANAL.

CLEANING. See DRY CLEANING; LAUNDRY.

CLEANING FLUID is any liquid used for dry cleaning. These liquids dissolve grease readily and do not damage clothes. They dry quickly, and leave almost no odor. All fluids must meet minimum fire-prevention standards. Chemically, cleaning fluids are organic compounds. Most of them are chlorinated hydrocarbons. Perchloroethylene (C_2Cl_4) is perhaps the most satisfactory, but carbon tetrachloride (CCl_4) is also widely used. See also DRY CLEANING.   W. NORTON JONES, JR.

CLEANLINESS. See BATHS AND BATHING (Modern Attitudes); HEALTH (Cleanliness); SANITATION.

CLEAR LAKE CITY, Tex., lies about 20 miles southeast of Houston. It houses workers from the nearby Manned Spacecraft Center of the National Aeronautics and Space Administration (NASA). The center plays an important role in the U.S. program to send men to the moon. Construction of the city began in the early 1960's. When completed in the 1980's, the city will have 150,000 persons. See also MANNED SPACECRAFT CENTER; NATIONAL AERONAUTICS AND SPACE ADMINISTRATION; TEXAS (Today).   G. W. SCHLESSELMAN

CLEARINGHOUSE is an institution maintained by an association of banks in a city. Its purpose is to settle quickly the claims which each bank has against the others. A clearinghouse enables banks to settle claims with the least possible transfer of cash.

The method used in the New York Clearing House served as a model for all later ones in America. This method permits each bank in the city to send at least two representatives to the clearinghouse. They are a *delivery clerk* and a *settling clerk*. Both clerks are assigned to a desk in a large room. When they arrive, they give the manager of the room a list of the amounts due their bank from each of the other banks. The list includes all checks, drafts, and other obligations. At 10 A.M. the delivery clerks begin moving from desk to desk. They deliver to each settling clerk the claims their banks have against his bank. Each settling clerk then draws up a statement which shows the balance his bank should pay or receive from each other bank. The manager checks the statements and reads out the amount each bank owes or is owed. The debtor banks pay the amount due to the clearinghouse manager. In turn, the manager pays the creditor banks. To clear checks, banks use the Federal Reserve Banks, which act as intercity clearinghouses. See FEDERAL RESERVE SYSTEM.

London banks used collectors called *walk clerks* in the 1600's. They would go to each bank and collect cash to cover credits. Two of these walk clerks happened to meet in a coffeehouse about 1670. They

CLEARWATER DAM

decided to save time and effort by arranging their exchange then and there. Other clerks soon learned of this scheme. Before long the coffeehouse had become the first clearinghouse. When the bankers found out, some of them ordered it stopped. But others realized that the idea had merit. They persuaded the rest to join them in engaging a room for the clerks. A set of clearing rules was later made, and a manager was placed in charge of the room. This beginning developed into the London Clearing House, the largest clearinghouse in the world.

New York City established the first American clearinghouse in 1853. Boston, Philadelphia, Pittsburgh, and Chicago founded theirs soon after. Every city of size or commercial importance now has one.　　　G. L. BACH

CLEARWATER DAM is part of a government flood-control project on the Black River near Piedmont, Mo.

HOW BANKS USE THE CLEARINGHOUSE
to settle their claims with one another

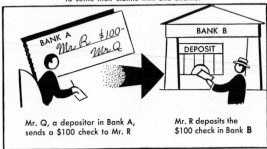

Mr. Q, a depositor in Bank A, sends a $100 check to Mr. R

Mr. R deposits the $100 check in Bank B

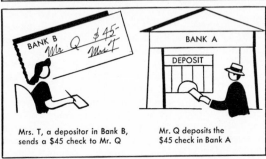

Mrs. T, a depositor in Bank B, sends a $45 check to Mr. Q

Mr. Q deposits the $45 check in Bank A

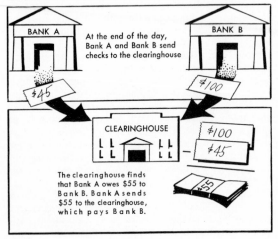

At the end of the day, Bank A and Bank B send checks to the clearinghouse

The clearinghouse finds that Bank A owes $55 to Bank B. Bank A sends $55 to the clearinghouse, which pays Bank B.

This earth-fill type dam is 4,225 feet long and 154 feet high. It was completed in 1948. Behind the dam is a reservoir that can control floods in an area of about 900 square miles. It provides a storage capacity of 5,580,000 gallons of water for flood control.　　　T. W. MERMEL

CLEAVAGE. See GEM (Qualities).

CLEAVELAND, MOSES. See CLEVELAND (Ohio).

CLEF. See MUSIC (The Language of Music).

CLEFT PALATE is a split in the palate, or roof of the mouth. It is *congenital* (present at birth) and results when the bones of the hard palate fail to join properly as the fetus develops. In most cases, doctors can join the two parts of the palate in an operation. A child with a cleft palate usually has normal mental powers, in spite of the defect. See also HARELIP; TONSIL (picture).

CLEISTHENES, *KLYS thuh neez*, was a statesman in ancient Athens. He established a democratic constitution there after Hippias, who held complete political power, was overthrown in 510 B.C. Cleisthenes was a member of the noble Alcmaeonid clan. This clan persuaded Cleomenes, the king of Sparta, to overthrow Hippias. After that, Cleisthenes gained public support by setting up a democratic form of government. He then reformed the Athenian tribal organization, ending the political and religious control of the noble clans. To protect the new democracy, he enacted laws providing for *ostracism* (banishment) for enemies of the state.　　　DONALD KAGAN

See also ATHENS (History).

CLEMATIS, *KLEHM uh tihs*, is any one of a group of herblike perennials and vines that grow throughout North America, Europe, and Asia. Several small-flowered kinds are called *virgin's bower*. The most popular species that grow in America include a large group of hybrid vine varieties that may climb 10 feet high and have flowers 6 inches across. The blossoms may be deep blue, violet, white, pink, or red. After the flowers fade, long feathery tufts remain on the vine.

Scientific Classification. Clematis belongs to the crowfoot family, *Ranunculaceae*. The best known American vine is genus *Clematis*, species *C. jackmanii*.　　　GEORGE A. BEACH

CLEMENCEAU, *KLAY MAHN SO*, or *KLEM un so*, **GEORGES** (1841-1929), a French statesman, led his country triumphantly through the last and most difficult period of World War I. In 1917, when he was 76, he became premier of France for the second time. He exercised powerful leadership with his slogan, "I make war!" and became known as "The Tiger of France." He presided over the Paris Peace Conference, where he insisted on severe terms for Germany and sought to obtain the left bank of the Rhine River for France. Clemenceau ran for president of France in 1920, but lost to Paul Deschanel. He resigned from his office as premier the day after he was defeated.

Clemenceau was born on Sept. 28, 1841, in La Vendée, France. Trained as a doctor, he traveled and taught for a time in the United States, where he married an American. When he returned to

Georges Clemenceau
Keystone

France, he became mayor of Montmartre, a section of Paris. He helped defend Paris against the Germans in 1870. He served as a deputy from 1876 to 1893, as premier from 1906 to 1909.   E. J. KNAPTON

CLEMENS, SAMUEL LANGHORNE. See TWAIN, MARK.

CLEMENT was the name of 14 popes of the Roman Catholic Church. The fifth and sixth were French, and resided at Avignon. Historically, the most important were Clement I, Clement VII, and Clement VIII. The dates of their reigns were:

Clement I, Saint	(88-97)	Clement VIII	(1592-1605)
Clement II	(1046-1047)	Clement IX	(1667-1669)
Clement III	(1187-1191)	Clement X	(1670-1676)
Clement IV	(1265-1268)	Clement XI	(1700-1721)
Clement V	(1305-1314)	Clement XII	(1730-1740)
Clement VI	(1342-1352)	Clement XIII	(1758-1769)
Clement VII	(1523-1534)	Clement XIV	(1769-1774)

Saint Clement I (? -99?) is commonly known as CLEMENT OF ROME. The third bishop of Rome after Saint Peter, Clement was the first of the early writers called "Apostolic Fathers." His *Epistle to the Corinthians* is an important source of early church history. It describes the organization of the early church and the primacy of the bishop of Rome.

Clement VII (1478-1534) belonged to the Medici family of Florence (see MEDICI). He reigned during the troubled early years of the Reformation. Weak and vacillating, Clement VII was ill-suited to govern the Church during such critical times. He refused to grant Henry VIII of England a divorce from his wife, Catherine of Aragon (see HENRY [VIII]). This refusal caused Henry to leave the Roman Catholic Church and found the Anglican Church.

In 1527, troops of the Holy Roman Emperor Charles V sacked Rome, and Clement was held prisoner for a time. Later, he was reconciled with the emperor, and he urged Charles to take strong measures against the Protestants in the Holy Roman Empire. Clement saw the need for reform in the church, but he failed to take vigorous action to accomplish it.

Clement VIII (1536-1605) was elected pope in 1592 at a critical time in church history. France and Spain were at war, and the pope had to avoid driving France into Protestantism and breaking with Spain. Clement reconciled King Henry IV of France with the Roman Catholic Church, and led in the mediations resulting in the Peace of Vervins between France and Spain. A lover of learning and a friend of scholars, Clement published revisions of the Vulgate, the breviary, and other liturgical books.   THOMAS P. NEILL and FULTON J. SHEEN

CLEMENTI, *clay MEN tee,* **MUZIO** (1752-1832), was an Italian pianist and composer. He composed *Gradus ad Parnassum* (1817), a collection of studies which is still used in developing piano technique. In addition, he composed more than 60 piano sonatas. The Irish composer and pianist John Field was among Clementi's many famous pupils. Clementi was born in Rome. He went to England at the age of 14, and remained there most of his life. Clementi was buried in Westminster Abbey.   ROBERT U. NELSON

CLEMM, VIRGINIA. See POE, EDGAR ALLAN.

CLEMSON UNIVERSITY is a coeducational, state-controlled university at Clemson, S.C. It has schools of agriculture, engineering, textiles, arts and science,

and education. Courses lead to bachelor's and master's degrees in most departments. There is also a program in industrial management. The library at Clemson University is a depository for certain United States publications. It also has a special collection of agricultural references.

Clemson, founded in 1889, has an extension division and a summer session. The home of John C. Calhoun stands in the center of the campus. For the enrollment of Clemson University, see UNIVERSITIES AND COLLEGES (table).

CLEOBULUS. See SEVEN WISE MEN OF GREECE.

CLEOPATRA, KLEE oh PAT ruh, or KLEE oh PAY truh, was the name of several Macedonian queens of Egypt. The most famous Cleopatra lived from 69 to 30 B.C. Some historians believe that she was Cleopatra VII. Others call her Cleopatra VI. But all agree that she was the last of the line of the Ptolemies, who had ruled Egypt for almost 300 years. Although not particularly beautiful, she was intelligent, witty, and ambitious. She attracted some of the greatest Romans of her day.

Cleopatra became queen in 51 B.C. when her father, Ptolemy XI Auletes, died. By the terms of his will, her brother, Ptolemy XII, then about 10 years old, was made joint ruler. In 49 B.C., young Ptolemy's guardians seized the power for him and drove Cleopatra from the throne. When Julius Caesar came to Alexandria in 48 B.C. in pursuit of Pompey, Cleopatra was secretly introduced into the palace, and Caesar fell in love with her. In a brief civil war that followed, her brother was defeated and drowned while trying to escape. A younger brother, Ptolemy XIII, then took the throne with Cleopatra. In 46 B.C., she went to Rome, where she stayed with Caesar until his death in 44 B.C. When she returned to Egypt, she had her brother put to death so that Caesarion, her son by Caesar, could rule with her as Ptolemy XIV.

She Meets Mark Antony. In 41 B.C., after the battle of Philippi, Cleopatra met Mark Antony at Tarsus in Asia Minor. She was dressed as Aphrodite, the Greek goddess of love. Antony at once fell in love with her and visited her at Alexandria. He married her in 37 B.C., after he deserted his wife Octavia, sister of Octavian, the future Emperor Augustus. Then Antony and Cleopatra cooperated closely to achieve their ambitions. He wanted to be sole ruler of Rome, and considered the wealth of Egypt a much-needed asset. She at the same time wished to bring Egypt into the empire as a partner rather than as a conquered province. Just as Cleopatra had once hoped to rule the Roman world as Caesar's queen, she now wished to rule as the favorite of Antony.

The result of this alliance was war between Antony and Octavian. Antony lost many of his Roman supporters, because they objected to the ambitions of Cleopatra. In 31 B.C., Antony lost the naval battle of Actium on the west coast of Greece. He and Cleopatra fled to Alexandria. While Octavian pursued them, Cleopatra led Antony to commit suicide by spreading a report that she had taken her own life. She established herself in a mausoleum built for her own burial. She then sent a message to Antony, telling him that when he received the message she would be dead. Before Antony died,

Cleopatra and Caesar met when he came to Egypt in 48 B.C. He fell in love with her, and took her to Rome to live with him.

Culver

he learned that Cleopatra was still living. His followers carried him to Cleopatra, and he died in her arms.

Her Death. Cleopatra then tried unsuccessfully to bring the cold-blooded Octavian under her spell. Rather than be carried off in humiliation to Rome, where Octavian could exhibit her, she killed herself. Tradition says she had an asp brought secretly to her in a basket of figs (see ASP). She placed the asp on her arm and died of its bite. But she may have used a horned viper, which is sometimes known as an asp, or a poisonous drug. Octavian, it is said, ordered that she have a magnificent funeral and that her body be laid next to that of Antony, according to her wishes. After her death, her son Caesarion was executed by the Romans to prevent him from claiming to be Caesar's heir, and the rightful ruler of the Roman Empire.

Cleopatra's reputation in history comes largely from the unscrupulous propaganda by Octavian, which made Antony appear the love-struck victim of an Oriental temptress. The Roman poets Virgil and Horace also adopted this version. Her story has been told many times in literature. It is dramatized in the famous play *Antony and Cleopatra* by William Shakespeare, in *All for Love* by John Dryden, and in *Caesar and Cleopatra* by George Bernard Shaw.　　　CHESTER G. STARR

Related Articles in WORLD BOOK include:

Actium, Battle of	Caesar, Gaius	Octavia
Antony, Mark	Julius	Ptolemy
Augustus	Horace	Virgil

CLEOPATRA'S NEEDLES are two famous *obelisks* (stone pillar structures) from ancient Egypt. One of them stands in Central Park in New York City. The other stands on the Thames Embankment in London. The Egyptian government presented the obelisks to the United States and England during the 1800's.

Cleopatra's Needles are misnamed. They have no connection with the Egyptian queen Cleopatra. The pillars bear the names of two Egyptian kings, Thutmose III, who lived about 1500 B.C.; and Ramses II (1200's B.C.). Cleopatra's Needles originally stood before the Temple of the Sun in Heliopolis. The Romans moved them to Alexandria in 23 B.C.

The obelisk in New York City stands 69 feet high. It is 7½ feet thick at the base, and it weighs 200 tons.　　RICARDO A. CAMINOS

See also OBELISK; THUTMOSE III.

CLEPSYDRA. See WATER CLOCK; CLOCK (introduction).

CLERESTORY, *KLEER stoh rih,* is a row of windows in the upper story of a building. In a church, the clerestory rises above the roofs of the aisles and ambulatory. The clerestory lets light into the church's interior. The clerestory windows of many cathedrals are made of beautiful stained glass.

CLERGYMAN. See MINISTER; PRIEST; RABBI.

CLERICAL WORK. See OFFICE WORK.

CLERK, SIR DUGALD. See DIESEL ENGINE (History).

CLERK OF COURT is an officer of a court of justice who performs many important administrative duties.

Cleopatra's Needle stands in Central Park in New York City. The 69-foot obelisk was brought from Egypt in 1880. It is more than 3,000 years old.

Ewing Galloway

The clerk keeps on file the court records, such as the *docket* (list of cases awaiting hearing). He issues the *summons* that calls a person into court, and the *judgment* that formally orders the unsuccessful party to do what the court has directed. He also certifies as correct any records of court proceedings that are needed in other legal proceedings.　　ARTHUR E. SUTHERLAND

CLERMONT was the first commercially successful steamboat. Designed and built by Robert Fulton, it sailed in regular passenger service on the Hudson River. Fulton sailed the wood-burning *Clermont* up the Hudson from New York City to Albany in 1807 on its first trip. The ship was registered as the *North River Steamboat of Clermont,* but it was generally called the *Clermont.* The 78-ton steamboat was 142 feet long and 14 feet wide. An English-built engine drove the boat's side paddle wheels. The *Clermont* was dismantled in 1815. For more details and picture, see FULTON, ROBERT.　　JOHN H. KEMBLE

CLERMONT, COUNCIL OF. See CRUSADES (How the Crusades Began).

CLERMONT-FERRAND, *KLEHR MAWN feh RAHN* (pop. 127,684; met. area 159,687; alt. 1,316 ft.), lies on a high plain in the Auvergne region of France, about 210 miles southeast of Paris. For location, see FRANCE (political map). The city contains the main plants of the Michelin Company, and is the center of the French rubber and automobile tire industry. It also is known for its university and for the mineral spring in the vicinity. In 1095 in this city, Pope Urban II preached the sermon that launched the First Crusade.　　EDWARD W. FOX

CLEVE, PER THEODOR. See HOLMIUM; THULIUM.

CLEVELAND

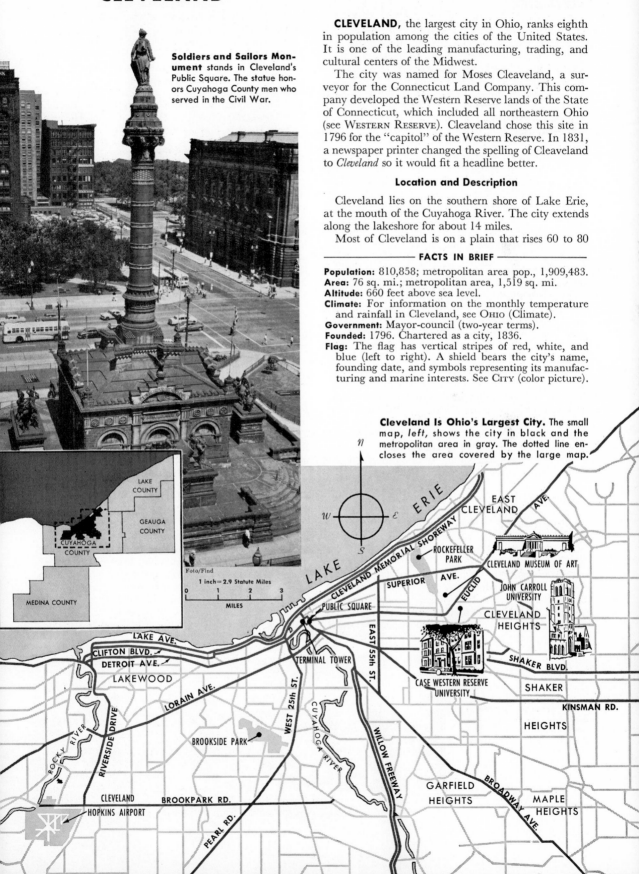

Soldiers and Sailors Monument stands in Cleveland's Public Square. The statue honors Cuyahoga County men who served in the Civil War.

CLEVELAND, the largest city in Ohio, ranks eighth in population among the cities of the United States. It is one of the leading manufacturing, trading, and cultural centers of the Midwest.

The city was named for Moses Cleaveland, a surveyor for the Connecticut Land Company. This company developed the Western Reserve lands of the State of Connecticut, which included all northeastern Ohio (see WESTERN RESERVE). Cleaveland chose this site in 1796 for the "capitol" of the Western Reserve. In 1831, a newspaper printer changed the spelling of Cleaveland to *Cleveland* so it would fit a headline better.

Location and Description

Cleveland lies on the southern shore of Lake Erie, at the mouth of the Cuyahoga River. The city extends along the lakeshore for about 14 miles.

Most of Cleveland is on a plain that rises 60 to 80

FACTS IN BRIEF

Population: 810,858; metropolitan area pop., 1,909,483.
Area: 76 sq. mi.; metropolitan area, 1,519 sq. mi.
Altitude: 660 feet above sea level.
Climate: For information on the monthly temperature and rainfall in Cleveland, see OHIO (Climate).
Government: Mayor-council (two-year terms).
Founded: 1796. Chartered as a city, 1836.
Flag: The flag has vertical stripes of red, white, and blue (left to right). A shield bears the city's name, founding date, and symbols representing its manufacturing and marine interests. See CITY (color picture).

Cleveland Is Ohio's Largest City. The small map, *left*, shows the city in black and the metropolitan area in gray. The dotted line encloses the area covered by the large map.

CLEVELAND

feet higher than Lake Erie. The half-mile-wide valley of the Cuyahoga divides the city into an East Side and a West Side. Iron and steel mills, oil refineries, lumber yards, loading machinery, warehouses, and other industries operate in this valley, called the *Flats*. An inner harbor has been formed on the river. Between 1940 and 1959, the city spent more than $20,000,000 to widen, deepen, and straighten the river. Now ore and coal vessels can travel more than 5 miles inland to the steel mills.

The Mall is a T-shaped park of about 100 acres that runs inland from Lake Erie in downtown Cleveland. The city's chief public buildings stand around it. These buildings include the Cuyahoga County Court House, the Underground Exhibition Hall, City Hall, Public Auditorium, Board of Education Building, Public Library, and Federal Building. The Federal Building, first of the group to be completed, was erected in 1910.

Public Square. The Federal Building also stands across from Monumental Park, commonly called the Public Square. Moses Cleaveland set the 4.4-acre square apart as a park. It now serves as a terminal for rapid-transit and bus lines. The Civil War Soldiers and Sailors Monument stands in the square. Statues of Cleaveland and of Tom L. Johnson, who was mayor in the early 1900's, also are in the square.

The Terminal Building Group is at the southwest corner of the square. Built at a cost of about $100,000,000, the group includes the Terminal Tower Building, Hotel Sheraton-Cleveland, Republic Building, Guildhall Building, Midland Building, Higbee Department Store, and the Post Office Building. The 773-foot-high Terminal Tower is one of the tallest buildings in the United States. An observation tower on the 42nd floor of the Terminal Tower offers an excellent view of Cleveland.

Streets. Cleveland's best-known street is Euclid Avenue, which extends from the Public Square through the eastern suburbs. The city's main shopping district lies along Euclid Avenue from the square to East 22nd Street. Euclid follows the shoreline of an ancient dried-up lake, which formed during the Ice Age. This lake was larger than any of the present-day Great Lakes. Indians and early white settlers wore the sandy ridge of the shoreline into a trail. When Cleveland became a village, the trail was cleared and laid out with mathematical accuracy. The settlers named it for Euclid,

an ancient Greek mathematician who was the *father of geometry*. Superior Avenue, another important thoroughfare, extends east to the city limits.

The principal East Side streets are Memorial Shoreway; St. Clair, Superior, Chester, Euclid, Carnegie, Cedar, and Woodland avenues; and Broadway. Important West Side highways include West Memorial Shoreway; Detroit, Franklin, and Lorain avenues; and West 25th Street. Suburbs of the city include Euclid, East Cleveland, Cleveland Heights, Shaker Heights, Garfield Heights, Parma, and Lakewood.

The People

The first settlers of Cleveland came from New England through the Mohawk Valley and along the shore of Lake Erie in the early 1800's. Between 1825 and 1830, many German and Irish workers settled in the city.

The early settlers were of Puritan stock. They established the first church in 1807. Roman Catholics now have the largest number of churches in the Cleveland area. They are followed by the Baptists, the Lutherans, and the Methodists.

Work of the People

Industries. Cleveland's 3,700 factories produce about $2,500,000,000 worth of goods a year. They turn out more than 14,000 different products. Cleveland ranks seventh among the nation's industrial centers.

Iron and steel products have the greatest value. They range from tiny bolts to mighty machines. The city also ranks high in the manufacture of motor-vehicle bodies and parts, and has large paint and varnish factories. Oil refining has been an important Cleveland industry since John D. Rockefeller, Sr., built his first oil refinery in the Flats in 1862. Cleveland also is an important center for the manufacture of batteries, clothing, chemicals, electrical equipment, knitted garments, lamp bulbs, and ships.

Transportation. Cleveland provides a connecting link between the East and the Midwest. Its harbor is one of the busiest on the Great Lakes. Major railroads and airlines serve the city. The Ohio Turnpike runs past the city's southern boundary.

Harbor. A five-mile-long stone breakwater forms Cleveland's outer harbor on Lake Erie. Cleveland is said to be the largest iron-ore receiving port in the world. Great Lakes freighters unload more than 13,000,000 gross tons a year. Other cargoes received at the city include automobiles, coal, grain, petroleum, sand and gravel, scrap metal, and sulfur. Cleveland is a major

The Cleveland Skyline is broken by the 52-story Terminal Tower. Municipal Stadium, *left foreground*, stands on the shore of Lake Erie.

inland port on the bustling Saint Lawrence Seaway.

Railroads. Five main-line railroads have terminals in Cleveland. Union Station in the Terminal Tower is one of the finest in the country. Three industrial rail lines also serve the city.

Airlines. Cleveland Hopkins Airport ranks as one of the largest in the world. All main east-west airlines use it. The Lewis Research Center of the National Aeronautics and Space Administration is at the airport. Burke Lakefront Airport is near downtown Cleveland.

Communication. Eleven radio stations and three television stations broadcast from Cleveland. Leading newspapers are the *Plain Dealer* and the *Press*.

Education

Schools. Cleveland has about 180 public schools and about 200 private and parochial schools. Case Western Reserve University, founded in 1826, is one of the oldest colleges in the Middle West. It occupies a beautiful campus in the University Circle district of Cleveland's East Side. Other institutions of higher learning include Cleveland-Marshall Law School, Cleveland State University, John Carroll University, St. John College of Cleveland, and Ursuline College for Women. Notre Dame College is located nearby. See also CLEVELAND INSTITUTE OF ART.

Libraries. In the late 1880's, the Cleveland Public Library became one of the first in the country to adopt the open-stacks plan. This plan gave the public access to book shelves. The library claims to have the largest chess collection in the world, and also owns special collections of folklore and Oriental material. The library maintains more than 30 branches.

Museums. The Cleveland Museum of Natural History owns one of the most complete collections of natural science in the United States. The Cleveland Health Museum, opened in 1940, is said to be the first permanent health museum in the country. The Western Reserve Historical Museum maintains records of the survey and settlement of the Western Reserve. It also has other displays. Dunham Tavern, built in 1842, once was an important stagecoach stop. It now houses pioneer relics collected from the Western Reserve.

An excellent collection of paintings, art objects, and sculpture may be seen at the Cleveland Museum of Art. One of its most valuable displays is the Guelph Treasure of medieval objects.

The Arts

The Cleveland Museum of Art sponsors a show of the works of local artists every May. The Cleveland Orchestra gives concerts in Severance Hall in the University Circle district. The Metropolitan Opera Association performs in Cleveland every spring.

Playhouse Square in the Euclid Avenue-14th Street district has five theaters that present stage and screen attractions. The Cleveland Play House is a resident professional theater group that gives plays at three theaters—the Brooks, Drury, and Euclid. About 30 little theater groups perform in the Cleveland area. The Lakewood Little Theater is perhaps the best known. The Cain Park Theater in Cleveland Heights has an outdoor amphitheater that seats 3,000.

Karamu House opened in 1915 as an experiment in racial understanding through the arts. People of any

race, creed, or color can come here to perform in plays, and attend art, music, and dance studios.

Recreation

The Cleveland Public Auditorium on the Mall has 16 halls for entertainments, concerts, and lectures. The Cleveland Municipal Stadium lies along the lakefront just north of the Mall. It seats over 78,000 spectators. The Cleveland Indians, who play baseball in the American League, and the Cleveland Browns of the National Football League play at the stadium.

Cleveland's park system covers about 2,600 acres. Lakes and woods give the parks great natural beauty.

Gordon Park lies on both sides of Doan Creek. A major attraction of the park is the Cleveland Aquarium. Rockefeller Park, a narrow strip of land four miles long, connects Gordon and Wade parks. John D. Rockefeller, Sr., presented the land to the city. A number of nationality groups in the city maintain special gardens in the Cleveland Cultural Gardens in Rockefeller Park. Wade Park includes the art and natural history museums. Brookside Park is the site of the Cleveland zoo. Other parks include Edgewater, Forest Hill, Garfield, Lakewood, Shaker Lakes, and Woodland Hills.

The Metropolitan Park District circles Greater Cleveland. It covers 15,000 acres of fine scenery. The main highways leading to Cleveland pass through it.

Government

Cleveland has a mayor-council form of government. Thirty-three councilmen form the legislative body. The city is the seat of Cuyahoga County.

Cleveland has been the home of many famous political leaders, including President James A. Garfield; John Hay, Secretary of State under President William McKinley; Senator Marcus A. Hanna; Newton D. Baker, Secretary of War under President Woodrow Wilson; and George M. Humphrey, Secretary of the Treasury under President Dwight D. Eisenhower. Garfield, Hanna, Hay, Rockefeller, and other leading citizens are buried in Lake View Cemetery.

History

Cleveland was incorporated as a village in 1814, 18 years after Moses Cleaveland established his settlement on the site. The community had a population of less than a hundred at the time. Development of the city began when the Ohio Canal, connecting Lake Erie with the Ohio River, was completed in 1832. The Ohio legislature granted Cleveland a city charter in 1836. Cleveland then had a population of about 6,000. The first railroad came to Cleveland in 1851, connecting the city with Columbus, the state capital. In 1852, the first boatload of iron ore from the Lake Superior region entered the Cleveland harbor. Great industrial development marked the history of the city during the last half of the 1800's, and continued in the 1900's. Major plants built in the mid-1900's included those manufacturing automobile bodies and parts, electronic equipment, and plastics.

In 1967, Cleveland voters elected Carl B. Stokes, the city's first Negro mayor. Stokes, a Democrat, defeated Republican Seth Taft.   RUSSELL W. KANE

GROVER CLEVELAND

Library of Congress

The United States Flag had 38 stars when Cleveland first took office in 1885, and 44 stars when he began his second term in 1893.

GARFIELD
20th President
1881

ARTHUR
21st President
1881 — 1885

B. HARRISON
23rd President
1889 — 1893

McKINLEY
25th President
1897 — 1901

22ND PRESIDENT OF THE UNITED STATES 1885-1889
24TH PRESIDENT OF THE UNITED STATES 1893-1897

CLEVELAND, GROVER (1837-1908), was the only President who served two terms that did not directly follow each other. He won the presidency in 1884, but lost it four years later to Benjamin Harrison. He ran against Harrison again in 1892 and won a second term.

Cleveland was the first Democratic President elected after the Civil War. This very fact showed that the emotions of the war had cooled enough to permit the return to a two-party system. Cleveland's victory also was a protest against the waste and corruption that had disgraced Republican administrations after the war. His honesty and common sense helped restore confidence in the government. These qualities had served him in his earlier successes as a lawyer, sheriff, and mayor, and as governor of New York.

As President, Cleveland had the courage to say "No." He said it often—to farmers who sought easy money to pay their debts, to manufacturers who wanted high protective tariffs, and to veterans who wanted bigger pensions. These "No's" made Cleveland unpopular in his time, but have added to the respect with which history holds him.

This big, good-humored man, called "Uncle Jumbo" by his relatives, occupied the White House during a time of swift social and economic change. The growing strength of labor unions and farm organizations created new problems for government. Cleveland lacked the experience and vision to find completely satisfactory answers to all the problems. He attempted to settle labor strikes by force—the legal force of court injunc-

tions and the physical force of army troops. He clung steadfastly to his faith in "sound" money and a low tariff as a cure for the nation's other economic ills. Although Cleveland's intentions were good, his methods fell short of success.

The era of the western frontier was drawing to a close when Cleveland took office. Settlers in the Southwest breathed easier when federal troops captured Geronimo, the fierce Apache chief. Jacob Riis shocked a complacent public with newspaper stories of how "the other half" lived in run-down slums.

During Cleveland's second term, the Duryea brothers built America's first automobile. A Kansas preacher, Charles Sheldon, wrote *In His Steps*, one of the world's all-time best sellers. Americans of the Gay 90's enjoyed Victor Herbert's early operettas. At the World's Columbian Exposition in Chicago, they applauded John Philip Sousa's band and rode the first and largest Ferris wheel ever built.

Early Life

Boyhood. Stephen Grover Cleveland was born on March 18, 1837, in Caldwell, N.J. He dropped his first name while still a boy. Grover was the fifth child in a family of four brothers and five sisters. His father, Richard Falley Cleveland, was a Presbyterian minister and a relative of Moses Cleaveland, the founder of Cleveland, Ohio. His mother, Ann Neal Cleveland, was the daughter of a publisher.

The family of a country minister led a hard life. The

IMPORTANT DATES IN CLEVELAND'S LIFE

1837 (March 18) Born in Caldwell, N.J.
1881 Elected mayor of Buffalo, N.Y.
1882 Elected governor of New York.
1884 Elected President of the United States.
1886 (June 2) Married Frances Folsom.
1888 Defeated for re-election by Benjamin Harrison.
1892 Elected to second term as President.
1908 (June 24) Died in Princeton, N.J.

Clevelands had little money and moved several times. Grover attended schools in Fayetteville and Clinton, N.Y., and went to work at the age of 14 as a clerk in a Fayetteville general store. He was only 16 when his father died, leaving him and his brothers to support his mother and sisters. Cleveland joined an older brother who was teaching at the New York Institution for the Blind in New York City. He taught there for a year.

Lawyer. When Cleveland was 17, he decided to go west to look for better opportunities. He planned to settle in Cleveland, Ohio, which attracted him because of its name. But he stopped in Buffalo, N.Y., to visit his mother's uncle, Lewis F. Allen, who persuaded him to stay there. Grover worked for his uncle for six months, then decided to become a lawyer. He worked as a clerk in the law office of Rogers, Bowen, and Rogers, and studied there. The serious, quiet youth worked hard for his $4 a week, which paid for room and board at the home of a fellow law clerk.

After being admitted to the bar in 1859, Cleveland continued to work for the same law firm. Two of his brothers served in the Union Army during the Civil War, but Cleveland's help was needed to support his mother and the other children. He paid a substitute to take his place in the army. Although this was legal

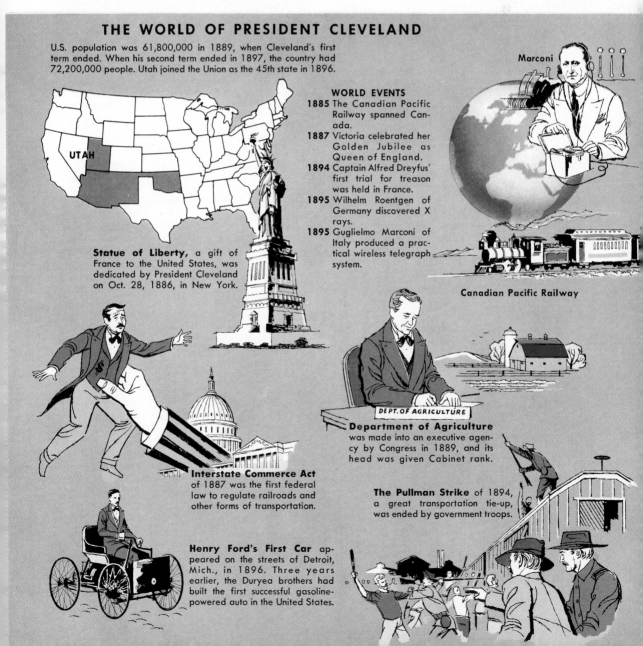

THE WORLD OF PRESIDENT CLEVELAND

U.S. population was 61,800,000 in 1889, when Cleveland's first term ended. When his second term ended in 1897, the country had 72,200,000 people. Utah joined the Union as the 45th state in 1896.

UTAH

Statue of Liberty, a gift of France to the United States, was dedicated by President Cleveland on Oct. 28, 1886, in New York.

WORLD EVENTS

1885 The Canadian Pacific Railway spanned Canada.
1887 Victoria celebrated her Golden Jubilee as Queen of England.
1894 Captain Alfred Dreyfus' first trial for treason was held in France.
1895 Wilhelm Roentgen of Germany discovered X rays.
1895 Guglielmo Marconi of Italy produced a practical wireless telegraph system.

Marconi

Canadian Pacific Railway

Interstate Commerce Act of 1887 was the first federal law to regulate railroads and other forms of transportation.

DEPT. OF AGRICULTURE

Department of Agriculture was made into an executive agency by Congress in 1889, and its head was given Cabinet rank.

The Pullman Strike of 1894, a great transportation tie-up, was ended by government troops.

Henry Ford's First Car appeared on the streets of Detroit, Mich., in 1896. Three years earlier, the Duryea brothers had built the first successful gasoline-powered auto in the United States.

Cleveland's Birthplace was the manse of the First Presbyterian Church of Caldwell, N.J. Cleveland, the minister's son, was born in the rear room on the first floor. The white clapboard house has been preserved as a museum.

Youngest First Lady in the nation's history was Frances Folsom Cleveland. She married the President in the Blue Room of the White House when she was 21 years old and he was 49. Cleveland called his wife by her nickname, "Frank."

and a common practice, the fact that Cleveland had not served in the war was later used against him by his political enemies.

Political Career

Minor Offices. Cleveland entered politics as a ward worker for the Democratic party in Buffalo. He served as ward supervisor in 1862 and later as assistant district attorney of Erie County. He was elected sheriff in 1870. During his term, the county had to hang two convicted murderers. Most sheriffs had delegated this distasteful task to deputies, but Cleveland sprang the traps himself. He explained that he would not ask anyone else to do what he was unwilling to do.

Cleveland returned to the practice of law after three years as sheriff. He relaxed by hunting and fishing with fellow lawyers. To relatives who wondered whether their stout "Uncle Jumbo" had ever thought of marrying, he replied: "A good many times; and the more I think of it the more I think I'll not do it."

Mayor of Buffalo. Like many cities, Buffalo suffered from a corrupt administration. In response to a growing demand for reform, Democratic leaders chose Cleveland to run for mayor in 1881. He won the election, and gave his political backers more reform than they had bargained for. Cleveland vetoed so many padded city contracts that he became known as the "veto mayor."

Governor of New York. Cleveland's reputation for honest administration became a valuable political asset. The Democrats nominated him for governor in 1882 as a candidate not owned by any political faction. He won easily.

Cleveland gave New York the same conscientious administration he had given Buffalo. He vetoed padded appropriation bills regardless of political pressure. He aroused a storm of protest when he killed a bill that

would have lowered streetcar fares in New York City. Cleveland explained that the bill violated the terms of a previous transit contract. Theodore Roosevelt, then a member of the state legislature, had advocated the bill, but later admitted that Cleveland had been right. When Cleveland later cooperated with Roosevelt to pass laws reforming the government of New York City, he earned the undying hatred of Tammany Hall, the Democratic political machine that controlled the city.

Election of 1884. Cleveland's reputation for good government made him a national figure. The Republican party nominated James G. Blaine for President in 1884, even though he had been implicated in a financial scandal (see BLAINE, JAMES G.). Many influential Republicans were outraged. They thought the time had come for a national reform administration. These Republicans, called *mugwumps*, withdrew from the convention and declared that they would vote for the Democratic candidate if he were an honest man (see MUGWUMP). The Democrats answered by nominating Cleveland. They chose Governor Thomas A. Hendricks of Indiana for Vice-President.

Good political issues were available to both parties in the campaign of 1884. Farmers were growing poorer, private interests were grabbing public lands and resources, and labor was becoming more dissatisfied. But neither party faced these issues. Instead, each attacked the other's nominee with scandalous personal stories.

The basic unrest of the people, their lack of faith in the honesty of previous administrations, and a series of campaign blunders by Blaine turned the tide. One of the most costly mistakes was made by a supporter of Blaine at a Republican rally in New York City. Samuel D. Burchard, a Presbyterian clergyman, declared that a vote for Cleveland would be a vote for "rum, Romanism, and rebellion." This remark appealed to popular prejudices that linked the Demo-

Place of Nominating Convention. Chicago

Ballot on Which Nominated..... 2nd

Republican Opponent.......... James G. Blaine

Electoral Vote................. 219 (Cleveland) to
182 (Blaine)

Popular Vote........... 4,874,986 (Cleveland) to
4,851,981 (Blaine)

Age at Inauguration........... 47

crats with whiskey, Roman Catholicism, and the Southern cause in the Civil War. Roman Catholics deeply resented the statement. Blaine later repudiated it, but the damage had been done. Cleveland, by a slim majority of 23,005 votes, became the first Democratic President to be elected since James Buchanan in 1856.

First Administration (1885-1889)

Cleveland, who faced a Republican Senate, made effective use of the presidential powers of veto, appointment, and administrative control. With these weapons, rather than with any strong legislative program, he moved to restore government efficiency.

Reforms. Cleveland ordered the members of his Cabinet to eliminate "abuses and extravagances" in their departments. As a result, the Department of the Navy tightened its supervision of shipbuilding and added several new vessels to the fleet, including the battleship *Maine*. The Department of the Interior forced western railroads to return to the public domain vast acreages of excess right-of-way land that they had held illegally. This land was forfeited because the railroads had failed to carry out their earlier agreements to extend their lines. The forfeited land equaled the combined areas of New York, New Jersey, Pennsylvania, Delaware, Maryland, and Virginia.

The spoils system had continued to flourish in spite of the Civil Service Act of 1883 (see SPOILS SYSTEM). Cleveland, like other Presidents of his era, was besieged by office seekers. He tried to steer a middle course between the reformers, who wanted him to extend civil service, and party politicians, who were hungry for jobs. He more than doubled the number of workers who held jobs through the merit system, although the total still included fewer than a fourth of all government employees. But his moderation satisfied neither the reformers nor the politicians.

Labor Problems were among Cleveland's gravest concerns. Farmers had heavy debts, and the Grange and Farmers' Alliances demanded reforms. Laborers suffered from low wages and harsh working conditions.

——— **VICE-PRESIDENT AND CABINET** ———

Vice-President................ *Thomas A. Hendricks
Secretary of State............ Thomas F. Bayard
Secretary of the Treasury...... Daniel Manning
Charles S. Fairchild (1887)
Secretary of War.............. William C. Endicott
Attorney General........... *Augustus H. Garland
Postmaster General.......... William F. Vilas
Don M. Dickinson (1888)
Secretary of the Navy........ William C. Whitney
Secretary of the Interior...... *Lucius Q. C. Lamar
William F. Vilas (1888)
Secretary of Agriculture....... Norman J. Colman (office
established in 1889)

*Has a separate biography in WORLD BOOK.

Employers in those days felt little sense of responsibility for their employees. The Knights of Labor, a labor group, grew to 700,000 members by 1886. Its strike at the McCormick-Harvester plant in Chicago led indirectly to the bloody Haymarket Riot (see HAYMARKET RIOT). Cleveland distrusted workers' movements, but he acted for the best interests of the nation as he saw them. He was the first President to devote an entire congressional message to the subject of labor, although nothing came of his proposal for a permanent government arbitration board.

Veterans' Affairs. Cleveland opposed many pension measures, defying the Grand Army of the Republic and other powerful pressure groups. The pension rolls had become full of fraud. Many healthy veterans claimed to be unfit for work, and widows continued to collect government money after they had remarried. Cleveland vetoed hundreds of dishonest claims. He also vetoed the Dependent Pension Bill, which would have extended pension coverage to all disabled veterans, whether or not their disabilities were connected with military service. This bill was later passed in 1890.

The Currency and the Tariff were the most important issues facing Cleveland during his first term. Dissension was growing between the bankers and industrialists of the East, and the farmers of the South and West. The industrialists wanted a high tariff to protect high prices. They also wanted what they called a "sound" money system, based on gold. Farmers wanted a low tariff so they would not have to pay high prices for imported manufactured goods. They had heavy debts, and wanted money to be "cheap" in comparison with goods. That is, the farmers wanted *inflation*, so they could pay their debts with less farm produce.

The Currency of the United States at this time was based on gold. But limited amounts of silver could be sold at the Treasury for gold at the fixed proportion of 16 to 1, or 16 ounces of silver for 1 ounce of gold. The Bland-Allison Act of 1878 required the Treasury to purchase and coin a minimum of $2,000,000 worth of silver a month. Meanwhile, new silver mines had been discovered, and the world price of silver fell. People could buy silver on the open market and make a profit by selling it to the government for gold. As a result, gold was rapidly drained from the Treasury.

Cleveland believed in a gold standard (see GOLD STANDARD). He asked Congress to repeal the Bland-Allison Act, but it refused. The government then issued bonds and sold them to banks for gold. But this helped matters for only a short time, because the drain on the Treasury's gold continued.

The Tariff. Cleveland felt that tariffs should be reduced, mainly because the government was collecting more money than it spent. His supporters advised him not to bring up this controversial subject. But, in his annual message in 1887, he dared to ask Congress to lower tariffs. Congress refused, but Cleveland focused national opinion on this problem.

Other Actions. The Presidential Succession Act of 1886 settled questions regarding succession to the presidency (see PRESIDENTIAL SUCCESSION). One of the most important bills of Cleveland's first term was the Interstate Commerce Act of 1887, which allowed the federal government to regulate interstate railroads.

Cleveland's Family. In June, 1886, Cleveland delighted the nation with his marriage to Frances Folsom (July 21, 1864-Oct. 29, 1947). The 21-year-old bride had been Cleveland's ward since her father died in 1875. He had been one of Cleveland's law partners. Cleveland was the only President to be married in the White House, and reporters pried into every detail with what he called "colossal impertinence."

The Clevelands had five children: Ruth (1891-1904), Esther (1893-   ), Marion (1895-   ), Richard F. (1897-   ), and Francis (1903-   ). Esther Cleveland was the first and only child of a President to be born in the White House.

Five years after Cleveland's death, Mrs. Cleveland married Thomas J. Preston, Jr., a Princeton professor.

Life in the White House. During Cleveland's first year in office, his younger sister Rose acted as his hostess. After his marriage, his young wife performed these official duties with ease and charm.

Cleveland was a hard-working President, particularly because he was unwilling to delegate responsibility. "He would rather do something badly for himself than have somebody else do it well," grumbled a political colleague. The President often stayed up until 2 or 3 A.M. going over official business, and sometimes answered the White House telephone himself.

As the Clevelands left the White House in 1889, Mrs. Cleveland told the servants: "I want you to take good care of all the furniture and ornaments in the house, for I want to find everything just as it is now when we come back again . . . four years from today."

Election of 1888. The tariff became the main issue in the election of 1888. Benjamin Harrison, the Republican candidate, opposed tariff reduction. Neither Cleveland nor the Democratic party waged a strong campaign. Cleveland's attitude toward the spoils system had antagonized party politicians. His policies on pensions, the currency, and tariff reform had made enemies among veterans, farmers, and industrialists. Even so, he had more popular votes than Harrison. But Harrison received a larger electoral vote and won the election. See HARRISON, BENJAMIN (Election of 1888).

Between Terms

New York Attorney. Cleveland moved to New York City in 1889 and returned to the practice of law. The Harrison administration reversed many of Cleveland's stringent policies. It boosted the tariff, increased the purchase of silver, and extended pension coverage. Both prices and government expenditures reached new heights. Cleveland, on the sidelines, sharply criticized Harrison's program.

Election of 1892. By the end of Harrison's term, many Americans were ready to return to Cleveland's harder policies. In 1892, the Democratic national convention nominated Cleveland and chose Adlai E. Stevenson, a former Illinois Congressman, as his running mate. The Republicans renominated Harrison and nominated Whitelaw Reid for Vice-President.

The campaign centered mainly on the issue of a sound currency. The new Populist party, formed by groups from the Grange, the Farmers' Alliances, and

--- CLEVELAND'S SECOND ELECTION ---

Place of Nominating Convention	Chicago
Ballot on Which Nominated	1st
Republican Opponent	Benjamin Harrison
Electoral Vote	277 (Cleveland) to 145 (Harrison)
Popular Vote	5,555,426 (Cleveland) to 5,182,670 (Harrison)
Age at Inauguration	55

the Knights of Labor, polled more than a million votes. But Cleveland won easily.

Second Administration (1893-1897)

Cleveland enjoyed greater popularity at the beginning of his second term than at any other time during his presidency. He had made no promises to anyone in order to become President again. He was free to handle the country's problems as he saw fit, with Democratic majorities in both houses of Congress. But a severe financial panic swept the country only two months after he took office. Its causes included a farm depression, a business slump abroad, and the drain on the Treasury's gold reserve.

At this crucial time, physicians found that Cleveland had cancer of the mouth. Government leaders feared that the nation's shaky financial situation would become worse if the public knew of the President's illness. To keep it a secret, Cleveland boarded a friend's yacht in New York Harbor in July, and a team of surgeons removed his left upper jaw while the ship steamed up the East River. The operation was completely successful. Cleveland wore an artificial jaw made of rubber, which changed his appearance only slightly. News of the operation gradually became public, although great efforts were made to keep it secret.

Labor Unrest grew more serious with the business slump. Cleveland was not hostile to labor. But his strong belief in order and his limited understanding of changing conditions led him to use force rather than to seek constructive solutions to the new problems that faced his administration.

One sign of discontent was "Coxey's Army," a group of unemployed men who demonstrated for government aid (see COXEY, JACOB S.). The Pullman strike of May, 1894, had far greater importance. Workers of the Pullman Company went on strike, and members of the American Railway Union, led by Eugene V. Debs, supported them by refusing to handle Pullman cars (see DEBS, EUGENE V.). A general railroad strike resulted. A federal court issued an injunction against the strikers

--- VICE-PRESIDENT AND CABINET ---

Vice-President	*Adlai E. Stevenson
Secretary of State	Walter Q. Gresham
	*Richard Olney (1895)
Secretary of the Treasury	John G. Carlisle
Secretary of War	Daniel S. Lamont
Attorney General	*Richard Olney
	Judson Harmon (1895)
Postmaster General	Wilson S. Bissell
	William L. Wilson (1895)
Secretary of the Navy	Hilary A. Herbert
Secretary of the Interior	Hoke Smith
	David R. Francis (1896)
Secretary of Agriculture	*Julius Sterling Morton

*Has a separate biography in WORLD BOOK.

because mail service had been interrupted. Disorders broke out near Chicago, and Cleveland sent federal troops, saying: "If it takes the entire army and navy of the United States to deliver a postal card in Chicago, that card will be delivered." The government broke the strike. Most people approved Cleveland's action. But Governor John P. Altgeld of Illinois, who had state militia standing ready, argued that the disorders were not serious enough to warrant federal troops. Some historians believe that Cleveland exceeded his constitutional powers and violated states' rights. See PULLMAN STRIKE.

Tariff Defeat. Cleveland resumed his campaign for tariff reform, and again asked Congress to lower import duties. While the Wilson-Gorman Bill was being debated, the President issued a statement accusing uncooperative Democrats of "party perfidy and party dishonor." His comments outraged many party members, and the bill as passed in 1894 fell far short of Cleveland's goal. He let it become law without his signature because it also provided for a federal income tax. The Supreme Court later declared the income tax provision unconstitutional.

Foreign Affairs. Many Americans in the 1890's felt that the United States should build a colonial empire. Cleveland wanted the United States to respect the rights of smaller, weaker nations. Events in Hawaii and Venezuela tested his principles.

Hawaii. At the end of Benjamin Harrison's administration, American settlers in Hawaii had brought about a revolution and asked the United States to annex the islands. Cleveland's second term began before the Senate could ratify the treaty of annexation. Cleveland felt that Americans in Hawaii had involved the United States in a dishonorable action, and he withdrew the treaty from the Senate. The islands continued independent until 1898.

Venezuela. Cleveland's most popular action during his second term was his firm stand in a boundary dispute between Great Britain and Venezuela. Britain had refused for several years to allow its claim to be decided by a board of arbitration. In 1895, Secretary of State Richard Olney sent a sharp note to Britain declaring that "the United States is practically sovereign on this continent, and its fiat is law upon the subjects to which it confines its interposition." In a message to Congress, Cleveland hinted that armed force might be necessary to settle the matter. England agreed to submit the Venezuela boundary to international arbitration, and a settlement was reached in 1899. But historians have criticized Cleveland's intervention as extreme and provocative.

Saving the Gold Standard. A severe financial panic in 1893 caused 15,000 business failures and threw 4,000,000 persons out of work. Cleveland felt that a basic cause of the panic was the Sherman Silver Purchase Act of Harrison's administration. In June, 1893, he called a special session of Congress to repeal the act. Congress did so, but the nation's gold reserves had dwindled alarmingly. The government floated four bond issues in the next three years to replenish them. J. P. Morgan and other financiers bought three of these bond issues, and Cleveland's opponents charged that he had betrayed the nation to Eastern bankers.

Meanwhile, the silver interests grew stronger. By the time of the Democratic convention in 1896, the "silverites" outnumbered the "goldbugs." To the dismay of Cleveland, who did not seek a third term, William Jennings Bryan won the Democratic presidential nomination. Bryan's famous "cross of gold" speech swung the party to the silver cause (see BRYAN, WILLIAM JENNINGS). Cleveland preferred the sound money policies of William McKinley, the Republican candidate, but he took no part in the campaign. His popularity had reached a low ebb at the end of his term, and he spoke of his "poor old battered name" when he left the White House in 1897.

Later Years

Cleveland spent his last years in Princeton, N.J. Public opinion about him gradually changed, and he regained respect. Cleveland served Princeton University as lecturer and as trustee, and enjoyed the company of Woodrow Wilson, president of the university. He wrote several magazine articles, and in 1904 published some of his lectures under the title *Presidential Problems*. He also helped reorganize the Equitable Life Assurance Society after financial scandals had damaged its reputation. People believed so strongly in him that his name restored their confidence.

After a three-month illness, Cleveland died on June 24, 1908. His last words were: "I have tried so hard to do right." He was buried in Princeton. OSCAR HANDLIN

Related Articles in WORLD BOOK include:

Harrison, Benjamin	President of the United States
Haymarket Riot	Stevenson, Adlai E. (1835-1914)
Hendricks, Thomas A.	World's Columbian Exposition

Outline

I. Early Life
  A. Boyhood   B. Lawyer

II. Political Career
  A. Minor Offices   C. Governor of New York
  B. Mayor of Buffalo   D. Election of 1884

III. First Administration (1885-1889)
  A. Reforms   E. Other Actions
  B. Labor Problems   F. Cleveland's Family
  C. Veterans' Affairs   G. Life in the White House
  D. The Currency and   H. Election of 1888
       the Tariff

IV. Between Terms
  A. New York Attorney   B. Election of 1892

V. Second Administration (1893-1897)
  A. Labor Unrest   C. Foreign Affairs
  B. Tariff Defeat   D. Saving the Gold Standard

VI. Later Years

Questions

How was Cleveland's marriage unique?

Why did Cleveland pay a substitute to serve for him in the Civil War?

Why did Cleveland execute two criminals himself?

How many Presidents have been defeated for re-election and later won a second term?

Who were the *mugwumps?* How did they affect Cleveland's nomination in 1884?

Historians have criticized two actions of Cleveland's second term which were popular at the time. Why?

Why was Cleveland's jaw operation kept secret?

What actions made him an unpopular President?

How did Cleveland feel about labor agitation? What did he do about it during his first term?

What words, spoken as he died, summed up his life?

CLEVELAND INSTITUTE OF ART

CLEVELAND INSTITUTE OF ART, in Cleveland, Ohio, was established in 1882. It offers four-year professional courses in advertising, ceramics, graphics, illustration, industrial design, painting, portraiture, sculpture, silversmithing, textile design, and weaving. The Cleveland Institute of Art also offers a five-year program leading to a bachelor of fine arts degree, and a five-year art education program in cooperation with Case Western Reserve University. The total enrollment is about 1,000.   JOSEPH MCCULLOUGH

CLEVELAND STATE UNIVERSITY. See UNIVERSITIES AND COLLEGES (table).

CLIBURN, VAN (1934-   ), is an American pianist. He gained world fame in 1958 by winning the International Tchaikovsky Competition in Moscow against pianists from 19 countries. When he returned to New York City, he received the first ticker-tape parade ever given a musician. HARVEY LAVAN CLIBURN was born in Shreveport, La., but later moved to Kilgore, Tex. When he was three, he began to study piano with his mother, a former concert pianist. Cliburn later attended the well-known Juilliard School of Music in New York City.   ROBERT U. NELSON

See also PIANO (picture).

CLICK BEETLE is the name used for any one of a group of beetles that spring and snap. There are about 300 different kinds of click beetles in the United States and Canada. Most of them are brown, but some are black, gray, or marked with bright colors.

The young of the click beetle are long, slender worms called *wireworms*. Wireworms bore into seeds of young corn, wheat, and other grains. They also feed on the roots of field and garden plants. See WIREWORM.

Some tropical click beetles can glow in the dark. One kind has two glowing spots on each side of its body. The dead bodies of tropical click beetles are sometimes worn as ornaments in Cuba. See BEETLE (Kinds of Beetles).

Scientific Classification. Click beetles are members of the order *Coleoptera*. They make up the click beetle family, *Elateridae*.   H. H. ROSS

CLIFF is a steep face of rock. Several processes of erosion form cliffs. Waves cut imposing and scenic cliffs along coast lines. Rivers create deep canyons with steep sides. Glaciers grind away the rock along valley walls and produce cliffs that appear after the glacier melts. Glaciers also pluck rock fragments away from high mountain slopes where snow collects to form walls around amphitheater-like basins.   A. J. EARDLEY

CLIFF DWELLERS were early Indians who built their houses in the high cliffs of the southwestern United States. Most cliff dwellings were built between A.D. 1000 and 1300, but the dry climate and protected locations have preserved many of them. Archaeologists have found wooden implements, bows and arrows, leather and cotton garments, sandals, food, and even the mummified bodies of the Cliff Dwellers. These discoveries told more about the life and customs of these people than scientists have learned about most people who lived before the era of writing.

Way of Life. Cliff Dwellers were short and black-haired. The backs of their heads were flattened, because their mothers strapped them to flat cradleboards

Sheer Rocky Cliffs Rise from the Pacific Ocean on the slopes of Neahkahnie Mountain, in northwest Oregon.

Ray Atkeson

Ray Atkeson

The "White House" of the Ancient Cliff Dwellers is the largest of nearly 100 such ruins. It stands in the Canyon de Chelly National Monument in Arizona.

when they were babies. In summer, both men and women wore simple skirts woven from cotton, yucca, and milkweed fibers. In winter, they wore fur robes and blankets made of cords wrapped with turkey feathers or strips of rabbit skin. Cliff Dwellers lived by farming on the plains at the foot of their cliff homes. They grew corn, beans, squash, tobacco, and cotton. They also domesticated the turkey. They hunted deer and mountain sheep, using weapons pointed with flaked stone. The people ate from skillfully made clay dishes and bowls, which they decorated with painted designs in red or black.

Cliff Dwellers had two main kinds of homes. Caves provided shelter for several groups, especially along river canyons. But most Cliff Dwellers lived in the famous two- and three-story cliff houses. They built these homes on protected ledges or in hollow spaces in cliff walls. They used sandstone blocks and laid them in mud mortar. They stacked the small rooms upon one another, and set each story back a few feet from the one beneath. Some cliff dwellings had room for 1,500 persons. There were few doors on the ground floor, and people used ladders to reach the first roof. In case of attack, the people drew the ladders up and fought from the housetops. Winding paths, ladders, or steps which were cut into the stone led up from the valleys below to the rock ledges on which the Cliff Dwellers' caves and houses stood.

All the villages had round underground chambers called *kivas*, which the people entered through a hatchway in the roof. Men held councils in them, and also used them for secret religious ceremonies and as clubhouses. Their plastered walls often had symbolic paintings in red, white, green, and yellow.

History. The Cliff Dwellers belonged to a group called the *Anasazi* (pronounced *AN ah SAH zee*) *culture.* The earliest members of this group, called *Basket Makers,* began farming in northern New Mexico and Arizona and southern Utah and Colorado about the time of Christ. Gradually they developed a type of many-storied dwelling called a *pueblo.* For this reason, all groups in Anasazi history after about A.D. 700 are called *Pueblo Indians.* Around the year 1000, certain groups of Pueblo Indians began moving up into the hills and building their homes in cliffs, perhaps for protection against groups of savage nomadic Indians. During the next 300 years, a period called *Classic Pueblo,* the Anasazi culture reached its highest point, among both these Cliff Dwellers and the other Pueblo Indians who had remained on the plains. The cliff-dwelling Indians abandoned their cliff houses by 1300, probably because of increased enemy attacks and a period of severe drought. They moved southward, along with their plains relatives, and built the pueblo villages that the Spanish found in the 1500's. For the story of these later Indians, see PUEBLO INDIANS.

See the Places to Visit sections of COLORADO, NEW MEXICO, and UTAH for the names of national monuments that have ruins of cliff dwellings.

CLIFFORD, CLARK McADAMS (1906-   ), served as United States secretary of defense under President Lyndon B. Johnson from March, 1968, to January, 1969. Clifford had previously served as special counsel to President Harry S. Truman from 1946 to 1950 and as an unofficial adviser to Presidents John F. Kennedy and Johnson.

Clifford was born in Fort Scott, Kans., and received a law degree in 1928 from Washington University in St. Louis. He served in the U.S. Navy during World War II and was appointed naval aide to President Truman in 1946 before leaving the service. In 1950, Clifford became a senior partner in one of the most successful law firms in Washington, D.C.

CLIFFS OF DOVER. See DOVER.

CLIFTON, N.J. (pop. 82,084; alt. 65 ft.), is an industrial and manufacturing center. It lies 12 miles northwest of New York City, between Paterson and Passaic, N.J. (see NEW JERSEY [political map]). Clifton, Passaic, and Paterson form a metropolitan area with a population of 1,186,873. Two railroads and several excellent highways carry Clifton's factory and mill products to markets in surrounding cities. These products include batteries, boxcars, chemicals, clothing, electronic equipment, metal products, pharmaceuticals, scales, and stained glass.

Clifton became a city in 1917. It has a council-manager form of government.   RICHARD P. McCORMICK

CLIMATE

CLIMATE is the usual weather in a certain area for a period of many years. Large and small areas all have climates. Each continent, country, city, and town has its own climate. Even an area as small as a city block or a flower garden has its own climate.

In describing the climate of an area, we usually consider the five most important conditions of the air. These conditions are (1) temperature, (2) wind, (3) sunshine, (4) humidity, and (5) rainfall (including rain, snow, sleet, and hail). *Climatologists*, or scientists who specialize in the study of climate, also include cloudiness, air pressure, and other conditions of the air.

How is climate different from weather? *Weather* is the condition of the air for a brief period of time. On a certain day, or during a certain week or month, the weather may be hot or cold, rainy or dry, windy or calm. But climate can be described only by the variety of weather conditions for many years. The climate of Chicago is hot in summer and cold in winter. Summer temperatures often rise above 90° F., and sometimes above 100° F. Winter temperatures often fall below 20° F., and sometimes below 0° F. Statements such as these describe the climate of a place. Weather is like each individual picture flashed rapidly, one after another, in a motion picture. Climate is the entire movie.

How Climate Affects Our Way of Life

Everywhere on earth, climate affects our way of life. It affects the kinds of clothing we wear, the kinds of food we raise, the kinds of houses we live in, and the kinds of transportation we use. It also affects the kinds of plants and animals that are native to an area.

People who live in a climate that is hot the year around, such as that of Panama, wear light clothing all year. Those who live in a climate with cold winters and warm summers, such as that of Minnesota, wear light clothing in summer and heavy clothing in winter. People of the Arabian desert wear robes that protect them from a climate that has hot days and cold nights.

Most food crops grow best in certain climates. Wheat thrives chiefly in areas that are neither too wet nor too dry, with warm to hot summers and cool to cold winters. Most rice comes from areas with warm, rainy climates. Citrus fruits need a mild, warm climate.

We build our houses for protection from the climate in which we live. Sturdy, well-insulated houses keep out cold in winter and heat in summer. Furnaces are needed in very cold climates. Air conditioners make homes cooler in hot climates.

Sometimes climate affects our methods of transportation. In hot, rainy climates, such as in the Congo, plants and trees grow so quickly that it is difficult to build and maintain roads or railroads. As a result, most people travel by boats along the rivers. In hot, dry climates, such as in the Sahara, people can easily travel on land because the plant life is sparse and slow-growing. Persons who live in cold, snowy climates may use sleds, snowshoes, or skis to travel on the snow.

Plant life differs from climate to climate. The cactus plants and the widely spaced bunch grass of desert climates are quite different from the evergreen forests of cold northern climates. The oak and hickory forests that grow in the climate of New England differ from the grass-covered prairies of the Midwest. Towering trees, with smaller trees and bushes beneath, thrive in hot, rainy climates, such as in most areas along the equator. But only tiny lichens and mosses grow in the cold lands near the North and South poles.

Animal life also varies with the climate. Antelope and giraffes live in the tropical grasslands, which have a rainy season and a dry season. Beavers and otters live in areas with warm summers and cold winters. Polar bears and penguins live in the cold polar lands. There are similar contrasts in the animal life of the sea. The cod and halibut are cold-water fish, but the tuna and the sailfish live in warm water.

Kinds of Climates

For general purposes, we can classify climates according to temperature and rainfall. Different areas may have the same *average* annual temperature or rainfall, but not the same kind of climate. In some regions, temperature and rainfall vary greatly from season to season. These seasonal variations are important in classifying climates.

The average annual temperature of San Francisco and St. Louis is the same, 55° F. But January temperatures average 49° F. in San Francisco, and only 32° F. in St. Louis. July temperatures average 57° F. in San Francisco, and 79° F. in St. Louis. The climate of San Francisco is warm and rainy with dry summers. St. Louis has a cold, moist climate.

The average annual rainfall in Tokyo and Calcutta is about the same—58 inches in Tokyo, and 62 inches in Calcutta. The rainfall in Tokyo is well distributed throughout the year. In Calcutta, almost all the rain falls in one season. Tokyo has a warm, rainy climate. Calcutta's climate is wet and dry tropical.

There are nine major kinds of climates. The table with this article classifies them according to temperature and rainfall.

Why Climates Differ

The *World Map* with this article shows the locations of the major kinds of climate. As shown on the map, climates may be roughly arranged by *latitude*, or dis-

The Nine Major Kinds of Climate

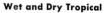

Rainy Tropical
Temperature
Hot throughout the year
Rainfall
Well distributed throughout the year

Wet and Dry Tropical
Temperature
Warm to hot throughout the year
Rainfall
Abundant only in one season

Semiarid
Temperature
Hot to cold
Rainfall
Little rain in any season

Desert
Temperature
Hot to cold
Rainfall
All seasons very dry

Warm Rainy
Temperature
Warm to hot summers, cool winters
Rainfall
Well distributed throughout the year

SPRING   SUMMER   AUTUMN   WINTER

Warm Rainy with Dry Summer
Temperature
Warm to hot summers, cool winters
Rainfall
Rainy winters, dry summers

SPRING   SUMMER   AUTUMN   WINTER

Cold Moist
Temperature
Cold winters, warm to hot summers
Rainfall
Some rain or snow in all seasons

SPRING   SUMMER   AUTUMN   WINTER

Polar
Temperature
Long, cold winters; short, warm summers
Rainfall
Little rain or snow

Ice Cap
Temperature
Very cold in winter, cold in summer
Rainfall
Little rain or snow

CLIMATES AROUND THE WORLD

Climate Creates Patterns of hot, cold, dry, and rainy regions throughout the world. Most of the warm regions are near the equator. The cold ones are near the poles. The climate of any large area may vary greatly. The Andes Mountains cross the equator but have a polar climate. The Sahara, one of the world's hottest, driest places, lies 1,800 miles north of the equator. But the Himalaya, which is about the same distance from the equator, has a polar climate.

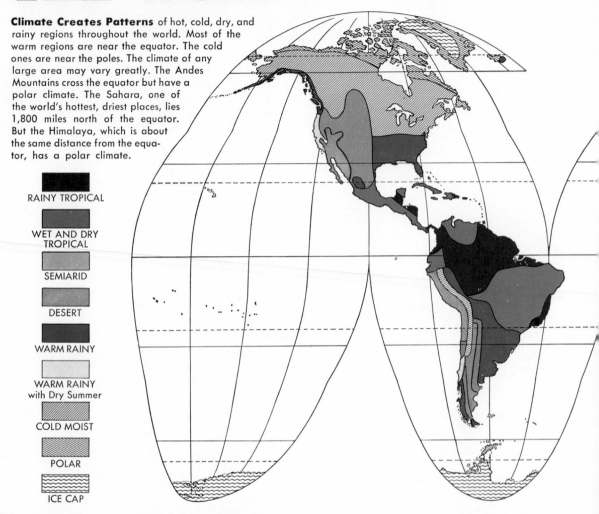

RAINY TROPICAL

WET AND DRY TROPICAL

SEMIARID

DESERT

WARM RAINY

WARM RAINY with Dry Summer

COLD MOIST

POLAR

ICE CAP

tance from the equator. However, this arrangement is far from consistent. For example, the northern Hudson Bay area in Canada has a polar climate. But it lies in the same latitude as the Alaskan coast, which has a warm, rainy climate. If the map were larger, still greater variations in climate would be apparent, because small climate regions in mountain areas could be shown. For instance, a small area of polar climate lies on top of the Andes Mountains along the equator. Such variations occur because latitude is only one of several factors that affect climate.

Latitude affects climate in two ways. It determines (1) the height of the noon sun and (2) the length of day. These factors, in turn, determine the amount of heat received from the sun. They vary throughout the year, depending on the latitude.

In the tropics, near the equator, the days are almost equally long throughout the year. The land receives much warmth every day because the sun is almost directly overhead.

At the other extreme, near the North Pole, the sun shines even at midnight during late spring and early summer. But it does not shine at all in late autumn and early winter.

In middle latitudes, between the tropics and the polar regions, the heat from the sun does not vary as much from season to season as in higher latitudes.

For a detailed explanation of how latitude affects the amount of heat an area receives from the sun, see WEATHER (Temperature Patterns).

Elevation affects climate because the temperature of the air usually becomes colder as elevation increases. Most hill and mountain locations are cooler than nearby lowland locations.

Terrain, or surface features of the land, affects climate in three ways. First, some surfaces are strongly

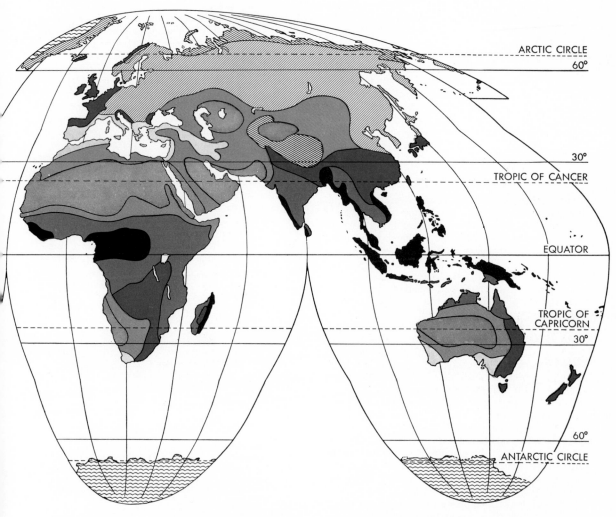

ARCTIC CIRCLE
60°

30°
TROPIC OF CANCER

EQUATOR

TROPIC OF
CAPRICORN
30°

60°
ANTARCTIC CIRCLE

heated by the sun and others are not. Surfaces such as sand, barren rock, and city pavements are strongly heated. They in turn heat the lower air. Bodies of water, grassland, and forests are less strongly heated by the sun. They may warm the lower air, but not as much as sand, rock, and pavements do.

Second, terrain influences the *wind*, or moving masses of air. Valleys channel the flow of the wind, bringing cooler or warmer air to some regions. Mountains block the wind or force it to rise so that it can move over the mountains.

Third, terrain may cause rainfall. When moist air rises to pass over mountains, clouds often form and rainfall results. Air becomes cooler as it rises, and cool air cannot hold as much moisture as warm air.

Oceans. The coastal regions of the continents have a mild climate because of the mild ocean air. In summer, the oceans do not become as warm as the land, and in winter they do not become as cold. Ocean air stays relatively cool in summer and relatively warm in winter. The west coasts of almost all continents in middle latitudes have especially mild ocean climates. In these areas the winds usually blow from west to east, bringing the mild ocean air over the land.

The oceans are also the source of rainfall. Winds pick up moisture as they pass over the oceans. When these winds move over the land, they bring clouds and rain. Coastal mountains that face ocean winds are very rainy. Much ocean air moves inland, sometimes at great heights. It is the source of rainfall even far from the coasts.

Cold Continental Areas. Dry, cold masses of air form in such areas as northwest Canada and Siberia. Winter temperatures of −50° F. or colder are common. When cold masses move away from the regions where they formed, they bring cold waves with them. They produce the cold winters that occur in most parts of the northern United States.

Hot Continental Areas. Dry, hot masses of air form in deserts and semiarid regions far from the coasts. Such regions include the deserts of the southwestern United States and the Sahara of Africa. As air masses move away from these regions they sometimes bring drought and heat waves.

Paths of Storms. In middle latitudes and near the polar regions, major storms move chiefly from west to east. These storm paths shift from season to season, and affect the amount of rainfall in the areas they pass through. For example, California has rainy winters because storms frequently cross the state during that season. California is dry in summer because the paths usually followed by moving storms have shifted far north of the state.

Changes in Climate

For hundreds of millions of years, the climates of different areas on earth have gone through great changes. At various times, *glaciers*, or huge sheets of ice, have moved down across the continents into regions that are now warm. The last Ice Age began about a million years ago. During the Ice Age, there were four major periods when glaciers covered much of Europe and North America. Each period lasted thousands of years. It was separated from the next period by a long, warmer time during which the ice melted. The last great ice sheet in North America was at its height about 25,000 years ago (see ICE AGE [Development]).

For the past 10,000 years, the general trend has been toward warmer and rainier climates in middle latitudes. There have been relatively short periods of 50 to 100 years when the climate became colder. From about 1850 to 1950, there was a small trend toward slightly higher temperatures in middle and high latitudes. Average temperatures became slightly colder in the mid-1900's. No one knows if this trend will continue.

Man can change the climate in a small area. He can increase the rainfall a bit in some mountainous areas by seeding the clouds with dry ice or special chemicals (see RAIN MAKING). Man also changes the climate slightly when he builds a city, destroys a forest, or plants crops in a barren field. But these small changes influence only the *microclimate*, the climate over a few acres or a few square miles.

Man may never be able to change the climate in major ways over really large areas. Atomic explosions might change the weather for a few years if thousands of them occurred in an atomic war. The explosions could increase dust in the air enough to lower the temperature slightly over large areas. But broad man-made changes in climate do not seem possible.

Studying Climate

The word *climate* comes from the Greek word *klima*, which means *slope*. The ancient Greeks believed that climate depended almost entirely on latitude. They thought the earth "sloped" away from the sun north of the Mediterranean Sea, and as a result the climate became colder and colder. South of the Mediterranean,

they thought, the earth "sloped" toward the sun and the climate grew hotter and hotter. Finally, there was a "torrid zone" at the southern end of the earth where it was too hot for human life.

Until the 1400's, most people believed that an uninhabitable torrid zone existed. Then Portuguese explorers sailed far south along the west coast of Africa and found people living in regions at the equator. Explorers such as Christopher Columbus, Sir Francis Drake, and Ferdinand Magellan extended the knowledge of climates in regions far from Europe.

During the 1500's and 1600's, scientists developed the barometer, thermometer, and wind gauge. These instruments measured certain conditions of the air, and helped scientists study climate and weather. By the 1880's, Charles R. Darwin and other scientists were observing and measuring climates in many parts of the world.

Today, high altitude balloons, space rockets, and artificial satellites carry instruments that help climatologists study the climate at great heights. New knowledge of the upper atmosphere indicates that changes in climate may be related to changes in the sun's radiation. It may become possible to predict changes in the sun's radiation far in advance. If this proves to be true, man may some day be able to predict climate as far ahead as a hundred or even a thousand years.

DAVID I. BLUMENSTOCK

Related Articles. See the section on climate in the various state, province, country, and continent articles, such as ALABAMA (Climate). Other related articles in WORLD BOOK include:

Outline

I. **How Climate Affects Our Way of Life**
II. **Kinds of Climates**
III. **Why Climates Differ**
    A. Latitude   E. Cold Continental Areas
    B. Elevation   F. Hot Continental Areas
    C. Terrain   G. Paths of Storms
    D. Oceans
IV. **Changes in Climate**
V. **Studying Climate**

Questions

What is the difference between climate and weather?
What are some ways that climate affects our food? Our clothing? Our homes?
Why did the ancient Greeks believe that no men lived far south of the Mediterranean Sea?
What are the five most important weather conditions in describing climate?
How might an atomic war lower temperatures?
How does distance from the equator affect climate?
How is the climate of an area affected by mountains? By valleys? By oceans?
How do space vehicles help the study of climate?
What is a microclimate?
What causes the cold winters that occur in most parts of the northern United States?

CLIMATRON. See MISSOURI (Places to Visit; picture).

CLINGMANS DOME is the highest peak in the Great Smokies and in Tennessee. The 6,642-foot-high mountain rises on the Tennessee-North Carolina boundary, about 35 miles southeast of Knoxville. For location, see TENNESSEE (physical map). The Clingmans Dome area is a resort region with a variety of plants, cool streams, and wooded mountain scenery. Perhaps the most spectacular trip in Great Smoky Mountains National Park is the climb from Gatlinburg, Tenn., past Newfound Gap to Clingmans Dome. E. WILLARD MILLER

See also TENNESSEE (color picture).

CLINICAL PSYCHOLOGY is concerned with the psychological adjustment of the individual to himself and his environment. Clinical psychologists deal with both normal and abnormal behavior. They administer and interpret psychological tests, and diagnose and treat mental disorders. They also study the structure and development of personality, and work to prevent serious disturbances in mental health.

Clinical psychology is an *applied* field of psychology. That is, it puts into practice the theories developed in the different fields of psychology. For example, clinical psychologists apply many findings of abnormal psychology when they diagnose and treat mental disorders. They also draw knowledge from the fields of learning, motivation, perception, personality, developmental psychology, physiological psychology, and social psychology. The chief activities of clinical psychology are (1) testing and diagnosis, (2) psychotherapy and consultation, and (3) research.

Testing and Diagnosis. Clinical psychologists are experts in the administration and interpretation of tests that measure aptitude, intelligence, and personality. Through their interpretation of test results, these experts help determine proper school placement for students of all ages. They also help employers determine people's aptitudes for certain kinds of jobs. Clinical psychologists also use personality tests in diagnosing mental disorders. See TESTING.

Psychotherapy and Consultation. Clinical psychologists treat only mental disorders that result from disturbed human relationships rather than from biological causes. They deal with brief, minor disturbances such as stress resulting from a school failure or grief due to the loss of a loved one. They also try to solve the prolonged problems of *neuroses* (mild personality disorders) and *psychoses* (severe personality disorders).

Psychotherapy is the clinical psychologist's chief tool in treating mental disorders. In most kinds of psychotherapy, the psychologist talks with the patient in a series of informal interviews. In most cases, the psychologist tries to help his patient understand the cause of his personality disturbance (see MENTAL ILLNESS [How Mental Illnesses Are Treated]).

Preventing mental disorders is an important goal of the clinical psychologist. He develops and takes part in consultation programs to educate the public in methods of improving and expanding mental health facilities. He also works with the clergy, teachers, and other persons who deal with children to help identify and solve psychological problems at an early stage.

Research. Clinical psychologists are trained to design and conduct scientific experiments. Through their knowledge and use of research techniques, they improve various methods of diagnosing and treating mental dis-

orders. They propose new theories on the structure and development of personality. They also develop and evaluate new testing methods. IRVING E. ALEXANDER

See also MENTAL ILLNESS with its list of Related Articles.

CLINKER. See CEMENT AND CONCRETE (How Cement Is Made).

CLINKER-BUILT VESSEL. See SHIP AND SHIPPING (The Vikings).

CLINTON, DE WITT (1769-1828), an American statesman, promoted the building of the Erie Canal. As early as 1809, he advocated building the canal. He served as a canal commissioner during the early years of its construction. The canal was completed in 1825, while Clinton was governor of New York. See ERIE CANAL.

Clinton was born in Little Britain, N.Y. He was graduated from Columbia College, and then studied law. He served as private secretary to his uncle, George Clinton, then governor of New York. He developed a strong interest in politics. In 1797, he was elected to the state assembly, and in the following year, he served in the state senate. In 1802, Clinton was sent to the United States Senate to fill a vacancy. The next year, he resigned his seat to become mayor of New York City. He

Brown Bros.
De Witt Clinton

was mayor from 1803 to 1815, except for two short intervals when he served in the New York Senate and was lieutenant governor of the state. In 1812, Clinton was an unsuccessful Federalist candidate for President of the United States. He served as governor of New York from 1817 to 1822 and from 1825 to 1828. During the time Clinton was governor, a school system was established. W. B. HESSELTINE

CLINTON, GEORGE (1739-1812), an American statesman and soldier, served as Vice-President of the United States from 1805 until his death. He served under two different Presidents, Thomas Jefferson and James Madison. Only one other Vice-President, John C. Calhoun, shares this record (see CALHOUN, JOHN C.).

Clinton also served as the first governor of New York. He was elected in 1777 after New York's constitutional convention, and won re-election six consecutive times, a record that still stands. Clinton strongly believed in states' rights, and at first opposed New York's ratification of the United States Constitution. Under the name "Cato," he published several letters against adoption of the Constitution. Alexander Hamilton started *The Federalist* papers largely to answer Clinton's objections (see HAMILTON, ALEXANDER).

Clinton was born in Little Britain, N.Y. He served as a brigadier general in the Continental Army in 1777. He also was a member of the New York Assembly and the Continental Congress. IRVING G. WILLIAMS

See also VICE-PRESIDENT OF THE U.S. (picture).

CLINTON, SIR HENRY (1730-1795), served as commander in chief of the British Army for four years during the Revolutionary War. He retreated from Philadelphia to New York, and stayed there about two years. Then in 1780 he invaded South Carolina and captured Charleston. He returned to New York, leaving Lord Cornwallis in command in the South. After Cornwallis surrendered in 1781 at Yorktown, Clinton resigned. He was blamed for Cornwallis' defeat. Clinton was born in Newfoundland. See also CORNWALLIS, CHARLES.   W. B. WILLCOX

CLIO. See MUSE.

CLIPPER SHIP was a fast, slender sailing vessel that was developed in the United States in the mid-1800's. To be classed a clipper, a ship needed a narrow *hull* (body) designed for speed, and many large sails mounted on tall *masts* (sail poles). Clipper ships were modeled after the "Baltimore Clippers," small, swift sailing ships developed on Chesapeake Bay for sea use. The name *clipper* came from the way the ships "clipped off" the miles. Traders used clipper ships to bring tea and opium from China, and wool and gold from Australia. Clipper ships carried passengers across the Atlantic Ocean, and around Cape Horn to California during the gold rush of 1849-1857.

The *Rainbow*, designed by John W. Griffiths and launched in 1845, was the first true clipper ship. It was much larger and faster than the earlier "Baltimore Clippers." Other famous clipper ships included the *Sea Witch* and the *Cutty Sark*.

Perhaps the most famous builder of clipper ships was Donald McKay, a Canadian. McKay did most of his work in East Boston. His ships included the *Flying Cloud, Stag Hound, Lightning, Sovereign of the Seas,* and *Great Republic.* When launched in 1853, the *Great Republic* was the largest sailing ship in the world. The 4,555-ton ship was 325 feet long and carried a crew of 130.

Some typical, fast clipper trips included a voyage across the Atlantic Ocean in 12 days, 6 hours by the *James Baines;* an 89-day, 4-hour voyage from New York City around Cape Horn to San Francisco by the *Andrew Jackson;* and a run of 465 miles in 24 hours by the

Champion of the Seas in 1854. More than 25 years passed before a steamship beat the *Champion of the Seas'* record. Square-riggers, ships designed to carry larger cargoes at slower speeds, gradually replaced the graceful clipper ships in the late 1800's.

In aviation, certain types of transoceanic passenger airplanes were called clippers (see AIRPLANE [color picture: Airplanes That Made History]).   ROBERT H. BURGESS

See also SHIP AND SHIPPING (color picture: Early Ships); MAINE (picture: Ships Built in Maine).

CLIPPERTON ISLAND is an isolated atoll in the northeast Pacific. It is 750 miles west of Acapulco, Mexico, and 1,300 miles northwest of the Galápagos Islands. Spanish explorers discovered the island, but it is named for John Clipperton, an English pirate who made it his headquarters. It now belongs to France. In 1943, the United States Navy occupied Clipperton Island for the duration of World War II.   EDWIN H. BRYAN, JR.

CLIPPING BUREAU. See PRESS CLIPPING BUREAU.

CLISTHENES. See CLEISTHENES.

CLIVE, ROBERT (1725-1774), BARON OF PLASSEY, was the British administrator and military leader who brought India into the British Empire.

Clive was born in Shropshire, England. He joined the English East India Company, Britain's trading company in India, in 1743. In 1747, he received a commission in the company's armed services. The British and French trading companies were struggling for control of India, and Clive won several important victories over the French and their Indian allies. In 1757, he led 3,200 troops to victory over 50,000 enemy troops at the Battle of Plassey. This important victory enabled the English to gain political control of Bengal, the richest province in India.

Clive returned to England in 1760 and entered Parliament. In 1773, some of Clive's enemies persuaded Parliament to investigate his career in India. The investigation showed that Clive had made a fortune, but that he had also rendered "great and meritorious service to his country." Sickness during the last year of his life caused Clive to become an opium addict. He committed suicide in 1774.   BRIJEN K. GUPTA

THE CLIPPER SHIP
UNDER PLAIN SAIL

1 Flying Jib	20 Mizzen-topgallant Staysail
2 Jib	21 Mizzen-royal Staysail
3 Fore-topmast Staysail	22 Mizzen Sail
4 Foresail	23 Lower Mizzen Topsail
5 Lower Fore-topsail	24 Upper Mizzen Topsail
6 Upper Fore-topsail	25 Mizzen-topgallant Sail
7 Fore-topgallant Sail	26 Mizzen Royal
8 Foreroyal	27 Mizzen Skysail
9 Fore-skysail	28 Spanker
10 Main-topmast Staysail	29 Boom
11 Main-topgallant Staysail	30 Stern
12 Main-royal Staysail	31 Bow
13 Mainsail	32 Bowsprit
14 Lower Main Topsail	33 Foremast
15 Upper Main Topsail	34 Mainmast
16 Main-topgallant Sail	35 Mizzenmast
17 Main Royal	
18 Main Skysail	
19 Mizzen-topmast Staysail	

French Clock of about 1770 had a hand to show the days of the week.

A French Clock of Gilded Bronze had a statue of George Washington on it.

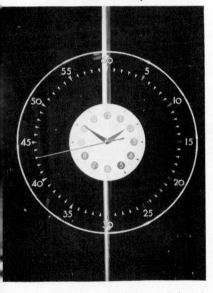

An Electric Clock has a dial made to resemble the dial of a telephone.

The Electric Clock uses a tiny motor instead of the complex mechanism of other clocks.

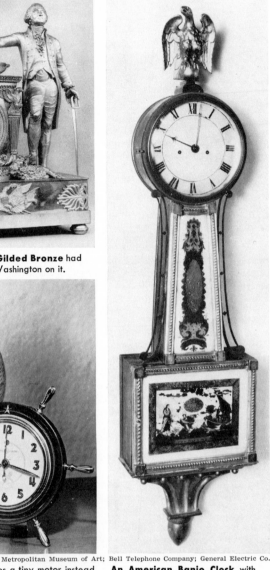

Metropolitan Museum of Art; Bell Telephone Company; General Electric Co.

An American Banjo Clock with a pendulum was made about 1815.

CLOCK is an instrument used for dividing the day and night into regular periods of time. The first clocks were the marked-off shadows of trees. When the shadow was short, the watchers could tell the time of day was near noon. When the shadows were long on either side, the day was either beginning or ending. Watching the shadows of a tree led to the making of the first sundial.

In order to measure time on cloudy days or during the night, the water clock or *clepsydra* was developed. This clock was used in China three thousand years ago. It was also known to the Egyptians, the Greeks, and the Romans. There were many forms of the water clock, but all of them worked about the same way. Water or some other fluid was made to run from one vessel to another. The amount of water that flowed could be measured to mark the passing of time.

In the 1300's Henry de Vick invented a clock which contained many of the important parts of the modern clock. It had wheels, a dial, and an hour hand. By 1700 a pendulum, a minute hand, and a second hand had been added to the clock. Since then the essential principles of clocks have not changed. Styles may vary, as in the tall grandfather clocks or the smaller mantle clocks. Clocks have become lighter and keep better time. Many modern clocks run by electricity.

Parts of a Clock

The essential parts of a clock are a set of wheels and a weight or spring which moves the wheels. The front of the clock contains a face and a set of hands which point out the hours and minutes. Before a clock can be made to run, it must be wound. In a clock which moves by

527

INTERESTING AND UNUSUAL CLOCKS

Metropolitan Museum of Art

A 200-Year-Old French Traveling Clock has a carrying case. The sturdily built clock was ideal for travelers.

French Clock of the 1700's had rotating bands instead of a dial.

German Clock of the 1500's was made of gilded bronze.

the energy produced by a falling weight, a chain or cord must be wound around a barrel or drum. As the weight falls, the drum turns. By means of gear teeth, the drum causes a small wheel, attached to a large wheel, to turn. This large wheel turns a small toothed wheel attached to still another larger wheel. A device called an *escapement* is connected to this second large wheel to keep the weight from falling too fast. This curved piece of metal has hooks called pallets on each end which fit into the second large wheel. The pendulum, as it swings from right to left, permits the second large wheel to move forward one tooth at a time as the device is tilted from side to side. The pendulum's swing is used to regulate the speed at which the wheels of the clock turn. The speed of the pendulum can be increased by moving its weight upward to shorten its pendulum. This makes the clock run faster. If the pendulum weight is lowered the pendulum swings more slowly and the clock runs more slowly.

One wheel turns around once every hour, and carries the long minute hand with it. The hour hand is moved by turning a small wheel with six teeth against a large wheel with 72 teeth. Thus, the minute hand turns twelve times while the wheel which moves the hour hand turns around once.

Spring Clocks. Clocks using only weights and pendulums were made for hundreds of years. This required that the clock remain in an upright position. Finally it was discovered that a small steel spring would provide enough energy to turn the wheels of the clock and thus permit the weight and the pendulum to be done away with. Spring clocks use a balance wheel instead of a pendulum to keep the wheels within the clock mechanism turning at an even rate. A balance wheel turns first in one direction and then in the opposite position. A small hairspring attached to the wheel provides a counterforce which sends it backward. Small clocks and watches use a mainspring to provide the energy to run them. In order to operate such a clock, the spring must be tightened or wound. Some clocks have springs that need to be wound only once every eight days. One special type of clock can run 400 days with one winding.

Striking Clocks. The part of a clock that strikes the hours is separate from the part that keeps time. Many of the early clocks had no hands to point out the hours. The escapement principle mentioned above was used to strike a bell or gong. People told time by listening to the number of strokes of a bell. The word clock is closely related to the German word *Glocke* and the French word *cloche*, which both mean bell.

The bell on a striking clock is struck by a hammer which is connected to a weight or spring which moves the hammer at certain times. Some clocks have hammers that strike a series of chimes. Others set a group of figures in motion at regular intervals.

Cuckoo clocks have small wooden birds that come out of the clock and whistle the hours. Alarm clocks have striking devices which sound at any desired time.

Electric Clocks. Some electric clocks depend for their power on an alternating current of electricity. This current vibrates at an even rate of sixty times per second, which serves to keep the clocks exactly on time. A num-

Front and Side Views of the Mechanism of a Clock

ber of different clocks in different places also may be kept on the same time by a central electrical control. This is done by sending out a current which is timed with the pendulum of the master clock. The swinging of the pendulum controls electrical impulses which keep the wheels of the other clocks moving properly.

Atomic Clocks are the most accurate in the world. Some of them will gain or lose only a few seconds in 100,000 years. Instead of a pendulum or vibrations of electric current, atomic clocks are tuned to vibrations of atoms or molecules. These vibrations are so stable that they almost always vibrate the same number of times for each second. Atomic clocks are exceptionally accurate because they are tuned to these stable vibrations.

The Metropolitan Museum of Art

An Old Grandfather Clock, made in Roxbury, Mass., has a long pendulum enclosed in the tall, oblong, wooden case.

Many atomic clocks are tuned to masers. In one clock of this type, microwaves passing through ammonia gas tune the clock to the frequency of the ammonia atom. See MASER.

The first atomic clock was developed by scientists at the National Bureau of Standards in the late 1940's. See ATOMIC CLOCK.

Naval Observatory Clocks in Washington, D.C., are extremely accurate. They furnish the standard time for the entire country. The clocks are kept in underground chambers and are in direct contact with solid ground. They are protected by glass cylinders and regulated by slight changes in the pressure of the surrounding air. These clocks have nickel-steel alloy pendulums that can withstand air temperature changes.   ARTHUR B. SINKLER

Related Articles in WORLD BOOK include:

Chronometer	Sundial
Horology	Time
Hourglass	Watch
Pendulum	Water Clock

CLOISONNÉ. See ENAMEL (Decorative).

CLOISTER, *KLOIS tur,* is a covered walk, often built around the courtyard of a monastery, church, or college building. *Arcades* (rows of arches on columns) support the roof of a cloister. The open space surrounded by a cloister is called a *garth.* The word *cloister* is often used to mean the courtyard and the covered walk.

A monastery is sometimes called a cloister because the cloister was the heart of many monastic communities during the Middle Ages. Monks worked and meditated in the courtyard, which often contained a garden and a well. They walked through the cloister to go from one building to another. A church often adjoined the monastery on one side of the cloister. Rooms of the monastery itself opened off the three other sides.

The Metropolitan Museum of Art, New York

The Cloisters, in Fort Tryon Park in New York City, have been reconstructed from the ruins of ancient European cloisters.

These rooms included the *sacristy,* where the sacred utensils were kept, and the *chapter house,* where the monks transacted official business. There was a *calefactory* (heated room) used for recreation, and a *parlor* where monks could talk if speaking were restricted elsewhere. A *refectory* (dining hall) usually ran along one side of the cloister, with a kitchen and pantry beyond. The windows of sleeping cells or a dormitory on the upper floor opened onto the cloister. There was also a library and study cubicles. The cloister often served as a graveyard for the monks.   ALAN GOWANS

See also NEW YORK CITY (Museums).

CLOISTERS. See METROPOLITAN MUSEUM OF ART.

CLOSED CIRCUIT. See ELECTRIC CURRENT (Electric Circuits).

CLOSED SEASON. See GAME.

CLOSED SHOP is a workshop or an industry in which only members of a labor union may be hired. In some closed shops, the union supplies all of the employees. When employees must be replaced, or new ones are needed, the employer obtains them through union headquarters. In a *union shop,* an employer may hire nonunion employees, but the new workers must join the union within a short period of time after they have been hired. The closed shop was declared illegal by the Taft-Hartley Act of 1947. However, the union shop is not illegal.   GERALD G. SOMERS

See also TAFT-HARTLEY ACT; OPEN SHOP; UNION SHOP.

CLOSURE. See CLOTURE.

CLOT. See BLOOD (Blood Clotting); ANTICOAGULANT; COAGULANT; FIBRIN.

CLOTH. See TEXTILE; COTTON (Making Cotton into Cloth).

CLOTHES DRYER. See LAUNDRY; APPLIANCES.

CLOTHES MOTH. See MOTH (Clothes Moths).

CLOTHIER'S BRUSH. See TEASEL.

CLOTHING
AROUND THE WORLD

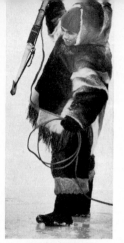

ESKIMO HUNTER

HALLOWEEN COSTUME   INDIAN CHIEFTAIN   MEXICAN CHARRO

CONSTRUCTION WORKER'S
PROTECTIVE CLOTHING

PERUVIAN FESTIVAL
COSTUME

MEXICAN
BULLFIGHTER

HAWAIIAN MUUMUU   GUATEMALAN INDIAN

R. Harrington, Three Lions; Harold Lambert; H. Armstrong Roberts; Gendreau; E. I. Du Pont
de Nemours & Co.; Hawaiian Visitors Bureau; Paul's Photos; Triangle; Wheeler Publishing Co.

CLOTHING. Suppose you asked several friends to list the things they need most. You would find that all their lists would include three important things—food, shelter, and clothing. Man cannot live anywhere without food. In most parts of the world he could not live long without some sort of shelter. People who live in cold regions must have clothing to stay alive. But even people who live in sunny regions require clothing.

How have people come to feel that they need clothing as much as food and shelter? Scientists find some answers to this question by studying primitive tribes that live today much as cavemen did thousands of years ago. For example, Charles Darwin, a British scientist, sailed around the world taking notes on the customs of various peoples and learned some surprising things about clothing. In Tierra del Fuego, a cold region at the southern tip of South America, he saw some people who did not wear clothing in spite of the cold rains and

sleet. He offered them some bright fabric, and was amazed when they tore it into rags and wrapped the rags around their heads. They were less interested in "dressing" than in "dressing up." It was their custom to wear bits of things for decoration. But wearing clothing as we do was not one of their customs.

As you look around you, it is easy to see how custom influences everyone. One woman passing you on the street may wear a dress, high-heeled shoes, and a feather hat. Another may wear a blouse and a skirt, a scarf on her head, and a pair of walking shoes. Both wear something on their heads, their bodies, and their feet. But the details of their clothing are much different. The woman with the feather hat and the high-heeled shoes is perhaps going to a concert. The other woman may be going to the grocery store. In such ways, custom influences what we all wear on different occasions. We usually feel uncomfortable if we violate custom. A girl

RUSSIAN BALLERINA

FRENCH DANCER
FROM TARASCON

SCOTTISH HIGHLANDER

LAPP HERDER

JAPANESE KIMONO

WEST AFRICAN WOMAN   BEDOUIN WOMAN   THAILAND DANCERS   PHILIPPINE SERPENTINA

Keystone; Keystone; James Sawders; Sovfoto; Kimura, Pix; Philippine Travel and Tourist Assn.; H. Armstrong Roberts; Leuenberger, Black Star; Trieschmann, Black Star

who wore her best party dress to school, for example, would feel overdressed and out of place. And a boy who wore blue jeans to church would also feel out of place.

Customs also vary from country to country. In most countries, men's clothes differ from the clothes that women wear. But Eskimo men and women usually dress exactly alike. Men in the United States wear trousers. But in parts of the Far East and in Scotland, men often wear clothing fashioned more like dresses or skirts. Women in the United States usually wear dresses or skirts. But in the Far East, women wear trousers every day. Arab women draw veils over their faces when they leave their homes. But among the Tuaregs of northern Africa, it is the men who veil their faces. Sometimes we can tell where a person is from by his clothes.

Clothes also may tell us what a person does for a living. Cowboys often wear large felt hats and high-heeled boots. Many railroad engineers wear striped blue

caps. Nurses, bus drivers, airplane pilots, and filling-station attendants all wear special types of uniforms.

Kinds of Clothing

Many clothing customs began for good reasons. Most are based upon either a need for protection or a desire for decoration. As a result, most clothing can be divided into (1) protective clothing or (2) decorative clothing.

Protective Clothing. Scientists believe that prehistoric man did not mind severe heat or cold. But today, most people dress partly to protect themselves.

In cold climates, people wear warm garments made of wool and fur and closely woven fabrics. They frequently wear a great deal of black. Black clothing helps keep the bodies of people warm, because this color absorbs the rays of the sun.

But in warm climates, people often wear white because it reflects the hot rays of the sun and makes them

53**1**

CLOTHING MATERIALS

Dressmakers often trim clothes with feathers and shells.

Grass and leaves furnish clothing in tropical countries.

Wool, hides, and animal hair are used to make material.

Cotton grows in the tropics and warm parts of temperate zones.

Linen fibers from flax have been used since ancient times.

Furs and hides of wild animals make warm suits in the North.

The clothing industry has developed many synthetic materials.

feel cooler. They also wear clothing of a fairly open weave, such as cotton or linen. These materials absorb perspiration and admit even a slight breeze. The people wear sandals, and their large, light hats of straw serve as sunshades. Some persons must choose clothing to protect themselves against both heat and cold. The people of the Arabian deserts wear flowing garments that shield their bodies from the fierce sun and blowing sand during the daytime. At night, the same garments protect their bodies against the cold.

In most temperate climates, people wear different kinds of clothing during cold and hot seasons. But they keep sweaters handy for cool summer nights, and cotton shirts or dresses for warm fall days.

Certain kinds of work also require forms of protective clothing. A soldier of today does not wear the heavy armor of the knights of old. But he may wear a steel or plastic helmet. Welders wear protective visors over their faces. Foresters and lumbermen wear heavy boots and trousers to guard against snakes and thorns. Jet pilots wear antigravity suits to protect them against sudden changes in air pressure. Men in outer space will wear special suits and helmets for protection.

Decorative Clothing. People like to beautify even their most useful clothing. New styles and fashions are designed to make clothes more attractive. Sweaters, dresses, suits, and even raincoats and snow boots come in gay designs and colors. Many women wear expensive furs for beauty rather than for warmth. The most casual outfit is more satisfying if it is becoming to the person wearing it.

Some kinds of clothes are largely decorative. Think of the costumes that you wear for a Halloween party or in a play. They may copy clothing that people of another country wear for protection. But for you these clothes are just decoration. Clubs and lodge groups may have uniforms that they wear to conventions or meetings. School bands, pep clubs, and majorettes wear bright and easily recognizable uniforms. Football uniforms are designed to be both protective and easy to identify.

Sometimes the members of a religious group continue to wear clothes like those worn when the group was founded. For example, the Mennonites have worn the same kind of dark, severe clothes for more than four hundred years.

Clothing Materials

Sources. Thousands of years ago, men did not have to decide what to wear each day. They probably wore the same thing every day—an animal skin draped around their shoulders or hips. It was a long time before they thought of cutting an animal hide into the shapes of sleeves, yokes, and trouser legs.

The earliest people were nomads who roamed the countryside looking for food and shelter. Some historians think these nomads paid little attention to their clothing. When people began raising crops, they began to stay more and more in one place. Soon they made two discoveries: how to make thread, and how to weave thread into fabric. Some authorities think that people who kept sheep and therefore had wool may have made *felt* before they thought of weaving wool into fabric. Felt is wool that has been dampened, pressed together, and allowed to shrink until it forms a dense, flat mass.

COSTUMES OF ANCIENT PEOPLES

1-3. CAVE MAN

4-8. EGYPT, 3000 B.C.

9. EGYPTIAN QUEEN, 3000 B.C.

10,12. CRETE, 1500 B.C.

11,13. PHOENICIA, 1500 B.C.

14,15,16. HEBREW, 960 B.C.

COSTUMES OF ANCIENT PEOPLES

1-4. ASSYRIA, 2100-1000 B.C.

5. BABYLONIA, 2100 B.C.

6. PERSIA, 500 B.C

7-9. GREECE, 550 B.C.

10,11,13. ROME, 50 B.C.

12. CENTURION, 50 B.C.

BYZANTINE AND FEUDAL COSTUMES

1-6. BYZANTINE, 428-1078   7-8. FEUDAL ENGLAND, 1400   9-14. FEUDAL FRANCE, 1416-1509

GOTHIC AND RENAISSANCE

2-7, 9-12. FRANCE, 1450-1550   1, 14, 15. ITALY, 1500   8, 13. ENGLAND, 1500

WESTERN EUROPE ENGLAND

1-6,8-11. 1600-1650   7. QUEEN ELIZABETH, 1600   12,13. 1700-1725

WESTERN EUROPE — FRANCE

3,4. FRENCH NOBILITY, 1675, 1650

1. PEASANT, 1676
2. COMMANDANT, 1662

8,9. REVOLUTIONARIES, 1793

5,6. NOBILITY OF THE COURT, 1700   7. KING LOUIS XIV, 1698

10. BALL COSTUME, 1774
11. ARMY OFFICER, 1715

1,2,3. DIRECTOIRE, 1795-1799   4. CONSULATE, 1799-1804

5,6,7. EMPIRE, 1804-1814

8. EMPIRE, 1810   9,10. LOUIS PHILIPPE, 1830-1848   11. 1855   12. 1859   13. 1875   14. 1890

NORTH AMERICA

1,2. PURITANS—
MASSACHUSETTS

3,4. FRENCH CANADIAN, 1668-1694

5,6. REVOLUTIONARY, 1770-1780

7,8. SOUTHERN PLANTATION, 1811

9,10,11. ALASKA ESKIMO   12. CANADA—HUDSON BAY   13,14,15. AMERICAN FRONTIER

Carl Link

LATIN AMERICA

1. MEXICO — TEHUANTEPEC

6. BRAZIL
7. GUATEMALA

2. MEXICO — PEON
3,4,5. MEXICO — UPPER CLASS
8. PANAMA
9. CHILE
10. ECUADOR

11,12,13. BOLIVIA   14. ARGENTINE   15,16,17,18. PERU — INCA INDIANS

EUROPE — NATIONAL COSTUMES

3,4,5. GERMANY—
BAVARIAN FOLK DANCERS

2. SWITZERLAND—APPENZELL

6,7. AUSTRIA—MERANER-TYROL

1. GERMANY—BLACK FOREST

8,9,10,11. NORWAY—REPPARFJORD LAPPS

12. NORWAY—HARDANGER BRIDE

13,15. SWEDEN—DALECARLIA

14 DENMARK

16. BELGIUM

22. EIRE (IRELAND)

19,20,21. SCOTLAND

23. WALES

17,18. THE NETHERLANDS

24,25. BASQUE · 26. FRANCE—NORMANDY · 27,28,29. FRANCE—BRITTANY

EUROPE — NATIONAL COSTUMES (continued)

3,4. SPAIN—ANDALUSIA

5. YUGOSLAVIA

6,7. ALBANIA

1,2. GREECE

(1. EVZONOI SOLDIER)

12. ITALY—NAPLES

13. PORTUGAL

14. SPAIN—ZAMORA

8,9. SPAIN—LEON

10,11. ITALY—SARDINIA

15. SPAIN—CATALONIA

16. PEASANT   18. UKRAINIAN   19,20. COSSACKS   21,22. POLAND

16

18

19

21

22

17

20

23

16-20. SOVIET UNION   23. CZECHOSLOVAKIA

17. RESIN

24   25   26   27   28   29

24. TURKEY   25. SERBIA   26,27. HUNGARY—BRIDAL PAIR   28,29. RUMANIA

THE ORIENT

3-6. CHINA— UPPER-CLASS FAMILY

1,2. BURMA   7. CHINA—MANCHU

8,9,10. CHINA— MONGOLIA

11,12. INDIA—MOSLEM   13. INDIA—SIKH   14,15,16. INDIA—UPPER-CLASS HINDU FAMILY   17,18. INDIA—PARSEE

21. HAWAII
22. PHILIPPINES

19,20. SIAM—DANCERS

24. BALI—DANCER

23. JAVA—DANCER

25,26,27. KOREA—UPPER-CLASS FAMILY   28,29. KOREA—BRIDAL COUPLE   30-33. JAPAN—UPPER-CLASS FAMILY

MODERN COSTUMES

1900

1904

1901

1905

1902

1929

1914

1913

1920

1925

1930

1926

1935

1939

1945

1945

1946

1948

1950

You may have seen a hat, skirt, or tablecloth made of felt. It was probably not hemmed, but simply cut off with shears. It did not unravel because it was not woven of threads. A woven fabric will eventually unravel if it is not hemmed.

You have probably let a yo-yo dangle on the end of its string, watching it whirl and twist the cord. In such a way wool, hair, or plant fibers were twisted into thread by the earliest methods. The dangling stick that twisted the thread was called the *spindle*. The fixed stick to which the mass of fibers was fastened was called the *distaff*. Women are still sometimes called "the distaff side," because they did the spinning. Of course, it has been many years since the average housewife made thread by hand for her family's clothing. See SPINNING.

We have a great variety of fabrics today. But there are still only three important methods of making fabrics. Felting and weaving are the oldest. The third method is knitting. See FELT; KNITTING; WEAVING.

One of the earliest plant fibers used to make fabric was linen. Linen thread is made of long fibers from the stalk of the flax plant. Linen is still considered one of the finest and most durable materials.

Other major materials for clothing are as ancient, or nearly as ancient, as felt, linen, and wool. At first, men wore clothes made of the uncured hides of fur-bearing animals. Then they began to scrape and cure hides to make leather. Eskimo women still chew animal skins to make soft leather. In Africa, the Masai tribe depends on its cattle herds for leather used in clothing, as well as for food. Cotton is the fluffy, white substance that bursts from the cotton boll when it is ripe. It was first cultivated about 5,000 years ago. Silk was made long ago. For hundreds of years, the Chinese jealously guarded their secret of how to spin silk from the cocoons of silkworms.

Many primitive peoples have worn plant fibers, leaves, or grasses without weaving them. The Hawaiian hula skirt made of ti leaves is such a garment. Some tribes have made garments from the inner bark of wild fig trees. They separate the bark, soak it, then pound it into a paperlike substance. We may smile at the idea of wearing wood. But some of our *synthetic*, or man-made, fabrics are made of wood or wood pulp. Most of us have also worn crepe-paper costumes on special occasions. They were handsome while they lasted, but not strong. Some scientists foresee a time when a disposable garment of durable paper will be practicable. We already have disposable paper handkerchiefs.

In addition to natural fibers for fabrics, scientists have developed new fibers from coal, petroleum, glass, milk, and wood. Rayon was one of the first synthetic fibers. Others include acetate, nylon, Orlon, Dacron, and Dynel. Some fabrics are a blend of natural and man-made fibers. Blending two or more fibers in a fabric is not so new as you might think. Pioneer women in America wove a material called *linsey-woolsey* made from linen and wool (see LINSEY-WOOLSEY).

Uses. Fabrics are important in designing dresses, coats, and suits. A designer may sometimes start with a piece of fabric and get from it his inspiration for a fashion. A piece of bulky tweed in a misty, soft color may inspire him to design a sports jacket. A filmy silk chiffon may lead him to design a draped party dress. Tweeds are excellent for sportswear because they wear well, are warm and absorbent, and can be dry-cleaned easily. Silk, on the other hand, is a more fragile fabric. It was a court fabric for hundreds of years. Some kings passed laws that common people could not wear silk. Actually, ordinary people in those days could scarcely have afforded to buy silks anyway. Many poorer people had only one or two outfits in their whole lives. They passed clothes on to their children. Clothing almost had to wear like iron to take so much use.

CLOTHING OF TODAY

BERMUDA SHORTS

IVY LEAGUE SUIT

LEVI'S

SPORT SEPARATES
Country Set

THREE-PIECE SUIT
Country Set

Levi Strauss and Co.

Bells on clothing were popular in Germany during the 1300's. Gentlemen went tinkling about the countryside with their clothes trimmed with hundreds of tiny bells.

Black Masks were fashionable for Englishwomen of the 1600's. The women wore masks on the street, keeping them in place with buttons held in their mouths.

Boiled Leather Shoes served as food in China during a famine of the 1500's.

Brilliant Ruffled Costumes were the usual dress of noblemen until the 1600's. Today, men tend to dress simply and women are often teased about their many changes in fashion. But in early days, men wore elaborate costumes, while women's styles were dark in color and changed little from year to year.

Buttons on men's suit-coat sleeves no longer actually "button." But they once kept a man's long, flowing cuffs out of the way when he worked or fought.

Children's Clothes were neither practical nor comfortable before 1900. Small boys dressed like their little sisters. Some wore long hair and dressy "Little Lord Fauntleroy" suits of velvet and lace.

Gloves were an important part of ladies' costumes in England during the 1500's. Queen Elizabeth I owned about 1,000 pairs of gloves, some trimmed with precious jewels.

Pointed Shoes with toes two or three feet long were fashionable for European men during the 1400's.

Slits in the backs of men's jackets originally permitted horsemen to spread their coattails while riding.

Velcro, a sort of sticky fastening, made its appearance in the late 1950's. Velcro is made of two strips of fabric. One is woven with hooklike loops, the other with a closer *pile*, or surface. When pressed together, they hold securely until pulled apart. The man who invented this device may have taken his idea from seeing how cockleburs clung to his trouser leg when he walked through a field.

Iris Brooke, *Western European Costume,* published by George G. Harrap & Co., Ltd.

Bells

Douglas Gorsline, *What People Wore,* N.Y., Viking, © 1952

Black Masks

Culver

Ruffs

United Shoe Machinery Corp.

Pointed Shoes

American Velcro, Inc.

Velcro

Today we do not expect to wear a piece of clothing so long. The growing habit of yearly changes in clothing fashions has led designers to use fabrics in experimental ways. A designer of highly styled clothing may even make evening dresses of tweed and sportswear of silk.

But designers still find certain textiles attractive for particular items. Felt and other wool fabrics, straw, and cotton go into most of our hats. Soft knit goods or leather make shapely, smooth-fitting gloves. Tweeds and smooth-faced wools are used in suits. Furs are always popular for coats or coat linings. They may be used as they come from the animal, or they may be dyed, plucked, sheared, or treated in some other way. Sometimes fur hairs are woven in a mixture with other fibers. Cotton, linen, silk, and wool are favorites for dresses. And cotton, sometimes combined with a synthetic, makes sturdy, durable clothing that is easy to care for. "Wash and wear" clothes appeal to travelers and mothers of young children. These clothes can be washed by hand or in a machine, dried quickly, and worn immediately. They need little or no ironing. Manufacturers make a variety of clothes in "wash and wear" fabrics. Even some men's suits are designed to be washed and worn without pressing. Most "wash and wear" clothing is made of man-made fibers, or it may be made of these fibers blended with natural ones.

Stretch yarn, which combines several synthetic fibers, is used in making elasticized tights, dancer's leotards, socks, gloves, swimsuits, and ski pants.

Style and Fashion

Style in clothes may mean the cut or design of a particular garment. Or it may refer to the kind of clothing worn during an historical period, such as "Grecian style." When we read that someone wore a dress in the Grecian style, we know that the dress was loose and flowing. It probably was gathered in with crisscross ribbon across the bodice and around the waist.

Style may also refer to dressing suitably for an occasion. Fashion, like style, may mean the line and cut of a particular garment, or it may mean the style or styles of the present time or of a past era (see FASHION).

The most advanced current fashions are called *high style*. Usually, high-style clothes look extreme when they first appear. But everybody may be wearing them by the next year.

A *fad* is a minor fashion that many persons accept, sometimes in a spirit of fun. It lasts only a short time. Sometimes you will see boys and girls everywhere wearing a particular kind of hat or cutting their hair a certain way. Soon the little hats will be thrown away and the hairdo will be changed for a more usual style.

War and peace, prosperity and hard times, scientific inventions, and many other factors may influence fashion. Take women's trousers. Amelia Bloomer was a leader in the movement for women's rights. She created and wore trousers for women in the United States (see BLOOMER, AMELIA J.). The baggy pants like those she originated still bear the name *bloomers*. She failed in her campaign to get women in all parts of the world to wear bloomers. But, when women began to work outside their homes and to take part in active sports, trousers for women seemed more sensible. In the 1930's, a few women wore beach pajamas with wide, loose legs, or knickers, somewhat like Mrs. Bloomer's bloomers. Many women who worked in factories during World War II found that close-fitting garments were safer to wear than skirts. Since then, tapered slacks, pedal-pushers, and Bermuda shorts have become accepted pants fashions for women.

A good fashion, whether a dance dress, a sweater, a suit, or slacks, is practical if it meets these tests: (1) it answers a definite need for the person buying it; (2) it is made of good fabric, and cut and fashioned well; and (3) it is attractive on the person who wears it.

How to Choose Clothes

A girl on a budget allowance should save most of her money for what are called basic clothes. She will buy at least one suit, a coat, a pretty "dress-up" dress, and the skirts, blouses, and sweaters that are a schoolgirl's best wardrobe friends. A boy usually invests most of his clothing allowance in a good suit, a coat, and sturdy school clothes.

Whatever you buy, you should carefully consider three things: quality, color, and style.

Quality. Whether you have lots of money for clothes or must watch every penny, you want to buy clothes of good, sound fabrics that can be cleaned or washed easily. The label should state clearly that the fabric will not shrink and the colors will not run. The wise shopper looks inside garments to see that they have ample, well-stitched seams and deep hems. She makes sure that the hem line is even all around, the buttonholes are neatly finished, and no loose threads dangle from the garment. She always chooses full-cut clothes that do not look tight or skimpy in any place.

Color is one of the first things you notice about a garment. Certain colors have great popularity one year, then go out of favor. Others seem to be popular almost every year. Red and blue are such colors. When choosing your wardrobe, you should buy major items of clothing—suits, coats, and winter dresses—in colors that will be good for a long time. You may buy less expensive items of clothing—hats, blouses, and summer dresses—in the season's unusual or special colors.

You should always choose colors that look right on *you*. A girl who does not look pretty in a bright new purple shade should not buy a dress in that color, however fashionable it may be. Skin color is the most important guide. To find her most attractive clothing colors, a girl should hold samples close to her face and choose the most becoming ones.

A Suitable Style. You must be certain that the way a garment is cut is suitable for you. Slim persons can wear bulkier fabrics with brighter or bigger designs than heavier persons can. A plump girl will look plumper if she wears stripes that go around, and slimmer if the stripes go up and down. A wide belt in a color that contrasts with the color of a dress is less flattering to a heavy figure than a narrow belt of the same color as the dress. A tall, thin girl may choose a full-skirted dress of wool tweed with a wide, contrasting belt. Her shorter, plumper sister may pick a slimmer-looking dress of wool jersey, with a narrow, matching belt.

To judge a certain style, look in a full-length mirror (a three-way mirror, if possible). Check the proportions of the garments in relation to your figure shape, the length of your legs, and the height of the heels you will wear with it.

Accessories complete your wardrobe. They include shoes, handbags, hats, jewelry, hosiery, neckwear, and gloves. Short, plump girls find that small, simple accessories are right for them. Taller girls may choose larger, more eye-catching ones. Whatever your build or height, you should be sure that your accessories are right for you. Young people look their best when they wear very little jewelry. They should have neat hairdos appropriate to their ages, and simple clothing. Some so-called "junk" jewelry can be fun. But a girl should own mostly "classic" jewelry, such as a string of pearls, hair barrettes, and charm and bangle bracelets.

Shoes should be selected for specific occasions. Oxfords, moccasins, or plain flats are good for school and casual wear—sneakers, or tennis shoes, for sports. White bucks and the ever-popular white saddle oxfords have become classics. Moccasins and flats can be more colorful as taste and clothes require. But black, brown, or tan are basic to every wardrobe. Girls' basic street or dress shoes can be black, brown, blue, or red—or white for summer—preferably with little heels.

A Planned Wardrobe. You may have seen a woman go to a crowded closet, look into it in despair, and say, "I have nothing to wear." It may have looked to you as though she had too much to wear. And you were probably close to the truth. A well-planned wardrobe includes the right clothes for different occasions, with the proper accessories to go with each outfit. A person who has a well-planned wardrobe does not need a great variety of clothing. A good rule in preparing a clothing budget is to list the types of your activities. Then note the kinds of clothing that each activity requires. Perhaps you already seem to have a number of garments in one basic color—blue, brown, or gray, for example. Then you may want to build your wardrobe around that one color. It is probably one you like and feel your best in.

Boys and girls in the fifth and sixth grades should have several complete outfits for school, enough knock-around clothing for active sports, and one or two outfits for dress-up occasions.

As they approach high school, young people need more party or date clothes. As they begin to hold summer jobs and look toward college or a regular job, they need some tailored clothes. Or they may need jeans to wear on rough or outdoor jobs.

How to Care for Clothes

The handsomest and best-made clothes will not stay attractive if you do not take care of them properly. With a little practice, caring for clothes can become a habit. It takes only a minute to hang up a dress or jacket properly. It takes less time to fold a sweater, and perhaps five minutes to give shoes a like-new shine. The results may be equal to adding dollars to your clothing allowance, because your clothes will last longer. And your general appearance will be improved.

Daily Care. Every child has heard his mother say, "Hang up your clothes!" He has probably wondered why she considered it so important. On the other hand, many a child has hung a sweater on a hanger, only to hear his mother say, "Don't hang *that* up!" Most clothes must be hung up between wearings to keep their shape and freshness. Stores sell special hangers for skirts and trousers, for suits, and for heavy coats. Small children can hang their clothes on hangers made to fit small necklines and shoulders. But you may have noticed that certain soft garments, such as sweaters, show the marks of hangers or stretch out of shape when hung on a hanger. Such knit garments should be neatly folded and placed in a box or drawer.

Boys and girls should learn to care for their own clothes. For boys, ties are usually the brightest articles of clothing. They should be hung up carefully after each wearing. Shirts should be laundered after each wearing. Girls' silk scarves that are allowed to get dingy look dreary, and dirty gloves are even worse. Set aside drawers, boxes, or closet sections for certain kinds of clothing, and form the habit of keeping those areas in careful order. If you have to paw through piles of disordered clothes to find a certain shirt or pair of socks, many clothes that went into the drawer carefully pressed will have to be pressed again before they can be worn. And too much pressing may shorten the lives of some garments.

Different fabrics require different pressing techniques and temperatures. Garments sometimes have special pressing instructions on their labels. A good rule is to test a small corner of each garment, or perhaps an inside seam, before pressing, to be sure the temperature of your iron is right.

Children can begin quite early to care for their shoes. Even small boys and girls can learn to smooth white polish on their saddle oxfords, to polish and buff their moccasins, and to wash their shoelaces snowy white. If you have enough shoes, it is better to wear one pair one day and another the next. Foot powder keeps shoes smelling fresh and clean. Shoe trees or racks help shoes keep their shape. Heels should be repaired as soon as they show signs of wearing down. Metal taps will help keep the soles from wearing out.

Cleaning. It is well to read all those little tags that dangle from a garment when you bring it home from the store. It is even better to read them before you buy the garment. The law requires manufacturers to tell you certain things about each piece of clothing. They tell you what fibers the garment is made of and the percentage of each fiber that went into it. For instance, a sweater may be 50 per cent wool and 50 per cent Orlon. The wool gives the sweater a warm, rich texture, and the Orlon makes it wash well, without shrinking or matting. The tags usually give directions for cleaning or washing and pressing.

Most woolen sweaters can be hand-washed in cool or cold water. They should be squeezed, not wrung, out. Some fabrics, such as corduroy or "wash and wear" fabrics, should be left to drip dry without squeezing or wringing. Velvet and felt garments can be freshened if hung in a steamy room. Hanging them in the bathroom after the shower has been allowed to run with hot water for a time is a good idea. Some garments that are wrinkled after a wearing may lose their wrinkles if carefully hung up overnight. You may be able to remove spots from a garment with a cleaning fluid before it has to go to a cleaner's for a more thorough cleaning.

Suede pocketbooks and shoes should be brushed before and after each wearing with a special brush designed for suede. Kid and calfskin shoes, pocketbooks, and belts should be polished to keep the leather soft and glossy. See Dry Cleaning.

Storing. Any clothing that is not worn often should be hung in a garment bag to keep out dust and moths. Hats which must hold a certain shape should be stuffed with tissue paper and stored in dustproof containers.

It is important to keep garments from being crowded together in a closet. Clothes should be hung where they can air between wearings. Air helps get rid of perspiration odors. Air is also important in preventing mildew. Sunlight is an excellent natural preventive against mold. But colored clothing should not be hung too long in direct sunlight, which might fade it.

Perhaps the worst enemy of woolen clothing and furs is the moth. In its larva stage, the moth can cause hundreds of dollars' worth of damage in a short time. Proper clothing care includes protecting woolens and furs from moths. Moth protection consists of (1) destroying existing moths, and (2) preventing other moths from infesting the garment. Moths can be destroyed simply by dry cleaning or laundering the garment. Moths dislike sunlight, so airing a garment in the sun will probably drive them away. Occasional airing is a good precaution in any case. After cleaning, the garment may be sprayed with a mothproofing chemical. Then it should be packed in a box or bag that is tightly sealed. Some woolens are mothproofed by the manufacturer and are so labeled. Dry cleaners can also mothproof garments when they are cleaned.

Clothing of Other Lands

Many nations have developed distinctive dress styles that we consider typical of them. For example, we think of kimonos in Japan and wooden shoes in The Netherlands. The people of some lands or regions still cling to their traditional costumes for everyday wear. The color pictures with this article show many of these costumes. But in most countries today, people wear clothing patterned after Western dress for daily use. They wear their traditional costumes only on ceremonial occasions. For descriptions of the clothing of various peoples, see the various country articles, such as Mexico (Way of Life).

The people of some lands have adapted new clothing styles to their ancient ones. The Eskimos provide us with an excellent example. The first white whalers arrived in Alaska in the 1850's. Since that time, the Eskimos of Point Barrow have changed many of their styles. The furs and skins of land and sea animals no longer make up an Eskimo's only source of clothing material. The sewing machine has become an Eskimo treasure. With it, Eskimo women stitch garments with thread. The Eskimos of Point Barrow also order clothing from Alaskan stores and from mail-order houses in other parts of the United States. Their clothes include Western-style winter coats, head scarves, and dresses for women.

But most Eskimos still wear long, hooded overgarments, called *parkas*, made of leather and fur. Parkas are often decorated with colored furs at the shoulders, hems, and cuffs. They may have extra-long sleeves so people can pull their hands inside in especially cold weather. Many Eskimos also wear mittens hung on cords around their necks, just as school children do. Eskimo women still carry their babies on their backs under their parkas.

Many Americans, including soldiers, have learned how cozy an Eskimo's parka can be in the frozen north.

How Clothing Is Made

The Clothing Industry is actually not one industry, but many. It includes the industries that produce women's, infants', and children's garments; men's and boys' wear; fur; embroidery; hats; bridal wear; accessories; findings (buttons, hooks and eyes, snaps, zippers, and thread); underwear and sleepwear; foundation garments; and sportswear. A fabrics industry may specialize in a certain kind of fiber, such as wool, cotton, silk, or a synthetic. Merchandising operations are also essential to marketing and selling clothing.

The four major clothing centers of the world are Paris, New York City, Rome, and London. The United States leads the world in manufacturing clothing. The industry ranks as the ninth largest in the country, employing over a million persons. More than 10,000 factories produce women's dresses, skirts, and suits, and about 1,400 make men's and boys' suits and coats. Canada has about 750 factories for women's clothing and about 570 for men's.

The largest number of garment factories in the United States is in the Middle Atlantic region. New York leads the states, with more than 6,000 factories that produce women's clothing and almost 600 that make men's wear. New York City is the clothing center of the United States. Other leading American clothing-manufacturing centers include, by rank, Philadelphia, Los Angeles-Long Beach, Chicago, Boston, Jersey City, Baltimore, Allentown-Bethlehem-Easton (Pa.), Cleveland, and Paterson-Clifton-Passaic (N.J.).

Most manufacturers have small factories. The average clothing company has fewer than 100 employees,

Wide World

Paris Fashion Houses set clothing styles for women throughout the world. At a spring fashion show, *above*, a model parades an afternoon dress before buyers and reporters from many lands.

Javanese Women create colorful garments by applying various dyes to fabrics in a method called *batik*. A woman uses hot wax to coat the areas of the design she does not wish to dye, *below*.

Standard Oil Co. (N.J.)

LEADING CLOTHING MANUFACTURING COUNTRIES
Value added by manufacture in 1965

Country	
United States $10,641,000,000	𝍢𝍢𝍢𝍢𝍢𝍢𝍢𝍢𝍢𝍢𝍢𝍢𝍢𝍢𝍢𝍢
Germany (West) $1,475,300,000	𝍢𝍢𝍢
Great Britain $1,199,000,000	𝍢𝍢𝍢
France $861,500,000	𝍢𝍢
Canada $605,600,000	𝍢𝍢
Japan $529,800,000	𝍢
India $464,800,000	𝍢
Italy $357,500,000	𝍢
Australia $298,100,000	𝍢
Spain $253,100,000	𝍢

Based on International Standard Industrial Classification, which includes footwear. Figures for Communist countries not available.

Source: Statistical Office of the UN.

MANUFACTURING CLOTHING

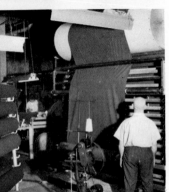

Examining the Cloth, *left,* inspectors look for stains, spots, or other imperfections.

Shrinking and Drying, *below left,* assure a better fit in the finished garment.

Cutting the Cloth, *right,* workers spread material and patterns on long, flat tables.

Sewing is usually done by machine, *below right.* Finishing touches are added by hand.

Delivering the Garments, workers push racks through the crowded streets, *opposite page.*

B. Kuppenheimer and Co., Inc.

although some firms employ as many as 1,000 persons.

The largest and most influential union connected with clothing is the International Ladies' Garment Workers' Union. The Amalgamated Clothing Workers of America, another large union, represents the makers of men's clothing. There are few strikes in the clothing industry, because of a strong spirit of cooperation between the companies and the unions. When a strike does take place, it usually ends within the industry in a friendly way. It is not unusual to hear of a clothing union lending money to a manufacturer to help him.

Manufacturing and Selling Clothing. The first step in the production of clothes is designing. Fashion designing, particularly women's fashions, is an important business. The jobs of many persons and the profits of many companies depend upon the sales of new styles. These styles begin in the minds of fashion designers in such great fashion centers as Paris, Rome, London, and New York. These designers work under great pressure. The clothing industry will sell more new garments if the designers can produce a style that is new and exciting. It must be pleasing to women, yet different from last year's style. A designer creates the idea for a garment and decides the colors and types of fabrics in which to make it. Next, he makes samples of the garment. Each season, buyers come from stores in many countries to see these samples. Attractive models parade the garments before the buyers. When a buyer sees a style he thinks customers will like, he buys it. In a few weeks, the new design is ready for its final test before the shopping public. If people buy it, a new fashion has been born. If they do not, the design soon disappears and another takes its place.

Ready-to-Wear Clothes. Many ready-to-wear clothes are made from a single design. Clothing factories receive orders for the clothes from the stores, then have patterns of the design cut in various sizes. These clothes are made almost entirely by machine. Department stores, clothing stores, specialty shops, and mail-order houses sell them to millions of customers. With mass production and distribution, clothing can be sold at prices almost everyone can afford (see Mass Production).

Manufacturers buy fabrics in large *bolts,* or rolls. Expert *examiners* unroll the bolts of material and inspect them for defects. Then workers called *spongers* shrink the fabrics with cold water or steam. After the fabrics dry, *spreaders* pile them on a large table. Workers called *markers* chalk-mark the outline of each pattern on the material. Then *cutters* use electric cutting machines or hand cutting tools to cut the various parts of the garments. *Sorters* number the pieces and put all the pieces for each garment in a bundle that also contains the necessary buttons and trimmings. *Machinists* then seam the pieces together. *Finishers* do all outside stitching, make buttonholes, and do any other work that appears on the outside of a garment. *Pressers* iron the wrinkles out of the completed garments and press the inside edges of seams flat. Finally, *shipping clerks* pack and ship the merchandise to stores in all parts of the United States and Canada. Probably someone else in a distant city is wearing a suit or dress just like yours.

Factories produce ready-to-wear clothes in certain standard sizes, based on age or figure type. In the United States, *children's sizes* range from 3 to 6X.

For Girls. Sizes 7 to 14 fit young girls, sizes 8 to 14 fit pre-teens, sizes 8 to 16 fit teens, and sizes 5 to 15 fit juniors. For *women,* there are three size groupings: misses', women's, and half sizes or "petites." *Misses' sizes* (numbered 6 to 20) fit the average youthful figure. *Women's sizes* (numbered 36 to 42) are cut a little larger. *Half sizes* (numbered $12\frac{1}{2}$ to $28\frac{1}{2}$) have shorter waists and are a little larger around. Some women can wear *junior sizes* (numbered 5 to 17), which have shorter waists and are a little smaller around.

For Boys, sizes 8 to 16 are next larger than children's sizes, 3 to 6X. *For men,* sizes are based on collar sizes

LEADING CLOTHING MANUFACTURING STATES AND PROVINCES
Value added by manufacture in 1965

State/Province	Value	
New York	$2,602,000,000	👕👕👕👕👕👕👕👕👕👕👕👕👕👕
Pennsylvania	$971,000,000	👕👕👕👕👕
New Jersey	$505,000,000	👕👕👕
California	$482,000,000	👕👕👕
Georgia	$351,000,000	👕👕
Massachusetts	$346,000,000	👕👕
Tennessee	$336,000,000	👕👕
Illinois	$295,000,000	👕👕
Quebec	$291,000,000	👕👕
North Carolina	$260,000,000	👕👕

Sources: Bureau of the Census; Dominion Bureau of Statistics.

and sleeve lengths for shirts, chest and waist measurements for suits, and waist and leg measurements for trousers.

Some manufacturers own factories that handle all the steps in manufacturing and distributing clothes. Others send their cut garments to *contractors* who sew them together and send them back to the manufacturer. Sometimes *jobbers* buy cut garments and complete the manufacturing and distributing process. Manufacturers may also sell their completed garments to *wholesalers* who sell them to stores and small retailers. Wholesalers do not sell to individual customers. *Retailers* own the stores where you buy your clothes. They sell clothing in relatively small lots, in contrast to wholesalers who sell them to dealers and merchants in huge lots.

Clothing Through the Ages

Prehistoric Times. Prehistoric man wore clothing as protection, as adornment, and as part of ritual. During the coldest periods of the Ice Age, furs may have made the difference between survival and death (see Ice Age; Prehistoric Man). Early man may also have worn the skins of animals to celebrate his victories over the beasts, to seek favor with the spirits of the hunt, and to gain strength and cunning from the animals.

Gradually, men learned to cut furs into pattern pieces and to fashion clothing that was fitted to their bodies. They may have splintered bones to make needles and used animal sinews as thread.

Ancient Times. Most of the information we have about ancient clothing comes from vases, statues, and *frescoes* (wall paintings) of the various periods. Often the original colors have faded. Maybe that is why we think of ancient peoples as clothed in white or light colors. Actually, most ancient peoples probably dressed in a blaze of color. They made dyes from plant and animal materials. They loved reds, yellows, and blues.

The Egyptians knew how to make cotton, linen, and wool clothing. They wrapped their mummies in long cloths of fine, sheer linen. At first, men wore *loincloths* or short, wrapped skirts called *shenti*. Later, they wore tunics and longer robes (see Tunic). A tunic was much like a simple doll dress—a rectangle of material, folded once, with a hole cut out for the neck. Some tunics were sewn down the sides. Others were wrapped around and tied with a sash. Women draped themselves in a length of cloth, sometimes adding a cape. Some wore straight skirts or dresses held at the shoulders with straps. Kings adorned themselves with ornamental belts, wigs, and headdresses. Slaves and children often went unclothed.

The Babylonians and Assyrians added fringes to the edges of their garments, perhaps to keep them from unraveling. Babylonian men and women wore a kind of skirt called a *kaunakes*. Some historians believe that the kaunakes was made of shaggy sheepskin. Others think it was made of cloth covered with twists of wool. All women and most men wore their hair long and braided. Assyrian kings wore long, fringed shirts and fringed aprons, often of linen.

The Hebrews wore many jewels. The men dressed in wool or linen tunics and fringed coats that opened down the front. Women wore slender tunics or robes.

The Persians were the first people to cut and fit garments, rather than simply drape themselves in pieces of fabric. They introduced coats with fitted, sewed-in sleeves. They also wore trousers that were full at the top and fitted at the ankle. They used leather and linen, and also imported silk for their garments.

The Cretans wore costumes unlike those of any other early peoples. Their clothes resembled the wasp-waisted, bustled look of the late 1800's. Women wore tightly laced belts or sleeved corselets that left their breasts bare. Their skirts were layers of material and appear to have been padded through the hips. They had neat aprons hanging down in front and back. Men also wore aprons and tight belts. They arranged their hair in a style similar

555

CLOTHING

to the pony-tail hairdos of schoolgirls in the 1950's. Women wore their hair somewhat shorter.

The Greeks wore soft, flowing garments. Important garments included the *chiton*, a rectangular piece of fabric wrapped around the body and fastened on the shoulders; the *himation*, a kind of cloak; and the *chlamys*, a shorter cloak that bared a man's fighting arm. At first, men wore their hair long and tied it with ribbons. Later, short hair became the style. Women wore their hair long, bound with ribbons, or in a simple bun. Jewelry included gold earrings, hair decorations, and brooches called *fibulas* for fastening garments at the shoulder. The Greeks took great pride in their fabrics. Some Greek towns gained fame for their finely woven materials, and others for embroidery.

The Romans had an enormous trade in clothing. They imported woolens from Gaul and Britain, linen from Egypt, printed cottons from India, and flowered silks and gold cloth from China and Persia. The Romans draped themselves in *togas* (semicircular cloaks) of wool (see TOGA). A Roman proudly wore his toga wrapped around his body and draped over one shoulder, leaving the other shoulder free. Men wore short tunics under their togas. Women had ankle-length tunics and *stolas* that were somewhat like Greek chitons. Boys wore a lucky charm, called a *bulla*, around their necks. Roman soldiers favored a circular cloak, sometimes hooded, called a *paenula*. Togas eventually came to stand for prestige and power. Only free male citizens were allowed to wear togas. The *palla*, a longer garment, replaced the short toga for women. Later, both men and women wore long-sleeved tunics called *dalmaticas*. Bright stripes banded the front and back of a dalmatica. Both the Romans and the Greeks wore sandals.

The Middle Ages. In the Byzantine, or East Roman, Empire, men and women dressed in similar semicircular capes called *paludamenta*. Knee-length tunics were popular for men, and women wore floor-length ones. Noblemen wore *hosa* (tights) and long, decorated scarves called *pallia*. Roman Catholic archbishops still wear a narrow type of pallium. Some types of hats worn in the Byzantine court have survived with little change for hundreds of years. The "Santa Claus" hat with its fur brim and drooping point ending in a ball or tassel is really a Byzantine style. See BYZANTINE EMPIRE.

Elaborate Byzantine clothing styles spread among various peoples in western Europe. Western rulers began to wear fancier clothes than their usual rough garments of cloth, leather, and fur. In turn, the people of the Byzantine Empire adapted the Western *bracco* (trousers) to their own use.

From about 400 to the 1400's, people made most of their clothes at home. Men raised sheep and flax, and women spun yarn and wove it into fabric. As towns grew, specialized shops run by master weavers, tailors, cobblers, and other craftsmen increased. During the 1100's, these craftsmen began to organize *guilds*, or simple labor unions (see GUILD). During the Middle Ages, individuals and families started to use identifying marks and colors in their clothes and possessions (see HERALDRY).

Clothing began to have a fitted rather than a loose look during the 1000's and 1100's. Women laced their dresses snugly at the waist, and wore long sleeves that widened at the wrists. Later, loose dresses bloused over a belt at the waist became stylish again. Women put up their hair instead of braiding it, and wore veils, called *wimples*, that fitted under the chin and jaw and were fastened on the crown of the head. Hoods with long tails called *liripipes* became fashionable for men.

Women adopted a *surcoat* (tunic) from the costume of the crusaders (see WORLD, HISTORY OF [picture: Thousands of Crusaders]). Most surcoats were cut out from under the arms down to the hips to show elaborate jeweled gowns underneath. Lords and ladies wore garments decorated with costly ermine and sable furs. The poor people lined their clothes with sheepskin, squirrel, and rabbit. The crusaders brought back silks and fabrics of metallic thread that only the rich could afford. Most people wore wool and linen.

The Renaissance. Towns flourished during the 1300's and 1400's, and merchants and craftsmen grew in number. Italian weavers gained fame for their glittering, beautifully woven textiles. The profits from silk-making made many Italian cities wealthy.

Clothing became more complicated. Women's clothing was cut and sewn to fit closely at the bodice, and had many new "finishing touches" such as buttons and *dagging*, a kind of scalloped edging. Women covered their heads with tall, peaked hats called *hennins* and other exaggerated hat shapes. Women did their best to hide their hair, but men wore theirs long.

During the early 1500's, men donned linen shirts and close-fitting upper garments called *doublets*. Later, they *slashed* their doublets (had slits cut in them) so they could pull their white shirts through in small puffs. They wore long, snug hose and broad, slashed shoes. Women's styles included low-necked dresses with skirts

Chlamys
Ancient Greece

Tunic and Paludamentum
The Middle Ages

Hood with Liripipe
The Middle Ages

Wimple
The Middle Ages

Hennin
The Renaissance

propped out stiffly over petticoats. Many skirts were split in front to show a *kirtle*, a rich underskirt. Women also had slashed sleeves.

Spanish fashions influenced styles throughout Europe in the late 1500's. Men wore tall hats, padded short breeches called *hose*, and bright stockings called *netherhose*. The *farthingale* became popular for women during the reign of Queen Elizabeth I. This heavy metal frame made skirts stand out so stiffly that women looked as though they were walking in boxes. Both men and women held their heads erect in great starched collars called *ruffs*. Men cut their hair short because of their ruffs, and women wore theirs up in frizzy curls. Women tried to beautify themselves by using many cosmetics and by dyeing their hair. Neither men nor women seem to have been very clean at this time. They considered frequent bathing unnecessary.

The 1600's. Gloves became popular for men and women, and shoes began to have heels in the 1600's. Men stopped wearing overstuffed hose and began to wear loose trousers, cut off just below the knee and ruffled. They still wore a sort of doublet. Slashing disappeared, but frills remained popular. The farthingale became less fashionable for women, and black began to replace bright clothing. Women wore three-quarter sleeves, showing bare arms for the first time since the beginning of the Middle Ages. Both men and women wore wide-brimmed hats trimmed with plumes. A well-dressed gentleman never went out without his sword.

The Puritans in England and the Puritan colonists who came to America favored dark, plain clothing and simple white caps for women. More elaborate clothing became stylish when Charles II took the throne. Englishmen began wearing *periwigs*, or huge, curled, powdered wigs. To wear them, they had to shave off their own hair. Men dressed in fussy clothes trimmed with ruffles, laces, and ribbons. Even their shoes had great bows and high red heels. In 1666, Charles II began to wear a Persian vest and a tunic-like coat. Men's vests and suit coats in the 1900's were patterned somewhat after this costume. Women shocked men by riding horseback in coats that closely copied those of the men.

The 1700's. The handicraft system began to break down after James Hargreaves invented the spinning machine in 1764 and Edmund Cartwright made the power loom in 1785 (see INDUSTRIAL REVOLUTION). English weavers produced large quantities of cloth at prices lower than those of guild craftsmen. More people could buy cloth outside their homes. But many continued to

make their own fabrics and clothes. Styles changed more rapidly than before. Only the nobility and the wealthy could keep up with the new fashions. Most people still wore comfortable, durable, woolen clothing.

French fashions influenced all Europe during the 1700's. Parisian designers sent fashion dolls, sometimes called *babies*, dressed in clothes to be copied in England, America, and other parts of the world. Girls and women wore tight corsets and great round *hoop skirts*. A *sacque* dress, fitted in front and loose in back, became popular. French noblemen and a few others wore paint and beauty patches as women did. Most men adopted simpler clothes. Wigs became smaller, and some soldier-kings wore their practical, fitted uniforms every day. Women piled their hair fantastically high above their foreheads, and powdered and decorated it. Elegant ladies sometimes carried little scratchers which they poked through their hair to scratch their heads.

During the French Revolution, men and women wore long coats, called *redingotes*, that opened down the front. Revolutionists generally wore long trousers instead of the knee-length breeches the aristocracy wore. Because of this, the revolutionists were called the *sans-culottes*, which means *without breeches*. From the French Revolution until about 1820, elegant women of France, England, and the United States again adopted Grecian-style clothing. Their dresses had low necklines and high, drawstring waistlines. This became known as the *Directoire* or *Empire* (pronounced *ahm-PEER*) style. Women wore sandals and short, curled hair and wide-brimmed bonnets. Women also began to carry handbags about this time. Men's clothing started to take on conservative lines. Men wore long-tailed coats, short vests, and knee-length breeches. Their accessories included *cravats*, or neckcloths, and *top hats*.

The 1800's. Elias Howe and Isaac Singer developed improved sewing machines in the 1850's. These and other new inventions gradually ended most handicraft production of clothing. At first, manufacturers made ready-to-wear clothes in only a few sizes. Most persons who could afford them still preferred clothes made by tailors and dressmakers. Others continued to wear homemade garments. But the clothing industry in the U.S. became firmly established by the end of the 1800's.

The 1800's brought many changes in style. *Crinoline*, a stiff cloth made of horsehair and linen thread, took its place in the fashionable world of the 1840's. In the 1870's, crinoline and hoop skirts gave way to *bustles*

Ruffs
The 1500's

Periwig
The 1600's

Farthingale
The 1500's

Bustle
The 1800's

that made skirts full in back. Women laced in their waists until they were as small as possible. Lines became slim and sleek rather than billowing. Paris designers introduced the first suits for women.

Men gave up variety and color in their clothes. In Western nations, all fashionable young men were wearing trousers by 1815. Checked trousers and simple narrow neckties became popular in the 1840's. Men wore suits of tweed and plaid by the 1880's. Hats included bowlers, caps, and high silk hats. Children's clothes became simpler and more suited to youthful activities.

The 1900's. Improved products and new manufacturing methods put the United States ahead of all other nations in manufacturing clothing. The ready-to-wear industry grew rapidly between 1890 and 1920. It soon produced most of the clothes worn in the United States. In the early days of the industry, employees worked long hours under poor conditions in *sweatshops* (see SWEATSHOP). Today, the industry boasts excellent working conditions.

During the early 1900's, women's clothes passed through more changes than they had in any previous period. For a few years around 1910, women wore *hobble skirts*. These were so tight at the bottom that women could hardly walk. About 1914, the *Gibson girl*, made famous by artist Charles Dana Gibson, became the feminine ideal. Her shirtwaist dress, in a modern version, is still a popular fashion. Clothing became simpler and less formal during World War I. In the 1920's, the silhouette was deliberately "boyish." Dresses were straight and ended at, or above, the knee. Rolled stockings became popular. Skirts became longer during the 1930's, then shorter again in the 1940's. During World War II, the silhouette was tailored and narrow. Shoulders were emphasized with padding. Slacks, pioneered by women working in war industries, became popular.

The "new look" of 1947 changed fashions considerably. Fitted bodices, full, long skirts, and crinolines returned. Nylon stockings and lingerie became available in large quantities for the first time. *Sheath dresses* and shorter hemlines became popular during the 1950's. In the late 1950's, loose-fitting *sack dresses, shifts,* and *A-line skirts* became popular. Also back in style were the high-waisted *Empire* lines. From England in the mid-1960's came the very short *miniskirts*.

Since the early 1900's, men had preferred double-breasted suits with wide lapels. During the 1950's, many men switched to *Ivy League* suits with narrow lapels, natural shoulders, and slim trousers. In the 1960's, colored, striped, and checked shirts were worn with business suits, along with wide ties in paisley print, stripes, or bright, swirling colors.

Both men and women dressed more casually during the 1950's and 1960's. They developed a greater interest in sportswear and wash-and-wear fabrics. Casual clothes for women included knee-length Bermuda shorts, tapered slacks, ski and stretch pants, and leotards. Men wore Bermuda shorts and slacks, and colorful sport shirts. *Turtle neck sweaters* and *tartan dinner jackets* also became popular. Improvements in sewing machines and in dress patterns, together with a "do-it-yourself" feeling, brought a revival of home sewing. With home sewing and with the variety of ready-made

clothing, more people than ever before are able to enjoy new fashions in clothing.

Career Opportunities

Fashion Designers hold important positions in the clothing industry. Persons who wish to enter this field may take fashion-designing courses in college, or attend special designing academies in New York City and other large cities. They must learn to design and draw new styles, to draft and cut patterns, to grade sizes, and to sew garments. Many designers begin as assistants in designing departments, as sample makers, or as artists in pattern houses. A talented designer may eventually become a partner in a large manufacturing firm.

Fashion Coordinators do a variety of jobs, from putting on an entire fashion show to selecting the shoes that a model will wear in a particular advertisement. Most large department stores have fashion coordinators who select merchandise, plan displays, and promote sales. A fashion coordinator must have a good knowledge of fashions.

Fashion Reporters and Artists specialize in presenting clothes attractively in magazines, newspapers, and direct-mail folders. They may work for publications, advertising agencies, or department stores. A copywriter must have a talent for writing and a knowledge of clothing design and materials. Copywriters usually find typing and a knowledge of secretarial skills important. Fashion editors select the merchandise to be shown in their publications, and may travel to Paris or other fashion centers to cover fashion shows. They must have superlative taste and the ability to anticipate fashion trends as they develop. Fashion illustrators need some knowledge of clothing construction in addition to a talent for drawing.

Garmentmakers. Persons interested in actual clothes-making can work as cutters, sewing-machine operators, fitters, finishers, tailors, or dressmakers. A person who wishes to enter any of these fields must be able to work quickly and efficiently with his hands. He might find some trade- or vocational-school training helpful. Tailors and dressmakers usually serve as apprentices before they can take their own positions.

Merchandising Positions. Young people may find positions as buyers, salesmen, heads of departments, and eventually officers in a store or chain of stores. Some may wish to open their own small retail stores. Many colleges and business schools offer specialized courses in business and management. Most large department stores offer junior-executive training courses in management to college graduates and occasionally to members of their staffs.

There is always room in the clothing industry for a small manufacturer with enough courage and capital to make a success of his own business. Individual skill and initiative have been responsible for much of the development of clothing down through the ages—from the first draped animal skin to the latest, most elegant fashion.　　　BETSY TALBOT BLACKWELL

Related Articles. See various country articles where clothing is discussed, such as JAPAN (Way of Life). See also the following articles:

ARTICLES OF CLOTHING

Derby	Glove	Hat
Fez	Handkerchief	Moccasin

Necktie　　　　Shoe　　　　　Turban
Parka　　　　　Stockings　　Uniform

Clothes Making and Care

Amalgamated Clothing　　　　　Knitting
　Workers of America　　　　　Laundry
Dressmaking　　　　　　　　　　Sewing
Dry Cleaning　　　　　　　　　　Spinning
Dyes and Dyeing　　　　　　　　Textile
Fashion　　　　　　　　　　　　Weaving
Garment Workers' Union,
　International Ladies'

Clothing Materials

Acrilan	Dynel	Organdy
Batiste	Fabrikoid	Orlon
Broadcloth	Faille	Percale
Brocade	Felt	Piqué
Buckram	Flannel	Rayon
Calico	Foulard	Sateen
Camel's Hair Cloth	Gabardine	Satin
Canvas	Gingham	Seersucker
Chambray	Grosgrain	Serge
Chenille	Haircloth	Shantung
Cheviot	Homespun	Shoddy
Chiffon	Jersey Cloth	Silk
Corduroy	Kersey	Swiss
Corfam	Khaki	Synthetics
Cotton	Lace	Taffeta
Covert	Lawn	Terry Cloth
Crepe	Leather	Tulle
Crinoline	Linen	Tweed
Dacron	Lisle	Velour
Denim	Madras	Velvet
Dimity	Moiré	Velveteen
Drill	Muslin	Voile
Duck	Nainsook	Wool
Duvetyn	Nylon	Worsted

Clothing in History

Armor　　　　　　　　　　Prehistoric Man (Food,
Colonial Life in America　　　Shelter, and Clothing)
　(Clothing; pictures)　　　Reformation (pictures)
Egypt, Ancient (Family Life;　Renaissance (pictures)
　color pictures)　　　　　Roman Empire (Family
Elizabeth I (pictures)　　　　Life)
Gauntlet　　　　　　　　　Tartan
Greece, Ancient (Family　　　Toga
　Life; color pictures)　　　Tunic
Linsey-Woolsey　　　　　　Western Frontier Life
Pioneer Life in America　　　(Clothing)
　(Clothing)

Other Related Articles

Batik	Jacquard
Button	Jewelry
Culture (pictures)	Lace
Embroidery	Modeling
Flax	Needle
Grooming, Personal (The	Pin
Importance of Clothing)	Sewing Machine
Hairdressing	Thread
Health (Clothing)	Twill
Indian, American (color pictures)	Zipper

Outline

I. Kinds of Clothing
　A. Protective Clothing
　B. Decorative Clothing
II. Clothing Materials
　A. Sources
　B. Uses
III. Style and Fashion
IV. How to Choose Clothes
　A. Quality　　　　　D. Accessories
　B. Color　　　　　　E. A Planned Wardrobe
　C. A Suitable Style

V. How to Care for Clothes
　A. Daily Care　　　B. Cleaning　　　C. Storing
VI. Clothing of Other Lands
VII. How Clothing Is Made
　A. The Clothing Industry　　C. Ready-to-Wear
　B. Manufacturing and　　　　　Clothes
　　　Selling Clothing
VIII. Clothing Through the Ages
IX. Career Opportunities

Questions

What is the difference between fad and fashion in clothing?

How do social conditions influence changes in clothing fashions?

What was the original reason for having slits in the backs of men's jackets or coats?

How does the information on a clothing tag or label protect the consumer?

What cities rank as the world's four major clothing centers?

How can a person build a coordinated wardrobe?

What specialists take part in the mass production and distribution of clothing?

How do customs influence types of clothes?

What important factors should be considered in selecting clothes?

Why are spinning and weaving considered twin discoveries?

Books to Read

ALLEN, AGNES. *The Story of Clothes*. Roy, 1958. A history for young readers that describes the evolution of clothing from earliest times.

BERK, BARBARA. *The First Book of Stage Costume and Make-Up*. Watts, 1954.

JUPO, FRANK J. *Nothing to Wear but Clothes*. Dutton, 1953. For young readers.

LEEMING, JOSEPH. *The Costume Book*. Lippincott, 1938. Folk costumes of 27 nations, costumes of 9 historical periods, and fairy tale costumes.

LESTER, KATHERINE M. *Historic Costume; A Résumé of Style and Fashion From Remote Times to the 1960's.* 5th Ed. Bennett, 1961.

RYAN, MILDRED G. *Dress Smartly: A 100 Point Guide.* Scribner, 1956. A discussion of the importance of good taste and intelligence in buying clothes.

SEVERN, WILLIAM. *If the Shoe Fits.* McKay, 1964. *Hand in Glove.* 1965. History, customs, legends of these articles of clothing.

WILCOX, R. TURNER. *Five Centuries of American Costume.* Scribner, 1963. *Folk and Festival Costume of the World.* 1965. A description of national costumes arranged alphabetically from Afghanistan to Yugoslavia, with a page of description and a page of illustrations for each country.

CLOTHING WORKERS OF AMERICA, AMALGAMATED. See AMALGAMATED CLOTHING WORKERS OF AMERICA.

CLOTHO. See FATES.

CLOTURE, or CLOSURE, shuts off debate in a legislative body. A legislature may vote to effect cloture. In the U.S. Senate, a two-thirds vote is required to do so. Free and open debate is necessary in a democracy in order to reach sound decisions and to protect minority groups. But if debate is unlimited, a minority in a legislature may prevent any action simply by continuing to debate. The Senate adopted a cloture rule in 1917, and amended it in 1959. The Senate has voted to use cloture only eight times since 1917. See also FILIBUSTERING.　　　　　EDWARD W. CLEARY

Van Bucher, Photo Researchers

High Cirrus Clouds look like tufts of hair. They are so high and cold that the water they contain is frozen into ice crystals.

Van Bucher, Photo Researchers

Medium-High Altocumulus Clouds, *above,* may appear as small cloud patches arranged in bands or irregular groups.

Peter Black, Tom Stack and Associates

A Towering Cumulus Cloud may rise thousands of feet and may develop into a cumulonimbus cloud that brings a thunderstorm.

Bernie Mendoza, Tom Stack and Associates

Some Cumulonimbus Clouds have rounded bumps on their undersides. Tornadoes sometimes come from these clouds.

Russ Kinne, Photo Researchers

Low Stratus Clouds cover the sky with a thick, even blanket. These clouds usually bring rain or snow.

CLOUD is a mass of small water droplets or tiny ice crystals that floats in the air. Fluffy white clouds floating across a blue sky, or the colors of clouds at sunset, are part of the beauty of nature. Clouds also play an important part in the earth's weather. The water that they bring as rain and snow is necessary to all forms of life. Clouds can also bring destruction or even death, in the form of hail or tornadoes.

Some clouds are great fleecy masses, and others look like giant feathers. Still others are dull gray or black sheets that darken the earth. Most clouds change

Reid A. Bryson, the contributor of this article, is Professor of Meteorology and Geography at the University of Wisconsin.

shape continually. They do so because parts of the cloud evaporate when touched by air that is warmer than the cloud. Cloud shapes also change because of the action of winds and air movements.

Kinds of Clouds

The name of a cloud may describe its appearance. For example, the term *strato* means *layerlike* or *sheetlike*. Clouds that appear as layers or sheets are called *stratus* clouds. The term *cumulo* means *pile* or *heap*, and *cumulus* clouds are piled-up masses of white clouds. The term *cirro* means *curl*, and *cirrus* clouds are curly white clouds. The term *nimbo* means *rain*, and *nimbus* clouds are dark gray rain clouds. These terms and a few others are used to form the names of the most common

Josef Muench

Cirrus Fibratus and Cirrus Floccus Clouds are thicker than the wispy cirrus clouds, and cover larger areas of the sky.

Ray Brod

Altocumulus Undulatus Clouds, *above,* appear in bands across the sky. The gaps between the bands may be wide or narrow.

Russ Kinne, Photo Researchers

Stratocumulus Clouds cover the sky with large, rounded masses within a few thousand feet of the ground.

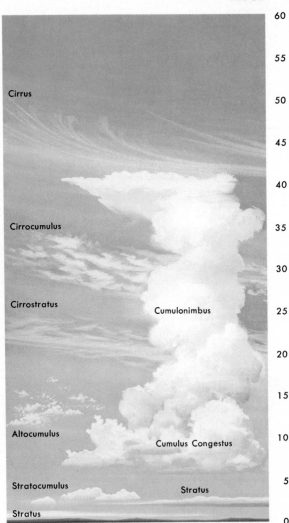

Scale indicates altitude above sea level in thousands of feet.
WORLD BOOK diagram by Herb Herrick

Different Clouds Are Seen at Various Altitudes above the earth. This diagram shows examples of some common clouds and their approximate altitudes. Many clouds are found only within a certain range of altitudes. Other clouds, such as the cumulonimbus, extend from very low to very high altitudes.

clouds. Clouds are grouped into classes according to their height above the ground.

Low Clouds. Two kinds of clouds, *stratus* and *stratocumulus*, are usually seen near the earth. The *bases* (lower edges) of most of these clouds are less than 6,000 feet above sea level. A stratus cloud looks like a smooth, even sheet. Drizzle often falls from it. A stratocumulus cloud is not as even in thickness as a stratus cloud. It has light and dark areas on the bottom, indicating, as its name suggests, that there are piles of clouds in the layer.

Middle Clouds, called *altostratus, altocumulus,* and *nimbostratus,* usually lie from 6,000 to 20,000 feet above the earth. Nimbostratus clouds sometimes may be closer to the ground. An altostratus cloud forms a smooth white or gray sheet across the sky. If the cloud is not too thick the sun may be seen through it. An altocumulus cloud appears in many shapes. It may be seen as unconnected piles or as a layer of clouds piled together. A nimbostratus cloud is a smooth layer of gray. Frequently, the cloud itself cannot be seen because of the rain or snow falling from it.

High Clouds, called *cirrus, cirrostratus,* and *cirrocumulus,* are formed entirely of ice crystals. Other clouds are mainly water droplets. Cirrus clouds are the delicate wispy clouds that appear high in the sky, sometimes higher than 35,000 feet. A cirrostratus cloud is a thin sheet of cloud. It causes a halo to appear around the sun or moon. This halo is the best way to recognize a cirrostratus cloud. Cirrocumulus clouds

HOW CLOUDS FORM

Clouds form when moist air rises and becomes cooler. The air usually rises by (1) convection, (2) lifting, or (3) frontal activity. Cool air cannot hold so much water vapor as warm air can, and the excess vapor changes into tiny drops of water or crystals of ice. These drops or crystals form clouds.

By Convection. Solar radiation heats the ground and the air next to it, *right*. The warm air becomes lighter and *convection* (a flow of air) carries this warm air upward. As the air rises, it becomes cooler. If the air is moist, some water vapor condenses and forms clouds, such as the cumulus clouds shown below.

Ray Atkeson

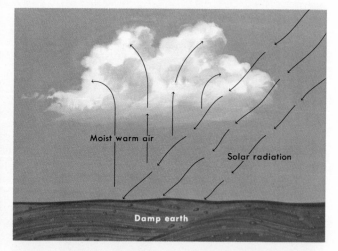

Moist warm air

Solar radiation

Damp earth

By Lifting. Warm, moist air blowing over mountains or hills is lifted, *right*. When the air rises, it cools and cannot hold all its water vapor. This vapor *condenses* (changes to drops of liquid) and forms clouds over the high ground, *below*. Clouds formed in this way cover the tops of some mountains permanently.

WORLD BOOK photo by Val L. Mitchell

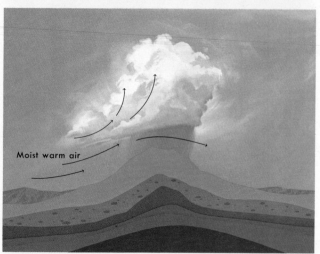

Moist warm air

WORLD BOOK diagram by Herb Herrick

By Frontal Activity. A weather front occurs when two masses of air at different temperatures come together. The diagram, *right*, shows cool air moving under warm air along a cold front. The warm air is cooled as it rises above the cool air. Many clouds form, *below*, along the front at all altitudes.

Robert H. Glaze, Artstreet

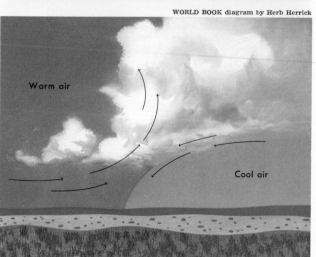

Warm air

Cool air

look like many small tufts of cotton hanging high in the sky. These clouds rarely form.

Clouds at More Than One Height. *Cumulus* and *cumulonimbus* clouds may rise to great heights while their bases are near the ground. Cumulus clouds are heaped-up piles of cloud. They may float lazily across the sky or change into the most spectacular of all clouds, the cumulonimbus. A cumulonimbus cloud may reach heights as great as 60,000 feet from its base, a few thousand feet from the ground. Its top of cirrus clouds spreads out in the shape of an anvil. This kind of cloud is often called a *thunderhead* because heavy rain, lightning, and thunder come from it. Sometimes hail or, on rare occasions, a deadly tornado comes from a cumulonimbus cloud.

How Clouds Form

Clouds form from water that has evaporated from lakes, oceans, and rivers, or from moist soil and plants. This evaporated water, called *water vapor*, expands and cools as it rises into the air. Air can hold only a certain amount of water vapor at any given temperature. When the temperature drops, some of the water vapor begins to *condense* (change to a liquid) into tiny droplets of water.

For water vapor to condense, particles so small they can be seen only through a microscope must be present. These particles, called *condensation nuclei*, become the centers of the droplets. Many condensation nuclei are tiny salt particles or small particles present in smoke. Most droplets measure from $\frac{1}{2,500}$ to $\frac{1}{250}$ of an inch in diameter.

If the temperature is cold enough, and other conditions are right, water vapor does not condense and form a liquid droplet. Instead, the water vapor turns directly to ice through a process called *sublimation*. For sublimation to occur at temperatures above $-40°$ F., small particles similar to condensation nuclei, with a shape somewhat like an ice crystal, must be present. These particles are called *freezing nuclei*.

A cloud often contains both water droplets and ice particles if the temperature is between 32° F. and $-40°$ F. Water droplets do not always freeze at the normal freezing temperature of water, 32° F. They may remain liquid down to a temperature of $-40°$ F.

Rain or snow forms when water evaporates from the liquid droplets and freezes on an ice crystal. The crystal grows larger until it falls out of the cloud. It falls to earth as a snowflake unless it enters a layer of air where the temperature is above freezing. Then the snowflake melts and becomes a raindrop.

Water vapor can rise to form clouds in several ways. When the sun warms the ground, the air next to the ground is heated. Because warm air is lighter than the same volume of cooler air, the warm air rises. This rise of warm air is called a *convection current*, and this method of cloud formation is called *convection*. As the air rises, it expands and becomes cooler. If enough water vapor is in the expanding air, the vapor will condense and form clouds.

Clouds also form by *lifting*. When warm, moist air moves up the side of a hill or over a mountain range, it is lifted and cools by expansion. This cooling causes the water vapor to condense and form clouds that hang over the mountains.

Weather fronts, where masses of warm and cool air meet, produce clouds by *frontal activity*. The water vapor in the rising warm air becomes cooler and condenses, creating the water droplets that form clouds.

Clouds and the Weather

Storms. Weather forecasters study clouds carefully because certain types often appear before storms. In many cases, a warm front or a low pressure system may be identified by these clouds, which form in a definite order over several days. First, a few wispy cirrus clouds appear in the west. Soon more appear and gradually merge into cirrostratus clouds that cover the sky. The cirrostratus clouds are later hidden by a lower layer of altostratus clouds that becomes thicker and hides the sun. Light rain or snow may begin to fall from the altostratus layer. The base of the clouds becomes still lower as nimbostratus clouds move in with heavier rain or snow. Cumulus and cumulonimbus clouds often develop within the nimbostratus ones, and the steady rain becomes a heavy shower.

As the storm moves past, the rain or snow ends but the sky remains overcast with stratocumulus clouds. These low clouds disappear as soon as fair weather returns.

A cold front brings clouds in a different order. Often, both middle and high clouds come before the front. The most striking feature of most cold fronts is a wall of large cumulus or cumulonimbus clouds along the advancing edge of cold air. As this wall passes overhead, the temperature falls. Heavy showers may also occur, and the direction of the wind usually shifts from the south to the northwest. After the line of clouds passes, many cumulus or stratocumulus clouds may remain for a short time. Clearing weather then occurs rapidly.

In summer, it is often possible to watch a thunderstorm form. The sky may be clear in the morning, or a few altocumulus clouds might be present. As the earth becomes warmer, small cumulus clouds appear and begin to grow. These clouds may become large, towering cumulus clouds that bring a little rain. As the towering cumulus clouds continue to grow, an anvil of cirrus clouds spreads out at the top and extends ahead of the main clouds. The clouds are now cumulonimbus, and a thunderstorm usually follows.

Heating and Cooling of the earth are also influenced by clouds. Most cloudy days are cooler than clear days because the clouds reflect much sunlight back into space. This reflected sunlight does not heat the earth. On the other hand, clouds have an opposite influence on the earth's temperature at night. The earth gives off heat toward space, causing the ground to cool off. Clouds intercept much of this heat and send it back toward the ground. For this reason, most cloudy nights are warmer than clear nights. The heat is trapped in the lower layer of air between the cloud and the ground. Therefore, low clouds trap much more heat than do higher clouds. REID A. BRYSON

Related Articles in WORLD BOOK include:

CLOUD CHAMBER

CLOUD CHAMBER is a device for tracing the paths of atomic particles. See WILSON CLOUD CHAMBER.

CLOUD SEEDING is a man-made method of causing rain. See RAIN MAKING.

CLOUDBURST is a sudden heavy rain falling for a short period of time in a small area. Cloudbursts are usually associated with thunderstorms. They occur most often in desert and mountain regions, and in the interiors of continents, such as the Great Plains of the United States. The uprushing air currents of a thunderstorm support a large amount of water in the form of raindrops. If the air currents are suddenly cut off, the mass of rain quickly falls out over a small area. Stream beds become torrents, and rivers form in valleys that are usually dry. During a cloudburst, several inches of rain may fall in 15 minutes. See also CLOUD; RAIN; WEATHER.   JAMES E. MILLER

CLOVE is the name given to the dried flower buds of a tropical tree. The dried buds are used as spices. The name comes from the French word for *nail* because of the shape of the flower bud. The clove tree grows wild in the Moluccas, or Spice Islands. Clove trees are also grown in Sumatra, Jamaica, the West Indies, and Brazil.

The clove tree, an evergreen, grows 15 to 30 feet tall. The large, smooth, oblong leaves taper to a point. The tree's purplish flowers grow on jointed stalks. The buds of these flowers, called *cloves*, are picked before they open. They have a reddish color when freshly picked, but turn dark brown when dried. Cloves have a fragrant odor and a warm, sharp taste.

Cloves are used chiefly in cooking. An oil taken from the buds and stem is used to flavor desserts and candies, and to scent soaps.

Scientific Classification. The clove tree belongs to the family *Myrtaceae*. It is classified as genus *Caryophyllus*, species *aromaticus*.   HAROLD NORMAN MOLDENKE

Cloves are the unopened flower buds of a tropical tree. The reddish buds grow on jointed stalks, *right*. When the buds are dried, *below*, they are dark brown and look like little nails. Dried cloves, used as a spice, have a warm, sharp taste.

St. Clair

Sweet Clover Has Small White or Yellow Flowers.

CLOVER is the name of several different kinds of legumes that grow wild in fields, on lawns, and along roadsides. Several kinds of clover are cultivated as food for livestock. Clover plants usually have three leaves, but sometimes more. Superstitious people believe that four-leaf clovers bring luck, and that five- and six-leaf clovers bring evil.

Most clover plants grow in the Northern Temperate Zone, although some are also found in South Africa and South America. They grow successfully in lowlands and also high up in the mountains. About 300 different kinds of clover plant are known.

Red Clover is the most important of all clovers. It is a weak perennial, which means it lives two or more years but is not long-lived. It grows from 6 inches to 2 feet tall. Farmers grow red clover to make hay, to provide pasture for farm animals, and to enrich the soil. This plant fixes nitrogen in the air by means of bacteria growing on its roots. When the plant is plowed under, this nitrogen makes the soil richer. About five times as much red clover as alfalfa is grown in the United States to feed livestock. Red clover flowers usually will not be fertilized unless a bumblebee pollinates them. When red clover was first planted in Australia, there were no bumblebees to carry the pollen. Not until bumblebees were introduced into the country would the red clover produce seed.

White Clover is a valuable pasture crop. Bees make expensive honey from the nectar in white clover blossoms. White clover is seldom grown alone. It is usually mixed with grasses and with other clovers. White clover, also a perennial, does not grow tall. Its stems creep along the surface of the ground and send down roots. For this reason, white clover spreads rapidly and provides an especially valuable plant for pastures and in lawns.

Alsike Clover is often called *Swedish clover*. It came to the United States from Sweden by way of England. The flowers range from white to pink and are borne on rounded heads. It grows well in a cool, moist climate and reaches a height of one to three feet.

St. Clair

Blossoms and Leaves of Red, *left,* and White Clover

Crimson Clover is much used for soil improvement and for livestock feed. Its flowers are often red, but sometimes may be white or yellow. Crimson clover must be planted from seed every year. It has often been called scarlet, or Italian, clover.

Other Kinds of clover include hop clover, rabbit-foot clover, Ladino clover, Japan clover, which is best-known as lespedeza, mammoth red clover, medicago, and strawberry clover.

Sweet Clover is not a true clover, although it is a legume. Sweet-clover plants are tall, erect plants somewhat like alfalfa in appearance. Four important kinds of sweet clover grow in the United States. White and yellow sweet clovers, which live for two years, are widely grown in the southern states. Their large roots penetrate deep into the soil. At the end of the second season, they decay and enrich the soil with nitrogen and decaying vegetable material. One kind of white sweet clover grows only for one year. Sour clover, a kind of sweet clover used almost entirely to improve the soil, is often called melilot.

Scientific Classification. Clover plants are in the pea family, *Leguminosae.* Red clover is genus *Trifolium*, species *T. pratense.* White clover is *T. repens;* alsike, *T. hybridum;* and crimson, *T. incarnatum.* White sweet clover is genus *Melilotus*, species *M. alba.* Yellow sweet clover is *M. officinalis;* sour clover, *M. indica.*   ROY G. WIGGANS

See also BUMBLEBEE; FLOWER (color picture, Flowers of Roadside, Field, and Prairie); LEGUME; LESPEDEZA; SHAMROCK.

CLOVERLEAF. See ROADS AND HIGHWAYS (Intersections).

CLOVIS I, *KLOH vihs* (466?-511), king of the Franks, became the first powerful ruler of the Merovingian dynasty, the founders of the French state. In 481, when Clovis inherited the royal title, he was only one of several Frankish kings. Then, in 486, he defeated the last great Roman army in Gaul. In one campaign after another, he defeated the Alamanni, the Visigoths, and the Burgundians. By 507 he ruled over most of Gaul,

western Germany, and the Low Countries of northwestern Europe.

Clovis was the first Germanic king to become an orthodox Christian. Most Germanic rulers either became Arian heretics or remained pagans. By his conversion to Christianity, Clovis won the support of his Catholic subjects, including the clergy.   WILLIAM C. BARK

See also ARIANISM; FLEUR-DE-LIS; FRANK; GOTH; MEROVINGIAN.

CLOWN is a comedian or buffoon in a circus. His make-up and costume are his own personal trademark, and no other clown may dress or make up in exactly the same way. The present-day circus clown had his prototype in the court jester of the Middle Ages. Clowns in early American circuses were talking and singing comedians. When circuses expanded their arenas to three rings, clowns were relegated to straight pantomime. In this role they reached their peak as comics.

American circuses feature clowns principally as punctuation points in their swift-paced shows. The clowns serve as comic relief between the tense performances of the aerialists, acrobats, equestrians, and trained animals. Many clowns have their own acts as comic, but expert, aerialists and bareback riders. Many clowns perform on either high or low wires.

Famous American clowns include Dan Rice, a talking and singing clown in the late 1800's. He numbered

Clown Emmett Kelly became famous as a sad-faced hobo who wandered quietly around the circus ring in tattered suit and hat.

Nick de Morgoli, Pix

President Abraham Lincoln among his fans and personal friends. Fred Stone, Bobby Clark, and Paul McCullough were circus clowns before they became stage comedians. Their success on the stage is often credited to their ability to get laughs in straight pantomime. Lou Jacobs, Paul Jung, and Felix Adler made up as *white-face* clowns. Otto Griebling adopted a hobo type, and Emmett Kelly became famous for his sad-faced tramp. Clowns in other countries include the Fratellinis, the Great Grock, Popoff the Russian, Robbins the banana clown, and Polidor. Long ago, P. T. Barnum, the great American promoter, remarked on the importance of clowns when he said that "Clowns are pegs used to hang circuses on." F. B. KELLEY

See also CIRCUS.

C.L.U. See INSURANCE (Careers).

CLUB is a group of persons organized for some particular purpose, such as social enjoyment and entertainment. A club is usually confined to one community, but there are many state and national groups. Membership is usually by invitation.

People join clubs for a number of reasons. Sometimes they merely believe in or favor the purposes of the club and wish to help support it. Sometimes they want fellowship. Some people value exclusiveness in a club, and are happy to become members of a group which seldom invites other people to join. Many people join clubs formed to celebrate a common experience, such as servicemen joining veterans' groups.

Modern clubs in England and the United States grew out of informal gatherings in the English taverns of the 1500's and 1600's. Groups of literary men and actors, along with the wealthy men who supported them, often met to talk and exchange views. One of the early London clubs met in the Mermaid Tavern in Cheapside. Among its members were Shakespeare, Ben Jonson, Beaumont, Fletcher, and Donne. Jonson established the Apollo Club at the Devil Tavern in 1624, and drew up bylaws for it. In 1764, Dr. Samuel Johnson and Sir Joshua Reynolds founded a club that still exists. It is called the Literary Club or simply The Club, and its first members included such distinguished figures as David Garrick, Edmund Burke, and Oliver Goldsmith.

Related Articles. Clubs and organizations are listed in WORLD BOOK under the key word in the name of the group. Example: LIONS CLUBS, INTERNATIONAL ASSOCIATION OF. See also COUNTRY CLUB; PARLIAMENTARY PROCEDURE; SERVICE CLUB; WOMAN'S CLUB.

CLUB MOSS is any one of a group of plants related to the ferns and horsetails. Club mosses are also called *ground pine*, or by the scientific name, *Lycopodium*. The plants are not true mosses. Club moss has a long rootstock that grows horizontally in the soil and produces erect green stems. The stems bear branches that divide and spread like a fan. The branches are covered with small green leaves that look like those of spruce or cedar. One to three cones develop at the tops of the branches. These cones contain spores for reproduction.

Scientific Classification. Club mosses are in the club moss family, *Lycopodiaceae*. They are all classified in the genus *Lycopodium*. ROLLA M. TRYON

See also FERN; HORSETAIL.

CLUBFOOT, or TALIPES, is an abnormal condition of the foot, usually present at birth. But it may develop later as the result of injury or poliomyelitis or other diseases. In the true clubfoot, the foot is bent downward and inward so that the person can walk only on his toes or on the outside of his foot. Sometimes the foot is bent in an upward and outward position so the person can use only his heel for walking. Doctors begin treatment early, sometimes when the baby is only a week old. They use massage, manipulate the foot into position, and use casts to hold the corrected position. In severe cases of clubfoot, surgery may be necessary to correct the condition. CLAUDE LAMBERT

R. W. Meyer
The Clumber Spaniel Has a Low, Heavy Body.

CLUMBER SPANIEL is a short, heavy hunting dog. It has a white coat with orange or lemon colored markings. The dog is quite heavy for its size. Males stand 17 to 18 inches high at the shoulder, and weigh from 55 to 65 pounds. Females weigh less.

The Clumber spaniel was developed in the 1800's in England, and it is still common there. It is named for Clumber Park, the home of a nobleman who developed the breed. The dog is uncommon in the United States. It is too slow to be useful in the larger hunting areas found in the United States. MAXWELL RIDDLE

CLUTCH. See TRANSMISSION; AUTOMOBILE (The Drive Train).

Club Mosses Are Very Attractive Plants. They are popular decorations in the house at Christmastime.
Nature Magazine; Hugh Spencer

CLYDE, *klide,* **RIVER,** is the principal commercial waterway in Scotland. The River Clyde rises in the Southern Uplands of Scotland and flows northward for 100 miles, draining the counties of Lanark, Renfrew, and Dumbarton. The picturesque Falls of Clyde near the town of Lanark once furnished the power for many mills in the Lowlands. Famous shipbuilding yards line the banks of the Clyde in Glasgow, the largest city in Scotland. The *Queen Mary, Queen Elizabeth,* and other famous ships have been built in Clyde shipyards. Below Glasgow, the river widens into the Firth of Clyde, an inlet of the sea that is over 50 miles long. See also FIRTH OF CLYDE. JOHN W. WEBB

CLYDESDALE. See HORSE (Draft; color picture).

CLYMER, GEORGE (1739-1813), was one of the Pennsylvania signers of the Declaration of Independence and of the United States Constitution. An early patriot, Clymer headed a committee to persuade Philadelphia merchants not to sell British tea sent over in 1773. He served on the Pennsylvania Committee of Safety, and in the first U.S. House of Representatives from 1789 to 1791. He also was president of the Philadelphia Bank and of the Academy of Fine Arts. Clymer was born in Philadelphia. ROBERT J. TAYLOR

CLYTEMNESTRA, *KLY tum NES truh,* in Greek mythology, was the wife of Agamemnon. While he fought in the Trojan War, she fell in love with his cousin Aegisthus. She and Aegisthus killed Agamemnon when he returned from Troy. Clytemnestra's son, Orestes, later killed her and Aegisthus. JOSEPH FONTENROSE

See also AGAMEMNON.

CNOSSUS. See KNOSSOS.

CNUT. See CANUTE.

COACH is a four-wheeled vehicle drawn by animals. Coaches served as the main means of public travel before the development of railroads. They were usually pulled by horses, and carried passengers, mail, and express freight between cities and towns. The word *coach* comes from *Kocs,* a town in Hungary where an early coachlike vehicle was built in the 1450's. However, Emperor Frederick III of Germany built one of the first real coaches in 1474. Railroad passenger cars are sometimes called *coaches.*

Coaches developed from the two-wheeled wagons and carts people had used since the time of the ancient Egyptians more than 5,000 years ago (see WAGON). Their use spread throughout Europe during the 1500's. But travel by horseback was considered more comfortable, because of the poor roads and riding qualities of coaches. For many years, coaches were used mainly for state occasions. The first public coach line in England went into operation about 1640. J. H. WHITE

See also STAGECOACH.

COACH is a person who drills athletes in the fine points of sports. The head coach is the team director in most sports. In professional baseball, the director is usually called a *manager.* Coaches teach techniques, conduct practice, determine strategy, and decide who will play. Coaching began in colleges in the mid-1800's. The first coaches were student athletes. Later, professional coaches were hired. Coaches of public school athletic teams are certified teachers. WALTER H. GREGG

COACH DOG. See DALMATIAN.

COAGULANT, *coh AG yoo luhnt,* is any substance that causes a fluid to clot, or thicken. Milk curdles because *rennin,* an enzyme, causes clots to form. One of the most important coagulant actions is the clotting of blood. Scientists have found many blood-clotting factors. The combined action of all of them produces a blood clot. If any one factor is missing, the tendency for blood to clot is reduced. Doctors then try to supply the missing substance. For example, in the blood disease *hemophilia,* doctors use an antihemophilic globulin to help the blood to coagulate. In other types of diseases, they may give the patient vitamin K or fibrinogen to induce the blood to clot and control hemorrhages. WILLIAM DAMESHEK

See also BLOOD (Blood Clotting); FIBRIN; VITAMIN (Vitamin K); ANTICOAGULANT; HEMOPHILIA.

COAHUILA, *KOH ah WEE lah* (pop. 1,093,366; area 58,522 sq. mi.), is a state in northern Mexico, across the Rio Grande from Texas. For location, see MEXICO (political map). Saltillo is its capital. Coahuila is a region of desert and mountains. Irrigation projects have made the area around the city of Torreón a rich cotton- and wheat-growing region (see TORREÓN). Coal mines lie near Nueva Rosita. Coahuila was one of the original states of Mexico, and included Texas until Texas won independence in 1836. CHARLES C. CUMBERLAND

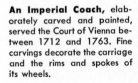

An Imperial Coach, elaborately carved and painted, served the Court of Vienna between 1712 and 1763. Fine carvings decorate the carriage and the rims and spokes of its wheels.

COAL is a soft black or brown rock. Its ability to burn makes it one of the most useful rocks dug from the ground. Coal can be burned to heat buildings. But its most important use is to produce steam to make electricity. Coal provides heat and steam for many other industries. Baked coal called *coke* is used in blast furnaces to produce steel. Coal also can be made into other kinds of fuel and hundreds of useful chemical products.

Coal, along with other valuable natural resources such as iron ore and petroleum, has helped make the United States the most important industrial nation in the world. The United States produces more coal than any other country except Russia.

Coal is sometimes called *buried sunshine*. This is be-

This article was critically reviewed by the National Coal Association.

cause coal captured the sunlight that fell on ancient forests long before there were men on the earth. When we burn coal today, we are using this captured energy from the sun.

In the United States, coal supplies more than one-fifth of the power and heat the nation uses. Coal furnishes an even larger percentage of energy in other industrial countries.

How Coal Was Formed

A chunk of coal looks black and smooth. But if you look at a piece of coal under a microscope you will see

HOW COAL WAS FORMED

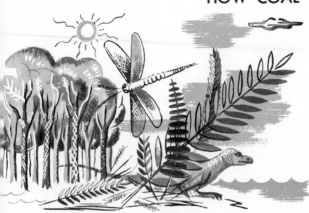

1. Dense Forests and Swamps covered much of the earth's surface hundreds of millions of years ago. They were filled with strange-looking trees, giant rushes, and wide-spreading ferns. Among the plants lived big lizards and giant insects.

2. As the Giant Plants Died, they fell into the swamps. The dead trees and ferns became tangled in a mass of decayed vegetable matter. This spongy, brown vegetable matter is called *peat*, the first material in the formation of coal.

566

that it is colored red and gold and arranged in layers. If you look closely at a piece of coal you may be able to see the markings of plants on it. These markings were made by the plants from which coal was formed. See accompanying illustrations, showing a fern fossil and the way coal was formed.

Time of Formation. Some coal was formed 400 million years ago. But most high-rank coal, such as that found in Pennsylvania, was formed more than 250 million years ago, during a time that geologists call the *Carboniferous Period* (see EARTH [table: Outline of Earth History]). Some coal is being formed in small quantities even now.

During the time that most coal was formed, the air was damp and steamy. Most of the plants were huge strange-looking ferns and trees that had no flowers. As these plants died, others grew on top of them. This happened time after time for thousands of years. The plants rotted and turned into a substance called *peat*, which looks like rotted wood. After a while, wide areas of the earth's surface sank. Streams and oceans poured in, carrying mud and sand which covered the peat. The pressure of the water above squeezed down the mass of peat and gradually formed it into coal. Geologists have estimated that a thickness of from five to eight feet of rotted plants and ferns was needed to form one foot of coal. Occasionally, the earth's crust *buckled* (folded). This movement greatly increased both pressure and heat beneath the surface. The increased pressure and heat formed the higher ranks of coal.

Coal Beds. Deposits of coal vary in thickness from a few inches to several hundred feet. Most coal is mined from beds which are from two and one-half to eight feet thick. These deposits are sometimes called *seams* (veins), but geologists prefer to use the word *bed*, because coal was formed in wide bedding areas. Coal deposits are sandwiched between layers of rock and dirt. The deposits may be level, sloping, or tipped on end, depending on whether they have been affected by the cracking and folding of the earth's crust. Many of the deposits in the mountain sections of the eastern part

Chicago Natural History Museum

A Fern Fossil. The plants that helped to form coal ranged from delicate mosses, ferns, and rushes to the largest trees. On this lump of coal may be seen a fragment of a fern.

of Pennsylvania are tilted at various angles.

Coal beds may lie deep in the ground or near the surface. In hilly or mountainous country, the coal often is exposed on the hillside. But it is likely to be covered with dirt or weathered from exposure to the air and hard to recognize. Excavations for buildings, railroads, or highways frequently uncover coal beds. Sometimes coal beds are found in drilling for water, oil, or gas. But the principal method of locating coal is to use core drillings. This is done by drilling out a *core* (column) from the earth's crust to indicate, layer by layer, what is under ground.

Chief Kinds of Coal

The plants which became coal took from the air the carbon they needed for their growth. They used a process made possible by sunlight. When the plants were squeezed together by water pressure, large amounts of oxygen and hydrogen were driven out, while the carbon

3. New Plants Grew on Top of the Old. Then they, too, died and became part of the mass of peat. Water sometimes covered the area. Different thicknesses (*1, 2, 3*) were caused by dirt and sand (*a, b*) being deposited between layers of peat.

4. Heat and Pressure caused different types of coal to be formed. Where the heat and pressure were greatest, usually as the result of folding of the earth's crust, the soft coal (bituminous) was formed into the hardest rank of coal (anthracite).

567

remained. Because coal has no fixed chemical formula, geologists classify it merely as a sedimentary rock. See ROCK (Sedimentary Rock).

Coal usually is divided into two main classes—*anthracite* ("hard" coal) and *bituminous* ("soft" coal). When anthracite was formed, it was squeezed under greater pressure than was bituminous. As a result, anthracite contains the highest percentage of carbon and the lowest percentage of moisture. Anthracite makes up only a small part of the world's supply of coal. About half of the world's coal reserve is bituminous coal. The rest of the reserve is still softer coal.

Anthracite generally lies deeper in the earth than bituminous. Nearly all the anthracite in the United States is found in eastern Pennsylvania. Small beds of this hard coal are also located in Alaska, Arkansas, Colorado, New Mexico, Virginia, and Washington.

Most of the anthracite is used as a fuel for household heating systems. When anthracite burns it produces almost no smoke. It sells for a higher price than bituminous coal, although the heating value of anthracite is slightly less than that of the better grades of bituminous coal.

Bituminous Coal is the most important and the most plentiful *rank* (type) of coal. It is the chief fuel in plants that generate electricity with steam. It also has other important industrial uses. It provides coke for the steel industry, and is the raw material for thousands of coke by-products including gas, light oils, and chemicals. Bituminous coal is also used to produce aluminum, cement, food, paper, and textiles. People use bituminous coal to heat homes and buildings.

Large deposits of bituminous coal are found in many states of the Union, both east and west of the Mississippi River. The most important bituminous coal beds in the United States are located in an area west of the Appalachian Mountains. This region extends from Ohio and Pennsylvania southwest to Alabama. Nearly 3 of every 4 tons of bituminous coal mined in the United States each year come from this eastern coal area.

Other Kinds of Coal are softer varieties which contain less carbon and more moisture than the better types of coal. They have limited uses. *Subbituminous coal* contains about 25 per cent moisture. It burns readily, and can be used for household heating and for industrial plants. Important deposits of subbituminous coal lie in Alaska, Arizona, Colorado, Montana, New Mexico, and Wyoming.

Brown coal and *lignite* are brownish-black coals that contain about one-half water. Lignite is the harder type of brown coal. There are large deposits of lignite in the northwestern United States and in western Canada. Peat is one of the earliest stages of coal. The remains of plants and ferns which have been preserved may be clearly seen in peat. Peat contains a very high percentage of water. Peat has been used as a fuel for hundreds of years in Ireland, England, and Germany.

How Coal Is Mined

Mining Methods. There are two general methods used to mine coal. These are (1) *strip* (surface) mining, and (2) *underground* (deep) mining. Miners usually use strip mining when the coal beds lie close to the sur-

face of the earth. Otherwise, they use underground mining. Almost 65 per cent of the coal mined in the United States comes from underground mines.

Strip (Surface) Mining. In this method, giant power shovels or other earth-moving equipment remove the *overburden*, the layer of earth and rock that covers the coal seam. When the coal is exposed, it is broken up, usually by explosives, and loaded by smaller power shovels into huge trucks. The trucks carry the coal to preparation plants. Strip mining is a fast, efficient way to mine coal. Production in strip mines averages more than 35 tons a man per day.

Underground (Deep) Mining includes several types of mines. The most important of these are (1) shaft mines, (2) drift mines, and (3) slope mines. Each type of mine is best suited to removing the coal from a particular type of coal bed.

Shaft Mines reach coal beds that lie far below the earth's surface. A hole is dug straight down to the coal. The coal miners then dig horizontal entries through the seams of coal. Miners, equipment, and coal are carried between the coal seam and the surface by an elevator system.

Separate shafts are dug to provide ventilation for the working rooms far beneath the ground. The average depth of shaft mines in the United States is 260 feet.

Drift Mines are used to reach coal beds in hillsides. The entrance is located where the coal is exposed on the hillside, and the tunnel is dug through the coal bed.

Slope Mines are also used to reach coal beds in hilly areas. Miners open a sloping tunnel through the ground to the coal bed level. The miners and their machines are moved in and out of the mine on cars that are pulled by electric locomotives along steel tracks. Coal is taken out of the mine in similar cars, or by conveyor belts.

Underground Mining Systems. Coal is mined according to a definite plan. It is mined in such a way as to remove as much coal as possible and allow it to be hauled to the surface easily for the most efficient, safest method of production.

The wall of the bed from which the coal is taken is called the *mine face*. In cutting into this mine face, there are two general mining systems: (1) the room-and-pillar system, and (2) the longwall system.

Room-and-Pillar Mines are composed of a series of rooms cut into the coal bed from numerous entries. The miners leave *pillars* (columns) of coal standing to help support the roof until they mine out a particular area. Then, as the miners move back to the main entry, they systematically remove the pillars and permit the roof to fall. This system is used in most of the underground coal mines of the United States.

Longwall Mines are common in Europe and are now found in the United States. In this system, coal is mined by a machine which is pulled back and forth across a face several hundred feet long. The loosened coal falls onto a conveyor belt which carries it away from the face. Movable steel props support the roof over the immediate work area, and as the miner works the machine deeper into the seam, the roof supports are advanced. The roof behind is allowed to fall. Miners, equipment, and coal move to and from the face through *haulageways* (tunnels) that open along each side of the face. One advantage of the longwall system is that

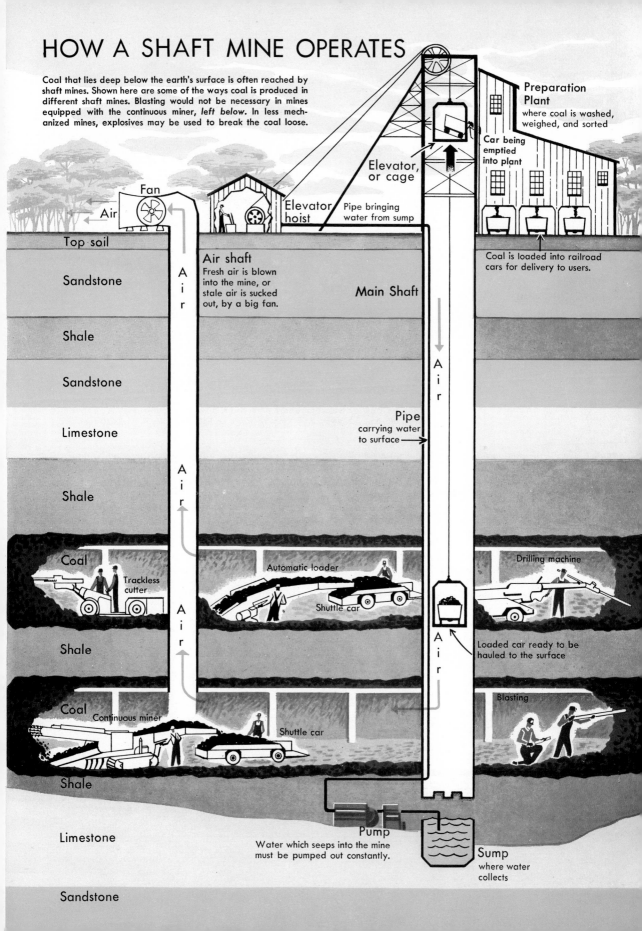

HOW A SHAFT MINE OPERATES

Coal that lies deep below the earth's surface is often reached by shaft mines. Shown here are some of the ways coal is produced in different shaft mines. Blasting would not be necessary in mines equipped with the continuous miner, *left below*. In less mechanized mines, explosives may be used to break the coal loose.

Preparation Plant where coal is washed, weighed, and sorted

Car being emptied into plant

Fan

Air

Elevator, or cage

Elevator hoist

Pipe bringing water from sump

Coal is loaded into railroad cars for delivery to users.

Top soil

Sandstone

Air shaft
Fresh air is blown into the mine, or stale air is sucked out, by a big fan.

Main Shaft

Air

Shale

Sandstone

Limestone

Pipe carrying water to surface →

Air

Shale

Coal

Trackless cutter

Automatic loader

Shuttle car

Drilling machine

Loaded car ready to be hauled to the surface

Shale

Air

Coal

Continuous miner

Shuttle car

Blasting

Shale

Pump

Water which seeps into the mine must be pumped out constantly.

Sump where water collects

Limestone

Sandstone

Strip Mines use huge excavators to remove earth and rock covering coal seams. The giant, *above*, has a wheel, *left*, that cuts away 3,500 tons of waste an hour and piles it over 420 feet away.

almost all the coal can be removed because no pillars are left standing.

Breaking Down the Coal. There are many methods of breaking coal from the mine face in lumps suitable for hauling to the surface of the mine. The coal was once broken off by men working with picks. But 95 per cent of all the coal is now mined in modern, mechanized mines. The slower hand labor of early mining methods has disappeared in such mines.

Undercutting. Before the coal wall is cracked, the miners usually cut out the mine face at the bottom of the coal bed so the coal can be shattered more easily by explosives. This undercutting may be done by hand, but more than 95 per cent of the undercutting in United States mines is done by machines. Cutting machines equipped with sharp, powerful blades, tear out the coal in a wide groove, or *kerf*. Some cutting machines are built to cut into the coal not only at the bottom, but also at the top and sides of the face. Another simple method of breaking down coal is called *shooting-off-the-solid*. The coal is blasted off the bed without any undercutting to help break it down. But a dangerously large explosive charge is needed in this method, and much dust and fine coal are produced.

SLOPE AND DRIFT MINES

This diagram shows two different ways that miners can reach coal. A *slope mine* uses a tunnel dug at a slant to reach coal that lies near the earth's surface, but not close enough for strip-mining methods. In a *drift mine*, the tunnel is dug into the side of a hill at the level of the coal seam.

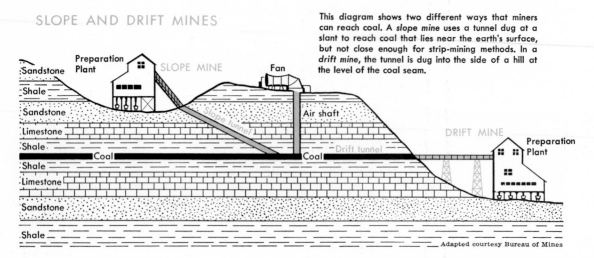

Adapted courtesy Bureau of Mines

Cracking the Coal Wall. If explosives are to be used in breaking down the coal, shot holes are drilled at intervals along the face of the coal bed. The explosives are inserted in these holes. When the explosion occurs, the coal wall cracks into pieces. Black powder and dynamite were once used as the chief explosives in coal mines. But they had a tendency to set fire to the gases and dust that accumulate in mines, and they have been discarded as too dangerous. Today, coal-mining companies in the United States widely use *permissible explosives* approved by the United States Bureau of Mines. The Bureau tests these explosives to make sure that they are safe for use in mines. Cylinders of compressed air or liquid carbon dioxide are also widely used in American mines. The cylinders are placed in the shot holes. When the compressed air or gas is released, it expands with such force that the coal wall is shattered as thoroughly as if dynamite had been set off. Compressed-air cartridges are widely used in Britain.

Continuous Coal-Mining Machines. Since World War II, many machines have been developed to mine coal mechanically. Use of these machines reduces accidents and reduces mining costs. A *continuous mining machine* can cut the coal loose and load it in one operation. Two men running this machine can mine coal at the rate of about 12 tons a minute.

At surface mines where a rising hillside makes overburden too thick to remove, miners may use a *coal auger.* A coal auger is a giant bit which can drill into a coal deposit and remove the coal from the holes it makes. The holes the auger bores may be 84 inches across and 200 feet deep.

A *push-button miner* with electronic remote controls can send a boring-type mining machine 1,000 feet under the ground while the operator stays on the surface. The giant device moves from one spot to another on tracks. It consists of a control station and spiral ramp on which the mining machine and portable conveyors are stored

until they are sent underground. See pictures of the push-button miner and auger later in this article.

Hauling Coal Out of a Mine. As the coal is mined, tracks are laid in the main haulageway. Cars loaded with coal are pulled over these tracks by small but very powerful electric locomotives. An increasing number of mines use conveyor belts to carry the coal to the surface. In most underground mines, low, flat loading machines gather the loose coal onto shuttle cars. The shuttle cars carry the coal to mine cars or to a conveyor belt. In surface mining, the loose coal is gathered up by large power shovels, and is loaded on trucks.

Sizing. Coal as it is taken from the mine is called *run-of-mine* coal. Pieces range in size from large chunks to a fine powder. Not much coal is sold in this *run-of-mine* form. Most coal is hoisted into a preparation plant where it is separated from impurities and sorted into various sizes by being passed through large screens. Each screen has openings of a certain size. Bituminous coal is classified by size. See the color illustration, *From Mine to Bin.*

Anthracite coal must be broken up to remove slate and other impurities embedded in it before it can be divided into sizes. In the anthracite industry, smaller sizes account for a major share of production. But larger sizes bring in more income, because they sell at higher prices per ton.

Powdered coal is used for many industrial purposes, but the most important use of it is in electric power plants. In some plants, coal is crushed into a fine powder and blown into 14-story tall furnaces where the powder flashes into flame. The flame's heat produces steam to make electricity. Powdered coal is also pressed into blocks called *briquettes* for use in home fireplaces. A binding material, such as tar or pitch, is mixed with the powdered coal to hold the briquettes together.

In Underground Coal Mines, Miners Ride to and from Their Work in Clean, Rapidly Moving "Man-Trip Cars."

National Coal Association

MINING
COAL

A Continuous Miner, *right,* bites into the face of a coal seam and chews out as much as 12 tons of coal a minute. The coal passes from the front of the machine to the rear end, *below,* where it flows into shuttle cars or onto a conveyor belt. This machine eliminates separate cutting, drilling, blasting, and loading operations.

A Cutting Knife on wheels, *right,* looks like a giant sawfish. The operator can make the sharp, powerful blades cut either a vertical or horizontal slot in a coal seam.

A Portable Coal Drill bores holes for compressed air cartridges or other kinds of explosive charges. Mines that do not have continuous miners use explosive devices to break down coal seams.

Preparing to Blast, a miner inserts an air cartridge into a hole in the coal seam. Compressed air is forced into the cartridge and bursts out with explosive force.

A Crawler-Type Loader, *right*, picks up coal that was blasted from the face of a seam and loads it in shuttle cars.

A Shuttle Car, such as this, *right*, hauls the coal from the face of the seam to a mine car or a conveyor belt that carries it to the surface.

A Push-Button Miner can be operated by one man from a desk in an electronic control station inside the spiral ramp. He pushes buttons to send a boring-type miner as far as 1,000 feet underground. The miner bites a hole 10 feet wide and 4 feet high. It pulls portable conveyors off the ramp as it eats into a coal seam. These conveyors feed the coal back to a conveyor-belt system on the surface.

Cleaning. Anthracite may have a quantity of slate mixed with the coal as it leaves the mine. After being broken into smaller sizes, the anthracite is sent through mechanical cleaners which automatically remove the slate. In many bituminous coal mines, little or no slate is found with the coal.

However, bituminous coal may contain clay and other impurities. About two-thirds of such coal is also cleaned mechanically. Such mechanical cleaning is done chiefly by machines called *jigs* and *dense-medium* washers. These machines separate the coal from the heavier impurities. Sometimes coal is treated with chemicals or sprayed with oil to settle the dust.

Grading. In its natural state, coal is classified by *rank*, which depends on its carbon and ash content, the amount of volatile, or gassy, matter and moisture it contains, and its heat value. As sold in the market, coal is classified by *grade*, which depends on its rank and such other characteristics as the size of the lumps and on special treatment which the coal has received. The grade of coal is important to customers, for it means that the coal will meet certain standards.

How Coal Is Transported

Shipping. After the coal has been processed at the preparation plant, it is usually loaded into railroad cars or coal barges. Sometimes coal is loaded for shipping directly from the car which has brought it to the mine surface.

Coal needs heavy transportation equipment because the fuel is so heavy and bulky. In the present day, railroad cars transport about 73 per cent of the coal produced in the United States. The fuel is carried in open-topped *gondola* or *hopper* coal cars. These cars carry

A Giant Coal Auger bores holes 42 inches wide and 200 feet deep into coal seams. A hydraulic crane lifts extra lengths of auger into place as needed. This machine, like the one in the picture at the top of the page, is another way of mining coal covered by too much earth and rock for strip-mining operations.

FROM MINE TO BIN

Run-of-mine coal, or coal as it comes up out of the mine, is not ready for use. It must be cleaned, screened, sorted into various sizes, and often crushed.

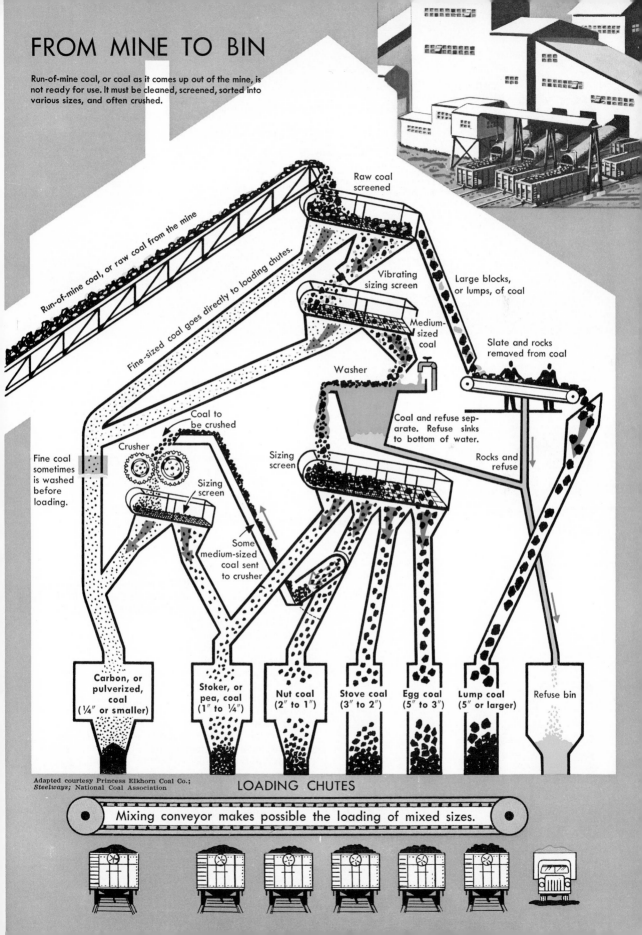

Run-of-mine coal, or raw coal from the mine

Raw coal screened

Fine-sized coal goes directly to loading chutes.

Vibrating sizing screen

Large blocks, or lumps, of coal

Medium-sized coal

Slate and rocks removed from coal

Washer

Coal to be crushed

Crusher

Sizing screen

Sizing screen

Some medium-sized coal sent to crusher

Coal and refuse separate. Refuse sinks to bottom of water.

Rocks and refuse

Fine coal sometimes is washed before loading.

Carbon, or pulverized, coal (¼″ or smaller)

Stoker, or pea, coal (1″ to ¼″)

Nut coal (2″ to 1″)

Stove coal (3″ to 2″)

Egg coal (5″ to 3″)

Lump coal (5″ or larger)

Refuse bin

Adapted courtesy Princess Elkhorn Coal Co.; *Steelways*; National Coal Association

LOADING CHUTES

Mixing conveyor makes possible the loading of mixed sizes.

TRANSPORTING COAL

Coal of various sizes is loaded from a mine preparation plant directly into railroad cars, *above*. Railroads carry the coal to large users, such as electric-power plants. Barges also haul great quantities of coal. A diesel towboat, *upper right*, pushes a string of barges along the Ohio River. Ships, *left*, carry coal across oceans and the Great Lakes.

up to 100 tons of coal, but some have been made which can carry as much as 145 tons of coal. Trucking of coal directly from the mines has been gaining importance. But railroads still carry almost six times as much coal from the mines as do trucks.

Several major railroads operate *unit* trains, made up entirely of coal cars that operate directly between mines and major consumers, such as electric-power plants. Unit trains can haul up to 15,000 tons of coal each trip. They are loaded and unloaded rapidly, and they save shippers money on freight rates.

Coal may also be shipped in pipelines in a soupy mixture called *slurry*, which can be burned without first separating and drying the coal.

Coal is also shipped by barge, because many mines and preparation plants are located on rivers and water transportation is cheaper than shipping by rail. Millions of tons of the coal mined in Pennsylvania and West Virginia are shipped this way on the Ohio River and its branches. Some coal produced in Ohio, Kentucky, Illinois, and Alabama is also shipped by river.

Many utility companies are building electric-power plants near mines and sending electricity over long-distance high-voltage lines to consuming areas. This eliminates the need to transport coal by railroad, barge, or truck, and reduces the cost of electric power.

Much of the coal mined in the Appalachian area is taken by rail to Lake Erie or to the Atlantic Coast, and from there it is shipped by boat. When the railroad cars reach the transfer point, they are run over huge docks onto rotary dumping machines or dumping pits. These dumping machines empty the coal either into

National Coal Association

freighters or onto conveyor belts that carry the coal to the ships.

The coal which is sent by boat on the Great Lakes is loaded at Toledo, Sandusky, Lorain, Ashtabula, and Conneaut, all in Ohio; and at Buffalo, N.Y. A modern lake steamer can carry 20,000 tons of coal.

From these points, the coal freighters go to various places in Canada and the United States. Many of the shipments are to Detroit; Chicago; Milwaukee; Superior, Wis.; and Duluth, Minn. Lake boats returning from Minnesota and Wisconsin usually bring back iron ore.

Most of the coal that is shipped along the Atlantic Coast is loaded at Hampton Roads, Va.; Baltimore; Philadelphia; and New York City. These so-called *tidewater* coal shipments go to ports in other countries, especially in western Europe. They also go to other ports in the Middle Atlantic states, and to the New England states. Canada ranks as the chief importer of United States coal. Italy and Japan also import large amounts. High-grade coking coals from the United States are in particular demand in European steel-producing centers.

Coal that arrives by ship is unloaded by huge cranes that scoop it out of the holds, and pile it for storage at the pier or load it on railroad cars for shipment farther inland.

Storing. Most large consumers of coal try to keep a supply on hand which will last several months beyond their immediate requirements. Sometimes coal is stored in the open, and sometimes in bins. Anthracite and bituminous coal may be kept for long periods of time without losing their heating or power values. But subbituminous coal must be stored or piled carefully to protect it from the weather, and lignite cannot be stored long because it dries out.

A major problem of coal distributors is having on hand the right grades and sizes of coal to meet the demands of the market. In coal yards there are usually a large number of bins, each containing a reserve supply of coal of a certain grade. Yet many retail deliveries are made directly from railroad cars. Retail dealers often combine coal distribution with other lines of business, including fuel oil and sometimes ice, lumber, and general hauling. These dealers usually deliver coal by truck.

Where Coal Is Found

World Coal Fields. Most of the world's coal fields have been located. About one-fifth of the world's coal supply lies in the United States. Russia and West Germany also have large coal deposits. Russia has deposits in both Europe and Asia. Its largest coal fields lie in the Donets Basin and in the Karaganda and Kuznetsk regions. The largest West German coal fields lie in the Ruhr region. Great Britain also has large coal deposits, especially in the region of the Pennine Chain and in Wales. In mainland China, especially large coal beds lie under the North China Plain and in central Manchuria. Poland has large coal fields near its southern border.

United States Coal Fields. The chief coal fields of the United States are spread over several wide areas. The great Appalachian coal area extends from Alabama to Pennsylvania and Ohio. A second huge coal area lies

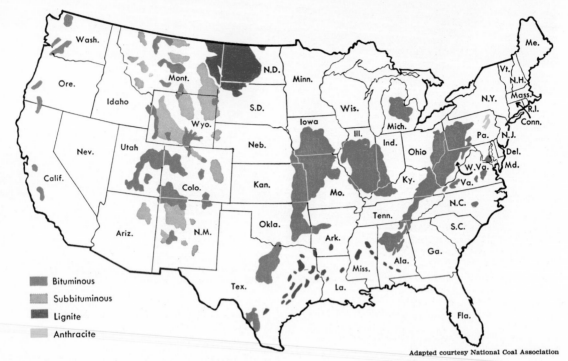

Main Coal Deposits of the United States, Outside Alaska and Hawaii, Showing the Kinds of Coal

Bituminous
Subbituminous
Lignite
Anthracite

Adapted courtesy National Coal Association

in Illinois, Indiana, and western Kentucky. Another large field crosses Iowa, Missouri, Kansas, Oklahoma, and Texas. The Northwestern Plains coal area includes parts of North and South Dakota and eastern Montana. The Rocky Mountain coal area lies in western Montana, Wyoming, Colorado, Utah, New Mexico, and Arizona. The Pacific Coast coal fields lie chiefly in Washington. Thirty-four of the 50 states of the United States have significant amounts of coal. Coal is mined in only 25 of these states.

Amount of Coal Mined. The United States is the world's second largest coal producer. It accounted for about 19 per cent of the total world output in the 1960's.

In the late 1960's, the United States was producing over 563 million tons a year. Of this amount, over 97 per cent was bituminous coal. Less than 3 per cent was anthracite. If the coal mined in the United States in a single year were used as paving material, it would build 12 superhighways 50 feet wide, 1 foot thick, and almost 3,000 miles long, about the distance between San Francisco and New York City.

West Virginia, Kentucky, and Pennsylvania mines supply over half of the bituminous coal, and Pennsylvania supplies all the anthracite in the country. The other chief coal-producing states are Illinois, Ohio, Virginia, Indiana, and Alabama. Although more than

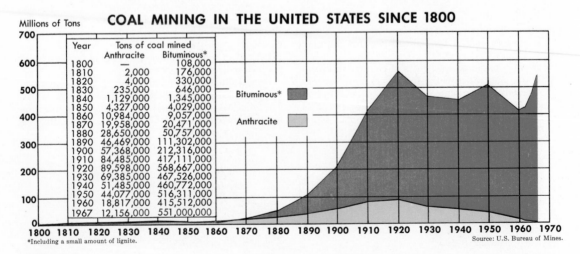

COAL MINING IN THE UNITED STATES SINCE 1800

Millions of Tons

Year	Tons of coal mined Anthracite	Bituminous*
1800	—	108,000
1810	2,000	176,000
1820	4,000	330,000
1830	235,000	646,000
1840	1,129,000	1,345,000
1850	4,327,000	4,029,000
1860	10,984,000	9,057,000
1870	19,958,000	20,471,000
1880	28,650,000	50,757,000
1890	46,469,000	111,302,000
1900	57,368,000	212,316,000
1910	84,485,000	417,111,000
1920	89,598,000	568,667,000
1930	69,385,000	467,526,000
1940	51,485,000	460,772,000
1950	44,077,000	516,311,000
1960	18,817,000	415,512,000
1967	12,156,000	551,000,000

Bituminous*

Anthracite

*Including a small amount of lignite.

Source: U.S. Bureau of Mines.

90 per cent of the coal mined in the United States came from coal fields east of the Mississippi River, eastern reserves make up only 40 per cent of the nation's total. The 14 Northeastern states use 6 out of every 10 tons of coal produced in the United States.

Other leading coal-mining countries are Russia, China (Mainland), Germany (East and West), and Great Britain. These countries and the United States mine about three-fourths of the world's output of coal.

For more detailed information on the coal deposits in various states and countries, see the Natural Resources sections of the articles on the states and countries.

World Coal Reserves are estimated to be about $9\frac{1}{2}$ thousand billion tons. More than 18 per cent of this reserve is in North America. Asia has 73 per cent and Europe has $6\frac{1}{2}$ per cent. United States coal reserves are estimated at more than 15 hundred billion tons. This includes beds down to 3,000 feet below the surface. Some good-quality coal deposits lie even below that depth, but these are not likely to be mined for many years. Today, beds are seldom mined that are more than a few hundred feet below the surface. It is estimated that there are 13 hundred billion tons of additional coal in unmapped and unexplored areas throughout the United States.

No one can tell exactly how long the coal resources of the United States will last. This will depend on a number of factors. These include the rate of consumption of American coal, the life expectancy of American reserves of oil and natural gas, the level of imports of these competitive fuels, and the future price of coal compared to other sources of energy. However, experts expect that the United States has enough coal to last, at present production rates, for about 1,500 years. This estimate includes billions of tons of subbituminous coal and lignite in the western United States. Even at increased rates, coal will last many years after such energy sources as oil and natural gas are gone.

Conservation of Coal

Coal that is consumed can never be replaced. Even the abundant coal resources of the U.S. must be used wisely. Little coal is used to heat homes. But industry needs more coal than ever before for power and heat. Producers and users must meet increasing demands for coal while guarding against waste.

The United States Geological Survey provides much needed information by mapping coal fields and estimating the coal resources of states. Newly discovered coal beds are analyzed to ensure that the coal will be used for the purpose for which it is best suited. Individual companies also conduct their own exploration and research to increase their own known reserves.

The United States Bureau of Mines estimates that 57 per cent of the coal in the ground in the United States will not be used because it cannot be mined. Coal pillars must be left in the mine to support roofs. Some coal cannot be mined because it lies under such restricted areas as towns, roads, and streams. However, United States mines have a higher percentage of recovery than do mines in other countries. United States mines average less than 300 feet in depth, and they have relatively level and thick seams. Many mines in other countries go down 3,000 to 4,000 feet and often have very thin seams and so increase mining costs.

LEADING COAL MINING STATES
Tons of coal mined in 1967

West Virginia	152,500,000 tons
Kentucky	99,500,000 tons
Pennsylvania	91,656,000 tons
Illinois	65,200,000 tons
Ohio	45,800,000 tons
Virginia	37,900,000 tons
Indiana	18,800,000 tons
Alabama	15,300,000 tons
Tennessee	6,750,000 tons
Colorado	5,425,000 tons

Source: U.S. Bureau of Mines

Up to 85 per cent of the coal in an underground mine may be recovered with the aid of modern equipment and methods. Huge surface mining shovels uncover coal that could not otherwise be mined. Augers bore into mountainsides to bring out coal too difficult and expensive to mine with picks and shovels. Underground machines recover higher percentages of coal.

Modern surface mining recovers coal that would otherwise be lost, but it leaves banks of land exposed to erosion. Responsible coal companies reclaim this land by planting trees or crops. Some of these areas

LEADING COAL MINING COUNTRIES
Tons of coal mined in 1967

Country	Tons
Russia	*656,000,000 tons
United States	563,256,000 tons
Germany (East)	*277,560,000 tons
China (Mainland)	*250,000,000 tons
Germany (West)	231,153,000 tons
Great Britain	192,824,000 tons
Poland	162,926,000 tons
Czechoslovakia	100,090,000 tons
India	80,912,000 tons
Australia	65,068,000 tons

*Estimate

Source: U.S. Bureau of Mines

WHAT WE GET FROM A TON OF COAL

We get POWER and HEAT if we burn the coal. Or we can change the coal into hundreds of useful products. When we roast one ton of coal in an airtight oven, we get ...

Hot gases

Roasted coal becomes coke

Tar and oil distilled from gases

Chemicals removed from gases

Remaining gases piped to users

...1,300 to 1,500 pounds of

...8 to 10 gallons of

...3 gallons of

...5 to 6 pounds of

...9,500 to 11,500 cubic feet of

COKE	COAL TAR	LIGHT OIL	AMMONIA	COAL GAS

LUMP COKE

Metallurgical coke
Copper smelting
Iron smelting
Lead smelting
Iron and Steel
  Casting

Heating purposes
Homes
Industry

Calcium carbide
Acetylene
  Chemicals
  Welding

Water gas
Heating purposes
  Homes
  Industry
  Chemicals

Other industrial purposes
Chemical processing
Lime burning
Beet sugar refining
Manufacture of
  mineral wool

SCREENINGS OR BREEZE
Iron ore agglomeration
Chemical processing
Steam generation

Tar acids
Carbolic acid
  Pharmaceuticals
Cresols
  Lysol
  Photo developer
  Plastics
Phenols
  Detergents
  Drugs
  Dyes
  Food
    preservatives
  Perfumes
  Rubber chemicals
  Weedkiller

Tar bases
Pyridine bases
  Antiseptics
  Disinfectants
  Paint thinner
Pyridine
  Clothes water-
    proofing
  Sulfa drugs
  Synthetic vitamins

Naphthalene
Insecticides
Fungicides
Plastic dolls
Explosives
Moth balls
Synthetic fibers

Heavy Oil
Dyes
Embalming fluid
Laxatives
Wood preservatives

Pitch
Electrodes
Insulation
Paving
Roofing
Storage batteries
Waterproofing

Benzene
Synthetic fibers
  Nylon
Aniline dyes
Food preservatives
Motor fuel
Plastics
Synthetic rubber
Tanning fluids

Toluene
Antiseptics
Fingernail polish
Printing ink
Saccharin
TNT explosive
Aviation gasoline
Detergents

Xylene
Motor fuel
Gasoline solvents
Herbicides

Solvent Naphtha
Rubber solvent
Electrical insulation
Linoleum
Varnish

Ammonium sulfate
Fertilizers
Chemicals

Ammonia liquor
Fertilizers
Explosives
Household ammonia
Refrigerant
Nitric acid

Diammonium phosphate
Fertilizer
Fire retardant

Heating purposes
Homes
Industry

Sulfur
Fungicides
Insecticides
Sulfuric acid

Cyanogen
Cotton finishing
Dyes

White-Hot Coke made from coal is dumped into a "hot car" for shipment to quenching towers.
National Coal Assoc.

yield valuable forest products. Still others have become public recreation areas and game preserves.

Some high-rank coal, especially coking coal, is less plentiful than other types. But much non-coking coal can be adapted for coking by processes such as crushing and removing impurities. By blending non-coking coal with coking coal and improving blast furnace methods, steelmakers can reduce the amount of coking coal needed to produce a ton of steel.

Conservation has been aided by the shift from beehive coke ovens to by-product coke ovens. The beehive ovens wasted coking by-products, but the by-product ovens save them.

Advances in transportation have increased coal-mining activity west of the Mississippi River. Coal pipelines, unit trains, and transmission of high-voltage electricity generated from coal at the mines may soon enable Pacific Coast consumers to use coal from the Rocky Mountains.

Efficient equipment for burning coal results in greater heating value and less waste. Modern air pollution control equipment helps to eliminate most of the smoke and soot, which indicate waste.

How Coal Is Used as Fuel

Coal supplies the fuel used to generate over half the electric power in the United States. The coal is burned under boilers containing water. Steam from the boiling water spins turbines which turn generators to produce electricity. One ounce of coal makes as much electricity as 100 tons of water falling one foot. The electric-utility industry uses nearly 300 million tons of bituminous coal a year. The aluminum industry, which consumes large quantities of electricity, is building plants in coal regions. This puts the plants close to low-cost sources of electric energy.

USES OF BITUMINOUS COAL—1968

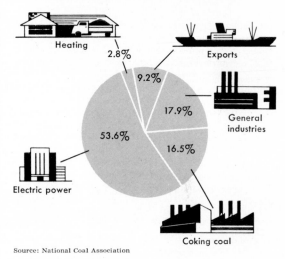

Heating 2.8%
Exports
9.2%
17.9%
General industries
53.6%
16.5%
Electric power
Coking coal

Source: National Coal Association

For every 47 tons of bituminous coal mined, only about one ton of anthracite is mined. Most anthracite is used for heating.

Steel is not usually made in large amounts without coke, which is bituminous coal with the tar and gases baked out. Imagine what life would be like without steel! There would be no automobiles, airplanes, trains, ocean liners, or skyscrapers. The U.S. iron and steel industry uses about 100 million tons of coal annually.

Coal is also widely used as a source of power and heat by other important industries. These include the chemical, cement, paper, and metal industries. Coal is also burned to provide the heat needed for many

COAL TO STEEL

In Making Steel, "skip cars" carry coke, iron ore, and limestone up inclines to be deposited in a blast furnace.
U.S. Steel Corp.

Pig Iron From the Blast Furnace is poured into an open hearth furnace for further refining. Temperatures may reach 3000° F.
Bethlehem Steel Corp.

schools, hospitals, hotels, and apartment buildings.

Coal is necessary even for the production of atomic energy. Millions of tons of coal are used each year to make the electricity needed to run United States uranium enrichment plants.

Coal has played a leading part in the course of history and in the struggles between nations. Wars have been fought to gain or keep coal fields. This is because industrial success depends to a large extent upon the amount of coal a country controls. The coal reserves of Alsace-Lorraine and of the Ruhr and Saar basins of Western Europe have been one of the causes of many conflicts in that part of the world. Victory or defeat in war may depend upon a nation's possession or lack of coal reserves because arms and munitions cannot be produced without coal.

Thick beds of coal have determined the location of cities. Coal has made great industrial centers of such cities as Birmingham, Ala., and Pittsburgh, Pa. These cities are near large deposits of coal.

Products from Coal

You use coal every day, although you may not recognize the coal as fingernail polish, a doll, moth balls, or the detergent with which you wash dishes. Chemicals obtained from coal are used to make these and thousands of other useful articles. Four of the main processes used to obtain valuable man-made products from coal are described below.

Carbonization consists of baking coal in an airtight oven. In this process, about two-thirds of the coal is changed into either *coke* or *char*, depending on the quality of the coal baked. Coke is particularly useful in making iron and steel, and as an industrial fuel. One-third of the coal baked turns into tar and gas. Coal tar is used in road surfacing and as a raw material that can be broken down into hundreds of useful chemicals. Coal gas, or coke oven gas, is used as a fuel gas and as a raw-material source of dyes and other industrial chemicals.

Hydrogenation is a process of treating coal with oil and hydrogen under heat and pressure, then separating the liquid mixture into useful products. Hydrogenation produces hydrocarbon gases such as ethane, propane, and butane. It produces low-priced pitch. And it turns out many valuable chemicals such as benzene, phenol, naphthalene, and aniline. These chemicals in turn are used to make everyday products such as dyes, perfumes, paints, and plastics. The hydrogenation process also can be used to produce fuel oil and gasoline. The first commercial use of the hydrogenation process in the United States was in 1952 at a plant built in West Virginia by the Union Carbide & Carbon Corporation. See HYDROGENATION.

Gas Synthesis, or the Fischer-Tropsch process, is a method of developing chemicals from coal by oxidation. The first step is to turn pulverized coal into a gas by exposing the coal to oxygen and superheated steam. The gas, a mixture of carbon monoxide and hydrogen, in turn is passed over various solid catalysts to change it into useful products. Cobalt catalysts have been used to change the gas into diesel fuel. Iron catalysts can change it into gasoline.

Gasification. Fuel gas is obtained from coal by two commercial methods which are described in the article GAS (Coke Oven Gas; Carbureted Water Gas). Experiments have been conducted in the United States and other countries with a process of burning the coal in the mine to produce gas, then piping the gas to the surface. The gas in turn can be used as a source of heat to make electric power, or can be broken down into liquid fuels such as gasoline.

Leading Coal Companies

Most mines are primarily owned by companies in the coal business. But some coal mines belong to steel companies, utilities, and other large industries that use a great deal of coal. These mines are called *captive mines.* Captive mines account for about 15 per cent of the coal produced in the United States.

The United States Steel Corporation is the largest captive mine owner in the United States. Its mines produce over 3 per cent of the total coal production in the United States. Peabody Coal Company of St. Louis and Consolidation Coal Company of Pittsburgh are the two largest owners of noncaptive mines and the two leading coal producers in the United States. Each mines about 11 per cent of the total U.S. coal production. Other large companies include the Island Creek Coal Company of Cleveland and the Pittston Company of New York City. Most major U.S. coal-producing and coal-sales companies work together through the National Coal Association of Washington, D.C. The association provides services in such fields as economics and transportation, government relations, law, marketing, public relations, and research.

The Mining Industry

Employment. The use of coal mining machines has made it possible for a far smaller number of miners to produce the coal the nation uses. For example, in 1923 more than 700,000 miners were employed in bituminous-coal mines of the United States. They produced almost 565 million tons of coal. In 1967, less than 132,000 bituminous miners produced about 551 million tons of coal. In the late 1960's, bituminous-coal mining employed about 12 times as many men as anthracite mining.

The United States coal miner produces more coal per day than does the average miner of any other country in the world. Bituminous miners in the United States mined an average of 19 tons per man every working day in the late 1960's, compared with an average of less than 3 tons per miner in Europe.

About 220,000 persons in the United States earn their living directly from the coal industry. In addition to the men who mine the coal and manage the mines, thousands of persons are engaged outside the mines in selling coal, transporting it, and handling it in coal-using industries.

Working Conditions. Before 1898, the length of the work week in the bituminous-coal mines of the United States was 60 hours. It was reduced to 52 hours during the period from 1898 through 1916, to 50 in 1917, to 48 between 1917 and 1932, and to 40 hours in 1933. Except for a few years during World War II, the 40-hour weekly schedule—eight hours per day and five days per week—has remained in effect.

BLACK MAGIC

BURNING 100 POUNDS OF COAL HELPS IN THE MANUFACTURE OF...

... 350 POUNDS OF CEMENT.

... 150 POUNDS OF PAPER, OR ENOUGH FOR 50 BIG SUNDAY NEWSPAPERS.

... 15 POUNDS OF ALUMINUM, ENOUGH FOR 120 FRYING PANS.

... 110 POUNDS OF STEEL, ENOUGH FOR 440 SOUP CANS.

MINING

A COAL MINER IN THE UNITED STATES MINES ABOUT 19 TONS OF COAL A DAY.

AIR

FOR EVERY TON OF COAL DUG, A MINE USES 6 TONS OF AIR FOR VENTILATION, ENOUGH TO FILL A 3-STORY BUILDING 50 FEET WIDE AND 100 FEET LONG.

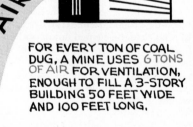

WATER

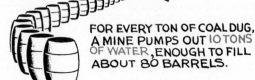

FOR EVERY TON OF COAL DUG, A MINE PUMPS OUT 10 TONS OF WATER, ENOUGH TO FILL ABOUT 80 BARRELS.

TRANSPORTATION

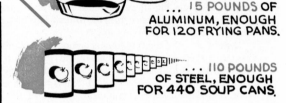

ONE OF EVERY 6 FREIGHT CARS USED BY THE RAILROADS HAULS COAL.

THE AMOUNT OF COAL MINED IN A YEAR IN THE UNITED STATES WOULD FILL A TRAIN LONG ENOUGH TO REACH AROUND THE EARTH ALMOST 3 TIMES.

Prepared with the cooperation of the National Coal Association

COAL

Weekly work schedules in the anthracite industry remained at 60 hours until April 1, 1903, when they were reduced to 54. A reduction from 54 hours per week to 48 took place on April 1, 1916, and from 48 hours to 35 on May 1, 1937.

During World War II, most miners worked long hours of overtime, but today the normal time worked by miners is 40 hours a week. Miners in the United States usually work about 220 eight-hour days a year.

In early days, coal-mining companies built many *company towns* to provide housing for their miners, and ran *company stores* to supply the miners' needs. This was considered necessary because mines were often located in areas far from cities and towns. There were several disadvantages in the company-town system. The miners sometimes felt that they were not free to live and to buy their goods where they pleased. As retail merchants and landlords, the mining companies had a heavy responsibility to the miners. The introduction of good roads, the automobile, and higher pay made it possible for many miners to live at a distance from the mines. This brought about a decline in company towns.

Unions. Most of the coal miners belong to the United Mine Workers of America. Under the leadership of John L. Lewis, this union became one of the strongest labor organizations in the United States. Lewis, who started working as a coal miner at the age of 12, became president of the United Mine Workers in 1920. He served as president of the union for the next 40 years, until he retired in January, 1960.

The union negotiates contract agreements with the mine operators. These agreements deal mainly with wage rates, hours of work, working conditions, and the royalties paid by the operators into the miners' welfare and retirement fund. This fund provides pensions for retired miners, medical care for miners and their families, and death benefits for miners' families.

Importance to Other Industries. All industries are likely to be seriously affected if anything interrupts the steady flow of coal from the mines. For example, if the great steel furnaces grow cold for lack of coal, a shortage of steel may cause shutdowns in automobile plants, building construction, shipyards, and hundreds of other manufacturing industries. All other industries may be greatly hampered, not only by a shortage of coal for their own use, but also by a shortage of automobiles, new buildings, and ships. Shutdowns spreading to these other industries may throw hundreds of thousands of persons out of work, with the result that they suffer hardships and cannot buy as much of the products of industry as they usually would. At the same time, coal-heated homes may be left without fuel. Without coal to provide energy to generate electricity, entire cities may be cast into darkness and various other essential community services may be cut off. Radio and television stations may go off the air for lack of power.

Thus, the normal operation of the coal industry is of great importance to the country. This is especially true in wartime. Government regulation of the United States coal industry was introduced in 1917, during World War I, but was lifted after peace was declared.

Regulation was revived in 1933. The federal government established minimum prices for coal and aided in the negotiation of wage-hour agreements. This type of regulation was discontinued in 1943 when wartime regulations setting maximum prices were in effect. Since 1946 little regulation has existed except for a time after the start of the Korean War. During several earlier periods of national emergency, the federal government took over operation of the mines when labor-management disputes interfered with coal production.

Mine Safety Measures

Protection Against Gases. Precautions against gas must be taken in many mines. There are many gases which displace the oxygen in the air, and make it unsafe to breathe. One of these dangerous gases is carbon dioxide. This gas often is found with deeply buried deposits of coal. Air which contains large proportions of carbon dioxide is called *chokedamp* or *blackdamp*. Chokedamp becomes a hazard when a section of the mine is cut off from a proper supply of fresh air. Constant ventilation of all parts of the mine prevents chokedamp.

An instrument known as the *flame safety lamp* is used to detect chokedamp. When chokedamp is present, the lack of oxygen makes the flame of the lamp burn lower. See SAFETY LAMP.

Another gas found in mines is carbon monoxide. It is sometimes called *afterdamp*, because it occurs only *after* a mine fire, an explosion, or the partial burning of explosives used in breaking down coal. Carbon monoxide is caused by the incomplete burning of the coal or coal dust. A carbon-monoxide detector, carried by a man wearing a gas mask, is used to test for the presence of this dangerous gas.

Probably the most common of the dangerous gases found in mines is methane. Explosions may result when only 5 to 15 per cent of methane is found in the air. The mixture of methane with air is called *firedamp*. Methane is formed by the same chemical changes which produced coal from organic matter. For this reason it is more often found in coal mines than in any other type of mine.

Firedamp can be detected by a flame safety lamp because it makes the lamp's flame burn higher. It can also be detected by an electrical methane-detecting device or by on-the-ground chemical analysis of mine air samples. Methane can be cleared out of coal mines by means of huge ventilating fans and ventilating doors to distribute fresh air to the working sections of the mines. In many mines, the weight of the air which is sent through the mine passages during a day is much greater than the weight of the coal taken from the mine during that same time.

For many years canary birds were used to detect gas in mines. If gas was present, the birds became sluggish and fell from their perches. Today, accurate mechanical or electrical detecting devices are used.

Protection Against Coal-Dust Explosions. Gas explosions in mines are usually confined to one part of the mine, and are not themselves the cause of widespread injury or loss of life. But gas may start much-feared coal-dust explosions. Under certain conditions, coal dust is highly explosive.

The breaking of the coal for loading into mine cars or onto conveyors results in the formation of many fine particles of coal dust. This coal dust can be made harmless by a simple process called *rockdusting* (see

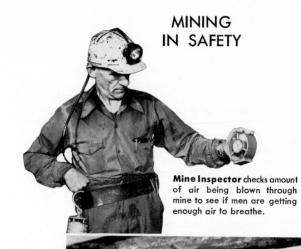

MINING IN SAFETY

Mine Inspector checks amount of air being blown through mine to see if men are getting enough air to breathe.

Safety Engineers talk over each mining operation with foremen and supervisors. A supervisor for each 10 to 12 miners helps to ensure safety in the mines.

Rockdusting, coating the surfaces of a coal mine with finely powdered limestone, reduces the danger of a minor gas explosion igniting the highly explosive coal dust.

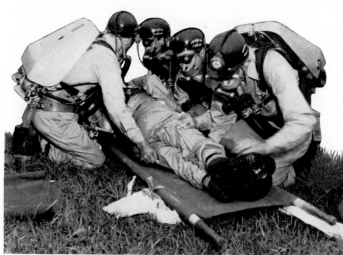

Mine Safety Team practices carrying miner on stretcher. A few minutes more or less in a mine disaster may mean many lives saved or lost.

Safety Fire Boss uses lamp to test for dangerous gases. If the lamp flame grows dim, the air has a dangerous amount of carbon dioxide. If the flame burns higher, the air has a dangerous amount of methane.

Western Kentucky Coal Co.; Bituminous Coal Institute; Pittsburgh Consolidation Coal Co.; National Coal Association

the picture of this process on the preceding page). In this process, powdered limestone is spread over all surfaces, effectively blanketing the coal dust. As another means of eliminating coal dust, water is used on the cutting and loading parts of mining machines.

Draining the Mine. Some mines are as dry as dust. But others, especially those located far below surface or under subterranean streams, are flooded with large quantities of water, which must be pumped out constantly. In such mines, drainage is a problem, and water may endanger the lives of the miners. In the anthracite region of Pennsylvania, as much as thirty-three tons of water may be pumped out for every ton of coal mined.

Sometimes, water in the mine comes in contact with sulfur-bearing rocks and other matter, causing acid to form. When this water is pumped from the mine, it may pollute nearby streams and water supplies. The United States Bureau of Mines conducts a research program to solve this problem in both operating and abandoned mines. The program is financed in part by the coal industry.

Protection Against Other Hazards. The greatest number of injuries in coal mines are caused by material falling from the mine roof. However, steel roof bolts which bind together the overlying layers of rock are used in most underground mines to prevent accidents. Steel and reinforced concrete pillars are sometimes used in main haulageways.

In the late 1960's, scientists reported that breathing high concentrations of extremely fine coal dust for several years can cause a disease known as *pneumoconiosis*. This disease, also called *black lung*, occurs when tiny coal particles coat the lungs of miners and interfere with breathing.

Safety Education. Coal mining today is safer than ever before. Some of this improvement has resulted from the development of improved safety devices, but safety education has also played an important part. Many mines have a safety director who meets regularly with the mine foremen and with employee groups to discuss safety measures. A single violation of the no-smoking rule may cause a disastrous fire or explosion. Failure to support the roof properly at a particular spot in the mine may cause a cave-in, trapping scores of miners. A good safety record depends on the cooperation of the mine operator and the miners in following safety measures. Many mines insist on giving their miners "pep talks" on safety practices. The talks concern the need for no-smoking rules and various other measures to insure greater safety for the miners. Posters placed at various locations about the mine warn the workers of the possibly disastrous results if they do not follow safety regulations exactly.

The United States Bureau of Mines, founded in 1910, studies the hazards of mining and advises mine operators on measures to prevent accidents. It also administers the federal Coal Mine Safety Act. As a result, deaths from explosions and certain other causes have been greatly reduced. The Departments of Mines in individual states, acting under state laws, have set up safety standards and regulations which also help to reduce the accident rate. Operators' associations and labor unions also aid in safety work and instruction of miners. Nearly all the mine accidents of recent years could have been prevented if safety regulations had been followed.

History of the Use of Coal

Early Use. The exact date of the first use of coal is not known. There is evidence that 3,000 to 4,000 years ago, in the Bronze Age, the people of Glamorganshire, Wales, used coal for funeral pyres to burn their dead. The Chinese probably used coal about 1,100 years before the Christian Era. King Solomon was probably familiar with the coal deposits of Syria, for coal is mentioned in the Book of Proverbs (26:21). It is also referred to in several later books of the Bible.

The Greeks used coal several hundred years before the birth of Christ. Aristotle, the Greek philosopher, mentioned it in his writings. But hundreds of years passed before coal had any great and lasting influence on the course of civilization.

Use in England. During the Middle Ages in England, coal was commonly thought to be a curse. People thought it filled the air with dangerous poisons that injured people's health. In 1306, King Edward I of England issued a proclamation that declared the use of coal punishable by death. At least one man was put to death for breaking this law. In early days, the methods of burning coal were so inefficient that smoke and bad odor filled the air. Many persons doubted that coal could ever be used successfully. The English were the first people to see the commercial value of coal and to use it widely.

The Industrial Revolution, which dates from the mid-1700's in Great Britain, was largely dependent on coal as the chief source of power to drive steam engines. See INDUSTRIAL REVOLUTION.

The word *coal* as used in the English language comes from the Anglo-Saxon *col*, which originally referred to charcoal. The spelling *cole* was used until about three hundred years ago, when the present spelling was adopted.

North America. Coal was discovered in North America in 1679. Father Louis Hennepin, a member of an early French exploring party, observed the black mineral along the Illinois River at a point about 80 miles southwest of the present city of Chicago. Some of the American Indian tribes, however, knew about coal long before this time. The Pueblo Indians of the Southwest used it in their pottery-making at an early date.

A colony of Huguenots, near what is now Richmond, Va., found a few pieces of bituminous coal near their colony in 1700. Fifty years later, a boy hunting crawfish discovered a rich bed in the region, and, before the end of 1750, mining operations were started. This was the first commercial mining of soft coal on the North American continent. In 1759, mining began in western Pennsylvania, and anthracite, now considered one of the finest of fuels, was discovered in eastern Pennsylvania in 1791. For a time this coal was believed to be useless. In some places the sale of anthracite was declared a fraud which was punishable by law.

With growing industrialization, especially after 1850, coal was increasingly used in the United States. The growth of railroads gave the coal industry one of its largest customers, and also stimulated the iron and steel industry, another large user of coal. In the 1890's, the development of steam-driven electric generators sparked the growth of the electric-power industry, the modern coal industry's largest customer.

During the 1960's, the U.S. government and the coal industry worked together in developing new uses of coal. Experimental projects included producing gasoline and pipeline gas from coal.

In recent years, oil and natural gas have been making an increasing contribution to America's fuel consumption, especially in transportation and home heating. All these fuels may eventually feel the impact of competition from atomic energy.

Critically reviewed by NATIONAL COAL ASSOCIATION

Related Articles in WORLD BOOK include:

SOME COAL PRODUCTS

Aniline	Coke	Nylon
Aspirin	Coke Oven Gas	Perfume
Benzene	Creosote	Plastics
Carbolic Acid	Dyes and Dyeing	Synthetics
Carbon	Gas (fuel)	Toluene
Coal Tar	Illuminating Gas	

OTHER RELATED ARTICLES

Damp	Lewis, John L.
Diamond	Lignite
Frick, Henry C.	Mining
Fuel	Peat
Hanna, Mark	Power
Heating (Coal and Coke)	Safety Lamp
Hydrogenation	United Mine Workers
Industrial Revolution	of America
Iron and Steel	West Virginia (pictures)
Jet	

Outline

I. **How Coal Was Formed**
   A. Time of Formation
   B. Coal Beds
II. **Chief Kinds of Coal**
   A. Anthracite
   B. Bituminous Coal
   C. Other Kinds of Coal
III. **How Coal Is Mined**
   A. Mining Methods
   B. Underground Mining Systems
   C. Breaking Down the Coal
   D. Hauling Coal Out of a Mine
   E. Sizing
   F. Cleaning
   G. Grading
IV. **How Coal Is Transported**
   A. Shipping
   B. Storing
V. **Where Coal Is Found**
   A. World Coal Fields
   B. United States Coal Fields
   C. Amount of Coal Mined
   D. World Coal Reserves
VI. **Conservation of Coal**
VII. **How Coal Is Used as Fuel**
VIII. **Products from Coal**
   A. Carbonization
   B. Hydrogenation
   C. Gas Synthesis
   D. Gasification
IX. **Leading Coal Companies**
X. **The Mining Industry**
   A. Employment
   B. Working Conditions
   C. Unions
   D. Importance to Other Industries

XI. **Mine Safety Measures**
   A. Protection Against Gases
   B. Protection Against Coal-Dust Explosions
   C. Draining the Mine
   D. Protection Against Other Hazards
   E. Safety Education
XII. **History of the Use of Coal**
   A. Early Use
   B. Use in England
   C. North America

Questions

What is a preparation plant?

Why was coal not widely used until long after its discovery?

How and when is coal believed to have been formed in the earth?

How is coal used in the production of nuclear energy?

What is a push-button miner?

What, in order, are the four largest coal-mining countries of the world? The four leading coal-producing states of the Union? How much coal is mined each year in the United States?

How long may the coal resources of the United States be expected to last?

What is meant by "hard" coal? "Soft" coal? Where in the United States is anthracite found? For what is anthracite used?

What are coking coals?

What are the chief types of coal mines, and how do they differ?

What are the chief safety precautions which must be taken in coal mines?

How is methane controlled in the modern coal mine?

What are some of the chief products of coal?

What is the principal means of transporting coal in the United States?

Where did French explorers first discover coal in North America?

Books for Young Readers

ADLER, IRVING and RUTH. *Coal*. Day, 1965. What coal is, where it comes from, and how it is changed into many other products.

BUEHR, WALTER. *Underground Riches: The Story of Mining*. Morrow, 1958. This book on mining in general has some material on coal formation and a chapter on coal mining.

COTHREN, MARION B. *Buried Treasure: The Story of America's Coal*. Coward-McCann, 1945.

PERRY, JOSEPHINE. *The Coal Industry*. Longmans, 1944. This basic book tells the history of coal and describes the mining industry.

Books for Older Readers

FRANCIS, WILFRID. *Coal: Its Formation and Composition*. 2nd ed. St. Martins, 1961. This summary of research work is designed for students in fuel technology and coal chemistry.

MITCHELL, DAVID R., ed. *Coal Preparation*. 2nd ed. American Institute of Mining and Metallurgical Engineers, 1950. A description of how coal is handled before it reaches the consumer.

NATIONAL COAL ASSOCIATION. *Bituminous Coal Facts*. National Coal Assn. Biennial report in text and tables of many aspects of the coal industry.

WILLIAMS, A. WYN. *Coal Manual for Industry*. Chilton, 1952. This book contains a description of the industrial uses of coal and of the equipment in which it is burned.

COAL AGE, or PENNSYLVANIAN PERIOD. See PENNSYLVANIAN EPOCH.

COAL GAS. See COKE OVEN GAS.

COAL OIL. See KEROSENE.

COAL TAR is a thick, black, sticky liquid. It is obtained as a by-product in the manufacture of coke and coke oven gas from soft coal. Coal tar is recovered by partially *condensing* (changing to liquid) the hot vapors from a coke oven or a coal gas producer. Further condensation produces light oils, such as *benzene* and *toluene*. Benzene is used as a solvent and in making perfumes and some gasolines, and toluene is used in making dyes, paints, explosives, and antiseptics.

Tar acids such as *carbolic acid* and tar bases such as *aniline* are other coal tar products. Carbolic acid and aniline are used to make dyes. *Creosote* and *pitch* are heavy liquid coal tar products. Creosote preserves wood, and pitch is used in the manufacture of roofing materials and paint. Perfumes, dyes, and drugs are made from coal tar products. Sir William H. Perkin, an English chemist, pioneered in coal tar chemistry by making mauve, the first dye. But *petrochemicals* (chemicals made from petroleum) are now replacing coal tar chemicals in industry and chemistry. CLARENCE KARR, JR.

Related Articles in WORLD BOOK include:

Aniline	Distillation
Aspirin	Dyes and Dyeing
Benzene	Naphtha
Carbolic Acid	Perfume
Coal (Products)	Perkin, Sir William H.
Coke	Phenacetin
Coke Oven Gas	Pitch
Creosote	Toluene

COALITION, KOH *uh* LISH *un*, is a combination of members of several political parties to run a country's government. A coalition is often used as a way of getting all parties to work together in a national emergency. During World Wars I and II, the British government was run by such a coalition. Coalition governments are most common in countries where there are many political parties and where a single party seldom wins a majority in the legislature or parliament. The term *coalition* is also used to describe an alliance of several nations against other countries. Coalitions of nations are often formed shortly before or during wars. Many European countries formed coalitions against France during the time of Louis XIV and during the Napoleonic wars. World Wars I and II were fought between coalitions of nations. ERIC SEVAREID

COANDA, HENRI MARIE (1885-   ), a civil aeronautics engineer and inventor, designed an airplane based on a jet-propulsion system. He crashed in it on takeoff near Paris in 1912. Coanda also developed a disk-shaped craft, based on an aerodynamic principle called the Coanda effect. Coanda was born in Bucharest, Romania. He studied at various schools, including the École Supérieure de l'Aéronautique. His other inventions include a device that is able to convert salt water to fresh water by using the energy of the sun. R. T. ELLICKSON

COAST AND GEODETIC SURVEY, JEE *oh* DEHT *ihk*, is a bureau of the United States Department of Commerce. Its main job is to gather information about the earth and sea and publish it in tables and maps useful to water and air navigators. The work is carried on by field stations, by survey parties, by a fleet of survey ships, and by the office of the bureau in Washington, D.C., which assigns duties to district offices.

Coast Survey, or *hydrographic* survey, measures the depths of water and the character of the sea bottom along more than 90,000 miles of shoreline of the United States and its dependencies (see HYDROGRAPHY). Its survey ships use electronic devices to *sound* (measure) the depths of the water (see FATHOMETER). Other electronic devices pinpoint the exact position of the sounding in relation to land so it can be charted. The survey locates reefs and shoals, wrecks, and other obstructions to navigation. It finds small obstructions by the *wire-drag method*, which consists of dragging a wire through the water behind two launches. Investigations carried on in connection with the hydrographic survey are used in publishing annual *Tide and Current Tables*. These tables give navigators essential advance information about the rise and fall of the tide and the ebb and flow of currents. See OCEAN (How the Ocean Moves); TIDE.

Geodetic Survey establishes exact positions on the earth's surface, taking into account the size and shape of the world. This survey determines the exact location and altitude of rivers, mountains, cities, and other important natural and cultural features. This information is supplied to engineers and surveyors for use in map-making, in establishing boundaries, and in planning and building such projects as dams, superhighways, and railroads.

Nautical and Aeronautical Charts are the principal products of the bureau. *Nautical charts*, or maps of water areas, are compiled from the results of the coast and geodetic surveys. The six main classes of nautical charts published by the bureau are: (1) *sailing*, (2) *general*, (3) *coast*, (4) *harbor*, (5) *intracoastal waterway*, and (6) *small-craft*. Supplementing these charts are publications called *coast pilots* which provide descriptive information that cannot be shown conveniently on the charts. *Aeronautical charts* (charts used by air navigators) include information gathered from the bureau surveys and from other sources. These charts show outstanding landmarks which help the aircraft navigator follow his course. The charts are printed in colors with navigational information for all types of aircraft. See CHART.

Magnetic and Seismological Observations are made by the bureau. Changes in the earth's magnetism are determined by observations at thousands of stations throughout the United States. The safety of navigation depends to a considerable extent on the navigator's knowledge of how the magnetism of the earth varies at different places and affects his magnetic compass. See COMPASS; MAGNET AND MAGNETISM.

Seismological observations (the recording of earthquakes) obtain information on the nature and distribution of earthquakes. These studies provide engineers with information which helps them build structures that can withstand earthquakes. See SEISMOGRAPH; SEISMOLOGY.

History. The bureau dates from February, 1807, when Congress authorized a survey of the coast of the United States. At President Jefferson's suggestion, a bureau of Coast Survey was established under the Treasury Department. By a Congressional Act in March, 1871, the work of the bureau was enlarged to include earth

COAST
AND GEODETIC
SURVEY

Coast and Geodetic Engineers, *right,* use sensitive instruments to make precise surveys of the United States. Recording equipment deep in the earth, *below,* sends back information used in locating an earthquake.

U.S. Coast and Geodetic Survey

Studying Ocean Currents, *below,* two survey divers prepare to observe the water at various depths.

measurements, or geodetic surveying. The name was changed to Coast and Geodetic Survey in 1878.

The bureau was transferred to the Department of Commerce and Labor in 1903, and to the Department of Commerce in 1913. Seismology was added in 1925, and aeronautical charting in 1926. In 1965, the Coast and Geodetic Survey became part of the Environmental Science Services Administration, a branch of the Department of Commerce (see Environmental Science Services Administration).

Throughout the years the bureau has helped develop new devices and methods for surveying. A tide-predicting machine used to forecast the times and heights of the tide for the *Tide Tables* was designed and built by the bureau in the early 1900's. The bureau developed a nine-lens aerial camera for map-making in the 1930's. During World War II, the bureau used *shoran* (short range navigation) to locate accurately survey ships in making soundings far from shore (see Shoran). Later the bureau invented the Electronic Position Indicator to extend the area covered by shoran. The new electronic technological aids increase the range, facility, accuracy, and productivity of almost all phases of Survey operations. H. Arnold Karo

Measuring Magnetic Fields, *below,* a scientist uses a magnetometer at the Fredericksburg Magnetic Observatory.

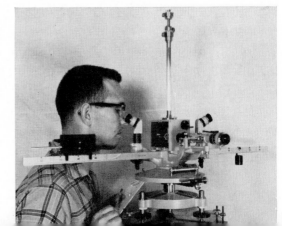

Coast Guard Cutters and icebreakers help out in Arctic waters, tracking icebergs and freeing ships. The Coast Guard aids seamen by gathering weather information, maintaining beacons and rescue stations, and patrolling the seaways.

St. John's Light Station, Mayport, Fla.

The Duties of the Coast Guard revolve around its role as the guardian of United States shores and waterways. Coastguardsmen are trained to pilot ships, plot courses, and perform skilled air and sea rescues. Through their actions, they proudly uphold the Coast Guard's motto, *Semper Paratus*, or *Always Ready*.

U.S. Coast Guard

COAST GUARD, UNITED STATES, is a branch of the armed services. It also serves as the chief agency for protecting life and property at sea and enforcing United States maritime laws. It fights smuggling, protects ships and ports, and rescues victims of sea disasters. Coast Guard ships patrol United States waterways, hunting icebergs, gathering weather information, and guiding ships. In peacetime, it operates as a branch of the Department of Transportation. In time of war, the Coast Guard becomes an active part of the United States Navy. The Coast Guard's many duties give special meaning to its motto, *Semper Paratus*, or *Always Ready*.

The Coast Guard is the nation's oldest continuous sea-going force. Since 1790, it has grown from a fleet of 10 cutters to an efficient force of ships and airplanes.

Coastguardsmen have fought in every war of the United States. They have rescued hundreds of thousands of men, women, and children from disasters, and have saved billions of dollars' worth of property from shipwrecks and floods. To perform their heroic work, coastguardsmen have gone to sea under the worst possible conditions. The many risks and dangers they face have led to the saying among coastguardsmen that "You have to go out, but you don't have to come back."

The Coast Guard has a peacetime strength of about 35,000 active and 32,000 reserve members. The Coast Guard emblem was adopted in 1927. "Semper Paratus" is the Coast Guard's famous marching song, and blue and white are its official colors.

What the Coast Guard Does

Protecting Life and Property. The Coast Guard has world-wide duties. Its ships, called *cutters*, patrol waterways. Its life-saving stations stand ready for emergencies. When accidents occur, rescue boats and aircraft go into action immediately. They rescue shipwrecked persons, search the waters for survivors, and tow damaged vessels to shore. The Coast Guard gives rescue assistance to any person or ship, regardless of nationality. It provides emergency medical aid to crews of all vessels at sea, and takes injured or critically ill seamen to shore bases for treatment. It also sends boats and men to help in relief operations.

Admiral Willard J. Smith, the contributor of this article, is Commandant of the United States Coast Guard.

Ships at sea depend on Coast Guard aids to navigation. Such guides as beacons, buoys, fog signals, lighthouses, lightships, and radio stations reduce the dangers of navigation. Loran stations use electronic devices to help ships determine their exact positions at sea (see LORAN). Coast Guard cutters report weather information to the U.S. Weather Bureau, which makes these data available to ships and planes. Icebreakers clear clogged harbors on the North Atlantic coast and on inland lakes, rivers, and canals. The International Ice Patrol, operated by the Coast Guard, locates icebergs in shipping lanes in the North Atlantic and warns ships about them (see ICE PATROL, INTERNATIONAL). The Alaskan Patrol offers protection in remote arctic regions. The Coast Guard's port-security program helps keep dangerous persons or cargoes from entering the United States.

Enforcing Sea Laws. The Coast Guard is responsible for enforcing all federal laws on the high seas and on the navigable waters of the United States. These include criminal laws, revenue and navigation laws, and nautical rules of the road. The Coast Guard is responsible for safety regulations for constructing and operating merchant ships. It signs crews on and off ships, and fixes safety rules for passengers and crewmen. The Coast Guard also establishes safety standards for yachts, motorboats, and other noncommercial vessels. The

Battling Giant Breakers, a motor lifeboat begins a rescue mission. Crew members must work in any kind of weather.

Rescuing Survivors, coastguardsmen haul in rubber life rafts tossed to victims of a shipwreck, *right*. Coast Guard lifeboats speed to save passengers from an airplane crash, *below*.

U.S. Coast Guard

Coast Guard Helicopters can take off at a moment's notice for emergency air-sea rescues or evacuation missions.

Lightships anchored at danger points along the coasts guide seamen. They carry fog signal devices and radio beacons.

U.S. Coast Guard; Wide World

Patrol Boats charge forward at top speed at the first sign of disaster.

U.S. Coast Guard

Radiomen keep constantly alert for distress signals from ships or pleasure craft. The men speed coast guard forces to the rescue.

Amphibious Search and Rescue Planes can take off from sea or land. The large planes use rockets for take-off power. They fly hundreds of miles to pick up stranded survivors.

U.S. Coast Guard

"How Salty Is the Sea?" Coastguardsmen take daily readings to find the sea temperature and the concentration of salt.

An Ice-Clogged Ship on Antarctic duty is pried loose with the help of 1,000 and 2,000 pound concrete blocks manned by coastguardsmen. The crewmen adopted a penguin, *far right*, as their mascot.

U.S. Coast Guard

Coast Guard Auxiliary, a voluntary association of yacht and motorboat sailors and owners, promotes safety.

The Coast Guard helps other federal agencies enforce their regulations in all possible ways. It polices oil pollution of waterways, and helps enforce laws concerning customs, immigration, internal revenue, quarantines, sponge-fishing in Florida waters, and the protection of fish and game. Under a program begun in 1963, the Coast Guard coordinates the work of several federal agencies to survey the entire U.S. coastline in order to prevent enemy infiltration.

—— **MAJOR COAST GUARD INSTALLATIONS** ——

Name	Location
*Alameda Coast Guard Base	Alameda, Calif.
Boston Coast Guard Base	Boston, Mass.
*Cape May Receiving Center	Cape May, N.J.
Coast Guard Curtis Bay Yard	Baltimore, Md.
Elizabeth City Air Station, Supply and Repair Base	Elizabeth City, N.C.
Galveston Coast Guard Base	Galveston, Tex.
Governors Island Coast Guard Base	Governors Island, N.Y.
Honolulu Coast Guard Base	Honolulu, Hawaii
Miami Coast Guard Base	Miami, Fla.
Mobile Coast Guard Base and Air Station	Mobile, Ala.
Portsmouth Coast Guard Base	Portsmouth, Va.
Terminal Island Coast Guard Base	Long Beach, Calif.
*United States Coast Guard Academy	New London, Conn.
Yorktown Coast Guard Reserve Training Center	Yorktown, Va.

*Has a separate article in THE WORLD BOOK ENCYCLOPEDIA.

Supporting the Navy. The Coast Guard stands ready to become part of the United States Navy in time of emergency. It resembles the Navy in organization and training, and cooperates closely with the Navy in many functions. The two services work together in Greenland, Iceland, and other arctic and antarctic regions. As part of the Navy in wartime, the Coast Guard maintains a port-security program, provides air-sea rescue services, escorts convoys, and mans troop transports.

Life in the Coast Guard

Training a Coastguardsman begins at "boot camp." The Coast Guard has training centers at Cape May, N.J., and Alameda, Calif., where recruits learn discipline and seamanship. A recruit is called a "boot" because in early days recruits wore leggings that looked somewhat like boots. Recruits receive 13 weeks of basic training. They take courses in communications, fire fighting, first aid, gunnery, military drill, physical education, and seamanship.

Recruits receive practical training on the drill field, the rifle range, and a 65-foot auxiliary schooner. Specially trained petty officers teach the courses. The Coast Guard also uses Navy materials and facilities in its training program. Coast Guard aviators are trained entirely by the Navy.

The Coast Guard tries to place men in positions for which they are best suited. It encourages them to take specialist courses. The men can earn ratings as electronics technicians, hospital corpsmen, journalists, oceanographers, photographers' mates, radiomen, and in other specialties. For further training, coastguardsmen can take correspondence courses from the Coast Guard and from the U.S. Armed Forces Institute.

Training an Officer. Most Coast Guard officers receive their training at the U.S. Coast Guard Academy at New London, Conn. A cadet takes a four-year course, and is graduated with a bachelor of science degree and a commission as an ensign in the Coast Guard. The academy organizes cadets into two battalions of four companies each. *First classmen* (members of the graduating class) serve as officers of the battalions. The highest honor a cadet can receive is to be chosen battalion commander in his first-class year. Members of each new class enter the academy during the summer, usually in late June or early July. These fourth classmen are called *swabs*. They spend their *swab summer* becoming adjusted to military life. Cadets spend part of each summer at sea, training aboard the bark *Eagle* and on major cutters. See UNITED STATES COAST GUARD ACADEMY.

A man with a bachelor's degree from an accredited college or university may take a special 16-week officer-candidate course at the Coast Guard Academy. Enlisted men with the proper qualifications may also take this course. Upon graduation, the men receive commissions as ensigns in the Coast Guard Reserve. An intensive 12-week officer's training course is open to qualified officers of the merchant marine. These men receive commissions in the Coast Guard after completing the course.

Careers in the Coast Guard include a variety of challenging positions. A coastguardsman has opportunities to become an expert in a specialized field. Coast Guard training also prepares men for civilian jobs when their enlistments end or when they retire from service. Applicants must be between the ages of 17 and 26. They must meet Coast Guard physical standards, and make a qualifying score on the Armed Forces Qualifications Test. They may have no more than one dependent.

Applicants to the Coast Guard Academy must be high-school graduates between 17 and 22 years old. They must be unmarried, meet rigid physical standards, and be of good moral character. Cadets are appointed on the basis of a nationwide competition each year. Applications to enter the competition should be sent to the Director of Admissions, U.S. Coast Guard Academy, New London, Conn. 06320.

Officers and enlisted men in the Coast Guard hold the same ranks and earn the same pay as those in the Navy. Coast Guard uniforms are similar to those of the Navy. But a Coast Guard officer wears a distinctive cap device and the Coast Guard shield instead of the Navy star. An enlisted man wears the Coast Guard shield on his lower right sleeve. See RANK IN ARMED SERVICES.

Ships and Weapons of the Coast Guard

Ships and Stations. The Coast Guard maintains a fleet of several hundred ships and boats that can perform various assignments. These vessels include cutters, fireboats, icebreakers, lifeboats, lightships, motorboats, surfboats, tenders, and tugs.

The service operates nearly 300 port-security offices, and more than 50 offices devoted to shipping-inspection duties. It also maintains light towers, navigational aids, and over 600 patrol and lookout stations, including more than 350 manned lighthouses.

Aircraft play a major part in Coast Guard operations. The Coast Guard has about a dozen kinds of aircraft for patrol work and extended searches. Coast Guard seaplanes can fly more than a thousand miles out to sea, land on the ocean, and pick up survivors of sea accidents. Helicopters are particularly important to the Coast Guard. They can rescue disaster victims in inland areas that could not otherwise be reached. The Coast Guard also uses helicopters in air-sea rescues, and in bringing help to flooded areas. During World War II, Coast Guard aircraft bombed submarines and rescued many survivors of torpedoed ships.

Ordnance. About 200 Coast Guard vessels are armed with guns. Weapons range from machine guns on small patrol vessels to 5-inch guns on large cutters. Many vessels also carry some antisubmarine warfare weapons. Coast Guard recruits receive small-arms training. The service also has a special training program for crew members of small armed vessels. It sends larger vessels to naval training centers for refresher training.

Organization of the Coast Guard

Coast Guard Headquarters are in Washington, D.C. The service operates as a branch of the Department of Transportation in peacetime. In wartime, or upon the direction of the President, it is subject to orders of the secretary of the navy. The commandant of the Coast Guard heads the service. An assistant commandant, a planning and control staff, and officers of various Coast Guard departments assist him. The United States and its possessions are divided into 12 Coast Guard districts, each headed by a district commander.

Regulars and Reserves. The *Regular Coast Guard* makes up the core of the service. It consists of officers and enlisted men who have chosen the Coast Guard as a full-time career. The *Coast Guard Reserve* is a supplementary group whose members may be called to active duty in time of emergency. Their training includes electronics, port security, and vessel manning.

Women in the Coast Guard are called SPARS. The name SPAR comes from the first letters of the Coast Guard motto, *Semper Paratus*, and its English translation, *Always Ready*. All women in the SPARS serve as

---
IMPORTANT DATES IN COAST GUARD HISTORY

1790 The United States Congress authorized the construction of 10 cutters for a Revenue Marine service.

1819 Congress authorized revenue cutters to protect United States merchant vessels against piracy, and to seize vessels engaged in slave trading.

1861 The cutter *Harriet Lane* fired the first shot from any vessel in the Civil War.

1863 The name of the service became the Revenue Cutter Service.

1898 The cutter *McCulloch* sent the first news of the victory over the Spanish fleet at Manila Bay.

1915 The Revenue Cutter Service and the Lifesaving Service were combined to form the United States Coast Guard.

1917 During World War I, the Coast Guard for the first time was ordered to serve as part of the Navy.

1939 The Lighthouse Service of the Department of Commerce was transferred to the Coast Guard.

1945 The icebreaker *Mackinaw* made the first winter trip through the Soo locks on Lake Superior.

1957 The cutters *Storis*, *Bramble*, and *Spar* completed the first trip through the deepwater northwest passage across the top of North America in one season.

reserves. The SPAR organization, established in 1942, reached a strength of 1,000 officers and 10,000 enlisted women during World War II. After the war, the Coast Guard discontinued all SPAR enlistments and training, and officially dissolved the organization. A number of SPARS returned to active duty during the Korean War. A small group of women reserves serves on active duty, most of them at Coast Guard headquarters. See SPARS.

History

The Revenue Marine was created in 1790 at the recommendation of Alexander Hamilton, first secretary of the treasury. Congress established this fleet of 10 small sailing vessels to stamp out smuggling and piracy along the coasts of the United States. Revenue Marine officers had permission to board all vessels that entered United States waters, and to examine their cargoes.

From 1790 until 1798—when the Navy was reorganized—the Revenue Marine served as the nation's only naval force. The service saw its first wartime activity from 1797 to 1800, when it cooperated with the Navy in fighting French privateers. The Revenue Marine also fought during the War of 1812. In 1831, the service began its first winter cruising to aid seafarers and ships in distress. The name of the service was changed to the Revenue Cutter Service in 1863.

New Duties. For many years, private organizations such as the Massachusetts Humane Society operated the only lifesaving services on the Atlantic Coast. In 1837, Congress authorized the use of public vessels to cruise the coast in rough weather and help navigators in distress. The government took over all privately operated lifesaving stations in 1871 and established the Lifesaving Service, operated by the Revenue Cutter Service. In 1878, the Lifesaving Service became an independent bureau of the Department of the Treasury. The Revenue Cutter and Lifesaving services were combined as the United States Coast Guard in 1915. The Federal Lighthouse Service became a part of the Coast Guard in 1939. The Bureau of Marine Inspection was transferred from the Department of Commerce to the Coast Guard in 1942.

World War I. On April 6, 1917, after the United States declared war on Germany, the Coast Guard's more than 200 officers and 5,000 men were ordered to go into action with the Navy. The Coast Guard served in the thick of the action, convoying cargo ships and screening transports. One of the war's great sea tragedies occurred on Sept. 26, 1917. The cutter *Tampa*, bound for England from Gibraltar, disappeared with a loud explosion. The entire crew of 111 coastguardsmen and 4 navy men was lost. Authorities believe that a torpedo hit the cutter. In proportion to its strength, the Coast Guard suffered greater losses in the war than any of the other United States armed forces.

World War II saw the Coast Guard serving as a specialized branch of the Navy. The service was responsible for handling and stowing explosives and other dangerous cargoes, and for protecting vessels and port facilities from fire, negligence, or damage. In 1942, a Coast Guard beach patrol captured eight German saboteurs who had been landed in the United States by submarine. The Coast Guard also furnished weather reports, provided cutters for convoy duty, manned its own vessels as well as many of the Army and Navy, took part

in Pacific operations, and developed beach-landing methods for the Allied invasion of Europe in 1944.

The Coast Guard Auxiliary was formed in 1939. During World War II, its members offered their boats and their services to the Coast Guard without pay. They wore uniforms and served under military discipline while on duty. The Coast Guard Reserve was established in 1941. During the war, about 10,000 reserve officers and 150,000 enlisted men were on active duty.

Recent Developments. In 1957, three cutters, *Storis*, *Bramble*, and *Spar*, were the first large vessels to sail the deepwater passage across the top of North America in one season. They shortened the route large ships must take to reach Baffin Bay and found a sea path that could be expected to be free of impassable ice during the summer. On the voyage, the cutters helped establish the Distant Early Warning (DEW) radar line in that part of the world (see DEW LINE). In the mid-1960's, the Coast Guard began operation of large ice-breakers that formerly belonged to the Navy. The ice-breakers support the Navy in polar operations. In 1966, the Coast Guard was transferred from the Treasury Department to the newly created Department of Transportation.

Vietnam War. In July, 1965, a Coast Guard squadron began patrolling the coastal waters of South Vietnam. The squadron's 26 cutters were assigned to prevent the flow of Communist troops and equipment from North Vietnam to South Vietnam.   WILLARD J. SMITH

Related Articles in WORLD BOOK include:

Beacon	Lighthouse
Breeches Buoy	Lightship
Buoy	Loran
Flag (color picture: Flags	National Defense
of the Armed Forces)	Navy, United States
Floods and Flood Control	SPARS
Ice Patrol, International	United States Coast
Icebreaker	Guard Academy

Outline

I. What the Coast Guard Does
   A. Protecting Life   B. Enforcing Sea Laws
      and Property   C. Supporting the Navy
II. Life in the Coast Guard
   A. Training a Coast-   C. Careers in the
      guardsman   Coast Guard
   B. Training an Officer
III. Ships and Weapons of the Coast Guard
   A. Ships and Stations   C. Ordnance
   B. Aircraft
IV. Organization of the Coast Guard
   A. Coast Guard Headquarters   C. Women in the
   B. Regulars and Reserves   Coast Guard
V. History

Questions

What is the Coast Guard motto? What does it mean?

What law-enforcement duties does the Coast Guard have?

How is the Coast Guard related to the Navy?

What is the *Regular Coast Guard?* A SPAR?

How does the Coast Guard aid navigators?

What kind of training do most Coast Guard officers receive?

What is the International Ice Patrol?

What kinds of services did the Coast Guard perform during World War II?

Why was the Coast Guard's forerunner, the Revenue Marine, established?

How are aircraft important to the Coast Guard?

COAST GUARD ACADEMY, UNITED STATES. See UNITED STATES COAST GUARD ACADEMY.

COAST RANGE is a series of mountains which forms the western coast of North America for about 2,500 miles. It extends from Kodiak Island, Alaska, through Canada to southern California. Twelve separate mountain ranges make up this coastal region. The Kodiak, Kenai, Chugach, and St. Elias ranges, and the Alexander Archipelago, a group of islands formed by the tops of sunken mountains, are in Alaska. The Queen Charlotte Islands and the Vancouver Range are in British Columbia. The Olympic Mountains rise in Washington, and the Oregon Coast Range extends from southern Washington to central Oregon. The Klamath Mountains rise in southern Oregon and northern California. The California Coast Range is in central California, and the Los Angeles Ranges rise along the coast of southern California.

The northern coast is sunk in great bays and straits from Shelikof Strait to Puget Sound. The southern coastline is high and regular, broken only by a few harbors. The highest peak in the Coast Range is Canada's Mt. Logan (19,850 feet).   JOHN H. GARLAND

See also UNITED STATES (The Pacific Ranges and Lowlands); OLYMPIC MOUNTAINS.

COASTAL PLAIN. See PLAIN; UNITED STATES (The Coastal Lowlands).

COAT OF ARMS. See HERALDRY.

COATI or COATIMUNDI, *koh AH tee MUN dih*, is a small animal that looks much like the raccoon. It has a silver-gray or brownish coat and a long, active, bushy tail. Coatis live in the forests of Mexico, Central and South America, and the southwestern United States. They grow about $2\frac{1}{2}$ feet long and weigh about 10 pounds. Their feet have long toes and sharp claws. Coatis eat insects and reptiles.

Scientific Classification. The coati is a member of the coati family, *Procyonidae*. It is classified as genus *Nasua*, species *N. narica*.   HAROLD E. ANTHONY

See also RACCOON; ANIMAL (color picture: Animals of the Tropical Forests).

COATSWORTH, ELIZABETH (1893-   ), is an American poet, novelist, and author of books for children. In 1931, she won the Newbery medal for *The Cat Who Went to Heaven*, a poetic story. She was born in Buffalo, N.Y., and was graduated from Vassar College and Columbia University.

COAXIAL CABLE is an electrical conductor that is used to transmit long distance telephone calls; coded, typed, or handwritten information; *facsimile* (electronic copy, such as maps, pictures, and charts); or other communications. It can transmit television programs, but most television is sent by radio relay.

A coaxial cable consists of from 8 to 20 *coaxials*. A coaxial is made up of a $\frac{3}{8}$-inch copper tube in which a copper wire is held in the center by plastic insulators. The insulators are spaced about one inch apart. The tube and the wire have the same *axis* (center), and are therefore called *coaxial*. The tube shields the signal from outside electrical interference and prevents the signal from losing its strength. The coaxial is wrapped with steel tape for strength, protection, and electrical shielding.

A.T. & T. Co.

A Coaxial Cable includes several tube-encased wires for communications and insulated wires for maintenance and control.

The cable includes several insulated wires, as well as the coaxials. The wires are used for control and maintenance. The cable is wrapped in a plastic and lead sheath. An 8-tube cable is about 2 inches in diameter and a 20-tube cable is about 3 inches in diameter. Electric signals are sensitive to changing temperatures, so most coaxial cables are buried in the earth which has a more constant temperature. Amplifiers that strengthen the signals may be placed as close as two miles apart.

Coaxials work in pairs. One coaxial carries signals in one direction, while the other handles signals in the other direction. One pair of tubes in a cable is usually kept in reserve for use in case of damage to another pair.

Today, a pair of coaxials can carry 3,600 separate signals at once. For example, a fully equipped, 20-tube cable, with a pair of tubes in reserve, can carry 32,400 two-way conversations simultaneously.

Two Bell Telephone engineers, Lloyd Espenshied and Herman A. Affel, invented the coaxial cable. The cable was successfully tested in 1936.   C. C. DUNCAN

See also CABLE; TELEPHONE; TELEVISION.

COBALT, *KOH bawlt* (chemical symbol, Co), is a tough, silver-white metallic element. The name *cobalt* is from the German word, *kobold*, meaning *underground spirit*. Georg Brandt of Sweden discovered the element in 1737.

Properties. Cobalt has the atomic number 27, and an atomic weight of 58.9332. It resembles nickel and iron in hardness and tensile strength, but it is stronger than iron and does not rust or tarnish. Its density is 8.9 and it melts at 1495° C. (2723° F.).

Sources. Cobalt occurs in compounds with arsenic, oxygen, and sulfur, and in ores that bear nickel, iron, copper, lead, and zinc. Large deposits of silver-nickel-cobalt ores are found in the Sudbury District of Ontario, Canada. Deposits also occur in Congo (Kinshasa), Zambia, and Morocco. There is little cobalt in the United States. Pennsylvania, Missouri, and Idaho have small deposits that occur mostly in pyrites.

Uses of Cobalt. Cobalt is chiefly used in alloys, especially in alnico and stellite. Alnico contains nickel and aluminum, and makes powerful permanent magnets for use in radio, television, and other electronic devices. Stellite contains chromium and tungsten. It is used to make drilling bits and cutting tools that stand considerable wear. Cobalt also goes into alloys used for jet engines and gas turbines, because it remains hard even at temperatures up to 1800° F.

Cobalt compounds, such as cobalt blue, ceruleum, new blue, smalt, cobalt yellow, and cobalt green, are used as pigments by artists and interior decorators, and in ceramics. The ceramics industry also uses large amounts of cobalt oxide for tinting glass and enamel. Vitamin B$_{12}$, an organic compound of cobalt, helps to prevent pernicious anemia (see VITAMIN). A radioactive isotope of cobalt, cobalt-60, has largely replaced radium in the treatment of cancer. It is both cheaper and easier to use than radium. Cobalt-60 also serves as a tracer for following the course of substances through the body. JOHN R. KOCH

See also ALLOY; COBALT-60; COBALT BOMB; ELEMENT, CHEMICAL.

COBALT-60 is a radioactive isotope of cobalt. It has an atomic mass number of 60. Its *half life* is 5¼ years. This means that half the atoms in a sample of cobalt-60 will decay to form atoms of nickel-60 in 5¼ years. As it decays, cobalt-60 gives off *beta particles* (electrons) and *gamma rays* of high energy. Cobalt-60 can be produced by bombarding atoms of ordinary cobalt with the neutrons in an atomic reactor, or by bombarding nickel or copper in a cyclotron. ROBERT L. THORNTON

See also ATOMIC REACTOR; COBALT BOMB; CYCLOTRON; RADIOACTIVITY.

COBALT BOMB. When cobalt is placed in an atomic reactor and exposed to neutrons, it becomes radioactive. This radioactive cobalt, cobalt-60, gives off high-energy radiations called gamma rays (see COBALT-60; GAMMA RAY). A cobalt bomb is a device in which cobalt-60 is used to produce an intense beam of gamma rays. It can be used in hospitals for treating cancer, in industry for examining metals for weak spots, and for other purposes where gamma rays are useful. See RADIATION (How Radiation Affects Life on the Earth); RADIOACTIVITY (Uses of Radioisotopes).

The term *cobalt bomb* also refers to an atomic bomb to which cobalt might be added. Scientists have never made such a bomb, but they believe it would produce large amounts of radioactive *fallout* (debris). During an atomic explosion, radioactive cobalt isotopes would be produced and scattered over a large area. A fallout of this kind would create a health hazard, and might prevent occupation of the exposed area for a long period of time. ROBERT L. THORNTON

See also FALLOUT; RADIATION SICKNESS.

COBB, IRVIN SHREWSBURY (1876-1944), an American humorist, was a novelist, short-story writer, dramatist, and newspaperman. He believed that "you had to poke fun at yourself before you could poke fun at anyone else without hurting his feelings." Cobb followed this formula in his humorous stories. He did not begin to publish until he was 37. His popular works include *Old Judge Priest* (1915), *Those Times and These* (1917), *A Laugh a Day* (1923), and his autobiography, *Exit Laughing* (1941).

Cobb was born in Paducah, Ky., on June 23, 1876. He became the managing

Irvin Cobb
U&U

editor of the *Paducah News* at 19. Later, he wrote for New York City newspapers as well as for the *Saturday Evening Post*. He also wrote for and acted in motion pictures. FREDERICK J. HOFFMAN

COBB, TY (1886-1961), was one of the greatest baseball players in history. Called the *Georgia Peach*, Cobb was born in Banks County, Georgia. His full name was TYRUS RAYMOND COBB. He began playing baseball for the Detroit Tigers in 1905. He played 24 seasons in the American League, 22 for Detroit, and 2 for the Philadelphia Athletics. He had a lifetime batting average of .367, and stole 892 bases. Cobb was an excellent strategist and a brilliant outfielder. He managed the Tigers from 1921 to 1926. Cobb was elected to the Baseball Hall of Fame in 1936. ED FITZGERALD

See also BASEBALL (picture).

COBBLE. See BOULDER.

COBDEN, RICHARD (1804-1865), was an English manufacturer and statesman who vigorously urged free trade. He believed that eliminating tariffs and other restrictions on trade would improve relations between nations and lead to world peace.

Cobden was born near Midhurst, Sussex. He became a partner in a textile business in 1828. Cobden helped organize the Anti-Corn Law League in 1838. England's corn laws were designed to keep the price of small grains high (see CORN LAWS). He was elected to Parliament in 1841, and helped repeal the corn laws in 1846. He also championed free trade and world peace. Cobden opposed Britain's part in the Crimean War (1853-1856), and this stand contributed to his defeat in 1857. Cobden was re-elected in 1859. VERNON F. SNOW

COBH, *kohv* (pop. 5,613; alt. 45 ft.), is a seaport in County Cork in southwestern Ireland. It lies on the south shore of Great Island in Cork Harbor. For location, see IRELAND (color map).

Cobh was built on a hillside in a half-circle facing the harbor. Ships traveling between Europe and the United States often make Cobh a port of call. Thousands of Irish immigrants have sailed to North America from Cobh. Saint Colman's Cathedral overlooks the harbor.

The city was called *Cove* until 1849. Then, during the British occupation of Ireland, it was named *Queenstown* in honor of Queen Victoria. The government renamed it *Cobh*, the Gaelic spelling of Cove, in 1922, after Ireland became free from British rule. T. W. FREEMAN

COBIA is a salt-water fish. See FISHING (table).

COBLENZ. See KOBLENZ.

COBOL. See COMPUTER (Writing a Program).

COBRA, *KOH bruh*, is any one of a group of poisonous "hooded" snakes. Cobras are nervous, and, when excited, flatten the neck by moving the ribs. This movement gives the appearance of a hood. In most snakes, the neck ribs are shorter than those farther back. But in cobras with large hoods, the neck ribs are the longest. These ribs are almost straight instead of curved like those of the body.

Cobras use their deadly poison in two ways. Some types bite their victims with poison fangs in the front of the upper jaw. Others also squirt the poison several feet directly at the eyes of the victim. In these kinds, the fangs are shaped so that the poison is sent forward when the cobra tilts back its head. This is called "spitting,"

Zoological Society of Philadelphia

The Spitting Cobra of Malaya can squirt poison directly at the eyes of its victim. The venom may cause blindness if it is not washed out immediately.

and is most highly developed in two African cobras and one East Indian. The venom does not harm humans unless it gets into their eyes. It causes severe irritation and even blindness if not washed out immediately. The bite may cause death in a few hours.

A full-grown Indian cobra is nearly 6 feet long, and about 6 inches around. Its color ranges from yellowish to dark brown. On the back of its hood it has a mark like a pair of spectacles. It is sometimes called "spectacled cobra."

Most cobras eat many kinds of animals, such as frogs, fishes, birds, and various small mammals. A dangerous enemy of the cobra is the tiny mongoose. This animal attacks and usually kills the snake. See MONGOOSE.

Cobras live in Africa, Southern Asia, and the East Indies, including the Philippine Islands. The *king cobra* of southeastern Asia is by far the largest of the group, and the longest poisonous snake known. It reaches a length of 18 feet. It has a narrow hood. Most king cobras retreat from men and will attack only when they are surprised while guarding their eggs.

Cobras are found in various types of country, and may even enter houses. Cobras are not so dangerous as generally believed, because of the way they attack. They prepare for battle by lifting up the front of the body without curving it like an S. An opponent can well judge how far a forward jab will reach. The S-curves of the rattlesnake and other vipers make the reach hard to judge. The cobra moves slowly compared to some snakes. A person can easily knock down a rearing cobra by swinging a level stick. The cobra's fangs do not deliver the poison nearly so well as the viper's. The cobra's are shorter, and cannot be folded back. But cobras often chew an object after they have seized it. This habit helps inject the poison.

The jugglers and snake charmers of India usually use the cobra because of its unusual hood and its nervous disposition. These men pretend to charm snakes with music. But snakes are deaf, and when they are being "charmed" they are only holding themselves on guard. They would do the same thing without the music.

Scientific Classification. The cobras belong to the terrestrial poisonous snake family, *Elapidae*. The Indian cobra is genus *Naja*, species *N. naja*. The king cobra is *Naja hannah*.   CLIFFORD H. POPE

See also ASP; SNAKE (color pictures: Indian Cobra, Indian Snake Charmer); SNAKE CHARMING.

COBWEB. See SPIDER (Tangled-Web Weavers).

COCA, *KOH kuh*, is one of a group of South American shrubs or small trees. Coca trees grow about 15 to 20 feet tall. The Huanuco coca is a greenish-brown plant with shiny, thick stems. The leaves are about 1 to 3 inches long with smooth edges. The Truxillo coca is pale green and has smaller leaves. Its leaves smell very much like tea leaves. The leaves of both plants taste bitter and produce a numbness of the tongue and lips when chewed.

The dried leaves of coca plants contain several drugs used in medicine, including cocaine, tropacocaine, and hygrine. The Indians of South America chew coca leaves with lime. The drugs in the leaves keep them from feeling tired or hungry, but they do not nourish the body. After a time, the chewing of these leaves becomes habit-forming, and ruins the health of the person.

Scientific Classification. Coca plants belong to the coca family, *Erythroxylaceae*. They are classified as genus *Erythroxylon*, species *E. coca*.   HAROLD NORMAN MOLDENKE

COCA-COLA COMPANY. See SOFT DRINK.

COCAINE, *koh KAYN* (chemical formula, $C_{17}H_{21}NO_4$), is a bitter drug which is made from leaves of the coca shrub. In large doses it is poisonous. Cocaine is a valuable drug if properly used, but it is one of the worst of the habit-forming drugs. When taken continuously, it ruins physical and mental health. It stimulates the heart and nervous system, and then dulls sensations. Continued use of cocaine causes loss of ability to sleep, nervous twitching, mental weakness, and finally death. A *cokefiend* (a person who takes cocaine) will lie, beg, or steal to get the drug.

Karl Koller, a German physician, started the practice of using cocaine as a local anesthetic. Synthetic drugs, similar to cocaine but safer, are now more often used. Cocaine is used as a local anesthetic in surgery of the nose and throat. When it is injected into the spinal canal it causes loss of feeling below the point of injection. Cocaine must be absorbed by mucous membranes in order to take effect. Cocaine was first prepared from coca leaves in 1844. In 1914, the Harrison Act made the sale of cocaine illegal in the United States except under a doctor's prescription.   A. K. REYNOLDS

See also ALKALOID; COCA; NOVOCAIN.

COCCOSPHERE. See PLANKTON.

COCCUS. See BACTERIA (Kinds).

COCCYX. See SKELETON (The Axial Skeleton).

COCHABAMBA, *KOH chah VAM bah* (pop. 95,576), is the third largest city in Bolivia. It lies in a small but thickly populated basin in the *Cordillera Real*, or *Royal Range*, of the Andes Mountains. For location, see BOLIVIA (color map). Cochabamba is in the center of one of Bolivia's richest agricultural areas. It was founded in 1574.   HAROLD OSBORNE

COCHIN CHINA. See VIETNAM (History).

COCHINEAL, *KAHCH uh NEEL*, is a natural dye obtained from the dried bodies of a tropical scale insect, the female *Coccus cacti*. Cochineal may be used to dye wool crimson, carmine, and scarlet. The insects are native to Mexico and Central America, but they have been taken to Spain, Algeria, and Java and raised there. They are brushed from the cactus plants on which they feed, and are killed by hot water or by dry heat. The bodies of 70,000 insects will yield only a pound of dye. Cochineal has been largely replaced by coal-tar dyes. See also CARMINE; DYES AND DYEING.   FRED FORTESS

Brown Bros.

Cochise, Chief of the Chiricahua Apaches, led his people in war against the United States for nearly 11 years.

COCHISE, *koh CHEEZ* (? -1874), an American Indian leader, was a chief of the Chiricahua Apaches. He came to notice in 1861 when an army officer tried to capture him under a flag of truce for a crime he had not committed. Cochise escaped and then led his tribe in a war against the white settlers. He was daring and used brilliant strategy in battles against the army.

A white man named Jeffords made friends with Cochise in 1862. In 1871, Jeffords led General O. O. Howard to Cochise's hiding place for an interview. Cochise accepted a reservation for the Chiricahua Indians through Howard. He moved his tribe to the reservation and died there in 1874. His burial place was kept secret and has never been found.

Cochise helped hold back the tide of white settlement in the Southwest. There have been several fictional accounts of his life. They show him as a man who fought for a cause in which he believed, but who used savage methods of waging war.　　　WILLIAM H. GILBERT

COCHLEA. See EAR (The Inner Ear; How We Hear; color diagram).

COCHRAN, JACQUELINE (1912-　　), is an American businesswoman and pioneer airplane pilot. She started flying in 1932, and was the only woman to enter the McRobertson London-Melbourne Race in 1934.

Jacqueline Cochran
Wide World

Miss Cochran also became the first woman to compete in the annual Bendix Trophy Race, which she won in 1938. During World War II, she organized and commanded the Women's Airforce Service Pilots (WASPs). She received the Distinguished Service Medal, the first civilian woman to be so honored. Miss Cochran became the owner of a cosmetics firm in 1935. She was born in Pensacola, Fla. ROBERT B. HOTZ

COCHRANE, MICKEY (1903-1962), rose to baseball fame as a catcher for the Philadelphia Athletics and catcher-manager for the Detroit Tigers. He ranks with Bill Dickey of the New York Yankees as one of baseball's two finest catchers. He was a masterful handler of pitchers, and had a lifetime batting average of .320. He was struck on the head with a baseball in 1937. This speeded the end of his playing career. Cochrane was elected to the Baseball Hall of Fame in 1947. GORDON STANLEY COCHRANE was born in Bridgewater, Mass. He attended Boston University.　　　ED FITZGERALD

COCK OF THE ROCK is a handsome South American bird with a rich orange plumage and a large crest that hides the bill. The wings and tail are black. The birds live in rocky ravines near mountain streams in the Andes from Colombia to Bolivia. They are also found in the mountains of the Guianas and in northern Brazil. At the mating season, the male birds gather together in a cleared spot in the forest where they dance and hop about to attract the females.

The cock of the rock makes its nest of plant fibers which it glues together with resin, and sticks to crevices of rocks. The birds feed on fruit and live in the thick undergrowth near the floor of the forest.

Scientific Classification. The cock of the rock belongs to the cotingas family, *Rupicolinae*. It is genus *Rupicola*, species *rupicola*.　　RODOLPHE MEYER DE SCHAUENSEE

See also BIRD (color picture: Birds of Other Lands).

COCKATOO, *KAHK uh TOO*, is a perching bird that belongs to the parrot family. It lives in Australia, Indonesia, and neighboring islands. The cockatoo looks like a parrot, but has a crest which it can raise and lower. The cockatoo's coloring may be combinations of white, black, red, rose, or gray. The common white cockatoo has a yellow or rose crest. The cockatoo has a powerful, curved bill and a thick tongue. It has strong feet with which it climbs about the branches of trees.

The cockatoo feeds on seeds, nuts, and fruits. It is a great pest in regions where there are many orchards.

Two Kinds of Cockatoos. The specimen at the left has blue eyes which contrast vividly with its white feathers. The Leadbeater cockatoo at the right has a salmon-pink inner wing.

N.Y. Zoological Society; H. Armstrong Roberts

Cockatoos are often seen in large flocks which fly swiftly. Cockatoos become tame and make amusing pets. They are not popular, however, because they rarely learn to talk, and often scream loudly.

Scientific Classification. Cockatoos belong to the parrot family, *Psittacidae*. The great black cockatoo is genus *Probosciger*, species *P. aterrimus*.   RODOLPHE MEYER deSCHAUENSEE

See also BIRD (color picture: Family Pets); FLORIDA (Places to Visit [Parrot Jungle]); PARROT.

COCKCROFT, SIR JOHN DOUGLAS (1897-1967), a British nuclear physicist, won the 1951 Nobel prize in physics with Ernest T. S. Walton for being the first to split atoms artificially. Cockcroft and Walton bombarded lithium atoms with protons accelerated to high speeds. Each lithium atom became two helium atoms. In World War II, Cockcroft directed air-defenses research, and organized atomic-energy research in Canada. He became director of research at the Harwell Atomic Energy plant in England in 1946. In 1961, he received the Atoms for Peace Award. Cockcroft was born at Walsden, Lancashire.   SIDNEY ROSEN

See also ATOM SMASHER; WALTON, ERNEST T. S.

COCKER SPANIEL, sometimes called the *American cocker*, is one of the most popular dogs in the United States. Cockers are favorite pets and show dogs. They are named for their ability to hunt birds called woodcock. However, relatively few cockers are now used as hunting dogs. Most cocker spaniels weigh 22 to 28 pounds and stand about 15 inches at the shoulder. Cockers have a soft, thick coat with *feathers* (long hairs) on the ears, chest, and legs. Many cockers have a solid colored coat. Pure black cockers are especially popular. Other solid colored cockers and mixed black and tan cockers are called *ascobs*. Cockers with red and white, black and white, or three-colored combination coats, are called *parti-colors*.   MAXWELL RIDDLE

See also DOG (color picture: Sporting Dogs).

COCKFIGHTING is a sport in which two *gamecocks* (fighting roosters) battle each other in a fight to the death. The sport is illegal in the United States, Canada, and many other countries. But it is sometimes carried

on secretly. Cockfighting ranks as a popular public sport in Spain, Latin America, and part of the Orient.

Gamecocks are specially bred to achieve physical power, speed of movement, courage, and the killer instinct. They usually are brightly colored and have long spurs on their legs. But breeders generally trim the spurs down, and attach artificial spurs to the gamecocks' legs. The spurs are usually steel or brass. The birds use the weapons to rip and tear at their opponents.

A cockfight takes place in an enclosed pit, usually outdoors. Spectators place bets on their favorite gamecocks. At the start of the fight, handlers hold their birds firmly and allow them to peck at each other. When the birds are angry, they are released and start to fight.

Cockfighting probably began in Asia thousands of years ago. The sport came to ancient Greece and Rome by way of India and China. It spread throughout Europe. During the 1700's, the sport became especially popular in England, where the training and breeding of fighting cocks became an important industry.   WALTER H. GREGG

COCKLE, *KAHK'l*, is a sea animal with a tough, protective shell. The cockle is a kind of clam. It has a round, grooved shell divided into two equal parts. The cockle moves about by using a long, muscular organ called a *foot*. This foot is strong enough to flip the animal several inches. Cockles live in shallow water along ocean coastlines in many parts of the world. They may be from one-half inch to 8 inches in diameter. The largest kinds of cockles are found on the Pacific coast of Central America.

Scientific Classification. Cockles are in the phylum *Mollusca* and the family *Cardiidae*.   R. TUCKER ABBOTT

COCKLEBUR, or CLOTBUR, is the name of several kinds of annual weeds belonging to the composite family. They all have spiny burs, inside of which are the seeds. There are usually two seeds in each bur. One seed will begin to grow, or germinate, a season before the other seed. The burs are covered with hooked prickles

L. W. Brownell
The Cocklebur Has Burs That Stick to Animals.

which stick to clothing. The poisonous seedlings can kill hogs and young cattle. Cockleburs are native to the American continent. They are found in low areas in fields and by roadsides. They are 1 to 3 feet tall, and their rough leaves are heart-shaped or irregular. Some of the flowers bear pollen, while others bear seeds. The pollen-bearing ones grow on the upper branches and the seed-bearing ones on the lower. To get rid of cockleburs,

Fierce Gamecocks Fight to the Death in the sport of cockfighting. Cockfighting is outlawed in many countries.
George Pickow, Three Lions

it is necessary to destroy the plants before the seeds ripen or to spray them with 2,4-D.

Scientific Classification. Cockleburs belong to the composite family, *Compositae*. Cockleburs make up the genus *Xanthium*.   LOUIS PYENSON

COCKNEY is a nickname for a citizen of London, particularly one from the East End area. According to the traditional definition, a cockney is anyone born within the sound of the bells of St. Mary-le-Bow Church. *Cockney* also applies to a dialect of English. Speakers change certain vowel sounds; for example, *lady* becomes *lydy* and *road*, *rowd*. They also drop the *h* at the beginning of words, and may add one in front of a word starting with a vowel; for example, *ard* for *hard* and *hanswered* for *answered*. The word *cockney* originally meant a misshapen egg.

See also LONDON (The People); BUTTON (picture).

COCKPIT OF THE REVOLUTION. See NEW JERSEY.

COCKROACH is a troublesome, unpleasant insect found throughout the world. It is closely related to grasshoppers and crickets. There are over 2,000 species of cockroaches.

The cockroach has a flattened, slippery body, covered with a shiny, leathery casing. It has long legs covered with bristles. The strong legs permit the cockroach to run rapidly. The cockroach is one of the fastest runners among insects. The insect has long *antennae* (feelers).

Cockroaches eat food, garbage, bookbindings, and other insects, such as bedbugs. They live in bakeries, groceries, office buildings, restaurants, hotels, flour mills, libraries, and homes. Swarms of them slip out at night through cracks in the walls and floors to look for food. Cockroaches are dirty and spread germs on everything they touch. Many kinds of cockroaches are found outdoors. They often can be found under stones and leaves or the loose bark of rotting logs and dead trees.

The most common kinds of cockroaches found in houses in America are the *Croton bug* or *German cockroach*,

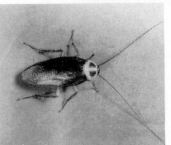

Cockroaches dislike bright light, and usually come out only at night. These insects reproduce in dirty, damp places.

Lynwood M. Chace

the *American cockroach*, the *Australian cockroach*, the *brown-banded cockroach*, and the *Oriental cockroach* or *black beetle*. The Croton bug is smaller than the other kinds, but it is more destructive. It also reproduces more rapidly than the others. It gets its name because it first was found in large numbers in the Croton waterworks system of New York City. The Croton bug is a pale yellow-brown with two stripes on the front part of the body. The other kinds of cockroaches vary in color from light to dark wood brown.

Cockroaches usually can be kept out of houses by keeping the rooms clean and dry. Cockroaches grow and reproduce best where there is dirt, grease, and mois-

ture. They can be killed by using roach powders that contain sodium fluoride, borax, sodium fluosilicate, rotenone, or pyrethrum. Roach powder should be dusted into crevices and hiding places around sinks and water pipes. The cockroach takes the poison into its body when it grooms itself. It scrapes the foreign particles and dust from its body with its legs and then draws its legs and feelers through its mouth.

Cockroaches can be trapped easily in large widemouthed jars. Food scraps should be placed in the jar and a paper funnel fitted into the top.

Scientific Classification. Cockroaches make up the cockroach family, *Blattidae*. The German cockroach is genus *Blattella*, species *B. germanica*.   URL LANHAM

See also ORTHOPTERA.

COCKSCOMB, *KAHX кoнм*, is a flower with heads of red and yellow blossoms shaped like a rooster's comb or like an ostrich plume. The cockscomb comes from tropical America, Asia, and the East Indies, but it now grows in all parts of the United States. It will bloom from midsummer until the fall frost if planted in light, rich soil that is kept damp.

Cockscomb Blooms are shaped like a rooster's comb.
U.S. Bureau of Plant Industry

Scientific Classification. Cockscombs belong to the amaranth family, *Amaranthaceae*. They are genus *Celosia*, species *C. argentea*, variety *cristata*.

See also AMARANTH; FLOWER (color picture: Fall Garden Flowers).

COCKSPUR. See HAWTHORN; SANDBUR.

COCKTAIL. See ALCOHOLIC DRINK (Compounded Liquors).

COCOA, *KOH koh*, is a reddish-brown powder made by grinding the *nibs* (kernels) of the seeds of the cacao tree. The cocoa is melted and pressed to remove the fat. Then it is ground and sifted into a powder. *Chocolate* is the cocoa mass with the fat left in. See also CACAO; CHOCOLATE.

COCOA, Fla. (pop. 12,294; alt. 25 ft.), gateway city to the Cape Kennedy long-range missile testing center, lies on the Indian River in Brevard County. For location, see FLORIDA (political map). Cocoa is in the center of the Indian River citrus-fruitgrowing region. But since the federal government established the John F. Kennedy (formerly Cape Canaveral) Space Center in 1949, most of Cocoa's residents have worked for the government. The United States launched its first earth satellite from Cape Kennedy in 1958.

Patrick Air Force Base also lies nearby. Other area activities include commercial and sport fishing; cattle and beef trading; and truck farming. Cocoa, incorporated as a village in 1895, received its city charter in 1913. The city has a mayor-council form of government.   KATHRYN ABBEY HANNA

J. C. Allen and Son; New York Botanical Garden

Food Value of the Coconut

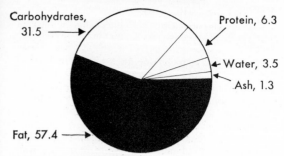

Carbohydrates, 31.5

Protein, 6.3

Water, 3.5

Ash, 1.3

Fat, 57.4

Coconut Palms have smooth trunks with featherlike leaves at the top. The coconuts grow in clusters among the leaves.

COCONUT PALM is the tall, graceful tree on which the coconut grows. It probably is native to southeast Asia and the islands of Melanesia in the Pacific Ocean. But man has introduced it to all the tropical and subtropical parts of the world. The coconut palm stands from 40 to 100 feet high. Large featherlike leaves spread from the top of its branchless trunk.

The coconut palm is one of the most useful trees. People in the tropics build houses and bridges from its wood. They use whole leaves to make thatch roofs, and strips of leaves to make hats, mats, and baskets. They make a sweet drink called *toddy* or *tuba* from the sap of the tree's blossoms. They also use this sap to make sugar, vinegar, and an alcoholic beverage.

The Coconut is the fruit of the coconut palm. Clusters of these large round fruits grow among the leaves of the tree. Each coconut has a smooth light-colored *rind*. Under the rind, there is a 1- or 2-inch *husk* of tough reddish-brown fibers. The husk and rind surround a brown woody shell that has three soft spots called *eyes* at one end. Workers usually cut away the rind and husk before shipping coconuts to market.

The coconut seed lies inside the shell. It is a ball of crisp, white, sweet-tasting coconut *meat* covered by a tough brown skin. Its hollow center holds a sugary liquid called coconut *milk*. The coconut seed is one of the largest of all seeds. It measures from 8 to 12 inches long and from 6 to 10 inches across.

A well-tended tree produces about a hundred coconuts a year. Each fruit takes about a year to ripen. Ripe coconuts fall from the tree. But on plantations, they are usually cut every two or three months.

Solid, dried coconut meat is called *copra*. Copra contains a valuable liquid fat that is made into soap, margarine, and cooking oil. Tropical lands produce millions of tons of copra each year. Each ton requires about 6,000 medium-sized coconuts. To make copra, workers split the coconuts open and dry them in the sun or in ovens. Some coconuts are dried by smoking.

Throughout the world, people enjoy eating crisp, juicy chunks of fresh coconut meat. Shredded and dried coconut meat adds a distinctive flavor and texture to candy bars and other foods. People in tropical lands also use the coconut husk. They weave its short stiff fibers (called *coir*) into mats, ropes, and brooms.

Growing Coconut Palms. In the tropics, people can plant coconut palms throughout the year. They half

The Seed of the Coconut lies inside a hard brown shell, *right*. A thick husk, *far right*, grows around the shell.

bury the coconut in a horizontal position. Within six months, a single leaf sprouts from one of the eyes and pushes through the husk. The young palm can be transplanted after one to four years. It will bear fruit in seven or eight years. Coconut palms need much water and a temperature of at least 72° F. most of the year.

Scientific Classification. The coconut palm belongs to the palm family, *Palmae*. It is genus *Cocos*, species *C. nucifera*.   HAROLD E. MOORE, JR.

See also COPRA; PACIFIC ISLANDS (picture); PALM (picture: The Coconut Tree); PHILIPPINES (picture); TRANSPORTATION (picture: A Raft of Coconuts).

LEADING COCONUT GROWING AREAS

Tons of coconuts grown in 1966

Philippines
1,774,700 tons

Indonesia
582,400 tons

India
297,600 tons

Ceylon
253,500 tons

Malaysia
194,600 tons

Mexico
187,400 tons

New Guinea (Australia)
102,200 tons

Mozambique
41,700 tons

New Hebrides
38,000 tons

Fiji Islands
28,200 tons

Source: *Production Yearbook, 1967,* FAO

COCOON, *kuh COON,* is a protective covering that encloses the pupa of many insects. The mature larva prepares the cocoon as a shelter around itself. Inside the cocoon, the larva changes to a pupa and eventually transforms into an adult insect. Among the insects that spend part of their lives in cocoons are ants, wasps, bees, and moths. Spiders spin silk cocoons around their eggs to protect them.

The chief substance of most cocoons is silk. But often the larva produces other substances from which it builds a cocoon. It may also use hairs from its own body, wood pulp, earth, or grains of sand. Some creatures use little or no silk in constructing their cocoons.

Most moth caterpillars (larvae) form cocoons. But many pass the pupal stage in the soil without a protective covering. A few butterfly caterpillars make flimsy cocoons. Perhaps the best-known cocoon is that of the domestic silkworm, which supplies most commercial silk. Some tussah silk obtained in India comes from the cocoons of large emperor moths.

Most moth caterpillars build their cocoons in inconspicuous places. They may choose a place under loose boards, beneath the bark of a tree, or among dead leaves or trash. *Cecropia, Promethea,* and *Cynthia* moth larvae build large cocoons that they fasten to tree twigs. These can easily be found in the winter when the trees are bare. The pupae spend the winter inside the cocoon. But the larva of many other kinds of moths does not

Hugh Spencer

The Cocoon of the Cecropia Moth, *left,* has been built on a tree's limb. The opened cocoon, *right,* shows the pupa inside.

change into a pupa until spring. The *woolly bear caterpillar,* the larva of the tiger moth, builds its cocoon in spring. Still other kinds pass the winter in the egg stage or as partly grown larvae.   ALEXANDER B. KLOTS

Related Articles in WORLD BOOK include:

Caterpillar	Metamorphosis	Silk (Raising
Chrysalis	Moth	Silkworms)
Larva	Pupa	

COCOS ISLANDS, or KEELING ISLANDS, are a coral group in the Indian Ocean. The Cocos Islands belong to Australia. They lie about 1,150 miles southwest of Singapore. The 27 islands have a total area of about 5 square miles and a population of 684. The chief product is *copra* (dried coconut meat). The Cocos Islands were once governed as part of the British colony of Singapore. In 1955, Great Britain turned the islands over to Australia. One of them is a refueling stop for several international airlines.   JUSTUS M. VAN DER KROEF

COCTEAU, *cock TOW,* **JEAN** (1889-1963), was a French avant-garde writer. As a playwright, author of ballet plots, screenwriter, novelist, and artist, he often used his talents to shock the public. But many of his shocking works also have great artistic merit.

Cocteau, like many other French writers, was drawn to the myths and dramatic plots of ancient Greece. He frequently used these materials in his plays. *Orpheus* (1925) is a study of the poet's agonizing search for inspiration and his struggle to gain acceptance for his work. *The Infernal Machine* (1934) is an adaptation of Sophocles' *Oedipus Rex.* Its theme is that the powers guiding the universe are hostile to humanity. In Cocteau's usual fantastic style, these plays use events out of time sequence, unexpected colloquial phrases, and symbols explainable in terms of modern psychology.

Cocteau's novels include *Les Enfants Terribles* (1929). His ballets include *Parade* (1917) with music by Erik Satie. Cocteau wrote and directed several motion pictures, including *The Blood of a Poet* (1932), *Beauty and the Beast* (1945), and *Orpheus* (1950).

Cocteau was born in Maisons-Laffitte. His publicized love affairs and his use of drugs made his private life as unconventional as his writing.   MALCOLM GOLDSTEIN

COD is one of the most important food fishes found in the sea. It lives along both shores of the North Atlantic Ocean, as far south as France and Virginia. The Alaskan cod of the North Pacific Ocean and Bering Sea is also important as food. Both are near relatives of the hake and haddock.

The cod has a slightly flattened body that tapers abruptly to the tail. It has five fins. It is usually greenish or olive on the back and sides, which are dotted with many small brown spots. The larger fish weigh from 20 to 35 pounds. The smaller weigh about 12 pounds. The largest cod ever caught off the New England coast by commercial fishermen was over 6 feet long and weighed $211\frac{1}{2}$ pounds.

The cod eats lobsters, shrimps, crabs, and other crustaceans, as well as mollusks, small fishes, and seaweed. It is such a greedy eater that it will swallow almost anything that comes its way. Pieces of rubber and leather, scissors, oil cans, glass, stones, and garbage have been found in the stomachs of captured fish. Along the northern coast of Europe, the cod lays its eggs in February, March, and April. On the American coast it lays its eggs from October to June. Summer and winter are spent in deep water, spring and fall near the shore. These fish produce an astonishing number of eggs. David Starr Jordan, an American biologist, estimated that if all the eggs laid during the life of a 75-pound fish developed into adults, the ocean would be filled with an almost solid mass of cod. A 21-pound cod produces 2,700,000 eggs in one spawning period.

The eggs are small, averaging one-nineteenth of an inch in diameter. They float in the upper layer of surface water, forming part of the plankton (see PLANKTON). The eggs are devoured by fishes, crustaceans, and other animals, thus cutting down the reproduction rate.

Cod Fishing. The chief cod fisheries of the world are those of Norway and Sweden, Great Britain, France, Canada, Iceland, and the United States. About 45 million pounds of codfish are caught annually

Trawling for Cod, a ship drags a bag-shaped net called a *trawl* behind it, *above*. When the trawl is full, winches haul up the fish and dump them into deck compartments, *right*.

by fishermen from the United States. American fishermen usually go to the Grand Banks of Newfoundland (ridges in the ocean where the water is only a few hundred feet in depth), and to the George's Bank, off Cape Cod. Nearly all the ships of the United States Atlantic cod-fishing fleet hail from Gloucester, Mass., which is the headquarters of the industry.

Fishermen usually fish for cod two or three weeks at a time. They usually use diesel-powered ships that can locate schools of cod by radar. A large bag-shaped net called a *trawl* is lowered into the water and dragged at a depth of about 2,100 feet for two or three hours. The fish swim into the mouth of the trawl. A successful catch may weigh a ton. The trawl is hauled up by powerful winches and the fish are released into compartments on the deck. Later, the fishermen clean the fish and store them in ice.

Marketing and Uses. Codfish is usually sold salted and dried. Cod-liver oil, obtained from the liver of the fish, is rich in vitamins needed by growing children. Since 1939, shark livers have partially replaced cod livers for oil. About 30,000,000 pounds of dried codfish

Codfish Rank Among the Most Important Food Fishes.

are prepared each year in the United States, but the export trade is for the most part carried on by Norway, Iceland, and Canada. The chief markets of the world are the countries of France, Spain, Portugal, Italy, and Brazil.

The importance of the cod in the early history of the United States is shown in the fact that it had a place on the seal of Massachusetts Colony, and today a gilded codfish hangs in the Massachusetts House of Representatives opposite the Speaker's desk, between two central columns. The abundance of the fish along the eastern shores of America was noted by the early voyagers and recorded in the stories of their travels.

Scientific Classification. Codfish belong to the codfish and hake family, *Gadidae*. The Atlantic codfish is genus *Gadus*, species *G. callarias*.   LEONARD P. SCHULTZ

See also COD-LIVER OIL; FISH (color picture, Salt-Water Fishes); FISHING (table, Game-Fishing World Records); POLLACK; SCROD.

The Food Elements Found in Fresh Codfish

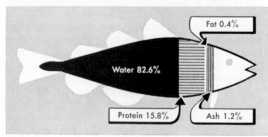

Fat 0.4%

Water 82.6%

Protein 15.8%   Ash 1.2%

COD-LIVER OIL is a thin, pale-yellow oil which is made from the fresh livers of codfish. It has a slightly fishy odor. Cod-liver oil contains large amounts of vitamins A and D, and is easily digested and used by the body. Cod-liver oil is a very important food for infants and young children because it prevents nutritional diseases such as rickets. Children who get poor food and little sunshine have the greatest need for cod-liver oil. The oil is very important in the treatment of such diseases as tuberculosis. Cod-liver oil may also have some value in healing tissues, and can be applied directly to the skin. Because cod-liver oil has a somewhat fishy taste, many persons find it easier to take in the form of emulsions or capsules. Some persons mix it with fruit juices. Austin Edward Smith

See also COD; RICKETS; VITAMIN.

CODA. See MUSIC (Terms).

CODDINGTON, WILLIAM. See RHODE ISLAND (History).

CODE, in law, combines all the laws on a given subject in a single statute or ordinance. It is passed by a legislative body, such as a state legislature, a county board of supervisors, or a village board. It is purely *statutory law*, as distinguished from the *common law* that arises from court decisions. In theory, it is possible for all the laws in a code to be new. That is, no law has ever been passed dealing with the particular subject. But in practice, a code nearly always represents a systematic and comprehensive revision of all the laws that the legislative body has passed on a given subject.

Statutes usually develop only as problems arise that point out the need for rules and regulations on particular points. Laws concerning automobiles are an example. The first rules set speed limits and required drivers to keep to the right. Then vehicles, and later drivers, were licensed. Stop signs, traffic lights, and other traffic regulations were established. Many cities passed their own regulations without regard to making them consistent with the state laws. Such piecemeal legislation left many gaps, uncertainties, and conflicts among the many separate regulations. As a result, most states revised their motor-vehicle laws, made them consistent, filled the gaps, and removed uncertainties. They enacted a single series of laws called a *Motor Vehicle Code*. Other well-known codes include state commercial codes and local or county building codes. Some villages combine all their laws into a *village code*. EDWARD W. CLEARY

CODE CIVIL. See CIVIL CODE; CODE NAPOLÉON.

CODE NAPOLÉON is the name often given to the code that contains the civil, as distinguished from the criminal, law of France. Napoleon Bonaparte appointed a commission of jurists to combine all French civil laws into one code. The code became effective in 1804. It became known as the *Code Napoléon* after he took the title of Emperor of the French. But its official name is *Code Civil*. See also CIVIL CODE.

CODE OF HAMMURABI. See HAMMURABI.

CODE OF JUSTINIAN. See JUSTINIAN CODE.

CODEINE, *KO deen* (chemical formula, $C_{18}H_{21}NO_3 \cdot H_2O$), is a drug which is made from opium. Codeine has the same properties as morphine, but is weaker. It relieves pain and produces sleep. It is used to treat severe coughs and asthma, intestinal pains, and neuralgia. A. K. REYNOLDS

See also MORPHINE; OPIUM.

CODES AND CIPHERS

CODES AND CIPHERS are methods of writing a message so that only persons with a key can read it. There are many methods of putting a message in secret form. The plain text can be *encoded* or *enciphered* to produce a *cryptogram*. The cryptogram or secret text can later be *decoded* or *deciphered*. Putting messages into code or cipher is called *cryptography*, a word that comes from Greek words for *hidden* and *writing*. *Cryptanalysis* is the art of breaking or solving codes and ciphers without the key. Cryptography and cryptanalysis make up *cryptology*.

Common Cryptographic Systems

Cipher Systems involve either transposition or substitution, or a combination of the two. In *transposition systems*, the cryptographer rearranges the elements of his plain text—usually single letters. For example, the message LEON ARRIVES WEDNESDAY might be enciphered as ANOEL EVIRR NDEWS YADSE. In this case, the system divides the original message into 5-letter groups, then reverses the order of the letters in each group. In *substitution systems*, the elements of the plain text—single letters or pairs of letters—retain their original positions, but are replaced by other elements. For example, LEON ARRIVES WEDNESDAY might be enciphered as EMHG YKKSTMN UMAGMNAYW. But cryptograms rarely keep their original word divisions. Instead, the cipher text is usually sent in 5-letter groups, in this case EMHGY KKSTM NUMAG MNAYW. Extra letters, called *nulls*, fill out the final 5-letter group if needed.

Code Systems are a specialized form of substitution in which the cryptographer treats syllables, words, phrases, and even whole sentences. Code systems employ *code books* that contain the code groups for a large number of words and phrases in a specialized vocabulary, such as that used in military operations. Each plaintext meaning has its own code group, usually composed of four or five letters or digits. For example, the code group BANAT might mean the word "attack," and the code group BANEV might mean the phrase "attack progressing satisfactorily." Code books also include *syllabary groups*, so cryptographers can encode proper names or other words that do not appear in the book itself. *California* might be encoded with the code groups for CAL, I, FOR, NI, and A.

Transposition Ciphers involve the use of a geometric design, such as a square or rectangle. The cryptographer inscribes the plaintext letters by one route in the design, then transcribes them by another route to form the cipher text. In *columnar transposition*, the cryptographer chooses a numerical key and writes his plaintext letters under it. He then takes the columns of letters in key-number order to form the cipher text. In the following example, the cryptographer uses the *key word* BREAKFAST, and gives each letter in it a number as it would appear in the alphabet. The first A is numbered 1, the second A is numbered 2, the B is numbered 3, and so on. The cryptographer then writes his plain text in rows under the numbers of the key. Suppose he wishes to report HEAVY ARTILLERY BARRAGE CAUSING SEVERE CASUALTIES AMONG OUR TROOPS. First he writes the key word, BREAKFAST, then the key numbers, and finally the text. When he takes the columns off in numerical order, he has his

```
      A B C D E   R E P U B            A B C D E   R E P U B
      F G H IJ K   L I C A N           F G H IJ K   L I C A N
P1    L M N O P   D F G H K   C1  P1   L M N O P   D F G H K   C1
      Q R S T U   M O Q S T            Q R S T U   M O Q S T
      V W X Y Z   V W X Y Z            V W X Y Z   V W X Y Z

      D E M O C   A B C D E            D E M O C   A B C D E
      R A T B F   F G H IJ K           R A T B F   F G H IJ K
C2    G H I K L   L M N O P   P2  C2   G H I K L   L M N O P   P2
      N P Q S U   Q R S T U            N P Q S U   Q R S T U
      V W X Y Z   V W X Y Z            V W X Y Z   V W X Y Z
```

Digraphic Substitution looks more complicated than it actually is. The cryptographer treats digraphs, or pairs of the letters of his plain text, as the elements for encipherment. He locates the first two letters in the plain sections of a four-square matrix (marked P₁ and P₂) and then finds the cipher text in the cipher sections at the opposite corners of an imaginary rectangle. The matrix *above left* is marked for the first two letters, and

the one *above right* for the second two letters. The matrix *below left* shows the third pair, and the one *below right* the fourth pair. In this case, the plain and cipher letters are the same for the fourth pair. Using this matrix, the final message would be enciphered as follows:

Plain: AT TA CK BE GI NS AT DA WN
Cipher: UN MO BT BE AA GQ UN RO XH

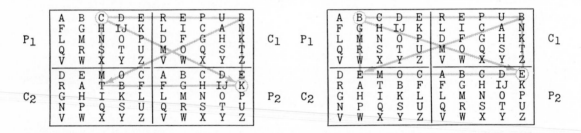

cipher text. To decipher the message, a cryptanalyst

```
B R E A K F A S T
3 7 4 1 6 5 2 8 9

H E A V Y A R T I
L L E R Y B A R R
A G E C A U S I N
G S E V E R E C A
S U A L T I E S A
M O N G O U R T R
O O P S
```

would simply reverse the process. The final cipher text in this example would begin VRCVL GSRAS EERHL, and so on.

Monoalphabetic Substitution Systems employ a single cipher alphabet, consisting of two parts, a *plain component* and a *cipher component*. In this example, the letters of a key word, MONARCHY, are placed first to produce a mixed sequence for the cipher:

```
Plain:  ABCDEFGHIJKLMNOPQRSTUVWXYZ
Cipher: MONARCHYBDEFGIJKLPQSTUVWXZ
```

To encipher the word AMMUNITION, the cryptographer would locate the cipher letters below the plain letters, MGGTIBSBJI.

Biliteral substitution uses a matrix such as this:

```
    A E I O U
B   A B C D  E
C   F G H IJ K
D   L M N O  P
F   Q R S T  U
G   V W X Y  Z
```

Here the plaintext letters have two-letter cipher equivalents. For example, ENEMY would be enciphered as BU DI BU DE GO. The cryptographer could use digits for the row and column designators, so that ENEMY might come out 10 38 10 37 59.

Polyalphabetic Substitution Systems employ more than one alphabet during encipherment. In the Vigenère table (named for Blaise de Vigenère, a French cryptographer of the 1500's who first described it in print), the plaintext letters appear in the row of letters at the top of the table, the key letters at the side, and the cipher letters within the square.

```
  A B C D E F G H I J K L M N O P Q R S T U V W X Y Z

A ABCDEFGHIJKLMNOPQRSTUVWXYZ
B BCDEFGHIJKLMNOPQRSTUVWXYZA
C CDEFGHIJKLMNOPQRSTUVWXYZAB
D DEFGHIJKLMNOPQRSTUVWXYZABC
E EFGHIJKLMNOPQRSTUVWXYZABCD
F FGHIJKLMNOPQRSTUVWXYZABCDE
G GHIJKLMNOPQRSTUVWXYZABCDEF
H HIJKLMNOPQRSTUVWXYZABCDEFG
I IJKLMNOPQRSTUVWXYZABCDEFGH
J JKLMNOPQRSTUVWXYZABCDEFGHI
K KLMNOPQRSTUVWXYZABCDEFGHIJ
L LMNOPQRSTUVWXYZABCDEFGHIJK
M MNOPQRSTUVWXYZABCDEFGHIJKL
N NOPQRSTUVWXYZABCDEFGHIJKLM
O OPQRSTUVWXYZABCDEFGHIJKLMN
P PQRSTUVWXYZABCDEFGHIJKLMNO
Q QRSTUVWXYZABCDEFGHIJKLMNOP
R RSTUVWXYZABCDEFGHIJKLMNOPQ
S STUVWXYZABCDEFGHIJKLMNOPQR
T TUVWXYZABCDEFGHIJKLMNOPQRS
U UVWXYZABCDEFGHIJKLMNOPQRST
V VWXYZABCDEFGHIJKLMNOPQRSTU
W WXYZABCDEFGHIJKLMNOPQRSTUV
X XYZABCDEFGHIJKLMNOPQRSTUVW
Y YZABCDEFGHIJKLMNOPQRSTUVWX
Z ZABCDEFGHIJKLMNOPQRSTUVWXY
```

The cryptographer writes a key word over and over

606

above his plain text. Then he looks down the column under his plaintext letter to find its cipher equivalent in the row that begins with his key letter. For example, if the key word is BLUE and the message is NINE PRIS- ONERS TAKEN, the cryptographer would write these three lines:

```
K:  BLUEB  LUEBL  UEBLU  EBL
P:  NINEP  RISON  ERSTA  KEN
C:  OTHIQ  CCWPY  YVTEU  OFY
```

In *digraphic substitution* the cryptographer treats pairs of letters, rather than single letters, as the elements of his plain text. In the *four-square matrix* shown here, he finds the first two letters of his message in squares P_1 and P_2. He uses these two points to form a rectangle, and finds the first two letters of cipher text in squares C_1 and C_2. He repeats the process for the other digraphs of his message, as shown in the illustration on the opposite page.

```
        A B C D E   R E P U B
        F G H IJ K   L I C A N
P1      L M N O P   D F G H K   C1
        Q R S T U   M O Q S T
        V W X Y Z   V W X Y Z

        D E M O C   A B C D E
        R A T B F   F G H IJ K
C2      G H I K L   L M N O P   P2
        N P Q S U   Q R S T U
        V W X Y Z   V W X Y Z
```

The German Army once used a *combined substitution-transposition cipher*, the so-called *ADFGVX system*. German cryptographers began by substituting letters in a 6x6 bilateral matrix containing the 26 letters and the 10 digits. They then inscribed the cipher text from this step into a transposition rectangle and took the columns of the rectangle in key order for the final cipher. In this example, the message ATTACK BEGINS AT DAWN is first enciphered as DGVXV XDGDX . . . , and this is written in

```
    A D F G V X
A   B 2 E 5 R L
D   I 9 N A 1 C
F   3 D 4 F 6 G
G   7 H 8 J Ø K
V   M O P Q S T
X   U V W X Y Z
```

```
G E R M A N Y
3 2 6 4 1 5 7
D G V X V X D
G D X G X A A
A F F X D A D
F V V D G V X
F D D G X F D
F
```

the rows of the transposition rectangle. The final cipher text will begin VXDGX GDFVD . . .

Some cryptographic systems employ *syllabary squares* or *code charts*, and may be considered primitive code systems. With this example of a syllabary square, a message could be encrypted as it would be in using the syllabary groups of a code book.

	1	2	3	4	5	6	7	8	9	Ø
1	A	1	AL	AN	AND	AR	ARE	AS	AT	ATE
2	ATI	B	2	BE	C	3	CA	CE	CO	COM
3	D	4	DA	DE	E	5	EA	ED	EN	ENT
4	ER	ERE	ERS	ES	EST	F	6	G	7	H
5	8	HAS	HE	I	9	IN	ING	IS	IT	
6	IVE	J	Ø	K	L	LA	LE	M	ME	N
7	ND	NE	NT	O	OF	ON	OR	OU	P	Q
8	R	RA	RE	RED	RES	RI	RO	S	SE	SH
9	ST	STO	T	TE	TED	TER	TH	THE	THI	THR
Ø	TI	TO	U	V	VE	W	WE	X	Y	Z

This square is only 10 x 10. If it were increased to such dimensions as 26 x 26, with letters to mark rows and columns, instead of the 10 digits, the square could

contain common words and perhaps even short phrases. It would then be classed as a *code chart*.

Mechanical Devices

Cipher Devices mechanically encipher or decipher messages, usually on the principles of polyalphabetic substitution. Some simply consist of two rotating concentric discs, each bearing a sequence of 26 letters. The cryptographer uses one disc to locate the plaintext letters, and the other for their ciphertext equivalents. Such a *cipher disc*, with normal alphabetic sequences, would be the equivalent of the Vigenère table. The cryptographer would set the particular key letter in the cipher component against "A" in the plain component. In order to provide successive shifts in the alphabets, as the code word BLUE did in the Vigenère table, the cryptographer might use a repeating numerical pattern such as 3-1-2-5-7-2-1, 3-1-2-5-7-2-1. Or he might begin at a prearranged initial setting and shift the discs by one position after enciphering or deciphering each letter. This *progressive alphabet system* would bring all of the alphabets into play in succession.

Sir Charles Wheatstone, a British scientist, invented a cipher device in 1867. It had two concentric discs and a gearing mechanism that automatically shifted the alphabets in an extremely irregular manner. The machine is known as the *Wheatstone cipher device*, but credit for the original invention belongs to an American, Decius Wadsworth. He built an identical device in 1817.

A French cryptologist, Étienne Bazeries, invented another type of cipher device in 1891. His *cylindrical cipher device* consists of 20 numbered discs on a central shaft, each bearing a different arrangement of the letters of the alphabet. To encipher a message, the cryptographer sets up the discs in a prearranged order. He arranges one row on the discs to form the first 20 letters of his message, then takes off any other row as the cipher text. He repeats the procedure for the rest of his message. To decipher the message, the cryptographer sets up the cipher message and examines the other rows for the one row that contains plain text all the way across. Bazeries was the first to describe this device in print. But credit for the original invention must again go to an American, Thomas Jefferson. In his papers, now in the Library of Congress, he described an almost identical device.

Cipher Machines are extremely complicated. They usually have a typewriter keyboard, and often need electric power. Some machines produce a printed tape with the enciphered or deciphered letters. Others, like teletypewriters, automatically encipher, transmit, and decipher at opposite ends of a circuit.

Concealment Systems

Concealment is not really a code or a cipher. It is a method of hiding a secret text in an otherwise innocent message or disguise. For example, the first letters of the words HAVE EXCELLENT LAUNCHING PLAN give the secret text HELP . In *open code systems*, the sender gives plaintext word equivalents to his secret text, then inserts them in an otherwise innocent message. In AUNT MARY LEFT FOR DETROIT ON FRIDAY, the words AUNT MARY might stand for "five troop ships," DETROIT might mean

CODES AND CIPHERS

"Southampton," and FRIDAY might be "Monday."

Francis Bacon devised a famous concealment system. Combinations of two elements, called *a* and *b*, represent the letters of the alphabet. These two elements may be two different styles of type in a book, the arrangement of red and black cards in a deck of playing cards, or the location of light and dark chocolates in a box. For example, a writer might put a dot or

A: aaaaa	G: aabba	N: abbaa	T: baaba
B: aaaab	H: aabbb	O: abbab U–V: baabb
C: aaaba I–J: abaaa	P: abbba	W: babaa
D: aaabb	K: abaab	Q: abbbb	X: babab
E: aabaa	L: ababa	R: baaaa	Y: babba
F: aabab	M: ababb	S: baaab	Z: babbb

underscore under some of the letters in the innocent sentence ALL IS WELL WITH ME TODAY in order to convey the message HELP.

All	is	well	w	ith	me	today
aab	bb	aaba	a	aba	ba	abbba
H		E		L		P

The *b* letters are exaggerated with underscores here.

Cryptanalysis

The art of cryptanalysis requires extensive study and experience, unusual perseverance, considerable imagination—and just plain luck. It may be impossible to solve a single short cryptogram, even if the system is fairly simple. But, if a cryptanalyst has enough time, enough messages, and enough information about the correspondents and the nature of their messages, he might be able to solve even a complex system.

Each language has its own individual characteristics and peculiarities. Cryptanalysts work with extensive tables of statistics of single letters, two- and three-letter combinations (called *digraphs* and *trigraphs*), and other elements of the language. They know, for example, that E, T, A, O, N, R, I, and S are the most frequent ones in English. They also use lists of frequent words and phrases and of *pattern words* that contain repeated letters, such as ATTACK and VESSEL, of the *abba* class, and DIVISION and ELEMENT, of the *abaca* class.

History

Cryptography goes back to the time of the ancient Greeks. The Spartans wound a belt in a spiral around a *scytale* (stick), wrote a message along the length of the stick, and unwound the belt. This in effect was the first transposition cipher. No one could read the message unless he had a stick exactly the right size. Julius Caesar used a simple substitution cipher. Each letter of the plain text was replaced by the letter three positions to the right in the normal alphabet. By his system, we would encipher CAB as FDE.

Gabriel de Lavinde wrote the first manual on cryptography in 1379. Sicco Simonetta wrote the first treatise on cryptanalysis in 1474.

In the 1600's, Cardinal Richelieu invented a *grille*. He would place a card with holes in it over a sheet of paper, write his secret message in the holes, then fill in the rest of the paper to look like an innocent letter. Only a man with an identical grille could read the words of the secret message. LAMBROS D. CALLIMAHOS

See also NATIONAL SECURITY AGENCY.

CODEX. See BOOK (Early Forms of Books); MANUSCRIPT (Parchment).

CODFISH. See COD.

CODICIL, *KAHD uh sil,* is an addition to a will. It may be written on the same piece of paper as the will or it may be a separate document. A codicil is regarded as part of the original will and revokes any part of the will which is not consistent with the codicil. It is believed that codicils were first made legal by the Emperor Augustus in ancient Rome. WILLIAM TUCKER DEAN

See also WILL.

CODLING MOTH is a small brown and bronze-colored moth. The caterpillars of this moth cause severe damage to apples. They also destroy such fruits as pears, quinces, and English walnuts. Originally a native of Europe, the codling moth now lives in all parts of the world.

In spring, the adult moths emerge from their cocoons under loose bark and trash. They lay their eggs on leaves and twigs. The *larvae* (caterpillars) bore into young apples. This usually causes the fruit to die and drop off. A second generation of larvae may bore into the sides of larger apples. In some areas, there is even a third generation.

The chief method of controlling codling moths is by a series of four to seven sprayings. The spray may contain lead arsenate, DDT, lime sulfur, fixed nicotine, or various other poisons. The exact schedule for spraying varies with the location. Orchards and packing sheds should be kept clean of all loose bark, fallen apples, and trash.

Scientific Classification. The codling moth belongs to the leaf roller family, *Tortricidae*. It is genus *Laspeyresia*, species *L. pomonella*. ALEXANDER B. KLOTS

See also MOTH (color pictures).

CODRUS. See ATHENS (History).

U.S. Agricultural Service

The Codling Moth, *above,* is less than an inch across from wingtip to wingtip. It lays its eggs on apple trees. The larvae burrow into developing apple fruits and eat the flesh, *below.* Codling moth larvae cause millions of dollars worth of damage every year.

USDA

CODY, JOHN PATRICK CARDINAL (1907-   ), archbishop of Chicago, was appointed a cardinal of the Roman Catholic Church in 1967 by Pope Paul VI. Cardinal Cody won recognition as a church administrator while archbishop of New Orleans and Chicago.

Cardinal Cody was born in St. Louis. He was ordained a priest in Rome in 1931 where he received doctorates in philosophy and theology at the North American College. He served for five years on the staff of the Vatican secretary of state in the 1930's. He was appointed archbishop of New Orleans in 1964 and archbishop of Chicago in 1965.   THOMAS P. NEILL

CODY, WILLIAM FREDERICK. See BUFFALO BILL.

COE COLLEGE. See UNIVERSITIES AND COLLEGES (table).

COEDUCATION means teaching both boys and girls, or men and women, in the same classrooms. Most public schools in the United States are coeducational. But many church-controlled and other private schools admit only males or females. Coeducation is still a rare practice in many countries, especially in secondary schools.

Before the mid-1800's, many persons opposed education for girls. Educators barred girls from some U.S. public schools. Sometimes girls could attend classes only during the lunch hour or after school hours, when boys were not present. But women's struggle for equal rights helped open schools and colleges to them.

Oberlin College at Oberlin, Ohio, became the first United States coeducational college. In 1835, it announced, "Young ladies attend recitations with young gentlemen in all the departments." Oberlin graduated three women with the bachelor of arts degree in 1841.

The state universities helped the cause of coeducation in the United States. It developed rapidly in the late 1800's. For instance, the University of Michigan opened its departments to women in 1870. Today, women may enter graduate and professional schools that were formerly open only to men.   R. FREEMAN BUTTS

COEFFICIENT. See ALGEBRA (Terms); FRICTION (Laws); HEAT (Expansion).

COELACANTH, *SEE luh kanth*, is a fish belonging to the group of *lobe-finned* fishes. Scientists believe that four-legged land animals developed from the lobe-finned fish hundreds of millions of years ago. They thought all lobe-finned fish had been extinct for many millions of years. But in 1938, a living coelacanth was caught off

The Coelacanth Is a Large, Blue, Oily Fish.
Wide World

South Africa. Others have been found near Madagascar. The coelacanth is a large, blue, oily fish.

Scientific Classification. The coelacanth belongs to the subclass *Crossopterygii*. They make up the coelacanth family, *Coelacanthidae*.   CARL L. HUBBS

See also EVOLUTION; PREHISTORIC ANIMAL (Animals with Backbones; Living Fossils).

COELENTERATE, *see LEN tur ayt*, is one of a group of soft-bodied animals. The group includes the fresh-water hydras, hydroids, jellyfish, sea anemones, and corals. These animals make up the phylum *Coelenterata*. There are about 9,000 *species* (kinds) of coelenterates, and most of them live in the sea.

The word *coelenterate* means *hollow intestine*, and in many of these animals a large digestive cavity occupies the interior of the body. The coelenterate body may be shaped like a cylinder, a bell, or an umbrella. Every coelenterate has at least two layers of cells that form its body wall. An outer layer makes up the body covering, and an inner layer lines the digestive cavity. Many coelenterates have a third, or middle, layer of cells.

A *medusa*, or jellyfish, is a coelenterate that has a bell- or umbrella-shaped body. Its mouth is at the underside of the body. Tentacles with special stinging cells hang downward from the body's ringlike edge. Medusas swim about freely in the sea.

A *polyp* is a coelenterate that has a body shaped like a hollow cylinder. A polyp lives with one end of its body attached to the sea bottom. The mouth and tentacles are on the other end. Polyps may exist singly or may live together in colonies. For example, hydras and sea anemones are single polyps, and hydroids and corals are colony-forming polyps.

Some coelenterates have both medusa and polyp stages in their lives. Buds on a polyp first develop into medusas. The medusas eventually break free and swim away. Then the medusas produce eggs and sperm that unite and develop into polyps.   ROBERT D. BARNES

Related Articles in WORLD BOOK include:

Coral	Medusa	Portuguese Man-of-War
Hydra	(jellyfish)	Sea Anemone
Jellyfish	Polyp	

COEUR D'ALENE, *kawr d'l AYN*, Ida. (pop. 14,291; alt. 2,155 ft.), lies on Lake Coeur d'Alene in northern Idaho (see IDAHO [map]). The main industries in the city and the scenic lake region include tourism and the manufacture of lumber. The Coeur d'Alene area is a hunting and fishing center. Farming, dairying, and mining are other major occupations in the surrounding region. Coeur d'Alene serves as the seat of Kootenai County, and has a mayor-council form of government.   WILLIAM S. GREEVER and JANET GROFF GREEVER

COEUR D'ALENE MOUNTAINS, sometimes called the BITTERROOT MOUNTAINS, form the northern part of the Bitterroot Range of the Rocky Mountains. They extend for about 40 miles along the Idaho-Montana border. For location, see IDAHO (color map).

The Coeur d'Alene Mountains look like a rolling upland cut by many streams, and have few prominent peaks. Ridge elevations vary between 5,200 and 6,800 feet above sea level.   HARRY H. CALDWELL

COEXISTENCE, in international relations. See COMMUNISM (Communism Today); COLD WAR.

COFFEE

Pan-American Coffee Bureau

Berries of the Coffee Tree. contain coffee beans. Ground and roasted beans are brewed with hot water to make coffee.

COFFEE, the drink made from the roasted and ground beans of the coffee tree, is the favorite hot drink in almost every country in temperate or cold climates.

The United States ranks as the largest consumer of coffee. Americans drink more than 500 million cups every day. The full, rich aroma of coffee adds much to the pleasure of drinking it. The *coffee break* has become an integral part of the business world. Each morning and afternoon, millions of workers pause for a few minutes of relaxation over a cup of coffee. The average American drinks the brew from about 15 pounds of coffee annually. Each year, the United States uses about 2,850,000,000 pounds, or about one-third of all the coffee grown in the world. Other leading coffee-consuming countries include France, Italy, Sweden, and West Germany. Brazil grows about one-third of the world's coffee crop. Its annual production averages more than 3 billion pounds. Coffee is vital to the economies of many Latin-American countries.

Coffee contains caffeine, a drug that acts as a stimulant to mental and physical energy. The drink tends to expand blood vessels mildly so that more blood flows to the heart and brain. See CAFFEINE.

From Bean to Cup

The Coffee Plant. The scientific name of the common coffee tree is *Coffea arabica*. It originally grew wild in Ethiopia. It now grows under cultivation in Java, Sumatra, India, Arabia, equatorial Africa, Hawaii, Mexico, Central and South America, and the West Indies.

Coffea arabica is a shrub with glossy, evergreen leaves. It reaches a height of 14 to 20 feet when fully grown. As a rule, coffee growers prune it to under 12 feet. The flowers of the *Coffea arabica* are white.

The coffee berry begins to grow while the tree is blossoming, and ripens from green to yellow to red. According to United States government research, the average coffee tree bears enough berries each year to make 1½ pounds of roasted coffee.

A coffee tree is usually five years old before it bears a full crop. The common variety grows best at altitudes of from 2,000 to 6,000 feet in a tropical climate. Most trees grow from seeds that are first planted in nursery beds. After a year, the seedlings are transplanted to prepared fields.

Preparation for Market. All berries must be hand-picked, because no one has yet found a way to harvest them successfully by machine. After the berries are picked, they are put through a *sluice* (bath of running water). Sticks, leaves, and the green and bad berries float on top. The good ones sink to the bottom.

Pulping. The good berries then go to a pulping house, where machinery removes the pulp. Each berry contains two *beans* (seeds). Each bean has a thin parchmentlike skin, and a second covering called the *silver skin*. When the beans are first uncovered, they are soft and bluish-green in color. Later, they become hard and the color changes to a pale yellowish tint.

After they leave the pulping machine, the coffee beans are run through a series of fermenting and washing tanks. The beans are then dried and left to cure for several weeks.

Hulling and Peeling make up the next step. Milling machines remove the parchment and the silver skin. As the beans come from the machine, a fan blows off the loose skins. The beans then go to a machine called the *separator*, which removes sand, dust, and small or broken beans. The beans are sorted until only the largest and best of the coffee beans remain.

LEADING COFFEE GROWING COUNTRIES
Pounds of coffee grown in 1968

Brazil
3,042,000,000 lbs.

Colombia
1,045,000,000 lbs.

Ivory Coast
569,000,000 lbs.

Angola
423,000,000 lbs.

Mexico
370,000,000 lbs.

Indonesia
331,000,000 lbs.

Uganda
327,000,000 lbs.

El Salvador
304,000,000 lbs.

Guatemala
238,000,000 lbs.

Ethiopia
231,000,000 lbs.

Source: *World Agricultural Production and Trade*, U.S. Department of Agriculture

Roasting. Most coffee is shipped in 132-pound burlap bags. At the roasting plant, the beans are emptied into chutes leading from an upper to a lower floor. An air-suction device removes dust and other materials. The beans lose weight during roasting. For example, 118 pounds of beans yields 100 pounds of roasted coffee. The coffee then goes to the blending machine, a giant cylinder that mixes different types of coffee.

From the blender, the beans flow by gravity to storage bins, then to roaster ovens. There, they are roasted at 900° F. for 16 to 17 minutes. Roasting develops the aromatic oils in the beans. The supervisor takes a sample to determine the exact moment to release the beans into cooling machines. The cooled coffee then goes through another cleaning process before being carried to bins where it is stored until ground. After being ground to *drip*, *regular*, or *fine* requirements, it is packed either in vacuum tins or in paper bags.

Instant Coffee. The processing of instant coffee grew greatly after World War II. In general, the procedure includes the brewing of coffee in huge containers, then evaporating the water from the brew. The remaining powder crystals are packaged, ready to become coffee again with the addition of boiling water.

A Good Cup of Coffee. Best brewing results are obtained by using one standard coffee measure, or two level tablespoons of coffee, to each cup. The water should be freshly drawn from the cold-water tap. Most coffee is made in *percolators*, *drip* pots, or *vacuum* coffee-makers, which strain boiling water through the coffee.

Kinds of Coffee

More than a hundred kinds of coffee are sold in the United States. They may be divided into three general groups—*Brazils*, *Milds*, and *Robustas*. The Milds include all Coffea arabica grown outside of Brazil. Coffee Robusta is a different kind of coffee, most of which grows in Africa. Most coffee is named for the region where it grows or the port from which it is shipped. *Mocha*, for instance, is shipped from the port of Mocha in Yemen. *Java* grows in and near Java.

American roasters place great importance on the taste of their blends. They pack different blends for different parts of the country. Coffee prepared for the South often has chicory added to it (see CHICORY).

Some persons find it more healthful to drink *decaffeinated coffee*. The removal of caffeine is a cold-water extraction, done with the aid of certain chemicals. Many people enjoy a *demitasse*, or half cup of black coffee, or a tall glass of *iced coffee*.

History

According to legend, coffee was discovered in Ethiopia when goatherds noticed that their flocks stayed awake all night after feeding on coffee leaves and berries. Coffee reached Arabia in the 1200's. *Coffee* comes from the Arabic word *qahwah*. Before its use as a beverage 700 years ago, coffee was a food, then a wine, and then a medicine. Coffee moved from Arabia to Turkey during the 1500's, and to Italy in the early 1600's. Coffeehouses sprang up throughout Europe in the 1600's and people met there for serious discussions. Coffee probably came to America in the 1660's. Coffee-growing was introduced in Brazil in the 1700's.

Coffee-exporting countries have tried for many years to control coffee prices and surpluses. At first, they agreed to export quotas that limited each country's exports. They also tried to control prices by stockpiling some coffee instead of exporting it. But in 1963, the United Nations arranged an International Coffee Agreement that included both exporting and importing countries. Exporting countries accepted export quotas. Importing countries agreed to observe a floor on prices and to limit their coffee purchases from countries that did not sign the agreement.

Scientific Classification. Coffee belongs to the madder family, *Rubiaceae*. The common coffee tree is genus *Coffea*, species *C. arabica*.   JOHN F. McKIERNAN

See also BRAZIL (pictures); CHICORY; COSTA RICA (pictures); EL SALVADOR (picture); SOUTH AMERICA (picture, Growing Coffee).

COFFER. See ARCHITECTURE (Architectural Terms).

United Press Int.

A Brazilian Woman, *above*, chops weeds in a crowded coffee tree field. New fields planted according to contour farming methods, *background*, can be cultivated with machines.

The Coffee Beans travel from the fermenting tanks to the drying area by sluiceways, *right*. Constantly flowing fresh water removes the gummy substance covering the beans.

Pan-American Coffee Bureau

The Coffee Beans Dry in the sun. Workers turn them constantly to assure uniform drying, *above left*.

Workers Sort the Beans and remove those that are discolored and defective, *above right*.

Bags of Green Coffee from Brazil are shipped to other countries to be processed and sold, *right*.

A Network of Beams Supports the Walls of a Cofferdam.

COFFERDAM is a temporary enclosure built in water. When the water is shallow, the cofferdam may be an earth dike. For greater heights, it is commonly made of two rows of piles, tied together. The space between them is packed with soil or rock. When the cofferdam is finished, the water is pumped out of the enclosure, leaving a dry foundation. Piers or other structures can then be built there. Cofferdams have been used to examine and repair sunken ships.   R. G. HENNES

See also CAISSON; PILE.

COFFIN. See FUNERAL CUSTOMS (Burial); SARCOPHAGUS.

COFFIN, ROBERT PETER TRISTRAM (1892-1955), was an American poet, essayist, novelist, and biographer. His book of verse, *Strange Holiness*, won the 1936 Pulitzer prize in poetry. As a professor and teacher, he had a great influence on other writers.

Over 40 of his books were published. They include *The Dukes of Buckingham* (1931), *Yoke of Thunder* (1932), *Red Sky in the Morning* (1935), *Saltwater Farm* (1937), *Primer for America* (1943), *Yankee Coast* (1947), and *Apples by Ocean* (1950). *Lost Paradise* (1934) is his autobiography.

Coffin was born in Brunswick, Me. He was graduated from Bowdoin College.   EDWIN H. CADY

COGNAC. See ALCOHOLIC DRINK (Distilled Liquors).

COGNATE. See ETYMOLOGY; LINGUISTICS.

COGWHEEL. See WHEEL AND AXLE (Uses).

COHAN, *koh HAN,* **GEORGE MICHAEL** (1878-1942), became a great American actor, theatrical director, song writer, and play-wright. Before he was 40, he was a leading producer and had created a popular form of musical play. Cohan starred in many of his own productions.

George M. Cohan

Culver

He began his stage career in his childhood. While only in his 20's, he won wide recognition for his acting, songs, and plays as a member of the Four Cohans, a family group. He wrote such popular songs as "Give My Regards to Broadway," "Over There," and "You're a Grand Old Flag." His plays include *Little Johnny Jones; Forty-Five Minutes from Broadway; George Washington, Jr.; The Song and Dance Man;* and adaptations of *The Miracle Man* and *Seven Keys to Baldpate.*

Cohan was also highly successful as the father in Eugene O'Neill's play, *Ah, Wilderness!* and as Franklin D. Roosevelt in the musical, *I'd Rather Be Right.* The motion picture, *Yankee Doodle Dandy,* told the story of Cohan's life. Cohan was born on July 3, 1878, in Providence, R.I. But, all his life, he considered July 4 as his birthday.   BARNARD HEWITT

COHEN, OCTAVUS ROY (1891-1959), an American author, became famous for his humorous short stories in Negro dialect. Many of his stories appeared in *The Saturday Evening Post.* Cohen also wrote motion-picture scenarios and radio scripts. His works include *The Crimson Alibi, Assorted Chocolates, Black and Blue, Lilies of the Alley, Carbon Copies, Borrasca,* and *Love Can Be Dangerous.* He was born in Charleston, S.C., and studied at Clemson College. He lived most of his life in Birmingham, Ala., a city he used often for the settings in his stories.   JOHN O. EIDSON

U&U

Octavus Roy Cohen

COHESION, *koh HE zhun,* is the force that holds a material together. At a low enough temperature, cohesion keeps the atoms or molecules of a material tightly together to make the material a *solid.* Heating the solid causes its atoms or molecules to vibrate faster and partially overcome the cohesive force. The atoms or molecules can then slide easily over each other and the material changes into a *liquid.* At still higher temperatures, the vibrations become so great that cohesion can no longer hold the atoms or molecules together. The material then becomes a *gas.*

The strength of different materials depends upon the strength of the cohesive forces between their molecules. The cohesive force may be greatly reduced by invisible cracks in the material. For example, glass fibers without cracks are 100 times stronger than ordinary glass which contains tiny surface cracks.

See also ADHESION; MOLECULE (Molecules and Matter); SURFACE TENSION.

COHN, FERDINAND JULIUS (1828-1898), was a German botanist and pioneer in bacteriology. He became the first to show that bacteria are plants. In 1872, he published the first systematic classification of bacteria into genera based upon morphology. With his help, Louis Pasteur disproved the theory of spontaneous generation (see SPONTANEOUS GENERATION). Cohn also contributed to the understanding of heat production by plants. He was born in Breslau, Germany (now Wrocław, Poland).   STANLEY E. WEDBERG

COHO. See SALMON (Coho Salmon).

COHORT. See LEGION; PRAETORIAN GUARD.

COHOSH. See SNAKEROOT.

COIFFEUR. See HAIRDRESSING.

COIL. See IGNITION; INDUCTION COIL.

The Value of a Coin depends upon its rarity rather than its age. A U.S. $50 gold piece, *above*, issued in honor of the Panama Canal opening, may cost as much as $1,000. Byzantine gold coins, *right*, made in the 1100's cost only about $20. The condition of a coin and the demand for it also affects its value.

COIN COLLECTING is a hobby that is popular with boys and girls, young and old, and citizens and rulers. *Numismatics* is the science of coins and medals. Hobbyists who collect old or rare coins are called *numismatists*. Both words stem from the Greek *nomisma* and the Latin *numisma*, meaning *a piece of money* or *a coin*. Numismatics once covered only coins. But today numismatics includes the collecting of medals, tokens, paper money, and related items.

Values in Coin Collecting

Education. Coins teach the hobbyist history, geography, economics, art, and related subjects. He can learn much about empires that no longer exist. Many coins commemorate historic events. Current coins bring life to geography lessons. For example, the debased coins of Rome and the worthless paper money of many countries at various times warn of the calamity of monetary inflation. Famous artists, sculptors, medalists, and engravers have designed coins and medals. They have created many beautiful, meaningful, and strikingly artistic designs.

Prices of Rare Coins rise or fall, depending on how much they are worn, their supply, and the demand for them. In a given United States series, the common coins may be low in price. Rare pieces can be costly. Scarce coins may sell for several thousand dollars each. Coins that are especially rare include the 1804 United States silver dollar, of which only six "originals" are known; the 1822 five-dollar gold piece, of which only three are known; and the 1894-S dime, of which only about six are known out of the 24 manufactured.

Developing a Collection

Starting a Collection is easy and inexpensive. The child who keeps a bus token from each city he visits has the beginning of a coin collection. Coins from other lands brought home by a soldier or a handful of Indian-head or Lincoln cents found in an old trunk make an excellent beginning. Additional coins may be obtained by taking them out of circulation, by trading with others, or by purchasing from a dealer's price list or auction.

Most American collectors limit their activities to American coins or paper money. Others prefer ancient or medieval coins, paper money and coins of other lands, tokens, medals, and odd and curious money. Hobbyists collect coins by dates, by mint marks, by countries, by types, by subjects or topics, and by metals. They keep them in such containers as trays in cabinets, holders, ordinary envelopes, and sealed plastic envelopes. The United States has about 100,000 serious collectors. Several million other Americans are interested in coin collecting to varying degrees.

Adding to a Collection. The coin collector should build his holdings with the best pieces he can afford. He is usually better off if he acquires the scarce pieces first. The most desirable coin is a proof that has been especially struck for the collector. Next in order is the *uncirculated* coin that is unused and is undamaged except for abrasions incurred in the normal contacts with other coins during manufacture. Coins are also described as being *very fine, fine, very good,* or *good,* depending on the amount of wear they have had. Certain uncirculated one-cent pieces from the 1900's in the United States are worth more than $100. These coins are more difficult to obtain than some ancient Roman coins, which are consequently worth perhaps 75 cents.

Coin Collections and Organizations

Famous Coin Collections include the one in the British Museum. The Smithsonian Institution in Washington, D.C., has a collection of more than 65,000 pieces, many of which are unique or rare. In New York City, famous collections include those of the American Numismatic Society and the Chase Manhattan Bank Money Museum.

A Chicago collector, Virgil Brand, owned what was supposed to have been the largest and most valuable

COINS OF OTHER LANDS

The First Coin containing silver was used in Greece, in the 600's B.C.

Decadrachm Was Coined about 413 B.C. in the Greek city of Syracuse in Sicily.

Shekel of Israel, coined in the time of the Maccabees, about 138 B.C.

Egyptian Coin of Cleopatra's Time. She reigned from 51 to 31 B.C.

Bohemian Joachimsthaler of about 1525. The word "dollar" is derived from it.

Mexican Two-Real Piece, 1535, was one of the first coins of the New World.

"Hog Money" of Bermuda, 1616, was named for hogs found on the islands.

Austrian Thaler of the period 1780-1880 has a bust of Maria Theresa.

French Five Franc Coin of 1811 has head of Napoleon I with laurel wreath.

COINS OF THE UNITED STATES AND CANADA

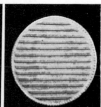

The Bar Cent was probably coined in England for the United States, 1785.

Fugio Cent, 1787, was the first coin issued by authority of the U.S. government.

A $50 Gold Piece, issued in California in 1851 during the Gold Rush.

U.S. Two-Cent Piece, 1864, was the first coin with motto "In God We Trust."

The $10 Gold Eagle was minted from 1907 to 1933. The Indian head wears a war bonnet.

Chase Manhattan Bank Money Museum

Canadian Silver Dollar of 1947 shows *voyageurs* (travelers) in canoe.

private collection of his time. Upon his death in 1926, an estimate of $3 million was placed on his collection. Secretary of the Treasury William H. Woodin owned an extensive collection. Other noted numismatists have included the Italian poet Petrarch, King Charles I of England, King Louis XIV of France, King Farouk I of Egypt, and King Victor Emmanuel III of Italy.

Numismatic Organizations. The American Numismatic Association, founded in 1891, ranks as the largest organization of its kind in the world. It has about 18,000 members in more than 450 affiliated clubs. The association's headquarters address is 3520 North Seventh Street, Phoenix, Ariz. 85014. It publishes a monthly magazine, *The Numismatist*. It holds an annual convention of coin collectors.

Numismatic organizations have been established in Australia, Canada, China, Cuba, France, Germany, Great Britain, India, Mexico, New Zealand, and other countries.

History

In ancient times, no such convenience as coined money existed. People carried on commerce and trade by simple barter and exchange. Even in American colonial days, wampum, tobacco, and other commodities served as mediums of exchange.

The Lydians of Asia Minor invented coined money in the 600's B.C. The first coins were made from *electrum*, a mixture of gold and silver as found in nature. In the more than 2,500 years since that time, thousands of coins of varying sizes and alloys have been made.

Some coin denominations stem from words whose original meanings referred to weights, such as *stater*, *shekel*, and *pound*. Other descriptive names come from

places, for example the *bezant* from Byzantium. The word *dollar* comes from the Bohemian *Joachimsthaler* of the 1500's. Some metals and alloys used in the manufacture of coins include gold, silver, copper, bronze, aluminum, tin, nickel, and platinum.

Before the 1900's, most numismatists concerned themselves with old coins. They collected ancient Greek and Roman coins and those from medieval times. But since the Civil War, collectors have become more interested in American coins. ELSTON G. BRADFIELD

See also GREECE, ANCIENT (color picture: Greek Coins); MONEY.

COIN MACHINE is a device that works when a coin is dropped into a special slot. The coin sets the mechanism in motion. There are many different types of coin machines. *Vending machines* sell merchandise such as candy, coffee, peanuts, cigarettes, and gum. *Automats* are sometimes installed in restaurants to sell food. *Juke boxes* are coin machines that play music on phonograph records. A *penny arcade* consists of a number of machines, such as *pinball machines*, that are gathered in one place and used for amusement.

See also VENDING MACHINE; SLOT MACHINE.

COIR. See COCONUT PALM.

COKE is a hard, grayish substance obtained when soft coal is heated in an airtight coke oven. It contains 87 to 89 per cent carbon, and is hard and *porous* (full of tiny holes). Coke produces intense, smokeless heat when it burns.

Coke is made by heating *pulverized coal* (coal ground to a powder) in an airtight oven. As the coal heats, it *decomposes* (decays). It cannot burn completely with-

FROM COAL TO COKE

Millions of tons of coke are made each year by baking coal in huge ovens at coking plants. A coke oven may be about 1 foot wide, 40 feet long, and 14 feet high, holding about 20 tons of coal. More than 100 coke ovens may sit side by side in a plant such as is pictured.

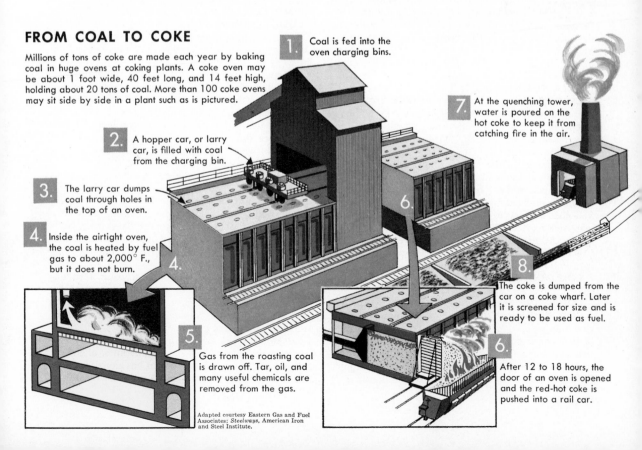

1. Coal is fed into the oven charging bins.

2. A hopper car, or larry car, is filled with coal from the charging bin.

3. The larry car dumps coal through holes in the top of an oven.

4. Inside the airtight oven, the coal is heated by fuel gas to about 2,000° F., but it does not burn.

5. Gas from the roasting coal is drawn off. Tar, oil, and many useful chemicals are removed from the gas.

6. After 12 to 18 hours, the door of an oven is opened and the red-hot coke is pushed into a rail car.

7. At the quenching tower, water is poured on the hot coke to keep it from catching fire in the air.

8. The coke is dumped from the car on a coke wharf. Later it is screened for size and is ready to be used as fuel.

Adapted courtesy Eastern Gas and Fuel Associates; *Steelways*, American Iron and Steel Institute.

out air. Coal tar and coke oven gas evaporate from the decomposed coal and are drawn out of the oven. The escaping tar and gas form the pores in the coke. The hot coke is then taken out of the oven and cooled with water at a *quenching tower* to keep it from burning in the air.

Coke is valuable in *smelting* (melting) iron ore. Coke used in smelting is called *metallurgical coke*. In the United States, about 90 per cent of metallurgical coke is made in giant coking plants with ovens equipped to save valuable coal tar and coke oven gas. Some metallurgical coke is made in older ovens called *beehive ovens* because of their shape. These ovens do not save the coal tar and coke oven gas.   CLARENCE KARR, JR.

See also COAL; GAS (Manufactured Gas); IRON and STEEL (The "Recipe"); PETROLEUM COKE.

COKE, *cook,* **SIR EDWARD** (1552-1634), was a brilliant English courtroom lawyer. He rose to prominence as speaker of Parliament in 1593. In 1594, he was selected over Sir Francis Bacon as Queen Elizabeth's attorney general, and in 1606 he became chief justice under King James I. As chief justice, Coke insisted that even the king was subject to the law. His famous *Institutes* and *Reports* (1600-1615) include many principles of modern law. Coke was born in Mileham, England, on Feb. 1, 1552.   DANIEL J. DYKSTRA

COKE OVEN GAS, or COAL GAS, is the gas obtained when coal is heated in an airtight place. It consists mainly of hydrogen and methane. Coke oven gas is burned to produce heat in industrial plants and in homes. It was formerly used for illumination.

Coke oven gas is made by heating coal in a *by-product coke oven* that heats to a temperature of about 2000° F. As the coal heats, coke oven gas and other by-products are given off in the oven. The gas leaves the oven through pipes and is stored in large tanks, or *gas holders*. See GAS (Coke Oven Gas).   CLARENCE KARR, JR.

COKER COLLEGE. See UNIVERSITIES AND COLLEGES (table).

COLA NUT. See KOLA NUT.

COLBERT, *kawl BEAR,* **JEAN BAPTISTE** (1619-1683), a French statesman, served King Louis XIV as superintendent of finance for 22 years. A believer in firm government control over the economic life of the country, Colbert worked to make France financially strong. He encouraged commerce and internal improvements such as canals and roads. He built a powerful navy and sent explorers and colonists to America. Many French industries received his support.

Colbert's efforts to keep the budget balanced failed when his rival Louvois, the war minister, persuaded Louis XIV to embark upon an expensive series of wars. Colbert was born in Reims.   RICHARD M. BRACE

See also LOUIS (XIV).

COLBY COLLEGE. See UNIVERSITIES AND COLLEGES (table).

COLCHICINE. See COLCHICUM.

COLCHICUM, *KOHL chi kum,* is a poisonous plant which grows wild in the moist meadowlands of England, Ireland, and of middle and southern Europe. It is sometimes called the meadow saffron. It has pale purple or white flowers which bloom in the autumn. Florists call the flowers, which look much like those of

the crocus, *autumn crocus*. Colchicum is easily grown when planted in light, moist, sandy loam.

Colchicine, a bitter drug taken from the colchicum plant, is used in small quantities to treat gout and rheumatism. Botanists also use the drug in experiments in heredity. Colchicine has the effect of doubling the number of chromosomes in a cell. This doubling causes the plant offspring to become much larger than their parents.

Scientific Classification. The colchicum plant belongs to the lily family, *Liliaceae*. It is genus *Colchicum*, species *C. autumnale*.   HAROLD NORMAN MOLDENKE

See also CROCUS.

The Pale Purple or White Flowers of Colchicum bloom in autumn. They look much like spring crocus blossoms.

J. Horace McFarland

COLD. See CLIMATE; HEAT (Convection).

COLD, COMMON. The common cold is any one of a number of distinct infections of the respiratory tract. Colds are the most widespread and prevalent of all diseases.

Although people consider them to be minor illnesses, research has shown that colds are a major cause of absenteeism among school children, military personnel, and industrial and professional groups. Experts estimate that the yearly cost of colds in the United States totals more than $5 billion. This includes time lost from work, wages lost, and the cost of treating colds and their complications.

The common-cold infections vary in severity from the mild cold without fever to extensive, fatal pneumonia. Scientists have made great progress in discovering the viruses that cause these illnesses. They have found that one of the reasons people have so many colds is that several different viruses can cause similar illnesses. Also, one cold does not give immunity against another.

People of all ages are susceptible to colds. But children, particularly preschool youngsters, seem to be most susceptible. Researchers have found that colds cause more than 30 million illnesses each year in American children of preschool age.

Symptoms. Colds are infections of the mucous membranes of the nose, throat, and, sometimes, of the air passages and lungs. When a person has a cold, his nose usually becomes stuffy and he has difficulty breathing.

The infection may spread to the ears and sinuses. Sometimes it spreads to the throat, causing soreness and often hoarseness. When colds spread to the air passages and lungs, they may cause bronchitis and pneumonia. Head colds are sometimes called *coryza*.

The simplest kind of cold usually lasts only one or two days. More severe colds may last longer, often causing fever and aches and pains throughout the body. Occasionally, the patient also has chills and loses his appetite. Colds are dangerous because they make people more susceptible to other infections.

Treatment. There is no specific treatment for colds. But a doctor often prescribes drugs to relieve the discomfort caused by cold symptoms. For example, he may give aspirin or other pain-relieving drugs to lessen muscular aches and pains. Rarely, he may prescribe nasal sprays, which shrink the mucous membranes and allow the patient to breathe easier. Antihistamine drugs have been used to treat certain types of colds, but these should be taken only if prescribed by a physician. A patient who has a fever should stay in bed. This not only provides rest, but it also isolates the patient from other persons.

Persons with colds should eat soft, nourishing foods. They should drink plenty of fluids such as fruit juices, tea, or plain water. If the cold persists or seems to get worse, a physician should be called. If complications begin to develop, the doctor will then be able to treat them early. Often he prescribes sulfa drugs and antibiotics to control complications.

Spread. Experts do not know all the ways in which cold germs spread. But doctors believe that a person can get a cold by breathing in the germs. Whenever a person with a cold coughs or sneezes, tiny droplets of moisture that contain cold germs spray out into the air. Anyone who breathes the air can "catch" the cold. For this reason, colds seem to spread most rapidly in places where many persons gather together, such as in schools, offices, theaters, or buses. A person should always cover his mouth and nose when he coughs or sneezes. Then germs of colds and other diseases cannot spray out into the air.

Prevention. Doctors do not know why some people seem to be more susceptible to colds than others. But they believe that certain conditions make it easier for people to "catch" colds. These conditions include chilling, overheating, exhaustion, and nervous fatigue. But, because viruses cause colds, exposure to a person with a cold is essential to transmission. Therefore, isolating persons who have colds is one of the best ways to prevent colds from spreading. Although scientists have developed several vaccines, none has proved effective against all types of colds.   CLAYTON G. LOOSLI

See also CATARRH; COLD SORE.

COLD-BLOODED ANIMAL is an animal that does not have built-in temperature controls. Scientists call these animals *ectothermic*, which means that they receive their heat from outside. Zoologists have shown that many of these animals maintain their body temperatures within fairly narrow limits by constantly moving about. For example, a lizard moves into the shade when it is too warm. It moves into the sun if it becomes too cool. All animals except mammals and birds are cold blooded. See also TEMPERATURE, BODY; WARM-BLOODED ANIMAL.   CLIFFORD H. POPE

U.S. Bureau of Plant Industry

A Two-Sash Cold Frame. Seedling plants are placed in cold frames to become hardier before they are transplanted.

COLD FRAME is a covered box built on the ground to protect growing plants. It has no bottom and may vary from 6 inches to 2 feet or more in height, depending on the kind of plant it contains. The top of a cold frame is made higher in the back to receive sunlight.

Different covers are used for different purposes. Glass or transparent plastic covers prolong the growing season by protecting plants from wind and cold. They may also be used to start plants early in the season. For plants that need shade, frames may be covered with spaced slats, burlap, or other material that reduces the amount of light entering the box. To protect plants during the winter, cold frames are covered with boards or straw mats.   HENRY T. NORTHEN

COLD LANDS. See ANTARCTICA; ARCTIC; CLIMATE.

COLD SORE is a skin infection that usually appears around the mouth. The sore, caused by a virus, is called *herpes simplex*. This disease may appear anywhere on the body. It may be started by a fever, a cold, or sunburn. When the infection develops about the lips, it is called a cold sore or *fever blister*. The sore begins as a patch of redness that tingles and burns. Small yellowish blisters form in the area. They run together, break, ooze, and make a crust before healing begins. Cold sores last from two to three weeks. Sometimes a cold sore comes back in the same place. No medicine will heal it, but a mild, nonirritating salve will ease the discomfort.   RICHARD L. SUTTON, JR.

COLD STORAGE is a method of storing foods and other perishable products by holding them at low temperatures above freezing and in moist air. Low temperatures prevent spoilage by checking the growth of bacteria and chemical reactions. Household refrigerators, and the walk-in refrigerators used by grocers, butchers, and restaurants are examples of small-scale cold storage. Refrigerated warehouses are examples of large-scale cold storage. Furs are also kept in cold storage during the summer. Florists use cold storage to store flowers, plants, and bulbs. Pharmacists, physicians, and scientists use it to preserve drugs, serums, medicines, and specimens for research.   JOHN T. R. NICKERSON

See also FOOD, FROZEN; REFRIGERATION; CUDAHY, MICHAEL.

THE EVENING SUN

BALTIMORE, FRIDAY, OCTOBER 16, 1964

Johnson Gets Peace Message From Russ Chief.

CHINA EXPLODES ATOM BOMB

LBI Gets Peace Message; Calls For

The New

NEW YORK, SUN

VOL. CX—No. 37,822.

EAST GERMAN TROOPS SEAL BORDER WITH WEST BERLIN TO BLOCK REFUGEE ESCAPE

U.S. ARMS B
FOR BERLI
HELD IN A

New York Times.

NEW YORK, FRIDAY, MAY 6, 1960.

SOVIET DOWNS AMERICAN PLANE; U.S. SAYS IT WAS WEATHER CRAFT; KHRUSHCHEV SEES SUMMIT BLOW

PREMIER IS BITTER

H-BL

COLD WAR

COLD WAR is the struggle between the Communist nations and the democratic nations. This struggle began after World War II ended in 1945. It is called the *Cold War* because it has not led to fighting, or "hot" war, on a wide scale.

The term *cold war* was used during the 1930's to describe Nazi Germany's methods of conquering nations with little fighting. After World War II, writers and political leaders began to use the term in its present meaning. Herbert Bayard Swope, an American jour-

nalist, suggested the term to statesman Bernard M. Baruch, who used it in a speech in April, 1946. A book called *The Cold War*, by the journalist Walter Lippmann, was published in 1947.

During World War II, the Communists and democracies fought as *allies* (partners) against the Axis powers—Germany, Italy, and Japan. The Allies defeated the Axis nations, but Great Britain, France, China, and Russia suffered terrible losses in gaining victory. The United States was by far the most powerful nation in the world. But Americans were tired of war and did not want to take on the burdens of world leadership. So the United States hastily reduced its armed forces.

Carol L. Thompson, the contributor of this article, is the Editor of Current History *magazine.*

618

No word of apology

Pueblo crew free

82 rel...

No 231

Phone 321 3000

SUN-TIMES

MONDAY, OCTOBER 29, 1962

80 Pages, 2 Sec.

Yorl

NDAY, AUGUST 13,

UILD-UP
N

The Crisis Breaks:
K Recalls Missiles

a Francisco Chronu...
THE VOICE OF THE WEST

CCCCAAA—   SAN FRANCISCO, THURSDAY, AUGUST 20, 1953   GA 1 1112 DAILY 10c SU...

AST IN RUSSIA

Burli... Train Wreck

Newspaper Headlines show that the Cold War is both a war of
nerves and a war of weapons. The threat of a nuclear war wiping out
the world is always in the background.

Wide World

On the other hand, the Soviet Union kept its huge
armies in uniform. It distrusted the democracies. Russia
wanted to be sure it had allies, and so it forced Eastern
European countries to accept dictators who had been
trained in Moscow. Russia also forced these countries
to join the Communist *bloc* (group of nations). In addition, the Russians supplied arms and money to Communist revolutionaries throughout the world.

By 1947, the United States had become aware of
the threat of Russian Communist expansion. The
amount of Communist *infiltration* (secret entry) in the
United States also alarmed many Americans.

Two great blocs came into being. The United States
led the *Free World* nations. This group included Can-

ada, France, Great Britain, West Germany, Japan, the
Philippines, and many other countries of Western Europe and Latin America. Russia led the Communist
bloc, which included Communist China (after 1949) and
the Communist nations of Eastern Europe. The Communist bloc was often called the *East*, and the Free
World bloc the *West*. The *nonaligned* or *neutral* nations—
those in neither bloc—included India, Sweden, Switzerland, Indonesia, Cambodia, and most African states.

During the late 1940's and the 1950's, the Cold War
became increasingly tense. Each side accused the other
of wanting to rule the world. Each side believed its
political and economic systems were better than the
other's. Each strengthened its armed forces. Both sides

618a

COLD WAR

HOW THE COLD WAR DIVIDES THE WORLD

The countries shown in gray on this map are associated with the United States or its allies. Countries in red are Communist, and most of them support Russia or China. Other countries are not on the side of either the United States or the Communist countries. Many of these neutral nations trade with both groups.

WORLD BOOK map-GJa

viewed the Cold War as a dispute between right and wrong. They saw every revolt and every international incident as part of the Cold War. This situation made it difficult to settle any dispute peacefully through compromise, with each side giving up something. Fear grew among all peoples that a local conflict would touch off a third world war that might destroy mankind.

The nature of the Cold War changed in the 1960's. Neither the East nor the West remained a *monolith* (united bloc). Communist China challenged Russia's leadership of the East. The Chinese accused the Russians of betraying Communism and being secretly allied with the United States. Some Communist countries followed China's leadership, and others remained loyal to Russia.

Among the nations of the Western bloc, France harshly criticized many U.S. policies. The French demanded independent leadership in Europe and among the non-aligned nations. Most European countries, including both East Germany and West Germany, began to search for new economic and political relationships with one another, regardless of American policies. Great Britain, because of economic and military weakness, withdrew as a military power in Asia and the Middle East. The United States and the Soviet Union tried even harder to avoid hot wars during the shift in the world balance of power.

For a discussion of the principles of Communism and democracy, see the WORLD BOOK articles on COMMUNISM and DEMOCRACY.

Goals in the Cold War

Each major power in the Cold War wants to strengthen itself and weaken its enemies. But the powers have different long-range aims. The United States and its allies want a world community of independent, non-Communist states. The Soviet Union and Communist China

each seek a world in which only its own brand of Communism can be developed.

The Democracies hope to preserve and encourage democratic ideals and a democratic way of life. They believe that respect for the individual leads to political democracy. In turn, political democracy helps the growth of freedom of expression, the right to vote freely, and government that represents the people. The Western nations believe that *capitalism*, or free enterprise, will raise living standards better and faster than Communism can (see FREE ENTERPRISE SYSTEM).

The Communist Powers believe the world will turn to Communism because, they say, capitalist democracy is collapsing. During the period that capitalism is weakening, the Communists believe the democracies will (1) fight each other and (2) struggle against the advance of Communism. To protect themselves against these actions, which they call "capitalist aggression," the Russians and Chinese support Communist dictatorships in the countries around them.

Russia believes the world may turn to Communism peacefully and gradually. China believes that a Communist society must be achieved by violence. But both Communist powers are sure of victory for Communism.

Weapons of the Cold War

The Cold War rivals use five main types of weapons: (1) military power, (2) the power of ideas, (3) economic power, (4) political power, and (5) scientific power.

Military Power. Both the United States and the Soviet Union store nuclear bombs, test new weapons, and develop missiles and antimissile defenses. Communist China, France, and Great Britain also have nuclear weapons. All the powers in the Cold War try to become so strong that the others will be afraid to start a general war.

618b

The Communists send weapons and military advisers abroad to spread Communism through revolutions or civil wars, often called "wars of liberation." During the 1950's, the Soviet Union used its military might to crush revolts against Russian control in East Germany, Hungary, and Poland. American military forces have been sent abroad to *contain* (prevent the spread of) Communism in Latin America, Korea, Lebanon, and Vietnam.

Russia and the United States also depend on military alliances and military bases. Russia keeps troops in many countries of Eastern Europe. It has a military alliance, the Warsaw Pact, with six Eastern European countries (see WARSAW PACT). The United States has troops and bases in Western Europe as part of the North Atlantic Treaty Organization (NATO), a military alliance (see NORTH ATLANTIC TREATY ORGANIZATION). In addition, the United States has *collective defense* agreements with more than 40 nations. In most of these agreements, an attack on one member nation is an attack on all. The United States also has military bases in Southeast Asia.

The Power of Ideas has become as important as military power. Both sides give out information and propaganda about their cultures and ways of life.

The democracies try to explain democratic goals and guidelines to the rest of the world. These nations attempt to show that they want freedom for all people. Many nations of the Free World have information programs. The United States Information Agency (USIA) sponsors a radio network overseas called the Voice of America (see UNITED STATES INFORMATION AGENCY; VOICE OF AMERICA). The United States also sponsors the Peace Corps and cultural exchange programs (see PEACE CORPS).

The Communist nations work to win over the free and the nonaligned nations to Communism. The Communists picture themselves as defenders of peace. They accuse the West of planning a third world war.

Economic Power. East and West both use economic power to support their large armies and to develop new weapons. They stress economic growth and strength be-

cause they believe a strong economy helps a nation convince other nations that its system is better.

Both sides use economic aid to try to strengthen friendly nations and to win friends among the neutral nations. They give food, clothing, money loans and grants, special trade rights, and technical advice to those nations.

In many underdeveloped countries, the Russians use aid programs that make these nations depend on the Soviet Union. Under a Russian *trade and aid* plan, surplus goods are sold to an underdeveloped nation. In return, that nation is allowed to sell its goods to Russia. Gradually, the underdeveloped nation finds it must continue to buy Russian goods so that it can continue to sell its goods to Russia. Communist China also offers foreign aid, but on a much smaller scale.

Western economic aid helps friendly nations strengthen their defenses against Communism. Beginning in 1948, the United States cut off almost all trade with Communist nations to keep them from becoming stronger. But many people believed that trade with Communist states would improve East-West relations and also widen the market for American goods. By the mid-1960's, the United States had resumed trade with some Communist nations.

Political Power. Both sides in the Cold War use *diplomacy* (relations with other nations) to ease differences and to form alliances. In the Warsaw Pact of 1955, Russia tried to unite the nations of Eastern Europe politically and militarily. The countries of Western Europe formed similar alliances, including the Western European Union, the Council of Europe, and NATO. These alliances had political, social, and cultural goals as well as military aims.

The United Nations (UN) is an important center of diplomatic activity. Both sides try to win support from neutral nations in the UN. See UNITED NATIONS.

The Russians and Chinese control many Communist political parties throughout the world. They use these parties to reach political goals. The parties operate legally in many countries and illegally in others. Most Communist parties operate secretly, and some members are really spies. Party members may join organizations that are liberal in character, and then try to control these groups. Communists often use sabotage, riots, strikes, or even murder to gain power. They believe all these actions are justifiable to hasten victory for Communism.

The United States and other Western countries use their *intelligence* (spy) agencies to achieve political goals. The U.S. Central Intelligence Agency (CIA) sometimes gives secret support to friendly governments or friendly groups within governments. The CIA also aids rebellions against Communist governments or governments that favor Communism.

Scientific Power. Each side points to scientific achievements as proof that its way of life is superior. Russia and the United States spend huge sums of money on scientific research. This research is devoted mainly to improving nuclear weapons, rockets, missiles, and spaceships. The East and West use these weapons to try to frighten each other.

Each side sponsors exchange programs in cultural

IMPORTANT COLD WAR TERMS

Arms Race is the effort of both the Communists and the Free World to produce more powerful weapons in greater numbers.

Balance of Terror refers to the approximately equal strength of the East and the West in nuclear arms.

Coexistence is the nonmilitary efforts of the East and the West to win the support of the neutral nations.

Containment is the West's policy of using political, economic, and military pressure to prevent the spread of Communism.

Escalation is intensified fighting, including an increase in the number of troops, types of weapons, or the area involved.

Iron Curtain refers to Russia's barriers against the West in travel and communication.

Limited War is (1) a war in which nuclear weapons are not used, or (2) a war confined to one area or country.

Massive Retaliation is a nuclear counterattack big enough to destroy a nation that has struck first.

Wars of Liberation are Communist-led or Communist-supported rebellions against non-Communist governments.

and scientific fields in underdeveloped nations. China also sends scientific advisers abroad.

The Coming of the Cold War

Historians do not agree on exactly when the Cold War began. Most believe it started shortly before or shortly after World War II ended in September, 1945. Others say it started with a speech by Premier Joseph Stalin of Russia in February, 1946. Stalin warned the Russian people that there would be wars as long as there were capitalist nations. He told the Russians they must "defend" themselves. Still other historians believe the Cold War began in 1947 when Russia tried to replace Germany and France as the strongest power in Europe. In response, the United States took strong action to prevent the spread of Communism.

The Alliance Breaks Up. In February, 1945, the leaders of the Allied *Big Three* met at Yalta in the Crimea. President Franklin D. Roosevelt of the United States and Prime Minister Winston Churchill of Great Britain reached agreement with Stalin on several issues. They set up *occupation zones* (areas controlled by the Allies) for postwar Germany, and worked out a plan to establish a new government in Poland. Stalin promised that Russia would go to war against Japan within three months after Germany surrendered. The three leaders also made plans to form the United Nations. See YALTA CONFERENCE.

Roosevelt died a few weeks after the Yalta Conference, and Harry S. Truman became President. Germany surrendered in May, 1945. The next month, delegates of 50 countries signed the United Nations Charter. See UNITED NATIONS (The San Francisco Conference).

Truman, Churchill, and Stalin met at Potsdam, near Berlin, in July, 1945. But just before the meeting, Churchill's Conservative Party was defeated in an election. Clement R. Attlee succeeded Churchill during the Potsdam Conference.

At Potsdam, the Allies agreed that the German people should be allowed to rebuild their lives "on a democratic and peaceful basis." However, serious disagreements arose. Great Britain and the United States charged that Russia was communizing the countries of Eastern Europe. Even before World War II ended, Russia had taken over the Baltic states of Latvia, Estonia, and Lithuania; parts of Poland, Finland, and Romania; and eastern Czechoslovakia. Russian troops occupied a third of Germany and all of Bulgaria, Hungary, Poland, and Romania. The Western nations also opposed a Russian proposal to give Poland nearly 40,000 square miles of German territory. See POTSDAM CONFERENCE.

The Iron Curtain Descends. During 1945 and early in 1946, Russia cut off nearly all contacts between the West and the occupied territories of Eastern Europe. In March, 1946, Churchill warned that "an Iron Curtain has descended across the continent" of Europe. He made popular the phrase *Iron Curtain* to refer to Russia's barriers against the West. Behind these barriers, the Russians steadily expanded their power.

In 1946, Russia organized Communist governments in Bulgaria and Romania. In 1947, Communists took control of Hungary and Poland. Communists seized full power in Czechoslovakia early in 1948. These countries became Russian *satellites* (nations controlled by Russia).

Albania already had turned to Communism. Enver Hoxha, who led the Communist National Liberation Army in an Albanian civil war during World War II, established a Communist government in 1944.

Yugoslavia also joined the Communist bloc. The Communist Party of Yugoslavia had helped drive out the Germans near the end of the war. Yugoslav Communists led by Marshal Tito then took over the government.

East and West also began to oppose each other in the United Nations. In 1946, the Russians rejected a U.S. proposal for an international agency to control atomic energy production and research. The Soviet Union

YEARS OF CRISIS

✳ 1946-1948	✳ 1947
Communists Take Over Eastern Europe	Truman Doctrine Announced By United States

Winston Churchill warned in a famous 1946 speech that an "Iron Curtain" had come down across Europe. President Harry S. Truman introduced the British prime minister to an audience at Westminster College in Fulton, Mo.

Winston Churchill Memorial and Library in the U.S.

The Greek Civil War ended in defeat for the Communist rebels. U.S. goods sent under the Truman Doctrine aided the victors.

United Press Int.

believed the United States already had a lead in atomic weapons and would have a monopoly if controls were approved.

See the History section of the articles on each Communist country mentioned in this section.

The West Holds the Line

The Containment Policy. In the fall of 1946, Greek Communists revolted against the Greek government. Great Britain had been giving military and economic aid to Greece. But the British told the United States they could no longer give enough help to the Greeks. The British also warned that they could not help Turkey resist Communist pressure.

In March, 1947, President Truman declared that the United States would help any free nation resist Communist *aggression* (attack). Congress granted his request for $400 million for aid to Greece and Turkey. With this aid, both Greece and Turkey successfully resisted Communism. The new American policy became known as the *Truman Doctrine*. Aimed at Soviet expansion in Europe, it developed into the *Containment Policy*, designed to *contain* (hold back) Communist expansion throughout the world.

The foreign ministers of the United States, Great Britain, France, and Russia met in Moscow in March and April, 1947. They tried to draw up a German peace treaty. But the ministers could not agree on ways to end the occupation or on how to unify Germany.

The failure of the conference convinced U.S. Secretary of State George C. Marshall that Russia would not help Europe recover from World War II. In June, 1947, Marshall proposed giving U.S. economic aid to all European nations that would cooperate in plans for their own recovery. This proposal grew into the European Recovery Program, or Marshall Plan, which began in 1948. The United States believed that a strong, stable Western Europe would block the spread of Communism.

Meanwhile, in September, 1947, Russia and eight other European Communist parties set up the *Cominform*, a new version of the Communist International. See MARSHALL PLAN; COMMUNISM (The Spread of Communism).

Czechoslovakia and Poland wanted to take part in the Marshall Plan, but Russia would not let them accept U.S. aid. Instead, Russia set up the Council for Mutual Economic Assistance (COMECON) in January, 1949. This organization was designed to unite the East European satellites economically and politically.

In June, 1948, the Western Allies announced plans to unify their German occupation zones and establish the West German Federal Republic (West Germany). West Germany was established in May, 1949. It had independence in some of its internal affairs, and it joined the Marshall Plan.

Also in June, 1948, Russia harshly criticized Tito, the Communist dictator of Yugoslavia. Tito then declared his country's independence from control by the Soviet Union.

The Berlin Blockade was Russia's answer to the West's plans for West Germany. In June, 1948, Soviet troops blocked all railroad, highway, and water traffic through East Germany to West Berlin. The city lay 110 miles inside the Russian occupation zone. The Russians thought the blockade would force the Western powers to leave Berlin. Then, the Russians believed, Europeans would lose faith in the United States.

Instead of pulling out of West Berlin, the Americans, British, and French set up the *Berlin airlift*. Day and night, for 11 months, Allied airplanes carried food and supplies to Berlin. The Russians lifted the blockade in May, 1949, and the Allies ended the airlift in September. The Berlin airlift showed the world that the United States would defend and support Western Europe. See BERLIN AIRLIFT.

The West Rearms. Military strength became more and more important in the late 1940's. During the

★ 1948	★ 1948-1949	★ 1949	★ 1949
Marshall Plan Started By United States	Berlin Blockade Set Up by Russia	NATO Pact Signed By 12 Countries	Communists Win Control of China

The Marshall Plan helped many European nations recover after World War II. This train carried U.S. goods to northern Greece.

Wide World

The Berlin Airlift of 1948-1949 defeated an attempt by the Russians to force the Western Allies out of West Berlin.

United Press Int.

Berlin blockade, the United States pledged continuing military aid to Western Europe. The United States, Canada, and 10 Western European nations signed the North Atlantic Treaty in April, 1949. This mutual defense treaty set up NATO. The NATO countries promised to defend West Germany and to prevent Russian expansion. In September, 1951, the United States signed the ANZUS mutual defense treaty with Australia and New Zealand (see ANZUS).

The nuclear arms race began on Aug. 29, 1949, when the Soviet Union tested an atomic bomb. Until then, the United States had been the only nation that knew how to make the atomic bomb.

Communist Expansion in Asia. During the 1940's, Communist strength increased in the Far East. The Russians had occupied Manchuria just before the end of World War II. After they left in 1946, the Chinese Communists took over most of northern Manchuria. The Russians also set up a North Korean "people's republic."

In China, Mao Tse-tung's Communist troops fought the nationalist armies of Chiang Kai-shek. The United States gave military aid to Chiang. Late in 1949, Chiang and his government fled to the island of Formosa (Taiwan). The conquest of China put a nation of more than 600 million persons into the Communist bloc.

The Korean War. At the end of World War II, Russian troops occupied North Korea and United States forces occupied South Korea. The North Koreans had a strong army. They received Russian military aid even after Soviet troops withdrew late in 1948. The United States withdrew its forces from South Korea in June, 1949.

North Korean troops invaded South Korea on June 25, 1950, and the Korean War began. On June 27, President Truman sent American forces to aid the South Koreans. At the request of the United States, the United Nations Security Council voted to send UN troops to help South Korea. The Russian delegation was *boycotting* (not attending) the council, and missed a chance to kill the decision by vetoing it. Seventeen nations contributed men to the UN force, and Chinese Communist troops aided the North Koreans.

Peace talks began in July, 1951. They went on for two years while bloody fighting continued. Finally, in July, 1953, representatives of the UN and the Communists signed a truce. In 1954, spokesmen for both sides met in Geneva, Switzerland, to discuss a political settlement. But they could not agree on a way to unite North and South Korea.

The Korean War was the first war in which troops of a world organization fought an aggressor nation. For the first time, Americans fought a "hot war" against Communism. Some historians believe the Korean War was a major turning point in the Cold War. It introduced limited warfare to the East-West conflict as a substitute to all-out—and possibly nuclear—war. Each side avoided attacking targets that could have led to expansion of the war. And each side limited the weapons it used and the territory in which it would fight. See KOREAN WAR.

To the Brink and Back

The Death of Stalin changed the character of the Cold War. The Russian leader died in March, 1953, two months after Dwight D. Eisenhower became President of the United States. The new rulers of Russia governed as a committee at first. Premier Georgi M. Malenkov and his associates adopted a softer policy toward Russia's satellites and the West. For example, they allowed the Russian wives of U.S. servicemen to follow their husbands to America. Russia also set up a cultural exchange program with the West. Soviet troops put down a revolt in East Germany in June, 1953, but Russia's softer course of action was obvious.

The arms race continued. The United States tested its first hydrogen bomb in November, 1952, and Russia set off its first H-bomb in August, 1953. Military

★ 1949	★ 1950-1953	★ 1953	★ 1953
Russia Explodes Atomic Bomb	Korean War—First Use Of UN Troops in Battle	Death of Stalin Alters Cold War	Russia Puts Down East German Revolt

The Korean War ended in 1953 with a truce signed at Panmunjom. Fighting had continued during two years of peace talks.

Wide World

Soviet Premier Joseph Stalin died in 1953. He was entombed with Lenin, *rear*, who had founded Russian Communism.

Pictorial Parade

alliances were strengthened during this period. In 1955, West Germany was allowed to join NATO. In response, Russia and its Eastern European satellites signed the Warsaw Mutual Defense Pact. Also in 1955, the United States announced its support of the military alliance of the Baghdad Pact, which later became the Central Treaty Organization. See CENTRAL TREATY ORGANIZATION; WARSAW PACT.

In January, 1954, the new U.S. secretary of state, John Foster Dulles, had outlined a new American military policy. The United States, he warned, would meet Communist aggression by "massive retaliation" with nuclear weapons. The United States, Dulles said, would strike back "at places and with means of our own choosing."

Cold War tensions increased in the Far East during 1954 and 1955. In Asia, the Chinese led the Communist push. The nationalist French Indochinese were led by Communists and supported by China. In the spring of 1954, after years of fighting, they defeated the French at Dien Bien Phu. A cease-fire agreement was signed in Geneva in July, 1954. It recognized the temporary division of Vietnam and gave North Vietnam to the Communists. Nationwide elections were to be held within two years. But neither the United States nor South Vietnam signed the agreement, and South Vietnam refused to hold the elections. The agreement also established the independence of Cambodia, Laos, and South Vietnam.

In September, 1954, the United States and seven other nations signed the Southeast Asia Collective Defense Treaty (see SOUTHEAST ASIA TREATY ORGANIZATION). This treaty was designed to prevent further Communist expansion in Southeast Asia. After the defeat of France in Indochina, the United States increased its aid to South Vietnam. The United States believed that if one Southeast Asian nation fell to Communism, the others would also topple over, one after another. This was called the "domino theory." But even with American support, South Vietnam could not defeat the Communist rebel forces, called Viet Cong, who were supported by North Vietnam. In 1955, the United States began sending military advisers to help the South Vietnamese government.

The United States also increased its support of the Chinese Nationalists on Formosa. In September, 1954, the Chinese Communists staged air and artillery attacks against the islands of Quemoy and Matsu. These islands, in the Formosa Strait, were held by the Nationalist Chinese. In 1955, Congress voted to let President Eisenhower use armed force if necessary to protect the Chinese Nationalists.

The Spirit of Geneva. In Europe, a thaw in the Cold War became apparent in 1955. The Western Allies and Russia signed a peace treaty with Austria in May. Russian troops left that country, and Austria became an independent, neutral nation. That same month, Premier Nikita S. Khrushchev of Russia apologized publicly to Tito and resumed trade with Yugoslavia.

Eisenhower and Khrushchev met in Geneva in July. Eisenhower proposed that the United States and Russia permit air inspection of each other's military bases. Such an "open skies" agreement would prevent either side from launching a surprise attack on the other. Khrushchev rejected the proposal. But both leaders agreed that an atomic war would be a disaster for both sides. Political observers began to write of a "big thaw" in East-West relations and called it the "spirit of Geneva."

After the Geneva conference, Russia announced a cut of 640,000 men in its armed forces. The Russians said they also had reduced the armies of their satellites. Khrushchev toured Afghanistan, Burma, and India, and offered them economic and technical aid.

Dulles still distrusted the Russians in spite of their softer line. In January, 1956, he told the American people that the United States had been on the brink of

★ 1955	★ 1956	★ 1957	★ 1957
Summit Conference Held in Geneva	Revolts Break Out In Hungary and Poland	Eisenhower Doctrine Announced by United States	Russia Launches Sputnik I

At the Geneva Conference, President Dwight D. Eisenhower, *second from left,* met with Russian, French, and British leaders.

United Press Int.

The Hungarian Revolution against Communist rule was crushed by Russian troops. Thousands of Hungarians were killed.

Paris Match

618g

war several times. "If you are scared to go to the brink, you are lost," Dulles warned. The use of "brinkmanship" had become part of U.S. policy.

In February, 1956, Khrushchev called for *peaceful coexistence* (competition without war) between East and West. He also began a campaign of *de-Stalinization* (removal of Stalinist influences) in Russia and its satellites. In April, 1956, Russia dissolved the Cominform.

Unrest in Eastern Europe. The new Soviet policy encouraged the peoples of Eastern Europe to expect more freedom from Russian rule. In Poland, riots and strikes broke out in Poznań in June, 1956, and spread to other cities. The rioters demanded a more liberal government and an end to Russian rule. A few months later, the Russians allowed Władysław Gomułka, a Polish Communist leader, to rejoin the Polish Communist Party. The Russians had jailed Gomułka in 1951 for trying to set up an independent Communist government in Poland. Khrushchev and other Russian leaders flew to Warsaw to confer with Gomułka in October, 1956. Faced with further rebellion, the Russians agreed to relax some controls in Poland. See POLAND (Communist Rule).

In Hungary, a revolt against Communism began in October, 1956. A rebel government led by Imre Nagy demanded withdrawal of all Russian troops. Early in November, Russian tanks rolled into Budapest. The fighting spread to all parts of the country, and thousands of Hungarian "freedom fighters" were killed. The Russians smashed the revolt in about two weeks. In spite of the new Soviet policy, Russia could not allow Hungary to break up the bloc of Eastern European satellites. See HUNGARY (Communist Hungary).

Trouble at Suez. During the period that Russia was putting down unrest in its Eastern European satellites, trouble was stirring in the Middle East. The United States was trying to prevent Communist expansion in that area. Both Russia and the West sought Egypt's

support by offering aid for its development plans. Each side offered to help build the Aswan High Dam. After Egypt courted Communist aid for the dam and bought Communist arms, the United States and Great Britain canceled their offers to help with the project. President Gamal Abdel Nasser of Egypt struck back by seizing the Suez Canal from international control. Nasser said Egypt would use the profits from operating the canal to build the dam "without pressure from any nation." But he did accept Russian aid.

In October, 1956, while Russia was involved with the Hungarian revolt, Israel invaded Egypt. Britain and France immediately joined in the attack. They wanted to return the Suez Canal to international control. The United States and Russia supported a United Nations resolution demanding an immediate truce. In addition, Russia threatened to send troops to help Egypt. The UN arranged a truce after a few days of fighting. But Russia, by backing Egypt against Israel, had won friends among the Arab nations of the Middle East.

New Challenges

Khrushchev's power in Russia reached its peak in the late 1950's. Sometimes the Russians followed a hard policy, mainly in response to China's challenge to Soviet leadership of the Communist bloc. At other times, Russia stressed peaceful coexistence, giving special attention to economic aid and scientific progress. But the Soviet Union continued to encourage riots, strikes, and revolts in non-Communist countries. And it still called for "wars of liberation." In the West, "peaceful coexistence" came to mean Communist efforts to conquer countries without a major war.

The Missile Gap. The Russians improved their ability to produce nuclear weapons, and the Free World feared a missile gap, or Soviet rocket superiority. In June, 1957, the Russians successfully tested an intercontinental ballistic missile (ICBM). That same year, they

★ 1958	★ 1960	★ 1960	★ 1961
United States Launches Explorer I	Russia Downs U-2 Spy Plane	Guerrilla Wars Erupt In Laos and South Vietnam	German Communists Build Berlin Wall

A U.S. Spy Plane was shot down over Russia in 1960, and the Russians canceled a summit meeting with the United States.

John Bryson, Rapho Guillumette

The Berlin Wall was built in 1961 by East German Communists to prevent East Germans from escaping to freedom in West Berlin.

United Press Int.

launched the first man-made earth satellite, *Sputnik I.* In January, 1958, the United States launched its first earth satellite. Russian rocket power was more advanced, but the two powers had clearly established a nuclear "balance of terror." A brief thaw in the Cold War followed. Russia stopped testing nuclear weapons in March, 1958, and the United States halted its tests in October.

The Eisenhower Doctrine was approved by Congress in March, 1957, because the United States feared Communist penetration in the Middle East. This policy permitted the President to "use armed force to assist any . . . nation . . . [in the Middle East] requesting assistance against armed aggression from any country controlled by international Communism."

In July, 1958, a revolution ended the rule of the pro-Western government of Iraq. The new government favored Communism. Nearby Lebanon feared a Communist revolution and asked the United States for aid. President Eisenhower quickly sent about 6,000 sailors and marines to help Lebanon. Great Britain sent 2,000 paratroopers to protect Jordan against Iraqi pressure. In spite of Russian protests, the American and British forces stayed in the Middle East for about three months.

The Far East. In 1958, the Chinese Communists again fired on Quemoy and Matsu, Formosa's offshore islands. Dulles warned that any attack on these islands would be considered aggression against Nationalist China, an ally of the United States. But occasional firing continued during the 1960's.

Germany. During the late 1950's, Europe remained the most important Cold War battleground. The Russians tried repeatedly to damage the reputation of the West in Germany. In November, 1958, they demanded peace treaties for East and West Germany. Such treaties would have ended the military occupation, and Western troops would have had to leave. The United States refused to yield to the Russian demand, and kept its

forces in Berlin. As a result, the Russians kept threatening to sign a separate peace treaty with the East German government.

The Spirit of Camp David. Another temporary thaw in the Cold War began in the spring of 1959. The foreign ministers of the United States, Great Britain, France, and Russia met in May. In July, Vice-President Richard M. Nixon visited Russia and met with Khrushchev. Two months later, Khrushchev visited the United States. He conferred with Eisenhower at Camp David in Maryland. Khrushchev was so friendly that observers spoke of the "spirit of Camp David," recalling the earlier "spirit of Geneva." Eisenhower and Khrushchev discussed a *summit* (top-level) conference to be held in Paris in 1960. The President accepted Khrushchev's invitation to visit the Soviet Union after the summit meeting.

The U-2 Incident abruptly ended the thaw. An American U-2 spy plane was shot down in Russia in May, 1960. The Russians captured the pilot, Francis Gary Powers, who confessed he was a spy. Eisenhower accepted personal responsibility for the flight. He admitted that U-2 planes had been flying over Russia taking photographs for four years.

When the summit conference began on May 15, Khrushchev demanded that Eisenhower apologize for the U-2 incident. Eisenhower refused, and Khrushchev angrily canceled his invitation for the President to visit Russia. Khrushchev then left the conference, which broke up the next day.

Africa. The Cold War struggle moved to Africa in July, 1960. Premier Patrice Lumumba of the Congo asked the UN to deal with a revolt in his newly independent nation. He charged that the Belgians were aiding the rebel Katangans. The Russians sided with Lumumba against a group led by Congolese President Joseph Kasavubu. The UN intervened in the dispute, keeping Russia and the West from direct military action

---

★ 1961	★ 1963	★ 1964	★ 1964
Castro Announces He Is a Communist	Atomic Test Ban Treaty Is Signed	Communist China Explodes Atomic Bomb	United States Bombs Bases in North Vietnam

Fidel Castro, *left,* declared his Cuban government was Communist, and was welcomed to Russia by Premier Nikita S. Khrushchev.

Wide World

U.S. Marines Entered the Vietnam War in 1965, increasing the number of American troops in Vietnam at that time to 27,000.

Francois Sully, *Newsweek*

in the troubled Congo. The Russians charged that the UN favored the West.

The Troika Proposal. In September, 1960, Khrushchev went to New York City for the meeting of the UN General Assembly. He again criticized the United States for the U-2 flights. The Russian leader showed his anger by taking off a shoe and pounding his desk with it.

Khrushchev tried to destroy the power of the UN to send troops into the world's trouble spots. He called for three secretaries-general—a *troika* (a Russian term for a vehicle drawn by three horses)—to replace the UN secretary-general. One would be a Communist, one from a neutral nation, and one from the West. The General Assembly defeated the proposal.

The Bay of Pigs. John F. Kennedy became President of the United States in January, 1961. Cold War tensions were high—in Europe, in Asia, and even on the doorstep of the United States, in Cuba.

The Cuban government of Fidel Castro had become openly Communist in 1960. Castro condemned the United States and began to receive military aid from Russia and other Communist countries. The Cuban government seized millions of dollars' worth of American property in Cuba. The United States ended diplomatic relations with Cuba in January, 1961.

In April, 1961, the United States sponsored an invasion of Cuba by anti-Castro Cubans at the Bay of Pigs. The attack was poorly planned and failed badly. The unsuccessful invasion strengthened Castro's control of Cuba, and the United States lost face.

The Berlin Wall. Kennedy and Khrushchev met in Vienna, Austria, in June, 1961. Khrushchev demanded a free Berlin and an end of the military occupation. The two leaders failed to reach agreement, and Khrushchev again threatened to sign a separate peace treaty with East Germany. The next month, Russia canceled cuts in its armed forces and increased its military spending.

Growing numbers of East Germans were fleeing to West Germany. On Aug. 13, 1961, the East German Communists began to build a wall of cement and barbed wire between East and West Berlin. To confirm the West's right to stay in West Berlin, the United States sent troops to the city by highway. American tanks enforced Western rights to enter East Berlin without showing papers to Communist border guards. Some East Germans escaped to West Berlin after the wall was built, but many were killed in the attempt. The wall remained, splitting Berlin in two. See BERLIN.

The Space Race Begins. On April 12, 1961, a Russian spaceman, Yuri Gagarin, made the first flight in space around the earth. Later that year, Alan B. Shepard, Jr., and Virgil I. Grissom piloted American spaceships in flight. In 1962, John H. Glenn, Jr., became the first American to circle the earth in space.

In September, 1961, Russia ignored an unofficial agreement against nuclear weapons tests, and resumed nuclear bomb testing in the atmosphere. The United States then resumed underground testing. American tests above ground were started again in April, 1962.

The Cuban Missile Crisis. In October, 1962, the United States learned that Russia had secretly installed missiles and missile bases in Cuba, about 90 miles from Florida. President Kennedy demanded that Russia remove the missiles and bases. He set up a naval "quarantine" of Cuba. Russia tried to bargain, and offered to remove the missiles if the United States would dismantle its military bases in Turkey. The United States refused. After a week of extreme tension, Khrushchev agreed to remove the missiles. See CUBA (History).

Easing Cold War Tensions

After the missile crisis in Cuba, Cold War tensions again eased. In July, 1963, the United States, Russia, and Great Britain approved a treaty to stop the testing of nuclear weapons in the atmosphere, in outer space,

---

★ 1966	★ 1966	★ 1967	★ 1968
France Withdraws Troops from NATO	China Accuses Russia of Betrayal	Johnson and Kosygin Meet in Glassboro, N.J.	Warsaw Pact Troops Invade Czechoslovakia

President Lyndon B. Johnson, *right,* and Russian Premier Aleksei N. Kosygin conferred in Glassboro, N.J., in 1967.

Pictorial Parade

Warsaw Pact Troops invaded Czechoslovakia in 1968 and stopped a government move to give the Czechs more freedom.

Keystone

and under water. In August, the United States and Russia set up a *hot line* between the White House and the Kremlin. This direct emergency communications link was installed to reduce the risk that a nuclear war might start by accident. In October, 1963, the UN unanimously adopted a resolution forbidding the use of nuclear weapons in outer space.

Direct relations between Russia and the United States also improved. In 1963, Russia faced a serious shortage of grain. Kennedy approved a plan to sell the Russians $250 million worth of American wheat. That same year, the two nations agreed to cooperate in space projects using weather and communications satellites.

President Lyndon B. Johnson, who became Chief Executive after Kennedy was assassinated in November, 1963, continued to work for peaceful coexistence. In April, 1964, Johnson and Khrushchev each revealed plans to cut down the production of materials used to make nuclear weapons. At the same time, Great Britain announced that it would stop making military plutonium, a radioactive element.

In June, 1964, the United States and Russia signed their first *bilateral* (two-nation) treaty. It provided that a *consul* (representative) of each nation would have an office in a city of the other country. The treaty also provided protection for Americans traveling in Russia, and for Russians traveling in the United States. The U.S. Senate approved the treaty in March, 1967, and Russia approved it in May, 1968. Also in 1964, Russia and the United States extended for two years an agreement providing for educational, scientific, and cultural exchanges. This agreement was renewed again in 1966 and in 1968.

The Shifting Cold War Battleground

The character of the Cold War changed again in the mid-1960's. The United States and Russia each had enough nuclear weapons to wipe out the entire world. Each had an antimissile defense system. In November, 1967, Russia was reported to have completed an orbital nuclear bomb system, which could penetrate U.S. antimissile defenses. But both powers realized that there would be no victor in an all-out nuclear war. At the same time, conflicts within both the Communist and Free World blocs changed the two-sided nature of the balance of power.

The Great Blocs Split. Following Russia's de-Stalinization campaign, the Soviet Union and Communist China began to move along different paths. Disagreements within the Communist bloc became more and more apparent during the 1960's. In 1960, at the third Congress of the Romanian Communist Party, the Russians and Chinese quarreled bitterly and openly. Russia soon cut off technical aid to China. When China attacked India in 1962, Russia supported India. Russia again backed India when Pakistan and India fought in 1965. China threatened India and aided Pakistan.

After Khrushchev fell from power in October, 1964, Russia's new leaders tried to heal the split with China. But Premier Aleksei N. Kosygin and General Secretary Leonid I. Brezhnev were unable to reunite the Communist bloc.

In 1966, China launched a "cultural revolution."

One aim of this revolution was to eliminate all Russian influence from China. The Chinese accused the Russians of betraying world Communism and being secret allies of the United States. Youthful Chinese called "Red Guards" rioted in the streets of major Chinese cities. They attacked the "enemies" of Mao Tse-tung, including all those believed to support the Soviet Union. China became a nuclear power when it exploded a hydrogen bomb in June, 1967, less than three years after its first atomic bomb test.

In March, 1969, Russian and Chinese troops began to fight each other on an island in the frozen Ussuri River. This river is the border between Chinese Manchuria and Russia's maritime territories. Both countries claimed they owned the island.

Some of Russia's satellites also shifted their loyalty. Albania had sided with China in 1961, and neither China nor Albania attended the 23rd Communist Party Congress in Moscow in 1965. Yugoslavia remained independent, with its own brand of "national Communism." Many other Communist countries, including Romania, Poland, and Cuba, loosened their ties with the Soviet Union.

Differences also sharpened among the Western nations. President Charles de Gaulle of France challenged the leadership of the United States and Great Britain. France established diplomatic relations with China in 1964, and sharply criticized U.S. policy in the Vietnam War. At De Gaulle's request, NATO moved its military headquarters from France in 1967, and the French withdrew their troops from the alliance. France also blocked Great Britain's entry into the European Economic Community (EEC), and refused to sign the nuclear test ban treaty.

In 1967, De Gaulle further strengthened France's relations with Russia and the nations of Eastern Europe. In June of that year, France sided with the Arabs against Israel in the brief Arab-Israeli War. In July, he called for independence for the Canadian province of Quebec. In August, 1968, the French exploded a hydrogen bomb.

The Growing Strength of Europe was another factor in the changing nature of the Cold War. More than 20 years after the end of World War II, the nations of Western Europe were enjoying prosperity. The EEC, also called the European Common Market, had become a powerful economic force. Leaders of the Western European nations were gradually increasing trade with Eastern European countries and Russia. Many Western European leaders were more worried about Germany's return to power than about Russia. The increasingly independent Eastern European states also worked for stronger trade relations with Western Europe.

Soviet-American Relations in the 1960's reflected the changing nature of the Cold War. On Nov. 4, 1966, Russia and the United States agreed to permit direct air service between Moscow and New York City. By January, 1967, they and 60 other nations had signed the first international treaty providing for the peaceful exploration and use of outer space. In August, 1967, the two powers submitted identical proposals for a treaty to prevent the spread of nuclear arms. Neither proposal provided for international inspection and controls. But in January, 1968, the United States and Russia reached agreement in the United Nations on such a provision. France refused to sign the treaty. The U.S. Senate approved the treaty in March, 1969. The treaty will go into effect when it has been *ratified* (formally approved) by the United States, Russia, Great Britain, and 40 other nations.

President Johnson and Premier Kosygin met for the first time in June, 1967. Kosygin went to the United States to address the UN General Assembly. The two leaders met in Glassboro, N.J., and discussed the Vietnam War, the Arab-Israeli dispute, and disarmament. Johnson and Kosygin reached no agreements, but they established cordial personal relations.

The Invasion of Czechoslovakia. Hopes for further easing of Cold War tensions in Europe were jolted in August, 1968, when Soviet, Bulgarian, East German, Hungarian, and Polish troops invaded Czechoslovakia. The invasion by these Warsaw Pact forces halted a move by the Czech government to give more individual freedom to the Czech people. Czechoslovak Communist Party leaders met with Soviet officials in Moscow. They then announced agreement on measures to "normalize the situation" in Czechoslovakia. In October, 1968, Czechoslovakia and Russia signed a treaty allowing Soviet troops to remain in Czechoslovakia. The agreements assured that Czechoslovakia would remain a Russian satellite. The invasion of Czechoslovakia caused the interruption of several cultural exchange programs between the West and the invading nations.

The Battle for the Neutral Nations continued in the 1960's, despite shifting power balances.

In Latin America, the United States still guarded

Crewmen of the U.S.S. *Pueblo* were freed in December, 1968, 11 months after the North Koreans captured the spy ship.

United Press Int.

against Communist aggression. In April and May, 1965, the United States, at the request of the Dominican Republic, sent troops to the Dominican Republic to prevent a Communist takeover during a revolt there. The crisis eased, and the troops were withdrawn.

In the Middle East, war broke out between Israel and the Arab powers in June, 1967. The United States supported the Israelis, and the Russians backed the Arabs. Russia helped arm the Arabs before the war began, but this aid did not prevent their defeat. During the six-day war, the United States and Russia used the hot line to prevent expansion of the fighting.

In Africa, most of the newly independent nations maintained their neutrality and took aid from all the major Cold War powers. No African country had a Communist government. After the fall of Ghana's president, Kwame Nkrumah, in February, 1966, Ghana expelled Russian scientific advisers, fearing Communist control. China also withdrew its advisers from Ghana.

The Vietnam War threatened to turn the Cold War into a general hot war. During the early 1960's, the United States stepped up its support of South Vietnam against the Communist Viet Cong forces. The United States blamed the struggle on Communist North Vietnam, viewing the war as "aggression from the north."

In August, 1964, North Vietnamese torpedo boats fired on two U.S. destroyers patrolling in the Gulf of Tonkin. The United States then began to bomb North Vietnam. Congress gave President Johnson broad powers to act to protect United States troops and security. North Vietnam then sent additional aid, including troops, to the Viet Cong. The United States gradually *escalated* (increased) its military effort, and by 1968, more than half a million American troops were in Vietnam. The Viet Cong and North Vietnamese received some support from Russia and China.

In late March, 1968, President Johnson announced that he had ordered a decrease in the bombing of North Vietnam. Johnson hoped this action would lead to serious peace talks. A little more than a month later, the President announced that the United States and North Vietnam had agreed on formal talks in Paris. Discussions began on May 13. In November, Johnson ended the bombing of North Vietnam. North Vietnam then said it was ready for more serious talks. South Vietnam declared that it would not deal with the Viet Cong, but a South Vietnamese delegation finally arrived in Paris in early December, 1968.

Early in 1969, American officials hinted that more progress toward peace was being made in secret sessions than in the formal talks. They would not reveal when or where the secret negotiations were being conducted. At the same time, both sides suffered heavy losses in South Vietnam as the fighting continued. See VIETNAM WAR.

Unrest in Southeast Asia. Incidents that reflected the Vietnam War took place in several other countries of Southeast Asia.

Malaysia, in 1964 and 1965, had been the target of an attempted invasion by guerrilla fighters from Indonesia. President Sukarno of Indonesia became increasingly hostile to the West. But Sukarno lost control of Indonesia in 1966. The country then became friendlier to the West and ended its quarrel with Malaysia.

Cambodia, on the border of Vietnam, struggled to remain neutral. Cambodia broke relations with the United States in 1965. North Vietnamese guerrillas constantly crossed Cambodia's borders and used Cambodian territory as a base for raids into South Vietnam. American and South Vietnamese troops crossed into Cambodia when chasing the Communists.

Laos also struggled for neutrality. In July, 1962, 14 nations, including the United States and Russia, had signed an agreement guaranteeing neutrality for war-torn Laos. In 1968, Communist guerrillas held about 40 per cent of Laos and warred against the central government. They were aided by North Vietnam.

Thailand openly supported the West in the war in Vietnam. In 1967, Thailand revealed that the United States was using bases there for bombing attacks on North Vietnam.

North Korea intensified border warfare against South Korea in 1967. In January, 1968, North Korea seized a United States spy ship, the U.S.S. *Pueblo*, and imprisoned its 82 surviving men. One had been killed during the seizure. The North Koreans freed the men in December, 1968.

Four months later, in April, 1969, North Korean jet fighters shot down a U.S. spy plane 90 miles off the coast of North Korea. All 31 crewmen were killed. President Richard M. Nixon declared that the United States would continue the flights, and that the planes would be protected.   CAROL L. THOMPSON

Related Articles in WORLD BOOK include:

WESTERN LEADERS

Adenauer, Konrad	Hammarskjöld, Dag
Attlee, Clement R.	Johnson, Lyndon B.
Chiang Kai-shek	Kennedy, John F.
Churchill, Sir Winston L. S.	Macmillan, Harold
De Gaulle, Charles A. J. M.	Marshall, George C.
Dulles, John Foster	Nixon, Richard M.
Eden, Anthony	Roosevelt, Franklin D.
Eisenhower, Dwight D.	Truman, Harry S.
Erhard, Ludwig	Wilson, Harold

COMMUNIST LEADERS

Brezhnev, Leonid I.	Kosygin, Aleksei N.
Bulganin, Nikolai A.	Lin Piao
Castro, Fidel	Malenkov, Georgi M.
Gomułka, Władysław	Mao Tse-tung
Ho Chi Minh	Stalin, Joseph
Kadar, Janos	Tito
Khrushchev, Nikita	Ulbricht, Walter

NEUTRAL LEADERS

Gandhi, Indira	Norodom Sihanouk
Nasser, Gamal A.	Nu, U
Nehru (Jawaharlal)	Suharto
Nkrumah, Kwame	Sukarno

CONFERENCES, ORGANIZATIONS, AND TREATIES

ANZUS	Potsdam Conference
Central Treaty Organization	San Francisco Conference
Cominform	Southeast Asia Treaty
Disarmament Agency,	Organization
United States	United Nations
North Atlantic Treaty	Warsaw Pact
Organization	Yalta Conference
Organization of American	
States	

PROGRAMS, STRATEGY, AND WEAPONS

Atomic Bomb	Hot Line	Peace Corps
Berlin Airlift	Intelligence Service	Point Four
Disarmament	International	Program
Foreign Aid	Relations	Rocket
Foreign Policy	Iron Curtain	Sputnik
Guided Missile	Marshall Plan	Spy

OTHER RELATED ARTICLES

Astronaut	Europe (The	Peace
Communism	Cold War)	Quemoy
Democracy	Korean War	Space Travel
Espionage	Neutrality	Vietnam War

Outline

I. **Goals in the Cold War**
　A. The Democracies
　B. The Communist Powers
II. **Weapons of the Cold War**
　A. Military Power　　　D. Political Power
　B. The Power of Ideas　E. Scientific Power
　C. Economic Power
III. **The Coming of the Cold War**
　A. The Alliance Breaks Up
　B. The Iron Curtain Descends
IV. **The West Holds the Line**
　A. The Containment　　D. Communist Expansion
　　　Policy　　　　　　　in Asia
　B. The Berlin Block-　E. The Korean War
　　　ade
　C. The West Rearms
V. **To the Brink and Back**
　A. The Death of Stalin
　B. The Spirit of Geneva
　C. Unrest in Eastern Europe
　D. Trouble at Suez
VI. **New Challenges**
　A. The Missile Gap　　G. Africa
　B. The Eisenhower　　H. The Troika Proposal
　　　Doctrine　　　　　I. The Bay of Pigs
　C. The Far East　　　J. The Berlin Wall
　D. Germany　　　　　K. The Space Race
　E. The Spirit of Camp　　　Begins
　　　David　　　　　　L. The Cuban Missile
　F. The U-2 Incident　　　Crisis
VII. **Easing Cold War Tensions**
VIII. **The Shifting Cold War Battleground**
　A. The Great Blocs Split
　B. The Growing Strength of Europe
　C. Soviet-American Relations
　D. The Invasion of Czechoslovakia
　E. The Battle for the Neutral Nations
　F. The Vietnam War
　G. Unrest in Southeast Asia

Questions

How do the long-term goals of the Communist nations and the democratic nations differ?

Where did U.S. troops fight troops of a major Communist power for the first time?

How did the death of Stalin affect the Cold War?

What was the "spirit of Geneva"? The "spirit of Camp David"?

What is the *Iron Curtain?* The *containment policy?*

How do the Cold War opponents use scientific power as a weapon?

Why did the Russians blockade Berlin in 1948? Why did they build the Berlin wall in 1961?

What was the U-2 incident? How did it affect the Cold War?

How has France challenged the United States and Great Britain for leadership of the West?

How did the attack on two U.S. destroyers in the Gulf of Tonkin affect American policy in Vietnam?

COLDEN, CADWALLADER (1688-1776), was a prominent official in colonial New York and a writer. He served as lieutenant governor of New York colony from 1761 until his death. He was a close friend of Benjamin Franklin, and wrote to scientists in several colonies. Besides books on physics and medicine, he published a history of the Iroquois Indians. Born in Scotland, Colden received a medical degree from the University of Edinburgh. He practiced medicine in Philadelphia for 10 years.   IAN C. C. GRAHAM

COLE, THOMAS (1801-1848), was a leader of the first American group of landscape painters, the Hudson River school. His most notable paintings are the four canvases of *The Voyage of Life* and the five titled *The Course of Empire*, elaborate allegories in romantic realism. Cole was born in Lancashire, England. He went to Philadelphia in 1819, and then to Ohio as a traveling portrait painter. In 1823, Cole re-

Culver

Thomas Cole

Courtesy of the Metropolitan Museum of Art, Gift of Mrs. Russell Sage, 1908

Thomas Cole's *The Oxbow* captured the beauty of American landscape. Cole pioneered the Hudson River school of American art.

turned to Philadelphia to study at the Pennsylvania Academy. He went to Europe in 1829 and again in 1841. Many scenes in his paintings came from his European studies.   EDWIN L. FULWIDER

COLE, TIMOTHY (1852-1931), an American wood engraver, reproduced the effects of painting better than anyone of his time. Born in London, he came to America with his parents as a child and studied in Chicago. In the 1870's, he moved to New York City, where he engraved illustrations for *Scribner's Magazine*. *Abraham Lincoln* (1928) is one of the best-known engravings made by Cole.   S. W. HAYTER

COLEOPTERA, the largest order of insects, contains more than 280,000 species. Members of this order include the beetles, weevils, and fireflies. See BEETLE with its list of Related Articles; FIREFLY; WEEVIL; INSECT.

COLERIDGE, SAMUEL TAYLOR (1772-1834), was a poet and philosopher-critic of the English romantic movement. His major poems are among the most original in English. His poem "The Rime of the Ancient Mariner" is one of the greatest in English literature. His literary criticism has influenced nearly all later critics.

His Life. Coleridge was born in Devonshire, the youngest of about 14 children of a clergyman. He studied at Cambridge University, where he met Robert Southey in 1794. The two young poets favored the principles of the French Revolution and planned to found a *pantisocracy* (a utopian society) in America. They also collaborated in 1794 on a drama opposing monarchy.

In 1795, Coleridge met William Wordsworth, and they became intimate friends. Together they published *Lyrical Ballads* (1798), which contains the first version of "The Rime of the Ancient Mariner." In 1798, Coleridge received an *annuity* (regular income) from the brothers Josiah and Thomas Wedgwood which enabled him to travel to Germany. There he absorbed ideas from German philosophers which influenced his own literary theories. On his return to England, Coleridge translated two plays by the German author Friedrich Schiller.

Detail of oil painting by Washington Allston, National Portrait Gallery, London

Samuel Taylor Coleridge

About 1800, Coleridge's health began to fail seriously. He had begun taking opium to relieve the pain of rheumatism. His marriage, never happy, also caused him increasing distress after he fell in love with Wordsworth's sister-in-law, Sara Hutchinson. Coleridge sought relief from his suffering in drugs and travel. He delivered a series of lectures in London on the principles of poetry. He then founded a short-lived periodical, *The Friend*. In 1813, he delivered another important series of lectures and successfully produced his play *Remorse* with the aid of Lord Byron. Coleridge spent his last years under a doctor's care, largely to control his addiction to opium.

His Writing. Coleridge's other famous poems are "Kubla Khan" and "Christabel." Coleridge said, possibly incorrectly, that "Kubla Khan" was inspired by an opium dream. "Christabel" is an unfinished narrative of medieval times. Each of the poems deals with the visionary and the supernatural. Each combines dreamlike vividness of imagery with a richness of literary references and intricate symbolism.

Coleridge blended keen psychological insights with precise pictures of natural scenes in his meditative lyrics, notably "Frost at Midnight," "This Lime Tree Bower My Prison," and "Dejection: An Ode."

In his literary criticism, Coleridge established the principle that a good poem is an organic, not a mechanical, unity. Therefore, a poem cannot be *paraphrased* (expressed in other words). He emphasized that poetry is creative or expressive, rather than imitative, and insisted that imagination, rather than reason, is the foundation of the fine arts.

Coleridge's best-known work of criticism, *Biographia*

Literaria (1817), contains valuable analyses of Wordsworth's poetry. Many of Coleridge's shrewdest critical comments appear in his notebooks, lectures, journalistic essays, and marginal comments on other writers' works. Coleridge was a devout man, and he wrote and talked much about religion, morality, and theology. His ideas on these topics influenced religious thought throughout the 1800's.   KARL KROEBER

COLETTE (1873-1954) was a French author who became admired in her old age as an outstanding French literary stylist. She did not try to put intellectual content into her books or to depict the world of men. She is supreme as a portrayer of girls and of women fond of love. Among her best books are *Chéri* (1920), *Le Blé en Herbe* (1923), *La Naissance du Jour* (1928), and *Gigi* (1944), which was made into a successful motion picture. Colette was born GABRIELLE SIDONIE COLETTE in St.-Sauveur-en-Puisaye. Between 1904 and 1916, she published under the pen name of *Colette Willy*. Later, she used the name *Colette* alone.   HENRI PEYRE

COLEUS is a large group of showy foliage plants, native to the African and Indian tropics. Coleuses grow 2 to 3 feet high and are valued for many-colored leaves.

Scientific Classification. The coleus belongs to the mint family, *Labiatae*. It forms the genus *Coleus*.

COLFAX, SCHUYLER (1823-1885), served as Vice-President of the United States from 1869 to 1873, during the first term of President Ulysses S. Grant. He also was an active leader of the Whig and Republican parties and a prominent member of Congress.

Colfax was elected to the United States House of Representatives in 1855, and remained there for 14 years. He joined the new Republican Party and became Speaker of the House in 1863. Colfax held the post until he was inaugurated Vice-President.

Schuyler Colfax

U&U

Colfax was born in New York City, but moved to South Bend, Ind., in 1836. He served there as deputy county auditor, and also published a newspaper in South Bend.   IRVING G. WILLIAMS

See also CREDIT MOBILIER OF AMERICA.

COLGATE UNIVERSITY is a private, nonsectarian, liberal arts college for men in Hamilton, N.Y. It was founded by Baptists in 1819 as a theological institution. All students take a special sequence of courses in general liberal arts as well as more specialized work. There are also many opportunities for independent study. Special study groups spend a semester each year studying the structure and problems of government in Washington, D.C., London, Buenos Aires, and other capitals. For enrollment, see UNIVERSITIES AND COLLEGES (table).   VINCENT M. BARNETT

COLIC, *KAHL ihk*, is a severe cramping pain in some abdominal organ. It frequently occurs in babies when indigestion and constipation cause gas to form in the intestines. The gas or an undigested particle of food irritates the intestine and produces a spasm. The gas and spasm are responsible for the pain. Lead and arsenic poisoning, blood diseases, stones in the gall bladder or kidneys, strangulation of the bowel, intestinal worms, and appendicitis also cause colic. Treatment depends on the cause. Relief is often obtained for a baby by holding him head up, and gently patting his back to help him expel the gas. Warm applications, light massage to the abdomen, enemas, or antispasmodic drugs also help in treating colic.   HYMAN S. RUBINSTEIN

COLIGNY, *koh LEE NYEE,* **GASPARD DE** (1519-1572), was one of the ablest French statesmen during the troubled period of religious wars. He was born in Châtillon-sur-Loing. A member of a great noble family, he became a Protestant and assumed a commanding position among the Huguenots. Although he had the title of "Admiral of France," his reputation as a fighting man resulted chiefly from land battles. His influence with the young King Charles IX aroused the fear of the Duc de Guise and Catherine de Médicis. They caused the massacre of the Huguenots on St. Bartholomew's Day. Coligny was the first to be killed.   WILLIAM C. BARK

See also CATHERINE DE MÉDICIS; HUGUENOTS.

COLIMA, *koh LEE mah,* is a small Mexican state. It has a population of 223,610 and an area of 2,106 square miles. Colima lies west of Mexico City, between the Pacific Ocean and the Sierra Madre mountains. For location, see MEXICO (political map).

A low coastal plain covers most of the state. Sandy beaches lie along the coast. Farmers in Colima grow corn, rice, sugar cane, and citrus fruits. Ranchers raise sheep, goats, and horses. The state was named for its capital, which was founded in 1522. Colima became a state in 1857.   CHARLES C. CUMBERLAND

COLINES, SIMON DE. See BOOK (Printed Books).

COLISEUM, an alternate spelling. See COLOSSEUM.

COLITIS, *koh LIE tihs,* is a disease involving inflammation of the colon or other parts of the large intestine. There are several different kinds of colitis. *Ulcerative colitis* may follow attacks of amebic or bacillary dysentery. But in many cases, doctors do not know the cause of the illness. Persons with ulcerative colitis may have rectal bleeding, diarrhea, cramping abdominal pain, fever, and loss of appetite. Ulcers form in the intestine. Surgical treatment may be required, depending on the severity of the condition. Doctors believe that when this type of colitis continues for a long time, the patient may become more susceptible to cancer of the colon than he otherwise would be.

Other kinds of colitis are *mucous colitis* and the *irritable bowel syndrome*, or *spastic colon*. These result from disturbances of the normal function of the colon. Persons with these conditions have severe diarrhea with the passage of mucus. A doctor should be consulted when any of these conditions occur.   E. CLINTON TEXTER, JR.

See also COLON; DIARRHEA; DYSENTERY.

COLLAGE, *kuh LAHZH,* is a picture or design made partly or entirely with pieces of paper, cloth, or other textured and figured materials attached to canvas or other backgrounds. This art technique first became popular in Paris early in the 1900's. Painters associated with the Cubist movement, such as Georges Braque, Pablo Picasso, and Juan Gris, created collages. Other artists later made use of the collage, and it has achieved

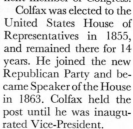

A Tiny Collage of cut paper wrappers, announcements, and tickets was composed by the German artist, Kurt Schwitters.

some recognition as a creative arts medium. Early examples of collages deteriorated rapidly because they employed newspaper and other fragile materials. Artists now give more attention to the durability of the materials. Earlier collages are rather stark in treatment. Recent ones try to create more appealing textural, spatial, and color relationships. RALPH MAYER

COLLAGEN DISEASES. See RHEUMATISM.

COLLAMER, JACOB (1791-1865), an American statesman, was Postmaster General for one year under President Zachary Taylor. He also served in the United States House of Representatives from 1843 to 1849 and in the United States Senate from 1855 until his death. Collamer, a Republican, was born in Troy, N.Y. He was graduated from the University of Vermont in 1810, and served in the Vermont legislature. ARTHUR A. EKIRCH, JR.

COLLARBONE is a long, slender, curved bone that connects the breastbone with a hooklike projection on

Collarbone, or Clavicle, Forms Part of the Shoulder.

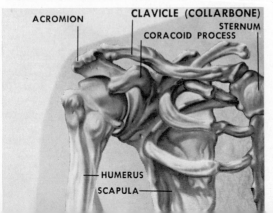

ACROMION
CLAVICLE (COLLARBONE)
STERNUM
CORACOID PROCESS
HUMERUS
SCAPULA

the shoulder blade. The technical name for the collarbone is *clavicle*. The breastbone is properly called the *sternum*, the hooklike projection, *acromion*, and the shoulder blade, *scapula*.

Man has two collarbones, one directly in from each shoulder. The bones are shaped somewhat like the italic letter *f*. Collarbones hold the arms in proper position at the sides of the body. When a person breaks a collarbone, his shoulder drops downward and forward toward the chest. Most broken collarbones are caused by falling on outstretched arms. A hard blow on the shoulder may dislocate the outer end of a collarbone.

Animals that walk on four legs, such as dogs, have no collarbones. Those that hang from trees, such as apes, have large collarbones. MARSHALL R. URIST

See also HUMAN BODY (Trans-Vision three-dimensional color picture).

COLLARDS, *KAHL erdz*, are the leaves of the collard plant, a vegetable related to the cabbage. The collard resembles kale, and can grow in warmer climates than ordinary kale (see KALE). It is usually grown in the southern United States. The collard plant may grow to a height of 2 to 4 feet. In warm climates, the seeds may be planted in September and the leaves picked the following spring and summer. Seeds may also be planted in summer and the leaves picked the following winter. Collards are cooked and eaten in the same way as spinach. The leaves of the plant may also be mixed in a stew or in a salad. Collard leaves provide a rich source of vitamin A.

Scientific Classification. The collard plant belongs to the mustard family, *Cruciferae*. It is classified as genus *Brassica*, species *oleracea*, variety *acephala*. JOHN H. MACGILLIVRAY

COLLATERAL. See BANKS AND BANKING (Terms).

COLLECTING is a popular kind of hobby. A person can choose to collect almost any type of article, and he can continue collecting different examples of this article all his life. Popular objects for collections include autographs, dolls, coins, stamps, and matchbook covers. Glassware, playing cards, post cards, antiques, buttons, china, and firearms also interest many collectors.

Stamp collectors are called *philatelists*. Collectors of rare books are *bibliophiles*, and rare coin collectors are *numismatists*. Other terms used to describe various kinds of collectors include: *antiquary* or *antiquarian* (relics of the past); *autographer* (autographs); *conchologist* (shells); *deltiologist* (post cards); and *phillumenist* (matchbook covers). Persons who collect rocks and minerals for a hobby are sometimes called *rock hounds*.

Collecting as a hobby often teaches the collector a great deal, because it demands a thorough knowledge of the article collected. A collection of costumed dolls, for example, helps the collector learn about the costumes worn in various places and at various periods in history. Some collectors combine two hobbies in one. They may build models from kits, and then collect them in the form of a complete series of model ships or airplanes. JACK WAX

See also HOBBY with its list of Related Articles on Collection Hobbies.

COLLECTIVE BARGAINING. See LABOR (Collective Bargaining).

COLLECTIVE FARM is a government-owned and government-planned farm in Communist countries. The government organizes collective farms to try to increase production and maintain control over the farm workers.

The land and most of the farm equipment belong to the government. The people who work on the farm must pay rent to the government out of the sale of the farm's products. The government determines the variety and quantity of crops to be grown in an area, and each farm has a committee which decides how to meet these goals. A typical collective farm may cover 1,200 acres and be farmed by 80 families. Every farm has a village where each family owns a small cottage, the plot surrounding it, and some livestock. Collective farming began in Russia in the late 1920's. See also the Agriculture sections of the articles on POLAND; RUSSIA; YUGOSLAVIA, and the Economy section of the article on BULGARIA.

COLLECTIVE OWNERSHIP. See SOCIALISM.

COLLECTIVE SECURITY is a principle of international diplomacy used by a group of nations to maintain peace. The principle requires group members to solve international disputes through discussion and to help defend a member state if it is attacked.

During the 1920's and 1930's, the principle was used by the League of Nations to work for peaceful settlement of international problems. Collective security was to replace *balance of power* (even distribution of strength so that one power cannot dominate) and the various alliances European diplomats had used since the late 1400's. Since 1945, the United Nations has tried to act as an agency of collective security, and has settled small disputes. But in many major cases, U.N. collective security has not worked. Instead, nations formed a number of regional agreements such as the North Atlantic Treaty Organization (NATO) and the Warsaw Pact.   ROBERT HUGH FERRELL

See also BALANCE OF POWER.

COLLEGE. See JUNIOR COLLEGE; UNIVERSITIES AND COLLEGES.

COLLEGE BOARDS. See COLLEGE ENTRANCE EXAMINATION.

COLLEGE DEGREE. See DEGREE, COLLEGE.

COLLEGE ENTRANCE EXAMINATION is a test or series of tests that help determine whether or not a person meets the admission requirements of a university or college. Entrance examinations are also useful for placement and guidance. Universities and colleges that use entrance examinations also have other standards for admission. These include satisfactory high school grades and recommendations from teachers, principals, and other persons.

Some universities and colleges give their own entrance examinations or examinations prepared by educational organizations. Many other schools require students to take either the *College Boards*, prepared by the College Entrance Examination Board, or the *ACT battery*, prepared by the American College Testing Program, Inc.

Kinds of College Boards. The College Entrance Examination Board gives two kinds of admissions tests—the Scholastic Aptitude Test (SAT) and the Achievement Tests. The *Scholastic Aptitude Test* is designed to test a student's ability to reason. The *Achievement Tests* are designed to test a student's achievement in such fields as mathematics, languages, and social studies. The College Board also gives a preliminary SAT to high-school juniors to help guide and prepare them for admission into college.

COLLEGE ENTRANCE EXAMINATION

All schools that use the College Boards require the Scholastic Aptitude Test. However, not all schools insist on the Achievement Tests. Schools that do require both tests usually ask prospective students to take three Achievement Tests in addition to the SAT.

The Scholastic Aptitude Test is a three-hour examination. The test consists of multiple-choice questions divided into two main groups—verbal and mathematics. Students may also be required to write an essay, called the *Writing Sample*. The Board does not grade the essay, but sends copies to universities and colleges that request an example of the student's writing ability.

The *verbal* sections place stress on the ability to read with understanding and the ability to understand word relationships. Following are two examples of the many kinds of questions asked in the verbal sections and the choice of answers.

Directions: Each question below consists of a word printed in capital letters, followed by five words lettered A through E. Choose the lettered word which is most nearly *opposite* in meaning to the word in capital letters.

1. UNFIT: (A) tight (B) qualified (C) chosen (D) serene (E) necessary
2. TANGIBLE: (A) radial (B) immaterial (C) minute (D) diffuse (E) unproved

The *mathematics* sections stress the ability to understand concepts and solve problems. Here are two samples of the mathematics problems.

Directions: In this section solve each problem, using the blank space at the right of the page for figuring. (In the actual test, ample space for computation will be allowed in the test book and no other paper will be allowed.) Then indicate the *one* correct answer in the appropriate space on the answer sheet.

1. In North Dakota the temperature has gone as high as 114° and as low as −45°. How many degrees difference is there between these two temperatures? (A) 69 (B) 79 (C) 114 (D) 159 (E) 169
2. A school has 2, 3, or 4 classes each semester in physics, with 20 to 30 students in each class. If 10% of the physics students failed in one semester, what is the greatest number who could have failed? (A) 3 (B) 6 (C) 8 (D) 10 (E) 12

The Achievement Tests are one-hour examinations in fourteen subject areas ranging from physics and mathematics to history and foreign languages. The achievement tests also use multiple-choice questions. These tests are designed to measure a student's knowledge of factual information in a specific subject. They also test his ability to reason with this information in order to solve problems relating to the subject.

The ACT Battery has two parts. The major part consists of four tests, covering (1) English, (2) mathematics, (3) natural sciences, and (4) social studies. The second part of the ACT battery is the Student Profile. The profile is a series of questions about the achievements, goals, and special interests of a student. The ACT battery is used for selection, placement, educational guidance, and scholarship awards. Emphasis is placed on intellectual skills, expression, and reasoning, rather than on detailed information.

Administration and Grading. Both the College Boards and the ACT battery are given five times yearly at several testing centers. Scores are sent to the university or college to which the student is applying and to the student's high school. There are no uniform "passing" or "failing" scores on entrance examinations. A score that disqualifies a person for one college may be high enough for admission to another.

Information on the entrance examinations required by a university or college should be obtained from that school. Information on the College Boards can be obtained from the College Entrance Examination Board, c/o Educational Testing Service, Box 592, Princeton, N.J. 08540; or Box 1025, Berkeley, Calif. 94704. Information on the ACT battery is available from the American College Testing Program, Box 168, Iowa City, Iowa 52240.   CHARLES O. NEIDT

COLLEGE MISERICORDIA. See UNIVERSITIES AND COLLEGES (table).

COLLEGE OF CARDINALS. See SACRED COLLEGE; POPE (The Sacred College); CONCLAVE.

COLLEGES, ASSOCIATION OF AMERICAN, is a national organization established in the United States to promote higher education in all its forms in liberal arts colleges. It was founded in 1915. Headquarters are at 1818 R Street NW, Washington, D.C. 20009.

            Critically reviewed by ASSOCIATION OF AMERICAN COLLEGES

COLLEMBOLA is an order of small insects. Most insects of this order move about by springing on a flexible tube that grows under their abdomen. For this reason, they are called *springtails*. The adult insects often gather in great numbers on the surface of snow and are sometimes called *snow fleas*. Most collembola eat decaying plants. But some kinds, called *garden fleas*, damage young garden plants. See also INSECT (table).

COLLES, ABRAHAM (1773-1843), was an Irish surgeon of the early 1800's. His name is still known in the medical field in connection with a common fracture of the wrist which he described in detail in 1814.

Colles was born near Kilkenny. He received his medical education at the University of Edinburgh. He then went to London, walking the distance of 400 miles in eight days. After spending some time there as an assistant to Sir Astley Cooper, one of the best surgeons of his day, Colles returned to Dublin. In 1804, he became professor of anatomy and surgery at the Irish College of Surgeons, a position he held for 32 years. His ability as a lecturer became well known.   GEORGE ROSEN

COLLIE is a dog first bred in Scotland to take care of sheep. It is one of the most intelligent and handsome of dogs. Its long hair grows thick on top, and soft and furry underneath. Its colors are brown and white, black, white and tan, gray, and all white. The collie has a long, narrow head and ears that stand up straight but droop at the points. Its bushy tail curls up at the tip. The dog is medium large. It is about 22 to 24 inches high at the shoulder, and weighs 50 to 75 pounds. Some have smooth, short coats. It is a helper, guard, and companion in farm work, especially in America.

Collies make excellent pets and companions, and are especially useful for protecting and herding livestock on farms. Some collies, such as the ones featured in the role of "Lassie," have become famous in motion pictures and television.   OLGA DAKAN

See also DOG (color picture: Working Dogs); SHEEP DOG; TERHUNE, ALBERT PAYSON.

COLLIMATOR. See SPECTROSCOPE.

COLLINS, MICHAEL (1930-   ), an American astronaut, was a crewman on the Apollo 11 mission, which made the first manned landing on the moon. Collins piloted the command module, *Columbia*, as it orbited 69 miles above the moon. His fellow astronauts, Neil A. Armstrong and Edwin E. Aldrin, Jr., landed on the moon on July 20, 1969, aboard the lunar module *Eagle*. See SPACE TRAVEL (Reaching the Moon).

Collins was born in Rome, Italy, while his father was stationed there with the U.S. Army. Collins graduated from the U.S. Military Academy in 1952, and was commissioned as an Air Force officer. He became an astronaut in 1963. Collins was the pilot of the Gemini 10 flight, in 1966.   WILLIAM J. CROMIE

See also ASTRONAUT (picture).

COLLINS, WILKIE (1824-1889), an English author, was one of the most successful writers of detective fiction in the 1800's. *The Woman in White* (1860) and *The Moonstone* (1868) are his best and most popular novels.

Some critics rank *The Moonstone* among the world's outstanding detective stories. Sergeant Cuff, a character in the novel, was one of the first detectives in English fiction. The book is about a diamond called the moonstone which is stolen from the forehead of an image of the moon-god of India. A curse, and sometimes murder, follows the diamond until it is returned.

WILLIAM WILKIE COLLINS was born in London. He became a lawyer in 1851, but never practiced law. However, he used his knowledge of law in writing his books. Collins gained his first literary success with *Antonina* (1850), a historical novel set in ancient Rome. In 1851, he met Charles Dickens and the two became close friends. Collins' first important mystery novel, *The Dead Secret* (1857), appeared in Dickens' magazine *Household Words*.   PHILIP DURHAM

National Portrait Gallery, London, Painting by Rudolph Lehmann

Wilkie Collins

COLLIP, JAMES BERTRAM. See BANTING, SIR FREDERICK GRANT.

COLLISION INSURANCE. See INSURANCE (Automobile).

COLLODI, CARLO (1826-1890), was the pen name of a writer and soldier, CARLO LORENZINI. His fame rests on *The Adventures of Pinocchio* (1883), a book he wrote for children. Pinocchio is a little wooden boy-puppet who wants to become a real boy. The story has been translated into several languages and made into a motion picture. Lorenzini was born in Florence, Italy. He fought for the independence of Italy from Austria. He also founded two humorous newspapers and wrote several novels.   F. J. CROWLEY

COLLODION, *kuh LO dih un*, is a heavy, colorless, clear liquid. Collodion consists of pyroxylin, or cellulose nitrate, which is dissolved in ether and alcohol. It is used for covering burns and wounds. Painted on the skin, it dries rapidly and forms a thin protective covering. Collodion is also used to make airtight seals, and to make filters in the study of viruses.

COLLODION COTTON. See GUNCOTTON.

COLLOID, *KAHL oid*, was a term originally applied only to gluelike substances, such as gelatin. These substances, when mixed with a liquid, pass through animal and vegetable membranes very slowly or not at all. This peculiarity of gelatinous substances was discovered by a Scottish chemist, Thomas Graham, in 1861. Graham noticed that substances in solution that readily pass through membranes, such as salt and sugar, usually crystallize, or form crystals, well. He suggested the division of all substances into two classes—*colloids* and *crystalloids*. Modern scientists prefer to speak of matter as being in the colloidal or crystalloidal state, since many substances can exist in both forms. The name colloid is retained, however, for convenience.

The particles in a colloidal state are very tiny. They range in size from about $\frac{1}{1,000,000}$ of a millimeter in diameter upward to about $\frac{100}{1,000,000}$ of a millimeter (a millimeter is about $\frac{1}{25}$ of an inch).

Colloidal particles give a substance several characteristic properties. The particles tend to remain in suspension and in constant motion. They carry an electrical charge, some particles being positive and others negative. The Cottrell method of smoke prevention, by use of electrically charged electrodes in chimneys, depends upon this property. Colloidal particles provide extensive surface for the adsorption of gases (see ABSORPTION AND ADSORPTION). Colloidal particles often provide color, such as the beautiful colors of sunsets. This characteristic of colloids is used to give color to glass and ceramics. Colloids also act as stabilizing agents that make emulsions possible (see EMULSION). Certain substances, known as *emulsifying agents*, form films of colloidal thickness about other substances. For example, milk is essentially an emulsion of butterfat in water with casein as an emulsifying agent. Colloids also have a part in the formation of *gels* (jellies). For example, pectin, found especially in unripe fruit, is commonly used to aid in producing fruit jellies through the formation of films about tiny drops of liquid.

Protoplasm, the life substance of cells, is a complex system of colloids (see PROTOPLASM). The body substances that digest food are also colloidal in nature.

See also LATEX.

COLLOQUIALISM. See LANGUAGE (table: Terms).

COLLOTYPE PRINTING. See PRINTING (Other Printing Processes).

COLLUSION is a secret arrangement between two or more persons to obtain something illegally. They may make an agreement to defraud, or cheat, a third person, or to obtain something to which they are not legally entitled from a court.

For example, a husband and wife may use collusion in obtaining a divorce. If the wife makes a false charge of cruelty and the husband falsely admits it, then they are both guilty of collusion. Usually collusion is not considered a crime in itself, but it may form the basis for some other offense. For example, it might form the basis for a perjury offense (see PERJURY).   FRED E. INBAU

COLOGNE, a toilet water. See COLOGNE; PERFUME.

COLOGNE (pop. 854,462; alt. 174 ft.) is a Rhine River port and industrial and trade center in western West Germany. For location, see GERMANY (political map). Its German name is KÖLN. Cologne became important early in the Middle Ages, when most people traveling north from Italy followed the Rhine route.

The Spires of the Magnificent Cologne Cathedral stand about 525 feet high. The Cathedral Bridge, *right*, crosses the Rhine River and leads to the Cologne suburb of Deutz.

Since the early 1800's, Cologne has been an important market place for western Germany. It is also an important governmental administrative center.

Cologne lies in a half-circle on the curving west bank of the Rhine. Across the river, Cologne's suburb of Deutz looks back at the ancient city. The old buildings and narrow streets of ancient Cologne formed a center around which the present city grew. Cologne spread so rapidly that in 1885 the old Roman walls were torn down to make space for more housing. A circle of boulevards, called the *Ringstrassen*, replaced the old walls.

The factories of Cologne produce textiles, sugar, tobacco, glue, chemical products, railroad cars, and diesel engines. The city's best-known product is a toilet water called *Eau de Cologne*, which has been made there for more than 200 years.

In ancient days, the town of Cologne belonged to the Teutonic tribe of Ubii. It became a Roman colony by A.D. 50 and was named Colonia Agrippina, after the wife of the Roman emperor Claudius (see AGRIPPINA THE YOUNGER). Its name was changed to Colonia, and later to Cologne and Köln. In the 1200's, Cologne became a free city of the Holy Roman Empire, with rights of self-government. It was one of the most powerful towns in the Hanseatic League (see HANSEATIC LEAGUE). At the beginning of the 1500's, new trade routes opened and Cologne lost its importance. During the 1800's, it developed into a manufacturing and shipping center. Construction of the Cologne Cathedral started during the 1200's, but the building was not completed until 1880, more than 600 years later.

During World War II, Allied bombers destroyed much of Cologne. The famous Cathedral was damaged, but escaped destruction. For several years after the war ended in 1945, the city was under British occupation. In 1949, Konrad Adenauer, a former mayor of Cologne (1917-1933), became chancellor of West Germany (see ADENAUER, KONRAD).   JAMES K. POLLOCK

See also RHINE RIVER.

Tom Hollyman, Photo Researchers

Cartagena, Colombia, once a major Spanish stronghold, lies on the Caribbean Sea. Old fortresses, churches, and walled parts of the city show the influence of Spanish occupation.

COLOMBIA, *koh LOM bee uh*, lies in the northwestern corner of South America. Its cool mountains and valleys have fertile soils and precious minerals. Vast pastures, thick forests, and tropical crops cover the hot, low plains. Colombia's natural wealth has attracted men since the days when explorers first touched the Ameri-

---

FACTS IN BRIEF

Form of Government: Republic.

Capital: Bogotá.

Official Language: Spanish.

Divisions: 22 departments, 3 intendancies, 5 commissaries, and 1 special district.

Head of State: President.

Area: 439,737 square miles. *Greatest Distances*—(northwest-southeast) 1,170 miles; (northeast-southwest) 850 miles. *Coastline*—580 miles along the Pacific Ocean; 710 miles along the Caribbean Sea.

Elevation: *Highest*—Cristóbal Colón, 18,947 feet above sea level. *Lowest*—sea level, along the coast.

Population: *1964 Census*—17,484,508; distribution, 53 per cent urban, 47 per cent rural. *Estimated 1970 Population*—21,093,000; density, 48 persons to the square mile. *Estimated 1975 Population*—24,691,000.

Chief Products: *Agriculture*—bananas, cacao, coffee, corn, manioc, potatoes, rice, sugar cane, wheat. *Mining*—coal, emeralds, gold, petroleum, platinum, salt, silver. *Manufacturing*—beverages, cement, chemicals, leather, steel, sugar, textiles, tobacco.

Flag: The flag has a yellow horizontal stripe above narrower blue and red stripes. Yellow is for independence, wealth, and justice; blue for loyalty, vigilance, and nobility; red for courage, honor, and generosity. See FLAG (picture: Flags of the Americas).

National Holiday: Independence Day, July 20.

National Anthem: "El Himno Nacional."

Money: *Basic Unit*—peso. See MONEY (table: Values).

can continent. At that time, they searched for the fabled treasures of El Dorado, the Indian chieftain who clothed himself in powdered gold. The searching parties started from the Caribbean seaport of Santa Marta, which was established in 1525 and is the oldest permanent settlement in South America. Today, the nation's wealth comes from such products as coffee and oil. Bogotá is the capital and largest city of Colombia.

The country was named for Christopher Columbus, although the Spanish explorer Alonso de Ojeda discovered it in 1499. Columbus came near Colombia in 1502, when he sailed along the Panama coast during his last voyage to America. The name of the country in Spanish, the official language, is RE-

Colombia lies in northwestern South America. The country covers about one-eighth the area of the United States.

1 INCH = 1,200 MILES

PÚBLICA DE COLOMBIA (REPUBLIC OF COLOMBIA).

For the relationship of Colombia to other American nations, see LATIN AMERICA; ORGANIZATION OF AMERICAN STATES; PAN AMERICAN UNION.

The Land and Its Resources

Location and Size. Colombia is the only South American country that faces both the Caribbean Sea and the Pacific Ocean. The Caribbean borders Colombia to the north for 710 miles. The Pacific borders it on the west for 580 miles. The *Color Map* shows that Venezuela borders Colombia on the northeast. Brazil borders the southeast. Peru and Ecuador lie to the south. The Isthmus of Panama forms part of the northwest border. Three islands in the Pacific and five in the Caribbean are part of Colombia. Colombia is the fourth largest country in South America.

Land Regions include mountains, coastal lowlands, and interior plains.

Mountains. The Andes Mountains enter Colombia at the country's southwest edge and fan into three distinct ranges. These ranges run through Colombia from southwest to northeast, in the same general direction as the coastline. The westernmost range is the Cordillera Occidental; the middle one, the Cordillera Central; and the eastern, or inland, range is the Cordillera Oriental. The Sierra Nevada de Santa Marta, a range separate from the Andes, rises in northeastern Colombia. There, snow-covered Cristóbal Colón, the country's highest peak, towers 18,947 feet above sea level. Deep valleys and basins lie between the rugged mountain ranges.

Coastal Lowlands extend along the shores of the Pacific Ocean and Caribbean Sea. The Pacific lowlands consist mostly of swamps and jungles. Few people live in this area. The Caribbean lowlands are fertile. Farmers

Robert C. West, the contributor of this article, is Professor of Geography and Anthropology at Louisiana State University. He wrote Pacific Lowlands of Colombia.

there cultivate many tropical crops, and large herds of cattle graze in the grassy areas.

Interior Plains. The eastern three-fifths of Colombia is a vast plain, almost at sea level. Jungle covers the southern part. There, half-civilized Indians live in isolated villages. The northern part of the great plain is called the *llanos*, and is covered by grass and scattered trees. See LLANOS.

Rivers. The Magdalena, Colombia's chief river, rises at a junction of the Cordilleras Central and Oriental. It flows northward to the Caribbean. River freighters and passenger ships can sail up about 700 miles of its 950-mile winding course. Other navigable rivers include the Atrato, Caquetá, Cauca, and Meta.

Natural Resources. Pools of petroleum lie underground in northern Colombia, near Barrancabermeja. Antioquia Department has gold and silver reserves. The only platinum mined in South America comes mainly from Chocó Department. Mines near the cities of Muzo and Chivor yield emeralds. Coal, iron ore, and limestone occur throughout several departments.

Climate in Colombia depends largely on altitude, and varies from extreme tropical heat to damp, biting cold. The Pacific lowlands are hot and muggy, and the Caribbean lowlands have hot but drier weather.

As the land slopes up into the foothills, the temperature stays hot and the rainfall becomes heavy. Low mountain ranges up to 3,000 feet have a year-round temperature of between 75°F. and 80°F. The high plateaus have frequent but light rains. There, the temperature hovers around 60°F.

Average January temperatures range from 58°F. in Bogotá to about 82°F. at Barranquilla. July temperatures average from about 57°F. at Bogotá to 84°F. at Barranquilla.

The jungle forests have heavy rains throughout the year. Colombia's swampy Pacific coast is the rainiest place in all the Americas. Each year, a small area along

Guajira Indian Women sew up large sacks of pure salt gathered on the northern coast of Colombia. Once each year, thousands of Indian families come to the coast to harvest tons of salt that have been evaporating for 10 months under the hot tropical sun.

Hamilton Wright

the Atrato River receives more than 350 inches of rain.

Life of the People

The People. Most of the people live in the green valleys and basins of western Colombia. This area makes up about two-fifths of the land. The vast eastern plains of Colombia average about one person to the square mile.

About 40 of every 100 Colombians are *mestizos* (persons of mixed white and Indian descent). About 30 of every 100 are whites, mostly of Spanish descent; about 15, mulattoes; 7, Indians; and 5, Negroes. Most Colombians belong to the Roman Catholic Church.

Cities. The leading cities of Colombia were among the first in the Western Hemisphere to be settled. Today, these cities have modern buildings and roads, as well as narrow, cobblestoned streets lined by old houses with carved doorways and brown-tiled roofs.

Bogotá, the capital and largest city, is a center of art and learning, and also has many factories. High in the Andes Mountains, northwest of Bogotá, lies Medellín, the second largest city.

Buenaventura, Colombia's leading port, is on a small island in a bay on the Pacific coast. Three-fourths of the country's coffee exports pass through this port. The ancient walled city of Cartagena, founded by the Spaniards in 1533, also lies on an island, in the Caribbean Sea. The industrial port city of Barranquilla lies on the Caribbean coast. See the separate articles on the Colombian cities that are listed in the *Related Articles* section of this article.

Work of the People

Agriculture is the chief industry in Colombia. But only about 4 per cent of the land is cultivated, and the average farm covers only 5 acres. Even the average coffee plantation in Colombia has only about 3,000 trees.

Indian farmers use primitive methods to grow scanty crops of corn, beans, and manioc, from which a bread

---

COLOMBIA MAP INDEX

*Does not appear on map; key shows general location.
†Does not appear on map; on island group in Caribbean Sea off coast of Nicaragua.

Source: Latest census (1964).

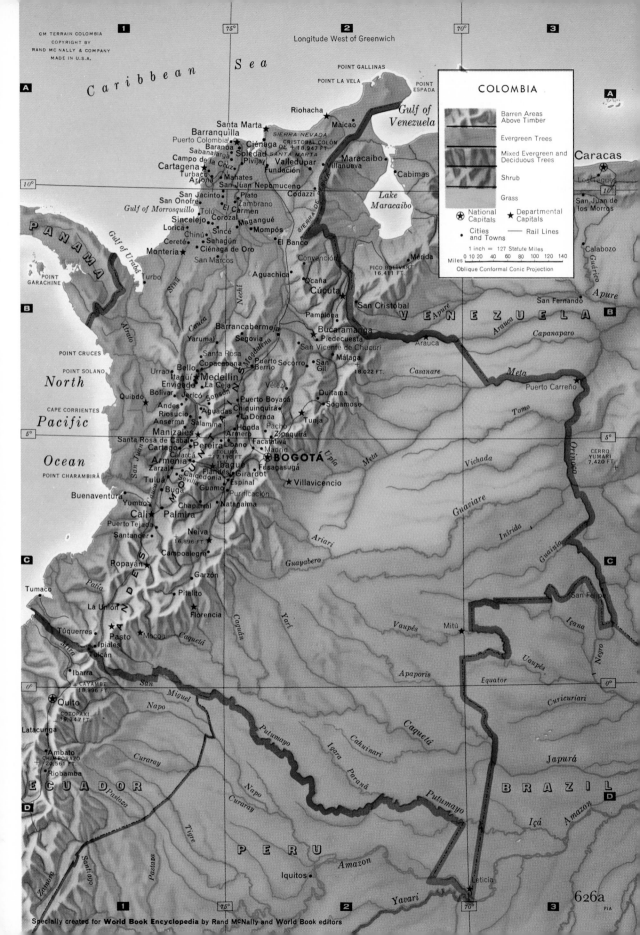

Big Skyscrapers in Cali, Colombia, tower above low, Spanish-style homes with their colorful tile roofs. The city is the main commercial center of the fertile Cauca Valley.

Hamilton Wright

is made. Planters use the latest scientific methods to grow coffee, bananas, rice, and sugar cane. Only Brazil grows more coffee than Colombia. Colombia also ranks high in the production of bananas and cacao beans. Other crops include cotton, fruits, potatoes, tobacco, and wheat. Cattle graze on grass in fertile valley bottoms, on mountain slopes, and on the plains.

Mining. Colombia ranks as one of the leading South American oil-producing countries. Drillers tap most of the oil from three fields—two near the Magdalena River at Barrancabermeja, and one at Catatumbo.

Colombia mines and dredges more gold than any other South American country. Miners take most of the gold from about 630 mines in Antioquia Department. Silver usually occurs with the gold. The area around the Atrato and San Juan rivers in Chocó Department yields platinum. Colombia is the only South American country with platinum deposits. Most of the world's emeralds are mined at Muzo and Chivor. Several departments mine coal, iron, and limestone. A soda plant operates near salt mines at Zipaquirá.

Manufacturing and Processing are not highly developed in Colombia, but they are growing steadily. The country has over 47,000 small manufacturing plants. Cotton and wool textiles are the most important manufactures. The first steel mill in Colombia opened in 1954 in Paz de Río in Boyacá Department. Other factories make processed foods, beverages, shoes, and chemicals.

Forest Industry. Trees cover almost 150 million acres. Valuable timber includes mahogany, dyewoods, cedar, and laurel. Cinchona tree bark yields quinine.

Transportation. About 2,000 miles of narrow-gauge railways and 12,500 miles of roads crisscross Colombia. Mountains have made road and railroad construction difficult. Landslides often destroy roadbeds during rainy periods. In 1961, Colombia completed a 418-mile

rail line, linking Bogotá and Santa Marta. It took nine years to lay the track through swampy rain forests.

Most of Colombia's markets are served by rail or road from the Magdalena River, the most important route for commerce since the early 1500's. This river still carries about 95 per cent of all the river traffic. Chief seaports include Buenaventura and Tumaco on the Pacific Ocean, and Barranquilla, Cartagena, and Santa Marta on the Caribbean Sea.

Communication. Twenty-two daily newspapers are published in Colombia. Bogotá's morning *El Tiempo* has the largest circulation. Colombia has two television stations and about 200 radio stations. The government operates postal, telephone, and telegraph services that reach even the most remote areas.

Education

Primary education in Colombia is free. A 1956 law requires every child over 7 to go to school for at least five years. More than 1,500,000 students attend elementary, high, commercial, and teacher-training schools, and other educational institutions. Teachers travel to isolated regions to teach children who cannot be reached in any other way. In 1947, Father José Salcedo, a Roman Catholic priest, founded a *radio school* in Sutatenza. About 250,000 farm families have learned to read and write by listening to his educational program.

The country has more than 50 institutions of higher learning. The National University at Bogotá, founded in 1572, is the oldest university in the country.

The Arts

Long before the arrival of the white man, the Indians showed a high degree of artistic ability. They used gold and silver in jewelry and in the decoration of

626b

Huge Oil Refineries line the Magdalena River in Barrancabermeja, a major petroleum drilling and refining center in the interior of Colombia. A pipeline carries oil to Cartagena on the Caribbean coast.

masks, ceremonial bowls, and goblets. Ancient ruins reveal beautifully carved stone objects. The conquering Spaniards used these skills in decoration and sculpture, especially in the churches. Modern Colombian art has Indian, Spanish, French, and Mexican influences.

Colombia has made its greatest cultural contributions through its poets, novelists, and journalists. Most of its presidents have been men of literary and journalistic fame. Probably the best-known writer is Jorge Isaacs, whose chief novel, *María*, was published in 1867.

Government

Colombia became a republic under the constitution of 1886, which was revised in 1910, 1936, and 1945. The national government resembles that of the United States. The people elect the president to a four-year term. Every citizen over 21 may vote. The president may serve more than one term, but not consecutively. He appoints 13 ministers to his Cabinet. The people also elect the Congress, consisting of an 80-member Senate, and a House of Representatives of 152 members. Senators serve four-year terms, and representatives hold office for two years. In 1957, Colombians voted to let the Liberal and Conservative parties each control half of the Congress and local legislatures until 1972. Under this system, Liberal and Conservative presidents alternate every four years. Members of other political parties cannot hold office.

Congress elects the vice-president for four years by a majority vote of both houses. A Supreme Court of 20 justices heads the nation's court system. Colombia is divided into 22 departments, 3 intendancies, 5 commissaries, and 1 special district. Each department has an elected assembly and a governor appointed by the president. The president appoints heads of intendancies and commissaries.

Colombia has an army of from 12,000 to 15,000 men, and a navy of about 6,000. A battalion of marines and a small air force also serve the country.

History

Early Days. The Chibcha Indians lived in Colombia before the coming of the white man. They farmed and made pottery. The Chibcha were easily overpowered by Spaniards who explored and settled the country.

The Spanish explorer Alonso de Ojeda discovered Colombia in 1499. The Spaniards named it New Granada, after the home province of Gonzalo Jiménez de Quesada, a Spanish lawyer who defeated the Indians and claimed the country for Spain in 1536. Spain established New Granada as a presidency under the viceroy (governor) of Peru in 1564. In 1740, Spain created the Viceroyalty of New Granada, including present-day Colombia, Venezuela, Ecuador, and Panama.

The New Republic. The people of New Granada made the first move to break free of Spain when new taxation caused an Indian uprising in 1781. Spanish troops quickly put down the rebellion. The New Granada patriot Antonio Nariño and others also rebelled against the harsh rule imposed by Spain. Nariño helped fan the flame of independence when he published a translation of the French book *The Rights of Man* in 1794.

In 1796, the viceroyalty was shaken by a revolt in Venezuela. Uprisings followed throughout New Granada. The Venezuelan patriot Simón Bolívar led the forces that finally overthrew the Spanish government in South America in 1819. That same year, Bolívar set up the Republic of Great Colombia. Panama voluntarily joined the republic in 1821, and Ecuador in 1822. General William Henry Harrison, who later became President of the United States, served as minister to Colombia from 1828 to 1829.

Political Revolts broke out in the new republic, and Venezuela and Ecuador established separate govern-

627

Hamilton Wright

Bunches of Colombian Bananas are washed by plantation workers before they are shipped to markets around the world.

and became president in 1953, was ousted in a short revolution. A group of military officers assumed control of the government. Alberto Lleras Camargo, candidate of the Conservative-Liberal coalition, was elected president in 1958, ending military control. Guillermo Leon Valencia of the Conservative party was elected president in 1962. During the 1960's, Colombia's industrial production declined, and unemployment and prices rose. Riots and strikes broke out in the country, and many persons criticized Leon Valencia's government for failing to ease the economic problems. In 1966, the voters elected Carlos Lleras Restrepo, a Liberal, as president.   ROBERT C. WEST

Related Articles in WORLD BOOK include:

Outline

I. **The Land and Its Resources**
  A. Location and Size C. Rivers   E. Climate
  B. Land Regions   D. Natural
                       Resources

II. **Life of the People**
  A. The People   B. Cities

III. **Work of the People**
  A. Agriculture   D. Forest Industry
  B. Mining   E. Transportation
  C. Manufacturing   F. Communication
     and Processing

IV. **Education**
V. **The Arts**
VI. **Government**
VII. **History**

Questions

What is unusual about Colombia's coastline?
What precious metal is found in Colombia that has not been discovered in any other South American country?
Where do most Colombians live? Why?
What is Colombia's chief industry?
Who were Jorge Isaacs? Simón Bolívar? José Salcedo?
What product makes up most of Colombia's exports?
What is the oldest permanent settlement in South America?
What three countries were once part of Colombia?
What did the Spaniards first call Colombia? Why?
What are Colombia's cultural contributions?

ments in 1830. The Republic of Great Colombia then reorganized as the Republic of New Granada, but suffered civil war and confusion until 1886. The constitution of 1863 restored the name Colombia to the country. The 1886 constitution took most of the power from the states and gave it to the central government.

The 1900's. Panama broke away from the Republic of Colombia in 1903. Colombia's failure to ratify the Hay-Herrán Treaty with the United States was the chief reason for the revolt. This treaty granted the right of way for a ship canal through the Isthmus of Panama. In 1922, the U.S. Senate approved a bill settling the dispute, and granted $25 million to Colombia.

During World War II, the United States used Colombian sea and air bases. Colombia broke off diplomatic relations with the Axis Powers in 1941. In 1943, it declared war against Germany. Colombia became a charter member of the United Nations in 1945.

The ninth Pan American Conference, which met at Bogotá in 1948, was disturbed by a four-day revolution. Communists were blamed for inciting the riots, which began on April 9. In May, Colombia broke off diplomatic relations with Russia.

Recent Developments. Colombia strengthened its industries during the 1950's with funds from the World Bank and technical aid from the United States. In 1957, Gustavo Rojas Pinilla, who had seized the government

COLOMBO, koh LUM boh (pop. 510,947; alt. 15 ft.), is the capital, seaport, and largest city of Ceylon. It lies on the west coast, and most of the island's shipping passes through its fine harbor. Colombo is the center of the country's tea, coconut, and cotton trade. It has been a major Asian port for hundreds of years. For location, see CEYLON (map).

Colombo is an old city, founded before the mid-1300's. The Portuguese who landed there in 1517 named it in honor of Christopher Columbus. The Dutch occupied the city from 1656 to 1796, and erected a number of buildings that still stand. Perhaps the most impressive is the Wolfendhal Church, built in 1749. Colombo is also the home of the University of Ceylon.

Camera Press, Pix

An Old Clock Tower in the Heart of Colombo's business district once served as a lighthouse for the city's harbor. The Portuguese built a fort on this site more than 400 years ago.

According to tradition, Buddha visited the temple of Kalaniya just outside Colombo. Commonwealth of Nations leaders set up the Colombo Plan there in 1950. ROBERT I. CRANE

COLOMBO PLAN provides assistance for economic development to countries of South and Southeast Asia. The assistance includes training personnel, scientific research in agriculture and industry, consultative services, and financial aid.

The Consultative Committee, which directs the program, has headquarters in Colombo, Ceylon. It consists of representatives from the 23 member countries: Afghanistan, Australia, Bhutan, Burma, Cambodia, Canada, Ceylon, India, Indonesia, Japan, Laos, Malaysia, the Maldive Islands, Nepal, New Zealand, Pakistan, the Philippines, Singapore, South Korea, South Vietnam, Thailand, the United Kingdom, and the United States.

Member countries within the region plan their own development programs with the advice of the committee. They pay most of the cost of these programs. Member countries outside the region contribute financial assistance and cooperate in other ways. The Colombo Plan Technical Cooperation Scheme is the chief means for technical cooperation.

Percy Spender, then foreign minister of Australia, proposed the idea of the Colombo Plan at a meeting of the Commonwealth Foreign Ministers at Colombo in January, 1950. The Consultative Committee held its first meeting in May, 1950, and published the principles of the plan in November. The Colombo Plan began operating in July, 1951. NORMAN D. PALMER

See also AUSTRALIA (In the 1950's and 1960's).

COLÓN, *koh LOHN* (pop. 64,892; alt. 25 ft.), is the second largest city in Panama. It stands on Manzanillo Island, which is actually a peninsula. Colón overlooks Limón Bay, at the Atlantic end of the Panama Canal. For location, see PANAMA (color map).

Colón has clean, wide streets, spacious residential areas, and busy shopping districts. It ships tropical fruits, hardwood lumber, and other products through the neighboring port of Cristóbal in the Canal Zone.

The Americans who built the Panama Railroad in the mid-1800's founded the city in 1852 and named it Aspinwall, after William H. Aspinwall, a promoter of the railroad. In 1890, the Panamanians changed the name to Colón in honor of Christopher Columbus. (*Colón* is Spanish for *Columbus.*) After the Panama Canal opened in 1914, the city became a leading commercial and tourist center. Today, Colón is an important international free trade zone. JOHN BIESANZ and MAVIS BIESANZ

COLÓN. See GALÁPAGOS ISLANDS.

COLON, *KOH lun*, is a mark of punctuation (:). Its primary function is to separate an introduction from what it introduces: a list, a long quotation, an illustration, or an explanation. A colon is used only when the words preceding it form a complete sentence, as in the second sentence of this article. An exception is that a colon may follow an introductory label, such as *thus.*

A colon also ends the formal opening of a business letter, may end the main headings of an outline, and may separate the independent parts of a long, complicated compound sentence. SUMNER IVES

See also PUNCTUATION.

COLON, *KOH lun*, is a part of the large intestine. This muscular tube carries *chyme* (food residue) from the *cecum* (the first part of the large intestine) to the *rectum* (the last part). The colon is divided into four sections. The *ascending colon* extends upward on the right side of the abdominal cavity. It joins the *transverse colon*, which extends across the cavity to the opposite side. This section meets the *descending colon*, which passes down the left side to join the S-shaped *sigmoid colon*. In human beings, the colon is about 5 feet long. It removes water and mineral salts from the chyme. Its strong muscles contract and relax to push the residue toward the rectum. Mucus covers the colon's inner surfaces to lubricate them and ease the passage of chyme. WILLIAM V. MAYER

See also HUMAN BODY (Trans-Vision three-dimensional color picture); COLITIS; DYSENTERY; INTESTINE.

COLON is a monetary unit used in two Latin-American countries, Costa Rica and El Salvador. In Costa Rica, it is a copper-nickel coin worth 100 centimos. In El Salvador, it is a paper note equal to 100 centavos. Its name comes from the Spanish name for Christopher Columbus, *Cristóbal Colón.* BURTON HOBSON

See also MONEY (table, Values of Monetary Units).

COLONEL. See RANK IN ARMED SERVICES.

COLONIAL ARCHITECTURE usually refers to the style of architecture common in the American colonies until the time of the Revolutionary War. See ARCHITECTURE (The 1700's); COLONIAL LIFE IN AMERICA (The Home).

COLONIAL DAMES OF AMERICA, NATIONAL SOCIETY OF THE, is a society of women organized in 1891 to create an interest in American colonial history. It seeks to stimulate a spirit of patriotism and a love of country. Membership is by invitation, and is based on descent from some ancestor who came to an American colony before 1750, and who, by distinguished services, contributed to the founding of the nation. The society was organized in Philadelphia. It has about 14,000 members. Headquarters are at 2715 Q St. NW, Washington, D.C. 20007. MARGUERITE APPLETON

COLONIAL LIFE IN AMERICA

Many different kinds of people lived in the 13 English colonies that became the United States. This picture shows just a few of them, including, *left to right,* an Indian, a Pilgrim, a New England farmer, a housewife, a town crier, and a Southern planter and his daughter.

COLONIAL LIFE IN AMERICA. The story of the American colonists is one of the great adventure stories of all time. It is the story of brave men and women who sailed across the Atlantic Ocean from Europe, conquered a wilderness, and founded a new nation. This story of courage and achievement took place in a remarkably short time. The colonial period lasted less than 170 years. It began with the settlement of Jamestown in 1607, and ended with the start of the Revolutionary War in 1775.

Most of the colonists were English. But America also attracted thousands of Dutch, French, Germans, Scotch-Irish, and Swedes. The colonists brought different customs and religious beliefs, but they shared a common goal. All were unhappy with life in the Old World and wanted to make a better life in the New World.

The English were latecomers to the Americas, but they were the first Europeans to live in the New World in large numbers. England hoped to compete with other European powers for the riches of the New World. Spain had already developed a huge colonial empire in Central and South America. France controlled Canada and much of the Mississippi Valley.

The Spanish and French were interested chiefly in re-

turning to Europe with furs, gold, and other riches. They also wanted to convert the Indians to Roman Catholicism. Their early settlements served as outposts for soldiers and traders, or as missions conducted by priests. On the other hand, the English colonies were settled by people from almost every walk of life. These people wanted to establish permanent homes in America.

In making America their homeland, the colonists were sometimes helped by the Indians. But often the Indians fought to keep their land. The colonists, fighting together and working together, overcame the Indians and the wilderness. They produced plenty of food and other vital products on their farms and plantations. They carried on a thriving trade with other countries. They built cabins and mansions, villages and cities. They established churches, schools, and local governments.

The colonists had to work hard, and they suffered many hardships. But during most of the colonial period, they had better living conditions and more freedom than any other people in the world.

This article deals entirely with the 13 original English colonies that became the United States. For the history of each colony, from settlement to statehood, see the separate WORLD BOOK articles on the states, such as GEORGIA (History). See also UNITED STATES, HISTORY OF (The Thirteen Colonies). For the history of other colonies in the New World, see CANADA, HISTORY OF; LATIN AMERICA (History).

The contributor of this article is Jane Carson, Research Associate at Colonial Williamsburg. The paintings and drawings are by H. Charles McBarron, a special consultant to the Smithsonian Institution.

COLONIAL LIFE IN AMERICA / *The Thirteen Colonies*

Between 1607 and 1733, the English established 13 permanent colonies on the Atlantic coast of North America. Most of the early settlements began as business projects, operated by individuals or companies organized by merchants. These men obtained permits from the king to colonize his lands in the New World.

The English colonizers had two main goals: (1) to make profits for themselves, and (2) to use the settlements to expand English trade and industry. They advertised America as a land of opportunity, and persuaded many Europeans to migrate to the colonies. Many merchants provided the settlers with transportation, land, and tools and other supplies.

Why the Colonists Came to America

America gave thousands of Europeans a chance to make a new start. The settlers knew they faced serious dangers and would suffer severe hardships. But they had important reasons for accepting the challenge of taming the wilderness.

Economic Opportunities. The settlers included many who could not find work in their European homelands. Everyone could find work in America. The New World had rich land to farm, and much timber to cut. Its waters and woodlands provided plenty of fish and game. All these were strong attractions for people who could not make a decent living in Europe.

Freedom of Worship. Some of the settlers, beginning with the Pilgrims, came to America chiefly because they were promised freedom of worship. Throughout the colonial period, other groups came to the English colonies to escape persecution because of their religious beliefs. These groups included Puritans, Quakers, Roman Catholics, Huguenots, and Jews.

631

THE THIRTEEN COLONIES IN 1763

This map shows the 13 British colonies that became the United States. Their population grew to nearly 2 million in a little more than 150 years after a small band of Englishmen established the first permanent settlement at Jamestown.

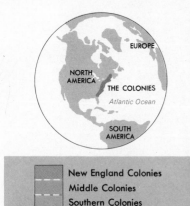

PROVINCE OF QUEBEC

Louisbourg

NOVA SCOTIA

NEW HAMPSHIRE
MAINE
Part of Mass.

Halifax

Lake Huron

Claimed by N.Y. & N.H.

Lake Ontario

Portsmouth

Lake Erie

NEW YORK
Boston • Salem
MASSACHUSETTS
Plymouth
Newport

(Reserved for the Indians by the Proclamation of 1763)

New Haven
New York City

PENNSYLVANIA
RHODE ISLAND
CONNECTICUT

Philadelphia
NEW JERSEY

Baltimore
Annapolis
DELAWARE
MARYLAND

VIRGINIA
Williamsburg

Jamestown • Norfolk

NORTH CAROLINA

New Bern

SOUTH CAROLINA

GEORGIA Charles Town

Savannah

EUROPE

NORTH AMERICA

THE COLONIES
Atlantic Ocean

SOUTH AMERICA

New England Colonies
Middle Colonies
Southern Colonies
Proclamation Line of 1763

Distance Scale
0 Miles   200   400
0 Kilometres   400   600

WORLD BOOK map–FHa

Land Ownership. Many settlers came to America because they were offered land free or at low cost. In those days, owning land gave a man a feeling of independence, and the promise of a good life for his children. Land ownership made a man a *freeholder*. A freeholder had certain rights in the community, generally including the right to vote.

There were several ways that land was distributed in the colonies. Under English law, all the land belonged to the king. The king issued permits, called *charters*, which allowed individuals or companies to colonize a certain area of land. Then each *proprietor* (individual owner) or company distributed the land to the settlers. In the early colonization of Virginia, the company gave each settler 100 acres of free land to develop. Later, the king took back the company's charter and established direct royal control over the colony. Under royal control, each new settler received some free land, usually 50 acres, and could purchase more for only five shillings an acre. Any person who paid the transportation of a new settler got 50 acres free.

In the New England Colonies, where settlements were called townships, the land was first assigned to each township. The township officials then divided the land among the settlers. Each settler got enough land near the village green for a house, garden, and cow shed. He also had a strip of farmland on the edge of the village, where he raised corn and other crops. A settler had the right to sell his land, or to buy more with the consent of the township officials.

In most of the other colonies, early settlers started as freeholders. Proprietors or companies gave a settler some land, and sold him more at bargain prices. In some colonies, individuals got large tracts of land by promising to develop the property. These promoters then brought

NOVA BRITANNIA.

OFFERING MOST

Excellent fruites by Planting in VIRGINIA.

Exciting all such as be well affected to further the same.

LONDON
Printed for SAMVEL MACHAM, and are to besold at his Shop in Pauls Church-yard, at the Signe of the Bul-head.
1609.

Bettmann Archive

Advertising helped sell shares of the stock companies that developed England's early settlements in the New World.

THE THIRTEEN COLONIES AND THE DATES
OF THEIR FIRST PERMANENT SETTLEMENTS

Virginia	1607	Delaware	1638
Massachusetts	1620	Pennsylvania	1643
New Hampshire	1623	North Carolina	c. 1653
New York	1624	New Jersey	1660
Connecticut	1633	South Carolina	1670
Maryland	1634	Georgia	1733
Rhode Island	1636		

NEW ENGLAND VILLAGE

Most New England settlers lived on the Atlantic Coast and earned their living chiefly as fishermen, shipbuilders, or seagoing traders. The rocky soil was not suitable for large farms, but New England had plenty of fine shipbuilding timber, and some of the best fishing waters in the world.

shiploads of settlers to the colony and gave them some land free. After the colony had been developed, the promoters could charge high prices for the remaining land.

Early Settlements

The English made an unsuccessful attempt to establish a colony in North America in 1585. That year, a group sponsored by Sir Walter Raleigh started a settlement on Roanoke Island, off the coast of what is now North Carolina. The settlers soon returned to England, and another group landed in 1587. This group disappeared mysteriously, and no one knows what happened to them (see LOST COLONY).

In 1606, a trading firm called the Virginia Company was granted a colonizing charter by King James. Two colonies were planned. One was to be located somewhere between present-day New York and the Carolinas. The other was to be someplace between New York and Newfoundland. The Virginia Company's plans led to the establishment of Jamestown and Plymouth. The experiences in these colonies served as a guide for future English colonization in America. ·

Jamestown was the first permanent English colony in America. The first colonists—all men or boys—landed on Jamestown Island on May 14, 1607. They set out to build a fortified outpost from which they could explore Virginia and trade with the Indians.

The Jamestown settlers expected to find gold and other treasures in the wilderness, but they found none. There was nothing they could send back to England for sale except lumber products. About 1612, the colonists learned how to raise and cure tobacco. The export of tobacco helped save the colony by providing a way for the colonists to support themselves.

Many serious difficulties almost ruined the settlement. The region was swampy and unhealthful. During the first year, about two-thirds of the settlers died of disease or starvation. More settlers were sent to Jamestown, but food was still scarce. So many died in 1609 that the year became known as the colony's "starving time."

Indian attacks added to the difficulties in founding the colony. The attacks stopped after the settlers signed a treaty in 1614 with Chief Powhatan, whose daughter Pocahontas had married John Rolfe. But the Indians broke the treaty after Powhatan's death in 1618. They killed many settlers in a massacre in 1622.

In spite of many tragedies and hard times, Jamestown survived. Farmers and their families replaced the explorers and traders. The Virginia Company also sent young women to Jamestown to marry the bachelors of the colony. There were two chief reasons for the survival of the Jamestown colony. First, the colonists learned how to produce their own food and supplies. Second, family life developed after women settled in the colony. For the story of the Jamestown settlement, see JAMESTOWN; VIRGINIA (History).

Plymouth was the second permanent English settlement in America. A group of Pilgrims—men, women, and children—established the colony in 1620 on the rocky southeastern shore of what is now Massachusetts. The Plymouth colonists called themselves Pilgrims because of their wanderings in search of religious freedom. The Pilgrims were farmers and skilled workmen. They wanted to raise their families in a place where they could live according to their religious beliefs. These beliefs required the Pilgrims to work hard and live simply.

Although the Pilgrims were quite different from the Jamestown settlers, they had many similar problems.

633

PHILADELPHIA MARKET

Certain days of each week were declared "market days" in every colonial city. On those days, the farmers of the surrounding countryside brought fresh meats, fruits, and vegetables to be sold in the city's special market areas. This painting was adapted from a print made in the late 1700's.

Their "starving time" came during the first winter, just after they landed in the New World. Only about half the 99 Plymouth settlers survived the bitter winter.

The Pilgrims were fortunate in their relations with the Indians of the region. Soon after the Pilgrims landed, they signed a friendship treaty with the Indians which lasted 50 years. They also had the help of a friendly Indian named Squanto. He taught them how to raise corn, and showed them the best fishing areas. See SQUANTO.

The story of how the Pilgrims established Plymouth Colony has become one of the most famous chapters of American history. This story is often told to show how courage and hard work can triumph over tremendous difficulties. The Pilgrims did not change their simple way of life as their colony developed. As a result, Plymouth never became prosperous. In 1691, it became part of the large colony of Massachusetts. For the story of how the Pilgrims developed their colony, see PLYMOUTH COLONY. See also PILGRIM.

Development of the Colonies

After English colonists had settled Jamestown and Plymouth, large areas of the Atlantic seacoast were colonized. The later colonists suffered hardships, but they had learned from the first settlers. There were no more "starving times" in colonial America.

The colonies are generally grouped according to location: (1) the Northern or New England Colonies, (2) the Middle Colonies, and (3) the Southern Colonies.

The Northern Colonies were Connecticut, Massachusetts, New Hampshire, and Rhode Island. Most New Englanders lived in villages and had small farms. The climate was too cool and the soil too rocky for large farms. New England Colonies had plenty of fine timber and some of the best fishing waters in the world.

The Middle Colonies were Delaware, New Jersey, New York, and Pennsylvania. Their climate favored large farms, where wheat and other grains were grown.

The Southern Colonies were Georgia, Maryland, North Carolina, South Carolina, and Virginia. The warm climate and rich soil of the south were fine for growing tobacco and rice. Life in the Southern Colonies developed chiefly on plantations.

Types of Colonies. No two colonies began or developed in exactly the same way. But there were three major types of American colonies: (1) *royal*, (2) *proprietary*, and (3) *corporate*. A royal colony was under the direct control of the king. A proprietary colony was controlled by an individual—the proprietor—under a grant from the king. A corporate colony was operated, as a rule, under a charter obtained from the king by a company's stockholders.

All the 13 English colonies were founded either as proprietary or corporate colonies. By the time the Revolutionary War began in 1775, eight of the colonies had become royal colonies—Georgia, Massachusetts, New Hampshire, New Jersey, New York, North Carolina, South Carolina, and Virginia. Three colonies—Delaware, Maryland, and Pennsylvania—were proprietary. The other two—Connecticut and Rhode Island—may be considered corporate colonies. Their charters were obtained by groups of colonists in America, not by stockholders in England.

Growth in the 1700's. The settlement of America increased rapidly during the late 1600's and the 1700's. Most of the new immigrants made their homes in the Middle Colonies, but others settled in New England or the Southern Colonies. The immigrants included

634

SOUTHERN PLANTATION

A colonial planter built his mansion to resemble a fine English country house. Behind the mansion were a kitchen, smokehouse, coach house, barns, and slaves' cabins. Most plantations were on a bay or river and had a wharf where their products could be loaded on ships.

large groups of Germans and Scotch-Irish. Like many of the early settlers, these groups had fled hard times and religious persecution in Europe. The Germans became known as the best farmers among the colonists. The Scotch-Irish won fame as the best Indian fighters.

The birth rate in America during the 1700's was probably higher than that of any other country. As a result of this high birth rate and increased immigration, the population of the colonies grew rapidly. It was about 250,000 in 1700, and increased to more than 1 million by 1750. The population doubled to over 2 million by 1770, and in 1775, there were nearly 2,500,000 persons in the colonies.

Population estimates made in 1770 show that the Southern Colonies had almost as many persons as New England and the Middle Colonies combined. The southern population was close to 1 million, New England's was about 571,000, and that of the Middle Colonies was about 556,000. Virginia was by far the largest colony, with over 447,000 persons. Massachusetts had more than 266,000 persons, and Pennsylvania was third, with over 240,000. Georgia, with about 23,000, had the smallest population.

As the population of the colonies increased, trade and manufacturing developed rapidly. These activities centered mainly in towns that had good harbors. Five towns became the most important American cities of the 1700's. They were, in order of size of population: Philadelphia, New York City, Boston, Charleston (called Charles Town in those days), and Newport.

Philadelphia was the busiest colonial port and the largest manufacturing center of the mid-1700's. In 1760, Philadelphia had over 23,000 people, and by 1775 its population had grown to about 40,000. New York City

had a population of about 25,000; Boston, 16,000; Charleston, 12,000; and Newport, 11,000.

Relations With the Indians

In some places, the Indians were friendly and helped the settlers. Elsewhere, the tribes tried to drive the colonists out of lands that had been Indian hunting grounds for thousands of years. Then terrible wars broke out. For a description of the battles, see INDIAN WARS.

The struggles between the colonists and the Indians became large-scale warfare because of fighting between England and France. In a series of wars from 1689 to 1763, the English and French sent troops to America and battled each other for land. In these wars, many English colonists fought French colonists who had settled in Canada and the Mississippi Valley. Each side had strong supporters among the Indian tribes. For that reason, the colonists called the wars the French and Indian Wars. England won, and France lost almost all its possessions in North America. For the details of these wars, see FRENCH AND INDIAN WARS.

After their victory, the English recognized the claims of the Indians to the western lands that the tribes occupied. In 1763, the English issued a proclamation which prohibited American colonists from settling west of the Appalachian Mountains. Land there was reserved for the Indians. The English hoped to prevent fighting between the colonists and the Indians.

Settlers who were ready to move to lands beyond the Alleghenies refused to obey the proclamation. Opposition by the colonists to the Proclamation of 1763 became one of the issues leading to the Revolutionary War (see REVOLUTIONARY WAR IN AMERICA [Events Leading to the Revolution]).

An engraving from *A Popular History of the United States*. Library of Congress

America's First Representative Legislature, the General Assembly, met at Jamestown in 1619. Its elected members, with the governor and council, made the laws of Virginia.

COLONIAL LIFE IN AMERICA / Society and Government

Colonial Society was made up of several classes. At the top were rich merchants and planters, and their families. They were called the "gentry" or the "better sort." The gentry lived in mansions and often traveled in comfortable carriages. The men used "Esquire" after their names, and their wives were addressed as "Madam." The gentry were well educated and included ministers, doctors, or lawyers who had attended a university.

Below the gentry were members of the "middling sort." Most of them were farmers or shopkeepers who owned property but were not wealthy. Some craftsmen and teachers were included in the "middling sort." The lowest rank, called the "meaner sort," consisted of poor people, including unskilled laborers, slaves, and *indentured servants*. An indentured servant was a person who came to the colonies under a contract to work for a master without wages. Instead of paying wages, the master paid for the servant's passage from Europe. The servant also received food, clothing, and housing. Most contracts covered a period of four to seven years.

Colonial society was the most democratic in the world, because members of the lower classes, except slaves, could easily rise to a higher class. A successful farmer could become the owner of a large estate. Then, if he sent his sons to college, they became members of the gentry. A craftsman or shopkeeper might become a wealthy merchant. An indentured servant, after serving the term of his contract, was given either land or craftsman's tools. He became a farmer or set up his own business. Skilled workers earned good wages, and could

invest their money in property or in some business.

Only slaves were forced to spend their lives at the lowest level of society. They were Negroes, originally brought from Africa and sold to wealthy colonists. Slaves and their children remained slaves unless their master freed them. But a free Negro generally found it hard to make a living. If he left home, he might be arrested as a runaway slave and sold into slavery again. He usually stayed in the neighborhood where people knew him, and worked for low wages. Most slaves worked in the Southern Colonies as farm laborers or house servants. In New England and the Middle Colonies, slaves usually worked in homes or shops.

Government. Each colony had a governor and a legislature. The king of England appointed the governor of royal colonies. In proprietary colonies, the proprietor named the governor. In Connecticut and Rhode Island, the people elected the governor. Most colonial legislatures consisted of two houses, and resembled the English Parliament in structure. Today, state legislatures still have that basic structure except for Nebraska, which has a one-house legislature.

A colonial legislature was called an Assembly, except in New England, where it was known as a General Court. The people elected the members of the lower house in all the colonies. In Connecticut and Rhode Island, the people also elected the members of the upper house. In Massachusetts, the upper house was elected by the lower house. In the other colonies, the king or the proprietor appointed the upper house.

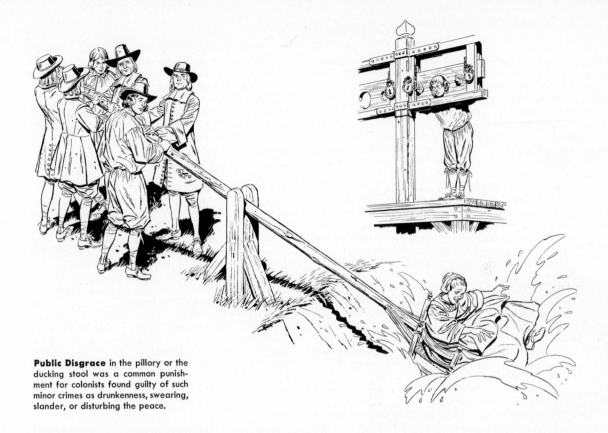

Public Disgrace in the pillory or the ducking stool was a common punishment for colonists found guilty of such minor crimes as drunkenness, swearing, slander, or disturbing the peace.

The laws passed by a colonial legislature had to be approved by the English government. Governors appointed by the king had the responsibility of carrying out his orders. The king expected them to enforce the laws of England, especially acts of Parliament that regulated colonial trade.

Voting Requirements differed in the various colonies, and changed from time to time. One of the most important requirements was property ownership. By 1750, most adult male citizens who owned property could vote. Land was considered the basic property, but other possessions could be substituted for it. A tenant farmer could vote if he owned valuable livestock, or a merchant who did not own his shop could vote if he owned valuable goods. Those who could not vote included women, indentured servants, slaves, and the very poor.

Most of the colonies limited voting and other rights of citizenship to members of a certain church group. In the royal colonies, all citizens had to be members of the Church of England, often called the Anglican Church. In colonies controlled by the Puritans, all citizens had to belong to the Congregational Church. As a result, Roman Catholics and Jews could not vote in most of the colonies.

The rules that governed citizenship and voting in the colonies seem highly undemocratic today. But in colonial times, these laws were broader than those of any other country, including England. The colonists based their laws on certain ideas that suited their social system and business life. They believed that men who owned property had a strong interest in good government. The gentry had the time, talent, and experience for public service, and the voters usually elected them to office. In most elections, about half of those qualified to vote went to the polls.

Local Government in the colonies was based on English county and town governments. In the south, the county court conducted most public business. This court consisted of justices of the peace, appointed by the governor. They levied taxes, supervised road construction and ferry service, and organized the *militia* (citizen soldiers). They also tried certain civil and criminal cases. In New England, the courts only tried cases. Citizens held town meetings at which they voted on local laws and elected town officials, called selectmen. The town meeting still exists in some New England towns (see TOWN MEETING). In the Middle Colonies, local governments consisted of both county and town units.

Law Enforcement in the colonies was the job of constables and sheriffs. Persons accused of a crime punishable by death were tried by certain high courts in the colonial capitals. Death by hanging was the customary penalty for such crimes as armed robbery, counterfeiting, murder, piracy, or treason.

Local courts with juries tried persons accused of such minor crimes as drunkenness, slander, swearing, theft, disturbing the peace, or breaking the Sabbath. Punishment included fines, public whipping, and suffering disgrace with the pillory, stocks, or ducking stool (see PILLORY; STOCKS; DUCKING STOOL).

637

Colonial households were large because grandparents, aunts, uncles, and cousins generally lived with the family. Servants also belonged to the family group. All members of the group worked together to support the household.

A colonial father decided important matters affecting the household. His wife, children, and servants obeyed him without question. By law and custom, he was responsible for the behavior and welfare of every member of the household.

Houses. The first settlers built houses that closely resembled those they had known in Europe. The colonists later changed their housing styles so they could make the best use of local building materials. The first cottages of Jamestown and Plymouth had thatched roofs, like English cottages. After the colonists found wood more plentiful than reeds or straw, wood shingles replaced thatch.

All the colonies had plenty of wood, and frame houses could be seen everywhere. In the Northern Colonies, where winters were very cold, the colonists built brick or stone chimneys inside the framework to supply warmth. In some homes, one chimney served several fireplaces. In the Southern Colonies, which had a generally mild climate, chimneys stood outside the framework of most homes.

Most early southern houses had $1\frac{1}{2}$ stories. A typical New England house of the 1600's had two stories in front and one in back. Some New England homes were built of the fieldstone that the colonists found in many areas. In areas near the Appalachian valleys, limestone was used to build many houses. Bricks were made in every colony during the 1700's, but wood cost less and remained the most popular building material throughout the colonial period.

Many houses in the Delaware and Hudson river valleys were of Scandinavian or Dutch design. The Swedish colonists who came to Delaware in 1638 built the first log cabins in America. The log cabin became the typical home of the pioneers who moved westward (see LOG CABIN). Most of the houses built by the Dutch settlers had $1\frac{1}{2}$ stories. Their doors were divided into upper and lower parts which opened separately. These doors became known as "Dutch doors."

Many wealthy colonial merchants and planters built homes in a style called Georgian architecture. Most Georgian houses were square or rectangular, with a central stair hall and many tall windows. The front door was large and impressive, and the main rooms had fine wood paneling. See GEORGIAN ARCHITECTURE.

The mansion of a typical southern plantation stood on a hill and overlooked a bay or river. It was surrounded by gardens, orchards, and shade trees, with a kitchen, laundry, and smokehouse nearby. Farther away were the stables and carriage house, and cabins where the slaves lived.

Some wealthy South Carolina colonists developed a type of town house that was especially suited for the climate of Charleston. A Charleston town house was only one room wide, but had three or four stories and several porches. Cool sea breezes swept through every room of these tall, narrow homes.

Furnishings of the first settlers were homemade, except for a few possessions brought from Europe. Many families made most of their own furniture and other household articles throughout the colonial period. Wealthy colonists imported their furnishings, generally from England. After colonial cabinetmakers developed their craft, the homes of the well-to-do had much fine American furniture.

The homemade furnishings of the settlers were plain and strong. Thick wooden planks, set on sturdy supports, served as a table. Blocks of wood, small barrels, or rough benches and stools were used as chairs. Mattresses were canvas bags, stuffed with straw and placed on the floor or on bedsteads made of log slabs.

Life in most colonial homes centered around the fireplace. The women prepared food there, and cooking utensils hung nearby. The fireplace provided most of the family's heat and light, and everyone gathered in front of it to eat, work, relax, or entertain visitors. A spinning wheel stood on the hearth.

The homes of most wealthy colonists had finely designed tables, chairs, beds, chests, and sofas. Some of this furniture came from the shops of such great English furniture designers as Thomas Chippendale, George Hepplewhite, Thomas Sheraton, and the Adam brothers. After 1750, colonial craftsmen copied many favorite English designs. They used native cherry, maple, pine, or walnut, and also mahogany imported from the West Indies.

The chairs and sofas of a Georgian mansion were richly upholstered in leather, tapestry, silk damask, or embroidered linen. Benjamin Franklin attached rockers to the legs of a chair that had a straight back made of slats. The slat-back American rocking chair became popular in many parts of the world.

Tables were graceful, and many had special features that saved space. These features included folding legs, and tops fitted with drop leaves. The drop leaves were hinged parts that rested on the legs when the table was being used. At other times, the legs were folded and the drop leaves lowered.

The most popular chests of drawers were "highboys" and "lowboys." A highboy was large and tall, with many drawers and short legs. A lowboy was a small, low chest of a few drawers. A lowboy often served as a side table. Tall cupboards stood in the halls, bedrooms, kitchen, and dining room. Some, called dressers, were divided into an upper section of open shelves, and a lower section with doors. The open shelves were used to display dishes and pewterware.

Most fine colonial bedrooms had a four-poster—a bed with a tall post at each corner. The four posts supported a *canopy* (overhead covering). Curtains hung from the frame of the canopy, and could be drawn together to keep out cold air. The mattress, stuffed with feathers, rested on woven ropes fastened to the bedstead several feet above the floor. The space between the floor and the mattress generally was used to store a child's bed during the day. This movable bed, called a trundle bed, was pulled out at night.

Some well-furnished colonial homes had a handsome clock. The most famous colonial clock was called a

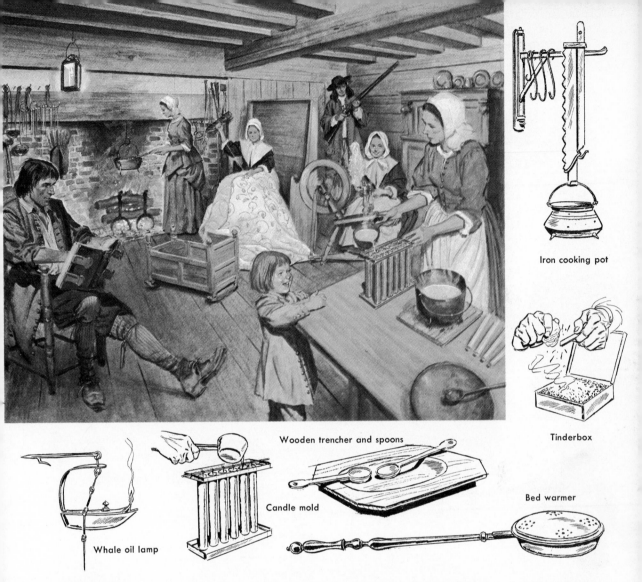

Iron cooking pot

Tinderbox

Wooden trencher and spoons

Bed warmer

Whale oil lamp

Candle mold

FARMHOUSE   Every member of the family shared in the tasks of a colonial household. The early settlers made most of their own clothing, furniture, and cooking utensils. In farmhouses throughout the colonies, the family gathered at nightfall to work in the light and warmth of the fireplace.

grandfather clock. It had a tall wooden case and stood on the floor. Other furnishings included candlesticks, chandeliers, and mirrors. The windows had heavy curtains made of brocade, damask, or linen. Floors were covered with imported carpets or colorful rugs, hand made in the home.

Clothing in colonial times varied according to a person's occupation or position in the community. A farmer and members of his family wore rough, homemade garments. A wealthy merchant or planter and his family had expensive clothing, made of imported materials and designed in fashionable English styles. Male servants who worked in the fields sometimes wore only breechcloths in summer.

Making clothing was an important task in most colonial households. On small farms, the women planted and tended a patch of flax, harvested the crop, spun the yarn, and wove it into linen. They wove woolen cloth

from yarn spun from the fleece of sheep. Linens and woolens were colored with dyes made from certain barks, berries, roots, or walnut hulls. The colonists tanned cowhide and deerskin, and made the leather into shoes or leggings.

In summer, workingmen wore breeches and a long linen shirt. In winter, they wore woolen or leather breeches, knitted stockings, and heavy shoes. For outdoor wear in cold weather, a man had a loose-fitting overcoat, leather leggings, woolen mittens, and a fur cap. A woman wore a dress of linen or wool, a petticoat, and a single undergarment called a shift. A cape or hooded cloak was worn outdoors. Children wore the same kind of clothes as adults.

A wealthy colonist ordered fashionable clothing from London, or from a local tailor who copied the latest English styles. A typical style of the times called for close-fitting breeches of brocade, silk, or velvet, fastened

639

Fire screen

Spectacles

Writing implements

Foot stove

LIVING ROOM

During the 1700's, many wealthy colonists built mansions in a style known as Georgian architecture. The living room had paneled walls and a large, richly decorated fireplace. Much of the furniture of a colonial mansion was made by skilled craftsmen who copied fashionable English designs.

at the knees with silver buckles. With the breeches, a gentleman wore a white linen shirt with lace ruffles at the neck and wrists. Over the shirt, he wore a long, brightly colored waistcoat and a knee-length coat. The coat had wide, flowing sides, and was decorated with gold braid and several rows of fancy buttons. Silk hose, and shoes with silver buckles completed the costume.

A fashionable gentleman wore a wig that he sometimes powdered white. Outdoors, he put a black *cocked hat* (a hat with the brim turned up) on top of the wig. During the late 1600's, wigs were large and expensive. A man who wore one was called a "bigwig." After 1750, many colonial men wore wigs. The most popular wig was small and resembled the wearer's natural hair. It was called a "tie" wig because a man pulled it back and tied it with a short ribbon.

Women of wealthy families wore a low-necked dress with a tight-fitting bodice, and ruffles at the elbows.

It had a full skirt, looped back to display a brightly colored embroidered petticoat. Under the dress, a hoop of steel or whalebone supported the skirt. A tightly laced corset pinched in the waist. A woman of fashion wore silk stockings and silk or leather shoes. She had several types of capes for outdoor wear.

During the 1600's, fashionable women generally wore simple hair styles. The hair was usually arranged so that a loose curl or two hung to the shoulder. Large, fancy hairdos became the fashion about 1760. Servants spent much time helping their mistress pile her hair high on a frame that she wore on her head.

Food was plentiful during most of the colonial period. After the first few years, the colonists kept themselves better supplied with food than any other people in the world. On their farms, they raised grain, cattle, hogs, sheep, chickens, fruits, and vegetables. In the fields and woodlands, they hunted deer, pigeons, squirrels, wild

640

Candelabrum

Candle snuffer
and wick trimmer

Wig powderer

Pannier, worn under hoop skirt

Snuffbox

Clay pipe and pipe-lighting tongs

DINING ROOM　　Wealthy colonists entertained in the style of the gentry of England. They often held large dinner parties at which the guests enjoyed a wide variety of fine foods and wines. The chandelier, dishes, silverware, and table linen were all imported from London.

turkeys, and other game. From the river and ocean waters, they took clams, oysters, lobsters, and many kinds of fish.

Corn was a basic food in almost every household. The people ate it in many forms, most commonly as corn bread. A woman mixed corn meal with water or milk, salt, and lard, and shaped it into buns. Then she baked or fried the buns on a hoe or on a griddle, or placed them in the ashes of the fireplace. Corn bread had different names in various parts of colonial America—ashcake, hoecake, johnnycake, or corn pone. Cooks also made corn hominy. Sometimes they roasted ears of corn in the husks.

Rye or wheat bread was made with yeast. In many homes, the women baked these breads in a small oven that was built into the fireplace or outside the house, against the hot chimney. They also baked bread in an iron bake kettle, which had a tight-fitting lid. The kettle

stood on a bed of hot coals, with embers piled around it and on top of the lid.

Meat or game was usually cooked with vegetables into a stew. Women made the stew in a large iron pot that hung over the fire on a pothook, fastened to a crane or a chimney bar. The iron pot had short legs and sometimes was placed on a bed of coals. Whole fowl or large cuts of meat were often roasted on sharp-pointed rods called spits. Handles on the spits allowed the meat to be turned above the fire.

The colonists had difficulty storing food for the winter because they had no methods of canning or refrigeration. They salted or smoked some meats, and dried or pickled certain vegetables. Root vegetables, and such fruits as apples or pears, were kept in cool, dry cellars. As a rule, the colonists depended on bread and meat for their food during the winter.

Most families ate bread and cold meat for breakfast

641

and supper. Dinner was served at noon or early in the afternoon. The colonists drank beer, cider, rum, or wine with dinner. In the 1700's, hot chocolate, coffee, or tea became popular.

Health of the colonists was poor by today's standards. Most of the people frequently suffered some type of illness, and they did not know how to treat or prevent many serious diseases. But no one in Europe or anywhere else knew how either. The general health of the colonists was no worse than in any other part of the world.

Contagious diseases sometimes spread rapidly and took many lives in the colonies. The settlers had epidemics of measles, smallpox, typhoid fever, bubonic

Detail from the frontispiece to Dilworth's *New Guide to the English Tongue*. Folger Shakespeare Library, Washington, D.C.

Children's Games in colonial times included many that are still popular. The youngsters shot marbles, flew kites, and played hopscotch, leapfrog, prisoners' base, and blindman's buff.

Shearing Sheep and cutting bristles from hogs supplied materials for many colonial household items. The sheep's wool was spun into yarn, and the hog bristles were used to make brushes.

From *Alle de Wercken*, 1657-59, by Jacob Cats. Folger Shakespeare Library, Washington, D.C.

plague, and yellow fever. Other widespread illnesses included dysentery, gout, influenza, pneumonia, rheumatism, scurvy, and tuberculosis.

Most colonists took medicines made of certain barks, herbs, or roots. These medicines, although believed to be powerful cures, usually failed. One helpful medicine was quinine, a bitter substance taken from the bark of the cinchona tree. The colonists used it for a common malarial fever called ague. Doctors still use quinine to treat certain types of malaria. Popular medicines were made from tobacco leaves and the roots of the ginseng plant and the sassafras tree.

There were few trained doctors and nurses during most of the colonial period. Most doctors studied medicine by helping experienced physicians. One of the first public hospitals in America was the Pennsylvania Hospital. It was chartered in Philadelphia in 1751, and still serves the community.

Recreation. The colonists combined work with play whenever they could. They often gathered to perform some task together and, at the same time, to enjoy games, contests, and other recreation. Neighbors got together to help a newcomer build a barn or a house. A barn or house raising was an opportunity for the men and boys to stage foot races, or shooting or wrestling contests. They also competed in plowing or corn husking. The women and girls held quilting bees, and everyone enjoyed spelling bees and singing groups. All these activities gave the people a chance to share good things to eat and drink, and to exchange news and gossip.

Weddings and holidays were important occasions for feasting and amusement. Many wedding celebrations lasted several days, during which the guests feasted, danced, and played card games. Christmas was a gay holiday season in most of the colonies. But some New England colonies followed the Puritan custom in England and outlawed the celebration of Christmas. They added Thanksgiving Day to the fall calendar as a harvest feast. Several colonies celebrated May Day as a spring festival.

Horse racing became popular in most of the colonies during the late 1600's. Virginians raised a special type of horse for their sport of *quarter racing*, a quarter-mile race along a straight path. Cockfighting was also popular in the south. Everywhere, fishing and hunting were favorite sports which kept colonial households well supplied with fresh foods.

The colonial tavern, sometimes called an "ordinary," developed as a favorite gathering place for men. The men gathered in the tavern to talk, smoke, eat and drink, play cards, or read a newspaper. Many taverns had a bowling green, a smooth, flat plot of grass where their customers could bowl.

Colonial children played many games that are still popular, including hopscotch, leapfrog, London Bridge, hide and seek, prisoners' base, and blindman's buff. Colonial toys included balls, dolls, marbles, kites, tops, rolling hoops, and jump ropes. Most toys were homemade, but rich children had doll tea sets or toy soldiers that were imported from England. Almost every household had several cats and dogs, and children who lived in the country made pets of young farm animals.

The Church strongly influenced the social and political life of colonial times. Most of the colonists were deeply religious. Many had come to America chiefly so they could worship according to their beliefs. In Europe, many religious groups had been persecuted for trying to establish new forms of worship.

Most colonial religious groups dated from the 1500's. They developed during the Reformation, a religious movement in Europe that resulted in the birth of Protestantism. King James I of England opened the way for religious freedom in the New World by allowing the Pilgrims to worship as they pleased. Many Puritans, Quakers, Baptists, Huguenots, and other persecuted groups then left Europe and established churches in the colonies. These groups did not always grant religious freedom to those who disagreed with them. The Puritans established the Congregational Church in New England. They denied citizenship to Quakers and others who believed in a different form of worship.

In most of the colonies, church officials performed important public services which today are generally the work of government agencies. They supervised education and care of the poor, and kept records of baptisms, marriages, and deaths. The people used their church building not only as a place of worship, but also for community gatherings. Before and after worship, the churchyard served as a social center for courtship, neighborly visits, and the exchange of news.

During most of the colonial period, church laws governed the behavior of the colonists in almost all activities. The courts enforced these laws. Rules governing behavior were particularly strict in New England. They required everyone to observe the Sabbath from Saturday afternoon until sundown on Sunday. Such tasks as cooking, shaving, cutting hair, or making beds were forbidden. Everyone was expected to spend the time in prayer. Certain strict Sabbath laws of the New Haven colony became famous as "blue laws." They

were given that name because they were bound in blue paper. Today, the term is used for restrictions on some activities or on certain forms of recreation on Sunday. See BLUE LAWS.

The colonists brought many ancient superstitions with them from Europe. These superstitions included the belief that certain women had evil powers, given them by devils. The women were accused of casting spells on their neighbors or practicing other forms of witchcraft. During the 1600's, the colonists persecuted many women as witches. Some of these women were imprisoned, and a few were executed. The persecution of suspected witches reached a climax in the famous Salem witchcraft trials of the early 1690's. See SALEM (Mass.); WITCHCRAFT.

Strong democratic ideas in religion spread through the colonies during the 1740's. That period is often called the time of the Great Awakening. Traveling preachers called evangelists held revival meetings in churches and open fields. The outdoor religious meetings attracted thousands of men and women of the lower classes of colonial society. The evangelists pleaded with the people to repent their sins and seek salvation. The experience of salvation, declared the evangelists, made all men equal in the sight of God.

The stirring sermons of George Whitefield and other famous evangelists aroused great excitement. But certain ministers of established churches opposed many evangelistic ideas. These ministers feared that strong ideas about equality might weaken their power to make church rules. In spite of such opposition, the Great Awakening developed a new interest in the importance of the common man. See GREAT AWAKENING.

The School. The children of rich colonists attended private schools or were educated by private teachers called tutors. The colonists established some public schools, but most children of poor families were taught by their parents at home. Some parents did not know

Preaching at Revival Meetings during a period known as the Great Awakening, George Whitefield, the famous evangelist, aroused excitement among colonists of the lower classes.

Bettmann Archive

Most Colonial Schoolchildren came from rich families. Poor children were usually taught at home by their parents. They learned skills that helped support the household.

Colonial Williamsburg

how to read or write, so they could not teach those skills. Most parents taught their children obedience, religious beliefs, and the skills they needed in daily life. Boys learned how to farm, raise cattle, and handle a gun. Girls learned such household tasks as sewing, spinning, and weaving, and how to cook and preserve food.

The first public school system supported by taxes was set up in New England in 1647. That year, a Massachusetts law called for every town with at least 50 families to establish an elementary school. Larger towns were expected to establish a secondary school, called a grammar school. But parents could still teach their children at home, and the wealthy could send theirs to private schools.

New England had many private schools called "dame" schools. Women, some of whom were widows, held these schools in their homes. They taught the alphabet, spelling, writing, and simple arithmetic. The children used *hornbooks* to memorize their lessons. A hornbook was a board with a sheet of paper pasted on it. On the paper were the alphabet, numerals, and the Lord's Prayer. A thin sheet of transparent horn covered the paper. See HORNBOOK.

Most of the colonies had some private schools that had been established as free schools. These schools were supported by charitable gifts for the education of the poor. Church groups operated many schools, and a minister often held classes in his home. Most of the students paid fees. In the south, planters hired tutors who became members of the plantation household.

If a student's parents could afford to send him to college, he prepared for it in a grammar school. There he studied Latin, mathematics, geography, science, philosophy, and English composition and literature. Many sons of wealthy colonists attended college in England. The first colonial college was established in Massachusetts in 1636. It became Harvard University.

In every colony, many poor children got some education by serving as *apprentices* (learners). Under the apprentice system, a boy's parents placed him with a master craftsman, tradesman, or professional man. The master taught his skills to the boy, and provided him with food, clothing, and lodging. He also gave the boy religious instruction and taught him to read and write. In return, the boy promised to work hard, study faithfully, and be obedient and well-behaved. For most boys, an apprenticeship was the only way to learn a craft, trade, or profession. Some sons of wealthy families also served apprenticeships, especially in becoming lawyers. Girls were "bound out" by their parents as household servants, or apprenticed to become housekeepers, cooks, or needleworkers.

An Apprentice learned to read and write while serving a master who also taught the boy the skills of a craft or trade.

The First College in the Colonies was founded in Massachusetts in 1636. It later became Harvard University.

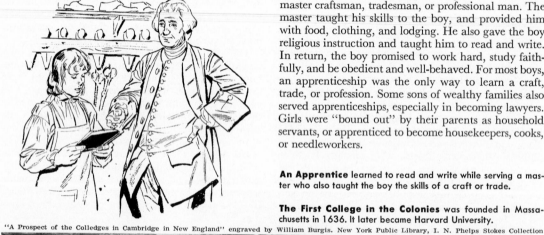

"A Prospect of the Colledges in Cambridge in New England" engraved by William Burgis. New York Public Library, I. N. Phelps Stokes Collection

Travel. Most of the early colonists rarely traveled far from home. As a rule, long journeys were made only by traders, or wealthy merchants or planters. These men generally traveled for business or pleasure by boat on rivers, bays, and the coastal waters. Freight and passengers were carried in many types of sailing vessels, including brigantines, schooners, shallops, sloops, and yawls. Large ships that sailed across the ocean carried small boats. These could be put over the side for travel on shallow inland waters.

Land transportation was slow and difficult. The first colonial roads were merely paths that followed ancient Indian trails through the woodlands. The colonists widened the paths for travel on horseback, and later for carts or wagons pulled by horses or oxen. Ferries carried travelers across rivers. Most of the wooden bridges built by the colonists could be used only by foot travelers, not by vehicles. By 1760, Philadelphia had two stone bridges.

The colonists put much effort into building roads. By 1760, a person could travel by road from New Hampshire to Georgia. At about the same time, stagecoach service linked Boston with Providence, and New York City with Philadelphia and Annapolis.

By the mid-1700's, comfortable passenger vehicles were being used in the towns by government officials and wealthy colonists. These vehicles included carriages, chariots, and coaches, drawn by four, six, or eight horses; two-horse chaises, curricles, and phaetons; and one-horse "riding chairs." Many carriages had richly carved wooden sides, and seats upholstered in leather or brightly colored cloth. Brass or silver ornaments decorated the harnesses.

Communication. During the 1600's, the colonists exchanged news chiefly by word of mouth. Someone would learn about an event from a peddler or a ship captain, and repeat the story to his neighbors. Friends exchanged news in letters that they often gave to travelers to deliver.

News was also spread by *postriders*, the first colonial mailmen. A postrider carried letters or messages, traveling on horseback along a certain route called a post road. On the way, he picked up news and passed it on to the men who welcomed him at taverns and post offices. In most towns, a town crier read official messages to the people.

Mail service operated irregularly in colonial times. Until 1700, it existed only in Massachusetts, New York, and Pennsylvania. In 1753, Benjamin Franklin of Pennsylvania and William Hunter of Virginia were appointed to manage the colonial postal service. Under their direction, post offices were established in all the colonies, and service improved greatly.

Newspapers came into general use after the mid-1700's. The first successful American newspaper, *The Boston News-Letter*, had started publication in 1704. During the next 60 years, newspapers were published in every colony except Delaware and New Jersey.

Bettmann Archive

A Town Crier read official announcements to the townsfolk until newspapers came into general use in the mid-1700's.

Colonial Stagecoaches began operating in the mid-1700's. Taverns provided food and lodging along the way.

Etching of an old Pennsylvania inn by E. T. Scowcroft. Free Library of Philadelphia

The task of building homes and communities in a rugged land demanded great energy and effort. The early colonists had little time for the arts or sciences. In 1743, Benjamin Franklin wrote that "the first drudgery of settling new colonies" was done and there could be "leisure to cultivate the finer arts and improve the common stock of knowledge." By the end of the colonial period, some colonists had made important contributions to literature and painting. Others were active in such scientific fields as astronomy and botany.

Literature. The earliest descriptions of colonial life were written to tell Europeans about the settlements in the New World. John Smith wrote about Jamestown and New England, William Bradford described the Plymouth Colony, and John Winthrop told of the Massachusetts Bay Colony.

Religious writings made up the bulk of colonial literature published in America during the 1600's. The first book printed in the colonies was a collection of psalms, published in 1640. Several ministers prepared this book, which became known as *The Bay Psalm Book*. Three religious leaders—Jonathan Edwards, Cotton Mather, and John Woolman—wrote many books and pamphlets during the 1700's.

Colonial poets also dealt chiefly with religious subjects. Michael Wigglesworth, a New England poet, wrote *Day of Doom*, the most popular literary work of the time. Anne Dudley Bradstreet, another New Englander, became America's first woman poet. She is best known for her collected poems, *The Tenth Muse Lately Sprung Up in America*.

Writings on political subjects became important in the mid-1700's. Dozens of revolutionary pamphlets and poems were circulated after Great Britain passed the Stamp Act of 1765 (see STAMP ACT). Benjamin Franklin was one of the most influential political writers, but he did not limit himself to politics. Franklin's witty proverbs helped make his *Poor Richard's Almanac* a favorite publication of the colonists. For a detailed account of colonial writers and their works, see the WORLD BOOK article on AMERICAN LITERATURE.

Painting. During the mid-1700's, several young colonists were trained by visiting European artists. These American artists, who went to Europe for further study and became world famous, included John Singleton Copley, Charles Willson Peale, Gilbert Charles Stuart, and Benjamin West.

Earlier artists, called *limners*, had little training. They traveled about and earned a living by painting portraits of wealthy colonists. Well-known limners included Charles Bridges, Gustavus Hesselius, Henrietta Johnston, John Smibert, and Jeremiah Theüs.

Science. During most of the colonial period, educated men had broad scientific interests. Many of these men worked to improve education and expand scientific study in the New World.

Benjamin Franklin won honors throughout the world for his scientific experiments and inventions. He led all the men of his day in the study of electricity. In 1752, Franklin flew a homemade kite during a thunderstorm, and proved that lightning is electricity. Then he invented the lightning rod, a way to tame electricity. See FRANKLIN, BENJAMIN (The Scientist).

Franklin also encouraged other scientists. In 1727, he formed the Junto, a debating club. Most of the members were interested in science as well as politics. They met regularly in Philadelphia to exchange ideas. In 1743, Franklin founded the American Philosophical Society, which became the chief center of colonial science.

John Bartram was the most famous botanist of the period. In 1728, he planted America's first botanical garden. Other noted colonial botanists included John Banister, John Clayton, Cadwallader Colden, John Mitchell, and Alexander Garden, for whom the gardenia was named.

Colonial scientists of the 1700's were well informed about new discoveries in astronomy, chemistry, meteorology, and physics. They often exchanged ideas with European scientists. Many performed laboratory experiments or kept records of rainfall, temperature, and the appearance of comets.

Documentary Script, surrounded by floral designs in color, was developed as an art by a number of German colonists.

Baptismal Certificate by Henrich Otto. Free Library of Philadelphia

Colonial Architecture has been preserved in the stately Governor's Palace reconstructed in Wiliamsburg, Va.

Colonial Williamsburg

Mrs. Thomas Van Alstyne by an unknown
artist. New York Historical Society

Woman's Portrait, by a colonial
artist with little training, has a glaring
error. The subject is shown with two
right hands.

Portrait of Isaac Royall and His Family by Robert Feke. Harvard Law School, Cambridge, Mass.

Painting of a Distinguished New England Family is a fine example of the
work of Robert Feke, a colonial artist whose portraits have become famous.

"The Duke's Plan of 1661," one of the earliest maps of a colonial city, was made
a few years before the English captured New Amsterdam and named it New York.

British Museum, London

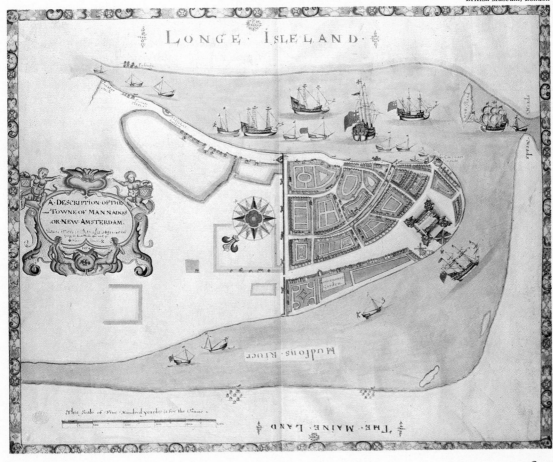

647

Planting Corn for Food, a skill learned from the Indians, saved many early settlers from starvation.

The Homemade Plow, *below left,* and the ancient mattock, *below right,* were important colonial farm tools.

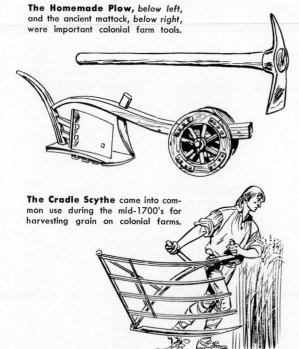

The Cradle Scythe came into common use during the mid-1700's for harvesting grain on colonial farms.

The Wedge-Shaped Iron Froe, a basic colonial tool, was often used to split logs into the slabs that made a sturdy table.

Throughout the colonial period, farming was the most important way of making a living. Farming meant survival for the first settlers. To stay alive, they had to produce food, along with materials for clothing and shelter. As their settlements grew, the colonists raised grains, tobacco, livestock, and other farm products for export. They also developed such industries as fishing and whaling, lumbering, shipbuilding, ironmaking, rum distilling, and flour milling. Colonial craftsmen made furniture, glassware, pottery, and metalware of pewter, iron, or silver.

Farming

Most colonial farmers were successful because they worked hard and land was plentiful. By today's standards, colonial farming methods were wasteful. The colonists usually planted the same kind of crop repeatedly, and the soil became exhausted after a few harvests. Then the farmers simply cleared more land. The most skillful farmers were the German settlers, who rotated their crops and added fertilizers to the soil. These methods kept their land highly productive.

Tools. The colonial farmer worked mostly with hand tools, including an ax, hoe, scythe, sickle, and spade. He also had a *mattock,* a kind of pickax with flat blades. The farmer used his mattock to break up soil or cut roots. These tools were not much better than the sharpened sticks used by the Indians. Some farmers had a homemade wooden plow. It was so heavy that four horses or oxen were required to pull it. Sometimes farmers used tools called harrows and drags, fitted with iron teeth, to break up the soil or prepare seedbeds.

Crops. In spite of wasteful methods and poor tools, the colonial farmer was as prosperous as any farmer of his day, anywhere in the world. Even in New England, with its rocky land and short growing season, a farmer

Great Supplies of Lumber were produced by all the colonies. The timber was used in building homes and ships, and in making millions of barrels for colonial trade and industry.

"Colonel Philip Skene's sawmill and blockhouse, Fort Ann, N.Y." from a sketch by Thomas Anburey. Library of Congress

was well-off. He produced enough vegetables, grain, and meat to feed his family, and usually had extra crops for sale.

Corn was the most important crop of early colonial times. The Indians showed the first settlers how to plant and cultivate it, and how to grind the kernels to make corn meal. Farmers in all the colonies raised corn. As colonial farming developed, wheat replaced corn as the chief grain. But farmers continued to raise large crops of corn to feed their livestock.

Wheat was the most valuable crop of the Middle Colonies. There, a farmer had the advantage of excellent soil and a highly favorable climate. The Middle Colonies exported so much wheat and wheat flour that they became known as the "bread colonies." These colonies also exported large quantities of beef and pork to Europe and the West Indies.

Many Maryland and Virginia farmers raised food crops, but specialized in growing tobacco. Most of the tobacco was exported to England and sold for a high price until about 1760. After tobacco prices fell, some planters raised corn or wheat instead. Maryland and Virginia had many mills that ground grain. Much flour and meal were shipped to the Northern Colonies, southern Europe, and the West Indies.

The farmers of Georgia and South Carolina developed two important crops—rice and indigo. About 1724, the South Carolina rice growers introduced irrigation systems, which increased the size of their crops. The indigo plant was the chief source of a blue dye. European textile industries used great amounts of the dye.

The Southern Colonies grew some cotton, but this crop did not become important until after the Revolutionary War. Some farmers in Pennsylvania and Virginia began to raise flax and hemp about 1750. These products were used in making clothing and rope. They

Huge Barrels that could easily be rolled aboard a ship were used for exporting such products as rum, tobacco, or naval stores.

Making Barrels and Casks for colonial trade required the skills of men called coopers.

Processing Tobacco in Virginia was illustrated by this picture which appeared in a London magazine of 1750. Most colonial tobacco was exported to English merchants.

"Tobacco Manufactory" from the *Universal Magazine*, London. Huntington Library, San Marino, Calif.

became especially important during the war, when most manufactured goods could not be imported.

Timber from all the colonies was used to produce valuable lumber and *naval stores*. In colonial times, naval stores consisted mainly of pitch and tar. These products were vital in building or repairing wooden sailing ships.

Trade and Industry

Colonial trade centered around the exchange of raw materials for European goods. English merchants were the chief customers of the colonists, and English manufactured goods were the settlers' main imports.

Trade of the colonists was strongly influenced by England's economic system, called *mercantilism*. Under this system, the English government protected the nation's industries against competition from the industries of other countries. A basic principle of mercantilism was government control of colonial trade. Parliament tried to strengthen that control by passing a series of laws called the *Navigation Acts*. Some of these laws required the colonists to trade almost entirely with merchants in England or in other English colonies, and to use English ships. Other laws tried to force the colonists to produce chiefly goods that would benefit English industries. The laws encouraged exports of iron, tobacco, and naval stores, which were greatly needed in England. The laws also prohibited the export of certain colonial farm products to England. The English feared these products would compete with English farm products. See MERCANTILISM; NAVIGATION ACT.

The colonists got around the restrictions by developing trade routes that linked colonial ports with southern Europe, the West Indies, and Africa. These three-cornered routes became known as the "triangular trade routes." On one of the routes, the colonists shipped fish, grain, lumber, and meat to southern Europe. There, the products were exchanged for fruit and wine. These were carried to England and traded for manufactured goods that went back to the colonies.

On another triangular route, American food products and lumber were traded in the West Indies for fruit, molasses, and sugar. These were taken to England and exchanged for manufactured goods, which went to America. Another route involved trading in rum and slaves. Rum, made in New England, was exchanged in Africa for Negro slaves. The slaves were exchanged in the West Indies for molasses, which went to New England to be used in making rum.

Fishing and Whaling became major industries in New England for two important reasons. First, the rocky New England land was not suitable for raising large crops. Second, New England ports were within easy sailing distance of the finest fishing and whaling waters of North America. These Atlantic coastal waters included the famous fishing area of the Grand Banks, off Newfoundland.

The principal colonial fishing centers were Boston, Gloucester, Marblehead, and Salem. The catches included cod, halibut, herring, and mackerel. Each year, thousands of tons of fish were salted and dried for export. The chief markets for the better grades of fish were in southern Europe. The poorer grades were generally sold in the West Indies to be used as food for the slaves who worked on sugar plantations.

Nantucket, New Bedford, and Provincetown became important whaling centers. Whales were valuable for their oil, used as fuel in lamps; and for whalebone, used as a stiffening material in women's clothing. For details of the early whaling industry, see WHALE.

Lumbering and Shipbuilding. From the time of the first settlements, lumbering was an important activity in all the colonies. Lumber products ranked among the chief exports of the colonists. The first export from Jamestown consisted of a cargo of clapboard and other building materials shipped to England in 1608.

The colonists used much lumber in building houses, riverboats, and seagoing vessels. Many wood products played an important part in other colonial industries. For example, millions of staves were used to make barrels, casks, and hogsheads for shipping fish, indigo, rice, tobacco, and whale oil.

New England was the center of the shipbuilding in-

COLONIAL TRADE ROUTES

Manufactured goods from England accounted for most colonial imports. Exports consisted mostly of raw materials. The maps on these pages include the famous "triangular trade routes." The colonists used these routes to get around English laws that were designed to control colonial trade.

Ships Sailing Directly to England carried colonial products that were in great demand by English industries.

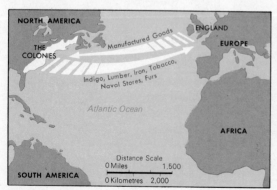

A Major Triangular Route included the West Indies. Goods traded there for colonial products were then taken to England.

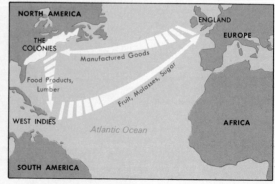

dustry, largely because of the demand there for fishing boats and merchant ships. The New England forests provided good shipbuilding timber, including cedar, maple, oak, and white pine. Virginia and the Carolinas also became important in the shipbuilding industry. The live oak trees of those colonies provided excellent ship timber.

The English encouraged colonial shipbuilding because their own best timber had been used up. By the end of the colonial period, about a third of England's merchant ships were being made in America.

Ironmaking. Iron ore, the most important metal found by the settlers, was mined in most of the colonies. The colonists obtained charcoal, the chief fuel used to smelt iron ore, from their large supplies of hardwoods. The ore deposits and fuel supplies made it fairly easy to develop ironmaking industries.

The first colonial blast furnace began operating about 1621 at Falling Creek, Virginia. The first successful ironworks was built 10 miles north of Boston in 1646. The site is now Saugus, Mass. By 1770, Hunter's ironworks at Falmouth, Virginia, was manufacturing $1\frac{1}{2}$ tons of pig iron daily. Colonial ironworks were producing about a seventh of the world's iron by 1775.

The colonies exported much iron to England in the form of iron bars. But the colonists themselves provided the most important market of the ironmaking industry. Every colonial village or large farm had a blacksmith shop where smiths hammered out iron nails, axes, hoes, and other farm tools. Large ironworks also manufactured these products. Other iron products included cooking pots, kettles, wire, and materials used in making or repairing metal parts of carriages and wagons.

Other Industries. Many industries developed because communities needed certain products or services. Almost as soon as a colonial village was established, someone set up a grist mill to grind grain into flour or meal. Next, perhaps, a blacksmith built a shop to make or repair farm tools. As the community grew, it needed coopers to make barrels. Other industries that developed as the result of community needs included brewing, brickmaking, glassmaking, papermaking, ropemaking, and tanning.

From *A Collection of Voyages*, 1704, by Awnsham and Churchill. Folger Shakespeare Library, Washington, D.C.

Colonial Whaling developed as an industry in the 1700's. But early New England settlers got valuable products, including oil for lamps, from stranded whales that they hauled ashore.

Charles Town, pictured about 1739, was the busiest seaport and richest city of the Southern Colonies. The city's wealth was based chiefly on large exports of rice, indigo, and deerskins.

New York Public Library, I. N. Phelps Stokes Collection

An Important Triangular Route was sailed by ships carrying goods exchanged in southern Europe to ports in England.

Ships of Colonial Slave Traders sailed a route that linked West Africa, the West Indies, and home ports in the colonies.

WORLD BOOK maps-FHa

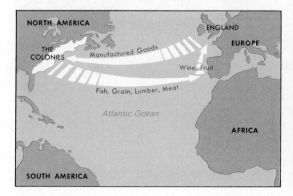

COLONIAL LIFE IN AMERICA

Money. The English government did not allow the colonists to mint coins. But Massachusetts built a mint anyway, and from 1652 to 1683 made various silver coins, including pine-tree shillings (see PINE-TREE SHILLING). Massachusetts and the other colonies sometimes were permitted to issue paper money. Coins came to the colonies chiefly through trade with the West Indies. Most of the coins were Spanish money, made of gold or silver. Colonial merchants weighed the coins on special scales, because customers frequently clipped or shaved the edges to get the precious metal.

The early colonists generally traded goods with each other to get the things they wanted. Sometimes furs and Indian wampum were used as part of this system of *barter* (see BARTER; WAMPUM). Certain crops often took the place of money in the colonies. Southerners used tobacco, and northerners used grain or cattle. People in Maryland and Virginia sometimes used tobacco notes. These notes resembled paper money, and their value was established by tobacco stored in warehouses. See MONEY (Money in the Colonies).

Crafts

During the early colonial period, most of the settlers made their own furniture and household articles. Wealthy colonists generally imported their furnishings from England. Later, skilled colonial craftsmen made many products of wood, iron, silver, pewter, glass, or leather. Some craftsmen copied European styles, but others developed a special American style. Examples of their work may be seen today in many museums.

Most craftsmen had shops in the cities or towns. In the Northern Colonies, some traveled from one community to another. Many customers supplied the raw materials used by a craftsman. In the south, many indentured servants were skilled craftsmen. After serving their period of indenture, many craftsmen set up their own shops.

Furniture. Most early colonial chairs, tables, beds, and chests were bulky and heavy. But the cabinetmakers improved their designs, and the furniture became lighter and more graceful. The styles that were developed to please various colonial tastes are described in FURNITURE (American Furniture).

Ironwork. Many articles made of iron by colonial blacksmiths are prized today as examples of fine craftsmanship. They include hinges, kettles, latches, locks, and weather vanes. A blacksmith was an important member of almost every community because he made and repaired tools and many other articles.

Silverware. The work of the silversmith was almost as important as that of the blacksmith. His customers considered silverware an investment because the metal itself had a high value. Valuable silver pieces included candlesticks, platters, bowls, coffee and tea pots, salt-cellars, and sets of tableware.

Almost every colonial town had a silversmith, but the main silversmithing centers were Boston, Philadelphia, and New York City. Three noted silversmiths were Bostonians—John Coney, John Hull, and Paul Revere.

Pewter was used in most colonial households in some form because it was cheaper than silver. Pewterware resembles silverware, and pewterers made the same kind of articles as silversmiths. See PEWTER.

Glass. The first successful American glass factory was established in Salem County, New Jersey, in 1739. Another began operating in Manheim, Pennsylvania, in 1765. These factories produced bottles, window panes, and much fine table glass that were sold throughout the colonies. See GLASS (Early American Glass).

Other Crafts. Craftsmen who worked with leather used hides that had either been imported or tanned in the colonies. Most of these craftsmen were saddlers and harness makers. They also made boots and shoes.

Gunsmiths developed their craft in all the colonies. The gunsmiths of Pennsylvania and western Virginia developed the "long rifle" used by many Revolutionary soldiers. Some colonial rifles were beautifully carved and inlaid with silver.

Colonial Williamsburg

Needlework picture by Dorothy Cotton. Henry Francis du Pont Winterthur Museum, Winterthur, Del.

Colonial Needlework is highly prized by collectors of antiques.

Spinning and Weaving were important home industries throughout the colonies.

Colonial Williamsburg

Made by John Coney. Museum of Fine Arts, Boston, Gift of Mrs. J. R. Churchill

Silversmithing was a leading craft in the colonies. Most towns had a silversmith, *left,* who made beautiful silver pieces, such as the sugar bowl, *above.*

Glassmaking, *left,* was slow in developing as a colonial craft. The first successful factory opened about 1739.

Stiegel Glass, named for Henry William Stiegel, a famous colonial glassmaker, is considered by some experts to be the most beautiful of all glassware. Stiegel applied patterns to his glass by molding, enameling, and engraving.

Sugar bowl and enameled tumblers by Henry William Stiegel. Corning Museum of Glass, Corning, N.Y.

Walter H. Miller

Furniture made by colonial cabinetmakers of the mid-1700's is noted for its graceful design. Some card tables, *left,* have needlepoint tops.

Pewterware, such as an engraved tankard, *right,* could be found in most colonial households. It was handsome and less expensive than silverware.

Pewter tankard made by Simon Edgell. Henry Francis du Pont Winterthur Museum, Winterthur, Del.

Museum of Fine Arts, Boston, William E. Nickerson Fund

653

Jamestown Festival Park on the James River in Virginia

Jamestown Foundation

Witch House in Salem, Mass.

Dick Hanley, Photo Researchers

Plimoth Plantation in Plymouth, Mass.

Plimoth Plantation

COLONIAL LIFE IN AMERICA / A Visitor's Guide to Colonial America

Every year, millions of visitors tour the region that once was colonial America. Throughout the region, historic sites offer interesting glimpses of colonial life. Almost every town or city has churches or houses that date from the 1700's and a few from the 1600's. In some places, a visitor may walk through the streets of an entire colonial community that has been rebuilt. Many public buildings and museums display colonial relics in cities that were important during colonial times— Boston, Charleston, New York City, Newport, and Philadelphia. Newport has over 300 colonial buildings.

PLACES TO VISIT

Following are brief descriptions of some especially interesting places to visit. See also the Places to Visit section of the WORLD BOOK article on each state.

Amstel House, in New Castle, Del., has exhibits of colonial arts, furnishings, and crafts. The house was built in the early 1700's.

Batsto is a partially restored colonial village in southeastern New Jersey. It includes an ironmaster's house, a blacksmith shop, a general store, and a glassware exhibit.

Ephrata Cloisters, in Ephrata, Pa., is a restored religious community built by German Seventh-Day Baptists in 1732.

Farmers' Museum, near Cooperstown, N.Y., has many colonial farm tools. Nearby is the **Village Crossroads,** a typical colonial village.

Fort Niagara, near Youngstown, N.Y., was the scene of fighting during the French and Indian Wars and the Revolutionary War. It was originally built in 1678.

Henry Francis du Pont Winterthur Museum, near Wilmington, Del., has a magnificent collection of early American furniture. Visitors must write for permission to go through this museum.

Jamestown Island, on the James River in Virginia, is the site of the first permanent English settlement in

Blacksmith Shop at Farmers' Museum in Cooperstown, N.Y.

Fort Niagara near Youngstown, N.Y.

Meeting House in Ephrata, Pa.

Saugus Ironworks in Saugus, Mass.

America. It is a National Park. Nearby, **Jamestown Festival Park** has reproductions of old James Fort and of the three ships that brought the first settlers to Jamestown in 1607.

Old Gaol Museum, in York, Me., was built in 1653, and is one of America's oldest buildings. It served as a *gaol* (jail) until 1860.

Old Narragansett Church, in North Kingstown, R.I., is the oldest Episcopal church in the northern United States. It was built in 1707.

Old Salem is a restored colonial village in Winston-Salem, N.C. Moravians founded the village in 1766.

Old Sturbridge Village, in Sturbridge, Mass., is a replica of a New England town in 1800.

Old Town Mill, in New London, Conn., is a colonial grain-grinding mill, built in 1650.

Plimoth Plantation, in Plymouth, Mass., is a reconstruction of the first Pilgrim settlement.

St. Mary's City, a village near Leonardtown, Md.,

was Maryland's first settlement, established in 1634.

Saugus Ironworks, in Saugus, Mass., is a reconstruction of America's first successful ironworks, built in the 1640's.

Shelburne Museum, in Shelburne, Vt., is a reconstruction of an early American village. The buildings house one of the world's most complete collections of articles used by the settlers.

Strawberry Banke, in Portsmouth, N.H., is a restoration of a colonial village, settled in 1630.

Whitehorse Tavern, in Newport, R.I., was built in 1673.

Williamsburg is a Virginia city whose colonial buildings have been restored. Colonial Williamsburg provides a glimpse of the buildings, gardens, furnishings, crafts, and social life of the 1700's.

Witch House, in Salem, Mass., was the home of Judge Jonathan Corwin, a judge at the witchcraft trials of the early 1690's. JANE CARSON

Related Articles. For the history of each colony, from settlement to statehood, see the separate state articles in WORLD BOOK, such as GEORGIA (History). See also UNITED STATES, HISTORY OF (The Thirteen Colonies), and the following articles:

COLONIZATION

Dutch West India Company
Jamestown
London Company
Lost Colony
Massachusetts Bay Colony
New England, Dominion of
New England Confederation
New Netherland
Ohio Company (The First)
Plymouth Colony
Plymouth Company
Williamsburg

GOVERNMENT AND LAW ENFORCEMENT

Blue Laws
Ducking Stool
Flag (color pictures: Flags in American History)
House of Burgesses
Mayflower Compact
Money (Money in the Colonies)
Pillory
Stocks
Town Meeting

EDUCATION AND COMMUNICATION

American Literature (Colonial Writing)
Education, History of (Colonial Days)
Freedom of the Press (picture)
Hornbook
Newspaper (picture: In Colonial Days)
School (picture: Colonial Schools)
Town Crier

BIOGRAPHIES

THE NEW ENGLAND COLONIES

Alden (John; Priscilla M.)
Andros, Sir Edmund
Bradford (family)
Bradford, William
Bradstreet, Anne D.
Brewster, William
Brown (family)
Carver, John
Cotton, John
Dudley, Thomas
Dyer, Mary
Eaton, Theophilus
Endecott, John
Faneuil, Peter
Hooker, Thomas
Hutchinson, Anne M.
Massasoit
Mather (family)
Philip, King
Randolph, Edward
Samoset
Sewall, Samuel
Shirley, William
Squanto
Standish, Miles
Uncas
Warwick, Earl of (1587)
Wentworth, Benning
White, Peregrine
Williams, Roger
Winslow, Edward
Winthrop (family)

THE MIDDLE COLONIES

Colden, Cadwallader
Franklin, Benjamin
Jemison, Mary
Johnson, Sir William
Leisler, Jacob
Minuit, Peter
Pastorius, Francis D.
Penn, William
Shikellamy
Stuyvesant, Peter
Van Rensselaer (family)
Zenger, John Peter

THE SOUTHERN COLONIES

Bacon, Nathaniel
Baltimore, Lord
Berkeley, Sir William
Byrd (family)
Dare, Virginia
Delaware, Lord
Dinwiddie, Robert
Oglethorpe, James E.
Pinckney (Elizabeth L.)
Pocahontas
Powhatan
Randolph (William)
Rolfe, John
Smith, John
Spotswood, Alexander

OTHER RELATED ARTICLES

Bacon's Rebellion
Charter Oak
Claiborne's Rebellion
Doll (Colonial Dolls)
French and Indian Wars
Georgian Architecture

Great Awakening
Indentured Servant
Indian Wars
Mayflower
Patroon System
Pennsylvania Dutch
Pilgrim
Pioneer Life
Plymouth Rock
Puritan
Salem (Mass.)
Shelter (Pioneer and Colonial Shelter)
Shot Tower
Thanksgiving Day
Witchcraft

Outline

I. The Thirteen Colonies
  A. Why the Colonists Came to America
  B. Early Settlements
  C. Development of the Colonies
  D. Relations With the Indians

II. Society and Government
  A. Colonial Society
  B. Government
  C. Voting Requirements
  D. Local Government
  E. Law Enforcement

III. The Home
  A. Houses
  B. Furnishings
  C. Clothing
  D. Food
  E. Health
  F. Recreation

IV. The Church and the School
  A. The Church
  B. The School

V. Travel and Communication
  A. Travel
  B. Communication

VI. Arts and Sciences
  A. Literature
  B. Painting
  C. Science

VII. Economy
  A. Farming
  B. Trade and Industry
  C. Crafts

VIII. A Visitor's Guide to Colonial America

Questions

How did the English settlers in the New World differ from the Spanish and French?

What were the three major types of English colonies?

How did most colonial boys learn a trade or profession?

What were two of the most important reasons for the survival of the Jamestown settlement?

Why were the Middle Colonies known as the "bread colonies"?

What were the five most important colonial cities of the 1700's?

How did the colonists get around the trade restrictions of the Navigation Acts?

What were the two most important crops of Georgia and South Carolina?

What were three chief reasons for discontented Europeans to migrate to the colonies?

What was the purpose of the Proclamation of 1763?

Books for Young Readers

AGLE, NAN H., and BACON, F. A. *The Lords Baltimore.* Holt, 1962.

AMERICAN HERITAGE. *Jamestown: First English Colony.* American Heritage, 1965.

BAILEY, CAROLYN S. *Children of the Handcrafts.* Viking, 1935. The arts and crafts taught to children in colonial days.

DALGLIESH, ALICE. *The Thanksgiving Story.* Scribner, 1954. *The Fourth of July Story.* 1956. *America Begins:*

The Story of the Finding of the New World. Rev. ed. 1959. These books are all intended for the early elementary grades. They combine pictures with a brief text and make historical events vivid and meaningful for young children.

DAVIS, BURKE. *America's First Army.* Holt, 1962.

DE ANGELI, MARGUERITE L. *Elin's Amerika.* Doubleday, 1941. A little girl of New Sweden in the 1600's.

EARLE, ALICE M. *Child Life in Colonial Days.* Macmillan, 1922. *Home Life in Colonial Days.* 1948.

EATON, JEANETTE. *Lone Journey: The Life of Roger Williams.* Harcourt, 1944.

EDMONDS, WALTER D. *Matchlock Gun.* Dodd, 1941. A boy fights off an Indian attack in colonial times.

FORBES, ESTHER. *Johnny Tremain.* Houghton, 1943. Paul Revere's apprentice in pre-Revolutionary times.

FOSTER, GENEVIEVE. *The World of Captain John Smith, 1580-1631.* Scribner, 1959.

GALT, THOMAS F. *Peter Zenger: Fighter for Freedom.* Crowell, 1951. A biography of the German immigrant who won the first victory for freedom of the press in the American colonies.

GRAY, ELIZABETH J. *Beppy Marlowe of Charles Town.* Viking, 1936. An English girl's adventures in South Carolina in the early 1700's.

HULTS, DOROTHY N. *New Amsterdam Days and Ways: The Dutch Settlers of New York,* Harcourt, 1963.

JUDSON, CLARA I. *Benjamin Franklin,* Follett, 1957.

LATHAM, JEAN L. *This Dear-Bought Land.* Harper, 1957. A vivid picture of the Jamestown settlement.

MORISON, SAMUEL E. *The Story of the Old Colony of New Plymouth (1620-1692). Knopf,* 1956.

NORTH, STERLING. *George Washington: Frontier Colonel.* Random House, 1957.

PEARE, CATHERINE O. *William Penn.* Holt, 1958.

PETERSHAM, MAUD F. and MISKA. *The Silver Mace: A Story of Williamsburg.* Macmillan, 1956.

SMITH, ERIC B., and MEREDITH, ROBERT, eds. *Pilgrim Courage.* Little, Brown, 1962. The story of the Pilgrims' voyage to America and their early struggles, based on William Bradford's journals and other first-hand sources.

SPEARE, ELIZABETH G. *The Witch of Blackbird Pond.* Houghton, 1958. Newbery medal winner. The story of a girl of 16 from Barbados who arrives in Connecticut in 1687 and whose adventures include being tried for witchcraft. Real historical characters appear, and the social background of the period is described.

TUNIS, EDWIN. *Colonial Living.* World Publishing Co., 1957. The author illustrates this history of colonial America with over 200 line drawings on subjects from house construction to costumes. *Colonial Craftsmen and the Beginnings of American Industry.* 1965. This book describes and illustrates the development of about 35 important trades, showing how they were organized and the kinds of tools used.

Books for Older Readers

ACHESON, PATRICIA C. *America's Colonial Heritage.* Dodd, 1957. This book shows how the European background of the colonists influenced their society and government.

BENÉT, STEPHEN VINCENT. *Western Star.* Holt, 1943. This narrative poem describes the Jamestown and Plymouth settlements.

BRIDENBAUGH, CARL. *Cities in the Wilderness: The First Century of Urban Life in America, 1625-1742.* 2nd ed. Knopf, 1955. *Cities in Revolt: Urban Life in America, 1743-1776.* 1955. These two volumes describe social, political, and cultural relationships in the development of the cities of colonial America. The books also describe the influence of urban life on the movement favoring independence from Great Britain.

CARSON, JANE. *Colonial Virginians at Play.* Colonial Williamsburg, 1965. For sale by University Press of Virginia. This book includes extensive quotations from intimate accounts of the colonial period, and many illustrations.

CHITWOOD, OLIVER P. *A History of Colonial America.* 3rd ed. Harper, 1961.

HAWKE, DAVID. *The Colonial Experience.* Bobbs, 1966. A general history of the American colonies that begins with the period of exploration and goes through the Revolutionary War.

LAMB, HAROLD. *New Found World: How North America Was Discovered and Explored.* Doubleday, 1955. A history of the exploration of North America to 1600.

LANGDON, WILLIAM C. *Everyday Things in American Life, 1607-1776.* Scribner, 1937.

VAUGHAN, ALDEN T. *New England Frontier: Puritans and Indians, 1620-1675.* Little, Brown, 1965.

WERTENBAKER, THOMAS J. *The First Americans, 1607-1690.* Macmillan, 1927. *Golden Age of Colonial Culture.* Cornell, 1959.

WRIGHT, LOUIS B. *The Cultural Life of the American Colonies, 1607-1763.* Harper, 1957. *Everyday Life in Colonial America.* Putnam, 1966.

COLONIAL NATIONAL HISTORICAL PARK. See NATIONAL PARK (National Historical Parks).

COLONNADE. See ARCHITECTURE (Greek).

COLONY. See ANIMAL (Animal Homes); ANT (The Ant Colony); BEE (The Honeybee Colony); WASP.

COLONY is a settlement established by people outside their native land, and ruled by the mother country. Nations establish colonies to find more room in which people can live, to increase trade by providing a market for manufactured goods, to gain sources of raw materials, to secure military advantages, and to increase the prestige of the mother country.

Climate has often decided how a colony develops. Temperate lands have attracted large numbers of colonists who have pushed out the inhabitants of the region. This occurred in the settlement of North America, where the new settlers drove the Indians farther and farther westward. Only a few colonists have left their native lands to settle in areas where the climate was either very hot or very cold. These few, instead of pushing out the inhabitants, took control of the colonized territory, as the Belgians did in the Belgian Congo.

Some colonies eventually become independent of the mother country. This happened when America broke away from England and became the United States. Canada, Australia, New Zealand, and India once were British colonies, but now are independent members of the British Commonwealth. Many former colonies of nations defeated in World Wars I and II became United Nations trust territories. Most of them are now self-governing.   WILLIAM T. R. FOX

Related Articles in WORLD BOOK include:

Africa (Colonial Rule; color map: Colonial Africa)
Asia (The Age of Colonialism; color map: Asia Before World War I)
Colonial Life in America
Commonwealth of Nations
Crown Colony
France (History)
Governor General
Great Britain (The Growing Empire)
Latin America (History)
Portugal (Overseas Provinces)
Trust Territory

COLONY, PENAL. See PENAL COLONY.

COLOPHON. See BOOK (Parts of a Book).

COLOR

Jean on a Wooden Horse, by Claude Monet, courtesy of Mr. Nathan Cummings, Chicago

Colors in Paint capture a wide variety of natural colors, and can be created by mixing only a few paints. The artist can make any color by blending the three primary colors of paint—red, yellow, and blue.

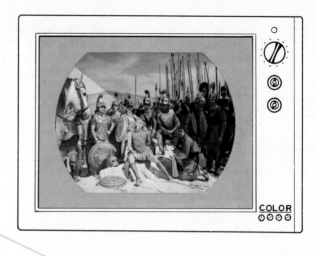

Colors in Light blend differently than colors in paint. Color television, for example, works by mixing colored lights. It can produce a wide range of colors by blending the three primary colors of light—red, green, and blue.

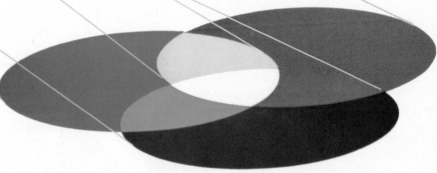

Illustrated by George V. Kelvin for WORLD BOOK

COLOR surrounds us everywhere. We see it in the sky, in the oceans, in the rocks, and in all plants and animals. Color adds beauty to our clothing and food. It makes our homes, schools, and offices attractive. We see it in paintings and photographs, in books and magazines, and in motion pictures and television shows. Advertisements and posters attract our attention with bright colors. Signs in yellow and black warn us of danger. Safety equipment is painted green, and fire trucks are red.

We use the names of colors in many common sayings. A person *sees red* when he loses his temper, or becomes *green with envy* at someone else's luck. He may *feel blue* (sad) because someone has *called him yellow* (a coward).

Ralph M. Evans, contributor of this article, is director of the Photographic Technology Division, Eastman Kodak Company. Faber Birren, the critical reviewer, is an industrial consultant on color. Artwork and photography by Arnold Ryan Chalfant & Associates for WORLD BOOK except where noted.

But *once in a blue moon* everything goes all right and he has a *red-letter day*.

Everything in the world has color. Our eyes see grass as green, an apple as red, and a beach as yellow-brown. We take these colors for granted, but we cannot prove that they exist. In fact, we know that dogs and many other animals cannot see colors. Still other animals, such as bees, see colors we do not see. All we know is that our eyes see color when light strikes them.

To learn about color, scientists have explored the nature of light. They know that white light, such as sunlight, can be broken up into the colors of the rainbow. They also know that these colors can be combined again to form white light.

Scientists have discovered many ways in which colors in light differ from the colors of a house, an apple, or an automobile. They believe that there are two ways to examine color. One way is to study the qualities of various colors as they appear in such things as paint. The other method is to study the way we see color.

Red   Yellow   Blue

Primary and Secondary Colors. A painter mixes pairs of the primary colors red, yellow, and blue to make the secondary colors orange, green, and violet, as shown *below*.

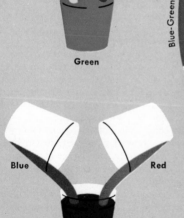

Red   Yellow

Orange

Yellow   Blue

Green

Blue   Red

Violet

COLOR IN PAINT

An artist can paint a sunset by starting with only three colors. He needs only red, yellow, and blue paint. He can mix these colors together to make others. For example, he can make orange for the glow of the sun by mixing red and yellow. He can make green for the grass by combining yellow and blue. And he can make violet for the shadows by mixing blue and red. The painter can go on to mix as many other colors as he needs. He simply combines his first three colors (red, yellow, and blue) with his three new ones (orange, green, and violet). He can make brown by mixing the orange with blue, and light yellow-green by blending yellow and green. He can make gray by mixing red and green.

Mixing colored light produces different results than mixing the same colors in paints. Blue and yellow paints mix to make green, but blue and yellow lights mix to make white. This and other information about colored light is explained in the section *Color in Light*.

The Color Wheel. We can arrange the painter's colors in a circle like the face of a clock to show how they are related. We start with red, yellow, and blue. These are called the *primary colors in paint* because we can use them to make the widest range of other colors. We put yellow at 12 o'clock, red at 4 o'clock, and blue at 8 o'clock.

Next, we put orange, violet, and green at 2 o'clock, 6 o'clock, and 10 o'clock on the circle. These colors are called *secondary* or *binary colors* because they are made by mixing the primary colors.

THE COLOR WHEEL

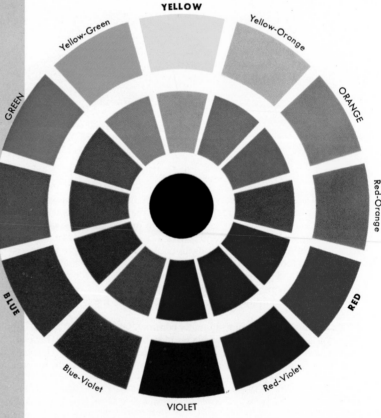

The outer circle shows the primary and secondary colors, separated by six intermediate colors. The inner circle shows darker colors obtained by mixing two colors that lie opposite each other in the outer circle.

Our clock face has spaces for six more colors. These colors are yellow-orange, red-orange, red-violet, blue-violet, blue-green, and yellow-green. These six colors are called *intermediate colors* because they lie between the primary and secondary colors.

Artists also speak of *tertiary colors*. These are soft colors formed by mixing the secondary colors together.

Any two colors directly opposite each other in the circle produce a black or dark gray when mixed together in equal parts. Such colors are called *complementary colors in paint*. When mixed together in unequal parts, complementary colors darken each other. For example, a little blue added to orange creates brown, and a little orange added to blue produces a darker blue.

The circle of paints can be expanded into a full *color wheel* such as the one shown here. The color wheel is one of the best ways to show how paint colors are related to each other. Some color wheels have only 10 colors, and others have as many as 100.

The Color Triangle. Two important paint colors, black and white, do not appear anywhere on the color wheel. We can see how black and white fit into the world of color by using a *color triangle*. A color triangle has a color at one angle, black at another, and white at the third. If a color from the color wheel, such as red, is mixed with white, the result is a *tint*—in this case, pink. If we mix red with black, the result is a *shade*—in this case, maroon. And if we mix red with both black and white, the result is a *tone*—in this case, rose.

Color Harmony is the use of combinations of colors to produce a pleasing effect. A woman may use color harmony when she selects the color of a hat to wear with a new dress. Interior decorators plan color schemes for the rooms of a home according to the principles of color harmony. Many persons use a color triangle or a color wheel to find attractive combinations of colors.

In a color triangle, the colors in any straight line form pleasing combinations. A pure color harmonizes with tints and white, with shades and black, or with tones and gray. A tint and a tone blend with black, and a shade and a tone go well with white. Groups of tints, shades, or tones also harmonize well.

In the color wheel, complementary colors, such as red and green, go well together. Such combinations often appear in nature, as in blue or violet flowers with orange or yellow centers. A color also goes well with the colors next to its complementary, such as red with blue-green and yellow-green. These are called *near comple-*

THE COLOR TRIANGLE

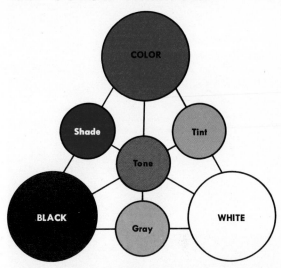

A color from the color wheel can be mixed with white to make a *tint*, or with black to make a *shade*. The color can also be blended with gray (a mixture of black and white) to produce a *tone*.

mentary or *split complementary colors*. Any three equally spaced colors, called *triads*, go well together, as in yellow-orange, red-violet, and blue-green.

Color harmony may also be achieved with *adjacent colors*. These colors lie next to each other on the color wheel. A color scheme called a *mutual complement* combines five adjacent colors (such as blue-green, green, yellow-green, yellow, and yellow-orange) with the complementary of the middle one (red-violet). A *double complement* combines two sets of complementaries, such as yellow-green and red-violet with yellow-orange and blue-violet.

There are no set rules of color harmony, because too many factors must be considered. If one color covers a large area and another near it covers only a tiny space, problems of harmony do not arise. The problems vary if one color covers a shiny area and the other covers a rough one. Any two colors could probably be made to blend harmoniously. For additional information on color harmony, see INTERIOR DECORATION (How to Use Color); CLOTHING (How to Choose Clothes).

COLOR HARMONY

The diagrams *below* show how three kinds of harmonizing colors can be found by connecting various positions on the color wheel.

Complementary Colors, such as yellow and violet, lie directly opposite each other on the color wheel.

Near-Complementary Colors, such as yellow and red-violet, or yellow and blue-violet, lie nearly opposite one another.

A Triad consists of three colors spaced an equal distance apart, such as the primary colors yellow, red, and blue.

COLOR IN LIGHT

THE SPECTRUM

Light travels in waves, just as radio signals and X rays do. Light waves are the only ones we can see. Scientists can measure the lengths of these waves. By examining colored lights, they have discovered that each has its own wavelength. Violet light has the shortest waves we can see—67,000 waves to the inch. Red light has the longest visible waves. But even these waves are so short that 33,000 of them measure only one inch. See LIGHT.

A narrow beam of white light spreads out into a beautiful band of colors when it passes through a transparent prism. This band contains the colors of the rainbow and is called the *spectrum*. The colors of the spectrum blend into each other, running from violet through blue, green, and yellow to red. The spectrum does not contain a true red—one that is neither yellowish nor bluish. Nor does it form a full circle of colors. The spectrum has no colors between red and violet, as the color wheel does.

By using a prism to form the spectrum, we learn that white light is a mixture of many colored lights. Thus, we can make colored lights from white light, and we also can make white light by mixing colored lights.

We can recombine the colors of the spectrum to form white light if we put a second prism close to the first one and use it to "collect" the colors. But suppose we put a mask over the first prism, letting only a tiny part of the spectrum come through. The light will have only one color. We cannot beam this *monochromatic* light through a second prism and divide it still further. In other words, we can divide white light to make colored lights, but we cannot divide narrow regions of the spectrum to make other colors.

A band of colors called a spectrum is formed when white light passes through a prism. The prism "bends" each color as it goes through. It bends violet light the most and red light the least.

PRIMARY COLORS IN LIGHT

We can form all colored lights by blending groups of colors from the spectrum. We blend the colors by passing them through a prism. If we take about a third of the spectrum at the red end, and blend its colors, the resulting light will be red. If we take about a third of the spectrum at the violet end, the blended light will be blue. And if we take the middle third of the spectrum, its colors will blend to form green.

These three colors—red, blue, and green—are the *primary colors in light*. The red and blue primaries of light are not exactly the same colors as the red and blue primaries of paint. In light, the blue primary is less green and the red primary is more orange. When we combine the three light primaries in equal parts, we produce white light, just as though we had combined all the colors of the spectrum. Many scientists define pure white light as a mixture of equal amounts of red, blue, and green light. These primary colors are used in creating color television (see TELEVISION [picture, How Color Television Works]).

Primary colors of light—red, green, and blue—can be mixed together to make white light. Each primary color may be thought of as a blend of the colors in one-third of the spectrum.

66ob

The principle of forming colors by combining parts of the spectrum is called *additive color mixture* or *color by addition*. It is one of two basic ways to mix colors, and can be used only with colors in light. The other basic way of mixing colors involves subtracting parts of the spectrum from white light. It is called *subtractive color mixture* or *color by subtraction*. It forms the basis for almost all present-day color photography (see PHOTOGRAPHY [Color Photography]).

When the spectrum falls on a colored surface, rather than a white one, the results are quite different. Instead of seeing the whole spectrum, we see only some parts of it. For example, red paper reflects most of the light waves at the red end of the spectrum. But it *absorbs* (does not reflect) almost all the light waves at the violet end. Yellow paper reflects red and green light, as well as yellow light, but absorbs most blue light.

In each of these cases, we have removed parts of the spectrum from white light to form colors. This process, color by subtraction, forms the closest link between color in light and color in objects. It explains why the colors in objects mix the way they do. If we put yellow and blue glass marbles in a plastic bag and hold them up to the light, they will appear green from a distance as the light shines through them. The yellow marbles transmit red, orange, yellow, and green light, but absorb blue and violet. The blue marbles transmit green, blue, and violet light, but absorb red, orange, and yellow. Green is the one color that both yellow and blue marbles transmit. In the same way, a mixture of yellow paint and blue paint makes green paint. In both cases, both yellow and blue subtract part of the spectrum. The remaining part is the new color.

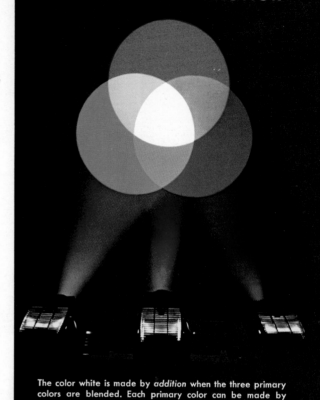

The color white is made by *addition* when the three primary colors are blended. Each primary color can be made by *subtraction* if white light is passed through a piece of colored glass that absorbs, or subtracts, all other colors.

COMPLEMENTARY COLORS IN LIGHT

The complement of a primary color is the color formed by blending the other two primaries.

Complementary colors in light are any two colors that form white light when combined. We can produce the three most important complementary colors in light by combining pairs of primaries. If we shoot a beam of red light and a beam of blue light onto a white screen together, they form a bluish red called *magenta*. If we beam blue and green lights onto the screen, we form a bluish green called *cyan*. With green and red lights, we form yellow. If we combine any one of these three complementary colors with the third primary color, we produce white light. For example, when we beam yellow light (made up of green and red) onto the screen and then add blue, the third primary color, we form white.

If we block off any color in the spectrum, the remaining colors will form its complementary. If we take out green, the remaining light is magenta. Scientists sometimes call yellow light by the odd name of *minus blue*. They mean that yellow light can be thought of as white light with the blue taken out.

Red and blue blend to make magenta, the complement of green.

Blue and green blend to make blue-green, the complement of red.

Green and red blend to make yellow, the complement of blue.

The purpose of this project is to learn how colors are created by adding and subtracting colored light. You can perform this demonstration with a color projector built from common materials.

To Create Color by Addition, turn the projector on so you see red, green, and blue circles, *left*. Where these circles overlap, the colors add to form new colors—yellow, blue-green, magenta, and white. Never run the projector for more than a few minutes. It becomes hot and must be allowed to cool.

Illustrated by Raymond Perlman for WORLD BOOK

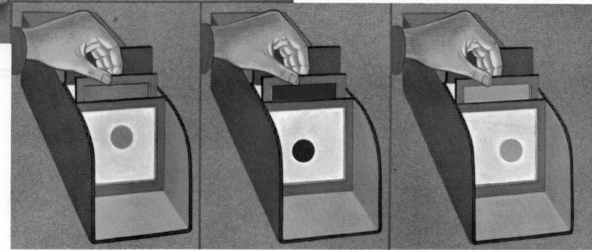

To Create Color by Subtraction, turn the projector on so that the red, green, and blue circles show. Then, insert colored filters one at a time. A red filter subtracts blue and green; a blue filter subtracts red and green; and a green filter subtracts red and blue. Subtracted colors may not disappear entirely from the screen because the simple filters may not work perfectly.

MATERIALS

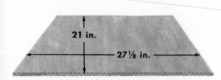

Stiff corrugated cardboard

2-pound coffee can open at both ends

3 cardboard tubes 1¼-inch diameter

100-watt bulb and socket

7 pieces of cardboard 5 inches square

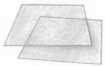

Tracing paper

Aluminum foil

Colored cellophane or gelatin 5 inches square

ASSEMBLY

Cut the projector housing from corrugated cardboard as shown, *right*. Fold and assemble as shown, *below*. First, tie the coffee can in place with string. Then assemble the tubes, permanent filters, and screen. Follow the dimensions as closely as possible, or the color circles may not overlap properly on the screen.

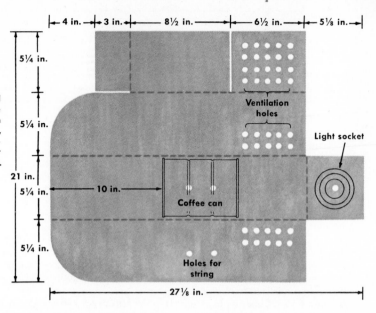

Ventilation holes

Light socket

4 in. · **3 in.** · **8½ in.** · **6½ in.** · **5⅛ in.**

5¼ in.

5¼ in.

21 in.

10 in.

Coffee can

5¼ in.

Holes for string

5¼ in.

27⅛ in.

Permanent Filters are mounted on a 5-inch-square piece of cardboard held by guide rails. Centers of the holes are ⅞ inch from the center of the square. Try various shades of red, green, and blue filters to get white where circles overlap on the screen.

Front Tube-Holder is a 5-inch-square cardboard sheet taped to projector housing 2½ inches from the front of the coffee can. The centers of the holes are ⅞ inch from the center of the square. The cardboard tubes are taped in place.

Rear Tube-Holder is a 5-inch-diameter cardboard circle taped to the front of the coffee can. The centers of the holes are 1⅜ inches from the center of the circle. The tubes are inserted through the holes so they extend 2 inches into the coffee can.

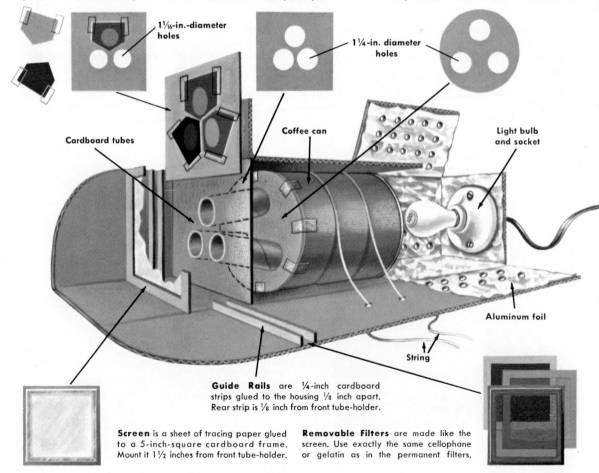

1¹⁄₁₆-in.-diameter holes

1¼-in. diameter holes

Cardboard tubes

Coffee can

Light bulb and socket

Aluminum foil

String

Guide Rails are ¼-inch cardboard strips glued to the housing ⅛ inch apart. Rear strip is ⅛ inch from front tube-holder.

Screen is a sheet of tracing paper glued to a 5-inch-square cardboard frame. Mount it 1½ inches from front tube-holder.

Removable Filters are made like the screen. Use exactly the same cellophane or gelatin as in the permanent filters.

66I

HOW THE EYE SEES COLOR

We are so used to seeing red apples that we rarely think about their color. But if we look at an apple in a dark room, it may seem dark gray. And if we look at it under a blue or green light, it will appear black. When we look at something, we see it in terms of the light reflected from it. A colored object usually reflects colored light into our eyes when we look at it. This is true whether we look at an apple, a painting, or a piece of colored cloth. Whenever we discuss colored objects, we are actually talking about colored lights—the rays of colored light reflected from objects.

Light reflected from an object travels to the sensitive area at the back of the eye, which is called the *retina*. An image forms there, and the nerves in the retina send this image to the brain. The retina has two kinds of cells that respond to light. They are (1) the rods and (2) the cones. The *rods* are extremely sensitive in dim light, but they do not respond to color. The *cones*, which respond only to stronger light, provide our color vision. In dim light, when only the rods respond, our eyes do not see color. See Eye (How We See).

A few persons can see only certain colors. Even fewer persons can see only white, gray, and black. These persons are *color blind* (see Color Blindness). Many animals have no color vision at all. They probably see objects as various shades of gray. This fact emphasizes that color is as much something happening in our eyes as it is something happening in the world around us.

HOW COLOR FOOLS THE EYE

Our eyes constantly play tricks on us. Many of these tricks are related to the way our eyes react to the colors around us. When we look from one area of color to another, our eyes adapt themselves to the change of color. The adaptation takes several steps, but we are not usually aware of them. We have learned unconsciously not to "see" them. When we do see one of these steps, we can hardly believe our eyes.

To See an Afterimage, stare at the center of the flag for about 30 seconds. Then look at a sheet of white paper. You will see an image of the flag with its proper colors.

Perhaps the best known visual effect that shows how our eyes adapt to color is the *afterimage*. If we stare at a colored area for about 30 seconds, then at a dot on a white or gray background, our eyes will "see" color in the blank area. The color we see will be roughly complementary to the color we first stared at. For example, it will be red if we looked at blue-green, or blue if we looked at yellow. The size of the afterimage depends on the distance from our eyes to the blank area. If the blank area is closer than the original colored area, the afterimage will be smaller than the original. But if we stare at the color and then look at a blank wall across the room, the afterimage will be much larger.

Another surprising visual effect is that the same color looks different on two different background colors. Gray looks much lighter when surrounded by black than when surrounded by white. Yellow seems to contain more red when placed on a green area than when placed on white. And a blue area placed on a green background seems to have more violet than when it appears on white. Scientists believe that we see greater differences between colors when we see them together than when we see them sepa-

All colored objects appear gray when seen in a dark room.

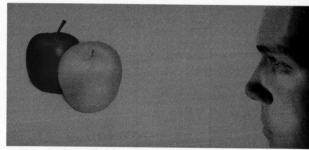

Under red light, red appears normal, but green looks black.

Under blue light, both red and green objects look black.

Under green light, green appears normal, but red looks black.

rately. They believe that the eye automatically becomes sensitive to one color when it sees the complementary color.

One of the commonest effects of color adaptation is that we usually accept a color as the same under both artificial light and strong sunlight. The yellowish color of light from an electric lamp changes most colors, but our eyes tend to see the colors unchanged. However, it is best to match colors only in daylight.

Probably the most interesting color illusion is to see color where no color exists. Narrow black lines placed close together seem to take on color if we stare at them long enough. When moved, as in a device called *Benham's disk*, they seem to have several colors. If the disk spins at a rate of 5 to 15 turns a second, the short curved lines are seen as colored rings. If the disk spins to the right, the inner rings appear red and the outer rings blue. If it spins to the left, the inner rings

Benham's Disk has only black and white markings, but it appears to have colored rings when it spins. You can draw the disk with black ink on white cardboard. Stick a pin through the center and hold one end of the pin as you spin the disk first in one direction and then the other.

seem blue and the outer ones red. An English newspaperman, Charles E. Benham (1860-1929), invented a spinning top in 1894 that showed this effect. But a German psychologist, G. T. Fechner (1801-1887), had demonstrated the effect in 1838. The effect is known as *Fechner's Colors*.

Reading Colored Letters may be easy or hard, depending on their contrast with the color of the background. In the example on the right, the letters seem to vibrate because the eye cannot focus on red and blue at the same time.

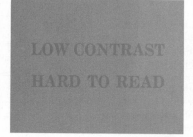

HIGH CONTRAST
EASY TO READ

LOW CONTRAST
HARD TO READ

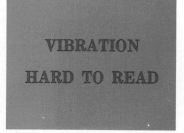

VIBRATION
HARD TO READ

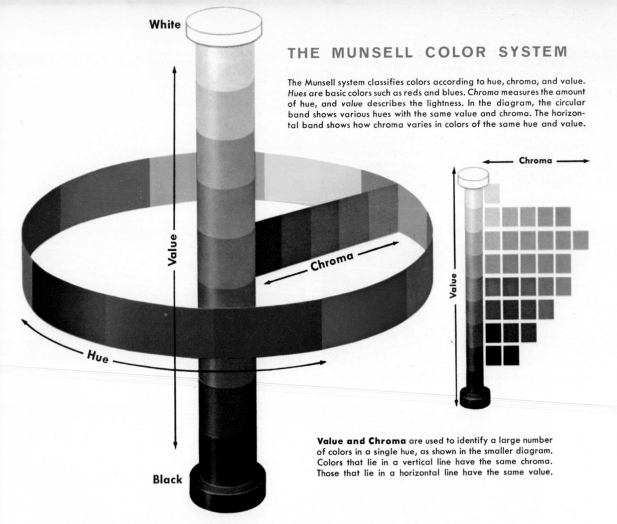

THE MUNSELL COLOR SYSTEM

The Munsell system classifies colors according to hue, chroma, and value. *Hues* are basic colors such as reds and blues. *Chroma* measures the amount of hue, and *value* describes the lightness. In the diagram, the circular band shows various hues with the same value and chroma. The horizontal band shows how chroma varies in colors of the same hue and value.

Value and Chroma are used to identify a large number of colors in a single hue, as shown in the smaller diagram. Colors that lie in a vertical line have the same chroma. Those that lie in a horizontal line have the same value.

CHARACTERISTICS OF COLOR

Color experts use three basic terms to describe colors in objects: (1) hue, (2) saturation, and (3) lightness. *Hue* is usually the basic name of a color. Red, for example, is a hue, but there are hundreds of reds. *Saturation* is the amount of hue in a color—there is a great deal of red in vermilion, but not much red in pink. *Lightness* indicates how light or dark a color is. Pink is almost as light as white. Vermilion is much darker.

Using these three terms, color experts can accurately describe two or three hundred colors. They estimate that about ten million colors exist. Each color differs from the others in some degree of hue, saturation, or lightness. Some of these colors have special names, because they differ so much from the colors suggested by their hue names. For example, brown is actually orange or red with low saturation and low lightness. Olive or olive drab is yellow or yellow-green with high saturation and low lightness. And pink is really bluish red with low saturation and high lightness.

Color Systems. Experts use the characteristics of color to organize all colors into logical systems. The American painter Albert H. Munsell (1858-1918) worked out the *Munsell Color System*, which arranges all colors on the

basis of their appearance. Munsell used the terms *value* for lightness and *chroma* for saturation. All the hues appear equally spaced around a circle, as in a color wheel. The value or lightness scale runs like an axle through the wheel. The chroma or saturation scales run like spokes from the central axle to the circle.

The German chemist Wilhelm Ostwald (1853-1932) developed another color system. It arranges colors on triangles and describes them in terms of purity, whiteness, and blackness. Variations on this system have been worked out by scientists in many countries.

In the United States, the National Bureau of Stand-

COLOR IN RELIGIOUS SYMBOLISM ———

Color	Symbolism
White	Symbol of light; signifies purity, joy, and glory.
Red	Symbol of fire and blood; signifies charity.
Blue	Symbol of heaven; signifies truth.
Green	Symbol of nature; signifies the hope of eternal life.
Purple	Signifies sorrow and suffering.
Black	Signifies death, in most countries.

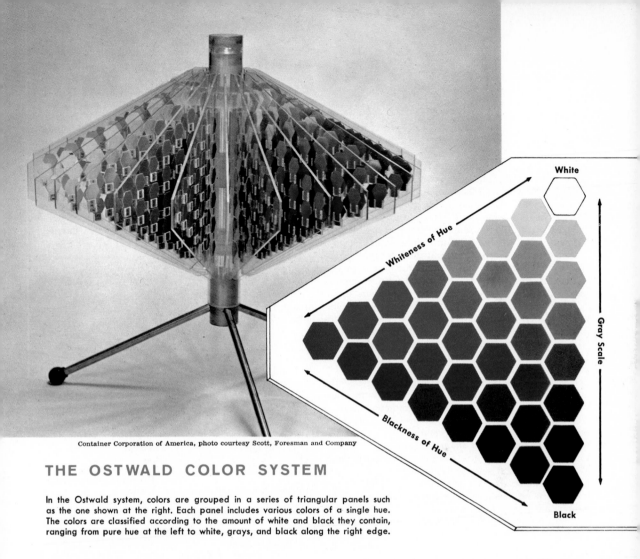

Container Corporation of America, photo courtesy Scott, Foresman and Company

THE OSTWALD COLOR SYSTEM

In the Ostwald system, colors are grouped in a series of triangular panels such as the one shown at the right. Each panel includes various colors of a single hue. The colors are classified according to the amount of white and black they contain, ranging from pure hue at the left to white, grays, and black along the right edge.

ards and the Inter-Society Color Council have worked out a system for naming colors. They have defined more than 270 colors, and related 7,500 other common names to the basic list.

Measuring Colors is one of the ways scientists study colors and color mixture. The science of color measurement is called *colorimetry*. Scientists use an instrument called a *spectrophotometer* to measure exactly how much colored light a colored object reflects or transmits. The instrument compares the colored light with the normal reflection from a white surface to obtain a *spectrophotometric curve* or *spectral reflectance curve*. Scientists use

the curves to predict accurately the light formed by either additive or subtractive color mixtures.

History of Color Studies

Early Theories about the nature of color developed in many countries of the ancient world. As early as the 1900's B.C., the Babylonians showed an interest in the subject. Most early theories assumed that color was one of the properties of an object, like hardness or weight. In the 400's B.C., the Greek philosopher Empedocles stated that each object gave off little particles that passed through the eyes. He believed that the

MEANING OF COLOR IN HERALDRY	
Color	**Signifies**
Yellow or gold	Honor and loyalty.
Silver or white	Faith and purity.
Red	Bravery and courage.
Blue	Piety and sincerity.
Black	Grief and sorrow.
Green	Youth and hope.
Purple	High rank and royalty.
Orange	Strength and endurance.
Red-purple	Sacrifice.

COLORS OF THE SEASONS AND MONTHS

Spring—pink and green.　　**Summer**—yellow and blue.
Autumn—orange and brown.　**Winter**—red and black.

January—black and white.	**July**—sky blue.
February—deep blue.	**August**—deep green.
March—gray or silver.	**September**—orange or gold.
April—yellow.	**October**—brown.
May—lavender or lilac.	**November**—purple.
June—pink or rose.	**December**—red.

eyes either produced a color reaction because of the particles, or recognized the particles as colored. Aristotle, a later Greek philosopher, seems to have been the first to realize that the eyes cannot see color without light. But he thought that color was created by something transparent between the object and the eyes.

Newton and Goethe. The English scientist Sir Isaac Newton (1642-1727) discovered the spectrum. He found that white light contains all the colors of the rainbow. Newton was the first to demonstrate that a prism cannot divide monochromatic light into a rainbow, as it does white light. He proved that colored lights, though different from one another, are alike in the ways they combine to form white light. Newton invented the color wheel. He put the pure hues of the spectrum on the outside and shaded them in to gray at the center. In all his work, he started with simple experiments and developed theories to explain them.

Johann Wolfgang von Goethe (1749-1832), the German poet, was fascinated by color. He worked out complicated theories about it. But Goethe regarded work with the spectrum and prisms as tricks to fool the eye. He thought of colored lights as darker than white light, and did not believe that they made up white light. He believed that all colored lights were formed of light and darkness. When Goethe announced his theories, most persons thought that they contradicted those of Newton. Actually, the two men disagreed on only a few points, but differed over interpretation.

The Three-Component Theory developed from Newton's work. In 1801, the English physicist Thomas Young (1773-1829) suggested that the eye has three kinds of color sensitivities. He believed that these sensitivities respond to what he called red, green, and violet light. Young later modified his theory and declared that nature has three basic sensations—red, green, and violet—that cause all colors.

A German physicist, Hermann von Helmholtz (1821-1894), enlarged Young's final theory. His work, published in 1867, made the three-component theory the basis for nearly all later work in color science. To honor both men, scientists call their combined work the Young-Helmholtz theory. It has been widely accepted, especially by physicists, because it fits in well with other theories about the behavior of light.

Helmholtz was not the only physicist who worked with Young's theories. In 1860, the Scottish physicist James Clerk Maxwell (1831-1879) became the first man to measure and define the spectrum accurately. The next year, while trying to prove Young's theory, Maxwell publicly produced the first color photograph.

The Opponent Color Theory followed somewhat the ideas of Goethe. Ewald Hering (1834-1918), a German physiologist, published this theory in 1874. He suggested that three pairs of opposing sensations produce all colors. The three pairs were blue and yellow, red and green, and black and white. Hering pointed out that no single color could contain both the colors in one of these pairs. The opponent color theory has been widely accepted, particularly by psychologists, because it fits in well with other theories of perception.

Recent Developments. Many scientists since Helmholtz and Hering have suggested color theories. No one has solved all the problems of color perception, and scientists continue to search for a satisfactory theory. For example, the American inventor Edwin H. Land (1909-   ) proposed a color theory in 1959. He demonstrated visual effects that were new and startling to most of his viewers. In one, he showed black-and-white photographs of the same scene, one made with a red filter and the other with a green filter. When he projected the red-filtered slide with red light and the green-filtered slide with white light, he seemed to produce full color. Land sought to explain these effects in his theory, and seemed to challenge all color work since Newton. But scientists familiar with the effects of color adaptation and visual perception argued that his demonstrations did not actually conflict with other theories about color.

RALPH M. EVANS

Critically reviewed by FABER BIRREN

Related Articles in WORLD BOOK include:

Outline

I. **Color in Paint**
   A. The Color Wheel
   B. The Color Triangle
   C. Color Harmony
II. **Color in Light**
   A. The Spectrum
   B. Color by Addition or Subtraction
   C. Primary Colors
   D. Complementary Colors
III. **How the Eye Sees Color**
IV. **How Color Fools the Eye**
V. **Characteristics of Color**
   A. Color Systems
   B. Measuring Colors
VI. **History of Color Studies**

Questions

Why is light needed before we can see colors?

What is *hue? Saturation? Lightness?*

How do complementary colors in light differ from complementary colors in paints?

Who discovered the spectrum?

What is an *afterimage?*

Why do blue and yellow paints combine to form a green color?

What are the primary colors of paint? Of light?

How can scientists predict the results of mixing different colors?

What are *tertiary colors?*

Why does color so often fool the eye?

COLOR BLINDNESS

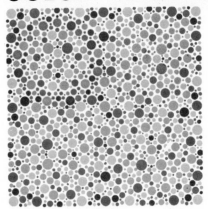

Testing Color Vision. These color patterns are examples of the figures used to find out whether persons confuse certain colors with others.

At the Left, persons who confuse both blue and yellow may not see the ○ and ✕.

At the Right, persons who confuse both red and green may not see the ○ and ▷.

These plates are copyrighted by American Optical Company and are reproduced here by permission. However, these reproductions do not present true testing conditions and cannot be used as a color vision deficiency test.

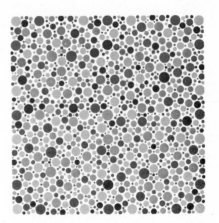

COLOR BLINDNESS, also called DALTONISM, is not being able to tell all colors apart. Most color-blind persons can see only two basic colors of the rainbow, and they confuse other colors. This kind of color blindness is called *dichromatic vision*. Most persons with dichromatic vision can see a fairly wide range of yellows and blues. But they tend to confuse reds with greens, and some reds or greens with some yellows. Only a very few persons are truly blind to all colors. They have *achromatic vision*. Persons with achromatic vision see the world in shades of white, gray, and black—somewhat like a black-and-white photograph.

More men than women are color blind. More than 4 of every 100 men are color blind, compared to about 1 of every 200 women. There is no cure for color blindness.

Many animals, including cats, dogs, and horses, probably do not see colors as we do. But the condition is normal in their eyes, not defective.

Many color-blind persons do not realize that their eyesight is defective. They have learned to use the color names that everyone else uses. These persons do not know that they do not see the colors that others see. They may be hampered in their everyday activities, and their condition may place them in danger. If they confuse red and green, for example, they may only be able to tell traffic signals apart by their brightness. Many armed forces refuse to accept color-blind persons for military service.

Most persons can be easily tested for color blindness. The *Hardy-Rand-Rittler* (*H-R-R*) and *Ishihara* tests indicate both the type and the degree of color blindness. In these and similar tests, colored triangles, squares, and other shapes lie buried in a jumble of dots. These dots vary in both color and intensity. As the person identifies the colored shapes, an examiner can determine his ability to see colors. Another test, the *Holmgren* test, measures the ability to match colors.

Scientists believe that color blindness is inherited. A color-blind man who marries a woman with normal vision has children with normal vision. But the defect is hidden in the daughters, and they can pass it on to their children. If a color-blind man marries a woman whose father is color blind, probably half of his children will be color blind. WILLIAM A. MANN

COLOR GUARD. See FLAG (Carrying the Flag).
COLOR ORGAN. See CLAVILUX.

by Arnold Ryan Chalfant & Associates for WORLD BOOK

To a Color-Blind Person, some colors look the same. A person who confuses red and green with other colors may say these pictures look the same or are equally colorful. Most persons with normal color vision would say the photograph on the right is the more colorful of the two.

667

Robert Koropp

Rocky Mountains Form a Backdrop for a Ranch near Hygiene

Skier at Aspen
Margaret Durrance, Photo Researchers

Cattle Drive near Pikes Peak
Howard Friedman, Photo Researchers

Denver at Night
Ronny Jacques, Photo Researchers

COLORADO

THE CENTENNIAL STATE

COLORADO is a state of unusual natural beauty. The scenic wonders of the Rocky Mountains and the cool, pleasant climate make the state a center for summer tourists. In winter, the deep, powdery snow of Colorado attracts skiers to world-famous resorts. More than 6 million visitors a year travel to such tourist areas as Aspen, Estes Park, and Colorado Springs.

But not all of Colorado is mountainous, and only part of the state's income comes from tourists. Most Coloradans live and work on the dry, flat plains that make up the eastern two-fifths of the state. Tunnels bored through the mountains bring water to the plains for busy cities and prosperous farms. Factories on the plains make manufacturing the leading economic activity in Colorado. These factories also make Colorado the leading manufacturing area in the Rocky Mountain States.

Herds of cattle and sheep graze on the mountains and plains. Irrigated farms produce rich crops of potatoes and sugar beets. Wheat fields spread across the plains.

Mining also has an important part in the state's economy. A series of mining booms has sparked Colorado's growth since the 1850's. The colorful story of Colorado gold and silver mining in the 1800's has become famous through music. The musical comedy *The Unsinkable Molly Brown* and the opera *The Ballad of Baby Doe* describe life during the great mining booms.

Today, petroleum is the state's most important mineral product. But miners still dig precious ores in mine shafts deep in the mountains. Colorado leads the nation in the production of molybdenum, a metal which makes steel tougher. The state ranks high in production of uranium, the raw material for atomic power.

The U.S. government owns more than a third of Colorado's land. The government controls grazing, logging, and mining on those lands. The U.S. Mint in Denver makes coins. One of the state's largest employers manufactures rockets and missiles for the government. The U.S. Air Force has its academy close to Colorado Springs, its defense headquarters in nearby Cheyenne Mountain, and its finance center in Denver.

The Spanish word *colorado* means *colored red*. The name was given first to the Colorado River, which flows through canyons of red stone. The state was named for the river. Colorado's nickname is the *Centennial State*. Colorado joined the Union in 1876, the *centennial* (100th anniversary) of the Declaration of Independence.

Denver is the capital and largest city of Colorado. For the relationship of Colorado to other states in its region, see the article on the ROCKY MOUNTAIN STATES.

The contributors of this article are Palmer Hoyt, editor and publisher of the Denver Post; *Tim K. Kelley, Chairman of the Department of Geography at the University of Colorado; and Michael McGiffert, Associate Professor of History at the University of Denver.*

--- FACTS IN BRIEF ---

Capital: Denver.

Government: *Congress*—U.S. senators, 2; U.S. representatives, 4. *Electoral Votes*—6. *State Legislature*—senators, 35; representatives, 65. *Counties*—63. *Voting Age*—21 years.

Area: 104,247 square miles (including 363 square miles of inland water), eighth in size among the states. *Greatest Distances*—(east-west) 387 miles; (north-south) 276 miles.

Elevation: *Highest*—Mount Elbert, 14,431 feet above sea level; *Lowest*—3,350 feet above sea level along the Arkansas River in Prowers County.

Population: *1960 Census*—1,753,947, 33rd among the states; density, 17 persons to the square mile; distribution, 74 per cent urban, 26 per cent rural. *Estimated 1965 Population*—1,959,000.

Chief Products: *Manufacturing*—chemicals; electrical machinery; food products; steel; stone, clay, and glass products. *Agriculture*—hay, livestock, sugar beets, vegetables, wheat. *Mining*—coal, gold and silver, molybdenum, petroleum, uranium, vanadium.

Statehood: Aug. 1, 1876, the 38th state.

State Motto: *Nil sine Numine* (Nothing without Providence).

State Song: "Where the Columbines Grow." Words and music by A. J. Fynn.

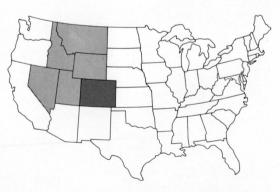

Colorado (blue) ranks eighth in size among all the states, and third in size among the Rocky Mountain States (gray).

669

Constitution of Colorado was adopted in 1876. It has been *amended* (changed) about 65 times. All amendments must be approved by the people in an election. They may be proposed by a two-thirds vote of the legislature, by a petition of the voters, or by a constitutional convention. A constitutional convention requires the approval of two-thirds of the legislators and a majority of those voting on the issue in an election.

Executive. The governor of Colorado serves a four-year term. A constitutional amendment passed in 1968 provided that candidates for governor and lieutenant governor must be elected as a team, beginning in 1970. Voters will then cast a single vote for the governor and lieutenant governor. The governor receives a salary of $20,000 a year.

The governor of Colorado has more power than the governors of many other states. For example, he may veto specific items in money bills, but sign the rest of the bill into law. The governor appoints the revenue director and the adjutant general. The people elect the secretary of state, treasurer, and attorney general to four-year terms. The legislature appoints the auditor to a five-year term. Under a constitutional amendment approved in 1966, the state reorganized the executive branch. Over 100 agencies, boards, and other units were consolidated into 17 departments. The plan went into effect in 1968.

Legislature, called the *General Assembly*, consists of a 35-member Senate and a 65-member House of Representatives. Senators serve four-year terms, and representatives serve two-year terms. The Assembly meets each year in January. Sessions in odd-numbered years may take up any subject. In even years, only money bills and bills from the governor can be considered.

In 1964, Colorado *reapportioned* (redivided) its legislature to provide equal representation based on population. The plan called for the subdistricting of counties electing more than one legislator. The state Supreme

Court ruled the subdistricts unconstitutional, and they were eliminated in 1965. The voters then initiated a constitutional amendment allowing subdistricts, and passed it in 1966. In 1967, the legislature acted on the amendment by dividing the state into single-member legislative districts.

Courts. Colorado's highest court is the Supreme Court, composed of a chief justice and six associate justices. The governor appoints the justices. After a justice serves for two years, he must win the voters' approval in an election. If approved, he serves a 10-year term. His later terms are for 10 years, but he must be voted in each time. Most major civil and criminal cases are tried in the state's 22 district courts. District judges are appointed and approved like justices, except their full terms are for six years. District courts may act as probate or juvenile courts, except in Denver where those courts are separate. Each county has a county court, and larger towns have municipal courts.

Local Government is carried on through 63 counties and about 250 cities and towns. The city and county of

Colorado Supreme Court sits in the Capitol in Denver. Thick maroon draperies form a backdrop for the judicial bench.

The Governor's Mansion, in Denver, is about eight blocks from the state Capitol. The building is constructed of red brick with white stone trimming. The mansion, completed in 1908, was given to the state in 1960 by the Boettcher Foundation of Denver.

The State Seal

Symbols of Colorado. On the seal, the triangular figure represents the "all-seeing" eye of God. The *fasces* (bound rods) are a symbol of power. The three mountains stand for the state's rugged land, and the pick and hammer for the importance of mining. The seal was adopted in 1877. On the flag, adopted in 1911, the red C stands for *Colorado*, which is Spanish for *colored red*. The golden ball is said to represent the state's gold production.

Flag and flower illustrations, courtesy of Eli Lilly and Company

The State Flag

Denver operate as a single government, with the same borders and the same officials. Each of the other 62 counties is governed by three commissioners elected by the voters to four-year terms.

Communities with more than 2,000 persons are called *cities*, and those with smaller populations are *towns*. Cities may adopt *home rule* charters, which give them greater control over their own affairs. Under certain conditions, home rule charters and laws passed under such charters may overrule state laws. Most of Colorado's cities use the mayor-council form of government. Several cities have city managers. All the towns have a mayor and a board of trustees.

Taxation. State taxes provide almost three-fourths of the state government's income. Income taxes, motor fuel and highway taxes, and a sales tax produce the largest amounts. About a fourth of Colorado's income comes from U.S. government grants and other programs.

Politics. Colorado voters have elected about as many Democrats as Republicans to Congress. Voters in Denver and Pueblo usually support Democrats. Voters in Denver's suburbs and in northeastern Colorado generally favor Republicans. Colorado has favored Republicans more often than Democrats in presidential elections. For Colorado's voting record in presidential elections, see ELECTORAL COLLEGE (table).

The State Bird
Lark Bunting

The State Flower
Rocky Mountain Columbine

The State Capitol is in Denver, the capital of Colorado since 1867. Earlier capitals were Colorado City (now Colorado Springs, 1862); and Golden and Denver (alternately from 1863 to 1867).
Colorado Dept. of Public Relations

The State Tree
Blue Spruce

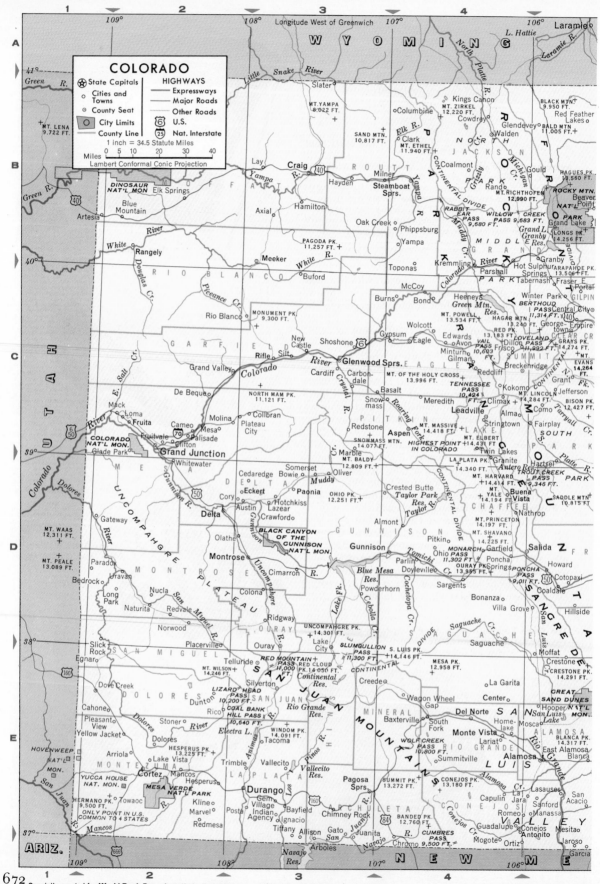

COLORADO

Legend

- ✪ State Capitals
- ○ Cities and Towns
- ◦ County Seat
- ⬡ City Limits
- County Line

HIGHWAYS
- Expressways
- Major Roads
- Other Roads
- ⑥ U.S.
- ㉕ Nat. Interstate

1 inch = 34.5 Statute Miles

Miles 0 5 10 20 30 40

Lambert Conformal Conic Projection

Specially created for **World Book Encyclopedia** by Rand McNally and World Book editors

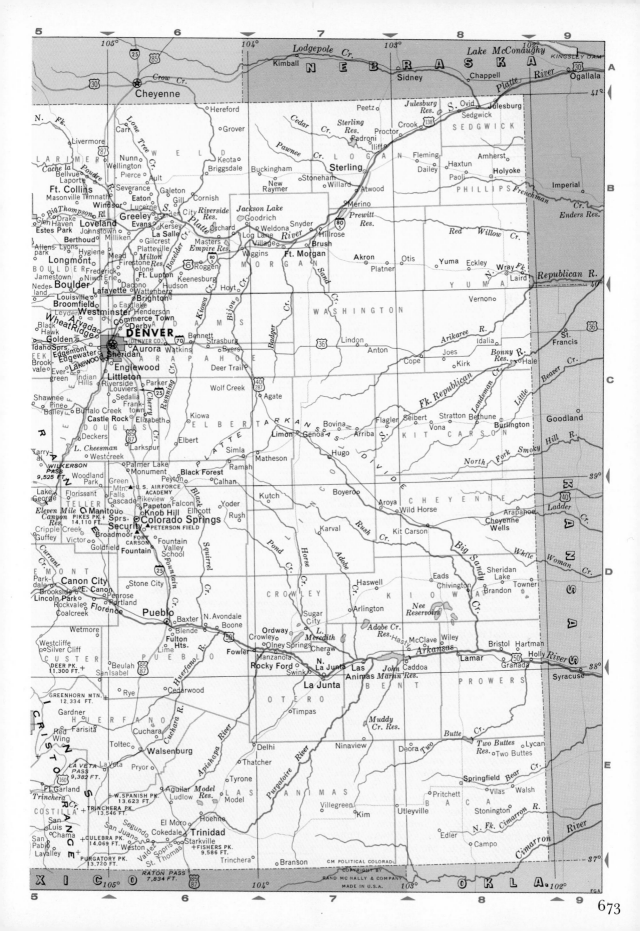

COLORADO / People

The 1960 United States census reported that Colorado had 1,753,947 persons. The population had increased 32 per cent over the 1950 figure, 1,325,089. The U.S. Bureau of the Census estimated that by 1965 the state's population had reached about 1,959,000.

Two of every three Coloradans live in one of the state's three Standard Metropolitan Statistical Areas, as defined by the U.S. Bureau of the Budget (see METROPOLITAN AREA). These are Colorado Springs, Denver, and Pueblo. For their populations, see the *Index* to the political map of Colorado.

Most of Colorado's cities grew up near the eastern edge of the mountains. Denver, the largest city, is a business, financial, and manufacturing center. Colorado Springs attracts many tourists, and serves several military bases, including the U.S. Air Force Academy. Pueblo has large steel mills. The largest city in western Colorado is Grand Junction. See the articles on the cities listed in *Related Articles* at the end of this article.

Most of Colorado's people are Protestants, but Roman Catholics form the largest religious group. Other large groups include Baptists, Methodists, Presbyterians, and members of the United Church of Christ.

POPULATION

This map shows the *population density* of Colorado, and how it varies in different parts of the state. Population density means the average number of persons who live on each square mile.

PERSONS PER SQUARE MILE

0 to 3	3 to 15	15 to 90	90 to 7,500

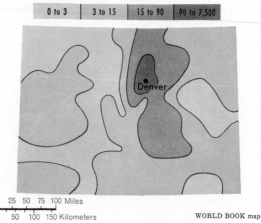

Denver

0 25 50 75 100 Miles
0 50 100 150 Kilometers

WORLD BOOK map

Place	Pop.	Loc.		Place	Pop.	Loc.
Hartsel	50	C 5		Laporte	800	B 5
Hasty	100	D 8		Lariat	900	E 4
Haswell	169	D 7		Larkspur	175	C 6
Haxtun	990	B 8		La Salle	1,070	B 6
Hayden	764	B 3		Las Animas	3,402.°	D 7
Heeney	15	C 4		Las Mesitas*	75	E 4
Henderson	200	C 6		Lasauses	200	E 5
Hereford	75	B 6		Lavalley	200	E 5
Hesperus	50	E 2		La Veta	632	E 5
Hillrose	157	B 7		Lay	15	B 3
Hillside	5	D 5		Lazear	60	D 3
Hoehne	200	E 6		Leadville	4,008.°	C 4
Holly	1,108	D 8		Leyden	25	C 5
Holyoke	1,555.°	B 8		Lime	80	D 6
Hooper	58	E 5		Limon	1,811	C 7
Hot Sulphur Springs	237.°	B 4		Lincoln Park	2,085	C 6
Hotchkiss	626	D 3		Lindon	40	C 7
Howard	43	D 5		Littleton	13,670.°	C 5
Hoyt	15	B 8		Livermore	20	B 5
Hudson	430	B 6		Logcabin*		B 5
Hugo	811.°	C 7		Log Lane Village	310	B 7
Hygiene	250	B 5		Loma	75	C 2
Idaho Springs	1,480	C 5		Longmont	11,489	B 5
Idalia	85	C 8		Long Park	25	D 2
Idledale*	350	C 5		Louisville	2,073	C 5
Ignacio	609	E 3		Louviers	250	C 6
Iliff	204	B 7		Loveland	9,734	B 5
Indian Agency	180	E 3		Lowrey*	25	B 5
Indian Hills	700	C 5		Lucerne	75	B 6
Ione	10	B 6		Ludlow	10	E 6
Ironton*	I	D 3		Lycan	5	E 8
Jacktown*	35	C 4		Lyons	706	B 5
Jamestown	107	B 5		Mack	150	C 2
Jansen*	350	E 6		Malta*		C 4
Jaroso	40	E 5		Manassa	831	E 5
Jefferson	50	C 5		Mancos	832	E 2
Joes	110	C 8		Manitou Springs	3,626	D 6
Johnstown	976	B 6		Manzanola	562	D 7
Juanita	15	E 3		Marble	5	C 3
Julesburg	1,840.°	B 8		Marvel	65	E 2
Juniper Springs*	10	B 3		Masonville	200	B 5
Karval	100	D 7		Masters	5	B 6
Keenesburg	409	B 6		Matheson	100	C 7
Keota	13	B 6		Mayday*	25	E 2
Kersey	378	B 6		McClave	120	D 8
Kim	350	E 7		McCoy	25	C 4
Kings Canon	10	B 4		Mead	192	B 6
Kiowa	195.°	C 6		Meeker	1,655.°	B 3
Kirk	100	C 8		Meredith	30	C 4
Kit Carson	356	D 8		Merino	268	B 7
Kittredge*	50	C 5		Mesa	90	C 2
Kline	35	E 2		Mesita	25	E 5
Knob Hill	3,400	D 6		Milliken	630	B 6
Kokomo (Recen)	74	C 4		Milner	40	B 3
Kremmling	576	B 4		Mineral Hot Springs*	10	D 5
Kutch	5	D 7		Minturn	662	C 4
Lafayette	2,612	C 5		Model	25	E 6
La Garita	50	E 4		Moffat	104	D 5
Laird	150	B 8		Mogote	85	E 4
La Jara	724	E 5		Molina	10	C 2
La Junta	8,026.°	E 7		Monarch*		D 4
Lake City	106.°	D 3		Monte Vista	3,385	E 4
Lake George	35	D 5		Montezuma*	17	C 4
Lakeside*	28	C 5		Montrose	5,044.°	D 3
Lakewood	40,000	C 5		Monument	204	C 6
Lamar	7,369.°	D 8		Morrison*	426	C 5
				Mosca	110	E 5

Place	Pop.	Loc.		Place	Pop.	Loc.
Mountain View*	826	C 5		Pueblo	91,181.°	D 6
Nathrop	25	D 4		Ramah	109	C 6
Naturita	979	D 2		Rand	15	B 4
Nederland	272	C 5		Rangely	1,464	B 2
Nevadaville*	10	C 5		Red Feather Lakes	50	B 5
New Castle	447	C 3		Red Wing	15	E 5
New Raymer	91	B 7		Redcliff	586	C 4
Ninaview	5	E 7		Redmesa	85	E 2
Niwot	200	B 5		Redstone	160	C 3
North Avondale	100	D 6		Redvale	10	D 2
North La Junta	1,000	D 7		Rico	353	E 2
Norwood	443	D 2		Ridgway	254	D 3
Nucla	906	D 2		Rifle	2,135	C 3
Nunn	228	B 6		Rio Blanco	5	C 3
Oak Creek	666	B 4		Riverside	180	C 5
Ohio	50	D 4		Rockvale	413	D 5
Olathe	773	D 3		Rocky Ford	4,929	D 7
Oliver	10	D 3		Roggen	50	B 6
Olney Springs	263	D 7		Romeo	339	E 5
Orchard	75	B 6		Rosedale*	70	B 6
Orchard City, see Eckert				Rosita	10	D 5
Orchard Mesa*	4,956	C 2		Royal Gorge*		D 5
Ordway	1,254.°	D 7		Rush	35	D 6
Ortiz	100	E 4		Rye	179	E 6
Otis	568	B 8		Saguache	722.°	D 4
Ouray	785.°	D 3		St. Thomas		E 5
Ovid	571	B 8		Salida	4,560.°	D 5
Padroni	150	B 7		San Acacio	95	E 5
Pagosa Springs	1,374.°	E 3		San Isabel		E 5
Palisade	860	C 2		San Juan	100	E 6
Palmer Lake	542	C 6		San Luis	800.°	E 5
Paoli	81	B 8		San Pablo	75	E 5
Paonia	1,083	D 3		Sanford	679	E 5
Papeton	2,300	D 6		Sargents	60	D 4
Paradox	25	D 2		Saw Pit*	30	E 3
Parkdale	35	D 5		Security	10,000	D 6
Parker	125	C 6		Sedalia	250	C 6
Parlin	25	D 4		Sedgwick	299	B 8
Parshall	100	B 4		Segundo	300	E 6
Peetz	218	B 7		Seibert	210	C 8
Penrose	175	D 5		Severance	70	B 6
Peyton	100	C 6		Shawee	100	C 6
Phippsburg	150	B 4		Sheridan	3,559	C 6
Pictou		E 6		Sheridan Lake	90	D 8
Pierce	424	B 6		Shoshone	15	C 3
Pikeview	200	D 6		Silt	384	C 3
Pine	35	C 5		Silver Cliff	153	D 5
Pitkin	94	D 4		Silver Plume*	86	C 5
Placerville	35	D 2		Silverton	822.°	E 3
Plateau City	35	C 3		Simla	450	C 6
Platner	25	B 7		Slater	5	B 3
Platteville	582	B 6		Slick Rock	200	D 2
Pleasant View	2,500	E 2		Snowmass	10	C 4
Poncha Springs	201	D 4		Snyder	150	B 7
Portland*	6	D 3		Somerset	150	D 3
Portland	73	D 5		Sopris	950	E 6
Powderhorn	10	D 3		South Fork	200	E 4
Pritchett	247	E 8		Springfield	1,791.°	E 8
Proctor	35	B 8		Starkville	261	E 6
Prospect Heights*	39	D 5		Steamboat Springs	1,843.°	B 4
Pryor	5	E 6		Sterling	10,751.°	B 7
				Stone City	35	D 6
				Stoneham	55	B 7
				Stoner	5	E 2
				Stonington	35	E 8
				Strasburg	600	C 6

Place	Pop.	Loc.
Stratton	680	C 8
Stringtown	90	C 4
Sugar City	409	D 7
Summitville	10	E 4
Superior*	173	C 5
Swink	348	D 7
Tabernash	250	C 5
Tacoma	10	E 3
Tarryall	15	C 5
Telluride	677.°	E 3
Thatcher	10	E 6
Thornton*	11,353	C 6
Tiffany	40	E 3
Timnath	150	B 6
Timpas	35	E 7
Tabe*	50	E 6
Toltec	50	E 6
Toponas	70	B 4
Towaoc	300	E 2
Towner	100	D 8
Trimble	20	E 3
Trinchera	75	E 6
Trinidad	10,691.°	E 6
Twin Lakes	40	C 4
Two Buttes	111	E 8
Tyrone	10	E 6
Uravan	750	D 2
Utleyville	5	E 7
Valdez	400	E 6
Vallecito	75	E 3
Vernon	50	C 8
Victor	434	D 5
Vilas	107	E 8
Villa Grove	25	D 5
Villegreen	10	E 7
Vona	130	C 8
Wagon Wheel Gap	10	E 4
Walden	809.°	B 4
Walsenburg	5,071.°	E 6
Walsh	856	E 8
Ward*	9	B 5
Watkins	100	C 6
Wattenberg	125	B 6
Weldona	150	B 7
Wellington	532	B 5
Westcliffe	306.°	D 5
Westcreek	5	C 5
Westminster	13,850	C 5
Weston	200	E 6
Wetmore	100	D 5
Wheat Ridge	21,619	C 5
Whitewater	150	D 2
Wiggins	400	B 6
Wild Horse	30	D 7
Wiley	383	D 8
Willard	25	B 7
Williamsburg*	57	D 5
Windsor	1,509	B 6
Winter Park	50	C 5
Wolcott	35	C 4
Woodland Park	666	C 5
Wray	2,082.°	B 8
Yampa	312	B 4
Yellow Jacket	30	E 2
Yoder	20	D 6
Yuma	1,919	B 8

*Does not appear on the map; key shows general location.   °County Seat.   Source: Latest census figures.

COLORADO / Education

Schools. The first school in Colorado was opened in 1859 by O. J. Goldrick. His students were the children of gold miners in the Cherry Creek area (now Denver). By 1862, many communities had public schools.

Today, the state department of education is headed by a five-member board of education. Board members are elected to six-year terms. They appoint a commissioner of education to direct the department. Local districts are run by elected school boards and appointed superintendents. Children in Colorado are required to attend school between the ages of 8 and 16. For the number of students and teachers in Colorado, see EDUCATION (table).

Libraries. Colorado's first public library was established in Denver in 1860. Today, Colorado has about 125 public libraries, including about 20 county libraries. The Colorado State Library has headquarters in Denver, with field offices in Pueblo and Grand Junction.

Museums. Denver has three outstanding museums. The Denver Art Museum owns several collections, including an Indian and Native Arts Museum. The Denver Museum of Natural History has displays about animals. The Colorado State Museum in Denver has exhibits on the early West. The state museum operates branches near Alamosa, and in Leadville, Montrose, Pueblo, and Trinidad.

── UNIVERSITIES AND COLLEGES ──

Colorado has 15 universities and colleges accredited by the North Central Association of Colleges and Secondary Schools. For enrollments and further information, see UNIVERSITIES AND COLLEGES (table).

Name	Location	Founded
Adams State College	Alamosa	1921
Colorado, University of	Boulder	1861
Colorado, Western State College of	Gunnison	1901
Colorado College	Colorado Springs	1874
Colorado School of Mines	Golden	1874
Colorado State College	Greeley	1889
Colorado State University	Fort Collins	1870
Denver, University of	Denver	1864
Fort Lewis College	Durango	1911
Loretto Heights College	Denver	1918
Regis College	Denver	1887
St. Thomas Seminary	Denver	1906
Southern Colorado State College	Pueblo	1963
Temple Buell College	Denver	1888
United States Air Force Academy	Colorado Springs	1954

COLORADO / A Visitor's Guide

Beautiful Colorado attracts more than 6,000,000 tourists a year. In summer, visitors enjoy the state's cool climate. Campers pitch their tents on forested mountain slopes or near beautiful mountain streams. High peaks test the skill of mountain climbers. Old mining towns and Indian cliff dwellings lure tourists interested in history. Fishermen cast for trout in the clear, swift streams. In autumn, hunters search for deer and other big game. In winter, skiers visit world-famous resorts such as Aspen, Arapaho Basin, Vail, and Winter Park. The ski season lasts from late November to April.

Fred M. Mazzulla

Opera House in Central City

Glen Fishback

Ancient Cliff Dwellings in Mesa Verde National Park near Cortez

PLACES TO VISIT

Following are brief descriptions of some of Colorado's many interesting places to visit.

Air Force Academy, north of Colorado Springs, trains the nation's air force officers. The Visitors Center at the south entrance shows films about the academy.

Bent's Fort, east of La Junta, was an early outpost for trappers. The old fort is a national historic site. A museum in La Junta features a model of the fort.

Buffalo Bill's Grave, on top of Lookout Mountain near Golden, honors the famous scout and showman William F. Cody (see BUFFALO BILL).

Central City, once a rich gold camp, is now a summer resort. A theater and opera festival is held each summer in the old-time opera house.

Garden of the Gods, near Colorado Springs, is a breathtaking cluster of huge red sandstone rocks. Thou-

sands of worshipers gather there on Easter Sunday for sunrise services. See GARDEN OF THE GODS.

Narrow Gauge Railroad, between Durango and Silverton, is the last passenger railroad of its type in the country. The tracks are set closer together than modern railroad tracks. Summer visitors can take a scenic 90-mile round trip through beautiful canyons.

Pikes Peak, west of Colorado Springs, is probably the most famous mountain in the Rockies, even though 31 Colorado peaks are higher. Visitors can reach the top of the mountain by automobile toll road, cog railway, on horseback, or on foot. See PIKES PEAK.

Royal Gorge, near Canon City, is a massive canyon cut by the Arkansas River. The gorge, more than a thousand feet deep, is crossed by the world's highest suspension bridge. See ROYAL GORGE.

Many Colorado cities and towns hold fairs and rodeos during the summer. Probably the outstanding event is the weeklong Colorado State Fair. It attracts thousands of visitors to Pueblo in August.

Many art, business, education, and religious groups hold meetings in Colorado each year. The Aspen Institute for Humanistic Studies sponsors many conferences. Estes Park is a popular location for meetings. Other annual events in Colorado include the following.

January-April: National Western Stock Show in Denver (January); Winter Carnival in Steamboat Springs (February); Easter Sunday Sunrise Services in the Garden of the Gods near Colorado Springs, and in Red Rocks Park near Denver.

May-August: Boat races near Salida (June); Pikes Peak Auto Race (late June); Rodeo in Greeley (first week in July); Opera Festival in Central City (opera in July, and a play in August); Aspen Music Festival (July and August); Rodeo in Monte Vista (late August); Pikes Peak or Bust Rodeo in Colorado Springs (August).

September-December: Rodeos in Durango and Rocky Ford (early September); New Year's Eve fireworks on Pikes Peak.

Margaret Durrance, Photo Researchers
Boat Races in the Rapids near Salida

Ragsdale, FPG
Pikes Peak Overlooks the Highway Through Ute Pass

Glen Fishback
Garden of the Gods near Colorado Springs

Ronny Jaques, Photo Researchers
United States Air Force Academy at Colorado Springs

U.S. Mint, in Denver, makes millions of coins each year. Tours of the mint must be arranged in advance by letter or telephone. See MINT.

National Parks, Monuments, and Forests. Colorado has two national parks—Rocky Mountain and Mesa Verde. Rocky Mountain National Park, in north-central Colorado, has 65 rugged mountains that rise above 10,000 feet. Mesa Verde National Park, near Cortez, preserves Indian cliff dwellings almost a thousand years old. See the separate articles in WORLD BOOK on each national park.

Six other areas of scenic beauty or historical interest have been designated as national monuments. These are Black Canyon of the Gunnison, Colorado, Dinosaur, Great Sand Dunes, Hovenweep, and Yucca House. See the separate articles on these places.

Twelve national forests cover about 14,320,000 acres in Colorado. Completely within the state are Arapaho, Grand Mesa, Gunnison, Pike, Rio Grande, Roosevelt, Routt, San Isabel, San Juan, Uncompahgre, and White River national forests. Manti-LaSal forest lies partly in Utah. For the areas and chief features of each national forest, see NATIONAL FOREST (table). In 1964, Congress set aside five areas of national forest land as national wildernesses. These areas will be kept in their natural condition.

Other Parks. The city of Denver maintains many mountain parks outside its city limits. Since 1963, Colorado has created state parks on land administered by the state fish and game commission. For information about these parks, write to Director, Game, Fish, and Parks Department, 6060 Broadway, Denver, Colo. 80216.

677

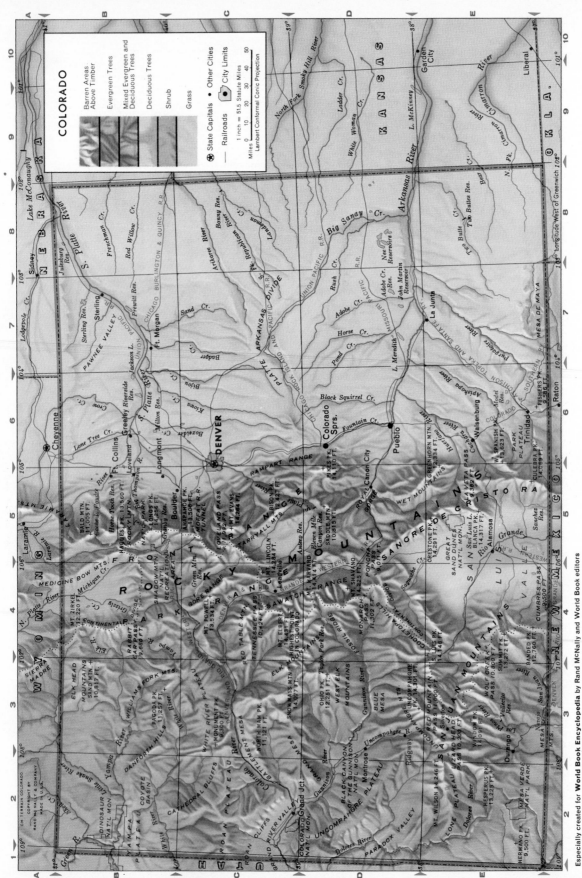

COLORADO

Barren Areas
Above Timber

Evergreen Trees

Mixed Evergreen and
Deciduous Trees

Deciduous Trees

Shrub

Grass

☆ State Capitals   ● Other Cities
── Railroads   ◉ City Limits

1 inch = 51.5 Statute Miles

Miles 0 10 20 30 40 50
Lambert Conformal Conic Projection

Especially created for **World Book Encyclopedia** by Rand McNally and World Book editors

COLORADO / The Land

Land Regions. Colorado has four main land regions: (1) the Colorado Plateau, (2) the Intermontane Basin, (3) the Rocky Mountains, and (4) the Great Plains.

The Colorado Plateau, along the western border, covers about a fifth of the state. It is an area of high hills, plateaus, deep valleys, and *mesas* (flat-topped hills with steep sides). Farmers raise a variety of crops in the valleys. Cattle and sheep graze on the grasslands of the mesas.

The Intermontane Basin, north of the plateau, is Colorado's smallest land region. It is a region of rolling hills and sagebrush plateaus wedged between mountain ranges near the northwest corner of the state. The word *intermontane* means *between mountains.* Herds of sheep graze on the plateaus, and forests cover the hills.

The Rocky Mountains cover the middle two-fifths of Colorado. They also rise in the state's northwestern corner. The Colorado Rockies have been called the *Roof of North America* because between 50 and 60 peaks reach 14,000 feet or more above sea level. These peaks are the tallest in the entire Rocky Mountain chain, which stretches from Alaska to New Mexico.

The Continental Divide runs through the Colorado Rockies. Streams east of the divide flow into the Atlantic Ocean. Those west of it flow into the Pacific. The Colorado Rockies are one of the country's most popular areas for mountain climbing, fishing, hunting, and skiing.

The Rocky Mountains of Colorado consist of five main mountain ranges: (1) the Front Range, (2) the Park Range, (3) the Sawatch Range, (4) the San Juan Mountains, and (5) the Sangre de Cristo Range. The easternmost group is the Front Range, which includes Mount Evans (14,264 feet), Longs Peak (14,256 feet), Pikes Peak (14,110 feet), and other mountains that rise to the west of Denver and Colorado Springs. The *Sangre de Cristo* (Blood of Christ) Range is just south of the Front Range. Together, the Front Range and the Sangre de Cristo Range form a mountain wall that faces the Great Plains to the east.

The Park Range, west of the Front Range, stretches from a point near the Wyoming border south to the beginning of the Arkansas River. South of the Park Range is the Sawatch Range, which includes Mount Elbert

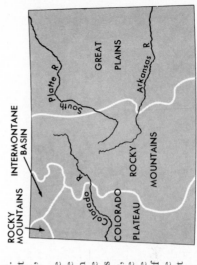

Land Regions of Colorado

COLORADO

(14,431 feet), the highest peak of the Rocky Mountains. The rugged San Juan Mountains occupy southwestern Colorado.

The mountains of Colorado surround many level, almost treeless areas called *parks*. The largest of these areas include North Park, Middle Park, South Park, and the San Luis Valley. See ROCKY MOUNTAINS.

The Great Plains cover roughly the eastern two-fifths of Colorado. Colorado's Great Plains region is part of the vast Interior Plain of North America that stretches from Canada to Mexico. It slopes gently upward from east to west toward the base of the Rocky Mountains. Farmers once thought the plains region was too dry for farming. However, irrigation projects in the valleys and dry farming on the higher lands have made

large-scale agriculture possible. (see DRY FARMING; IRRIGATION).

Rivers and Lakes. More important rivers begin in Colorado than in any other state. These rivers provide water for many states. Three major tributaries of the Mississippi-Missouri river system rise on the eastern slope of the Rocky Mountains. These are the Arkansas, South Platte, and Republican rivers. West of the Rockies, the Colorado River begins at Grand Lake, flows through Middle Park, and winds southwest into Utah. The Colorado drains a twelfth of all the land of the United States. Several of the chief tributaries of the Colorado, including the Uncompahgre, Gunnison, San Juan, and Dolores rivers, also rise in the state. The Rio Grande starts in the San Juan range, and flows east and south into New Mexico. The North Platte River flows north from North Park into Wyoming.

Rivers add much to Colorado's scenic beauty. Many

have carved deep gorges, or tumble down mountains in lovely waterfalls and cascades. The Royal Gorge of the Arkansas River, west of Canon City, is more than 1,000 feet deep. A bridge 1,053 feet above the floor of the Royal Gorge is the highest suspension bridge in the world. In some places, the Black Canyon of the Gunnison River in western Colorado is 2,400 feet below the surrounding land.

Many beautiful lakes lie in the mountains. Grand Lake, formed by glaciers, covers about 600 acres near the town of Grand Lake. It is Colorado's largest natural lake. Summit Lake, 12,740 feet above sea level, is one of the highest lakes in the country. Many artificial lakes have been created by damming the rushing mountain streams. John Martin Reservoir, formed by a federal flood-control project on the Arkansas River, is the largest lake. It covers more than 29 square miles when full. The water is used for irrigation.

Independence Monument, *center,* and other unusual rock formations are part of the Colorado National Monument near Grand Junction. These scenic formations are in the Colorado Plateau region.

Alpha Photo Assoc.

Summer Wildflowers brighten a level area high in the Rocky Mountains near Boulder. Colorado's Rocky Mountains region has many peaks that tower 14,000 feet or more above sea level.

Ragsdale, FPG

The Continental Divide forms a backdrop to the moderately sloping Great Plains region near Denver. This gently rolling land ends abruptly at the base of the mighty Rocky Mountains.

Ronny Jaques, Photo Researchers

COLORADO / Climate

Colorado's climate is generally dry and sunny. But because of the great differences in altitude, temperatures vary widely in short distances. The mountains are almost always cooler than the plains and plateaus. Burlington, on the plains, has an average January temperature of 28° F. Leadville, in the mountains, has a January average of 18° F. Average July temperatures are 74° F. in Burlington and 55° F. in Leadville. Colorado's highest temperature, 118° F., occurred at Bennett on July 11, 1888. Taylor Park Dam in Gunnison County had the lowest, −60° F., on Feb. 1, 1951.

Colorado's average yearly *precipitation* (rain, melted snow, and other forms of moisture) is about 15 inches. This moisture is not distributed evenly. The western slopes of the mountains get the most rain and snow. The San Luis Valley, in the south, is the driest area.

The dry air makes Colorado's climate comfortable. The sun warms the thin air quickly, especially at high altitudes. Colorado also has the *chinook*, a warm wind that occasionally blows down the eastern slopes of the mountains in winter. A chinook can raise temperatures on the plains by 20 degrees or more in a short time.

SEASONAL TEMPERATURES

JANUARY

AVERAGE OF DAILY LOW TEMPERATURES

Degrees Centigrade	Degrees Fahrenheit
-9 to -4	16 to 24
-13 to -9	8 to 16
-18 to -13	0 to 8
-22 to -18	-8 to 0

AVERAGE OF DAILY HIGH TEMPERATURES

Degrees Fahrenheit	Degrees Centigrade
44 to 52	7 to 11
36 to 44	2 to 7
28 to 36	-2 to 2
20 to 28	-7 to -2

JULY

AVERAGE OF DAILY LOW TEMPERATURES

Degrees Centigrade	Degrees Fahrenheit
13 to 18	56 to 64
9 to 13	48 to 56
4 to 9	40 to 48
0 to 4	32 to 40

AVERAGE OF DAILY HIGH TEMPERATURES

Degrees Fahrenheit	Degrees Centigrade
84 to 96	29 to 36
72 to 84	22 to 29
60 to 72	16 to 22

AVERAGE YEARLY PRECIPITATION
(Rain, Melted Snow, and Other Moisture)

Inches	Centimeters
20 to 28	51 to 71
12 to 20	30 to 51
4 to 12	10 to 30

0   100   200 Miles
0   100   200   300 Kilometers

MONTHLY WEATHER IN DENVER AND PUEBLO

		JAN	FEB	MAR	APR	MAY	JUNE	JULY	AUG	SEPT	OCT	NOV	DEC
DENVER	Average of:												
	High Temperatures	42	45	51	61	69	81	87	85	77	66	53	45
	Low Temperatures	16	19	25	34	43	52	58	57	48	37	26	18
	Days of Rain or Snow	6	6	8	9	11	7	9	9	5	6	5	4
PUEBLO	Days of Rain or Snow	5	4	6	7	10	7	9	9	4	4	4	3
	High Temperatures	45	49	55	65	73	84	90	88	81	69	55	47
	Low Temperatures	14	19	25	35	45	54	60	59	49	37	23	16

Temperatures are given in degrees Fahrenheit.

Source: U.S. Weather Bureau

WORLD BOOK maps

Brilliant Yellow Aspens Attract Autumn Visitors to resort areas near the city of Aspen. The trees are bare in winter, and bright green leaves cover the branches in summer.

Margaret Durrance, Photo Researchers

68oa

Colorado's economy is divided roughly along the natural lines of its land. East of the mountains lie the major manufacturing centers and the chief crop growing areas. In the mountains, many kinds of metals are mined. On the western side of the state are major grazing areas, orchards, and uranium mines. Oil occurs in places on both sides of the mountains.

The federal government and tourists play a major part in Colorado's economy. The U.S. government owns more than a third of the land in Colorado. It is an important factor in the state's economy because it controls grazing, logging, mining, and recreation on this land. Tourism ranks high as an income producer. Visitors spend more than $400,000,000 a year in the state.

Natural Resources. Mineral deposits, a pleasant climate, rich soils, vast evergreen forests, and water are Colorado's greatest natural resources.

Soil. The soils of the eastern plains and the valleys of the western mountains are among the most fertile in the nation. These soils contain the minerals needed by growing plants. The eastern soils are brown. During years of good rainfall, they produce excellent crops. In dry years, the soil becomes powdery, and crops are poor. The high mountains and some western plateaus have thin, stony soils called *lithosols*.

Minerals. Vast deposits of coal, molybdenum, natural gas, petroleum, uranium, vanadium, and zinc help support Colorado's economy. Huge oil shale and uranium deposits offer promise of future mineral development. Supplies of building materials such as gravel, sand, and stone seem large enough for the state's future needs.

Forests. About 20,000,000 acres, or nearly a third of Colorado's land, is covered by forests. But only about 8,000,000 acres can be cut for commercial use. Some forests are unsuitable because they are too far from transportation or too low in quality. Others have been set aside for conservation purposes. About 6,000,000 acres of the commercial forests are on U.S. government land.

Almost all the commercially valuable trees are *softwood* (evergreens suitable for construction lumber). However, Colorado imports lumber each year because not enough is produced in the state. Leading lumber trees include various kinds of firs, pines, and spruces.

Plant Life. Because of the large differences in altitude and moisture, Colorado's land has a wide variety of plant life. Plants include many kinds of cactus, greasewood, sagebrush, and yucca in the drier areas. The chief grasses are buffalo and grama grass. Spring wild flowers include buttercups, sand lilies, wild geraniums, and yarrows. Summer brings columbines, dogtooth violets, Indian paintbrushes, mountain lilies and daisies, and wild irises and roses.

Animal Life of Colorado includes about 400,000 deer, elk, and other big game animals. Pronghorn antelope live on the plains. Fur-bearing animals include bears, beavers, bobcats, foxes, martens, rabbits, and skunks. Under the dry plains, prairie dogs dig elaborate systems of tunnels. Game birds include several kinds of grouse, pheasants, and quail. Colorado game fish include bass, catfish, crappies, perch, and trout.

Water is precious in the dry West. The control of water sources is a continuing concern to the people of the entire region. Six major rivers rise in Colorado. By agreement with other states, and with Mexico, Colorado cannot use more than its share of the water in these streams.

Distribution of water within the state is uneven. The *Western Slope* (the land west of the Continental Divide) covers slightly more than a third of the land area. But it gets more than two-thirds of the *surface water* (runoff from rain and snow). The *Eastern Slope*, with almost two-thirds of the land area, gets less than a third of the surface water. There have been bitter legal and political fights over water rights within the state.

Many dams and tunnels have been built for *transmountain diversion* of water. Western Slope water is brought through tunnels in the mountains for use on the dry but heavily-populated Eastern Slope. Some of this water goes to homes and factories. The rest is used to irrigate the fertile soil of the plains. These projects help solve eastern Colorado's water problems. The future growth of Colorado, both in manufacturing and agriculture, depends on the amount of water available.

Manufacturing, including processing, accounts for more than half the value of all goods produced in Colorado. Goods manufactured in the state have a *value*

PRODUCTION IN COLORADO

Total yearly value of goods produced—$2,211,146,000

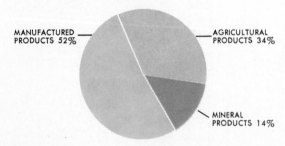

MANUFACTURED PRODUCTS 52%

AGRICULTURAL PRODUCTS 34%

MINERAL PRODUCTS 14%

Note: Manufacturing percentage based on value added by manufacture. Other percentages based on value of production.

Source: Latest available U.S. Government statistics

EMPLOYMENT IN COLORADO

Average yearly number of persons employed—633,050

	Number of Employees
Wholesale & Retail Trade	132,000
Government	122,400
Manufacturing	94,100
Services	91,600
Agriculture	67,000
Transportation & Public Utilities	44,800
Construction	38,400
Finance, Insurance & Real Estate	27,900
Forestry & Mining	14,850

Source: Employment statistics supplied by employers to government agencies

added by manufacture of about $1,152,000,000 yearly. This figure represents the value created in products by Colorado's industries, not counting such costs as materials, supplies, and fuels.

Colorado has more than 3,500 manufacturing plants, but most of them are small. Only about 200 plants have more than a hundred workers. But, Colorado is the leading manufacturing state in the Rocky Mountain region.

Colorado's two largest manufacturing industries produce food products and steel. Food processing accounts for about a fifth of the value added by manufacture. This industry includes about a hundred packing, processing, and shipping plants for meat. About 15 refineries make sugar from sugar beets. Almost a hundred plants can or freeze foods. Pueblo is the center of Colorado's steel industry.

Defense work is also important in Colorado. Most of the defense work takes place at the Martin Company missile plant south of Denver, and at a government plant at Rocky Flats near Boulder. The Martin plant produces long-range Titan missiles. The Rocky Flats plant works under the Atomic Energy Commission. Details of work done at the Martin and the Rocky Flats plants are not published. But the plants rank among Colorado's largest employers.

Other large factories make chemicals, luggage, mining and electrical machinery, paper, petroleum products, and rubber products. Building materials such as clay, glass, lumber, and stone products are processed in many locations. Grand Junction is the center of the Western Slope's uranium processing industry.

Agriculture in Colorado earns about $751 million a year. Colorado has more than 33,000 farms. They range from large ranches of many square miles to small *truck* (vegetable) farms.

Livestock and livestock products account for almost two-thirds of the value of all Colorado farm products. The state ranks among the leaders in production of sheep, but cattle raised there have a much greater dollar value. Grazing of cattle on ranches has been important for many years. Colorado farmers also *finish* (fatten) cattle in *feed lots*. Operators of feed lots put range cattle in relatively small pens. There, the cattle

are fattened on special feed. They gain weight faster because they do not have to hunt for their feed. These animals bring better prices in the market. The area around Greeley has the most feed lots.

The chief field crops, in order of importance, are wheat, sugar beets, and hay. Most of Colorado's wheat is grown on the eastern plains by dry-farming methods. Sugar beets grow best on irrigated land in northern Colorado. Hay is grown in many areas, including some high mountain valleys.

Colorado ranks high as a producer of vegetables. Potatoes are grown in the San Luis Valley of southern Colorado. Much of this valley area is irrigated with water from wells. Other major vegetable crops, in order of value, are dry beans, onions, and lettuce. Colorado farmers also grow high-quality celery and cantaloupes.

Other important agricultural products include flowers and fruits. Colorado carnations are sent to many other states, and have become famous for their size and beauty. Apples, peaches, and cherries grow in the western part of the state, usually in irrigated orchards.

Mining in Colorado produces about $300 million a year, or a seventh of the value of all goods produced in the state. Petroleum, molybdenum, coal, and sand and gravel lead in value, in that order.

A feature of Colorado's mining industry is its wide distribution. Of the 63 counties, all but Denver County have income from mining.

Petroleum and other mineral fuels account for almost half of Colorado's mining income. About half the oil comes from the Rangely field in Rio Blanco County in northwestern Colorado. Colorado coal provides fuel for steel mills in Colorado and Utah, and for some electric power plants. Natural gas and natural gas liquids also are important products of Colorado mining.

Molybdenum is Colorado's most valuable metal. This metal makes steel hard and tough. It also has uses in rockets where tough, heat-resistant metal is needed. Colorado's major molybdenum deposit lies at Climax, two miles high among the rugged mountain peaks. This deposit, the largest known source of molybdenum in North America, produces about two-thirds of the U.S. supply.

FARM, MINERAL, AND FOREST PRODUCTS

This map shows the areas where the state's leading farm, mineral, and forest products are produced. The major urban areas (shown in red) are the state's important manufacturing centers.

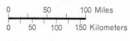

0   50   100 Miles

0   50   100   150 Kilometers

WORLD BOOK map

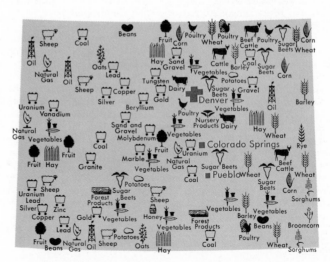

COLORADO

About 70 mines in 22 counties produce copper, gold, lead, silver, and zinc. Usually, all or most of these metals come from the same ore. The value of copper, lead, and zinc produced is much higher than that of gold or silver.

Colorado is among the leading states in uranium ore production. More than 350 mines produce this ore. Mesa, Montrose, and San Miguel counties, on the Colorado Plateau, lead in uranium ore production.

Large quantities of building materials are available almost everywhere in Colorado. Colorado limestone is used in making cement. Sand and gravel are found in almost every county. Production of these basic materials totals about 20,000,000 tons a year. Stone quarries produce basalt, granite, marble and sandstone. Other mineral products include clay, gem stones, gypsum, lime, mica, perlite, pumice, and salt.

Colorado has another enormous mining prospect. This is oil shale, which could become a rich source of petroleum. The shale, a type of rock, is found in a vast deposit in northwestern Colorado and nearby areas of Utah and Wyoming. It lies on or near the surface, and can be mined with huge power shovels. Colorado has about a trillion and a half tons of oil shale. In 1964, a group of oil companies began experiments with this shale at a plant near Rifle.

Electric Power. More than 80 per cent of Colorado's electricity is produced by steam power, mostly from coal. Water power provides the rest. About two-thirds of the power comes from privately owned plants. Colorado's power production almost tripled between 1950 and 1960. New dams and new steam generating plants continued to raise Colorado's power capacity during the 1960's. For Colorado's kilowatt-hour production, see ELECTRIC POWER (table).

Transportation. Colorado has special transportation problems because of its mountains. Colorado has more miles of mountain roads than any other state. The highest road in the United States climbs to the top of 14,264-foot Mount Evans near Denver. About 24 highways across the mountains are kept open by snow plows during the winter months. Colorado has about 79,000 miles of roads, more than half of them paved.

Colorado has air service from seven airlines. Denver's Stapleton International Airport, the chief commercial airport, is one of the busiest fields in the United States. Colorado has about 125 public and private airports.

Thirteen railroads use Colorado's 3,783 miles of track. The 6.4-mile Moffat Tunnel, one of the longest railroad tunnels in the country, cuts the travel time between Denver and Salt Lake City by several hours.

Communication. Colorado's oldest newspaper is the *Rocky Mountain News*, first published in Denver in 1859. Today, Colorado has about 170 papers, including 27 dailies. Leading papers include the *Colorado Springs Gazette-Telegraph*, *Denver Post*, *Grand Junction Sentinel*, *Pueblo Chieftain*, and *Rocky Mountain News*.

The state's first commercial radio station, KFKA in Greeley, began broadcasting in 1921. KFEL-TV (now KCTO-TV) in Denver, Colorado's first television station, began operation in 1952. Today, the state has 11 TV stations and about 75 radio stations.

68od

Union Colony Founded. In 1870, Nathan C. Meeker began a cooperative agricultural community in the South Platte Valley. Because the colony was sponsored by Horace Greeley, noted editor of the *New York Tribune*, the town that grew out of it was named for him.

Highest Automobile Road in the U.S. winds in a series of hairpin curves to the top of 14,264-foot Mount Evans, in the Rockies west of Denver.

"West Point of the Air," the U.S. Air Force Academy, moved to its new home near Colorado Springs in 1958.

COLORADO / History

Indian Days. Indians roamed the plains of present-day Colorado before white men arrived. Early explorers found the Arapaho, Cheyenne, Comanche, Kiowa, and Pawnee tribes on the plains. The Utes lived in the mountain valleys.

Exploration and Settlement. Spanish explorers who came in the 1500's were the first white men to visit the Colorado region. The Spaniards failed to find gold, and left without attempting to settle the area. In 1682, the explorer Robert Cavalier, Sieur de la Salle, claimed for France an area that included what is now eastern Colorado. In 1706, Juan de Ulibarri, a Spanish official, claimed the region for Spain.

In 1803, the United States bought present-day eastern and central Colorado as part of the Louisiana Purchase. During the next 20 years, Americans explored

HISTORIC COLORADO

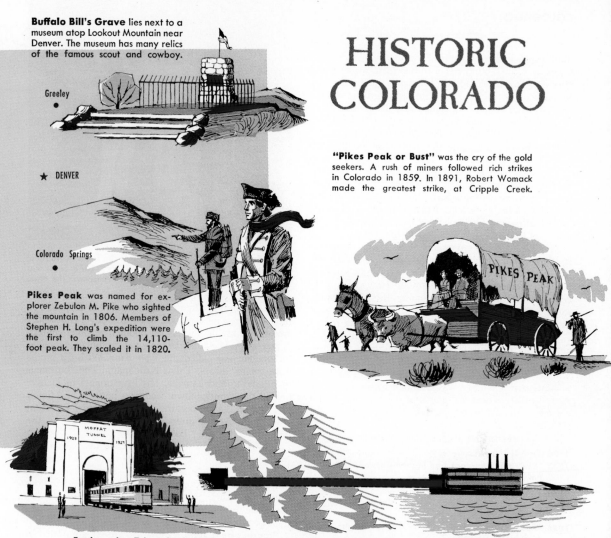

Buffalo Bill's Grave lies next to a museum atop Lookout Mountain near Denver. The museum has many relics of the famous scout and cowboy.

Greeley •

★ DENVER

Colorado Springs •

Pikes Peak was named for explorer Zebulon M. Pike who sighted the mountain in 1806. Members of Stephen H. Long's expedition were the first to climb the 14,110-foot peak. They scaled it in 1820.

"Pikes Peak or Bust" was the cry of the gold seekers. A rush of miners followed rich strikes in Colorado in 1859. In 1891, Robert Womack made the greatest strike, at Cripple Creek.

PIKES PEAK

Engineering Triumphs. In 1927, the 6-mile Moffat Tunnel, 40 miles west of Denver, was completed at a cost of $18,000,000. The tunnel greatly shortened the traveling distance to the Pacific Coast. The 13-mile Alva B. Adams Tunnel, completed in 1947, carries water through the Rocky Mountains. It cost $12,800,000, and is part of the Colorado-Big Thompson irrigation project, which covers 720,000 acres in eastern Colorado.

much of the region. Zebulon M. Pike, an army officer, entered the Colorado area in 1806. Pike's record of the trip describes the mighty mountain that was named for him—Pikes Peak. Another officer, Major Stephen H. Long, led an exploring party in 1820. The first permanent American settlement was Bent's Fort, built in 1833 by the Bent and St. Vrain Fur Company. The fort, near the site of present-day La Junta, was used as a base by Kit Carson and other famous frontiersmen.

Mexico won control of western Colorado from Spain in 1821. The United States took control during the Mexican War (1846-1848). The United States kept the land under the terms of the treaty that ended the war.

The Gold Rush. Colorado had few settlers until the late 1850's. Then, in 1858, prospectors found gold along Cherry Creek, near the site of present-day Denver.

Gold hunters rushed into the area. "Pikes Peak or Bust" became the slogan of the prospectors as they traveled the long, hard trail to the Colorado gold fields. The rush reached its height by the end of 1859, when about 100,000 persons had reached the area.

Governing the booming area became a major problem. The Indians claimed that the land had been given to them by various treaties. The miners ignored the Indian claims and set up what they called the Jefferson Territory. Congress refused to recognize the Jefferson Territory, and created the Colorado Territory in 1861. William Gilpin was appointed as the first territorial governor. See JEFFERSON TERRITORY.

Territorial Days. Indians and whites fought many small clashes and three important battles during the 1860's and 1870's. In 1864, troops of the Colorado

68oe

militia attacked a peaceful Cheyenne village at Sand Creek and killed hundreds of Indian men, women, and children. This battle became known as the Sand Creek Massacre. The U.S. government criticized the attack, and paid the Indians for their losses. In 1868, a large force of Indians attacked 50 army scouts on the Arikaree River in eastern Colorado. The scouts fought for several days on Beecher Island in the river. They finally were saved by other troops.

The last big Indian battle in Colorado was the Meeker Massacre in 1879. In this fight, the Ute Indians killed their reservation agent, Nathan C. Meeker, and ambushed a body of troops. After the battle, a respected Ute chief named Ouray helped calm the Indian warriors and settle their problems with the whites.

Many settlers started ranches and farms along the streams. Crude irrigation systems were developed along the eastern edge of the mountains, and in the San Luis Valley. Horace Greeley, a famous New York City editor who believed in developing the West, sponsored a farming colony in Colorado in 1870. Greeley made popular the expression, "Go west, young man."

In 1870, the Denver Pacific Railroad linked Denver with the main line of the Union Pacific at Cheyenne, Wyo. This line connected Colorado and the East. The Kansas Pacific built its line to Denver later in 1870.

Statehood. Colorado was admitted to the Union on Aug. 1, 1876. Territorial governor John L. Routt was elected as the first state governor.

———— **IMPORTANT DATES IN COLORADO** ————

1706 Juan de Ulibarri claimed the Colorado region for Spain.

1803 The United States acquired eastern Colorado as part of the Louisiana Purchase.

1806 Zebulon M. Pike explored Colorado.

1848 The United States took western Colorado after the Mexican War.

1858 Gold was discovered at Cherry Creek, near the site of what is now Denver.

1859 The Colorado gold rush attracted thousands of prospectors and settlers.

1861 Congress created the Colorado Territory.

1870 The Denver Pacific Railroad was completed to Denver.

1876 Colorado became the 38th state on August 1.

1879 The Meeker Massacre marked the end of serious Indian fighting.

1899 The state's first beet-sugar factory began operating.

1906 The U.S. Mint in Denver issued its first coins. Congress established Mesa Verde National Park.

1915 Rocky Mountain National Park was established.

1927 The Moffat Tunnel, a railroad tunnel through the mountains, was completed.

1956 The Upper Colorado River water storage project was approved by Congress.

1958 The U.S. Air Force Academy's permanent campus opened near Colorado Springs.

1959 The Colorado-Big Thompson irrigation system was completed.

1962 Ground was broken for the three-dam Curecanti water storage project.

1966 North American Air Defense Command completed its underground operations center in Cheyenne Mountain.

Denver Public Library Western Collection

Silver Bricks were laid from the street to the Teller House Hotel when President U. S. Grant visited Central City in 1873. Silver was used instead of gold because gold was so common in the area.

A new mining boom brought wealth to Colorado in the early years of statehood. This time silver caused the growth. Leadville and Aspen boomed as silver centers.

Horace A. W. Tabor became the symbol of this colorful era. He was called the *Silver King*. With his profits from several mines, Tabor built magnificent buildings in Leadville and Denver. His investments in Denver helped that frontier town become a business and financial center. Tabor became a U.S. Senator. President Chester A. Arthur attended Tabor's wedding to the beautiful Elizabeth "Baby" Doe.

In 1893, business slumped all across the nation. For this reason, the U.S. government canceled its agreements to buy large amounts of silver. Silver prices dropped. In Colorado, many silver mines closed and the miners lost their jobs. Other businesses suffered because the unemployed persons could not afford to buy their products.

Progress as a State. Colorado's growth continued in spite of the state's troubles. A major gold discovery at Cripple Creek softened the blow of the silver crash. Farmers began to experiment with different crops, and expanded their irrigation systems. Sugar beets and potatoes became valuable Colorado crops. The state's first sugar refinery opened in Grand Junction in 1899. In 1902, construction started on a railroad over the Continental Divide. In 1906, the U.S. Mint in Denver produced its first coins.

By 1910, Colorado had almost 800,000 persons. Agriculture had replaced mining as the state's most important industry. Colorado had more acres of irrigated land than any other state. The food processing industry grew as canneries and more sugar refineries were built.

The 1910's and 1920's. The development of automobiles in the early 1900's caused rapid growth in two Colorado industries—oil and tourism. The family car made vacation travel easier, and Colorado's splendid scenery attracted thousands of tourists. Cars also increased the demand for petroleum products. Colorado's first oil wells were drilled in the Arkansas Valley during territorial days, but production was small. Later, new

National Center for Atmospheric Research

Colorado Scientists study the earth's atmosphere at an observation station near Climax. During the 1960's, major scientific centers in Colorado have carried on space-age research.

oil fields were discovered. By 1920, oil had become Colorado's most important mineral product.

The state government kept pace with the advances in industry. For example, a plan of workmen's compensation was passed in 1915. In 1927, the famous Moffat railroad tunnel was completed with state funds.

The Depression and the 1940's. Colorado's economy suffered during the Great Depression of the 1930's. Farm prices dropped sharply, and stayed low. A long period of dry weather began on the eastern plains. Wind whipped the dry, powdery soil into huge dust clouds, and dust storms darkened the sky. The state and federal governments began programs to restore the wind-damaged land, and to help the unemployed. In 1935, the Colorado legislature voted a 2 per cent sales tax to raise money for old-age pensions. Highway construction and other programs helped put men back to work.

In the 1940's, Colorado's economy boomed. After the outbreak of World War II in 1939, the government established a number of military bases in Colorado. Military payrolls in Colorado jumped from $3 million in 1940 to $152 million in 1945. The war also produced a great demand for Colorado's oil and metals.

After World War II ended in 1945, the state's population increased rapidly. Land became more valuable, particularly near the growing cities. Construction began in 1945 on the Cherry Creek Dam and reservoir near Denver. Private groups rebuilt the old mining town of Aspen. It became famous as a winter ski resort, and as an art, education, and health center.

In 1947, the Alva B. Adams Tunnel was completed. It brought water from western Colorado to the area east of the mountains for a huge irrigation system, the Colorado-Big Thompson Project.

The 1950's. In 1954, manufacturing replaced agriculture as Colorado's most important industry in value of products. The biggest developments were related to national defense programs. Uranium mining and milling became important industries on Colorado's Western Slope. Colorado Springs became the headquarters of the North American Air Defense Command. The U.S. Air Force Academy's permanent campus near Colorado Springs opened in 1958. A huge missile plant was built south of Denver in the late 1950's.

In 1956, Congress approved construction of a system of dams to form the Upper Colorado River water project. This project was designed to increase the use of the Colorado River for irrigation, for generating power, and for cities. The Colorado-Big Thompson Project, completed in 1959, irrigates more than 720,000 acres. Its six hydroelectric plants produce power.

Agriculture in Colorado suffered in the mid-1950's from droughts on the plains, but better farming methods held down wind damage.

Colorado Today faces the problems of rapid population growth. Colorado's climate and scenery make it an attractive place to live. Since 1945, the state has ranked among the nation's fastest growing areas. Suburbs have grown up around Denver. These suburbs and Denver shared many problems, but each city could meet only its part of a problem. The beginning of an area-wide approach to the problems came in 1963. That year, a metropolitan system of sewage control was established. Denver also acted to share its plentiful water supply with other cities. Problems still to be solved include air pollution, area planning, taxation, and zoning.

Colorado's manufacturing industries have continued to grow. Machinery and transportation equipment manufacturing increased in importance in the 1960's.

Dams and irrigation projects costing more than $300

THE GOVERNORS OF COLORADO

	Party	Term
1. John L. Routt	Republican	1876-1879
2. Frederick W. Pitkin	Republican	1879-1883
3. James B. Grant	Democratic	1883-1885
4. Benjamin H. Eaton	Republican	1885-1887
5. Alva Adams	Democratic	1887-1889
6. Job A. Cooper	Republican	1889-1891
7. John L. Routt	Republican	1891-1893
8. Davis H. Waite	Populist	1893-1895
9. Albert W. McIntire	Republican	1895-1897
10. Alva Adams	Democratic	1897-1899
11. Charles S. Thomas	Democratic	1899-1901
12. James B. Orman	Democratic	1901-1903
13. James H. Peabody	Republican	1903-1905
14. Alva Adams	Democratic	1905
15. James H. Peabody	Republican	1905
16. Jesse F. McDonald	Republican	1905-1907
17. Henry A. Buchtel	Republican	1907-1909
18. John F. Shafroth	Democratic	1909-1913
19. Elias M. Ammons	Democratic	1913-1915
20. George A. Carlson	Republican	1915-1917
21. Julius C. Gunter	Democratic	1917-1919
22. Oliver H. Shoup	Republican	1919-1923
23. William E. Sweet	Democratic	1923-1925
24. Clarence J. Morley	Republican	1925-1927
25. William H. Adams	Democratic	1927-1933
26. Edwin C. Johnson	Democratic	1933-1937
27. Ray H. Talbot	Democratic	1937
28. Teller Ammons	Democratic	1937-1939
29. Ralph L. Carr	Republican	1939-1943
30. John C. Vivian	Republican	1943-1947
31. W. Lee Knous	Democratic	1947-1949
32. Walter W. Johnson	Democratic	1949-1951
33. Dan Thornton	Republican	1951-1955
34. Edwin C. Johnson	Democratic	1955-1957
35. Stephen L. R. McNichols	Democratic	1957-1963
36. John A. Love	Republican	1963-

million promise improved use of Colorado's water supply. Major projects include the Curecanti storage system of three dams, and the Frying Pan-Arkansas project to bring water to the eastern plains. Several scientific centers have brought space-age research to Colorado. The National Bureau of Standards laboratory moved to Boulder in the late 1950's. It expanded rapidly during the 1960's. The National Center for Atmospheric Research was established in Boulder in 1961 by a group of universities.

In June, 1965, severe floods along the Arkansas and South Platte rivers caused damage estimated at over $500 million.

In 1966, the North American Air Defense Command completed its underground combat operations center in Cheyenne Mountain, near Colorado Springs. The underground center was built at a cost of more than $142 million.

PALMER HOYT, TIM K. KELLEY, and MICHAEL McGIFFERT

COLORADO / Study Aids

Related Articles in WORLD BOOK include:

BIOGRAPHIES

Bonfils, Frederick G.	Pike, Zebulon M.
Carpenter, M. Scott	Sabin, Florence R.
Dempsey, Jack	Teller, Henry M.
Greeley, Horace	Whiteman, Paul
Guggenheim (family)	

CITIES

Aspen	Grand Junction	Leadville
Colorado Springs	Greeley	Pueblo
Denver		

HISTORY

Arapaho Indians	Indian Wars
Cheyenne Indians	Jefferson Territory
Cliff Dwellers	Ute Indians
Comanche Indians	Westward Movement

PHYSICAL FEATURES

Arkansas River	John Martin Dam	Rocky Mountains
Cherry Creek	Moffat Tunnel	Royal Gorge
Dam	Mount Evans	Sangre de Cristo
Colorado River	Mount of the	Mountains
Dust Bowl	Holy Cross	Shadow Mountain
Garden of	Pikes Peak	Dam
the Gods	Rio Grande	

PRODUCTS

For Colorado's rank among the states in production, see the following articles:

Bean	Onion	Sugar Beet
Lead	Sheep	Uranium
Molybdenum	Sugar	Wool

OTHER RELATED ARTICLES

Easter (picture)	United States Air Force
Ent Air Force Base	Academy
Rocky Mountain States	Western Frontier Life

Outline

I. Government
  A. Constitution
  B. Executive
  C. Legislature
  D. Courts
  E. Local Government
  F. Taxation
  G. Politics
II. People
III. Education
  A. Schools
  B. Libraries
  C. Museums
IV. A Visitor's Guide
  A. Places to Visit
  B. Annual Events
V. The Land
  A. Land Regions
  B. Rivers and Lakes
VI. Climate

VII. Economy
  A. Natural Resources
  B. Manufacturing
  C. Agriculture
  D. Mining
  E. Electric Power
  F. Transportation
  G. Communication
VIII. History

Questions

How are eastern Colorado's water problems being solved?

What are two main mineral products of Colorado?

Where is the highest road in the United States?

Where are most of Colorado's cities?

Why is Colorado called the Centennial State?

Why was H.A.W. Tabor important to the city of Denver?

How and when did the slogan "Pikes Peak or Bust" originate?

What is Colorado's most important agricultural activity?

What products come from Colorado's leading manufacturing industries?

What mountains are called the *Roof of North America?* Why?

Books for Young Readers

BARNES, NANCY (pseud. of Helen S. Adams). *Wonderful Year.* Messner, 1946.

BLOCH, MARIE H. *Tony of the Ghost Towns.* Coward-McCann, 1956.

GEORGE, JOHN L. and JEAN C. *Dipper of Copper Creek.* Dutton, 1956.

KELLEY, TIM K. *Living in Colorado.* Rev. ed. Pruett Press, 1964.

PRITCHETT, LULITA C. *The Cabin at Medicine Springs.* Watts, 1958. Pioneering in the late 1800's.

Books for Older Readers

ARPS, LOUISA W. *Denver in Slices.* Sage, 1959.

BORLAND, HAL. *High, Wide and Lonesome.* Lippincott, 1956. Life on a homestead in eastern Colorado.

Colorado: A Guide to the Highest State. Rev. ed. Hastings, 1951.

HAFEN, LE ROY R. and A. W. *The Colorado Story: A History of Your State and Mine.* Old West Publishing Co., Denver, 1953.

LAVENDER, DAVID S. *Bent's Fort.* Doubleday, 1954. The business ventures of the Bent brothers in the Southwest from the 1830's to the 1860's. *Red Mountain.* 1963. A novel of mining days in southwest Colorado.

MOODY, RALPH. *Little Britches.* Norton, 1950. *Home Ranch.* 1956. Life on a Colorado ranch.

SPRAGUE, MARSHALL. *Money Mountain: The Story of Cripple Creek Gold.* Little, Brown, 1953. *Massacre: The Tragedy at White River.* 1957.

UBBELOHDE, CARL. *Colorado: A Students' Guide to Localized History.* Teachers College Press, 1965.

WOLLE, MURIEL V. *Stampede to Timberline: The Ghost Towns and Mining Camps of Colorado.* Sage, 1962.

COLORADO, UNIVERSITY OF, is a state-supported coeducational school at Boulder and Denver, Colo. The Boulder campus has the colleges of arts and sciences, engineering, pharmacy, and music; the extension division; the schools of business, nursing, law, journalism, education, and architecture; and the graduate school. The schools of medicine, nursing, and the medical division of the graduate school are in Denver. Courses lead to bachelor's, master's, and doctor's degrees. A Creative Arts Festival every summer includes activities in drama, music, creative dancing, and fine arts. There are army, navy, and air force ROTC units on campus. The Boulder campus has a high-altitude observatory and the Sommers-Bausch Observatory. The Denver campus includes the Cancer Research Building and the Medical Center. The university was chartered in 1861. For enrollment, see UNIVERSITIES AND COLLEGES (table). QUIGG NEWTON

COLORADO, WESTERN STATE COLLEGE OF. See UNIVERSITIES AND COLLEGES (table).

COLORADO BEETLE. See POTATO BUG.

COLORADO COLLEGE is a coeducational liberal arts school at Colorado Springs, Colo. Bachelor's and master's degrees are offered in most departments. A fine arts course is given in connection with the Colorado Springs Fine Arts Center. The college was founded in 1874. For enrollment, see UNIVERSITIES AND COLLEGES (table).

COLORADO DESERT occupies about 2,000 square miles of southeastern California west of the Colorado River. The Santa Rosa Mountains and Coast Ranges separate it from the Pacific Ocean. The Mojave Desert lies to the north and west of the Colorado Desert. For location, see CALIFORNIA (color map). Parts of the Colorado Desert lie 245 feet below sea level. The desert includes the Salton Sea in southern California, formed in 1905 when irrigation engineers lost control of the Colorado River (see SALTON SEA). Hoover Dam and other Colorado River dams furnish water to the Colorado Desert's Imperial and Coachella valleys (see IMPERIAL VALLEY). GEORGE SHAFTEL

COLORADO NATIONAL MONUMENT, in western Colorado, includes many strange rock formations, such as Devil's Kitchen, Window Rock, and Monolith Parade. Prehistoric remains and a preserve of deer, buffalo, and elk may also be seen on the 17,000-acre monument, which was established in 1911. C. LANGDON WHITE

COLORADO RIVER, one of the major rivers in the United States, is 1,450 miles long. It flows across 1,360 miles of the United States and 90 miles of Mexico. It rises in the Rocky Mountains of Colorado, and flows southwestward into Utah. The Colorado is joined by the Green River in eastern Utah, then continues southwestward into Arizona. After merging with the Little Colorado River in northern Arizona, the river swings west through the Grand Canyon. The Virgin River of Nevada joins its course beyond the Grand Canyon. The Colorado then turns south, and flows across the Mexican border to the Gulf of California. Arizona's Williams and Gila rivers merge with the river north of the Mexican border. The Colorado River drains an area of about 250,000 square miles.

The Grand Canyon of the Colorado River presents an outstanding example of the effects of wind, water, and weather on the earth's surface. For millions of years,

Location Map of the Colorado River

the river worked its way into layer after layer of rock, gradually deepening and broadening its channel. Sand, pebbles, and boulders carried by the river produced a constant grinding action. The action of wind and temperature and the gradual elevation of the Colorado plateau added to the effect of the grinding. The Grand Canyon now consists of a great gash in the earth more than a mile deep and between 14 and 18 miles wide in some places.

Many rapids and waterfalls lie along the course of the Colorado. The waters carry tons of silt and sand. Until Hoover Dam was built, the river deposited these materials in its lower river valley, forming a rich delta country. The Hoover Dam, completed in 1936, helps check floods and erosion, and provides a dependable supply of water and electric power. Davis, Parker, and Imperial dams, which lie downstream from Hoover Dam, also help regulate the flow of water. In 1956, Congress passed a bill providing for the construction of four major power dams and a number of water-supply units on the Colorado and its branches. Construction began in 1957 on the Glen Canyon Dam, one of the four major dams. The Navajo and the Flaming Gorge dams were completed in 1963, and the Glen Canyon Dam about a year later. The Colorado-Big Thompson Project diverts water from the Colorado River and stores it. The water is used to irrigate 720,000 acres of land in north-central Colorado.

Plans were announced in 1963 to develop recreation areas and wildlife preserves along both banks of the lower Colorado River. The plans affect about 400,000 acres of land between Hoover Dam and the Mexican border along about 265 miles of the river. ALICE B. GOOD

See also AQUEDUCT (Present-Day); GRAND CANYON NATIONAL PARK; HOOVER DAM; POWELL, JOHN W.

COLORADO RIVER forms a major drainage system of central Texas. It rises at the edge of the Staked Plains and flows southeast 840 miles into the Gulf of Mexico at Matagorda Bay. The river drains an area as large as Tennessee. Six artificial lakes furnish water for power and irrigation. They are Buchanan, Inks, Lyndon B. Johnson, Marble Falls, Travis, and Austin. Austin, the capital of Texas, is on the river. H. BAILEY CARROLL

COLORADO SCHOOL OF MINES. See UNIVERSITIES AND COLLEGES (table).

COLORADO SPRINGS

COLORADO SPRINGS, Colo. (pop. 70,194; met. area 143,742), is a tourist and recreation center. It lies 5,980 feet above sea level, east of Pikes Peak. A major gateway to the Rocky Mountains, it is famed for its rugged mountain setting. Colorado Springs has a healthful year-round climate, with an average of more than 300 days of sunshine. It is the third largest city in the state. For the location of Colorado Springs, see COLORADO (political map).

The city is the home of Colorado College and the Colorado Springs Fine Arts Center. Points of interest include the Garden of the Gods, Pikes Peak, and the Will Rogers Shrine of the Sun Memorial. The United States Air Force Academy is north of the city. Other military installations include Ent Air Force Base, Cheyenne Mountain Combat Operations Center of the North American Air Defense Command (NORAD), and Fort Carson, home of the 5th Infantry Division.

Colorado Springs has about 200 manufacturing firms which make such products as tools, plastics, furniture, and airplane equipment. The largest motion-picture advertising studio in the world is in the city.

Colorado Springs was founded in 1871. It has a council-manager form of government, and is the seat of El Paso County.   HAROLD H. DUNHAM

COLORADO STATE COLLEGE is a state-supported coeducational school in Greeley, Colo. Founded in 1889, it has undergraduate and graduate programs in liberal arts and teacher training. There are divisions of arts, education, health and physical education, humanities, music, sciences, and social studies. For enrollment, see UNIVERSITIES AND COLLEGES (table).

COLORADO STATE UNIVERSITY is a coeducational state-supported land-grant school in Fort Collins, Colo. It has schools of agriculture, engineering, home economics, science and arts, veterinary medicine, and forestry and range management. Courses lead to bachelor's, master's, and doctor's degrees. It began as the Agricultural College of Colorado in 1870, and was known as the Colorado Agricultural and Mechanical College from 1951 to 1957. For enrollment, see UNIVERSITIES AND COLLEGES (table).   WILLIAM E. MORGAN

COLORED PEOPLE. See NEGRO; RACES OF MAN; AFRICA (People).

COLORED PEOPLE, NATIONAL ASSOCIATION FOR THE ADVANCEMENT OF. See NATIONAL ASSOCIATION FOR THE ADVANCEMENT OF COLORED PEOPLE.

COLORING, PROTECTIVE. See PROTECTIVE COLORATION.

COLOSSEUM, *kahl uh SEE um,* or FLAVIAN AMPHITHEATER, is perhaps the finest surviving example of ancient Roman architectural engineering. It stands near the center of present-day Rome. The Colosseum is shaped like a present-day football stadium. It could seat about 45,000 spectators. Such spectacles as fights between gladiators and between men and wild animals were held there.

The four-story Colosseum is 161 feet high, about 600 feet long, and 500 feet wide. Awnings could be hung from the walls to protect spectators from the sun. Half columns decorated the *façade* (outer part) of the Colosseum, and archways separated the columns. The fourth-story walls have rectangular windows and rectangular *pilasters* (flat columns attached to the walls). The oval-shaped *arena* (sand-covered area) on the floor of the Colosseum is 282 feet long, and 207 feet across at its widest point.

Originally, the arena could be flooded for water spectacles. Later, however, cages for men and animals were installed beneath the arena. A wall separated the spectators from the arena. The seats for spectators rested on sloping concrete supports as in many stadiums today.

Construction of the Colosseum started during the reign of Emperor Vespasian, who ruled from A.D. 69 to 79. Construction was completed in A.D. 80, during the reign of Titus.   WILLIAM P. DONOVAN

See also ROMAN EMPIRE (picture: At the Colosseum); ROME (picture: Ancient Rome).

COLOSSIANS, EPISTLE TO THE, the 12th book of the New Testament, was written by the Apostle Paul about A.D. 62. The *epistle* (letter) warned against teachings that tried to reduce the importance of Christ. It was addressed to Christians in Colossae (now central Turkey). Paul was a prisoner, probably in Rome, at the time. See also PAUL, SAINT.   W. W. SLOAN

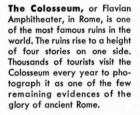

The Colosseum, or Flavian Amphitheater, in Rome, is one of the most famous ruins in the world. The ruins rise to a height of four stories on one side. Thousands of tourists visit the Colosseum every year to photograph it as one of the few remaining evidences of the glory of ancient Rome.

COLOSSUS OF RHODES. See Seven Wonders of the World.

COLOSSUS OF THE NORTH. See Latin America (Relations with the United States).

COLOUR is the spelling used in Britain and Commonwealth countries for *color*. See Color.

COLT. See Horse (Horse Terms).

COLT, SAMUEL (1814-1862), developed the first successful repeating pistol. The pistol, patented in 1836, had a cylinder of several chambers that could be discharged in succession by the same locking and firing mechanism (see Revolver). Colt established a permanent factory at Hartford, Conn., where he also produced arms used during the Mexican War and the Civil War. After Colt's death, his company made the famous six-shooters that were used throughout the West. Colt was born in Hartford. Charles Edward Chapel

See also Western Frontier Life (color picture).

Bettmann Archive
Samuel Colt

COLTER, JOHN (1770?-1813), an American trapper, discovered and explored the Yellowstone region. He was born near Staunton, Va., and spent his early days on a farm. In October, 1803, he enlisted for the Lewis and Clark expedition near Maysville, Ky. He stayed with the expedition until 1806. He was a good marksman, and could withstand great fatigue.

Colter left the expedition in 1806 to become a mountain man. He planned to join two companions and remain in the upper Missouri River area for at least two years in pursuit of his fortune. For a considerable period, Colter was lost to civilization. He probably spent his time in the West, wandering along the Missouri River and through the Rocky Mountains. The scene of his greatest activity was along the Yellowstone River. He associated closely with many Indian tribes.

In 1807, Colter was in the Yellowstone basin on a fur-hunting expedition. During this period, he made his famous exploring journey into the wild countryside and discovered the great thermal springs area that is now Yellowstone National Park. He also discovered several passes through the Rocky Mountains.

Colter's exploits in the mountains have been a basic source of information about American frontier expansion in that region. He returned to St. Louis in 1810 and retired as a mountain man. Thomas D. Clark

COLTRANE, JOHN WILLIAM (1926-1967), was a famous jazz saxophonist and composer. His sometimes violent style made him one of the most controversial and widely imitated jazz musicians of the 1960's. Coltrane was also one of the first jazz performers to reflect the influence of the music of India.

Coltrane was born in Hamlet, N.C. He played in the bands of Dizzy Gillespie and Johnny Hodges during the early 1950's. He achieved greater recognition as a frequent soloist with the Miles Davis quintet between 1955 and 1960. Coltrane formed his own quartet in 1960, and scored a popular success with a recording of the song "My Favorite Things." Previously a tenor saxophonist,

he played the soprano saxophone on this record. Coltrane did much to popularize the soprano saxophone among jazz musicians. Leonard Feather

COLT'S-TAIL. See Fleabane.

COLTSFOOT is a wild plant of Europe and Asia. It also now grows in northeastern United States and in Canada. The coltsfoot has light-yellow flowers which look like dandelion blossoms. The flowers bloom in March or April, and are borne on stems which have no leaves. The leaves appear after the flowers have died. They are large and broad, and downy on the underside. The leaves are rounded at first, but later become shaped like a heart or a colt's foot. The *false coltsfoot* and the *beetleweed* are not true coltsfoot plants. The false coltsfoot is sometimes called the wild ginger or coltsfoot snakeroot, and belongs to the birthwort family.

Leaves of the Coltsfoot plant are used to make a popular home remedy for chronic coughs, and to treat certain lung diseases. Its yellow flowers look like dandelion blossoms.

Bureau of Plant Industry, USDA

Scientific Classification. The coltsfoot belongs to the composite family, *Compositae*. It makes up the genus *Tussilago*. Harold Norman Moldenke

COLUM, PADRAIC (1881-   ), was an original member of the group of Irish writers that made Dublin's Abbey Theatre famous. He wrote three important plays for the Abbey—*Broken Soil* (1903, revised as *The Fiddler's House*), *The Land* (1905), and *Thomas Muskerry* (1910). Each is a realistic study of peasant or provincial life and each was intended as part of a connected "comedy of Irish life through all the social stages."

Colum was born in County Longford, and moved to the United States in 1914. He then began writing young people's books based on myth and folklore. These books include *The King of Ireland's Son* (1916), *The Adventures of Odysseus* (1918), and *The Children of Odin* (1920). Colum's verse—from *Wild Earth* (1907) to *Collected Poems* (1953)—is a subtle rendering of simple speech and song patterns. His verse is clear in style and nostalgic in feeling. Martin Meisel

COLUMBA, SAINT. See Missions and Missionaries.

COLUMBIA. Long before the Revolutionary War, many people felt that America should have been named Columbia after its discoverer, Christopher Columbus. During the war, poets in the 13 colonies used the name Columbia to describe the new nation that was to become the United States. The word was first used by Phillis Wheatley, a Negro slave poetess in Massachu-

685

COLUMBIA

Columbia

setts, in a poem honoring George Washington. Philip Freneau popularized the term in several poems during and after the war. It appeared first in law in 1784 when King's College in New York City became Columbia College. Towns, counties, and institutions throughout the United States have since adopted the name.

Many artists have symbolically pictured Columbia as a tall, stately woman dressed in flowing garments and holding an American flag. A blue, flaglike drape with white stars is usually part of her costume. During the 1800's, Columbia appeared on the prows of ships, in patriotic paintings, and in pageants representing the spirit of the American Revolution. The bronze *Statue of Freedom*, on top of the Capitol in Washington, D.C., is often incorrectly called a statue of Columbia.   MERRILL JENSEN

COLUMBIA, Mo. (pop. 36,650; alt. 730 ft.), is the home of the University of Missouri and two women's junior colleges, Christian and Stephens. It ranks as one of the medical centers of the Middle West, with the university's schools of medicine and nursing, the university hospitals, the Ellis Fischel State Cancer Hospital, and the Boone County Hospital. The state historical society maintains its library in the city. It has a council-manager form of government. Columbia lies in central Missouri, about 130 miles west of St. Louis (see MISSOURI [color map]).   NOEL P. GIST

COLUMBIA, S.C. (pop. 97,433; met. area 260,828; alt. 190 ft.), is the capital of the state and the seat of Richland County. It stands on the east side of the Congaree River, just below the junction of the Broad and Saluda rivers. Columbia is near the center of the state. For location, see SOUTH CAROLINA (color map).

State, federal, and county offices in Columbia employ about 19,000 persons. The city serves as the distributing center for many industries of state-wide importance. Over 250 industrial plants are in the area. Chief manufactures include chemicals, concrete products, electronics equipment, lumber, metal products, processed foods, and textiles. The printing and publishing industry is also important. The State Farmers Market in Columbia has made the city a leading farm-marketing center of the southeast.

South Carolina's Capitol, called *State House*, is the leading point of historic interest in Columbia. Architects modeled the building after the U.S. Capitol in Washington, D.C. Construction of the present building began in 1855. The army of Gen. William T. Sherman damaged the partially completed building in 1865. But the state restored the Capitol for use in 1869, and the structure was finished in its present form in 1907.

Columbia has several churches of historic interest. The First Baptist Church, built in 1859, served as the meeting place of the Secession Convention in 1860. The parents of Woodrow Wilson lie in the graveyard of the First Presbyterian Church. The Washington Street Methodist Church stands on the supposed site of the first Christian house of worship built in Columbia.

Other points of interest in Columbia include the boyhood home of Woodrow Wilson, the executive mansion, and the Town Theatre, one of the oldest little theaters in the country. Institutions of higher learning in the city are: the University of South Carolina, Columbia College, Allen University, Benedict College, Columbia Bible College, and Lutheran Theological Seminary.

The South Carolina legislature selected Columbia's site in 1786. The legislature bought four square miles of land and reserved a space in the center of the square-shaped site for the Capitol. It also planned two 150-foot-wide streets to divide the square into four sections, with 100-foot-wide streets arranged at right angles. The legislature governed the city until 1805. Several annexations have increased the original site to about $18\frac{1}{2}$ square miles. Columbia has a council-manager form of government.   JULIAN J. PETTY

See also SOUTH CAROLINA (color picture, State Capitol).

The Domed State House at Columbia, S.C., *center*, is a gray granite building of Italian Renaissance design.

COLUMBIA BROADCASTING SYSTEM, INC. (CBS), is a large radio- and television-broadcasting system and electronics manufacturer in the United States. William S. Paley organized the company in 1927. It has grown from the original 16 radio stations to include six separate divisions active in informing and entertaining the American people or in developing and manufacturing electronics equipment. Headquarters are in New York City.

CBS Television and *CBS Radio* networks operate hundreds of stations throughout the United States. But each division functions as a completely separate network, maintaining its own officers, staffs, and studios. CBS owns only a few stations in each network. But it has over 190 affiliate stations. The radio and TV networks give large portions of their air time to educational, cultural, religious, and civic programs. Each has its own news reporters in many parts of the world. In 1952, CBS Television opened large television producing facilities called Television City in Hollywood, Calif.

Columbia Records, another division of CBS, is one of the world's largest producers of phonograph records. *CBS-Columbia, Inc.,* a manufacturing division, makes television and radio sets. *CBS-Hytron,* another manufacturing division, produces many kinds of electronic tubes for radio and television sets and also for other uses.

CBS Laboratories, a research division, carries on research programs designed to aid the other CBS divisions. It also cooperates with other organizations. Several medical schools teach surgery with color television and other equipment designed by the CBS Laboratories division. CBS also owns the New York Yankees baseball team.

COLUMBIA COLLEGE. See UNIVERSITIES AND COLLEGES (table).

COLUMBIA PLATEAU. See PACIFIC COAST STATES (Land Regions); IDAHO (Land Regions).

COLUMBIA RIVER is an important waterway of the Pacific Northwest region of the United States, and of southwestern Canada. It ranks as one of the world's greatest salmon streams, and is famous for the hydroelectric plants, irrigation projects, and beautiful scenery along its course. It is 1,214 miles long, and drains an area of about 259,000 square miles. About 220,000 square miles of this area lie in the United States.

Course. The Columbia River rises on the western slopes of the Rocky Mountains in the Canadian province of British Columbia. From its source in Lake Columbia, it flows northwestward for 180 miles through a wild, forested region. Waters from the thaws of large snow and ice fields feed the Columbia in this area. Then it makes a sharp curve to the south into Washington. The Kootenay and Pend Oreille rivers join the Columbia north of the international border. In Washington, the Columbia sweeps westward and southward along the Big Bend. Just below the point where the Snake River joins the Columbia, it turns westward to form the boundary between Washington and Oregon to the Pacific Ocean. The river passes through the Cascade Mountains by way of the deep Columbia Gorge. For the location of the Columbia River, see WASHINGTON (physical map).

Ports. The mouth of the Columbia River forms the main Pacific Coast harbor between San Francisco and the Strait of Juan de Fuca. Astoria, Ore., is an important fishing port at the entrance to the river. The major river port is Portland, Ore., lying on the Willamette River near where it joins the Columbia. The leading river ports in Washington are Vancouver and Longview. Canal and lock systems permit small vessels to

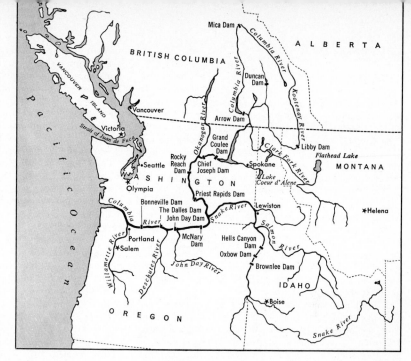

The Historic Columbia River drains an area of 259,000 square miles in the highly productive Pacific Northwest region.

travel past power dams on the lower part of the Columbia River and sail up the Snake River as far as Lewiston, Ida.

Hydroelectric Development. The Columbia River Basin has more than one-third of the potential water power of the United States, and is one of the world's great water-power regions. Federal and private agencies have built large power dams on the Columbia and its tributaries. The John Day Dam, under construction between The Dalles and McNary dams, will produce about 700,000 kilowatts more energy than the Grand Coulee, the largest dam on the river. About 25 dams on the Columbia provide power, limited flood control, recreation areas, and water for irrigation throughout the Columbia Basin.

In 1964, the United States and Canada reached final agreement on a multimillion dollar joint power and flood-control treaty. Canada will build the Duncan, Mica, and Arrow dams in British Columbia, largely with U.S. money. The United States will build Libby Dam in Montana. Goals of the treaty include an end to flood damage, and providing cheaper sources of power for both countries.   HOWARD J. CRITCHFIELD

See also BONNEVILLE DAM; GRAND COULEE DAM; GRAY, ROBERT; SALMON.

COLUMBIA RIVER HIGHWAY is one of the most famous automobile routes in the Pacific Northwest. It extends from Pendleton, in northeastern Oregon, to Astoria, Ore., on the Pacific Coast. It follows part of the old Oregon Trail. The road is 322 miles long and forms the western end of U.S. Highway No. 30. Scenic spots include the Hood River and Bonneville Dam. Work on the road began in 1913, and was completed in 1915. The last of five reconstruction jobs to modernize the highway was finished in 1956.   MATTHEW C. SIELSKI

COLUMBIA UNION COLLEGE. See UNIVERSITIES AND COLLEGES (table).

COLUMBIA UNIVERSITY

COLUMBIA UNIVERSITY is a privately endowed university in New York City. Its campus is at Morningside Heights, in upper Manhattan. Columbia ranks among America's leading universities in liberal arts and professional studies.

Its Divisions include Columbia College; the schools of architecture, arts, engineering and applied science, international affairs, law, and social work; and graduate schools of arts and sciences, business, journalism, and library service. The university's faculty of medicine includes the college of physicians and surgeons, and schools of public health, nursing, and dental and oral surgery. The university also has a School of General Studies that offers special adult education programs. Columbia College is the university's undergraduate school of liberal arts for men. About 2,700 men are enrolled in this college. All other divisions of the university admit both men and women.

Affiliated Institutions. Three colleges in New York City are affiliated with Columbia University. Barnard College was established by the trustees of Columbia University as an undergraduate school for women. It awarded its first bachelor's degrees in 1893. Barnard students now attend classes at Columbia and receive degrees from Columbia University. Barnard is named for Frederick A. P. Barnard, the tenth president of Columbia University. Teachers College is a graduate school of education. It offers programs leading to master's and doctor's degrees. Teachers College was established in 1887 and became part of Columbia University in 1898. It granted its first degrees in 1901 (see TEACHERS COLLEGE, COLUMBIA UNIVERSITY). The College of Pharmaceutical Sciences offers programs leading to bachelor's, master's, and doctor's degrees. It was chartered in 1829, and became affiliated with Columbia University in 1904.

Other Facilities. The university operates regional institutes, centers, and programs. These offer graduate studies and conduct research in such fields as Communist affairs, computer technology, oceanography, nutrition sciences, urban environment, war and peace studies, and applied social research.

Students operate a daily newspaper and an FM radio station. The university has cooperative programs with many museums, hospitals, libraries, and other institu-

Columbia University occupies a huge campus at Morningside Heights, a residential section of Upper Manhattan in New York City.

Columbia University

tions in New York City. Butler Library is one of the largest university libraries in the United States. It contains about 4 million volumes, 50,000 periodical titles, rare manuscripts, and historical documents.

History. Columbia was the fifth college founded in the United States in colonial days. King George II of England chartered it as King's College in 1754. King's College stood for many years near the present site of New York City city hall. A medical school was added in 1767, and the buildings were used as a hospital during the Revolutionary War. The school reopened as Columbia College after the war. Columbia moved to a temporary site in midtown New York City in 1857, and planned to move to what is now Rockefeller Center. It never moved there, but Columbia University still owns the land on which Rockefeller Center stands.

Columbia added schools of law and mines, and the faculties of political sciences, philosophy, and pure science. With the founding of the school of architecture in 1896, Columbia became a university. In 1897, the university moved to its present site at Morningside Heights.

For the enrollments of Columbia University and the three affiliated colleges, see UNIVERSITIES AND COLLEGES (table). DAN CARLINSKY

See also BARNARD, FREDERICK A. P.; BUTLER, NICHOLAS MURRAY; AMERICAN ASSEMBLY, THE.

COLUMBIAN EXPOSITION. See WORLD'S COLUMBIAN EXPOSITION.

COLUMBIAN ORDER. See TAMMANY, SOCIETY OF.

COLUMBINE is a graceful plant that grows wild in Europe, Asia, and North America. Gardeners plant many kinds as border plants. The common *wild columbine* bears red and yellow nodding flowers on rigid, slender stems. Each blossom has five long-spurred petals and many large stamens.

Bees and hummingbirds like columbine because the flower petals hold large amounts of nectar. The plants grow each year from underground rootstocks and bloom from April to July.

The *Rocky Mountain columbine*, or *blue and white columbine*, is the state flower of Colorado. The beautiful blue and white flowers may be 2 inches across. The long, slender spurs curve outward and end in tiny knobs. The *short-spurred columbine* bears blue or purple flowers. Their bluish spurs are quite short, bend inward slightly, and end in a hook.

Scientific Classification. Columbines belong to the crowfoot family, *Ranunculaceae*. The wild columbine is genus *Aquilegia*, species *A. canadensis*. The Rocky Mountain columbine is *A. caerulea*, and the short-spurred columbine is *A. brevistyla*. ROBERT W. HOSHAW

See also FLOWER (color picture: Flowers of the Woodland).

COLUMBINE is the young and lively sweetheart of Harlequin in comedy and pantomime. Columbine originated in Italian comedy of the 1500's. See also PANTOMIME; HARLEQUIN; PIERROT.

COLUMBITE, *koh LUM bite*, is a mineral ore. It is an oxide of niobium, iron, and manganese, and has the chemical formula $(Fe,Mn)Nb_2O_6$. It is the chief source of the element niobium. Its composition varies greatly, with the element tantalum (Ta) often taking the place of all or part of the niobium. When there is more tantalum than niobium, the mineral is called *tantalite*.

Columbite is black, and occurs in blocklike crystals in coarse granite rocks called *pegmatites*. See also NIOBIUM; TANTALUM.   CORNELIUS S. HURLBUT, JR.

COLUMBIUM. See NIOBIUM.

COLUMBUS, Ga. (pop. 116,779; met. area 217,985; alt. 265 ft.), is a textile center and one of the largest cities in the state. It serves as a trading center for the Chattahoochee Valley. A large Army base, Fort Benning, lies nine miles south of Columbus. The city is on the west-central boundary of Georgia, across the Chattahoochee River from Phenix City, Ala. (see GEORGIA [political map]).

Industry and Commerce. Water power helped make Columbus the South's first city to become an industrial center. Water still powers the city's factories. The Chattahoochee River falls 120 feet in a distance of only three miles near the city, and powers three hydroelectric plants. Cotton-textile manufacturing is the most important industry. Other products include textile machinery, soft drinks, farm implements, marble and granite, brick, tile, wood and paper products, chemicals, candy, and peanut products.

Cultural Activities. Columbus has about 60 public schools. The University of Georgia maintains an off-campus center in Columbus. Columbus also has two public libraries, the Columbus Museum of Arts and Crafts, and a symphony orchestra.

History and Government. The Georgia legislature established Columbus on the site of an old Indian village in 1827. It became a cotton-milling center by 1845. The city served as a chief supplier of shoes and swords for Confederate soldiers during the Civil War. Union forces captured Columbus in one of the last battles of the war in April, 1865. Columbus, the seat of Muscogee County, has a council-manager form of government.   ALBERT B. SAYE

COLUMBUS, Ohio (pop. 471,316; met. area 754,924; alt. 780 ft.), is the state capital and home of Ohio State University. It is a central Ohio industrial center.

Location, Size, and Description. Columbus lies at the junction of the Scioto and Olentangy rivers in the approximate center of the state. All major cities of Ohio lie within 150 miles of the capital. Columbus is the third largest city in Ohio. It covers an area of about 92 square miles, on both sides of the rivers. For location, see OHIO (political map).

Columbus has many attractive parks and residential sections. A 10-acre park known as Capitol Square surrounds the gray limestone Capitol in the middle of the city. The building's rotunda contains noted paintings of *Perry's Victory on Lake Erie* and *The Signing of the Treaty of Greene Ville*. The McKinley Memorial and other statues of famous Americans stand on the Capitol grounds. The Ohio state fairgrounds and the Ohio State University campus and football stadium lie on the north side of the city. Fort Hayes, the headquarters of the 20th U.S. Army Corps Reserve and home of the Ohio National Guard, occupies 80 acres a few blocks northeast of Capitol Square. The Columbus General Depot, one of the largest army installations for servicing and supplying engineer and quartermaster units, is located in the eastern part of the city. Lockbourne Air Force Base operates 11 miles southeast of Columbus.

The People. About 97 per cent of the people in Columbus are native-born Americans. Negroes make up

The Ohio State Capitol in Columbus, *center,* stands in a landscaped 10-acre park in the downtown section of the city.

about 16 per cent of this figure. The foreign-born residents come chiefly from Germany, Great Britain, and Italy. Famous persons who were born in Columbus, or who lived there, include Senator John W. Bricker, General Curtis E. LeMay, Eddie Rickenbacker, and author James Thurber.

Industry and Commerce. Columbus ranks fourth among Ohio cities as an industrial center. It lies near large deposits of coal, oil, and natural gas. About 800 manufacturing plants operate in its industrial area. Chief products include aircraft and aircraft parts, automobile body hardware, ball and roller bearings, burial caskets and vaults, circuit breakers, and coated fabrics. Other manufactures include fabricated metal products, food products, mining machinery and equipment, plastic products, radio and television tubes, refrigerators, and steel castings. North American Rockwell Corp., which employs about 8,500 persons in the manufacture of military aircraft and missiles, ranks as the largest industry in Columbus.

Columbus is the home of several scientific research organizations, including the Battelle Memorial Institute, Ohio State University, and the Edward Orton, Jr., Ceramic Foundation. The Battelle Institute conducts specialized research in industrial problems, and leads all other organizations of its kind in volume of research. See BATTELLE MEMORIAL INSTITUTE.

Transportation. Seven major airlines provide transportation to and from Columbus. City-owned Port Columbus airport lies seven miles east of the business district. Five large railroad lines and seven bus lines serve Columbus.

History. The first settlers in the Columbus region settled on the west side of the Scioto River in 1797. They named their village Franklinton. In 1812, the land directly opposite the town of Franklinton, on the east bank of the river, was selected as the site of the state capital. In the same year, the state legislature adopted the name Columbus for the city, after America's discoverer. In 1834, Columbus received a city charter, and in 1871 annexed the greater part of Franklinton across the river. A new city charter in 1916 provided for government by a mayor and council. Columbus is the seat of Franklin County.   JAMES H. RODABAUGH

See also OHIO (picture: The State Capitol).

689

Christopher Columbus

The Flagship *Santa María* led Columbus' tiny fleet. The ship, with Columbus aboard, ran aground on a coral reef off Cap-Haïtien, Haiti. Columbus' men built a fort from the wreckage. This model represents only one scholar's idea of what the *Santa María* looked like. No one really knows.

COLUMBUS, CHRISTOPHER (1451-1506), discoverer of America, was one of the greatest seamen and navigators of all time. He was a self-made and self-educated man with one idea—to reach the East by sailing west. Wise men of olden times and the Middle Ages had always believed this to be possible. In trying to do so, Columbus opened the New World to the use and knowledge of Europeans. He never reached the East, but he proved that it could be done.

Years of Preparation

Early Life. Columbus was born between August 25 and October 31, 1451, in Genoa, then the capital of an independent Italian republic. The family name was *Colombo*. In English, he is known by the Latin form of his name, *Columbus*. He called himself *Cristóbal Colón* after he settled in Spain. His father, Domenico Colombo, was a wool weaver who took a leading part in the affairs of his local guild. His mother, Susanna Fontanarossa, was the daughter of a wool weaver.

Christopher was the eldest of five children. The next brother, Bartholomew, planned the great voyage with Christopher and became his right-hand man in all his enterprises. The youngest brother, Diego, helped him to rule Hispaniola.

As a youth, Christopher helped his father at the loom. But he had always longed to go to sea. Genoa was an important seaport. Genoese ships traded through the Mediterranean region, and many small boats sailed between Genoa and other coastal towns. Christopher undoubtedly caught a ride aboard some of these boats when he was young and learned how to use oars and sails.

He had little schooling. The Genoese dialect that he spoke was almost a different language from Italian, which he never learned to read or write. When he went abroad and had to speak Spanish, he learned to read and write it. He also taught himself Latin because all geography books were written in Latin. No record is left about what sort of boy he was. But judging from his later life, he was dreamy and sensitive.

Early Voyages. The chance to go to sea came sometime between his nineteenth and twentieth birthdays, when he shipped aboard a Genoese galley. The galley had been chartered by King René of Provence to punish the Barbary pirates. After that Columbus made one or two voyages to the island of Chios in the Aegean Sea. Then came a voyage that almost cost him his life. His ship, the *Bechalla*, formed part of a convoy bound from Genoa to England. On August 13, 1476, the convoy was attacked by a hostile fleet off Lagos, Portugal. Christopher was wounded and his ship sank. Jumping into

Samuel Eliot Morison, the contributor of this article, is a former professor of history at Harvard University and winner of a Pulitzer prize for his biography of Christopher Columbus, Admiral of the Ocean Sea.

Christopher Columbus has been painted by many artists, but they differ widely on how he looked. This portrait could have been painted during Columbus' lifetime by the Italian artist Sebastian del Piombo. The King and Queen of Spain granted Columbus the privilege of bearing a coat of arms, *above*, in 1493, following the success of his first voyage.

The Metropolitan Museum of Art, New York, Gift of J. Pierpont Morgan, 1900

The Niña became the flagship after the *Santa María* was wrecked. The *Niña* was probably about 70 feet long and had a beam (width) of about 23 feet.

The Pinta, on Oct. 12, 1492, was the first ship to sight land. Smaller than the *Santa María*, the *Pinta* was probably only about 75 feet long.

by Vories Fisher for WORLD BOOK (ship models courtesy Museum of Science and Industry, Chicago)

the sea, he grabbed a long oar. Using the oar as a life preserver, he managed to reach shore. A few months later he was on a Portuguese vessel which stopped at Galway in Ireland. The vessel sailed north of Iceland in February, 1477, before returning to Lisbon.

By the spring of 1477, Christopher was in Lisbon, the liveliest city in Europe. There his brother, Bartholomew, kept a shop which sold charts and nautical instruments. The Portuguese had discovered the Azores, colonized the Madeiras, and sailed down the coast of Africa almost to the equator. They had invented a handy type of ship, the caravel, which could gain ground against the wind instead of merely scudding before it (see CARAVEL). They were trying to reach the Indies (which at that time meant India, China, the East Indies, and Japan) by sailing around Africa. What they wanted in the Indies were gold, gems, drugs and spices, which reached Europe only by long, costly, overland caravans. While the Portuguese seamen were trying to reach the Orient the hard way, around Africa, Columbus thought of what he believed to be the easy way, sailing due west.

The Great Idea

What Columbus Wanted to Do. Columbus was not trying to "prove the world was round," as so often has been said. He didn't have to. Thinking people knew the world was round. Columbus was simply trying to find a short sea route to the Indies. Paolo Toscanelli, a learned man of Florence with whom Columbus corresponded, believed that Japan lay only 3,000 nautical miles west of Lisbon, Portugal. Columbus expected, by sailing 2,400 miles west along the latitudes of the Canary Islands, to reach a group of islands near Japan where he would be accepted as lord and master by the natives. There he planned to establish a great trading city where the products of the East and the West would be exchanged. In the Philippine Islands, which the Spaniards occupied some sixty years after his death, his original dream was achieved.

First Attempts to "Sell" His Plan. Columbus had a hard time selling his simple plan because the learned men to whom it was referred had a more nearly correct idea of the size of the world than he. The airline route from the Canaries to Japan is about 11,000 nautical miles. (America did not come into the argument because nobody suspected the existence of America.) The big mistake Columbus made was in estimating the size of the globe and the width of the Atlantic. This mistake made him think that Japan was about where the Virgin Islands are located.

Columbus asked for a great deal. He wanted three ships equipped and maintained at the king's expense, a large share in the trade, the governorship of any lands he might discover, the title of Admiral, and noble rank. He wanted all these privileges to be passed on to his sons. None of the Portuguese discoverers had asked for so much. King John II of Portugal did not care to invest in an enterprise which his experts declared to be impractical, so he refused Columbus' request in 1482.

In the meantime, Columbus had traveled to Madeira and the Gulf of Guinea in Portuguese ships, and had become a captain. About 1479 he married a Portuguese lady, Felipa de Perestrello. They lived in the Madeiras.

Felipa died shortly after their only child, Diego, was born. She was buried in the Carmo church in Lisbon.

Success in Spain. In 1485 Columbus went to Spain to offer his services to King Ferdinand and Queen Isabella, at the same time Bartholomew was trying to interest Henry VII of England and Charles VIII of France. Christopher took little Diego from Portugal to Spain. About five miles from Palos was a Franciscan friary called *La Rábida*, which conducted a school for small boys. Columbus decided to leave Diego there while he went to court. Father and son made the long, dusty walk together. At the door of La Rábida they ate a piece of bread and drank a jug of water. While arrangements were being made to leave Diego, Columbus met Friar Antonio de Marchena, who became his loyal supporter and recommended him to Queen Isabella.

The queen, a handsome and intelligent young woman, was sympathetic and put Columbus on the royal payroll. Her experts, however, took the same view of his plan as did the Portuguese. Besides, Ferdinand and Isabella were busy fighting the Moors. Not until they had conquered Granada, the last Moorish stronghold in Spain (January 2, 1492), were they ready to do business. The experts told the sovereigns to dismiss Columbus, but Louis de Santangel, the royal treasurer, persuaded the queen that she was missing a great opportunity. She sent for Columbus at once, and even offered to pawn the crown jewels to raise money. But the treasurer supplied most of the funds (about $14,000) to fit out the fleet. Isabella kept her jewelry and won a new world.

Columbus was riding a mule homeward when the queen's messenger caught up with him. He was given everything he asked for—ships, honors, titles, and percentage of trade. No discoverer was ever promised so much before his performance. No discoverer's performance so greatly exceeded his promise.

First Voyage to America

Ships and Crew. Columbus had three vessels on his first voyage. They were the *Santa María* and two smaller vessels, the *Pinta*, and the *Niña*. The vessels in which Columbus sailed on all his voyages were made of wood and had no engines or motors, and very few comforts, as compared to the great ocean liners of today. The *Santa María* was manned by 40 men, the *Pinta* by 26 men, and the *Niña* by 24 men. There were bunks for only a few of the officers. The cooking was done with wood in a firebox on deck. These ships had good compasses, but no log to measure distance and no instrument for "shooting a star" except a crude quadrant that was not accurate when the ship rolled. Columbus navigated by dead reckoning. He knew just enough celestial navigation to measure latitude from the North Star (see LATITUDE).

Sailing Westward. The fleet sailed from Palos, Spain, Aug. 3, 1492. Nine days later it reached the Canary Islands. The sailors loaded provisions there, and made repairs. The ships left San Sebastian September 6. The last land sighted was Ferro, one of the Canary Islands, on September 9. Columbus set the course due west. He had fair trade winds and smooth seas most of the way across. The only trouble came from the crew. For the most part they were honest men, and there is no evidence that they feared "falling off the edge of the earth." But they were afraid they would be unable to beat back against the wind which always seemed to blow from the east. After three weeks of sailing, the longest anyone had ever sailed in one direction out of sight of land, it was hard for Columbus to persuade them to carry on. "The Admiral cheered them as best he could, holding out good hope of the advantages they might have," wrote his earliest biographer. He told the crew that he "had sailed to go to the Indies and would continue until he found them, with the Lord's help." Either he or Captain Pinzon of the *Pinta* cried "*Adelante! Adelante!*" *(Sail on! Sail on!)*

The Discovery. On October 10, everyone agreed to sail on for three more days and then return if land were not found. The island which Columbus named San Salvador, in the Bahamas, was sighted by moonlight at 2 A.M. October 12. Before noon that day Columbus landed on the beach at Fernandez Bay and took possession of a New World (as it proved to be) for Spain. He believed and always insisted that this was an island of the Indies, near Japan or China. He also believed that the gentle Arawak, who offered the "men from Heaven" all they had, were Indians (see ARAWAK INDIANS). Men knew within 30 years that Columbus was wrong, but everyone has continued to call the native inhabitants of America "Indians" and the islands he first discovered, the "West Indies."

The three ships stayed only a few days at San Salvador. On Oct. 28, 1492, the fleet entered Bahía Bariay, Cuba, which Columbus believed to be part of China. They explored ten or twelve harbors from Punta Brava to Cape Maisi, and sent men up-country to Holguín in the hope that this native village was Peking, and that they could present a letter from Ferdinand and Isabella to the emperor of China. They found no emperor but saw natives smoking cigars—the first time Europeans had seen tobacco. From Cape Maisi the fleet crossed the Windward Passage and sailed along the north coast of the island of Hispaniola. The climate and trees reminded Columbus so much of Spain that he named it *Española* (Little Spain).

On Christmas Eve the *Santa María* was wrecked on a reef near the present Cap-Haïtien, in the Republic of Haiti. The local Indian chief helped save the cargo and seemed so friendly that Columbus decided to build a fort and leave forty men to hunt for gold. Columbus then started home on the *Niña*, sailing from Samaná Bay, Jan. 16, 1493. With him he took several Indians he had captured.

The Hard Voyage Home. The homeward voyage was very rough. The *Niña* and the *Pinta* were separated in a storm west of the Azores. The *Niña* so nearly sank that Columbus sealed up an account of his discoveries in a cask and threw it into the water. The *Niña* called at the Portuguese island of Santa Maria in the Azores. There the governor thought Columbus was lying and that he had been poaching in Africa. He arrested Columbus' crew on their way to church, but let them go when Columbus threatened to shoot up the town. On her way to Spain the *Niña* was overtaken by another storm that ripped off all her sails and forced her into Lisbon. There Columbus had the satisfaction of visiting King John II and exhibiting some of the Indians who had survived the voyage. The *Niña* finally reached her home port of Palos March 15, 1493. Later the same day the *Pinta* also arrived at Palos.

Triumphant Return to Spain. Columbus rode horseback across Spain, with some of his officers and the captive Indians, to report to Ferdinand and Isabella at Barcelona. They gave him a grand reception, and confirmed his title of *Admiral of the Ocean Sea*, which meant that he had the right to judge admiralty cases (piracy, shipwreck, wage disputes, and the like) anywhere in the Atlantic Ocean. He also was given the title *Viceroy of the Indies*. He was ordered to organize a second voyage, to colonize Hispaniola and explore further.

Later Voyages

Second Voyage to America. On his second voyage, Columbus commanded 17 ships, carrying about 1,000 colonists, all men, to the New World. This "handsome fleet," as the Admiral called it, sailed from Cadiz, September 25, called at the Canaries, and made the ocean crossing in the excellent time of 21 days. They reached the West Indies Nov. 3, 1493, at an island Columbus named Mariagalante after his flagship. The fleet passed Dominica, Guadeloupe, Antigua, Nevis, St. Kitts, St. Croix, the Virgins, Puerto Rico, and other islands. In three weeks' sailing they reached Cap-Haïtien. All the men Columbus had left there the previous Christmas had been killed by the Indians, whom they had mistreated. When Columbus heard this sad news, he turned eastward and founded Isabela, on the north coast of Hispaniola. This was the first European

Columbus Probably Was Born in This House in Genoa, Italy, between Aug. 25 and Oct. 31, 1451. The house is located near the city's eastern gate. Columbus left in 1476 to go to sea, and never returned. But he left Genoa a small legacy in his will.

Wide World

Columbus' First Voyage 1492

Aug. 3, 1492. *Santa María*, *Niña*, and *Pinta* sail from Palos, Spain.

Aug. 12. The ships reach San Sebastian in the Canary Islands, and stay there until September 6.

Sept. 9. Sailing westward, the fleet loses sight of land at nightfall.

Sept. 16. Crewmen see the first patches of floating seaweed in mid-ocean.

Sept. 23. A "dove" is sighted.

Sept. 24. The fleet meets variable winds and calms. Sailors believe they sighted land, but find they are mistaken.

Sept. 30. Ships complete three weeks with no sight of land. This was the longest voyage yet made out of sight of land.

Oct. 7. Another mistaken shout of "Land Ho!" creates great disappointment.

Oct. 10. The sailors are on the point of mutiny, but agree to sail on for two or three more days.

Oct. 12. Columbus discovers America when land is sighted. He goes ashore on San Salvador (now Watlings Island) in the Bahamas.

Dec. 24. Columbus' flagship *Santa María* is wrecked off Cap-Haitien.

Jan. 16, 1493. The *Niña* and *Pinta* begin their homeward voyage. Columbus sails on the *Niña*.

Jan. 23. The two ships cross the path of their outbound voyage.

Feb. 8. The ships meet strong headwinds.

Feb. 12. A great storm endangers the *Niña*.

Feb. 13-14. The *Niña* and the *Pinta* are separated during the night by the storm.

Feb. 15. The *Niña* arrives at Santa Maria island in the Azores. After waiting 10 days, the *Niña* sails without the *Pinta*.

March 3. The *Niña* reaches Lisbon, and stays there 10 days.

March 15. The *Niña* returns to its home port, Palos, and the *Pinta* arrives there a few hours later.

Atlantic

Ocean

NORTH AMERICA

BAHAMA ISLANDS

Oct. 12

WATLINGS ISLAND

Oct. 10

Oct. 7

Sept. 30

Dec. 24

Jan. 23

Jan. 16, 1493

CUBA

HISPANIOLA

Columbus First Landed on Oct. 12, 1492.
Landing of Columbus by John Vanderlyn, Library of Congress

SOUTH AMERICA

colony in America. Leaving his brother Diego in charge, he took the *Niña* and two caravels to explore the southern coast of Cuba during the summer of 1494.

On the same voyage he discovered Jamaica. Returning to Isabela, he found the colonists fighting among themselves and with the Indians. After defeating the Indians and restoring order, he returned to Spain in June, 1496.

In Spain, Columbus found that many Spaniards who had returned from the New World complained that he was a cruel taskmaster. This was not true. He had been too lenient. The Spaniards were not satisfied and said there was no gold in Hispaniola. There was some, but not enough to satisfy them. The king and queen believed Columbus. They agreed to send new men to the colony and gave Columbus one ship and two small caravels, to make a third voyage of discovery.

Third Voyage to America. Columbus departed from Sanlúcar, Spain, on May 30, 1498. He selected a southerly route, thinking it would lead him to lands where more gold could be found. The fleet ran into the doldrums around 9° north latitude and was becalmed for eight days, while the men suffered from the heat

(see DOLDRUMS). Then the southeast trade wind sprang up and carried the three ships to the island of Trinidad, on July 31. Sailing through the treacherous Serpent's Mouth, they crossed the Gulf of Paria to the coast of Venezuela. In one of the little harbors on the Paria Peninsula (probably Yacua) on Aug. 5, 1498, Columbus went ashore, possibly the first time since the 1000's that Europeans set foot on the American continent. "I believe that this is a very great continent which until today has been unknown," wrote Columbus in his journal. He called the continent an "Other World."

Columbus in Disgrace. The prediction of Columbus proved true, but it did not help him. He found the Hispaniola colony seething with discontent because there was not enough gold to make everyone rich in a year. The Spaniards claimed they could not eat "Indian food" like corn and cassava. He tried to quiet the rebels by giving them land and letting them enslave the Indians to work it, but that failed to satisfy many. Large numbers went home, where they demanded back pay and the Admiral's head. Columbus' son, Diego, and his

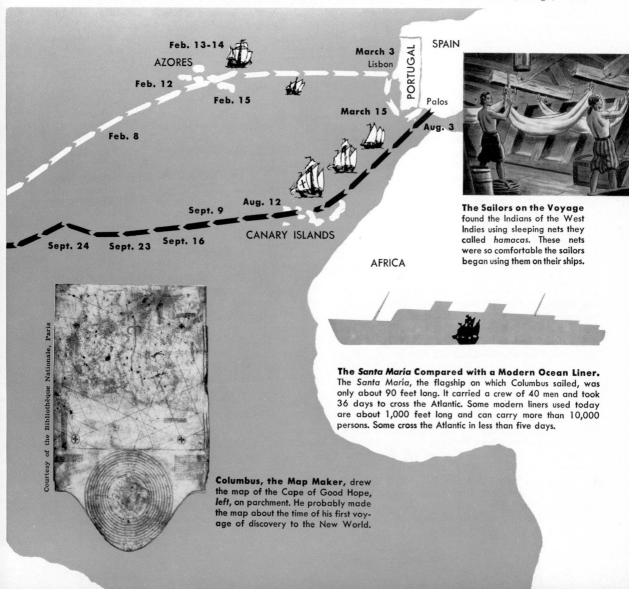

Feb. 13-14 AZORES
Feb. 12
Feb. 15
Feb. 8
March 3 Lisbon
PORTUGAL
SPAIN
March 15
Palos
Aug. 3
Sept. 9
Aug. 12
Sept. 24 Sept. 23 Sept. 16
CANARY ISLANDS
AFRICA

The Sailors on the Voyage found the Indians of the West Indies using sleeping nets they called *hamacas*. These nets were so comfortable the sailors began using them on their ships.

The *Santa María* Compared with a Modern Ocean Liner. The *Santa María*, the flagship on which Columbus sailed, was only about 90 feet long. It carried a crew of 40 men and took 36 days to cross the Atlantic. Some modern liners used today are about 1,000 feet long and can carry more than 10,000 persons. Some cross the Atlantic in less than five days.

Courtesy of the Bibliothèque Nationale, Paris

Columbus, the Map Maker, drew the map of the Cape of Good Hope, *left,* on parchment. He probably made the map about the time of his first voyage of discovery to the New World.

second son, Ferdinand, whose mother was Beatriz Enríquez de Harana, were pages at court. Whenever they appeared in the streets they were followed by a gang of rascals shouting, "There go the sons of the Admiral of the Mosquitoes, of him who discovered lands of vanity and delusion, the grave and ruin of Spanish gentlemen!"

In 1500, King Ferdinand and Queen Isabella sent Francisco de Bobadilla to settle the troubles at Santo Domingo, the new capital of Hispaniola. He put Columbus and his two brothers in chains and shipped them to Spain for trial. There they were released by order of the king and queen. But Ferdinand and Isabella sent out Ovando as governor of Hispaniola. Ovando took a fleet of thirty ships and 1,500 new colonists.

Fourth and Last Voyage. As a last chance to regain his fortunes, the Admiral asked for ships to make a new voyage of discovery. This the king and queen granted, mainly to get rid of him. On May 9, 1502, Columbus set sail on his fourth, last, and most adventurous voyage to America. He commanded four caravels, *La Capitana*, *Santiago de Palos*, *La Gallega*, and *Vizcaína*.

His 13-year-old son, Ferdinand, went with him. Ferdinand's account of the voyage, written many years later in a biography of his father, is the best we have. Ferdinand had plenty of playmates aboard, for his father preferred strong, lively boys to old salts who were always grumbling and wanting to go home. At least one-third of the people on this voyage were boys between twelve and eighteen years old.

The purpose of this voyage was to discover a passage to the Indian Ocean between Cuba and the "Other World" found four years before. Columbus believed that South America lay a short distance southeast of China. This was a common belief until Magellan's ship returned from a voyage around the world in 1522. The fleet crossed from the Canaries to Martinique in twenty-one days, and then sailed to Santo Domingo. Columbus noticed the signs of a West Indies hurricane about to break and sent a captain ashore to warn Ovando. Ovando, however, laughed at Columbus and sent a big fleet to sea. It was struck by the hurricane, and 20 ships were sunk with all their crews. Several ships struggled back to Santo Domingo. But only one, which happened to be carrying all the gold Columbus' agent had collected in Hispaniola, reached Spain safely. In the meantime, the four ships led by Columbus came through the hurricane with little damage. The ships met in the port of Azua west of Santo Domingo.

From Azua they sailed past Jamaica to southern Cuba and crossed the Caribbean to the Bay Islands off the coast of Honduras. It was July 30, 1502. For the rest of the year they sailed east and south along the coast of Central America, looking for the strait that was not there. They had to buck headwinds and foul weather along the Mosquito Coast. Everyone was tired and soaked to the skin. Columbus said this was the longest and grimmest tempest he had ever been through.

Ferdinand wrote about a storm off the coast of Panama: "What with the heat and the wet, our hardtack became so wormy that, God help me, I saw many sailors who waited till darkness to eat it so they would not see the maggots."

On reaching Almirante Bay in the present Republic of Panama, Columbus learned that another ocean lay only a few days' march across the mountains. But he had not found a strait leading to that ocean. He spent New Year's Day, 1503, anchored off the site of the present United States Naval Base at Coco Solo, Canal Zone. But the explorers never learned how near the Pacific Ocean was.

The Indians of Costa Rica and Panama were more civilized than any that Europeans had met before. Columbus, by trading cloth, beads, and various small wares, obtained a valuable load of copper and gold objects such as masks, great disks, and bird-shaped pendants. After passing Porto Bello and finding no strait, he turned westward again and tried to found a colony in the province of Veragua where gold was plentiful and easy to mine.

The local Guaymi Indians were willing to trade, but did not want the Spaniards as permanent guests. The local chief, El Quibián, was friendly at first, but soon got ugly. Bartholomew, Columbus, and Diego Méndez captured El Quibián as a hostage. The Indian chief jumped overboard and escaped. Then he led his warriors to attack the village that the Spaniards were building beside the Belén River. The Indians killed a number of Spaniards, including Captain Diego Tristán of the *Capitana* before they were driven off. Columbus could not leave the rest to certain death. He took them all aboard and started home on April 16, 1503.

Columbus had to move slowly along the coast as far east as possible, because his ships were leaking badly from holes eaten in the planking by *teredos* (shipworms). Abandoning the two least seaworthy ships, he cut across the Caribbean. On June 25, the waterlogged *Capitana* and *Santiago* were beached at St. Ann's Bay on the north coast of the large island of Jamaica.

There Columbus was marooned for a year. He sent Captain Diego Méndez in an Indian dugout canoe to Hispaniola for help. Méndez reached Hispaniola, but Governor Ovando blocked efforts to get a ship, because he feared that Columbus might get his job as governor. In the meantime, the admiral had to put down a mutiny of his men. In order to obtain food from the Indians, he used the famous eclipse trick. He learned from his almanac that there would be a total eclipse of the moon on February 29, 1504. Columbus told the Indians that God would punish them by removing the light unless they promised to supply the Spaniards with plenty of cassava, corn, and fish. The Indians did not take too much stock in this, but before the eclipse was complete they "with great howling and lamentation came running from every direction to the ships laden with provisions, praying the admiral to intercede with God on their behalf." Columbus promised to do his best, and after that the Spaniards were given plenty of food in return for glass beads, rings, and other articles.

Finally, on June 29, 1504, Columbus and 100 survivors, out of 135 who had left Spain, sailed from Jamaica in a little caravel chartered by Méndez. The admiral's last voyage ended at Sanlúcar, Spain, on Nov. 7, 1504.

The Admiral's Last Days

Before Columbus was allowed to come to court to tell his adventures, Queen Isabella died, and King Ferdinand would do nothing for him. The admiral was fifty-three years old and in failing health. He had suffered from arthritis during the last two voyages and now could scarcely move. He had enough money to live on, but wanted the governorship and his rightful share in American trade restored to him. The few remaining months of his life were spent either in bed or painfully traveling by muleback to be near the king in the hope he would relent. On May 20, 1506, in a humble dwelling at Valladolid, the "Discoverer of America and Admiral of the Ocean Sea" died. With him at the end were his two sons, Captain Méndez, and a few faithful servants. He was buried in Valladolid. His grandson took his remains to Santo Domingo. The tomb in the cathedral of Seville covers the ashes of his son Diego.

Estimates of Columbus

Appearance and Character. Columbus was described in 1501 as "a tall man and well built, ruddy, of a great creative talent, and with a long face." His son Ferdinand added: "He had an aquiline nose and his eyes were light in color: his complexion too was light, but kindling to a vivid red. In youth his hair was blond but when he came to his thirtieth year it all turned white." He was simple in dress, and moderate in eating and drinking. His manners were pleasant but dignified.

Columbus had a mystic belief that God intended him to make great discoveries in order to spread Christianity. He said his prayers several times daily and attended Mass whenever possible. Although he often seemed greedy for money and titles, it was to save his descendants from the poverty he had endured as a young man. As a seaman, he was one of the greatest in history. Anyone could have reached America by sailing west long enough, but few men with the means Columbus had could have found the way back to Spain, or have reached the desired island on later voyages. Columbus had great moral and physical courage. Again and again he faced mutinous sailors, armed rebels, frightful storms, and fighting Indians without flinching. His tenacity was so great as to be a fault. A man of one idea, and that a radical one, he was regarded as tiresome by most people and was hated by many. Also he had an unfortunate habit of saying "I told you so" about the success of his first voyage, which made some people eager to trip him up.

The World's Debt to Columbus. In 1492 most thinking men in the Old World were feeling very gloomy about the future. Thirty years later a great renewal of human spirit had commenced. Columbus had not only discovered a new world, but his success had encouraged other discoverers and opened new windows to science and to all knowledge. To few men in modern history does the world as we know it owe so great a debt as to Christopher Columbus.   SAMUEL ELIOT MORISON

Related Articles in WORLD BOOK include:

Outline

I. Years of Preparation
A. Early Life
B. Early Voyages

II. The Great Idea
A. What Columbus Wanted to Do
B. First Attempts to "Sell" His Plan
C. Success in Spain

III. First Voyage to America
A. Ships and Crew
B. Sailing Westward
C. The Discovery
D. The Hard Voyage Home
E. Triumphant Return to Spain

IV. Later Voyages
A. Second Voyage to America
B. Third Voyage to America
C. Columbus in Disgrace
D. Fourth and Last Voyage

V. The Admiral's Last Days

VI. Estimates of Columbus
A. Appearance and Character
B. The World's Debt to Columbus

Questions

What did Columbus hope to prove by making his first voyage?

Why did Columbus have such a hard time "selling" his plan for a voyage westward?

How did Queen Isabella get money to send Columbus on his first voyage?

What were the names of the three ships Columbus took on his first voyage to America? How many men accompanied Columbus on the first voyage?

What did Columbus hope to find on his last voyage?

How many voyages did Columbus make to America?

Who wrote the best account of Columbus' last voyage?

How did Columbus once use the "eclipse trick" to obtain food from the Indians?

How much did Columbus know about celestial navigation?

When Columbus spoke of "the Indies," what countries did he mean?

Why did Columbus once threaten to shoot up a Portuguese village?

COLUMBUS, KNIGHTS OF. See KNIGHTS OF COLUMBUS.

COLUMBUS DAY honors the day Christopher Columbus discovered America. It is celebrated on October 12, a legal holiday throughout the United States. Most schools hold programs and special events on that day. Cities and organizations sponsor parades and hold banquets.

The first Columbus Day celebration was held in 1792, when New York City celebrated the 300th anniversary of the landing. In 1892, President Benjamin Harrison called upon the people of the United States to celebrate Columbus Day on the 400th anniversary of the event. Columbus Day has been celebrated annually since 1920.

Although the land Columbus discovered was not named after him, many monuments honor him. The Republic of Colombia in South America bears his name. So do towns, rivers, streets, and public buildings. The name *Columbia* has also been used as a poetic personification of the United States (see COLUMBIA). The Columbus Memorial Library in Washington, D.C., contains 90,000 volumes on the 21 American republics.

Many Latin-American countries also celebrate October 12 as the *Día de la Raza* (Day of the Race). It honors the Spanish heritage of the peoples of Latin America. Celebration ceremonies feature speeches, parades, and colorful fiestas.   ELIZABETH HOUGH SECHRIST

COLUMN

COLUMN, *KAHL um,* is a vertical structure or pillar designed chiefly to support a weight above. It usually serves both to strengthen and to decorate a building. It may be constructed of any material, such as stone, wood, metal, marble, or brick. A typical column consists of three parts, the *base, shaft,* and *capital.* The shaft is the central upright portion. It is usually cylindrical in shape, but it may be modeled on any regular geometrical figure. The base forms the lowest part. It supports the shaft, which is crowned by the capital.

Early architecture used various kinds of columns. The Egyptians favored the heavy, massive type of column, represented by the great central pillars of the Hall of Karnak (see EGYPT, ANCIENT [color picture: The Temple of Amon-Re at Karnak]). The Persian column, like the Greek, was generally tall and slender.

The Greek Orders. The Greeks developed the column to a high degree. Their styles of base, shaft, and capital may be separated into three classic orders of architecture: Doric, Ionic, and Corinthian.

The Doric Column is the oldest and simplest of the three types. It has a plain shaft without a base, which tapers slightly upward, the height from 5 to 7 times its lower diameter. Along the shaft, 16 to 20 vertical, shallow grooves, or *flutes,* meet in sharp edges. The capital has two parts of equal thickness. The upper, a square block, or plinth, called the *abacus,* rests on the lower, a circular pillowlike tablet called the *echinus.* Above the capital is the *entablature,* which consists of three parts. The most celebrated example of Doric architecture is the stately Parthenon, on the Acropolis of Athens (see GREECE, ANCIENT [color picture: The Parthenon in Athens]; PARTHENON).

The Ionic Column was invented by the Asiatic Greeks. It is a more slender, graceful, and decorative structure than the Doric. Its shaft rises from a circular or polygonal base to a capital adorned with an echinus and *volutes* (scrolls) connected by a horizontal band. Its height ranges from $7\frac{1}{2}$ to $9\frac{1}{2}$ times its diameter. Along

the shaft are 24 flutes, separated by narrow *fillets* (flat surfaces). Among the finest examples of Ionic columns is the Erechtheum at Athens (see ACROPOLIS).

The Corinthian Column is the most ornamental. A variation of Ionic, it has a slender, fluted shaft but a more elaborate capital. The capital consists of a bell-shaped core surrounded by two or three rows of acanthus leaves (see ACANTHUS). Above these leaves, pairs of branching scrolls meet at the corners in spiral volutes. The monument of Lysikrates at Athens is an example.

The Roman Orders. The column became an architectural feature of wonderful variety and beauty under the Romans. Five orders are usually assigned to them: Tuscan, Doric, Ionic, Corinthian, and Composite.

The *Tuscan* is an elementary Doric, with a column seven diameters in height. The *Roman Doric* column is borrowed from the Greek. It generally has a simple molded base that rests on a square plinth. The Romans adopted the Greek Ionic with little change. But the Corinthian was enriched and elaborated to become a distinct Roman order. The Romans added the *Composite* to these four. The Composite combined elements of the Doric and Corinthian orders.

The Romans favored columns designed to serve as memorials to famous persons and events. They erected massive towerlike columns fitted with interior staircases. A famous example is Trajan's Column in Rome.

Columns of Later Periods. In early Christian and medieval European architecture, the column was used freely and in a variety of forms. Most of the capitals come from the Corinthian and are called *Corinthianesque.* The interior of the Cathedral of Notre Dame in Paris uses a combination of arch and shaft. The Renaissance revived Roman-style columns. The colonnades of Saint Peter's Church in Rome are of special note. Architecture today has adopted classic and Renaissance columns to give an effect of grandeur. The Treasury Building in Washington, D.C., is an example.   KENNETH J. CONANT

See also pictures of columns with ARCHITECTURE; POMPEII; ROME; VATICAN CITY.

COLUMNIST. See JOURNALISM (Special Assignments).

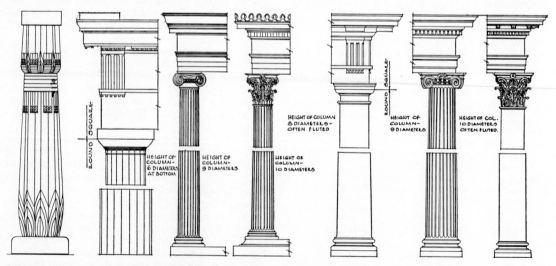

Columns Used in Early Architecture include, *left to right,* an Egyptian column; the three Greek orders, Doric, Ionic, and Corinthian; and the three Roman orders adapted from the Greeks.

Examples of the Doric and Ionic columns can be seen on the Acropolis in Athens. The Corinthian column was used in the monument of Lysikrates, which is also located in Athens.

COMA, *KOH muh,* is a state of deep and complete loss of consciousness. The word comes from the Greek word *koma,* meaning *deep sleep.* Persons in this state ordinarily cannot be aroused by stimulants such as spirits of ammonia, light slapping, or a pinprick. Head injuries, tumors, and strokes may cause coma. Persons who take poisons or an overdose of sleeping drugs often develop a coma. Doctors treat coma according to its cause. For example, if it is caused by a poison, the doctor gives an antidote. LOUIS D. BOSHES

COMANCHE INDIANS, *koh MAN chee,* were a southern Plains tribe that hunted bison from the Platte River of Nebraska down into Mexico. They became the most expert of all Indian horsemen in the American Southwest.

Because the Comanche moved about constantly, they lived in skin tepees which could be carried easily. They plundered peaceful Indians, and later stole horses from Spanish and American settlements. They terrorized ranch owners by swooping down at night and yelling and waving blankets to stampede the horses. They rode bareback, but kept a loop of horsehair braided into the horse's mane. When enemy arrows or bullets came thick, a warrior threw his body into this loop and rode against the horse's side or even underneath him, keeping only one heel on the horse's back for support. Westerners claimed that a Comanche could shoot as straight in this position as he could while he was riding upright.

By the Treaty of Medicine Lodge, the U.S. government established a reservation for the Comanche in southwestern Oklahoma in 1867. They received land and the privileges of citizenship. They became farmers and stockmen, and gradually adopted most of the white man's ways. BERTHA P. DUTTON

See also INDIAN, AMERICAN (table: Indian Tribes).

COMB JELLY. See CTENOPHORE.

COMBAT, TRIAL BY. See TRIAL BY COMBAT.

COMBAT ENGINEER. See ENGINEERS, CORPS OF.

COMBINATIONS. See PERMUTATIONS AND COMBINATIONS.

COMBINE is a farm machine which moves across a field, cutting and threshing in one operation such crops as small grains, soybeans, and grass seed. This combined harvester and thresher is either self-propelled or is pulled by a tractor. The combine threshes the seed from the stalks of straw, collects the seed into a tank or sacks, and leaves the straw lying on the ground. The first combine was used in Michigan in 1837, but the machine did not come into general use until about 1917. The first extensive use of the combine was on the large wheat fields of the West. Smaller combines were manufactured suitable for use on smaller farms, so that combines are now used in all parts of the U.S. where grain is raised.

Before the combine came into general use, most small-grain crops were harvested with *binders,* which cut and bound the straw and grain into bundles. The bundles of grain then were threshed with a stationary threshing machine. A. D. LONGHOUSE

Related Articles in WORLD BOOK include:
Agriculture (picture:
  A Modern, Self-
  Propelled Combine)
Reaping Machine
  (pictures)
Rice (picture: Powerful
  Combines)
Threshing Machine
Wheat (picture: A Combine)

Western Ways

Comanche Indians wear elaborate feather headdresses and bells for special ceremonial dances. The Comanche were once a warlike tribe in the American Plains regions. But today they work as farmers and ranchers in the Southwest.

COMBUSTION is any chemical reaction that gives off heat and light. The *rapid* union of oxygen with any substance is combustion. Combustion is usually thought of only in connection with fire, but it includes many other chemical reactions. Combustion occurs, for example, when chlorine burns in hydrogen gas, or in the burning of any substance in chlorine.

The speed of combustion determines the temperature of the burning substance. If coal burns slowly, the temperature is lower than if it burns rapidly. But the amount of heat given off by the burning of a certain amount of coal is always the same, whether combustion occurs rapidly or slowly. The kindling temperature is the lowest temperature at which a substance burns. The temperature of combustion is the highest temperature

699

reached during combustion. The heat of combustion, measured in calories, is the total amount of heat given off when a substance burns. See CALORIE.

Spontaneous combustion occurs when the burning substances have not been ignited by a match or some other burning object. Heaps of rags soaked with oil, or piles of coal that contain moisture sometimes begin to burn without being ignited. In these examples, spontaneous combustion is caused by the rapid union of oxygen with carbon and hydrogen in the oil or coal. This rapid reaction raises the temperature of the rags or coal above the kindling temperature, and the substance begins to burn.   RALPH G. OWENS

See also DUST EXPLOSION; FIRE; OXIDATION; OXYGEN.

COMECON. See COMMON MARKET.

COMEDY, *KAHM uh dih,* is the light and amusing branch of the drama. A comedy usually has a happy ending, unlike a *tragedy,* which usually ends in disaster. The term *comedy* also includes exaggerated forms of comic entertainment that are called *farce* and *burlesque.*

One of the purposes of comedy is to provide delightful entertainment for theater audiences. Another is to show people how silly they can be. All first-class comic dramatists are serious writers who hope to improve people by showing them their faults in an amusing way. Some of the greatest plays ever written are comedies.

Comedies differ from country to country because the senses of humor of the various peoples are apt to be different. For example, French comedy is usually light-hearted and witty. Scottish comedy is *whimsical* (playful and sweet). English comedy is often clever, but gentle. German comedy may be fantastically exaggerated. Irish is satirical. American comedy is noisy and full of jokes. Comedy often depends on local situations for its appeal. For that reason, a comedy that is extremely successful in one period or place might not be considered at all funny in another. But great comedy always contains elements that are meaningful to all ages.

Comedy developed from ancient Greek festivals in honor of Dionysus (called Bacchus in Rome), the god of revelry (see BACCHUS). In the earliest Greek comedies, a witty fellow simply indulged in ridicule. Later, a plot was added. Greek comedy reached its highest development in the plays of Aristophanes. Two Romans, Plautus and Terence, adopted plots from Greek comedies.

There have been comic playwrights in every period of history when the theater existed. William Shakespeare was the greatest writer of comedy in England in the 1600's. His most famous comedies include *As You Like It, A Midsummer Night's Dream,* and *Twelfth Night.* Molière was the comic genius of France in the late 1600's. In the 1700's, Oliver Goldsmith and Richard Brinsley Sheridan in England and Pierre de Beaumarchais in France were important authors of comedy. Modern masters of comedy include English playwrights George Bernard Shaw, Sir James Barrie, Noel Coward, and Oscar Wilde; Americans Philip Barry, William Saroyan, Thornton Wilder, Moss Hart, and George S. Kaufman; and French writers Jean Giraudoux and Jean Anouilh.   GLENN HUGHES

See also BURLESQUE; DRAMA; HUMOR; TRAGEDY.

COMEDY OF ERRORS, THE. See SHAKESPEARE, WILLIAM (Types of Plays; table: The First Period; Music).

COMEDY OF MANNERS. See ENGLISH LITERATURE (Restoration Drama).

COMENIUS, *koh ME nih us,* **JOHN AMOS** (1592-1670), was a Czech educator and bishop. His *Orbis Sensualium Pictus (Visible World)* (1658), was the first textbook in which pictures were as important as the text. He favored broad general education, rather than the narrow training of his day which emphasized the study of languages. He urged the establishment of more schools and universities. Comenius was born in Moravia. See also LITERATURE FOR CHILDREN (Puritan Times).   CLAUDE A. EGGERTSEN

Screen Gems

Slapstick Comedy for television viewers is provided by The Three Stooges, a well-known burlesque team. Burlesque is one of the most exaggerated forms of comedy.

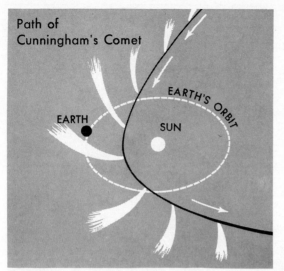

Path of Cunningham's Comet

EARTH

EARTH'S ORBIT

SUN

The Tail of a Comet Always Points Away from the Sun.

COMET, *KAHM eht*, is a heavenly body that looks like a star with a tail. Some comets do not have tails, and look like hazy, round spots of light. But most comets have three parts: a nucleus, a head, and a tail. The bright central nucleus may be nearly as large as the earth, which is about 7,900 miles in diameter. The head, or *coma*, surrounding the nucleus, may be from 30,000 to 100,000 miles in diameter. The tail, which looks like a bright streak behind the comet, may sometimes be 100 million miles long, or farther than the distance from the earth to the sun. The light of a comet is partly reflected sunlight and partly the *luminescence* (glow) of particles caused by sunlight.

Theories of Comets. It has long been believed that comets are masses of tiny solid particles held together loosely by gravitation. But this theory does not fit all the observed facts. Some astronomers have put forth another theory. They suggest that comets are formed in cold outer space from interstellar particles containing such compounds as methane, ammonia, and water. These probably exist as icy water in outer space. The astronomers believe that such "ices" make up perhaps 70 to 80 per cent of the mass of a comet. The other 20 or 30 per cent is a rocky and metallic material that is formed from interstellar dust. This rocky material resembles meteoric particles in composition. It is imbedded in the icy material.

As the comet travels in its path, or orbit, it sooner or later gets near enough to the sun to have the outer layers of the icy material evaporate, due to the heat of solar radiation. This evaporation releases the meteoric particles. The escaping gases and meteoric material stream off into space along the comet's orbit. This release of material accounts for the streams of meteors that are observed when the earth crosses the paths taken by certain comets. See METEOR.

Paths of Comets. Comets travel around the sun in egg-shaped paths called *ellipses*. The time it takes a comet to make a complete orbit is called its *period*. Encke's comet has a period of only three and a third years. Halley's comet has a much longer period, one of about 77 years.

Some comets travel in such long orbits that they are near the sun only once in thousands of years. But all comets are parts of the sun's family, just as are the earth

Visual Education Service

Halley's Comet appears about every 77 years. It was last visible to the naked eye in 1910, and should reappear about 1986.

and the other planets. Most comets cannot be seen without a telescope, and then only for short periods when they are near the sun. They may be visible for a few days or for a few years.

Famous Comets. The most famous comet to be seen as a brilliant, awe-inspiring heavenly sight was Halley's comet, in 1910. This comet was named for Edmund Halley (1656-1742), who in 1682 predicted its return in 1759, 1835, and 1910, and was right each time. Halley showed that the comet had appeared in 1066, 1456, 1531, and 1607. See HALLEY'S COMET.

Another comet, Biela's, broke in two in 1846 and has since disappeared. A very bright comet, Donati's, with two curved tails, appeared in 1858. In February and March, 1942, Whipple's comet could be seen easily without a telescope, among the stars of the Big Dipper. In 1957, the Arend-Roland comet appeared. It was the first bright comet since Halley's comet reappeared in 1910. Humason's comet, discovered in 1961, had unusual brightness, even when far from the sun.

Before science explained what comets are, men feared them greatly. In 1456, Halley's comet frightened everyone in Europe so much that Christian churches added a prayer to be saved from "the Devil, the Turk and the comet." In 1910, the earth passed through the tail of Halley's comet without any noticeable effect. Even if the earth ran into the head of a comet, there might be only a shower of meteors.   CHARLES ANTHONY FEDERER, JR.

See also SOLAR SYSTEM (diagram).

COMIC OPERA. See OPERA (Forms).

FAMOUS COMETS		
Name	First Seen	Period of Orbit (Years)
Halley's Comet	240 B.C.	77
Tycho Brahe's Comet	1577	....
Encke's Comet	1786	3.3
Biela's Comet	1806	6.7
Great Comet of 1811	1811	3,065?
Pons-Winnecke Comet	1812	6.26
Great Comet of 1843	1843	512.4
Donati's Comet	1858	2,040
Schwassmann- Wachmann Comet	1927	16.15
Arend-Roland Comet	1957	....
Humason's Comet	1961	2,900
Ikeya-Seki Comet	1965	....

Chi. Trib.-N.Y. News Syn.
Little Orphan Annie

Chi. Trib.-N.Y. News Syn.
Dick Tracy

Detective Comics, Inc., © 1946
Superman

King Features Syn. © 1945
Blondie

Field Enterprises, Inc.
Steve Canyon

COMICS are a series of drawings that tell the sequences of a story or an incident in picture form. They were originally meant to be funny, and were called *funnies*.

Kinds of Comics. Many comics involve humorous characters who get into and out of amusing situations. Others are adventure stories in picture form. The heroes and villains of these strips move from one exciting episode to another. Some comics present the daily but dramatic doings of businessmen, housewives, doctors, ministers, newspaper reporters, career girls, and many other persons. Other comics retell stories from the Bible or from history. Still others retell legends and folk tales. Many readers follow their favorite comic strip year after year. During World War II, the armed forces used comics as teaching devices. Manufacturers often use comics to advertise their products.

Creating and Selling Comics. Many comic strips are the work of one person who writes the story and draws the pictures. But more often, one person conceives the plot and develops the conversation and narrative, and another person draws the pictures.

Comic strips are usually drawn several weeks before they appear in print. Writers must have a store of ideas ready to put into work. Many artists and writers sell their comic strips to a *syndicate*, or distributing company. The syndicate sells the strip to newspapers. In this way a strip appears at the same time in hundreds of newspapers in all parts of the country and in foreign publications as well. Some comic characters have gained world-wide fame as a result of newspaper syndicates that sell comic strips in many parts of the world (see NEWSPAPER SYNDICATE).

History. The first widely known comic strip was "Hogan's Alley," by Richard F. Outcault. It appeared in the 1890's, and its hero was known as *the Yellow Kid*. A rival newspaper hired Rudolph Dirks to draw "The Katzenjammer Kids." Frederick Burr Opper, another early artist, drew comic strips and political cartoons for Hearst papers from 1899 to 1936. He created "Happy Hooligan," "Alphonse and Gaston," and "Our Antediluvian Ancestors."

Comic books appeared in the early 1930's. At first they consisted mainly of reprinted comic strips. But today they contain especially written and drawn material. Due to the large amount of material needed, an entire staff of artists and writers is often needed to produce a single comic book.

Comics enjoy great popularity. Millions of readers find entertainment and relaxation in following their comic-strip heroes.   MARJORIE H. BUELL

Some popular comic strips are described in the following list.

Blondie was created in 1930 by Murat Bernard "Chic" Young. Blondie is the boss of the Bumstead household, and Dagwood is her good-natured husband. Their two children, Alexander and Cookie, act like millions of other children. Daisy, the dog, and her puppies play an important part in the amusing situations that occur. Young was born in Chicago in 1901.

Bringing Up Father was created in 1912 by George McManus. The characters are henpecked Jiggs and his "society" wife Maggie. McManus was born in St. Louis, Mo., in 1884, and died in 1955.

Dick Tracy, a detective action strip, was created by Chester Gould in 1931. Dick Tracy is a symbol of law and order. Other characters in the strip include Junior, Tracy's young helper, and Tess Trueheart, now Mrs. Tracy. The name of a character often describes his personality, occupation, or physical appearance. Gould was born in Pawnee, Okla., in 1900.

Gasoline Alley began as a single cartoon in 1919. The characters were a group of men who met on Sunday in the alley behind their houses to talk about their automobiles. In 1921, the creator of the cartoon, Frank O. King, changed it to a comic strip and began the trend from straight comedy to storytelling. The strip concentrated on the adventures of Walt Wallet and Skeezix, who had been left on Walt's doorstep as an infant. King was born in Cashton, Wis., in 1883. He died in 1969.

The Gumps deals mainly with the adventures of Andy Gump, his wife Min, and their son Chester. The strip was created in 1917 by Joseph Medill Patterson, then president of the Chicago Tribune-New York News Syndicate. It was first drawn by Robert Sidney Smith, who was born in Bloomington, Ill., in 1877. When Smith died in 1935, Gus Edson took over his work. Edson was born in Cincinnati, Ohio, in 1901. He died in 1966.

Joe Palooka was created in 1930 by Hammond Edward "Ham" Fisher. The strip was inspired by the artist's acquaintance with a good-natured prize fighter. Joe Palooka was the first comic character to put on a soldier's uniform in World War II. When Joe enlisted in the army, President Franklin D. Roosevelt personally thanked Fisher for helping to make the draft popular. Fisher was born in Wilkes-Barre, Pa., in 1900, and died in 1955.

Li'l Abner is the creation of Al Capp (Alfred Gerald Caplin). The strip began in 1934. Li'l Abner, a hillbilly, is the son of Pappy and Mammy Yokum of Dogpatch, U.S.A. Daisy Mae was the hero's faithful but unappreciated girl friend until 1952, when Li'l Abner finally married her. Capp is responsible for Sadie Hawkins' Day, a sort of annual leap-year day, when the girls pursue the boys. See CAPP, AL.

Mutt and Jeff was created by Harry Conway "Bud" Fisher in the early 1900's. "Augustus Mutt" began as a sports-page cartoon in the *San Francisco Chronicle*. "Mutt and Jeff" is the oldest continuously published comic strip. Fisher was born in Chicago in 1885. After his death in 1954, the strip was continued by Al Smith.

Peanuts was created by Charles Monroe Schulz in 1950. His perplexed and frustrated hero, Charlie Brown, is the main character of the strip. Charlie Brown's friends include Schroeder, a musical genius who plays a toy piano; Lucy and her baby brother Linus; and Snoopy, an almost-human dog. Schulz was born in Minneapolis in 1922.

Steve Canyon was created in 1947 by Milton Arthur Caniff. Steve, a colonel in the U.S. Air Force, flies his way through exciting but realistic adventures. See CARTOON (Caniff, Milton Arthur).

Superman was created in 1938 by Jerry Siegel. The original artist was Joe Shuster. Superman has superhuman powers. He is a combined Sherlock Holmes, Hercules, Robin Hood, and Sir Galahad. He can do anything. Superman, who was born on another planet, poses as Clark Kent, a meek newspaper reporter. Siegel was born in Cleveland in 1914.

See also CARICATURE; CARTOON.

COMINFORM, short for **Com**munist **Inform**ation Bureau, was established in 1947. Its chief purpose was to spread Communist propaganda. The Cominform's main publication was its newspaper, *For a Lasting Peace, for a Peoples' Democracy*. Out of the Cominform developed the Warsaw Pact. This was the Communists' answer to the North Atlantic Treaty Organization (NATO), established by non-Communist countries in 1949. The Cominform was dissolved in 1956.   WILLIAM B. BALLIS

COMINTERN, short for **Com**munist **Intern**ational, often called the *Third International*, was founded in 1919. V. I. Lenin established it to organize revolutions through Communist parties in every country. Communist groups from various countries sent delegates to congresses in Moscow. The Russians dissolved the Comintern in 1943. See also COMMUNISM (The Comintern); INTERNATIONAL, THE.   WILLIAM B. BALLIS

COMITIA, *koh MIHSH ih uh*, were assemblies of the people of ancient Rome. The oldest assembly, the *Comitia Curiata*, confirmed the selection of kings and approved important decisions. Both the *Comitia Centuriata* and the *Comitia Tributa* elected officials, voted on issues, and made laws. The Comitia Centuriata, organized according to wealth, dealt with the more important issues and officials. The Comitia Tributa, organized according to tribes, became the most important lawmaking body.   FRANK C. BOURNE

COMMA (,) is a mark of punctuation. Its chief uses include: (1) separating the parts of a compound sentence joined together with *and, but, or, nor, for, so,* or *yet;* (2) setting off a phrase or clause preceding a subject —*After leaving, he felt sad;* (3) setting off a nonrestrictive modifier or a phrase in apposition—*Bob, who was next, had no trouble. Jim, the boss, spoke last;* (4) separating each item in a series—*to strive, to seek, to find;* and (5) separating the parts of a date, the parts of an address, or the parts of a name.   SUMNER IVES

See also PUNCTUATION (The Comma).

COMMAGER, *KAHM uh jur,* **HENRY STEELE** (1902-), an American educator and historian, won high praise for his books, *The Growth of the American Republic* (with Samuel E. Morison, 1931), and *America: the Story of a Free People* (with Allan Nevins, 1942). Commager and Nevins also wrote *The Heritage of America* (1939). Commager edited *Documents of American History* (1934), and wrote frequently for periodicals on public issues. He was born in Pittsburgh, Pa., and was graduated from the University of Chicago.

The Bobbs-Merrill Co., Inc.
Henry Steele Commager

He became a professor of history at Amherst College in 1956.   MERLE CURTI

COMMAND. See AIR FORCE, UNITED STATES (Organization); ARMY, UNITED STATES (Organization of the Army); NAVY, UNITED STATES (Organization of the Navy).

COMMANDER. See RANK IN ARMED SERVICES.

COMMANDER IN CHIEF has supreme command of a nation's armed services. In the United States, the President is the commander in chief of the Army, Navy, and Air Force. The title of *commander in chief* may also be given to an officer commanding a theater of operations, a major naval fleet, a unified command of units from two or more of the military services, or a specified command assigned to a specific task.   THOMAS E. GRIESS

See also PRESIDENT OF THE UNITED STATES.

COMMANDER ISLANDS, also known as the KOMANDORSKIYE ISLANDS, are a Russian group in the Bering Sea, east of the Kamchatka Peninsula. The group covers about 715 square miles, and consists of Bering and Medny islands and two tiny islets. The islands are mountainous, and largely covered with tundra vegetation (see TUNDRA). The people fish, and operate fox and seal fur farms. See also BERING, VITUS.   THEODORE SHABAD

COMMANDMENTS, TEN. See TEN COMMANDMENTS.

COMMANDO is the British term for a soldier who is trained to take part in surprise attacks. Such soldiers were called *Rangers* in the U.S. Army during World War II. Today, U.S. soldiers who qualify for difficult commando-like training can become members of the Army *Special Forces*. The U.S. Air Force has similar *Special Operations* units (formerly *Air Commandos*).

The word *commando*, originally Portuguese, was first used in South Africa during the Boer War to describe surprise actions. Prime Minister Winston Churchill suggested the name for the British *combined operations units* that staged hit-and-run raids during World War II. Commando raids destroyed war plants and materials, rescued Allied agents, or tried out invasion tactics.

Famous commando operations during World War II included a raid on St. Nazaire, France, in March, 1942. Commandos destroyed the largest dock in western Europe, preventing the Germans from using it for the battleship *Tirpitz*. Canadian and British commandos staged the largest raid, on Dieppe, France, on Aug. 19, 1942. The commandos held out for nine hours, but they suffered heavy losses. Units of United States Special Forces and Special Operations were used in the Vietnam War during the 1960's.   CHARLES B. MacDONALD

See also ARMY, UNITED STATES (Special Forces); RANGERS; WINGATE'S RAIDERS.

COMMEDIA DELL' ARTE. See PANTOMIME.

COMMEMORATIVE COIN. See MONEY (U.S. Money Today).

COMMENCEMENT. See GRADUATION.

COMMENSALISM. See SYMBIOSIS.

COMMENTATOR. A radio or television speaker who comments on sports, politics, and general news is called a *commentator*. News broadcasters report the news; commentators try to interpret it.   EARL FRANKLIN ENGLISH

See also JOURNALISM (In Radio and Television).

COMMERCE, *KAHM urs*, is the buying and selling of merchandise. It usually refers to large-scale transactions, particularly between different places or communities. In the United States, matters of commerce are supervised by the Department of Commerce and by state commerce commissions. For more information, see TRADE and BUSINESS with their Related Articles.

COMMERCE, CHAMBER OF. See CHAMBER OF COMMERCE; CHAMBER OF COMMERCE OF THE UNITED STATES.

COMMERCE, DEPARTMENT OF, is an executive department of the United States government. The secretary of commerce, a member of the President's Cabinet, heads the department. The department develops and fosters domestic and foreign commerce. It promotes the nation's manufacturing and shipping industries. It provides services to business and industry, and is responsible for advancing the country's scientific and technical development. The department represents the needs of government to business, and of business to government.

Functions. The Department of Commerce collects, analyzes, and distributes commercial statistics. It conducts population and agricultural censuses and coastal and geodetic surveys. It compiles and publishes nautical and aeronautical charts. It establishes weights, measures, and standards for commodities, and issues patents and registers trademarks. It provides weather forecasts. It distributes scientific and technical data. It administers the merchant marine.

The Secretary of Commerce is appointed by the President with the approval of the Senate. He administers all functions assigned to the department. He advises the President on policies and programs that affect the industrial and commercial aspects of the nation's economy. He serves as the President's principal contact with the business world.

The undersecretary of commerce is the chief assistant of the secretary and serves as acting secretary of commerce in his absence. The secretary's staff also includes five assistant secretaries of commerce.

Organization. The Department of Commerce has headquarters in Washington, D.C. The assistant secretary of commerce for science and technology supervises the Environmental Science Services Administration, the Patent Office, the National Bureau of Standards, the Office of State Technical Services, and the Office of Telecommunications. The assistant secretary for domes-

SECRETARIES OF COMMERCE		
Name	Year Appointed	Under President
George B. Cortelyou	1903	T. Roosevelt
Victor H. Metcalf	1904	T. Roosevelt
Oscar S. Straus	1906	T. Roosevelt
Charles Nagel	1909	Taft
William C. Redfield	1913	Wilson
Joshua W. Alexander	1919	Wilson
*Herbert C. Hoover	1921	Harding, Coolidge
William F. Whiting	1928	Coolidge
Robert P. Lamont	1929	Hoover
Roy D. Chapin	1932	Hoover
Daniel C. Roper	1933	F. D. Roosevelt
*Harry L. Hopkins	1938	F. D. Roosevelt
*Jesse H. Jones	1940	F. D. Roosevelt
*Henry A. Wallace	1945	F. D. Roosevelt, Truman
*Averell Harriman	1946	Truman
Charles Sawyer	1948	Truman
*Sinclair Weeks	1953	Eisenhower
Frederick H. Mueller	1959	Eisenhower
*Luther H. Hodges	1961	Kennedy, L. B. Johnson
*John T. Connor	1965	L. B. Johnson
Alexander B. Trowbridge	1967	L. B. Johnson
Cyrus R. Smith	1968	L. B. Johnson
Maurice H. Stans	1969	Nixon

*Has a separate biography in WORLD BOOK.

THE PRESIDENT

Department of Commerce

The Department of Commerce encourages U.S. foreign and domestic trade. The departmental seal, *left above*, was adopted in 1913. It appears on the cornerstone of the Department of Commerce building, *above*, which stands on Fourteenth Street in Washington, D.C.

SECRETARY OF COMMERCE

UNDERSECRETARY OF COMMERCE

| United States Travel Service | Maritime Administration | Office of Foreign Direct Investments | Office of Minority Business Enterprise |

Assistant Secretary for Administration	Assistant Secretary for Domestic and International Business	Assistant Secretary for Science and Technology	Assistant Secretary for Economic Affairs	Assistant Secretary for Economic Development
	Bureau of International Commerce	Patent Office	Bureau of the Census	Economic Development Administration
	Office of Field Services	National Bureau of Standards	Office of Business Economics	
	Business and Defense Services Administration	Environmental Science Services Administration		
	Office of Foreign Commercial Services	Office of State Technical Services		
		Office of Telecommunications		

tic and international business advises the secretary of the department's responsibilities concerning industry, trade, investment, and related economic activities. He has charge of the Business and Defense Services Administration, the Bureau of International Commerce, the Office of Field Services, and the Office of Foreign Commercial Services. The assistant secretary for economic affairs advises the secretary on broad, long-range economic programs. He directs the Office of Business Economics and the Bureau of the Census. The assistant secretary for economic development directs the Economic Development Administration. There is also an assistant secretary for administration.

The United States Travel Service encourages people of other countries to visit the United States. The Maritime Administration promotes and supports the maritime industry of the United States. The Office of Foreign Direct Investments controls investments by U.S. businessmen in foreign countries. The Office of Minority Business Enterprise helps Negroes, Mexican-Americans, Puerto Ricans, and American Indians become managers and owners of their own companies.

History. Congress established the Department of Commerce and Labor on Feb. 14, 1903, at the request of President Theodore Roosevelt. The department consisted of eight bureaus that handled matters on corporations, labor, census, statistics, fisheries, navigation, immigration, and standards. On March 4, 1913, Congress set up a separate Department of Labor and a new Department of Commerce (see LABOR, DEPARTMENT OF).

Since then many bureaus and agencies have been transferred to or from the department. For example, Congress assigned it the Patent Office from the Department of the Interior in 1925. In 1939, the Bureau of Fisheries went to the Department of the Interior. In 1940, the Weather Bureau, which had been under the Department of Agriculture, became part of the Department of Commerce.

In 1949, Congress transferred the Bureau of Public Roads from the Federal Works Agency to the department. In 1950, the Maritime Administration was created within the Department of Commerce. In 1963, the Bureau of International Commerce and the Office of Foreign Commercial Services were created to handle the department's international activities.

In 1966, Congress transferred several agencies from the department to the newly created Department of Transportation. The agencies include the office of the undersecretary for transportation, the Bureau of Public Roads, the Great Lakes Pilotage Administration, and the St. Lawrence Seaway Development Corporation. The Office of Minority Business Enterprise was established in the department in 1969. The Department of Commerce has about 25,000 employees.

Critically reviewed by the DEPARTMENT OF COMMERCE

Related Articles in WORLD BOOK include:

Census, Bureau of the
Coast and Geodetic
　Survey
Environmental Science Serv-
　ices Administration
Flag (color picture:
　Flags of the United
　States Government)

Maritime
　Administration
Merchant Marine
National Bureau of
　Standards
Patent Office
Weather Bureau, U.S.

COMMERCIAL. See ADVERTISING (Television; Radio; Preparing Advertisements).

COMMERCIAL ART includes many types of art used for business purposes. It is often called *advertising art*, because much commercial art is used in selling products and services. Commercial art is different from *fine*, or *original art*, such as painting and sculpture, because commercial art must be reproduced by printing or other methods.

Commercial artists work for advertising agencies, department stores, manufacturers, motion-picture studios, publishers, television stations, and many other types of businesses. They create art for such things as advertisements, books, magazines, packages, filmstrips, and trademarks. The art work in WORLD BOOK is produced by commercial artists. Commercial art studios offer a variety of art services, and range in size from only a few to more than 100 employees. Some artists work independently, and are paid according to each assignment. They are called *free-lance artists*. About 400,000 persons work

COMMERCIAL ART

Photos from University of Illinois

Commercial Artists create finished illustrations that can be reproduced in advertisements, books, and magazines.

Trademarks Help to Identify Products.

Magazine Advertisement

Booklet Design

in some phases of commercial art in the United States.

The early commercial artists were self-taught or had some training in fine art. These artists worked on design, drawing, lettering, and all steps in preparing a piece of art work for reproduction. Educational training aimed at providing specialized courses in commercial art was not developed until about 1930.

In recent years the field has expanded and developed greatly. Today, many commercial artists specialize in such specific parts of commercial art as design, illustration, photography, and photo retouching. Specialists within these areas include fashion illustrators, product illustrators, book illustrators, technical illustrators, cartoonists, film animators, and other types of illustrators.

Some commercial artists become art directors. Art directors do little art work themselves, but they plan and direct the work of others. Many commercial artists specialize in one field of commercial art, such as the design of advertisements.

Commercial art is a relatively new profession. Few people were employed in the field before 1900, and educational training for a professional career in commercial art was not available until about 1930. Today, there are many commercial art schools that offer four-year training programs, and many colleges and universities offer degrees in commercial art.   RICHARD S. COYNE

Related Articles in WORLD BOOK include:

Advertising	Etching	Photoengraving and
Cartoon	Illustration	Photolithography
Design	Lettering	Photography
Drawing	Lithography	Poster
Electrotyping	Packaging	Rotogravure
Engraving		

COMMERCIAL ATTACHÉ. See ATTACHÉ.

COMMERCIAL EDUCATION. See BUSINESS EDUCATION.

COMMERCIAL LAW. See BUSINESS LAW.

COMMISSAR is a Communist title for a Russian official. V. I. Lenin, Joseph Stalin, and Leon Trotsky were *people's commissars*, the most important group. In 1918 commissars were appointed to watch over officers and troops so that they acted according to Communist party wishes. Political instructors succeeded army commissars in 1942, and *ministers* replaced people's commissars in 1946.   WILLIAM B. BALLIS

COMMISSION is the fee earned by an agent who performs a service or does business for someone else. The amount of the commission is usually a certain percentage of the amount of the business. The percentage is agreed upon beforehand.

COMMISSION, MILITARY, is a written order giving an officer rank in the armed services. In the United States, the President commissions officers with the approval of the Senate. An officer accepts the commission voluntarily, and it does not have to be renewed. In wartime, the President may remove an officer from the commissioned list for cause. A board of officers handles dismissals.

The term *in commission*, when referring to a ship or an aircraft, means that the vessel or airplane is ready for active service.   THOMAS E. GRIESS

COMMISSION FORM OF GOVERNMENT. See CITY AND LOCAL GOVERNMENTS.

COMMISSION OF FINE ARTS. See FINE ARTS, COMMISSION OF.

COMMISSIONER OF EDUCATION. See EDUCATION, OFFICE OF.

COMMISSIONER OF INTERNAL REVENUE is the head of the Internal Revenue Service. See INTERNAL REVENUE (The Internal Revenue Service).

COMMITTEE FOR ECONOMIC DEVELOPMENT (CED) is a private organization that makes recommendations on ways to improve the United States economy. CED is a nonprofit, nonpolitical, and nonpartisan organization. Its suggestions are chiefly aimed at achieving full employment, higher living standards, and a more stable economy. It is made up of 200 trustees who are business and educational leaders. The committee makes its recommendations through a series of publications called *Statements on National Policy*. It also publishes papers by outstanding scholars on economic problems. CED was created in 1942. It has offices in New York City and Washington, D.C.

Critically reviewed by the COMMITTEE FOR ECONOMIC DEVELOPMENT

COMMITTEE FOR INDUSTRIAL ORGANIZATION. See CONGRESS OF INDUSTRIAL ORGANIZATIONS.

COMMITTEE OF PUBLIC SAFETY. See FRENCH REVOLUTION (The Convention).

COMMITTEE OF THE WHOLE is a committee composed of all the members of an organization. Usually a large group will ask a small committee to investigate a matter and make a report to the whole group. But sometimes the whole group wants to consider the matter, and meets as a committee of the whole. The advantage of meeting in this manner, or as a committee of the whole, is that the discussion can be informal, because no official action can be taken.

After its discussion, the committee of the whole ends the meeting by *rising from the committee*. The group then returns to its regular rules and ways. The chairman of the committee of the whole gives an official report of any decisions to the group.

The committee of the whole is a device often used by legislative bodies. Any member of either branch of the United States Congress can act as chairman of a committee of the whole.

In the Canadian House of Commons, the chairman of the committee of the whole is the deputy speaker. In the British House of Commons, a regular chairman other than the speaker is chosen.   THOMAS A. COWAN

COMMITTEE ON SPACE RESEARCH. See SPACE TRAVEL (Steps in the Conquest of Space).

COMMITTEES OF CORRESPONDENCE were organized by towns, counties, and colonies before and during the Revolutionary War in America. The first Committee of Correspondence was appointed by the town of Boston in 1772 at the suggestion of Samuel Adams. The committee's purpose was to keep in touch with other New England districts in their struggle to uphold the rights of the colonists. The first colonial committee was appointed by Virginia in 1773. The Committees of Correspondence played an important part in drawing the colonists together in preparation for their struggle with Great Britain.   JOHN R. ALDEN

See also COMMITTEES OF SAFETY.

COMMITTEES OF SAFETY sprang up in the colonies to carry on necessary functions of government during the Revolutionary War in America. They provided the transitional government after colonial governors had been overthrown and before the colonies could set up their first state governments. In Connecticut and New Hampshire, the committees continued their work even after the state governments had begun operating.

On July 18, 1775, the Second Continental Congress urged the colonies to set up committees of safety. The new committees took over much of the work of the earlier committees of correspondence, which had carried on vigorous programs of propaganda against the British since 1772.

See also COMMITTEES OF CORRESPONDENCE.

COMMODITY CREDIT CORPORATION (CCC) is a corporation within the U.S. Department of Agriculture. It is wholly owned by the U.S. government. The CCC is managed by a board of directors, subject to the general supervision and direction of the Secretary of Agriculture. The corporation has capital stock of $100 million held by the United States, and is authorized to borrow up to $14½ billion.

The CCC conducts many programs designed to support and protect farm income and prices, assist in the maintenance of balanced and adequate supplies of agricultural commodities, and assist in their orderly distribution. For these purposes, the CCC conducts price support, export, and storage programs. In carrying out these programs, it engages in buying, selling, lending, and other activities. It makes available the materials and facilities needed for the production and marketing of agricultural commodities. The CCC also obtains agricultural commodities for sale to other government agencies, foreign governments, and relief agencies, and to meet domestic requirements.

In carrying out most of its operations, the CCC uses the facilities and personnel of various agencies of the Department of Agriculture. The CCC was created in 1933.

COMMODITY EXCHANGE. See BOARD OF TRADE.

COMMODITY EXCHANGE AUTHORITY is an agency of the United States Department of Agriculture. Its purpose is to administer the Commodity Exchange Act. The objectives of this act are to prevent manipulation of prices of grains and other agricultural products, and to guard against false and misleading information that might affect prices. It protects persons who use the commodity markets from cheating, fraud, and unfair practices. This agency reviews the rules and regulations of the commodity markets and licenses the merchants and brokers. The Commodity Exchange Authority was established in 1923 as the Grain Futures Administration.

Critically reviewed by the COMMODITY EXCHANGE AUTHORITY

COMMODITY STABILIZATION SERVICE. See AGRICULTURAL STABILIZATION AND CONSERVATION SERVICE.

COMMODORE. See RANK IN ARMED SERVICES (table: Grade and Pay for Officers).

COMMON CARRIER is a person or company that transports passengers and goods by water, land, or air, for a fee. The term includes truck lines, express companies, bus lines, street railways, railroads, steamboat companies, air transport, and pipelines. Telephone and telegraph companies have also been included by law, although they do not transport goods. Storekeepers who maintain a delivery service solely for their customers are not common carriers.

The common law has placed the carrier under two great obligations. First, its service is compulsory, for it must serve everybody who is able to pay. Second, it is liable for loss or injury to goods or passengers carried. These obligations have been regulated by law. Commerce between states is under federal control. States control common carrier operations within their borders.

It is generally stated that common carriers are responsible for any loss or accident except those due to an "act of God or of the public enemy." In this sense, an "act of God" means any unavoidable accident that occurs through no fault of a human being. A train being struck by lightning is an example of an "act of God." The term *public enemy* includes any government that is at war with the government of the common carrier. Robbers, bandits, and rebels are not regarded as public enemies in this sense.

Passenger carriers ordinarily are required to accept as passengers any persons who offer to pay the required fare. But they need not carry drunken or disorderly persons, anybody with a contagious disease, fugitives from justice, or those who take passage for the purpose of committing crime. FRANKLIN M. RECK

See also FEDERAL COMMUNICATIONS COMMISSION; INTERSTATE COMMERCE COMMISSION.

COMMON LAW is the body of rules found in the written records of judges' decisions. It is law made by judges, rather than by legislatures. Early in England's history, judges had to decide legal cases according to what they felt most persons would think was right. They discovered what most persons thought by following the customs of the community and the common beliefs of the people. If an earlier judge had decided the same kind of case, his decision was often accepted as correct. When a large number of judges had decided the same question in the same way, the decision became law. It would be changed only if the customs and beliefs of the community changed.

Lawyers learned common law by reading reports in which judges gave reasons for their decisions. By reading many decisions of the same kind, a lawyer could see how a rule developed and how it was applied. Most modern law schools still teach law in this way.

The law of Commonwealth countries and the United States is called *common law*, as opposed to the *civil law* of European countries. American law is based on English common law, but it has been changed by legislation and by the courts. ERWIN N. GRISWOLD

See also CIVIL LAW; EQUITY; LAW; STATUTE.

COMMON MARKET is an economic union of nations. Nations form common markets to stimulate industrial growth, increase employment, and put more goods and services within the consumer's reach. To do this, common markets stimulate trade among members by eliminating tariffs and other trade barriers within the organization.

For information on how a common market operates, see EUROPEAN COMMUNITY.

Common markets include:

Arab Common Market. Founded: 1964. Members: Egypt, Iraq, Kuwait, Jordan, and Syria.

Council for Mutual Economic Assistance (COMECON). Founded: 1949. Members: Bulgaria, Czechoslovakia,

East Germany, Hungary, Mongolia, Poland, Romania, and Russia.

East African Community. Founded: 1967. Members: Kenya, Tanzania, Uganda.

European Economic Community (EEC), also called the *European Common Market*. Founded: 1957. Members: Belgium, France, West Germany, Italy, Luxembourg, and The Netherlands. See EUROPEAN COMMUNITY.

European Free Trade Association (EFTA). Founded: 1959. Members: Austria, Denmark, Great Britain, Norway, Portugal, Sweden, and Switzerland. See EUROPEAN FREE TRADE ASSOCIATION.

General Treaty for Central American Economic Integration. Founded: 1960. Members: Costa Rica, El Salvador, Guatemala, Honduras, and Nicaragua.

Latin-American Free Trade Association (LAFTA). Founded: 1961. Members: Argentina, Bolivia, Brazil, Chile, Colombia, Ecuador, Mexico, Paraguay, Peru, Uruguay, and Venezuela.

COMMON PLEAS, COURT OF. See COURT OF COMMON PLEAS.

COMMON SCHOOL. See MANN, HORACE.

COMMON SENSE. See PAINE, THOMAS.

COMMON STOCK. See STOCK, CAPITAL.

COMMONS, HOUSE OF. See HOUSE OF COMMONS.

COMMONS, JOHN ROGERS (1862-1945), pioneered in the development of many applied fields of economics. He worked especially in labor economics and labor history, and in the promotion of progressive social legislation. His writings include *Institutional Economics* (1934) and *Legal Foundations of Capitalism* (1924). He was born at Hollandsburg, Ohio.   H. W. SPIEGEL

COMMONS RIDING. See SCOTLAND (What to See).

COMMONWEALTH is a name sometimes used in referring to a state, to a country, or to a group of states and countries. The word originally meant a group of persons banded together for the common good or public welfare. The United States may be called a commonwealth. Pennsylvania, Massachusetts, Virginia, and Kentucky use the word *commonwealth* as part of their official titles. Puerto Rico is a commonwealth of the United States.

Australia is made up of several states. Its official name is The Commonwealth of Australia. The Commonwealth of Nations includes such countries as Great Britain, Canada, Australia, and New Zealand.

See also AUSTRALIA; COMMONWEALTH OF NATIONS; ENGLAND, COMMONWEALTH OF; PUERTO RICO.

COMMONWEALTH DAY. See VICTORIA DAY.

COMMONWEALTH FUND is a charitable foundation established in 1918 to promote the welfare of mankind. At present, the foundation gives most of its income to the promotion of health, chiefly through aid to medical education. It also sponsors the Harkness Fellowships, annual awards which permit young university graduates from Great Britain, Western European countries, Australia, and New Zealand to study in the United States.

The Commonwealth Fund makes grants from income totaling about $5 million a year. The fund was established by a gift from Mrs. Stephen V. Harkness. Her son, Edward S. Harkness, served as president of the fund from 1918 until his death in 1940. Headquarters are at Harkness House, 1 East 75th Street, New York, N.Y. 10021. For assets, see FOUNDATIONS (table).

Critically reviewed by the COMMONWEALTH FUND

COMMONWEALTH OF NATIONS is a group of countries and their dependencies that share a common history of having lived under British law and government. The group is often referred to simply as the COMMONWEALTH. The countries in the Commonwealth cover about a fourth of the earth's land surface. About one of every four persons lives in a Commonwealth nation or territory.

In addition to historical ties, Commonwealth nations are joined together economically. They form the world's largest *preferential* trading organization. Members of the Commonwealth enjoy *Commonwealth Preference* when trading with the United Kingdom. This means that the United Kingdom permits certain products to be traded without the usual tariffs (see TARIFF). Commonwealth members account for more than a fourth of the trade among non-Communist nations.

Commonwealth nations cooperate closely with each other, but each nation has an independent foreign policy that reflects its own views and interests.

All Commonwealth members were once monarchies, and gave allegiance to the king, or queen, of England. They regarded the British ruler as their own monarch. Later, some members, such as India, became republics, and considered the British Crown only as a symbol of the Commonwealth.

Independent Members of the Commonwealth are those countries with complete self-government. They include Australia, Barbados, Botswana, Canada, Ceylon, Cyprus, Gambia, Ghana, Guyana, India, Jamaica, Kenya, Lesotho, Malawi, Malaysia, Malta, Mauritius, Nauru, New Zealand, Nigeria, Pakistan, Sierra Leone, Singapore, Swaziland, Tanzania, Trinidad and Tobago, Uganda, the United Kingdom, and Zambia. All of the independent members are equal in the Commonwealth. Even the United Kingdom has no special powers.

Representatives of independent members meet annually at the Commonwealth Conference in London to discuss matters of common interest to member nations. The conference usually convenes in the spring. Conclusions reached at the conferences are not binding on the member nations. The conference gives Commonwealth members a chance to express their ideas to the rest of the world.

Each independent member is governed by its own executives and elected assembly, makes its own laws, and manages its relations with other countries. It can collect taxes, impose tariffs, and enter into trade agreements. It exchanges diplomats with other countries. It makes its own treaties and declares war by itself.

Except for the United Kingdom itself, all member-nations that are monarchies have a governor-general appointed by the Crown. In choosing this official, the Crown acts on the advice, not of the British government, but of the government of the country to which the governor-general is appointed. As these nations see it, the king or queen has to live somewhere, and happens to live in England. Therefore, a governor-general must represent the Crown in each of the other monarchies. Like the ruler, he has no real power to govern. He is mainly a symbol of the Commonwealth.

Associated States, formed in 1967, are in the West Indies. They include Antigua, Dominica, Grenada,

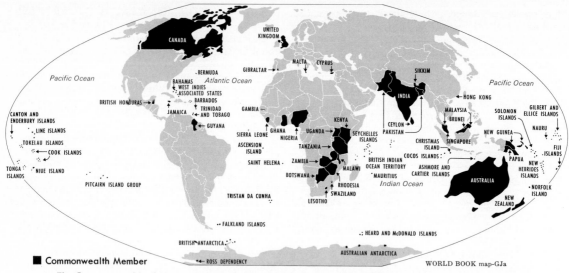

The Commonwealth of Nations, Shown in Black, Is One of the Largest Political Alliances in the World.

■ Commonwealth Member

WORLD BOOK map-GJa

THE COMMONWEALTH OF NATIONS

Members	Location	Status
INDEPENDENT MEMBERS		
Australia	Pacific Ocean	Monarchy
Barbados	Caribbean Sea	Monarchy
Botswana	Africa	Republic
Canada	North America	Monarchy
Ceylon	Indian Ocean	Monarchy
Cyprus	Mediterranean Sea	Republic
Gambia	Africa	Monarchy
Ghana	Africa	Republic
Guyana	South America	Monarchy
India	Asia	Republic
Jamaica	Caribbean Sea	Monarchy
Kenya	Africa	Republic
Lesotho	Africa	Monarchy
Malawi (Nyasaland)	Africa	Republic
Malaysia	Asia	Federation
Malta	Mediterranean Sea	Monarchy
Mauritius	Indian Ocean	Monarchy
Nauru	Pacific Ocean	Republic
New Zealand	Pacific Ocean	Monarchy
Nigeria	Africa	Republic
Pakistan	Asia	Republic
Sierra Leone	Africa	Monarchy
Singapore	Asia	Republic
Swaziland	Africa	Monarchy
Tanzania	Africa	Republic
Trinidad-Tobago	Caribbean Sea	Monarchy
Uganda	Africa	Republic
United Kingdom	Atlantic Ocean	Monarchy
Zambia	Africa	Republic

WEST INDIES ASSOCIATED STATES

Antigua, Dominica, Grenada, St. Christopher (St. Kitts)-Nevis-Anguilla, St. Lucia	Caribbean Sea	Associated States

DEPENDENCIES OF THE UNITED KINGDOM

Members	Location	Status
Bahamas	Atlantic Ocean	Colony
Bermuda	Atlantic Ocean	Colony
British Antarctic Territory	Antarctica	Colony
British Honduras	Central America	Colony
British Indian Ocean Territory	Indian Ocean	Colony
British Virgin Is.	Caribbean Sea	Colony

Members	Location	Status
Canton and Enderbury Islands	Pacific Ocean	Condominium
Cayman Islands	Caribbean Sea	Colony
Central and Southern Line Islands	Pacific Ocean	Colony
Channel Islands	English Channel	Crown Dependencies
Falkland Islands	Atlantic Ocean	Colony
Fiji Islands	Pacific Ocean	Colony
Gibraltar	Europe	Colony
Gilbert and Ellice Islands	Pacific Ocean	Colony
Hong Kong	Asia	Colony
Man, Isle of	Irish Sea	Crown Dependency
Montserrat	Caribbean Sea	Colony
New Hebrides Is.	Pacific Ocean	Condominium
Pitcairn Is. Group	Pacific Ocean	Colony
Rhodesia	Africa	*Self-governing Colony
Saint Helena	Atlantic Ocean	Colony
St. Vincent	Caribbean Sea	Colony
Seychelles Islands	Indian Ocean	Colony
Solomon Islands (British)	Pacific Ocean	Protectorate
Turks and Caicos Is.	Caribbean Sea	Colony

DEPENDENCIES OF AUSTRALIA

Antarctica (Aust.)	Antarctica	Territory
Christmas Island	Indian Ocean	Territory
Cocos Islands	Indian Ocean	Territory
Heard and Mc-Donald Islands	Indian Ocean	Territory
New Guinea	Pacific Ocean	Trust Territory
Norfolk Island	Pacific Ocean	Territory
Papua	Pacific Ocean	Territory

DEPENDENCIES OF NEW ZEALAND

Cook Islands	Pacific Ocean	Territory
Niue Island	Pacific Ocean	Territory
Ross Dependency	Antarctica	Territory
Tokelau Islands	Pacific Ocean	Territory

DEPENDENCY OF INDIA

Sikkim	Asia	Protectorate

*In 1965, Rhodesia declared itself independent.

708b

St. Christopher (St. Kitts)-Nevis-Anguilla, and St. Lucia. They are self-governing in all matters except defense and foreign affairs, which are the responsibility of Britain. The states can break this tie at any time.

Dependencies are Commonwealth areas that do not have complete self-government. The dependencies are administered by independent Commonwealth members. Each dependency is developing toward self-government. The Crown appoints the governors of the British dependencies. The governors are responsible to the British secretary of state for the Commonwealth. But the British parliament has the final responsibility for the government of the British dependencies.

Dependencies include: *colonies, crown dependencies, protectorates, protected states, states, federations, trust territories,* and *condominiums.*

Colonies are territories that have been annexed to the British Crown. This means that persons living in the colonies are British citizens. They are sometimes called *Crown Colonies.* A governor appointed by the British government is the highest official in each colony. He holds all political power in some colonies. But some colonies have elected assemblies, and in them the governor's power is limited. Some of the colonies have become practically self-governing. Most colonies are ruled as though they were parts of Great Britain.

Crown dependencies are self-governing territories annexed by the British Crown. They are not bound by acts of the British Parliament unless named.

Protectorates are governed the same as colonies, except that the British Crown has not annexed them. Residents of protectorates are not citizens of Great Britain, but are under British protection. A *commissioner* appointed by the Crown is usually the highest British official.

Protected States are independent countries that have made treaties with Great Britain for protection. These protected states control their own internal affairs, but permit the British government to manage their defense and foreign relations. The people who live in protected states are not citizens of Great Britain. Each state has its own executive officials. A commissioner represents the Crown in protected states.

States are like protected states, except that states control their defense and foreign relations jointly with the Crown. A governor represents the Crown.

Federations consist of several dependencies of the United Kingdom that have joined together under a federal government.

Trust Territories are former colonies of nations that have been defeated in war. For example, some of Germany's colonies in Africa and the Pacific Ocean were put under control of Commonwealth nations after World War I. They were called *mandates* by the League of Nations. After World War II, these former colonies were called *trust territories* by the United Nations. The Commonwealth nations administer these trust territories until their people gain independence.

Condominiums include areas controlled jointly by two nations that have interests there. For example, the British Commonwealth and France jointly administer the New Hebrides Islands. Each country is represented by a *resident commissioner.*

History. The Commonwealth of Nations began to take form in the early 1900's. At that time, self-governing countries within the British Empire came

together for *Imperial Conferences.* The United Kingdom was the chief member at these conferences until 1922. At that time, Canada and South Africa refused to join the United Kingdom in war against Turkey. This forced the nations within the Empire to reconsider their relationship with Great Britain. In 1926, representatives of the principal parts of the Empire convened an Imperial Conference in London. They defined Commonwealth nations as "united by a common allegiance to the Crown, and freely associated members of the British Commonwealth of Nations." This declaration was made legal by the Statute of Westminster, in 1931.

After World War II, the Commonwealth underwent new changes. Some newly independent nations became republics and renounced their allegiance to the Crown. Other nations, such as Ireland, Burma, and South Africa, left the Commonwealth entirely.

In 1965, a Commonwealth Secretariat was established. It initiates and coordinates Commonwealth activities. The Secretariat is responsible for convening Commonwealth conferences. The headquarters of the Secretariat are in London.   Ross N. Berkes

Related Articles. All of the countries and most of the dependencies in the accompanying table have separate articles in WORLD BOOK. Other related articles include:

Colony	Flag (color pictures)	Territory
Condominium	Governor General	Trust Territory
Crown Colony	Protectorate	

COMMUNAL SOCIETIES, *KAHM yoo nuhl,* emphasize collective ownership and cooperative work. They discourage members from pursuing individual objectives. No one owns private land, and each person is responsible to some extent for the care and well-being of everybody else. The clearest cases of communal societies exist among primitive peoples.

In the 1800's, such European thinkers as the Comte de Saint-Simon, Robert Owen, Charles Fourier, Étienne Cabet, and Pierre Joseph Proudhon reacted against the liberalism and individualism of the time. They sought a cure for the evils in society through some form of communal society that would prevent unearned wealth but would allow some private ownership. These ideals inspired many communities in Europe and the United States. Other thinkers, such as Karl Marx, wanted to set up a communal society in which everyone was absolutely equal and no one owned private property (see COMMUNISM). Examples of present-day communal societies include collective farms such as the *kibbutzim* of Israel (see ISRAEL [Agriculture]).   John F. Cuber

Related Articles in WORLD BOOK include:

Amanites	Hutterites	Oneida Community
Brook Farm	New Harmony	Shakers
Doukhobors		

COMMUNE, *kahm YOON,* is the smallest district of local government in France and some other countries. It resembles the *township* in the United States. The French commune has a mayor *(maire)* who governs the town with the help of deputies and a council. A commune may be a small village or a large city. Usually 12 communes make up a *canton,* the next largest political division. See also CANTON.   Robert E. Dickinson

COMMUNICABLE DISEASE. See DISEASE (introduction; How Diseases Spread; table).

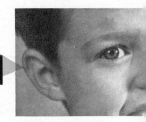

COMMUNICATION

Communication reaches us by means of hearing and seeing, and sometimes by means of tasting, smelling, and touching. We communicate by talking, writing, signaling, gesturing, singing, drawing, and even by dancing. Man has developed such devices as radio, television, telephones, and motion pictures to communicate with people beyond the ordinary limits of sight and sound.

SEE

HEAR

SMELL   TASTE   TOUCH

Ewing Galloway

COMMUNICATION means sharing information. We communicate with each other in many ways. A baby cries when it is hungry. We wave hello or good-by to our friends. Even animals use sounds and movements to share information. For example, a dog barks and wags its tail to show joy. Machines also communicate. A dial on the dashboard of an automobile indicates the temperature of the engine. Important methods of communication include letters, books, magazines, newspapers, signs, radio and television broadcasts, advertisements, and motion pictures.

Wilbur Schramm, the contributor of this article, is Director of the Institute for Communication Research at Stanford University and author of Responsibility in Mass Communication *and* Television in the Lives of Our Children.

Communication is a basic human activity. If it suddenly disappeared, our whole way of life would crumble. We would have no governments and no elections, no laws and no courts, no cities and no nations, no schools, no advertising, and almost no entertainment.

Communication has made the world "smaller." Radio can send the human voice around the world faster than it can be shouted from one end of a football field to another. Persons talking by telephone between Pittsburgh and Paris can hear each other as quickly as if they were talking in the same room. Without modern means of communication, it would take months, or even years, to share information with people in far parts of the world who can now be reached in a few seconds.

The Importance of Communication

In Daily Life, communication is with us from the time we wake up until we go to bed. The ringing of the alarm clock tells us it is time to get out of bed. A cheery voice from the kitchen tells us that breakfast is ready. As we walk to school or drive to work, traffic lights tell us whether we can cross streets safely. In school, books and teachers help us share information about our world. On the job, high-speed communication makes modern business and industry possible. Newspapers tell housewives about bargains in neighborhood shopping centers. Radio and television weather reports help us plan what to wear.

Communication also protects us. Radio broadcasts alert policemen so they can rush to the scene of a crime or accident. Fire alarms send fire trucks speeding on their way to battle blazes. The scream of an ambulance siren warns traffic so that doctors can bring sick persons to hospitals quickly and safely.

In Business and Industry, salesmen rush their orders to factories by telephone and telegraph. Stock tickers flash the news of ups and downs in stock-market prices. Newspapers and magazines bring businessmen up-to-date information on business conditions.

Advertising is one of the most important means of business communication. Every time we pick up a newspaper, read a magazine, or tune in a radio or television program, we see advertisements. These tell us about products we may want to buy or things we may want to do. Modern advertising reaches millions of people at the same time. If an ad is successful, it makes a large number of persons want to buy the same product. This enables manufacturers to use modern mass-production methods to turn out thousands of the same

product cheaply and quickly. Therefore, communication also helps make products available at low cost.

In Agriculture, speedy communication helps protect crops against floods, frosts, and other hazards. The farmer was once isolated, but today, broadcasts keep him in touch with developments. If orange growers in Florida or California hear a warning of an approaching cold wave, they can quickly light smudge pots to keep frost from their orchards. Blizzard warnings enable cattlemen to protect their grazing livestock.

Communication helps farmers in other ways. Newspapers, magazines, and government bulletins bring news of the latest developments in agriculture. A government bulletin might tell a farmer about a new insect killer. Communication also brings the latest news about crop and livestock prices. These enable farmers to sell their products when they can earn the most money. The telephone enables farm families to call their neighbors, or, in an emergency, to summon help.

In Transportation. Communication and transportation are so closely linked that they are difficult to separate. Before the mailman can deliver a letter, for example, it must be transported from one place to another. Airplanes, trains, and ships carry mail across oceans and continents. Trucks and mailmen take the mail from post offices to homes. Newspapers, magazines, and books would be almost useless if they were not transported from one place to another.

Communication often makes transportation possible. Semaphore signals tell train engineers whether the track ahead is clear. Radio and radar guide airplanes to safe landings. Charts help sailors bring their ships into harbors. Road signs and road maps keep us from getting lost when driving or hiking. In these and many other ways, communication and transportation depend on each other. See TRANSPORTATION.

Kinds of Communication

Gestures and Signals. Much of our communication is face to face and without words. We smile. We frown. We tip our hats. We hold up our hands in one way to say that we want to recite in class, and hold them up in another way to say "stop." A person may squeeze a friend's hand to communicate sympathy or love. We share a variety of information about how we feel by the expressions on our faces and the tones of our voices.

People have also learned to use signals so that they can communicate over greater distances. Woodsmen may make cuts in trees or build piles of stones to show others a path through a forest. Primitive tribes send smoke signals. Doorbells signal the arrival of visitors. Students listen for the buzzer that tells them when a class begins and ends. When the telephone rings, we know someone is calling us. See SIGNALING.

Pictures and Symbols. In the caves of prehistoric men, explorers have found colorful, lifelike drawings of prehistoric animals and hunters. One explorer came across a crude image of a bear made of clay in a prehistoric cave in France. Bears were probably dangerous enemies of cave men. The explorer guessed that the cave dwellers danced around the clay bear and jabbed it with sticks.

These cave pictures and sculptures illustrate a great

Airmail

Billboards

Phonograph

Baby's cry

Telephone

Mail

Doorbell

Clock

TV

Radio

Arm wave

Dog's bark

Magazines

Bells

"KEEP SMILING" ICE CREAM

COMMUNICATION IN EVERYDAY LIFE

Communication plays a part in almost everything we do at home, in school, at work, and at play. The brown circles indicate sound communication, and the blue, sight communication.

advantage in communication that man has over animals. He can make better *symbols* (things that stand for other things). *Words* are the easiest of all symbols to use, whether written or spoken. Words are the names given to everything we see and know. See SYMBOL.

Language and Writing. After the development of words, the development of language became the next great step in communication. Language is a systematic way of using words so that people can share information efficiently. Every language has two elements: (1) a group of words whose meaning is understood by everyone who uses the language, and (2) an accepted way of linking these words so they can be used together. The English language has dictionaries that tell what words mean. It also has a system of grammar that tells how these words can be put together in sentences.

Not all written languages use words. The ancient Egyptians wrote a language that used pictures called *hieroglyphics* (see HIEROGLYPHIC). Mathematics is a kind of number language. It has certain meanings for each of its symbols, with patterns of relationships between them. Multiplication tables and axioms of geometry show relationships among numbers (see MATHEMATICS).

Language and writing give us a way to communicate more than simple experiences. A person need not communicate only about hunger, food, and cold. With language and writing, he can discuss scientific theories and write poetry. He can record his history as he makes it.

Language and writing have also made it possible for people to share information even if they are not close together. A person can write a letter to a friend thousands of miles away. He can put up a sign that says "Stop" without having to be there to hold up his hand. He can take a series of electrical buzzes, use them to mean words, put them on a telegraph line, and communicate with people on the other side of the world. He can speak sentences into a microphone and be heard on every continent. See LANGUAGE; WRITING.

Mass Communication is the sharing of information with many people in many places with the help of machines. Machines produce the books, magazines, newspapers, radio programs, television programs, and films that are the *media* (means) of mass communication. A newspaper brings a reporter's knowledge of an event to thousands of readers. Millions of persons can watch a baseball game on television. Motion-picture

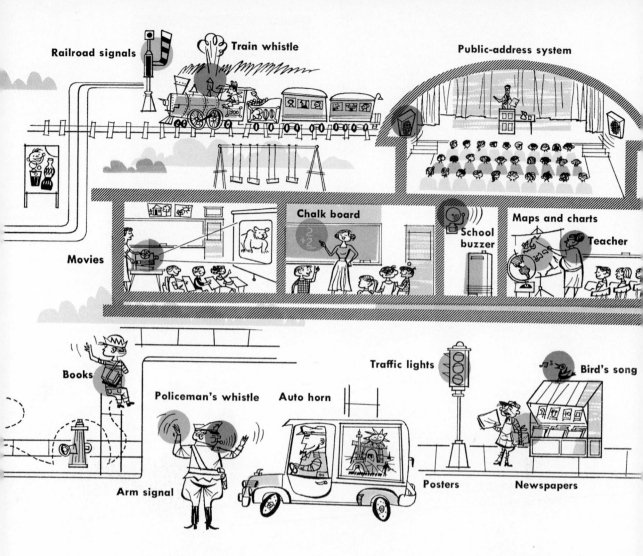

Railroad signals

Train whistle

Public-address system

Movies

Chalk board

School buzzer

Maps and charts

Teacher

Books

Policeman's whistle

Auto horn

Traffic lights

Bird's song

Arm signal

Posters

Newspapers

audiences in all parts of the world can enjoy the excitement of a movie drama.

Sharing the information delivered by mass communication takes up more of the time of people in the United States and Canada than any other activity except working and sleeping. Mass communication teaches us many of the things we know about the world we live in. Cameras, microphones, and teletypes serve as eyes and ears to tell us about wars, politics, sports events, and scientific discoveries. Libraries and reference books bring us the accumulated knowledge of the ages. Weather, news, and market reports help us predict future events. Mass-communication media make new plays, music, and other kinds of entertainment available everywhere, not just in a few large centers.

Development of Communication

We do not know just when man first learned to talk. Nor do we know who was the first man to use a sound to describe an object or an event, and make someone else realize that the sound was its name. Perhaps this first talker was playing with his voice, as small children play with their fingers and toes. Perhaps he was imitating some sound of nature. But he began language when he connected a sound with a particular thing.

After men began to talk, thousands of years must have passed before there was any written language. In different parts of the world, men fitted names to things and put together their own forms of language. More than a thousand language "communities" developed in which men still speak their own tongue. This huge number slows communication and makes understanding difficult.

Written Language. In very early times, man probably began to try to keep records and to communicate over long distances. After he had fire, he developed smoke signals. He sent messengers and questioned travelers. Traveling minstrels brought him news as well as songs (see MINSTREL). He had simple business dealings and built little markers to indicate the boundaries of his property. He also put knots in cords or notches in sticks to record what was owed him. Hunters drew pictures in the sand or on cave walls to record their triumphs, or perhaps to show younger men how to hunt. As man's language developed, he began to string pictures together to make picture stories. Finally, his

Oriental Institute, University of Chicago

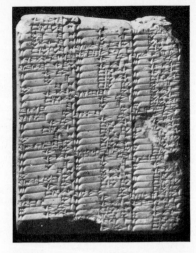

COMMUNICATION
THROUGH THE YEARS

Ancient Forms of Writing included Egyptian hieroglyphics, *left*, a picture language, and Babylonian cuneiform, *above*, a system of wedge-shaped writing. Both developed about 3000 B.C.

Indians Used Smoke Signals to send long-distance messages. The number and spacing of the smoke puffs had various meanings.

Printing in the 1500's was a laborious job. Printers set and inked the type by hand and printed on crude presses.

Culver Service

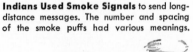

IMPORTANT DATES IN COMMUNICATION

c.3000 B.C. The Egyptians developed a picture language called *hieroglyphics*. At the same time, the Sumerians were writing on clay tablets with *cuneiform*, a system of writing that used wedge-shaped signs.

c.2500 B.C. The Egyptians used papyrus sheets for written records.

c.1500 B.C. The Semites devised an alphabet.

600's B.C. The Assyrians and Babylonians established libraries, including the Royal Library at Ninevah.

322 B.C. Aristotle made one of the first attempts to bring all existing knowledge together in a series of books.

c.300 B.C. The Hindus invented numerals.

c.200 B.C. Parchment was developed in western Asia.

63 B.C. Marcus Tullius Tiro, a Roman slave, invented a system of shorthand.

c. A.D. 70's Pliny the Elder edited his *Natural History*, the oldest reference work in existence.

c.105 The Chinese used paper and ink.

c.450 Block printing was practiced in Asia.

c.800 The Arabs adopted our present number system from India.

c.868 The oldest preserved block-printed book, *The Diamond Sutra*, was printed.

c.1440 Gutenberg invented movable metal type.

1539 The first printing press in the Western Hemisphere began operating in Mexico City.

1622 European newsletters developed into printed news-sheets called *corantos*, which were somewhat like newspapers. The first English coranto, the *Weekly News*, was published.

1639 Stephen Daye established the first press in the American colonies in Cambridge, Mass.

1665 The first English newspaper, the *London Gazette*, appeared.

1702 The first daily newspaper in English, the *Daily Courant*, was published in London.

1704 The *Boston News-Letter*, America's first newspaper that lasted more than one issue, was published.

1731 The first magazine, the *Gentleman's Magazine*, was published in London.

1741 The first magazine in America, the *American Magazine*, appeared in Philadelphia.

Monks in the Middle Ages Copied Books by Hand. They carefully copied manuscripts letter by letter. Because of the time this took, books were scarce until printing developed.

Johannes Gutenberg, Inventor of Movable Metal Type, made printing possible. The famous Gutenberg Bible, *right,* one of the earliest books printed in Europe, dates from before 1456.

The Secret of Making Paper from Wood was discovered by the French scientist René Antoine de Réaumur in the early 1700's. He observed how wasps chewed up wood to make paperlike nests.

Daguerreotype Pictures, invented in 1839, were one of the first successful means of photography. They used copper plates coated with silver iodide that had to be exposed several minutes.

IMPORTANT DATES IN COMMUNICATION

1755 Samuel Johnson published *Dictionary of the English Language,* one of the first English dictionaries.

1783 The first daily newspaper in America, the *Pennsylvania Evening Post and Daily Advertiser,* was founded in Philadelphia.

c.1803 The Fourdrinier brothers in England perfected a machine for making paper.

1814 The cylinder press was developed.

1828 Noah Webster published the first comprehensive American dictionary.

1826-39 Joseph Niépce and Louis Daguerre of France invented a method of photography.

1833 The first public library was established at Peterborough, N.H.

1837 The Massachusetts legislature established free public education under state supervision.

1844 Samuel Morse sent the first public telegraph message.

1858 The first transatlantic cable was laid.

1867 Christopher Latham Sholes, Carlos Glidden, and S. W. Soulé made the first practical typewriter.

1876 Alexander Graham Bell invented the telephone.

1877 Thomas A. Edison invented the phonograph.

1889 George Eastman developed a practical photographic film.

1894 Motion-picture projectors were perfected.

1895 Guglielmo Marconi invented the wireless telegraph.

1918 The world's first regular air-mail service was established between New York City, Philadelphia, and Washington, D.C.

1923 Pictures were televised between New York City and Philadelphia.

1927 Sound pictures appeared in American theaters.

1941 Commercial television began in the United States.

1957 The first artificial earth satellite sent back information from space.

1959 Russian and American rockets sent back information from beyond the moon.

1962 Television programs were relayed between the U.S. and Europe via the satellite *Telstar I.*

1965 The U.S. launched the first commercial communications satellite, called *Early Bird.*

715

COMMUNICATION

ability to speak grew greater than his ability to record what he knew. Then he took a great step toward written language. He could already speak and draw pictures. Now he began to make a picture equal a word.

It took a long time to draw every picture in detail. So, about five or six thousand years ago, man learned to simplify his pictures. The simplified pictures became the first written language. This language was rather awkward to use, because there was no good material to write on. Words had to be cut in stone, scratched on wax tablets, or marked in clay before the clay hardened. But picture writing was greatly superior to any earlier means of communication. Now man could record a promise, write history, and send messages great distances without depending on a messenger's memory.

The Alphabet. After man had a picture language, it took him about two thousand years to develop an alphabet. The Semitic peoples of Syria and Palestine probably developed the first alphabet about 1500 B.C. The Semites used picture-symbols of about 20 simple objects to represent the different sounds in their speech. These symbols included ones for ox, house, hand, fish, and teeth. By combining these symbols in a line, they could write any spoken word. This alphabet became the pattern for the Greek and Roman alphabets. It also formed the basis of our English alphabet. See ALPHABET and the separate articles for each letter of the alphabet.

The invention of the alphabet ranks as one of the great events in human history. As the alphabet spread throughout the world, it freed men from the burden of learning a different symbol for each word. As a result, learning to read became much easier, and more people learned. Writing was simpler, and more was written. The use of the alphabet encouraged study and discovery. Writing became a convenient tool for commerce and news gathering. Laws could be published widely.

The Growth of Communication was very rapid between the development of the alphabet about 1500 B.C.

COMMUNICATION THROUGH THE YEARS

"What Hath God Wrought!" was the first public telegraph message sent by Samuel F. B. Morse on May 24, 1844. This picture shows a reenactment of the famous event.

John Hancock Mutual Life Insurance Co.

The Pony Express served as the fastest means of transcontinental communication during its short life in 1860-61.

Library of Congress

The First Successful Transatlantic Cable opened in 1866. The painting *below* shows the men who laid the cable awaiting a reply from Ireland.

Bettmann Archive

Ewing Galloway

The First Practical Typewriter looked like a piano. It was invented in 1867 by Christopher Sholes, Carlos Glidden, and S. W. Soulé.

and the beginning of printing from movable metal type about A.D. 1440. The Egyptians were using papyrus paper by 2500 B.C. (see PAPYRUS). Parchment paper was being used in the Mediterranean area by 200 B.C. (see PARCHMENT). The first libraries, probably built by the Assyrians, appeared in the 600's B.C. The Greeks established libraries throughout the ancient world, including the one at Alexandria founded in the 200's B.C.

Some of the world's greatest literature came from Greece, Rome, and the eastern Mediterranean region between 1000 B.C. and A.D. 400. Postal service began with messenger service provided by Cyrus the Great in the Persian Empire during the 500's B.C. Pliny the Elder developed an encyclopedia in the A.D. 70's. During the A.D. 100's, Ptolemy drew parallels of latitude and longitude on the early maps.

The Romans had what might be called the first newspaper, which they posted each day outside the Senate. They called it the *Acta Diurna*, or daily proceedings of the Senate. It was a handwritten newspaper, and

─── FAMOUS FIRST WORDS ───

"What hath God wrought!" Samuel F. B. Morse sent this message from Washington, D.C., to Baltimore over the world's first commercially practical telegraph line on May 24, 1844.

"Europe and America are united by telegraphy. Glory to God in the highest, on earth peace, and good will toward men." On Aug. 16, 1858, this transatlantic message was sent over the first submarine telegraph cable, laid by Cyrus Field.

"Mr. Watson, come here. I want you." Alexander Graham Bell spoke these words, the first communication by telephone, in a hot Boston attic in 1876.

"Good morning, Mr. Edison. Glad to see you back. I hope you are satisfied with the kineto-phonograph." When Thomas A. Edison returned from Europe in 1889, his assistants had a surprise for him. Edison glued his eye to a peephole and saw motion pictures of an assistant synchronized with a phonograph speaking these words.

"S." On Dec. 12, 1901, the repeated sound of this letter in Morse code came clearly to Guglielmo Marconi in St. John's, Newfoundland. This signal, the first long-distance wireless message, came from Cornwall, England.

A New York-to-Chicago Call became possible in 1892 when Alexander Graham Bell, *left*, opened the first long-distance telephone line to link the two cities.

The Linotype Machine, *right*, invented by Ottmar Mergenthaler in 1884, replaced hand setting of type. This speeded up printing newspapers, magazines, and books.

A. T. & T. Co.

Chicago Sun-Times

RCA

Westinghouse

Guglielmo Marconi, the "Father of Radio," developed the wireless telegraph in 1895. This was the ancestor of TV and radio.

Listening to Radio in 1920 required the use of earphones to pick up the weak signals received by the early sets.

DuMont

The Modern Miracle of Television brings sight and sound to millions of homes. TV studios such as this were unknown before the 1940's when television first became practical.

UNUSUAL
MEANS OF COMMUNICATION

Homing Pigeons have been messengers for thousands of years. They carry messages on their backs or legs.

Chicago Public Library
The Blind Read with Their Fingers using the Braille system of dots on paper.

United Press Int.; Illinois Bell Telephone Co.

Telephones on Wheels aid doctors, salesmen, and other busy persons. Car telephones work by radio.

LISTEN

SUN

TALK

MOON

Bettmann Archive
Communicating with Drum Beats is an important means of sending messages from place to place used by some tribes in Africa.

Indian Sign Language uses hand signals to stand for ideas or things. The signals gave Indians a universal language.

only a few copies of the paper were made each day.

Monks of the Middle Ages wrote beautiful books on parchment with ink and color. These books could be made by hand only, one at a time. There was no economical way to make more copies of books until printing from movable type developed. See BOOK (picture, Copying Manuscripts).

Printing from Movable Type. Printers in China, Japan, Korea, and India had printed from carved wooden blocks for more than a thousand years before printing was known in Europe. Both paper and ink had been invented in China as early as the A.D. 200's. They reached Europe by way of the Moslem countries. The people of Korea even knew of movable type.

Europe's first printer was Johannes Gutenberg. He did four important things: (1) he used ink and paper developed in Asia; (2) he designed a press similar to that used for squeezing wine grapes; (3) he cast metal type so that it could be used over and over again; and (4) he used the alphabet from the Mediterranean countries. Gutenberg put these four ideas together into a single operation. He had to design and cast only 26 letters to print anything that had been written. Without the

alphabet, he would have faced the same difficulties as Asian printers who had to work with thousands of picture-symbols. See GUTENBERG, JOHANNES.

Printing developed in western Europe at a time when people wanted knowledge, news, and commercial information. Europeans had just discovered the Americas. Great scientific discoveries were being made. More persons had become interested in government and trade. Presses were soon founded in most European countries. A press was opened in Mexico City in 1539, and Stephen Daye established one in Cambridge, Mass., in 1639. These presses printed religious books, schoolbooks, and newspapers. See PRINTING (History).

Through the ages, news has been reported by travelers; by government reports such as the *Acta Diurna;* by town criers; by professional newsletter writers; and, finally, by newspapers, magazines, radio, and television. For the first hundred years after the development of movable type, newsletters enjoyed great popularity. For a large fee, an English tradesman could subscribe to a letter with the business news from Hamburg. For a smaller fee, Venetians could buy a page of notes issued by the government of Venice. This Venetian newsletter

Communications Satellites such as *Early Bird, right,* can carry telephone, television, and other electronic communication. *Early Bird* relays messages between Europe and the United States.
Communications Satellite Corp.

Wide World

Sign Language for the Deaf uses hand signals to stand for letters and numbers. Here, deaf persons use signs to auction items at a bazaar.

Pneumatic Tubes carry messages short distances in department stores, newspaper plants, and other places. Air pressure shoots message tubes through the pipes.
Kelly Systems, Inc.

Communication with Machines is done by means of punched cards that feed information to a computer. This card gives payroll information to a computer that automatically prepares a pay check.
International Business Machines Corp.

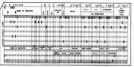

became so popular that it had to be printed. About 1609, a German newsletter appeared in print. The first news sheet in England was printed in 1621. The British colonies in America had no printed newsletter or newspaper until 1690, when Benjamin Harris published a newspaper in Boston. It was called *Publick Occurrences Both Forreign and Domestick.* The colonial government suppressed it after one issue. The first daily paper in America, the *Pennsylvania Evening Post and Daily Advertiser,* began in 1783 in Philadelphia. See NEWSPAPER (History).

The Surge of Printing brought a wave of interest in democracy, literacy, and education in America and western Europe. As more persons learned to read, they became more concerned with government. Now they had ways to communicate their dissatisfactions. Printing became a weapon in the English, French, and American revolutions. These revolutions gave the common man much more importance in government. To take advantage of this new importance, he not only had to be able to read the news and editorials, but also to have the knowledge and thinking ability that comes from education. Free public education developed. As more people

became educated, they needed more printed materials. Political, intellectual, educational, and communication revolutions all occurred together.

Printing is really only the use of a machine to reproduce language. It could be called *machine-duplicated* communication. Until the mid-1800's, almost every improvement in mass communication consisted of ways to improve machine-duplication and to use it for more things. During the early 1800's, people learned to operate presses with steam power. Others learned to etch plates with acid and to print pictures from them. About 1803, two brothers in England, Henry and Sealy Fourdrinier, invented a machine for making paper fairly cheaply and quickly. In 1828, Noah Webster produced the first comprehensive American dictionary. Three Milwaukeeans invented the typewriter in 1867. Until 1884, each piece of type was set by hand. In that year, Ottmar Mergenthaler of the United States invented the *linotype,* which uses a keyboard like that of a typewriter to set type mechanically.

Great efforts were made to speed the circulation of news and mail. For example, the daring young riders of the Pony Express braved wind, rain, snow, desert,

William Eccles

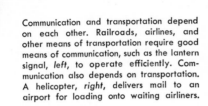

Communication and transportation depend on each other. Railroads, airlines, and other means of transportation require good means of communication, such as the lantern signal, *left*, to operate efficiently. Communication also depends on transportation. A helicopter, *right*, delivers mail to an airport for loading onto waiting airliners.

mountains, and hostile Indians to carry the mail from the Missouri frontier to California. They usually took 10 days to race over the route, but sometimes made it in 8 or 9 days by cutting stops. They set a new record in 1860 when they carried the news of President Abraham Lincoln's election from Fort Kearney, Neb., to Fort Churchill, Nev., in six days. But this was almost the end of the Pony Express. The telegraph was bringing a new era to communication. See PONY EXPRESS.

Electronic Communication has made it possible to send messages over long distances in a fraction of a second. The first major development in electronic communication was the telegraph, invented in the 1830's. It sends coded electric messages over wires.

In 1876, Alexander Graham Bell invented the telephone, the first device to transmit the human voice over electric wires. Thomas A. Edison invented a machine called the *phonograph* that recorded sound. Guglielmo Marconi found a way to send signals through the air without using electric wires. By 1907, Lee De Forest had developed the vacuum tube that made it practical to send the human voice through the air electronically.

The 1800's and early 1900's brought another exciting chapter in communication history. As early as 1826, men had learned how to take photographs. They were taking colored pictures as early as 1861. Photography developed somewhat slowly, because pictures had to be taken on glass plates rather than film. George Eastman provided a workable camera film in 1889. During the 1890's, Thomas A. Edison, C. Francis Jenkins, and others developed motion pictures. In 1927, people began to see—and hear—the first sound pictures.

Motion-picture and broadcasting techniques were combined to create television. TV began on an experimental basis in the early 1920's, and commercially during the 1940's.

During the 1950's and 1960's, methods were developed for sending communications over long distances by means of communications satellites. The first satellites, such as *Echo*, simply reflected radio and television waves from one ground station to another. Later, satellites were equipped with solar-powered amplifiers

that picked up the waves and rebroadcast them to the receiving station. The first commercial communications satellite, called *Early Bird*, began operating in 1965.

The Communication Industry has become one of the most important in the world. This growth has been closely related to an increase in *literacy* (the ability to read and write). When Gutenberg developed movable type about 1440, probably fewer than 10 of every 100 adults in the world could read. In the 1800's, only about 20 of every 100 adults were literate. Today, more than 97 of every 100 persons in the United States above the age of 8 can read. About the same proportion of persons can read in Russia, Canada, and most of the countries of western Europe. In some of these nations, the percentage is even higher. Only a few underdeveloped nations have a literacy rate as low as that of the entire world during the early 1800's.

The United States has the largest system of mass communication in the world. It uses almost two-thirds of the world's supply of newsprint, and has more than half of the world's radio and television sets. The United States has about 1,800 daily newspapers, 8,000 weeklies, 8,500 magazines, 4,000 radio stations, and 600 television stations. Each year, the American book industry publishes more than 15,000 books, and the motion-picture industry produces about 150 feature films.

The communication industry has grown not only in size, but also in the number of persons it reaches. Newspapers, radio, television, and magazines reach millions of people in the United States every day. The book industry sells nearly half a billion books a year. The people of the United States spend over $14 billion a year on mass communication, including advertising and public relations. But Americans spend many times this amount on all communication, including telephones, telegraph, and postal service.

The communication industry has become highly developed in many other countries. Great Britain, for example, publishes about 600 copies of daily newspapers for every 1,000 persons. This compares with about 350 newspapers for every 1,000 Americans. Great Britain and Germany, and probably Russia, publish

Mobile Television Units are housed in trucks that bring TV cameras and crews to locations for on-the-spot news stories.
NBC

Transportation Provides Communication Links. Ships laid the first transatlantic telegraph cables in the 1800's.
Brown Bros.

more books than the United States. Even though Canada has a small population compared to the United States, it has an important and fast-growing communication industry. Canadians make more telephone calls per person than the people of any other country.

Recent Developments have brought revolutionary changes in communication. Man has developed machines such as radar that can peer into fog or darkness and tell him what lies ahead. Instruments used in airplanes tell pilots whether they are on course, and whether their planes are flying level. Pilots can make safe landings in bad weather, using only the information from their instruments. See AIRCRAFT INSTRUMENTS; RADAR.

The development of electronic computers has enabled engineers to design machines that run other machines. Scientists can feed information and problems into computers and receive answers. Some computers have been designed to play chess and to translate languages. In 1959, the United States Air Force and other organizations announced the development of a computer that could design a product and direct other machines how to make it. See AUTOMATION; COMPUTER.

The first man-made radio messages from space came from Sputnik I, the world's first artificial satellite launched by Russia in 1957. In 1959, Russian and U.S. rockets sent back messages from beyond the moon. The first radio communication with space travelers took place in 1961 and 1962 with the Russian cosmonauts Yuri Gagarin and Gherman Titov and U.S. astronaut John Glenn (see SPACE TRAVEL).

On Oct. 1, 1965, United States scientists set a record for communication distance. They sent a radio signal 191 million miles to the *Mariner IV* spacecraft and received a return signal. *Mariner IV* was farther from the earth than Mars was at the time.

Problems of Communication

It is not always easy to communicate exactly what we mean. We often find that we are misunderstood or cannot get our message across. This difficulty in communicating can produce serious, and even disastrous, results. For example, a person driving a car who mis-

understands a policeman's signal might become involved in an accident. A garbled radio message might cause an airplane pilot to miss vital landing instructions. Even in sports, poor communication can produce disheartening results. A football player who misunderstands the instructions of his quarterback might cause his team to lose a game.

Misreading a message has sometimes changed the course of history. On Dec. 7, 1941, Japanese planes appeared on American military radar nearly half an hour before they attacked Pearl Harbor. But the Americans misread the radar's message, and thought the planes were friendly. If the Americans had interpreted the message correctly, they might have been able to get enough planes into the air to fight off the Japanese.

Problems of Personal Communication. The first problem to be solved in any system of effective communication is *delivering the message.* When two persons want to share information, one of them creates a message. He sends it and assumes that the other has received it. Suppose that Mr. Adams writes a letter and puts it in the mailbox. If he has put a stamp on the envelope, if he has put the right address on it, and if nothing happens to it in the mails, the letter will reach the address of Miss Brown. If Miss Brown remembers to look in the mailbox, if she does not drop the letter and lose it, if she is not too busy, and if she cares to read Mr. Adams' letter, the message will be received.

Next, *the message must get attention.* Does a boy hear his mother calling him? Do you hear the telephone ring? Do you catch the little gesture with which your friend gives special meaning to what he says? How many books in the library have you never taken from the shelves? Those unread books are messages that have never come to your attention. You tune in only a few of the many television and radio programs from which you can choose. You read only a fraction of the news.

Third, *the message must be interpreted.* In some ways, this is the most difficult problem of communication. For a while, the message exists away from both the sender and the receiver. It has a life of its own. It may be a letter going through the mails, sound impulses in

COMMUNICATION

the air caused by speech, or ink marks on paper. It may be electric impulses broadcast in the air, shadows cast on a motion-picture screen, or paint on canvas.

The person who receives a message always interprets it in terms of his own experiences. If the sender and receiver have not had the same experiences, the message may not mean exactly the same thing to the receiver. If the sender has had an unpleasant experience with school, and the receiver has had only pleasant experiences, a message about school will not mean the same thing to both of them. A message in German means nothing to one who does not speak German.

The study of meanings of words is called *semantics* (see SEMANTICS). Students of semantics find that different persons give different meanings to the same message. There have been experiments in which the same face has been described by different people as happy, sad, angry, pleasant, friendly, and unfriendly. This is because people have had different experiences which they relate to that particular facial type.

Another basic problem in communication is that *the message must be accepted and acted upon*. Suppose a mother calls her son in to dinner. Even if the boy hears the message and understands it, he still may not come. Perhaps he has become too absorbed in a game of baseball. Or perhaps he is not hungry, or simply feels like disobeying. We do not buy all the goods which advertisements urge us to buy. We do not believe all we hear. In general, the more strongly we feel about something, the less likely we are to let a message change our minds about it. For example, researchers have learned that many more Republicans than Democrats tend to read Republican campaign advertisements, and vice versa.

Problems of World Communication resemble those of personal communication. But they are more difficult because of the distances and differences that separate people in various parts of the world. People in countries that lie far apart often hear little about each other. Some governments *censor* messages (see CENSORSHIP).

Nearly 3,000 languages are spoken throughout the world. One person could never hope to understand all these languages. Few persons can understand even two of them well. So language is a barrier to the sharing of information throughout the world.

Culture is an even greater barrier. *Culture* means the rules and patterns by which people live (see CULTURE). Cultures differ greatly in different countries, and people rely on vastly different experiences to interpret messages. In India, for example, the cow is a sacred animal and the people would not think of eating its flesh. When the Indians read about *roast beef*, they may be sickened and disgusted. Americans might have a pleasant sensation of good food. Different experiences with government may make words such as *freedom* and *democracy* mean different things in different countries.

Almost every nation tries to persuade other nations to accept its point of view. This persuasion often takes the form of private talks or notes exchanged between representatives of the governments. These exchanges form part of *diplomacy* (see DIPLOMACY). Persuasion by means of public messages is called *propaganda*. It faces the same problems as other types of communication in trying to be effective. Governments spend considerable

money and effort on propaganda. See PROPAGANDA.

A number of international organizations have been established to improve world communications. For example, the United Nations provides a place in which nations can discuss their mutual problems.

Government and Communication

In the United States, the government has as little as possible to do with the communication system. In fact, the various communication media check on various government functions. Obviously, if the newspapers or broadcasting systems are to check on the government, they should not be controlled by the government. The Communications Satellite Act, passed by Congress in 1962, specified that a private corporation be created to develop a communications satellite system. It limited the government's role in the organization.

The chief power of the U.S. government over media is the right to assign frequencies for radio and television stations (see RADIO [Radio Waves; In the United States]; TELEVISION [Channels]). The government was not permitted to do even this in the early days of radio. But, when many stations came on the air, broadcasts began to interfere with each other. Finally, both the public and the station owners demanded that the government assign frequencies to keep the stations apart.

The Federal Communications Commission assigns radio and television frequencies (see FEDERAL COMMUNICATIONS COMMISSION). The Federal Trade Commission investigates reports of misleading advertising in order to protect the public (see FEDERAL TRADE COMMISSION). Copyright laws enable authors to register their work so it cannot be stolen (see COPYRIGHT). Other laws protect the public against obscene material in print, on the screen, or on the air (see MOTION PICTURE [In the United States]).

The government operates the postal service at a low cost to users. It provides especially low rates for newspapers, books, and magazines, so they can be easily available. The government also regulates utilities such as the telephone and telegraph industries.

The government interferes little with the content of communication. The Federal Communications Commission is forbidden by law to censor radio or TV programs. Whenever censorship commissions or the U.S. Post Office have suppressed material not obviously obscene or sacrilegious, the press and the public have protested loudly. Many courts, including the Supreme Court of the United States, have rendered decisions enforcing the rights of free speech and free press. See FREEDOM OF SPEECH; FREEDOM OF THE PRESS.

Most mass media have their own advisory or regulatory commissions and their own professional organizations to keep watch on the content of communication. The motion-picture industry, for example, has the Motion Picture Association of America. The National Association of Broadcasters maintains offices that read scripts and see and hear programs of its members. The radio and television industries, and newspaper, magazine, and book publishers have their own professional organizations, some of which discuss ethics.

In Other Democracies. The philosophy of keeping communications free from governmental control also exists in Canada, Great Britain, and many nations of western Europe and Latin America. Like the United

States, these countries have a political philosophy based on a faith in a "free market place of ideas." This means that if the different viewpoints on a question are freely available, men will be able to choose between truth and error. As a result, conflicting viewpoints on important matters must be fully and fairly represented.

In some democracies, the ownership of the means of communication differs from that of the United States. In Great Britain, for example, the British Broadcasting Corporation (BBC), a public organization, handles all radio broadcasts and operates a television network. Britain also has private TV stations. But, in spite of this government ownership, British law and tradition have enabled broadcasting to remain as free as that of the United States. Canada has a similar system, with the government-owned Canadian Broadcasting Corporation (CBC) owning several radio and television stations. Canada also has many private stations. See GREAT BRITAIN (Communication); CANADA (Communication).

In Dictatorships, the mass-communication media are controlled by censorship rules and other restrictions. Anything which the government does not want the public to know cannot be published or broadcast. The government usually owns the broadcasting systems in these countries. It decides who can own and operate newspapers, and sometimes suppresses or confiscates papers it does not like. In Russia and other communist nations, the mass-communication media function as a branch of the governments.   WILBUR SCHRAMM

Related Articles. See the Communication section in the various state, province, and country articles, such as COLORADO (Communication); NEW BRUNSWICK (Communication). See also the following articles:

Advertising	Magazine	Public Relations
Alphabet	Mathematics	Publishing
Book	Motion Picture	Radar
Braille	Music	Radio
Computer	Newspaper	Reading
Education	Painting	Signaling
Encyclopedia	Phonograph	Speech
Invention	Photography	Symbol
Language	Post Office	Telegraph
Laser	Printing	Telephone
Library	Propaganda	Television
Literature	Public Opinion	Writing

Outline

I. The Importance of Communication
II. Kinds of Communication
    A. Gestures and Signals C. Language and Writing
    B. Pictures and Symbols D. Mass Communication
III. Development of Communication
IV. Problems of Communication
    A. Problems of Personal Communication
    B. Problems of World Communication
V. Government and Communication
    A. In the United States   C. In Dictatorships
    B. In Other Democracies

Questions

How does the ability of people to read and write affect the communications in a country?

How can a machine communicate with men?

What effect did the development of modern printing have on political life in Europe and America?

How does culture affect communication?

What country has the largest system of mass communication in the world?

What nation makes the most phone calls per person?

What was the *Acta Diurna?*

What were Gutenberg's greatest achievements?
What are four problems of personal communication?
What is the chief power of the United States government over mass media?

Books for Young Readers

BATCHELOR, JULIE F. *Communication: From Cave Writing to Television.* Harcourt, 1953.
BENDICK, JEANNE and ROBERT. *Television Works Like This.* 3rd ed. McGraw, 1959.
COLBY, CARROLL B. *Communications: How Man Talks to Man Across Land, Sea, and Space.* Coward, 1964.
EPSTEIN, SAMUEL, and WILLIAMS, BERYL. *The First Book of Codes and Ciphers.* Watts, 1956.
FLOHERTY, JOHN J. *Get That Story: Journalism—Its Lore and Thrills.* Rev. ed. Lippincott, 1964.
HOGBEN, LANCELOT. *The Wonderful World of Communication.* Doubleday, 1959.
LAMBERT, ELOISE. *Our Language: The Story of the Words We Use.* Lothrop, 1955.
ROGERS, FRANCES, and BEARD, ALICE. *Heels, Wheels, and Wire: The Story of Messages and Signals.* Rev. ed. Lippincott, 1953.
SCHNEIDER, HERMAN and NINA. *Your Telephone, and How It Works.* 3rd ed. McGraw, 1965.

Books for Older Readers

AMERICAN RADIO RELAY LEAGUE, INC. *Radio Amateur's Handbook.* Revised annually. Amer. Radio.
DUNLAP, ORRIN E. *Communications in Space: From Wireless to Satellite Relay.* Rev. ed. Harper, 1964.
FLOHERTY, JOHN J. *Men Against Distance: The Story of Communications.* Lippincott, 1954. *Television Story.* Rev. ed. 1957.
JOHNSON, ROY I., and others. *Communication: Handling Ideas Effectively.* McGraw, 1956.
KERMAN, STEPHEN D. *Color Television and How It Works.* Sterling, 1962.
KIVER, MILTON S. *Television Simplified.* 6th ed. Van Nostrand, 1962.
NEAL, HARRY E. *Communication: From Stone Age to Space Age.* Messner, 1960.
SCHRAMM, WILBUR, ed. *Mass Communications.* 2nd ed. Univ. of Illinois Press, 1960. *Mass Media and National Development.* Stanford Univ. Press, 1964.
SIMON, IRVING B. *Story of Printing.* Harvey, 1965.
WELLS, ROBERT. *Messages, Men and Miles: Electronic Communications: How They Work.* Prentice-Hall, 1958.

COMMUNICATIONS SATELLITE is an artificial earth satellite used to send television, radio, telephone, and other electronic communications to any part of the world. Giant rockets launch communications satellites into orbits that reach thousands of miles above the earth. Transmitting stations on the ground then beam signals to the satellites by means of special antennas. The satellites send the signals back to earth. The signals can be picked up by receiving stations halfway around the world from the transmitting station.

Communication by satellite is more reliable than communication by short wave radio, and it has better quality. It also can handle a wider range of radio frequencies.

Kinds of Communications Satellites. A communications satellite is called *passive* or *active*, depending on the way it sends signals back to earth.

Passive communications satellites simply reflect signals, as a mirror reflects light. The United States launched *Echo I*, the first passive communications satellite, in 1960. Echo I was a huge, 100-foot plastic balloon with a thin coating of metal. This silvery satellite could be

COMMUNICATIONS
SATELLITES

Artificial Satellites send radio messages to earth. The *Explorer VI* satellite, launched Aug. 7, 1959, has paddle wheels that convert solar energy to electricity to power its communication equipment.

"Spacemail" for the Future may be possible using stationary satellites that would orbit over one spot on earth. A TV-like scanner would convert written messages to radio signals. An antenna would send these to a satellite that would retransmit them to a receiver. Here, a facsimile machine converts the signals to printed messages for delivery.

TV by Way of Space uses satellites as relay stations. In the *Echo* system, *right*, TV signals are bounced off *Echo* satellites. The satellites only reflect these signals.

The *Telstar* Satellite System uses a satellite, *below*, that receives, amplifies, and retransmits TV signals. Both the *Echo* and *Telstar* systems require several satellites to transmit around the world. In addition to TV programs, satellites can relay telephone conversations, telegraph messages, and photographs.

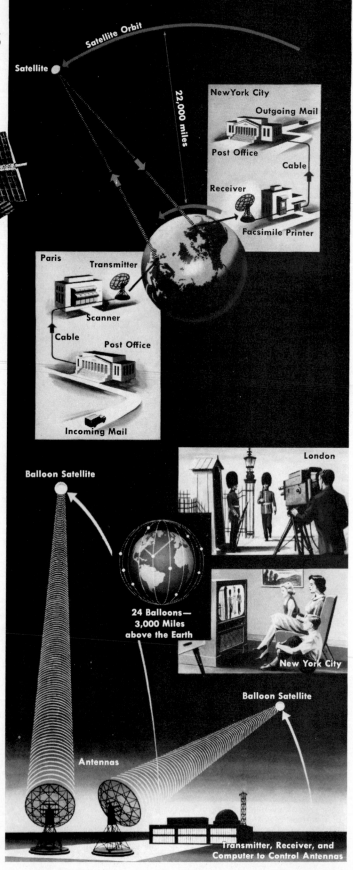

seen moving across the sky like a bright star. Echo I circled the earth until mid-1968, when it re-entered the atmosphere and burned up. It had been punctured and torn out of shape by tiny particles that speed through space. *Echo II* was launched in 1963.

The signals sent to a passive satellite must be strong, because radio waves weaken as they travel into space and back to earth. The satellite must also be large, to reflect a sufficient portion of the radio energy. Even then, the receiving stations must use sensitive equipment in order to detect the weak reflected signal. But passive communications satellites are reliable. They are not dependent on batteries that can go dead or electronic equipment that can fail. They can reflect signals from many ground stations at the same time.

Active communications satellites carry a radio receiver and transmitter. They receive signals from earth, *amplify* (strengthen) them, and then transmit them back to earth. The electronic equipment in an active satellite gets its power from sunlight by means of solar batteries (see SOLAR ENERGY).

The United States launched several experimental active satellites during the 1960's. These included *Telstar*, *Relay*, and *Syncom*. These satellites relayed many television programs between the United States and Europe. The satellites were small, measuring only a few feet in their largest dimension.

In 1965, the Communications Satellite Corporation (Comsat) of the United States launched the first commercial communications satellite. Called *Early Bird*, it is an active satellite with 240 telephone channels. It can also carry television broadcasts between the United States and Europe. *Early Bird* orbits the earth once every 24 hours, so it remains in one spot above the Atlantic Ocean at the equator. In 1965, Russia orbited its first communications satellite, *Molniya I*.

Communications Satellite Systems consist of a series of orbiting satellites and a group of sending and receiving stations located around the earth. A series of satellites is necessary because a single satellite can serve less than one-third of the earth's surface at one time. The sending and receiving stations must be able to point their antennas directly at a satellite to complete a transmission. If the satellite is below the horizon, a ground station can neither send messages to it, nor receive messages from it. Scientists and engineers have proposed various kinds of systems that would enable most ground stations to use at least one satellite at any given time.

Random orbit system uses a large number of satellites placed in various orbits around the poles and the equator. Sending and receiving stations track one satellite across the sky until it nears the horizon. Then the stations switch to another satellite and follow it.

Synchronous orbit system uses satellites launched to an altitude of 22,300 miles. At this altitude, the motion of the satellite is *synchronized* with the rotation of the earth. That is, the satellite completes one orbit while the earth makes one revolution. As a result, the satellite remains fixed over one position on the earth's surface. Three of these satellites placed properly can link stations in any two parts of the world. *Early Bird* is an example of a synchronous satellite.

Reflecting wire system consists of an orbiting ring made up of millions of tiny wires, each about an inch

long. The wires can reflect radio waves much like a single large reflector. Two orbiting rings can provide world-wide communications for any spot on earth. One ring would circle the earth in a north-south direction, the other in an east-west direction. In 1963, the United States placed an experimental reflecting ring in orbit in a project called *West Ford*.

History. Arthur C. Clarke, an English writer, proposed the idea of using satellites for communication in 1945. He suggested manned satellites placed in synchronous orbits. Radio operators in the satellites would receive messages and relay them to earth. In 1955, John Robinson Pierce, an American scientist, proposed the use of unmanned passive and active satellites in both synchronous and random orbits.

The first message was transmitted from a satellite in 1958 as a part of *Project Score*. In this project, a satellite broadcasted a recording of a Christmas message by President Dwight D. Eisenhower. In the early 1960's, the United States launched a series of successful experimental communications satellites. The Communications Satellite Corporation, established in 1962, began to build a communications satellite system in 1965.   JOHN ROBINSON PIERCE

See also SPACE TRAVEL (Artificial Satellites); MAINE (picture: Communications Satellite Station).

COMMUNICATIONS SATELLITE CORPORATION (COMSAT) was established to develop a commercial communications satellite system. This system will make it possible to transmit telephone conversations, television pictures, messages, and business data across oceans and continents.

Congress authorized the establishment of the corporation in 1962. The bill defined the corporation's objectives and specified the responsibilities of the President and various government agencies to the corporation. The law requires that stock be issued to communications companies and to the general public. The companies select six members, public stockholders select six, and the President appoints three to the board of directors.

The corporation was organized by 13 incorporators appointed by the President. In 1965, the corporation launched *Early Bird*, the world's first commercial communications satellite.   JOSEPH V. CHARYK

COMMUNION, *kuh MYOON yun,* in Christian churches, is the *sacrament* (holy ceremony) of the Last Supper. At the Last Supper, after pronouncing a blessing over bread and wine, Christ said to His disciples, "Take, eat. This is my body . . . This is my blood . . . This do in remembrance of me." Most Protestants call the sacrament *Communion,* or *The Lord's Supper.* The Eastern Orthodox Church uses the name *Holy Eucharist.* In the Anglican churches the ceremony is called *Holy Communion.* These two names are also used by Roman Catholics.

Some Protestant churches observe the ritual monthly or weekly. Others observe it every three months. Roman Catholics must receive communion during the Easter season, and often they receive weekly or daily communion. Communion, for Catholics, is an integral part of the Mass.   FULTON J. SHEEN

See also MASS; ROMAN CATHOLIC CHURCH (The Sacraments); SACRAMENT; TRANSUBSTANTIATION; VIATICUM.

Sovfoto

Communists Celebrate the Russian Revolution of 1917 by holding huge parades. Marchers in Moscow's Red Square carry portraits of Karl Marx and V. I. Lenin.

COMMUNISM

THE COMMUNIST COUNTRIES OF THE WORLD

This map shows in red the countries with Communist governments. Communist rule has spread over large parts of the world since the Russian Revolution of 1917. Today, about a third of the world's people live in a country that has a Communist form of government.

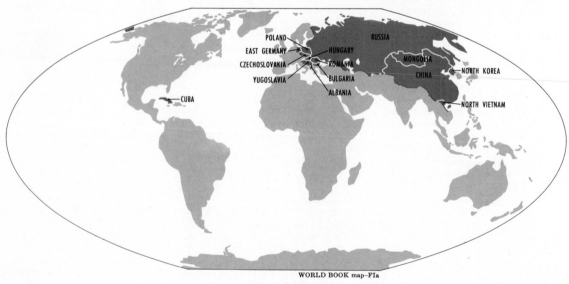

WORLD BOOK map–FIa

COMMUNISM is a term that has several meanings. It can be a form of government, an economic system, a revolutionary movement, a way of life, or a goal or ideal. Communism is also a set of ideas about how and why history moves, and in what direction it is headed. These ideas were developed mainly by V. I. Lenin from the writings of Karl Marx. Lenin was a Russian revolutionary leader of the early 1900's. Marx was a German social philosopher who lived in the 1800's.

Communism has become one of the most powerful forces in the world. Its rise has shaped much of history since the early 1900's. Many persons consider Communism the greatest threat to world peace. Others look on it as the world's greatest hope.

According to Communists, their long-range goal is a society that provides equality and economic security for all. For the present, Communists call for government ownership—instead of private ownership—of factories, machines, and other basic means of production. They also call for government planning of economic activity, and for strict rule by the Communist Party.

COMMUNIST PARTY MEMBERSHIP

This table shows the estimated number of Communist Party members in each Communist country and in several non-Communist countries. The table also shows the per cent of the population of each country that belongs to the party. There are about 45 million Communist Party members in the world.

Country	Communist Party Members	Per Cent of Population
COMMUNIST COUNTRIES		
Albania	66,000	3
Bulgaria	611,000	7
China	21,000,000	3
Cuba	60,000	1
Czechoslovakia	1,698,000	12
East Germany	1,610,000	9
Hungary	540,000	5
Mongolia	49,000	4
North Korea	1,600,000	14
North Vietnam	760,000	4
Poland	1,860,000	6
Romania	1,518,000	8
Russia	12,471,000	5
Yugoslavia	1,046,000	5
NON-COMMUNIST COUNTRIES		
Argentina	60,000	*
Australia	5,000	*
Canada	4,000	*
Chile	30,000	*
Finland	49,000	1
France	290,000	1
Great Britain	33,000	*
Greece	27,000	*
Indonesia	150,000	*
India	125,000	*
Italy	1,575,000	3
Japan	250,000	*
Sweden	29,000	*
United States	12,000	*
West Germany	7,000	*

* Less than 1 per cent.
Sources: U.S. Department of State; UN.

Alexander Dallin, the contributor of this article, is Adlai E. Stevenson Professor of International Relations at Columbia University, and editor of Diversity in International Communism *and* Soviet Conduct in World Affairs.

Communists seek a world ruled by Communists everywhere. But different kinds of Communism have slowly developed, varying more and more from one another. Communist methods of gaining and holding power range from war and violent revolution to propaganda and education. Today, Communism has two principal meanings. First, it describes the parties that work to take over non-Communist countries. Second, it means the group of nations ruled by Communists.

Fourteen nations have Communist governments. The largest of these nations are the Soviet Union and China. More than a billion persons, or about a third of the world's population, live under Communist rule. Communist parties also operate in most non-Communist countries.

Communist states are dictatorships whose rulers permit little public or organized criticism. Communist leaders seek the support of the people, but they do not depend on it to stay in power as officials in democracies do. Communism permits little of a person's life to remain outside the party's control. Such a form of government is often described as *totalitarian*.

The terms *Communism* and *socialism* frequently get confused. Communists usually refer to their beliefs and goals as "socialist," and Russia's official name is the Union of Soviet Socialist Republics. But socialists (often called *social democrats*) do not consider themselves Communists. Socialism may or may not be based on the teachings of Marx, but socialist beliefs are not based on the teachings of Lenin. Communism is based on the teachings of both Marx and Lenin. Communists and socialists both seek public ownership or control of the principal means of production. But most socialists favor democratic and peaceful methods to achieve their goals, while Communists are generally prepared to use force if necessary.

Communists speak of socialism as the present stage of development in most Communist countries. They consider it a very imperfect version of the "higher" Communist society they claim to be building. Therefore, when we speak of Communist countries, we do not mean that they have achieved full Communism. We merely mean that these countries are ruled by Communists.

The ideas of Marx and Lenin have been the common foundation on which Communists have built. In practice, some of these ideas have been whittled down or ignored by Communists themselves. For various reasons, Communists have not been able to enforce total control. Especially in the 1960's, some Communist states have followed more moderate and flexible policies.

This article presents a broad survey of Communism—what it is, how it works, and how it has developed. For a detailed description of life in a particular Communist country, read the WORLD BOOK article on that country. For a more complete understanding of Communism and other political or economic systems, read the articles on COLD WAR; DEMOCRACY; ECONOMICS; FREE ENTERPRISE SYSTEM; GOVERNMENT; and SOCIALISM.

MAIN FEATURES OF COMMUNISM

Communism varies much from one Communist country to another. But certain basic features of Communism are more or less the same in all these countries.

The Communist Party is the Communists' main instrument for gaining and using power. In a Communist country, the Communist Party is the only party with any power. Communists allow no political rivals, and voters have no real choice among candidates. They may vote for or reject the party's candidate, but often they cannot vote for anyone else.

The Communist Party in most countries is modeled after the Communist Party of the Soviet Union. It has strict membership requirements and is extremely demanding of its members. The party is highly *centralized*. That is, the top leaders make the important decisions. The Communist Party demands strict obedience of its members. After it has adopted a policy, all members must accept the "party line" until the leaders change it. For a discussion of the structure of a typical Communist Party, see RUSSIA (The Communist Party).

In most Communist countries, less than 8 per cent of the people belong to the Communist Party. The party seeks to sign up as members all those who hold important positions in such fields as education, government, and the military. In this way, the party can have some control over these fields. Communism teaches that Communists form a select group that is better trained and more responsible and reliable than any other. But for many persons, membership in the party is largely a way to get—and keep—a job.

Communism and Government. In Communist countries, party leaders play a key role in all major government decisions, and in seeing that they are carried out. The party is a link between the structures that support the ruling system, including the government, the police, the military, agriculture, and industry.

Most Communist countries have an elected national legislature, but these legislatures have little power. They usually pass without question all laws proposed by the Communist Party leaders. The extent to which the party itself runs a country varies according to time and place. For example, the party plays a far smaller role in Yugoslavia and Cuba than in Russia or China. But in each Communist country, a few persons occupy top positions in both the party and the government.

In spite of the high degree of Communist organization and discipline, things do not always go smoothly. Bitter disputes often occur within the leadership of Communist parties and nations. Many of these disputes involve high-ranking Communists who take different sides in an argument over policy or a struggle for power. When a Communist Party leader opposes other leaders —for example, from industry or the military—the party leader almost always wins.

Communism and the Economy. Running the economy is a major responsibility of Communist governments. Communism prohibits the use of hired labor for private gain. In most Communist countries, the state owns most of the land, banks, natural resources, industry, and large-scale trade and transportation. The government also operates all mass communication, including broadcasting, television, publishing, and motion-picture production.

Individuals in a Communist country can own property, but the amount and kind vary from one country to another. Normally, a person may own his home, household goods, and personal savings. He also may own such personal items as books, musical instruments, a radio, and a television set. In some cases, he may cultivate his own small plot of land and own some livestock. But this practice varies greatly from country to country. Individuals can spend their money largely as they wish, but their choice is limited to what the government decides to produce or make available.

Major economic decisions are made by government planners. These decisions must agree with the policies of the Communist Party. The planners decide what and how much should be produced, and what prices should be charged for goods and services. In the United States and other capitalist countries, such decisions are usually made by individuals or corporations. The government planners must determine (1) what raw materials will be produced, (2) when and where they will be produced, (3) to whom and at what prices they will be sold, (4) what products they will be used for, and (5) how the finished products will be distributed. The planners must be sure that the right kinds of resources and skilled labor are at the right place at the right time. Compare this system to the American system as described in the article on ECONOMICS.

The farmland in most Communist countries is owned by the state. Farm workers on *state farms* receive wages from the government for their work. Farmers on *collective farms* are paid a share of the production and profits. The government lends the land to the collective farm. Most of it is worked jointly, but families on collective farms may cultivate small plots of land for themselves, and sell their products as they wish.

Communist China has experimented—rather unsuccessfully—with large agricultural *communes*. In communes, large numbers of people are organized, as in an army, and told what to do. Meals are served in common dining halls, and young children are cared for in nurseries operated by the government. In contrast, most farmland in Poland and Yugoslavia is now privately owned and cultivated.

The farm population has often been neglected or abused by Communist governments, and in earlier years the peasants strongly resisted Communist policies. Detailed government planning has also frequently held back farm managers in their attempts to use land and workers in the best way. Increasing agricultural production has been one of the major problems of Russia, China, and other Communist countries.

Labor unions in Communist countries exist mainly to help meet production goals. Unions also administer social insurance and operate vacation facilities. They have some influence on safety, job classifications, and employee complaints, but not in hiring workers. Labor unions in almost all Communist countries are forbidden to strike against or picket the employer—the state.

Economic Change. There is no doubt that most Communist countries have made rapid progress in building up their industries. There are several reasons for their rapid industrial growth. For one thing, most of these countries had little industry when the Communists took over. The new rulers made industrialization one of their major goals. A Communist system can shift people and resources around more easily than a private enterprise system. For a while, at least, it can concentrate on developing such heavy-industry products as steel and machine tools while neglecting consumers' demands for more and better food, clothing, and housing.

However, planning and centralization have also created problems. In the late 1960's, Russia and many East European Communist countries tried different schemes to improve production and efficiency. One method was to give company directors greater freedom. The directors were offered bonuses for meeting or bettering the production, sales, and profit goals set for their firms. Communist governments also began to let customers have greater influence on the goods produced, and on the services made available to them.

In Russia and Eastern Europe, many earlier economic notions have been given up. The governments no longer strive for equal income or equal wealth for all. Instead, they try to reward higher or better output with extra cash. Management has borrowed many ideas from American business. The ways of organizing and running Communist economies have become more and more varied, and experimentation continues. But in all cases, the leaders keep central control over natural and human resources.

LIFE UNDER COMMUNISM

Life under Communism varies from one country to another. The following section deals mainly with life under Communism in Russia and Eastern Europe.

Making a Living. The standard of living in the Soviet Union and the Communist countries of Eastern Europe is lower than that of the United States and Canada. But the differences were even greater before the Communists took over. Families spend a much smaller part of their budget on housing than American families do. They also spend less on vacations and leisure. Clothing is more expensive than in the United States. But education and medical services are free. Such items as toys, household gadgets, bicycles, and cameras are scarcer and more expensive. Few families can afford a car. A far higher percentage of women have jobs in the Communist countries than in America. Like the men, most of the women work six days a week.

Some persons in Communist countries make much more money than the rest. They include high party and government officials; and scientists, writers, and actors and other performers. However, the differences in income between the highest and lowest paid persons are much less than in the United States, and no one may—legally—accumulate a great fortune. In general, money plays a smaller part in Communist countries, and many people there believe that Americans are "money mad."

Education receives a great deal of attention in Communist countries. Communist schools stress science, mathematics, and languages. Training in science and engineering tends to be better—and more popular—than in the humanities and social sciences.

In the social sciences, students are taught only the official version. They have little chance to learn about or discuss other points of view. Some facts in history textbooks are changed to agree with the party line. Other facts are simply not mentioned at all. Since the

mid-1950's, however, some untruths have been removed from Soviet and East European textbooks.

Leisure and Culture. Communists emphasize organized group leisure-time activity. Many persons belong to music, art, or folk dancing clubs. Such activities as scouting, arts and crafts, amateur theater, and stamp collecting are also organized into groups. These activities are often tied in with Communist youth organizations, which combine recreation and political instruction. Party leaders consider youth groups important in gaining support and, later on, party members.

Communist governments also encourage young people to take part in sports. Communist athletes compete against men and women from non-Communist countries in the Olympic Games and other international contests. There are many opportunities for such cultural activities as concerts, plays, and poetry readings. Many of these activities have a political theme. Persons in Communist countries have little opportunity to travel abroad. But it has become easier to see foreign movies, hear foreign radio broadcasts, and—in some countries—to get foreign books.

Personal Freedom. Communists consider their goal, their party, and the state more important than individual rights and liberties. In Communist countries, there are usually huge gaps between official claims of freedom and conditions as they actually exist. For example, Russia has a constitution that assures citizens freedom of speech, press, and assembly; and the right to a job and to leisure. The constitution guarantees freedom of religious worship and freedom of "anti-religious propaganda." It promises equal rights for all, regardless of race, sex, or nationality.

But the Russian government and party have violated or ignored many of the rights set forth in the constitution. Citizens may be punished if they publicly criticize the policies or leaders of the Communist Party. The government does not allow persons to establish organizations or newspapers that oppose it. Books, magazines, newspapers, and movies are valuable tools for promoting the party line. Writers who criticize Communist leaders are not allowed to publish their work.

Communists try to discourage religious worship because they consider religion a force that acts against Communism. Church membership may make it more difficult for a person to advance in his job, and impossible to join the Communist Party. In several countries—and especially in Poland and the Soviet Union—there has been much discrimination against Jews, even Jewish members of the Communist Party.

Such restrictions exist in varying degrees in other Communist countries, but the trend since the mid-1950's has been toward allowing greater personal freedom. This was not the case during the rule of Joseph Stalin, the undisputed leader of world Communism from the late 1920's to the early 1950's. Stalin ordered millions of Russian peasants murdered when they resisted government attempts to seize their land. During World War II, five of Russia's nationalities were abolished and their members exiled because Stalin suspected these people of disloyalty. The peak of mass terror came between 1935 and 1938 in Russia, and again from 1948 to 1952 in Russia and Eastern Europe.

COMMUNISM

Stalin's successors gave up terror as a major weapon to control the people. The secret police have lost much of their power, and most forced labor camps have been closed. But in a milder way, all Communist states continue to use threats and terror. See STALIN, JOSEPH.

ORIGINS OF COMMUNISM

Modern Communism is based on the theories of Marx as interpreted and modified by Lenin. These theories are often called *Marxism-Leninism*. Marx and Lenin took many of their ideas from earlier writers.

Early Communism. The word *communism* comes from the Latin word *communis*, which means *common* or *belonging to all*. The idea of *communal* property dates at least from the time of the early Greeks. In the 300's B.C., the Greek philosopher Plato expressed communal ideas in his book *The Republic*. Plato proposed that a ruling class own everything in common, putting the welfare of the state above all personal desires. A number of early Christian groups had some form of community ownership of property.

Thomas More, an English statesman and philosopher, suggested in his book *Utopia* (1516) that all citizens share equally the wealth produced by industry. During the French Revolution (1789-1799), some extremists favored a revolutionary dictatorship to abolish private property. In the 1800's, communal ideas were practiced in a number of settlements. Such settlements in the United States included New Harmony in Indiana, Brook Farm in Massachusetts, and Oneida Community in New York.

Marxism. Marx's basic ideas were first expressed in the *Communist Manifesto* (1848), which he wrote with Friedrich Engels, a German economist. Marx believed the only way to ensure a happy, harmonious society was to have the workers in control. His ideas were partly a reaction against hardships suffered during the 1800's by workers in France, England, and Germany. Most factory and mine workers were poorly paid, and had to work long hours under unhealthful conditions.

Marx was convinced that the triumph of Communism is inevitable. He taught that history follows certain unchangeable laws as it advances from one stage to the next. Each stage is marked by struggles that lead to a higher stage of development. Communism, Marx declared, is the highest and final stage of development.

According to Marx, the key to understanding the stages of historical development is knowing the relationship between different classes of people in producing goods. He claimed that the owners of wealth are the ruling class because they use their economic power to force their will on the people. He held that *class struggle* is the means by which history moves from one stage to the next. Marx assumed that the ruling class would never willingly give up its power, and that struggle and violence were therefore inevitable.

Marx called for the abolition of *capitalism*, an economic system in which the chief means of production are privately owned. Under capitalism, Marx believed, a struggle takes place between the *bourgeoisie* (pronounced BOOR zhwah ZEE) and the *proletariat* (pronounced PROH luh TAIR ee uht). The bourgeoisie are the owners of factories and other means of production, and the proletariat are the workers. Marx argued that workers do not receive full value for their labor under capitalism, because the owners keep the profits. He believed that capitalism would someday destroy itself. Wealth would be in the hands of only a few persons, and the workers' living standards would continually grow worse. Finally, the workers would revolt and seize control of industry and the government.

According to Marx, the workers would establish a *dictatorship of the proletariat* that would work to set up a classless Communist society. Everyone would live in peace, prosperity, and freedom. There would be no more need for governments, police, or armies, and all these would gradually wither away.

History has not moved as Marx expected it to. Capitalism has not collapsed. Wealth has become more widely distributed, and the poor have not become poorer nor a larger part of the population. No Communist country has been able to abolish social classes. Just as in non-Communist countries, some persons have more wealth and power than others. Conflicts and crime have not vanished in Communist society. Contrary to Marx's expectations, all workers do not show brotherly feelings for each other. Instead, national and racial hatred have often proved stronger than class ties.

COMMUNISM IN RUSSIA

Before 1917. Marx had expected his theories to be tested in Germany, Great Britain, or some other highly industrialized country. But it was in relatively backward Russia that Communists were first successful in setting up a Communist-controlled government.

During the late 1800's, Russia began to come out of its age-old backwardness. Although the country was still largely agricultural, its industry began to flourish. As industrialization increased, revolutionary activity grew. Radical Western ideas—including Marxism—became popular. In 1898, Marxists founded the Russian Social Democratic Labor Party. The party split into two groups in 1903. The *Bolsheviks* (members of the majority), led by Lenin, wanted the party to consist of a small group of disciplined revolutionaries. The *Mensheviks* (members of the minority) wanted the party to have wider membership and to reach decisions through democratic methods. In 1918, Lenin's group became the Russian Communist Party (Bolsheviks).

Lenin abandoned the Marxist idea that proletarian revolutions could be carried out only in highly industrialized countries with a large working class. He believed that backward areas with a small industrial proletariat offered a revolutionary movement certain advantages. According to Lenin, the Communist Party would plan the revolution. It would lead the workers and speak for them. To achieve its immediate goals, the party would seek temporary partners, including peasants and poor shopkeepers. After these goals had been reached, the party would feel free to turn against its former partners and form new alliances to achieve other goals. Thus, Lenin's theory of revolution actually called for the dictatorship of the Communist Party.

In 1905, thousands of Russians revolted against the czar, but the revolution was put down by the army. During the following years, the czar failed to bring about any basic reforms. World War I (1914-1918) created additional heavy problems for Russia. The nation suffered heavy troop losses on the front, and severe food shortages at home. In March, 1917 (February in the old Russian calendar, which was replaced in 1918), the people overthrew the czar. A democratic *provisional* (temporary) government was set up.

Communism Under Lenin. In November, 1917 (October in the old calendar), the Bolsheviks, led by Lenin, seized power and established a Communist government. When the Bolsheviks took over the government, they had fewer than 100,000 members in a country of over 160 million people. They succeeded for several reasons. For one thing, the provisional government had little experience. Its leaders did not want to withdraw from the war, and they could not carry out reforms while the war was still going on. The Bolsheviks also succeeded because of their effective organization, their appeal to the people, their willingness to act, and the clever leadership of Lenin.

Lenin led Russia from 1917 until his death in 1924. Soon after he came to power, Russia made peace with Germany, but from 1918 to 1920 Russia was torn by civil war between Communists and non-Communists. The Communists defeated their rivals, who were divided and poorly organized. From the start, Lenin used force and terror against his political opponents. By 1921, conditions had become grave throughout the country. Peasant and sailor revolts broke out, and famine threatened. The World War, revolution, and civil war had brought Russia near economic collapse.

In 1921, realizing the need for a change in policy, Lenin introduced the New Economic Policy (NEP). The NEP called for getting along with certain groups that were considered enemies of Communism. These included tradesmen, peasants, and middle-class engineers, scholars, and army officers. Russia's economy recovered steadily under the NEP.

By the time Lenin died, Russia had become a one-party state. All opposition had been banned, and all public organizations—such as workers' councils and trade unions—had been turned into tools of the Communists. See LENIN, V. I.

Communism Under Stalin. For several years after Lenin died, leading Communists in Russia struggled for power. Through plotting and trickery, and by shifting alliances, Joseph Stalin defeated his rivals one by one. After 1928, he had complete control of the Communist Party and the Russian government. For the next 25 years, Stalin ruled with an iron hand. The Russian economy and Russia's influence abroad grew rapidly—but at a great cost of human life and personal freedom in Russia.

In Stalin's view, no area of life could be outside the grip of the leader. Everything—even truth and morals—was a weapon at his service. In the mid-1930's, Stalin began a campaign of terror to eliminate all opposition. He claimed to be *purging* (purifying) the Communist Party. Stalin ordered most of his earlier Communist associates arrested or put to death. Thousands of party officials, army officers, and factory managers were labeled "enemies of the people" and forced to confess imaginary crimes. The secret police terrorized the Rus-

sian people. Millions were sent to forced labor camps. See STALIN, JOSEPH (Rule by Terror).

For more detailed information on the development of Communism in Russia, see RUSSIA (History).

THE SPREAD OF COMMUNISM

The Comintern. Throughout the 1920's and 1930's, Russia remained the world's only Communist country. Local Communists were active in many countries, but suffered severe setbacks in China, Germany, Poland, and Spain.

The Bolsheviks thought the Russian Revolution of 1917 would spark revolution in other countries. But none succeeded, and the Bolsheviks soon realized that world revolution required careful direction and organization. In 1919, the Russian Communists helped establish the *Comintern* (Communist International). The Comintern united all the Communist parties of the world in a disciplined revolutionary organization. The Comintern actually became a tool of the Soviet leadership. All its attempts to promote revolution in other countries failed. Stalin had little faith in the Comintern, and it was officially dissolved in 1943.

World War II (1939-1945) provided opportunities for Communist gains in many countries. In 1939 and 1940, Russia took over Latvia, Lithuania, and Estonia, plus parts of Poland, Finland, and Romania. All this territory became part of the Soviet Union.

Toward the end of the war, Russian troops helped free many countries from German and Japanese control. Wherever possible, Russia set up Communist-controlled governments. Bulgaria, Czechoslovakia, East Germany, Hungary, Poland, Romania, and North Korea became independent "people's democracies." But these countries were actually Russian *satellites* (countries controlled by Russia). The satellites adopted Soviet political and economic practices, and followed the foreign policy of the Soviet Union.

In some other countries, Communists who had led national resistance movements during the war took power with little or no Soviet help. Local Communists took over the governments of Yugoslavia and Albania, and, later, North Vietnam. Communists also became strong political forces in France and Italy, but were unable to take control there. In Greece, Indonesia, Malaya, Burma, and the Philippines, Communists made bids for power but lost in fighting civil wars.

In China, the Communists and Nationalists joined forces to help defeat the Japanese, who had invaded the country in 1937. In the 1940's, the Chinese Communists gradually gained the upper hand over the Nationalists. By 1949, they had taken complete control of mainland China. See CHINA (Communist Victory).

In 1947, nine European Communist parties set up the *Cominform* (Communist Information Bureau). The Russians controlled the Cominform and tried to use it to keep the other parties in line. Yugoslavia was expelled in 1948 after President Tito refused to take orders from Russia. The Cominform then lost most of its effectiveness, and was finally dissolved in 1956.

Stalin died in 1953, but other Communists continued to use armed force to spread or maintain Communism. Russian troops crushed revolts in East Germany in

1953 and in Hungary in 1956. Fidel Castro became dictator of Cuba in 1959, and two years later declared his government to be Communist.

The Cold War. In the late 1940's, the United States and its allies promised to come to the aid of non-Communist countries that were attacked by a Communist country. The struggle between the Communist and non-Communist powers became known as the *Cold War*. The chief weapons of the Cold War are propaganda, plus economic, military, and political power.

Since the beginning of the Cold War, most Communist attempts at expansion have failed. The Western powers won a victory in 1949, when they broke Russia's blockade of West Berlin. They took another important stand in the Korean War (1950-1953), after South Korea had been attacked by Communist-ruled North Korea. Between 1958 and 1962, Russia again applied pressure on the Western powers to withdraw from Berlin, and again failed.

In 1962, Soviet Premier Nikita S. Khrushchev tried to gain a sudden military advantage by placing long-range missiles in Cuba. A firm stand by the United States forced him to remove the missiles rather than risk nuclear war. During the 1960's, the United States and a few other nations joined forces in an attempt to prevent a Communist takeover of South Vietnam. The Soviet Union and China supplied Communist North Vietnam with war materials. See COLD WAR.

Why Communism? The spread of Communism is usually thought of in terms of force and revolution. However, millions of persons have freely chosen to become Communists. Many of these have become disappointed and dropped out of the Communist Party.

Communism has different appeals for different in-dividuals and groups. Its main attraction for some is its claim to provide simple answers and solutions in difficult situations. Some persons join the party to avoid being outsiders, and to feel they are part of a meaningful group. Others join to ride the "wave of the future." They believe that Communist victory is inevitable.

The appeals of Communism seem to be strongest in countries where some of the following conditions exist. (1) There are huge differences in income and social position between the poor and the rich, and the poor feel these differences. (2) Communism is the only effective movement fighting for change, reform, or revolution. (3) The existing government does not command the strong loyalty of the people, and its institutions do not stand up well under stress. (4) Many persons feel deprived and discriminated against socially and economically, and as national or racial groups. (5) Communists are not looked on as criminals or lunatics, but as one of several accepted types of revolutionaries.

COMMUNISM TODAY

Since Stalin's death in 1953, no one man or country has been the leader of world Communism. Russia has lost its leadership of the world movement, which has split into a number of separate groups.

In the 1960's, there was also a growing willingness in Russia and Eastern Europe to depart from standard Communist practices and to experiment with new policies and techniques. Communist doctrine seemed to be losing its importance, especially for young people. There was increasing interest in safe and comfortable living, and less interest in revolutionary activity. This was not true in Africa, Asia, and Latin America, where at least some Communist groups were working for radical social and political change.

The Splintering of World Communism began in the mid-1950's. It was made possible largely by a more permissive attitude by Russia toward the Communist countries of Eastern Europe. By the mid-1960's, most of these nations had cast off the features that had earned them the label of Soviet "satellites." Their governments began making more and more of their own major decisions, and often ignored Soviet advice. Such independence has been demonstrated by Yugoslavia since 1948, and by Romania from 1964 on.

In 1968, Czechoslovakia defied Soviet warnings and undertook far-reaching reforms under new Communist Party leader Alexander Dubček. These reforms included freedom of the press and tolerance of groups openly critical of Communist policies. But developments that followed indicated that Russia was again setting limits on change and dissent in Eastern Europe. In August, 1968, Soviet, Bulgarian, East German, Hungarian, and Polish troops invaded Czechoslovakia to try to stop the reforms. Soviet troops remained in Czechoslovakia, and government censorship was gradually reimposed. In April, 1969, Dubček was replaced as party leader.

A serious challenge to Russia's leadership came from China. The Soviet-Chinese dispute was kept secret at first. After it burst into the open in the early 1960's, every Communist party had to take sides.

Some of the issues in the quarrel between Russia and China concerned different interpretations of Commu-

A Split in the Communist Movement took place in the 1960's after China accused Russia of betraying the ideals of Marx and Lenin. Chinese demonstrators burned images of Russian leaders.

Kyodo News Service, Tokyo

nist teachings. Nikita S. Khrushchev, premier of Russia from 1958 to 1964, concluded that Communist governments could rule effectively without using large-scale terror. He also stressed "peaceful coexistence" with non-Communist countries. Khrushchev considered forcible revolution as only one of many methods for achieving worldwide Communism. He stressed economic aid and the example of Soviet economic advancement under Communism.

China accused the Soviet Union of betraying Marxism-Leninism. The Chinese called the Russians cowards for arguing that the threat of nuclear war made large-scale wars unthinkable as means for furthering Communist aims. The Chinese urged Communists to follow their example and take over through guerrilla-type civil wars. They supported programs of direct action and condemned peaceful coexistence.

The Russians and Chinese also differed on many questions involving their national needs. Both wanted to be the world spokesman for Communism. In 1960, Russia stopped giving economic and military assistance to China. China and Albania scolded Russia for seeking better relations with the United States. China, Albania, Cuba, North Korea, and North Vietnam refused to sign the nuclear test ban treaty negotiated by Russia and the United States in 1963. China also demanded that Russia return vast territories taken from China more than a century ago. In 1969, China and Russia engaged in a series of armed border clashes over possession of an island in the Ussuri River.

By the late 1960's, the unity of world Communism appeared to be beyond repair. In each country, the party was adapting Communism to its own needs.

Communism in Non-Communist Countries. Communist parties exist—legally or illegally—in about 90 countries. Their total membership is estimated at 45 million. Of these, fewer than 3 million party members live in non-Communist countries.

In the United States, the Communist Party has little influence. The party was founded in 1919. It may have had as many as 100,000 members during the Great Depression of the 1930's. During the 1930's, some American intellectuals supported the ideals of Communism and believed that the capitalist economy was about to collapse. The party lost many members after World War II because of Soviet policy and the Cold War. Many others left the party after the story of Stalin's crimes was exposed in Russia in 1956. In 1968, party leaders claimed to have 13,000 members. Other estimates placed the membership as low as 5,000.

Some people argue that party membership is not an accurate measure of Communist strength. Although there no doubt are secret Communist agents and sympathizers in the United States, the danger is often exaggerated. Most political experts believe that Americans should be aware of the dangers of Communism, but that American society has little to fear as long as citizens prize their freedoms and fulfill their civic duties.

In Other Countries. The Communist Party is extremely small in Canada. In most Latin-American countries, Communist organizations are illegal. In others, including Brazil and Mexico, the parties are badly split. Among the Western European nations, Italy, France,

and Finland have strong Communist parties. The party is illegal in Spain, Portugal, and Greece, but there is some Communist influence in those countries. There are few Communists in Africa or the Middle East.

In Asia, the Japanese Communist Party is influential among intellectuals, but has been unable to attract large numbers of voters. The Communist Party of Indonesia had over 2 million members before its leaders supported an attempt in 1965 to take over the government. Many thousands of its members were killed after this uprising, and the party was outlawed. In India, Communists are bitterly split into rival parties. In South Vietnam, Communist influence is exerted through the Viet Cong, who control the National Liberation Front (see VIETNAM WAR).   ALEXANDER DALLIN

Related Articles in WORLD BOOK include:

BIOGRAPHIES

Brezhnev, Leonid I.	Kosygin, Aleksei	Owen (family)
Castro, Fidel	Lenin, V. I.	Stalin, Joseph
Engels, Friedrich	Mao Tse-tung	Tito
Khrushchev, Nikita S.	Marx, Karl	Trotsky, Leon

OTHER RELATED ARTICLES

Bolshevik	Materialism
Brainwashing	Menshevik
Cold War	New Harmony
Collective Farm	Oneida Community
Dictator	Politburo
Government	Russia
Imperialism	Smith Act
International, The	Socialism
Internationale, The	Totalitarianism

Outline

I. Main Features of Communism
  A. The Communist Party
  B. Communism and Government
  C. Communism and the Economy
  D. Economic Change

II. Life Under Communism
  A. Making a Living   C. Leisure and Culture
  B. Education   D. Personal Freedom

III. Origins of Communism
  A. Early Communism   B. Marxism

IV. Communism in Russia
  A. Before 1917
  B. Communism Under Lenin
  C. Communism Under Stalin

V. The Spread of Communism
  A. The Comintern   C. The Cold War
  B. World War II   D. Why Communism?

VI. Communism Today
  A. The Splintering of World Communism
  B. Communism in Non-Communist Countries

Questions

Why is Communism sometimes called totalitarian?
How does socialism differ from Communism?
What did the word *communism* mean originally?
Who were the Bolsheviks? The Mensheviks?
Who planned the Bolshevik Revolution of 1917?
What led to the Soviet-Chinese dispute?
Who wrote the *Communist Manifesto?*
What was the Comintern? The Cominform?
Why do Communists oppose capitalism?
How did the Soviet Union use World War II to advance Communist goals?

COMMUNIST MANIFESTO. See COMMUNISM (Marxism); MARX, KARL H.

COMMUNIST PARTY. See COMMUNISM.

COMMUNITY

Standard Oil Co. (N.J.)

A Village Community contains many smaller family, school, and neighborhood communities. It forms a part of many larger and larger communities, linked to them by common interests.

COMMUNITY. Each of us belongs to several communities at the same time. Suppose you examine a letter mailed by someone in another nation to a friend in the United States. It might be addressed like this:

> Mr. John Brown and Family,
> 11 Sutton Place,
> Central City,
> California,
> U.S.A.

Each line of this address identifies one of five different communities to which John Brown belongs. These are (1) the Brown *family* community, (2) the Sutton Place *neighborhood* community, (3) the Central City *local* community, (4) the California *state* community, and (5) the *national* community of the United States.

Each community is a part of the next larger community in the series. And each larger community is made up of the many smaller ones. Several other things are true of all communities. (1) Each community is made up of people who have similar customs and ways of looking at life and who think of themselves as belonging to that community. For example, every member of the Brown family feels that he is a part of the Brown family community. In a similar way, he feels that he

belongs to his neighborhood, town, county, state, and nation. (2) The people of each community live in a particular space that can be defined. The Brown family lives in a house at 11 Sutton Place. The people of Central City all live within certain city limits. (3) Each community has created laws or institutions to serve its people. The Brown family has certain rules of behavior, and Central City has its own laws. (4) Each community has a common language, or at least a system whereby its people can communicate with one another. (5) Each community has certain problems that unite its people in a common cause. For example, the people on Sutton Place may be working for a new school, or the people of California for a better state park system.

Expanding Communities

The Family Community. A typical family includes two parents and one or more children. But it might be a childless couple. Or it might consist of several generations living under one roof. Although the family is the smallest community, it is also the oldest and most important. The family must teach children the basic values of life, and begin their education. We depend upon the family for love, affection, and encouragement.

The School Community. For most children, the school is the next expanding community. It is made up of

728

children from many families, and so is larger than a family community. A school serves a person for only a few years of his life. Because of this, it differs from the other communities to which a person "belongs" throughout his life.

The Neighborhood Community is a group of families who live close together. They deal with each other in face-to-face contacts. They have common problems, and cooperate in various activities.

The Local Community consists of several neighborhoods. It might be a village, including the farm families who depend on the village. Or it might be a group of neighborhoods within a city area.

The County Community is more closely defined than the local community. It is a specific political unit, and provides specific services for its members. These services include those of the county recorder, the county tax collector, the county superintendent of schools, and the county sheriff. The county community also provides many activities through private groups like the county medical association or county grange. In Louisiana, this community is called a *parish*.

The Metropolitan Community includes at least one central city of 50,000 or more persons surrounded by several local communities closely dependent on each other. The people of metropolitan communities have many troublesome problems, such as transportation, water supply, sewage, and law enforcement.

The State or Province Community welds together many smaller communities. It establishes laws and services for a large number of people. The state or province community also has many private agencies, such as state chambers of commerce, state athletic leagues, provincial bar associations, and the like. Most persons take great pride in their state or province, and feel great loyalty to it.

Regions of States or Provinces are less rigidly defined geographically than some other communities. But they are important from the standpoint of the lives and customs of the people. New Englanders, for example, differ in many ways from Southerners or Westerners. The differences may involve social attitudes, economics, politics, and even food. States or provinces within a region must often act as a unit. For example, New Jersey and New York state set up the *Port of New York Authority* to manage the problems of transportation and port facilities in the region around New York City (see PORT OF NEW YORK AUTHORITY). Water-distribution agreements among various Western states are another example of this type of cooperation. THE WORLD BOOK ENCYCLOPEDIA has separate articles on each of the several regions of states in the United States. See UNITED STATES (table: Geographic Regions).

The National Community includes all the smaller communities within its boundaries. Although large and varied, it is one of the most highly organized communities. People identify themselves strongly with their national community. They are citizens of the United States, Canadians, English, Germans, or Russians. The United States consists of 4 regional communities; 50 state communities; thousands of metropolitan, county, and local communities; millions of neighborhood communities; and about 50,000,000 family communities.

International Communities are made up of groups of various national communities.

The Inter-American Community consists of the many nations that make up North, Central, and South America. The Americas have a growing awareness of their common interests, and cooperate through various organizations. See ORGANIZATION OF AMERICAN STATES; PAN AMERICAN UNION.

The Atlantic Community includes nations grouped about the Atlantic Ocean and Mediterranean Sea. Wars and trade among the peoples of these areas, and modern technology, have paved the way for ties that bind them increasingly together. After World War II, they joined together for purposes of mutual defense (see NORTH ATLANTIC TREATY ORGANIZATION). Other associations formed by these nations include the European Community and the European Free Trade Association.

The Pacific Community includes lands around the Pacific Ocean—North America, South America, Asia, Australia, and the Pacific Islands. This community covers two thirds of the world's water and land area. On its land live 1,500,000,000 persons who lack a common language and do not as yet have common values or institutions. But modern trade, communications, and transportation are bringing these peoples closer together. SEATO is a move in the direction of a common defense policy (see SOUTHEAST ASIA TREATY ORGANIZATION).

Other International Communities include the Communist Community, the Arab Community, the South American Community, and the African Community. In various ways, the people of these areas fulfill the definition of a community. The Communist Community, for example, is comprised of peoples who to some extent have a sense of belonging, maintain their own types of institutions, and have common problems. See INTERNATIONAL RELATIONS.

The World Community. All the peoples of the earth conform more and more in many ways to the definition of a community. The advances of science and technology have brought wide acceptance of this fact. The United Nations, for example, is a recognition of the emerging community made up of the peoples of the entire world. The Universal Postal Union, the International Bank, the International Court of Justice, and the International Bureau of Weights and Measures are other indications that mankind has begun to think of itself as belonging to an all-inclusive community. See WORLD.

Activities of the Community

Although communities vary greatly in size and population, they all carry on much the same activities. These activities can be grouped into eight general kinds: (1) protection, (2) trade and industry, (3) transportation, (4) communication, (5) education, (6) recreation, (7) government, and (8) religion and the arts. Let us look at the ways the various expanding communities conduct these activities.

Protection and conservation of health, life, resources, and property are the responsibility of every community. For example, the family community keeps matches away from small children, heats the house, and supplies food. The state or province community provides high-

Family

School

Neighborhood

Local

County

Metropolitan

State or Province

Region of States or Provinces

Family

School

Neighborhood

Local

County

Metropolitan

State or Province

Region of States or Provinces

National

International

World

Expanding Communities

Expanding Communities include all the peoples of the world. Some communities, such as the international community, are quite new, but the family community is as old as mankind.

World

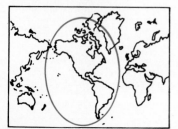

International

National

way-safety patrols. State-wide insurance companies offer insurance against loss. The national community maintains an army and navy, and encourages conservation of natural resources. See PROTECTION, with its list of Related Articles.

Industry and Trade form part of the life of every community. The local community may produce milk, poultry, and vegetables. It may manufacture furniture or build its own houses. States and regions of states often specialize in producing certain types of products, and trade them for the products of other states. Every community exchanges goods and services. The neighborhood exchanges baby-sitting services, or perhaps maintains a barbershop or local drugstore. Each community also consumes goods and uses services. See TRADE; INDUSTRY.

Transportation. Communities provide various types of transportation. The school may provide buses to bring children to classes. The state builds highways. The national community provides interstate highway systems and waterways. National airlines and railroads carry people and goods. See TRANSPORTATION.

Communication. The size of the community has expanded with the growth of communication facilities. Primitive communities extended only as far as a man could walk. But today's ideas are exchanged quickly from one part of the world to another. Each community has its own communication system. The family and neighborhood may communicate mainly by word of mouth. A local or national community has newspapers, magazines, radio, and television. See COMMUNICATION.

Education. Schools form only part of the educational effort of communities. The family is the first to teach the young. In the home, a baby learns to talk, walk, and follow directions. The neighborhood provides further education in play groups, the church, and the library. In larger local communities, television and publishing become important educational influences. The national community provides many programs of education in such fields as agriculture, home economics, and military science. The United Nations conducts educational programs on an international scale. See EDUCATION.

Recreation. People today have more leisure time than ever before. They spend much of this time within their family communities. Families participate in such activities as games, household projects, reading, and music. The neighborhood or local community furnishes motion pictures, athletics, concerts, and social events. State and national communities maintain great systems of parks and forests. The Olympic Games provide recreation for the international community. See AMUSEMENTS; RECREATION.

Government. A pupil who helps elect a representative to a student council participates in government within the school community. Every business company, every luncheon club, and every labor union must agree upon rules and regulations. In that sense, they all form some kind of government at their own community level. As a community grows in size, government organization becomes more complicated. A family government may be informal. But a reading of the Constitution of the United States shows how complicated the government of a national community can become. Nations of the world join together to form such governmental organizations as the United Nations and the North Atlantic Treaty Organization.

Religion and the Arts. People in all parts of the world worship in churches, temples, and synagogues. They find pleasure and inspiration at musical concerts and theatrical performances. Families may read aloud together from great literature that expresses or mirrors human ideals and values. Family groups may sing, paint, or dance together. Neighborhood families may gather together to worship. Local communities provide studios and instructors for people who wish to paint, dance, or make music together. Libraries are maintained on local, state, and national levels. Many churches reach across national boundaries into the international community.

Community Improvement

Each of the communities of man changes constantly. Some grow old and weak through these changes. But others become larger, stronger, and more complicated. By studying these changes, a community may be able to guide its growth in such a way that it will be a better place in which to live.

If a man and wife have several children, the size of their family community will grow and they may need a larger house. By studying their budget, and by saving wherever possible, the family may be able to have a bigger home. As the children approach college age, they will need extra money for additional educational expenses. Again, by planning ahead, the family may be able to meet these needs.

Planning is just as necessary for a local community. A growing city needs a larger water supply to provide water for its new homes and factories. So the city government hires experts who predict how much more water will be needed. It hires engineers to design the new water system. Then it consults financial experts who recommend the best way for the city to raise the necessary money. Eventually, by good planning, the city solves the problems caused by its growth.

As the population of a school community increases, it may become necessary for the school district to erect a larger building, buy new equipment, and hire more teachers. School boards everywhere study the growth of their school communities and plan ahead to meet these needs. Sometimes a school district must call for help from the larger community of which it is a part. Perhaps they will need to increase taxes, which are collected by the county community. Or perhaps they must obtain authority for the tax change from the state community.

State communities are becoming more aware of the need for the region of states community to plan solutions to problems that extend over state boundaries. Many state compacts or interstate authorities have been established to study and act on such problems as transportation, water supply, and irrigation. The national community plans ahead to meet its military, recreation, and conservation demands.

Every person should study the needs of each of the various communities to which he belongs. All these communities contribute in some way to his welfare. And each demands certain loyalties and responsibilities

COMMUNITY

in return. Sometimes these responsibilities seem to conflict with each other. For example, a metropolitan community might need a new highway to solve a serious transportation problem. The best route for this highway may be through your own neighborhood. Your neighbors complain that the new highway will lower property values in the neighborhood community. Which community should you be loyal to—your neighborhood, or your larger metropolitan community? As the complexity of the expanding communities increases, it becomes increasingly important for a person to learn how he can be a good citizen in each and every one of the communities he belongs to.   PAUL R. HANNA

Related Articles in WORLD BOOK include:

COMMUNITY LEVELS

City and Local Governments	Nation	Town
County	Province	Tribe
Family	School	Village
Metropolitan Area	State Government	World
	Suburb	

COMMUNITY LIFE AND ACTIVITIES

Adult Education	Farm and Farming	Public Health
Art and the Arts	Fire Fighting	Recreation
Citizenship	Government	Religion
City Planning	Human Relations	Safety
Civics	Industry	Service Club
Civilization	Juvenile	Shelter
Club	Delinquency	Social Security
Communication	Playground	Social Settlement
Conservation	Police	Trade
Culture	Post Office	Transportation
Education	Protection	United Funds

COMMUNITY IN HISTORY

Aegean Civilization	Inca
Assyria (The People; Way of Life)	Indian, American (Life of the Indians)
Babylon	Middle Ages (Life of the People; Medieval Towns)
Babylonia (Way of Life)	
Colonial Life in America	
Egypt, Ancient (Family Life; City Life)	Pioneer Life in America
Feudalism	Roman Empire (City Life; Country Life)
Greece, Ancient (The People; Family Life)	Western Frontier Life

Outline

I. Expanding Communities
   A. The Family Community
   B. The School Community
   C. The Neighborhood Community
   D. The Local Community
   E. The County Community
   F. The Metropolitan Community
   G. The State or Province Community
   H. Regions of States or Provinces
   I. The National Community
   J. International Communities
   K. The World Community

II. Activities of the Community
   A. Protection
   B. Industry and Trade
   C. Transportation
   D. Communication
   E. Education
   F. Recreation
   G. Government
   H. Religion and the Arts

III. Community Improvement

Questions

What are the eight basic human activities carried on in most communities?

In what way does the school community conduct each of these activities?

What is the largest community? The smallest?
What are the common characteristics of communities?
Why does everyone belong to several communities?
How can communities be improved?
How can community life be developed?
How can community leaders be developed?
How do our community responsibilities sometimes seem to conflict with each other?
Why are larger communities growing in importance?

COMMUNITY ACTION PROGRAM. See ECONOMIC OPPORTUNITY, OFFICE OF.

COMMUNITY CHESTS. See UNITED FUNDS.

COMMUNITY COLLEGE. See JUNIOR COLLEGE.

COMMUNITY PROPERTY is the property husbands and wives own together under the laws of eight states—Arizona, California, Idaho, Louisiana, Nevada, New Mexico, Texas, and Washington. The laws differ in detail, but generally consider any property received through the efforts of a husband or his wife as the joint property of both. This does not include gifts and legacies to only one or the other, or property one owned before the marriage. When the husband or wife dies, half the property goes to the survivor. Only the other half of the property can be willed. In case of divorce, most states require the husband and wife to divide their community property evenly.   WILLIAM TUCKER DEAN

COMMUTATION OF SENTENCE. See PARDON.

COMMUTATIVE LAW. See ALGEBRA (Fundamental Laws); SET THEORY (Using Set Theory).

COMMUTATOR. See ELECTRIC GENERATOR (Direct-Current Generators).

COMMUTER. See METROPOLITAN AREA; SUBURB.

COMO, LAKE. See LAKE COMO.

COMORO ISLANDS, *KAHM oh roh*, are a group of small, mountainous islands owned by France. They lie in the Mozambique Channel midway between northern Madagascar and the southeastern coast of Africa. The main islands are Grande Comore, Anjouan, Moheli, and Mayotte. Moroni, the capital, lies on Grande Comore. The four main islands cover 838 square miles, and have a population of 288,000. The islands have a 230-mile coastline. Most of the people are Moslems. They produce coffee, cacao, sisal, vanilla, perfume plants, rice, and coconut palms. The islands are represented in the French Senate by one member, and in the French National Assembly by two members. A president and an eight-member council, who are elected by the Territorial Assembly, govern the islands. The Assembly is elected by the people.   HIBBERD V. B. KLINE, JR.

See also MALAGASY REPUBLIC (map).

COMPACT CAR. See AUTOMOBILE (World War II and after).

COMPANY. See ARMY, UNITED STATES (table: Levels of Command).

COMPANY, in business. See CORPORATION; HOLDING COMPANY; JOINT-STOCK COMPANY; LIMITED COMPANY; PARTNERSHIP.

COMPARATIVE ANATOMY. See ANATOMY; EVOLUTION (Comparative Anatomy).

COMPARATIVE PSYCHOLOGY is the psychology of animals—the study of their intelligence, needs, sensory capacities, and characteristic ways of behaving.

Animals are studied in their natural environments and in such special environments as laboratories and zoos. The natural environment is of particular interest because the animal is equipped to survive there. In the

A Brightness Discrimination Experiment requires an elephant to choose the brighter of two panels by pressing the panel with its trunk. When the animal makes the correct choice, it is rewarded with peanuts delivered automatically into the food cup.

M. E. Bitterman

laboratory, selected features of the environment are varied systematically, and their effects on behavior are measured precisely. Although naturalists sometimes criticize laboratory studies as "artificial," implying that the information obtained is not to be trusted, this criticism is misleading. Some of the most penetrating insights into the behavior of animals have been achieved by making radical changes in their natural environments. For example, rearing a chick in complete isolation shows that social stimuli are necessary for its normal development.

Why Animals Are Studied. Animals are studied because of curiosity about them, and also for practical reasons. Information about the migration and spawning of salmon is not only interesting in itself but also has great economic importance.

Experiments with animals also provide information about man under conditions in which human experiments are not practical. For example, the brains of rats can be stimulated with electrical currents passing through fine wires embedded in the brains by surgery. Experiments of this type have yielded much information about how the brain regulates such basic drives as hunger and thirst. Experiments with rats also have provided valuable information about the psychological effects of drugs.

The results of animal experiments can be applied to man only if it can be assumed that experiments with human beings would yield the same results. Whether they would or not is uncertain. The assumption that they would can sometimes be justified because of (1) the structural resemblances between man and the higher animals, and (2) the similar results of experiments that can be performed with both men and animals.

Methods of Studying Animals. A great deal is learned about men simply by asking them questions, but that method is not available in the study of animals. If the ability of a monkey to detect small differences in brightness is to be determined, the animal first must be trained to respond differently to objects of different brightness. One method is to show the animal a pair of differently illuminated panels, and to reward it with a raisin for pressing the brighter panel. After the monkey has learned to choose the brighter one, the experimenter

gradually reduces the difference in brightness between the two panels until wrong choices become as frequent as correct ones. At that point, the limit of the animal's capacity to discriminate has been reached.

Some animals respond differently to certain great differences in stimulation without special training. An octopus is much more likely to attack a moving object than a stationary one. But special training usually is necessary to provide a more detailed picture of sensory capacity.

A kind of information obtained from men by questioning, but which cannot be obtained from animals even by indirect methods, is information about consciousness. The fact that an animal responds differently to two lights of different color does not tell what the colors are for the animal, or whether it experiences color at all. The psychologist does not ask, therefore, what an animal "sees," but only about its ability to discriminate among visual stimuli.

Problems Studied. Any single instance of behavior is the product of several different psychological processes. A monkey's performance in an experiment on brightness discrimination involves more than its ability to detect a difference in brightness. Essential also are an interest in raisins and an ability to learn how to get them in the experimental situation. A comparable experiment could not be performed with a jellyfish, because the jellyfish is incapable of learning. The behavior of such a simple animal is determined entirely by its inherited structure. If that behavior is not appropriate to the environment in which the animal finds itself, the animal simply does not survive.

Comparative psychologists are particularly interested in the ability of animals to learn about their environments and discover new ways of dealing with them. In experiments on classical conditioning, they study the ability of animals to learn about sequences of environmental events. In experiments on instrumental conditioning, they study the ability of animals to learn about the consequences of their actions. See LEARNING (How We Learn).

The intelligence of an animal is closely related to the structure of its brain. Environments change, and some animals adjust more easily than others to these changes. Suppose a rat has been rewarded for pressing the brighter of two panels. If the experimenter then decides to reward the rat for pressing the dimmer panel instead, it will have considerable difficulty learning to press that panel. After the rat has begun to press the dimmer panel, it may have some difficulty shifting back to the brighter panel if the experimenter changes the conditions again. In general, however, the rat accomplishes each shift more easily than the previous one, until it is able to change its behavior almost as soon as the conditions change. A fish, whose brain is much simpler than a rat's, is a less flexible animal. It finds the hundredth change as difficult as the first.   M. E. BITTERMAN

COMPARISON

COMPARISON, in grammar, is the inflection of an adjective or adverb. Its purpose is the expression of a greater or smaller degree of the quality the word denotes. *Inflection* means changing the ending of a word. The pronominal, demonstrative, and limiting adjectives may not be changed to a greater or less degree.

The Three Degrees of adjectives or adverbs are the positive, comparative, and superlative. The *positive* is the simple degree, as in, "This book is *heavy*"; "This book is *interesting*." The corresponding adverbs, *heavily* and *interestingly*, are also in the positive.

The *comparative* is used when two objects are being compared, as in, "This book is *heavier* (or *less heavy*) than the other," or, "*more interesting* (or *less interesting*) than the other." The corresponding adverbial forms, such as *more heavily* and *less interestingly*, are also in the comparative degree.

The *superlative* is used to point out the one among three or more objects that has the highest or lowest degree of the quality referred to: "This is the *heaviest* (or *least heavy*) book," or, "the *most interesting* (or *least interesting*) book." The corresponding adverbial forms, such as *least heavily* and *most interestingly*, are also in the superlative degree. The superlative is also used in the intensive sense of *very*, without implying comparison.

If the suffixes *er* and *est* are added to the positive form, the change is described as *comparison by endings*. If the adverbs *more*, *most*, *less*, or *least* are prefixed, the change is described as *comparison by adverbs*.

Irregularly Compared Adjectives include some of the most common adjectives in English—words that have come down from Old English, or Anglo-Saxon, forms. The following list contains some of them.

Positive	Comparative	Superlative
bad, ill, evil	worse	worst
far	farther	farthest
good, well	better	best
in, *adv.*	inner	inmost, innermost
little	less	least
much, many	more	most
near	nearer	nearest, next
old	older	oldest, eldest

Adjectives and Adverbs Without Comparison include those which it is impossible to compare without violating their meaning. These include *perpendicular*, *square*, *eternal*, *unique*, *perfect*. There can be nothing more perfect than a perfect object. The correct phrase is *more nearly perfect*.

Other and *else* are often used to distinguish the elements that are to be compared. For example, if Robert's height is being compared with that of the other boys in the class, we must set Robert apart from the group. We say, "Robert is taller than *any other boy* (or *anybody else*) in his class"; not, "Robert is taller than *any boy* (or *anybody*) in his class."

Common Errors include use of the superlative when only two objects are being compared. "Helen is the *prettiest* of the twins," is incorrect for "Helen is the *prettier* of the twins."

Another error occurs in the use of an excluding word such as *other* when the superlative *includes* the object of the comparison. "Of *all other* persons, I like him the least," should be, "Of *all* persons, I like him the least."

The double comparative, such as "more happier," is as wrong as the double negative. The error is common in words such as *preferable*, which is itself a comparative.

The superlative should not be used if only one person or thing is involved or mentioned. "He is the *shortest of any boy* in the room," is wrong for, "He is the *shortest boy* in the room."   CLARENCE STRATTON

See also ADJECTIVE; ADVERB; INFLECTION.

COMPASS, or PAIR OF COMPASSES, is a mathematical tool. It consists of two pointed legs that are joined at

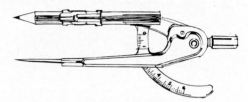

The Compass Is a Handy Tool used in geometry, and in such occupations as architecture, carpentry, and engineering.

the top so the legs can be moved closer together or farther apart. A pencil or penpoint may be attached to one leg to draw circles or arcs. Compasses are used to construct many kinds of geometric figures, such as right triangles and *polygons* (many-sided figures). Compasses also may be used as *dividers*, to measure length or other dimensions.

Early Egyptians and Babylonians used the compass, with a ruler, to discover many mathematical principles. See also GEOMETRY (Constructions); MEASUREMENT (picture).

COMPASS is a device for determining directions. The simplest form of the compass is a magnetic needle that turns. The needle is mounted on a pivot so that it can move freely. It always points in the direction of the magnetic north and south poles. A simple pocket compass helps a person find his way when he is lost, and when there are no landmarks to guide him. All he needs to know is the direction in which he should be going. If he must walk west to reach the nearest town, he goes in a direction at right angles to the left of the end of the needle which points north.

Boxing the Compass means naming the 32 points, or directions, marked on the face of a compass. The *cardinal points* are north, east, south, and west. The *intercardinal points* are northeast, southeast, southwest, and northwest. Below is the way a person would "box the compass." The 16 main points are in black type.

North	**East-northeast**
North by east	East by north
North-northeast	**East**
Northeast by north	East by south
Northeast	**East-southeast**
Northeast by east	Southeast by east
Southeast	**West-southwest**
Southeast by south	West by south
South-southeast	**West**
South by east	West by north
South	**West-northwest**
South by west	Northwest by west
South-southwest	**Northwest**
Southwest by south	Northwest by north

Southwest   **North-northwest**

Southwest by west   North by west

Old-style compasses were marked with the 32 points of the compass. Newer compasses are marked with the 16 main points and with the 360 degrees of a circle, starting with 0 at north, 90 at east, and 180 at south.

The Mariner's Compass is a large magnetic compass used aboard a boat or ship. It has several magnets fastened on a flat disk, called a *compass card*. This compass card is marked with the points and degrees of direction. The card rests on a pivot so it can turn freely inside the glass-covered compass bowl and can always point toward magnetic north. The compass bowl is filled with a nonfreezable liquid mixture of alcohol and water or glycerin and water. This liquid mixture floats the card and at the same time *damps* (slows) the movement of the card so that it does not constantly swing from side to side with the motion of the ship. A black vertical line, called a *lubber's line*, is marked inside the compass bowl. The compass bowl is mounted so that the lubber's line is toward the bow of the ship. Thus, the compass-card point opposite the lubber's line indicates the direction the ship is heading.

Deviation. The magnetic compass points toward the North Magnetic Pole. But if it is placed close to a metal object, it will be drawn toward that object. The angle formed between the North Magnetic Pole and the direction the compass points is called *deviation*.

When a mariner's compass is installed on a ship, it is mounted on a *gimbal* (supporting frame) in a stand called a *binnacle*. The binnacle has magnetic devices that correct major errors of deviation in the compass. After these corrections have been made, the navigator *swings the ship*. That is, he heads the ship in different directions, checking the direction by various landmarks. As he does this, he notes how many degrees of deviation the compass shows from the exact direction of the ship. For instance, by sighting toward a lighthouse on the east, the navigator can tell that the ship is heading exactly east, but his compass may show the ship is heading two degrees south of east. Later, when the ship is out of sight of land, the navigator will know that if he wants to head directly east he should steer a course two degrees south of east on his compass.

Ewing Galloway

A Gyrocompass Repeater on deck picks up information on the ship's course from the gyrocompass below deck.

Variation. Because the magnetic compass points toward the North Magnetic Pole, it seldom points toward the true North Pole at the same time. The difference on the compass between the direction of the North Magnetic Pole and the true North Pole is called *variation* or *declination*. The variation of a compass is different at different places on the earth. The variation also changes at different times of the year and in different years. Therefore, to use a magnetic compass with complete accuracy, a person must have a *declination chart*, which shows exactly what variation correction must be made in reading the compass.

History. Chinese and Mediterranean navigators probably first used magnetic compasses to guide their ships in about the 1000's or 1100's. These compasses were simple pieces of magnetic iron, usually floated on straw or cork in a bowl of water. About the 1300's, the compass card was marked off into 32 points of direction. During the following years, navigators learned more about deviation or variation of compasses in various parts of the world, and came to use magnetic compasses with greater accuracy.

When iron and steel vessels appeared in the late 1800's, it became more difficult to make accurate readings on magnetic compasses aboard ships. As a result, the gyrocompass was developed. It is not affected by magnetism, and points toward true north. Large ships today carry both magnetic compasses and gyrocompasses. Ordinary magnetic compasses are not satisfactory in aircraft, so various gyroscopic and special magnetic compasses have been developed for use in aviation. Radio has also been used for compasses. After World War II, scientists developed special gyroscopes for compass use in the polar regions.   PAUL W. BIGELOW

Taylor Instrument Companies

A Pocket Compass can save lives. A person lost in the woods may walk in circles unless he has a compass to guide him.

COMPASS PLANT

John H. Gerard

The Yellow Flower Heads of the Compass Plant look much like sunflowers. This coarse plant sometimes grows 10 feet tall.

COMPASS PLANT is a coarse plant that grows in the Midwestern United States. It reaches a height of 10 feet, and is covered with short, rough hairs. The leaves are about 1½ feet long, and cut into several lobes. The *petioles*, or leaf stalks, bend so that the leaves usually point in a north-south direction. In this way, the leaves escape the strong midday sun, but get the full early morning and late afternoon sunlight. The compass plant is known as the *pilotweed* in some Midwestern States.

Scientific Classification. The compass plant belongs to the composite family, *Compositae*. It is genus *Silphium*, species *S. laciniatum*.   JULIAN A. STEYERMARK

COMPENSATION. See DAMAGES; UNEMPLOYMENT INSURANCE; WAGES AND HOURS; WORKMEN'S COMPENSATION.

COMPETITION, in economics. See MONOPOLY AND COMPETITION.

COMPLEMENT, in set theory. See SET THEORY (Operations with Sets).

COMPLEMENTARY COLOR. See COLOR (Color in Paint; Color in Light).

COMPLEX. See MENTAL ILLNESS (Terms; Kinds); OEDIPUS COMPLEX.

COMPOSER is a person who invents musical ideas and writes them down for others to perform. The composer is often distinguished from the improviser, who invents as he plays. Composers of popular songs and dance music are usually called *songwriters*.

Composers must study many different fields of music, such as harmony, counterpoint, form, and orchestration, in order to gain experience and develop an ear for music. They often perform, conduct, or improvise while study-

ing. But they learn most by studying other composers' scores, and through personal experience in writing music. Many composers plan musical ideas as a painter sketches a picture. Ludwig van Beethoven's notebooks show that his ideas developed and improved in this way.

Composers are the most creative of musicians, and have introduced many new techniques and styles. Composers historically important as innovators include Beethoven, Claudio Monteverdi, Joseph Haydn, Richard Wagner, Igor Stravinsky, and Arnold Schönberg. They developed new ideas that shaped the progress of music. Other composers consolidated earlier established methods, and are recognized as masters of a particular style or period. Such composers include Giovanni Palestrina, Johann Sebastian Bach, Wolfgang Amadeus Mozart, and Johannes Brahms.

Early composers usually performed their own music. Since about 1850, however, composers have specialized more, major works have grown longer, and music has become more complex. For these reasons, composers seldom perform their own music in public, but rather have it played by specially trained performers. Another reason why composers seldom perform their own works is the modern tendency for audiences and performers to show more interest in music of earlier times. When music was composed for immediate use and performers sought new scores for their audiences, the competent composer was highly respected. But, for the last 100 years, living composers have found it difficult to gain recognition for their serious works. Mechanical reproductions of music have created a large audience, but the increase has favored the composers of light music.

The adventurous composer who introduces new ideas into serious music has always had difficulty in gaining acceptance. His greatest works usually become popular only after his death. Sometimes 50 years may pass before such a composer attains recognition. GRANT FLETCHER

See also the list of biographies of composers in the Related Articles in the MUSIC article.

COMPOSERS, AUTHORS AND PUBLISHERS. See AMERICAN SOCIETY OF COMPOSERS, AUTHORS AND PUBLISHERS.

COMPOSITE FAMILY, *kum PAHZ it*, also called COMPOSITAE, is the largest and the most highly developed family of flowering plants. It consists of more than 20,000 *species* (kinds) of herbs and shrubs. Composite plants have efficient methods of reproduction. They can produce many seeds, and have good methods of scattering them.

Each flower head is a composite of many small flowers. The heads are usually made up of two kinds of flowers, the *ray* and the *disk* flowers. In the sunflower, for example, ray flowers form the yellow outer fringe of the flower head. Disk, or tubular, flowers make up the inner brown disk. The seed coverings of composite plants vary greatly. The seeds of the thistle and dandelion are tipped with feathery hairs and are carried by the wind. Other seeds have bristles, scales, or barbs, and are carried on the fur of animals.

Only a few composite plants, including endive, chicory, lettuce, and artichoke, are used as food for man. Some, such as calendula, camomile, wormwood, tansy, and arnica, are used to make drugs. Chrysanthemums, asters, and dahlias are grown for their beauty. Weeds and wild flowers of the composite family include ragweeds, goldenrod, sagebrush, thistles, and burdock.

Many flowers of the composite family have separate articles in WORLD BOOK. For a list of these flowers, see FLOWER (table, Families [Composite]).

Scientific Classification. The composite family is in the order *Campanulales*. Some classifications divide it into several families. GEORGE H. M. LAWRENCE

COMPOSITION is the expression of organized thoughts in writing. Oral composition is the expression of organized thoughts in speech. A prime method for both writing and speaking well is to strive first to speak well and then to write as you speak.

Composition of written reports or letters is one of the most important tasks in modern life. Aside from its use in business, composition is important in school, as well as in club activities, discussion groups, and similar activities of community life.

A clear, concise letter will bring a reply sooner than a "gabby" letter. Business letters deserve special attention, because there is no assurance that there will be even one interested reader. Good ones may open up limitless business opportunities for the writer.

Preparing a Composition

Choosing a Subject is difficult for some persons. Boys and girls often complain that they have nothing to speak or write about. Yet whenever two or three are in a group, tongues wag and ears open. Boys and girls also hold lengthy telephone conversations or write pages and pages of letters to friends. Their natural desire to share knowledge, ideas, and opinions with others merely needs improvement.

To write a composition, you must know what you are trying to say. Limit your topic. Don't try to solve all the problems of the universe on one sheet of paper. Don't describe all your pets or all your friends. You need not describe an entire storm to tell how you were drenched on the way home from school.

Sources. Much of what you write can come from your own knowledge and experiences. When you need more information, the encyclopedia is a good starting point. But you must often go to specialized books or to other people for specific information. You may take notes on the material in other sources. But if you copy directly, be sure to use quotation marks to indicate that these are not your own words, but the words of some other writer.

Outlining is important to the finished composition. Try to express in one sentence exactly what you hope to accomplish in your composition. Decide where and how you are going to end your composition before you begin. Select a starting point and move directly from that to the chosen ending. The route should be a straight one. The first event is followed by the second, or the cause leads directly to the result or effect. A fact may be traced backwards to its cause. A number of circumstances may be related by starting with the least important one you want to tell about, and working up to the most important.

Put the plan on paper before starting the composition. Jot ideas down as they pass through your mind. Then arrange them in the proper order and change, cross out, or add words. Make sure that you have included all the necessary steps so that your reader will understand the subject as clearly after reading your composition as you

do while writing it. Take out facts which have no relation or are loosely connected with the topic in mind. This makes for *unity*. The finished outline must hold together. This quality in any kind of a composition is called *coherence*. The plan need not be long.

Writing the composition is simpler with the outline before you. It eliminates much of the confusion over what to say and when to say it.

Writing a Composition

Effective Sentences. Make every sentence proceed naturally from the one which it follows. There should be no contradictions, no "backwater" remarks, such as: "When I saw him I was frightened; at least I felt shy." Avoid many connecting words that add little to the meaning. "The title of this book is *Tom Sawyer*. It was written by Mark Twain. It was about the Mississippi Valley" can become "*Tom Sawyer* by Mark Twain takes readers to the Mississippi Valley"—11 words instead of 20. Your sentences should bring interesting facts close together and not "string them out."

At every point you should know exactly where you are in all your material so that your readers and listeners will also know. Use such expressions as *next, afterwards, likewise, unexpectedly, as a result, meanwhile, moreover, however,* and *on the other hand* to show relations of sentences and ideas. Make your concluding sentence a carefully worded and exact one.

Expressive Words. Use words that express precisely what you intend to say. Avoid such indefinite expressions as "She had a *peculiar* kind of red dress on." What made it peculiar? Beware of exaggeration. Did the high waters sweep *everything* away? How many objects? Name some. The word to use is the word which most closely expresses the meaning or feeling intended. Sometimes the strongest word you can think of to express your meaning is the shortest one.

Do not be content with any word which does not exactly fit your need. Ask other persons. Look in books. Read the dictionary entry for the word that does not satisfy you; you may find a hint of the word you need. Use concrete and colorful words as much as you can. But beware of using words which seem out of place with the topic and the intention of your composition.

Correct Usage. A writer is not understood unless he follows the rules of spelling, capitalization, and punctuation. Every new topic means a new paragraph. The first line of the paragraph begins to the right of the regular margin to show a new section is beginning.

Testing. One of the most important tests of a good composition is in the fulfillment of the theme. Before starting to work, know what you want to accomplish in the composition. This is your *theme*. After the composition is completed, read it and then ask yourself, "Did I accomplish what I set out to do?" J. N. HOOK

Related Articles in WORLD BOOK include:

Alliteration	Hyperbole	Paragraph
Antonym	Irony	Punctuation
Capitalization	Language	Simile
Figure of Speech	Letter Writing	Spelling
Grammar	Onomatopoeia	Synonym
Heteronym	Outlines and	Vocabulary
Homonym	Outlining	Writing (career)

COMPOSITION

COMPOSITION, in the arts, has a number of special meanings. In music, it means either the act of putting notes or sounds together to form a piece, or the completed work itself. In the graphic arts, composition means setting type, either by hand or by machine. In painting and the other visual arts, composition means putting together lines, shapes, colors, light and dark areas, patterns, textures, and other elements. There are two basic approaches to composition in the visual arts—*spatial* (composition in space) and *pictorial* (composition in the work as a whole).

Spatial Composition is a way of giving depth and solidity to a work of art. A sculptor works in three dimensions—height, width, and depth—but a painter has only the flat surface of his canvas to work with. If he wants to give the impression of depth in his landscape, he must use visual tricks such as perspective to gain the effect he wants. He makes the distant objects in his scene smaller and more blurred than the objects in the foreground. He uses brighter colors and sharper lines for near objects, and duller colors in the background. He arranges the lines and planes so they seem to lead backwards toward the horizon. See PERSPECTIVE.

Pictorial Composition is a way of keeping all the elements in a painting from falling apart. If a painter is too skillful in this use of spatial composition, his work may seem more like a real scene outside a window than it will like what it is—a three-dimensional scene in two dimensions. Or, if he uses a bold pattern and emphasizes strong, bright colors, his work may seem more like the design for fabrics or wallpaper than it will like a painting. By using all elements of painting, and not just a few, a painter can create a valuable work of art.

Two of the most important modes of composition are *representation* and *design*. We often think of a painting as only a picture of something, a representation of an object or emotion. Painters often think of their works only in terms of design—balance and contrast, rhythm and repetition (see DESIGN). Many great paintings strike a balance between representation and design. They give us a picture of something we can recognize, unified and given added meaning by a rich, complex design. But not all painters have been interested in both representation and design, and most painters have been more interested in one mode than another.

See also PAINTING (How Do Painters Paint?).

COMPOSITION OF FORCES. See FORCE.

COMPOST, *KAHM post*, is a mixture of soil and partly decayed plants. It may also include commercial fertilizer and manure. Compost is used to make garden soils more fertile and improve production. It may also be spread around plants as a mulch (see MULCH).

Coffee grounds, garden-plant clippings, grass clippings, leaves, including the outer leaves of vegetables, and manure are good materials for compost. Spread them in a layer about 6 inches deep and sprinkle this with commercial fertilizer. Then cover the layer with about an inch of soil and start a new layer of compost. The mixture should be watered frequently to speed decay. Allow the compost to decay for about 6 months before using it.   WILLIAM RAYMOND KAYS

COMPOUND is a chemical combination of two or more elements. The different elements join to form compounds in much the same way that letters of the alphabet may be linked to form words. Hundreds of thousands of possible compounds can be formed from the 103 elements. The atoms of these elements combine to form molecules of a new substance, the compound. Many compounds occur in nature. Others are man-made.

The properties and appearance of a compound are usually quite different from those of the elements it contains. For example, the element sodium (Na) is a soft, shiny metal that reacts violently with water and many other substances. Another element, chlorine (Cl), is a greenish, poisonous gas. But when these two elements are combined in the proper proportions, the result is the compound sodium chloride (NaCl), or common table salt. In the same way, two gaseous elements, hydrogen and oxygen, make up water, H_2O. Sugar, $C_{12}H_{22}O_{11}$, is a white, sweet-tasting solid. But it consists of carbon, a black, tasteless solid, and hydrogen and oxygen, two colorless, odorless, tasteless gases.

A compound has a definite, unchanging composition. Water contains two atoms of hydrogen to each atom of oxygen, and it always consists of 11.19 per cent hydrogen and 88.81 per cent oxygen by weight. Pure sugar, or sucrose, always contains 42.11 per cent carbon, 6.48 per cent hydrogen, and 51.41 per cent oxygen.

A compound should not be confused with a mixture. A compound always has the same composition by weight, and its atoms are always arranged in a definite manner. A mixture, on the other hand, can be made from varying proportions of substances. Also, a compound is formed by chemical reaction, whereas a mixture is not.

When a compound is prepared, a chemical reaction always takes place. Heat, light, or electrical energy may either be used up or produced. For example, sunlight supplies the energy by which sugar or starch is made in the photosynthesis of plants. But hydrogen and oxygen combine with explosive violence to form water. Chemical reactions also occur when a compound is broken down into its original elements.

Chemists prepare some compounds by direct union of the elements. However, they usually make the desired compound from other compounds. This sometimes involves complex chemical reactions. Thousands of useful compounds are made from the hydrocarbon compounds present in petroleum and natural gas.   JAMES S. FRITZ

Related Articles. See CHEMISTRY with its list of Related Articles on specific chemical compounds. See also:

Acid	Element, Chemical	Molecule
Atom	Homolog	Radical
Base	Isomer	Salt, Chemical

COMPOUND EYE is an eye that consists of many units. Insects and crustaceans have compound eyes. See also ANT (Head); BEE (Eyes); CRUSTACEAN; EYE (Animals Without Backbones); INSECT (Senses).

COMPOUND MOTOR. See ELECTRIC MOTOR (Kinds; picture: Types of Electric Motors).

COMPRESS. See BANDAGE.

COMPRESSED AIR. See AIR (Air Compression); PNEUMATIC TOOL.

COMPRESSION. See GASOLINE ENGINE (High and Low Compression); HEAT (Sources).

COMPRESSIVE STRENGTH. See STRENGTH OF MATERIALS.

COMPRESSOR. See PUMP; JET PROPULSION (Turbojet); SUPERCHARGER; WIND TUNNEL.

COMPROMISE OF 1850 was a series of acts passed in 1850, by which the United States Congress hoped to settle the strife between opponents of slavery in the North and slaveowners of the South. These laws helped delay civil war for about 10 years.

The main problem was whether the territory the United States received as a result of the Mexican War should have slavery. To satisfy the South, the Compromise gave Texas $10 million to abandon its claims to New Mexican territory, and to set up a stricter federal law for the return of runaway slaves. To please the North, the slave trade was abolished in the District of Columbia, and California entered the Union without slavery. The territories of New Mexico and Utah were organized, but the slavery question was left to each of them to settle.

Daniel Webster, Henry Clay, and Stephen A. Douglas led in winning the passage of the Compromise laws. John C. Calhoun led the opposition. For a few years, the Compromise seemed to have ended the friction. Businessmen wanted peace so prosperity would continue. But many northerners thought the Fugitive Slave Law was too harsh, and some states interfered with its enforcement. Many slaves escaped to Canada by the *underground railroad*. Slavery did not become a major issue again until Congress passed the Kansas-Nebraska Act of 1854, making slavery legal in territories where it had been prohibited.   JOHN D. HICKS

See also FUGITIVE SLAVE LAW; KANSAS-NEBRASKA ACT; OMNIBUS BILL; UNDERGROUND RAILROAD.

COMPTON, Calif. (pop. 71,812; alt. 65 ft.), is an industrial city midway between Los Angeles and Long Beach (see CALIFORNIA [political map]). Compton has over 160 manufacturing plants. Its chief products include aircraft parts, oil-drilling tools, pipe, aluminum castings, heaters, structural steel, coffee, and roofing materials. Two railroads and an airport serve the city. Its fine school system includes Compton District Junior College and about 30 public schools. The city has three county libraries and a civic symphony orchestra.

A group of miners, unsuccessful in the California gold rush, founded Compton in 1867. One founder was Griffith Dickinson Compton. The city was rebuilt after an earthquake destroyed it in 1933. Compton has a council-manager form of government.   GEORGE SHAFTEL

COMPTON is the family name of two brothers who made important contributions to atomic science.

Karl Taylor Compton (1887-1954) made many discoveries in the field of electrical discharge in gases. He was also an administrator and a director of scientific research. He was chairman of the board that evaluated the Bikini atomic bomb tests in 1946. In 1948, Compton became head of the Research and Development Board of the National Military Establishment, which reported on countermeasures against the atomic bomb. President Harry S. Truman named him to the National Security Training Commission in 1951.

Compton was born in Wooster, Ohio, and was graduated from the College of Wooster. He taught physics and, from 1915 to 1930, headed a group of research workers in atomic physics at Princeton University. He served as president of the Massachusetts Institute of Technology from 1930 to 1948.

Arthur Holly Compton (1892-1962) headed one of the groups that produced the atomic bomb, and made important discoveries in the fields of X rays and cosmic rays. He shared the 1927 Nobel physics prize for one of his discoveries, called the *Compton effect*. His experiments with the scattering of X rays showed that these rays may behave as particles. These experiments helped to prove the quantum theory.

Compton was born in Wooster, Ohio, and was graduated from the College of Wooster. He taught physics at Washington University from 1920 to 1923 and at the University of Chicago from 1923 to 1929. He served as chancellor of Washington University from 1945 to 1953. In 1956, Compton published *Atomic Quest: A Personal Narrative*, which is an account of the World War II plutonium project.   RALPH E. LAPP

See also ATOMIC BOMB; COSMIC RAYS; PLUTONIUM; QUANTUM THEORY; X RAYS.

COMPTON-BURNETT, IVY (1892-   ), an English novelist, ranks among the most accomplished literary stylists of her time. In achieving style, she largely ignores description, plot, and exciting action. Instead, she uses highly polished dialogue to reveal the essential nature and inner thoughts of her characters. All her characters speak brilliantly—whether they are adults or children, masters or servants. Many of her books center around intricate family relationships. They are all set in the late Victorian upper-class atmosphere in which Miss Compton-Burnett was raised. *Bullivant and the Lambs* (1948), *Mother and Son* (1955), and *The Mighty and Their Fall* (1962) are typical of her many novels. Miss Compton-Burnett was born in London.   JOHN ESPEY

COMPTON EFFECT. See COMPTON (Arthur H.).

COMPTROLLER. See BANKS AND BANKING (Terms).

COMPTROLLER GENERAL OF THE UNITED STATES is one of the most important financial officers of the government. He has control and direction of the General Accounting Office, a legislative agency that checks on government spending for the Congress.

The comptroller general rules on the legality of the use of federal funds and settles claims for and against the government. His decisions are usually final, but may be reviewed by Congress or the Supreme Court.

The President appoints the comptroller general to a 15-year term. He cannot be reappointed, and only Congress can remove him from office.

Critically reviewed by the GENERAL ACCOUNTING OFFICE

See also GENERAL ACCOUNTING OFFICE.

COMPTROLLER OF THE CURRENCY is the United States government official who oversees the operations of the more than 4,800 national and District of Columbia banks. He and his staff make sure national bank laws are obeyed. They also inform the public of regulations governing bank operations. The comptroller approves all new national banks, their consolidations, and their branches. National bank examiners on his staff regularly examine the banks to determine whether they are in sound financial condition.

The comptroller's office is part of the Department of the Treasury. It was created in 1863 by the act that established the national banking system.

Critically reviewed by the OFFICE OF COMPTROLLER OF THE CURRENCY

COMPULSION. See NEUROSIS.

COMPULSORY MILITARY SERVICE. See DRAFT, MILITARY.

Computers by the Dozen fill the testing center of a computer manufacturer. Here, specialists test new *programs* (sets of instructions) which computers follow when solving problems.

COMPUTER

COMPUTER is a machine that handles information with amazing speed. It works with such information as names and addresses, book titles, lists of items sold in stores, mathematical problems, and weather forecasts. A computer handles information in the form of numbers. It solves problems dealing with words by changing them into problems dealing with numbers. The fastest computers can do millions of arithmetic problems in a few seconds.

Businessmen use computers for bookkeeping and accounting. A computer keeps track of sales, customer payments, and the amount of stock in warehouses. It figures out employees' wages and prints their paychecks. Many banks have computers to record the amount of money deposited or withdrawn by each customer. Engineers use computers to check the design of buildings, bridges, and dams. Astronauts use computers to keep their spaceships on course. Computers make the connections between telephones in some areas.

In some industries, computers control machines that make products. A computer turns the machines on and off, and adjusts their operation when necessary. Machinery controlled by computers is used in making bakery goods, chemicals, steel products, paper, and many other items. Computers also set type for printing newspapers and books. For more information on the use of computers in industry, see the article on AUTOMATION in WORLD BOOK.

Computers have been called "electronic brains." But a computer cannot think. A human operator must put *data* (facts and figures) into a computer. Then he must tell the computer what to do with the information.

Special machines are used to put information and instructions into a computer. One of the most important of these machines is similar to a tape recorder. It records information in the form of tiny magnetic spots on a plastic tape. This machine "reads" the tape and sends the information to the computer in the form of electric signals. A piece of magnetic tape about an inch long could hold the names, addresses, and telephone numbers of 15 persons.

A computer has a *memory* that stores information, and an *arithmetic* (pronounced AR ith MEHT ick) unit which performs mathematical operations. These parts of a computer contain most of the electronic equipment that makes the computer work. A computer is connected electrically with tape machines, automatic typewriters, and printing machines that record the information produced by the computer.

A computer operator sits at a desklike unit called a *console*. On parts of the console are tiny lights that flash when the computer is operating. These lights tell what operation the computer is performing at any moment. A computer works noiselessly most of the time. But when the high-speed printing machines operate, they sound almost like machine guns. Some of these printers can print enough information in one minute to fill four pages of a telephone directory.

Most computers that can do many kinds of jobs fill a large room with all the necessary equipment. Computers that do only special jobs, such as helping to guide space vehicles, may be as small as table radios.

Evan F. Linick, the contributor of this article, is Manager, Research and Development for the Software Resources Corporation.

Computers may be classified according to the jobs they can do. A *general purpose computer* can perform many kinds of jobs. General purpose computers may be used in banks, department stores, libraries, or schools. A *special purpose computer* is designed for just one job, such as helping to guide a space vehicle.

Computers also may be classified into two types according to the way they work. These types are: (1) *digital computers* and (2) *analog computers*. Each type operates in a different way. The operation of these computers is explained in the following two sections.

Digital Computers solve problems by counting *digits* (numbers). These machines can add, subtract, multiply, and divide. Electronic digital computers differ from adding machines and other ordinary figuring machines because they can automatically do many problems, one after the other. For example, a computer may first add two numbers, then subtract a third number from the sum of the first two, and finally multiply the result by a fourth number—all in one continuous operation. A digital computer also can compare two numbers to find if both are equal or if one is larger than the other.

Before a digital computer can solve any problem, it must be given two kinds of information. First, it must have all the numbers to be used in solving the problem. Second, the computer must have a set of instructions, called a *program*, that tell it what to do with the numbers. The numbers and the instructions are stored in the memory of the computer.

A human operator puts the necessary numbers and the program into the computer. The machine then performs a series of operations with the numbers, according to the instructions of the program.

Most digital computers are general purpose computers. Manufacturers produce a variety of standard models, each of which can do many basic jobs in almost any business or industry. These computers are so widely used that the word *computer*, when used alone, usually means a general purpose, digital computer.

The rest of this article, except for the following section on analog computers, describes the parts and operation of general purpose, digital computers.

Analog Computers solve problems by measuring one quantity in terms of some other quantity. Most well-known instruments operate on this principle. For example, a thermometer measures temperature in terms of the length of a thin line of liquid in a glass tube. The longer the line, the higher the temperature. An automobile speedometer measures speed by means of a pointer moving across a dial. The faster the car is going, the farther the pointer moves. An analog computer might use electrical hookups to represent the speed and direction of an airplane, and to measure the effect of wind on the plane. The computer's electrical hookups act as an *analogy* (likeness) of the flying airplane. The analogy gives an analog computer its name.

Crewmen learning to pilot airplanes or spacecraft are trained in machines controlled by analog computers. Guided by a computer, a training machine duplicates situations that might occur on a real flight.

Quantities such as electrical voltage cannot be measured exactly. As a result, analog computers are not so exact as digital computers, which work with numbers digit by digit. Most analog computers are special purpose computers. They may solve their special problems faster than a digital computer could.

SIMPLE DIGITAL COMPUTERS

Digital computers solve problems by counting, just as a person does when he counts on his fingers. A cash register is a mechanical digital computer. It contains wheels that turn to certain positions to represent numbers. The register adds by counting the turns that the wheels make.

SIMPLE ANALOG COMPUTERS

Analog computers measure one quantity in terms of another quantity. A thermometer indicates temperature in terms of the length of a thin line of liquid. The line gets longer as the temperature rises. A bathroom scale indicates weight by the distance a dial moves.

A general purpose, digital computer consists of five main parts. Each part does a special job. (1) *Input equipment* sends data and instructions into the memory. (2) The *memory* stores data and instructions until they are needed. (3) The *control unit* gets instructions from the memory and tells the arithmetic unit what to do with the data. (4) The *arithmetic unit* gets data from the memory and performs the operations ordered by the control unit. (5) *Output equipment* records the desired information and delivers it from the computer.

Input Equipment works with punched cards, magnetic ink records, magnetic tape, and other kinds of records that contain data and instructions.

Punched cards carry information in the form of patterns of holes. Operators put the holes in the cards with *key punch* machines similar to typewriters. A common type of card has room for holes that represent 80 letters or numbers and other symbols.

Machines called *card readers* take information from the punched cards. These machines can "read" more than a thousand cards a minute. They put the information from each card into the form of electric signals. The signals are sent to the computer's memory. Then they are usually recorded on magnetic tape for storage.

Magnetic ink records consist of information printed with magnetic ink on checks or other documents. Magnetic ink looks like ordinary printing ink, but it contains a metal powder that can be magnetized. When magnetized, numbers printed with this ink can be read by a machine. This machine produces electric signals that carry data into the computer's memory.

Magnetic tape used in computers is similar to that used in tape recorders. Computer tape carries information in the form of small magnetic spots. Spots representing more than a thousand letters and numbers can be recorded on one inch of tape. Machines called *tape units* put data and instructions on the tape. These machines get the information from punched cards and other input records. Tape units also are used to read information from magnetic tape and send it into the memory.

Other input equipment includes machines that handle *punched paper tape*, and automatic readers called *optical scanners*. Punched paper tape carries information in the form of patterns of holes, as do punched cards. Optical scanners work somewhat like the human eye. They "look" at printed records and produce electric signals that represent the information. The signals may then be recorded on magnetic tape.

Some input machines put magnetic spots on cards, cylinders, or disks. Such machines can "find" information stored in them faster than a magnetic tape unit can. A tape machine must read a whole reel of tape to find information stored near the end of the tape. A disk type storage unit contains many disks. To find a particular piece of information, the machine selects and reads a single disk. One disk holds much less data than a reel of tape, so desired information can be found faster.

Memory receives information from input machines and holds it until needed by other parts of the computer. One kind of memory consists mainly of thousands of small rings called *cores*. Each core can be magnetized in either a clockwise or counterclockwise direction.

Operator's Console, *above,* keeps track of the basic operations performed by the computer equipment shown on these pages.

Input. Just as a bookkeeper reads a check, *above,* to put information into his head, a tape unit, *below,* reads magnetic tape to put information into a computer. The bottom photo shows the part of the machine that reads the tape.

When magnetized one way, a core stands for a 1. When magnetized the opposite way, it stands for a 0. The memory "remembers" any number by magnetizing a group of cores in a certain combination of 1's and 0's. This method of using 1's and 0's to represent any number is called the *binary numeration system* (see NUMERATION SYSTEMS [The Binary System]). The memory also remembers words by substituting numbers for letters.

A single memory core can store one *binary digit* (a 1 or a 0), also called a *bit*. Many cores are needed to represent most numbers or words. The memory is divided into sections with a certain number of cores. A number called an *address* identifies each section so that the computer can find stored information when it is needed.

Control Unit guides the computer in performing operations with stored data. This unit selects *instructions* from the memory. An instruction consists of a series of numbers. It includes a code number that tells what operation is to be performed, such as addition or subtraction. The instruction also includes addresses that tell where data for the operation are stored in the memory. After the control unit selects an instruction, it commands the arithmetic unit to perform the proper operation. Then it selects another instruction and gives

Memory. A bookkeeper stores data in an account book, *above*. Similarly, a computer stores data in its memory, *below*. Rings in the memory, *bottom*, are magnetized to represent numbers.

Processing. A bookkeeper uses a calculator, *above*, to do mathematical operations. A computer's arithmetic unit, *below*, performs similar operations with data stored in its memory. Thousands of electronic circuits, *bottom*, do the job.

Output. A bookkeeper writes his answers in an account book, *above*. A computer may print its data on a long sheet, *below*. A row of printing wheels, *bottom*, prints a line at a time.
WORLD BOOK photos by Edward F. Hoppe

Esso

the arithmetic unit another command. The control unit repeats these operations until the job is finished.

Arithmetic Unit gets data from the memory. It stores the data temporarily in its own storage devices, called *registers*. The registers connect with electronic circuits that perform mathematical operations according to commands from the control unit. After an operation has been completed, the answer appears as new data in the registers. The answer is transferred to the memory for storage until it is needed for another operation or is sent to output equipment.

Output Equipment includes card and tape punches, magnetic tape units, automatic typewriters, high-speed printers, and other machines that display information.

Card and tape punches put information on punched cards and punched paper tape. Magnetic tape units record data on magnetic tape. Output information is put on punched cards, paper tape, and magnetic tape so it can be put back into the computer easily when needed. Generally, automatic typewriters are used to print only small amounts of information because they can type only one character at a time. High-speed printers can print a whole line of more than 100 letters and numbers at a time, and 1,000 lines a minute. High-speed printers record information on a continuous, folding sheet of paper that may be 100 feet long.

Other output devices include instruments that display information in the form of graphs, and machines that produce engineering drawings based on computer data. Some output equipment shows information on a screen similar to a television screen. A computer's output may be sent over telephone lines, or by radio signals, to equipment thousands of miles from the computer.

COMPUTER / Programming a Computer

A computer by itself cannot solve any problem. A computer specialist called a *programmer* must tell the machine exactly what to do. He writes a set of instructions called a *program* that tells the computer what data to use and what operations to perform with the data. Preparing these instructions is called *programming*.

Most programs are so long and complicated that even an experienced programmer can make mistakes when writing them. He checks his program carefully and then tests it on the computer. If the computer does not work properly, the programmer must find his mistakes and correct them. Programmers refer to mistakes as "bugs," and call the testing procedure "debugging."

Planning a Program begins with a detailed description of the job the computer is to do. The programmer might get the job description from scientists and engineers who want to solve mathematical problems. Or he may get it from *systems analysts* (experts who plan information handling systems). The job description tells what input information is necessary, what processing must be done, and what the output should be.

A programmer or a systems analyst uses the job description to prepare a diagram that shows how all the parts of the job fit together systematically. This diagram is called a *systems flow chart*. The chart maker uses symbols to stand for punched cards, magnetic tapes, reports produced by output equipment, and other records and operations. He connects these symbols with lines to show how information will flow from input equipment, through the computer, to output equipment.

The systems flow chart helps the programmer prepare another diagram called an *operations flow chart*. In this chart, he breaks the job down into detailed steps that show the exact operations the computer must perform.

Writing a Program. The operations flow chart helps the programmer write the instructions that make up the program. The programmer writes the instructions on special forms called *coding sheets*. For most jobs, key punch operators then put the instructions on punched cards. Machines read the cards and send the program to tape units that record it on magnetic tape.

The programmer writes the program in a "language" consisting of certain words and symbols. The language he uses depends on the particular computer he is working with and on the job to be done. Computer languages include COBOL (COmmon Business Oriented Language), used in processing business data, and FORTRAN (FORmula TRANslation), used in solving problems of algebra. COBOL and FORTRAN are called *compiler languages*. They allow the programmer to write instructions using simple, common expressions.

Suppose that a computer is to update customers' accounts by subtracting a *credit* (amount of a payment) from the total amount each customer owes. The COBOL instruction for this operation would be:

SUBTRACT CREDIT FROM TOTAL

Programmers also use another kind of language called an *assembly language*. Assembly languages are somewhat harder to use than compiler languages because they involve symbols as well as words. The instruction above, when written in an assembly language, might be:

S CREDIT, TOTAL

The symbol *s* stands for *subtract*. The words *credit* and *total* represent addresses that tell where data for the operation are stored in the memory.

The computer cannot work directly with instructions written in compiler or assembly languages. The instructions must be translated into a *machine language* consisting of binary digits. Here is how the above instruction might appear in machine language:

011111   011110100010   000000101110

The first group of digits is an operation code meaning *subtract*. The next two groups are addresses of numbers stored in the memory. To perform the operation, the computer subtracts the number stored in the first address from the number stored in the second address.

Computer operators do not have to translate compiler and assembly languages into machine language. The computer does the translation itself. It usually records the program in machine language on magnetic tape. When the job is to be performed, the computer reads the tape and stores the program in its memory, along with other input information.

HOW A COMPUTER HANDLES CHECKING ACCOUNTS

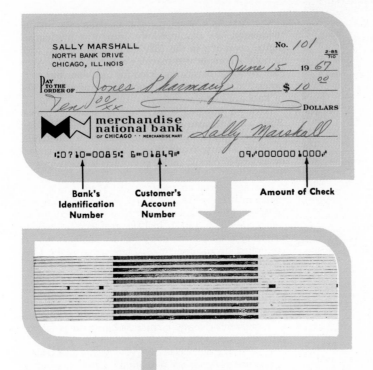

SALLY MARSHALL
NORTH BANK DRIVE
CHICAGO, ILLINOIS

No. *101*

2-85
710

June 15 19 67

PAY TO THE ORDER OF *Jones Pharmacy* $ *10 00*

Ten 00/xx DOLLARS

merchandise
national bank
OF CHICAGO · · MERCHANDISE MART

Sally Marshall

⑆0710⑆0085⑆ 6⑈01849⑈ 09⑆000000 1000⑆

Bank's Identification Number

Customer's Account Number

Amount of Check

A Personal Check, *left,* has numbers printed in magnetic ink in the lower left-hand corner. These numbers identify the check writer's bank and account. After a check has been cashed, it goes to the bank, where a clerk uses a machine to add in magnetic ink the amount written on the check. These numbers go in the lower right-hand corner. Numbers printed in magnetic ink can be read by another machine at the bank. It reads thousands of checks and records the numbers on computer tape.

Computer Tape carries information in the form of invisible magnetic spots. If these spots could be seen, they would appear as shown, *left.* This section of tape, shown actual size, holds information from more than 25 checks.

WORLD BOOK photo

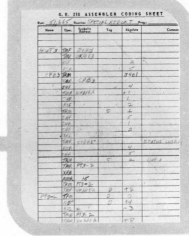

The Bank's Computer, *left,* reads the tape and subtracts the amounts of cashed checks from the customer's account. A computer program, *right,* guides the computer and tells what information must be printed in bank reports and statements.

Reports and Statements are printed by the computer. A daily report, *below left,* lists the checks handled for each account. A customer's monthly statement, *below right,* lists checks, deposits, and the amount remaining in the account.

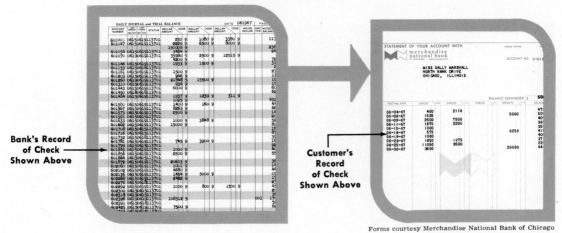

Bank's Record of Check Shown Above

Customer's Record of Check Shown Above

Forms courtesy Merchandise National Bank of Chicago

COMPUTER / History

University of Pennsylvania

ENIAC, the first electronic digital computer, began operating in 1946. The U.S. Army Ordnance Corps used it to solve artillery problems. This computer contained about 18,000 vacuum tubes.

Autonetics

A Miniature Electronic Circuit, *above,* is tinier than a dime, but contains as many parts as a six-transistor radio. Such circuits power the shoebox-size computer of a guided missile.

Computerized Drawing Board, *below,* displays drawings stored in its memory. A designer can change any part of a drawing by touching the screen with a pointer and pressing a button.

General Motors Corp.

The First Computers. Charles Babbage, an English mathematician, developed the idea of a mechanical digital computer in the 1830's. He designed and tried to build a complicated machine called an *analytical engine.* Babbage never completed his machine. But computers today are based on many of the principles used in Babbage's design.

About a hundred years later, in 1930, Vannevar Bush, an American electrical engineer, built the first analog computer. He called his machine a differential analyzer. During World War II (1939-1945), engineers developed electronic analog computers to help aim anti-aircraft guns.

The first digital computer, called Mark I, was completed in 1944 by Howard Aiken, a Harvard University professor. Mechanical and electrical devices controlled the operation of Mark I. In 1946, engineers at the University of Pennsylvania built the first digital computer controlled by vacuum tubes. They called it the Electronic Numerical Integrator and Computer (ENIAC).

Perhaps the most important computer advancement during the 1940's was the work of John von Neumann, an American mathematician. Von Neumann developed the idea of storing the computer program in the machine's memory. Early computers had used programs, but did not store them in their memories.

In 1951, the builders of ENIAC developed UNIVAC I, the first of a variety of computers that were mass-produced during the 1950's. The manufacture of computers had become an industry.

Three Generations of Computers. Computer manufacturers speak of "generations" of computers. The computers of the 1950's made up the first generation. These machines could perform thousands of calculations a second. Vacuum tubes controlled the electronic circuits of first generation computers.

Second generation computers were developed in the early 1960's. These computers could perform 10 times as many calculations a second as first generation machines. The use of *transistors* (tiny amplifiers) instead of vacuum tubes made second generation computers smaller and more dependable than the earlier machines.

In 1965, manufacturers announced the production of third generation computers. These machines could do a million calculations a second—100 times as many as second generation machines. Third generation computers had miniature electronic circuits that greatly reduced their size and increased their dependability.

Computers of the Future will be used more and more to give immediate answers to problems. Persons already can get certain kinds of information from a computer by speaking into a telephone and receiving a spoken reply. Other systems include computers that make telephone calls to other computers and exchange data with them. Someday, the services of single computers will be shared by businessmen, engineers, and scientists. Each "customer" will communicate directly with the computer by telephone or by means of a keyboard machine similar to a typewriter. The computer will handle many questions at the same time. It will give each questioner a spoken reply, a typed answer, or information projected on a screen similar to that of a television set.

COMPUTER/*Careers*

The development of computers has created career opportunities in such fields as automation, electronic data processing, and systems analysis. These fields deal with general principles of information handling and management that apply to all businesses. Computer specialists use their skills wherever computers help do a job. These experts can choose from an almost unlimited variety of jobs in education, government, industry, or science.

A computer specialist is basically a problem solver. He must have imagination so he can visualize difficult situations and find solutions to problems. He also should be creative so he can suggest new ideas and new ways of doing things.

Above all, a computer expert needs training. This training may begin with a high school course in computer programming or with similar introductory courses. It should include at least a strong background in high school mathematics.

A college degree is desirable for almost every job in the computer field. College students may take courses in computer programming, computer languages, data processing, and systems analysis. At a university, these courses may be offered by the department of computer science, or by the departments of business, engineering, or mathematics. Many engineering schools include computer programming as a standard part of second- or third-year studies. A computer specialist may spend several months in on-the-job training to complete the preparation for his particular job.

Jobs associated with computers include: (1) computer operator, (2) computer programmer, (3) design engineer, (4) service engineer, and (5) systems analyst.

Computer Operator controls the computer and its input and output equipment. He works at a control unit called a *console*. The computer operator takes care of data files and computer programs stored on punched cards or magnetic tape. He keeps records telling what jobs the computer does and how long each job takes. The operator also may schedule new jobs.

Computer Programmer writes the instructions that the computer follows in doing a particular job. For a detailed description of the programmer's job, see the section on *Programming a Computer* in this article.

Design Engineer works on the research and development of computers and of their input and output equipment. He tries to design new machines that are faster and smaller than existing machines, but able to do even more work. He also tries to improve machines to make them easier for programmers and operators to use. The job of computer design engineer requires at least a bachelor's degree in a field such as electronics. Many design engineers have master's or doctor's degrees.

Service Engineer keeps computers in working order. Most service engineers are employed by computer manufacturers to work with their customers.

Systems Analyst determines how a computer will fit into the overall picture of the people and machines that do a particular job. He must know everything about the job and about the equipment that is to do the job. The systems analyst not only serves the persons who want a job done, but also helps the programmers and operator who actually do it. EVAN F. LINICK

National Science Teachers Assoc.

High School Programmers use their school's computer to "debug" one of their own programs. Many high schools offer courses in electronic data processing and in programming.

COMPUTER/*Study Aids*

Outline

I. **Kinds of Computers**
   A. Digital Computers   B. Analog Computers
II. **Parts of a Digital Computer**
   A. Input Equipment   D. Arithmetic Unit
   B. Memory   E. Output Equipment
   C. Control Unit
III. **Programming a Computer**
   A. Planning a Program   B. Writing a Program
IV. **History**
V. **Careers**
   A. Computer Operator   D. Service Engineer
   B. Computer Programmer E. Systems Analyst
   C. Design Engineer

Questions

What is a computer *program?*

How do computer memory rings store information?

What common computer language is used in processing business data?

How do analog computers represent numbers?

How do electronic digital computers differ from adding machines and other figuring machines?

What information does each instruction of a computer program include?

What is "debugging"? Who performs this job?

How do *compiler languages* such as COBOL and FORTRAN differ from *machine language?*

How did second generation computers differ from first generation computers?

What are the main parts of a general purpose, digital computer?

COMPUTER-ASSISTED INSTRUCTION. See EDUCATIONAL PSYCHOLOGY.

COMSAT. See COMMUNICATIONS SATELLITE CORPORATION.

COMSTOCK LODE consisted of several immensely rich veins of silver and gold in Nevada. One part alone produced nearly $200 million worth of ore. Ethan and Hosea Grosh of Pennsylvania discovered silver near the site in 1856, but died before developing their claim. The claim was rediscovered in 1859, and a great stampede began. The lode took its name from Henry J. P. Comstock, one of the 1859 claimants. Virginia City, Nev., grew up on the site of the lode.   WALKER D. WYMAN

See also NEVADA (The Comstock Lode).

COMTE. See COUNT.

COMTE, *kawnt,* **AUGUSTE** (1798-1857), was a French social thinker and philosopher. He founded the philosophy known as *positivism,* and originated a concept of social science which he called sociology.

Comte sought to discover the laws that he believed governed the evolution of the mind. In his book, *The Course of Positive Philosophy* (1830-1842), he framed his "law of the three states." This law advanced the idea that men try to understand phenomena in three ways. Comte believed that men first seek a *theological* (supernatural) explanation; then a *metaphysical* (abstract) explanation; and finally a *positive* explanation. The positive explanation is derived from an objective examination of the phenomena themselves. Comte believed that students should concern themselves only with phenomena that have an objective, "positive," existence. This belief forms a basis of positivism.

Comte regarded all social thought as an interrelated whole, the laws of which can be found by assembling what he considered the facts. His ideas have influenced students of historical and social theory, and of criminology, and such authors as Herbert Spencer and John Stuart Mill, who were seeking a "science of society." Comte was born at Montpellier.   E. J. KNAPTON

See also SOCIOLOGY (Beginnings).

COMUS was the god of mirth in Greek mythology. He was the friend of Dionysus (Bacchus) and the satyrs.

CONACHER, LIONEL, CHARLIE, and **ROY.** See HOCKEY (Famous Hockey Players).

CONAKRY, *KAHN uh kree* (pop. 43,000; met. area 109,000; alt. 75 ft.), is the capital, chief seaport, and commercial center of Guinea. It lies on Tombo Island (see GUINEA [map]). A bridge connects it with the mainland. The chief exports of Conakry include bananas and palm kernels.   ALAN P. MERRIAM

James Bryant Conant
Wide World

CONANT, JAMES BRYANT (1893-   ), is an American scientist, educator, and diplomat. As a professor of organic chemistry at Harvard University, he helped unravel the mysteries of such molecules as *chlorophyll* (green coloring matter in plants) and *hemoglobin* (red coloring matter in blood). From 1930 to 1949, he served on the Board of Scientific Directors of the Rockefeller

Institute. During World War II, he was chairman of the National Defense Research Committee. He served as president of Harvard University from 1933 to 1953. He served as ambassador to West Germany from 1955 to 1957. He later made studies of schools and teacher education for the Carnegie Foundation. In 1963, he became chief educational consultant in Europe for the Ford Foundation. Conant's books on chemistry and on his philosophy of education have had wide influence. They include *The American High School Today* (1959) and *The Education of American Teachers* (1963). Conant was born in Dorchester, Mass.   HERBERT S. RHINESMITH

CONCENTRATION CAMP is a place where political enemies, real or assumed, are imprisoned, usually without trial. The term was first used by Great Britain for prison camps it set up during the Boer War in Africa around 1900. Russian secret police imprisoned millions of persons in labor camps after 1928, during Joseph Stalin's dictatorship. During World War II, the United States and Canada held thousands of persons of Japanese ancestry in special camps (see WORLD WAR II [Internment of Aliens]). But the best known concentration camps were those set up in Nazi Germany before and during World War II.

After the Nazis came to power in 1933, they used concentration camps to imprison political enemies and to terrorize the German people. Most early prisoners were

The Nazi Concentration Camp at Auschwitz, Poland, opened in 1940. About 2½ million persons were executed there during World War II.

Elliott Erwitt, Magnum

Communists and other political opponents. Many, however, were Jews arrested on false charges. Prisoners were almost always treated brutally, and many of them died. By 1939, the Nazis had six camps, including those at Dachau and Buchenwald.

When World War II began, the number of camps quickly increased to 22. They were filled with persons of all European nationalities, and included prisoners of war as well as civilians. An estimated 7 to 8 million persons were imprisoned by the Nazis between 1933 and 1945. Some prisoners were sent to manufacturing plants to work. Others were forced to perform dangerous or degrading tasks in the camps or other places.

In 1942, the Nazis decided to rid Europe of all Jews. By the war's end, they had murdered about 6 million. At first, they used firing squads. Later, they used special gas chambers to kill large groups of victims at a time with poison gas. Others died as the result of experiments performed on them by doctors and scientists. About $2\frac{1}{2}$ million persons were executed at Auschwitz, an extermination camp in Poland. Many others died, chiefly of starvation, at Buchenwald, in Germany.

Allied forces reached the camps in 1945. They found thousands of unburied dead, and survivors who were crippled, insane, or dying of disease or starvation. During the Nuremberg Trials after the war, many Nazi leaders were convicted of crimes against humanity. Some were executed. GEORGE G. WINDELL

See also AUSCHWITZ; BELSEN; BUCHENWALD; DACHAU.

CONCEPCIÓN, *cone sehp SYOHN* (pop. 187,251; alt. 75 ft.), Chile's third largest city, is on the banks of the Bío-Bío River, six miles from the Pacific Ocean (see CHILE [color map]). A railroad connects Concepción with its port, Talcahuano, nine miles away. The city is a shipping and processing center for farm products.

CONCEPT, *KAHN sept,* is a person's idea of a class of objects, such as *cat, horse,* and *house,* or of ideas, such as *democracy, love, liberty,* or *God.* A concept is a consciousness of those qualities that make an object or idea what it is or appears to be. Much of philosophy consists of man's attempts to define concepts. All nouns are man-made concepts.

A person may form concepts as the result of such things as observation, reading, or personal experience. A child may get his first idea of what cats are like by observing the size, color, and other features of his own pet kitten. When he sees another cat, he reconstructs his idea to leave out those qualities not common to both cats. After he has seen many cats, he learns that all cats have certain common features. He blends these features into his *concept* (general idea) of *cat.*

A person can form concepts without having any direct experience with what the concepts stand for. Such concepts may be learned from other persons or from reading. Most Americans form their ideas of such concepts as *Communism* or *Hinduism* in this way.

The meaning given to a concept may be different among various groups of people. The meanings of *socialism* or *morality,* for example, differ widely because persons in various parts of the world associate different aspects of human behavior with these concepts. Generally, persons who have common experiences and common purposes in developing a concept assign about the same meaning to the concept. Scientists have tried to standardize the meanings of concepts in science.

But even these meanings change as new knowledge is obtained. For example, the concepts of *relativity* and *atom* have changed radically. HADLEY CANTRIL

See also THOUGHT AND JUDGMENT (Concept Attainment).

CONCEPTUS. See EMBRYO (Fertilization).

CONCERT is a performance of music before an audience. Originally, amateur groups performed music in private homes (see CHAMBER MUSIC). But noblemen hired such composers as Bach, Handel, and Mozart to write and perform for them. These men were known in their time as performers, but we remember them as composers. Great performers such as Frédéric Chopin, Franz Liszt, and Niccolò Paganini drew large audiences to their concerts. Paying to attend public concerts became common in the 1800's. Artists also began giving *recitals* (solo concerts) then. GRANT FLETCHER

CONCERTINA, *KAHN sur TEE nuh,* is a musical instrument in which metal reeds are made to vibrate by air pressure produced by means of a bellows. The player

David Wexler & Co.

The Concertina is more popular in Europe than in the United States. It produces a sound somewhat like that of an accordion.

presses small keys or plugs in the end plates of the instrument. These keys open valves that control the reeds. The treble concertina used the most is a small, six-sided instrument with a range of about $3\frac{1}{2}$ octaves. There are also tenor, bass, and contrabass concertinas. Charles Wheatstone patented the concertina in 1829. See also WHEATSTONE, SIR CHARLES. CHARLES B. RIGHTER

CONCERTO, *kohn CHEHR toh,* is a musical composition in which a solo instrument, such as a violin, plays with orchestral accompaniment. A concerto usually has three movements, and resembles the sonata in form (see SONATA). Concertos may be written for more than one soloist. Beethoven wrote a triple concerto for piano, violin, violoncello, and orchestra. RAYMOND KENDALL

CONCH, *kahngk,* is a large, heavy sea snail with a spiral shell. The name *conch* comes from a Greek word meaning *shell.* Conchs live in the world's shallow seas.

Conch shells have many uses. They can be ground up to make *porcelain* (china), or burned to make lime. Some conch shells are used to make buttons and cameos. The shell of an East Indian species, the *Triton's trumpet,* is used as a horn. The egg cases of certain conchs look like leathery wafers strung on a cord. These strings of egg cases are called *sea necklaces.* The meat of

American Museum of Natural History

The Conch has a meaty body that can move in and out of the spiral shell. The animal uses a claw on its body to move about.

the pink conch of the West Indies is used to make chowder or salad.

Scientific Classification. Conchs are in the phylum *Mollusca* and the class *Gastropoda*.   R. TUCKER ABBOTT

See also MOLLUSK; SHELL (color picture).

CONCHOLOGY. See SHELL (Collecting Shells).

CONCILIATION is a method of settling conflicts between two parties peacefully. Conciliation involves the efforts of a third party. If the opposing parties agree to the procedure, the third party tries to arrange a compromise. A third party may be another state or an international organization. Conciliation is an important function of the United Nations. Sometimes conciliation succeeds only in stopping hostilities between belligerents, as in the case of the Arab-Israeli conflict. *Mediation* and *good offices* are similar procedures in which a third party tries to help settle a dispute.   WILLIAM T. R. FOX

See also UNITED NATIONS (Achievements and Problems).

CONCLAVE, *KAHN klayv*, is the assembly and place of meeting of the cardinals of the Roman Catholic Church for the election of a pope. The word in French or Latin means a *room which may be locked*. In a wider sense, it also refers to any private meeting. Long ago the clergy and the people chose the popes, but often amid great confusion. The present method dates back to 1274. Soon after the death of a pope, the cardinals meet in the city in which he died. The public may view the meeting place on the first day. Thereafter the cardinals are locked in and allowed no communication with the outer world until after the election.   FULTON J. SHEEN

See also CARDINAL; POPE; SACRED COLLEGE.

CONCORD, Mass. (pop. 3,188; alt. 130 ft.), is an attractive residential town noted for its historic and literary attractions. Boston lies 19 miles to the southeast. For location, see MASSACHUSETTS (political map).

Concord's largest industries engage in the manufacture of electronic test equipment and in metallurgical research. The Concord grape originated in Concord.

A group of Puritans founded Concord in 1635. Concord became a center of pre-Revolutionary War activity and a storage area for military supplies. Minutemen

from the surrounding countryside rallied to oppose British forces searching for these supplies. In the fight at North Bridge on Apr. 19, 1775, the patriots resisted the British advance, and finally forced their retreat to Boston. Today, a replica of the bridge and a statue of a minuteman by Daniel Chester French mark the battleground. See MINUTEMAN (pictures).

Concord was the center of American writing in the mid-1800's. Bronson Alcott, Louisa May Alcott, Ralph Waldo Emerson, Nathaniel Hawthorne, Henry Thoreau, and Margaret Sidney lived and wrote there. Visitors are welcome at Emerson House; at the Old Manse of Hawthorne and Emerson; at Orchard House, where Louisa May Alcott wrote most of *Little Women;* at The Wayside, where Hawthorne lived, and Margaret Sidney wrote *The Five Little Peppers;* and at the Antiquarian Museum, which has antiques of famous persons. Nearby are Thoreau's Walden Pond, and Sleepy Hollow Cemetery, where most of the writers who lived in Concord are buried. Concord is governed by a town meeting and town manager.   WILLIAM J. REID

CONCORD, N.H. (pop. 28,991; alt. 290 ft.), is the capital and third largest city in the state. It is located on the Merrimack River in south-central New Hampshire (see NEW HAMPSHIRE [political map]). Called Penacook when it was founded in 1727, it took the name Rumford in 1733, and assumed its present name in 1765. Concord became the state capital in 1808.

The chief economic activities of Concord center around granite quarries, printing plants, and factories that make electronics products, leather belting, and wood products. Concord is a major retail trade center. Concord has about 20 public schools, the state historical society, and state and city libraries. The last home of President Franklin Pierce stands in Concord. The city has a mayor-council government.   J. DUANE SQUIRES

For the monthly weather in Concord, see NEW HAMPSHIRE (Climate). See also NEW HAMPSHIRE (color picture: State Capitol).

CONCORD, BATTLE OF, on April 19, 1775, marked the second clash between the patriots and the British in the Revolutionary War in America. The opening battle of the war had been fought at nearby Lexington, Mass. During the previous winter, the Americans had gathered

The Old Manse in Concord, Mass., served as the setting for Nathaniel Hawthorne's book, *Mosses from an Old Manse.*

Keith Martin

Culver

Patriots at the Battle of Concord defended "the rude bridge that arched the flood" against a force of British regulars who marched from Boston to destroy an American store of arms.

military supplies in case of war. The British government ordered its commander in chief in Boston, Lieutenant General Thomas Gage, to destroy the supplies at Concord. On the night of April 18, Gage sent 700 troops under Lieutenant Colonel Francis Smith to carry out this command. But Paul Revere and William Dawes warned the countryside that the British were coming.

After a clash at Lexington early the next morning, the British continued on to Concord, six miles beyond. They destroyed the patriots' supplies, then headed back toward Boston. Hundreds of Americans had gathered at Concord, and fired at the British from all sides. Smith's men eventually reached Charlestown, near Boston. The British suffered 273 casualties. The Americans had 95 casualties in the two battles at Lexington and Concord.   MERRILL JENSEN

See also REVOLUTIONARY WAR IN AMERICA (picture).

CONCORD COLLEGE. See UNIVERSITIES AND COLLEGES (table).

CONCORDAT, *kahn KAWR dat,* is an agreement, especially one between the pope and a civil government, to regulate the affairs of the Roman Catholic Church within that state.

A concordat may be announced by a decree from the pope, called a *papal bull,* or by a formal treaty. Pope Pius XI made an important concordat with the Italian government in 1929. It regulated ecclesiastical affairs with Italy.   FULTON J. SHEEN

See also PAPAL STATES; POPE; TREATY.

CONCORDAT OF WORMS. See ROMAN CATHOLIC CHURCH (History).

CONCORDIA COLLEGE. See UNIVERSITIES AND COLLEGES (table).

CONCORDIA SENIOR COLLEGE. See UNIVERSITIES AND COLLEGES (table).

CONCORDIA TEACHERS COLLEGE. See UNIVERSITIES AND COLLEGES (table).

CONCRETE. See CEMENT AND CONCRETE.

CONCRETION is a mass of minerals that have become cemented together to form a deposit in sedimentary rock. Concretions are formed in various sizes. They range from a fraction of an inch to several feet.

CONCURRENT FORCES. See MOTION (Newton's Laws).

CONCUSSION is a condition that results from a violent blow or shock. For example, when a person receives a violent blow on the head, concussion of the brain may result. The blow interferes with the normal function of the brain. The person becomes dizzy and nauseated, and usually loses consciousness.

CONDE. See COUNT.

CONDEMNATION OF REAL PROPERTY. See EMINENT DOMAIN.

CONDENSATION, *kahn den SAY shun,* is the process by which a substance changes from a gas into a liquid. Condensation of a gas to a liquid takes place when the temperature of the gas is lowered below its boiling point. When the temperature of steam drops below 100° C., the steam changes into droplets of water. Some gases condense so easily that either cooling them or increasing the pressure will change them into their liquid state. Other gases condense at such low temperatures that they require both cooling and high pressure to change them to a liquid state. Every known gas can be condensed into liquid form.

Helium is the most difficult to condense. Its boiling point is −268.9° C. Air, under high pressure, begins to condense at −140° C. Under certain conditions, a gas may condense directly to the solid form. A familiar example of this is the formation of snow crystals from the water vapor in the atmosphere. Snow crystals form when the temperature of the atmosphere is below the freezing point.   LOUIS MARICK

See also DEW; DISTILLATION; GAS (matter); LIQUID.

CONDENSED MILK is a form of canned concentrated milk. It is made by evaporating about 60 per cent of the water from fresh whole milk or skim milk. Condensed milk was invented by Gail Borden. He received a patent in 1856 for the commercial manufacture of condensed milk. Evaporated milk, which has no added sugar, has largely replaced condensed milk (see EVAPORATED MILK).   GLENN H. BECK

CONDENSER, sometimes called a *capacitor,* is an apparatus that stores electricity. The term *condenser* is also used for an apparatus that changes gas or vapor, such as steam, into liquid (see CONDENSER, STEAM). The electric condenser consists of two conductors of

The Leyden Jar is an old type of electrical condenser. A spark will flash between these two Leyden jars when they have been charged enough to overcome the air's resistance.

W. M. Welch Mfg. Co.

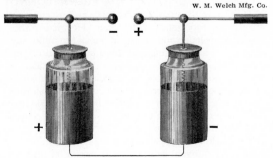

electricity, separated by a nonconductor. The simplest form of electric condenser is called a *paper-condenser*. It has a sheet of waxed paper between two sheets of aluminum foil. The three sheets are wound into a compact unit. The nonconducting wax paper that insulates the aluminum foil is called a *dielectric*.

If the wound sheets of aluminum foil and wax paper are attached to a battery, no charge will pass through them, but a charge will be stored up in the dielectric. This charge is called an *electrostatic* charge, because it does not flow past the condenser. If the battery is disconnected, the current will flow back into any circuit that includes the condenser for a short while. When an electric force resists an electric current, the force is called a *counter electromotive force*. The force of a charged condenser equals the applied voltage.

Condensers are classed according to the material used to insulate them. *Air condensers* have an air space between aluminum plates. They are used for tuning in radio sets. *Glass condensers* can store charges of high voltage. *Mica condensers* have a plate made of mica to insulate the conductors. They are used for high-voltage currents. *Electrolytic condensers* have two metal conductors in a liquid or moisture-retaining material. Under an electric charge, the atoms in the liquid form *ions*, or become electrically charged. The ions are drawn to the metal conductors and, with the metal, form a new substance which coats the metal so that a current can pass through in only one direction. Electrolytic condensers are used in the electric *filters* that form a part of the circuits of radio sets. PALMER H. CRAIG

Related Articles in WORLD BOOK include:

Capacitance	Electrolyte	Leyden Jar
Electric Current	Farad	Mica
Electrolysis	Insulator, Electric	

CONDENSER, STEAM, is a device used on steam turbines to increase the amount of work they can do. A steam condenser consists of a chamber filled with pipes. Cool water flows through the pipes. Steam leaving the turbine passes through the chamber and is cooled by the pipes. This condenses the steam into a liquid and creates a low-pressure area in the chamber.

Without a condenser, steam escaping from a turbine would have to push against atmospheric pressure of 14.7 pounds per square inch. But the pressure in the condenser is only about 0.7 pounds per square inch. Thus, more of the energy of the steam can be converted to work, because it does not have to push against the higher atmospheric pressure. OTTO A. UYEHARA

See also CONDENSATION; TURBINE (Steam Turbines).

CONDILLAC, *KAWN DEE YAHK*, **ÉTIENNE BONNOT DE** (1715-1780), a French philosopher and psychologist, stressed the importance of the senses. He tried to show that all knowledge and all operations of the mind, such as thinking and judging, can be traced to an original awareness of the senses. To make this idea clear, he used the example of a statue gradually coming to life, as one sense organ after another comes into operation. Condillac's chief work was *Treatise on the Sensations* (1754). He was born in Grenoble. W. T. JONES

CONDIMENT, or SEASONING, is anything used to give relish to food and to gratify the taste. Condiments are usually pungent substances, as pepper or mustard.

CONDITIONED REFLEX. See REFLEX ACTION.

CONDOMINIUM. See HOUSING (Condominium Housing).

CONDOMINIUM, *KAHN doh MIN ih um*, is joint rule or sovereignty over a territory. This type of rule is rare. The Republic of Sudan was once under the joint sovereignty of Great Britain and Egypt. Great Britain, Germany, and the United States shared control of Samoa, a group of 14 islands in the South Pacific Ocean, from 1889 until 1899. The islands were then divided between Germany and the United States. The German group is now independent Western Samoa.

Great Britain and France rule the New Hebrides. The United States and Great Britain share control of tiny Canton and Enderbury Islands. The word *condominium* is from two Latin words, meaning *together* and *domain*. See also COMMONWEALTH OF NATIONS; SAMOA; SUDAN. WILLIAM T. R. FOX

CONDON, EDWARD UHLER (1902-   ), an American physicist, became noted for his contributions to theoretical physics. In 1928, he helped apply new quantum theories to radioactive processes (see QUANTUM THEORY). Condon was born at Alamogordo, N.Mex., near the site of the first atomic-bomb test. He received a Ph.D. degree from the University of California in 1926. He taught at Princeton University and at the University of Minnesota, and became a professor at Washington University in 1956. RALPH E. LAPP

CONDOR is a large vulture. The condor of North America, called the *California condor*, is the largest land bird on the continent. It reaches a length of 45 to 55 inches, has a wingspread of $8\frac{1}{2}$ to 10 feet, and weighs between 20 and 25 pounds. Only about 40 California condors are still living today. They live in a sanctuary in Los Padres National Forest in southern California.

The California condor has a long hooked beak that extends almost straight out from its flat forehead. It has a bald yellow head and reddish neck. A ruff of long, pointed black feathers circles the base of the neck. Dark gray feathers cover most of the condor's body and wings. White feathers are under each wing.

Like other vultures, the condor feeds chiefly on the bodies of dead animals. It usually nests in caves high on cliffs. The female lays one egg on the bare floor of the cave. The egg is about $4\frac{1}{2}$ inches long and $2\frac{1}{2}$ inches wide, large enough to hold more than a half pint of water. The egg is plain white with a greenish or bluish tint. California condors are rare. This is because the large animals they eat are scarce; and many condors have been killed by man. They are also rare because of a slow rate of reproduction. A condor does not breed until it is six years old and lays only one egg every two years. Young condors grow slowly.

The *South American condor* is about the size of the California condor. It lives high in the Andes Mountains, and may fly as high as 20,000 feet. The female lays two white eggs. The bird appears on the coat of arms of Bolivia, Chile, Colombia, and Ecuador.

Scientific Classification. Condors are in the American vulture family, *Cathartidae*. The California condor is genus *Gymnogyps*, species *G. californianus*. The South American condor is *Vultur gryphus*. OLIN SEWALL PETTINGILL, JR.

See also BIRD (Young Birds; color picture: Wings in Flight); VULTURE.

CONDUCT. See BEHAVIOR; ETIQUETTE.

CONDUCTING is the art of leading a musical group in performance. A conductor usually uses hand motions that give the beat and guide the performers in tempo and dynamics. A conductor must be a skilled musician. He must have an exceptional ear for rhythm and pitch, and know the music of both past and present.

The use of hand motions to direct musical performers dates back to early times. Hand signals called *cheironomy* were used in Gregorian chants before musical notation became highly developed. The signals reminded the singers of the pitches and rhythms they had learned by ear. In small musical groups, one player usually kept the performers together. When large numbers of musicians began to perform together, they found it necessary to have one principal leader. In the 1600's, the composer often served as leader, conducting from the keyboard. Later, the leading violinist sometimes waved his bow to give signals while playing. About 1820, Louis Spohr, a German violinist, began using a small stick to conduct in public. This gave rise to the baton (see BATON). The tradition of specialized conducting became established by about 1850. Today, the conductor holds a position of great authority.   GRANT FLETCHER

See also ORCHESTRA with its Related Articles, which has a list of biographies of conductors.

CONDUCTION. See HEAT (How Heat Travels).

CONDUCTOR, ELECTRICAL. See ELECTRIC CURRENT (Conductors).

CONDUCTOR, RAILROAD. See RAILROAD (Careers in Railroading).

CONDUIT. See VOLCANO (How Volcanoes Are Formed; picture).

CONDUIT, *KAHN diht*, is a tube or sheath that encloses and protects electrical wires. The form of conduit used depends on the size and number of wires and on the purpose for which the wires are used. In the typical small home, nonmetallic conduits, usually plastic,

protect pairs of wires. Pairs of wires may also be held in a flexible metal sheath called *BX cable*. In larger structures, such as factories, conduits consist of hollow metal tubes that are several inches in diameter. Sometimes a metal *raceway* (trough) acts as a conduit. A flexible waterproof conduit often protects the wire in places where moisture or weather might harm the wiring. In almost all cases, the connections for wires in conduits are made only at junction boxes.   SAMUEL SEELY

CONE, a part of the eye. See EYE (The Eyeball); COLOR (How the Eye Sees Color).

CONE is a solid figure whose base lies on a plane and is bounded by a closed curve, and whose *lateral surface* (side) tapers uniformly to a point called the *vertex*. The cone that occurs in most practical problems is called a *right circular cone*. Its base is a circle. The line drawn from the vertex to the center of the base is perpendicular to the base. This perpendicular line is called the *altitude* of the cone. A line from the vertex to a point on the circumference of the base is the *slant height*. If you cut off the top of a cone with a plane parallel to the base, the portion of the cone that remains is called a *frustum*.

The Area of the Lateral Surface of a cone equals the circumference of the base of the cone multiplied by half of the slant height. If L stands for the area of the cone's lateral surface, r for the radius of the base, and s for the cone's slant height, then $L = (2\pi r)(\frac{1}{2}s)$ or $L = \pi rs$.

The Volume of a Cone equals one-third that of a cylinder with the same base and altitude. If V stands for the volume, B for the area of the base, and h for the altitude, $V = \frac{1}{3}Bh$, or $V = \frac{1}{3}\pi r^2 h$.

The Area of the Lateral Surface of a Frustum equals the product of half the slant height and the sum of the circumferences of the bases. If L stands for the area of the frustum's lateral surface, R for the radius of the upper base, s for the slant height, and r for the radius

A Liquid-Tight Conduit protects the electrical lines to this motor photographed under water at Silver Springs, Fla.

Anaconda Metal Hose Division of The American Brass Co.

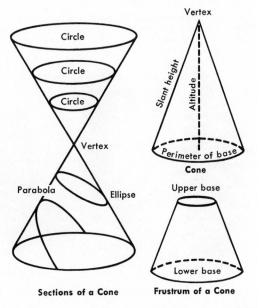

Sections of a Cone

Frustrum of a Cone

of the lower base, then $L=\frac{1}{2}s(2\pi r+2\pi R)$ or, $L=\pi s(r+R)$.

The Volume of the Frustum of a cone is found by multiplying one-third of the altitude by the sum of the areas of the two bases, plus the square root of their product. Thus, $V=\frac{1}{3}h(\pi r^2+\pi R^2+\sqrt{\pi r^2\times\pi R^2})$ or, $\frac{1}{3}h\pi(r^2+R^2+rR)$. The volume of the frustum may also be found by completing the cone. It is the volume of the top cone subtracted from the volume of the entire large cone.   MILES C. HARTLEY

See also CIRCLE; CYLINDER; ELLIPSE; HYPERBOLA; PARABOLA.

CONE-BEARING TREES, sometimes called CONIFERS, make up a large group of trees and shrubs that have naked seeds. Such plants, called *gymnosperms*, do not produce a pod or other fruit that must break open to set the seeds free. The seeds fall out from between the scales of cones. Most cone-bearing trees grow in temperate climates. The leaves are usually small, evergreen, and needle-shaped. A few cone-bearing trees that grow in subtropical climates have long, leathery leaves. On most cone-bearing trees the leaves stay on the tree for several years. Common cone-bearing trees include the pines, hemlocks, spruces, firs, junipers, cedars, larches, redwoods, yews, and cypresses.

The trees bear their seeds in cones. All of the trees have male and female flowers. Both are usually on the same tree. The male flowers give off pollen. They are arranged in catkinlike clusters called *strobiles* (see CATKIN). Each female flower has a seed-producing cone at the top. When the female flowers are pollinated, they develop into cones. In some cone-bearing trees, it takes only a few months for the cones to ripen. In others, such as the pine tree, it takes two years. Some cone-bearing trees, such as the juniper, have cones that look like berries. The yew has very small cones and only one large seed. Its male and female flowers grow on two different plants.

When the seeds are fully formed, they fall from the cones. They grow into new trees.

Scientific Classification. The yew belongs to the yew family, *Taxaceae*. The remaining gymnosperms are in the pine family, *Pinaceae*.   K. A. ARMSON

Conestoga Wagons replaced horse pack trains, and were the long-distance freight carriers before the railroads were completed.

Related Articles in WORLD BOOK include:

Arborvitae	Evergreen	Piñon
Balsam Fir	Fir	Redwood
Bristlecone	Ginkgo	Sequoia
Pine	Gymnosperm	Spruce
Cedar	Hemlock	Yew
Cycad	Juniper	
Cypress	Larch	
Douglas Fir	Pine	

CONESTOGA WAGON was a sturdy, colorful covered wagon used by American pioneers. It was named for the Pennsylvania town where it was first built in the middle 1700's. Conestogas carried most of the freight and people that moved west over the Alleghenies from the time of the Revolutionary War until about 1850. These wagons were sometimes called the *camels of the prairies*.

Both ends of the wagon were built higher than the middle. The white canvas roof was high and rounded. Wheels with broad rims prevented bogging down in mud. These could be removed and the wagon could be used as a boat. Conestoga wagons were drawn by teams of from four to six horses.   JOHN J. FLOHERTY

See also PENNSYLVANIA DUTCH; WESTERN FRONTIER LIFE (color picture).

CONEY. See CONY.

White Pine   Hemlock   Balsam Fir   Arborvitae   Larch

Every Cone-Bearing Tree Has a Distinctive Type of Cone Which Helps to Identify It.

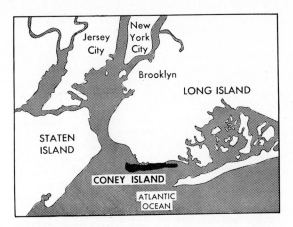

Coney Island, at the southwest end of Long Island, attracts millions of visitors each year during the summer months. People flock to the amusement park there to see freak shows and museums, to play games, and to enjoy the many rides.

CONEY ISLAND is a popular New York seaside resort. Actually it is an island in name only, since land has been filled in connecting it with Brooklyn. Coney Island is famous in history as the place where Henry Hudson landed in 1609. Thousands of people seek relief there from the heat of summer. The *map* shows that Coney Island lies at the southwestern end of Long Island, about nine miles away from the southern tip of Manhattan Island. It is nearly five miles long at the widest part, and three-quarters of a mile across. Coney Island may be reached by automobile, bus, subway, or boat. Sometimes more than a million people visit "Coney" in a day. In the immediate vicinity are Brighton Beach, West Brighton, Sea Gate, and Manhattan Beach.

A true outing at Coney Island includes a trip along the Boardwalk, a wide thoroughfare which stretches along the beach for more than a mile. The patrons crowd the souvenir stands, see side shows, and visit the New York Aquarium. They also swim, dance, play games of chance, and take thrilling rides. There is little activity at Coney Island in winter.   WILLIAM E. YOUNG

CONFECTION. See CANDY.

CONFEDERATE ARMY SOCIETIES. See CONFEDERATE VETERANS, UNITED; DAUGHTERS OF THE CONFEDERACY, UNITED.

CONFEDERATE MEMORIAL DAY honors Confederate soldiers who died during the Civil War. Arkansas, Maryland, Virginia, and West Virginia celebrate this day annually on May 30, which is Memorial Day in the North. Alabama, Georgia, Florida, and Mississippi celebrate the day on April 26. North Carolina and South Carolina observe May 10, and Kentucky, Tennessee, and Louisiana observe June 3, the birthday of Jefferson Davis.

The tradition of decorating the graves of Confederate soldiers began during the Civil War. The Memorial Day observance in the North grew out of these customs. General John A. Logan is credited with naming May 30 as Memorial Day. In 1868, he ordered all Grand Army of the Republic posts to decorate the graves of Union soldiers on May 30.   RAYMOND HOYT JAHN

See also MEMORIAL DAY.

CONFEDERATE STATES OF AMERICA was the name taken by six southern states when they organized their own government at Montgomery, Ala., in February, 1861. The states *seceded* (withdrew) from the government of the United States in 1860 and 1861 because they feared that the election of Abraham Lincoln, a Republican President, might lead to restrictions on their right to do as they chose about the question of Negro slavery. The first state to leave the Union was South Carolina on Dec. 20, 1860. Mississippi, Florida, Alabama, Georgia, and Louisiana followed South Carolina's lead in January, 1861. In March, 1861, Texas also seceded, and later in that year Virginia, Arkansas, North Carolina, and Tennessee joined the ranks to make 11 Confederate States of America in all.

The idea of a state leaving the Union was not new, and the South did not invent it. Throughout the United States, persons who believed in the doctrine of states' rights had long argued that a state had a right to withdraw from the Union whenever it chose. They argued that individual states had formed the Union and therefore could also dissolve it. Some persons in the New England states wanted to leave the Union during the War of 1812, because the war was unpopular there.

Government. Organization of a government for the Confederacy began on Feb. 4, 1861, when delegates from six of the seven seceding states met at Montgomery, Ala., and set up a temporary government. Jefferson Davis of Mississippi was elected President of the Confederacy, and Alexander H. Stephens of Georgia was chosen Vice-President. Both were to serve for one year. With the adoption of a permanent constitution, their terms of office were extended to six years. Six prominent Southerners became members of the first Cabinet, and Montgomery was named the temporary capital. After Virginia seceded, the Confederate Congress voted on May 21, 1861, to move its capital to Richmond. The move was accomplished on May 29.

The Constitution of the Confederacy, adopted in March, 1861, was modeled after the United States Constitution. But it contained six important differences:

1. The term of the President and Vice-President was six years. The President was not allowed to succeed himself.

2. Cabinet members received seats in Congress, with the privilege of debate. But they could not vote.

3. Foreign slave trade was ended, but not slavery.

4. Congress was forbidden to make appropriations for internal improvements, to levy a protective tariff, or to give bounties.

5. A two-thirds vote of both houses of Congress was necessary to admit a new state into the Confederacy or to make appropriations not requested by the heads of departments through the President.

6. The President could veto single items in appropriation bills.

The Confederate States hoped for a peaceful withdrawal from the Union. A number of persons in the Confederacy and in the Union worked hard to avoid war. But their efforts failed, and war began with the attack on Fort Sumter on April 12, 1861.

The Border States were the slave states that lay between the North and the deep South. When the war began, both the Union and the Confederacy made strong

753

Secretary of State	Robert Toombs (1861)
	Robert M. T. Hunter (1861)
	Judah P. Benjamin (1862)
Secretary of the Treasury	Christopher Memminger (1861)
	George A. Trenholm (1864)
Secretary of War	Leroy P. Walker (1861)
	Judah P. Benjamin (1861)
	George W. Randolph (1862)
	Gustavus Smith (Acting)(1862)
	James A. Seddon (1862)
	John C. Breckinridge (1865)
Secretary of the Navy	Stephen R. Mallory (1861)
Postmaster General	John H. Reagan (1861)
Attorney General	Judah P. Benjamin (1861)
	Thomas Bragg (1861)
	Thomas Watts (1862)
	George Davis (1864)

efforts to gain their support. North Carolina, Virginia, Arkansas, and Tennessee joined the Confederacy. Delaware, Maryland, Kentucky, and Missouri stayed in the Union. But the western counties of Virginia seceded from the South later in the war, and formed the state of West Virginia. And secessionist groups set up separate state governments in both Kentucky and Missouri, even though these states stayed in the Union. These groups also sent delegates to the Confederate Congress. This accounts for the 13 stars in the Confederate flag even though only 11 states actually joined the Confederate States of America.

Foreign Relations. Great Britain, France, The Netherlands, Spain, and Brazil were among the countries that recognized the Confederate States as a belligerent, but not as a nation. Recognition of southern belligerency meant that Confederate ships received the same privileges granted to vessels of the United States in foreign ports or on the high seas.

The Confederacy suffered great financial disadvantages. The wealth of the nation, before secession, lay mainly in the North, and the South lacked adequate resources for taxation. The Confederate government had to issue paper money early in the war. This money soon became almost valueless. The people of the Confederate States gave generously to their government, and willingly bought government bonds. But their loyal financial support could not create resources that did not exist within the boundaries of the Confederacy.

Progress of the War favored the Confederacy in the first months. The defeat of the Union forces at Fredericksburg, in December, 1862, led the Emperor of France, Napoleon III, to offer his services as peacemaker between the Union and the Confederacy. The Union rejected this offer. In 1863, the tide began to turn against the Confederacy. The Union armies could get more materials and supplies from the industrial North than the Confederate armies could obtain from the agricultural South. The North kept its army supplied with ammunition, food, and clothing, while the army of the South often lacked these supplies. Union ships blockaded Southern ports. The only way the South could bring in necessary supplies from overseas was to run the blockade. But Southern soldiers fought bravely until there was no longer any hope of victory.

The Confederate Congress met in frequent sessions during the war, mainly to follow the bidding of President Davis, who made free use of his war powers. The Davis government lasted until the fall of Richmond, on April 3, 1865. Danville, Va., served as the capital after the fall of Richmond. When the Army of Northern Virginia surrendered on April 9, 1865, the Confederate States of America came to an end. The men of the Confederacy defended to the best of their ability a way of living that to them seemed right. But they yielded to superior force. The road to reunion in spirit between the North and the South was long and hard, but by the beginning of the 1900's resentment and ill will had been largely forgotten.   JOHN D. HICKS

Related Articles. See the History sections of the articles on the states of the Confederacy. See also:

Benjamin, Judah P.	Johnston, Joseph Eggleston
Border State	Lee, Robert E.
Breckinridge, John C.	Mallory, Stephen R.
Civil War	Memminger, Christopher G.
Confederate Memorial Day	Nullification
Davis, Jefferson	Randolph (George W.)
Emancipation	Seddon, James A.
Proclamation	Semmes, Raphael
Flag (Flags of the	States' Rights
United States)	Stephens, Alexander H.
Fort Sumter	Walker, Leroy P.
Gordon, John Brown	West Virginia (History)

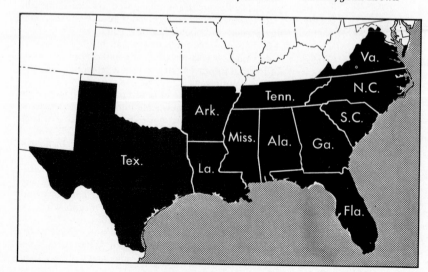

The Confederate States of America was formed by eleven states during the Civil War.

CONFEDERATE VETERANS, UNITED, was an organization of men who fought for the Confederate States of America during the Civil War. It was founded in 1889 at New Orleans to preserve the friendships formed during the war, and to help Confederate Civil War veterans, their widows, and their orphans.

CONFEDERATION. See ARTICLES OF CONFEDERATION; CANADA, HISTORY OF (Confederation).

CONFESSION, in religion. See ALTAR; ROMAN CATHOLIC CHURCH (Penance).

CONFIRMATION is a religious ceremony practiced by several faiths. In the Roman Catholic, Eastern Orthodox, and Lutheran churches, and in the Church of England, it is associated with baptism. Confirmation is the second sacrament of the Roman Catholic Church. Roman Catholics believe that it confers the grace of the Holy Spirit on baptized persons. During confirmation in Protestant churches, the baptized renew and confirm the promises made for them at baptism. In Judaism, boys are confirmed at the age of 13 in a ceremony called *Bar Mitzvah*. Some temples have similar ceremonies for girls called *Bas Mitzvah*. Many also hold a confirmation exercise on Shabuot (see SHABUOT). BERNARD RAMM

See also BAPTISM; BAR MITZVAH; BAS MITZVAH; ROMAN CATHOLIC CHURCH (The Sacraments).

CONFLICT OF INTEREST occurs if an individual has a financial or other interest in a company doing business with his employer. For example, a person working for a government agency that awards contracts to private industry may have a financial interest in a company bidding for these contracts. A conflict of interest occurs if the government employee favors the company in which he has an interest. The conflict-of-interest issue often arises when businessmen take positions in government. Full-time government employees are required to give up all outside financial interests that might conflict with their official duties. ROBERT A. DAHL

CONFUCIANISTS practice the system of ethics, education, statecraft, and religion first taught by the Chinese philosopher Confucius. This system, called *Confucianism*, is practiced by about 350 million persons.

Confucianists believe that men realize heaven's preordained harmony and justice when they observe the duties and responsibilities of the five basic relationships: ruler and subject, father and son, husband and wife, elder and younger brother, and friend and friend. Each relationship involves specific duties and manners.

In developing this ideal, Confucianists have made important contributions to the culture of China. They gave China its ethical ideal of the *superior man*, who has self-respect, magnanimity, sincerity, earnestness, and benevolence. They also fostered a distinctive type of education that tried to mold the individual so that the virtues of the superior man became his inner nature. Confucianists influenced the practice of statecraft by instilling higher officials with a sense of responsibility for the people's welfare. Confucianists emphasized the traditional practices of Chinese religion. The emperor offered annual prayers and sacrifices on behalf of the people of China, and lesser princes who ruled provinces worshiped local spirits. GEORGE NOEL MAYHEW

See also CONFUCIUS; RELIGION.

CONFUCIUS, *kahn FYOO shus* (551?-479? B.C.), became famous as a *sage* (wise man) of China. He said, "What you do not like done to yourself, do not unto

Confucius, the great philosopher and teacher of China, became one of the most influential men who ever lived.

Brown Bros.

others," several hundred years before Jesus pronounced the Golden Rule. His goal was to help men develop a moral sense of responsibility toward others. He taught them to be gentlemanly and kind, and to show respect to their elders and superiors. The principles Confucius taught are still the ideals of millions of people.

Confucius was born into a poor but respected family of the state of Lu. His father died shortly after the boy's birth. Though poor, his mother gave him the best education available. At the age of 15, he decided to become a scholar. Confucius mastered the teachings of sages. He decided that he must restore the faith and practices of the prophet-emperors and sages of old.

By the time Confucius was 21, students began to come to him. He taught that the secret of good government lay in choosing honest and educated officials.

He was at one time appointed to a high position in the government of Lu, and his well-governed district became the wonder of his time. But he soon had to resign because of a jealous noble. He traveled from place to place trying to find a prince who would accept his teachings of just and honest government. But Confucius was misunderstood and ignored by most rulers of his time.

Although Confucius taught for 50 years, he died practically unknown. Later the *Five Classics*, which record his teachings, became the Confucian Bible and were used in Chinese schools. CLIFTON E. OLMSTEAD

See also CONFUCIANISTS.

CONGENITAL DISLOCATION. See DISLOCATION.

CONGLOMERATE. See ROCK (Clastic Sediments).

CONGO
(BRAZZAVILLE)

* ⊛ National Capital
* • Other City or Town
* — Road
* ┼┼┼ Rail Line
* ┼ Highest Known Elevation
* ⌒ River

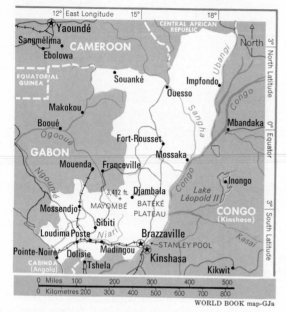

WORLD BOOK map-GJa

CONGO (BRAZZAVILLE) is a hot, humid country in west-central Africa. The equator runs through the country. Thick forests of trees and tangled bushes and vines cover over half of Congo (Brazzaville). Only elephants, crocodiles, and other wild animals live in much of this area. Congo (Brazzaville) is larger than New Mexico, but it has fewer people than the city of Baltimore, Md.

Congo (Brazzaville) was once a territory in French Equatorial Africa, and it was called Middle Congo. It became independent in 1960. Its name in French, the official language, is RÉPUBLIQUE DU CONGO (REPUBLIC OF THE CONGO). But it is usually called Congo (Brazzaville) to distinguish it from its neighbor, Congo (Kinshasa), which has the same official name. Brazzaville is the capital and largest city.

Congo (Brazzaville) has few valuable minerals, and most of its soil is poor. But the country is a transportation center. Pointe-Noire, on the Atlantic coast, is an important port. The inland countries of the Central African Republic, Chad, and Gabon use this port to bring in and send out goods.

R. J. Harrison Church, is Professor of Geography at London University and the author of West Africa and Africa and the Islands.

756

Government. Congo (Brazzaville) is a republic, with a president as head of state. All citizens over 18 years of age may vote. The people elect the 55 members of the National Assembly to five-year terms. Assembly members and local government councils elect the president to a five-year term. The president appoints the prime minister and other ministers. The National Movement for the Revolution, the only political party allowed in the country, determines government policies.

People. Most of the country's 897,000 people live either on the southern border near Brazzaville, or on the coast in and around Pointe-Noire. Pointe-Noire and Dolisie are other important cities.

The people belong to four main groups: (1) the Kongo, (2) the Batéké, (3) the M'Bochi, and (4) the Sangha. Each of these groups is composed of several tribes. About 45 of every 100 persons belong to the Kongo group, farmers who live west and southwest of Brazzaville. About 20 of every 100 belong to the Batéké group, hunters and fishermen who live north of Brazzaville. About 10 of every 100 are M'Bochi. Once fishermen, the M'Bochi now work as clerks and technicians in the towns. The Sangha live in the northern forests.

About half the people practice *fetish* religions. They believe that all things, even lifeless objects such as stones, have spirits. About 4,500 are Moslems, and most of the rest are Christians.

Most of the older Congolese cannot read or write, but about 75 of every 100 children now receive some elementary education. The Center of Administrative and Advanced Technical Studies in Brazzaville offers higher education to Congolese and to students from the Central African Republic, Chad, and Gabon.

Land. Congo (Brazzaville) covers 132,047 square miles, and is split into six main geographical regions. They are (1) the Coastal Plain, (2) the Mayombé Escarpment, (3) the Niari Valley, (4) the Stanley Pool Region, (5) the Batéké Plateaus, and (6) the Congo River Basin.

The Coastal Plain extends about 40 miles inland from the Atlantic Ocean. There are *lagoons* (lakes) near the coast, but the region is generally dry and treeless.

The Mayombé Escarpment, and a series of plateaus

FACTS IN BRIEF

Capital: Brazzaville.

Official Language: French.

Official Name: Republic of the Congo.

Form of Government: Republic. *Head of State*—President (5-year term).

Area: 132,047 square miles. *Greatest Distances*—(north-south) 590 miles; (east-west) 515 miles. *Coastline*—100 miles.

Population: No complete census. *Estimated 1970 Population*—897,000; distribution, 64 per cent rural, 36 per cent urban; density, 7 persons to the square mile. *Estimated 1975 Population*—961,000.

Chief Products: *Agriculture*—bananas, cassava, coffee, palm kernels and oil, peanuts, plantains, rice, rubber, sugar cane, sweet potatoes, yams. *Forestry*—limba, mahogany, okoume. *Mining*—lead.

Flag: A yellow diagonal stripe separates two triangles (green and red). See FLAG (picture: Flags of Africa).

Money: *Basic Unit*—franc. See MONEY (table: Values).

rising to between 1,600 and 2,600 feet above sea level, lie inland, behind the coastal plain. River valleys are cut deeply into these heavily forested ridges.

The Niari Valley, a richer farming region, lies beyond the Mayombé Escarpment. It is covered by wooded land and *savannas* (grassy plains).

The Stanley Pool Region, east of the Niari Valley, consists of a series of bare hills. Most of the land there has been cleared for farming. Stanley Pool is a lake formed by the widening of the Congo River.

The Batéké Plateaus are grass-covered elevated plains in the central part of the country. Deep, forested valleys containing tributaries of the Congo River separate them.

The Congo River Basin in the north includes large swampy areas. The Ubangi, the main Congo tributary, forms the country's northeastern border.

Most of Congo (Brazzaville) has a hot, humid climate, with rainfall throughout the year. Parts of the Congo River Basin have about 100 inches of rainfall a year, and temperatures average from 75° to 78° F. The Batéké Plateaus average less than 60 inches of rain a year. Temperatures there vary between 70° and 80° F. The coastal area is cooler and drier than the rest of the country, because of the cold Benguela ocean current that flows along the coast.

Economy. Except for its forests, Congo (Brazzaville) has few natural resources. It has few industries.

Most of the Congolese raise bananas, corn, rice, and other crops to feed their own families. Lumber is the chief export, and most of it comes from the Mayombé ridges and the northern forests.

Congo (Brazzaville) has one of the longest transportation systems in Africa. The Congo-Ocean railroad, a 320-mile line linking Brazzaville and Pointe-Noire, and its branch line form the only railroad. Boats can use the Congo and Ubangi rivers north of Stanley Pool at Brazzaville, but rapids below Stanley Pool prevent boats from getting to or from the ocean. The Congo-Ubangi river system carries goods and passengers as far as Bangui, capital of the Central African Republic, a distance of 700 miles. Most of the exports and imports of the Central African Republic and Chad move over the river system and the Congo-Ocean railroad. Some of Gabon's trade moves over the branch of the Congo-Ocean railroad. This shipping trade is important to the Congo (Brazzaville) economy. Building and maintaining roads is difficult because of the heavy rains and thick forests.

History. Little is known of the early African kingdoms that ruled what is now Congo (Brazzaville). Portuguese explorers first landed there in the 1400's. European traders bought slaves and ivory along the coast in the 1600's and 1700's. Pierre Savorgnan de Brazza, an Italian explorer working for France, reached the area in 1875. Henry M. Stanley, the famed English explorer, sailed down the Congo River from its source to the ocean in 1876 and 1877. In 1880, Brazza and Makoko, the Batéké king, signed a treaty that placed the area on the north side of the Congo River under French protection. This area, then called Middle Congo, became a territory in French Equatorial Africa in 1903. In 1910, it was linked with the territories of Gabon, Chad, and Ubangi-Shari (now the Central African Republic). Middle Congo gained internal self-government in 1958. It became independent on Aug. 15, 1960.

Fulbert Youlou became the first president, but the army and trade unions forced him to resign in 1963. A socialist government then took control, and Alphonse Massamba-Débat became president. The government nationalized industries, and recognized such Communist governments as those of China, North Korea, and North Vietnam. In 1968, military leaders took control of the government, and removed Massamba-Débat from office. Major Marien Ngouabi became president and head of state in 1969. R. J. HARRISON CHURCH

See also BRAZZAVILLE; CONGO RIVER; FRENCH EQUATORIAL AFRICA.

Brazzaville, Capital of Congo (Brazzaville), Stands Beside Stanley Pool, On the Congo River.

Camera Press, Ltd.

CONGO
(KINSHASA)

✦ Capital

• Other City or Town

── Road

↦ Rail Line

▲ MOUNTAIN

∼ River

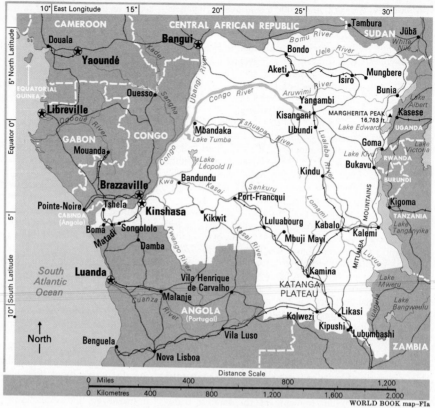

WORLD BOOK map–FIa

CONGO (KINSHASA), the third largest country in Africa, straddles the equator in central Africa. It is larger than the part of the United States that lies east of the Mississippi River.

The Congo is a hot, rainy country. Tropical rain forest covers the central area. The Congo's mining industry is one of the world's major producers of copper and industrial diamonds. But most Congolese are poor farmers.

Belgium's King Leopold II controlled this area as the Congo Free State from 1885 to 1908. Then, it became a Belgian colony, the Belgian Congo. The Congo became independent in 1960, and it has been troubled by political unsteadiness much of the time since then.

The country's name in French, the official language, is RÉPUBLIQUE DÉMOCRATIQUE DU CONGO (DEMOCRATIC REPUBLIC OF THE CONGO). It is called *Congo (Kinshasa)* to distinguish it from neighboring *Congo (Brazzaville)*. Kinshasa, formerly called Léopoldville, is the capital and largest city.

Government

The Congo has been under military rule since 1965. Lieutenant General Joseph Mobutu, the Congo's presi-

dent, heads the government and the army. Mobutu has tried to base his government on a constitution that Congolese voters approved in 1967, the third constitution since 1960. It centers power in the president and the national government.

People

The people of the Congo belong to widely varying groups or tribes. For example, more than 200 different languages are spoken in the Congo. For easy communication, many Congolese speak Swahili and Lingala in addition to their tribal language.

Most Congolese cities have an administrative and commercial center, with a number of modern buildings. A spacious, attractive section of comfortable bungalows stands at one end of the city. This was once the European section. Today, the remaining Europeans share this section with Congolese civil servants and political leaders. The African section of the city is a busy, overcrowded area of one-story, cinder-block houses. The people living there earn low wages, if they have jobs at all. They buy their food in a large, open market place.

Most farmers live in villages and raise crops in the surrounding fields. They live in square or rectangular houses that have thatched roofs and walls made of mud plastered over a framework of branches. The more prosperous houses may have corrugated iron or tin roofs. The farmers' main food crops are cassava, corn, and rice.

M. Crawford Young, the contributor of this article, is Associate Professor of Political Science at the University of Wisconsin, and the author of Politics in the Congo.

Most educated Congolese are Christians. The Roman Catholic Church has over 4 million members there. There are about 800,000 Protestants and 300,000 Moslems. The rest of the people practice traditional African religions.

Political unrest blocked efforts to expand education. In 1960, about 1½ million pupils attended primary school, but fewer than 200 completed secondary school. The Congo has three universities—in Kinshasa, in Lubumbashi, and in Kisangani.

FACTS IN BRIEF

Form of Government: Republic (military rule).

Divisions: 8 provinces, each headed by a governor appointed by the president for unlimited terms; central district of Kinshasa.

Capital: Kinshasa.

Head of State: President, elected by the people to a seven-year term.

National Assembly: About 300 deputies, elected by the people to five-year terms; one house.

Courts: *Highest*—Supreme Court. *Other*—two appeals courts; local courts.

Voting Age: 18 (men and women).

Local Government: About 25 districts, headed by district commissioners; about 125 territories headed by territorial administrators; 800 to 900 local units headed by chiefs.

Official Language: French.

Area: 905,568 square miles. *Greatest Distances*—(north-south) about 1,300 miles; (east-west) about 1,300 miles. *Coastline*—30 miles.

Elevation: *Highest*—Margherita Peak, 16,763 feet above sea level. *Lowest*—sea level along the coast.

Population: No complete census. *Estimated 1970 Population*—17,456,000; distribution, 78 per cent rural, 22 per cent urban; density, 19 persons to the square mile. *Estimated 1975 Population*—19,463,000.

Chief Products: *Agriculture*—cacao, cassava, coffee, cotton, palm products, rice, rubber, tea. *Mining*—coal, cobalt, copper, gold, industrial diamonds, manganese, tin, zinc.

Flag: A yellow star (for unity) lies on a blue field next to a diagonal red stripe (for blood of national heroes) edged in yellow (for natural riches). Adopted: 1963. See FLAG (color picture: Flags of Africa).

Money: *Basic Unit*—zaire. See MONEY (table: Values).

Land

The Congo River is the central geographic feature of the country (see CONGO RIVER). Central Congo is a swampy, heavily forested region that straddles the equator. A zone of tropical rain forest stretches across the Congo for about 160 miles on either side of the equator. Sparsely wooded grasslands lie north of the rain forest. Open grassy plains with forested valleys lie south of it.

The land rises steadily to a series of mountain ranges in the east and the Katanga Plateau in the southeast. Margherita Peak (16,763 ft.), the highest point in the Congo, lies in the snow-capped Ruwenzori Range, the highest eastern range. Much of the Katanga Plateau is 5,000 feet above sea level. A series of large lakes lies on the Congo's eastern border.

The climate is warm and humid in central and western Congo, and mild in the higher eastern regions. Daytime temperatures in central Congo stay close to 90° F. The Congo has from 20 to 80 inches of rain a year.

Economy

The Congo's economy depends on rich mineral deposits. In the late 1960's, minerals provided about 80 per cent of the country's export income. The Congo is a leading producer of copper, found in southern Katanga province. It is the leading producer of industrial diamonds, found chiefly in Kasai-Oriental province, and cobalt. Other important mineral deposits in the Congo are coal, gold, manganese, tin, and zinc.

The Congolese government has part-ownership in

United Nations

Copper, Most Valuable Congo Export, is mined in Katanga province, *below.* Other metals are separated from the copper ore, and then the copper is refined in smelting plants such as the one in Lubumbashi, *right.*

Pictorial Parade

CONGO (KINSHASA)

Wide World

A Typical Congolese Farmer's House has a thatched roof and walls made of mud plastered over a framework of branches. About three-fourths of the Congolese people are farmers.

some of the large Belgian corporations that operate the mining industry. In 1967, it dissolved Union Minière du Haut Katanga (UMHK) and took over the UMHK mines. A new Belgian firm operates these mines for the Congolese government.

About 75 per cent of the people are farmers. European-owned plantations produce and process cacao, coffee, palm products, rubber, and tea. The Congo exports coffee, cotton, minerals, and rubber, chiefly to Belgium. It imports manufactured goods, principally from the United States.

The Congo has 85,000 miles of roads, and 3,000 miles of railroads. The Congo River and its tributaries provide the country with 7,200 miles of navigable waterways. Matadi is the chief seaport.

History

The famous Kingdom of the Kongo flourished in what is now the Congo in the 1400's and 1500's. The Portuguese arrived in Kongo in the 1400's and converted the kingdom to Christianity. But Kongo fell apart when the Portuguese began taking slaves in the 1500's. After the 1500's, other powerful states grew up in the Congo, but they declined by the 1800's.

Henry M. Stanley, an American explorer, crossed the Congo in the 1870's. Also in the 1870's, Arab and Swahili traders from Zanzibar set up outposts in east-central Congo. In 1885, King Leopold II of Belgium took personal control over a vast area he called the Congo Free State. The king's agents treated the Congolese brutally. Protests in Great Britain and the United States against Leopold's policies forced Belgium to make the Congo a colony, which was called the Belgian Congo, in 1908.

Under Belgian Rule, the Congo began to prosper. Unlike other African states at the time, there was no visible independence movement in the Congo. But in 1956, two Congolese groups called for independence. Then

the economic boom the Belgian Congo had enjoyed ended in 1957.

In January, 1959, riots occurred in Léopoldville (now Kinshasa). After the riots, Belgium's King Baudouin promised independence for the Congo, but he did not set a date. Independence movements expanded rapidly, and the Congolese demanded immediate independence. In January, 1960, Belgian and Congolese leaders set June 30, 1960, as the Congo's independence day.

Independence. National elections were held in May, 1960, but none of the nine major political parties won a majority in parliament. Two prominent leaders, Joseph Kasavubu and Patrice Lumumba, agreed to form a government with Kasavubu as president and Lumumba as prime minister. But the new government lacked unity. When the Congo became independent, Europeans held almost all important positions, controlling civil service and the economy. All army officers were Europeans.

The government broke down less than a week after independence. Army units near Léopoldville (Kinshasa) mutinied. In the panic that followed, almost all European army officers and civil servants fled the country. Inexperienced Congolese replaced them, and confusion followed. Moise Tshombe, president of Katanga province, declared Katanga independent. Belgian troops occupied important cities to protect fleeing Europeans and the Tshombe government. The Congolese government appealed to the United Nations to restore order. UN troops began to arrive on July 15, and they stayed there until June 30, 1964.

On Sept. 5, 1960, President Kasavubu dismissed Lumumba. Joseph Mobutu, an army colonel, then set up a provisional government made up of university students at Léopoldville (Kinshasa). Lumumba was imprisoned, but his followers set up a rival government at Stanleyville (now Kisangani) headed by Antoine Gizenga. South Kasai province also declared itself independent. By November, 1960, there were four governments in the Congo. Then in January, 1961, Lumumba was taken to Katanga and assassinated.

In February, 1961, a civilian cabinet headed by Joseph Ileo replaced the provisional government of university students. With UN help, a new government under Prime Minister Cyrille Adoula ended the Katanga secession and reunited the country in January, 1963.

Followers of Lumumba led revolts against the central government in 1964. By September, the central government had lost control of one-fourth of the Congo. But the Congolese army, strengthened by white *mercenaries* (hired soldiers) and aid from the U.S. and Belgium, overcame the rebels.

Recent Events. Kasavubu dismissed Adoula on June 30, 1964, and appointed Tshombe prime minister. Voters approved a new constitution in June, and elected a parliament in early 1965. But neither Tshombe nor his successor Evariste Kimba could end the disunity in the country.

Then Lieutenant General Joseph Mobutu seized power on Nov. 25, 1965. He dissolved all political parties, and has strengthened the central government. In erasing the last traces of colonialism, the government renamed many of its cities in 1966. Thus, Léopoldville became Kinshasa; Élisabethville became Lubumbashi; and Stanleyville became Kisangani. Katanga troops mutinied in 1966, and mercenaries started a revolt in

1967. But the Congolese army defeated both forces and drove the mercenaries into Rwanda.　M. CRAWFORD YOUNG

Related Articles in WORLD BOOK include:

Africa (pictures)　Katanga　　　Lake Tanganyika
Belgian Congo　　Kinshasa　　　Stanley and Livingstone
Copper　　　　　Lake Albert

CONGO RIVER is the fourth longest river in the world, and the second largest in the volume of water it carries. It drains an area of about 1,400,000 square miles in west-central Africa. Ships can travel up the Congo for 1,000 of its 2,718 total miles. Railway portages provide transportation along the river where rapids obstruct navigation.

The Congo rises in southeastern Congo (Kinshasa). It is called the Lualaba River at its source, and has many other names before it becomes the Congo just after crossing the equator. Important branches include the Aruwimi and Ubangi rivers from the north and the Lomami and Kasai rivers from the south.

The Congo River widens to form Stanley Pool just before it rushes over some 30 rapids below Kinshasa. The river drops about 800 feet between Kinshasa and Matadi, which lies 90 miles from the sea. The Congo has no delta, unlike other African rivers. It empties its muddy waters into the South Atlantic through a deep channel that extends far into the ocean.

Portuguese navigators discovered the mouth of the Congo River in 1482. But Europeans knew nothing about its upper course until Henry M. Stanley explored the region between 1874 and 1877.　HARRY R. RUDIN

See also RIVER (color chart, Longest Rivers); STANLEY AND LIVINGSTONE.

CONGREGATION OF THE INDEX. See INDEX LIBRORUM PROHIBITORUM.

CONGREGATIONAL CHRISTIAN CHURCHES merged with the Evangelical and Reformed Church in 1961 to form the United Church of Christ (see UNITED CHURCH OF CHRIST). A small number of the congregations of the Congregational Christian Church voted against the merger.

CONGRESS, *KAHNG grehs*, comes from the Latin word *congressus*, which means *a meeting*. Any group of people who represent organizations, regions, or nations, and who meet together to discuss their problems, may be called a congress. In the United States, the word *congress* usually refers to the Congress of the United States. An *international congress* is a conference attended by representatives of various nations. Such a congress may meet either to lay down peace terms at the end of a war, or to settle problems in time of peace. The name *congress* was given to several important international conferences which took place in the 1800's to determine boundaries and arrange political settlements in Europe. The most important of the congresses were as follows:

Congress of Vienna (1814-1815), which divided up Napoleon's empire after the Napoleonic Wars.

Congress of Paris (1856), which settled the problems that grew out of the Crimean War. This congress also was an important step in the growing unity of Italy.

Congress of Berlin (1878), which took away from Russia Balkan land it had won from Turkey during the Russo-Turkish Wars.　PAYSON S. WILD, JR.

See also BERLIN, CONGRESS OF; CONGRESS OF THE UNITED STATES; CONTINENTAL CONGRESS; VIENNA, CONGRESS OF.

CONGRESS OF THE CONFEDERATION

CONGRESS HALL. See PHILADELPHIA (Independence Hall National Park).

CONGRESS OF INDUSTRIAL ORGANIZATIONS (CIO) was an association of labor unions active from 1938 to 1955. In 1955, it merged with the American Federation of Labor (see AMERICAN FEDERATION OF LABOR AND CONGRESS OF INDUSTRIAL ORGANIZATIONS). Most of the CIO unions had members only in the United States, but a few international unions also had chapters, or locals, in Canada. Most of the CIO unions were *industrial unions*, rather than *craft unions*. The CIO organized all workers in a plant into one union rather than just the workers in one particular craft.

The CIO was originally a committee of the American Federation of Labor called the *Committee for Industrial Organization*. In 1935, eight presidents of AFL unions formed the CIO to carry on an organizing drive in mass-production industries. The CIO signed up unskilled as well as skilled workers. Some AFL leaders opposed the idea of industrial unions. But the CIO set up organizing committees and organized industrial unions in steel, automobile, rubber, and other major industries. The AFL refused to accept the new unions, and expelled the unions that had taken part in the CIO. In 1938, the CIO formed its own federation and changed its name to the *Congress of Industrial Organizations*.

In its 1938 constitution, the CIO stated its main purposes as: (1) to organize the unorganized; (2) to improve wages, hours, and working conditions; (3) to establish peaceful labor relations by forming unions strong enough to bargain with large industries; (4) to maintain collective bargaining and wage contracts; and (5) to secure legislation for the welfare of workers.

The Political Action Committee (PAC) of the CIO worked in national politics. State and city industrial councils were active in state and local politics. The CIO supported pro-labor political candidates and legislation in line with its main purposes.

CIO membership grew from about 4,000,000 in 1938 to about 6,000,000 in 1945. In 1949 and 1950, the CIO expelled 11 affiliated unions that it found guilty of being dominated by communists or communist sympathizers.

After many attempts at a merger, the CIO and AFL finally united in 1955. By then the craft vs. industrial union conflict had become less important. More than half of the AFL's members were in industrial unions. Rivalry among labor leaders lessened after the deaths in 1952 of William Green, president of the AFL, and Philip Murray, president of the CIO. When the two organizations merged, the CIO had about 5,800,000 members, the AFL about 10,200,000.　JAMES B. CAREY

See also DUBINSKY, DAVID; LABOR (Labor Unions in the U.S.); LEWIS, JOHN L.; MURRAY, PHILIP; REUTHER, WALTER PHILIP.

CONGRESS OF RACIAL EQUALITY. See CORE.

CONGRESS OF THE CONFEDERATION, established by the Articles of Confederation, operated the United States government from Mar. 1, 1781, to Mar. 4, 1789. It replaced the Continental Congress, although many persons continued to call it that. The Congress of the Confederation was replaced by the Congress established by the United States Constitution. See also ARTICLES OF CONFEDERATION; CONTINENTAL CONGRESS.

CONGRESS
OF THE UNITED STATES

CONGRESS OF THE UNITED STATES is the law-making branch of the federal government. Its legal name is THE CONGRESS, but most people call it simply CONGRESS. Its most important task is making laws. But Congress does much more than make laws. For example, Congress plays an important part in amending the United States Constitution. Congress also conducts investigations. In addition, it reviews the work of the executive and judicial branches of the government.

Congress is closer to the American people than is either the executive or the judicial branch of the government. The people elect the members of Congress directly. Each member of Congress tries to serve and to reflect the desires of his *constituents* (the voters he represents). The people elect the President only indirectly, through the Electoral College (see ELECTORAL COLLEGE). They do not elect any federal judges.

How Congress Is Organized

Congress is a *bicameral* (two-house) legislature. It consists of the *Senate* and the *House of Representatives* (usually called simply the *House*). All members of Congress are *congressmen*. But this term usually refers only to members of the House. In each house, the party with the most members is called the *majority party*. The party with the least members is called the *minority party*.

The Senate. The *formal* (official) organization of the Senate is given in Article I, Section 3 of the Constitution (see UNITED STATES CONSTITUTION). The Vice-President of the United States is the formal head of the Senate. He has the title of *President of the Senate*. The Senate elects one of its members from the majority party to be *president pro tempore* (temporary president). He presides whenever the President of the Senate is absent. Other officials of the Senate include the secretary, sergeant at arms, chief clerk, chaplain, secretary for the majority party, and secretary for the minority party. These officials are not senators.

The organization of the Democratic and Republican parties in the Senate is called the *informal* (unofficial) organization of the Senate. This organization is not mentioned in the Constitution. The leaders of the Democratic and Republican parties are chosen by their parties in a party *caucus* (conference). The senators of each party elect a *floor leader*. The floor leader is his party's chief officer in the Senate. Each party also elects a *whip*, who ranks second to the floor leader. See SENATE.

The House of Representatives, like the Senate, has both a formal and an informal organization. The formal organization of the House is specified in Article I, Section 2 of the Constitution. The presiding officer is the *speaker of the House*. The majority party nominates the

John H. Ferguson, the contributor of this article, is Professor of Political Science at Pennsylvania State University.

Lyndon B. Johnson, the critical reviewer of this article, was President of the United States from 1963 to 1969 and majority leader of the U.S. Senate from 1955 to 1961.

United Press Int.

early adjournment gives senators and representatives time to campaign for re-election. In odd-numbered years, Congress sometimes does not adjourn until mid-summer or late summer. After Congress has adjourned, the President can call a *special session*. The President can adjourn Congress only when the two houses cannot agree on an adjournment date.

The Senate and the House usually meet separately. They occasionally meet together in a *joint session* in the chamber of the House of Representatives. The Constitution requires Congress to hold a joint session to *canvass* (examine) the electoral votes after a presidential election. Both houses also meet together when the President addresses Congress in person. No legislation can be *enacted* (passed into law) at a joint session.

How Congress Makes Laws

The Power to Legislate. The Constitution gives Congress all the lawmaking powers of the federal government. But it does not give all these powers in the same way. The *expressed powers* of Congress are listed in Article I, Section 8 of the Constitution. These powers are the most important ones. They deal with such subjects as taxation, borrowing money, and declaring war. Other expressed powers concern foreign and domestic commerce, national defense, coinage, weights and measures, and the courts.

The *implied powers* are not listed in the Constitution. But Article I, Section 18 of the Constitution says that Congress can pass all laws that are "necessary and proper" for carrying out the expressed powers. Congress has the expressed power to pass tax laws. It has the implied power to set punishments for persons who break the tax laws. Ever since the Constitution was written, authorities have argued over what action could be properly implied.

Other powers of Congress do not come from the Constitution. Congress has these *inherent powers* because the United States is a *sovereign* (independent) nation. For example, some authorities say that Congress uses its

speaker, and the entire House elects him. Nonmember officials of the House include the clerk, sergeant at arms, doorkeeper, postmaster, and chaplain.

Informal organization is more significant in the House than in the Senate. The membership of the House is much larger than that of the Senate. One Representative cannot influence the House as greatly as one senator can influence the Senate. Each representative must work closely with his fellow party members to accomplish his party's program. Party policy is set in caucuses. Each party has a floor leader and a whip. See HOUSE OF REPRESENTATIVES.

Agencies Under Congress. Five government offices report directly to Congress. These are (1) the Architect of the Capitol, (2) the Botanic Garden, (3) the General Accounting Office, (4) the Government Printing Office, and (5) the Library of Congress.

When Congress Meets. A new Congress comes into existence every two years upon the election of a new House of Representatives. About a third of the Senate comes up for election every two years. The Senate is called a *continuing body* because there is never a completely new Senate. Beginning with the first Congress (1789-1791), regular sessions of Congress have been numbered consecutively.

Congress holds one regular session each year. Regular sessions begin on January 3 unless Congress sets a different date. They usually end on July 31, but Congress can change this date also. In even-numbered years, Congress usually adjourns in early summer. An

---

FACTS IN BRIEF ABOUT CONGRESSMEN

Qualifications: A candidate for the Senate must be: (1) at least 30 years old, (2) a citizen of the United States for at least 9 years, and (3) a resident of the state from which he seeks election.

A candidate for the House of Representatives must be: (1) at least 25 years old, (2) a citizen of the United States for at least 7 years, and (3) a resident of the state from which he seeks election.

Nomination: Candidates for the Senate and the House are nominated by primary election or by party convention.

Election: A senator is elected by the voters from all parts of his state. A representative may (1) be elected by the voters of one congressional district of his state, or (2) be elected *at large* (by voters throughout the state).

Term: Senators are elected to six-year terms, and representatives are elected to two-year terms. A member of Congress can serve an unlimited number of terms.

Income: Every member of Congress receives a salary of $42,500 a year. Members also receive free office space and allowances for office expenses, staff salaries, travel, and similar expenses.

Removal from Office: Members of Congress may be expelled by a two-thirds vote of their house.

Congressional Committees often hold hearings on matters connected with bills they are considering. The committees may call witnesses to answer questions and give information. This helps the congressmen decide what action to take on the bills.

inherent powers when it grants or cancels a person's citizenship, or when it prevents undesirable persons from entering the country. See SOVEREIGNTY.

Congress is limited in the way that it uses its powers. For example, the Supreme Court can rule that an act of Congress violates the Constitution. If the court declares an act unconstitutional, the act is no longer the law of the land, unless the court later reverses its decision. See SUPREME COURT OF THE UNITED STATES (Authority of the Supreme Court). The Constitution also limits Congress by prohibiting it from taking certain actions. Congress cannot change state boundaries or state constitutions. Nor can it deny *due process of law* to individuals (see DUE PROCESS OF LAW). Finally, Congress is limited by the power of public opinion. Members of Congress know their actions must reflect the general will of the people.

The Committee System. Committees of Congress do most of the work of preparing legislation. The House has 21 *standing* (permanent) committees and the Senate has 16. There are also four other kinds of committees: (1) *subcommittees* of the standing committees; (2) *special* and *select* committees, appointed for a limited time or purpose; (3) *joint* committees made up of members of both houses; and (4) *commissions* and *boards* that handle various other matters.

Democrats and Republicans in each house have special committees that nominate members of the standing committees. All the members of each house then choose the committee members from among the nominees. Both Democrats and Republicans serve on each committee. But the majority party has a majority of the members of every committee.

The chairman of each committee is selected by a custom called the *seniority rule*. The congressman from the majority party who has been on the committee the longest time is automatically named chairman. Many committee chairmen come from states in which one party is much stronger than the other. These states do not often change congressmen. Their congressmen are re-elected time after time, and build up seniority.

Critics of the seniority rule claim that it rewards length of service, not ability or party loyalty. But other authorities say the seniority rule is an automatic way of choosing committee chairmen. It eliminates fights over who will be the chairmen.

In both houses of Congress, nearly every *bill* (piece of legislation) goes before a standing committee for action. The committees can take one of three actions:

(1) *report* (recommend) a bill favorably in its original form, (2) report the bill with proposed changes, or (3) *pigeonhole* (fail to report) the bill.

Passing a Bill. After a bill has been reported by a committee, it is placed on the *legislative calendar* of the house that is considering it. The calendar shows the order in which bills have been reported by committees. The House has separate calendars for the two types of bills it considers: (1) public bills and (2) private bills. *Public bills* deal with matters of general concern, such as taxation, national defense, and foreign affairs. *Private bills* deal with specific places, groups, or persons, such as paying damages to a man who was hit by a government-owned truck. The Senate puts all bills on the same legislative calendar. The Senate also has an *executive calendar* that includes executive actions such as treaties and presidential nominations.

In both houses, a *simple majority vote* (one more than half) is enough to pass most bills. On major matters, the Senate takes a *roll call vote*. Each senator says "Aye!" or "Nay!" when his name is called. The House of Representatives uses four methods of voting: (1) voice vote, (2) standing vote, (3) teller vote, and (4) roll call vote. In a *voice vote*, all in favor say "Aye!" and then all opposed say "Nay!" In a *standing vote*, all in favor stand, then all opposed stand. In a *teller vote*, all in favor file past one teller who counts them, and all opposed file past another teller. In a *roll call vote*, each member says "Aye!" or "Nay!" when his name is called. The first three methods are quick, but only a roll call vote records how an individual member voted.

Before the President can sign a bill, both houses of Congress must pass it in identical form. If the House and the Senate pass different versions of the same bill, a special *conference committee* tries to settle the differences. Five representatives and five senators serve on most of these committees, but the number often varies. The presiding officer in each house appoints the members who are to serve on the conference committee.

Congress can enact a bill even if the President vetoes it. The vetoed bill becomes law if, after the President's veto, both the Senate and the House repass it by a two-

STANDING COMMITTEES OF CONGRESS	
Senate	**House of Representatives**
Aeronautical and Space Sciences	Agriculture
Agriculture and Forestry	Appropriations
Appropriations	Armed Services
Armed Services	Banking and Currency
Banking and Currency	District of Columbia
Commerce	Education and Labor
District of Columbia	Foreign Affairs
Finance	Government Operations
Foreign Relations	House Administration
Government Operations	Interior and Insular Affairs
Interior and Insular Affairs	Internal Security
Judiciary	Interstate and Foreign Commerce
Labor and Public Welfare	Judiciary
Post Office and Civil Service	Merchant Marine and Fisheries
Public Works	Post Office and Civil Service
Rules and Administration	Public Works
	Rules
	Science and Astronautics
	Standards of Official Conduct
	Veterans' Affairs
	Ways and Means

WHERE CONGRESS WORKS

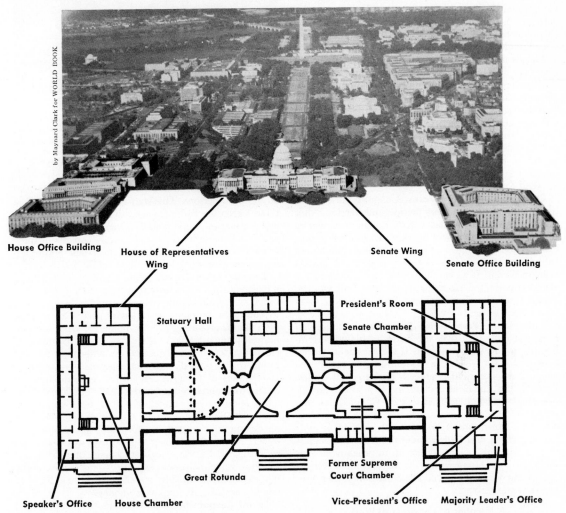

by Maynard Clark for WORLD BOOK

House Office Building

House of Representatives Wing

Senate Wing

Senate Office Building

Statuary Hall

President's Room

Senate Chamber

Speaker's Office   House Chamber

Great Rotunda

Former Supreme Court Chamber

Vice-President's Office   Majority Leader's Office

The United States Capitol in Washington, D.C., is the meeting place of the Senate and the House of Representatives. President George Washington laid the cornerstone in 1793. Since then, the Capitol has been remodeled many times. Congress first met there in 1800. It had previously met in Federal Hall in New York City and in Congress Hall in Philadelphia.

thirds majority of those members voting. See UNITED STATES, GOVERNMENT OF (illustration: How a Bill Becomes Law).

Other Duties of Congress

Congress has six major nonlegislative duties. These deal with (1) amending the Constitution, (2) conducting investigations, (3) reviewing the operations of the executive branch, (4) *canvassing* (examining) electoral votes, (5) determining presidential disability, and (6) impeaching and trying federal officials.

Amending the Constitution is the most important nonlegislative power. Congress may propose amendments, or else it may call a constitutional convention to propose them. Congress usually indicates whether the states must vote on a proposed amendment (1) by

state legislatures or (2) by special state conventions.

Conducting Investigations. Congress can investigate any subject that affects any of its powers. Under its power to declare war, for example, Congress can investigate groups that might be harmful to the United States.

The entire House or the entire Senate can conduct an investigation. But congressional committees usually do so. An investigating committee can call witnesses and require them to produce information. The House or the Senate can give its committees the power to issue warrants for the arrest of persons who do not obey congressional orders. Congress can punish these persons for *contempt*, but usually the courts try contempt cases and prescribe penalties (see CONTEMPT).

Reviewing Government Actions. Congress has a constant influence on the operations of the executive

758c

branch of the government. Congress *appropriates* (sets aside) money for the executive departments, and can call on department heads to explain their budgets. Congressional committees also can investigate the activities of federal agencies. Also, if the office of Vice-President becomes vacant, the President names a new Vice-President, who must be confirmed by Congress.

The Senate has an especially strong check on two powers of the President. The Constitution requires that the Senate must (1) approve all treaties made by the President and (2) give its advice and consent when the President appoints certain government officials. These officials include ambassadors, justices of the Supreme Court, Cabinet and sub-cabinet officers, federal district judges, federal district attorneys, and postmasters. If a senator objects to an appointee from his home state, the Senate seldom approves the appointment. This custom is called *senatorial courtesy*.

Canvassing Electoral Votes. Congress must check the official outcome of every presidential election. After the Electoral College has voted, Congress canvasses the results and announces the vote. In most elections, these actions are largely ceremonial. The public knows the winner long before Congress makes the official announcement. If no candidate wins a majority of the electoral votes, the House elects the President and the Senate elects the Vice-President. See ELECTORAL COLLEGE (The College in Action).

Determining Presidential Disability. A disabled President must turn over the duties of his office temporarily to the Vice-President. If the President refuses, Congress may appoint a commission to determine whether the President is able to discharge his duties. Later, if the President declares he is again fit for office, and the commission disagrees, Congress has the power to decide the issue. See UNITED STATES CONSTITUTION (Amendment 25).

Impeaching and Trying Federal Officials. Congress seldom uses this power. When an impeachment does take place, the House brings the impeachment charges against the accused official. The Senate then tries him. See IMPEACHMENT.

A Member of Congress at Work

Responsibilities of His Office. During sessions, most members of Congress use the morning hours to take care of office work, to meet visitors, and to attend committee meetings. Most senators serve on two standing committees, and most representatives serve on one. Senators and representatives may also serve on subcommittees and special committees.

Senate and House sessions begin at noon and last through the afternoon. Sometimes they extend into the evening. But the legislator usually spends little time at these sessions. A bell signal in his office calls him for debates or votes.

Telephone calls, letters, and visits—many of them from constituents—take up a great deal of the legislator's time. Many persons who contact a member of Congress want to give their views on various bills. Others inquire about jobs, contracts, passports, immigration, or appointments to the military academies.

Every legislator has assistants to aid him in his work.

Courtesy of American Telephone and Telegraph Co.

The First Continental Congress met in Philadelphia in 1774. Patrick Henry addressed the delegates, who were more interested in winning fair treatment from Britain than in independence for the colonies. The Congress was especially concerned about Britain's treatment of the colonies on trade and taxation.

A senator receives an allowance to hire an office staff of about 10 persons. This staff usually includes two or three legislative and administrative assistants and several secretaries. Representatives receive smaller allowances. A representative's staff usually consists of three or four secretaries. The speaker of the House and representatives with special duties have additional aides.

Congressional Travel. Most members of Congress have an office both in their home town and in Washington, D.C. Legislators often travel home to talk with voters, to study local problems, to talk with party leaders, or to plan campaign strategy. Trips home are especially important when a legislator is seeking renomination or re-election. Congressmen receive an allowance for one round trip to their district each session.

Members of Congress also travel to campaign for others, to attend meetings, and to make public speeches. They often have to travel as part of their committee work. The Senate and House sometimes send members on distant trips to gather information or to take part in ceremonies. Critics refer to such trips as *junkets*. The *critics* suggest that many legislators make these trips only to enjoy travel at public expense. Congressmen argue that experience gained by traveling helps them legislate wisely and save the taxpayers' money.

Social Responsibilities. Members of Congress and their families attend many important ceremonies. These include the President's inauguration, the ritual of swearing in new members of Congress, and various ceremonies honoring national heroes and events. A legislator also meets important visitors from other countries and attends official parties and receptions.

Many *lobbyists* (persons who try to influence legislators) try to have frequent social contacts with members of Congress. They try in this way to persuade legislators to favor a group or a cause. Legislators must be careful to avoid accepting any favors that could be interpreted as bribes. See LOBBYING.

History of Congress

Early Days. The First Continental Congress was the country's first national legislature. It met in Philadelphia in 1774. The Second Continental Congress, which met in Philadelphia in 1775, governed throughout the Revolutionary War. It operated until 1781, when the Congress of the Confederation was formed.

Many persons continued to use the name Continental Congress when referring to the legislature. The Continental Congresses and the Congress of the Confederation were *unicameral* (one-house) legislatures. See CONTINENTAL CONGRESS; ARTICLES OF CONFEDERATION.

In 1787, a Constitutional Convention met to strengthen the national government. The convention delegates had many problems. One of the most difficult was the need to compromise the conflicting demands of small and large states. The small states feared that the large states would dominate them. They insisted that all states should have equal representation in the national legislature. But the large states, with more people, thought this would be unfair. The solution, known as the *Connecticut Compromise*, provided for a two-house legislature. In one house (the Senate), each state received equal representation. In the other (the House), representation was based on population. See UNITED STATES CONSTITUTION (The Constitutional Convention).

Reforms in Congress. Although Congress has grown much larger, its form has changed little. Amendments 17 and 20 to the Constitution made important changes. Amendment 17, in 1913, gave the people the right to elect their senators. Previously, senators had been elected by state legislatures. Amendment 20, in 1933, abolished the lame duck session (see LAME DUCK AMENDMENT).

Disputes have raged over many other features of Congress. One of the most stirring arguments concerned the power of the speaker of the House. This dispute came to a climax in 1910, when Joseph G. Cannon (1836-1926) of Illinois was speaker. Until then, the speaker had appointed all House committees. As a result, he had almost complete control over the House. In 1910, the House adopted a resolution that gave the entire House the power to appoint committees.

In 1946, Congress passed the Legislative Reorganization Act. This act increased the efficiency of Congress. Among other actions, it cut the number of standing committees and gave Congress greater control over lobbying. In 1955, the House adopted new rules for investigating committees. These rules provided added protection for the civil liberties of witnesses.

In 1964, the Supreme Court of the United States ruled that all congressional districts must be "substantially" equal in population. This decision was directed at the problem of *apportionment* (distribution) of House members. In the past, a rural district with 250,000 persons and an urban district with 500,000 persons might each elect one representative. This meant that the citizens in the rural district had greater representation than those in the urban district. After the 1964 decision, several states changed the boundaries of their districts so that all their House members represented nearly equal numbers of persons.

Unsolved Problems still exist. One such problem is to improve the cooperation between the President and Congress. This issue becomes particularly difficult when the President belongs to one political party, and the majority of legislators belong to the other party.

Another problem is *gerrymandering* (shaping legislative districts in an unfair way). Federal regulations might discourage state legislatures from this practice. See GERRYMANDER.

Some critics claim that members of Congress spend too much time on petty matters, such as private bills. They say the legislators should have more aides to do research and to handle routine work on such matters. Other critics make the following points: (1) Legislators would get more done if the District of Columbia were allowed to govern itself. (2) The Senate could save much time and money if it would outlaw the filibuster (see FILIBUSTERING). (3) The House could pass laws more quickly and easily if it reduced the power of the Rules Committee. (4) The quality and quantity of work done by committees might be improved if Congress appointed chairmen on the basis of ability, not seniority. But regardless of their criticisms, most authorities agree that the Congress of the United States is one of the most successful legislative bodies in the world. These authorities point out that the men and women who have served in Congress have, on most issues, carried out the will of the majority of Americans.   JOHN H. FERGUSON

Critically reviewed by LYNDON B. JOHNSON

Related Articles. See the articles on HOUSE OF REPRESENTATIVES and SENATE. Other related articles include:

Capitol	Speaker
Congressional Page	Territory
Congressional Record	United States, Government of
Franking and Penalty Privileges	United States, History of
General Accounting Office	United States Botanic Garden
Government Printing Office	United States Constitution
Legislature	Vice-President of the United States
Library of Congress	
President of the United States	

Outline

I. How Congress Is Organized
   A. The Senate
   B. The House of Representatives
   C. Agencies Under Congress
   D. When Congress Meets

II. How Congress Makes Laws
   A. The Power to Legislate
   B. The Committee System
   C. Passing a Bill

III. Other Duties of Congress
   A. Amending the Constitution
   B. Conducting Investigations
   C. Reviewing Government Actions
   D. Canvassing Electoral Votes
   E. Determining Presidential Disability
   F. Impeaching and Trying Federal Officials

IV. A Member of Congress at Work
   A. Responsibilities of His Office
   B. Congressional Travel
   C. Social Responsibilities

V. History of Congress

Questions

Why is Congress the branch of government closest to the people?

Why are there two houses of Congress?

What is a *joint session? Senatorial courtesy?*

What is the role of a congressional committee in passing laws?

How does Congress take part in amending the Constitution?

How does Congress influence the President's treaty-making power?

What are *delegated powers? Implied powers?*

In what ways is the power of Congress limited?

What suggestions do critics make for improving the efficiency of Congress?

What are six nonlegislative duties of Congress?

CONGRESSIONAL COMMITTEE. See CONGRESS OF THE UNITED STATES (The Committee System).

CONGRESSIONAL LIBRARY. See LIBRARY OF CONGRESS.

CONGRESSIONAL MEDAL OF HONOR. See DECORATIONS AND MEDALS (Military Awards).

CONGRESSIONAL PAGE is a boy who works as a messenger in the United States Senate or House of Representatives. Pages carry messages between the Capitol and the Senate and House office buildings, and run errands for the senators and representatives. Senate pages must also see that the senators' desks and documents in the Senate chamber are in order before each session.

Senators and representatives appoint a limited number of boys from their home districts to work as pages. The boys receive a salary of $1,800 a year. They attend a special high school located in the Library of Congress. Classes are held daily from 6:30 A.M. to 9:45 A.M.

CONGRESSIONAL RECORD is a printed account of what is done and said in Congress daily. Each member of Congress finds on his desk in the morning a copy of the *Record* for the day before.

A printed account of what happens in Congress has been published since 1799. Up to 1824, it was known as the *Annals of Congress*, and from 1825 to 1837 as the *Register of Debates*. In 1837 the *Congressional Globe* was first printed. The present *Congressional Record* was started in 1873.

The *Congressional Record* prints everything said in Congress, except during executive sessions of the Senate. Congressmen may make changes in their speeches before they are printed in the *Record*. The congressmen also can have material other than speeches before Congress printed in the *Record*. The *Record* is sent free to depository libraries, and anyone may subscribe to it or even buy separate parts of it from the Superintendent of Documents, Government Printing Office, Washington, D.C. 20402. WILLIAM G. CARLETON

CONGRESSMAN or **CONGRESSWOMAN** is a member of the Congress of the United States. The term generally is used in referring to a member of the House of Representatives. See ADDRESS, FORM OF; CONGRESS OF THE UNITED STATES.

CONGRESSMAN AT LARGE. See HOUSE OF REPRESENTATIVES (Apportionment).

CONGRESSWOMAN, FIRST. See RANKIN, JEANNETTE.

CONGREVE. See MATCH (History).

CONGREVE, WILLIAM (1670-1729), was an English dramatist who wrote witty, sophisticated comedies. The best of his five plays are *Love for Love* (1695) and *The Way of the World* (1700). They contain lively and clever speeches rather than memorable characters or comic situations. They have a polished prose style and a civilized, realistic view of life.

The Way of the World presents a satirical picture of a cultured, worldly high society. The play laughs at hypocrites, boors, would-be wits, fools, and aging coquettes. Though one of Congreve's best, this comedy failed. It was too subtle and sophisticated for its audience. Congreve's most popular play during his lifetime was *The Mourning Bride* (1697), his only tragedy. It contains the famous line "Music hath charms to soothe a savage beast."

Congreve was born in Yorkshire, and grew up in Ireland. He entered law school in London in 1691, but preferred writing and the leisurely life of a man about town. He wrote little after 1700. THOMAS H. FUJIMURA

CONGREVE, SIR WILLIAM (1772-1828), developed the rocket used by British troops in the Napoleonic Wars. By 1808, he had made a weapon lighter, cheaper, and more powerful than the smooth-bore cannon. The rocket was chiefly effective for its noise and glare. The "rockets' red glare" in "The Star-Spangled Banner" refers to Congreve rockets used in the War of 1812. Congreve was born at Woolwich. ROBERT E. SCHOFIELD

CONIC PROJECTION. See MAP.

CONIFER. See CONE-BEARING TREES.

CONJUGATION, *KAHN joo GAY shun*, is the complete list of the *inflections* (various forms) of a verb—in voice, mood, tense, number, and person. Everyone uses all these forms constantly. The verb itself has few forms, but other words may be used with it. For example, *walk* has only four different forms: *walk, walks, walked,* and *walking.* But other words may be added to make verbs, as in *am walking, will walk, did walk, could walk.* The verbs used with any one pronoun (such as *he*) make a *synopsis* (a shortened conjugation).

Other forms are not heard so often. The *subjunctive* mood in the present tense includes *if I be hidden,* and in the past tense includes *if he were hidden.* Such forms are used to indicate uncertainty. For example, "If I were made wealthy I should be surprised."

Another form is the *emphatic* form: *he does eat, we do eat, you did eat.* The *progressive* form tells that an action is going on, was going on, or will be going on. For example, *I am eating, he was eating, I shall be eating.*

In questions, verbs have different forms, usually made by adding the helping verbs *do, does,* or *did.* Examples are *do you know, does he ask, did she appear?*

In the present and past tenses, helping verbs are used to make the negative forms with the negative adverb *not.* For example, *I am not whispering.* CLARENCE STRATTON

See also INFLECTION; VERB.

CONJUGATION OF THE VERB *HIDE*

Principal Parts

Present: hide	*Past:* hid	*Past Participle:* hidden

Tenses	**Active Voice - Indicative Mood**		
Present	I *hide,* you *hide,* he *hides;* we, you, they *hide*		
Past	I, you, he; we, you, they *hid*		
Future	(time to come) I *shall,* you, he *will;* we *shall,* you, they *will hide*		
	(determination) I *will,* you, he *shall;* we *will,* you, they *shall hide*		
Present Perfect	I *have,* you *have,* he *has;* we, you, they *have hidden*		
Past Perfect	I, you, he; we, you, they *had hidden*		
Future Perfect	(time to come) I *shall,* you, he *will;* we *shall,* you, they *will have hidden*		
	(determination) I *will,* you, he *shall;* we *will,* you, they *shall have hidden*		

Passive Voice - Indicative Mood

Present: I am hidden	*Past:* I was hidden	*Future:* I shall be hidden

CONJUGATION is a biological process of reproduction. In the paramecium and certain other protozoa, conjugating organisms exchange *gamete* (reproductive) nuclei only. During the process, two organisms connect by a bridge of *protoplasm* (cellular material). A single nucleus passes through this bridge from each organism to the other. Then, the individuals separate and continue to reproduce by *fission* (splitting). In certain algae, one whole cell fuses with another of similar size. Still other algae form *conjugation tubes* that connect cells of two filaments or two cells of the same filament. The contents of one cell move through the tube and fuse with the contents of the other. Then, the cell undergoes *meiosis* (reduction division of the nucleus). Only one functional cell results from this division, and it grows into a new filament.   NEAL D. BUFFALOE

CONJUNCTION is a word used to connect words, phrases, clauses, and sentences. The term comes from two Latin words that mean *joined with*. There are two kinds of conjunctions, *coordinating* and *subordinating*.

Coordinating Conjunctions connect two words, phrases, clauses, or sentences that are grammatically equal. The following examples illustrate coordinating conjunctions. Words—"He ate bread *and* butter." Phrases—"In red coats *and* with loud drums, the soldiers came marching." Clauses or sentences—"He reads well, *but* his sister reads better."

The principal coordinating conjunctions are:

Expressing addition: and, also, both, as well as, moreover, further, likewise.

Expressing separation or choice: either, or, neither, nor, else, whether, otherwise.

Expressing opposition: but, yet, still, only, nevertheless, whereas.

Expressing effect or result: therefore, hence, consequently, so, so that, thus.

Conjunctions in Pairs are called *correlative conjunctions* and occur in the following constructions.

Both . . . and: *Both* John *and* Mary attend school.

Not only . . . but also: He *not only* reads *but also* writes.

Either . . . or: *Either* I must go now *or* I cannot go at all.

Neither . . . nor: *Neither* the child *nor* the man went.

Whether . . . or: *Whether* it rains *or* shines, I intend to go.

Though . . . yet: *Though* he was tired, *yet* he walked on.

Subordinating Conjunctions join a subordinate clause to the principal clause of a sentence—elements that are not grammatically equal. "He can read better *than* I can." *Than* is a subordinating conjunction connecting the subordinate clause *I can* (*read* is understood) with the principal clause.

The commonest subordinating conjunctions are:

Expressing time and place: when, as, since, while, before, ere, after, until, where.

Expressing cause or reason: because, since, as, whereas, inasmuch as, for.

Expressing condition or supposition: if, unless, though, although, provided, in case, even if.

Expressing purpose or result: that, so that, lest, in order that, so . . . as.

Expressing comparison: than (after comparative), as . . . as, so . . . as.

Common Errors include carelessness in using the correlatives and the comparative *than*. "John is *as* old but not taller *than* Richard" is incorrect for, "John is *as* old *as*, but not taller *than*, Richard." Many persons use a plural verb after two singular nouns connected by *or* or *not*. "Either John or Joe *are* coming" is wrong for "Either John or Joe *is* coming."   CLARENCE STRATTON

CONJUNCTIVA. See EYE (Parts of the Eye).

CONJUNCTIVITIS, *kahn JUNK tih VI tihs*, is any inflammation of the membrane covering the outer layer of the eyeball and the inner lining of the eyelids. This membrane is called the *conjunctiva*. In conjunctivitis, a person's eyes become red and watery and pus may form.

Acute conjunctivitis, also called *pinkeye*, is caused by bacteria and viruses that can be spread to others by using the same towel. Doctors cure bacterial conjunctivitis by treating the eye with antibiotics or sulfonamides. Viruses that can infect the conjunctiva include those that cause colds and measles. Viruses that cause such diseases as herpes and trachoma sometimes infect the conjunctiva and *cornea* (the clear tissue over the colored part of the eye). Victims may lose part or all their sight. The conjunctiva can also become inflamed by smoke, certain eye drugs, and substances that cause allergies such as hay fever.   WILLIAM F. HUGHES

See also ALLERGY; TRACHOMA.

CONJURING, *KUN jur ing*, is a form of entertainment based on pretending to do things everyone knows are against the laws of nature. The conjurer is an especially trained actor. He depends on skill with the hands, psychology, and, often, mechanical apparatus. He counts on the fact that the mind does not notice many things that the eye sees.   JOHN MULHOLLAND

CONN. See IRELAND (Early Days).

CONNAUGHT, DUKE OF (1850-1942), ARTHUR WILLIAM PATRICK ALBERT, the third son of Queen Victoria, served as governor general of Canada from 1911 to 1916. Before going to Canada, he opened the first parliament of the Union of South Africa on behalf of the king. Connaught served in Canada during the Fenian Raid in 1870. He also served in Egypt, India, and Ireland. He was promoted to the rank of general in 1893 and to field marshal in 1902. From 1907 to 1909, he commanded British forces in the Mediterranean. Connaught was born in London. At 16, he entered the Royal Military Academy.   LUCIEN BRAULT

Brown Bros.

The Duke of Connaught

CONNAUGHT TUNNEL is the longest double-track railway tunnel in North America. It carries the Canadian Pacific Railway five miles through Mount Macdonald in the Selkirk range of southeastern British Columbia. Inside the concrete-lined tunnel, trains run on the left-hand track to give engineers a maximum view ahead. Work began on the tunnel in 1913, and was completed in 1916.   RODERICK HAIG-BROWN

Historic Village Green and Church in Litchfield

CONNECTICUT, *kuh NEHT ih kut,* is the third small-est state. Only Delaware and Rhode Island have smaller areas. In spite of its small size, Connecticut is an important industrial state and a favorite vacationland. Hartford, the capital and largest city of Connecticut, is known as the *Insurance Capital of the World.* Over 30 insurance companies have headquarters in Hartford.

Connecticut leads the states in making helicopters, jet aircraft engines, and submarines. Connecticut also leads in the production of ball and roller bearings, pins and needles, silverware, small firearms, and thread. It ranks among the leaders in manufacturing electric out-lets and switches, hardware, propellers, typewriters, watches and clocks, and other products.

The mighty Connecticut River cuts through the cen-ter of the state. The river flows into Long Island Sound, Connecticut's outlet to the Atlantic Ocean. The word *Connecticut* comes from an Algonkian Indian word meaning *on the long tidal river.* Most of the state's big

industrial cities are west of the Connecticut River. They stretch from Hartford in central Connecticut to Stam-ford near the southwestern border. New York City lies south of Connecticut. Thousands of Connecticut men and women commute to work in the giant metropolis.

Connecticut's rural areas and small towns contrast sharply with its industrial cities. Many towns center around a *green* (public park). Near the green may stand a small white church, a town meeting hall, a tavern, and several colonial houses. Forests, rivers, lakes, water-falls, and a sandy shore add to Connecticut's beauty.

The people of Connecticut played important parts in the history and industrial development of the United States. Connecticut delegates to the Constitutional Convention of 1787 worked out the *Connecticut Compro-mise.* The compromise broke a deadlock over how many men each state should elect to the U.S. Congress. The compromise also earned Connecticut the nickname of the *Constitution State.* Connecticut provided large quan-

CONNECTICUT

THE CONSTITUTION STATE

The contributors of this article are Bob Eddy, Editor of
The Hartford Courant; *Joseph B. Hoyt, Chairman of the*
Social Science Department at Southern Connecticut State Col-
lege, and author of The Connecticut Story; *and Albert E.*
Van Dusen, State Historian of Connecticut, Professor of History
at the University of Connecticut, and author of Connecticut.

——— FACTS IN BRIEF ———

Capital: Hartford.

Government: *Congress*—U.S. Senators, 2; U.S. Representatives, 6. *Electoral Votes,* 8. *State Legislature*—senators, 36; representatives, 177. *Counties,* eight (Connecticut has no county governments). *Towns,* 169.
Voting Age, 21 years.

Area: 5,009 square miles (including 139 square miles of
inland water), 48th in size among the states. *Greatest*
Distances: (east-west) 90 miles; (north-south) 75 miles.
Shoreline, 618 miles.

Elevation: *Highest,* 2,380 feet above sea level, on the
south slope of Mount Frissell. *Lowest,* sea level along
the Long Island Sound shore.

Population: 2,535,234 (1960 census), 25th among the
states. *Density,* 506 persons to the square mile. *Dis-*
tribution, urban 78 per cent; rural, 22 per cent. *Esti-*
mated 1965 Population, 2,886,000.

Chief Products: *Manufacturing,* chemical products, clocks
and watches, electrical machinery, fabricated metal
products, firearms, hardware, non-electrical machinery, plastics and rubber products, textiles, transportation equipment. *Agriculture,* dairy products (especially milk), fruit, greenhouse and nursery products,
hay, poultry products, tobacco, vegetables. *Mining,*
clays, feldspar, sand and gravel, stone. *Fishing Industry,*
clams, lobsters, oysters, scallops, shad.

Statehood: January 9, 1788, the 5th state.

State Motto: *Qui transtulit sustinet* (Latin for *He who trans-*
planted still sustains).

Connecticut Development Commission

Autumn Scene near Goshen

Connecticut Development Commission

Constitution Plaza in Hartford

tities of food, clothing, and other supplies to the Colonial Army during the Revolutionary War. For this reason, George Washington honored Connecticut with
another nickname—the *Provisions State.*

Eli Whitney made Connecticut the birthplace of
mass-production manufacturing. Working in Hamden,
he showed the advantages of using interchangeable
parts in gunmaking. Whitney's methods led to the high-
speed industrial production methods of today. Steel
manufacturing began in Hartford County. Connecticut
men were also the first Americans to make bicycles,
dyed silk, friction matches, printing type, repeating
pistols, rubber shoes, and vulcanized rubber. The first
insurance policies covering accidents, automobiles, and
aircraft were written in Hartford. The *Nautilus,*
launched in Groton in 1954, was the world's first nuclear-powered submarine.

For the relationship of Connecticut to other states in
its region, see NEW ENGLAND.

Connecticut (blue) ranks 48th in size among all the states, and
5th in size among the New England States (gray).

Constitution of Connecticut was adopted in 1965. It replaced an earlier constitution adopted in 1818. Colonial Connecticut's first constitution was the Fundamental Orders of 1639. Connecticut governed itself under the Fundamental Orders until it received a royal charter in 1662. The charter was the constitution until 1818.

An *amendment* (change) to the constitution may be proposed by the legislature or by a constitutional convention. An amendment proposed by the legislature must be approved by a majority of the members of each house, and by a majority of electors voting on the amendment in a general election. If the amendment is approved by a three-fourths majority of each house, electors vote on it in the next general election. If it is approved by a majority of less than three-fourths of each house, it must be approved again by a majority in the next regular session of the legislature. Then it is voted on in a general election.

A constitutional convention may be called by a two-thirds vote in each house of the legislature, or by a majority of electors voting on the question. An amendment proposed by a convention must be approved by a majority of the electors.

Executive. The governor of Connecticut is elected to a four-year term. He receives a $35,000 annual salary. The governor may be re-elected any number of times. For a list of all the governors of Connecticut, see the *History* section of this article.

The voters also elect the lieutenant governor, attorney general, comptroller, secretary of the state, and state treasurer to four-year terms. The governor, with the approval of either house of the legislature, appoints most other top executive officials. These officials include the commissioners of agriculture, banking, finance, health, highways, insurance, labor, taxes, and welfare.

Legislature, called the *general assembly*, consists of a 36-member senate and a 177-member house of representatives. Voters in each of Connecticut's 36 senatorial districts elect one senator. Voters in each of the state's 177 assembly districts elect one representative. Senators and representatives serve two-year terms.

The legislature meets in odd-numbered years. Sessions begin on the first Wednesday after the first Monday in January. They must end by the Wednesday after the first Monday in June. Special sessions, which may be called by the governor, have no time limits.

In 1965, Connecticut *reapportioned* (redivided) its legislature to provide equal representation based on population. For a discussion of reapportionment, see the *Connecticut Today* section of this article.

Courts. The supreme court is Connecticut's highest court. It is a court of appeals, and has a chief justice and five associate justices. The superior court is the state's highest trial court. It has 35 justices. Supreme and superior court justices are nominated by the governor and appointed by the legislature. They serve eight-year terms.

Connecticut also has a court of common pleas, a circuit court, and a juvenile court. The judges of these courts are nominated by the governor and appointed by the legislature. Judges who serve in the common pleas court, circuit court, and juvenile court serve four-year terms. The judges of Connecticut's 125 probate courts are elected by the people. Probate court judges also serve four-year terms.

Local Government in Connecticut is centered in 169 *towns*. Connecticut towns are similar to *townships* in other states. That is, they are geographic districts that may include several communities and large rural areas under one government.

Most small Connecticut towns use the town meeting form of government. This pure form of democracy allows citizens to take a direct part in government. Each year, town voters meet to elect officials, approve budgets, and decide other business. The chief town officials are called *selectmen*. See TOWN MEETING.

Some towns have heavily populated areas called *boroughs* and *cities*. Most of Connecticut's 12 boroughs have a government that is independent of the town government. In most of the state's 23 cities, the city and town governments operate as one unit—called a *city government*. The most common form of city government is the mayor-council type. Some cities use the council-manager form. Connecticut cities operate under state charters. All chartered cities have *home rule*—they are free to amend their own charters. Connecticut and

Morton J. Boardman

The Governor's Mansion, surrounded by six acres of landscaped grounds, overlooks Hartford. The house was built for private use, but was bought by the state in 1943. Many of the mansion's furnishings date from the 1700's.

The State Seal

Symbols of Connecticut. On the state seal, the three grape-vines symbolize the transplanting of the culture and traditions of Europe to the colony of Connecticut. The seal was adopted in 1931. The grapevines also appear on the state flag, which was adopted in 1897. Earlier flags, dating back to the 1770's, used the grapevine symbol, but were not official state flags.

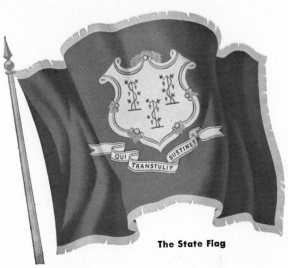

The State Flag

Rhode Island are the only states that do not have county governments. Counties in these states are divisions of court systems.

Taxation provides about four-fifths of the Connecticut government's income. Almost all the rest comes from federal grants and other U.S. government programs. Sales and gross receipts taxes bring in the largest percentage of the state's income. These taxes include, in order of importance, a general sales and gross receipts tax, and taxes on motor fuels, public utilities, tobacco products, insurance, and alcoholic beverages. Other Connecticut taxes include corporation net income taxes, estate and gift taxes, and license fees.

Politics. Connecticut gave early support to the Republican party after the party was formed in 1854. In presidential elections between 1856 and 1932, Connecticut voted for 15 Republicans and only 5 Democrats. The voters chose about three times as many Republicans as Democrats for governor during the same period. The Democrats gained strength during the 1930's. Since 1960, registered Democratic voters have outnumbered registered Republicans in Connecticut. For Connecticut's electoral votes and voting record in presidential elections, see ELECTORAL COLLEGE (table).

The State Bird
Robin

The State Flower
Mountain Laurel

State Capitol in Hartford was completed in 1879. It is built of granite and marble. New Haven and Hartford were twin capitals from 1662 to 1873, when Hartford became the only capital.
Connecticut Development Commission

The State Tree
White Oak

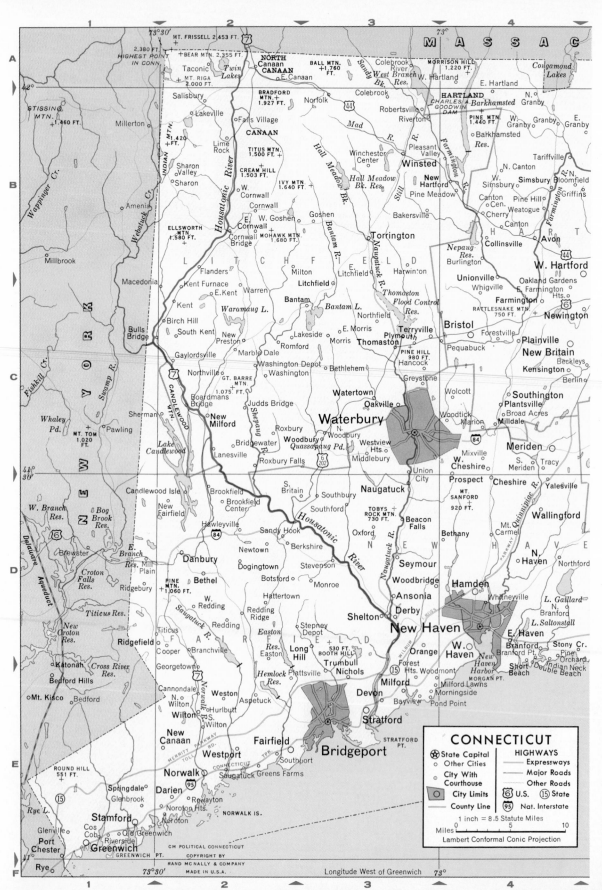

Map labels (reading roughly top to bottom, left to right):

Grid columns: 1 2 3 4

73°30′
MT. FRISSELL 2,453 FT.
MASSAC

2,380 FT. HIGHEST POINT IN CONN.
+ BEAR MTN. 2,355 FT.
BALL MTN. + 1,760 FT.
Colebrook River Br. Res.
MORRISON HILL 1,220 FT.
Congamond Lakes

Taconic
Twin Lakes
NORTH Canaan CANAAN
E. Canaan
Sandy Bk.
West Branch
W. Hartland
E. Hartland

42°
MT. RIGA 2,000 FT.
Salisbury
BRADFORD MTN. + 1,927 FT.
Norfolk
Colebrook
HARTLAND
CHARLES A. GOODWIN DAM
Robertsville
Riverton
Barkhamsted
N. Granby
E. Granby

STISSING MTN. + 1,460 FT.
Millerton
Lakeville
CANAAN
1,420 + FT.
Falls Village
Mad R.
Pleasant Valley
PINE MTN. 1,440 FT.
W. Granby
Granby

Lime Rock
TITUS MTN. 1,500 FT.
Winchester Center
Skiff R.
Barkhamsted Res.
N. Canton
Tariffville

Sharon Valley
CREAM HILL 1,503 FT.
W. Cornwall
Cornwall
IVY MTN. 1,640 FT.
Goshen
Hall Meadow Bk. Res.
New Hartford
Pine Meadow
Winsted
Simsbury
Simsbury
Bloomfield
Griffins

Sharon
W. Goshen
Cornwall
E. Cornwall
MOHAWK MTN. 1,680 FT.
Bantam R.
Torrington
Bakersville
W. Simsbury
Canton Cen.
Pine Hill
Weatogue
Canton

ELLSWORTH MTN. 1,580 FT.
Cornwall Bridge
Flanders
Milton
Litchfield
Harwinton
Nepaug Res.
Burlington
Collinsville
Cherry
Canton
Avon

Kent Furnace
Warren
Bantam
Litchfield
E. Litchfield
Thomaston Flood Control Res.
Unionville
Whigville
Oakland Gardens
E. Farmington
W. Hartford

E. Kent
Kent
Waramaug L.
Bantam L.
Northfield
Farmington
RATTLESNAKE MTN. 750 FT.
Newington

Birch Hill
South Kent
New Preston
Lakeside
E. Morris
Morris
Thomaston
Terryville
Plymouth
Hancock
PINE HILL 980 FT.
Forestville
Pequabuck
Bristol
Plainville
New Britain

Bulls Bridge
GT. BARRE MTN. 1,075 FT.
Washington Depot
Washington
Bethlehem
Greystone
Wolcott
Southington
Plantsville
Broad Acres
Kensington
Berlin
Beckleys

Gaylordsville
Northville
Boardmans Bridge
Judds Bridge
Watertown
Oakville
Waterbury
N. Woodbury
Woodtick
Marion
Milldale
Meriden

Sherman
New Milford
Roxbury
Woodbury
Westview Hts.
Middlebury
Mixville
W. Cheshire
S. Meriden
Tracy

Lake Candlewood
Lanesville
Bridgewater
Quassapaug Pd.
Union City
Prospect
Cheshire
Yalesville

Candlewood Isle
Brookfield
S. Britain
Southbury
Naugatuck
MT. SANFORD 920 FT.
Wallingford

New Fairfield
Brookfield Center
Southford
TOBYS ROCK MTN. 730 FT.
Beacon Falls
Bethany
Mt. Carmel

Hawleyville
Sandy Hook
Oxford
Bethany
N. Haven
Northford

Danbury
Newtown
Berkshire
Housatonic River
Seymour
Hamden
Whitneyville
L. Gaillard
N. Branford
L. Saltonstall

Bethel
Dogingtown
Stevenson
Woodbridge
Ansonia
Derby
New Haven
E. Haven
Branford
Stony Cr.

PINE MTN. 1,060 FT.
Botsford
Monroe
Shelton
Orange
W. Haven
Branford Pt.
Short Beach
Pine Orchard
Indian Neck

W. Redding
Hattertown
Stepney Depot
530 FT. BOOTH HILL
Trumbull
Nichols
Forest Hts.
Woodmont
New Haven Harbor
Double Beach

Redding
Redding Ridge
Long Hill
Milford
Milford Lawns
Morningside

Titicus
Ridgefield
Cooper
Branchville
Easton Res.
Easton
Plattsville
Devon
Bayview
Pond Point

Georgetown
Cannondale
Weston
Aspetuck
Hemlock Res.
Stratford
STRATFORD PT.

N. Wilton
Hurlbutt
Wilton
S. Wilton
Bridgeport

New Canaan
Westport
Fairfield
Southport
Saugatuck
Greens Farms

ROUND HILL 551 FT.
Norwalk
NORWALK IS.
Springdale
Glenbrook
Darien
Rowayton
Noroton Hts.
Noroton

Stamford
Glenville
Cos Cob
Old Greenwich
Riverside
Greenwich
GREENWICH PT.

Port Chester
Rye

Longitude West of Greenwich
73°

CM POLITICAL CONNECTICUT
COPYRIGHT BY
RAND McNALLY & COMPANY
MADE IN U.S.A.

Legend box:

CONNECTICUT

⊛ State Capital
○ Other Cities
◉ City With Courthouse
City Limits
County Line

HIGHWAYS
Expressways
Major Roads
Other Roads
⑥ U.S. ⑮ State
�95 Nat. Interstate

1 inch = 8.5 Statute Miles
Miles 0 ——— 10
Lambert Conformal Conic Projection

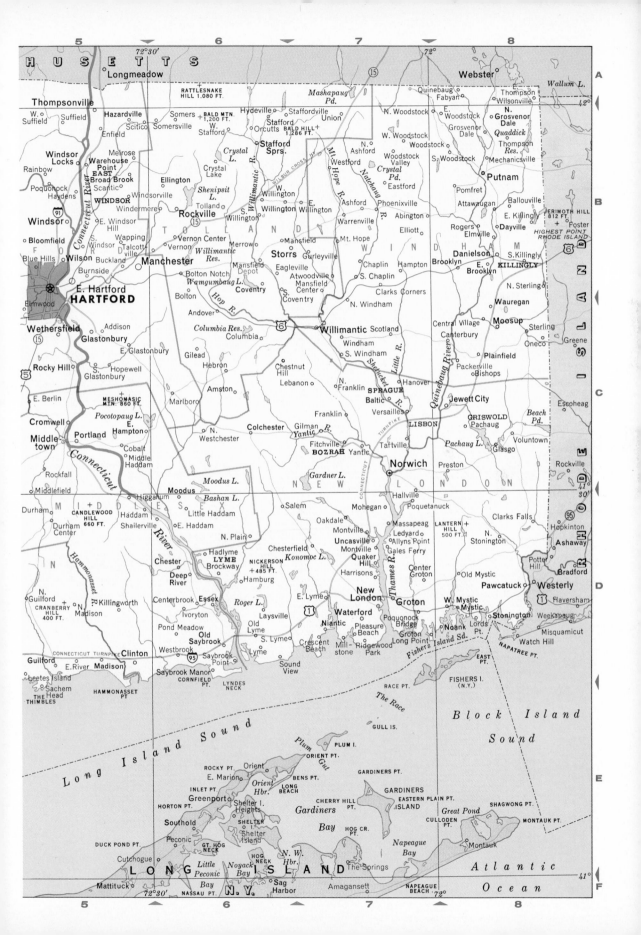

CONNECTICUT MAP INDEX

Population

2,886,000 .Estimate 1965
2,535,234 1960
2,007,280 1950
1,709,242 1940
1,606,903 1930
1,380,631 1920
1,114,756 1910
908,420 1900
746,258 1890
622,700 1880
537,454 1870
460,147 1860
370,792 1850
309,978 1840
297,675 1830
275,248 1820
261,942 1810
251,002 1800
237,946 1790

Metropolitan Areas

Bridgeport 337,983
Hartford 549,249
Meriden 51,850
New Britain 129,397
New Haven 320,836
New London-Groton-Norwich 170,981
Norwalk 96,756
Stamford 178,409
Waterbury 185,548

Counties

Fairfield ..653,589..D 2
Hartford ..689,555..B 4
Litchfield .119,856..B 2
Middlesex ..88,865..D 5
New Haven 660,315..D 3
New London .185,745..C 7
Tolland ....68,737..B 6
Windham ..68,572..B 7

Cities and Towns

Abington .....130..B 7
Amston ....300..C 6
Andover ......200 (1,771▲)..C 6
Ansonia ...19,819..D 3
Ashford, 50 (1,315▲) B 7
Aspetuck .....125..E 2
Attawaugan ...350..B 8
Avon ....5,273..B 4
Bakersville ...150..B 3
Ballouville ...125..B 8
Baltic ....1,366..C 7
Bantam ......833..C 3
Barkhamsted ..60 (1,370▲)..B 4
Bayview ......300..E 3
Beacon Falls 2,886..D 3
Beckleys ......150..C 5
Berlin ......3,500 (11,250▲)..C 5
Bethany ....2,384..D 4
Bethel ......8,200..D 2
Bethlehem ....600 (1,486▲)..C 3
Bloomfield ..5,000 (13,613▲)..B 5
Blue Hills ..4,000..B 5
Boardmans Bridge ......165..C 2
Bolton, 500 (2,933▲) B 6
Bolton Notch .250..B 6
Botsford ......150..D 2
Bozrah (Town of) (1,590▲)..C 7
Branchville ...200..D 2
Branford ...2,371 (16,610▲)..D 4
Branford Point ....300..D 4
Bridgeport 156,748.°E 3
Bridgewater ..250 (898▲)..C 2
Bristol .....45,499..C 4
Broad Brook 1,389..B 5
Brookfield ....500 (3,405▲)..D 2
Brookfield Center .....400..D 2
Brooklyn .....900 (3,312▲)..B 8
Burlington ...700 (2,790▲)..B 4
Canaan .....1,146..A 2
Canaan (Town of) (790▲)..B 2
Candlewood Isle ....200..D 2
Cannondale ...300..E 2
Canterbury ...175 (1,857▲)..C 8
Canton, 400 (4,783▲) B 4
Canton Center, 175..B 4
Center Groton .150..D 7
Centerbrook ...600..D 6
Central Village 800..C 8
Chaplin, 130 (1,230▲) B 7
Cheshire ....4,072 (13,383▲)..D 4
Chester .....1,414 (2,520▲)..D 6
Clinton .....4,166..D 5
Cobalt ....200..C 5
Colchester ..2,260 (4,648▲)..C 6
Colebrook ....125 (791▲)..B 3
Collinsville ..1,682..B 4
Columbia .....200 (2,163▲)..C 6
Conning Towers* ...3,457..D 7
Cornwall .....150 (1,051▲)..B 2
Cornwall Bridge .....200..B 2
Coventry (South Coventry) .3,568 (6,356▲)..B 6
Cromwell ....6,780..C 5
Crystal Lake ..640..B 6
Danbury ...39,382..D 2
Danielson ...4,642..B 8
Darien .....18,437..E 2
Dayville ......900..B 8
Deep River ..2,166 (2,968▲)..D 6
Derby ......12,132..D 3
Double Beach .300..D 4
Durham ......700 (3,096▲)..D 5
Durham Center 350..D 5
Eagleville .....200..B 6
East Berlin ...400..C 5
East Brooklyn ....1,213..B 8
East Canaan ..570..A 2
East Farmington Heights ...1,800..C 4
East Glastonbury ....375..C 5
East Granby ..200 (2,434▲)..B 5
East Haddam .500 (3,637▲)..D 6
East Hampton ....3,000 (5,403▲)..C 5
East Hartford .....43,977..B 5
East Hartland, 330..B 4
East Haven, 21,388..D 4
East Killingly 560..B 8
East Lyme ...850 (6,782▲)..D 7
East Morris ..125..C 3
East River ...200..D 5
East Thompson ....170..A 8
East Windsor (Town of) (7,500▲)..B 5
East Windsor Hill ....900..B 5
East Woodstock ....150..B 8
Eastford, 350 (746▲) B 7
Easton, 600 (3,407▲) D 2
Ellington .....400 (5,580▲)..B 6
Elmville .....350..B 8
Enfield .....3,000 (31,464▲)..B 5
Essex 1,470 (4,057▲) D 6
Fabyan ....170..A 8
Fairfield ...46,183..E 2
Falls Village ..500..B 2
Farmington .2,500 (10,813▲)..C 4
Fitchville .....500..C 7
Forest Heights, 250 E 3
Franklin, 50 (974▲) C 7
Gales Ferry ...450..D 7
Gaylordsville ..200..C 2
Georgetown ..1,100..D 2
Germantown* 2,893..D 2
Gilman ....150..C 7
Glasgo ....150..C 8
Glastonbury .3,400 (14,497▲)..C 5
Goshen, 400 (1,288▲) B 3
Granby, 700 (4,968▲) B 4
Greenmanorville* .....1,200..B 5
Greystone .....100..C 3
Greenwich .53,793..E 1
Griswold (Town of) (6,472▲)..C 8
Grosvenor Dale 530..B 8
Groton .....10,111 (29,937▲)..D 7
Groton Long Point ....350..D 7
Guilford ....2,420 (7,913▲)..D 5
Haddam ......350 (3,466▲)..D 5
Hadlyme ......302..D 6
Hamburg ......150..D 6
Hamden ...41,056..D 4
Hampton 300 (934▲) B 7
Hanover ......250..C 7
Hartford ..162,178.°B 5
Hartland (Town of) (1,040▲)..B 4
Harwinton ....500 (3,344▲)..B 3
Hawleyville ...150..D 2
Haydens ......125..B 5
Hazardville .4,000..B 5
Hebron, 200 (1,819▲) C 6
Higganum ....900..D 5
Hydeville .....100..B 6
Indian Neck, 1,000..D 4
Ivoryton ......950..D 6
Jewett City ..3,608..C 8
Kensington ..4,500..C 4
Kent, 400 (1,686▲)..C 2
Kent Furnace .100..C 2
Killingly (Town of) (11,298▲)..B 8
Killingworth ..150 (1,098▲)..D 5
Lakeside ......200..C 2
Lakeville .....950..B 2
Lanesville .....100..C 2
Laysville ......275..D 6
Lebanon ......300 (2,434▲)..C 7
Ledyard ......250 (5,395▲)..D 7
Leetes Island .400..D 5
Lime Rock ....220..B 2
Lisbon (Town of) (2,019▲)..C 7
Litchfield ..1,363 (6,264▲).°C 3
Lords Point ..120..D 8
Lyme (Town of) (1,183▲)..D 6
Macedonia ....130..C 2
Madison .....1,416 (4,567▲)..D 5
Manchester 42,102..B 5
Mansfield ....100 (14,638▲)..B 6
Mansfield Center .....600..B 7
Mansfield Depot ......130..B 6
Marble Dale ..175..C 2
Marion ....350..C 4
Marlboro (Marlborough) ...700 (1,961▲)..C 6
Massapeag ....100..D 7
Mechanicsville 130..B 8
Melrose ....100..B 5
Meriden ....51,850..C 4
Merrow ....75..B 6
Middle Haddam ....500..C 5
Middlebury 2,000 (4,785▲)..C 3
Middlefield ...400 (3,255▲)..C 5
Middletown, 33,250.°C 5
Milford ....41,662..E 3
Milford Lawns, 575..E 3
Mill Plain ....170..D 1
Milldale ......950..C 4
Millstone .....125..D 7
Mixville ......400..C 4
Mohegan ......300..D 7
Monroe .....1,000 (6,402▲)..D 3
Montville ...1,060 (7,759▲)..D 7
Moodus .....1,103..D 6
Moosup .....2,760..C 8
Morningside ..375..E 3
Morris, 150 (1,190▲) C 3
Mystic ......2,536..D 8
Naugatuck .19,511..D 3
New Britain, 82,201 C 4
New Canaan, 13,466 E 2
New Fairfield 200 (3,355▲)..D 2
New Hartford ......1,034 (3,033▲)..B 4
New Haven, 152,048.°D 4
New London, 34,182.°D 7
New Milford 3,023 (8,318▲)..C 2
New Preston ...900..C 2
Newington .17,664..C 5
Newtown ....1,261 (11,373▲)..D 2
Niantic .....2,788..D 7
Nichols (part of Trumbull) ....E 3
Noank ......1,116..D 8
Norfolk, 850 (1,827▲) B 3
North Bloomfield ..500..B 4
North Branford ...450 (6,771▲)..D 4
North Canaan (Town of) ....(2,836▲)..A 2
North Canton .250..B 4
North Franklin 202..C 7
North Granby .200..B 4
North Grosvenor Dale ......1,874..B 8
North Haven ...15,935..D 4
North Stonington ..800 (1,982▲)..D 8
North Westchester .100..C 6
North Windham ...250..C 7
North Woodbury ..150..C 3
North Woodstock ..350..B 8
Northfield ....350..C 3
Northford .....300..D 4
Northville .....155..C 2
Norwalk ...67,775..E 2
Norwich ...38,506.°C 7
Oakdale ......150..D 7
Oakland Gardens ....300..C 4
Oakville ....6,000..C 3
Old Lyme .....800 (3,068▲)..D 6
Old Mystic ....500..D 8
Old Saybrook 1,671 (5,274▲)..D 6
Oneco ....300..C 8
Orange ......8,547..D 3
Oxford, 400 (3,292▲) D 3
Pachaug ......150..C 8
Pawcatuck ..6,000..D 8
Pequabuck ...300..C 4
Pine Meadow .400..B 4
Plainfield ...2,044 (8,884▲)..C 8
Plainville ..13,149..C 4
Plantsville ..2,793..C 4
Plattsville ....400..E 2
Pleasant Valley ....B 4
Pleasure Beach ....1,264..D 7
Plymouth .....950 (8,981▲)..C 3
Pomfret ......600 (2,136▲)..B 8
Pond Meadow .150..D 6
Pond Point ...350..E 3
Poquetanuck ..200..D 7
Poquonock ....400..B 5
Poquonock Bridge ....3,000..D 7
Portland ....7,496..C 5
Preston, 200 (4,992▲) C 8
Prospect ...4,367..C 4
Putnam .....6,952 (8,412▲).°B 8
Quaker Hill .1,671..D 7
Quinebaug ....350..A 8
Rainbow ......250..B 5
Redding ......200 (3,359▲)..D 2
Redding Ridge 325..D 2
Ridgebury ....175..D 1
Ridgefield ..2,954 (8,165▲)..D 2
Ridgewood Park ....280..D 7
Riverton ......240..B 3
Rockfall ......550..C 5
Rockville ....9,478..B 6
Rocky Hill ..7,404..C 5
Rogers ....758..B 8
Roxbury, 225 (912▲) C 2
Sachem Head .200..C 5
Salem, 300 (925▲)..D 6
Salisbury .....368 (3,309▲)..B 2
Sandy Hook ..950..D 2
Saybrook Manor ......300..D 6
Saybrook Point ....500..D 6
Scantic ....100..B 5
Scitico ....225..B 5
Scotland, 250 (684▲) C 7
Seymour ...10,100..D 3
Shailerville ...230..D 6
Sharon, 800 (2,141▲) B 2
Shelton ....18,190..D 3
Sherman, 250 (825▲) C 2
Short Beach ..950..D 4
Simsbury ...2,745 (10,138▲)..B 4
Somers, 950 (3,702▲) B 6
Somersville ...500..B 6
South Britain .300..D 3
South Chaplin .150..B 7
South Coventry .....B 6
South Glastonbury ......1,000..C 5
South Kent ...150..C 2
South Killingly 150..B 8
South Lyme ...250..D 6
South Willington ..300..B 6
South Windham ...380..C 7
South Windsor 900 (9,460▲)..B 5
South Woodstock ..400..B 8
Southbury ....800 (5,186▲)..D 3
Southford ......262..D 3
Southington 14,000 (22,797▲)..C 4
Southwood Acres* ....3,000..B 5
Sprague (Town of) ....(2,509▲)..C 7
Stafford ......350 (7,476▲)..B 6
Stafford Springs ...3,322..B 6
Staffordville ..400..B 6
Stamford ....92,713..E 1
Stepney Depot .700..D 3
Sterling, 450 (1,397▲) C 8
Stevenson .....200..D 3
Stonington ..1,622 (13,969▲)..D 8
Stony Creek ...950..D 4
Storrs ....6,054..B 7
Stratford ...45,012..E 3
Suffield .....1,069 (6,779▲)..B 5
Taconic ....200..A 2
Talcottville ..670..B 6
Tariffville ....650..B 4
Terryville ...5,231..C 3
Thomaston ..3,579 (5,850▲)..C 3
Thompson ......500 (6,217▲)..B 8
Thompsonville .....19,000..B 5
Tolland ......400 (2,950▲).°B 6
Torrington .30,045..B 3
Tracy ....300..C 4
Trumbull ...20,379..E 3
Uncasville ...1,381..D 7
Union, 70 ..(383▲)..B 7
Unionville ...2,246..B 4
Vernon ....500 (16,961▲)..B 6
Vernon Center ......100..B 6
Versailles .....300..C 7
Voluntown ....500 (1,028▲)..C 8
Wallingford 29,920..D 4
Wapping ......400..B 5
Warehouse Point .....1,936..B 5
Warren, 100 (600▲) C 2
Warrenville ...100..B 6
Washington ...500 (2,603▲)..C 2
Washington Depot ......503..C 2
Waterbury 107,130.°C 3
Waterford ..5,000 (15,391▲)..D 7
Watertown ..5,500 (14,837▲)..C 3
Wauregan .....950..C 8
Weatogue .....200..B 4
West Cornwall, 200..B 2
West Goshen ..150..B 2
West Granby .375..B 4
West Hartford .62,382..B 5
West Hartland ....200..A 4
West Haven 43,002..D 4
West Mystic .3,268..D 8
West Redding 250..D 2
West Simsbury ...170..B 4
West Stafford .300..B 6
West Suffield .400..B 5
West Willington ..300..B 6
West Woodstock ..100..B 7
Westbrook ....950 (2,399▲)..D 6
Westford .....230..B 7
Weston .....3,000 (4,039▲)..E 2
Westport ...20,955..E 2
Westview Heights .....900..C 3
Wethersfield 20,561..C 5
Whigville ......250..C 4
Whitacres* ..1,000..B 5
Willimantic 13,881.°C 7
Willington .....100 (2,005▲)..B 6
Wilson ......2,500..B 5
Wilsonville ....150..A 8
Wilton ......3,500 (8,026▲)..E 2
Winchester Center (Winchester) 250 (10,496▲)..B 3
Windermere ....75..B 6
Windham ......350 (16,973▲)..C 7
Windsor ....12,000 (19,467▲)..B 5
Windsor Locks ....11,411..B 5
Windsorville ..180..B 5
Winsted .....8,136..B 3
Wolcott .....1,500 (8,889▲)..C 4
Woodbridge 5,182..D 3
Woodbury ...1,000 (3,910▲)..C 3
Woodstock ....200 (3,177▲)..B 8
Woodstock Valley ......100..B 7
Woodtick .....400..C 4

*Does not appear on the map; key shows general location.
▲Population of entire town (township), including rural area.
°Court House.
Source: Latest census figures.

CONNECTICUT /People

The 1960 United States census reported that Connecticut had 2,535,234 persons. The population had increased about 26 per cent over the 1950 figure, 2,007,280. This was the largest percentage of increase among the six New England states and three Middle Atlantic states that make up the northeastern United States. The U.S. Bureau of the Census estimated that by 1965 Connecticut's population had reached 2,886,000.

More than 2 million people, or about 80 per cent of Connecticut's population, live in nine Standard Metropolitan Statistical Areas (see METROPOLITAN AREA). These areas are Bridgeport, Hartford, Meriden, New Britain, New Haven, New London-Groton-Norwich, Norwalk, Stamford, and Waterbury. For their populations, see the *Index* of the political map of Connecticut.

Hartford is Connecticut's capital and largest city. Other large cities, in order of population, include Bridgeport, New Haven, Waterbury, and Stamford. See the separate articles on Connecticut cities listed in the *Related Articles* at the end of this article.

Most of Connecticut's people were born in the United States. Italians make up the largest of the groups born in other countries. Roman Catholics form the state's largest single religious group. Other large religious groups include Baptists, Episcopalians, Methodists, and members of the United Church of Christ.

CONNECTICUT /Education

Schools. Connecticut's Yale University, founded in 1701, is the third oldest U.S. university. Only Harvard University and the College of William and Mary are older. The Litchfield School was one of the first law schools in the United States. It operated in Litchfield between 1784 and 1833. In 1817, Thomas H. Gallaudet founded the first free American school for the deaf, in Hartford. The school now operates in West Hartford as the American School for the Deaf.

John Higginson, a teacher and minister, founded Connecticut's first school about 1637. A law passed in 1650 required Connecticut towns with more than 50 families to have an elementary school. The law also required towns with more than a hundred families to have a *secondary* (high) school. Money for Connecticut's first school fund came from the sale, in 1795, of the Western Reserve—a strip of land that Connecticut owned in what is now northeastern Ohio.

A commissioner of education and a nine-member board of education supervise Connecticut's public-school system. The governor appoints the board members to six-year terms, and the board members elect the commissioner to the same term.

Connecticut law requires children between the ages of 7 and 16 to attend school. For the number of students and teachers in Connecticut, see EDUCATION (table).

Libraries. The Yale University Library, founded in 1701, is the oldest library still operating in Connecticut. Its 4½ million volumes make it one of the world's largest libraries. The Scoville Memorial Library in Salisbury was founded in 1803 as the Bingham Library for Youth.

POPULATION

This map shows the *population density* of Connecticut, and how it varies in different parts of the state. Population density means the average number of persons who live on each square mile.

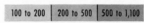

PERSONS PER SQUARE MILE

| 100 to 200 | 200 to 500 | 500 to 1,100 |

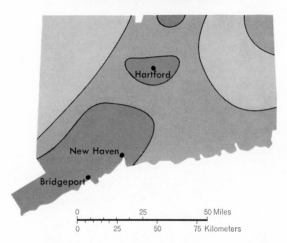

WORLD BOOK map

UNIVERSITIES AND COLLEGES

Connecticut has 19 universities and colleges accredited by the New England Association of Colleges and Secondary Schools. For enrollments and further information, see UNIVERSITIES AND COLLEGES (table).

Name	Location	Founded
Albertus Magnus College	New Haven	1925
Annhurst College	South Woodstock	1941
Bridgeport, University of	Bridgeport	1927
Central Connecticut State College	New Britain	1849
Connecticut, University of	Storrs	1881
Connecticut College	New London	1911
Eastern Connecticut State College	Willimantic	1889
Fairfield University	Fairfield	1942
Hartford, University of	West Hartford	1957
New Haven College	West Haven	1958
Quinnipiac College	Hamden	1929
Saint Alphonsus College	Suffield	1963
Saint Joseph College	West Hartford	1925
Southern Connecticut State College	New Haven	1893
Trinity College	Hartford	1823
United States Coast Guard Academy	New London	1876
Wesleyan University	Middletown	1831
Western Connecticut State College	Danbury	1904
Yale University	New Haven	1701

In 1810, Salisbury began using taxes to support the library. Some historians believe it was the first free, tax-supported public library in the United States.

CONNECTICUT

Today, Connecticut has over 200 public libraries and many school and special libraries. The largest public libraries are in Bridgeport, Hartford, and New Haven. The State Library in Hartford houses the state archives, many books about Connecticut, and a special law collection. Hartford has special law and insurance libraries.

Museums. Yale's Peabody Museum has world-famous natural history exhibits. The Yale Art Gallery is the oldest university art museum in the United States. Other fine art museums are in Farmington, Hartford, Middletown, New Britain, New London, and Norwich. Children's museums are in Canton, Hartford, New London, Stamford, and Waterbury. The American Clock and Watch Museum in Bristol displays timepieces made in the 1700's and 1800's. The New Haven Colony Historical Society exhibits the original model of Eli Whitney's cotton gin. The society also owns valuable prints and early American portraits.

U.S. Coast Guard

Parading the Colors, cadets at the U.S. Coast Guard Academy in New London march on the parade grounds.

Yale University, in New Haven, is the third oldest U.S. university. Harkness Tower rises above the campus.

C. T. Albertus

CONNECTICUT / *A Visitor's Guide*

Southern Connecticut's seashore offers vacationers swimming, fishing, boating, and beautiful scenery. Inland, many summertime visitors hike and ride horseback across the state's wooded hills and valleys. Hunters follow winding forest trails in search of rabbits, raccoons, squirrels, and other small game. Fishermen try their luck in Connecticut's rivers, streams, and lakes. In winter, the state's snow-covered hills provide skiing and other winter sports. Tourists and students of American history also may visit many historic sites, museums, and colonial buildings.

A Summer Day at Rocky Neck State Park

Connecticut Development Commission
Old Town Mill in New London

PLACES TO VISIT

Following are brief descriptions of some of Connecticut's many interesting places to visit.

Cathedral Pines, in Cornwall, is often called one of America's most beautiful forests. This white pine woodland is so thick in some places that sunlight seldom reaches the ground below the trees.

Colonial Buildings are among Connecticut's most famous landmarks. Almost every Connecticut town has at least one example of Colonial architecture. *Whitfield House,* in Guilford, is the oldest house in the state. It was begun in 1639, and may also be the oldest stone house in New England. Three buildings stand as shrines to Nathan Hale, the famous Connecticut patriot. *Nathan Hale Homestead* in South Coventry was the home of Hale's parents. In East Haddam and New London

Mystic Seaport in Mystic

The best-known annual event in Connecticut is probably the American Shakespeare Festival in Stratford. Plays by William Shakespeare, England's greatest dramatist, are performed in a building patterned after the *Globe*, a London theater of Shakespeare's time. The Shakespeare Festival lasts from mid-June to early September. County fairs are held in various Connecticut towns from early August to early October.

Other annual events in Connecticut include the following.

March-May: Spring Flower and Garden Show Meet in Hartford (March, no fixed date); Children's Services Horse Show in Farmington (about May 18 to 20).

June-July: Yale-Harvard Boat Race in New London (mid-June); Laurel Festival in Winsted (mid-June); Barnum Festival in Bridgeport (first week in July); Litchfield Open House (second week in July).

August-October: Mystic Outdoor Art Festival (second week in August); American Dance Festival in New London (third week in August); Greater Hartford Open Golf Tournament in Wethersfield (September); Connecticut Antique Show in New Haven (late September); Danbury State Fair (first week in October).

Trolley Museum in East Haven

Whitfield House in Guilford

Connecticut Development Commission
Shakespeare Festival Theater in Stratford

are the *Nathan Hale Schoolhouses*, where Hale taught school from 1773 to 1775. Other Connecticut colonial buildings, with the location and original completion date of each, include *Stanley-Whitman House* (Farmington, 1660); *Pardee-Morris House* (New Haven, 1685); *Mansfield House* (Ansonia, before 1690); *Buttolph-Williams House* (Wethersfield, 1692); *Denison House* (Mystic, 1717); *Judson House* (Stratford, 1723); *Nathaniel Allis House* (Madison, 1739); *Glebe House* (Woodbury, 1750?); *Webb House* (Wethersfield, 1752); *Shaw Mansion* (New London, 1756); and *Dickerman House* (Hamden, 1770).

Groton Monument, in Groton, is a granite tower 134 feet high. It commemorates the Battle of Fort Griswold in 1781. British troops, led by the traitor Benedict Arnold, massacred patriots they captured in the battle.

Mystic Seaport and Marine Museum, in Mystic, recall Connecticut's seafaring tradition. The seaport has been rebuilt to look like a whaling village of the 1800's. The *Charles W. Morgan,* New England's last wooden whaling ship, is in the harbor. The *Australia,* the oldest American schooner still afloat, is also there.

Old Town Mill, in New London, is an old grain-grinding mill set in scenic surroundings. The mill was built in 1650 and rebuilt in 1712.

Trolley Museums exhibit trolleys that date from the late 1800's and early 1900's. Visitors may ride on some of the trolleys. The museums are the Branford Trolley Museum in East Haven, and the Connecticut Electric Railway Association Museum in Warehouse Point.

State Parks and Forests. Connecticut has 82 state parks and 28 state forests. For information on them, write to Superintendent of State Park and Forest Commission, Park Department, State Office Building, 165 Capitol Ave., Hartford, Conn. 06115.

Land Regions. Connecticut has five main land regions: (1) the Taconic Section, (2) the Western New England Upland, (3) the Connecticut Valley Lowland, (4) the Eastern New England Upland, and (5) the Coastal Lowlands.

The Taconic Section covers the northwestern corner of Connecticut between the Housatonic River and the New York border. This region also extends north into Massachusetts. It includes the highest point in Connecticut, on the south slope of Mount Frissell.

The Western New England Upland occupies most of western Connecticut, and parts of Massachusetts and Vermont. In Connecticut, the region lies between 1,000 and 1,400 feet above sea level. The land slopes from northwest to southeast. Many rivers flow between the region's ridges and steeply sloping hills.

The Connecticut Valley Lowland extends through the center of Connecticut and north into Massachusetts. It averages 20 miles in width. Lava ridges, including Hanging Hills, Mount Lamentation, and Talcott Mountain, rise from 300 to 600 feet above the rivers of the region.

The Eastern New England Upland covers most of eastern Connecticut. The entire Eastern New England Upland stretches from Connecticut to Maine. The Connecticut portion is heavily forested, and includes narrow river valleys and low hills. Few of the hills rise as high as 1,200 feet. The land slopes gradually from northwest to southeast.

The Coastal Lowlands are part of a larger region of the same name that covers the entire New England coast. In Connecticut, the region is a narrow belt, from 6 to 16 miles wide, along the southern shore. The Coastal Lowlands are somewhat lower and smoother than the rest of the state. They are broken by low ridges, and beaches and harbors along the coast.

Coastline. The Coast and Geodetic Survey, which measures the coastline of the United States, defines Connecticut's southern boundary as a *tidal shoreline.* This 618-mile shoreline includes bays and the mouths

Land Regions of Connecticut

TACONIC SECTION

WESTERN NEW ENGLAND UPLAND

CONNECTICUT VALLEY LOWLAND

EASTERN NEW ENGLAND UPLAND

COASTAL LOWLANDS

Connecticut River

Housatonic River

Tobacco Grown in the Shade is Connecticut's most valuable farm crop. This special tobacco is raised in the Connecticut Valley Lowland region, and is used as the outer wrapping of cigars.

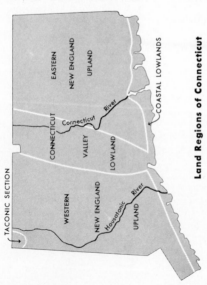

Connecticut Development Commission

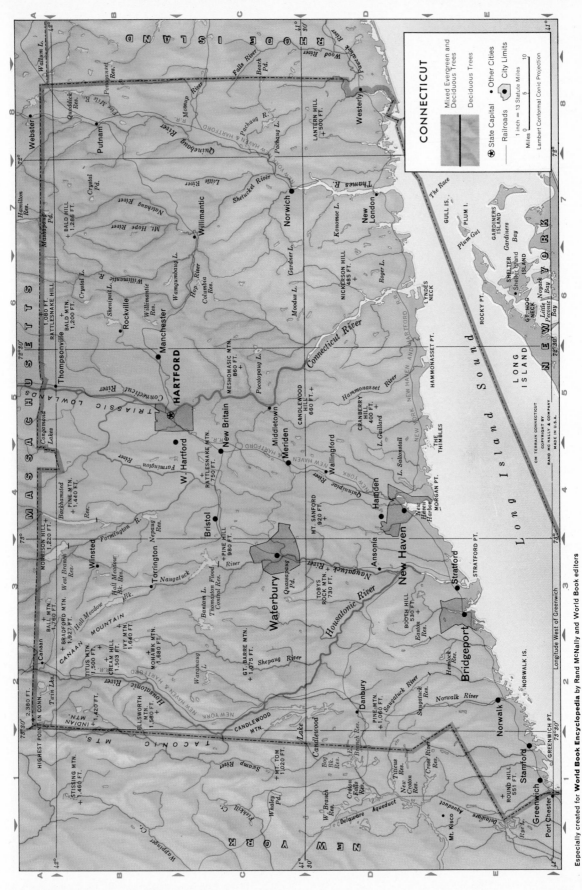

CONNECTICUT

Mixed Evergreen and
Deciduous Trees

Deciduous Trees

⊛ State Capital   • Other Cities

Railroads   ◉ City Limits

1 inch = 13 Statute Miles

Miles
0   5   10

Lambert Conformal Conic Projection

R H O D E   I S L A N D

M A S S A C H U S E T T S

N E W   Y O R K

N E W   Y O R K

Long Island Sound

LONG ISLAND

Especially created for **World Book Encyclopedia** by Rand McNally and World Book editors

CONNECTICUT

Larry Keighley, Alpha Photo Assoc.

of many rivers. The Connecticut shore has many fine harbors, including Greenwich, Stamford, Norwalk, Bridgeport, New Haven, and New London. Long Island, a part of New York south of Connecticut, helps protect Connecticut's shore from Atlantic storms.

Several small islands lie off the Connecticut coast. The largest, Mason's Island, covers about 1½ square miles near Mystic. Other islands include the Norwalk Islands off Norwalk, and The Thimbles near Branford.

Mountains. Connecticut's highest mountains are all in northwestern Litchfield County. The highest point in the state, on the south slope of Mount Frissell, has an altitude of 2,380 feet. The top of Mount Frissell is in Massachusetts. Other mountains include Bear Mountain (2,355 feet), Mount Gridley (2,200 feet), Mount Riga (2,000 feet), and Bradford Mountain (1,927 feet).

Rivers, Waterfalls, and Lakes. The Connecticut River flows south through the center of the state. It is Connecticut's chief river. Some ocean-going ships can sail on the Connecticut as far north as Hartford, 50 miles inland. The Housatonic River and its chief tributaries, the Naugatuck and Shepaug rivers, drain the Western New England Upland. The Thames and the Quinebaug are the chief rivers of eastern Connecticut. Connecticut has many small waterfalls. Kent Falls, the largest, plunges about 200 feet along a distance of about a quarter of a mile near Kent.

Over 5,000 lakes and ponds dot the Connecticut landscape. Most of them are small. Several of the largest ones are used as reservoirs, and others provide recreation activities. The largest lake, Lake Candlewood, is man-made. It was created to store water for generating power. The state's other lakes include Bantam, Pachaug, Shenipsit, Twin Lakes, and Waramaug.

Salt Marshes make up part of the Coastal Lowlands region of Connecticut. This area near the Atlantic Ocean is flatter and lower than other parts of the state. It has many harbors.

The Connecticut Turnpike runs through the broad river valleys and low hills of the Eastern New England Upland region. This traffic interchange provides an exit to the city of Norwich.
Eric M. Sanford, Alpha Photo Assoc.

The Broad Connecticut River flows through the central part of the state. This ferry crosses the river near Chester. Some ocean ships can go up the river as far as Hartford.
Eric M. Sanford, Alpha Photo Assoc.

Forested Hills Rise Above the Fields in Connecticut's Western New England Upland region. The stony soil is best suited for growing hay and other feed crops for livestock.
Arthur Griffin, Alpha Photo Assoc.

CONNECTICUT/Climate

Connecticut's weather is rarely very cold or very hot. January temperatures average 27° F., and July temperatures average 72° F. The state's record low temperature, −32° F., was recorded in Falls Village on Feb. 16, 1943. The record high, 105° F., was recorded in Waterbury on July 22, 1926.

Yearly precipitation (rain, melted snow, and other forms of moisture) in Connecticut averages about 46 inches. The average rainfall is distributed fairly evenly throughout Connecticut.

Snowfall averages from about 25 inches yearly in the southeast to 35 inches in the western and central sections of the state. The highest places in the northwestern part of Connecticut sometimes receive 80 inches of snow annually.

Winter Sportsmen take advantage of the snowfall on Mohawk Mountain near Cornwall. Some parts of northwestern Connecticut receive as much as 80 inches of snow annually.

Connecticut State Highway Dept.

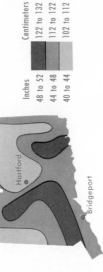

AVERAGE
YEARLY PRECIPITATION
(Rain, Melted Snow, and Other Moisture)

Inches		Centimeters
48 to 52		122 to 132
44 to 48		112 to 122
40 to 44		102 to 112

SEASONAL TEMPERATURES

JANUARY

AVERAGE OF DAILY HIGH TEMPERATURES

Degrees Fahrenheit	Degrees Centigrade
38 to 42	3 to 6
34 to 38	1 to 3
30 to 34	-1 to 1

AVERAGE OF DAILY LOW TEMPERATURES

Degrees Fahrenheit	Degrees Centigrade
20 to 24	-7 to -4
16 to 20	-9 to -7
12 to 16	-11 to -9

JULY

AVERAGE OF DAILY HIGH TEMPERATURES

Degrees Fahrenheit	Degrees Centigrade
80 to 84	27 to 29

AVERAGE OF DAILY LOW TEMPERATURES

Degrees Fahrenheit	Degrees Centigrade
60 to 64	16 to 18
56 to 60	13 to 16

WORLD BOOK maps

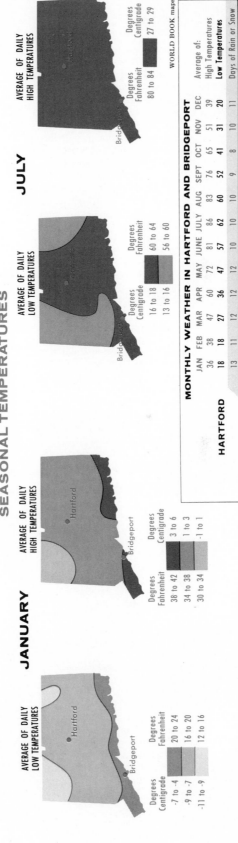

| | 0 | 25 | 50 | 75 | 100 Miles |
| 0 | 25 | 50 | 75 | 100 | 125 | 150 Kilometers |

MONTHLY WEATHER IN HARTFORD AND BRIDGEPORT

		JAN	FEB	MAR	APR	MAY	JUNE	JULY	AUG	SEPT	OCT	NOV	DEC
HARTFORD	Average of:												
	High Temperatures	36	38	47	60	72	81	86	83	76	65	51	39
	Low Temperatures	18	18	27	36	47	57	62	60	52	41	31	20
	Days of Rain or Snow	13	11	12	12	13	11	10	10	9	8	10	11
BRIDGEPORT	Average of:												
	High Temperatures	37	37	45	55	67	76	82	80	74	64	52	40
	Low Temperatures	22	21	29	37	48	58	63	63	56	45	35	25

Temperatures are given in degrees Fahrenheit.

Source: U.S. Weather Bureau

769

Manufacturing is by far Connecticut's most important economic activity. Agriculture ranks second, followed by the tourist industry. Manufacturing is centered in Fairfield, Hartford, and New Haven counties. More than half the state's industrial labor force works in 10 cities—Bridgeport, East Hartford, Groton, Hartford, New Britain, New Haven, Norwalk, Stamford, Stratford, and Waterbury. Farms and the tourist trade thrive in many parts of Connecticut. Millions of tourists contribute about $100,000,000 yearly to the economy.

Natural Resources. Unlike many other states, Connecticut does not depend chiefly on its own natural resources for the raw materials of its industries. The state has many forests, but they are not commercially important. Connecticut lacks large deposits of valuable minerals, and much of the soil is unsuitable for farming.

Soil. Some of the soils at Connecticut's low elevations are dry. But they produce good vegetable and tobacco crops. Much of the soil in the uplands is stony. It is best suited for growing grass that can be made into hay or used as cattle feed.

Forests cover more than 60 of every 100 acres of land in Connecticut. Unlike many other states, Connecticut does not use its forests to support a wood-processing industry. Most of the state's trees are too small to be valuable in industry. Connecticut forests are used mainly as recreation areas. Connecticut trees include the ash, beech, birch, elm, hemlock, hickory, maple, oak, red and white pine, and poplar.

Plant Life. The mountain laurel, Connecticut's state flower, grows throughout the woodlands and along roads. Many persons in western Connecticut call this flowering shrub *ivy*. Pink and white dogwood grow throughout Connecticut. Bayberry, sheep laurel, and sweetfern cover many fields.

Animal Life of Connecticut consists chiefly of small creatures. The animals most prized by hunters and trappers include foxes, hares, minks, muskrats, otters, and rabbits. The fresh-water duck is Connecticut's most common game bird. Partridges, ring-necked pheasants, and ruffed grouse are also hunted. Orioles, sparrows, thrushes, and warblers live in the state.

Connecticut waters in Long Island Sound have many clams, flounders, lobsters, and oysters. Shad is the leading fish of the state's inland waterways.

Minerals. Stone—especially a kind of basalt called traprock—and sand and gravel are Connecticut's leading minerals. Deposits of clays, feldspar, gypsum, and mica are also found in the state.

Manufacturing accounts for almost 96 per cent of the value of goods produced in Connecticut. Goods manufactured there have a *value added by manufacture* of about $4,210,000,000 a year. This figure represents the value created in products by Connecticut industries, not counting such costs as materials, supplies, and fuel.

Manufacturing industries employ about 417,000 workers, or 42 per cent of Connecticut's labor force. This percentage is higher than that of any other state. The chief kinds of manufactured goods are, in order of importance: (1) transportation equipment, (2) non-electrical machinery, (3) electrical machinery, and (4) fabricated metal products.

PRODUCTION IN CONNECTICUT

Total yearly value of goods produced—$4,390,024,000

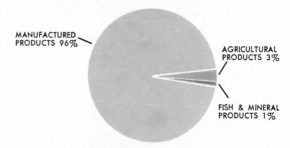

MANUFACTURED PRODUCTS 96%

AGRICULTURAL PRODUCTS 3%

FISH & MINERAL PRODUCTS 1%

Note: Manufacturing percentage based on value added by manufacture. Other percentages based on value of production.

Source: Latest available U.S. Government statistics

EMPLOYMENT IN CONNECTICUT

Average yearly number of persons employed—994,405

	Number of Employees
Manufacturing	416,900
Wholesale & Retail Trade	171,500
Services	128,000
Government	101,700
Finance, Insurance & Real Estate	56,800
Construction and Mining	50,200
Transportation & Public Utilities	43,600
Agriculture & Fishing	25,705

Source: Employment statistics supplied by employers to government agencies

Transportation Equipment has a value added of about $780,500,000 yearly. Connecticut leads the states in making helicopters, jet aircraft engines, and submarines. It ranks high in propeller production. Factories in Bloomfield, Bridgeport, Plainfield, and Stratford turn out helicopters. Jet aircraft engines are made in East Hartford, North Haven, Southington, and Stratford. Groton is a major submarine-making center, and propellers come from Windsor Locks. Small boats are built in Essex, Mystic, and Noank.

Non-Electrical Machinery has a value added of about $677,158,000 annually. Factories in many parts of Connecticut make machine tools such as grinders, lathes, and planers. Connecticut makes more ball and roller bearings than any other state. It is also a leading manufacturer of office machines, especially typewriters. Hartford factories produce the most office machines.

Electrical Machinery has a yearly value added of about $467,966,000. Connecticut leads the states in making electrical conductors, outlets, and switches. The state's wide variety of electrical products also includes generators, household appliances, lighting fixtures, and motors.

Fabricated Metal Products have a value added of about $425,255,000 yearly. Connecticut leads the states in making silverware, and ranks high in hardware production. Other metal products include bolts, nuts, rivets, washers, and valve and pipe fittings. Silverware comes

FARM AND MINERAL PRODUCTS

This map shows where the state's leading farm and mineral products are produced. The major urban areas (shown in red) are the important manufacturing centers.

```
0   5   10  15  20  25  Miles
0   10  20  30  40  Kilometers
```

WORLD BOOK map

from Meriden and Wallingford. New Britain and New Haven are important hardware centers.

Other Products. Connecticut leads the states in rolling and drawing copper, and in making fasteners, needles, pins, small firearms, and thread. The state ranks high in clock and watch production. Connecticut's long list of manufactured goods also includes brooms and brushes, chemicals, clothing, and plastics and rubber products.

Agriculture accounts for over 3 per cent of the value of goods produced in Connecticut. The state's farmers earn about $159,600,000 a year. Connecticut's 8,300 commercial farms average about 107 acres in size.

Dairy products, especially milk, and poultry products, especially eggs, each earn about 25 per cent of Connecticut's farm income. *Broilers* (chickens 9 to 12 weeks old) are another important product.

Tobacco, Connecticut's leading field crop, accounts for about 13 per cent of the total farm income. Many farmers in the Connecticut Valley raise shade-grown tobacco, the most expensive tobacco leaf grown in the United States. It is used as the outer wrapping of cigars. Farmers also grow the more common broadleaf tobacco. Many tobacco farmers rotate the crop with potato and corn crops. Apples are by far the most important fruit grown in Connecticut. Other fruits include peaches, pears, and strawberries.

Greenhouse and nursery products earn about 10 per cent of Connecticut's farm income. These products include ornamental shrubs, flowers, and vegetable plants.

Mining contributes about $19,754,000 a year to the value of goods produced in Connecticut. This figure represents less than half of 1 per cent of the state's total production. Sand and gravel are Connecticut's most valuable minerals. Stone, especially traprock, ranks next in importance. Clays, feldspar, gemstones, granite, limestone, and mica are also mined.

Fishing Industry has relatively little importance in Connecticut today. About 47,000 acres of oyster beds lie in Long Island Sound off the Connecticut coast. Fishermen catch oysters, flounders, and lobsters in the

Sound, and dig for soft-shelled clams on the sandy shore. Shad fishing is centered on the Connecticut River, and scallop fishing near Niantic.

Electric Power. Steam-powered plants, fueled by coal or oil, supply more than 90 per cent of Connecticut's electric power. Most of the rest comes from hydroelectric plants. A small part of the power is generated by atomic energy. For Connecticut's kilowatt-hour production, see ELECTRIC POWER (table).

Transportation. Connecticut has about 18,000 miles of roads and highways, most of which are paved. The 129-mile Connecticut Turnpike crosses the state from the New York border, near Greenwich, to the Rhode Island border, near Killingly.

The Hartford and New Haven, Connecticut's first important railroad, began service between New Haven and Meriden in 1838. Today, the New Haven Railroad (formerly the New York, New Haven, and Hartford), and the Central Vermont Railway operate on almost 800 miles of track in Connecticut. The New Haven line carries thousands of Connecticut commuters to and from their jobs in New York City.

More than 60 airports serve Connecticut. Bradley Field in Windsor Locks provides direct air passenger service between Connecticut and 50 large U.S. cities.

Bridgeport, New Haven, and New London are important seaports. The state's coastal ports handle about 13,000,000 tons of cargo yearly.

Communication. About 25 daily newspapers and 60 weekly and semiweekly newspapers are published in Connecticut. The *Connecticut Courant* (now the *Hartford Courant*) began publication in 1764. It is the oldest continuously published newspaper in the United States. The *Courant* and the *Bridgeport Post, Hartford Times, New Haven Journal-Courier,* and *New Haven Register* are among Connecticut's chief newspapers.

Connecticut has 46 radio stations and 7 television stations. The state's first radio station, WDRC, opened in Hartford in 1922. The first television station, WNHC, began operating in New Haven in 1948.

Indian Days. Between 6,000 and 7,000 Indians lived in what is now Connecticut before the white man came. The Indians belonged to several tribes of the Algonkian Indian family. The Pequot, the most powerful tribe, lived in the south near the Thames River. The Mohegan (or Mohican), a branch of the Pequot tribe, lived near present-day Norwich. Uncas, the Mohegan chief, was characterized as an ideal Indian in James Fenimore Cooper's novel *The Last of the Mohicans.* Other Connecticut tribes included the Niantic, Paugusset, Quinnipiac, Saukiog, Siwanog, Tunxis, and Wangunk.

Dutch Exploration. Adriaen Block, a Dutch explorer, sailed up the Connecticut River in 1614. Block claimed Connecticut for the Dutch. The Dutch did not act on this claim until 1633 when they built a small fort—called the *House of Hope*—on the present site of Hartford. But the Dutch never settled permanently in Connecticut. They claimed parts of Connecticut off and on until 1674, when the English finally drove them out.

English Settlement. Englishmen from Massachusetts made Connecticut's earliest permanent settlements. Windsor, the first one, was founded in 1633. Other early settlements included Hartford, New Haven, New London, Saybrook, and Wethersfield. Hartford, Wethersfield, and Windsor united in 1636 to form the *Connecticut Colony* (also called the *River Colony*).

Many early Connecticut settlers left Massachusetts in search of political and religious freedom. The most famous of these settlers was Thomas Hooker, a Congregationalist minister and the chief founder of Hartford. In 1638, Hooker preached a sermon calling for government based on the will of the people. The Connecticut

Yankee Peddlers traveled far and wide during the 1700's. They spread the fame of the state's craftsmen by selling such Connecticut products as brassware, buttons, clocks, combs, firearms, hats, pins, and tinware.

HISTORIC CONNECTICUT

The Fundamental Orders of Connecticut were adopted in 1639. These laws set forth the idea of government by consent of the people.

IMPORTANT DATES IN CONNECTICUT

1614 Adriaen Block claimed Connecticut for the Dutch.

1633 The first English settlement in Connecticut was made at Windsor.

1636 The towns of Hartford, Wethersfield, and Windsor united to form the Connecticut Colony.

1637 Connecticut and other colonies defeated the Pequot Indians in the Pequot War.

1638 A group of wealthy Puritans founded New Haven.

1639 The Connecticut Colony adopted the Fundamental Orders.

1662 The Connecticut Colony received a charter from England. It served as Connecticut's constitution until 1818.

1665 The Connecticut Colony and the New Haven Colony united.

1687 Colonists preserved the Connecticut charter by hiding it, presumably in the Charter Oak in Hartford.

1776 Connecticut passed a resolution in favor of independence from Great Britain on June 14.

1788 Connecticut became the 5th state when it ratified the U.S. Constitution on January 9.

1910 The U.S. Coast Guard Academy was moved to New London.

1954 The first atomic submarine was launched at Groton.

1960 The U.S. census showed that Connecticut was the fastest-growing northeastern state between 1950 and 1960.

1965 Connecticut apportioned its legislature on the basis of population. Connecticut adopted its present constitution.

Colony put Hooker's principle into practice in 1639, when it adopted the *Fundamental Orders* as its law. The Fundamental Orders gave voters the right to elect government officials. The Fundamental Orders are sometimes called the *first written constitution.*

The Pequot War. The Connecticut colonists feared the Pequot Indians because small bands of the tribe had attacked their settlements. The Pequot feared the colonists as a threat to Pequot supremacy in the region. Captain John Mason, aided by Mohegan and Narraganset warriors, led a small army against the Pequot at Mystic in 1637. Mason's men burned a Pequot fort, killing hundreds of Indians. That same year, colonists defeated the remaining Pequot in a fight near Fairfield. See INDIAN WARS (The Pequot War).

Expanding the Colony. By 1660, several new towns had joined the Connecticut Colony. The new towns included Fairfield, Farmington, Middletown, New London, Norwalk, Saybrook, and Stratford. In 1638, New Haven had been founded as an independent colony. It was originally a Puritan *theocracy* (church-state).

Litchfield

The Charter Oak may have served as a hiding place for Connecticut's charter. Settlers supposedly hid it from an English governor in 1687 to protect their freedom.

★ HARTFORD **"The Insurance Capital of the World,"** Hartford, is the home of more than 30 companies, which together provide every kind of insurance.

Mass Production got its start in Connecticut when Eli Whitney became the first manufacturer to use standard parts to make guns.

• Groton

America's First Law School was founded at Litchfield in 1784. Its graduates included 17 U.S. Senators and 10 state governors.

• New Haven

The *Nautilus*, the first atomic submarine, was built at Groton. The state's shipyards once produced whalers and clipper ships.

Yale University, at New Haven, was founded in 1701. It is the nation's third oldest institution of higher learning.

Beginning in 1643, the towns of Branford, Guilford, Milford, Stamford, and Southold (on Long Island) joined the New Haven Colony. As a result, Connecticut consisted of two colonies—the Connecticut Colony and the New Haven Colony.

In 1662, John Winthrop, Jr., of the Connecticut Colony received a charter from the king of England. The charter gave the colony a strip of land 73 miles wide stretching from Narragansett Bay to the Pacific Ocean. This area included the entire New Haven Colony. At first, New Haven strongly objected to being made part of the Connecticut Colony. But the two colonies united in 1665.

Colonial Life. The earliest Connecticut colonists were farmers. Most of them raised only enough food for their own needs. Each family made most of its own clothing, household utensils, and farm tools.

During the late 1600's, Connecticut began exporting farm products to other lands, especially to the West Indies. Manufacturing started in Connecticut during the early 1700's. Clockmaking, shipbuilding, and silversmithing were the first important industries. Two brothers, Edward and William Pattison, made the first tinware in North America in the 1740's. The Pattison brothers became the first of Connecticut's famous *Yankee peddlers*. These house to house salesmen traveled far and wide in small carts selling a variety of Connecticut products. The peddlers were such shrewd businessmen that stories arose accusing them of selling wooden nutmegs. These stories gave Connecticut the humorous nickname of the *Nutmeg State*.

Defending the Colony. Sir Edmund Andros, named by the English king as governor of several other New England colonies, twice tried to gain control of Connecticut. In 1675, he sent troops to seize a fort in Saybrook. But his forces withdrew because Connecticut resisted strongly and the soldiers wanted to avoid a bloody battle. In 1687, Andros arrived in Hartford and demanded Connecticut's charter. But the people refused to give it to him. They supposedly hid the charter in a large oak tree, later called the Charter Oak (see CHARTER OAK).

The Revolutionary War. During the 1760's, Great Britain passed a series of laws that caused unrest in Connecticut and the other American colonies. Some of these laws set up severe taxes and restricted colonial trade. A few Connecticut men urged loyalty to Britain in spite of the laws. But the great majority favored independence.

After the Revolutionary War began in Massachusetts in 1775, hundreds of Connecticut men joined the patriot forces. Governor Jonathan Trumbull and Nathan Hale rank among the most famous Connecticut patriots. Trumbull was the only colonial governor to hold office throughout the Revolution. He worked hard to supply men, food, and equipment for the patriot army. He became a close friend and trusted adviser of General George Washington. Often, when in need of advice or supplies, Washington said: "We must ask Brother Jonathan." *Brother Jonathan* was Washington's nickname for Trumbull (see BROTHER JONATHAN). Nathan Hale was hanged by the British as a spy. His dying words won him lasting fame: "I only regret that I have but one life to lose for my country."

Connecticut passed a resolution favoring independence from Britain on June 14, 1776. On July 4, the 13 colonies adopted the Declaration of Independence. On July 9, 1778, Connecticut *ratified* (approved) the Articles of Confederation, the forerunner of the United States Constitution. The colony became a state on Jan. 9, 1788, when it ratified the U.S. Constitution. Connecticut was the fifth state to join the Union.

Roger Sherman of Connecticut broke a deadlock that threatened to break up the Constitutional Convention of 1787. Convention delegates from large states wanted a state's representation in Congress to be determined by population. Delegates from small states wanted all states to have equal representation in Congress. Sherman worked out the *Connecticut Compromise*, which the Convention approved. The compromise established the present two-house U.S. Congress. Representation in the House of Representatives is based on population. All the states have equal representation in the Senate.

During the 1780's, Connecticut gave up claims to most of the western land that the colony had been granted in the 1662 charter. Connecticut kept only its claim to the Western Reserve. The state sold this piece of land in northeastern Ohio to the Connecticut Land Company in 1795. The money was used for education.

The 1800's. Until the 1850's, most of Connecticut's people continued to work on farms. But before 1900, Connecticut had become a thriving industrial state.

Connecticut owes much of its industrial importance to the inventors who worked there. Perhaps the most important of these inventors was Eli Whitney. Whitney is best known as the inventor of the cotton gin. But he was also the father of mass-production manufacturing. While working in Hamden about 1800, Whitney built machine tools that made interchangeable gun parts. Until then, all gun parts were handmade, and part of one gun usually would not fit another gun.

In 1808, Eli Terry of East Hartford became the first person to make clocks by mass production. In 1810, Rodney Hanks and his nephew, Horatio Hanks, built the nation's first silk mill in Mansfield. Samuel Colt of Hartford invented the first successful repeating pistol, and obtained a U.S. patent for it in 1836. Colt made pistols and other firearms in his Hartford factory. In 1839, Charles Goodyear of Connecticut found a way to *vulcanize* (strengthen) rubber. He patented his method in 1844. Connecticut men also pioneered in making bicycles, cigars, copper coins, nuts and bolts, pins and needles, silk thread, and rubber shoes.

Improved transportation helped Connecticut grow industrially. Fifteen railroad companies were organized in the state between the 1830's and 1850's. Steamships began serving Connecticut ports in the early 1800's. With these facilities, industries could import large quantities of raw materials inexpensively. Connecticut's industrial growth also was aided by thousands of Canadian and European immigrants. These workers provided relatively inexpensive factory labor.

The 1900's. Great numbers of immigrants settled in Connecticut during the late 1800's and early 1900's. By 1910, about 30 per cent of the state's population was made up of persons born outside the United States. Most of the immigrants settled in cities, where they found jobs. By 1910, almost 90 per cent of Connecticut's people lived in urban areas.

In 1910, the U.S. Coast Guard Academy was moved to New London from headquarters in Maryland and Massachusetts. The U.S. Navy opened a submarine base in nearby Groton in 1917. After the United States entered World War I in 1917, many of the nation's largest munitions factories operated in Connecticut. About 67,600 Connecticut men served in the armed forces during the war.

Connecticut industry continued to grow during the 1920's. At the same time, the Republican party controlled Connecticut politics. The Great Depression of the 1930's slowed industry and caused widespread unemployment in Connecticut. The depression swung many Connecticut voters over to the Democratic party. Democrat Wilbur Cross won election as governor four times during the 1930's. Economic conditions improved when the depression eased in the late 1930's.

During World War II (1939-1945), Connecticut was an important supplier of war materials. The state's factories made airplane engines, propellers, shell cases, and submarines.

The Connecticut legislature approved a sales tax in 1947, and raised corporation taxes in 1953. These taxes helped pay for rising education costs and other state services. In 1954, the *Nautilus*, the world's first nuclear-powered submarine, was launched at Groton. The American Shakespeare Festival, now a major U.S. cultural event, began in Stratford in 1955. Also in 1955, two floods caused over $200,000,000 worth of property damage and took nearly 120 lives in Connecticut.

Connecticut adopted a direct primary voting law in 1955. This law gives Connecticut voters a voice in choosing candidates for state elections. The next year, Governor Abraham Ribicoff launched a vigorous traffic-safety campaign based on strict enforcement of the state's driving laws. A law passed in 1957 required persons 16 or 17 years old to take a course in driver education before they could receive a driver's license. In 1963, the law was amended to allow parents to teach their children to drive.

Connecticut Today ranks among the most prosperous states. Its people have one of the nation's highest average annual incomes. Much of the prosperity has resulted from the state's thriving industry.

Connecticut industry has kept pace with Nuclear Age and Space Age developments of the 1950's and 1960's. The building of nuclear submarines is one of Connecticut's most important industries. Re-entry vehicles for spacecraft are made in Stratford. Small tape recorders made in Middletown can send signals back to earth from outer space. These recorders are not much bigger than saucers. The search for new products has made industrial research important in Connecticut. Each year, Connecticut firms spend millions of dollars on studies of ways to develop new products.

A 1963 state report showed that 32 Connecticut communities had planned, started, or completed urban-renewal projects. The cost of these projects was estimated at $380 million. Urban-renewal has wiped out slums in many large Connecticut communities. For example, the site of Hartford's Constitution Plaza was a slum until an urban-renewal project made it an attractive business district.

The 1960's brought political changes to Connecticut. In 1964, Connecticut redrew its Congressional districts. Each of the five districts, regardless of population, had elected one Congressman to the U.S. House of Representatives. A sixth had been elected by the

Robert L. Perry, FPG

Nuclear-Powered Submarine, the *Thomas A. Edison,* glides through the water after its launching at a Groton shipyard in 1961.

state as a whole. The state created six new Congressional districts with fairly equal populations.

Connecticut faced further political problems during the 1960's. In 1964, a federal court ruled against Connecticut's system of electing legislators. Under this system, 10 per cent of Connecticut's voters could elect a majority of the state representatives. This was possible because many thinly populated areas elected the same

THE GOVERNORS OF CONNECTICUT

	Party	Term			Party	Term
Under Articles of Confederation			26. James E. English		Democratic	1867-1869
1. Jonathan Trumbull	Federalist	1778-1784*	27. Marshall Jewell		Republican	1869-1870
2. Matthew Griswold	Federalist	1784-1786	28. James E. English		Democratic	1870-1871
3. Samuel Huntington	Federalist	1786-1788	29. Marshall Jewell		Republican	1871-1873
			30. Charles R. Ingersoll		Democratic	1873-1877
Under United States Constitution			31. Richard D. Hubbard		Democratic	1877-1879
1. Samuel Huntington	Federalist	1788-1796	32. Charles B. Andrews		Republican	1879-1881
2. Oliver Wolcott	Federalist	1796-1797	33. Hobart B. Bigelow		Republican	1881-1883
3. Jonathan Trumbull II	Federalist	1797-1809	34. Thomas M. Waller		Democratic	1883-1885
4. John Treadwell	Federalist	1809-1811	35. Henry B. Harrison		Republican	1885-1887
5. Roger Griswold	Federalist	1811-1812	36. Phineas C. Lounsbury		Republican	1887-1889
6. John Cotton Smith	Federalist	1812-1817	37. Morgan G. Bulkeley		Republican	1889-1893
7. Oliver Wolcott, Jr.	Toleration	1817-1827	38. Luzon B. Morris		Democratic	1893-1895
8. Gideon Tomlinson	National		39. O. Vincent Coffin		Republican	1895-1897
	Republican	1827-1831	40. Lorrin A. Cooke		Republican	1897-1899
9. John S. Peters	National		41. George E. Lounsbury		Republican	1899-1901
	Republican	1831-1833	42. George P. McLean		Republican	1901-1903
10. Henry W. Edwards	Democratic	1833-1834	43. Abiram Chamberlain		Republican	1903-1905
11. Samuel A. Foot	National		44. Henry Roberts		Republican	1905-1907
	Republican	1834-1835	45. Rollin S. Woodruff		Republican	1907-1909
12. Henry W. Edwards	Democratic	1835-1838	46. George L. Lilley		Republican	1909
13. William W. Ellsworth	Whig	1838-1842	47. Frank B. Weeks		Republican	1909-1911
14. Chauncey F. Cleveland	Democratic	1842-1844	48. Simeon E. Baldwin		Democratic	1911-1915
15. Roger S. Baldwin	Whig	1844-1846	49. Marcus H. Holcomb		Republican	1915-1921
16. Isaac Toucey	Democratic	1846-1847	50. Everett J. Lake		Republican	1921-1923
17. Clark Bissell	Whig	1847-1849	51. Charles A. Templeton		Republican	1923-1925
18. Joseph Trumbull	Whig	1849-1850	52. Hiram Bingham		Republican	1925
19. Thomas H. Seymour	Democratic	1850-1853	53. John H. Trumbull		Republican	1925-1931
20. Charles H. Pond	Democratic	1853-1854	54. Wilbur L. Cross		Democratic	1931-1939
21. Henry Dutton	Whig	1854-1855	55. Raymond E. Baldwin		Republican	1939-1941
22. William T. Minor	American		56. Robert A. Hurley		Democratic	1941-1943
	(Know-Noth-		57. Raymond E. Baldwin		Republican	1943-1946
	ing)	1855-1857	58. Wilbert Snow		Democratic	1946-1947
23. Alexander H. Holley	American and		59. James L. McConaughy		Republican	1947-1948
	Republican		60. James C. Shannon		Republican	1948-1949
	(Know-Nothing		61. Chester Bowles		Democratic	1949-1951
	Republican)	1857-1858	62. John Lodge		Republican	1951-1955
24. William A. Buckingham	Republican	1858-1866	63. Abraham A. Ribicoff		Democratic	1955-1961
25. Joseph R. Hawley	Republican	1866-1867	64. John N. Dempsey		Democratic	1961-

*Term began in 1769

number of representatives as did heavily populated areas. In addition, one senator was elected from each senatorial district, even though the districts had widely unequal populations. In 1965, Connecticut *reapportioned* (redivided) its legislature to provide equal repre-

sentation on the basis of population. Voters in each of 177 districts elect one representative. Voters in each of 36 senatorial districts elect one senator. All districts are nearly equal in population.

In 1965, Connecticut adopted its present constitution. The constitution requires that the legislature be reapportioned after each federal census.

BOB EDDY, JOSEPH B. HOYT, and ALBERT E. VAN DUSEN

CONNECTICUT/Study Aids

Related Articles in WORLD BOOK include:

BIOGRAPHIES

Andros, Sir Edmund
Arnold, Benedict
Barnard, Henry
Benton, William
Bowles, Chester
Colt, Samuel
Deane, Silas
Dodd, Thomas J.
Eaton, Theophilus
Ellsworth, Oliver
Gallaudet (Thomas H.)
Gibbs, Josiah W.
Hale, Nathan
Hooker, Thomas
Humphreys, David
Huntington, Samuel

Johnson, William S.
Putnam, Israel
Ribicoff, Abraham A.
Sherman, Roger
Thomas, Seth
Trumbull (Jonathan)
Uncas
Warner, Seth
Welles, Gideon
Whitney, Eli
Williams, William
Winthrop (John, Jr.;
  John III)
Wolcott
Woolley, Mary Emma
Yale, Elihu

CITIES

Bridgeport
Danbury
Greenwich
Groton
Hartford

Litchfield
Manchester
Meriden
Naugatuck

New Britain
New Haven
New London
Norwalk

Stamford
Waterbury
West Hartford
Willimantic

HISTORY

Charter Oak
Colonial Life in America
Hartford Convention

Mystic Seaport
New Netherland
Western Reserve

PHYSICAL FEATURES

Connecticut River
Housatonic River

Long Island Sound
New England

OTHER RELATED ARTICLES

New London Naval Submarine Base
United States Coast Guard Academy

Outline

I. Government
　A. Constitution
　B. Executive
　C. Legislature
　D. Courts
　E. Local Government
　F. Taxation
　G. Politics

II. People

III. Education
　A. Schools
　B. Libraries
　C. Museums

IV. A Visitor's Guide
　A. Places to Visit
　B. Annual Events

V. The Land
　A. Land Regions
　B. Coastline
　C. Mountains
　D. Rivers, Waterfalls, and Lakes

VI. Climate

VII. Economy
　A. Natural Resources
　B. Manufacturing
　C. Agriculture
　D. Mining
　E. Fishing Industry
　F. Electric Power
　G. Transportation
　H. Communication

VIII. History

Questions

Why is Connecticut called the *Constitution State?*
What is Connecticut's chief economic activity?
How did Connecticut's population growth in the 1950's compare with that of other northeastern states?
What were the *Fundamental Orders?*
How did Connecticut provide its first school fund?
What technique first used in Connecticut led to modern manufacturing methods?
Who was *Brother Jonathan?*
Which city in Connecticut is called the *Insurance Capital of the World?*
What defense products are made in Connecticut?
How does Connecticut seek to teach safe driving techniques to teen-agers?

Books for Young Readers

HUMPHREVILLE, FRANCES T., and VAN DUSEN, ALBERT E. *This is Connecticut.* Singer, 1963.
Litchfield Associates. A Guide to Historic Sites in Connecticut. Text by Eric Hatch. Wesleyan Univ. Press, 1963.
STILES, DAN (pseud. of George C. Haig). *The Face of Connecticut.* Sugar Ball Press, 1962.

Books for Older Readers

BRADBURY, BIANCA. *Goodness and Mercy Jenkins.* Washburn, 1963.
BRAINARD, NEWTON C. *The Hartford State House of 1796.* The Connecticut Historical Society, 1964.
HOYT, JOSEPH B. *The Connecticut Story.* Readers Press, 1962.
VAN DUSEN, ALBERT E. *Connecticut.* Random House, 1961.

CONNECTICUT, UNIVERSITY OF, is a state-supported coeducational university at Storrs, Conn. Schools and colleges at the university include agriculture, business administration, education, engineering, fine arts, home economics, liberal arts and sciences, nursing, pharmacy, physical education, and physical therapy. The university has branches in Avery Point, Hartford, Stamford, Torrington, and Waterbury, and maintains schools of dentistry, insurance, law, medicine, and social work in Greater Hartford. The university has an extension division and summer sessions. Courses lead to bachelor's, master's, and doctor's degrees. The university was founded as a land-grant college in 1881. For enrollment of the University of Connecticut, see UNIVERSITIES AND COLLEGES (table). DONALD W. FRIEDMAN

CONNECTICUT COLLEGE. See UNIVERSITIES AND COLLEGES (table).

CONNECTICUT COMPROMISE. See UNITED STATES CONSTITUTION (The Compromises).

CONNECTICUT RIVER rises in northern New Hampshire, and forms the boundary between that state and Vermont. It then cuts across Massachusetts and Connecticut to empty into Long Island Sound. It is 407 miles long. Industrial towns grew up along its middle course to take advantage of the power from the river's falls and rapids. Important industries along the river include textile mills and paper plants. Some ocean-going ships can travel the Connecticut between Hartford, Conn., and Long Island Sound.   JOHN H. GARLAND

CONNECTING ROD. See PISTON; AUTOMOBILE (diagram: How an Automobile Runs); GASOLINE ENGINE (Pistons).

CONNECTIVE TISSUE is the supporting tissue of the body. It also helps to hold the body organs in place. Connective tissue is made up of cells, fibers, and intercellular substance. There are six forms of connective tissue in the body of an adult human being: (1) loose, or areolar, tissue; (2) fat; (3) dense fibrous tissue; (4) bone; (5) cartilage; and (6) blood-forming tissue.

Loose, or *areolar*, *tissue* is like a spider web. It supports, penetrates, separates, and allows motion between all the different parts and organs within the body. Its cells are called *fibroblasts*. Its white fibers are called *collagen*, and its yellow fibers, *elastic*. Cells that contain drops of fat make up the *fatty tissues*. The fibers of *dense fibrous tissue* are arranged in bundles to form the ligaments and tendons. The cells that make up *bone* contain deposits of minerals.   IRVIN STEIN

See also BLOOD; BONE; CARTILAGE.

CONNELLY, MARC (1890-   ), is the author of *The Green Pastures* (1930), perhaps America's most popular religious drama. The play has an all-Negro cast and is written in the homespun language of the Negro South. It takes place in heaven, and God (called "De Lawd" in the play) is the chief character. "De Lawd" changes from the Old Testament God of wrath to a God of mercy. The play is filled with humor and the recognition of the dignity of man. It won a Pulitzer prize in 1930.

Connelly and George S. Kaufman earlier collaborated to write several lively, satirical comedies. But their most significant collaboration was *Beggar on Horseback* (1924), an expressionistic dream play adapted from a German script. The play shows the forces in everyday life that oppose the creative person.

Connelly was born MARCUS COOK CONNELLY in McKeesport, Pa.   THOMAS A. ERHARD

CONNOR, JOHN THOMAS (1914-   ), served as secretary of commerce from January, 1965, to January, 1967. Connor was president of Merck & Co., a drug manufacturer, from 1955 to 1965. He served as general counsel of the Office of Scientific Research and Development from 1942 to 1944. In 1945, he became a special assistant to Secretary of the Navy James Forrestal. Connor was born in Syracuse, N.Y. He graduated from Syracuse University and Harvard Law School.   CARL T. ROWAN

CONNOR, RALPH. See GORDON, CHARLES WILLIAM.

CONQUISTADORS, *kahn KWIS tuh dawrz*, were Spanish explorers who conquered various regions of Latin America during the 1500's. *Conquistador* is a Spanish word meaning *conqueror*. The most famous con-quistadors included Hernando Cortes, who took Mexico, and Francisco Pizarro, who conquered Peru. See also EXPLORATION AND DISCOVERY (Spanish Explorations).

CONRAD, CHARLES, JR. See ASTRONAUT.

CONRAD, JOSEPH (1857-1924), was a Polish-born author who wrote in English. He became famous for his novels and short stories about the sea.

Conrad was born JÓZEF TEODOR KONRAD NALECZ KORZENIOWSKI near Kiev, in what was then Russian Poland. He left Poland at the age of 16 and arrived in England at the age of 20, unable to speak English. During the next 16 years, he worked his way up from deckhand to captain in the British Merchant Navy and so mastered his adopted language that he was able to write some of its greatest novels. He retired from the navy in 1894.

Conrad used the varied experiences of his life in many of his works. From his voyages in the Indian Ocean and Malayan Archipelago came some of his best-known novels. He began with *Alamayer's Folly* (1895) and *An Outcast of the Islands* (1896), both set in Borneo. Such later masterpieces as *The Nigger of the "Narcissus"* (1897), *Lord Jim* (1900), *Typhoon* (1903), *Victory* (1915), and *The Shadow Line* (1917) are also set in the eastern seas. Several of his short stories, including "The Secret Sharer" and "Youth," are set there, too. Conrad's story "Heart of Darkness" is based on his voyage up the Congo River, and *Nostromo* (1904) uses memories of his early voyages in the Caribbean.

The people of Conrad's day infuriated him by thinking of him as merely a writer of sea stories. But Conrad knew his works really dealt with universal problems. He used the concentrated little world of a ship to treat the general problem that obsessed him: How can society endure against all the destructive forces of the individual ego and the modern world? *Nostromo*, for example, gives an epic picture of the clash between capitalism and revolution in South America. He also wrote two absorbing novels about revolutionaries in Europe, *The Secret Agent* (1907) and *Under Western Eyes* (1911).

Conrad was not particularly interested in character for its own sake. He was most interested in men who were actively pursuing their aims in life. Some, like the captain of the "Narcissus," triumph over weakness and evil. More often, Conrad's heroes yield to the powers of weakness and evil in themselves and others. But Conrad was not exactly a pessimist. He affirmed the value of the old-fashioned virtues—courage, fidelity, and discipline. He was modern in realizing how enormously difficult it is to practice such virtues.   IAN WATT

CONSCIENCE, *KAHN shuns*, is a sense of right or wrong. It enables us to apply the general moral law to particular cases, so that we can know whether a certain action is good and should be done, or is bad and should be avoided. A person may know that lying is wrong. If he repeats a story that he judges to be a lie, he is acting against his conscience.   JAMES COLLINS

CONSCIENTIOUS OBJECTOR. See PACIFISM.

CONSCIOUSNESS is the state of awareness, and is the opposite of unconsciousness, a state in which there is no experience. See PSYCHOANALYSIS; PSYCHOLOGY (History); SUBCONSCIOUS; SUBLIMINAL.

CONSCRIPTION. See DRAFT, MILITARY; ARMY.

Rapho-Guillumette

Conserving the Soil insures food for the future. *Contour plowing* across sloping land and *strip cropping*, or planting different crops in alternate rows, helps keep rain from washing soil away.

Wildlife Conservation saved the bison, or American buffalo, from destruction. Hunters killed all but about 550 of these mighty animals by the late 1800's. But game laws and other measures protected the herds. About 10,000 bison now live in the western U.S.

Conservation

CONSERVATION means the protection and wise use of our natural resources. We cannot control the supply of air we breathe or the sunshine that warms the earth. But we can influence the supplies of our other natural resources—soil, water, forests, minerals, and wildlife. Conservation means guarding these resources so they may be used wisely by the greatest number of people.

We like to think of our world as large enough and rich enough to provide good homes for everyone. Unfortunately, the supply of most resources is limited. Water covers about seven-tenths of the earth's area and so makes it useless for growing crops. Much of the actual land surface is either too cold, too dry, too wet, or too mountainous for crop farming. This leaves only about one acre of cultivated land to provide food for each of the more than three billion persons on the earth.

Our natural resources are not only limited, but many of them can also be easily damaged or destroyed. Men cut down trees and mine metals for use in building and manufacturing. They destroy forests to clear the land for farming. They pollute streams and make the water unfit for use. They overwork the soil and make it useless for growing more crops.

Whenever possible, we must replace the resources we use. A good forester cuts trees only where other trees will grow to replace them. The wise farmer adds to his soil the plant foods that crops take from it. Conservation is concerned not only with the resources we need today, but also with resources for the future. In each generation, every person's share of the world becomes smaller because our population is growing rapidly. Every morning finds about 175,000 more persons on earth than there were the morning before. We have a real duty to use our resources wisely so that the people who come after us will be able to use them, too.

Conservation also means safeguarding human resources. Our well-being depends not only on soil, trees,

William A. Garnett

Conserving Water means making the most of each drop. Dams, such as Grand Coulee in Washington, store water for irrigation projects and use it to generate electric power.

Human Resources are a nation's strength. The battle against tuberculosis is an important part of conservation.
Chicago Tuberculosis Institute

Mineral Conservation fights waste by reusing our resources. A pile of scrap metal is melted down and used again.
U.S. Steel Corp.;
Grand Rapids *Herald Review*

Weyerhaeuser Timber Co.

Forests of Tomorrow require planning today. Block cutting of Douglas firs ensures a continuous supply of future wood. Uncut trees scatter seeds that sprout quickly in cutover areas.

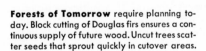

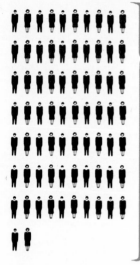

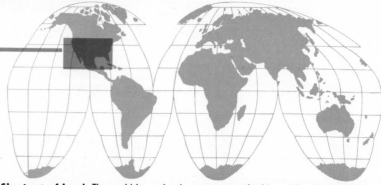

Shortage of Land. The world has only about one acre of cultivated land to provide food for each of the 3,616,000,000 persons who live on the earth. If all this land were in one place, it would cover only the area shown in blue on the map, *above.*

Each Figure Represents 50,000,000 Persons

The Booming World Population makes it vital to conserve our resources for future generations. In the last 200 years, the number of persons living on the earth has increased more than four times.

Sources: *Demographic Yearbook, 1967, UN; Production Yearbook, 1967, FAO*

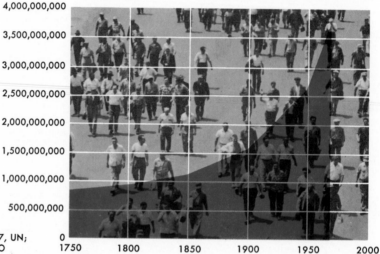

and minerals. It also depends on our health and on the services we receive from others. We must try to see that all the things men make—houses, roads, machines—are well cared for. Conservation of human and natural resources helps make and keep our homes, our country, and our world better places in which to live.

Conservation concerns national, state, and local governments. It also concerns the doctor who saves human lives and the teacher who helps develop students into useful citizens. The forest ranger in his lonely fire tower and the farmer planting his crops both work for conservation. So do the social worker, the city planner, the game warden, and the policeman on the corner. To each of us, conservation means personal responsibility for the wise use of natural and human resources in our homes and communities. Because of this, conservation should be everybody's business.

Kinds of Conservation

There are eight chief kinds of conservation: (1) soil conservation, (2) water conservation, (3) forest conservation, (4) wildlife conservation, (5) conservation of grazing lands, (6) mineral conservation, (7) conservation for recreation, and (8) conservation of human resources.

Each type of conservation has its own problems and solutions. But different resources depend on one another. An example is the *balance of nature* between soil, water, and wildlife. Plants and animals only "borrow" the foods they need. When they die and decay, they give the elements they have used back to the soil. See BALANCE OF NATURE.

Soil Conservation. Most of the food that supports life comes from the soil, either directly or indirectly. President Theodore Roosevelt once said: "When the soil is gone, man must go. And the process does not take long." The earth is a great ball of rock about 8,000 miles in diameter. But its thin surface of soil averages only 2 or 3 feet thick. The depth of the *topsoil*, the fertile top layer, is usually thin enough to be measured in inches. See SOIL.

It takes nature several hundred years to build an inch of topsoil. But erosion can wash or blow away this inch in a few years or even weeks. Rain falling on an acre of barren, sloping land can wash away as much as 60 truckloads of soil in a year. Such washing away is called *sheet erosion.* Water can also carve gullies in hillsides. Wind may blow the topsoil off both sloping and level land. In the United States, erosion has destroyed an estimated more than 50 million acres of farmland since colonial times. This is an area larger than Nebraska. Erosion has partially destroyed another 50 million acres and threatens about 100 million acres.

Other processes besides erosion can make soil lose its fertility. Heavy rainfall can *leach out* the minerals that plants need to grow. In leaching, rain water seeps through the soil and carries dissolved minerals below the roots of most plants. Farmers can also ruin their land if they grow crops without *fertilizing*, or returning needed food elements to the soil.

Wise farmers add chemical and natural fertilizers to the soil to maintain the food supply needed by growing plants. They plow animal manure and green plants into the ground to increase the plant food and humus (see Humus). *Crop rotation* is an important way of keeping soil fertile. When a farmer rotates his crops, for example, he may alternate corn with other crops that use different elements from the soil. He avoids planting the same crop on the same land year after year. See Cropping System.

Soil conservation tries to keep the soil deep and productive. In *contour plowing*, a farmer plows his furrows across a slope, rather than up and down. The furrows catch the rain water and keep it from running off the hill. Some farmers lay out their fields in *stairstep terraces* on a hillside. Deep gullies can be controlled by planting trees or grasses, or by building dams to hold back water and soil. One of the best ways to prevent erosion is to keep land covered with closely growing plants such as wheat, grass, and trees.

Water Conservation. Man and most animals need a constant supply of water to live. Farmers need water for their crops. Hydroelectric dams hold back needed water and provide power for homes and industries.

Trees, grasses, and other plant life play an important part in the natural circulation of water, and thus help conserve it (see Water [color illustration: The Water Cycle]). Without plants most water would run off as soon as it falls, taking away valuable soil. Rapid runoff would cause frequent floods, and leave little water during dry seasons.

Nature has many ways of conserving and controlling water. But man often upsets the water balance in his desire to grow more crops. He drains ponds, swamps, and wet lands. He plows under the natural sods, cuts timber, and dredges and straightens streams. These changes reduce natural storage of water and speed runoff.

Water can be held on the land by planting vegetation. Forests and grass should be planted where there are no natural growths. Dams built across rivers help hold back the water. Reservoirs behind the dams store water during wet seasons for use in dry seasons. Dams help prevent floods by controlling the flow of water.

Many towns and cities get their water from nearby lakes and rivers. Some communities dump sewage and garbage into the water, making it unfit to drink. Water pollution is one of our most serious problems. Progressive cities have sewage-treatment plants (see Sewage). These plants return only safe water to the streams or lakes. Many states have laws that prohibit companies from dumping raw industrial wastes, such as liquids from a metal-plating factory, into streams. These wastes often endanger the supply of drinking water. They also kill fish. Most industrial wastes can be treated to make them harmless.

Forest Conservation is closely related to water and soil conservation. Trees slow the runoff of rain and check erosion. This helps keep loose soil from clogging rivers and streams. Trees planted along the edges of fields can check the force of the wind and help prevent soil erosion. Forests provide homes for wildlife and offer opportunities for recreation. Well-managed forests supply wood products of various kinds, and provide jobs for workers in the forest-products industry. See Forest and Forest Products (Forestry and Conservation); Tree (Trees in Conservation).

In many regions, man has wasted the forests so badly that they cannot fully serve these useful purposes. Men sometimes cut trees without planting new ones. Grazing animals may injure trees, and insects and diseases may cause them to die. Fires often damage or kill trees, and burn the humus out of the soil. Many such destructive fires are caused by a carelessly tossed match or cigarette.

Well-protected forests can serve man indefinitely. Lumbermen in the United States, Canada, and many other countries have learned the importance of harvesting trees in such a way that the land will continue to provide lumber. They replant where necessary, and do not cut down young trees or seed trees.

The Forest Service of the United States Department of Agriculture cooperates with the states and private landowners to conserve forests. Their efforts include fire prevention and fire fighting, control of disease and insects, technical services to timber owners and loggers, and forestry research.

Wildlife Conservation. Wild animals play an important part in the balance of nature, and furnish us with many important products. Birds and other small animals help control insects. Wild animals provide fur,

---

CONSERVATION TERMS

Erosion is the wearing away of soil by water or by wind.

Farm Plan preserves the soil, vegetation, and water of a farm to achieve maximum conservation.

Habitat includes food, shelter, and all other things that affect wildlife.

Humus is the partially decayed remains of plants and animals in the soil.

Irrigation is the artificial watering of plants.

Land Drainage is the artificial removal of water from land by means of ditches or pipes.

Plant Cover is the combination of all plant life—mosses, grasses, shrubs, trees—on any soil surface.

Runoff is rain or melted snow that does not evaporate or soak into the ground, but runs into rivers, lakes, and oceans.

Strip Cropping means raising different crops in alternating strips to control erosion.

Sustained Yield is the cutting and care of woodland so it will produce a forest crop continuously.

Terracing means plowing or shifting the soil so it lies in horizontal plots that check the flow of water and resist erosion on hillsides.

Urban Renewal is the replacement of old buildings in a city with new, modern ones.

Vegetated Waterway is a part of a field that is planted with grass to prevent erosion.

Watershed is the land from which water drains into a river. *Watershed management* means the control of the plant cover and soil to achieve a regular flow of clear water into the river.

food, and recreation. They also make our surroundings more interesting.

Hunters have killed great numbers of wild animals for sport and food. Forest fires destroy wildlife. Plowing natural grasslands and draining lakes and swamps destroy the nesting and feeding places of many birds. Some birds, such as the passenger pigeon, have completely disappeared (see PASSENGER PIGEON). Others, such as the whooping crane, the California condor, and the trumpeter swan, are in danger of dying out (see CONDOR; CRANE; SWAN).

It is just as important to keep some animals from becoming too plentiful as it is to keep others from being wiped out. For example, animals such as the mountain lion that feed on other animals should not be allowed to become too numerous. But they play a valuable part in the balance of nature, and should not be destroyed completely. We even need to control the number of harmless animals, such as deer. Too many of these animals may crowd other wildlife out of their habitats by eating too much of the available food. Animals can also damage trees and crops. For example, a large number of crows can ruin a corn crop.

·················soil conservation

T.V.A.

Erosion Takes Its Toll of unprotected farm land. Rain water running down the slopes of this farm can wash away 60 truckloads of topsoil a year and carve deep gullies.

Soil Conservation Service, USDA

Contour Plowing conserves water and prevents erosion. The deep furrows run across the slope of the land. Rain water collects in the troughs and soaks into the ground instead of running off.

Wind Erosion caused the "Dust Bowls" of the Great Plains. In times of drought, wind picks up the dry or sandy soil and carries it across the land in violent dust storms.

We can best protect game and fish by taking care of the places where they live. This enables wildlife to live well, raise their young ones, and hide from their enemies. Partridge, for example, need food patches, brushy undergrowth for shelter, and shrubs and trees in which to hide from hawks. Young trout need clean, cool water to thrive and grow. Squirrels need trees in which to build their nests. Migrating birds need feeding and resting places on their journeys. The federal and state governments have established hundreds of wildlife refuges throughout the United States to give animals a safe place in which to live.

Fish and game laws keep fishermen and hunters from killing too many animals. In the late 1800's, for example, only about 550 bison (American buffalo) remained of the great herds that once roamed the United States. Hunters had killed the rest. Game laws and other protective measures saved these mighty animals. About 10,000 bison now live in various parts of the western United States. See WILDLIFE CONSERVATION.

Conservation of Grazing Land. A large part of the western United States consists of lands on which only grass and bushes grow. These *dry grazing lands* lack enough rain to grow trees. They often have years of almost no rain at all. More than half the United States is grazing land, most of it in the dry areas west of the Mississippi River. Ranchers use this land to graze sheep and cattle. Livestock also grazes on woodlands, cleared lands, and planted fields in the East, the South, and parts of the West.

Americans have mistreated much of their grazing lands. The main damage came from years of overgrazing. Livestock have destroyed much of the original plant cover in some areas. Fires have also injured the grass and

Strip Cropping helps prevent wind erosion. On this Montana farm, rows of wheat alternate with rows of *fallow*, or idle, land. The wheat helps break the force of the wind, preventing it from blowing the fallow soil. Wheat farmers often let half their land lie fallow each year in order to give it a chance to soak up rain.

·····water conservation

Too Little Water. Years of drought turned this Arizona water hole into a cracked, sun-baked mud flat. Man cannot prevent drought. But careful use and planning can help provide a supply of precious water for times of need.

Too Much Water. Rain-swollen rivers flooded this Oklahoma farm. Floods not only destroy lives and property, but they also carry away valuable soil. Because of this, dams, reservoirs, and other flood-control projects are an important part of conservation.

Life, © 1951 Time, Inc.

soil. Coarse, useless plants such as mesquite have sprung up in the grazing land in some regions of the West. In other areas, grazing has speeded up the normal erosion. Much wildlife has been destroyed or greatly reduced. The loss of plant cover has also reduced the value of the land as a *watershed*, or drainage area.

Planting trees and careful grazing can restore and preserve much of the eastern grazing lands. But the dry West presents a more difficult problem. It may take 20 to 50 years for grass to return to an area where it has been destroyed. The federal government owns about a third of the dry western grasslands, and has taken the lead in protecting these areas. The federal Bureau of Land Management limits the number of livestock that ranchers can graze on the public lands (see PUBLIC LANDS). It has also taken steps to replant grasslands, control erosion, and provide watering places for livestock.

Mineral Conservation. Without minerals, we would have few conveniences of modern life. Minerals provide steel for automobiles, copper for telephone wires, and aluminum for airplanes. Coal and petroleum are burned for power and heat. Uranium and other radioactive

elements produce atomic power. It took nature millions of years to make minerals. But a bed of coal that took a million years to form can be mined and burned by man in a few years. See MINERAL.

We can conserve minerals by mining them carefully, reusing them when possible, and finding substitutes for those that are scarce. Scientists have discovered methods of refining petroleum so that little is wasted or unused. They also have found efficient ways to extract metals from ores so that the loss is small. Plastics provide an important substitute for minerals. The reuse of scrap metals also helps conserve minerals.

Conservation for Recreation has become more important than ever before. Industrial progress, such as automation, gives us more spare time to enjoy the outdoors. Modern transportation makes it possible to reach forests, lakes, mountains, and beaches quickly and easily.

But the number of recreational areas has decreased as the need has grown. Private owners have closed many scenic spots. Other areas have been spoiled by misuse or neglect. Expanding cities have taken over beautiful countryside. As a result, our remaining recreational areas

Water Conservation at Its Best is shown in this drawing. Trees and plants hold water on the land and prevent floods. The reservoir stores water and serves as a recreational area. The dam controls the river's flow and puts it to work turning generators in the powerhouse. An irrigation canal carries water to thirsty farm land. The waterworks pumps water from the river, purifies it, and sends it to city homes. A sewage treatment plant makes waste harmless before returning the water to the river. This insures safe water for cities downstream.

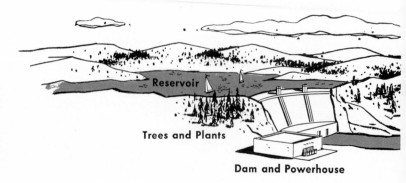

Reservoir

Trees and Plants

Dam and Powerhouse

have become more and more valuable and should be preserved for the enjoyment of all.

Nearly all natural resources have recreational value. For example, a river can provide a home for fish, power for homes and industry, and water for drinking. It can also supply a place for swimming, fishing, boating, and other recreation. Western grazing lands serve as good hunting areas. Reservoirs created mainly to control floods and maintain waterways can also be used for water sports. For example, Lake Mead behind Hoover Dam is a popular recreation area.

Almost every city or town has at least one park. Most state governments try to establish state parks within about 30 miles of every citizen. The National Park Service operates 31 national parks that cover more than 13,500,000 acres. National forests and monuments are also important recreational areas. See NATIONAL FOR- EST; NATIONAL MONUMENT; NATIONAL PARK.

Conservation of Human Resources. People are the most important resource of any nation. The health, happiness, and well-being of every person concerns not only the person himself, but his community as well.

Care for health and the fight against disease are important parts of human conservation. Scientists such as Emil von Behring, the German bacteriologist who discovered a diphtheria vaccine, and Jonas E. Salk, the American bacteriologist who discovered the polio vac- cine, rank among the greatest conservationists. But a child who eats properly and gets the sleep he needs is also a conservationist. Each person has a responsibility to conserve his own health and energy. Accident pre- vention, in both homes and industry, is an important conservation measure in which everyone can help.

Human resources also include everything that people make. Manufactured articles should be protected and carefully used. This prevents the waste of the human energy, skill, and knowledge that went into making them. It also reduces the drain on natural resources.

As cities grow older, slums begin to appear. It costs much money and effort to replace tumble-down build- ings with new ones. *Urban-renewal* projects build new housing to replace old, unsightly, and unsanitary build- ings. These projects encourage people to take pride in their homes.

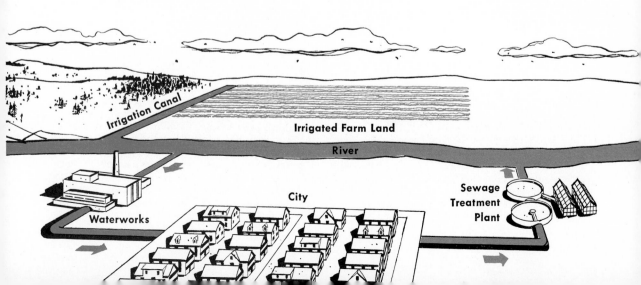

....forest conservation

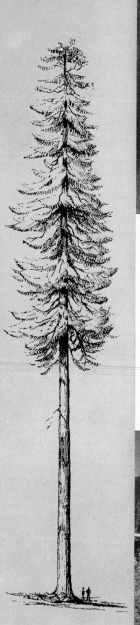

Raging Forest Fires destroy valuable timber and threaten lives and property. They also ruin the fertility of the soil and destroy the forest as a home for wildlife. Once they start, forest fires are hard to fight. But man can prevent most forest fires with care and planning.

The Results of Conservation. These logs symbolize what wise forestry practices can do. The forest that produced these logs will serve as a continuous source of wood for future years.

Careless Cutting produces ruin and waste. Wise lumbermen never cut down an entire forest. They leave trees to scatter seeds and reforest the land. Cutover land loses its value as a watershed. Trees hold water on the land. On land such as this, water runs off quickly, causing floods and washing away the soil.

The home, church, and school serve as the most important organizations and agencies that promote human conservation. They help mold character, prevent crime and delinquency, and teach people how to live happy, useful lives.

How Conservation Is Achieved

Individuals can do much to promote conservation. But people have to work together in order to care for our natural resources properly. They can work with their neighbors in community conservation projects, or take part in projects carried on by state and federal governments. Nations join to fight waste and promote conservation on an international level. Special organiza-tions work for conservation and help educate citizens in preventing waste and destruction of natural resources. Schools also play an important part in conservation by teaching young people its importance.

Community Cooperation. Some of the responsibility for conservation rests on local communities—the county, city, town, and village. Citizens often band together in *conservation districts* for various purposes. These districts are sponsored by state and federal governments. Farmers join *soil-conservation districts* to get technical assistance and to work out efficient farm-management plans. In the United States, more than 2,700 soil-conservation districts attack soil erosion on a community-wide basis. Farmers in dry areas often form *irrigation* *districts* and *water-users associations*. These organizations enable farmers to share the costs of storing and distributing water. In regions where land is to be drained for farming, a number of farmers may unite to form *drainage districts*. In some states, *water-conservation districts* work to reduce flood damage and to make better use of the water supply. *Levee districts* help local residents prevent floods.

Urban-renewal and neighborhood-improvement programs require the cooperation of all interested citizens. Some states grant charters to neighborhood redevelopment corporations made up of private citizens. These corporations attack the problems of neighborhood blight by such means as condemning and selling old or unsanitary buildings.

State and Federal Governments. In the United States, the right to regulate the management of natural resources belongs, by law, to the states. For example, a state can pass laws to reduce waste of natural gas and to control the amount of petroleum taken from the ground. State laws govern conservation districts. Many states own forests that they manage according to planned conservation practices.

Each state government has departments that protect and manage wildlife resources, and regulate hunting and fishing. Many states have agencies devoted to forest and water conservation. These departments not only do much conservation work, but also conduct active programs of conservation education.

The federal government and the states share in water-resource research, in the cost of forest-fire control, and in tree planting. The federal government also joins with local communities to share the costs of reducing stream pollution and in the removal of slum areas in cities. The U.S. Extension Service provides trained men and women to help farmers plan conservation programs. The Extension Service centers its work at state land-grant universities and colleges. Agricultural experiment stations at these schools encourage correct land-use practices.

In addition to working with state and local governments, the federal government has responsibility for a vast range of conservation activities. The Forest Service of the U.S. Department of Agriculture manages the national forests. The department's Soil Conservation Service works with soil-conservation districts. The Fish and Wildlife Service of the Department of the Interior works with the states on wildlife conservation. It also maintains waterfowl refuges and fish hatcheries. The department's Bureau of Reclamation constructs irrigation and flood-control projects. Other conservation agencies in the Department of the Interior include the National Park Service and the Geological Survey, which studies water and mineral resources. The Department of Health, Education, and Welfare pays special attention to the conservation of human resources. The Corps of Engineers of the U.S. Army has charge of flood control along major rivers.

International Cooperation. Nations often work together to solve mutual conservation problems. The United States and Canada cooperate to conserve the halibut fisheries off the coast of British Columbia. Treaties between the two countries limit the amount of fish that can be taken from these waters. A joint commission studies the fishery problems and establishes and enforces regulations. A treaty between the United States and Canada protects waterfowl that migrate between the two countries.

Canada, Japan, Russia, and the United States have a treaty that controls the hunting of fur seals in the northern Pacific Ocean. Many nations have joined in an international agreement to conserve whales. The waters of the Rio Grande are the subject of an agreement

Selective Cutting makes room for new growth. This forester uses a paint gun to mark a tree for cutting. This twisted tree would make a poor saw log, but it can be used for wood pulp.

Texas Forest Service

Plowing a Fire Line around a forest helps protect it from fires. This open space prevents flames from leaping from tree to tree. Fire lines are an important means of fire protection.

American Forest Products Industries, Inc.

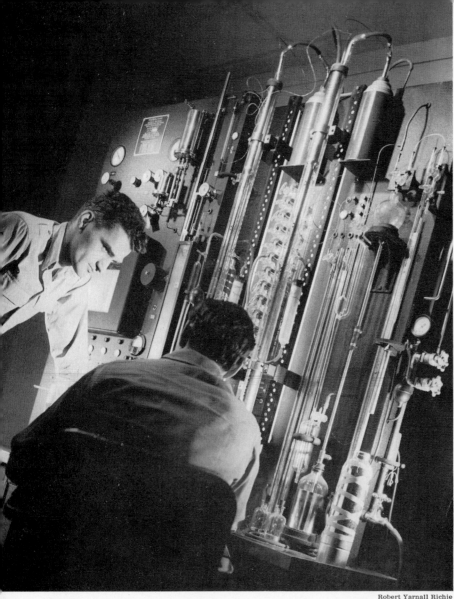

·······mineral

conservation

The Battle Against Waste
is often fought in the laboratory. These petroleum scientists
use a miniature refinery to plan
ways to get the most out of a
barrel of oil. Men cannot make
minerals. But research such as
this can find means to make the
best use of mineral resources.

Robert Yarnall Richie

between the United States and Mexico. The Falcon Dam, completed in 1953, was built by the two countries to store the river's water and help prevent floods.

In 1949, the United Nations held a world conference on the scientific use and conservation of natural resources. The UN has a continuous program of studies and activities in the field of international resources. The World Health Organization; the Food and Agriculture Organization; and the United Nations Educational, Scientific, and Cultural Organization (UNESCO) deal with special conservation problems on a world scale.

Special Organizations also do effective work in conserving resources. These nongovernmental organizations include the American Forestry Association and the National Wildlife Federation, which promote the intelligent management and wise use of forests and wildlife. The Izaak Walton League is especially concerned with fish conservation. The National Audubon Society helps promote public understanding of the value and need for soil, water, plant, and wildlife conservation. The

Garden Club of America does much to guard the outdoor beauty of the United States.

Some organizations specialize in conservation research and education. These organizations include the American Association for the Advancement of Science, the Conservation Foundation, the Friends of the Land, the National Education Association, the National Safety Council, and Resources for the Future, Inc. Other important conservation organizations include the National Association of Soil Conservation Districts, the National Reclamation Association, and the National Rivers and Harbors Congress.

Most of these organizations are run by and for adults. But many of them welcome young people. Many youth organizations take an active part in conservation work. Conservation is a merit-badge subject of the Boy Scouts of America. The Girl Scouts and the Camp Fire Girls also study it. Farm youth groups such as the 4-H Clubs and the Future Farmers of America stress conservation in their educational programs.

Conservation Education. Conservation is an important school subject in the United States. Many school subjects contribute to an understanding of the need for and the processes involved in conserving natural resources. Classroom projects and field trips are two special ways that students learn about conservation.

Classroom Projects help make conservation more meaningful. Students in chemistry and general-science classes sometimes test samples of soil from their yards and gardens. Classes may make plaster models that show how erosion occurs and can be prevented. Biology students make aquariums that illustrate the balance of nature between fish, water, and plants. Geography classes sometimes make maps that show the locations of forests and forest areas destroyed by fire. Art classes make picture exhibits to show the importance of various kinds of conservation. Students throughout the country plant trees on Arbor Day (see ARBOR DAY). In some schools, students work in school gardens that raise vegetables for their lunchrooms. Raising pets and collecting minerals are other examples of classroom projects related to conservation.

Field Trips serve as an effective and interesting way to learn about conservation. Some states operate camps as part of their regular school programs. In these camps, young people learn some of the problems involved in conservation of land and wildlife. Students may make trips to sewage-disposal plants. They learn how engineers remove impurities that would pollute the water supply. Students sometimes take trips to farms to see soil conservation at work. See NATURE STUDY.

Conservation in the United States

Early Efforts. When the first colonists settled in America, they found a land of great natural wealth. The pioneers had no idea that good farm land, forests, and wildlife would ever become scarce. Some of the early farmers, such as those of southeastern Pennsylvania, continued the careful farming methods they had learned in Europe. But most of the settlers moved on to unused land when their farms wore out.

Some leaders became concerned about what was happening to the natural resources. Thomas Jefferson favored contour plowing to hold soil in place. George Washington worried about soil erosion on his Mount Vernon estate. His workers dug mud from the shore of the Potomac River and used it to fill in eroded fields.

During the 1700's and 1800's, individuals and private organizations sometimes protested the waste of natural resources and promoted efforts to conserve them. The naturalist and writer Henry Thoreau wrote articles urging the establishment of wilderness areas where wild animals might live in safety. The bird paintings of John J. Audubon helped create a world-wide interest in birds. The judge and geographer George Perkins Marsh (1801-1882) wrote *The Earth as Modified by Human Action*. This great book, written in 1864, helped arouse wide interest in conservation problems.

In spite of the efforts of these and other men, the resources of the eastern United States were gradually reduced during the 1800's. Timber became scarce along the East Coast. Only the opening of the western forest areas prevented a timber shortage in the United States. In the West, pioneers cut down or burned the forests, plowed up grasslands, and killed many kinds of wild-

life. Wasteful hunting methods wiped out almost all the buffalo. Miners dug minerals in such a way that only part of the copper, iron, and coal was removed.

As wildlife declined, state governments passed fish and game laws. Steps were taken to conserve scenic resources. In 1872, the government established Yellowstone National Park, the first national park in the world. Also in that year, J. Sterling Morton, a Nebraska politician who later became U.S. Secretary of Agriculture, started the custom of Arbor Day. In 1891, Congress passed a law giving the President the right to set aside areas as forest reserves. In 1898, Gifford Pinchot, one of the outstanding leaders of the conservation movement, became head of the division of forestry in the Department of Agriculture. Under Pinchot's leadership, the division took an increasingly important part in forest conservation. It became the Forest Service in 1905.

National Policy. In spite of these early efforts, the conservation movement did not make much progress until President Theodore Roosevelt, with Pinchot's help, gave it his powerful support. Roosevelt added more acres to the national forests than did all other presidents before and after. He also regulated grazing in national forests. In 1908, he called the first White House conference of governors to consider conservation problems. As an outgrowth of this conference, 27 states established conservation commissions within two years. Also in 1908, Roosevelt appointed the National Conservation Commission, headed by Pinchot. This commission included 49 prominent men of science, industry, and politics. The group made the first inventory of natural resources in the United States.

Delegates from the United States, Canada, Newfoundland, and Mexico met at the North American Conservation Conference in Washington, D.C., in 1909. This meeting helped publicize the need for conservation. The delegates approved a broad statement of conservation principles. The following year, the geologist and educator Charles R. Van Hise published the first textbook on conservation, *The Conservation of the Natural Resources of the United States*.

Congress passed the Week's Law in 1911. This act made it possible to enlarge national forests by purchasing areas from which water drains into navigable streams. President Woodrow Wilson signed the bill that established the National Park Service in 1916. He also signed the first migratory bird treaty with Canada in 1916. The treaty went into effect in 1918.

Several men played an important part in helping to establish and promote a national conservation policy during and after this period. The naturalist John Muir wrote of the natural beauty of the West and the need to care for it. Muir helped establish Yosemite National Park. The cartoons of Jay N. "Ding" Darling fought for conservation of wildlife and other resources. Newspapers throughout the country printed Darling's cartoons. Fairfield Osborn, Paul B. Sears, and other scientists also made important contributions to conservation through their books and as leaders of conservation groups.

The 1930's and 1940's saw an increase in conservation on the national level under President Franklin D. Roosevelt. During the depression of the 1930's, thousands of unemployed men and youths worked on federal

United Press Int.

Wildlife Refuges protect birds and other animals. Ducks on their way south for the winter rest and feed safely at this water-fowl refuge located near Washington, D.C.

·············*wildlife conservation*

"Planting" Fish with an Airplane is a quick and efficient way to restock out-of-the-way lakes and ponds. Young fish are raised in a hatchery, then placed in special tanks in the plane. When the plane reaches the lake, the fish are dumped into the water. Almost all the fish survive the 100-foot drop.

New York State Conservation Dept.

conservation projects. From 1933 to 1942, the Civilian Conservation Corps (CCC) continuously employed between 175,000 and 500,000 young men in the protection and improvement of natural resources. They planted more than 2,000,000 acres of forests, and fought countless fires. See CIVILIAN CONSERVATION CORPS.

Congress established the Tennessee Valley Authority in 1933 to preserve and develop the resources of the area. That same year, the Department of the Interior set up a Soil Erosion Service. The service was transferred to the Department of Agriculture in 1935 as the Soil Conservation Service. The Taylor Grazing Act of 1934 ended the unregulated grazing of public grazing lands. From 1933 to 1943, the National Resources Board, later the National Resources Planning Board, made studies of the nation's resources and their best use. The Flood Control Act of 1936 established the first national policy on flood control.

By the time the United States entered World War II in 1941, the conservation movement included all efforts to preserve the country's natural resources. Rationing, scrap-metal drives, and other wartime activities helped drive home the message of conservation. They showed how a nation depends on its resources.

Recent Developments. Progress has been made in all phases of conservation during recent years. Soil-conservation districts have increased in number. Lumber companies have adopted policies of forest conservation and increased the number of tree farms. Federal, state, and local governments have made special efforts to prevent flood damage, to reduce stream pollution, and to meet the water-supply needs of various parts of the country. Natural gas is being produced with relatively little waste, and improved refining techniques have vastly increased the number of products obtained from petroleum. Improved technology has enabled industry to use magnesium, titanium, and other substances once believed useless. Urban-renewal and public-health programs have taken important steps toward the conservation of human resources.

In 1954, Congress passed the Watershed Protection and Flood Prevention Act. This law provided for greater cooperation between federal, state, and local governments in reducing flood damage. In 1955, the Department of the Interior began a 20-year program to restore most of the federal grazing lands in the West. In 1957, the Forest Service undertook its five-year "Operation Outdoors" to improve and expand national forest facilities for outdoor recreation.

Conservation in Other Countries

Canada has thick forests, rich mineral deposits, rushing streams, and plunging waterfalls that make it one of the world's most prosperous countries. But, as in the United States, the early settlers carelessly wasted Canada's natural resources. They cut much of the great forest belt that stretches from the Atlantic Coast to the Pacific Coast, giving little thought to the future needs of the country.

Forest fires have also caused heavy losses. Damage to the forests injured wildlife and muddied the rivers and streams. Erosion is common on the farm lands of southern Canada. The dry parts of western Canada need irrigation. Some grazing lands are overgrazed and eroded. Canada ranks as a great vacationland, but careless tourists often leave waste and litter that spoil the beauty of recreation areas.

During the early 1900's, Canadians realized the need for conservation. The country has developed many conservation programs. The federal and provincial governments work with private industry to preserve the country's resources. The provincial forest services and wood pulp and paper companies have made excellent progress in fire control. Animal preserves, and laws that limit hunting, trapping, and fishing help protect Canadian wildlife. The provincial governments have established model fur farms to improve methods of raising valuable fur-bearing animals. Large-scale irrigation projects have turned dry sections of Alberta, Saskatchewan, and British Columbia into regions of fertile farmland.

Latin America, like the United States and Canada, has had conservation problems ever since the days of early settlement. Soil erosion is widespread. Steep slopes have been farmed and badly eroded in the mountainous region that extends from northern Mexico to the tip of South America. Soil erosion has also hit the rolling uplands of southeastern Brazil. Dust storms blow across the drier parts of Argentina. People throughout Latin America cut trees to make charcoal, and loggers remove the forests in many areas. As a result, soil washes from the forest areas. Streams fill with silt and are less useful for irrigation and water supply. In most of the wooded regions, farmers burn over small plots of woodland, grow crops on them for a year or two, then abandon the land for a freshly burned area. This process destroys both forest and soil unless the people allow the land to rest long enough for trees to grow again. Wildlife suffers from the damage to forests, soil, and rivers.

Several Latin-American countries have undertaken important projects to conserve their resources. Mexican schools have an active program of conservation education. Large-scale irrigation projects in Mexico have

turned more than 5,600,000 barren acres into fertile farmland. The government has also established experimental farms and agricultural schools, and has loaned money to farmers to buy fertilizer.

Other Latin-American countries that have undertaken irrigation projects include Peru, Ecuador, Venezuela, Chile, Brazil, and Costa Rica. Venezuela has taken important steps to conserve petroleum, its chief mineral resource. Engineers use modern mining methods in order to waste as little of the country's valuable oil as possible.

Europe has imported large quantities of food for more than a hundred years. This is partly because of the large population, and partly because of widespread soil damage. Southern Europe especially suffers from poor conservation. As long as 500 years ago, sheep and goats destroyed trees and shrubs and ruined the soil by overgrazing in much of Italy, Spain, and Greece. Rains washed the soil to the valleys, creating swamps where malarial mosquitoes thrived. Mining exhausted the small mineral deposits.

Central and northern Europe have also suffered loss of minerals and forest cover. But both nature and man have been kinder to these areas. The rains are lighter than in Southern Europe, and they do not wash the soil away so quickly. Sweden and Norway have had forest-conservation programs since the 1860's. Denmark and Belgium have shown how to use fertilizer to make rich farmland from poor, sandy soil. The Netherlands and Belgium lead the world in diking and draining portions of the sea, creating some of the richest farmland on earth. French farmers save and use every available bit of animal manure for fertilizers. French foresters keep forests growing on mountain slopes and sand dunes. The Germans work hard at all branches of conservation. For example, they have drained and fertilized the poorer, wet lands of the country's north-

United Press Int.

...........*human*

conservation

Urban-Renewal Projects replace old, run-down housing with modern apartments. Crime and disease breed in slums. Housing projects, such as this one in Chicago, give people healthful, comfortable homes.

CONSERVATION

ern plain to make farmland. Switzerland checks floods in mountain streams by caring for forests.

In southern Europe, the Italians have drained and enriched the soil in the Po Valley in the northern part of the country. Land reclamation programs have been successful in southern Italy and in Greece.

Russia has conservation problems similar to those of the United States and Canada. Fires and logging have damaged the country's great northern forest. Water-eroded gullies cut through the fertile plains of the Ukraine region in southwestern Russia. Wind erosion and dust storms threaten the dry eastern plains. Since World War II, the Russians have plowed vast areas of grassland to plant wheat. This plowing has increased the danger of wind erosion. But Russia has begun a large-scale program of conservation and resource development. It includes planting trees in dry areas and controlling rivers to prevent flood damage. One of the largest programs attempts to control the mighty Volga River and store the spring floodwaters for irrigation and to generate electric power.

Asia has an exceptionally great need for conservation. Two-thirds of the world's population lives in Asia on resources that have been greatly reduced and damaged over a period of several thousand years.

The Japanese are perhaps the most active conservationists in Asia. In Japan, more than 101 million persons live in an area the size of California. More than three-fourths of the land is too mountainous for permanent cultivation. However, the Japanese conserve their land carefully. The hills and mountains are kept covered with forests. The soil is heavily fertilized with waste from homes and cities, and with commercial fertilizers.

Most of China's forests have disappeared. The soils have washed away from the hill lands. Many families live on river lowlands where they suffer from floods. However, careful methods of planting and fertilizing have preserved the fertility of much of the soil that might have become worn out from centuries of farming. Many Chinese farmers raise crops on terraces carved out of the hillsides. These terraces allow farmers to cultivate the steep slopes, and help prevent further soil erosion.

India has developed large-scale irrigation projects that furnish water to more than 67 million acres of farmland. Wood is scarce in some parts of India. In these areas, many persons use animal manure as fuel rather than as fertilizer. As a result, much of the soil is poor in plant nutrients. India, Burma, and Pakistan have well-developed forest services to protect their timberlands and to create new timber reserves for the future.

In southwestern Asia, grazing by goats, sheep, and cattle has destroyed much of the grass cover. Irrigation works have fallen into disuse during times of political trouble. In Israel, where the soil was more than three feet deep in Biblical times, the hills are rocky and bare. However, Israel has made rapid strides in conservation. Irrigation projects have turned desert wasteland into rich farmland, and the Israelis have drained swamps and lakes to provide soil for crops. In Iraq, the government has used part of the profits from the petro-leum industry to build irrigation ditches and drain areas with marshes.

Africa has serious conservation problems throughout the continent. Grazing animals have destroyed much of the forest in Algeria, Morocco, and Tunisia. Soil erosion has also become a serious problem in northwestern Africa. Centuries of fire and overgrazing have damaged much of the grassland and desert shrub that cover most of the continent. Only scattered patches of virgin forest remain in central Africa. Throughout the continent, Africans have difficulty finding a sufficient amount of safe drinking water.

Some steps have been taken to solve Africa's resource problems. In Egypt, dams and irrigation canals have been built to control and use the precious water of the Nile River. Egypt's irrigation system provides water for more than 4 million acres of farmland. Irrigation projects have also been started in northwestern Africa.

Preservation of wildlife has become a major conservation problem in Africa. Governments have established game preserves that cover more than 3 of every 100 acres south of the Sahara desert. Strict game laws protect lions, elephants, and other wild beasts that live in these preserves. The largest preserve, Kruger National Park in South Africa, covers an area of about 8,000 square miles. This is about the size of Massachusetts. Between 35,000 and 40,000 persons visit Kruger National Park annually.

Careers in Conservation

Conservation offers many kinds of careers for persons interested in the problem of preserving natural resources. Thousands of experts are needed to devote their lives to conservation problems. An interest in the outdoors leads some persons to careers in forestry, soil conservation, wildlife management, and similar occupations. People who prefer laboratory work may enjoy such jobs as water purification and biological studies. Other careers await in conservation education, and in city and regional planning. Membership in such organizations as the Boy Scouts, Girl Scouts, Four-H Clubs, and the Future Farmers of America can help young people choose the conservation careers that will give them the greatest satisfaction.

Forestry offers a fine opportunity for a conservation career. In the United States, membership in this rapidly growing profession increased from only 10 persons in 1898 to about 20,000 in the mid-1960's. Foresters protect woodlands from fire, insects, and disease. They also direct the care and use of forest land so that it will continue to produce good crops of trees. In addition, foresters safeguard the wildlife, water, and soil of the forest lands. They supervise grazing in forest areas. Foresters work for the United States Forest Service, state forest services, and private industry.

An applicant for a forest-ranger job should have a college degree in forestry. More than 25 universities and colleges offer forestry degrees. A few schools also offer graduate forestry degrees for persons interested in research at forest experimental stations. Students of forestry study such subjects as chemistry, biology, botany, lumbering, and *dendrology* (the history and identification of trees).

Soil Science attracts young persons who enjoy active, outdoor lives. Soil conservationists supply farm-

American Forest Products Industries, Inc.

Forestry and Conservation. The manager of a tree nursery gives visiting students a close look at a tiny pine tree seedling as he explains the importance of tree replacement programs.

ers and ranchers with information on soil and water. They are employed by the Soil Conservation Service and other agencies of the U.S. Department of Agriculture, and also by state agricultural experiment stations. They are also employed by many farm cooperatives and private industries.

A soil scientist should have a college degree with a major in soils or in closely related subjects that concern land use. Students of soil science study such subjects as plant pathology, plant physiology, genetics, and biological chemistry.

Wildlife Management jobs range from laboratory studies of microscopic plants and animals to policing fields and streams. The Fish and Wildlife Service, the Forest Service, the National Park Service, and other agencies employ experts in wildlife management.

Good fishermen and woodsmen may find jobs in wildlife conservation after finishing high school. But the best jobs require a college education. More than 50 colleges and universities in the United States provide training in wildlife management. Persons with degrees in ornithology, entomology, zoology, and biology also find jobs in this field.

Civil Engineering plays an important part in many conservation programs. These include building roads for loggers or doing construction work connected with soil conservation. But civil engineers are especially concerned with the development, use, and conservation of water resources. They build dams, reservoirs, power plants, and water-supply systems. The Bureau of Reclamation and the Corps of Engineers of the United States Army are among the government agencies that employ engineers to work on such problems as flood control, irrigation, and water pollution. Civil engineers

are employed by state and local governments and by private industry. They must have a college degree.

Other Professions. Teachers play an important part in conservation by instructing students in good conservation practices. Colleges, universities, and some high schools give .courses in conservation. These are usually taught by persons who majored in geography or biology. Sometimes majors in economics or political science teach this subject. Most state departments of conservation also employ persons who are specialists in conservation education. These positions require college training in conservation.

Persons with college degrees in regional planning or geography can find work with city and regional planning agencies. These groups study such problems as water supply, the establishment and care of parks, and urban renewal. Postgraduate work in city and regional planning is also desirable.   J. RUSSELL WHITAKER

Related Articles in WORLD BOOK include:

CONSERVATION LEADERS

Darling, Ding	Pinchot, Gifford
Miner, "Jack," John T.	Roosevelt, Theodore
Muir, John	Sears, Paul B.
Osborn (Fairfield)	Van Hise, Charles R.

SOIL AND WATER CONSERVATION

Cropping System	Ground Water	Sewage
Drainage	Irrigation	Soil
Erosion	Reclamation	Soil Bank
Floods and	of Land	Water
Flood Control		

FOREST AND WILDLIFE CONSERVATION

Animal (How Man	Fishing (Fish Conservation)
Protects Animals)	Forest and Forest Products
Arbor Day	Fur (Fur Conservation)
Beaver	Game
Bird (How We Protect	Tree Farming
Birds)	Wildlife Conservation
Fish (Fish Conservation)	

CONSERVATION OF HUMAN RESOURCES

Baby	Juvenile	Public Health
Child	Delinquency	Recreation
Child Labor	Labor	Safety
Crime	Life	Sleep
Education	Medicine	Social Security
Freedom	Nutrition	Social Work
Handicapped	Peace	Standard of Living
Health	Population	World
Housing	Protection	

CONSERVATION AND GOVERNMENT

Agriculture,	National Forest
Department of	National Monument
Central Valley Project	National Park
Civilian Conservation	Reclamation, Bureau of
Corps	Soil Conservation Service
Interior, Department of	Tennessee Valley Authority
the	UNESCO
Missouri River Basin	World Health Organization
Project	

CONSERVATION ORGANIZATIONS

American Association for the	Four-H Clubs
Advancement of Science	Future Farmers of
American Forestry Association	America
Audubon Society, National	Girl Scouts
Boy Scouts	Izaak Walton League
Camp Fire Girls	of America

CONSERVATION

National Wildlife Federation

Wild Flower Preservation Society of America

OTHER RELATED ARTICLES

Aviation (Conservation)
Balance of Nature
Coal (Conservation)
Ecology
Fire Prevention
Natural Resources
Petroleum (Petroleum Conservation)
Plant Quarantine

Questions

Why does a wise farmer not plant the same crop year after year?

How have the United States and Canada cooperated in conservation projects?

How long does it take to build an inch of topsoil?

In what way is soil conservation related to water conservation?

What are two reasons why it is important to protect wildlife?

What is the balance of nature?

What can be done to preserve mineral resources?

What are some youth organizations that help promote wise conservation practices?

What part did Theodore and Franklin Roosevelt play in conservation?

What are the eight chief kinds of conservation?

Books for Young Readers

FLOHERTY, JOHN J. *Forest Ranger.* Lippincott, 1956. History of the Forestry Service.

HARRISON, C. WILLIAM. *Forest Fire Fighters and What They Do.* Watts, 1962. Work of the U.S. Forest Service, with career suggestions.

HITCH, ALLEN S., and SORENSON, MARIAN. *Conservation and You.* Van Nostrand, 1964. Lists suggestions for saving natural resources.

PLATT, RUTHERFORD, and ALBRIGHT, H. M. *Adventures in the Wilderness.* American Heritage, 1963.

SHIPPEN, KATHERINE B. *Great Heritage.* Viking, 1947.

Books for Older Readers

ADAMS, ANSEL, and NEWHALL, NANCY. *This Is the American Earth.* Sierra Club, 1960. A plea for the conservation of scenic resources, with many photographs.

BUTCHER, DEVEREUX. *Seeing America's Wildlife in Our National Refuges.* Devin-Adair, 1955.

CARSON, RACHEL. *Silent Spring.* Houghton, 1962. A biologist's warning against insecticides.

CLEPPER, HENRY E., ed. *Origins of American Conservation.* Ronald, 1966. Covers wildlife, forests, fisheries, and soil.

DOUGLAS, WILLIAM O. *A Wilderness Bill of Rights.* Little, Brown, 1965.

FARB, PETER, and the Editors of LIFE. *The Land and Wildlife of North America.* Time, Inc., 1964. Numerous photographs.

McMILLEN, WHEELER. *Bugs or People?* Appleton, 1965. A reasoned answer to opponents of pesticides.

SEARS, PAUL B. *Deserts on the March.* 3rd ed. Univ. of Oklahoma Press, 1959.

SMITH, GUY HAROLD, ed. *Conservation of Natural Resources.* 3rd ed. Wiley, 1965. Nineteen specialists focus attention on land and water resources.

UDALL, STEWART L. *The Quiet Crisis.* Holt, Rinehart & Winston, 1965. Plea for preserving our cities and countryside.

CONSERVATION OF ENERGY. See ENERGY (The Conservation of Energy).

CONSERVATION OF MASS, LAW OF. See MASS.

CONSERVATION OF MATTER, LAW OF. See MATTER (Conservation of Matter).

CONSERVATION OF MOMENTUM. See MOMENTUM.

CONSERVATION OF PARITY. See PARITY.

CONSERVATISM is a political attitude or philosophy that places great emphasis on tradition. Conservatives rely on history as a guide to wisdom and goodness, and have great respect for historical institutions and traditional values and ideas. Therefore, they seek progress in line with proven values of the past. But the word *conservatism* is confusing because its meaning varies with time, place, and circumstance.

Principles of Conservatism. Conservatives take a limited view of what politics can achieve. They believe that the aim of politics, or government, is to help promote a good life for man in society. But most conservatives doubt that the good life can be brought about mainly by political means. They believe that all political problems are basically moral problems, and they feel that legislation cannot significantly change human attitudes. Conservatives believe that man's potential for evil is as great as his potential for good, and they doubt that evil will disappear with social reform or education.

Conservatives believe that rights are something a person earns, rather than something he is given. They emphasize the performance of duties as the price of rights. Conservatives believe in the desirability of maintaining social classes. They believe that all men have equal rights, but they deny that all are born with equal abilities or to equal wealth, advantages, and influence in society. They maintain that only a few are natural leaders, and that their leadership is essential to social order. For these reasons, conservatives consider political and economic leveling foolish. They feel such leveling is bound to fail.

Conservatives see a necessary link between the enjoyment of freedom and the institution of private property. They maintain that abolishing private property would destroy individual liberty. Therefore, many conservatives consider Socialism and Communism the greatest threats to modern society.

History. The name *Conservative* was first used around 1830. It was applied to the descendants of the old British Tory party, and the words *Tory* and *Conservative* are used interchangeably in Great Britain today. But conservative ideas were expressed as early as the 1700's in the writings and speeches of the British statesman Edmund Burke. Early U.S. conservatives included John Adams and Alexander Hamilton. Conservatism arose partly as a reaction to the excesses of the French Revolution and the belief that man could become perfect through political revolution. Conservatives argued that social change must be brought about within the framework of traditional ideas and institutions.

The word *conservative* as used in the United States today is often confusing. Many persons in the U.S. who call themselves conservatives advocate a return to the principles and theories of liberalism of the 1800's. They oppose almost all government regulation of the economy, and are economic liberals in the tradition of Adam Smith. Traditionally, however, conservatives have opposed both economic liberalism and socialism. They have tried to steer a middle course between the extremes of individualism and collective ownership, and they have generally favored a strong central government. A true conservative should also be distinguished from a *reactionary*. A reactionary wants to revolutionize existing society according to a model in past history. A true conservative is never revolutionary. He wants to preserve the best in the past and continue it into the future. JOHN H. HALLOWELL

See also LIBERALISM; RIGHT WING.

CONSERVATIVE PARTY is one of the two main political parties in Great Britain. The second is the Labour Party. Historically, the Conservative Party took the place of the Tory party that appeared in England during the late 1600's and flourished until the middle 1800's. Benjamin Disraeli, a founder of the Conservative Party, worked for a new program for the Conservatives. He wanted the working class given the right to vote. He also sought to pass social legislation in favor of the workers and worked for stronger bonds between Great Britain and its empire.

Disraeli succeeded in "educating" his party. Conservatives passed the Reform Bill of 1867, which increased the number of working class voters. After World War I, Conservatives helped reorganize the British Empire to achieve equality between Great Britain and the dominions. Winston Churchill, a Conservative, led the National Coalition Government during World War II. In 1951, the Conservative Party returned to power as an independent political group. It won a decisive victory in 1959. JAMES L. GODFREY

See also DISRAELI, BENJAMIN; LIBERAL PARTY; PEEL, SIR ROBERT; TORY.

CONSERVATOR, in law. See RECEIVER.

CONSERVATORY is a school that teaches all branches of music. The old Italian religious conservatories taught orphans music and speaking. A conservatory was founded in Naples before 1490.

Perhaps the most famous conservatory is the French *Conservatoire de Musique*, established in 1795. All the larger cities in America have conservatories of music.

The term is also applied to indoor botanical gardens (see BOTANICAL GARDEN). CHARLES B. RIGHTER

CONSIGNEE AND CONSIGNOR. See BILL OF LADING.

CONSISTORY. See POPE (The Sacred College).

CONSOLATION OF PHILOSOPHY. See BOETHIUS, MANLIUS SEVERINUS.

CONSOLIDATED SCHOOL is the result of joining two or more school districts and combining their school populations. This term is generally used in rural or suburban areas. The need for more adequate school facilities in areas where the population is scattered led to the consolidation of independent school districts in many parts of the United States. Often, as many as six districts with inadequate schools have been combined to make two or three larger districts. Such consolidation insures a more varied curriculum, and better libraries and teaching staffs. R. FREEMAN BUTTS

CONSONANT, *KAHN soh nunt*, is a letter or sound which in speech requires hindering of the breath by the tongue, teeth, or lips. There are two kinds of sounds. The open sounds with free breath are called *vowels*. The closed sounds, called *consonants*, are made with the breath wholly or partly checked. *Stopped consonants* require complete stoppage of the breath. They are *b, d, g, k, p, t. Open consonants* require only partial stoppage of breath. They are *l, m, n, r, w, y.* The *spirants* are open consonants that require friction in the oral passages. They are *f, j, s, v, z. H* is an *aspirant*, or *breathed*, consonant. CLARENCE STRATTON

See also PRONUNCIATION; VOWEL.

CONSORT. See PRINCE CONSORT; QUEEN.

CONSPIRACY, *kahn SPIHR uh sih*, is an agreement between two or more persons to do something that is against the law. It is not always necessary that the planned act be committed or that any person be defrauded or injured. The act of *conspiring* sometimes constitutes the crime. Each person involved is criminally responsible for everything that results, whether it was intended or not. Conspiracy is punishable by fines as high as $10,000, or imprisonment for as long as 14 years. If loss of human life results from a conspiracy, the crime of murder may be charged. FRED E. INBAU

CONSTABLE is a police officer in a rural community of the United States. He may arrest persons suspected of crime. But his main job is to carry out court orders. The word *constable* comes from the title of an official of the Eastern Roman Empire called the *comes stabuli*, or count of the stable. In France, the constable was once a member of the king's household, or a commander of the king's armies. In England, all policemen are called constables. H. F. ALDERFER

CONSTABLE, JOHN (1776-1837), is generally considered one of the greatest English landscape painters. He originated the kind of landscape painting that still looks most natural. Painters before him had painted landscapes in brown tones. When Constable used green for grass and leaves, his color seemed bright and vivid. He achieved this naturalness because he painted preparatory studies outdoors. Landscape painters who influenced him, such as the French artist Claude (Lorrain) and the Dutch masters, painted in studios.

Constable painted quiet views of the countryside near London and Suffolk. He painted summer, spring, and autumn scenes, but never winter scenes. Although his paintings lack imagination in subject and style, their naturalness in showing everyday scenes seemed romantic to peo-

John Constable

ple of his day. He painted in both oil and water color.

Constable became famous in France when his painting *The Hay-Wain* won a prize at the Paris Salon exhibition of 1824. This painting appears in color in the PAINTING article. French romantic painters, such as Eugène Delacroix, began to imitate some of Constable's methods. Constable's best-known paintings include *The Cornfield, Hampstead Heath, View of Suffolk, Weymouth Bay,* and *Salisbury Cathedral from the Meadows.*

Constable was born in Suffolk, England, the son of a miller. As a boy, he drew the countryside around his father's mill, where he worked. He later said these placid scenes made him an artist.   LESTER D. LONGMAN

CONSTANCE, COUNCIL OF. See POPE (The Troubles of the Papacy); SIGISMUND.

CONSTANCE, LAKE. See LAKE CONSTANCE.

CONSTANCE, PEACE OF. See FREDERICK (I) Holy Roman Emperor.

CONSTANCE MISSAL, a book of Masses for the German diocese of Constance, is one of the earliest books printed in Europe. Scholars believe that Johannes Gutenberg printed it about 1450, several years before he produced his famous 42-line Bible. The letters of the Missal are cruder than those of the Bible. The Pierpont Morgan Library in New York City owns the only copy of the book in the United States. Two other copies are in Munich, Germany, and Zurich, Switzerland.

CONSTANŢA, *kawn STAHN tsah* (pop. 152,324; met. area 202,024; alt. 45 ft.), is the only Romanian seaport on the Black Sea. See ROMANIA (color map). The city has a modern harbor. A pipeline brings petroleum from the oil fields to Constanţa, which has large oil-storage tanks. Railroads connect Constanţa with the chief cities of the Danube Basin. Two fashionable Black Sea pleasure resorts, Mamaia and Eforie, are located near Constanţa.   ALVIN Z. RUBINSTEIN

CONSTANTINE was the name of one pope and of one antipope of the Roman Catholic Church.

Constantine I (?-715) became pope in 708. He was able to break the antipapal power of Felix, archbishop of Ravenna, and to maintain smooth relations with the Byzantine emperors. Constantine was born in Syria.

Constantine II (?-769), an antipope, was the brother of Toto, the duke of Nepi. At the death of Pope Paul I in 767, Toto, by force, had his brother elected pope, though Constantine was only a layman. Constantine was inept, and Toto dominated him. After 13 months, a legitimate election was held, and Stephen III was elected pope. Constantine was blinded and expelled from Rome.   GUSTAVE WEIGEL and FULTON J. SHEEN

CONSTANTINE was the name of two Greek kings.

Constantine I (1868-1923) succeeded his father, George I, in 1913. During World War I, Constantine believed the Germans would win and he wanted Greece to remain neutral. Because of this, the Allies drove him into exile in 1917. He was recalled in 1920, when the Greek Army invaded Turkey. But the Greeks were defeated, and the king went into exile again in 1922 (see GREECE [History]). Constantine was born in Athens.

Constantine II (1940-   ) became king in 1964 after the death of his father, King Paul I. During World War II, Constantine lived in exile with his father and his uncle, King George II. In December, 1967, Constantine unsuccessfully tried to overthrow the military junta that had been ruling Greece since the preceding April. The king and his family went into exile in Italy. The junta named a *viceroy* to act in place of the king. Constantine was born in Psikhikón.   R. V. BURKS

CONSTANTINE, Algeria (pop. 184,200; met. area 223,259; alt. 2,170 ft.), is a trading and mining center, and the capital of an Algerian political department. The original city was destroyed in A.D. 311, but Constantine the Great, whose name it bears, rebuilt it. Constantine lies about 225 miles east of Algiers, the capital. It is connected by railroad with the port of Skikda. See also ALGERIA (map).   KEITH G. MATHER

CONSTANTINE I, THE GREAT, *KAHN stan tine,* was the first emperor of Rome to become a Christian. He was born about A.D. 275 and died in 337. During his reign, Christians gained freedom of worship, and the Christian church was recognized as a legal body. The Eastern Orthodox Churches regard Constantine as a saint. He rebuilt Byzantium (now Istanbul, Turkey), renamed it Constantinople, and made it his capital. The empire's strength began to shift from Rome to the eastern provinces. Some historians consider this the beginning of Byzantine history.

Constantine made many gifts to the Christian church, including huge estates which he gave to the church in Rome. He built the first great Christian cathedral, the Lateran Basilica in Rome. Constantine built other famous churches in and near Rome, and in Antioch (now Antakya, Turkey), Constantinople, and Jerusalem.

Constantine's official name was FLAVIUS VALERIUS AURELIUS CONSTANTINUS. He was born in Naissa (now Niš, Yugoslavia). His father, Constantius, became emperor of the western provinces in 305. Constantius died and Constantine succeeded him in 306. The system of shared rule between two senior and two junior emperors, started by Emperor Diocletian, broke down completely. Seven claimants struggled for power. In 312, Constantine attacked Maxentius, his major rival in the west. Constantine later told how a vision before the battle had

promised him victory if he fought under the sign of the cross. He ordered the Greek letters *chi* and *rho,* the first two letters of Christ's name, to be marked on his soldiers' shields. With these letters on their shields, Constantine's forces defeated Maxentius at the Milvian Bridge, which crosses the Tiber River. As a result of his vision, Constantine became a strong supporter of Christianity. The Arch of Constantine, built in Rome about 315, honors Constantine's victory over Maxentius.

In 313, Constantine arranged a partnership with Emperor Licinius, ruler of the eastern provinces. They met in Milan and issued a

Visual Education Service

Constantine the Great is shown with his mother, Helena, in this painting by Cima.

statement of policy called the *Edict of Milan* which gave freedom of worship and equal rights to all religious groups. Constantine recognized the Christian church as a legal body with rights to hold property, and returned property to Christians that had been seized. For more than 10 years, Constantine and Licinius ruled the empire between them, each trying to gain supremacy. In 324, they clashed and Constantine became sole ruler. Constantine made Constantinople his capital and the center of Roman government.

In 325, Constantine presided over the first great *ecumenical* (general) council of the Christian church. The council met in Nicaea, in what is now northwest Turkey, to deal with disputes among Christians, especially with the Arian heresy which placed Christ on a lower level than God. More than 300 bishops from all parts of the empire attended. The council condemned Arianism and drew up a statement of essential beliefs, called the *Nicene Creed* (see NICENE COUNCILS). Constantine died in 337, after being baptized a Christian on his deathbed. The empire was passed to his sons, Constantius, Constans, and Constantine II.   RAMSAY MacMULLEN

See also BYZANTINE EMPIRE (Establishment).

CONSTANTINE PALAEOLOGUS. See BYZANTINE EMPIRE (Final Decline).

CONSTANTINOPLE. See ISTANBUL.

CONSTELLATION, *KAHN stuh LAY shun*, is a group of stars within a definite region of the sky. By knowing the positions of the constellations, it is possible to locate stars, planets, comets, and meteors. For thousands of years, man has used his knowledge of the constellations to guide himself from place to place during journeys over the surface of the earth. See STAR.

Each constellation has a definite time of the year when it *culminates* (reaches its highest point in the sky). At latitudes too far north or south of the equator, many constellations do not culminate high enough to be seen. The constellations appear to move westward as the earth rotates around the sun. For this reason, certain constellations can be seen only during one of the seasons of the year (see ASTRONOMY [Skies of the Seasons]).

In 1928, the International Astronomical Union fixed the boundaries of the 88 constellations in the sky. The Greeks recognized and named 48 constellations. Many of these same constellations were also recognized by the Arabs, the Egyptians, and the Babylonians. Since the 1700's, astronomers have named the 23 constellations in the extreme Southern Hemisphere.

The names of the constellations are given in Latin, because Latin was once the language of learning. The names of the constellations used by the Greeks, Egyptians, and other peoples were translated into Latin. For convenience, the ancients named the constellations after a certain figure that its stars seemed to form in the sky. For example, the stars in Ursa Major, the Great Bear, seemed to form a bear. Today, the stars have changed positions somewhat and so they do not form clear outlines of the figures (see FIXED STAR).   I. M. LEVITT

Related Articles in WORLD BOOK include:

Andromeda	Boötes	Cepheus
Aquarius	Cancer	Cygnus
Aries	Canis Major	Draco
Auriga	Capricornus	Gemini
Big and Little	Cassiopeia	Hercules
Dippers	Centaurus	Leo

Libra	Perseus	Scorpius
Lyra	Pisces	Southern Cross
Orion	Pleiades	Taurus
Pegasus	Sagittarius	Virgo

CONSTELLATION, a 36-gun frigate built in 1797, was the first United States Navy ship to capture a foreign warship. It captured the French frigate *L'Insurgente* on Feb. 9, 1799 during the undeclared war between France and the United States (1798-1800). Thomas Truxtun, who had supervised the construction of the *Constellation*, commanded the ship. His naval victories made him a national hero. In the early 1960's, the *Constellation* was restored in Baltimore, Md., where it was originally launched. It was designated a national historic landmark in 1964.   MERRILL JENSEN

See also NAVY, U.S. (Undeclared War with France).

CONSTIPATION, *kahn stuh PAY shun*, is a condition in which the bowel does not rid itself of waste materials in a normal manner. Constipated persons do not have regular bowel movements, and may have pain or tenderness over the colon. They also may suffer from headaches and backaches. Constipation may be caused by weakness of the bowel muscles, by a diet that does not supply enough bulky foods, or by the too frequent use of laxatives. Constipation may also accompany an illness that affects the tissues or nerves of the bowel.

When constipation results from a faulty diet, the patient should eat more green vegetables and fruits, and other foods that contain roughage. He also should drink ample quantities of water and attempt to establish a regular time each day to have a bowel movement. Constipation may be a symptom of a serious disease. If it persists, or is accompanied by rectal bleeding, it should be investigated by a physician.   E. CLINTON TEXTER, JR.

See also LAXATIVE.

CONSTITUTION is a statement outlining the agreed basic principles of formal organizations ranging from national governments to private clubs. A typical constitution establishes the structure and purposes of the organization and the rights of its citizens or members. It also defines the powers of officers, how they are selected, and how long they can stay in office. Constitutions may also be called *Articles of Union* or *Charters* (see CHARTER).

In Western political philosophy, the principles of constitutional government often have been based on a belief in a *higher law*—a body of universal principles of right and justice that is superior to detailed, everyday law. In modern democracies, a constitution's function is to put all men—including the rulers—under law.

Government constitutions may be *written* or *unwritten*. The United States has a written constitution. The British constitution is unwritten. It consists of tradition and custom concerning the powers of the monarch, Parliament, and the courts. Many parts of the British constitution were taken from written documents such as the Magna Carta. However, the constitution itself has never been written out in a single document. The British constitution can be modified by Parliament.

Most modern governments have constitutions based on a single document. In most democracies, the written constitution can be changed only by a special process, such as a special election. Such special amending procedures reflect the belief that a constitution should deal with basic principles, and that special deliberation should be required before these principles can be modified or replaced.

Most countries in the world now have nondemocratic or military governments. In these governments, a constitution can be changed by *fiat* (a command or decree) of the ruling group. In countries with such governments, a constitution is more a statement of purpose than a statement defining powers.

In actual operation, constitutions in most democratic countries are unwritten in the sense that the formal document is not the only vital element. Custom and how various governmental bodies interpret the constitution are equally important and sometimes dominant. Under power called *judicial review*, U.S. courts may declare acts of government *unconstitutional* if the acts are considered to conflict with the basic law of the constitution. Most countries have important *nonlegal* rules which do not come from the written constitution or court interpretation. If these nonlegal rules are an essential part of the system of government, they are part of the "constitution" in the broad sense of the term. For example, most aspects of the political party system and the rules for nominating the President in the United States are not specified in the written constitution or subject to court action.   ROBERT G. DIXON, JR.

See also BRITISH NORTH AMERICA ACT; GREAT BRITAIN (Government); UNITED STATES CONSTITUTION; GOVERNMENT; BILL OF RIGHTS.

CONSTITUTION is a famous frigate of the United States Navy. Its popular name is *Old Ironsides*. The frigate was built at a Boston shipyard between 1794 and 1797. It was 204 feet long and had a displacement of 2,200 tons. The hull was made of oak from Massachusetts, Maine, and Georgia, and the masts of white pine. It could carry provisions for a crew of 475.

The *Constitution* was launched on the third attempt on Oct. 21, 1797. It was unharmed in battles with the Barbary powers in 1803 and 1804. In the War of 1812,

The **Constitution,** better known as *Old Ironsides,* one of the most famous vessels in the United States Navy, is viewed by thousands of people each year in the Boston Naval Shipyard.

U.S. Navy

798

the vessel fought and won a battle near Cape Race against the *Guerrière*, an English warship. It was during this battle that the ship earned its nickname. A sailor is said to have seen shot from the British guns bouncing off the *Constitution's* sturdy sides, and exclaimed that the ship had sides of iron. Isaac Hull, an American naval officer, commanded the frigate. After other severe and victorious battles, the *Constitution* was condemned in 1830 as unseaworthy and was ordered destroyed.

The poem "Old Ironsides," by Oliver Wendell Holmes, in which he wrote:

> Oh, better that her shattered hulk
> Should sink beneath the wave,

aroused public sentiment, and the vessel was rebuilt and restored to service in 1833. In 1855, it was put out of commission at Portsmouth Navy Yard and used as a training ship, but was again rebuilt in 1877. In 1897, a hundred years after its launching, the ship was finally drydocked and repaired, to be preserved as a memorial.

Thirty years later, American children raised money to recondition the vessel for a tour of United States ports. In 1930 Congress appropriated $300,000 to complete the work. On July 31, 1931, *Old Ironsides* was commissioned into active service. After sailing 22,000 miles, it returned to the Boston Naval Shipyard on May 7, 1934.   JOHN D. HICKS

See also WAR OF 1812 (picture).

CONSTITUTION DAY commemorates the signing of a constitution. In the United States, it falls on September 17. On that day, in 1787, delegates from 12 states signed the document that established a new form of government for the nation. Constitution Day is not a national holiday. But many American communities observe it with ceremonies, programs, and meetings.

The signing of the Constitution of the United States climaxed a four-month session of debates in Independence Hall in Philadelphia. George Washington presided over the session that began on May 25. The convention proposed to ensure the rights that the Declaration of Independence had declared inalienable. The Constitution became one of the most important documents in history. It has served as a model for nearly every country that has adopted a constitutional form of government. These countries celebrate the adoption with their own Constitution Day.   RAYMOND HOYT JAHN

CONSTITUTION OF THE UNITED STATES. See UNITED STATES CONSTITUTION.

CONSTITUTION STATE. See CONNECTICUT.

CONSTITUTIONAL CONVENTION. See UNITED STATES CONSTITUTION (The Constitutional Convention).

CONSTITUTIONAL UNION PARTY was an American political party formed late in 1859 by former members of the Whig party. At a convention held in Baltimore in May, 1860, the party nominated John Bell and Edward Everett for President and Vice-President. A platform of national unity was adopted. The candidates lost, and the party died out. See also WHIG.   DAVID DONALD

CONSTITUTIONALISM. See POLITICAL SCIENCE (Constitutionalism).

CONSTRUCTION, BUILDING. See BUILDING CONSTRUCTION.

CONSTRUCTION BATTALION. See SEABEES.

CONSTRUCTION ENGINEER. See ENGINEERING (Engineers at Work).

CONSUL, *KAHN sul,* is an official appointed by the government of one country to look after its commercial interests in a city of another country. A consul differs from a diplomatic representative in that he attends primarily to business matters, while the diplomat is interested primarily in political relations (see AMBASSADOR). United States consuls issue birth, death, and marriage certificates to Americans temporarily within their jurisdiction, regulate shipping, and insure justice to American citizens who are traveling abroad.

The Consular Service of any leading country is divided into three ranks: consuls-general, consuls, and commercial agents. The consuls-general have charge of all consuls in a district. The commercial agents, although they have the same duties and powers as consuls, are not officially recognized by the government. The powers and duties of consuls are often determined by treaty.

Roman Consul. The title *consul* was given to the two highest magistrates of the Roman republic. The insignia were the purple-bordered toga, a staff of ivory, and an ornamental chair. The title, without the function, was retained under the empire. See LICTOR.

During the French Republic, from 1799 to 1804, the three chief magistrates were consuls. Napoleon Bonaparte, the first consul, held all the real power in the government. PAYSON S. WILD, JR.

CONSULATE. See CONSUL; NAPOLEON I (First Consul of France).

CONSULTING ENGINEER. See ENGINEERING (Engineers at Work).

CONSUMER AND MARKETING SERVICE is a Department of Agriculture agency that provides service to consumers and regulates the marketing of food and fiber. The service inspects meat and poultry for wholesomeness. It offers grading services for all major farm products for quality. The service provides daily information on market conditions and prices. It administers marketing laws and regulates meat, poultry, fruit and vegetable marketing practices. It conducts the National School Lunch Program, Special Milk Program, and the Food Stamp Program. It buys surplus foods and distributes them to institutions, schools, and needy families. It also advises consumers monthly on which foods are in plentiful supply. The agency was established in 1953 as the Agricultural Marketing Service. It took its present name in 1965.

Critically reviewed by CONSUMER AND MARKETING SERVICE

CONSUMER COOPERATIVE. See COOPERATIVE.

CONSUMER CREDIT. See CREDIT; INSTALLMENT PLAN.

CONSUMER EDUCATION is the knowledge that people must have in order to get the highest possible standard of living from the money they spend. It tells the buyer what to look for in anything he buys, who and what he can trust, and whether or not the guarantee offered on a product is a good one. Some guarantees cover parts and the operation of a product for an extended time. Others are almost worthless.

Some buyers believe that a high price means high quality. But there need be no connection at all between price and quality.

Other consumers depend on the retailer for information concerning a product. The retailer has to know something about the products he puts up for sale. But he believes almost as much of the advertising he reads as the customer. Also, the retailer may stock a product simply because a rival has it.

Advertising should be reliable. Consumers are helped by factual advertising. Factual advertising tells them that a product will do certain things. Some advertising, however, simply draws attention to a product and makes no claims.

The educated consumer knows that brand names, trademarks, and labels are also a kind of advertising. Labels often contain useful information, especially those on food products. The buyer should read these labels carefully and be sure he understands what they say before making a purchase. The brand name is important when it represents a manufacturer with a good, established reputation.

Grading of goods by government or private agencies is another guide for consumers. Goods are rated according to certain standards for consumers. For example, the United States government grades meat, vegetables, and canned fruit.

Another aid to the purchaser is the *stamp* or *seal of approval*. For example, the Underwriters Laboratories approves housing materials and household fixtures and appliances that meet rigid standards.

Many private organizations test products and sell their findings or offer them free of charge to consumers. At present, the private testing agencies are the only ones that provide information about the quality of commodities. The National Bureau of Standards sets up standards for governmental purchasing and tests goods which the federal government buys. The consumer benefits only indirectly by this organization.

Professional and civic organizations, and consumer research groups publish books, pamphlets, magazines, and newspaper articles that are helpful to consumers. Television, motion pictures, and radio are widely used in schools and for adult groups. Many schools offer courses on consumer education.

The federal government and many state governments have agencies working actively in consumer protection and education. Federal government agencies include the Food and Drug Administration, the Federal Trade Commission, and several branches of the Agricultural Research Service. The Food and Drug Administration has power to act against manufacturers who ship useless or harmful foods, drugs, or cosmetics across state lines. The Federal Trade Commission has the power to stop false or misleading advertising. STEWART B. HAMBLEN

Related Articles in WORLD BOOK include:

Advertising	Fur (Names of Fur)
Better Business Bureau	Price
Budget	Pure Food and Drug Laws
Consumption	Shoe (Shoes and Health)
Cosmetics	Stockings
Federal Trade	Textile (Testing Fabrics;
Commission	Regulations)
Food and Drug	Trademark
Administration	

CONSUMERS LEAGUE, NATIONAL. See NATIONAL CONSUMERS LEAGUE.

CONSUMPTION, a disease. See TUBERCULOSIS.

CONSUMPTION, *kun SUMP shun,* in economics, is the use of goods and services to satisfy needs and desires. Most business activity is aimed at providing goods and services for consumption. Examples of consumption include eating food, wearing clothing, and using soap. People who use goods and services are called *consumers*.

The amount of goods and services that a family consumes depends almost entirely on its income. After taxes are deducted, Americans spend over 90 per cent of their yearly incomes on consumer goods and services. The following table shows the relation between income and consumption at various income levels for American families living in cities.

Income	Per Cent of Families	Average Income	Average Consumption
Less than $3,000	13	$ 2,191	$ 2,540
$3,000-$5,999	39	4,725	4,675
$6,000-$9,999	36	7,675	6,910
More than $9,999	12	14,335	10,960

Families with low incomes tend to spend a larger part of their earnings for essentials such as food and housing than do families with higher incomes. Those with the lowest incomes spend more than they earn and are forced into debt. As incomes rise, families tend to spend a larger part of their earnings for such items as clothing, education, and entertainment. John Maynard Keynes, a noted British economist, was one of the first to emphasize the close relationship between income and consumption (see KEYNES, JOHN MAYNARD).

About two-thirds of all the goods and services produced in the United States each year are used by consumers. The remaining third is used by the government or invested in buildings, manufacturing machinery, and other forms of capital. In Great Britain, consumers also use about two-thirds of the goods and services produced. In the Soviet Union, only slightly over half of the country's goods and services are consumed.　ROBERT DORFMAN

See also INCOME; DISTRIBUTION; PRODUCTION; STANDARD OF LIVING; CONSUMER EDUCATION.

CONTACT FLYING. See NAVIGATION (Piloting).

CONTACT LENS. See LENS, CONTACT.

CONTAGIOUS DISEASE. See DISEASE (introduction; How Diseases Spread).

CONTAMINATION. See POLLUTION.

CONTÉ, NICOLAS. See PENCIL.

CONTEMPT, in law, is willful disregard or disobedience of public authority, such as a court or legislative assembly. Contempt is usually shown by failure to obey specific demands, or by insults. There are two kinds of contempt of court: those committed in the presence of the court, which disturb or interrupt its proceedings, and those that result from a refusal to comply with an order of the court. Both are punishable by fine or imprisonment. See also ATTACHMENT.　FRED E. INBAU

CONTINENT is a part of the earth's surface that forms one of the great dry-land masses of the world. It usually has extensive plains or plateaus and one or more mountain ranges, and is surrounded or nearly surrounded by water. The continents of the world are Asia (17,119,000 square miles), Africa (11,704,000 square miles), North America (9,416,000 square miles), South America (6,889,000 square miles), Antarctica (5,100,000 square miles), Europe (4,063,000 square miles), and Australia (2,967,909 square miles). Technically, Europe is not a continent, but a large peninsula of Asia. It is part of what may be called the Eurasian continent, with a

total area of 21,182,000 square miles. The continents cover about three-tenths of the world's total surface. See also the separate articles in WORLD BOOK for each continent.　J. ROWLAND ILLICK

CONTINENTAL, a type of paper money. See MONEY (New Nation, New Currency).

CONTINENTAL ARMY. See ARMY, UNITED STATES (History).

CONTINENTAL ASSOCIATION was an agreement adopted by the First Continental Congress on Oct. 20, 1774. It provided that each colony would (1) stop all importing from Great Britain by Dec. 1, 1774; (2) discontinue the slave trade effective Dec. 1, 1774; (3) stop consumption of all British and some foreign products by Mar. 1, 1775; and (4) stop all exports to Britain and the West Indies by Sept. 10, 1775. The association was operating in 12 colonies by April, 1775.

CONTINENTAL CODE. See MORSE CODE.

CONTINENTAL CONGRESS was a convention of delegates from the American colonies that first met in Philadelphia on Sept. 5, 1774. The meeting grew out of a desire for unity which had spread through the colonies. All the colonies saw danger to themselves in the acts of Parliament aimed against Massachusetts, especially the Boston Port Bill. See BOSTON PORT BILL.

The First Continental Congress was attended by 56 delegates representing 12 colonies. Georgia sent no delegates but agreed to support any plans made at the meeting. Leaders of the Congress included Samuel Adams, George Washington, Peyton Randolph, Patrick Henry, Richard Henry Lee, John Adams, John Jay, Joseph Galloway, and John Dickinson. Peyton Randolph of Virginia was chosen president of the Congress, and equal voting power was given to each of the 12 colonies.

The first Congress was more interested in fair treatment from Great Britain than in independence. It set forth the position of the colonies toward taxation and trade in a Declaration of Rights, adopted on Oct. 14, 1774. The Congress recognized that it was not practical for the colonies to seek representation in Parliament. But it claimed the right of each colonial assembly to draw up its laws on all subjects except trade with other countries.

Probably the boldest act of the Congress was to set up the Continental Association, which bound the colonists not to trade with Great Britain or use British goods until British trade and taxation policies had been changed. The delegates made plans to hold another Congress the following May, if necessary.

Second Continental Congress. British colonial policy did not change, and the colonies drew close to war with the fighting between Massachusetts farmers and English troops at Lexington and Concord. The Second Continental Congress met in Philadelphia on May 10, 1775. New delegates of note were Benjamin Franklin, Thomas Jefferson, and John Hancock. The Congress took on the duties of a government, uniting the colonies for the war effort. An army was organized and George Washington was appointed Commander in Chief. On July 8, 1775, the Congress issued a Declaration setting forth the need to take up arms and the reasons for doing so. Two days later, it made a final, futile appeal to the king in an effort to right matters without war.

With the outbreak of war, the Second Continental

Delegates of the First Continental Congress, Held at Carpenters' Hall, Philadelphia, Prayed for Guidance.

Congress encouraged the colonies to set themselves up as states. On July 4, 1776, it adopted the Declaration of Independence. Then it set about drawing up an outline for a permanent union of states which resulted in the Articles of Confederation. The Second Congress operated under great difficulties, because it was a group without legal authority except when it acted with the consent of the states. But it continued to work until March 1, 1781, when a Congress authorized by the Articles of Confederation took over. This new Congress was known as the *Congress of the Confederation*.

In addition to Peyton Randolph, who served as president twice, the presidents of the Continental Congress were: Henry Middleton, John Hancock, Henry Laurens, John Jay, Samuel Huntington, Thomas McKean, John Hanson, Elias Boudinot, Thomas Mifflin, Richard Henry Lee, Nathaniel Gorham, Arthur St. Clair, and Cyrus Griffin. JOHN R. ALDEN

See also ARTICLES OF CONFEDERATION; CONGRESS OF THE CONFEDERATION; CONTINENTAL ASSOCIATION; DECLARATION OF INDEPENDENCE.

CONTINENTAL DEPOSIT. See OCEAN (The Land Beneath the Sea).

CONTINENTAL DIVIDE is the term used to designate the line separating areas drained to opposite sides of a continent. In North America it is also called the *Great Divide*, and separates westward-flowing and eastward-flowing waters (see GREAT DIVIDE). In South America, the continental divide follows the western portion of the Andes mountains. In Europe, the divide separates streams flowing to the Atlantic and Arctic oceans on the north and to the Mediterranean and Black seas on the south. In Asia, the term is applied to the separation between drainage into the Arctic and Pacific oceans on the north and east and drainage into the Indian Ocean on the south. The African divide separates the drainage into the Atlantic Ocean from the drainage into the Indian Ocean. E. WILLARD MILLER

See also DIVIDE (diagram; picture).

CONTINENTAL DRIFT is the theory that the continents are slowly changing their positions on the surface of the earth. According to the theory, North and South America are drifting away from Europe and Africa at a rate of about one inch per year. Australia is drifting away from Antarctica at a similar rate.

The theory is based on the observation that certain coastlines of the continents would fit together like pieces of a jigsaw puzzle if the continents could be brought together. The Atlantic coastlines of North and South America seem to match those of Europe and Africa. The coastlines of Africa and Asia on the Red Sea also seem to match each other.

The first good explanation of the matching coastlines was suggested in 1912 by the Austrian scientist Alfred Wegener. Wegener suggested that all the continents once fitted together and formed one large continent. The continent split into several pieces about 200 million years ago, and the pieces have been drifting apart ever since. Wegener could not explain why the drift occurs.

Many scientists now hold the theory that drift is caused by slow convection currents which flow in the solid earth just like those in a pan of hot water. The heat of the earth's center sets currents of rock in motion that break the cooler crust of the earth open in some places, or push it up to form ridges. The current then moves away from these high spots, carrying the continents with it. After the rock cools, it sinks back toward the center of the earth. Some scientists think the deep trenches in the Pacific Ocean floor indicate places where the rock sinks.

Evidence for the Theory. Matching of opposite coastlines provides the most important evidence supporting the theory of continental drift. But scientists have also found other supporting facts. For example, they have found that there were once large amounts of ice at places now near the equator. Coal has been found near the North and South poles, indicating that these areas

CONTINENTAL DRIFT

Before the Continents Drifted, they may have been fitted together in a single, huge continental land mass that might have looked like this about 200 million years ago.

After the Continents Drifted, they took their present shape and position. Some scientists believe that the continents drifted apart on opposite sides of the mid-ocean ridges, *dotted lines.*

were once warm enough for plants to grow. Magnetic studies of rocks indicate that some rocks formed at different latitudes from where they are found today. Other magnetic studies suggest that the Atlantic and Indian oceans have widened, while the Pacific has shrunk.

Studies indicate that the Atlantic Ocean floor is much younger than the land. Radioactive dating methods show that the oldest rocks from the ocean floor are only about 150 million years old, compared to about $3\frac{1}{2}$ billion years for rocks on the continents. The layer of mud on the ocean floor is thin, indicating that the mud has been forming for only a short time. These studies indicate that the Atlantic is widening by parting along the mid-ocean ridge. Also, studies of Iceland, the only is-

Rock Currents May Cause Continental Drift. Heat deep within the earth may cause rock to rise beneath the mid-ocean ridges, move the continents as it flows, then sink as it cools.

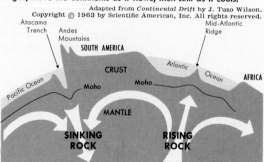

land that lies across the Mid-Atlantic Ridge, indicate that the island is slowly widening and that lava is filling cracks beneath the surface.

Evidence Against the Theory. The strongest argument against the theory of continental drift is based on gravity measurements from spacecraft and on studies of earthquake waves. The measurements indicate that most of the earth's inner rock is too rigid to flow and move the continents. In addition, some scientists doubt that the shapes of opposite coastlines really match very closely. They point out that ice at the equator may have come from glaciers on former mountains there, and that the earth's climate may once have been warm enough for coal-forming plants to grow near the poles. The lack of old rocks on the ocean floor may indicate only that the oldest rocks have become so deeply buried that they have not yet been found.

Recent evidence has favored drift. But more evidence is needed to establish with certainty whether or not the continents are drifting. For example, information is needed about how accurately opposite coastlines match each other. More measurements are needed of the age and magnetic properties of rocks from the ocean floor and from below the ocean floor. More accurate data must be obtained on theories of the rock currents believed to be causing drift. Even if drift has happened, more work is needed to discover the detailed patterns of past continent movements.   J. TUZO WILSON

CONTINENTAL SHELF. See OCEAN (The Land Beneath the Sea; map).

CONTINENTAL SYSTEM sought to choke off Great Britain's trade with the rest of Europe in the early 1800's. Napoleon I adopted the system as a means of economic warfare against Britain. Napoleon began the system with his Berlin Decree of Nov. 21, 1806. The decree declared Britain to be in a state of blockade. His Milan Decree of 1807 extended the blockade to neutral ships that stopped in Britain. Napoleon fought the Peninsular War in a vain effort to enforce the system. But these attempts proved to be a major factor in his losing Russia as an ally. See also NAPOLEON I (Dominates Europe).   ROBERT B. HOLTMAN

CONTINO, ANTONIO. See BRIDGE OF SIGHS.

CONTOUR FARMING. See AGRICULTURE (Soils and Water); CONSERVATION (color pictures).

CONTOUR MAP. See MAP (pictures: How Contour Maps Are Made).

CONTRABAND, *KAHN truh band,* in commerce, means *trade forbidden by law.* The word *contraband* most often refers to goods useful in war, such as arms or ammunition. The warships of a country at war may search for, seize, and destroy contraband goods that are being shipped to its enemy in neutral ships.

In modern total warfare, almost anything is "useful for military purposes" and may be declared contraband. During World War I, Great Britain declared cotton to be contraband, because Germany used it in the manufacture of explosives. During World War II, Germany and Great Britain each published contraband lists of many items. Unless there are treaties defining exactly what articles are contraband of war, this law often leads to embarrassment.   TELFORD TAYLOR

See also BLOCKADE.

CONTRABASS. See BASS (musical instrument).

CONTRACEPTION. See BIRTH CONTROL.

CONTRACT is an agreement made by two or more persons that is enforceable by law. It consists of voluntary promises to do or not to do certain things. When persons make a contract, their promises become legal obligations.

Contracts are vital to the economic systems of the United States, Canada, and other countries where private enterprise is encouraged. Much of the wealth of free enterprise nations takes the form of such contracts as bonds and promissory notes. Most business activities in these countries depend on contracts. These contracts include promises to deliver or pay for goods, perform or pay for services, pay wages or rent, exchange real estate, and construct homes, factories, and office buildings.

Freely made economic decisions are basic elements of the free enterprise system. As a result, a leading principle of contract law is that persons may agree with each other on any terms they think fit. But an agreement that would upset public order is unenforceable. For example, the courts would not enforce an agreement to bribe a public official. The courts also refuse to enforce an agreement if one party has clearly taken unfair advantage of another. The laws bar some persons, chiefly minors or the mentally incompetent, from assuming obligations under contract.

The making of a contract usually involves two important acts, (1) making an offer and (2) accepting the offer. The acts may be verbal or in writing. However, the law requires certain contracts to be made in writing. These include agreements to sell real estate and agreements that cover a long period of time.

Before a contract is formed, the parties usually negotiate the terms of the agreement. One party makes one or several offers. As soon as the other party accepts an offer, the negotiations are over. Under United States law, the moment of acceptance is decisive. At that time, the contract is concluded. Government agencies usually negotiate contracts under special rules. They invite all interested parties to submit *bids* (offers). Then they accept the most favorable bid.

Most contracts are enforceable only if all parties get something out of the agreement. What a contracting party gets is called a *consideration*. When a loan contract is made, the money advanced by the lender is the consideration received by the borrower. The borrower's promise to return the money with interest is the consideration received by the lender. A promise for no consideration is not an offer to make a contract. For example, if two friends promise each other to meet for lunch, no consideration is involved. They merely agree to a social engagement, not to a contract.

A contract is said to be *discharged* after the obligations of the agreement have been fulfilled. If either party violates the agreement, a *breach of contract* occurs. In that case, a court ordinarily awards money, called *damages*, to the other party. In enforcing contracts, the courts try to carry out the plain intention of the agreement. W. F. YOUNG, JR.

See also BONA FIDE; BOND; LEASE.

CONTRACT BRIDGE. See BRIDGE (card game).
CONTRACTION, POETIC. See ELISION.
CONTRACTOR. See BUILDING TRADE (The Contracting System); ARCHITECTURE (Overseeing the Construction).

CONTRALTO, *kuhn TRAL toe,* is the lowest voice a woman can sing, and falls in the lower register of an alto voice. Some parts in music are written either for a woman singing contralto or for a man singing the same part. He is called a *countertenor.*
CONTREDANSE. See DANCING (During the 1600's).
CONTRERAS, BATTLE OF. See MEXICAN WAR (Scott's Campaign).
CONTROL GROUP. See EXPERIMENTATION, SCIENTIFIC.
CONTROL ROD. See ATOMIC REACTOR (illustration).
CONUNDRUM. See RIDDLE.
CONURBATION. See GREAT BRITAIN (Population); METROPOLITAN AREA.
CONVECTION. See HEAT (How Heat Travels).
CONVENT is a religious community of either men or women who have taken strict vows and live under religious rule. The term is usually applied to an order or society of female Christian nuns, and especially to the building in which they live.

In an *enclosed* convent, the sisters and novices are fully isolated from the outside world. In their cloistered life, they seek their own salvation and that of others through a program of worship, prayer, and contemplation. The Carmelite and Dominican Nuns of the Perpetual Adoration (Second Order) are contemplative orders. *Unenclosed* convents include active orders, societies, and institutes that conduct schools, maintain hospitals, run children's and old people's homes, and take part in other types of social services. Examples are the Little Sisters of the Poor and the Sisters of Charity and Christian Instruction. To some degree, almost all orders seek to combine the two ways of life. The head of a convent is usually called *mother superior*, but may have a different title, such as *abbess.*

Buddhist and Taoist nuns also live in convents. They devote themselves completely to contemplative lives, but are not as fully isolated from society as the Christian contemplative orders. R. PIERCE BEAVER

See also CLOISTER; MONASTICISM; NUN.

CONVENTION is a meeting held by a large organization, usually national in scope, to consider problems, draft policies, and plan future activities. Local chapters send representatives, called *delegates.* Most organizations, such as the American Legion, hold a convention every year. All delegates may meet together for one or more sessions, but the delegates usually transact most convention business during smaller sectional meetings.

Political parties customarily hold conventions to plan campaigns and select candidates for elections. In the United States, the major political parties hold national conventions every four years to select presidential and vice-presidential candidates. W. HAYES YEAGER

See also POLITICAL CONVENTION.

CONVERSATION is the spoken exchange of ideas and opinions with others. The ability to engage in interesting conversation is one of the greatest assets a person can have. It is an aid to business and social success, and helps one to enjoy more fully the company of others.

Thomas Hardy, the English novelist, once sat next to another famous writer at a dinner party in London. The two had never met before their hostess introduced them. Halfway through the meal the only words the men had

CONVERSATION

spoken to each other were, "How do you do?" Suddenly Hardy looked up from his plate and asked, "Do you talk?" The other gruffly replied, "No." "Neither do I," grunted Hardy, and they finished the dinner in silence. Hardy was a great novelist, but not a conversationalist.

Making Conversation Interesting. The person who has a rich store of knowledge and a variety of interests has the foundation for entertaining and holding the interest of other people. Sentences that sparkle cannot spring from an empty person any more than milk can be poured from an empty pitcher. The person who has absorbed ideas from books and from people is listened to with pleasure. The inner richness which develops from study and reading and keen observation encourages confidence, the seed of personality and eloquence.

Sincerity and naturalness are marks of the good conversationalist. The man who speaks sincerely can often gain listeners even if his words do not flow easily. And the person who talks in a natural, relaxed manner about interesting subjects wins an audience in the same way that a smooth-stroking tennis player attracts spectators. The jerky, halting speaker creates a feeling of uneasiness in his listeners. Their attention will not focus on sentences that have not been clearly organized. Thoughts should first be framed in the mind, then spoken smoothly and easily.

The skilled talker is not too grave. He spices his conversation with humor. He is enthusiastic without being deadly earnest. Every person likes to be amused as well as informed. The conversationalist who combines wit with ideas that make sense is always in demand as a formal or informal entertainer.

Voice Quality. A pleasant tone of voice adds finish to conversation just as a beautiful frame completes a picture. Many young persons speak loudly and harshly. Others speak rapidly and in so low a tone that their words are lost. Words should be spoken clearly and should not be run together. Full tones and sharply sounded consonants add power to the voice and give it the ring of authority.

A pleasant tone is especially important in telephone conversation, because the voice is the speaker's only method of expressing his feelings. He cannot use facial expressions or a hearty handshake to convey his sincerity and interest.

The Art of Listening. Sometimes a person can be a good conversationalist without saying a word. Listening is half of every conversation, and courtesy demands that a person be a good listener. The duties of a listener are simple but are frequently overlooked. The good listener gives all his attention to the conversation. He looks the speaker in the eye, but does not glare at him hypnotically. He smiles to show his appreciation of a clever remark, and always follows the ideas of the talker closely. He asks questions when the speaker is finished, not before. The good listener restrains himself when tempted to interrupt. And the man who can bellow with hearty laughter at the end of a funny story is the best listener of all.

An eager listener stimulates his companions to their best conversation. The person who masters the art of intelligent listening as well as talking is rare and delightful company.

Topics of Conversation. "What can we find to talk about?" is a question frequently asked of youth counselors by boys and girls. The most pleasant topic is one that interests both talkers. The more interests a person has, the more subjects he enjoys discussing. When a girl who likes to dance meets a boy who specializes in fancy steps, there is no groping for conversation. The two are attracted to each other because of a mutual interest, and conversation comes easily. The person who is actively interested in a variety of fields can talk and listen intelligently in any group. Wherever he goes, he finds people interested in some of the things he likes, and the conversation flows.

If you want to have a lot to talk about, develop many hobbies and interests. If you are not interested, you cannot be interesting.

Do not offend the person with whom you are talking. What you do not say will sometimes win you more friends than what you do say. Everybody has a few "sore spots," or topics he would rather not discuss. It is your duty to be on the lookout for these and to avoid them. Think before you speak. If there is doubt in your mind about a subject, do not bring it up. If you must bring it up, do so tactfully.

The Language of Conversation. Everyone must adjust his language to the person or group with which he is talking. Boys use one kind of language on the playground, another in class recitation, and still another at home. The language of the North Woods guide is rough and suitable to his environment, but when he moves to the city he faces a difficult language adjustment. Many of the best conversationalists have developed their speech to the point where it is simple and yet colorful, and will fit into any group with little adjustment.

Striking phrases and unusual words add color to a conversation. Reading is one of the best methods of building a strong vocabulary. A companion method is the practice of looking up unusual words in a good dictionary. But the best method of all is listening to interesting persons.

Related Articles in WORLD BOOK include:

Etiquette	Introductions	Speech	Voice
Humor	Language	Vocabulary	

CONVERSE COLLEGE. See UNIVERSITIES AND COLLEGES (table).

CONVERSION. See PETROLEUM (Refining).

CONVERTER is a device used to convert electrical energy from alternating current to direct current. An *inverted converter* changes direct current to alternating current. See also ELECTRIC CURRENT.

CONVERTIBILITY, *kuhn VUR tuh BILL uh tih,* is the privilege of exchanging the currency of one nation for that of another. This privilege plays an important role in international trade. For example, an importer from nation A buying goods from nation B must find a way to pay for them. This is much easier if the two currencies are convertible, because all he needs to do is go to his bank and purchase a check for an equivalent amount in B's currency. Otherwise, he can buy goods only to the extent that he has B's currency. One problem in achieving true world-wide convertibility is the difference in economic strength and stability among nations. See also MONEY (Money Around the World; table: Values of Monetary Units); INTERNATIONAL TRADE (Financing International Trade).   LEONARD C. R. LANGER

804

CONVERTIPLANE is an aircraft designed to fly horizontally, and also to land and take off vertically. Such aircraft can usually *hover* (remain motionless) in the air. They are also known as *VTOLs* (vertical take-off and landing) and *STOLs* (short take-off and landing). The term *V/STOL* (vertical or short take-off and landing) includes all types of convertiplanes.

Convertiplanes have great commercial and military possibilities because they need only a small landing space compared to that for conventional aircraft. With convertiplanes, commercial airlines could operate from the tops of buildings or small landing areas in the heart of a city. One of the problems of military aircraft operations is the difficulty of building and maintaining suitable airfields. Military convertiplanes, however, could operate in any area where there was room enough to land or where a small landing field could be easily built.

How They Work. A variety of systems have been developed for achieving both horizontal and vertical flight. In general, however, there are two basic types.

One type has two separate propulsion systems—one for vertical flight and the other for horizontal flight. For example, the Sikorsky Stowed Rotor VTOL covers the helicopter rotors it uses for vertical flight when it reaches speeds over 150 mph.

The second type of convertiplane often looks more like a conventional aircraft. It uses only one propulsion system for both horizontal and vertical flight. It has jet, propeller, or ducted fan engines mounted in the fuselage or on the wings. They operate by tilting or rotating the wings, engines, or the entire aircraft to fly in the desired direction. Or they may use vanes or flaps to deflect the jet thrust or air blast from the engines downward for vertical flight. The Ryan XV-5A is an example of this second type of aircraft. It has a ducted fan mounted on each wing. See DUCTED FAN PRINCIPLE OF FLIGHT.

History. Active experiments on convertiplanes began in 1937 with models tested by Gerard Herrick of New York City and E. Burke Wilford of Philadelphia. In 1955, the U.S. Department of Defense reported testing the first successful convertiplane, the McDonnell XV-1. Since then, many airplane manufacturers have built numerous experimental convertiplanes with steadily better performance. In 1942, convertiplanes were not available at any price. In 1952, they cost twice as much as a conventional plane. Today, they cost 30 to 40 per cent more than ordinary aircraft.   LESLIE A. BRYAN

See also AUTOGIRO; HELICOPTER.

A Convertiplane such as the Hawker Siddeley *Harrier, below,* can fly from any small, open area. It takes off and lands vertically, like a helicopter. But once in the air, it flies like an ordinary plane. The plane has four exhaust nozzles that direct the exhaust from its jet engine toward the ground for take-off or landing and swivel horizontally for level flight.

Hawker Siddeley Aviation Ltd.

CONVEYOR BELT

CONVEYOR BELT is a device that *conveys* (carries) large quantities of material from place to place. It consists of an endless belt that is looped over two pulleys. One of the pulleys is called the *drive pulley*, and supplies the power that keeps the belt moving. Most conveyor belts are powered by an electric motor.

The belt travels over a series of rollers that reduce friction and support the belt. The material moves along the belt at a moderate speed in a straight line. A conveyor belt can carry material at a much steeper grade, or slant, than can a truck or a railroad train. The steepness of the grade is limited only by the slant at which the material will slide down the belt.

Conveyor belts such as those used in mines and quarries may be a mile or more in length. The longest conveyor belt in the world—$5\frac{1}{2}$ miles in length—is located in Oklahoma. The belt is used to carry limestone from a quarry to a cement mill.

Types of Conveyor Belts. The belt of a conveyor may be flat and wide, and the materials simply placed on the belt to be carried away. But for moving bulk material, such as sugar or salt, the belt forms a trough so the material can be moved without spilling. Other conveyor belts consist of chains that have buckets hanging from the chain. Some chain belts have either hooks or scoops that pick up the material and carry it along.

Many times, a conveyor belt makes up only a part of a much larger conveyor system. If the system must change directions or turn a corner, the material is dropped from one belt to another belt that moves in the desired direction. In such a system, each belt is called a *flight*. Different flights are needed for each change of direction required.

Uses. Conveyor belts play an important part in mass production. Automobiles, for example, move along the assembly line on a conveyor system (see ASSEMBLY LINE). Workers stand in one place, and the materials to be worked on move past them. In airports, conveyor belts carry luggage from the ticket counter to the baggage room. Many buildings now use moving sidewalks, which consist of a ramplike conveyor belt with handrails. An escalator is a conveyor belt designed to form stairs as it moves around as an endless belt. In meatpacking plants, conveyor belts carry the carcasses of the animals from one station to another to be processed.

Conveyor belts are widely used to load and unload ships, trucks, and railroad cars. One such system moves over 6,000 tons of coal an hour. A steady stream of coal is dumped from railroad cars to the belt. The belt carries the coal to a loading tower that distributes the coal to the various parts of the ship. Mines transport their ores to ships or factories in much the same way.

CONVEYOR BELT

Trough Conveyor Belts move tremendous tonnages of bulk material efficiently and rapidly. The dock conveyor, *below,* carries iron ore, limestone, and coal from ships to blast furnace storage areas.

Link-Belt Company

A Moving Sidewalk, *left,* which is actually a flat conveyor belt, can carry up to 15,000 persons an hour.

H. Armstrong Roberts

A Conveyor Belt moves dolls past assembly-line workers in a factory.

Many industries use special types of conveyor belts to make their products. Large bakeries, for example, use conveyor belts to speed up the baking of bread. The mixed dough is placed in pans and put on an endless belt that passes through a walled oven over 100 feet long. It takes the belt about 30 minutes to carry the pans through the oven. The continuous movement of a number of these belts allows large bakeries to bake over 30,000 loaves of bread an hour.   R. G. HENNES

See also AUTOMOBILE (Assembling; diagram: Assembling an Automobile); CABLE CAR.

CONVOLVULUS, *kuhn VAHL vyoo luhs,* is a *genus* (group) of plants in the morning-glory family. Scientists know of about 200 kinds. Some, such as bindweed, are weeds. Scammony and others are used in medicines. Still other kinds of convolvulus are grown for their beauty.

Related Articles in WORLD BOOK include:

Bindweed	Moonflower	Scammony
Dodder	Morning-Glory	Sweet Potato
Jalap		

CONVOY is a group of merchant ships sailing under the protection of one or more warships. Attacks by German submarines made it necessary for almost all Atlantic shipping to move in convoys during World Wars I and II. During World War II, the United States built the *destroyer escort* for convoy duty, and the British and Canadians developed the *corvette.* These warships were light destroyers, armed with depth charges and light guns. The Allies also built special aircraft carriers, called *escort carriers,* to provide air protection against submarine attack.   THEODORE ROPP

See also AIRCRAFT CARRIER; CORVETTE; DESTROYER.

CONVULSIONS are violent, completely involuntary contractions of the muscles. They may be signs of damage to brain tissue, such as might result from injury, infections, or tumors. They also may occur during many physical or mental illnesses. In young children, convulsions often accompany acute infections and fever. Convulsions of various degrees occur in epilepsy.

Convulsions vary in form or degree. Sometimes the whole body becomes rigid. Or the person may twist and turn his body, and the muscles of his face, legs, and arms may twitch. In some types of epilepsy, only one limb, or even just a part of it, may be involved in the convulsion. Treatment of convulsions depends on the cause. A doctor should always be called for a patient with convulsions.   LOUIS D. BOSHES

CONWAY CABAL. See CABAL.

Conveyor Belts can operate economically up and down steep grades, in narrow tunnels, and across wide valleys and rivers, *below.*

Link-Belt Company

N.Y. Zoological Society

The Tree Hyrax lives a solitary life in the forest. The male "talks" with its neighbors by letting out a long, swelling howl.

CONY, *KOH nih,* or CONEY, also called HYRAX, is a rabbit-sized animal resembling a guinea pig. It lives in Africa and southwestern Asia. Conies have short legs, ears, and tails, and they have broad nails on their paws. They are related to the hoofed animals. Some conies live in rocky hills, and others live in trees. The cry of the species that lives in West Africa has been described as "agonized screeching." Conies are mentioned in the English version of the Bible. In addition to hyraxes, certain other rabbit-like animals as well as some rabbits and fishes are called *conies.* The term *coney* is also a trade name for a particular kind of rabbit fur.

Scientific Classification. The cony belongs to the order *Hyracoidea.* The cony is a member of the coney family, *Procaviidae.*   FRANK B. GOLLEY

See also FUR (Rabbit); PIKA.

CONYNE, SILAS J. See KITE (The Conyne Kite).

COOCH'S BRIDGE. See DELAWARE (The Revolutionary War).

COOK, FREDERICK ALBERT (1865-1940), an American explorer, claimed that he discovered the North Pole in April, 1908. His story was questioned when Robert Edwin Peary returned from a polar expedition in September, 1909. Danish scientists investigated, and announced that Cook did not have sufficient proof of claims. His claim that he reached the summit of Mount McKinley, Alaska, also was disputed. Cook was imprisoned in 1923 for fraudulent use of the mails. He was born in Callicoon Depot, N.Y.   JOHN E. CASWELL

COOK, JAMES (1728-1779), a British navigator, became a famous explorer of the Pacific Ocean. He made three voyages to the South Pacific region and mapped the area with scientific accuracy and remarkable precision. His first valuable service was a survey of the Saint Lawrence River and the Newfoundland Coast. This work won the attention of the British government, and Cook received command of three expeditions to the South Pacific. He left Plymouth, England, in 1768 on his first voyage. He sailed around Cape Horn and reached New Zealand, where he mapped the North and South islands. In 1770, Cook sailed along the east coast

Brown Bros.

Captain James Cook landed at Tanna in the New Hebrides Islands in 1774. He mapped the region, fixing the location of many islands in the South Pacific. The spot where Cook was killed, at Kealakekua Bay, Hawaii, *right*, is marked by a bronze tablet.

of Australia. He claimed a large area for Great Britain and named it New South Wales. Cook returned to England in 1771.

Cook started on a second voyage in 1772 to investigate whether or not a continent extended from the South Pacific to the South Pole. Geographers had speculated on the existence of such a continent for hundreds of years. Cook made important discoveries on this voyage. He became the first person to sail across the Antarctic Circle, and discovered the large island of South Georgia. His pioneer work led him to conclude that a frozen continent lay farther south in the Antarctic. Later explorers proved him to be right.

On his third voyage, from 1776 to 1779, Cook proved that there was no direct water route from the Pacific Ocean to Hudson Bay. He left England, sailed eastward

through the Cape of Good Hope, and reached New Zealand in 1777. He continued northeastward, discovered the Sandwich Islands (now Hawaii), and landed on the western coast of North America in 1778 (see HAWAII [History]). Cook sailed up the coast, made charts, explored the vicinity of Bering Strait, and then returned to Hawaii. He was killed by the islanders in 1779.

Cook was born in Marton, Yorkshire. He joined the British navy as a seaman, and rose rapidly to positions of command and responsibility.   JAMES G. ALLEN

See also BRITISH COLUMBIA (Discovery); CANADA, HISTORY OF (color picture: Captain James Cook).

COOK, MOUNT. See MOUNT COOK.

COOK COUNTY. See CHICAGO (Greater Chicago).

COOK ISLANDS lie in the South Pacific Ocean, about 1,800 miles northeast of New Zealand. For location, see PACIFIC ISLANDS (color map). The islands are a dependency of New Zealand. They cover 93 square miles and have a 90-mile coastline. The main islands include Rarotonga, Mangaia, Atiu, Aitutaki, Mauke, and three small islets. The capital is Avarua, on the northern shore of Rarotonga. Manihiki and several other islands to the north are administered by the Cook Islands. The islands have fertile soil and a mild climate. Their chief exports include copra, fruits, and tomatoes. Most of the 21,000 people are Polynesians.

Captain James Cook discovered the islands in 1773. Great Britain took control in 1888, and assigned administrative control of them to New Zealand in 1901. A new constitution gave the people of the islands control of their internal affairs in 1965.   EDWIN H. BRYAN, JR.

COOKE, JAY (1821-1905), an American financier, was the chief financial agent for the United States during the Civil War. He sold war loans, which totaled well over $1 billion. Cooke was born in Sandusky, Ohio. He worked his way up from a clerkship in a Philadelphia bank to the establishment of his own banking firm in 1861. In 1873, the failure of his company helped bring on a general financial panic. In 1878 and 1879, Cooke made another fortune in western silver mines.   KENNETH W. PORTER

COOKE, WILLIAM F. See TELEGRAPH (Development).

Underwood & Underwood

SAUCES AND
DRESSINGS

For Desserts

CARAMEL SAUCE

PUT half cup sugar in sauce-pan on fire, let it get light brown, then add little water, and boil for few moments, then add half-pint cream, yelks of two eggs; stir until it comes to boil, then remove from fire, and when nearly cool season with vanilla.

COLD SAUCE

Cream butter and sugar together, add wine or brandy and little nutmeg, and beat until it looks white.

From *Gay Nineties Cook Book* by F. Meredith Dietz and August Dietz, Jr., © 1945 The Dietz Press, Inc.

Trying Her Hand at Cooking delights many a girl at an early age, *right*. Recipes in today's cookbooks give more specific directions than those listed in cookbooks around 1900, *above*.

Rae Russell

COOKING is the art and science of preparing foods for the table, usually by heating them until they are changed in flavor, tenderness, appearance, and chemical composition. Cooking develops flavor, and makes many foods more attractive in appearance. It also makes some foods easier to digest. Because the effect of food is so important to health, cooking has developed into a science, and is so taught in schools and colleges.

History of Cooking

It is not known when, how, or by what people the art of cooking was first discovered. But records found on the walls of the Egyptian tombs of about 4000 B.C. prove that cooking was known at that time. Until people learned to build fires, no food was heated intentionally. Perhaps the people had tasted food cooked by molten lava from erupting volcanoes, or by forest fires. But until fire and heat could be controlled there could be little cooking. Charles Lamb, in "A Dissertation on Roast Pig," has a delightful explanation of how cooking began. He said that a house in China burned down, and a pig was accidentally roasted. In some very hot climates, such as the deserts in the southwestern part of the United States, some food was cooked by baking or drying on flat stones placed in the hot sun. The Indians baked their thin corn cakes in this manner.

The first broiling was done by placing the food on a stick and holding it over hot coals. Later this stick was made of an iron rod or *spit* which was put over the fire. The food was pushed on the stick, and turned frequently to cook it on all sides and to keep it from burning. Cooking on a flat stove with a fire built around it was also known very early. As people continued to learn about cooking, they dug pits in the ground, lined them with stones, and built fires on them. After the stones were heated the food was placed on them, covered with green leaves, and left to cook.

Boiling, which is cooking in water, could not be done until the invention of containers which held water and which were not destroyed by heat. Among the earliest pots were those of soapstone used by the Egyptians

about 1600 B.C. Later the Eskimos used similar pots. Skin bags and birch-bark kettles were used early by the American Indians. Cooking was done by dropping hot stones into the containers of food. As the stones cooled off, more hot ones were added.

The ancient Egyptians knew at least six forms of cooking, including baking, broiling, roasting, boiling, frying, and stewing. The ancient Jews also knew a great deal about cooking. The book of Genesis in the Bible tells the story of Rebekah who prepared kid so that it tasted like venison and gave it to Isaac (Genesis 27). Assyrian and Babylonian carvings of about 750 B.C. show cooking being done over a pan of charcoal, called a *brazier*.

The Romans, who were famous for their banquets, prepared food by cooking it over charcoal on grills, or on stone hearths. Permanent types of ovens have been found among the ruins of Pompeii. The manuscripts of the Middle Ages tell us that boiling and broiling were the two most common methods of cooking at that time. A type of bread was often made in an oven which resembled a beehive. Such ovens were found only in the "great houses" of the wealthy or in public bakeries of Europe until long after America was discovered. In colonial North America, however, nearly every home had an oven of its own, because homes were usually far apart and the forests were full of dangers.

Closed stoves of brick or porcelain tile have been in use in northern European countries since the end of the Middle Ages. Cast-iron stoves were used in Alsace as early as 1490. But it was not until the 1800's that cook-stoves became popular. Before that time, the people in America and other countries cooked in kettles over the fireplace or on an open fire outdoors. Ovens for baking were built into the fireplace. Dutch ovens, large cylinders with shelves and open on one side, were set beside the fire. Roasting was done on spits.

Modern Improvements in Cooking

The methods of cooking changed as equipment for cooking became better in design and materials. Women

809

TYPES OF COOKING

Baking   Boiling   Poaching   Deep-fat frying

learned to save the juices which dripped from the meat as it was being roasted, and to make sauces to serve with it. They learned to use seasonings of various kinds, and how to combine foods to give new and tastier dishes that were more pleasing in appearance. The appearance of food has a powerful effect on the appetite.

Modern methods of cooking are based on the methods of earlier times. But they are carried on with the aid of modern cooking utensils of metals, glass, or enamel, and with modern equipment. Such equipment includes mechanically operated stoves, beaters, refrigerators, and many electrical appliances. Gas, kerosene, coal, electricity, and wood are the main sources of energy or heat used in cooking.

Recipes. Until very recently, recipes told one to take a "handful" of this ingredient, "fat the size of a walnut," a "pinch" or a "smidgen" of seasoning, and perhaps "enough liquid to make a dough." Sometimes the recipe said to "use your own judgment." Naturally, an inexperienced person had a difficult time learning to cook. With tested recipes and equipment of standard sizes, there can be little doubt in the cook's mind about the amounts of ingredients to use, or the methods of preparation. The texture and flavor of foods are controlled to a large degree by the skill and cleverness with which the ingredients are combined. The skill of the greatest chefs can now be duplicated in the home kitchen.

Making More Foods Available. Another important change in cooking has come about by the development of transportation. Foods once unknown in one part of the world are to be found regularly in food stores now. They can be shipped in refrigerated trucks or trains and by air. Cold storage, fast freezing, canning, and modern methods of dehydration have also provided a wider variety of foods which can be used in the home all the year round. Canned foods and commercially packaged foods are often partly cooked. For this reason, food preparation does not take as much time as it did before.

There are many special directions for preparing foods, both fresh and stored. Foods kept in cold storage may be used exactly as fresh foods are. Those which are fast-frozen must be thawed before they can be used in some recipes. But vegetables which are to be heated,

seasoned, and served in the same form in which they are packed may be put on the stove while they are frozen. More food value is retained by this method. They usually contain enough moisture so that none need be added during cooking. The liquid in which foods are canned should be used in soup, or boiled down to the needed amount and served with the foods, since it contains minerals and vitamins needed by the body.

Dehydrated foods have been dried by the sun or by heat to preserve them, shrink them in size, and make them lighter in weight. Most dried foods are soaked before they are cooked. Water is added to them to replace that which was evaporated.

Methods of Cooking

Cooking is done by several means, all of which use either dry or moist heat. Methods using dry heat are roasting, baking, broiling, pan-broiling, and frying. The first four mentioned use air in connection with the heat. Frying uses fat. Moist heat employs water or steam. Boiling, simmering, stewing, steaming, waterless cooking, and pressure cooking apply moist heat.

It is usually desirable to retain as much of the natural flavor and color as possible in cooking vegetables and fruits. This often means cooking them in as little water as possible only until they are tender. This method preserves the food value. Alkalies such as soda should not be added to vegetables. They increase the speed of cooking, but that is all.

Roasting is done by placing the food in the oven or over coals, and cooking until it is tender. Tough cuts of meat should not be prepared in this way. Dry heat tends to harden the connecting tissues. It gives tender cuts a very delicious flavor, since they retain most of their juices. Meats should be roasted at a low temperature, usually one between 300° and 350° F. Such temperatures do not evaporate the juices. The meat does not taste dry, and there is little shrinkage. A thermometer may be inserted in the middle of the largest muscle of the roast, not too near a bone. It will tell when the meat is cooked to the proper degree at the center.

Baking is similar to roasting. It is used for preparing many types of cakes, breads, vegetables, fruits, main dishes, and meats. The food is placed in the oven at

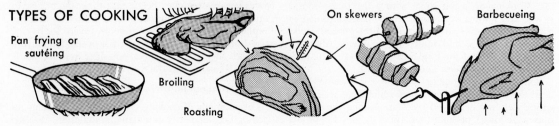

TYPES OF COOKING

Pan frying or sautéing   Broiling   Roasting   On skewers   Barbecueing

the temperature recommended in the recipe used and cooked until done. Excess moisture in the food is evaporated during the cooking process. Other changes also take place. Oven temperatures are sometimes indicated as slow, medium, or hot. A *slow* oven temperature ranges from 250 to 325° F., and is used for baked dishes containing a large amount of egg or cheese. A *medium* oven ranges from 325 to 400°, and is used for cakes, some breads, and most vegetables. A *hot* oven, over 400°, is used for most breads, rolls, quick breads, pie shells, and other similar foods.

Broiling is done by placing the food on racks immediately under a flame or electric unit, or directly over hot coals. The food is cooked on one side until it is done halfway through. Then it is turned over, and continued until the food is cooked to the desired degree. This method is used for very tender cuts of meat and for certain fruits and vegetables. It is the method most frequently used at picnics for "weenie roasts." A hot skillet is used to *pan-broil*. The food is placed in it, and grease or moisture is poured off as it collects.

Frying is cooking food in fat. At first the term applied to deep-fat frying, and the word *sauté* was used for the preparation of food in a small amount of fat. But frying has gradually come to mean cooking foods in any amount of fat. French-fried potatoes, doughnuts, and many other foods are prepared by the deep-fat method, which uses a kettle full of oil or fat. Most tender foods may be prepared in a small amount of fat.

Boiling and Simmering are methods of cooking foods in enough water to cover them. They differ only in the temperature used. Water at sea level boils at 212° F. Foods cooked at a lower temperature are said to be *simmered. Stewing* is cooking food at simmering temperatures in a small amount of water. This method is particularly good for tough cuts of meat. The water and low cooking temperatures soften the connective tissue and make the meat tender.

Braising is the term used in meat cookery by which the meat is first browned, then has a small amount of water added.

Steaming is a method of cooking in which a small amount of water is reduced to steam. The steam surrounds the food and cooks it. Steam cooking may be done by various methods. The food may be placed in a small amount of water in a covered pan and heated. Vegetables may be placed in a parchment bag, sealed, and dropped into a pot of boiling water. The moisture on the vegetables turns to steam and cooks the food. Double boilers are sets of two pans which fit together so that water may be converted into steam in the lower pan to cook the food in the upper pan. Other steamers are built like portable ovens, with pans of water beneath the shelves. Steam under pressure, as produced in the pressure cooker, is used to cook foods very quickly. The pressure, which is registered on a gauge on top of the cooker, is measured in pounds. There is a temperature rise in the cooker with increasing pressure. Pressure cookers may be purchased in sizes ranging from two quarts to twenty or more quarts. The larger sizes usually have racks with sets of pans. Several kinds of foods requiring similar cooking times can thus be prepared at once.

Seasoning. To the epicure, the difference between excellent food and good food is often in the seasoning.

H. Armstrong Roberts

Fresh Fruits and Vegetables, cooked just before being served, often have more flavor than canned and frozen products.

Salt and pepper are used by most persons, but other seasonings may be used. A group of small plants, called *herbs*, are dried or used fresh to give delightfully different flavors. In this group of plants are mint, basil, thyme, parsley, sage, dill, tarragon, mustard, cress, savory, and horse-radish. Leeks, garlic, onions, and shallots are also used for seasoning. Flowers have been frequently added for flavoring. Petals of violets, roses, marigolds, and nasturtiums are used, as well as poppy, caraway, anise, and other seeds. The leaf of the bay tree is another seasoning. Herbs make foods more appetizing. Often a blend of several herbs is more satisfying than one alone. Prepared seasonings, such as mustard, catchup, and horse-radish, are also used on foods, either while they are being prepared or just before they are eaten.   HELEN MARLEY CALAWAY

CALVIN
COOLIDGE

The United States Flag had 48 stars when Coolidge took office.

WILSON
28th President
1913 — 1921

HARDING
29th President
1921 — 1923

HOOVER
31st President
1929 — 1933

F. D. ROOSEVELT
32nd President
1933 — 1945

Harris & Ewing

30TH PRESIDENT OF THE UNITED STATES 1923-1929

COOLIDGE, CALVIN (1872-1933), was a shy, silent New England Republican who led the United States during the boisterous Jazz Age of the 1920's. He was the sixth Vice-President to become President upon the death of a chief executive. Coolidge was vacationing on his father's farm in Vermont when President Warren G. Harding died in 1923. The elder Coolidge, a notary public, administered the oath of office in the dining room. Never before had this ceremony been performed by such a minor official or by a President's father.

In 1924, Coolidge was elected to a full four-year term. He enjoyed great popularity and probably could have been re-elected. But he decided to retire. His terse announcement became his most famous statement: "I do not choose to run for President in 1928." Herbert Hoover succeeded him.

Americans respected the views of the closemouthed Coolidge, although he seldom said anything very original or profound. His reputation for wisdom was based on his dry wit and robust common sense. He issued few unnecessary public statements and rarely wasted a word.

Coolidge, who had risen to fame as governor of Massachusetts, served as President during the Roaring 20's. Prosperity stimulated carefree behavior and a craving for entertainment. The nation's "flaming youth," featured in the novels of F. Scott Fitzgerald, set the pace. Sports figures became national heroes as Babe Ruth hit 60 home runs in one season and Gene Tunney

defeated Jack Dempsey in the famous "long-count" bout. Charles A. Lindbergh made the first solo flight across the Atlantic Ocean. Motion pictures began to talk, with Al Jolson starring in *The Jazz Singer*. George Gershwin brought jazz into the concert hall with his *Rhapsody in Blue*. Americans defied Prohibition, and Al Capone and other gangsters grew rich by bootlegging liquor. A popular song summed up the whole era: "Ain't We Got Fun?"

The solemn, frugal Coolidge seemed to be a misfit from another era. But people voted for him even if they did not imitate his conduct. They cherished him for having the virtues of their pioneer forefathers.

Early Life

Childhood. Calvin Coolidge was born on Independence Day, July 4, 1872, in Plymouth Notch, a village near Woodstock in central Vermont. He was named for his father, John Calvin Coolidge, but his parents called him *Calvin*, or *Cal*. He dropped the name *John* after leaving college.

Calvin's parents had been childhood playmates in Plymouth Notch. His father was descended from an English family that came to America about 1630. When Calvin was 4 and his sister, Abigail, was 1, his father bought a small farm across the road from the family store. Cal helped with the farm chores and studied in a small stone schoolhouse nearby.

The elder Coolidge served three terms in the Vermont

house of representatives and one term in the state senate, and held many local public offices. He passed his political shrewdness on to his son.

Education. Coolidge's mother, Victoria Josephine Moor Coolidge, died when he was 12 years old. The next year he entered Black River Academy at nearby Ludlow. He was graduated in 1890. His sister, who also attended the school, had died of an intestinal ailment a short time before. He took a short course at St. Johnsbury Academy, and entered Amherst College in 1891.

Coolidge made his first appearance as an orator in

1892, when he delivered the Independence Day address in his home town. As a college student, he showed great interest in political campaigns. He earned only fair grades during his first two years, but was graduated *cum laude* in 1895.

Coolidge then read law with the firm of Hammond and Field in Northampton, Mass. He passed the Massachusetts bar examination in 1897, and about seven months later opened his own office in Northampton.

Political and Public Activities

Entry into Politics. Coolidge became an active worker for the Republican party in 1896. He was elected to the Northampton city council in 1898, and became city solicitor in 1900. He won re-election in 1901, but lost in 1902.

In 1904, Coolidge met his future wife, Grace Anna Goodhue (Jan. 3, 1879-July 8, 1957), a teacher at the Clarke School for the Deaf in Northampton. She was gay, talkative, and fun-loving—just the opposite of the quiet Coolidge. Shortly after their marriage on Oct. 4,

---

IMPORTANT DATES IN COOLIDGE'S LIFE

1872 (July 4) Born in Plymouth Notch, Vt.
1905 (Oct. 4) Married Grace Anna Goodhue.
1906 Elected to Massachusetts house of representatives.
1909 Elected mayor of Northampton, Mass.
1911 Elected to Massachusetts senate.
1915 Elected lieutenant governor of Massachusetts.
1918 Elected governor of Massachusetts.
1920 Elected Vice-President.
1923 (Aug. 3) Became President of the United States.
1924 Elected to full term as President.
1933 (Jan. 5) Died in Northampton, Mass.

THE WORLD OF PRESIDENT COOLIDGE

U.S. population was 122,000,000 in 1929, and there were 48 states in the Union.

Radiotelephony Service

WORLD EVENTS
1924 Civil war raged in China.
1925 Locarno Conference resulted in establishing a neutral Rhineland.
1927 Radiotelephony connected New York City and London.
1928 The Kellogg-Briand Peace Pact was signed in Paris.

First Diesel Locomotive in regular service began operating in New York City (1925).

U.S. Marines landed in Nicaragua to help stabilize that nation's government (1926).

Kellogg-Briand Pact

First Flight Over North Pole was made by Richard E. Byrd and Floyd Bennett (1926).

Charles Lindbergh flew nonstop across the Atlantic from New York City to Paris (1927).

First Round-the-World Flight carried 2 U.S. Army biplanes 26,345 miles (1924).

First "Talking" Motion Picture, *The Jazz Singer,* was produced (1927).

Grace Coolidge had a fun-loving personality in contrast to her husband, "Silent Cal."

1905, he arrived home from his office with a bag containing 52 pairs of socks, all with holes. When his bride asked if he had married her to darn his socks, Coolidge, with characteristic bluntness, replied: "No, but I find it mighty handy." The couple had two sons, John (1906-), who became a business executive, and Calvin, Jr.. (1908-1924).

Coolidge was elected to the Massachusetts house of representatives in 1906, and was re-elected the next year. He won election as mayor of Northampton in 1909, and was returned to office in 1910. From 1912 to 1915 Coolidge served in the state senate, with two terms as president of that body. He was elected lieutenant governor in 1915, and twice won re-election. He was elected governor in 1918.

As Governor, Coolidge became nationally famous during the Boston police strike of 1919. In defiance of police department rules, a group of Boston policemen had obtained a union charter from the American Federation of Labor. Police Commissioner Edwin U. Curtis suspended 19 of the union's leaders, and the next day almost three-fourths of Boston's more than 1,500 policemen went on strike.

Bands of hoodlums roamed Boston for two nights, smashing windows and looting stores. Coolidge mobilized the state guard, and order was restored. When Curtis fired the 19 suspended policemen, Samuel Gompers, president of the AFL, protested to Coolidge. In reply, Coolidge made his famous declaration: "There is no right to strike against the public safety by anybody, anywhere, any time."

Coolidge won re-election in 1919 by a record vote. In 1920, he received some votes for the presidential nomination at the Republican national convention that chose Senator Warren G. Harding of Ohio. The delegates gave Coolidge the vice-presidential nomination on the first ballot. Harding, friendly and easy-going, and Coolidge, silent and unsmiling, won an overwhelming victory over their Democratic opponents, Governor James M. Cox of Ohio and Assistant Secretary of the Navy Franklin D. Roosevelt.

Vice-President. At Harding's invitation, Coolidge regularly attended meetings of the Cabinet. He was the first Vice-President to do so.

Even in the social whirl of Washington, Coolidge remained unchanged. He rarely smiled, almost never laughed, and sat silently through official dinners. At one affair, a woman told him she had bet that she could get more than two words out of him. Replied Coolidge: "You lose."

Early on the morning of Aug. 3, 1923, while vaca-

Coolidge's Birthplace in Plymouth Notch, Vt., is now the rear of this store. The house was once separate from the store.

tioning on his father's farm, Coolidge was awakened with the startling news of Harding's death. He dressed and knelt in prayer, then walked downstairs to the dining room. There, by the light of a kerosene lamp, his father administered the presidential oath at 2:45 A.M. After that, President Coolidge went back to bed—and slept. Years afterward, when asked to recall his first thought upon becoming President, he replied: "I thought I could swing it."

Eighteen days later, Coolidge had a second oath of office administered by a justice of the Supreme Court of the District of Columbia. Attorney General Harry M. Daugherty had questioned the validity of the first oath, because Coolidge's father had authority to swear in only state officials of Vermont.

Coolidge's Administration (1923-1929)

Cabinet. Only three members of Harding's Cabinet remained in office throughout the Coolidge administration. They were Secretary of the Treasury Andrew W. Mellon, Postmaster General Harry S. New, and Secretary of Labor James J. Davis. Herbert Hoover, Secretary of Commerce under Harding, served until he resigned in 1928 to run for President.

Corruption in Government. Coolidge entered the White House just as the Teapot Dome and other scandals of the Harding administration became public. Coolidge made no effort to shield the guilty, and his personal honesty was never questioned. In 1924, he forced the resignation of Attorney General Daugherty

--- **VICE-PRESIDENT AND CABINET** ---

Vice-President...............	*Charles G. Dawes
Secretary of State...........	*Charles Evans Hughes
	*Frank B. Kellogg (1925)
Secretary of the Treasury.....	*Andrew W. Mellon
Secretary of War.............	John W. Weeks
	*Dwight F. Davis (1925)
Attorney General............	Harry M. Daugherty
	*Harlan F. Stone (1924)
	John G. Sargent (1925)
Postmaster General..........	Harry S. New
Secretary of the Navy........	Edwin Denby
	Curtis D. Wilbur (1924)
Secretary of the Interior......	Hubert Work
	Roy O. West (1928)
Secretary of Agriculture......	Henry C. Wallace
	Howard M. Gore (1924)
	William M. Jardine (1925)
Secretary of Commerce.......	*Herbert Hoover
	William F. Whiting (1928)
Secretary of Labor..........	James J. Davis

*Has a separate biography in WORLD BOOK.

and other high officials who had been connected with the scandals. See HARDING, WARREN GAMALIEL (Government Scandals); TEAPOT DOME.

"Constructive Economy." Coolidge continued Harding's policy of supporting American business at home and abroad. He favored a program of what he called "constructive economy," and declared that "The business of America is business." The government continued high tariffs on imports in an effort to help American manufacturers. Although Congress reduced income taxes, revenue from taxes increased and the administration reduced the national debt by about a billion dollars a year. Congress also restricted immigration beyond what it had done in 1921. Coolidge vetoed the World War I veterans' bonus bill, but Congress passed it over his veto.

A paradox of the Coolidge era was that the President stood for economy and a simple way of life, and yet enjoyed great popularity with a public that largely had thrown thrift to the winds. Some economists warned that this period of prosperity would end in a dreadful depression. But most Americans believed that good times had come to stay. Coolidge did not try to stop the speculation which contributed to the stock-market crash of 1929 seven months after he left office.

Farmers did not share in the general prosperity. Farm prices had fallen, and the purchase of farm products by other nations had declined because of a world-wide surplus of agricultural products. Coolidge twice vetoed a bill to permit the government to buy surplus crops and sell them abroad. Coolidge also pocket-vetoed a bill that would have let the government operate the Muscle Shoals power facilities as an electric power project (see MUSCLE SHOALS; VETO).

"Keep Cool with Coolidge." Coolidge had no important rivals for the Republican presidential nomination in 1924. After naming him on the first ballot, the party's national convention chose Charles G. Dawes, Director of the Bureau of the Budget, for Vice-President. The Democrats nominated John W. Davis, former ambassador to Great Britain, for President, and Governor Charles W. Bryan of Nebraska for Vice-President. Dissatisfied members of both parties formed the Progressive party. They nominated Senator Robert M. LaFollette of Wisconsin for President and Senator Burton K. Wheeler of Montana for Vice-President.

Both Democrats and Progressives urged defeat of the Republicans because of the Harding scandals. Republicans replied with the slogan "Keep Cool with Coolidge." Coolidge and Dawes received more than half of the popular votes cast in the election. On March 4, 1925, Chief Justice William Howard Taft became the first former President to administer the presidential oath of office. Coolidge's inaugural address was the first to be broadcast by radio.

--------- COOLIDGE'S ELECTION ---------

Place of Nominating Convention..Cleveland
Ballot on Which Nominated.......1st
Democratic Opponent ....John W. Davis
Electoral Vote...................382 (Coolidge) to
      136 (Davis)
Popular Vote....................15,718,211 (Coolidge)
      to 8,385,283 (Davis)
Age at Second Inauguration......52

Foreign Affairs were marked by two main achievements: the improvement of relations with Mexico and the negotiation of the multilateral Kellogg Pact to outlaw war (see KELLOGG PEACE PACT). Coolidge appointed Dwight W. Morrow as ambassador to Mexico. Morrow settled some old disputes and also obtained valuable concessions from Mexico for American and British owners of oil property.

Although Coolidge opposed joining the League of Nations, he favored membership in the World Court. But the Senate placed what he called "unworthy" conditions on membership, and the President let the matter drop. Earlier, in 1923 and 1924, Dawes had directed an international committee that worked out a plan by which Germany could pay its World War I *reparations* (compensation for damages). See DAWES PLAN.

Life in the White House offered an interesting contrast between the taciturn Coolidge and his gay, charming wife. The difference was particularly noticeable at official receptions.

The President had an interest in many behind-the-scenes details of running the White House. He enjoyed appearing unexpectedly in the kitchen to inspect the iceboxes and to comment on future menus. He once protested mildly because he thought 6 hams were too many for 60 dinner guests. Coolidge also liked to play practical jokes on the staff. He would ring for the elevator, then stride quickly down the stairs, or push all the buttons on his desk just to see all his aides run in at once.

Tragedy struck the Coolidges shortly after his nomination in 1924. Their son Calvin developed a blister on a toe while playing tennis with his brother on the White House courts. The resulting infection spread, and the 16-year-old youth died of blood poisoning. "When he went," Coolidge wrote in his autobiography, "the power and the glory of the presidency went with him." In 1926, the President's father died.

"I Do Not Choose to Run . . ." The Coolidges traveled to the Black Hills of South Dakota for a summer vacation in 1927. On August 2, the day before the fourth anniversary of his presidency, Coolidge called newsmen to his office in the Rapid City high school. He handed each reporter a slip of paper on which appeared the words: "I do not choose to run for President in 1928."

Coolidge's announcement caught the nation by surprise, because he had given no clue as to his plans. Coolidge wrote in his autobiography that "The chances of having wise and faithful public service are increased by a change in the presidential office after a moderate length of time." He also mentioned the "heavy strain" of the presidency, and expressed doubt that Mrs. Coolidge could serve four more years as First Lady "without some danger of impairment of her strength."

Coolidge had a typical response when reporters asked him to comment upon leaving the capital: "Good-by, I have had a very enjoyable time in Washington."

Later Years

The Coolidges returned to Northampton, but the stream of tourists past their home made it impossible to enjoy a quiet life. In 1930, Coolidge bought an estate

815

in Northampton called The Beeches, which had iron gates to keep curious visitors at a distance.

Coolidge published his autobiography in 1929, first in magazine installments, then in book form. The next year he began writing a series of daily newspaper articles called "Thinking Things Over with Calvin Coolidge." He wrote chiefly about government, economics, and politics. He had become a life trustee of Amherst College in 1921, and was named a director of the New York Life Insurance Company in 1929.

The stock-market crash in October, 1929, and the resulting nationwide depression distressed Coolidge, who felt that he might have done more to prevent it. But, following the renomination of Herbert Hoover in 1932, he said that the depression would have occurred regardless of which party had been in power.

Coolidge became increasingly unhappy as the depression deepened during the fall and winter of 1932. On Jan. 5, 1933, Mrs. Coolidge found him lying on the floor of his bedroom, where he had died of a heart attack. He was buried beside his son and father in the Plymouth Notch cemetery.

Mrs. Coolidge sold The Beeches and built another home in Northampton where she lived until her death on July 8, 1957. Coolidge had written: "For almost a quarter of a century she has borne with my infirmities, and I have rejoiced in her graces."

Authoritative works on the life of Calvin Coolidge include *Calvin Coolidge, The Man From Vermont* by Claude M. Fuess, and *A Puritan in Babylon* by William Allen White.   GEORGE H. MAYER

Related Articles in WORLD BOOK include:

Dawes, Charles G.
Harding, Warren G.
Hoover, Herbert
Mellon, Andrew W.
Morrow, Dwight W.

President of the United States
United States, History of
    (Boom and Bust)
Vice-President of the United
    States

Outline

I. **Early Life**
   A. Childhood
   B. Education
II. **Political and Public Activities**
   A. Entry into Politics
   B. As Governor
   C. Vice-President
III. **Coolidge's Administration (1923-1929)**
   A. Cabinet
   B. Corruption in Government
   C. "Constructive Economy"
   D. "Keep Cool with Coolidge"
   E. Foreign Affairs
   F. Life in the White House
   G. "I Do Not Choose to Run . . ."
IV. **Later Years**

Questions

What were some unusual features about Coolidge's inaugurations as President?

What made Governor Coolidge nationally famous?

Why did Coolidge abandon the idea of trying to get the United States into the World Court?

When was the slogan "Keep Cool with Coolidge" used?

Why was Coolidge so popular with the people?

How did the investigations of corruption in government affect Coolidge?

In what ways did Coolidge's outlook on life differ from that of the American people as a whole?

What was Coolidge's most famous statement?

How did Coolidge squelch a woman who had bet that she could get him to chat with her?

What tragedy struck Coolidge during his presidency?

COOLIDGE TUBE, another name for X-ray tube. See X RAYS.

COOLING SYSTEM. See AIR CONDITIONING; AUTOMOBILE (The Cooling System).

COON. See RACCOON.

COON, CARLETON STEVENS (1904-   ), an American anthropologist, became a leading authority on the peoples and cultures of North Africa and the Middle East. He made many expeditions to these areas. His best-known books include *Races of Europe* (1939) and *Story of Man* (1954). Coon taught anthropology at Harvard University from 1939 to 1948, when he became associated with the University Museum, Philadelphia. He was born in Wakefield, Mass.   DAVID B. STOUT

COONEY, BARBARA (1917-   ), an American illustrator, won the Caldecott medal in 1959 for her illustrations in *Chanticleer and the Fox*. Other books she illustrated include *Rocky Summer* (1948), *Kildee House* (1949), *Yours with Love* (1952), and *Snow Birthday* (1955). She also wrote and illustrated *King of Wreck Island* (1941). She was born in Brooklyn, N.Y.

COONHOUND is a dog that has been bred especially for raccoon hunting. It stands from 23 to 27 inches high. It has a highly developed sense of smell, which makes it an ideal dog for trailing raccoons. Only the *black and tan coonhound* is recognized as a pure breed by the American Kennel Club. There also are five other coonhounds, differing chiefly in color. The black and tan's black coat is marked with tan on the head, chest, and legs. See also DOG (color picture: Hounds).   OLGA DAKAN

COOPER. See BARREL.

COOPER, JAMES FENIMORE (1789-1851), is generally considered the first important American novelist. He invented the sea-romance type of adventure story and the story of wilderness flight and pursuit. His best sea stories include *The Pilot* (1823) and *The Red Rover* (1827). *The Leather-Stocking Tales*, which include his five best-known novels, are his best frontier stories. Cooper won fame for rapid-fire narratives and well-defined characters.

Brown Brothers
James Fenimore Cooper

His Works. Cooper's stories are still read in many parts of the world. *The Leather-Stocking Tales* were *The Pioneers* (1823), *The Last of the Mohicans* (1826), *The Prairie* (1827), *The Pathfinder* (1840), and *The Deerslayer* (1841). The hero of these novels, a frontiersman, has various names, including Natty Bumppo, Hawkeye, Deerslayer, or Leather-Stocking. The novels tell the story of Leather-Stocking and his Indian friend Chingachgook, a Mohican chief. *The Deerslayer* describes the hero and his Indian friend as young men on their first warpath. In *The Last of the Mohicans* and *The Pathfinder*, they are famous scouts. *The Pioneers* tells of Chingachgook's death and of Leather-Stocking's journey westward. The hero dies as an old trapper among the Plains Indians in *The Prairie*. The whole series has been called an American epic of the expanding frontier.

Cooper wrote 50 books, including 33 novels, during

his 30-year literary career. In his later years, he wrote many travel books, political works, and a history of the U.S. Navy. He is recognized as one of the most important social critics of his day.

His Life. Cooper was born on Sept. 15, 1789, in Burlington, N.J., into a large Quaker family. In 1790, the family moved to Cooperstown, a village Cooper's father had founded in New York. Cooper grew up as the son of a great landowner, near the frontier of the settlement. The settlers had daily contact with the Indians. Cooper's impressions of this community furnished material for his stories. Lake Otsego at Cooperstown became the setting of two novels.

Cooper entered Yale College but was expelled in his third year for a prank. He went to sea for a time as a cabin boy, then joined the navy. In 1811, he was married, retired from the navy, and settled in Cooperstown.

Cooper liked to read aloud to his family. One day he threw aside the book he was reading and declared, "I could write a better book than that myself." His wife dared him to try. The result was *Precaution* (1820), a novel patterned on the works of Jane Austen and set in England. It sold fairly well, although it was not a very good novel. Cooper then wrote one of his best and most famous works, *The Spy* (1821). This was the story of Harvey Birch, an unsung hero of the Revolutionary War. It was widely translated. ARVID SHULENBERGER

See also LAST OF THE MOHICANS.

COOPER, JOHN SHERMAN (1901-   ), a Kentucky Republican, won election to the United States Senate five times between 1946 and 1966. In 1946, 1952, and 1956, he was elected to fill vacancies caused by Senate resignations or deaths. Cooper was a member of the United Nations General Assembly in 1949, a special consultant to the secretary of state in 1950, and ambassador to India and Nepal in 1955 and 1956. Cooper was born in Somerset, Ky. He served in the Kentucky house of representatives from 1928 to 1930. THOMAS D. CLARK

COOPER, LEROY GORDON, JR. (1927-   ), a United States astronaut, became the first person to make two orbital space flights. He made 21 revolutions of the earth in 1963 and 120 revolutions in 1965. Virgil I. Grissom made two space flights before Cooper did, but Grissom's first flight did not take him into orbit around the earth.

Cooper's first flight, in a Project Mercury spacecraft, lasted 34 hours and 20 minutes. He released a metal ball equipped with flashing lights to test how far away he could sight it. He estimated he could see the lights up to 18 miles away. Cooper also recorded a prayer of thanks.

The Gemini 5 spacecraft that Cooper used for his second flight was the first one to use *fuel cells*. Fuel cells are devices that produce electricity from the chemical reaction between a fuel and oxygen (see FUEL CELL). Cooper made this flight with astronaut Charles Conrad. It lasted almost eight days (190 hours and 55 minutes). Cooper and Conrad proved that astronauts can withstand weightlessness without harm on the trip to the moon.

Cooper was born in Shawnee, Okla., served briefly in the marine corps, then attended the Naval Academy Preparatory School and the University of Hawaii. He received a U.S. Army commission, transferred to the U.S. Air Force, and was graduated from the Air Force Institute of Technology. Later, Cooper became a test pilot. JOHN J. PETERSON

See also ASTRONAUT.

COOPER, PETER (1791-1883), an American inventor, manufacturer, and philanthropist, built the first American steam locomotive to operate on a commercial railroad. He also played an important part in developing the American iron industry. Cooper helped Cyrus Field lay the underseas Atlantic Cable, and founded the

Brown Bros.

Peter Cooper

The *Tom Thumb* was the first steam locomotive to operate commercially in America. Peter Cooper completed it in 1830. He raced it against a horse-drawn car. But *Tom Thumb* lost when a power belt slipped off.

Baltimore and Ohio Railroad

PETER COOPER'S "TOM THUMB" 1829-30 BALTIMORE & OHIO R. R.

Cooper Union for free instruction in art and science.

Cooper began earning a fortune in the 1820's, when he successfully manufactured glue, isinglass, and gelatin. He remained in this business all his life. By 1830, when he built the famous locomotive, "Tom Thumb," he also operated an ironworks in Baltimore (see TOM THUMB). He pioneered in the manufacture and sale of structural iron beams. His son, Edward, and his son-in-law, Abram Hewitt, helped him in this phase of the business. During the 1850's and 1860's, Cooper helped promote telegraph and cable companies.

Throughout his life, Cooper took an active interest in civic affairs. He worked effectively for public education, improved water supplies, and better police and fire protection. In national politics, he was a Democrat and a follower of Andrew Jackson. After the Civil War, he strongly supported political and social reforms. He ran for President when 85 on the Greenback ticket (see GREENBACK PARTY). Cooper published the book *Ideas for a Science of Good Government* (1883).

Cooper was born in New York City, but spent his youth in Peekskill, N.Y. He soon showed a talent for mechanics and invention. Although he had only a limited education, he received a practical training by helping his father in hatmaking, brewing, and other trades. At 17, he was apprenticed to a coachbuilder, and he later worked as a mechanic.   ROBERT H. BREMNER

See also RAILROAD (Race of Tom Thumb).

COOPER UNION. See UNIVERSITIES AND COLLEGES (table).

COOPERATIVE, *koh AHP ur AY tiv*, is a business enterprise, jointly owned by a group of persons and operated without profit for the benefit of the owners.

There are several types of cooperatives. Some are for the purpose of selling goods produced by the members of the organization. These are often called *marketing cooperatives*. Others are for the purpose of buying goods to resell to members, and sometimes to the general public as well. These are called *consumer* or *farmer-purchasing cooperatives*. Still others furnish loans (see CREDIT UNION), provide apartment housing at cost, produce goods, or perform various other services.

Men have worked together to gather crops and to produce goods since earliest times. Some men have claimed that all should share the benefits of their work on an equal basis. Others point out that nearly every time such a scheme has been tried, the workers tend to lose initiative, and to become lazy and dissatisfied. Robert Owen, a British factory owner of the late 1700's and early 1800's, was the first person in modern times to experiment with a business organized for the benefit of workers and consumers. He had little success. In the same period, William King, a British physician, recommended that workers own their machines.

Chief Kinds of Cooperatives

Consumer Cooperatives. The modern consumer-cooperative movement started in Rochdale, England, on Dec. 21, 1844, when 28 poor weavers opened a tiny grocery store on Toad Lane. Each put a pound sterling of their money in a fund to rent the store and purchase flour, sugar, butter, and oatmeal, at wholesale prices. These pioneers in cooperation introduced coopera-

tive business practices which have become known as the Rochdale Principles. These are now followed by all true cooperative organizations. One of the principles is that membership should be open to all. Also, each member shall have only one vote, no matter how many shares he owns. The purpose of this is to insure democratic control. Another principle is that any money earned by the business be given back to the members in the form of a saving. The rules also limit the amount of interest paid on shares of stock. Frequently it is limited to 4 per cent. Trading is on a cash basis.

The Rochdale store grew until its membership totaled over 45,000 and its capital to over half a million pounds. The movement has since spread to other parts of the world. The central cooperative organizations are united in an International Cooperative Alliance.

Marketing Cooperatives grade, process, and sell farm produce for the highest price. Each member contributes money to help finance the association. The cooperative pays returns to the farmer according to the amount of produce he sells through the organization. These cooperatives also offer many services which they can perform more easily than the farmer can. Among them are packing, storing, trucking, advertising, and testing.

Marketing cooperatives generally specialize in the handling of a single product. There are separate cooperatives for wheat, cotton, dairy products, livestock, tobacco, wool, citrus fruits, or poultry.

Cooperatives in the United States

Consumer, marketing, and *service* cooperatives are among the principal types in the United States. New York and Connecticut had "associated or cooperative dairying" as early as 1810. Cooperative cheese factories started in New York in 1850. Similar organizations started in Wisconsin and Illinois in the next 10 years.

The National Grange and Farmers' Alliance promoted cooperatives. By 1890, farmers had about 1,000 cooperatives. The Farmers Educational and Cooperative Union, begun in 1901, and the American Farm Bureau Federation, founded in 1920, have both supported cooperation. Manufacturing cooperatives have been set up, with the workers owning and controlling their factories, but have not been very successful.

For many years small individual groups in the United States have employed cooperative methods for purchasing. Labor and farm organizations, such as the Knights of Labor and the Grange, have at times sponsored cooperative stores. Immigrant groups, particularly the Finns, Swedes, Bohemians, and Slavs, brought their ideas on consumer cooperation and used them.

Growth of Consumer and Farmer-Purchasing Cooperatives. After World War I, many farmers in the United States received low prices for their products and paid high prices for their purchases. This situation resulted in a rapid development of farmer-purchasing cooperatives among farmers. They first purchased feed, seed, and fertilizer from wholesalers and distributed them among themselves. Many farmers found that by owning their warehouses and factories they could get better service at a saving. Some cooperatives began to distribute oil and petroleum products. A number of farmers also started to purchase their groceries and household supplies through consumer cooperatives.

Membership in consumer and farmer purchasing cooperatives is now more than 2,500,000. Their total business amounts to over two billion dollars a year. Consumer cooperatives co-ordinate their work through the Cooperative League, founded in 1916.

Today, farmers purchase about one-fifth of their farm supplies through cooperatives.

At the end of World War II, the 2,500 cooperative stores in the United States supplied merchandise to about half a million families. Over half of these stores specialized in groceries with the uniform "Co-op" label and grading. The labels indicate government grading of the food product according to its quality. Cooperative grocery stores are found in all parts of the United States. They purchase through a central business organization called National Co-operatives, Inc., which also serves cooperatives in Canada.

One of the greatest advances in cooperative purchasing has been in oil. Cooperatives now market 16 per cent of all rural petroleum products. They own more than twenty oil refineries, 1,000 miles of pipelines, and 2,000 oil wells. Over 1,500 cooperative service stations furnish gasoline and oil to about half a million families. Other cooperatives include bookstores, cafeterias, and bakeries.

Growth of Marketing Cooperatives. Two general types of marketing cooperatives exist in the United States. One is the combined, or federated, type. This consists of an association of previously independent cooperatives. The local units own the stock, elect directors, and control the federation. The other type is an association which serves an entire region from one central office. It may operate over a large territory. Each member signs a contract to deliver his produce to his local shipping point. Many of the national federations and regional associations belong to the National Council of Farmer Cooperatives. Its headquarters are in Washington, D.C. It represents 5,000 local cooperative associations and about 2,600,000 patrons.

The federal government encourages marketing cooperatives. The Farmer Cooperative Service of the United States Department of Agriculture also assists them. The Farm Credit Act of 1933 provided for the establishment of twelve Banks for Cooperatives which make loans to these organizations. The Capper-Volstead Act of 1922 made it clear that they did not violate the antitrust laws, and defined their legal basis. But cooperatives are subject to the same trade regulations governing other business organizations, groups, or individuals.

Service Cooperatives. About half a million families have insured their lives and automobiles through cooperatives. Mutual insurance companies have insured property for millions of U.S. families. More than 2 million farms get light and power from cooperative rural electric associations. Cooperative methods are also used in housing, telephone service, banking, medical care, burial associations, loan societies, and camps.

Cooperatives Throughout the World

Scandinavian Cooperatives. Wherever people have been allowed to establish free institutions, cooperatives have appeared. In Sweden, they compete with both the giant privately owned companies and with government control, and hence are often referred to as the "middle way." Their business amounts to about 15 per cent of the total retail trade. They charge low prices and return only small refunds to members. This policy has enabled them to lower the prices of many products. The cooperatives of Finland do about 40 per cent of the total retail business of the country. Almost 90 per cent of the farm marketing is cooperative in Denmark.

Canadian Cooperatives. In Canada, the marketing of wheat takes place through large cooperative wheat pools. They were first organized in 1923 in Alberta as a result of needs which arose during World War I. Farmers made contracts for a period of five years to deliver all their wheat to be sold through the pool. Over one-fourth of the people of Saskatchewan are members of such wheat pools. Farm and household equipment, oil and gasoline, and many other products are sold through cooperatives in Canada. The volume of business through cooperatives expanded in the 1960's.

Cooperatives in Great Britain. About 11 million people belong to cooperatives in Great Britain. Their stores range in size from tiny shops to those with business amounting to a million dollars each month. The local societies are federated into huge regional organizations supplying goods at wholesale. They own factories, farms, plantations, and an ocean-going fleet.   C. MAURICE WIETING

Related Articles in WORLD BOOK include:

Consumer Education	Food (The Food Industry)
Farm Credit Administration	Grange, National
(Banks for Cooperatives)	Housing (Cooperative
Farmer Cooperative Service	Housing)
Farmers Union, National	Owen (family)

COOPERATIVE ALLIANCE, INTERNATIONAL. See COOPERATIVE (Consumer Cooperatives).

COOPERSTOWN, N.Y. (pop. 2,553; alt. 1,290 ft.), is a resort village on Otsego Lake, about 80 miles west of Albany. William Cooper visited the site in 1785 and settled there in 1789. His son, James Fenimore Cooper, set two of his famous *Leatherstocking Tales* in the beautiful country that surrounds Otsego Lake.

Abner Doubleday, an American army officer, laid out a diamond for the game of baseball at Cooperstown in 1839.

Interesting places to visit include the National Baseball Museum and Hall of Fame, the Farmers' Museum, and Fenimore House. See also BASEBALL (History).   WILLIAM E. YOUNG

The Baseball Museum and Hall of Fame at Cooperstown features such items as this painting of Babe Ruth.

Pittsburgh Plate Glass Co.

COORDINATES. See ALGEBRA (Functions).

COOSA RIVER is formed by the junction of the Oostanaula and Etowah rivers near Rome, Ga. The Coosa flows west and south until it joins the Tallapoosa River north of Montgomery, Ala., to form the Alabama River. For location, see ALABAMA (physical map). The river is 300 to 500 feet wide, and drops about 450 feet during its 286-mile course. The Alabama Power Company has built several dams on the river.   J. ALLEN TOWER

COOT

COOT, or MUD HEN, is a dark gray water bird that looks like a duck. The American coot lives in southern Canada, the United States, Mexico, and South America. The European coot is sometimes seen in North America. The name *coot* is also used for about six kinds of wild ducks.

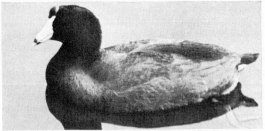

Allan D. Cruickshank

The Coot Is More at Home in Water than on Land.

The coot is from 13 to 16 inches long, and weighs about a pound. Most of its body is dark, with a white patch under the tail. Its large, clumsy feet have lobes or scallops for swimming. The saying *silly as a coot* probably comes from the bird's clumsiness.

Scientific Classification. The American coot belongs to the rail family, *Rallidae*. It is genus *Fulica*, species *F. americana*. The European coot (or mud hen) is classified as *F. atra*. GEORGE J. WALLACE

COOTIES, MILITARY ORDER OF THE. See VETERANS OF FOREIGN WARS OF THE UNITED STATES.

COP. See POLICE (In the United States).

COPAL. See TALLOW TREE.

COPENHAGEN, KOH p'n HAY gun (pop. 872,541; met. area 1,378,460; alt. 45 ft.), is Denmark's capital and largest city. Its official name is København. Old parts of the city lie on the eastern coast of the island of Sjaelland, at the head of a harbor which gave the town its early name of *Købmandehavn* (Merchant's Harbor). Its suburbs now occupy part of the island of Amager,

just east of Sjaelland. The city is as far north as Moscow, but winds blowing across the North Sea make its climate milder.

Appearance. Copenhagen is an old city crowded with new buildings of stone and concrete. It has an airport, factories, railroads, and wide boulevards. Narrow cobblestone streets lined with gabled houses twist through the older sections of the city.

Copenhagen and its suburbs have more than a fourth of Denmark's population. More than half the country's shipping passes through its harbor. Exports include manufactured articles such as lace, needlework, and Copenhagen's famed porcelain and silverware. Fishing boats line the harbor, and live fish are sold in the markets.

Copenhagen has many parks, statues, fountains, and beautiful buildings, some of them dating back to the 1600's. The *Børsen* (Exchange), built in the early 1600's, has a spire shaped like four great dragons whose tails twine up to the peak. Four palaces are set around a great, open square. One of them is the home of the King of Denmark. Nearby is the Marble Church, begun by Frederick V in 1749. Its dome is almost as large as the dome of St. Paul's in London. In the Bispebjerg area is a church built in memory of Nikolai F. S. Grundtvig, a Danish theologian and poet. The University of Copenhagen, founded by Christian I in 1479, is one of the oldest universities in Europe.

History. The history of Copenhagen was the history of Denmark for many years, because the country centered around the town. In 1043, Copenhagen was a fishing village. By the 1100's it had grown into a town because of the trade through its fine natural harbor. In 1416, Copenhagen became the capital of the country. Part of the early wealth of Copenhagen came from duties put upon ships that sailed through the straits between Denmark and Sweden. The city stood firm against an attack by Swedish forces under King Charles X from 1658 to 1659, against an English bombardment in 1807, and against various other enemy attacks. German troops occupied Copenhagen from 1940 to 1945. JENS NYHOLM

See also DENMARK (pictures; map); FREE PORT.

COPEPOD is a small crustacean of the order *Copepoda*. Copepods may live in fresh or sea water. They are part

Authenticated News

Copenhagen's Rådhusplads is a large square in the heart of the city. The city hall, *right*, faces the square. It was opened in 1905.

of the *plankton*, or mass of small organisms that drift near the surface of water. They serve as an important part of the diet of many fish, especially herring.

See also CRUSTACEAN; PLANKTON; ANIMAL (color picture: Animals of the Oceans).

COPERNICUS, *koh PUR nih kus*, **NICOLAUS** (1473-1543), was an astronomer of German and Polish descent. He founded present-day astronomy with his theory that the earth is a moving planet.

In Copernicus' time, astronomers accepted the theory Ptolemy had formulated 1400 years earlier. Ptolemy had said the earth was the center of the universe, and had no motion. He also thought that the observed motion of the heavenly bodies was real motion.

But Copernicus doubted Ptolemy's theory. He believed that the earth hurtles rapidly through space, and that man does not see this motion because he travels with the earth. Copernicus said the motions described by Ptolemy did not occur. What man sees in the heavens is affected by the earth's motion. Real motions in the heavens must be separated from apparent motions.

Copernicus skillfully applied this new idea in his masterpiece, *Concerning the Revolutions of the Celestial Spheres* (1543). In this book, Copernicus demonstrated how the earth's motions could be used to explain the motions of other heavenly bodies. His theory laid the foundations for the telescopic discoveries of Galileo, the planetary laws of Johannes Kepler, and the gravitation principle of Sir Isaac Newton.

Copernicus was born in the city of Thorn (now Toruń, Poland), and attended the University of Kraków. Through the influence of his uncle, a bishop, he was appointed a canon of the cathedral chapter of Frauenburg (now Frombork, Poland). The income from this position supported him for the rest of his life. The chapter gave him permission to continue his education in Italy. Copernicus received a master's degree from the University of Bologna and a doctor's degree from the University of Ferrara. He also studied medicine.

When he returned to Poland, he acted as medical adviser to his uncle and served as canon. He held this office until his death.   EDWARD ROSEN

See also GALILEO; KEPLER, JOHANNES; NEWTON, SIR ISAAC; PTOLEMY.

COPLAND, *COPE lund*, **AARON** (1900-   ), is a leading American composer. Folk themes and tunes influenced much of his music, as in his ballets *Billy the Kid* (1938), *Rodeo* (1942), and *Appalachian Spring* (1944). Copland won the Pulitzer prize for music in 1945 for *Appalachian Spring*. He composed his first opera, *The Second Hurricane* (1936), and an orchestral work, *An Outdoor Overture* (1937), to be performed by school children. His orchestral works include *Symphony No. 3* (1946) and *Concerto* for clarinet and orchestra (1948). Copland also wrote chamber music and piano music, including a piano *Fantasy* (1957). Copland composed several motion-picture scores, including *Our Town* (1940). He also wrote books on music, including *What to Listen for in Music* (1939).

Copland was born in Brooklyn, N.Y., of immigrant Lithuanian parents. He studied music in New York City and Paris. He won two Guggenheim fellowships and many other awards. Copland became influential in encouraging American music, both in the United States and in Europe.   HALSEY STEVENS

COPLEY, JOHN SINGLETON (1738-1815), is generally considered the greatest portrait painter in colonial America. His many superb portraits capture the character of Americans in settings of everyday life. He painted with remarkable directness and vitality, making rich use of color, texture, and light and shade.

Copley was born in Boston, and began his professional career when he was 15. He had few opportunities to study art, but he had great talent and desire and soon developed his stunning style. In 1766, he sent *Boy with a Squirrel* to a London exhibition. The painters Sir Joshua Reynolds and Benjamin West praised this charming portrait and recommended that Copley study in Europe. Copley was having great success in America, so he put off going to London until 1774. He settled there permanently, and his portraits soon took on the brilliant brushwork and rich atmospheric quality characteristic of British painting.

In 1778, Copley began a career as a painter of historical subjects, fulfilling a lifelong ambition. He painted many historical works, but only two of them— *Watson and the Shark* (1778) and *The Death of Lord Chatham* (1781)—were successful. After 1781, Copley's work gradually declined. In old age, he longed to return to America, but remained in London until his death.

In the past, critics praised Copley's straightforward, vivid American portraits and were critical of the lavish portraits and large historical paintings he did in England. Today critics still praise his American works, and they view his English works with less disfavor than in the past.   EDWARD H. DWIGHT

See also HANCOCK, JOHN (picture).

John S. Copley's painting of Pennsylvania Governor and Mrs. Thomas Mifflin shows the style of colonial portraiture.

The Historical Society of Pennsylvania

COPPER

COPPER (chemical symbol, Cu) has been one of man's most useful metals for more than 5,000 years. Today, the uses of this reddish-orange metal range from rain gutters for houses to electronic guidance systems for space rockets.

Copper is the best low-cost conductor of electricity. As a result, the electrical industry uses about half the copper produced, chiefly in the form of wire. Copper wire carries most of the electric current for homes, factories, and offices. Large amounts of copper wire are used in telephone and telegraph systems, as well as in television sets, motors, generators, and other kinds of electrical equipment and machinery.

Combined with other metals, copper forms such alloys as brass and bronze (see BRASS; BRONZE). Copper and its alloys can be made into thousands of useful and ornamental articles. In the home, copper serves as the basic material for lighting fixtures, locks, pipe, plumbing fixtures, doorknobs, drawer pulls, candlesticks, and clocks. Other commonly used copper products include lamps, mailboxes, pots, pans, and jewelry. And perhaps the most familiar copper objects are the pennies that jingle in our pockets and purses.

Chemical compounds of copper help improve soil and destroy harmful insects. Copper compounds in paint help protect materials against corrosion from weather. Also, copper in small amounts is vital to all plant and animal life.

In ancient times, the chief source of copper for the peoples near the Mediterranean Sea was the island of Cyprus. As a result, the metal became known as *Cyprian metal*. Both the word *copper* and the chemical symbol for the element, *Cu*, come from *cuprum*, the Roman name for Cyprian metal.

Properties of Copper

The physical characteristics of copper make it a valuable industrial material. These include (1) conductivity, (2) malleability, (3) ductility, and (4) resistance to corrosion.

Conductivity. Copper is perhaps best known for its ability to conduct electricity. Silver is the only better conductor, but silver is too expensive for common use. Copper alloys do not conduct electricity nearly as well as pure copper. Impurities in refined copper also greatly reduce electrical conductivity. For example, as little as $\frac{5}{100}$ per cent arsenic cuts the conductivity of copper by 15 per cent. Copper is also an excellent conductor of heat. This property makes it useful in cooking utensils, radiators, and refrigerators.

Malleability. Pure copper is highly *malleable* (easy to shape). It does not crack when hammered, stamped, forged, die-pressed, or spun into unusual shapes. Copper can be *worked* (shaped) either hot or cold. It can be rolled into sheets less than $\frac{1}{500}$ of an inch thick. Cold rolling changes the physical properties of copper and increases its strength.

Ductility. Copper possesses great *ductility*, the ability to be drawn into thin wires without breaking. A copper bar 4 inches square can be heated, rolled, and

Frank R. Milliken, the contributor of this article, is executive vice-president, Kennecott Copper Corporation.

drawn into a round wire thinner than a human hair. Such a wire would be more than 20 million times longer than the bar used to make it.

Resistance to Corrosion. Copper is quite resistant to corrosion. It will not rust. In damp air, copper turns from a reddish-orange to a reddish-brown color. After long exposure, copper becomes coated with a green film called *patina*. The patina protects the copper against further corrosion.

Other Properties. Copper has an atomic number of 29, and an atomic weight of 63.54. It melts at 1083° C. ($\pm$ 0.1° C.), and boils at 2595° C. Copper has a density of about 560 pounds per cubic foot and a specific gravity of 8.92 (see DENSITY; GRAVITY, SPECIFIC). It is about 14 per cent heavier than iron. Cold-rolled copper has a tensile strength between 50,000 and 70,000 pounds per square inch (see STRENGTH OF MATERIALS). Copper keeps its strength and toughness up to a temperature of about 400° F.

Copper Ores

Most copper comes from about seven kinds of ores. These ores also may contain other metals, such as lead, zinc, gold, cobalt, platinum, and nickel. Copper ores usually contain less than 4 per cent copper. Five tons of ore may yield as little as 20 pounds of copper.

The chief copper ores are *sulfides* (sulfur compounds). They include bornite; chalcocite, or copper glance; and chalcopyrite, or copper pyrites. *Oxidized ores*, such as azurite, cuprite, and malachite, also yield valuable amounts of copper. Almost pure copper, called *native* copper, rarely occurs in nature. Native copper supplies only a small percentage of the world's total copper production, however.

Sources of Copper

Over $5\frac{3}{4}$ million tons of copper are mined each year throughout the world. Copper deposits have been found in every continent. But about half the world's copper comes from the large mountain ranges extending from Alaska to the tip of South America.

In some places, miners dig copper ore from mines far below the earth's surface. Elsewhere, they remove it from great open pits at the surface. In *open-pit* mining, large power shovels or other machines remove the ore from wide "steps" that measure 40 to 70 feet high. Most copper in the United States comes from open pits. See MINING (Kinds of Mining); UTAH (picture: Bingham Canyon Copper Mine).

The United States mines about a fourth of the world's copper. But it uses more copper than it mines, and imports large amounts, chiefly from Chile. About half the copper mined in the United States comes from Arizona. The Keweenaw Peninsula in Michigan is one of the few remaining sources of native copper.

Canada mines about 9 per cent of the world's copper. Most of it comes from Ontario and Quebec. The Sudbury district in Ontario has the largest deposits in Canada. British Columbia, Manitoba, and Saskatchewan also produce important amounts.

Other Areas. Russia, Chile, and Zambia are the largest copper producers after the United States. Each accounts for over 10 per cent of the world's supply. Russia does not publish production figures. Its rank as the second largest copper producer is based on estimates.

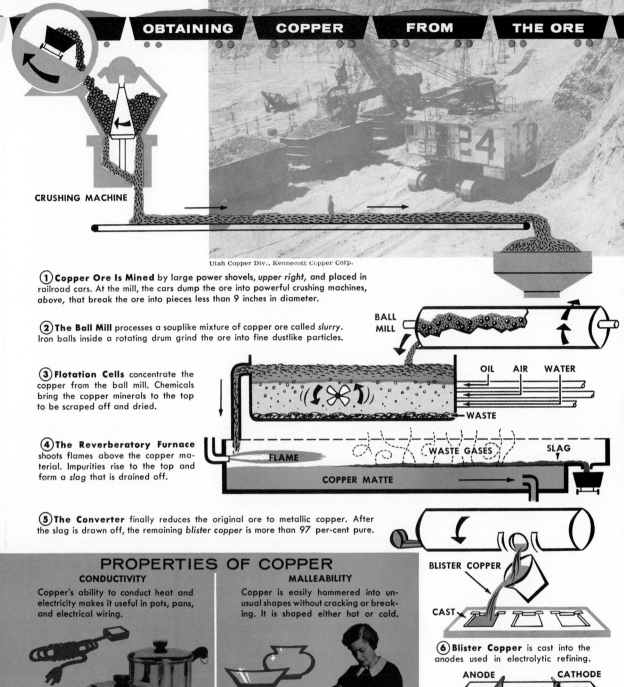

CRUSHING MACHINE

Utah Copper Div., Kennecott Copper Corp.

① Copper Ore Is Mined by large power shovels, *upper right,* and placed in railroad cars. At the mill, the cars dump the ore into powerful crushing machines, *above,* that break the ore into pieces less than 9 inches in diameter.

② The Ball Mill processes a souplike mixture of copper ore called *slurry.* Iron balls inside a rotating drum grind the ore into fine dustlike particles.

BALL MILL

③ Flotation Cells concentrate the copper from the ball mill. Chemicals bring the copper minerals to the top to be scraped off and dried.

OIL   AIR   WATER

WASTE

④ The Reverberatory Furnace shoots flames above the copper material. Impurities rise to the top and form a *slag* that is drained off.

FLAME   WASTE GASES   SLAG

COPPER MATTE

⑤ The Converter finally reduces the original ore to metallic copper. After the slag is drawn off, the remaining *blister* copper is more than 97 per-cent pure.

BLISTER COPPER

CAST

PROPERTIES OF COPPER

CONDUCTIVITY

Copper's ability to conduct heat and electricity makes it useful in pots, pans, and electrical wiring.

Revere Copper and Brass Inc.

MALLEABILITY

Copper is easily hammered into unusual shapes without cracking or breaking. It is shaped either hot or cold.

Copper & Brass Research Assn.

⑥ Blister Copper is cast into the anodes used in electrolytic refining.

ANODE   CATHODE

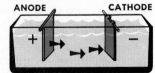

+   −

⑦ Electrolytic Refining produces 99.9 per-cent pure copper. An electric current causes the copper on the anodes to deposit on the cathodes.

99.9% PURE COPPER

DUCTILITY

Copper is drawn into thin wires and rods that withstand great stresses without breaking or becoming weaker.

RESISTANCE TO CORROSION

Copper is ideal for materials that touch water, such as downspouts, because the metal does not rust.

LEADING COPPER MINING STATES AND PROVINCES
Tons of copper mined in 1966

Arizona 740,000 tons	🚃🚃🚃🚃🚃🚃🚃🚃🚃🚃🚃
Utah 265,000 tons	🚃🚃🚃🚃
Ontario 209,000 tons	🚃🚃🚃🚃
Quebec 173,000 tons	🚃🚃🚃
Montana 128,000 tons	🚃🚃🚃
New Mexico 109,000 tons	🚃🚃
Nevada 79,000 tons	🚃🚃
Michigan 73,000 tons	🚃🚃
British Columbia 58,000 tons	🚃
Manitoba 31,000 tons	🚃

Sources: U.S. Bureau of Mines; Dominion Bureau of Statistics.

LEADING COPPER MINING COUNTRIES
Tons of copper mined in 1966

United States 1,429,000 tons	🚃🚃🚃🚃🚃🚃🚃🚃🚃🚃🚃🚃
Russia 880,000 tons	🚃🚃🚃🚃🚃🚃🚃
Chile 724,000 tons	🚃🚃🚃🚃🚃🚃
Zambia 687,000 tons	🚃🚃🚃🚃🚃🚃
Canada 510,000 tons	🚃🚃🚃🚃
Congo (Kinshasa) 348,000 tons	🚃🚃🚃
Peru 194,000 tons	🚃🚃
South Africa 137,000 tons	🚃🚃
Japan 123,000 tons	🚃🚃
Australia 117,000 tons	🚃🚃

Source: U.S. Bureau of Mines.

Russian copper deposits lie chiefly in the Ural and Caucasus mountains and in the state of Kazakhstan. Congo (Kinshasa) and other parts of Africa also have large deposits of copper. Important copper deposits also occur in Australia, China (mainland), Japan, Mexico, Peru, the Philippines, and South Africa.

Obtaining Copper from the Ore

At the mine, large power shovels load the ore, often in the form of big boulders, into railroad cars or into trucks. These vehicles carry the ore to nearby mills and smelters.

All ores do not go through exactly the same processes. There are variations, depending on the type of ore. But all the processes are designed to separate valuable minerals from the ore and waste rock, to extract copper and any other metals that may be present in the resulting mixture, and to purify the metals that are produced.

In a typical process, the ore is sent to the mill, where it is crushed and the waste rock removed. The resulting material is then sent to the smelter, where the metallic copper is removed. This copper may contain other metals, such as gold, silver, and nickel, that must be removed by refining.

Milling starts in a *concentrator*, where the crushed ore is ground into fine particles. Then water is added to the crushed ore to form a souplike mixture called *slurry*. The slurry passes into *ball mills*, which are rotating, drum-shaped cylinders half-filled with iron balls. As the cylinders rotate, the balls grind the ore into particles small enough to pass through a screen with 10,000 openings to the square inch.

The slurry next goes through a *flotation process* that concentrates the mineral-bearing particles. The slurry first passes into containers called *flotation cells*. There, chemicals and oil are added, and the entire mixture is agitated by paddles or air jets to make it bubble. One chemical makes the bubbles stable. Another chemical coats the mineral particles so that they stick to the bubbles. The bubbles rise to the top of the cell with the mineral particles and form a froth. This froth is scraped off and dried. The product is now called *copper concentrate*, and may contain from 15 to 33 per cent copper. The waste material, called *tailings*, does not become attached to the bubbles, and is emptied from the lower part of the flotation cell.

Leaching is used to recover copper from ores that do not react to the chemicals used in the flotation process. In leaching, water containing sulfuric acid or other chemicals circulates through the ore and dissolves the copper. The copper-bearing solution then passes through troughs containing pieces of iron. Some of the iron dissolves, and replaces the copper in the solution. The copper is deposited on the remaining pieces of iron. From time to time, the pieces of iron are agitated and washed to remove the copper, and more iron is added as needed. Copper obtained by leaching is called *precipitate copper*, and is from 60 to 90 per cent pure. Such copper is usually smelted and refined. But it is sometimes sold for use without further refining.

Smelting removes most of the remaining impurities from the copper. In smelting, copper concentrate (sometimes precipitate copper is added) first goes through a *reverberatory furnace*. Such a furnace may process as much as 350 tons of copper concentrate at one time. A firebox at one end of the furnace shoots flames over the concentrate, changing it into a bubbling mass. The heat helps drive off some impurities in the form of gas. Other impurities rise to the top of the molten mass to form *slag*, which consists mostly of iron, lime, and silica. The slag is skimmed off and discarded. The new mixture, called *copper matte*, contains from 25 to 50 per cent copper. It still has impurities in the form of iron sulfide and other metals.

The copper matte next goes through a *converter*. In

the converter, blowers force air through the molten copper matte, and silica is added. The silica combines with the impurities, forming slag. The slag is again skimmed from the top. The new mixture is called *blister copper*, because the surface swells into blisters as the copper cools. Blister copper is from 97 to 99.5 per cent pure.

When blister copper does not contain significant amounts of gold or silver, it may be refined in a *fire-refining furnace*. This furnace removes most of the remaining impurities, mainly oxygen. In a process called *poling*, workers force green pine logs into the *melt* (furnace load) of molten copper. The logs create a blazing, bubbling turmoil in the hot copper. As the logs burn, oxygen and other gases are removed from the copper. The resulting copper is 99.9 per cent pure.

Electrolytic Refining. Copper to be used in electrical conductors must be electrolytically refined to a purity of more than 99.9 per cent. To do this, blister copper is cast into cakes about 3 feet square and 3 inches thick. The cakes serve as *anodes* (positive poles) in the electrolytic process. For a discussion of the chemical principles involved in this process, see ELECTROLYSIS.

The copper anodes are put into tanks containing a solution of copper sulfate and sulfuric acid. They are suspended alternately with *cathodes* (negative poles) which are thin sheets of pure copper called *starter sheets*. When an electric current passes through the tank, the anode bars gradually dissolve, depositing copper more than 99.9 per cent pure on the cathodes. Most of the remaining impurities in the anodes settle to the bottom of the tank and form a *sludge*. Processors use various methods to recover small amounts of gold, silver, platinum, and other metals from the sludge. After electrolysis, the copper cathodes are usually melted in an electric furnace, and cast into various shapes and sizes, such as bars, cakes, ingots, and billets.

Making Copper Products

Fabricating plants, such as brass and wire mills, make semifinished forms including sheets, tubes, wires, and rods. They make these forms from copper bars, cakes, ingots, and billets. Manufacturers of copper products buy the semifinished forms from these plants.

Copper Sheets are rolled from copper cakes that measure about 25 inches wide, 8 inches thick, and up to 72 inches long. The cakes are heated in a furnace to about 1700°F., then rolled on a hot mill into sheets about $\frac{1}{2}$ inch thick. Other mills finish the sheets by rolling them to exact thicknesses. The sheets are then cut into pieces of the required size to make such products as roofing sheets, cooking utensils, and photoengraving plates (see ENGRAVING).

Copper Tubes are made from copper billets that vary in diameter from 3 to 9 inches and are up to 52 inches long. Workers heat the billets in a furnace, then pierce them to produce a rough pipe. The pipe shells thus formed are forced through dies and over other devices to produce tubes of the required size. Manufacturers use the tubes to make plumbing pipes, household gas lines, and electrical conduits.

Copper Wire is made from copper bars that measure about 54 inches long and 4 inches square. After being heated in a furnace, the bars are rolled on a mill to form rods about $\frac{1}{4}$ inch thick. The rods are then pulled through the dies of wire-drawing machines. These dies reduce the rods to the desired wire sizes. Most copper wire is used to carry electric current.

Extruded Copper. Some copper is *extruded* (squeezed) through a hole in a die to form the desired shape. Copper can be extruded into rods, tubes, and other special shapes. These are made into hinges, door pulls, and other pieces of hardware.

History

Copper was one of the first metals known to man. It came into use because early peoples found it in native condition and could easily beat it into tools, weapons, and ornaments.

Early Civilizations. Copper was probably first used about 8000 B.C. by people living along the Tigris and Euphrates rivers, where Iraq lies today. As early as 6000 B.C., the Egyptians knew how to hammer native copper into sheets to make tools and ornaments. Copper was later used by many peoples, including the Chinese, the Inca of Peru, and the American Indians.

About 3800 B.C., men discovered how to melt and alloy copper with tin to make bronze. About 3500 B.C., they learned to smelt copper from ore. From about 3000 B.C. to about 1100 B.C., bronze became important (see BRONZE AGE). Much later, the Romans used swords made of bronze in their conquests. The process of combining zinc with copper to make brass was probably discovered sometime between 1000 B.C. and 600 B.C.

Industrial Developments. From early times until the A.D. 1800's, ample high-grade ore was available, and methods for processing and using copper changed only slightly. By the late 1800's, the rapid growth of electric lighting and telephone and telegraph systems had greatly increased the demand for copper, which dwindling deposits of high-grade ore could not meet. Also, most native copper deposits had been used up.

Geologists had located large ore deposits in the United States and Chile. But the copper content of the ore was so low that the ore could not be processed at a profit. About 1900, a young American mining engineer, Daniel C. Jackling, realized that low-grade ores could be processed cheaply by using mass-production methods. His process involved the use of steam shovels to strip off surface rock. Other special mass-production equipment was used for smelting and refining. New techniques for separating copper from the ore also increased the supply of available copper.

The Kennecott Copper Corporation is the leading copper producing company in the United States. The leading Canadian company is the International Nickel Company, Incorporated.   FRANK R. MILLIKEN

COPPER GLANCE. See CHALCOCITE.

COPPER PYRITES. See COPPER (Copper Ores).

COPPERHEAD is a poisonous American snake, one of the pit vipers. It is also known as the *pilot snake* and *rattlesnake pilot*. Its body has broad chestnut-red bands between coppery red ones. Most copperheads are about $2\frac{1}{2}$ feet long. The largest grow to about 4 feet.

The copperhead bites people more often than the banded and diamondback rattlesnakes, because it is silent and smaller, and is not so quickly noticed. The bite is seldom fatal to adults, but can seriously poison children who weigh less than 75 pounds. This reptile eats mostly rodents and other small mammals. Sometimes it eats insects and frogs. It usually bears from three to seven young in August or September.

The copperhead lives south of a line from the northeastern tip of Massachusetts through Pittsburgh to the southeastern corner of Nebraska. From there the line passes southwest to the upper Rio Grande in Texas, and then just misses New Mexico. In this area any snake is likely to be called a copperhead if its markings resemble one. But the copperhead can be told from other kinds of snakes in a number of ways. It has no rattle on the tip of its tail. It has a pit in front of and below each eye. The snake's nostril is in front of the pit.

Scientific Classification. The copperhead belongs to the pit viper family, *Crotalidae*. It is genus *Agkistrodon*, species *A. mokasen*. CLIFFORD H. POPE

See also SNAKE (color picture); VIPER.

COPPERHEAD was a name given to Northern Peace Democrats who criticized President Abraham Lincoln's Administration during the Civil War. Loyal Unionists claimed the Copperheads were pro-Southern and reminded them of the poisonous snakes with the copper-colored heads. Copperheads cut the head of Liberty from the copper cent and wore it as a badge.

Copperheads opposed Lincoln's attempts to free the slaves in the South. They spoke out against political arrests and the military draft and favored compromise with the Confederate States to end the war. The movement reached its peak early in 1863. But Union military victories and Republican election victories in 1864 helped to end the Copperhead movement. FRANK L. KLEMENT

See also SONS OF LIBERTY; SEYMOUR, HORATIO; VALLANDIGHAM, CLEMENT L.

COPPIN STATE COLLEGE. See UNIVERSITIES AND COLLEGES (table).

COPRA, *KAHP ruh,* is the dried meat of the coconut. Copra is valuable for its oil, used in the manufacture of soap, candles, and other articles. Copra is one of the main exports of islands in the Pacific. The oil is pressed out after the copra has been dried in the sun, in ovens called *kilns,* or by the use of hot air. The remaining cake, called *coconut-stearin,* is used, like cottonseed-oil cake, for fodder and manure. Copra yields from 50 to 65 per cent of its weight in oil when dried. Hot-air drying sometimes makes copra produce as much as 75 per cent of its weight in oil. Thirty average coconuts produce about a gallon of oil. See also COCONUT PALM. C. L. MANTELL

COPTS, *kahpts,* are members of the Coptic Orthodox Church. The name *Copt* is taken from the Greek word *Aegyptios,* meaning *Egyptians.* The Copts are descended from ancient Egyptians who were converted to Christi-

Spaa, Pix

Monks of the Coptic Church worship daily in their ceremonial robes. Usually, they hold a cross and read from the Coptic Bible.

anity in the A.D. 100's and 200's. The converts developed their own Coptic language. It combined the Greek alphabet with Egyptian vocabulary and symbols. They used the language in religious writings and translations of the Bible. A dialect of this language is still used in the church liturgy, although Arabic is the dominant language spoken today. The Copts originated monasticism, which later spread to other churches.

At first, the *patriarchate* (ruling division) of Alexandria was one of the most powerful in Christendom. But disputes concerning the nature of Christ led to a split between Rome and Alexandria. The Egyptian church adopted a *monophysite doctrine* that asserted the single nature of Christ. In 451, the Council of Chalcedon condemned this doctrine as heresy. The Coptic Church broke away from Rome and Constantinople, and has remained independent under the patriarch of Alexandria. When the Moslems conquered Egypt in 642, many Copts were converted to Islam. Today, about 3,500,000 Ethiopians belong to the Coptic Orthodox Church. About 1,200,000 Egyptians are members. An ancient Coptic community also exists in Jerusalem. KEITH C. SEELE

COPYHOLD. See VILLEIN.

COPYING MACHINE. See DUPLICATOR; PHOTOGRAPHIC COPYING; PRINTING (Electrostatic Printing).

COPYREADER. See JOURNALISM (Journalists at Work).

COPYRIGHT is the legal right an author has to protect his writings against copying. It also extends to dramatic, musical, and artistic works. In the United States, *copyright* usually means *statutory copyright,* a grant of rights by Congress as set forth in the United States Copyright Law. It also means a recognized right not specified in the Copyright Law. This right is called *common-law copyright.* Generally, common-law copyright is in effect before a work is published, and statutory copyright becomes effective after it is published.

Common-Law Copyright. Prior to publication, an author has the sole right to decide what shall be done with his work. No one may publish it without his permission, unless he sells a copy of his manuscript without restriction or makes his work public without qualifying for statutory copyright. Common-law copyright ends when statutory copyright begins.

Statutory Copyright. Many copyright laws have been enacted in the United States since the first Federal Copyright Act of 1790. The present copyright law was enacted in 1909, *codified* (systematized) in 1947, and later amended. It grants statutory copyrights for 28 years and allows owners to extend the copyright for another 28 years. An applicant must state to which of the following classes the work belongs:

(a) Books, including composite and encyclopedic works, directories, gazetteers, and other compilations.

(b) Periodicals, including newspapers.

(c) Lectures, sermons, addresses for oral delivery.

(d) Dramatic compositions or musical dramas.

(e) Musical compositions.

(f) Maps.

(g) Works of art or models or designs for works of art.

(h) Reproductions of a work of art.

(i) Drawings or plastic works of a scientific or technical character.

(j) Photographs.

(k) Prints and pictorial illustrations, including prints or labels used for articles of merchandise.

(l) Motion-picture photoplays.

(m) Motion pictures other than photoplays.

Other Privileges. A statutory copyright carries with it the right to print, reprint, publish, copy, sell, and, in some instances, to perform and record the copyrighted work. If it is a literary work, the owner may translate it into other languages or dialects, or make any other version of it. The copyright owner also has the right to arrange or adapt it, if it is a musical composition, and to complete, execute, or finish it, if it is a model or design for a work of art.

The copyright owner of works in classes (a), (c), and (e) has the sole right to read or perform the work publicly for profit. The copyright owner of items in class (d) controls both profit and nonprofit performances.

How to Obtain a Statutory Copyright. The Copyright Office does not grant statutory copyrights. It merely registers claims.

For Works Reproduced in Copies for Sale or Public Distribution. First, publish the work with the notice of copyright. This should consist of either the word "Copyright," the abbreviation "Copr.," or the symbol ©, accompanied by the name of the copyright owner. If the work is a printed literary, musical, or dramatic work, the notice should include the year in which the copyright was secured by publication. For example, "Copyright 1960 by John Doe." On copies of works specified in classes (f) through (k), the notice may consist of the symbol © accompanied by the initials, monogram, mark, or symbol of the copyright owner. His name must also appear somewhere on these copies. In a book or other printed publication, the notice of copyright should appear on the title page or the page immediately following. In a periodical, the notice should be on the title page or the first text page of each separate issue, or under the title heading. In a musical work, the notice should appear on the title page or first page.

Second, promptly after publication, send two copies of the best edition of the work to the Copyright Office, with application and fee for registration. In the case of contributions to periodicals, send one complete copy of the periodical containing the contribution.

For Works Not Reproduced in Copies for Sale or Public Distribution. Send an application and fee for registration to the Copyright Office with one of the following:

One manuscript or typewritten copy, in the case of dramatic or musical compositions or of lectures or other works prepared for oral delivery.

One print in the case of photographs.

One photograph or other identifying reproduction in the case of works of art (such as paintings, drawings, or sculptures), models or designs for works of art, or scientific or technical drawings or plastic work.

A title, description, and one print from each scene or act in the case of motion-picture photoplays.

A title and description, with not less than two prints taken from different sections, in the case of motion pictures other than photoplays.

If the works are later reproduced for publication, the author should send two complete copies of the best edition to the Copyright Office, accompanied by an application and fee for registration.

Fees. The fee set by law for registration of any work is $6. Renewal of any copyright costs $4. Checks or money orders should be made payable to the Register of Copyrights. Forms and specific instructions can be obtained from the Copyright Office, Library of Congress, Washington, D.C. 20540.

International Copyright. The United States and 51 other countries are parties to the Universal Copyright Convention signed at Geneva, Switzerland, in 1952. A person may obtain copyright protection in every country that has agreed to the convention by publishing his work first in one of the countries (or anywhere in the world if he is a citizen of one of the countries) with the prescribed notice. This notice should consist of the symbol © with the name of the copyright owner and the year of first publication. Each country is then bound to protect the work according to its own laws. The United States maintains reciprocal copyright relations with many countries that have not signed the Universal Copyright Convention. U.S. citizens who want copyright protection for their works in one of these countries must comply with its copyright laws and regulations.

Many European countries are members of the Bern Union, the *Union Internationale pour la Protection des Oeuvres Littéraires et Artistiques*. It has headquarters in Bern (Berne), Switzerland. Any country in the Union grants citizens of any other member country the same rights it gives its own citizens. An author who lives in some other country may obtain these rights by publishing his work first, or at the same time, in a member country.

The United States has joined with several American republics in copyright conventions to protect literary property in the Western Hemisphere. The most important of these conventions now in effect was signed at Buenos Aires in 1910. The most recent Inter-American Copyright Convention was signed at Washington, D.C., in 1946.   RICHARD FERGUSON

See also PATENT; TRADEMARK.

COQUELIN, BENOÎT CONSTANT

COQUELIN, *kawk LAN,* **BENOÎT CONSTANT** (1841-1909), a French actor, became famous as the original Cyrano in Edmond Rostand's romantic drama, *Cyrano de Bergerac.* Coquelin also was a leading spokesman for the technical approach to acting. He scored his first great acting success in 1861 in Pierre de Beaumarchais' comedy, *The Marriage of Figaro.* Coquelin was born in Paris.   CLIFFORD E. HAMAR

COQUINA. See LIMESTONE.

CORACLE, *CAWR uh k'l,* is an oval-shaped, basket-like boat. Its frame is made of narrow strips of wood that are covered with canvas or tarred cloth. Coracles are used on the inland waters of Wales and Ireland. The Sioux bull-boat and the *kufa* of Iraq resemble the coracle (see IRAQ [picture: Round Kufas]).   ROBERT H. BURGESS

CORAL, *KOHR al,* is a limestone formation formed in the sea by millions of tiny animals. Coral formations may look like branching trees, large domes, small irregular crusts, or even like tiny organ pipes. The living coral-forming animals color the formation in beautiful shades of tan, orange, yellow, purple, and green. When the animals die, they leave limestone "skeletons" that form the foundations of barriers and ridges in the sea called *coral reefs.*

Coral reefs look like lovely sea gardens, because many colorful sea animals live among the corals. These animals include fishes, starfish, mollusks, and sea anemones. Sometimes coral masses build up until they rise above the water to form *coral islands.* The grinding, battering sea helps to build coral islands. It breaks up the coral growths and piles them up. Often, soil lodges on the coral and vegetation begins to grow. Many Pacific islands were formed this way.

Coral Reefs are found mostly in warm and tropical seas, because the coral-forming animals cannot live in water colder than 65° F. Reefs abound throughout the South Pacific, in the East Indies and the Indian Ocean to Ceylon, and around Madagascar on the southeastern African coast. They also form along the tropical eastern coast of Brazil, through the West Indies, along the Florida coast, in the Bahamas, and at Bermuda. There are three types of coral reefs: (1) fringing reefs; (2) barrier reefs; and (3) atolls.

Fringing reefs are submerged platforms of living coral animals that extend from the shore into the sea.

Barrier reefs follow the shoreline, but are separated from it by water. They form a barrier between the water near the shore and the open sea. A barrier reef may consist of a long series of reefs separated by channels of open water. Such reefs usually surround volcanic islands of the South Pacific. The Great Barrier Reef of Australia, more than 1,250 miles long, is the most magnificent coral reef in the world.

An *atoll* is a ring-shaped coral island in the open sea. It forms when coral builds up on a submerged mudbank or on the rim of the crater of a sunken volcano. The atoll surrounds a body of water called a *lagoon.* One or more channels connect the lagoon to the open sea. Many coral islands of the South Pacific are atolls.

Coral reefs do not develop on the East Coast of North America north of Florida and Bermuda. But small patches of coral grow as far north as New England. Certain corals grow as far north as the Arctic Circle.

How Coral Is Formed. The animals that form coral belong to the same animal group as the hydras, jellyfish, and sea anemones. Most individual coral animals, called *polyps,* are only a fraction of an inch in size. A small percentage of them are as much as a foot in diameter. A coral polyp has a cylinder-shaped body. At one end is a mouth surrounded by tiny *tentacles.* The other end attaches to hard surfaces on the sea bottom.

Most coral polyps live together in colonies. The *stony corals* attach themselves to each other with a flat sheet of tissue that connects to the middle of each body. Half of the coral polyp extends above the sheet and half below. Coral polyps build their limestone skeletons by taking calcium out of the seawater. Then they deposit *calcium carbonate* (limestone) around the lower half of the body. As new polyps grow, the limestone formation becomes larger and larger.

Coral polyps reproduce either from eggs or by *budding.* Small, knoblike growths called *buds* appear on the body of an adult polyp, or on the connecting sheet, from time to time. These buds grow larger, separate from the parent, and begin to deposit their own limestone in the colony. Budding helps the colony increase its size. New colonies form when the adult polyps of an old colony produce eggs. The eggs grow into tiny forms that swim away. Then the developing animals settle to the sea bottom and begin to form new colonies by budding.

Precious and Gorgonian Corals. Other kinds of coral, in addition to stony corals, are found in the world's oceans. These corals are also colonies of polyps, but the skeletons they form are internal rather than external. *Precious* coral is a *species* (kind) valued for jewelry. It has a hard *core* (internal skeleton) that can be polished. Polishing brings out beautiful red, rose, or pink colors. Craftsmen carve the coral into beads and other ornaments. Precious coral grows in bushlike formations in the Mediterranean Sea and the Sea of Japan.

The *gorgonian* corals have internal skeletons of a flexible, horny substance. These corals look like bushes, fans, or whips. They may be soft yellow, rose, purple, brown, tan, or black. In clear West Indian waters, they look like sea gardens as they wave back and forth on the reefs.

Scientific Classification. Corals are in the phylum *Coelenterata* and the class *Anthozoa.*   ROBERT D. BARNES

Related Articles in WORLD BOOK include:

Atoll	Barbados	Limestone
Australia (color	Bermuda	Polyp
picture: Col-	Gem (color picture)	Sea Fan
orful Coral	Great Barrier Reef	
Formations)		

CORAL SEA is the part of the Pacific Ocean between the northeast coast of Australia, the Solomon Islands, and the New Hebrides Islands. It has an unusually large number of coral atolls and bank reefs. The boundaries of this sea are so indefinite that the name could be applied to large parts of the Southern Pacific. The reefs along the western shores of the Coral Sea have the finest specimens of coral (see CORAL).

United States and Japanese naval forces fought a key World War II battle in the Coral Sea. Neither side won a clear-cut victory, but the Japanese offensive was checked for the first time in the war.   F. G. WALTON SMITH

See also PACIFIC ISLANDS (color map).

Living Rose Coral, *left,* stretches out its tentacles in search of food. When corals die, they leave behind their rigid, protective shells, *below.*

Robert C. Hermes

Visual Education Service

Reef-building Corals Grow in Warm Seas.

Visual Education Service

Fan Coral Has the Daintiness of Lace.

Lynwood M. Chace

Mushroom Coral Is Produced by One Large Polyp.

Ralph Buchsbaum

Brain Coral Has Its Polyps Arranged in Rows.

CORAL SNAKE

CORAL SNAKE is the name given to several closely related poisonous snakes of the Western Hemisphere. They are found in the southern United States, Mexico, Central America, and tropical South America. Coral snakes have small, blunt heads and bodies.

Coral snakes are poisonous. They do not strike as most other snakes do, but they bite. They are dangerous if stepped on or handled. They are snake-eaters.

The *South American* coral snake is about 4 feet long. It is common in tropical South America. Its body is made up of circles of bright red separated by rings of dark purple. There are two narrow circles of light yellow in each of the purple ones. The scales are shiny and polished. This snake has a red snout. Behind the snout are a black band and a broad red band.

The *eastern* coral snake, or *harlequin*, generally ranges from 20 to 40 inches in length. It lives in the southeastern United States and in extreme northeastern Mexico. Its body is encircled by broad black and red bands separated by narrow yellow ones. The snake has a black snout. Just behind the snout is a wide yellow band followed by a black band. Some of these coral snakes are covered with black spots that hide much of the red color. Some nonpoisonous snakes look like coral snakes because they have similar coloring. But coral snakes have red and yellow bands next to each other. The harmless snakes have red and black bands together.

The *western*, or *Arizona*, coral snake is about 18 inches long. It lives in the lower parts of southern Arizona, in southwestern New Mexico, and in northern Mexico. It also has a black snout. Behind the snout is a white or yellow band followed by a red band.

Scientific Classification. Coral snakes belong to the poisonous land snake family, *Elapidae*. The South American coral snake is genus *Micrurus*, species *M. lemniscatus*. The eastern coral snake is *M. fulvius*, and the western, or Arizona, is *Micruroides euryxanthus*.   CLIFFORD H. POPE

See also SNAKE (color pictures).

CORAX. See ORATORS AND ORATORY (Beginnings).

CORBEL. See ARCHITECTURE (Beginnings).

CORBETT, JAMES JOHN (1866-1933), became the world heavyweight boxing champion in 1892. He was regarded as one of the first scientific boxers. A bank teller, Corbett became a professional boxer in 1884, and won the heavyweight title from John L. Sullivan. He lost it to Bob Fitzsimmons in 1897. After trying twice to regain the championship, he retired from the ring and became an actor. Corbett was born in San Francisco, Calif. See also BOXING (picture).   LYALL SMITH

CORBUSIER. See LE CORBUSIER.

CORCORAN, WILLIAM WILSON (1798-1888), an American banker and philanthropist, gave part of his fortune to establish the Corcoran Gallery of Art in Washington, D.C. Corcoran also donated many liberal gifts to religious and educational institutions in the District of Columbia and in Virginia. He was born in Georgetown, now in Washington, D.C.   ROBERT H. BREMNER

CORCORAN GALLERY OF ART, in Washington, D.C., has collections of paintings, sculpture, drawings, tapestries, and ceramics. It houses one of the world's most important collections of American art, and displays works by Gilbert Stuart, John Singer Sargent, Winslow Homer, and Thomas Sully, among others. The

Photograph courtesy Corcoran Gallery of Art
The Corcoran Gallery of Art, founded by William W. Corcoran, is one of the oldest art institutions in the U.S.

W. A. Clark Collection is devoted to masterpieces from Europe and the Middle East.

The gallery operates an art school offering instruction to about 750 students. It also organizes exhibitions, the most important of which is the Biennial Exhibition of Contemporary American Painting.

William Wilson Corcoran, a banker and philanthropist, founded the gallery in 1859. It is a self-supporting institution.   Critically reviewed by the CORCORAN GALLERY OF ART

CORD is a unit for measuring firewood. It is commonly defined as a pile of wood 4 feet wide, 4 feet high, and 8 feet long. Because fireplaces are smaller than they once were, wood dealers sometimes sell a *face cord*. This is 4 feet high and 8 feet long. But it may be 2 feet wide, or some other convenient measure. The cord is not rec-

A Cord of Wood Is 128 Cubic Feet
(8 feet x 4 feet x 4 feet)

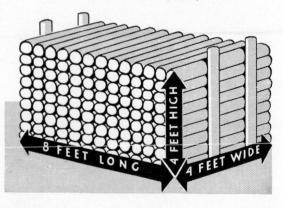

8 FEET LONG   4 FEET HIGH   4 FEET WIDE

ognized as a legal measure by the United States government.   PHILLIP S. JONES

See also WEIGHTS and MEASURES (Wood Measure—United States).

CORD AND CORDAGE. See ROPE.

CORDAY, *kawr DEH,* **CHARLOTTE** (1768-1793), a French patriot, killed Jean Paul Marat during the Reign of Terror in 1793. She was tried in a Revolutionary court, and, four days later, she was guillotined. Miss Corday sympathized with the Girondists, a group of representatives in the French legislature (see GI-RONDIST). When the Girondist leaders were arrested by their rivals, Miss Corday resolved to kill Marat, an opponent in the legislature. She obtained an interview with him. While he was in his bath, where he spent several hours each day seeking relief from a skin disease, she stabbed him to death. Charlotte

Chicago Historical Society

Charlotte Corday

Corday was born in Normandy, France. RICHARD M. BRACE

See also MARAT, JEAN PAUL.

CORDIAL. See ALCOHOLIC DRINK (Compounded Liquors).

CORDILLERA, *KAWR dill YAIR uh,* or *kawr DILL er uh,* is a group of mountain ranges, usually the principal mountain group of a continent. The word cordillera comes from the Spanish word *cuerda,* which means *cord* or *chain.* Spaniards use the word to mean any mountain chain. The term *cordillera* once was used in America to mean only the Andes Mountains. American geographers now use the term to mean any group of mountain systems, such as the western cordillera of North America, which includes the Sierra Madre, the Rockies, the Sierra Nevada, the Cascade Range, the Coast Ranges, and the Great Basin ranges. South America, Asia, and Europe also have great cordilleras. SIGISMOND DeR. DIETTRICH

CORDITE, *CORE dite,* is one of the original smokeless powders used to propel projectiles from guns. The name *cordite* refers to the cordlike lengths in which it is made. Cordite is composed of 30 per cent nitroglycerin, 65 per cent nitrocellulose, and 5 per cent petrolatum. The British government adopted the original cordite formula in 1887. This cordite burned with so much heat it damaged gun barrels. JULIUS ROTH

CÓRDOBA, *KAWR thoh vah* (pop. 580,000), in northern Argentina, is the country's third largest city. It is the capital of an Argentine province also called Córdoba. For location, see ARGENTINA (color map).

The city lies 1,240 feet above sea level, in an irrigated grazing section. Córdoba is a center for livestock, wool, and hides markets. Founded in 1573, it is the oldest major city in Argentina. GEORGE I. BLANKSTEN

CORDOBA is the unit of paper money in Nicaragua. One hundred centavos make one cordoba. It is named after the Spanish explorer, Francisco Fernández de Córdoba (1475?-1526). For the cordoba's value in dollars, see MONEY (table: Values).

CÓRDOBA, *KAWR doh vah* (pop. 207,009; alt. 330 ft.), is an ancient Moorish city in Spain, and the capital of Córdoba province. It lies 86 miles northeast of Seville in the south-central part of the country. For location, see SPAIN (color map).

Romans occupied Córdoba in 206 B.C. It reached its peak of importance in the 900's as a world-famous cen-

ter of Moorish art and culture. A mosque is Córdoba's chief landmark. It was built as a Moslem house of worship in the 700's, and was made into a Roman Catholic cathedral in 1238. More than 1,000 pillars of granite, onyx, marble, and jasper support its arches.

Nearby farms produce cereals, grapes, olives, and vegetables. Córdoba is the home of soft, fine-grained cordovan leather. WALTER C. LANGSAM

CÓRDOBA, FRANCISCO FERNÁNDEZ DE. See EXPLORATION AND DISCOVERY (table).

CORDUROY, *KAWR duh roy,* is a cotton or rayon fabric with raised ribs of the cloth running lengthwise. The name probably comes from the French phrase *cord du roi,* meaning *king's cord.* Corduroy with wide ribs is called *wide-wale corduroy.* The type with narrow ribs is *pin-wale corduroy.* Corduroy is made 36 inches wide for use in sportswear, boys' clothes and suits, and dresses and jackets for women. Corduroy is made 50 inches wide for draperies and upholstery. It may be in one color or a variety of printed patterns. KENNETH R. FOX

CORDUROY ROAD. See ROADS AND HIGHWAYS (Early American Roads).

CORE, in geology. See EARTH (Inside the Earth).

CORE, or CONGRESS OF RACIAL EQUALITY, is an organization that has used nonviolent action to oppose racial segregation. It sponsored "Freedom Rides" and "sit-in" campaigns in efforts to break down segregation in the southern states. CORE operates through local committees. The organization was founded in 1942 in Chicago. It has headquarters at 38 Park Row, New York, N.Y. 10038.

CORELLI, *koh REHL ih,* **ARCANGELO** (1653-1713), was an Italian composer. The violin at that time was replacing the viol. Corelli understood what the violin could do, and he wrote sonatas and concertos especially for string orchestra. His work laid the foundation for future developments in the use of string instruments. Corelli directed concerts at the Roman palace of Pietro Cardinal Ottoboni. PERCY M. YOUNG

COREOPSIS, *KOH ree AHP sis,* is a large group of plants related to the sunflower. They are commonly called *tickseed.* The plants may be from 1½ to 4 feet high.

Coreopsis Flowers Look Like Daisies and may have one or two layers of petals. The blooms are usually red or yellow.

J. Horace McFarland

CORFAM

The leaves are often *lobed* (cut out). Coreopsis flowers look like daisies. The flat fruits are small and dry and look like bugs. *Coreopsis* is the Greek word for *bug*. Most coreopsis plants are perennials and live for several years. But some are annuals and live only one season. The annual coreopsis is often called *calliopsis*. The yellow, red, or maroon flowers grow on slender stems.

Scientific Classification. Coreopsis plants belong to the composite family, *Compositae*. They form the genus *Coreopsis*. A common annual is *C. calliopsidea*.   MARCUS MAXON

CORFAM is a synthetic material that is used in the manufacture of shoes, belts, handbags, luggage, and other products that are often made of leather. It is a trade name of the Du Pont Company. Corfam is the first man-made shoe upper material to breathe like leather. The material contains millions of tiny pores per square inch that permit foot perspiration to be released to the outside air. Corfam weighs less than leather, resists scuffs, repels water, and can be easily cleaned with a damp cloth. The product was developed by Du Pont researchers and was first marketed in 1964.

Critically reviewed by the DU PONT COMPANY

CORFU, *kawr FOO*, or in Greek, KÉRKIRA (pop. 101,770), is the northernmost of the Ionian Islands. The mountainous island covers 229 square miles, and lies off the western coast of Greece (see GREECE [color map]). It produces olives, citrus fruit, and wine. Corfu has also become an important tourist center. Colonized about 700 B.C. by the Corinthians, Corfu was one of the causes of the Peloponnesian War. The Ionian Islands were ceded to Greece by Great Britain in 1864. See also IONIAN ISLANDS. HARRY N. HOWARD

CORGI. See WELSH CORGI.

CORI is the name of two Czech scientists. CARL FERDINAND CORI (1896-   ) and GERTY THERESA RADNITZ CORI (1896-1957), husband and wife, shared the 1947 Nobel prize for physiology and medicine. They showed how an enzyme converts animal starch into blood sugar. Their work made possible an understanding of sugar diabetes. Both were born in Prague (now Praha), Czechoslovakia, and were graduated from the German University there. They became American citizens in 1928.   HERBERT S. RHINESMITH

CORIANDER, *KOH rih AN dur*, is an annual herb that grows in the countries around the Mediterranean Sea. The plant is about 3 feet high and has small white flowers. Its seeds have a pleasant odor when ripe, and they taste sweet after they have been dried out. The seeds are used as a spice in curries, sauces, and liqueurs, and to make small round candies. They are used in Europe more than in the United States or Canada. But the United States usually imports about 1,400,000 pounds of coriander seeds a year. Coriander-seed oil is used to flavor food, and as a medicine. About 500 pounds of coriander seeds yield 5 pounds of oil.

Scientific Classification. Coriander belongs to the parsley family, *Umbelliferae*. It is genus *Coriandrum*, species *C. sativum*.   HAROLD NORMAN MOLDENKE

CORINTH, *CAWR inth*, was one of the most important cities of ancient Greece. It was founded in prehistoric times on the isthmus that connects the Peloponnesus with the rest of Europe (see GREECE, ANCIENT [color map]). According to Homer, it was the home of Bellerophon, Medea, and Sisyphus.

Corinth was favorably situated for trade by land. It also had good harbors at Cenchreae and Lechaeum, on either side of the isthmus. By 750 B.C., Corinth had become the wealthiest city of ancient Greece. Except for two periods (454-404 B.C. and 146-44 B.C.), it maintained economic supremacy for about 1,300 years.

In 734 B.C., Corinthians founded colonies at Corcyra (now Corfu), an Ionian island west of Greece, and at Syracuse in Sicily. In 581 B.C., they instituted the Isthmian Games, an international festival held every second year (see ISTHMIAN GAMES). The games honored their principal god, Poseidon (Neptune). Corinth was famous for its skilled workers in bronze and clay, and for its naval architects. Because of commercial rivalry with Athens, Corinth was the chief instigator of the Peloponnesian War (see PELOPONNESIAN WAR).

The Romans destroyed the city in 146 B.C., but later rebuilt it by order of Julius Caesar. Emperor Augustus

Ewing Galloway

Relic of Ancient Corinth, these Doric columns were once part of the Temple of Apollo. Each column is a single stone 23½ feet high and over 17 feet around at the base. The Apostle Paul, on one of his visits to Greece, saw people worship heathen gods in this temple.

Ewing Galloway

Corinth Canal links the Gulf of Corinth with the Saronic Gulf. It is about 4 miles long, 79 feet wide, and 26 feet deep.

made it capital of the Roman province of Achaea. Saint Paul visited Corinth in A.D. 51 and founded a church there (see CORINTHIANS, EPISTLES TO THE).

In the Middle Ages, the city was largely confined to its citadel, Acrocorinth. American archaeologists began excavations in Corinth in 1896.   DONALD W. BRADEEN

CORINTH CANAL flows between the lower part of Greece and the northern mainland. It provides a waterway between the Gulf of Corinth and the Saronic Gulf. The town of Isthmia lies at the eastern end of the 4-mile-long canal, and Poseidonia is at the western end. A French company began building the canal in 1882, and Greece finished it in 1893. An unsuccessful attempt to build such a canal had been made by the Roman Emperor Nero in A.D. 67.   C. BRADFORD WELLES

CORINTHIAN COLUMN. See COLUMN.

CORINTHIANS, *koh RIHN thi unz,* **EPISTLES TO THE,** the seventh and eighth books of the New Testament, were written by the Apostle Paul probably about A.D. 54.

The first *epistle* (letter) was sent from Ephesus, in present-day Turkey, to a Christian church which Paul had organized in Corinth, Greece. The epistle was written after word came to Paul that the church was split into four divisions, each claiming a different leader. It included suggestions for solving this and other problems. A famous passage is Chapter 13, which deals with Christian love.

Paul wrote the second epistle in two parts. Chapters 10 to 13 include a severe letter which Paul wrote after the first epistle failed to unite the Corinthian church. Even his authority and sincerity had been challenged. Chapters one to nine are a later letter written from Macedonia expressing gratitude that friendliness had been re-established.   W. W. SLOAN

See also PAUL, SAINT.

CORINTO, *koh REEN toh* (pop. 9,177; alt. 5 ft.), the main Pacific Ocean port of Nicaragua, is the western terminus of the government railroad. About 85 per cent of the republic's agricultural exports pass through the city. These include coffee, sugar, animal hides, and lumber. Corinto is on an island which is connected to

the mainland by a bridge. For the location of Corinto, see NICARAGUA (color map).   ROLLIN S. ATWOOD

CORIOLANUS, *KAWR ih oh LAY nus,* **GAIUS MARCIUS,** was a general of the early Roman Republic. He was given his last name as a reward for his skill and bravery in capturing the town of Corioli from the Volscians, bitter enemies of Rome.

During a famine in 491 B.C., Coriolanus suggested that no grain be given to the poor unless they gave up their right to elect *tribunes* (representatives). The people became indignant over this, and exiled Coriolanus. He joined the Volscians to get revenge, and led their army to the gates of Rome. He was about to capture the city when his mother and wife persuaded him to spare Rome. The angry Volscians then killed Coriolanus. William Shakespeare told the story of this warrior in his tragedy of *Coriolanus.*   HERBERT M. HOWE

CORIOLIS FORCE, *KAWR ih OH lis.* An object moving over the earth or any other rotating body tends to move in a straight line. But the earth rotates beneath the moving object. To someone rotating along with the earth, the path of the object appears to curve, as if it were pushed. Objects tend to drift to the right in the Northern Hemisphere and to the left in the Southern Hemisphere. This push is called the *Coriolis force,* or the *Coriolis effect.* It was named after the French mathematician Gaspard G. Coriolis, who first analyzed it. The Coriolis force mainly affects objects moving above the earth that are not affected by the forces of friction. Such objects as airplanes, rockets, bullets, and air masses have curved paths. The Coriolis force is important to the weather and the direction of the wind. See also AIR (Air Movement); WEATHER (Air Movement).

CORIUM. See SKIN.

CORK, *kawrk* (pop. 122,146; met. area 128,420; alt. 56 ft.), is the second largest city in the Republic of Ireland. The main part of Cork is on an island between two arms of the Lee River, but the rest of the city spreads over the hillsides that border the river. For location, see IRELAND (color map).

Cork has large iron foundries, shipbuilding yards, an

Patrick Street in Cork is the site of the Father Matthew statue, which honors Ireland's famous temperance leader.

Camera Press, Pix

833

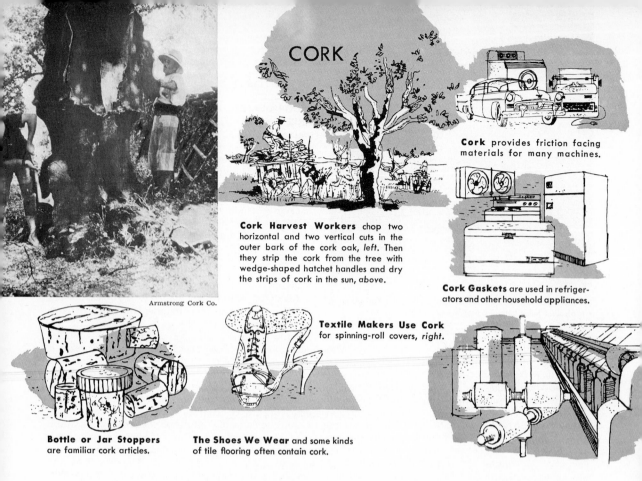

CORK

Cork Harvest Workers chop two horizontal and two vertical cuts in the outer bark of the cork oak, *left*. Then they strip the cork from the tree with wedge-shaped hatchet handles and dry the strips of cork in the sun, *above*.

Armstrong Cork Co.

Cork provides friction facing materials for many machines.

Cork Gaskets are used in refrigerators and other household appliances.

Textile Makers Use Cork for spinning-roll covers, *right*.

Bottle or Jar Stoppers are familiar cork articles.

The Shoes We Wear and some kinds of tile flooring often contain cork.

automobile plant, and factories that produce fertilizers, flour, leather, paper, and woolen and linen goods. The city's many fine buildings include the Roman Catholic Church of Christ the King and Saint Finbar's Church of Ireland Cathedral. The University College is located in Cork.

Saint Finbar, an Irish bishop, founded a church at Cork in the 600's. Viking raiders began the first permanent settlement in the 800's. The city's four miles of *quays*, or artificial river banks, and its beautiful, broad streets, including Patrick Street, Grand Parade, and South Mall, were built in the 1700's. When Great Britain granted Ireland home rule in 1921, Ireland gave the British permission to use Cork Harbor as a naval base. The British withdrew their forces in 1938.   T. W. Freeman

CORK is a lightweight, spongy substance obtained from the bark of the cork oak tree. It does not absorb water readily and can be compressed a great deal, but springs back when released. Men used cork as early as 400 B.C. The Romans wore cork sandals to keep their feet warm, and used cork to float anchors and fishing nets. Cork bottle stoppers have been manufactured since the 1600's.

The Tree. The cork tree is a live oak. This means that it is green the year round. It grows abundantly in Portugal and Spain, where most of the world's cork is produced. Algeria is the third most important country in cork production. The cork oak has been planted in parts of California, and in some of the southeastern states, but the total yield of cork there is small. The outer layer of the bark is composed of dead cells whose thin walls have become thickened and waxy. These cells are so compact that each may be in contact with 14 others. The cork tree lives from 300 to 400 years, but seldom grows more than 50 feet high.

Gathering Cork. A cork tree must be approximately 20 years old before its bark is thick enough to be stripped. The first layer removed is called the *virgin bark*. Workers strip the bark during June, July, and August. Each tree can be stripped about once every 10 years. The best cork comes after the second stripping.

A cork stripper uses a long-handled hatchet to cut long, oblong sections of bark from the top of the lowest branches to the bottom of the tree. The sections of bark are pried off carefully with the wedge-shaped handle of the hatchet. The inner layer continues to produce more cork after each stripping. Cork will never grow again on a spot where the inner layer of bark has been bruised by the stripper's hatchet.

Preparation for Market. The slabs of stripped cork are boiled, and a rough, gritty outer layer is scraped off. The boiling dissolves tannic acid from cork, and softens the material so that the slabs can be straightened out and packed in bundles. Before being loaded on ships, cork is sorted according to quality and thickness.

Uses. Most cork is used for insulation. For this purpose, it is ground and pressed into boards and pipe coverings. In this form, cork covers the walls and freezing pipes of thousands of cold-storage plants, meat-packing factories, ice-cream plants, and oil refineries.

Cork floats in water, and is used in making buoys and floats for fishing nets. Linoleum is made by mixing cork powder with linseed oil and spreading this paste over canvas or burlap. Floors are made soundproof with cork. One of its principal uses is for "corks," or bottle stoppers. Thin cork gaskets seal metal bottle caps. Cork is also used in waterproof coats, in balloon fabric, as filling for automobile tires, and as wadding for shotgun cartridges. Cork shavings are burned to make *Spanish black*, or *cork black*, a paint used by artists.

Scientific Classification. The cork oak tree belongs to the beech family, *Fagaceae*. It is genus *Quercus*, species *suber*.   HARRY E. TROXELL

See also INSULATION; OAK; PORTUGAL (Cork); TANNIC ACID.

CORLISS, GEORGE HENRY (1817-1888), an American engineer, helped perfect the steam engine. His refinements included a more reliable governor that cut off steam from the engine according to the load put upon it (see GOVERNOR). Corliss also designed the largest engine built up to that time, for the Philadelphia Exposition of 1876. Corliss was born in Easton, N.Y. He started his career as an engineer with an engine firm in Providence, R.I. Later, he became the head of his own company.   RICHARD D. HUMPHREY

CORM is a short, thick, underground stem from which other plants can be grown. It resembles a bulb. But most of the corm consists of stem tissue. A corm has smaller and thinner leaves than a bulb. Unlike the bulb, the corm stores food in the stem, instead of in the thickened leaves. Small corms are called *cormels*. See also BULB; STEM.

CORMORANT, *KAWR moh runt*, is a large, web-footed bird that catches fish by diving under water. Different kinds of cormorants are found throughout the world. Most of them live on seacoasts, but they are often seen on large rivers and lakes. The cormorant is related to the pelican. The large kinds are more than 30 inches

long. All have long, powerful bills with a hook on the end. The cormorant has powerful wings. Its tail feathers spread out like a partly opened fan.

One of the most common cormorants of North America, the *double-crested cormorant*, perches in trees, on rocks, and on the ledges of sea cliffs. Hundreds of these birds live around the Bay of Fundy in Nova Scotia and New Brunswick. With their feathered bodies, long necks, and flat heads, they look like rows of bottles sitting on the cliffs. The double-crested cormorant has bronze-tinted feathers. During the nesting season it has a crest of white curved feathers behind each eye. It has an orange throat. The *common cormorant* is larger and has white feathers bordering the throat.

N.Y. Zool. Soc.

The Cormorant is related to the large-beaked pelican.

Cormorants can stay under water a long time when they dive for fish. They swim with their webbed feet. These birds fly close to the water looking for fish, or they perch on a branch over the water and wait for fish to appear. Cormorants dive into the water to catch the fish.

Scientific Classification. Cormorants belong to the family *Phalacrocoracidae*. The common cormorant is genus *Phalacrocorax*, species *carbo*. The double-crested cormorant is *P. auritus*.   ALEXANDER WETMORE

See also BIRD (Bird Pets); PELICAN.

Fishermen in the Orient Have Long Used Cormorants to catch fish. They tie long cords to the birds to keep them from flying away with the fresh fish they catch.

Pix

The Cormorant dives into the water to catch fish for its owner with its long hooked bill. A metal ring around its neck prevents the bird from swallowing the fish.

Yomiuri Shimbun, Tokyo

CORN

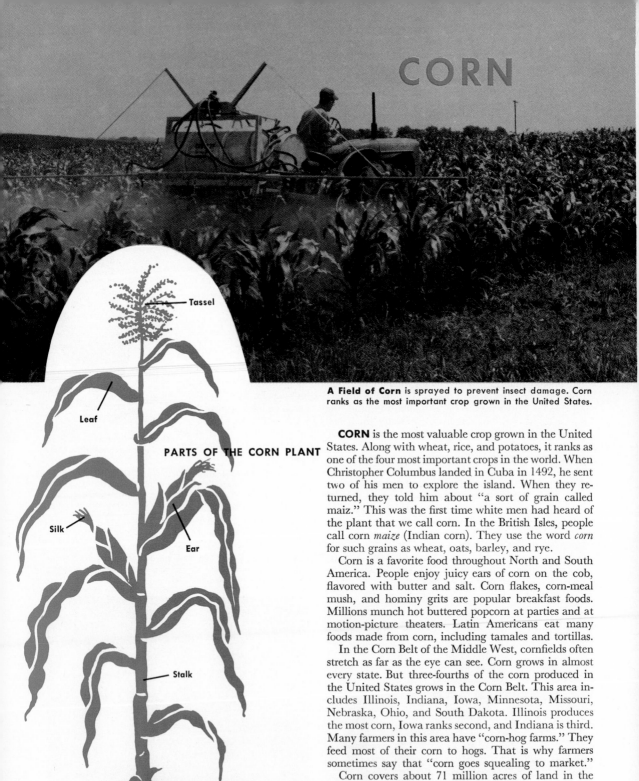

A Field of Corn is sprayed to prevent insect damage. Corn ranks as the most important crop grown in the United States.

PARTS OF THE CORN PLANT

Tassel

Leaf

Silk

Ear

Stalk

Prop Roots

Roots

CORN is the most valuable crop grown in the United States. Along with wheat, rice, and potatoes, it ranks as one of the four most important crops in the world. When Christopher Columbus landed in Cuba in 1492, he sent two of his men to explore the island. When they returned, they told him about "a sort of grain called maiz." This was the first time white men had heard of the plant that we call corn. In the British Isles, people call corn *maize* (Indian corn). They use the word *corn* for such grains as wheat, oats, barley, and rye.

Corn is a favorite food throughout North and South America. People enjoy juicy ears of corn on the cob, flavored with butter and salt. Corn flakes, corn-meal mush, and hominy grits are popular breakfast foods. Millions munch hot buttered popcorn at parties and at motion-picture theaters. Latin Americans eat many foods made from corn, including tamales and tortillas.

In the Corn Belt of the Middle West, cornfields often stretch as far as the eye can see. Corn grows in almost every state. But three-fourths of the corn produced in the United States grows in the Corn Belt. This area includes Illinois, Indiana, Iowa, Minnesota, Missouri, Nebraska, Ohio, and South Dakota. Illinois produces the most corn, Iowa ranks second, and Indiana is third. Many farmers in this area have "corn-hog farms." They feed most of their corn to hogs. That is why farmers sometimes say that "corn goes squealing to market."

Corn covers about 71 million acres of land in the United States, more than any other crop. Every year the nation's farmers harvest about $5 billion worth of corn. The United States usually produces about 50 per cent of the world total. Other large corn producers are Brazil, China, Mexico, Russia, and Yugoslavia. Canada grows corn chiefly in the provinces of Ontario, Manitoba, and Quebec.

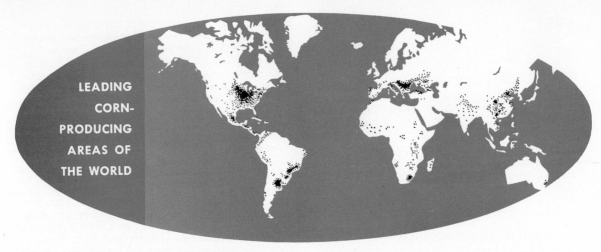

LEADING
CORN-
PRODUCING
AREAS OF
THE WORLD

Farmers in the United States feed the largest part of the corn crop to their livestock. They sell the rest to industries for use in processed food and industrial products, including corn syrup, cornstarch, and plastics.

Uses of Corn

Livestock Feed. Farmers feed about four-fifths of the corn grown each year to hogs, cattle, sheep, and poultry. Hogs eat almost half the corn crop. Hogs once had to eat from 5 to 6 pounds of corn in order to gain a pound. Improved feeding methods have reduced this amount to 3 to 4½ pounds of corn. Corn provides the base for many kinds of poultry feeds and dairy feeds. Every year, about 85 million tons of corn and cornstalks are made into *silage*, a fermented livestock feed (see Silo).

Corn production is closely related to hog and cattle raising, because these animals depend chiefly on corn for food. The Corn Belt states usually raise more than half the hogs in the United States, and nearly half the cattle. The price that farmers can receive for their corn helps them decide what to do with it. As corn prices rise, for example, farmers usually sell more corn and raise fewer hogs. They receive more money by selling the corn than they would by feeding it to the hogs and then selling the hogs. If corn prices fall, farmers generally raise more hogs and feed the corn to them, because the hogs would bring in more money than the corn.

Food for Man. Americans eat an average of about 45 pounds of corn per person every year. Many kinds of food are made from the kernels. Corn also provides food indirectly. We eat it in the form of meat and meat prod-

LEADING CORN GROWING STATES
Bushels (56 pounds) of corn grown each year

Illinois 888,524,000 bu.	
Iowa 855,231,000 bu.	
Indiana 406,692,000 bu.	
Minnesota 307,657,000 bu.	
Nebraska 281,895,000 bu.	
Ohio 234,020,000 bu.	
Missouri 187,165,000 bu.	
Wisconsin 126,347,000 bu.	
South Dakota 94,748,000 bu.	
Michigan 94,467,000 bu.	Includes corn used for grain, but not for silage, hogging down, grazing, or forage.

Based on a 4-year average, 1964 through 1967.

Source: U.S. Department of Agriculture

LEADING CORN GROWING COUNTRIES
Bushels (56 pounds) of corn grown in 1967

United States 4,722,200,000 bu.	
Brazil 515,700,000 bu.	
China (Mainland) *455,900,000 bu.	
Mexico 334,600,000 bu.	
Russia 314,900,000 bu.	
Yugoslavia 287,000,000 bu.	
Romania 267,700,000 bu.	
Argentina 259,800,000 bu.	
South Africa 223,200,000 bu.	
India 216,500,000 bu.	Includes corn used for grain, but not for silage, hogging down, grazing, or forage.

*Latest available information, a 4-year average, 1960-64.

Source: U.S. Department of Agriculture

CORN

ucts that come from animals raised on corn. Corn, in one form or another, makes up more of our diet than any other farm crop.

We eat corn just as it comes from the ear in succotash, chowder, pudding, popcorn, fritters, parched corn, and as roasted or boiled corn on the cob. We sometimes eat soft, white hominy, made by treating the whole grains with lye and washing them carefully. Manufacturers flavor hominy, roll it out, and toast it to make corn flakes. Corn kernels are coarsely ground to make corn meal. Foods made from corn meal include corn bread, cookies, tamales, and waffles. Corn kernels are high in food value. They provide a rich source of fats, proteins, and carbohydrates. A pound (about 3 ears) of sweet

corn, boiled on the cob, contains about 550 calories.

Corn refining is the process of separating the kernel into its parts. The basic products of refining are starch, sugar, syrup, and oil. *Corn oil* is used as a salad oil and cooking oil, and in other food products such as margarine and shortening. *Cornstarch* is used to thicken puddings, gravies, and sauces. It is also used in such products as candy, chewing gum, and baked goods. *Corn syrup*, made by heating cornstarch in closed tanks, sweetens many foods and is used as a spread for bread.

Other Products. Factories manufacture hundreds of important corn products that we do not eat. Manufacturers make wallboards and certain kinds of paper from cornstalks. Ground cobs can be substituted for cork. Corncobs are sometimes burned as fuel. Corncob meal may be used for fertilizer, for cleaning furs, and for polishing metal. Cobs are an ingredient of *furfural*, a chemical used in making phonograph records, buttons, and similar articles (see FURFURAL). Smokers sometimes enjoy pipes made from corncobs.

Industries use corn meal in making adhesives, cork products, felts, cleaning compounds, plywood, and many other products besides foods. Starch, refined from corn meal, is used to stiffen and finish paper, yarns, and fabrics. Starch also plays a part in the manufacture of cosmetics, explosives, electric batteries, and drugs.

Corn sugar has uses in leather tanning, rayon and paper manufacturing, and other industries. Manufacturers make ethyl alcohol from corn sugar or syrup. Ethyl alcohol is an important ingredient in smokeless powder, shatterproof glass, synthetic rubber, brake fluids, and plastics (see ALCOHOL).

Doctors sometimes use injections of *dextrose*, or refined corn sugar, for patients who have had major operations or suffer severe injuries (see DEXTROSE). Corn sugar supplies a quick source of energy for the human body. Dextrose may also be an ingredient of certain drugs. Druggists sometimes use cornstarch in pills and tablets. Corn syrup sweetens cough sirup and other liquid medicines. Manufacturers use corn oil in soaps, glycerine, paints, varnishes, and rubber substitutes.

CORN PRODUCTS

Food for Man

Baked goods	Ice cream	Sausage
Baking powder	Icings and candy	Shortening
Breakfast foods	Jams and jellies	Syrup
Catsup	Margarine	Tamales
Chewing gum	Popcorn	Vinegar
Cooking oil	Puddings	Yeast
Corn flour	Salad dressing	

Food for Livestock

Corn bran	Fodder	Gluten meal
Corn grain	Germ cake and meal	Oil cake and meal
Corn meal	Gluten feed	Silage

Other Products

Adhesives	Fertilizer	Photographic film
Antifreeze	Fuel	Plastics
Antiseptics	Furfural	Safety glass
Ceramics	Insulating	Soaps
Cork substitute	materials	Solvents
Dyes	Paints	Synthetic fibers
Ether	Paper and	Varnishes
Explosives	paperboard	Whisky
Felt	Pastes	

Kinds of Corn

The six main kinds of corn have different types of kernels. These kinds are: (1) dent corn, (2) sweet corn, (3) flint corn, (4) popcorn, (5) flour corn, and (6) pod corn. The term "Indian corn" may be used to mean any of these kinds of corn. But the corn that the Indians taught the early settlers to grow was flint corn. Dent corn and flint corn are commonly called "field corn" because they are fed to animals. Broomcorn and Kafir corn are plants that resemble corn. But they are not corn as the term is used in the United States.

Hybrid corn is produced by crossing two types of purebred corn. Breeders can produce hybrids of any of the different kinds of corn. Most breeding of hybrid corn has been done with dent corn.

Dent Corn is the most common commercial variety. It makes up about 9 of every 10 bushels of corn grown in the United States. Each kernel of dent corn has a small dent on the top. This dent is made when the hard and soft starch in the kernel shrink unequally as it dries. Farmers harvest dent corn when the seeds become hard and ripe. Most dent corn is hybrid corn.

Dent corn may be used as a livestock feed on the

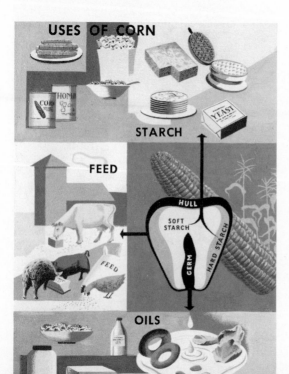

USES OF CORN

STARCH

FEED

HULL

SOFT STARCH

GERM

HARD STARCH

OILS

THE SIX MAIN KINDS OF CORN

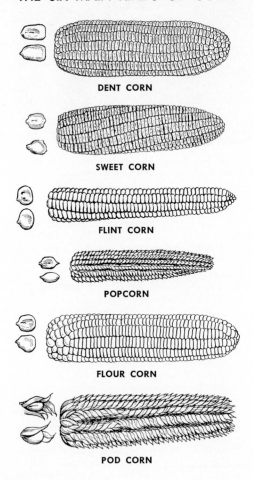

DENT CORN

SWEET CORN

FLINT CORN

POPCORN

FLOUR CORN

POD CORN

Flint Corn has hard kernels with a smooth coat. They vary in color from white through golden yellow to deep red. The ears sometimes appear on the stalk close to the ground. Flint corn can grow in cold climates because it ripens in less time than other kinds of corn. Wisconsin, the New England States, and other northern states grow flint corn. Argentina, a leading world producer of corn, grows almost no other type of corn but flint. Argentina exports much of its corn. Flint corn can be shipped and stored with less spoilage than other kinds.

Popcorn is one of the favorite "fun foods" of Americans. People eat it plain with salt and butter, or cover it with caramel or white sugar sirup. Popcorn has small, hard kernels that are either rice-shaped with pointed ends or flat with rounded ends. A tough outer coat covers each kernel. When the kernels are heated rapidly, the moisture inside them turns to steam. This steam builds up a great pressure within the kernel. This pressure bursts the kernel's outer shell, and the entire inside of the kernel puffs out. Other kinds of corn crack and parch when heated, but do not pop. Indiana, Iowa, Illinois, and Ohio lead in growing popcorn. See PoPCORN.

Flour Corn, or soft corn, is one of the oldest types of corn. It has soft, starchy kernels. The Indians in the southwestern United States mainly grow flour corn. They can grind the kernels by hand because flour corn has softer kernels than other kinds of corn. Flour corn ripens late in the season. It grows in the warm areas of South America, but is not grown commercially in the United States.

Pod Corn has a separate covering around each kernel. In all other corns, the kernel has no separate covering. Some scientists believe pod corn may be the ancestor of all other types of corn. Pod corn has never been grown commercially, because the husks on each kernel make it hard to use.

The Corn Plant

Corn is really a grass, but an unusual one. It belongs to the group of six true grains, or cereals, that includes wheat, barley, oats, rice, and rye. The corn plant usually grows 3 to 10 feet tall and has many short *ear shoots*, or branches. But the giant corn of the Jala Valley in Mexico has ears 3 feet long. Its strong stalks can be used to make fences.

Stalk. The tough, jointed *cornstalk*, or stem, resembles bamboo. It has a central core of *pith* (soft, spongy tissue). A root system with many branches supports the green stalk. Sometimes *prop roots* grow out of the stalk several inches above the ground to help support the plant against the wind. The *tassel* grows at the top of the cornstalk. It contains hundreds of small flowers that produce pollen. Most corn flowers are pink, but they may be green, yellow, red, or purple.

Leaves. At each joint of the stem, a long, swordlike leaf curves gracefully outward and downward, ending in a pointed tip. The lower part of the leaf partly encloses the stem, forming a *sheath*. The *blade* (upper part of the leaf) is long, narrow, and pointed.

Ears of corn grow from the places where the leaves join the stalk. A corn plant may have one ear, or as many as eight. *Husks* (a special kind of leaf) enclose and

farm where it grows. Or the farmer may sell the corn to manufacturers, who can make many different food and industrial products from it. Farmers in all parts of the Corn Belt grow dent corn.

Sweet Corn is grown chiefly for people to eat. Farmers must pick it at just the right time to ensure the best flavor. Sweet corn tastes best when picked while a milky fluid fills the kernels. It is not as good after the kernels have begun to harden and the corn is getting ripe.

Unless it is kept refrigerated, sweet corn quickly loses its flavor after harvesting. This happens because heat turns the sugar in the kernels to starch. Refrigerated trucks and railroad cars make it possible to carry fresh sweet corn far from the places where it grows. Canned and quick-frozen sweet corn last indefinitely, and can be shipped throughout the world. Most sweet corn grows in the northern states. Wisconsin, Minnesota, and Illinois lead in sweet corn production. The center of the corn-canning industry is just north of the Corn Belt. Minnesota, Wisconsin, northern Illinois, and Maine lead in the canning of sweet corn.

Sweet corn is a good source of energy. It contains twice as much sugar as dent corn. It is also a good source of vitamins A and C. Sweet corn may have white or yellow kernels. It has smaller stalks and ears than dent corn.

Planting Corn on this Indiana farm is done with a tractor-drawn machine that plants four rows of seed at a time.

Cultivating a Cornfield controls weeds and loosens the soil. Corn needs cultivation only when it is young.

protect each ear. An ear consists of a *corncob* covered with rows of *kernels*, the seeds of the corn plant. An even number of rows usually grow on the ear. An ear may have 8, 10, 12, or more rows of kernels. Each kernel has what looks like a silk thread that runs from the kernel up the row, and sticks out of the husk at the end of the ear. This thread is called the corn *silk*.

Every kernel has three parts: (1) the *hull*, or outer covering; (2) the *germ*, or young embryo corn plant; and (3) the *endosperm*, which makes up the rest of the kernel. When the kernel is planted, the young plant uses the endosperm as food as it begins to grow. The endosperm is made of *hard starch* and *soft starch*. Different kinds of corn have different amounts of these two kinds of starch in their kernels. See CORNSTARCH.

Natural Pollination. In midsummer, the wind shakes pollen out of the tassels and blows it about like dust. Some of the pollen grains fall on the sticky threads of corn silk hanging out of the young ears.

When a pollen grain lands on the silk, it sends out a tiny pollen tube that grows down the silk to an egg cell in the young kernel. There, a male cell from the pollen grain *fertilizes*, or unites with, the egg cell. As the fertilized egg cell grows, the whole kernel becomes the seed. Corn cannot reproduce successfully for more than a few years without man's help. If corn grows wild, the heavy seeds all fall too close to the parent plant.

Hand Pollination, or **Hand Breeding,** is the transfer of pollen by hand from the tassel to the silk. Breeders cover the tassels of certain corn plants with paper bags before the tassels are ready to shed their pollen. They place bags over the young ears of other corn plants before the silk is ready to receive pollen. They *detassel*, or remove the tassels from these plants. The tassels and ears continue to grow in the bags. When the silk is ready, breeders carefully dust the pollen from the tassel onto the silk of the ear. They protect the pollinated ear with a bag so that no more pollen can reach it. After the kernels ripen, they are labeled and stored for use as seeds.

By using hand breeding, instead of allowing the wind to pollinate the plants, breeders can control the reproduction of corn. They also can *cross-fertilize* one plant with another to obtain the best qualities of each.

Hybrid Corn

More than nine tenths of the corn grown in the United States is hybrid. Its use is rapidly increasing in other important corn-growing areas of the world. Hybrid corn plants produce up to one third more corn than do the best varieties developed by other methods of breeding. Hybrids are also bred to have a greater ability to withstand drought, diseases, and pests. All the ears of hybrid corn ripen at the same time. Hybrids have stronger stalks and roots than other types of corn. The plants are more uniform and stand up better, and the ears can be more easily harvested with mechanical equipment. No hybrid has all these desirable qualities, but each type has some of them.

To produce hybrid corn, breeders first produce *pure strains*, or plants that have the same characteristics year after year. They do this by *inbreeding*, or fertilizing a plant with pollen from the same plant. Breeders take pollen from the tassel of a corn plant and place it on the silk of an ear of the same plant. Plants grown from seeds produced by inbreeding are called *inbreds*. After inbreeding for several years, inbred plants tend to be the same year after year. For example, the seeds of small plants produce only small plants. These plants are pure strains. But most inbreds do not grow as well as cross-fertilized plants. Some are weak, and others grow only one small ear. Because of their small yields, inbreds are used only for breeding. However, by cross-fertilizing plants from two different inbred lines, breeders can produce plants that are better than either parent.

The main kinds of hybrid corn seed are *single-cross* seed, which is produced by crossing two inbred lines, and *double-cross* seed, which results from crossing two single crosses. Double-cross hybrid seed can be produced more cheaply than single-cross hybrid seed, because it yields more seed for the land and labor used. Corn from a crop of hybrid corn cannot be used for seed, because it produces a crop with a lower yield. New hybrid corn seed must be produced and used every year. Since the 1930's, the production of hybrid seed has become an important commercial industry in the Corn Belt. In the 1950's, breeders found a way to prevent some of the parent plants from producing pollen. This eliminates the need for detasseling.

Growing Corn

Farmers plant field corn in the early spring, about 10 days after the average date of the final killing frost. The plants grow rapidly during the warm summer. They may grow as much as three to five inches a day during the three-week period before the tassels shed their pollen. In the Corn Belt, corn plants grow "knee-high by the Fourth of July," and head-high three weeks later. Growers harvest corn in the late summer or early

Harvesting Corn is an easy job with a mechanical picker that picks the ears, removes the husks, and drops the ears in a wagon.

Farmers Store Corn in *cribs*. Temporary cribs, such as these, have no roofs. But for long storage, a roof is needed.

fall, depending on the climate and the breed of corn.

Corn plants grow best in a climate that provides rain during the growing season and warm weather for a month or so after pollination. The Corn Belt of the United States supplies all these conditions. Here, a large area of fertile land receives 8 to 10 inches of rain during the four months after corn planting. After the tassels appear, Corn Belt temperatures usually range from 70° to 80° F. for 30 days or more. The level or gently rolling land of the Corn Belt allows farmers to use laborsaving machinery in the cornfields.

Planting. Corn plants need rich, well-drained soil. Farmers can improve poor soils with manure or artificial fertilizers. Sometimes, corn growers plant crops of legumes or grasses, called *green manures*, and plow them under to enrich the soil. Or they may grow corn in rotation with oats, clover, alfalfa, and other crops. The clover and alfalfa, like other legumes, enrich the soil for plants that follow them. See CROPPING SYSTEM.

Farmers plant corn in different ways. The most common methods are hill checking, power checking, drilling, listing, and bedding. In *hill-check* plantings, two to four seeds are dropped into hills spaced three to four feet apart. This type of planting lets the farmer cultivate all around the hills. In *power-check* planting, two or more seeds are dropped into hills arranged in rows. The farmer can adjust the distance between the hills in each row to any spacing he desires. In *drilled* plantings, the kernels are dropped individually with any desired spacing. Farmers in drier areas use *listing*, or lister planting. A machine called a *lister* opens a furrow and drops the seed into it. *Bedding* resembles listing except that the seeds are planted on the ridges instead of in the furrows. Some Southern farmers use bed planting on soils that are poorly drained at planting time. Power-checked, drilled, listed, and bedded corn can be cultivated only between the rows. The number of corn plants on an acre should range from 6,000 to 24,000, depending on soil fertility, water supply, and other conditions.

Cultivation. Farmers cultivate their cornfields mainly to control weeds. Corn growers usually cultivate their fields twice. They cultivate while the weeds and corn plants are small. After the corn has grown 25 to 30 inches high, it can compete successfully with the weeds for food and sunlight. Then, it does not need further cultivation. The use of chemical weed killers to control weeds has increased rapidly since the late 1940's (see WEED [Weed Control]).

Harvesting Corn. Most farmers harvest their corn with machines. Mechanical *pickers* have almost replaced the older method of *husking* (removing the husks) by hand. Some growers use machines called *picker shellers* that pick and shell the corn in one operation. Sometimes, farmers turn their livestock loose in the fields to eat the ripened corn and fatten for market. When hogs harvest corn in this way, the process is called *hogging off*. Unless the farmer limits the range of his animals, this method of harvesting can be wasteful. In some parts of the country, farmers cut and *shock* (stack) the corn plants. They feed the shocked corn to their livestock during the winter months. Farmers sometimes cut down the cornstalks when the stalks are green and the ears are hard. Then, they chop the material and place it in silos to produce silage.

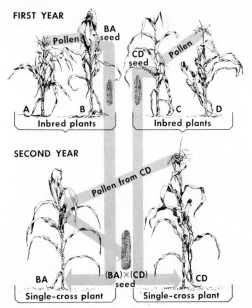

USDA

Hybrid Seed Corn is produced by double crossing. The four inbred strains are not good producers. Fertilizing plant B with pollen from plant A and plant C with pollen from plant D results in single-cross *hybrid* seed, BA and CD. The plants grown from this seed are better producers than the inbred plants. Still better results can be obtained from a second cross. Fertilizing plant BA with pollen from plant CD results in the *double-cross* seed corn, (BA) × (CD). This seed is sold to farmers for planting.

ENEMIES OF CORN

USDA; Hugh Spencer; Bur. of Plant Industry

Corn Smut, *above,* is a fungus disease that turns the kernels of corn into swollen masses of black powder.

The European Corn Borer, *left,* the larva of the moth shown above it, eats its way through corn.

P. S. Tice

The Corn Ear Worm is a greenish-brown caterpillar that does serious damage to corn, cotton, and other valuable crops.

Ears of field corn are usually stored in ventilated bins called corn *cribs.* These cribs have roofs to protect the corn from rain or snow. Corn with much moisture must be dried before it is stored in a crib, or it becomes moldy. In northern areas, where insects do not seriously damage stored corn, farmers store the ears with the husks removed. In the South, some farmers store the ears with the husks still on the ears. The husks help reduce damage by certain insects.

Enemies of Corn. More than 350 kinds of insects feed on the roots, stalks, leaves, and kernels of corn. These pests include the corn-ear worm, chinch bug, grasshopper, white bug, and European corn borer. Insects take a heavy toll of the corn crop each year. Farmers fight them by spraying or dusting powerful insecticides on the plants. They sometimes mix the insecticides with soil or fertilizer to kill certain pests.

Many kinds of diseases, especially smut and rot, attack corn plants (see ROT; SMUT). A combination of disease-free soil, vigorous varieties of corn, and rich, fertile land usually prevents disease and pest trouble.

Farmers protect stored corn from rats and mice by lining the walls and floor of the cribs with wire netting, and by covering the doors and openings with mesh.

Some farmers use poisons. Insecticides sprayed on the stored corn help prevent damage by the granary weevil, grain moth, rice weevil, and other insects. These insects attack corn mainly in Virginia, Kentucky, Missouri, and other southern states.

Processing Corn

Milling is the grinding of corn or other seeds. If the grain is soaked and treated chemically before grinding, the process is called *wet milling.* The process of grinding grain while it is dry is called *dry milling.*

Wet Milling. The principal products of wet milling are starch and oil. Cornstarch is important as a food and as a raw material in many industries. Corn oil is used as food for both people and livestock. The wet-milling industry uses about 145 million bushels of corn every year. Wet millers use mostly yellow dent corn. They can use corn with a fairly high moisture content, because they treat the corn with water.

By-products of wet milling include *zein,* a protein used as a source of many plastics, and *waxy cornstarch,* which is cornstarch made from a special hybrid corn called waxy corn. Some wet-milling processes produce lactic acid, used in the preparation of such foods as cheese, pickles, and sauerkraut. Gluten meal, made from the endosperm of corn kernels, and germ meal, made from the germ, are important livestock feeds.

The water in which wet-milled corn is soaked before preparation is called *steepwater.* It has many uses. It provides a food on which molds and bacteria may grow. Scientists extract penicillin and other antibiotic drugs from the molds, and use the bacteria in yeast production. Steepwater also contains *inositol,* one of the B vitamins.

Dry Milling separates the corn kernel into its parts— hull, endosperm, and germ. Repeated grinding reduces the endosperm to particles of any desired size. The sizes most commonly used include those for hominy grits, corn meal, and corn flour. Grits, or coarse hominy, may be boiled and used as a breakfast cereal, or rolled flat and toasted to make corn flakes. Corn meal is used in bread, griddlecakes, and many other foods. Corn flour has the smallest particles of ground corn. It is used in pancake mixes, as a filler in various meat products, and in baking as a substitute for wheat flour. By-products of dry milling include corn oil and livestock feed.

Dry millers use about 101 million bushels of corn each year. Some corn meal is produced by a method called the *old process.* This meal is sometimes called *water-ground,* because many mills use water to provide power. Millers using the old process grind whole corn between rotating stones. Leaving the germ in the meal improves the flavor and nutritional values, but limits the time that the meal stays fresh. Most corn meal sold commercially is made by the *new process.* New-process meal, made from hulled corn kernels with the germ removed, keeps longer than old-process meal. Steel rolls and cylinders and other equipment grind new-process meal.

Distilling and Fermentation industries include manufacturers of ethyl and butyl alcohols, acetone, and whisky. These industries use about 30 million bushels of corn each year. They use the products of both wet and dry milling. Malt and yeast ferment corn, and produce ethyl alcohol and carbon dioxide. The products of fermentation may be distilled to purify them. The grain that remains is used for livestock feed. Acetone and butyl-alcohol manufacturers allow bacteria to ferment corn meal. Acetone and butyl alcohol are used in manufacturing rayon, plastics, and other products. By-products of distilling and fermentation include carbon dioxide, corn oil, vitamin and protein concentrates, and grain germ mixtures. See DISTILLING; FERMENTATION.

Livestock-Feed Manufacturing uses more shelled corn than any other industry. This industry also uses such by-products of corn processing as gluten meal, oil meal, and germ meal. The manufacturers grind and mix corn with other feed materials to make various livestock and poultry feeds.

History

Indian Corn. Botanists believe that corn first grew somewhere in North America. Fossilized pollen grains from corn plants found in Mexico may be more than 60,000 years old. Ears of corn about the size of strawberries have also been discovered in Mexico. They may be 3,000 years old.

No one in Europe knew about corn before Columbus sailed to America in 1492. But, when the early explorers arrived from Europe, they found that the American Indians were growing corn from Canada to the southern tip of South America. The Indians grew all the main types of corn that are raised today. They also raised varieties of corn with red, blue, pink, and black kernels. Some kernels had bands, spots, or stripes. The kernels ranged in size from no larger than a grain of wheat to as big as a quarter. Corn played an important part in the religious life of many American Indian tribes. They held elaborate ceremonies when planting and harvesting it, and used corn patterns to decorate pottery, sculpture, and other works of art.

Indians showed the early settlers from Europe how to plant and grow corn. Corn became of first importance to the life of the pioneers (see PIONEER LIFE IN AMERICA [Food]).

Early American colonists often used corn as money. People paid their rent, taxes, or debts in corn, and even traded it for marriage licenses. In settlement after settlement, corn kept people from starving in difficult times.

Improving Corn. Until about 1900, corn grown in the United States was not much different from some of the corn grown by the Indians. But farmers worked to improve the quality of their corn. They tried to grow bigger ears, stronger plants, and more ears on each plant. At first, corn growers simply sowed seeds from the best plants. After many years of selecting only the best seeds, farmers could grow corn that was somewhat better than that grown from ordinary seeds. But even then the results were not always satisfactory.

In the early 1900's, farmers began pollinating corn by hand. They improved the yield of corn by selecting good plants to breed. But they still could not produce uniform plants. George H. Shull (1874-1954), an American geneticist, began studying corn in 1905. He produced the first hybrids while studying heredity in corn. Shull established pure strains of corn by inbreeding, and produced hybrids by crossing the pure strains. Hybrids came into common use about 1933. Scientists continue to try to improve the quality of corn by breeding new hybrids.

Economic Problems. The development of hybrid corn and improved farming methods have helped increase

U.S. corn production from about 25 bushels an acre in the early 1930's to about 78 bushels an acre in the late 1960's. Total corn production increased from about 2,300,000,000 bushels a year to about 4,722,000,000 bushels a year during that period. Machinery enables farmers to plant, cultivate, and pick more corn. Fertilization and crop rotation improve the soil and increase the yield from each acre. New insect-killing chemicals destroy many of the insect pests that attack corn.

This increase in production often results in the production of more corn than the American people can use. The surplus reduces the profits of farmers, because prices drop. In 1933, Congress passed the first law establishing a price-support program for corn and other crops. Several laws passed since that time have continued this program. Under the program, the government lends money to farmers or agrees to purchase their crops at a given price, called parity (see PARITY). To receive these price supports, the farmer must agree to grow only as much corn as the government determines. The government tries to avoid large surpluses by limiting the amount of corn grown.

Scientific Classification. Corn belongs to the grass family, *Gramineae*. It makes up the genus *Zea*, which includes only the species *Z. mays*. But there are many varieties. For example, dent corn is *Z. mays*, variety *indenta*. Sweet corn is *Z. mays rugosa*.   G. F. SPRAGUE

Related Articles in WORLD BOOK include:

Acetone	Corn Oil	Iowa (color picture)
Alcohol	Corn Syrup	Maize
Chinch Bug	Cornstarch	Popcorn
Corn Borer	Farm and	South Dakota (color
Corn Ear	Farming	picture: Corn
Worm	Furfural	Palace)
Corn Meal	Hominy	Starch

Outline

I. Uses of Corn
   A. Livestock Feed   C. Other Products
   B. Food for Man
II. Kinds of Corn
   A. Dent Corn   C. Flint Corn   E. Flour Corn
   B. Sweet Corn   D. Popcorn   F. Pod Corn
III. The Corn Plant
   A. Stalk   C. Ears   E. Hand
   B. Leaves D. Natural Pollination   Pollination
IV. Hybrid Corn
V. Growing Corn
   A. Planting   C. Harvesting Corn
   B. Cultivation   D. Enemies of Corn
VI. Processing Corn
   A. Milling   C. Livestock-Feed
   B. Distilling and Fermentation   Manufacturing
VII. History

Questions

Why does popcorn pop?

What are the parts of a kernel of corn?

What is the main use of corn? What kind of corn is used for this purpose?

What is the Corn Belt? Why is it well suited for growing corn?

What kinds of corn did the American Indians grow?

What are some different methods of planting corn?

What is hybrid corn? How is it produced?

What is the role of the tassel in reproduction? What is the role of the silk?

What characteristics do breeders try to develop in hybrid corn? Why?

What is the leading corn-growing state?

CORN

CORN is a small, hard, shiny thickening of the *epidermis* (outer layer of the skin). This thick growth presses on the *dermis* (deeper skin layer) and causes it to become thin and tender. Pressure and friction cause corns. Therefore, corns often develop over the joints of the toes of persons who wear shoes that do not fit properly. But corns may form anywhere on the body where pressure and friction injure the skin. A *soft corn* is one located between the toes. Here the thickened skin remains soft because it is constantly bathed with sweat.

Corn plasters do not cure corns. To cure a corn, a person must remove the things that caused it to form. But he may use plasters to relieve pain. Most of them contain chemicals that soften the outer horny accumulation and relieve pain. Because of the danger of infection, paring corns with sharp instruments should be done only by a doctor.   RICHARD L. SUTTON, JR.

See also CALLUS.

CORN BELT. See CORN (introduction; Growing Corn).

CORN BORER, also called the *European corn borer,* is a serious insect menace to corn crops. The borer is the larva of a night-flying moth. It is pinkish with small brown spots. The female moths begin to lay eggs on corn leaves in early June. The tiny borers feed on the young leaves and tassels. As they grow larger, the borers feed on the stems and ears. One or more generations of borers appear each year, depending on the length of the growing season. In winter, the larvae live in old corncobs, stems, and stubble. The corn borer prefers to eat corn and sorghum. But it attacks other plants, including celery, potatoes, beans, beets, flowers, and weeds.

Farmers destroy corn borers during the winter by feeding cornstalks to livestock, or by shredding or burning the stalks. They plant late in the season to avoid the first flight of the moths, and use hybrid corn plants that are not affected by the corn borer. In some cases, farmers use insecticides.

Scientific Classification. The European corn borer belongs to the snout moth family, *Pyraustidae.* It is genus *Pyrausta,* species *P. nubilalis.*   E. GORTON LINSLEY

See also CORN (picture); MOTH (color picture).

CORN CRAKE. See RAIL.

The Corn Borer came to the United States from Europe about 1910, and had become a serious pest by 1926. It has spread over most of the Eastern and Midwestern states, and causes damage to the corn crop in the shaded areas on the map.

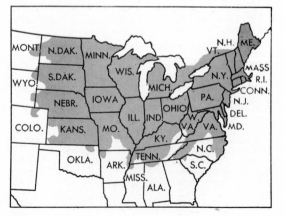

844

CORN EAR WORM, or BOLLWORM, ranks among the worst insect pests in the United States. It costs nearly $100 million a year to fight it. Most corn ear worms are greenish-brown with dark stripes. They measure about $1\frac{1}{2}$ inches long. The adult is a grayish-brown moth.

On corn, the moths usually lay their eggs on the silk. The eggs hatch in two to eight days. As far north as Kentucky, three broods of corn ear worms appear each year—in June, July, and August. Farther north, two broods are normal. To the south, as many as five broods may occur. Corn ear worms also attack cotton, tomatoes, alfalfa, beans, and other crops.

Insecticides, including DDT and toxaphene, help protect such crops as sweet corn, cotton, and tomatoes. Practical methods have not been developed for field corn.

Scientific Classification. The corn ear worm belongs to the owlet moth family, *Noctuidae.* It is genus *Heliothis,* species *H. obsoleta.*   E. GORTON LINSLEY

See also CORN (picture); MOTH (color picture).

CORN-HOG FARMING. See AGRICULTURE (Raising Animals); CORN; HOG.

CORN-HOG STATE. See IOWA (Agriculture).

CORN LAWS were measures passed in England between the 1400's and mid-1800's to control the price of small grains, called *corn* in England. The first corn laws prevented grain exports. By the 1500's, landowners could export grain if English prices fell too low. As the population grew in the 1700's, grain imports were permitted if prices rose too high.

By the 1830's, however, industry was developing in Great Britain, and support grew for the free trade proposals of economist Adam Smith. Landowners had lost support in Parliament. The Anti-Corn Law League, a group of factory owners and workers, demanded that the laws be repealed so bread would be cheaper. Parliament repealed the corn laws in 1846. Food imports then increased, and British agriculture eventually declined.   LACEY BALDWIN SMITH

See also PEEL, SIR ROBERT.

CORN MEAL is made by *milling* (grinding) the *kernels* (seeds) of the corn plant. It may be used in making baked foods and such products as adhesives, cleaning products, and soaps. Manufacturers refine corn meal to produce laundry starch and sizing for fabrics and paper. See also CORN (Uses); CORNSTARCH.

CORN OIL is a vegetable oil product of whole grain corn. About half of the germ, or *embryo*, of each corn grain is oil. To obtain the oil, processors soak the grains in a weak sulfurous acid solution. The softened grain is then cracked and mixed with water, and the oily germ floats off as a layer above the water. After refining, corn oil is used principally as a cooking and salad oil, and in paints and linoleum. See also CORN (Uses).

CORN PONE. See BREAD (Kinds).

CORN SMUT. See SMUT; CORN (picture).

CORN SNAKE. See SNAKE (color picture).

CORN STATE. See IOWA.

CORN SUGAR. See CORN (Other Products).

CORN SYRUP is a thick, sweet liquid made from the starch of corn. It is also called *liquid glucose* or *commercial glucose.* Corn syrup consists of a mixture of dextrin, maltose, and dextrose. It is a chief sweetening agent for candies, gums, and jellies, and is often used to sweeten pancakes and waffles. It varies in color from water-white, to yellow or light brown.

CORNEA. See Eye (The Eyeball).

CORNEAL TRANSPLANTATION. See Eye Bank.

CORNEILLE, *cor NAY y'*, **PIERRE** (1606-1684), was a French playwright. He is often called the father of French tragedy, but he is more truly the founder of French heroic comedy. Corneille favored tragicomedy and melodrama over the conventional tragedy of his day.

Corneille is best known for his tragicomedy *The Cid* (1636). The French Academy condemned the play for breaking several "classical" rules. These "classical" rules held that a play should consist of a single plot in a single location within a day's time. Violence was also prohibited on stage. Although *The Cid* broke these rules, it enjoyed great popularity. It was the first French drama to center interest on the characters' inner psychological conflict rather than on details of the plot. It also brought to the French stage a new lyrical language in keeping with the passionate nature of Corneille's heroes.

The subjects of most of Corneille's plays are taken from Roman history. Most of his leading characters, like their ancient models, show great pride, patriotism, honor, and stern courage. They are fearless, remorseless, and subject to violent emotions such as hatred, revenge, and superhuman ambition. Many of Corneille's plays show the influence of Spanish drama, especially in the passionate, boastful, and violent nature of their heroes.

Corneille's other famous plays include *Horace* (1640), *Cinna* (1641), *Polyeucte* (1642), and *Rodogune* (1644). He described his drama theories in the prefaces to his plays and especially in his *Discourses on Tragedy* (1660). Corneille was born in Rouen.   Jules Brody

CORNELIA was the mother of the Gracchi, political reformers of ancient Rome. See Gracchus.

CORNELIAN. See Carnelian.

CORNELL, EZRA (1807-1874), was an American businessman and philanthropist. He rose with the rapidly growing telegraphic communications industry, and helped organize the Western Union Telegraph Company. He became a wealthy man, and in his later years devoted his energies and fortunes to educational projects. He is particularly remembered for helping found Cornell University (see Cornell University).

Cornell was born in New Britain, N.Y. His father was a poor potter, and he received little education. After several false starts in various fields, Cornell invented a machine that solved Samuel F. B. Morse's problem of laying cable for his first telegraph line. Cornell then became one of the leading builders of telegraph systems. He retired from business at the age of 51.   Richard D. Humphrey

Katharine Cornell
Culver

CORNELL, KATHARINE (1898-   ), an American actress, won fame for the quality of her acting and her fine choice of plays. She became famous in *A Bill of Divorcement* (1921). Beginning with *The Green Hat* (1925), her husband, Guthrie McClintic, direct-ed her performances. Her greatest success came in *The Barretts of Wimpole Street* (1931), which she performed almost a thousand times. She also won praise for her acting in *Romeo and Juliet, Saint Joan, Candida, The Wingless Victory, The Three Sisters,* and *Antigone.* Her autobiography, *I Wanted to Be an Actress,* was published in 1941.

Miss Cornell was born in Berlin, Germany, of American parents. Even as a child, the theater fascinated her, and she determined to make it her career. At the age of 18, she began acting with the Washington Square Players in New York City.   Mary Virginia Heinlein

CORNELL COLLEGE. See Universities and Colleges (table).

CORNELL UNIVERSITY is a private school that gets New York state support. The main campus at Ithaca has colleges of arts and sciences, engineering, and architecture. It also has schools of law, hotel administration, education, a general graduate school, and graduate schools of nutrition and business and public administration. The campus has four units of the State University of New York. They are the colleges of agriculture, home economics, the veterinary college, and the school of industrial and labor relations. The medical college and the school of nursing are part of the New York Hospital-Cornell Medical Center in New York City. The agricultural experiment station is at Geneva, and the aeronautical laboratory is at Buffalo. Students in the schools of industrial and labor relations, hotel administration, and agriculture are required to work in their chosen fields during the summer months. Statler Hall, at Ithaca, is the "practice inn" for the School of Hotel Administration.

Five of the 45 members of the board of trustees are appointed by the governor of New York. Cornell was founded in 1865 as a land-grant university. It was named for its founder, Ezra Cornell, an American businessman and philanthropist. For enrollment, see Universities and Colleges (table).   John Mason Potter

See also Cornell, Ezra; New York (color picture).

The Cornell University Library Clock Tower dominates the wooded campus overlooking Cayuga Lake at Ithaca, N.Y.

Cornell University

CORNER BROOK, Newfoundland (pop. 27,116; alt. 95 ft.), is an important newsprint-producing center and the second largest city in the province. It is located on the west coast of Newfoundland in the Bay of Islands near the mouth of the Humber River (see NEWFOUNDLAND [political map]). Corner Brook is the center of one of the world's largest pulp and paper mills. The mill was established in 1925, and produces about 1,200 tons of newsprint and pulp daily. Cement and gypsum are also manufactured in the city. The Humber River is famous for its salmon fishing. Corner Brook has a mayor-council form of government.　　FRED W. ROWE

CORNERING THE MARKET was a technique formerly used to accumulate all or most of the available supply of a particular stock or commodity. The buyer did this in order to raise the price of the stock or commodity at will. Cornering seriously affected stock-market speculators who *sold short*, or sold stock that they did not own but planned to buy later at lower prices. The market corner forced those who needed a particular stock to go to the controlling group and pay extraordinarily high prices. Various stock exchanges and the Securities and Exchange Commission have outlawed cornering. They limit the prices at which a speculator may sell short, because these practices have caused serious fluctuations in the stock market.　　G. KEITH FUNSTON

See also BLACK FRIDAY; GOULD (Jay); MARKET.

CORNERSTONE forms a part of the corner or angle in a building wall. It usually lies at the foundation of a main angle of the building. It is one of the most important stones in the building because of the support it provides, and because of what it symbolizes. It has both ceremonial and historical significance.

Laying the cornerstone is often done in formal dedication ceremonies. Many cornerstones have been hollowed out and filled with documents, newspaper clippings, and other items of interest to persons who may tear down the building, perhaps hundreds of years later.

A cornerstone may have inscribed on it the date when construction of the building began or was completed. It may also bear the names of the officials of the company or government office constructing the building and the names of the architects and contractors.

CORNET, *KAWR net*, or *kawr NET*, is a brass-wind treble instrument with a cupped mouthpiece. It looks somewhat like a trumpet, with a main tube almost 5 feet long, but it lacks the trumpet's power and brilliance. The tube has three valves operated by sliding rods, or pistons. The tone is produced by the vibration of the player's lips. The pitch is controlled in part by the lips and in part by the pistons. The cornet has a range of about two and one-half octaves. It is used in military and concert bands. It is sometimes used in amateur orchestras in place of the trumpet.

The cornet evolved from the small coiled continental posthorn in the early 1800's in France. Its earliest appearance seems to have occurred during the première of the Italian composer Rossini's opera *William Tell* in 1829. See also TRUMPET.　　CHARLES B. RIGHTER

CORNFLOWER. See BACHELOR'S-BUTTON; FLOWER (table: National Flowers).

CORNHUSKER STATE. See NEBRASKA.

CORNICE. See ARCHITECTURE (table: Architectural Terms [Entablature]).

CORNING, N.Y. (pop. 17,085; alt. 935 ft.), is a glass-making center on the Chemung River in the south-central part of the state (see NEW YORK [political map]). It is often called the *Crystal City*. Products made at the glass works include huge telescope lenses, light bulbs, laboratory apparatus, heat-resisting glass, the famous Steuben glass, and tubes for neon and fluorescent lights. Corning was incorporated as a village in 1848, and as a city in 1890. In 1951, the Corning Glass Works opened the Corning Glass Center, which has exhibits on the history of glass. Corning has a mayor-council government. See also GLASSWARE (Present-Day Art Glass).　　WILLIAM E. YOUNG

CORNPLANTER (1740-1836) was a Seneca Indian chief. He fought the colonists during the Revolutionary War, but later supported the United States. Trusted by both Indians and settlers, Cornplanter helped arrange several treaties that brought peace to the frontier. The grateful Pennsylvania legislature voted a grant of land to Cornplanter near what is now Warren. The Cornplanter tract is now covered by the waters of a huge dam built to control floods on the upper Allegheny River. Cornplanter was born in what is now New York state, near the Genesee River.　　S. K. STEVENS

CORNSTALK (1720?-1777) was a Shawnee Indian chief during colonial days. He led an uprising against the white settlers in western Virginia in 1774. Cornstalk was defeated at Point Pleasant, Va., in October, 1774, by troops sent by Lord Dunmore, the British governor of Virginia. He then made a treaty with Dunmore that lasted until 1777. Then, the British began inciting the Indians to attack white settlers. Cornstalk went to Point Pleasant to warn the settlers, but they held him as a hostage. After the Indians ambushed a soldier, the settlers killed Cornstalk and his son. A monument to Cornstalk stands in Point Pleasant.　　JAMES GAY JONES

CORNSTARCH is a fine white flour made by grinding and refining grains of corn. It is made of corn from which the seed-bearing part, called the *germ*, has been removed. The corn is ground in a process called *wet milling*. The cornstarch is then dried in ovens for marketing. Since only 10 per cent of moisture remains in the cornstarch after the drying process, it is often mixed with other foods to protect them from moisture. Manufacturers use cornstarch in bakery products, baking powder, candies, and salad dressing. Cooks use it to thicken gravies and puddings. Cornstarch is also used in asbestos products, explosives, paints, and textiles. See also CORN (Milling).　　LEONE RUTLEDGE CARROLL

CORNU, PAUL. See HELICOPTER (Manned Flights).

CORNUCOPIA is a horn of plenty, symbol of nature's productivity. According to Greek mythology, there are two stories about its origin. In one, Hercules and a river-god had a contest. When the river assumed the form of a bull, Hercules wrenched off one of its horns and filled it with flowers for the goddess of plenty. In the other account, the infant Zeus was fed by the milk of a goat. Zeus gave one of the goat's horns to his nurses as a memorial of their care. The horn could be filled with whatever the owner wished. CHARLOTTE E. GOODFELLOW

See also SYMBOL (picture).

CORNWALL. See ENGLAND (Location; color map: The 38 Counties of England).

CORNWALL, Ont. (pop. 45,766; alt. 192 ft.), stands on the north bank of the St. Lawrence River in eastern Ontario (see ONTARIO [political map]). Its industries include a chemical factory and rayon and paper mills. Canada's St. Lawrence Seaway Authority headquarters are in Cornwall. Cornwall was founded in 1784 by the United Empire Loyalist settlers. It was chartered as a city in 1945.   D. M. L. FARR

CORNWALLIS, *kawrn WAHL ihs,* **CHARLES** (1738-1805), FIRST MARQUIS CORNWALLIS, was a British general in the Revolutionary War. His surrender at Yorktown in 1781 ensured the American triumph.

Cornwallis helped capture New York in 1776, then pursued General George Washington across New Jersey. He became second in command to Sir Henry Clinton in 1778. In 1780, he directed the southern campaign. Invading North Carolina, he defeated General Nathanael Greene at Guilford Courthouse. Then, against Clinton's wishes, he moved into Virginia. Finally, a French fleet and French and American troops surrounded him at Yorktown. His forces surrendered on Oct. 19, 1781.

Cornwallis was commander in chief and governor-general of India from 1786 to 1793 and again in 1805. He also served as viceroy and commander in chief of Ireland from 1798 to 1801. Cornwallis was born in London on Dec. 31, 1738.   W. B. WILLCOX

CORNWALLIS, EDWARD (1713-1776), a British soldier and colonial official, led 2,500 settlers to Nova Scotia in 1749 and founded Halifax. The city became Nova Scotia's capital in the same year. He served as governor and captain-general of Nova Scotia from 1749 to 1752. Cornwallis served in the British army from 1731 to 1748. He was appointed governor of Gibraltar in 1762 and served there until his death. Cornwallis was born in London.   CHARLES BRUCE FERGUSSON

See also CANADA, HISTORY OF (color picture).

COROLLA. See FLOWER (The Parts of a Flower).

CORONA, *koh ROH nuh,* in astronomy, refers to the faintly luminous area around the sun that is visible during total eclipses. Its light comes partly from sunlight reflected off particles near the sun, and partly from radiation of certain gaseous atoms, such as iron, nickel, calcium, and argon that have lost many of their electrons. The temperature of the corona is probably more than 1,000,000° C. The corona varies in size. Sometimes it extends into space for several diameters of the sun.

Visual Education Service

The Sun's Corona, as Seen During a Total Eclipse

The name *corona* is also given to a part of certain flowers that lies between the *corolla* (petals) and the stamens. In architecture, the corona is the upper, projecting part of a cornice.   R. WILLIAM SHAW

See also ECLIPSE; SUN (picture: The Corona).

Brown Bros.; Yale University Art Gallery

Lord Cornwallis, *above,* led British troops in many Revolutionary War battles. But he sent another general to surrender his troops to General George Washington at Yorktown. The scene, *right,* from John Trumbull's painting *The Surrender of Lord Cornwallis* shows French and American officers, including Washington, lined up to receive the British surrender.

Francisco Coronado, shown in a painting by N. C. Wyeth, set out in 1540 to search for seven cities that were said to be stocked with gold and gems. Instead, he discovered parts of the Rio Grande, the Grand Canyon, and central Kansas.

CORONADO, KOH roh *NAH thoh,* or KAHR oh *NAH doh,* **FRANCISCO VÁSQUEZ DE** (1510-1554), a Spanish explorer, led an expedition into the American Southwest, in search of the Seven Cities of Cibola and Gran Quivira. Explorers and Indians reported these cities to be rich in gold. Coronado, with a force of 300 Spaniards and several hundred Indians, began his search early in 1540. He visited what is now Arizona and New Mexico, and found Indian pueblos, but no golden cities.

The following spring, Coronado led his army across the Great Plains into what is now Kansas. He discovered the Palo Duro Canyon near present-day Amarillo, Tex. He saw big buffalo herds grazing on the plains. He found Indians called Quiviras, but no sign of gold.

Although Coronado failed to find the cities, his exploration of the Southwest proved valuable. The expedition discovered the Continental Divide, which runs through the Rocky Mountains. Some of his men, on a separate trip, discovered the Grand Canyon.

Coronado was born in Salamanca, Spain. He went to Mexico in 1535, and became governor of New Galicia, northwest of Mexico City, in 1538.   RICHARD A. BARTLETT

See also KANSAS (Exploration).

CORONARY SCLEROSIS. See ARTERIOSCLEROSIS.

CORONARY THROMBOSIS is a condition in which a clot forms in an artery or branch of an artery of the heart. The clot may often cut off the blood supply to the heart muscle (see HEART [Arteriosclerosis; Heart Attacks]). The pain from coronary thrombosis is called angina pectoris (see ANGINA PECTORIS). It begins under the breastbone and may move to a shoulder and down the arm. It is usually on the left side. There is also shortness of breath, coughing, rapid pulse, and a drop in blood pressure. Coronary thrombosis may be caused by bleeding due to an injury or operation, hardening of the arteries, or other blood diseases.   JOHN B. MIALE

CORONATION is a ceremony at which a king, queen, or pope publicly receives a crown as a symbol of rule. The ceremony is usually rich in color and tradition. Most coronations have religious as well as political features, and a religious official often performs the ceremony. During the proceedings, the new ruler also receives other official marks of royalty. When accepting this power, he usually makes a solemn pledge to rule wisely.

The British Coronation includes many features common to coronation ceremonies in other countries. The British ceremony takes place in Westminster Abbey. The new monarch is conducted from the west door of the Abbey along the nave to the crossing, where the ceremony is performed. First the monarch sits in a Chair of Estate. The *regalia*—the crown, orb, scepter, rod, swords of state, spurs, ring, and bracelets used in the ceremony—are placed on the altar. The Archbishop of Canterbury then presents the monarch to the people in the abbey as the true ruler of the realm. The monarch takes the coronation oath, swearing to rule justly and to support the Church of England. The monarch receives a Bible, which is placed on the altar. The celebration of the communion service of the Church of England then begins.

The service is interrupted after the Creed, the cloak is removed, and the monarch moves to King Edward's Chair, also called the Coronation Chair. Here the monarch is anointed and clothed in a cloak of gold cloth. The spurs of St. George, a symbol of knighthood, are presented. The Sword of State is taken from its scabbard and carried before the monarch during the rest of the ceremony. *Armills* (bracelets) are put on the wrists of the monarch. While sitting in King Edward's Chair, the monarch receives the *orb,* a globe of gold surmounted with a cross signifying the rule of Christ over the world.

The Archbishop of Canterbury Placed the Crown on the Head of Queen Elizabeth II During Her Coronation.

Queen Elizabeth II, Wearing Her Coronation Robes and St. Edward's Crown, Received Pledges of Allegiance.

Eight Perfectly Matched Horses Drew the Royal Coach in Queen Elizabeth II's Coronation Procession.

The Coronation Ring, symbolizing the marriage of the ruler and the kingdom, is placed on the monarch's right hand. The monarch receives a rod with a dove to hold in the left hand. The dove symbolizes the Holy Ghost. The monarch holds a scepter with a cross in the right hand. On top of the scepter is the *Star of Africa*, the largest cut diamond in the world. After the monarch receives these various symbols of authority, the Archbishop of Canterbury places the crown of St. Edward on the monarch's head.

The guns of the Tower of London fire a salute in honor of the coronation. The peers and peeresses, who were bareheaded until this moment, place their coronets and caps on their heads. The monarch moves to the throne after receiving a blessing from the archbishop. Nobles, carrying the Jewelled Sword of State, the Sword of Temporal Justice, the Sword of Spiritual Justice, and the Sword of Mercy, which has a blunted point, surround the throne. The monarch gives the rod and scepter to an attendant, then receives homage and fealty from representatives of the clergy and the public.

The monarch then leaves the throne, removes the crown, and offers the archbishop the bread and wine for Holy Communion. An altar cloth and an ingot of gold are placed on the altar. The monarch takes Holy Communion and returns to the throne. Then the monarch receives the crown, the scepter, and the orb, and leaves the throne. After walking in procession down the nave, the monarch leaves the Abbey through the west door. A banquet follows the coronation. In earlier times a fully armed knight, the King's Champion, rode into the banquet hall to challenge anyone who questioned the monarch's right to the throne.

The British coronation ceremony is quite ancient. The earliest record of the ceremony used in the coronation of an English king dates from about the A.D. 750's. King Edward I (1272-1307) made the Coronation Chair to contain the *Stone of Scone* (or *Stone of Destiny*), the Coronation Stone of ancient Scottish kings.

Development. Ancient Germanic tribes elected their rulers. The newly elected king received a spear, and a diadem of silk or linen was placed on his forehead. As the king sat upon a shield, his warriors lifted him to receive the acclamation of his followers.

Religious pageantry, taken from the Bible, influenced coronation ceremonies after the birth of Christianity. According to a custom mentioned in the Bible, kings were anointed with *chrism*, a mixture of oil and balm. People thought that chrism gave the anointed ruler special miraculous powers. In England, popular belief held that a person who even touched the king's clothes could be cured of illness. In some coronation ceremonies, the ruler was ordained as one of the lower ranks of the clergy. The Holy Roman emperor became a subdeacon and canon of St. Peter's Church and St. John Lateran in Rome.   I. J. SANDERS

Related Articles in WORLD BOOK include:

CORONER, *KAHR oh nur,* is an officer whose chief duty is to investigate any death which appears not to be from natural causes. In many states, he must be a physician, and may also serve as medical examiner. The coroner may be assisted by a jury of six or more men in his attempt to discover the cause of death. The report made by the coroner and the jury is used as a basis for possible arrests. The first coroners were those of early France and England. They guarded the fines collected by the king, or crown, and were called *crowners*. From this title came *coroner*. See also INQUEST.   H. F. ALDERFER

COROT, *KAW ROH,* **CAMILLE** (1796-1875), was a French landscape and figure painter. His work formed an artistic bridge between the tradition of classical composition of the early 1800's and the Romantic movement's concern with nature which led to Impressionism (see IMPRESSIONISM).

Corot began to study painting against his parents' wishes. In 1825, he went to Italy, where he became concerned with the play of light and color values. He began painting in solid masses in order to produce light and dark patterns of color. Corot's early work shows the influence of the French landscape painters, Claude (Lorrain) and Nicolas Poussin, and of the Dutch landscape painters of the 1600's.

Brown Bros.
Camille Corot

Corot returned to France in 1828 and traveled a great deal, because a small income left him free from economic worries. He came under the influence of a group of nature painters in the village of Barbizon. Corot was called "the lyric poet" of this group. He changed his style, and began painting everything as if seen through a delicate gray veil, accented by a few details of bright color. Corot's style underwent a final change in 1871. He again painted in the style of his youth, but his works were now drenched in Impressionist light and color. His painting, *Dance of the Nymphs*, appears in color in the PAINTING article.

Corot painted portraits for his own pleasure throughout his career. He also painted religious pictures. His portraits, along with his early and last paintings, are considered his best works. Corot was born JEAN BAPTISTE CAMILLE COROT in Paris, the son of a successful hairdresser.   ROBERT GOLDWATER

CORPORAL. See RANK IN ARMED SERVICES.

CORPORAL. See GUIDED MISSILE (Ballistic Missiles).

CORPORAL PUNISHMENT is any punishment applied to the body of the offender. It originally included death, mutilation, branding, bodily confinement, and flogging. See also TORTURE.

CORPORATION is an organization that can own property and make contracts as if it were a person. The property and contracts belong to the organization, not to the individuals who form it. Those who invest in a corporation have *limited liability*. If the corporation fails, they can lose no more than their investment, because the corporation's debts are not their debts.

In the United States, a corporation cannot be formed without the permission of the state or federal government. National banks must get federal government approval, but most corporations are chartered by a state government. A corporation set up in one state can do business in other states if its officers file certain forms and pay required fees in those states.

Corporations are formed under *general incorporation laws*. Persons wishing to form a corporation file *Articles of Incorporation*, stating the purpose and makeup of the organization. A state official then issues a certificate that permits the corporation to exist.

Stock Corporations own most large businesses and many small ones. A stock corporation is made up of persons who invest in the business by buying shares of the corporation's *capital stock*. These investors are called *stockholders*. The corporation distributes profits among the stockholders. These individual portions of the profits are called *dividends*.

The persons who form a corporation decide how many shares of stock will be issued and how much each will cost. After the corporation is formed, a stockholder usually may sell his stock to anyone else. The price generally depends on how well the company is doing (see STOCK, CAPITAL).

A corporation is governed by a board of directors, elected by the stockholders. Ordinarily, each stockholder can cast one vote for every share of stock he owns. As a result, a person owning 51 per cent of the stock can outvote all other stockholders, no matter how many there are. Some corporations issue certain *nonvoting stock*. Owners of this stock cannot vote.

The voting stockholders elect directors at regular meetings. If a stockholder does not wish to cast his vote in person, he may give another person written permission to cast it for him. That person is called a *proxy* (substitute). The written permission is also called a proxy. Sometimes, groups of stockholders compete for control of a corporation. Each group tries to collect proxies from other stockholders. The group holding the most proxies can elect the directors it favors.

The directors establish the policies of a corporation. The policies are carried out by officers, such as a president, vice-president, secretary, and treasurer. In most corporations, the directors choose the officers. In some, the stockholders elect the officers.

Parent and Subsidiary Corporations. A corporation may own all or most of the stock of another corporation. The corporation owning the stock is generally called a *parent corporation*, or *holding company*. The other corporation is called a *subsidiary*. Most subsidiaries are businesses that are related to the business of the parent company. For example, a corporation that makes automobiles may have a subsidiary that makes automobile parts.

Membership Corporations are formed without issuing stock. Instead of stockholders, they have members who elect the directors. Membership corporations include churches, cooperatives, country clubs, and community service organizations, such as the Red Cross or the Young Men's Christian Association (YMCA). They often are called *nonprofit corporations*.

Municipal Corporations include cities, counties, or school districts that run the business of communities.

As a rule, their governing bodies, such as city councils or school boards, are elected by the voters of the community.   ROBERT E. RODES, JR.

Related Articles in WORLD BOOK include:

Bond	Limited Company
Bylaw	Manufacturing (tables)
Cartel	Monopoly and
Charter	Competition
Excess-Profits Tax	Partnership
Franchise	Proxy
Holding Company	Stock, Capital
Investment	Trust
Joint-Stock Company	

CORPS, *kohr,* is an army unit consisting of two or more divisions. The name comes from *corpus,* the Latin word for *body.* A corps is normally composed of about 65,000 to 90,000 men, but the size can vary. A corps is usually commanded by a lieutenant general. A corps can conduct major military operations.

The word *corps* also refers to the United States Marine Corps and to the branches of the United States Army, such as the Medical Corps and Signal Corps.

See also ARMY (Major Armies of the World); ARMY, UNITED STATES (table: Army Levels of Command).

CORPS OF ENGINEERS. See ENGINEERS, CORPS OF.

CORPUS CHRISTI, *KAWR pus KRIHS tee,* Tex. (pop. 172,056; met. area 266,594; alt. 35 ft.), is a port on Corpus Christi Bay, about 230 miles southwest of Galveston (see TEXAS [political map]). A 21-mile channel links the city and the Gulf of Mexico. Canal and barge lines, trunk-line railroads, and highways and airlines serve the port. The city lies on the Gulf Intracoastal Canal, which follows the coastline from Carrabelle, Fla., to Brownsville, Tex. Corpus Christi has important oil-refining and shipping industries, and is a trade center for a large agricultural area. The natural-gas reservoir of the region gives Corpus Christi the lowest power cost of any coastal city in the United States. The city enjoys a semitropical climate and is a vacation center. The city was founded in 1839. In 1946, it adopted a council-manager government.   H. BAILEY CARROLL

For information on monthly temperature and rainfall in Corpus Christi, see TEXAS (Climate).

CORPUS CHRISTI, a feast. See SPAIN (Way of Life).

CORPUS CHRISTI, UNIVERSITY OF. See UNIVERSITIES AND COLLEGES (table).

CORPUS CHRISTI NAVAL AIR STATION, Texas, houses the headquarters of the Naval Air Advanced Training Command. The station covers 5,258 acres, and lies eight miles from the center of Corpus Christi. After basic training, naval pilots receive advanced training in multi- and single-engined fleet aircraft there and at other air stations. The base was set up in 1941. During World War II, it trained more than 35,000 naval aviators.   JOHN A. OUDINE

CORPUS JURIS CIVILIS. See JUSTINIAN CODE.

CORPUSCLE, *CORE pus'l,* in physiology, is a term used for a small mass or body. It is often used to mean *cell,* especially in referring to the red cells and white cells of the blood. Certain parts of the nervous system, such as the nerve endings in the skin that respond to pressure, are called *corpuscles* (see BLOOD [Parts]).

CORPUSCULAR THEORY. See LIGHT (Nature).

CORRAL. See COWBOY (Branding Cattle).

The Louvre, Paris

Correggio painted *The Marriage of Saint Catherine* when he was about twenty-eight years old. This painting is considered one of his masterpieces. It shows his rhythmic use of lines and the graceful, almost sentimental beauty of his figures.

CORREGGIO, *kohr RED jo* (1494-1534), an Italian artist, became the greatest painter of the city of Parma. At the peak of the Renaissance, Correggio ranked with Michelangelo, Titian, and a few other outstanding artists. His soft surfaces and daringly twined forms have little appeal to those with a taste for simplicity. But his painting *Holy Night* and his dome frescoes in Parma are famous for their originality. He was born ANTONIO ALLEGRI in Correggio, and was known by that town's name.   CREIGHTON GILBERT

Brown Bros.
Correggio

CORREGIDOR, *kuh REHG uh door,* a rocky fortified island, lies at the entrance to Manila Bay on the island of Luzon. It is sometimes called the *Gibraltar of the Pacific.* During the early days of World War II, United States and Filipino troops made a determined stand on Corregidor against overwhelming Japanese forces. Their surrender to enemy troops on May 6, 1942, marked the end of organized U.S. resistance in the Philippines. The Japanese held Corregidor until U.S. troops freed Luzon in February, 1945. The U.S. ceded Corregidor to the Republic of the Philippines in 1947. In 1963, the United States and the Philippines agreed to develop Corregidor into a battlefield park as a World War II memorial.   STEFAN T. POSSONY

CORRESPONDENCE. See LETTER WRITING.

CORRESPONDENCE SCHOOL is an educational institution that furnishes home-study material through the mail. Over 3,500,000 persons are enrolled in more than 750 home-study schools in the United States. About 75 per cent of the courses are of the vocational type.

Colleges and universities provide correspondence courses for nearly 200,000 persons. They coordinate their programs through the National University Extension Association. Government agencies, the armed forces, religious institutions, and business and industry provide courses for over 1,700,000 persons.

Nearly 1,500,000 persons are enrolled in private home-study schools. The National Home Study Council was organized in 1926 by a group of home-study schools. It works with the National Commission on Accrediting and the Federal Trade Commission to maintain sound educational standards and business practices. The 59 accredited schools in the council have an enrollment of about 1,200,000 persons.

The University Extension movement in England first used the correspondence plan in 1868. The earliest practical courses in the United States were developed in 1892 by President William R. Harper of the University of Chicago. The Blackstone School of Law in Chicago, and the International Correspondence School in Scranton, Pa., founded in 1891, are pioneer correspondence schools still in existence.　Thomas J. McLernon

See also Extension Service.

CORRESPONDENT. See Foreign Correspondent; War Correspondent.

CORROBOREE is an Australian aborigine dance festival. See Australia (picture, Aborigine Tribesmen).

CORRODENTIA is an order of destructive insects commonly called book lice, bark lice, or dust lice. They infest homes, libraries, and museums, damaging books by eating the paste and glue in the bindings. Out of doors, they eat refuse. See Book Lice; Insect.

CORROSION, *kuh ROH zhun,* is the gradual chemical breakdown of metals or rocks. A corroding metal or rock reacts slowly with some substance such as oxygen or an acid. This reaction alters the metal and often makes it useless. Corrosion in iron and steel is called *rusting.* Metals laid underground may be corroded by chemicals in the soil. Gases, such as sulfur dioxide in smoke, sometimes cause corrosion. Corrosion may be dangerous when it occurs in gas pipes or in high pressure boilers. See also Oxidation; Rust.

Corrosion can often be prevented by coating the metal with paint. The metal may be mixed with another substance to produce an alloy that does not corrode. Corrosion can also be prevented by covering the metal with a noncorroding metal.

CORROSIVE SUBLIMATE. See Bichloride of Mercury.

CORRUPT PRACTICES are unethical techniques used by politicians to gain a political advantage in an election. The term is most commonly used in referring to federal and state legislation, called *corrupt practices acts,* that govern campaigns and elections. These laws prohibit such activities as bribery, ballot-box stuffing, tampering with voting machines, and threatening or impersonating voters. Many of these laws also govern party campaign finances. They control the amount of money the candidate and the party may spend on each election, how the money may be raised, and how it may be spent. They often require political parties to publish a financial report outlining expenditures for a particular campaign. The laws that limit campaign spending have been easy to evade. But in U.S. elections, especially those for national offices, most other corrupt practices have ended.　Robert A. Dahl

CORRUPTION OF BLOOD. See Attainder.

The Island of Corsica Lies in the Mediterranean Sea.

CORSICA, *KAWR sih kuh* (pop. 275,465), is a French island in the Mediterranean Sea. It lies nine miles north of the island of Sardinia, between southeastern France and northwestern Italy. Corsica's name in French, the official language, is Corse. The island is one of the *departments* (main administrative districts) of France. It is famous as the birthplace of Napoleon.

Size and Description. Corsica has an area of 3,368 square miles, and ranks as the fourth largest island in the Mediterranean. Its 275-mile coastline is high and craggy, and there are few natural harbors. The wild, rocky interior is covered with scrub and cut by narrow, fertile valleys. Ajaccio, the capital of Corsica, lies on the western side of the island beside the Gulf of Ajaccio. Bastia, Corsica's largest city, lies on the eastern side of the island.

Economy. Corsica has a mild climate, and crops flourish in the rich soils of the valleys. Farmers raise olives, grapes and other fruits, grains, vegetables, and tobacco. Cork, pine, oak, and chestnut trees cling to the steep slopes of the mountains. Corsicans grind chestnuts into meal to make bread. Wool for clothing comes from sheep that graze in the mountains. Along the coast, the people fish for sardines and hunt for coral. Miners quarry granite and marble in the mountains. Some iron, lead, and copper are also mined. Since World War II, Corsica's principal exports have been wool and cheese. The island's fastest-growing source of income is the increasing tourist trade. Tourists enjoy the pleasant climate, the rugged scenery, and the colorful Corsican villages.

History. Corsica was first settled about 560 B.C. by Phoenicians, who called the island *Cyrnos.* It was conquered in turn by Etruscans, Carthaginians, and Romans. Its Roman conquerors renamed the island Corsica. Vandals captured Corsica in A.D. 469, but it was recaptured by Rome, under Justinian the Great, in 534. Later, the island came under the rule of Charlemagne.

Pope Gregory VII assumed sovereignty of Corsica in 1077, and granted it to the Bishop of Pisa to control. About 300 years later, Corsica came under the control of the Italian city of Genoa. In 1768, the Genoese ceded the island to the French, who lost it to the British in 1794. In 1796, Napoleon sent an expedition to Corsica to re-establish French control. France has held the island since then, except for a brief occupation by British soldiers in 1814, and the occupation by Italians and Germans during World War II. Allied forces freed the island in 1943, and it again became part of the French Republic.　Edward W. Fox

CORTES. See Spain (Government).

Hernando Cortes, *above,* explored and conquered Mexico for Spain in the early 1500's. Cortes held the Aztec Emperor Montezuma hostage, *left,* while he and his men forced the Indians to bring them large quantities of gold and silver.

Brown Bros.

CORTES, *KAWR tehz,* or *kor TAYS,* **HERNANDO** (1485-1547), was a Spanish adventurer who conquered Mexico. He was probably the greatest Spanish conqueror in the Americas. His name is often spelled CORTEZ.

Cortes was born in Estremadura, Spain. He went to Santo Domingo in the West Indies in 1504, and took part in the conquest of Cuba in 1511. The governor of Cuba became interested in the mainland to the west of the island. He chose Cortes to command the small fleet and army that he was sending to the area to explore and look for treasure.

Cortes and his expedition of about 650 men explored the coast of Yucatán and, early in 1519, landed on the coast of Mexico. There, Cortes founded the settlement of Veracruz. He scuttled all his ships except one, which he sent to Spain to report to the king concerning the plans for conquest. He destroyed the vessels because he wanted to add their crews to his small army.

Conquest of the Aztec. Cortes left soldiers to guard Veracruz, then led the main force overland to Tenochtitlán (Mexico City), the capital of the powerful and highly civilized Aztec Indians. The Aztec had conquered most of the nearby tribes. Cortes was received graciously by Montezuma, the Aztec ruler, who secretly feared the white men. But Cortes soon made Montezuma a prisoner and used him to govern the country. A larger Spanish expedition landed at Veracruz, and Cortes persuaded most of the men in it to join him.

The Aztec, angered by Montezuma's submission to Cortes, renounced his rule and attacked the Spaniards in Tenochtitlán. Cortes had superior weapons and slaughtered Aztec warriors by the thousands, but they were so numerous that he had to withdraw from the city. The Aztec pursued him, but he finally defeated them in a great battle on the plain of Otumba. Cortes and his soldiers won the rich country of Mexico for Spain on July 7, 1520.

The Spaniards retired to a friendly Indian city, where Cortes received reinforcements from the West Indies and from many Indian groups who hated the Aztec because of their bloodthirstiness and cruelty. With this increased army, Cortes captured Tenochtitlán in 1521 and ended the Aztec nation.

Later Work. Cortes spent the next few years spreading Spanish rule over other cities and districts. He governed Mexico, then called New Spain, for a time. The king of Spain entitled him Marquis of the Valley. In 1536, he commanded an expedition that founded the first settlement in Lower California.

Cortes eventually fell out of favor with the king and returned to Spain in 1540 to plead his own cause. He failed in his attempt to have his rights restored, and died at a small village near Seville.   CHARLES E. NOWELL

See also AZTEC; MONTEZUMA.

CORTEX. See BARK; GLAND (The Adrenal Glands).

CORTEX, CEREBRAL. See BRAIN (The Cerebrum).

CORTISONE, *KAWR tuh sohn,* is one of a large family of compounds that are normally made in the *cortex,* or outer portion of the adrenal glands. Cortisol is another closely related member of the family. Cortisone is essential for normal life. It has a marked effect on the formation and use of sugar in the body. It increases resistance to cold and other stresses. In patients who have lost the use of their own adrenal glands, these compounds restore strength, health, and a feeling of well-being.

Cortisone was first used at the Mayo Clinic in Rochester, Minn., by Philip S. Hench and Edward C. Kendall to treat patients with rheumatic fever and one form

An Important Source of Cortisone is a wild Mexican yam. Its roots yield a substance used for making this synthetic hormone.

United Press Int.

of rheumatism. These men received the 1950 Nobel prize in physiology and medicine for their work with this substance. (They shared the prize with Tadeus Reichstein, who first isolated cortisone.) Further investigation showed that cortisone was valuable in treating many other diseases. Among these were allergic and inflammatory conditions, asthma, disorders of the eyes and skin, and diseases of the gastrointestinal tract and the kidneys. Cortisone can be used effectively in more different diseases than any other substance.

The adrenal glands were the only source of cortisone for 12 years after the substance was discovered. Cortisone was expensive and the supply was small. But in 1948, scientists produced cortisone from a compound in the bile of cattle. Cortisone is the most complicated substance that manufacturers have been able to make in quantity. EDWARD C. KENDALL

Related Articles in WORLD BOOK include:

ACTH	Hench, Philip S.	Kendall, Edward C.
Gland	Hormone	Reichstein, Tadeus

CORTOT, *core TOE,* **ALFRED** (1877-1962), a French pianist, writer, and teacher, played many concerts in Europe and America. In 1919 he helped found the École Normale de Musique in Paris. Among his books are *French Piano Music* (1930-1932) and *Alfred Cortot's Studies in Musical Appreciation* (1937). Cortot was born at Nyon, Switzerland. ROBERT U. NELSON

CORUNDUM, *koh RUN dum* (chemical formula, Al_2O_3), is the second hardest pure mineral. Only diamond is harder. Corundum occurs as transparent nuggets in loose gravel, and as rough nontransparent grains in rocks.

Varieties of transparent corundum are polished and used as gemstones. Gemstones from corundum include the ruby, sapphire, Oriental amethyst, Oriental emer-

ald, and Oriental topaz. The colors of the gemstones are caused by impurities in the corundum. For example, the red of the ruby is caused by the presence of chromium oxide, and the blue of the sapphire by iron and titanium. Gemstone corundum comes from Africa, India, the Malagasy Republic, and Russia.

Nontransparent corundum is used as an *abrasive* (grinding, smoothing, and polishing material). Emery, a common abrasive, is a natural mixture of corundum and other minerals. Abrasive quality corundum and emery are mined in Turkey and Greece. WILLIAM C. LUTH

Related Articles in WORLD BOOK include:

Abrasive	Emery	Ruby
Amethyst	Gem	Sapphire
Emerald	Hardness	Topaz

CORVETTE, *kawr VET,* is a warship about 150 feet long used for convoy duty. It can operate in rough waters for long periods of time. The corvette is larger than a subchaser, but smaller than a frigate or a destroyer. In early sailing days, a corvette was a flush-deck warship, or a vessel whose deckline had not been broken by raised sections. In European navies, it ranked below a frigate in size. It usually had one row of guns. A large American sloop-of-war almost equaled a small corvette in size. WILLIAM W. ROBINSON

CORWIN, NORMAN (1910-   ), became a noted American writer and radio and television director and producer. Such radio programs as *Words Without Music* (1938), *Ballad for Americans* (1941), and *The People, Yes* (1941) made broadcasting history. His telecast, *Between Americans,* won the Freedom Award in 1951. Corwin was born in Boston. BARNARD HEWITT

CORYMB. See INFLORESCENCE.

CORYPHENE. See DOLPHIN.

CORYZA. See COLD, COMMON.

COSGRAVE, WILLIAM THOMAS (1880-   ), served as president of the Irish Free State's executive council from 1922 to 1932. He lost to Eamon de Valera's party, which wanted complete independence from England. He criticized the 1937 constitution, which established the republic of Eire. But he joined De Valera in supporting President Douglas Hyde's election in 1938.

Born in Dublin, Ireland, Cosgrave went to prison for his part in the 1916 *Easter Rebellion.* Later he served in the revolutionary government from 1919 to 1921. He became president after the head of the Free State, Arthur Griffith, and his successor, Michael Collins, had died in quick succession. ALFRED F. HAVIGHURST

See also DE VALERA, EAMON; IRELAND (The Irish Free State).

COSIMO DE' MEDICI. See MEDICI.

COSINE. See TRIGONOMETRY.

COSMETICS, *kahz MET icks,* include all substances, preparations, devices, and treatments used to cleanse, to alter the appearance, or to promote the attractiveness of the face and body. They are made for both men and women. Cosmetics include beauty products for the hair, scalp, body, face, and hands. Soap and perfume are related to cosmetics, as are dentifrices, deodorants, and *depilatories* (hair-removing preparations). *Cosmetic treatments* include hairdressing, permanent waving, manicuring, special baths, and massage.

The manufacture of cosmetics is an important in-

855

dustry in the United States. It employs thousands of persons, and has retail sales of more than $1,500,000,000 a year. Cosmetics have become one of the most heavily advertised consumer products in the world. In addition, many publications print articles featuring the use and application of cosmetics.

Uses of Cosmetics

The face and hair are the most conspicuous parts of the human body. A great variety of cosmetic aids have been designed especially to make these parts of the body more attractive.

Face. People use *creams* to cleanse and soften the skin. Creams may also provide a smooth surface for the application of powder. They are made of fats, oils, and waxes, and are usually lightly perfumed. *Lipstick* is made of similar substances colored in various shades of red. *Face powder* consists principally of harmless mineral compounds that are ground fine and thoroughly blended. They are tinted in a variety of shades, and usually perfumed. *Bath powders* consist largely of *talc* and other absorbent substances. *Dry rouges* are powders mixed with coloring and a binding substance that holds the powder in cake form. *Lotions* cleanse the skin, bleach it, or tighten it slightly. They usually contain water, alcohol, glycerin, oil, and perfume.

Hair. There are many products available for persons who wish to change the color of their hair. These materials include bleaches, and temporary and permanent dyes. *Bleaches*, usually hydrogen peroxide with ammonia, lighten the shade of the hair. Most *temporary dyes* are powders, composed of mild acid and dyes, which can be dissolved in water and applied as rinses. The coloring can usually be removed from the hair by shampooing. *Permanent dyes* are divided into three classes: *vegetable substances*, such as henna, camomile, and wood extracts; *metallic compounds*, such as salts of lead, silver, copper, and nickel; and *coal-tar* (organic) *compounds*, of the same general type as those used to dye furs. The coal-tar dyes produce the most natural shades, but should be used with caution because they may irritate the scalp. These dyes should be used only by persons who have a professional knowledge of the proper methods of hair coloring.

History

The history of cosmetics goes back thousands of years. The Bible, for example, describes the practice of anointing the head or body with oil. Among the ancient Egyptians, physicians used cosmetics. The most famous figure associated with cosmetics was Cleopatra, the last queen of Egypt, who was noted for her skill in making and using cosmetics.

Physicians supplied cosmetics to the Greeks, then to the Romans, the Arabs, and the peoples of Western Europe. The word *cosmetics* comes from the Greek word *kosmetikos*, meaning *skilled in decorating*. Each of these groups added something to the art of cosmetics. But finally physicians became too busy to practice the art of adornment, and eventually tradesmen supplied the growing demand for beauty aids.   S. R. Friedman

See also Glycerin (Uses); Grooming, Personal; Hairdressing; Theater (pictures).

Fordham University

The Beginning of High-Altitude Cosmic-Ray Research took place in the early 1900's when Victor F. Hess of Austria, made several balloon flights to measure the intensity of the rays.

COSMIC RAYS are particles of high energy that originate in outer space. Many can penetrate thousands of feet of rock. The rays from radium, nuclear bombs, or X-ray machines can penetrate only a few inches of lead. The study of cosmic rays sends scientists to all parts of the earth. They climb to the tops of high mountains, descend into the deepest mines, and drift miles above the earth in balloons to learn about this radiation. Instruments that study cosmic rays have been sent far out into space in rockets and satellites. The study of cosmic rays was one of the most important parts of the International Geophysical Year (see INTERNATIONAL GEOPHYSICAL YEAR).

What Cosmic Rays Are

The rays detected in deep mines, at the surface of the earth, and even on high mountains are *secondary* cosmic rays. The *primaries* come from outside the earth's atmosphere. They crash into the nuclei of atoms of the air, and create a variety of secondary particles. Some of these, in turn, produce still more particles. Most primary particles lose their identity in the part of the atmosphere more than 10 miles above the earth.

The Secondaries are composed of all the known subatomic particles, including mu-mesons, pi-mesons, neutrons, electrons, and positrons (see ATOM [Inside the Atom]). High-energy X rays, or gamma rays, are also present. At sea level, about 10 secondaries pass through a square inch of the surface of the earth every minute. The intensity of the bombardment increases up to several hundred secondaries in a square inch each minute about 10 miles above the earth.

The Primaries are atomic nuclei with energies from a few hundred million to about 1,000,000,000,000,000,000 ev, or electron volts (see ATOMIC ENERGY [table]). The largest atom smashers achieve energies near 30,000,-000,000 ev. About 87 per cent of the primaries are *protons* (nuclei of hydrogen atoms). About 12 per cent are helium nuclei. The rest are nuclei of heavier elements.

Variations in Intensity. Between 50 and 200 primary cosmic rays pass through an area of 1 square inch each minute. This range in intensities results partly from a *latitude effect*. Primary cosmic rays bear electric charges,

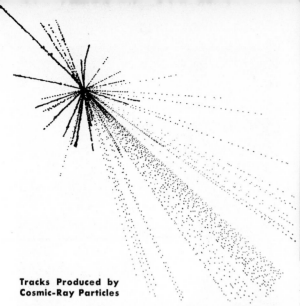

Tracks Produced by Cosmic-Ray Particles

Marcel Schein

Peter Meyer, The University of Chicago

Modern Cosmic-Ray Research uses unmanned balloons. The balloons carry sensitive measuring instruments aloft. Radio signals from the ground release the instruments on parachutes.

so the magnetic field of the earth deflects them. The particles have a wide range of energies. Near the equator, only high-energy particles can penetrate the magnetic field. But at the poles, particles of lower energies can penetrate. The intensity of radiation is lowest near the equator. It increases steadily toward the poles. At the equator, the primary cosmic-ray intensity is only a third to a fourth of its value at the poles. Usually, a "cut-off" latitude exists, beyond which intensity of cosmic radiation does not increase toward the poles. This occurs because no particles have energies lower than that required to penetrate the earth's field at the cut-off latitude. The cut-off energy varies.

How the Sun Affects Cosmic Radiation

When eruptions on the sun occur most frequently, the cosmic-ray intensity is usually less than when the sun is not active (see Sun [The Stormy Surface of the Sun]). For example, 1957 was a year of great solar activity. In that year, the total cosmic-ray intensity was about a third of the total intensity in 1954, a year of little solar activity. The sun has an 11-year cycle of activity, and so do cosmic rays. Effects of shorter duration also exist. For example, the intensity may drop sharply in a few hours and build up slowly over a period of days. Scientists believe that both the 11-year cycle and the short-term effects result from variations in solar activity. But a different mechanism causes each. Physicists do not understand in detail the ways that solar activity influences cosmic rays. They believe that material ejected from the sun produces these effects. Short-term effects probably occur when this material interacts with the magnetic field of the earth. The 11-year cycle is probably caused by larger-scale events, which will be explained later in this article.

Cosmic Rays from the Sun. Large increases in cosmic-ray intensity sometimes accompany giant explosions, or solar flares, on the sun. The solar flare of Feb. 23, 1956, increased cosmic-ray intensity about 50 times the normal at some places. Particles came from the sun a few minutes after the flare was seen. They had energies up to at least 30,000,000,000 ev. The intensity remained above normal many hours after the flare ceased.

Solar System Barrier. Physicists believe that a barrier exists in the solar system beyond the orbit of the earth. Some cosmic rays pass through this barrier. But it reflects others. This takes place in much the same manner as light from a city is reflected by clouds above it. If the barrier did not exist, cosmic-ray intensity would return to normal shortly after the flare ceased. The particles would escape directly into the galaxy. The barrier causes them to be scattered back and forth in the inner part of the solar system before they finally escape.

This same barrier should also affect cosmic rays traveling towards the solar system from the rest of the galaxy. It probably contains magnetic fields that deflect and reflect particles. Physicists believe that material ejected from the sun produces the barrier. The quantity of material ejected depends on the sun's activity. The barrier is stronger at times of increased solar activity, and lets fewer cosmic rays through. Changes in strength of the barrier probably produce the 11-year cycle of intensity and the variations in cut-off energy.

Energies of Cosmic Rays

Physicists believe that a magnetic field extending throughout the galaxy affects the paths of the cosmic rays. Particles spend about 10,000,000 years wandering in the galaxy before escaping from this field. The cosmic rays are probably accelerated to their high energies during the time they spend in the field.

Acceleration probably occurs when the particles "collide" with moving irregularities in the magnetic field. When a particle collides head on with a moving object it gains energy. For example, in table tennis, a moving ball gains speed after it strikes a paddle moving towards it. But, if the ball strikes a paddle moving away from it, the ball loses speed. The ball corresponds to a cosmic-ray particle and the paddle to a moving irregularity in the magnetic field of the galaxy. You might think that because a particle gains energy in one kind of collision and loses it in another, there would be no over-all gain or loss of energy. But a moving particle makes more head-on collisions with moving objects than overtaking collisions. Scientists believe that equal numbers of

857

magnetic irregularities move in opposite directions through any region of the galaxy, like automobiles on a highway. A cosmic ray encounters more irregularities head-on than it overtakes, the same way that a motorist on a highway sees more cars coming toward him than in the direction he goes. Thus, over a long period of time, cosmic rays are slowly accelerated.

Effects of Cosmic Rays

Cosmic radiation affects both individuals and the human race as a whole. A human being can probably tolerate a radiation dose of $\frac{1}{100}$ roentgen, the unit of radiation, each day without damage to his body. The dosage from cosmic rays at sea level amounts to about $\frac{1}{1,000}$ roentgen each day. Even at the highest altitudes at which man lives, the dosage remains well below the danger level. However, at extremely high altitudes, or beyond the atmosphere, the dosage probably exceeds the amount that man can tolerate. The heavy nuclei in the primaries, although of low intensity, may produce serious biological effects. This represents a hazard for space travelers (see RADIATION SICKNESS; SPACE TRAVEL [Dangers in Space]).

The effects of cosmic rays on man come about through *mutation*, or changes in heredity. Heat and chemicals cause about 90 per cent of all mutations (see MUTATION). Radiation causes the rest. Of this fraction, cosmic rays cause about a fourth.

History

Scientists discovered cosmic rays in the early 1900's. At that time, the electroscope was commonly used for observing radioactivity (see ELECTROSCOPE). This instrument discharges in the presence of radioactivity. Scientists found that even when they shielded an electroscope with lead from all known radioactive materials, it continued to discharge. At first, they thought that traces of radioactivity on the earth caused the leakage of radiation into the electroscope. But when electroscopes were flown in balloons to escape such effects, scientists found that the rate of leakage increased up to the highest altitudes reached at that time, 30,000 feet. This indicated that rays from the atmosphere or beyond caused the leakage.

In the late 1920's, scientists found that the intensity of cosmic rays varies with latitude. This indicated that primary cosmic rays are electrically charged particles. New instruments showed that the secondaries are charged particles and gamma rays. In the 1930's, physicists discovered new subatomic particles, the positron and mu-meson, in secondary cosmic rays (see MESON). In the late 1940's, they discovered more types of secondary particles. Special photographic films carried to high altitudes by balloons showed that primaries consist of protons and the nuclei of heavier elements. In the 1950's, research centered on the effects of the sun on cosmic rays.   K. B. FENTON

Related Articles in WORLD BOOK include:

Atom	Ion Counter	Radiation
(Inside the Atom)	Light	Radioactivity
Delta Ray	(Electromagnetic	Wilson Cloud
Geiger Counter	Waves)	Chamber

COSMOLOGY. See METAPHYSICS (Branches).

COSMONAUT. See ASTRONAUT.

J. Horace McFarland

Cosmos Flowers have white, pink, crimson, or orange petals with a bright yellow center. The leaves are delicate and feathery.

COSMOS, *KAHZ mahs*, are tall, late-summer flowers that are native to Mexico and the American tropics. Their flowers range from white and pink to red and orange, and may be double or single. Cosmos are in the daisy family.

Seeds may be planted outdoors after the ground warms, or indoors in early spring and then transplanted a few weeks before summer. Cosmos are well adapted to full sun, and to light soil that is not too rich. Most varieties need protection from wind because they are so tall. They make good background plants or fillers among shrubs. They also provide excellent cut flowers.

Scientific Classification. Cosmos belong to the composite family, *Compositae.* They make up the genus *Cosmos.* The familiar garden plants are *C. bipinnatus*, the yellow cosmos is *C. sulphureus.*   ROBERT W. SCHERY

See also COMPOSITE FAMILY; FLOWER (color picture, Fall Garden Flowers).

COSMOS is a term used to refer to everything in creation, from the smallest atoms to the most distant celestial bodies. The ancient Greeks originated the term. To them, the cosmos was a well-ordered, harmonious system. The earth, the sun, and the planets made up their cosmos.

Today, we know that the sun is only one of about 100 billion stars that form the Milky Way. This galaxy is one of about 1 billion galaxies that make up the observable universe.   I. M. LEVITT

See also GALAXY; UNIVERSE.

COSMOTRON, *KAHZ moh trahn*, is the name scientists have given to a high-energy atom smasher, or *nuclear accelerator*, built at the Brookhaven National Laboratory on Long Island, New York. It has a huge circular magnet weighing 2,200 tons. Sandwiched inside the magnet is a vacuum chamber 60 feet in diameter. Protons produced in a Van de Graaff generator are injected into the cosmotron vacuum chamber at 5 million electron volts (5 Mev) of energy. These charged particles are accelerated again and again as they speed around the 60-foot orbit, until they finally reach over 2 billion electron volts (2 Bev) of energy. Then, the protons have energies about equal to those which are found in cosmic rays. Hence the name *cosmotron*.

An even higher energy machine called a *bevatron*, at the University of California, works on the same principle. RALPH E. LAPP

See also ATOM SMASHER with its Related Articles.

COSPAR. See SPACE TRAVEL (Steps in the Conquest of Space).

COSSACK, *KAHS ack*, is the name given to a group of about 3 million Russians living in southern and eastern parts of Russia. They are Slavic peoples who became border defenders against the Tartars in the 1400's (see SLAV). They gained a reputation as daring horsemen and mercenary soldiers who recognized no authority but their own. The name comes from a Tartar word meaning *free laborer*, later applied to those who lived in the no man's land beyond the state. Eleven groups developed, the Don and Kuban Cossacks being the largest. See COSSACKS, DON.

Cossacks were an elite corps in the armies of the czars and received special privileges, including exemption from taxes. After the Revolution, they fought on the side of the White armies, trying to overthrow the new government. Their historical organization was broken up after the Red, or Bolshevik, armies won the civil war. Many were killed or deported.

Cossack cavalry units served effectively against German tanks in World War II. WILTON MARION KROGMAN

See also CLOTHING (color picture: Europe).

COSSACK ASPARAGUS. See CATTAIL.

COSSACKS, DON, were one of the largest and most powerful groups of Cossacks in southern Russia before the Russian Revolution. When the Bolsheviks, or Reds, took over the government, the Don Cossacks joined the forces opposing them, called the *Whites*. The Whites lost the civil war that followed, and many fled or were deported. One enterprising leader, Serge Jaroff (1896-   ), formed a group to sing Russian folk songs and liturgical music. His *Don Cossack Chorus* won wide ac-

claim in tours through Europe, and finally settled in the United States. Their performances, which feature strong rhythms and good control of dynamics, brought Russian folk music to many who had never heard it before. See also SHOLOKHOV, MIKHAIL A.

COST. See PRICE.

COST OF LIVING is the amount of money needed to buy a standard amount of goods and services of daily living. Needs of individual persons and families vary. Everyone needs food, clothing, and shelter, but needs go beyond these bare necessities. The cost of living includes the cost of transportation, reading, recreation, rent, electricity, gas, fuel, home furnishings, medical and personal care, taxes, and many other things.

When salaries and wages keep step with the prices of goods and services, the worker's buying power remains stable. When prices rise, persons with low incomes or fixed incomes, such as pensions, fall behind in buying power. Increases and decreases in the cost of living come from many things. Rising incomes, spending, abundance of credit, industrial expansion, and cost of new equipment tend to make prices go up. When more goods than money are available, prices go down.

The Bureau of Labor Statistics is the fact-finding agency of the United States government in the field of labor economics. It collects and analyzes data on employment, wages, and productivity. It also makes surveys throughout the United States on the cost of living, and reports its findings through its publications. Workers, businessmen, and other governmental agencies supply information on the amount and kinds of goods people buy and on changing standards of living. The bureau collects information regularly from about 1,350 reporters and from about 4,500 establishments in 46 cities and towns. They report on rents, on retail prices of food, clothing, and home furnishings, and on miscellaneous goods and services. The bureau prepares a cost of living or consumer price index that summarizes this information. KENNETH E. BOULDING

See also INFLATION AND DEFLATION; WAGES AND HOURS.

COST OF LIVING

The Consumer Price Index, prepared by the U.S. Bureau of Labor Statistics, measures the cost of living in the United States. The index shows changes in prices of goods and services purchased by city families. The bureau collects prices for about 300 items in 46 cities. In 1962, the bureau changed the base from 1947-1949 to 1957-1959.

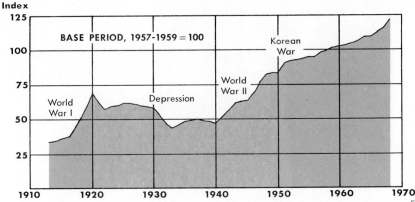

Year	Index
1915	35.4
1920	69.8
1925	61.1
1930	58.2
1935	47.8
1940	48.8
1945	62.7
1950	83.8
1955	93.3
1960	103.1
1961	104.2
1962	105.4
1963	106.7
1964	108.1
1965	109.9
1966	113.1
1967	116.3
1968	121.2

Source: U.S. Bureau of Labor Statistics

COSTA RICA

COSTA RICA, *KAHS tuh REE kuh,* is the second smallest country in Central America. It received its name from early Spanish adventurers who came in search of gold. The name means *rich coast* in Spanish. Costa Rica is the only Central American nation whose people are mostly of European (Spanish) descent. The name of the country in Spanish, the official language, is REPÚBLICA DE COSTA RICA, or REPUBLIC OF COSTA RICA. San José is the capital and largest city.

Costa Rica is a beautiful land of towering mountains, high plateaus, and hot coastal plains. Most of the people are farmers. They raise coffee, bananas, and other crops in the rich volcanic soils, aided by the mild climate. Most of its income comes from the export of coffee and bananas. For the relationship of Costa Rica to other American nations, see CENTRAL AMERICA; LATIN AMERICA; ORGANIZATION OF AMERICAN STATES; PAN AMERICAN UNION.

The Land and Its Resources

Location and Size. Nicaragua lies to the north of Costa Rica, and Panama to the south. The *Color Map* shows that Costa Rica has a 120-mile coastline on the Caribbean Sea and a 485-mile coastline on the Pacific Ocean. Costa Rica covers 19,575 square miles. El Salvador is the only Central American country that is smaller.

Land Regions. Sea-level coastal plains stretch inland from the shores of the Pacific and Caribbean, and rise steeply to central highlands with towering volcanic peaks. The coastal plain along the Caribbean makes up about three-tenths of the area of the country. It has swampy soils and thick hardwood forests. Fewer than a tenth of the people live in this area. The coastal plain along the Pacific Ocean is dry in northwestern Guanacaste province. Farmers there raise grains and cattle. In the south, large plantations produce millions of bananas a year. About two-tenths of the people live on the Pacific coastal plain.

The mountains crossing central Costa Rica, from northwest to southeast, have three *cordilleras* (ranges): the Guanacaste, Central, and Talamanca. These mountains rise more

A Huge Costa Rican coffee plantation lies beside the Pan American Highway a little north of San José, *far left.*
Herbert Lanks, Pix

Ripe Coffee Berries are picked by hand and dropped into large baskets. Women and girls usually do this work.
Hancock, Gendreau

COSTA RICA

Evergreen Trees

Mixed Evergreen and Deciduous Trees

⊛ National Capitals   ★ Provincial Capitals
• Cities and Towns   — Rail Lines
—·—·— Provincial Boundaries

1 inch = 37 Statute Miles

Miles 0 5 10   20   30   40

Lambert Conformal Conic Projection

Longitude West of Greenwich

Specially created for **World Book Encyclopedia** by Rand McNally and World Book editors

COSTA RICA MAP INDEX

*Does not appear on the map; key shows general location.
*Population of metropolitan area, including suburbs.
Source: Census figures and official estimates.

86oa

COSTA RICA

1 INCH = 1,200 MILES

by Rand McNally for WORLD BOOK

Costa Rica is about one-170th as large as the U.S. It lies between Nicaragua and Panama in Central America.

than 12,000 feet, forming walls around level basins and tablelands with elevations of between 3,000 and 4,000 feet. The largest of these tablelands, the *Meseta Central* (Central Plateau) covers about 3,500 square miles and is the principal coffee-producing area. About seven-tenths of the population live in this section.

Natural Resources. The fertile soil of the Central Plateau ranks as Costa Rica's chief natural resource. Dense hardwood forests, including rosewood, mahogany, cedar, and ebony, grow throughout the country. Quinine is made from the bark of cinchona trees (see QUININE). The chief minerals are gold and salt.

Climate. The coastal lands under 3,200 feet have a hot climate, with annual temperatures ranging between

---

FACTS IN BRIEF

Form of Government: Republic. *Head of State*—President.

Capital: San José.

Official Language: Spanish.

Divisions: Seven provinces.

Area: 19,575 square miles. *Greatest Distances*—(north-south) 170 miles; (east-west) 170 miles. *Coastline*—485 miles on the Pacific; 120 miles on the Caribbean.

Elevation: *Highest*—Chirripó Grande, 12,861 feet above sea level; *Lowest*—sea level along the coasts.

Population: *1963 Census*—1,378,705; distribution, 66 per cent rural, 34 per cent urban. *Estimated 1970 Population*—1,767,000; density, 90 persons to the square mile. *Estimated 1975 Population*—2,099,000.

Chief Products: *Agriculture*—bananas, cacao, cattle, coffee, cotton, sugar cane. *Manufacturing*—leather goods, rope, rubber products, sugar, textiles. *Mining*—gold, salt.

Flag: The *national flag*, representing the country, has horizontal blue, white, red, white, and blue stripes. The *state flag*, used by the government, has Costa Rica's coat of arms on the red bar. Both flags were adopted in 1848. See FLAG (picture: Flags of the Americas).

National Holiday: Independence Day, September 15.

National Anthem: "Himno Nacional."

Money: *Basic Unit*—colon. See MONEY (table).

77° F. and 100° F. The Caribbean side receives much rainfall, averaging about 300 rainy days a year. The Pacific side has a rainy season that lasts from May to November. The Central Plateau, with a temperate climate, has moderate rainfall. Temperatures there vary between 59° F. and 77° F. In regions above 6,000 feet, temperatures range between 41° F. and 59° F.

Life of the People

The People. Costa Rica has a population of 1,767,000. About 98 of every 100 persons are whites descended from Spanish pioneers, and dark-skinned *mestizos* of mixed white and Indian descent. Most of the people live in the largest cities and throughout the Central Plateau. Many mestizos farm along the Pacific Coast.

Family Life resembles that in other Latin-American countries (see LATIN AMERICA [Way of Life]). Most Costa Ricans have large families who work together to cultivate the fields and harvest the crops. Food prices are so high that most families spend half of their incomes on food. The people of farm communities live in cottages with thick, white stucco walls and red or pink tile roofs. In the cities, people live in houses and apartments of Spanish-style architecture.

Most Costa Ricans belong to the Roman Catholic Church, the state church. The chief religious holiday is the Fiesta of Our Lady of the Angels, on August 2.

Cities. San José, the capital and largest city of Costa Rica, is also the center of economic and social life. Limón, on the Caribbean, serves as the main banana-shipping port, and Puntarenas is the principal Pacific port. See ALAJUELA; PUNTARENAS; SAN JOSÉ.

Work of the People

Agriculture employs about 55 of every 100 Costa Rican workers. About three-fifths of the farmers own their own farms. But most farms cover less than 2 acres and provide a poor living for their owners. The other two-fifths of the farmers work on large plantations or rent small farms. Coffee and bananas rank as the most important crops. Coffee grows throughout the country, especially on the uplands of San José, Cartago, Alajuela, and Heredia provinces. Bananas grow on the coastal plains. Cacao is also an important export crop. Cocoa comes from the seeds of cacao pods. Rubber trees thrive on large coastal plantations.

Since the early 1950's, the government has encouraged farmers to plant sugar cane, fruits, and vegetables. Farmers also grow rice, corn, beans, and tobacco for local use. They raise beef and dairy cattle throughout the country. Abacá and hemp are also grown.

Manufacturing and Processing. The chief manufacturing industry is sugar refining. Costa Rica has more than 20 sugar mills. Other manufactured products include cigarettes, clothing, hardwood furniture, leather goods, ropes, rubber products, shoes, soaps, and textiles.

Transportation. Costa Rica has more than 700 miles of narrow-gauge railroad track. Four railroads connect the Caribbean coast with the Pacific coast via San José. Public roads cover about 4,700 miles. The Pan American Highway runs north and south through the country. Most of it is paved. Several airlines and shipping lines also serve Costa Rica.

Communication. Telephone and telegraph lines connect most of the cities. Costa Rica has about 40 radio

Central Park in San José stands near the city's cathedral, *left background*. San José is Costa Rica's largest city and the center of the country's economic and cultural life.

A Costa Rican Family uses a hand-painted oxcart for transportation. Most families living in rural areas work together to cultivate and harvest the crops.

Puntarenas, the principal Pacific seaport of Costa Rica, lies on a narrow strip of land that juts into the Gulf of Nicoya.

stations. The country's six daily newspapers are all published in San José.

Education

The law requires children between the ages of 7 and 14 to attend school. About 80 of every 100 Costa Ricans can read and write. The national university, the University of Costa Rica, was founded in 1843 at San José as the University of Santo Tomás.

Government

The Costa Rican constitution, adopted in 1949, provides for a system of checks and balances similar to that of the United States government (see UNITED STATES, GOVERNMENT OF [Separation of Powers]). The president heads the government, and appoints a cabinet of eight ministers. He is elected to a four-year term, and cannot be re-elected until eight years after the end of a term. The one-house national legislature has 45 members. Representatives are elected for four-year terms on the basis of proportional representation by provinces. The Supreme Court has 17 justices elected to eight-year terms by the legislature.

Costa Rica is divided into seven provinces for local government. The president appoints the governor of each province to a four-year term.

The law requires all persons 20 years of age and over to vote. The chief political parties are the National Liberation, National Republican, and National Union.

History

Early Days. Christopher Columbus discovered Costa Rica in 1502. A small group of Spaniards headed by Columbus' brother, Bartholomew, landed on the coast and established the first white colony near present-day Limón. By 1530, Spain had conquered the Chorotega and Boruca Indians who lived in Costa Rica. For the next 300 years, Costa Rica was a Spanish colony.

Independence and Confederation. Costa Rica and other Central American colonies broke away from Spain in 1821. They joined the Mexican Empire the next year. In 1823, the Central American states withdrew from Mexico, adopted a constitution, and formed the United Provinces of Central America. But this union

began to fall apart in 1838. Its president, Francisco Morazán, fled to exile in South America (see MORAZÁN, FRANCISCO). In 1842, Morazán overthrew Costa Rica's government, became president, and attempted to revive the confederation. A counterrevolution ousted his regime within several months. In 1844, the country adopted a new constitution. In 1856, William Walker, an American adventurer, tried to seize control of several Central American countries, including Costa Rica (see WALKER, WILLIAM). President Juan Rafael Mora ousted Walker, and became a national hero (see MORA, JUAN R.).

The development of the coffee industry after 1850 led to great progress. The government used the coffee revenue from world markets to improve communication and transportation, to build schools and railroads, and to import manufactured goods.

Revolutions. Since 1900, Costa Rica has had several revolutions. In 1917, Federico Tinoco overthrew the government and took over the presidency. Revolutionaries ousted Tinoco in 1919, and Julio Acosta became the new leader. Under Acosta and his successors, Costa Rica became the most democratic and orderly Central American republic.

Otilio Ulate won the presidential election of 1948, but the national assembly refused to allow him to take office. Colonel José Figueres led a revolt to support Ulate, and took over the government. Ulate was inaugurated as president in 1949.

Recent Developments. Ulate reduced the public debt and changed the army into a civil police force. José Figueres served as president from 1953 until Mario Echandi won office in 1958. A new hydroelectric dam and generating station began operating at La Garita in 1957. During the 1950's, Costa Rica nationalized its banks and began to develop land and industry with government assistance.

Francisco J. Orlich was elected president in 1962. Also in 1962, Costa Rica joined the General Treaty for Central American Economic Integration, a common market designed to promote trade. José Joaquin Trejos-Fernandez, a mathematics and economics professor, was elected president in 1966, in his first try for political office.   WILLIAM S. STOKES

Related Articles in WORLD BOOK include:

Outline

Questions

Who discovered Costa Rica? When?
What does the name *Costa Rica* mean?
What is Costa Rica's chief natural resource?
Who is the national hero of Costa Rica?
What are Costa Rica's main agricultural products?
Where do most of the people of Costa Rica live?
What American tried to seize Costa Rica in 1856?
When was Costa Rica a part of the Mexican Empire?
What are the three climate zones of Costa Rica?
When did Costa Rica adopt its constitution?

Debutantes Bow at a Cotillion in Raleigh, N.C. The Girls Perform a Traditional Figure Dance.

COSTAIN, THOMAS BERTRAM (1885-1965), a Canadian-American novelist and historian, began writing books at the age of 54. He produced many widely read historical novels. His novels include *For My Great Folly* (1942), *The Black Rose* (1945), *The Moneyman* (1947), *High Towers* (1949), *The Silver Chalice* (1952), and *The Tontine* (1957). *The White and the Gold* (1954) is a history of Canada to 1763. *The Last Plantagenets* (1962) completed a four-volume history series called "The Pageant of England." Born in Brantford, Ont., Costain worked as a newspaper and magazine editor before becoming an author. HARRY R. WARFEL

COSTELLO, *KAHS tuh lo,* **JOHN ALOYSIUS** (1891-
), served as Prime Minister of the Republic of Ireland from 1948 to 1951 and from 1954 to 1957. In 1948 he headed a party coalition that took the leadership Eamon De Valera had held for 16 years. De Valera held political control between Costello's two terms, and, in 1957, his victory ended Costello's second term. Costello was born in Dublin and received a law degree. He served as Attorney General of the Irish Free State from 1926 to 1932. ALFRED F. HAVIGHURST

Consulate General of Ireland
John A. Costello

See also DE VALERA, EAMON; IRELAND (The Republic of Ireland).

COSTUME. See CLOTHING.

CÔTE D'AZUR, *KOHT DAH ZYUR,* is the eastern end of the Mediterranean Coast of France. This area includes part of the French Riviera, a famous vacation resort (see RIVIERA). The name *Côte d'Azur,* meaning *azure coast,* was given to this region because of the beautiful deep blue of the sea and the sky. Groves of palm and orange trees and gardens of brilliant tropical flowers line the shore. This part of the Mediterranean Coast is a health resort area and playground for travelers from all parts of the world. W. R. MCCONNELL

COTEAU. See SOUTH DAKOTA (Land Regions).

COTILLION, *koh TILL yun,* is a ballroom dance similar to the quadrille. It permits an endless variety of steps, and often consists of complicated figures. A head couple leads the rest of the dancers through the various steps and patterns. At least four couples do the dance, but any number of additional couples may join in. The cotillion is usually the last dance of a ball. It was one of the most popular dances of the 1800's. The term *cotillion* also refers to a gathering of people for social dancing. WALTER SORELL

COTOPAXI, *KOH toh PAK see,* in the Andes Mountains of Ecuador, is the highest active volcano in the world. It is 40 miles south of Quito, Ecuador. Its nearly perfect cone, with slopes of about 30 degrees, rises 19,344 feet above sea level, and is covered with glaciers and snow fields. Its crater is about 2,600 feet across. During the last 400 years, it has erupted more than 25 times. Lava and hot ash cause snow on the flanks of the cone to melt rapidly, sending big flows of mud pouring down the mountainside. An explosive eruption occurred in February, 1942. GORDON A. MACDONALD

See also MOUNTAIN (color picture, Mountains of the World).

COTTAGE INDUSTRY was an economic system widely used during the Industrial Revolution. The worker agreed to make products, such as clothes, for someone who planned to sell them. The worker usually worked at home, but he often rented working space outside his home. The worker was not the employee of the person who sold the goods. He merely agreed to do the work, and could later refuse additional work. The system is also known as the *domestic system* or the *putting-out system.* See also INDUSTRIAL REVOLUTION (Before the Revolution).

Cotton

Cotton Grows on One of Every 25 Acres of Cropland in the United States.

COTTON is the most important fiber that man uses to make clothing. More than three of every four persons in the world wear cotton clothing. Cotton can be made into more kinds of products—from diapers to explosives —than any other fiber. The United States uses over 5 billion pounds of cotton a year, an average of about 25 pounds for each person.

More than 9½ million Americans depend on cotton for at least part of their livelihood. Farmers, business-men, and industrialists have invested more than $24 billion in producing and processing cotton. Cotton grows on one of every 25 acres of cropland in the United States. The United States produces far more cotton than any other nation. Farmers in Asia, Latin America, Africa, and Europe also grow large crops of cotton.

Eli Whitney invented the *cotton gin* in 1793. This machine made it possible to *gin* cotton, or remove the cotton seeds from the fibers, more cheaply. With it, one man could do the work once done by 50 men picking out seeds by hand. Before the Civil War, cotton ranked as the only important crop of the South. Slaves toiled in the cotton fields of great plantations, cultivating and picking the snowy crop.

Cotton still ranks as the main source of income for southern farmers. But now they also raise other crops,

as well as livestock. Fluffy white cotton bolls cover the fields of the cotton-producing states during autumn. Many places in the South have celebrations in honor of cotton. For example, Memphis, Tenn., holds an annual Cotton Carnival.

Uses of Cotton

All parts of the cotton plant are useful. The most important part is the *lint* (fiber) used in making cotton textiles. *Cottonseed* provides oil and forms the base of many food products. The *linters*, or short fuzz on the seeds, are used in making cushioning, paper, plastics, and other products. Farmers plow under the *stalks* and *leaves* as humus to improve soil structure.

Cotton-Fiber Products. Lint is used to make all kinds of clothing, from hats to shoes. Cotton has strength and toughness for work clothes. But it can also be spun into fine cloth for dressy gowns. Household goods made of cotton include rugs, towels, and bed sheets. Other cotton-fiber products include bandages, book-bindings, and auto seat fabrics. Chemists have made

Dabney S. Wellford, the contributor of this article, is the Director of the Information Service for the National Cotton Council of America.

International Harvester; Rod Heinrichs/Grant Heilman

cleaned, bleached, and sterilized are used as medical cotton.

Kinds of Cotton

There are four main kinds of cotton: (1) American upland, (2) Egyptian, (3) Sea-island, and (4) Asiatic. The various kinds of cotton plants resemble each other in most ways. But they differ in such characteristics as color of flowers, character of fibers, and time of blooming. Each main kind has several varieties with different characteristics. Some varieties of cotton grow best on irrigated land. Some have lint $1\frac{3}{4}$ inches long, and others have lint only $\frac{1}{2}$ of an inch long. Some varieties have stronger fibers than others. Some are easier to harvest by machine than other varieties. Some grow best in certain parts of the world.

—————— **PRODUCTS FROM COTTON FIBER** ——————

Abrasives	Filter cloth	Slip covers
Adhesive tape	Gloves	Suits
Awnings	Handkerchiefs	Tablecloths
Bags	Hose	Tarpaulins
Bathing suits	Hosiery	Tents
Bedspreads	Insulating	Thread
Bedticking	material	Towels
Blankets	Luggage	Trousers
Blouses	Overalls	Twine
Bookbindings	Pajamas	Umbrellas
Carpets	Pillowcases	Underwear
Coats	Play clothes	Uniforms
Conveyor belts	Sheets	Upholstery
Diapers	Shirts	fabric
Draperies	Shoelaces	Window shades
Dresses	Shoes	Zipper tape

—————— **PRODUCTS FROM COTTONSEED** ——————

Artificial leather	Glycerin	Paints
Cattle feed	Linoleum	Salad oil
Chemicals	Margarine	Shortening
Cosmetics	Mellorine	Soap
Fertilizer		

—————— **PRODUCTS FROM COTTON LINTERS** ——————

Absorbent cotton	Lacquer and	Phonograph
Adhesives	enamel	records
Cellophane	Linoleum	Plastics
Celluloid	Mattresses	Thermal
Cellulose	Mops	insulation
Cushioning	Paper	Varnish
Explosives	Photographic	Weatherproofing
	film	materials

Cotton farmers in cool temperate regions must plant their crops every year. But in the hot, moist tropics, cotton plants may live and bloom for several years. Some of these plants grow over 10 feet high.

American Upland Cotton is raised in almost every cotton-producing country. This hardy plant produces a large yield under various growing conditions. Upland cotton makes up two-thirds to three-fourths of the world's cotton crop. It can be made into many kinds of fabrics, from coarse to fine. It is used both for heavy canvas and for expensive shirts.

The upland cotton plant may grow from 1 to 7 feet tall. It has creamy-white flowers, and strong, white fibers $\frac{7}{8}$ to $1\frac{1}{4}$ inches long.

Egyptian Cotton was developed from stocks that originated in South and Central America. *Karnak*, the most famous variety, has strong fibers about $1\frac{1}{2}$ inches long. It is now being rapidly replaced by *Menoufi*, a higher-yielding variety. Growers in the United States

cotton fireproof, waterproof, rotproof, shrinkproof, and wrinkle-resistant. Specially treated cotton shirts and dresses can be washed and dried without ironing.

Cottonseed Products. Oil is the most important product made from cottonseed. In some cotton-oil mills, machines crush the kernels of the seed and squeeze out the oil. Other mills roll out the kernel so that it looks like oatmeal. These mills then use chemicals to dissolve the oil out of the seed. *Refined* (purified) cottonseed oil forms the base for such products as margarine, salad oil, shortening, and a frozen dessert made of vegetable fat called *mellorine*. The remains of the refining process are used in still other products, such as soap, linoleum, and phonograph records.

Meal remains after the oil is removed from the cottonseed. The proteins in this meal make it a valuable food for farm animals. The *hull*, or outer covering of the cottonseed, is used for cattle feed, chemicals, and as mulching material.

Cotton-Linters Products. Many industries use chemically treated linters as raw materials for such products as plastics, photographic film, paper, and sausage casings. Explosives manufacturers use linters in guncotton (see GUNCOTTON). Linter fibers are also used to stuff mattresses, cushions, and pads. Linters that have been

865

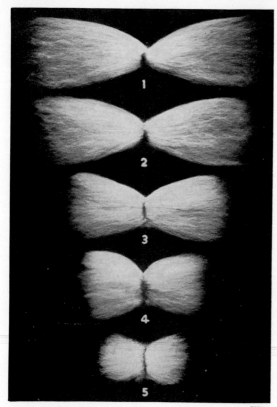

The Chief Commercial Types of Cotton are: (1) Sea-island; (2) Egyptian; (3) American upland long-staple; (4) American upland short-staple; and (5) Asiatic.

and Peru have developed several varieties called American Egyptian cottons. *Pima S-2*, an American-Egyptian variety, has uniform fibers about $1\frac{3}{8}$ inches long.

Egyptian cotton has lemon-colored flowers and long, silky, light-tan fibers. It is made into clothing, balloon cloth, typewriter ribbons, and other fine fabrics.

Sea-Island Cotton first grew on the Sea Islands off the coast of South Carolina, Georgia, and northern Florida. Farmers in the United States once grew it, but the boll weevil ruined the crops. Today, most Sea-island cotton comes from the West Indies, where the boll weevil is not a serious pest.

Sea-island cotton is one of the most valuable and costly kinds of cotton. Its silky fibers are about $1\frac{3}{4}$ inches long. It can be made into high-quality textiles. But it is expensive to raise, because it grows slowly and has a low yield and small bolls. The plant has brilliant yellow flowers and white lint. Technically, Sea-island is closely related to Egyptian cotton. But growers consider it a separate kind of cotton, because of its commercial importance.

Asiatic Cottons grow mainly in China, India, and Pakistan. Chinese and Indian cottons have short, coarse, harsh fibers, and low yields. They are used for blankets, padding, filters, and coarse cloth. Varieties of American upland cotton are rapidly replacing the Asiatic cottons, because they have fibers of better quality.

The Cotton Plant

The plant described in this section is American up-

land cotton, the most widely grown kind. Other kinds of cotton plants resemble American upland. This plant grows upright and has branches spreading in all directions. It has broad leaves with three to five lobes. Its *taproot* (long main root) may grow as deep as 4 feet into the ground.

The Flower. White flowers blossom from the *squares* (buds). The flowers open in midmorning and begin to wither the next day. They turn pink, blue, and finally purple as they dry and fall off the plant. The flowers must be pollinated during the few hours they remain open. Cotton plants usually pollinate themselves (see POLLEN AND POLLINATION).

At first, only one or two flowers open each day. The first flowers bloom low on the plant, near the main stem. As the plant becomes larger, several flowers open daily. These flowers open higher on the plant and farther out on the branches. Flowering starts in summer and may last until the autumn frosts.

The Boll, which contains the cotton fibers, begins to form while the flower withers. A boll matures in 45 to 60 days. It grows to about the size of a golf ball. At full size, it is green and almost round, with a pointed tip. At this stage, the boll cracks in four or five straight lines from the tip. Then it splits open, showing four or five *locks* (groups of 8 to 10 seeds with fibers attached). The open dried boll, which holds the fluffed-out cotton, is called the *burr*.

Cotton-Growing Regions

The United States ranks as the chief cotton-growing country. It produces about $10\frac{3}{4}$ million bales of cotton a year. Each bale weighs about 500 pounds, including packaging. U.S. farmers produced 526 pounds of cotton lint per acre in 1965, an all-time high yield. In the 1920's, the United States grew more than half the world's cotton. The nation grew about the same amount of cotton in the 1960's as it did in the 1920's, but it now produces only about one-fifth of the world's total. This is because other countries are growing much more than they once did. The United States produces about $1\frac{1}{4}$ million more bales of cotton than Russia, the next largest producer.

The *Cotton Belt* of the United States includes 14 states: Alabama, Arizona, Arkansas, California, Georgia, Louisiana, Mississippi, Missouri, New Mexico, North Carolina, Oklahoma, South Carolina, Tennessee, and Texas. Texas leads the states in cotton production.

The cotton-textile industry in the United States uses about $9\frac{1}{2}$ million bales of cotton a year. Mills in the Southeast and in New England spin this cotton into textile products that are sold throughout the world. The United States exports an average of $4\frac{3}{4}$ million bales of cotton each year. The nation imports about 225,000 bales every year. This is mainly special cotton with long fibers, which is not widely grown in the United States, or short, coarse Asiatic cotton.

Other Countries. Cotton grows in many countries in Asia, including Afghanistan, Burma, China, India, Iran, Israel, Pakistan, Asiatic Russia, Syria, Thailand, and Turkey. In South America, farmers raise cotton in Argentina, Brazil, Colombia, and Peru, among other countries. The principal Central American cotton-producing countries are El Salvador, Guatemala, Honduras, Mexico, and Nicaragua. The leading cotton-growing countries in Africa include Chad, Congo (Kinshasa), Egypt, Mozambique, Nigeria, Sudan, Tanzania, and Uganda. In Europe, cotton grows in Bulgaria, Greece, European Russia, southern Spain, the lower part of the Italian peninsula, and Yugoslavia. Australia also produces cotton.

How Cotton Is Grown

Today's farming methods have largely changed cotton growing. Once, it was produced almost entirely by hand and mule labor. Today, it is produced scientifically, with little labor and large amounts of supplies and equipment. In 1930, a farmer worked about 270 hours to produce one bale of cotton. Today, it takes him an average of about 22 hours.

Cotton grows best in fertile, well-drained soil that gets adequate moisture during the growing season. Farmers prefer dry weather after the bolls open. Cotton requires a warm to hot climate with about 180 frost-free days during the growing season.

Preparing the Soil. After harvesting a crop, cotton growers shred the stalks and plow them into the soil, or leave them on the surface to prevent erosion. In spring, they plow the soil. Then they use machines called *middlebusters* to prepare *beds* (low ridges) in which they plant the cotton seeds. Some farmers plant seed on a flat field, others between the beds.

Cotton needs fertile soil, so most growers use large amounts of fertilizer. In most situations, the fertilizer is placed a few inches to the side and below the seed. Many farmers rotate cotton with other crops. Farmers sometimes grow winter legumes or other cover crops in cotton fields between seasons (see LEGUME). Good cover crops add or help maintain organic soil matter as well as provide protection against erosion. Legumes may add nitrogen, an element needed by cotton plants.

Planting and Cultivating. In the United States, most farmers plant cotton in April or May. Farmers use two-, four-, six-, or eight-row tractor-mounted planters to open *furrows* (grooves) in the earth. The planters drop the cotton seeds into the ground, apply fertilizer, close the furrows, and press down the soil. This is done in one operation. Many farmers also apply weed-control chemicals and soil fungicides during the planting operation. Some planters sow seeds in solid *bands* (rows), but most drop the seeds at regular intervals, called *hills*. Rows normally are about 40 inches apart.

When solid band planting is used, the farmer thins the crop after the seedlings are a few inches high to prevent crowding. Thinning is usually done with a hoe, and is called *chopping*. Groups of two or three cotton plants are left in hills or clusters 6 to 10 inches apart. From 30,000 to 60,000 plants remain in each acre.

Chemicals may now be used on cotton planted in hills to control weeds and avoid the need to cultivate by hand or with tractors. Flamers may be used to burn small weeds near the base of the cotton plant in combination with tractor cultivation.

Control of Pests and Disease. In an average year, a cotton farmer loses 1 bale of every 8 because of insect damage, and 1 bale of every 7 or 8 because of disease.

The most harmful insect pests include the boll weevil, bollworm, pink bollworm, lygus, thrips, and aphid. Powerful dust or liquid insecticides can control all these pests except the pink bollworm. But no single spray or dust destroys all insects. The farmer uses the poisons that will kill the insects which attack his plants. Airplanes or machines on the ground apply the insecticides in a fine, mistlike spray or powdery dust that drifts onto all parts of the cotton plant (see INSECTICIDE).

Cotton growers try to keep the pink bollworm under control by isolating infected fields, sterilizing seeds and cotton, and by using machines that chop up leaves and other trash from the cotton. Shredding stalks as soon as the crop is harvested and plowing them under helps control the pink bollworm and the boll weevil.

Stages in the Growth of the Cotton Plant include the *square*, or bud, *center*; the fully opened flower, *left*; and the boll, *right*. Leaflike bracts surround the bud, flower, and boll.

The Cotton Plant at Harvesttime looks as if it has clusters of fluffy snowballs. The ripened bolls pop open exposing the cotton fibers which are ready for picking by machine or hand.

National Cotton Council

WHERE COTTON GROWS IN THE WORLD

The United States produces about one-fifth of all the cotton raised in the world. Other cotton-producing areas include Russia, eastern China, western India, eastern Brazil, Pakistan, and northern Mexico. Each dot represents 50,000 bales of cotton.

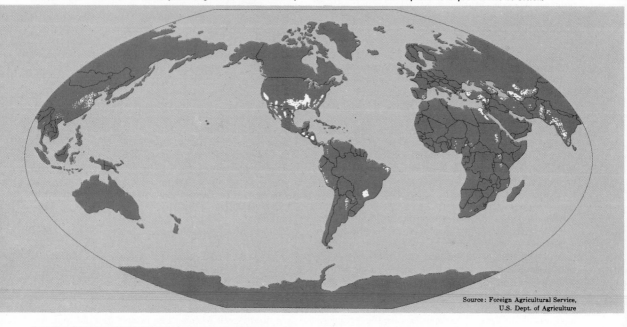

Source: Foreign Agricultural Service,
U.S. Dept. of Agriculture

LEADING COTTON GROWING COUNTRIES
Bales (500 pounds) of cotton grown in 1968

United States
10,822,000 bales

Russia
9,500,000 bales

China (Mainland)
6,400,000 bales

India
5,000,000 bales

Brazil
3,300,000 bales

Pakistan
2,400,000 bales

Mexico
2,300,000 bales

Egypt
1,930,000 bales

Turkey
1,850,000 bales

Sudan
850,000 bales

Source: *Foreign Agriculture Circular*, "Cotton," Feb., 1969, U.S. Dept. of Agriculture

Small worms called *nematodes*, which can only be seen with a microscope, attack the roots of the cotton plant. They cut off the plant's food and water supply, so that it wilts or becomes stunted, and produces a smaller yield. Nematodes can be controlled by fumigating the soil or planting resistant crops in rotation.

There are two kinds of cotton diseases: (1) diseases of the *seedlings* (young plants), and (2) diseases of the older plants. Treating the seeds or spraying the seedbed with fungicides before planting controls seedling diseases (see FUNGI; FUNGICIDE). Fungicides also protect sprouting cotton. Diseases of older cotton plants, such as wilt and blight, may be partially controlled by using disease-resistant varieties.

Picking Cotton. In the United States, machines harvest almost three-fourths of the cotton crop. The rest is picked by hand. In the Cotton Belt, thousands of workers travel daily from towns and cities to nearby farms to pick cotton. The pickers remove cotton fibers and seeds from the burrs by hand. They put the cotton in large sacks that they drag along the ground behind them. Late in the season, pickers may *snap* the cotton (pick the burrs along with the seeds and fibers).

Russia

Novosti from Sovfoto

Mainland China

Eastfoto

Grant Heilman

United States

WHERE COTTON GROWS IN THE UNITED STATES

The leading cotton-producing areas are in Texas, California's San Joaquin Valley, the Mississippi River Valley, and southern Arizona. Each dot represents 25,000 bales.

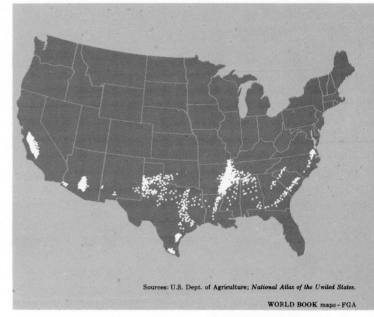

Sources: U.S. Dept. of Agriculture; *National Atlas of the United States.*

WORLD BOOK maps – FGA

Machine harvesting is done by *stripping* or *picking*. Stripping machines are used in areas where soil, climate, and variety cause the cotton plant to be relatively small. This is the cheapest method of harvesting. Most stripping is done in Texas and Oklahoma. As the stripper moves along the rows of cotton plants, two long, revolving rollers break off the bolls, twigs, and leaves. So much trash remains in the cotton picked by a stripper that it must be cleaned by gins specially equipped for the purpose.

Farmers in other parts of the Cotton Belt use picking machines. These pickers pull the cotton from the bolls in one or two rows of cotton at a time. A one-row mechanical picker can do the work of about 40 hand pickers. Mechanical pickers use revolving spindles to pick the cotton. Some pickers have slender grooved rods as spindles. Others have larger cone-shaped, barbed spindles. As the mechanical picker moves down the row, the rapidly revolving spindles reach into all parts of the plants. The barbs or grooves in the spindles catch the cotton and pull it out of the burr. A stationary stripper mechanism or revolving rubber *doffers* remove the cotton from the spindles. Then the cotton is blown

LEADING COTTON GROWING STATES

Bales (500 pounds) of cotton grown in 1968

Texas
3,537,000 bales

California
1,580,000 bales

Mississippi
1,522,000 bales

Arkansas
1,034,000 bales

Arizona
724,000 bales

Louisiana
545,000 bales

Alabama
400,000 bales

Tennessee
323,000 bales

Oklahoma
265,000 bales

Georgia
262,000 bales

Source: *Cotton Situation*, March, 1969, U.S. Dept. of Agriculture

India

Government of India

Brazil

FAO

Sudan

Bern Keating, Black Star

Four-Row Cotton Planter prepares furrows and drops seeds into them. Wheels press the soil firmly over the seeds.

National Cotton Council

Tractor-Mounted Cultivator works on four rows at a time. The tractor has a flame cultivator at the rear, used to burn weeds.

into a large steel basket on the picker machine.

Most growers spray or dust their fields with chemicals about 10 days before picking cotton by machine. The chemicals kill the leaves, which drop off the plants. This removal of the leaves is called *defoliation*. Defoliation helps keep mechanically picked cotton clean and free from leaves.

Marketing Cotton

Ginning and Baling. Cotton gins remove the cotton fibers from the seeds. At the gin, seed cotton passes through the *drier*, a machine that dries the cotton. *Burr machines* and *cleaners* remove burrs, leaves, and other trash. Then the cotton goes to machines called *gin stands*, which pull the lint off the seeds. Lint is further cleaned in *lint-cleaning machines*.

Next, the lint goes to the *bale press*, which packs it into 500-pound bales. These bales measure about 56 by 28 by 45 inches, or about the size of a large home refrigerator. Six yards of jute or other bagging material covers each bale. Six steel ties bind each bale.

Trucks carry the bales from the gin to a warehouse for storage. In order to save freight charges, compressing machines squeeze each bale to nearly half its original size. A railroad boxcar can carry 100 or more compressed bales. Bales for export are compressed to almost one-third their original size. A crew of 25 men operating a huge machine can compress about two bales a minute.

Classing. Cotton buyers and sellers judge cotton on the basis of samples cut from the bales. In the United States, most farmers send their samples to government classing offices. These offices are part of the Department of Agriculture. They are located in areas of high cotton production. Skilled classers judge the value of the cotton on the basis of grade, staple, and preparation.

Grade shows the amount of trash in the sample, the color of the fiber, and any discoloration due to insects and disease. The chief grades of white fibers are, from best to poorest: (1) Good Middling, (2) Strict Middling, (3) Middling, (4) Strict Low Middling, (5) Low Middling, (6) Strict Good Ordinary, and (7) Good Ordinary.

Staple is the length of the lint. Classers pull a cotton sample between their thumbs and forefingers several times to straighten the fibers. They discard most of it until a pinch of well-aligned fibers remains. *Staple length* is the average length of these fibers.

Preparation shows the quality of the ginning. Poor

ginning produces cut or snarled fibers. A mechanical device is often used to determine fiber fineness. The strength of the fiber may be measured mechanically, although this is done less frequently.

Selling. Farmers normally sell their cotton (1) at the gin, (2) to cotton merchants in nearby towns, or (3) to buyers or agents for textile mills. Any place where cotton is bought and sold for immediate delivery is called a *spot market*. Some farmers belong to cooperative marketing associations that sell their cotton.

Eighteen southern cities, the chief spot markets, have *cotton exchanges*. All accredited cotton merchants in these markets belong to the exchanges. The exchanges make rules for the local market, settle disputes between merchants, and post the prices and cotton-market news from throughout the world. The U.S. Department of Agriculture publishes prices daily from 15 markets.

New York has a *futures exchange*. There, agreements are made to buy or sell cotton at a stated price at a stated future time. A merchant or spinner who buys cotton on the spot market can protect himself against the risk of a change in price by selling a futures contract in a futures exchange. When he sells his cotton or cloth, he buys back his futures contract. This is called *hedging* against a price change (see BOARD OF TRADE [Hedging]).

Making Cotton into Cloth

Cleaning. When cotton arrives at a textile mill, workers remove the steel ties and bagging that hold the bales together. *Blending machines* open the bales and mix and break up the compressed layers of cotton. Several blenders feed cotton into *cleaning machines*, which further mix the cotton, break it into smaller pieces, and remove trash.

The cotton is sucked through a pipe to *picking machines*. Beaters in these machines strike the cotton repeatedly. They knock out dirt, and separate lumps of cotton into smaller pieces. The picking machines form the lint into a *lap* (long rolled sheet).

Cotton then goes to a *carding machine*, where the fibers are separated. Trash and short fibers are removed. Some cotton goes through a *comber* that takes out more short fibers and makes a stronger, more lustrous yarn.

Spinning. The spinning processes basically do three jobs: (1) they *draft* the cotton, or reduce it to smaller and smaller structures; (2) they *straighten* and *parallel* the fibers; and (3) they put *twist* into the yarn. Several

Airplanes Spray or Dust Cotton Fields with insecticides and *defoliants,* or chemicals that cause the leaves to drop off the plant.

At the Cotton Gin, machines called *gin stands* pull the cotton fibers off the seeds. Other machines clean the fibers.

Bale Presses at the gin pack the cotton into 500-pound bales. Presses at the warehouse compress the bales even more.

In the Cotton Classing Room, skilled classers examine samples of cotton to determine the grade and staple of the fibers.

Carding Machines straighten the cotton fibers. Then the fibers are brought together to form a *sliver,* or loose rope.

Spinning Frames twist the fibers to make a fine, strong yarn. Many yarns are tied end to end to form one long yarn.

A Mechanical Loom automatically weaves hundreds of yarns into cloth. One weaver can tend up to 40 mechanical looms.

Chemicals are Added to Printed Cloth to make sure that the colors of the pattern remain bright permanently.

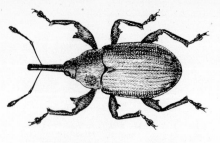

ENEMIES OF COTTON

Boll Weevil Larvae feed on the fibers in the boll, causing great damage to cotton crops.

Aphids and Bollworms attack cotton. Aphids, *left*, suck juices from leaves and stems. Bollworms, *above*, attack the leaves and bolls.

Nematodes may attack the cotton roots and keep the plants from getting food from the soil.

USDA

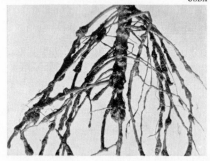

different machines perform these jobs. See SPINNING; SPINNING JENNY.

Yarn is the final product of spinning. It must be twisted to give it strength and to make the fibers cling together. Many yarns are tied end to end to form one long yarn. Yarns to be woven lengthwise in cloth are *warped* (wound side by side) on a gigantic spool called a *beam*. Several hundred yarns can be wound on each beam. Several beams fit into a *slashing machine*. This machine unwinds the yarns and feeds them through a vat of *sizing* (a mixture of starch, gum, and resins). Then it dries and rewinds the yarns. Sizing strengthens the yarns and protects them during weaving. Looms weave yarn into cloth (see WEAVING [How Cloth Is Woven]).

Finishing. After inspectors check the cloth, the sizing is dissolved in hot water and washed away. Some cloth passes through a gas flame that singes the fuzz off its surface. Boiling the cloth in an alkaline solution in a tightly closed *kier* (large vat) removes any natural waxes, colored substances, or discolorations. Then the cloth is bleached in hypochlorite or peroxide. Manufacturers put some cloth into a strong solution of sodium hydroxide to *mercerize* it (see MERCERIZING). Mercerization adds luster to the cloth and makes it stronger. The cloth may then pass through a machine that prints various designs on it. Cloth intended to be solid-colored goes through a *dye bath*.

Colored yarns are used to weave designs into some fabrics. These yarns are kiered, bleached, and dyed before warping and sizing. Wrinkle-resistant and easy-care cloth passes through mixtures of chemicals that link the fiber molecules and give them desired qualities.

History

Early Days. The Aztec Indians grew cotton for textile purposes nearly 8,000 years ago in Mexico. Asiatic cottons first grew wild in East Africa. About 5,000 years ago, the people in what is now Pakistan cultivated cotton. The Persians brought cotton-growing methods from India. The ancient peoples used cotton for clothing, for bindings for sandals, and even for harnesses for elephants. Greek and Roman travelers described cotton plants as the fleece of tiny lambs growing on trees. The Greek historian Herodotus wrote about a tree in Asia that bore cotton "exceeding in goodness and beauty the wool of any sheep."

The army of Alexander the Great first brought cotton goods into Europe in the 300's B.C. The cloth cost so much that only the very rich could afford it. In the A.D. 700's, Moslem invaders brought cotton-manufacturing processes to Europe. Italians and Spaniards wove some cotton, but the art spread northward slowly.

The English began to weave cotton in the 1600's. They imported raw cotton from the countries bordering the eastern edge of the Mediterranean Sea. Later they imported cotton from the southern colonies in America. In the 1700's, English textile manufacturers developed machines that made it possible to spin thread and weave cloth in large quantities (see INDUSTRIAL REVOLUTION). Then they began to export cotton cloth.

In America, early explorers found that Indians knew how to make cotton clothing. In the early 1600's, southern colonies began growing cotton. The colonists wove cotton into coarse cloth for their own use. Large-scale cotton growing began in the late 1700's.

English manufacturers tried to keep cotton-mill machinery out of the United States. They wanted the United States to sell its raw cotton to England and buy back finished cloth. Samuel Slater, an English textile worker and mechanic, learned how these machines were made. He came to the United States in 1789. Slater supervised the building of cotton mills in New England in the 1790's. One of these mills, Old Slater Mill, built in 1793, still stands in Pawtucket, R.I. (see RHODE ISLAND [Places to Visit]; SLATER, SAMUEL).

Cotton manufacturing in New England grew rapidly. In 1793, Eli Whitney invented the cotton gin, which made it possible to send more cotton to the mills.

The demand for cotton increased, and the southern cotton industry expanded. Cotton became so important to the South that people called it "King Cotton" and sang songs about it. Slave traders brought Negroes to the United States to provide the farms and plantations with cheap labor. The great plantations of the Old South had many slaves and often covered 2,000 to 3,000 acres. But most southern farmers had small farms and only a few slaves or none at all. Southern farmers felt strongly that they could not make money from growing cotton without the cheap labor provided by slaves. This became one of the causes of the Civil War.

Cotton Mills Move South. After the Civil War, Southerners began to build their own factories to make cotton cloth. Land was cheap and taxes were low. Southern laborers worked for lower wages than the workers in northern mills. By the 1920's, the South was producing more cotton cloth than New England. This move to the South continued through the 1940's and 1950's. Today, most cotton mills are located in the southeastern states, near cotton-farming areas. These states have ample power and labor to run the mills.

Technical Advances. Until the late 1800's, most cotton seeds were thrown away as waste. The value of cottonseed as a source of oil was recognized as early as the late 1700's. But there was no machinery to extract the oil. John Lineback of Salem, N.C., patented the first cottonseed-hulling machine in 1814. But practical machinery to crush the seeds and produce oil and other products did not go into operation until the mid-1800's. Today, about 95 per cent of the cottonseed crop is crushed. Farmers use the rest for planting.

Today, cotton must compete with the many synthetic fibers. To help in this competition, chemists have developed ways to improve cotton cloth. Chemicals applied to the cloth make it permanently crisp, wrinkle-resistant, waterproof, resistant to mildew, stronger, and more lustrous. Well over one-fourth of the cotton cloth is now treated in this way.

Manufacturers may combine cotton fibers with wool, rayon, linen, and synthetic fibers to produce cloth with special qualities. New weaves and chemical finishes have made it possible to produce textured cotton, cotton tweeds and suiting materials, silky cottons such as faille and chiffon, tufted cotton for rugs, and many other kinds of textiles.

Economic Problems that face the American cotton farmer include competition from the man-made fiber industry. Producers of synthetic fibers spend large sums for research and advertising, something the individual farmer cannot do. Through a price-support program, the federal government will loan a farmer the price-support value of his cotton crop when the market price falls below the support level. The government takes the crop as security. If the market price rises sufficiently later in the same season, the grower may pay off the loan and sell his cotton on the market. Otherwise, the government takes possession of the cotton. Because of the loan program, the market price is normally a little above the support price. Farmers are not allowed to plant more cotton acreage than the federal government allots to them.

Since 1956, the U.S. government has subsidized exports of raw cotton at about 6 to $8\frac{1}{2}$ cents per pound. This has made it possible for U.S. producers to keep their customers in other lands. The Agriculture Act of 1964 provided a two-year subsidy on cotton used in the United States. This subsidy was set at the same rate as the export subsidy. It offset the low prices of cotton that was used to make imported cotton products. It also helped farmers compete on better terms with the makers of synthetic fibers.

Scientific Classification. Cotton is in the bombax family, *Bombacaceae*. Cotton makes up the genus *Gossypium*. There are about 20 species, but only 4 of them are cultivated. American upland cotton is genus *Gossypium*, species *G. hirsutum;* Egyptian and Sea-island cottons are *G. barbadense;* and the Asiatic cottons are *G. herbaceum* and *G. arboreum*. Each of these four species includes several varieties.   DABNEY S. WELLFORD

Related Articles in WORLD BOOK include:

COTTON CLOTHS

Batiste	Denim	Mosquito Netting
Broadcloth	Dimity	Muslin
Brocade	Drill	Nainsook
Buckram	Duck	Organdy
Calico	Foulard	Percale
Cambric	Gabardine	Piqué
Canvas	Gauze	Poplin
Chambray	Gingham	Sateen
Chenille	Haircloth	Seersucker
Cheviot	Huck	Shantung
Chintz	Jersey Cloth	Swiss
Corduroy	Khaki	Terry Cloth
Covert	Lace	Ticking
Crepe	Lawn	Velveteen
Cretonne	Lisle	Voile
Crinoline	Madras	

OTHER RELATED ARTICLES

Boll Weevil	Pink Bollworm	Virginia
Cellulose	Rayon	(picture)
Cotton Gin	Spinning	Weaving
Farm and Farming	Textile	Whitney, Eli
Guncotton	Thread	

Outline

I. Uses of Cotton
  A. Cotton-Fiber Products   C. Cotton-Linters
  B. Cottonseed Products   Products

II. Kinds of Cotton
  A. American Upland   C. Sea-Island Cotton
     Cotton   D. Asiatic Cottons
  B. Egyptian Cotton

III. The Cotton Plant
  A. The Flower   B. The Boll

IV. Cotton-Growing Regions
  A. The United States   B. Other Countries

V. How Cotton Is Grown
  A. Preparing the Soil   C. Control of Pests
  B. Planting and Culti-   and Disease
    vating   D. Picking Cotton

VI. Marketing Cotton
  A. Ginning and Baling B. Classing C. Selling

VII. Making Cotton into Cloth
  A. Cleaning   B. Spinning   C. Finishing

VIII. History

Questions

What is the leading cotton-growing country?

What important invention decreased the cost of producing cotton?

What is the most important cottonseed product?

What is the *Cotton Belt?*

How are airplanes often used in growing cotton?

How large is a bale of cotton?

What is a *cotton exchange?*

What is a *spot market?* a *futures exchange?*

How do explosives manufacturers use cotton?

Name two ways that the United States government has helped the cotton grower.

COTTON, JOHN

Brown Bros.

John Cotton

COTTON, JOHN (1584-1652), a Puritan clergyman, greatly influenced the religious and political life of early New England. Religious persecution forced him to flee from England to America in 1633. He became the "teacher" at First Church in Boston. He opposed Roger Williams' idea of individual freedom of conscience (see WILLIAMS, ROGER). Born in Derby, England, and educated at Cambridge University, Cotton served as vicar of St. Botolph's Church in Boston, England, from 1612 to 1633.   EARLE E. CAIRNS

COTTON BELT. See COTTON (Cotton-Growing Regions).

COTTON GIN is a machine invented in 1793 by Eli Whitney for separating cotton fiber from the seed. The cotton gin helped make cotton the chief crop of the southern United States. Before the invention of this machine, it took a person a full day to hand pick the seeds from a pound of cotton fiber. The word *gin* comes from the Old French *engin*, meaning *engine*.

Modern gins use the same principle as the first machine. Harvested cotton is fed through a row of about 70 saws that make from 350 to 500 revolutions a minute. The saws have a 12-inch diameter, and are placed about $\frac{5}{8}$ of an inch apart. The teeth on the saws pull the cotton from the seeds. Ginning ribs between the saws prevent the seeds from passing through. Brushes or air jets remove the fiber on the teeth of the saws.

Hand-harvested cotton comes to the gin relatively clean. But machine-picked cotton contains much more

The Cotton Gin Invented by Eli Whitney helped to shape the course of American history. In this model of the machine, the metal teeth used to tear the cotton fibers away from the seed are visible on the cylinder toward the right.

U.S. National Museum

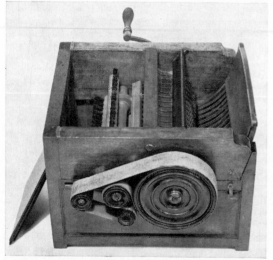

leaf and stem trash. For this reason, the modern gin must use additional equipment to clean the fiber. In 1955, the United States Department of Agriculture developed a *precleaner extractor* to remove much of this trash before the actual ginning. The machine consists of a vertical column with four rows of saws, one above the other. As the saws rotate, they drag the cotton over *grid bars* that scrub off the trash. Brushes remove the cotton from the teeth of the saws.   A. D. LONGHOUSE

See also COTTON; WHITNEY, ELI.

COTTONMOUTH is another name for the *water moccasin*, a poisonous snake that lives in the southeastern United States. See WATER MOCCASIN.

COTTONSEED OIL is an edible oil used in salads and cooking or made into margarine and shortening. Manufacturers remove the hulls from cottonseed. They steam the seeds and place them in hydraulic presses, which extract the oil. A ton of cottonseed provides about 310 to 320 pounds of oil. The defatted seeds and hulls are used as food for livestock. See also COTTON (Cottonseed Products); OIL (Fixed); VEGETABLE OIL.

COTTONTAIL. See RABBIT.

COTTONWOOD is a group of large, spreading, poplar trees that grow in the United States. These trees grow quickly and make good shade trees, but are short-lived. Early in spring, their small, greenish flowers

The Wide-Spreading Cottonwood Tree grows in most parts of the United States. The tree thrives in moist soil, and often grows to a height of 100 feet or more along riverbanks.

U.S. Forest Service

Cottonwood Trees have long, drooping clusters of many small flowers. Male and female flowers are on different trees. The tree gets its name from the cottony seeds, which float in air.

J. C. Allen and Son

L. W. Brownell

Cottonwood Leaves look clean and shiny all summer long. They are shaped like a triangle, and have wavy, toothed edges.

pounds. In 1912 he founded the Research Corporation and endowed it with his many patent rights in the field of electrical precipitation. Earnings from these finance new scientific research and the training of future scientists. Born in Oakland, Calif., Cottrell studied at the universities of California and Berlin, and received his Ph.D. from the University of Leipzig. HERBERT S. RHINESMITH

COTYLEDON, *KAHT ih LEE dun,* is the name given to the first leaves formed from a seed. These first leaves store and digest food for the new plant that is forming. The cotyledons are really part of the seed. They are usually thick and blunt. When a seed begins to sprout, a tiny stem and roots develop from the different tissues in the embryo of the seed. As the embryo grows, it uses up all the food stored in the seed. The cotyledons help in this process by digesting the stored food and moving it to the embryo.

In some plants, such as beans, the *cotyledons* (seed leaves) cling to the stem and develop green coloring matter. Then they begin to manufacture food for the new plant through photosynthesis (see PHOTOSYNTHESIS). When the plant grows other leaves, the cotyledons dry up and fall off. In other plants, as in peas, the cotyledons do not come above ground.

There are two types of cotyledon formation in the seeds of *angiosperms* (flowering plants). One type of seed has two cotyledons and is called a *dicotyledon.* A bean is a typical two-cotyledon seed. The rest of the seed, which consists of a *plumule* (tiny shoot) and the hypocotyl (tiny root), is tucked between the two cotyledons. Reserve food is stored in the two fleshy cotyledons. After a bean is soaked in water, the skin can be peeled off, and the bean can be split into two parts. The two thick parts of the bean are the cotyledons. In other dicotyledons, the cotyledons are thin and the food of the seed is stored outside of them.

The other kind of seed of flowering plants, a *monocotyledon,* has a single cotyledon next to the plumule and hypocotyl. Reserve food is stored outside the cotyledon. A kernel of corn is a typical single-cotyledon seed. ARTHUR W. GALSTON

See also ANGIOSPERM; DICOTYLEDON; GERMINATION; MONOCOTYLEDON; SEED.

droop in long clusters called *catkins,* and form masses of cottony seeds. The cottonwoods' shiny green leaves are shaped like a triangle, and have wavy, toothed edges. The thick, dull gray bark splits into ridges and long furrows. Cottonwoods grow in moist soils, especially along rivers.

The eastern cottonwood grows throughout the eastern regions of the United States. *Black cottonwood,* the tallest western broadleaf tree, grows along the Pacific Coast. The whitish or light brown wood of these trees is soft and weak. Manufacturers use it for boxes and crates, furniture, pulpwood, and excelsior. Cottonwood is the state tree of Kansas and Wyoming.

Scientific Classification. Cottonwoods belong to the willow family, *Salicaceae.* The eastern cottonwood is genus *Populus,* species *deltoides.* The black cottonwood is *P. trichocarpa.* ELBERT L. LITTLE, JR.

See also CATKIN; LEAF (picture, Kinds of Leaves); POPLAR; TREE (pictures, Tree Shapes; Autumn Colors).

COTTRELL, FREDERICK GARDNER (1877-1948), an American chemist, invented the Cottrell Electrical Precipitator in 1910. Using up to 100,000 volts, this machine removes smoke and other impurities from big industrial smokestacks. Valuable by-products are recovered, and clean air results.

Cottrell also developed helium production for airships and became an expert on nitrogen fixation, or changing nitrogen in the air into more useful com-

Cotyledons are present in the seeds of all flowering plants. Many kinds of seeds, including those of corn, contain only one cotyledon, *below left.* But a great many other plants, including the broad bean, have seeds with two cotyledons, *below right.* Botanists use this difference in classifying flowering plants.

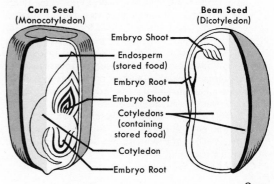

Corn Seed (Monocotyledon)

Bean Seed (Dicotyledon)

Embryo Shoot
Endosperm (stored food)
Embryo Root
Embryo Shoot
Cotyledons (containing stored food)
Cotyledon
Embryo Root

COUBERTIN, KOO behr TAN, **PIERRE DE** (1862-1937), BARON COUBERTIN, a French sportsman, revived the Olympic Games in 1896. The games had not been held since the Roman Emperor Theodosius abolished them as a public nuisance in 392. Coubertin founded the International Olympic Committee in 1894, and served as its director until 1925. He was born in Paris. See also OLYMPIC GAMES.   RICHARD G. HACKENBERG

COUGAR. See MOUNTAIN LION.

COUGH is a sudden, explosive expelling of air from the lungs. The air is forced out through the mouth, in contrast to sneezing in which the air comes through the nose (see SNEEZING). Coughing and sneezing are important body defenses, because they help rid the breathing channels of harmful irritants. But they can also spread infection or disease.

When irritating substances enter any part of the respiratory system, a special set of nerves is stimulated. These nerves act to cause a short, deep intake of air. The *glottis*, or opening of the larynx, closes. This creates great air pressure in the lungs. Suddenly the glottis opens and the captured air rushes out in a blast, pushing before it any foreign substance in its path. A person can make himself cough whenever he wants. But he finds it difficult to stop a cough that results from irritating substances.   ALBERT P. SELTZER

COUGHLIN, KAWG lin, **CHARLES EDWARD** (1891-), an American Roman Catholic priest, became well-known before World War II for his political activities. In radio addresses and his paper, *Social Justice*, he favored inflation and isolationism. His bishop reproved him for his activities. Born in Hamilton, Ont., he was assigned to the Shrine of the Little Flower at Royal Oak, Mich., in 1926. Father Coughlin retired from the shrine in 1966.   MATTHEW A. FITZSIMONS

COULEE. See GRAND COULEE DAM; WASHINGTON (Land Regions).

COULOMB, koo LAHM, is the unit that measures the quantity of electricity flowing past a section of an electric circuit in one second when the current is one ampere.

An electric current carrying one coulomb per second is called a current of one *ampere*. Ampere is the unit of rate or strength of flow. The name *coulomb* was given to the unit to honor the French physicist Charles A. de Coulomb.   E. R. WHITEHEAD

See also AMPERE; ELECTRIC MEASUREMENT; FARAD.

COULOMB, koo LAHM, **CHARLES AUGUSTIN DE** (1736-1806), a French scientist, inventor, and army engineer, made fundamental contributions in the fields of friction, electricity, and magnetism. He formulated *Coulomb's Law*, which states that the force between two electric or magnetic charges varies inversely as the square of the distance between them. He invented a number of instruments for measuring magnetic and electric forces. He also published papers on friction in machinery. The unit for the quantity of electricity, the coulomb, was named in his honor.

Coulomb was born in Angoulême. He was educated in Paris and entered the French Army. After nine years of army service in the West Indies, he devoted himself to scientific research.   ROBERT W. ABBETT

COUMARIN. See ANTICOAGULANT.

COUNCIL. Many councils of various types are listed in THE WORLD BOOK ENCYCLOPEDIA under the key word. Example: HEALTH COUNCIL, NATIONAL.

COUNCIL, CITY. See CITY AND LOCAL GOVERNMENTS (Forms of Local Government).

COUNCIL BLUFFS, Iowa (pop. 52,957; alt. 990 ft.), has been a railroad center since President Lincoln fixed the eastern terminus of the Union Pacific Railroad near the city in 1863. The city stands on the east side of the Missouri River, opposite Omaha, Nebr. (see IOWA [political map]). It was at first a military post. Between 1846 and 1852 the town became an outfitting place for the wagon trains of the Mormon migration and the California gold rush. The city is the principal trading center of southwestern Iowa, serving particularly as a grain market. Council Bluffs has a council-manager government.   WILLIAM J. PETERSEN

COUNCIL FOR MUTUAL ECONOMIC ASSISTANCE. See WORLD (map: Major Economic Organizations of the World).

COUNCIL GROVE, Kan. (pop. 2,664; alt. 1,235 ft.), is a trading center on the Neosho River, about 120 miles southwest of Kansas City. When the Santa Fe Trail crossed the river here, pioneers and Osage Indians held a council in a grove. From the council came the name *Council Grove*. The town was incorporated in 1858. It has a mayor-council government.   WILLIAM F. ZORNOW

COUNCIL OF BLOOD. See ALVA, DUKE OF.

COUNCIL OF ECONOMIC ADVISERS. See ECONOMIC ADVISERS, COUNCIL OF.

COUNCIL OF FOREIGN MINISTERS. The foreign ministers of various nations sometimes conduct negotiations when mutual problems are considered too important for routine diplomacy. They may meet to discuss questions of international politics, or they may make personal visits to the heads of other governments. Sometimes a meeting of foreign ministers precedes a top-level conference of government heads. The ministers may then work out an agenda for the heads of state to follow.

Many international organizations have special councils of foreign ministers. These organizations include the Anzus Council, Arab League, Central Treaty Organization, Council of Europe, European Community, North Atlantic Treaty Organization, Organization of American States, Southeast Asia Treaty Organization, and Western European Union.

Meetings between foreign ministers played an important role in international relations from the end of the Thirty Years' War in 1648 until World War I. Since that time, meetings between the heads of governments, sometimes called "summit conferences," have tended to overshadow the work of the foreign ministers. But the foreign minister is still one of the most important officials in any government.

COUNSELING. See VOCATIONAL GUIDANCE (Counseling; Vocational Guidance as a Profession); GUIDANCE.

COUNSELOR. See LAWYER.

COUNT is a title of honor going back to the days of the Roman Empire. The Latin word *comes* means *companion* or *follower*, and was used to indicate the companions of the Roman proconsuls. From this came the Spanish title *conde*, and the French *comte*. *Count* came into the English language as a translation of foreign titles equal to the English *earl*. See also EARL.

COUNTER REFORMATION was a movement in the Roman Catholic Church that took place between 1560 and 1648. During this time, the church reformed abuses within its own organization and tried to stamp out Protestantism. There had been many voices calling for disciplinary reforms even before the Protestant Reformation. But no general reform was accomplished before the Council of Trent was called in 1545. This Council continued with some interruptions until 1563. It clearly outlined and reaffirmed Roman Catholic doctrines.

Much of the work accomplished during this period is to be credited to the Jesuits. They established Roman Catholic missions and made many advances in the religious education of the people. Other movements to check the growth of Protestantism were accompanied by violence. The Thirty Years' War was the result of the attempt to repress Protestantism in Germany. It ended with the Peace of Westphalia in 1648.

Protestantism had only a feeble existence in Spain and Italy. The Counter Reformation was accompanied by the work of the Inquisition in those countries. All direct attempts to return England as a nation to Roman Catholicism had at last to be abandoned. FULTON J. SHEEN

Related Articles in WORLD BOOK include:

Inquisition	Roman Catholic Church
Jesuit	Thirty Years' War
Reformation	Trent, Council of

COUNTERFEITING, *KOWN ter fiht ing*, is the production of any article in imitation of another, but especially the unlawful production of imitations of money. Printing and coining money is the function of a national government. One who counterfeits commits a crime against the government.

Technically, counterfeiting is different from *duplication.* Counterfeiting is the imitation of the coins in less valuable material. In duplication, coins of the same metallic value are made by unauthorized persons. In the United States, counterfeiters are tried in federal district courts. Prison sentences range from 5 to 20 years, and fines from $5,000 to $10,000. FRED E. INBAU

See also MONEY (Printing Paper Money); SECRET SERVICE, UNITED STATES.

COUNTERGLOW. See ZODIACAL LIGHT.

COUNTERPOINT is the combination of several melodies at once. Music today is usually written with a single melody and supporting chords. Counterpoint is written with several melodies that form chords when they are played together. Singing several popular songs together creates a *quodlibet.* Any harmonies in it are purely accidental, but the harmonies in counterpoint are intentional. Counterpoint is also called *polyphony,* from the Greek words *poly,* or *many,* and *phony,* or *voices.* Contrapuntal music includes the canon and the round, such as "Three Blind Mice," and the fugue.

Counterpoint developed about 1100. Monks at that time sang *organum,* with several parts parallel to the melody of a plain chant. Later the separate voices were allowed to move in different directions and new styles of counterpoint developed. Counterpoint then reached high points in the 1500's, with the music of Giovanni Palestrina of Italy and William Byrd of England, and in the 1700's, with the fugues of Johann Sebastian Bach. GRANT FLETCHER

See also CANON; FUGUE; ROUND.

COUNTESS. See EARL.

COUNTING. See ARITHMETIC.

COUNTRY is a term that means any independent nation with a definite name and a geographic boundary. About 145 countries are generally recognized as independent. The number has steadily increased since World War II as more colonies have become independent. In size, the countries of the world range from Vatican City, which covers 108.7 acres, to Russia, which spreads out over 8,649,500 square miles. There are eight huge countries, each with more than 1,000,000 square miles, and about 55 large ones covering from 100,000 to 1,000,000 square miles. There are about 30 medium-sized countries with over 40,000 square miles; about 35 that include between 3,000 and 40,000 square miles; and about 15 small ones covering less than 3,000 square miles. For lists of countries of the world, see the various continent articles, such as AFRICA (table: Independent Countries); also WORLD (table: Independent Countries of the World).

In a second meaning, the term *country* may refer to a region that is not necessarily a political unit and does not usually have exact boundaries. The Bluegrass Country of Kentucky is an example of this meaning of country. SAMUEL N. DICKEN

See also BOUNDARY.

COUNTRY CLUB provides golfing facilities and other services for its members. The name arose because a golf course requires a great deal of acreage. As a result, such clubs had to be established on the outskirts, or country-side, of a community. Most early country clubs were formed almost solely for golfing.

The members themselves as a group own most country clubs. Such clubs are known as *private clubs,* because only the members and their guests may use the facilities. They are not operated to make a profit. *Semiprivate clubs* have fewer restrictions on membership and guest privileges, and are conducted as profit-making businesses. About 3,000 private country clubs operate in the United States. Most clubs have swimming pools, tennis courts, and dining rooms, in addition to golf courses.

COUNTRY LIFE. See FARM AND FARMING.

COUNTS, GEORGE SYLVESTER (1889-), an American educator and author, became a leading authority on education in Russia. He made several trips there to study schools. His books include *The Education of Free Men* (1941) and *The Challenge of Soviet Education* (1957). He taught at Yale, the University of Chicago, and Teachers College, Columbia University, from 1927 to 1956. After World War II, he served on the United States Educational Commission to Japan. Counts was born near Baldwin City, Kans. JOHN S. BRUBACHER

COUNTY is usually a division of local government. Almost all the states of the United States are divided into counties. Louisiana has *parishes* that correspond to counties, and Alaska has *boroughs.* Connecticut has *towns,* and Rhode Island has *cities* and *towns.* Connecticut is also divided into eight counties and Rhode Island into five counties, but these counties are only divisions of the state court systems. The form of county organization and the number and powers of county officers vary from state to state. State legislatures determine the county boundaries.

In counties where large cities occupy the entire

county area, city and county governments may be combined. Denver, Honolulu, and San Francisco, for example, have combined city and county governments. Some cities are not part of any county, and do not form a part of county government. In these cities, municipal officials perform many of the duties which are ordinarily performed by county officials. Baltimore and St. Louis are examples of two cities which have governments of this kind.

Importance. The importance of county government varies with the section of the country. The county is especially important in the South and West. It is unimportant in New England, where the town is the center of local influence (see TOWN). In the Midwest and in the Middle Atlantic States, the county often shares authority with the township (see TOWNSHIP). County revenues are raised chiefly by taxes on personal property and real estate. State governments remit some parts of state-collected taxes to counties.

The number and size of counties vary from state to state and from region to region. The United States has 3,043 organized counties. Texas, with 254, has the largest number of counties. The number and type of county officers also vary from state to state.

County Governments usually have a *decentralized* administration, with no executive head. The main county institution is an elective board. In southern and western states, this board is generally called a *board of commissioners*. It consists of from 2 to about 15 members who are elected at large. In other states, especially in the Midwest and the East, the governing body is usually called a *board of supervisors*. It has from 15 to 100 members who are elected from districts, wards, or townships. County officers are usually elected for terms of from 2 to 4 years. They may include county commissioners or supervisors, sheriff, prosecuting attorney or district attorney, coroner, registrar of wills, recorder of deeds, clerk of courts, jury commissioner, controller or auditor, surveyor, engineer, and others.

Duties. County governments may administer justice, assess and collect taxes, record official documents, and register voters. They may also administer roads, public education, zoning, and licensing. Some counties manage such functions as sewage disposal, jails, and relief systems. Some counties may also maintain parks, airports, hospitals, libraries, electric service, and water service.

Of all forms of local government, the county has resisted change most strongly. But some counties have adopted the county-manager system, and a few counties have consolidated in order to promote greater efficiency in their operations.

The word *county* comes from the French *comte*, which was derived from the Latin *comitatus*, meaning *body of companions*. The French county was the domain of a count. The English began to call their *shires* counties about 1400. The English colonists brought the county system with them to America.　　　DAVID FELLMAN

Related Articles in WORLD BOOK include:

Assessor	County Agricultural	District
Board of	Extension Agent	Attorney
Supervisors	County Home Extension	Sheriff
Coroner	Agent	Shire

COUNTY AGRICULTURAL EXTENSION AGENT is an official who advises farmers on better ways to carry out their work. He works with community leaders to help rural citizens take part in area development programs. The federal, state, and county governments cooperate in employing a county agent. The agents work as part of the extension service of the state land-grant university and the U.S. Department of Agriculture.

The county agent tells the farmer about new farming methods and shows him how to apply them to his local situation. The agent also helps the farmer with farm management, soil conservation, and marketing problems. He works with young people as well as adults, and trains local leaders. He gives advice to farm cooperatives and other groups that serve farmers.

A person who wants to become a county agricultural extension agent should have a bachelor of science degree in agriculture. He should also have a broad understanding of farming, and the desire to help people help themselves.　　Critically reviewed by FEDERAL EXTENSION SERVICE

See also AGRICULTURAL EDUCATION; COUNTY HOME EXTENSION AGENT; FARM AND FARMING (The County Agent); FOUR-H CLUB.

COUNTY GOVERNMENT. See COUNTY.

COUNTY HOME EXTENSION AGENT is a woman who advises members of rural communities on homemaking and family welfare matters. She gives instruction in nutrition and in the preparation and preservation of foods. She teaches both adults and young people how to manage a home, clothe the family, and care for children. She also gives advice on family relationships, and helps local leaders develop and carry out community improvement projects.

Federal, state, and county authorities cooperate in employing a home agent, as they do in the case of a county agricultural agent. A district or state leader supervises her work. A committee of local citizens determines most of the work program to be carried out each year by the home agent. The agent sends annual reports to state and federal extension services.

A girl who plans to become a home agent should study for a bachelor of science degree in home economics at a college or university.

Critically reviewed by FEDERAL EXTENSION SERVICE

See also AGRICULTURAL EDUCATION; COUNTY AGRICULTURAL EXTENSION AGENT; FOUR-H CLUB.

COUPÉ. See BUGGY.

COUPERIN, *koo PRAN,* **FRANÇOIS** (1668-1733), a French composer, musician, and teacher, won fame as a composer of sacred works and of music for the harpsichord. The harpsichord was the most important keyboard instrument of his time. He wrote a famous textbook, *The Art of Playing the Harpsichord.* He dedicated it in 1716 to the six-year-old King Louis XV of France.

Johann Sebastian Bach, the famous composer, greatly admired Couperin. Bach arranged one of Couperin's trios for the organ, and used some of the ideas expressed in Couperin's book in teaching his eldest son.

Couperin was born in Paris, a member of a family which produced about a dozen excellent musicians. He studied music with his father, Charles. In 1685, at the age of 17, he won a competition for the highly coveted post of organist to the king of France. Soon afterwards, he began teaching the royal children, including the crown prince.　　KARL GEIRINGER

The Stone Breakers by Gustave Courbet shows his concern with the realities of everyday life. Courbet used this realistic style in his most famous works.

The Art Institute of Chicago

COUPLET, *CUP let,* is a rhyme of two lines. The *heroic couplet* is an English metrical form in iambic pentameter, used in sequence.

A *closed* couplet emphasizes the rhyme, and completes a thought within two lines. For example:

A perfect Judge will read each work of Wit
With the same spirit that its author writ:
Survey the Whole, nor seek slight faults to find
Where nature moves, and rapture warms the mind . . .

In an *open* couplet, clauses and sentences end anywhere, and the rhyme is not emphasized. For example:

A thing of beauty is a joy forever:
Its loveliness increases; it will never
Pass into nothingness; but still will keep
A bower quiet for us, and a sleep
Full of sweet dreams, and health, and quiet breathing.

John Dryden and Alexander Pope used the closed couplet brilliantly. Other poets used open couplets with great skill. They include Geoffrey Chaucer, George Chapman, and John Keats.

Less common forms include the *short couplet*, or four-stress lines; the *long couplet*, or six-stress lines; and couplets as a stanzaic form. CHARLES W. COOPER

See also METER; POETRY; RHYME.

COUPON. See BOND (picture); RATIONING.

COURANTE. See DANCING (The Renaissance).

COURBET, *KOOR BEH,* **GUSTAVE** (1819-1877), a French painter, is famous for his efforts to develop realism in French painting during the 1800's. He painted his early works, such as *Man with the Leather Belt,* in a romantic style (see PAINTING [In the 1800's]). But, in 1849, he exhibited *Burial at Ornans* and *After Dinner at Ornans,* both of which showed events of his day. These paintings, and others of untraditional "realist" subjects, such as *The Stone Breakers, Young Ladies of the Village,* and *Young Ladies by the Seine,* caused a scandal when they were exhibited.

In 1855, Courbet organized his own exhibit when the Salon, the official group sponsoring public exhibitions of paintings, refused to let him display his work. Courbet painted the *Studio* for the show. He called the picture "a real allegory of seven years of my artistic life," and painted himself surrounded by his friends and favorite subjects for painting.

He was born JEAN DÉSIRÉ GUSTAVE COURBET in Ornans, France. In 1840, he moved to Paris, where he attended free drawing classes and copied paintings in the Louvre. He became involved in the Commune of Paris in 1871 and was imprisoned for his activities (see COMMUNE). He died in Switzerland. ROBERT GOLDWATER

COUREURS DE BOIS, *koo RUR duh BWAH,* were French-Canadian frontiersmen of the late 1600's and the early 1700's who made their living trading for furs with the Indians. Canada was a colony of France, and private fur traders were required to get a license from the government at Quebec. The government issued very few licenses, and most coureurs de bois engaged in trading illegally. The term *coureurs de bois* means *Vagabonds of the Forest.* The adventurous life of the coureurs de bois attracted many young men who were bored with farming.

The coureurs de bois sold brandy to the Indians, and the missionaries frowned on their activities. But these adventurers learned Indian languages and customs. They provided a link between the Indians and the French that helped to cement the alliance against the English during the French and Indian Wars. P. B. WAITE

COURNAND, *coor NAN,* **ANDRÉ FREDERIC** (1895-), an American physician, shared the Nobel prize in physiology and medicine in 1956. Cournand, Dickinson W. Richards, Jr., and Werner Forssmann won the award for developing a research method called *cardiac* (heart) *catheterization,* and for using a *catheter* (thin tube) in studying the heart and lungs and their blood vessels. Cournand was born in France. He came to the United States in 1930. OSCAR A. THORUP, JR.

See also FORSSMANN, WERNER; RICHARDS, D. W., JR.

COURSE INDICATOR. See AIRCRAFT INSTRUMENTS (The Deviation Indicator).

COURSE OF STUDY. See CURRICULUM.

The System of Courts in the United States

FEDERAL COURTS

The decisions of administrative agencies usually are reviewed in the Courts of Appeals. Sometimes they are reviewed in District Courts.

United States District Courts

REVIEW

APPEAL

REVIEW

United States Courts of Appeals

Administrative Agencies
such as the Federal Trade Commission and the Tax Court of the United States

COURT is a government agency with the power to settle disputes between individuals or organizations. All courts use officials called *judges*. Some courts have *juries* as well as judges. The administrative work of the court is done by the *clerk* of the court. Courts also may have *marshals*, *sheriffs*, and *bailiffs*, to assist in enforcing the decisions of the court, and in keeping order during proceedings before the court.

The word *court* may also mean the place where judges and other persons regularly meet to settle legal disputes, or it may mean the gathering itself.

How a Court Works

To illustrate the workings of a British or American court, let us take an example of a dispute which the parties are unwilling to settle privately.

Suppose that you fall on a flight of stairs after visiting a friend at his apartment. You have broken your leg and suffered bruises, and you believe the accident resulted from the carelessness of the owner of the apartment house. You or your lawyer will talk to the owner and try to work out a settlement without going to court. But many cases cannot be settled by private talks. Let us assume yours is not settled.

If there were no courts, you would have to pay the costs of the accident, such as hospital bills, yourself, or use force to make the apartment house owner pay. But this is not always fair, and the government provides a court where you can tell your side of the dispute, and the owner can tell his. You will submit a written statement of your side of the event. This is called the *complaint*. Because you begin the lawsuit, you are called the *plaintiff*. The owner will be called the *defendant*,

and the written report of his side of the story is called his *answer*. If he does not file an answer, he ordinarily will be considered at fault, and must pay you. By comparing the two sides, the lawyers and the court can see just where the difference of opinion lies.

When the trial is held, you and the owner produce *evidence*, either written or given by witnesses, in an effort to show the truth in the case. A jury usually decides questions of fact, such as whether the carpeting on the stairs was torn or loose. If both sides wish it, the judge alone may decide questions of fact. The judge decides questions of law.

After all the evidence is in, the judge tells the jury about the rules of law in the case. Then the jury decides who wins. The jury's decision is called a *verdict*. The jury also decides how much money you are entitled to if you win the case. The court then gives a *judgment* embodying the verdict of the jury. If the court finds that the owner was careless, he will be ordered to pay you. But if the owner is not found at fault, you must bear the expense yourself.

System of Courts in the United States

There are two systems of courts in the United States. One is maintained by the states, and the other by the federal government. The state courts began as courts of the American colonies. They became state courts when the colonies became states. The federal court system was provided for in the United States Constitution to interpret the Constitution, to settle disputes which go beyond the limits of one state, and to settle disputes among the various states.

Federal Courts. The Constitution provides that "the

Lower Courts of the Land

STATE COURTS

Justices of the Peace

Magistrates' Courts

Police, Traffic, and Small Claims Courts

In many states, a person has a choice between these lower courts and trial courts. Usually a case heard in the lowest courts cannot be appealed to higher courts.

SUPERIOR COURTS

Municipal Courts

County, District, or Superior Courts

Probate Courts

Special Trial Courts
such as traffic courts, juvenile courts, and womens' courts

Cases may be appealed from trial courts to higher state courts.

The Highest Court in the Land

United States
Court
of Claims

United States
Court
of Customs
and Patent
Appeals

United
States
Customs
Court

REVIEW

APPEAL

REVIEW

Supreme Court of the United States

judicial power of the United States shall be vested in one Supreme Court, and in such inferior courts as the Congress may from time to time ordain and establish" (Article III, Section 1). Federal courts handle cases involving the Constitution, federal laws, and cases in which the United States is a party. They also try cases between citizens of different states, cases in which other countries or their citizens are parties, and cases concerning ships at sea, called *admiralty* cases.

The system of federal courts is governed by a statute called the Judicial Code. The trial court, where cases are first heard, is called the *district court*. The United States and its possessions have about 90 district courts. The courts in Guam, the Virgin Islands, and the Panama Canal Zone are known as *territorial courts*. District courts in Puerto Rico are called *courts of the United States*. The *courts of appeals* rank above the district courts. One appellate court is located in each of the 11 judicial circuits into which the country has been divided. The highest federal court is the *Supreme Court of the United States*.

Cases tried in the federal courts usually are heard first in district courts, but there are special types of cases in which higher courts may have *original jurisdiction*. When federal cases are appealed, they usually go from the district court to a court of appeals. On rare occasions, they may go directly to the Supreme Court. In addition to reviewing trials in the district courts, the courts of appeals also review orders issued by administrative agencies such as the Securities and Exchange Commission and the Federal Trade Commission. Cases from state supreme courts also may go to the Supreme Court if some question of federal law is involved.

There are federal courts with special authority for certain kinds of cases, such as the *Court of Claims*, where individuals may sue on some claims against the federal government; the *United States Customs Court;* and the *Court of Customs and Patent Appeals*.

State Courts are much like federal courts in their methods of procedure. The lowest state courts often are the *magistrates' courts* in cities, and those of justices of the peace in villages and rural communities. Usually a person may choose to have his case heard in these courts, or in state trial courts. If he chooses these lower courts, he usually gives up his right to appeal. *County courts, municipal courts*, and other state superior courts are usually next higher. In many states, there is an intermediate court of appeals above the county or district courts. Appellate courts usually review the decisions of state administrative agencies. The highest court in a state is usually called a *supreme court*.

Other Court Systems

France and many of the nations of Europe use a system of civil law. In many cases, this makes court procedures quite different from those in English-speaking countries. For example, the *Assize* courts, which handle grave criminal cases and misdemeanors in connection with the press, are the only courts in France which have juries. Most French courts have panels of

Cases from state supreme courts may be reviewed by the Supreme Court of the United States if some question of federal law is involved.

REVIEW

Cases may be appealed to the intermediate appellate courts, if the state has them, or go directly to the Supreme Court of the state.

Intermediate Appellate Courts

APPEAL

REVIEW

APPEAL

REVIEW

**State Administrative
Agencies**
such as state commerce
commissions

Decisions of state administrative agencies are reviewed by the Supreme Court of the state. Some decisions may be reviewed by state intermediate appellate courts.

Supreme Courts of the States

judges. The rules for admitting evidence are very broad, and no person can refuse to testify on the grounds that he may incriminate himself.

Both France and West Germany allow citizens to sue their governments for damages. Great Britain did not make this provision until 1947. Courts in West Germany are a mixture of German forms and English and American ideas. In East Germany, the Communists have used the courts as tools to increase their power. Courts in many European countries cannot declare an act of the legislature unconstitutional.

The courts of Canada include the Supreme Court, the Exchequer Court, and the provincial courts. The governor-general appoints all judges of these courts.

International Courts

International courts differ in two ways from the courts within a country. First, nations, and not private citizens or corporations alone, come to an international court for justice. Second, no nation is forced to make use of international courts, or to abide by their decisions. But many persons believe international courts should have the power to enforce their decisions.

The Permanent Court of Arbitration was set up by The Hague Peace Conferences of 1899 and 1907. It consists of a group of experts on international law. When a problem arises in which arbitration is needed, five judges are selected from this group to act as arbitrators. The International Court of Justice now is a part of the United Nations. It meets at the Hague to settle any disputes brought before it. See INTERNATIONAL COURT OF JUSTICE; INTERNATIONAL LAW.

History of Courts

The structure of the court systems of the United States and Canada is based in general on that of England. The earliest English courts were local ones. They were organized in villages, manors, and counties. Their origins go back beyond any recorded history.

During the 1000's and the 1100's in England, the king and a group of officials and noblemen traveled about the country, holding court. The officials who followed the king were called his *court*. The king was regarded as the source of justice, but he himself could not handle all the cases that were brought to him. Instead, he appointed some of the officers who accompanied him to hear cases and administer justice for him. These men were the early judges. Separate church courts handled cases involving members of the clergy and religious matters. See CANON LAW.

In the 1200's a system of central courts became established in England. The king sent judges out into the country at regular intervals to hold court. The people recognized these as the king's courts, even though the king himself was not present. The earliest of the king's courts was the *Court of the Exchequer*, which collected the king's revenues. Next the *Court of Common Pleas* was set up. But at all times, cases were heard before the king himself, or, in Latin, *coram rege*. The king had advisers to help him decide these cases. Out of this grew the *Court of King's Bench*. The greatest court was Parliament, which is still known in Great Britain as the *High Court of Parliament*. The highest tribunal in Great

Britain today is a committee of the House of Lords. Ranking below it are the *Court of Appeal*, *High Court of Justice*, and the county and borough courts.

The courts of the Exchequer, Common Pleas, and King's Bench continued in Great Britain until 1875, when they were consolidated in the High Court of Justice. The Court of Appeal was set up as an intermediate appellate court between the High Court and the House of Lords.

In America, provincial courts were set up in all 13 colonies. After the Revolutionary War in America, each state set up a court system modeled after the British courts.   ERWIN N. GRISWOLD

Related Articles. See the Government section of the various state, province, and country articles, such as CALIFORNIA (Government). See also CANADA, GOVERNMENT OF; UNITED STATES, GOVERNMENT OF. See also the following articles:

COURTS

Appellate Court	District Court
Court-Martial	International Court of
Court of Appeals	Justice
Court of Claims	Juvenile Court
Court of Common Pleas	Parlement
Court of Domestic Relations	Supreme Court of the
Court of Military Appeals	United States
Customs Court, United States	Territorial Courts

OFFICERS

Bailiff	Justice of the	Public
Chief Justice	Peace	Defender
Clerk of Court	Lawyer	Puisne
District Attorney	Marshal	Receiver
Judge	Notary Public	Sheriff
Jury and Trial by Jury		

PROCEDURES AND WRITS

Affidavit	Equity	Inquest	Subpoena
Appeal	Evidence	Judgment	Suit
Arraignment	Fine	Mandamus	Summons
Attachment	Forfeiture	Oath	Venire
Bail	Garnishment	Petition	Warrant
Brief	Habeas Corpus	Quo Warranto	Witness
Demurrer	Indictment	Sentence	Writ
Deposition	Injunction		

OTHER RELATED ARTICLES

Court Reporter	Law
Crime	Law Enforcement
Justice, Department of	Star Chamber
Kangaroo Court	United States Constitution

COURT, in sports, is a flat, smooth surface for playing games. It is made of dirt, wood, cement, or other material, and usually has marked boundaries. Sports played in courts include racket games, handball, and basketball.

COURT, INNS OF. See INNS OF COURT.

COURT-MARTIAL is a military court which tries offenses against the rules of the armed forces. At one time in the United States, the code of justice used in the courts of the army and air force differed from that used in navy courts. But with the unification of the armed services, a Uniform Code of Military Justice went into effect on May 31, 1951. This code combined and revised the rules and regulations of the different services. No matter what branch of the service the accused may belong to, the court procedure is the same.

There are three types of courts-martial. A *general court-martial* may try any cases subject to the military code and may impose any prescribed punishment, including the death sentence. A *special court-martial* may try cases involving noncapital offenses made punishable

At a United States Army Court-Martial the president of the court reads its decision to the accused soldier and his lawyers.

by the code. A *summary court-martial* has jurisdiction to try and sentence persons guilty of the more minor military offenses described by the code.

A serviceman who commits a serious offense comes up for a pretrial investigation of the charges against him. If the investigation shows that it is warranted, a court-martial is assembled. In a serious offense, the accused can be represented by either civilian or military officer-lawyers. All charges are automatically reviewed by trained legal staffs after the trial. Serious charges can be appealed to the Court of Military Appeals, which is composed of three civilian judges appointed by the President (see COURT OF MILITARY APPEALS).

Officer-lawyers on duty at a court-martial must be certified by the judge advocate general of their branch of the service in order to act as defense and trial counsels. Only fully qualified persons are allowed to act as "law officers." A law officer at a general court-martial is similar to the judge in a civil court. Enlisted men may request to have one third of their trial courts composed of other enlisted men.   JOHN W. WADE

See also UNIFORM CODE OF MILITARY JUSTICE.

COURT OF APPEALS is a high federal or state court. The U.S. Court of Appeals ranks next to the Supreme Court of the United States as a reviewing authority. Several states also have courts of appeals.

The U.S. Court of Appeals hears most appeals from district courts and federal administrative agencies. It also reviews the decisions of some agencies. In some cases, the party who feels himself wronged has a right to appeal directly to the Supreme Court of the United States. In a few cases, the parties have a right to ask the Supreme Court to review a decision of a court of appeals.

The Court of Appeals divides its work into 10 judicial circuits. A star indicates the District of Columbia Circuit.

COURT OF MILITARY APPEALS

But in most cases, the Supreme Court only reviews cases that present an important question of law.

In the early days in the United States, federal judges traveled from place to place to try cases and to hear appeals. The route which was assigned to the court was called the *circuit*. Today the circuits are geographical areas. Each circuit has one court of appeals.

The circuits are numbered one through ten. The eleventh circuit covers only the District of Columbia. The First Circuit includes Puerto Rico, the Third includes the Virgin Islands, the Fifth includes the Panama Canal Zone, and the Ninth includes Alaska and Hawaii. The judges of the First, Fifth, and Ninth Circuits travel to these places to hear cases.

Only three judges ordinarily sit to decide each case, although more than three judges are assigned to some circuits. A justice of the Supreme Court is assigned to each circuit as the *Circuit Justice*. In early times, he often helped decide cases at the court of appeals level, but now he rarely does this. The chief judge has a position on the court of appeals like that of the chief justice of the Supreme Court. The chief judge assigns tasks to the other judges.   ERWIN N. GRISWOLD

See also CIRCUIT RIDER; COURT (Federal Courts); DISTRICT COURT; SUPREME COURT OF THE UNITED STATES.

COURT OF CHANCERY. See EQUITY.

COURT OF CLAIMS is a special court which settles claims against a state or government. Congress created the United States Court of Claims in 1855. The court has a chief justice and four judges appointed by the President. Usually no one can sue the U.S. government without its consent. But the government agreed to be sued on certain claims when this court was established. Congress appropriates money to pay for judgments of this court. See also CLAIM.   ERWIN N. GRISWOLD

COURT OF COMMON PLEAS was a court in England in which civil cases were heard. The courts were probably first set up in the 1200's. Cases brought by common citizens were called *common pleas*. This distinguished them from cases brought by the government, which were called *pleas of the crown*. The Court of Common Pleas existed until 1875, and then its duties were assigned to the High Court of Justice.   ERWIN N. GRISWOLD

COURT OF DOMESTIC RELATIONS is a special court which deals with problems of the family. Its procedure is less formal than that of most courts and is often much like that of a court of equity, although it may also have the powers of a criminal court in some cases. The matters handled by the court differ from place to place but may include action for divorce, nonsupport of wife or child, adoption, guardianship, and crimes against children. Sometimes the court handles cases dealing with neglected or delinquent children.   JOHN W. WADE

See also EQUITY; JUVENILE COURT.

COURT OF EQUITY. See EQUITY.

COURT OF LIONS. See ALHAMBRA.

COURT OF MILITARY APPEALS is a civilian court of the Department of Defense. It reviews questions of law in any court-martial of a general or flag officer, and in any court-martial resulting in a death sentence. It also may review other courts-martial decisions. The court's decisions in matters of law are final. The President appoints the three judges. See also COURT-MARTIAL.

COURT PLASTER

COURT PLASTER is thin silk treated with a solution of isinglass, alcohol, glycerin, and water. At one time it was used to cover skin cuts and blemishes. Now, cosmetics or sterile adhesive bandages are used. The term comes from the old custom of ladies at court wearing specks of black plaster on the face.   Austin Edward Smith

COURT REPORTER is a stenographer who records the testimony given at a trial or other legal proceeding. He records every word spoken except discussions that the judge or attorneys indicate should be "off the record." If testimony is given that may not be admitted as evidence, the judge can instruct the court reporter to "strike that from the record."

Court reporters take notes in shorthand or on a machine, and later transfer them to a typewritten record. Newspaper reporters who cover court news are often called *court reporters*.

COURTESY. See Etiquette.

COURTOIS, *koor TWAH*, **BERNARD** (1777-1838), a French chemist, discovered the element iodine in 1811. Courtois obtained heavy violet vapors by adding strong sulfuric acid to the ashes of seaweed. The vapors condensed to form black crystals. Sir Humphry Davy named the element iodine.

Courtois was born in Dijon, France. He studied at the École Polytechnique.   Paul R. Frey

COURTSHIP OF MILES STANDISH, THE, is a long narrative poem by Henry Wadsworth Longfellow about the Pilgrims of Plymouth Colony. It tells how Captain Miles Standish courted Priscilla Mullens, "the Mayflower of Plymouth." Standish lacked the courage to ask Priscilla to marry him, though in battle he feared nothing. He persuaded his friend, the young and handsome John Alden, to tell her of his offer. John himself

Priscilla Mullens Listens to John Alden while he pleads the cause of his friend, Captain Miles Standish. Because she knew John Alden also loved her, she is said to have asked him, "Why don't you speak for yourself, John?"

loved Priscilla. But he was a loyal friend of the captain, so he carried out the mission.

The story is based on tradition rather than known facts. One of the descendants of John Alden published a prose version (1812-1814). This version tells that John soon visited Priscilla again on his own behalf, and that later they were married. Standish was supposed never to have forgiven his friend. But the poem relates that he went to fight the Indians, and returned on the wedding day to wish the bride joy.   Norman Foerster

See also ALDEN (John); PLYMOUTH COLONY; STANDISH, MILES.

COUSIN is a person outside your immediate family related to you by blood and descended from the same ancestor. The chart shows how cousins are related.

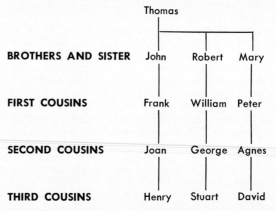

Thomas

BROTHERS AND SISTER	John	Robert	Mary
FIRST COUSINS	Frank	William	Peter
SECOND COUSINS	Joan	George	Agnes
THIRD COUSINS	Henry	Stuart	David

First cousins are children of brothers and sisters, so Frank, William, and Peter are first cousins to each other. *Second cousins* are children of first cousins, so Joan, George, and Agnes are second cousins, and so on. A *first cousin once removed* is the child of your first cousin, so George and Agnes are Frank's first cousins once removed. Henry and Stuart are Peter's first cousins twice removed, and so on. See also FAMILY (Family Relationships).

COUSTEAU, *koo STOH*, **JACQUES-YVES,** *zhahk ivez* (1910-   ), a French undersea explorer, helped invent the Aqua-Lung, which enables a person to breathe under water (see AQUA-LUNG). He explored the ocean depths, using Aqua-Lungs and watertight cameras. He described his experiences in *The Silent World* (1953) and *The Living Sea* (1963). He salvaged cargo from many sunken ships. While working on a Greek vessel that sank about 230 B.C., he used underwater television to maintain contact between divers in the water and scientists aboard ship. He was among the first to use the bathyscaph, which enabled him to make observations two miles below the surface (see BATHYSCAPH). He was born at St.-André-de-Cubzac, France.   Frank Goodwyn

COUSY, BOB (1928-   ), ranks among the outstanding all-around players in basketball history. A 6-foot, 2-inch guard, Cousy played for the Boston Celtics of the National Basketball Association (NBA) from the 1950-1951 season through the 1962-1963 season. He helped lead the Celtics to six NBA championships. Cousy won fame for his skillful dribbling and accurate passing. He led the league in *assists* (passes to teammates that result in scores) every season from the 1952-1953 season through the 1959-1960 season. Also a fine shooter, Cousy averaged $18\frac{1}{2}$ points per game during his career.

ROBERT JOSEPH COUSY was born in New York City. He won All-America honors at College of the Holy Cross in 1950. From 1963 to 1969, he was the basketball coach at Boston College. In 1969, Cousy became coach of the Cincinnati Royals in the NBA.   HERMAN WEISKOPF

COUVADE. See FAMILY (The Couvade).

COUZENS, JAMES JOSEPH (1872-1936), a Michigan Republican, served as mayor of Detroit from 1919 to 1922, and as a United States senator from 1922 to 1936. A philanthropist and public reformer, Couzens set up a fund of about $10 million to encourage better care of children in Michigan and elsewhere throughout the world. Couzens was born in Chatham, Ont. In 1903, he helped organize the Ford Motor Company. He became its business manager and vice-president.   SIDNEY GLAZER

COVARRUBIAS, *KOH vahr ROO vyahs,* **MIGUEL,** *mee GHEL* (1904-1957), a Mexican painter, became internationally known for his caricatures of famous persons. His paintings of Negro, Mexican, and Balinese types revealed a keen appreciation of the characteristics of peoples of various lands, and are documents in ethnology and anthropology, as well as in art. His map murals of Pacific regions also are famous.

Covarrubias' works include *The Prince of Wales and Other Famous Americans* (caricatures, 1925), *Negro Drawings* (1927), *The Island of Bali* (1937), *Mexico South* (1946), and *Indian Art of Mexico and Central America* (1957).

Covarrubias was born in Mexico City, and was largely self-taught as an artist.   NORMAN RICE

COVENANT. See JUDAISM (Service to God).

COVENANT, ARK OF THE. See ARK OF THE COVENANT.

COVENANTERS, *KUV uh nun turz,* was the name given to members of a religious group in Scotland. They bound themselves by a series of agreements, or covenants, to uphold the Presbyterian faith. The most important of the early covenants was drawn up in 1580. At this time, Roman Catholics were making a serious effort to regain Scotland for their church. The *National Covenant* of 1638 was a revival of this agreement. It was adopted and signed at Edinburgh as a result of the efforts of King Charles I and Archbishop Laud to force the Scots to accept English forms of worship.

The Solemn League and Covenant of 1643 was practically a treaty between England and Scotland. It was

From *The Island of Bali* by Miguel Covarrubias, © 1936, 1937 Alfred A. Knopf, Inc.
Miguel Covarrubias painted in flat, decorative, almost poster-like patterns in the illustrations for his book *The Island of Bali.*

signed by the General Assembly of the Church of Scotland and by the commissioners of the English Parliament. It established the Presbyterian Church in England, Scotland, and Ireland. Charles II later rejected both of these covenants.   W. M. SOUTHGATE

COVENTRY, *KAHV un tree* (pop. 333,830; alt. 270 ft.), is an automobile and industrial city in England. It lies in Warwickshire (see GREAT BRITAIN [political map]). The city appears often in old legends. Lady Godiva and her husband are supposed to have founded a Benedictine monastery there on the ruins of a convent built in the 800's and destroyed by the Danes in 1016. Coventry once had many buildings of historic interest, including three churches whose spires could be seen for miles around. During World War II, most of the center of the city was destroyed by a German air raid. Dedication of Coventry's new cathedral in 1962 climaxed the rebuilding of the city.   JOHN W. WEBB

COVERDALE, MILES (1488?-1568), a bishop of Exeter, England, became famous for his English translation of the Bible in 1535. He used Tyndale's English version of the New Testament and the Old Testament through

H. Zinram, London

Coventry Cathedral rises near the ruins of the old church, *left,* which is kept as a memorial. The modern cathedral was completed in 1962 at a cost of more than $4 million. The old church, built in the 1300's, was destroyed by a Nazi air raid in 1940.

Chronicles. He translated other portions from the Latin and from Martin Luther's German translation. Coverdale also helped produce the Bible of Cromwell, or *Great Bible*, and edited Cranmer's Bible. He was born in Yorkshire, and educated at Cambridge. GEORGE L. MOSSE

See also BIBLE (The Bible in Modern Tongues).

COVERED BRIDGE. See NEW BRUNSWICK (Places to Visit); OHIO (color picture).

COVERED WAGON. See CONESTOGA WAGON; PIONEER LIFE IN AMERICA (Crossing the Plains).

COVERT, *KUV ert*, is a cloth woven with raised lines that run diagonally across the surface of the fabric. The yarns of covert cloth are often woven in white and in color to give it a speckled appearance. Cotton covert, 35 inches wide, is used to make suits, trousers, and play clothes. Wool covert, 54 inches wide, is used in making such items of wearing apparel as coats, suits, riding habits, and raincoats.

COVINGTON, Ky. (pop. 60,376; alt. 515 ft.), an industrial center, is the third largest city in the state. It lies at the junction of the Ohio and Licking rivers, across the Ohio River from Cincinnati, Ohio. For location, see KENTUCKY (political map).

Covington's most important manufactures include iron and steel products, machine tools, packaging machines, electric equipment, time locks, parking meters, paper products, bags, asphalt, lithograph and art products, and lumber products. Other important industries include meat packing, brewing, distilling, and fruit packing. Covington has one of the world's largest X-ray equipment laboratories.

Greater Cincinnati Airport lies outside Covington. Three railroads, Ohio River barge lines, and highways also serve the city.

Covington was incorporated in 1815, and named after General Leonard Covington, a hero of the War of 1812. It has a council-manager government. THOMAS D. CLARK

COW is a female adult animal of the bovine group. The term *cow* is also used for the female of other mammals, including moose and seals. Cows, bulls, and steers are called *cattle* (see CATTLE).

COW PARSNIP is a large, coarse plant which belongs to the parsley family. It grows from 4 to 8 feet high. The cow parsnip has large, hairy leaves. Its small white flowers grow in huge clusters. The plant becomes a troublesome weed when it is allowed to grow in damp soil near water. The cow parsnip may be eaten in place of celery, but is usually used as fodder.

Scientific Classification. The cow parsnip belongs to the parsley family, *Umbelliferae*. It is classified as genus *Heracleum*, species *H. maximum*.

HAROLD NORMAN MOLDENKE

COWARD, NOEL (1899-), gained distinction as an actor, playwright, director, and composer for the stage and motion pictures. He became best known for his sparkling dialogue in such comedies

Noel Coward

Larry Fried, Pix

as *Hay Fever* (1925), *Private Lives* (1930), *Tonight at 8:30* (1935), and *Blithe Spirit* (1941). His songs include "Some Day I'll Find You" and "I'll See You Again." He has written two autobiographical books, *Present Indicative* (1937) and *Future Indefinite* (1954). His novel *Pomp and Circumstance* appeared in 1960.

Coward was born in Teddington, England. His first success as a writer came with *The Vortex* in 1924. His acting and singing were limited mainly to the leading roles in his own plays and revues. RICHARD MOODY

COWBIRD is a migratory North American bird. It is a kind of blackbird. It makes its home from Mexico as far north as southern Canada. Its full name is the *brown-headed cowbird.*

Cowbirds lay their eggs in the nests of other birds and leave the youngsters for the foster parents to raise. The female cowbird chooses a nest that belongs to some small bird, and usually lays only one egg in it while the other birds are away. Then she flies off and does not return. The young cowbird is much larger than the other young birds in the nest, and generally grabs most of the food. As a result, the other youngsters sometimes starve. The foster parents do not seem to realize that they are raising an outsider. But if the egg is discovered, especially when placed in the nest of a yellow warbler, the other bird covers it and builds another nest on top of the old one. Cowbird eggs are white with brownish specks.

The male cowbird is about 8 inches long, and is seen more often than the smaller female. It has shining black feathers and a brown head. The female has a dull, brownish-gray color. Cowbirds feed on insects, worms, seeds, and berries. The cowbird's call is a shrill, grating whistle, sometimes followed by a few sharp notes.

Scientific Classification. The brown-headed cowbird belongs to the icterid family, *Icteridae*. It is genus *Molothrus*, species *M. ater*. ALBERT WOLFSON

See also BIRD (Foster Parents in the Bird World; picture: Bird Nests).

The Cowbird lays its eggs in other birds' nests, then lets the foster parents hatch them and feed and care for the young.

Allan D. Cruickshank, N.A.S.

COWBOY

The American Cowboy has always been a symbol of the strength and vigor of the colorful "Wild West."

COWBOY. Men who take care of large herds of cattle are called *cowboys* or *cowhands*. American cowboys gained fame in the days of the western frontier. The dangerous lives they led, the sad songs they sang, and the colorful vocabulary they used have all become a part of American folklore.

Cowboys are known by various other names. Early cowboys were called *cowpokes* or *cowpunchers*, because they used sticks to poke cattle onto loading ramps. *Wranglers* are cowboys who look after the horses on a ranch. Mexicans call a cowboy a *vaquero*, and this name has become *buckaroo* in English. The South American name for cowboy is *gaucho*. Many cowboys today prefer to be called *cowhands*, because they are hired *hands*, or workers, who tend cows. Cowboys usually call all cattle *cows*, regardless of whether the animals are young or old, steers or cows.

Western cowboys became important in the late 1860's after the Civil War. They worked on ranches in Texas, Montana, and other Western States. They spent long, hard weeks driving cattle from the ranches to railroad towns where the cattle were shipped east. Many cowboy songs and tales originated on these "long drives" along western trails.

There have probably never been more than about 100,000 cowboys. But their lonely jobs, their difficult work, and their part in building the West have given cowboys an importance far beyond their numbers.

For a description of cowboy life today, see RANCHING.

A Cowboy's Equipment

His Horse was a cowboy's most precious possession in frontier days. It was his only means of transportation. On the trails, a sure-footed horse might mean the difference between life and death for a cowhand. If a herd stampeded, the cowboy depended on his horse to help *head* the cattle (get them under control). A horse was so valuable that a cowboy might give all the water in his canteen to his horse, even if it meant that he himself had to go thirsty.

All cowboys had to be good horsemen, because they actually "lived in the saddle." Cowhands must still be able to ride well. Almost every cowboy owned a horse of his own, and possibly a spare one. But, on the ranch, he might have about six horses for his own use. These horses belonged to the ranch owner, who assigned them to the cowboys. No cowboy was allowed to ride a horse assigned to another man. A day on the trail might involve so much work that a horse often needed several days to recover. Most cowboys saved their best horses for night work, because neither horse nor rider could afford to make mistakes in the darkness.

A horse wrangler kept ranch horses together. He made sure that the right horse was ready when a cowboy needed it. Cowboys on a ranch sometimes held *horse roundups* to count their horses. At one time or another, most cowboys took turns at *breaking* (taming) wild horses. But younger cowboys usually did most of the breaking. Montana cowboys were known as the best "bronc busters."

Cowhands still use heavier and larger equipment than horsemen in the East. A Western saddle is large and roomy. It has a sturdy *pommel* (horn) that the cowboy can lash his rope to or hold on to when necessary. The *cantle* (back of the saddle) curves up to give the rider better support. A cowhand can even take short naps in his saddle without fear of falling off. He can also use his saddle as a pillow when he stretches on the ground. See SADDLE.

The early Spanish explorers brought the horse to North America. Some of their horses broke loose and ran wild on the western plains. Gradually, the Indians captured horses and learned to use them for their fast hit-and-run attacks on each other and on white men. Mexican vaqueros began to tend cattle from horseback. When the American cowboy came along, he learned to use the horse as an aid both in fighting and in handling cattle. Wild horses usually ran in packs, like wolves, ready to be taken by anyone smart enough and fast enough to catch and tame them. The earliest horse used was the *mustang*, which originally came from Arabia. Mustangs were smaller than average horses, but had greater endurance. They also had what the cowboys called "cow sense" in directing and searching out the cattle. See HORSE (color pictures).

His Clothing evolved from practical needs, and has changed little since early days. The cowboy started

THE WORKING COWBOY

Union Pacific

Charles J. Belden

A Good Horse and a Strong Rope have long been regarded as the two things a cowboy must have for his work.

The Cowboy's Equipment, *below*, includes boots and chaps, to protect his legs and feet, and spurs and quirt, to control his horse.

Saddles represent a major investment, and each cowhand picks his with great care. The hands no longer "live in the saddle," but they still need strong, well-made saddles and harnesses.
F.S.A.

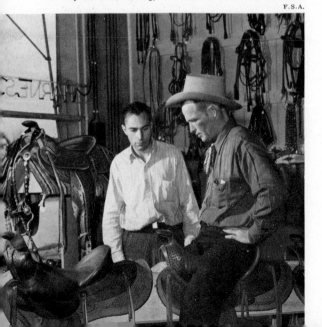

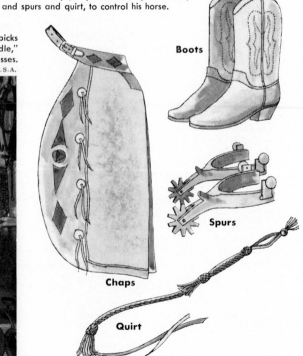

Boots

Chaps

Spurs

Quirt

Ross Santee
From *Arizona Highways*

A **Ranch Outfit** of the Old West, *left*, included horse-drawn wagons and strings of saddle horses for the cowboys on the range. The hands often "rode fence," repairing breaks in the barbed wire, *below*. Today's hands often ride herd on their cattle from a jeep, *bottom*.

Look Magazine

wearing his trousers tight because he did not want loose cloth flapping or catching brush as he chased cattle. His trousers are still called *Levi's*. He began wearing leather *chaps* to keep thorns and branches from tearing his trousers, and to protect his legs from rubbing during the long hours he spends in the saddle. His broad-brimmed *sombrero* (hat) was designed to keep the sun and wind out of his eyes, and to have enough brim to catch water in the rain. The hat's deep crown helped keep it on the cowboy's head when he rode madly after a stampeding herd. It could also be used as a bucket. A sombrero was made large enough and sturdy enough to serve as a sort of whip. The cowboy could wave it to direct a surging herd of cattle, to urge his horse on, or to

send signals to his companions a couple of hills away.

The cowboy's high-heeled boots also began for practical reasons. The heel gave him a hold in the stirrup. The length of the boot supported his ankles and provided warmth. A cowboy's neckerchief or bandana could be pulled over his face as a filter against dust.

An early cowboy's equipment always included a knife and a gun. The knife served a variety of purposes, from mending bridles to spearing a piece of hot *chuck* (food). The pistol was usually a Colt revolver with about a seven-inch barrel (see REVOLVER). The cowboy used it to frighten cattle and make them move, and to defend the herd from bandits. Some cowboys carried Winchester rifles. The rifles had better range and accuracy,

"Dick" Whittington

Bronco is a wild horse.
Chuck is food.
Cinch is a band that goes around a horse's body to hold a saddle or a pack.
Dogie is a calf whose mother has left it.
Hackamore is a halter.
Kidney Pad refers to a small saddle used by Easterners.
Maverick is an unbranded cow whose owner is unknown.
Muley is a hornless cow. Cowboys do not like to herd muleys.
Mustang means any wild horse.
Necktie Social was a hanging in early days.
Nester was a squatter who settled on government land, usually to farm.
On the Dodge means hiding from the police.
Outlaw is any animal that is particularly wild. The term may also be used for a criminal.
Paint is a horse with irregular patches of white.
Quirt is a cowboy's whip.
Remuda is a range outfit's collection of saddle horses. No mares are permitted in a remuda.
Road Agent is cowboy slang for a robber.
Rustler is a cattle thief.
Shindig is a cowboy dance.
Sold His Saddle. If a man has "sold his saddle," it means that he is disgraced.
Stetson is any cowboy hat, regardless of the manufacturer.
String is a cowboy's *mount*, or line, of horses.
Tenderfoot is a person who is new to a job.
Waddy is a temporary hand hired when a ranch is short of help.

Roping a Calf takes speed, strength, and skill. The cowhand must hold the frightened animal down until he can tie its legs. Roping is a favorite display at rodeos.

but were bulkier and less handy. The knife is still useful, and, in wilder areas, cowhands still carry guns.

His Rope was an early cowboy's most important tool. He used it to catch cattle, to hold his horse, to pull his wagons across muddy rivers and swamps, to tie his packs in place, and to kill snakes. As Ramon F. Adams said in his book *Western Words*, the cowboy "does everything with his rope except eat with it."

Early ropes were made of horsehair, grass, or henequen. Most ropes today are made of nylon. A rope may be from 30 to 70 feet long. It has a small *honda knot*, or fixed loop, at one end. The cowboy passes the other end of the rope through this knot to form a loop. Then he can pull the rope tight or slack it off after he has caught an animal. Cowboys in the Southwest use the word *lariat* (from the Spanish *la reata*, meaning *the rope*). Pacific Coast cowboys sometimes use the word *lasso* to mean *to rope*. See KNOTS, HITCHES, AND SPLICES.

The Life of a Cowboy

Cowboys often live lonely lives. Most ranches lie far from even the smallest towns. A cowhand may go for months without seeing anyone besides the dozen or so men with whom he works. Early cowhands labored long hours, especially on the trail. They always suffered from lack of sleep, and often from broken bones caused by spills from a horse.

On the Ranch, the cowboy of early days served as an odd-job man, doing whatever was necessary. He might pitch hay, hunt stray animals, clear brush, break horses,

or mend *gear*, or equipment. He lived in a bunkhouse with the other hands, apart from the main house, where the ranch owner lived. The cowboy's main job was to watch and protect the cattle as they grazed on the range. He often *rode fence*, or patrolled the range to see whether any fences needed repairing. Even today, when a cowhand works out on the range, he camps wherever night overtakes him. He spreads his bedroll on the ground to sleep in. A cowboy always sleeps with "one ear cocked," listening for any unusual activity or restlessness in the herd.

Cowboys ate a limited variety of food, including fresh beef, salted pork and bacon, beans, and sourdough biscuits. A ranch cook, or *cookie*, prepared the food and rode the range with a *chuck wagon* (see CHUCK WAGON). The men ate from tin plates while sitting on the ground, resting on rocks, or standing. They drank scalding hot coffee from tin cups or cans. They ate few fresh fruits, and drank little fresh milk. This still holds true in many areas.

Most cowboys spent their spare time talking, playing cards, reading, or just being bored. On the trail, they were usually too tired at night to do more than swap a few tall tales or play some practical joke. On the rare occasions when a cowboy did leave the ranch and go to town, he visited a barber, shopped, and talked with other cowboys. On the whole, in spite of motion-picture attitudes, most cowboys behaved as well as any other people who had been away from civilization for months.

The Roundup is a business period when a ranch owner

The Chuck Wagon carries much more than just food. When cowhands live on the range, they carry their bed rolls on the wagon. It also has room for other equipment.

gets an accurate idea of how many cattle he actually owns. In early days, cattle from various ranches in an area grazed together on the great open range. Twice a year, cowboys rounded up the cattle, and herded them to a central place. Men from each ranch sorted out their own cattle according to the animals' markings. Then they *branded*, or marked, new calves, selected older cattle to go to market, and separated diseased or undersized animals from the regular herd. Roundups occupied an important place in a cowboy's life. They required more skill than any other phase of his work. As a result, there was a certain rivalry about a roundup, somewhat like that of an athletic contest.

A roundup was also a social event. As many as 10 ranches might be represented at a single roundup. That would mean visiting with old friends as well as working. On northern ranges, as in Montana and Wyoming, roundups might attract as many as 300 cowboys. The cowboys often held a large celebration called a *rodeo* after they finished their work (see RODEO). They competed in bareback riding, steer wrestling, calf roping, and other tests of skill. Rodeos are popular today, but are more commercialized.

Branding Cattle was an early means of reducing the chance of their being lost or stolen. Each ranch still has its own *brand*, or scar design, placed in a certain position on all its cattle. Cattle owners register their brands with county or state authorities. For example, a brand may be described as a *clover leaf* placed *right side, flank;* or the letter *R* placed *left side, jaw.* Brands are respected throughout the West. In early days, a calf could wander off the range in Texas and travel all the way to Montana. Anyone who found the calf in Montana would check to see whose brand it bore. He would then arrange to return the calf to its owner. Sometimes a dishonest cowboy would try to change the brand on a stray cow to make it appear that the stray wore his brand. But if a thief were caught tampering with another man's brand, he usually met swift and stern justice.

Branding is an important feature of a roundup. After the cattle from each ranch have been herded into a *corral*, or enclosed yard, the cowboys ride among them to select new calves to be branded. This process is called *cutting out.* Both horse and rider need great skill to isolate a lone calf from a milling herd. Once a calf has been cut out, the men drive or drag it to a fire. A number of branding irons are kept red-hot in the flames. Some of the men drag the animal into position by the fire, and others apply one of the branding irons to its side. The resulting burn leaves a permanent scar in the animal's flesh. One man keeps *tally*, or scores the number of animals branded by each outfit.

Cowhands sometimes make other markings and clips on their cattle in order to recognize them easily. The most common markings are knife cuts on the animal's ears or on its *dewlap*, the skin under its neck. Each ranch has its own mark registered with the proper agency. Old-time ranch owners branded their horses, but most horses were not marked.

The Cattle Drive. Perhaps the most tiring work of an

early cowboy was trailing a herd from the range to market. This "long drive" might mean moving hundreds of cattle several hundred miles. The cattle plodded along with riders ahead, behind, and on both sides. The cowboys had to be able to get the herd across rivers, find watering places for it, guard it against Indian attack, protect it in bad weather, and head off stampedes that might scatter the cattle several miles. Cowboys often sang songs to pass away the hours. A man on night watch would enjoy crooning softly to the herd. No matter how poor his voice, it seemed to have a soothing effect on the cattle.

At the end of the trail lay the "cow town," where the cowboys delivered their herds. Most cow towns had a cemetery called *Boot Hill*. These Boot Hill cemeteries were filled with cowboys who had played a little too hard in the cow towns, and wound up getting shot.

History

The name *cowboy* goes back to the Revolutionary War in America, but it has little to do with the cowboys of today. The first "cowboys" were Tories, or Americans who were loyal to England. They were called cowboys because they often lured American patriots into traps in the brush by tinkling cowbells as if they were lost cattle. These men operated in Westchester County, near New York City. Later, the name cowboy came to be used only for cowhands who tended cattle in the West.

Beginnings. Cattle raising became an important industry in the United States in the late 1860's. Ranchers in Texas raised Longhorn steers that they sold in the East at a profit. Cowboys trailed herds to railroad towns where dealers shipped the cattle to Chicago and other meat-packing centers. Ranchers found that trailing the herds was a cheap way of transporting them to the railroads. In addition, the cattle usually fattened along the trails. Cowboys often used the Chisholm Trail, which ran from the Mexican border through Austin and Waco, Tex., to Abilene, Kans. Some favored the Western Trail, which led to Dodge City, Kans., still called "the cowboy capital of the world." The Shawnee Trail ran east to Kansas City and St. Louis, Mo. See ABILENE; DODGE CITY.

During the 1870's and 1880's, more and more cattlemen began driving herds north to be sold for beef. They also drove cattle into such northern areas as Montana, Wyoming, and the Dakotas, to stock the ranges there. These ranges had been left open to grazing when buffalo herds were destroyed and Indian tribes were placed on reservations. Some cattlemen bought cattle in Texas and drove them west to California and Arizona. But most California cattle came directly from Mexico.

Cattlemen could make large profits during the 30 years after the Civil War. A steer that cost $5 in Texas or Wyoming would be worth about $40 to $50 in Chicago. The cattle industry enjoyed a boom, and some cattlemen made huge fortunes (see WESTERN FRONTIER LIFE [The Cattle Boom]). The boom had for the most part ended by the middle of the 1880's. But while it lasted, it advertised the cattle industry and brought fame to the cowboy who tended the herds. Cattle raising became more of a regular business in the 1900's. With the growth of railroads and the closing of the trails, cow-

boy life lost much of its color, glamor, and adventure.

Cowhands Today differ in two ways from earlier cowboys. First, they have more specialized jobs. They can do some particular types of work better than cowboys of the 1880's. But most of them are not so experienced in all-round work. Second, today's cowboys on large ranches generally use machines for many jobs that earlier cowboys had to do themselves. A pick-up truck carries cowboys from ranch headquarters to the range. Trucks move the cattle from one range to the next. A special truck delivers food that is fresh and hot to cowboys working on the range. Helicopters search through the thick brush for stray cattle. Machines dig ditches or holes for fence posts. The use of machines has also given cowboys more leisure time than they ever had before.

But in many ways, the cowhand's work has not changed much since early days. Cowboys must still know how to ride. They must be able to work long hours, in all kinds of weather, and on little food. And they must know how to handle cattle.

The National Cowboy Hall of Fame was opened in Oklahoma City, Okla., in 1965. It honors outstanding Americans who had a part in developing the West. The hall is sponsored by the 17 Western States. It includes an art gallery for Western photographs and paintings, and a shrine. Each of the Western States has a section in the shrine to honor its heroes. A large research library of Western history is planned. About 140 persons have been elected to the Hall of Fame, including Will Rogers, the Oklahoma humorist; Theodore Roosevelt, President of the United States, who was a rancher in the Dakotas during his early life; Charles Russell, a Montana artist who painted many scenes from cowboy life; James McClure, a New Mexico rancher and rodeo official; and Charles Goodnight, a pioneer cattleman of Texas, who founded the old Goodnight Trail.   JOE B. FRANTZ

Related Articles in WORLD BOOK include:

Bronco	Oklahoma (picture,	Roosevelt,
Chuck Wagon	*The Cowboy*)	Theodore
Gaucho	Oregon (picture,	Saddle
Hawaii (picture,	Branding Cattle)	Texas (pictures)
Hawaiian	Ranching	Western Frontier
Cowboys)	Rodeo	Life
Horse	Rogers, Will	Westward
Indian Wars		Movement

Outline

I. A Cowboy's Equipment
   A. His Horse   B. His Clothing   C. His Rope

II. The Life of a Cowboy
   A. On the Ranch   C. Branding Cattle
   B. The Roundup   D. The Cattle Drive

III. History

Questions

What are some items of a cowboy's clothing? What purposes do they serve?

What is (1) a chuck wagon? (2) a cowpuncher? (3) a "cow town"?

What kind of work did early cowboys do on the ranch? On the range?

What was the "long drive"? Why was it important?

Why do ranchers hold roundups?

How do cowboys brand cattle?

What was the cattle boom? When did it occur?

How are cowboys of today like those of early days? How are they different?

Why were early cowboys called *cowpokes*?

What city is called "the cowboy capital of the world"?

COWELL, HENRY (1897-), an American composer, created a sensation in the 1920's by his unusual approach to piano playing. By striking large numbers of notes together, he produced dense and dissonant effects which he called *tone clusters.* Cowell explained his theories in his book *New Musical Resources* (1930). He founded the *New Musical Quarterly*, a journal that supported the cause of American composers. His compositions include hymns and many symphonies. Cowell was born in Menlo Park, Calif.   WILLIAM FLEMING

COWLES, *KOLZ*, is the name of an American family of newspaper editors and publishers.

Alfred Cowles (1832-1880) was one of five partners who, with Joseph Medill, bought the *Chicago Daily Tribune* in 1855. Cowles was born in Mantua, Ohio.

William Hutchinson Cowles, Sr. (1866-1946), a son of Alfred Cowles, bought the *Spokane* (Wash.) *Spokesman* in 1893 and combined it with the *Review*, a rival paper. Cowles was born in Evanston, Ill., and began his newspaper work in Chicago. He became a director of the Associated Press in 1912.

Cheney Cowles (1908-1943), a son of William Hutchinson Cowles, became executive editor of the *Spokesman-Review* in 1938 and managing editor of the *Spokane Daily Chronicle* in 1939. Cowles held various positions on these newspapers, including that of financial editor. He was born in Spokane, and was graduated from Yale University.

William Hutchinson Cowles, Jr. (1902-), brother of Cheney Cowles, became president of the Spokane Chronicle Company in 1936 and of the Cowles Publishing Company in 1946. The latter company publishes the *Spokesman-Review* and various farm journals. Cowles was born in Sands Point, N.Y., and was graduated from Yale University.   JOHN E. DREWRY

COWLEY, ABRAHAM (1618-1667), was an English poet and essayist whose first volume of verse was published when he was 15. His major publications include *Poetical Blossoms* (1633), *The Mistress* (1647), and his unfinished epic *Davideis* (1656). Cowley began as a love poet strongly influenced by John Donne and his followers. Many of Cowley's love poems lack a personal note, and some are marred by fantastic imagery. Later, however, he began imitating the *Odes* of the Greek poet Pindar. This new style produced his best poem, "Ode to the Royal Society."

Cowley was born in London. As a follower of Charles II, he lived in exile during the Puritan revolution but was in great favor after the Restoration in 1660. Cowley helped form the Royal Society in 1660 and was one of its first members.   RICHARD S. SYLVESTER

See also METAPHYSICAL POETS.

COWPEA, also called the BLACK-EYED PEA, is a member of the pea family. It grows wild in Asia, but is cultivated in the United States. It is a trailing or bushy vine, but does not climb. The flowers of the cowpea are yellowish-white to purple, and usually grow in pairs. In the South, the cowpea is usually grown for forage. Some kinds of cowpeas are a popular food, eaten in the pod or shelled. They also may be used in soups and stews. See also PLANT (picture: Vegetables Unknown to Our Forefathers).

Scientific Classification. The cowpea belongs to the pea family, *Leguminosae*. It is classified as genus *Vigna*, species *V. sinensis*.   WAYNE W. HUFFINE

COWPENS, BATTLE OF. See REVOLUTIONARY WAR IN AMERICA (The War in the South).

COWPER, *KOO per*, **WILLIAM** (1731-1800), was an English poet who wrote the familiar saying, "I am monarch of all I survey." Some of his poems, such as "There Is a Fountain Filled with Blood" and "God Moves in a Mysterious Way," have become well-known hymns. He interpreted the religious awakening of his day in England. His nature poetry foreshadowed the English romantic movement.

Brown Bros.

William Cowper

Cowper was born in Hertfordshire. After attending Westminster School, he studied law in London and was admitted to the bar in 1754. But he did not enjoy the practice of law. While preparing for a clerkship in the House of Lords, he fell into a fit of depression and developed a mental illness that recurred throughout his life. In 1765, he went to live with Morley Unwin, a clergyman, whose simple family life in Huntington suited Cowper's temperament. After Unwin's death, Cowper went with Mrs. Unwin and her children to Olney in 1767. There, he wrote his *Olney Hymns* (1779), which includes "Oh! For a Closer Walk with God."

Cowper became famous in 1785 when he published "The Task," a long poem in blank verse. Some of the descriptions of nature in this poem resemble what William Wordsworth wrote several years later. In the same volume with "The Task" was "The Diverting History of John Gilpin," a rollicking poem about a "linen-draper bold." Cowper wrote a variety of poems, including "Table Talk," "Truth," and "Alexander Selkirk."   GEORGE F. SENSABAUGH

See also ENGLISH LITERATURE (The Romantic Age).

COWPOX. See VACCINATION.

COWPUNCHER. See COWBOY.

COWRIE, *COW ree*, or COWRY, is a sea snail with a shiny, colorful shell. It lives in the shallow waters of warm seas. Cowries may be from a half-inch to 6 inches long. The top of the shell looks like a colorful egg, and the underside of the shell has a long, narrow opening bordered by many small teeth. There are more than 150 kinds of cowries. Some kinds are extremely rare and are worth hundreds of dollars to shell collectors. Cowries were once used as money in China, India, and Africa. One kind was worn as a badge of office by chieftains in the Fiji Islands. See SHELL (color pictures).

Scientific Classification. Cowries are members of the phylum *Mollusca*. They belong to the cowrie family, *Cypraeidae*.   R. TUCKER ABBOTT

COWSLIP is any one of four plants: the marsh marigold; the shooting star, or American cowslip; the Virginia cowslip; and the European cowslip.

Marsh marigold grows in swampy places. Its bright yellow flowers appear from April to June. People often eat the leaves and stems of these plants for greens. *Virginia cowslip* is also called *Virginia bluebell*. Its bell-shaped flowers grow in clusters and always seem to be nodding.

Shooting star is the common name for a group of plants known as American cowslips. The flowers of these plants have an interesting shape. The petals bend backward, and the pistil and yellow stamens form a pointed tip that seems to shoot out of the flower. *European cowslip* grows in meadows throughout Europe. It has beautiful, fragrant clusters of large yellow or purple flowers.

Scientific Classification. Marsh marigold belongs to the crowfoot family, *Ranunculaceae*. It is classified as genus *Caltha*, species *C. palustris*. Virginia cowslip belongs to the borage family, *Boraginaceae*. It is classified as *Mertensia virginica*. Shooting star and European cowslip belong to the primrose family, *Primulaceae*. Shooting stars make up the genus *Dodecatheon*. The European cowslip is classified as genus *Primula*, species *P. veris*.   ROBERT W. HOSHAW

See also FLOWER (color picture: Flowers That Grow in Wet Places [Marsh Marigold]); PRIMROSE.

COX, JAMES MIDDLETON (1870-1957), an American politician and newspaper publisher, was the Democratic candidate for President in 1920. He and his running mate, Franklin D. Roosevelt, were defeated by a Republican landslide that elected Warren G. Harding as President and Calvin Coolidge as Vice-President.

Cox began his political career by serving in the U.S. House of Representatives from 1909 to 1913.

Wide World
James M. Cox

He was elected governor of Ohio in 1912, 1916, and 1918. Cox owned newspapers and radio and television stations in Ohio, Georgia, and Florida. In 1933 he served as a delegate to the World Monetary and Economic Conference in London. He wrote an autobiography, *Journey Through My Years* (1946).

Cox was born in a log-cabin farmhouse near Jacksonburg, Ohio. He left school at the age of 16, but through wide reading earned a license to teach. He bought his first newspaper at the age of 28.   GEORGE M. WALLER

COXEY, JACOB SECHLER (1854-1951), gained fame as the leader of *Coxey's Army*, a group of unemployed men. During the depression of the 1890's, Coxey urged a huge road-improvement program to create employment. He organized an "army" to attract national attention, and marched out of Massillon, Ohio, with 100 men.

Coxey expected 100,000 more to join the ranks by the time he marched into Washington, D.C. But, when the group paraded in Washington on May 1, 1894, less than 500 men were in line. The "army" collapsed after Coxey was arrested by the police for walking on the Capitol lawn. Coxey was born in Selinsgrove, Pa.   J. R. CRAF

COYOTE, *KY oat* or *ky OH tee*, is a wild animal of the dog family. It is noted for its eerie howl, usually heard in the early evening. The coyote lives in regions of

E. R. Kalmbach, U.S. Fish & Wildlife Service
The Coyote's Howl can be heard far away on quiet nights. The animal varies the long, sad howl with short barks and whines.

western North America from Panama to Alaska. Ranging from 16 to 21 inches high at the shoulder, it has a bushy tail and erect ears. Its soft fur is light yellow or yellowish-gray, and may be tipped with black. The coyote is sometimes called the *prairie wolf*.

The coyote eats gophers, rats, rabbits, and animals it finds dead. Because it also kills and eats stray sheep or calves, it is often hunted by farmers and ranchers. However, many wildlife experts believe that coyotes do more good by destroying rodents than they do harm as killers of livestock. They are fast enough to catch jack rabbits, which eat the grass that is needed for food by sheep.

Scientific Classification. The coyote is a member of the dog and wolf family, *Canidae*. It is classified as genus *Canis*, species *C. latrans*.   WILLIAM O. PRUITT, JR.

See also ANIMAL (color picture: Animals of the Deserts).

COYPU, *COY poo*, is a large rodent that lives near water. Its soft undercoat, called *nutria*, is a valuable fur. Coypus look and act like beavers. They are about 3 feet long, including the tail, and weigh about 20 pounds. Their hind feet are webbed. They have strong cheek muscles and sharp teeth, which they use to cut down plants. Coypus use plants for food and to build nests. Coypus live in lakes and ponds, and usually burrow into the banks to make their homes. Coypus originally lived in South America and are still common

The Coypu's Valuable Fur Is Covered with Coarse Hair.
N.Y. Zoological Society

there. They have been introduced into Europe and North America, where they are raised for their fur. There are coypu (or nutria) farms in many parts of the United States and Canada. See also FUR (Nutria).

Scientific Classification. Coypus belong to the hutia and coypu family, *Capromyidae*. They are genus *Myocastor*, species *M. coypus*.   DANIEL H. BRANT

COYSEVOX, *kwahz VOH,* **ANTOINE** (1640-1720), was the leading French sculptor during the latter part of the reign of Louis XIV. Coysevox produced much of the sculpture that decorated the gardens and state apartments of the palace of Versailles. Much of his work reflected the tastes of Louis XIV. It is in a rich, ornamental style, reflecting a desire for dignity and grandeur.

Coysevox also made many portrait busts. Several of those he did later in his career are more informal and lively than his earlier decorative sculpture. This informality in his work reflected the developing taste of the 1700's.

Coysevox was born in Lyon, the son of a master woodworker. A picture of his statue *Mercury* appears in color in the SCULPTURE article.   ROBERT R. WARK

COZZENS, JAMES GOULD (1903-   ), an American novelist, won a Pulitzer prize for *Guard of Honor* (1948). His novels *S.S. San Pedro* (1931) and *The Last Adam* (1933) became book-club selections. In 1957, he published *By Love Possessed*, perhaps his most popular work. In 1960, this novel received the Howells medal from the American Academy of Arts and Letters as the most distinguished work of American fiction published during the previous five years. Cozzens was born in Chicago and attended Harvard University. In his sophomore year, he published his first novel, *Confusion* (1924). Surprised by its success, he left Harvard to devote all his time to writing novels.   JOHN O. EIDSON

CPA. See CERTIFIED PUBLIC ACCOUNTANT.

CRAB is an animal that is covered by a hard shell, and that has jointed legs. It lives in shallow waters along the shore, and also in deep waters. Many kinds of crabs are valued by man as food. There are about 4,500 different kinds. Some kinds, such as fiddler crabs, live in burrows in the banks of salty tidal streams. Some other kinds of crabs live in fresh water or in burrows up to several miles ashore.

The smallest crabs are the tiny pea crabs. The female pea crabs live in the sheltering shells of live oysters. The shape and relative size of the big claws of crabs differ greatly among the species, according to their habits. Male pincer crabs have one pincer much larger than the other. Hermit crabs live in empty sea shells and close them tightly, using one claw as a door. The color, form, and texture of claws, legs, and bodies run through many shades and shapes, and from smooth to rough and spiny. Some crabs are swimmers, and have paddles on the last pair of legs. Many crabs run sideways on the sand or rocks of the seashore. Crabs eat other small crustaceans and arthropods, and organic matter.

The *blue crab* is the most common crab sold as food in eastern American markets. When these crabs have shed their shells, and the new ones have not yet hardened, they are sold as the extra-choice *soft-shelled crabs.* Two types of edible crabs live on the Pacific Coast. The *Alaska king crab*, also called *Japanese crab*, is a good tasting crab that is caught by both American and

U.S. Fish and Wildlife Service
The Ghost Crab lives in burrows high up on sandy ocean beaches. This amusing creature runs sideways on the tips of its claws.

The Lyre Crab, *right,* takes its name from the lyrelike shape of its shell. Lyre crabs have thick, round bodies.

The Edible Crab, *left,* lives on the sandy bottom in shallow water. It is often seen around wharves and piers.

The Stone Crab, *right,* is one of the best-tasting food crabs. It has a hard shell.

The Bristly, or Horse, Crab, *left,* comes from the northwest waters of North America. It has a rough surface.

Japanese fishermen. One of the largest crabs, its 12-pound body supplies much meat. The *dungeness crab* is caught in shallow water from California to Alaska, and canned in Oregon, Washington, and Alaska. Crabs are taken in nets and wicker traps.

Scientific Classification. Crabs are in the phylum *Arthropoda.* They belong in the class *Crustacea* and the order *Decapoda.*   J. LAURENS BARNARD

Related Articles in WORLD BOOK include:

Animal (color picture: Coconut Crab)	Blue Crab Chile (picture: Crab Fishermen)	Fiddler Crab Hermit Crab Washington
Arthropod	Crustacean	(color picture)

CRAB APPLE

CRAB APPLE is a tree that bears apples two inches or less in diameter. These trees grow wild from Siberia to northern China, and in North America. They are grown in North America and other regions for their edible, round fruit. Crab apple trees are also popular as ornamentals. The trees usually are up to 20 feet

Crab Apple Trees Blossom from March Through June, depending on the region in which they live. The fragrant flowers are white, pink, or deep rose, *above*. The tart apples may be eaten fresh or made into delicious jellies, *below*.

tall, but some may grow 40 feet tall. They have large white to deep pink flowers that have a spicy fragrance.

The fruits vary from pure yellow through shades of yellow-red to pure red. Some crab apples taste bitter, but many are pleasantly tart and are eaten fresh. They are good for making jellies, butter, and pickles. Crab apples are very adaptable. They often crossbreed with other crab apples and with the common apple. Some crab apples and crab apple hybrids are so winter-

hardy they are used as rootstocks for common apples in cold climates.

Scientific Classification. Crab apples belong to the rose family, *Rosaceae*. The prairie crab apple is classified as genus *Malus*, species *M. ioensis*. The showy crab apple is *M. floribunda.*   REID M. BROOKS

CRAB NEBULA. See ASTRONOMY (color picture: Wonders of the Milky Way).

CRABBE, BUSTER. See SWIMMING (Famous Swimmers).

CRACKING. See PETROLEUM (Conversion).

CRACÓW. See KRAKÓW.

CRADLE OF LIBERTY. See BOSTON (introduction; The Freedom Trail).

CRADLES OF CIVILIZATION. See CIVILIZATION (Cradlelands); ASIA (History).

CRAFT. See HANDICRAFT.

CRAFT GUILD. See GUILD.

CRAIG, EDWARD GORDON (1872-   ), an English stage designer, producer, and author, strongly influenced theater production and the art of stage settings after 1910. He founded a theater arts journal, *The Mask* (1908), and the School for the Art of the Theatre (1913) at the Arena Goldoni in Florence, Italy. His best-known book is *On the Art of the Theatre* (1911). Craig also wrote *The Art of the Theatre* (1905), *Toward a New Theatre* (1913), *Scene* (1923), and *Ellen Terry and Her Secret Self* (1931).

Craig was the son of the famed actress Ellen Terry (see TERRY, ELLEN ALICIA). He was born in Stevenage, England, on Jan. 16, 1872. He was graduated from Bradfield College, in England.   BARNARD HEWITT

CRAIK, DINAH MARIA MULOCK (1826-1887), an English novelist and poet, became popular with young people as well as adults. Her chief work, *John Halifax, Gentleman* (1857), expresses noble religious ideals. Perhaps her best-known children's book is *The Little Lame Prince* (1874). In 1881, she published *Thirty Years' Poems*.

Dinah Craik was born in Stoke-on-Trent, England. Her father was a minister of a small congregation. She started writing to support a brother. LIONEL STEVENSON

CRAMP is a condition in which either a single muscle or a group of muscles contracts, causing discomfort or pain. There may be only a single *spasm* (contraction of the muscle). Then the cramp begins and ends quickly and abruptly. The muscle spasms may continue over a long period. Cramps may involve any area of the body. Perhaps the best-known cramps are those of the stomach and intestines. These cramps may result from poor eating habits, or from chilling the stomach. They often cause common stomach-aches. Cramps are also characteristic of many diseases.

Cramps often result when certain muscles are used too much. For example, a person who writes for a long time may develop writer's cramp. Cramps sometimes result from hard, muscular work in a hot place. Foundrymen and firemen may develop cramps in their arms and legs. Athletes often develop cramps in the muscles they use most strenuously. For example, a runner may develop cramps in his legs, or a baseball pitcher may have cramps in his pitching arm. Doctors treat cramps with heat and massage, and give medicines to relieve pain. They may also administer drugs that relax the muscles.   LOUIS D. BOSHES

CRANACH, *KRAH nahk*, **LUCAS, THE ELDER** (1472-1553), one of the leading German painters of the Renaissance, painted many portraits of the great men of his time. His portraits include those of King Christian II of Denmark, the Holy Roman Emperor Charles V, and such Protestant reformers as Martin Luther and Philipp Melanchthon. Cranach also painted many religious and mythological subjects, and became well known for his humorous versions of Greek mythology.

Cranach was born in the Franconian town of Cranach (now Kronach, Bavaria). He took his name from the town, and his real name is not known. Cranach lived most of his life in Wittenberg, where he was court painter. Cranach's three sons were minor artists. One of his sons was called Lucas Cranach the Younger (1515-1586). LESTER D. LONGMAN

CRANBERRY is an edible red berry that grows on a trailing vine. The cranberry vine grows in marshy or swampy land in the cool regions of the United States and Canada. It has small, oval, evergreen leaves and tiny pink flowers. Its fruits, the cranberries, may be round or oblong, depending on the variety. They grow on small, slender stems. The plant is called *cranberry*, or *craneberry*, because the slender stems of the fruit curve like the neck of a crane.

People use cranberries for sauces, jellies, and juice. They often grind the raw berries with other fruits to make relishes. Many families enjoy stringing the colorful raw berries and decorating their Christmas trees with them.

Cranberry vines grow best in low-lying bog lands with acid soil. Growers remove wild growth from the bog, spread sand several inches deep over the area, then plant the vines. The plants grow from cuttings about 5 to 10 inches long. Workers push these cuttings through the sand layer so that the new roots will form in the soil beneath. They leave about 18 inches between the plants. After the plants begin to grow, they cover the area like a mat. Growers often flood their bogs early in winter to protect the plants from damage that might be caused by heating and thawing. Flooding at other times of the year prevents damage from insects and dry weather. Pesticides are also used to control insects. Leaf-eating insects damage cranberry plants.

Cranberry harvesting begins late in September. Pickers use special scooplike rakes to gather the berries. They place the berries in boxes, which are taken to packing houses. Machines separate the sound berries, blow out the chaff, and grade them. Packers put the berries in boxes or plastic bags for shipment to the market. Massachusetts and Wisconsin produce great quantities of cranberries. New Jersey and Washington are also important cranberry-growing states.

Scientific Classification. Cranberries belong to the heath family, *Ericaceae*. The large, or American, cranberry is genus *Vaccinium*, species *V. macrocarpon*. The small, or European, cranberry is *V. oxycoccus*. C. M. CHANEY

CRANBROOK ACADEMY OF ART. See UNIVERSITIES AND COLLEGES (table).

CRANE is a large bird, with a long neck and long legs. Cranes in flight can be distinguished from herons. Cranes fly with necks stuck out straight, and herons fly with necks curved. The largest crane in North America is called the *whooping crane* because its loud, deep call can be heard a mile or more away. The loud

call is aided by the whooping crane's large windpipe, which is nearly 5 feet long. The whooping crane is about 4 or 5 feet high. It has a wingspread of 6 or 8 feet. Its feathers are white and the wings are tipped with black. Whooping cranes once ranged widely in the United States, but now there are less than 50 alive. They nest in northern Canada, and spend the winter in Texas.

There are three other kinds of cranes in North America. They are all brown or gray, and are about 3 feet high. Their wingspread is about 6 feet. They have a small patch of bare red skin on their foreheads. One of them is the *little brown crane*, which breeds in the icy region of the Arctic Circle and spends the winter in the southwestern United States and Mexico. The *sandhill crane* is slightly larger. It breeds in Canada and in the Northern States west of the Great Lakes, and

Gathering Cranberries, workers use a special wooden scoop, *top*. Experienced pickers can rake the cranberries from the vines quickly. Some large cranberry growers use motor-driven picking machines. The fruit grows on small, slender stems, *below*. It is used to make sauces, jellies, puddings, and pies.

Allan Grant, Graphic House; L. W. Brownell

The Crowned Crane has a spreading tuft of black-tipped white and yellow bristles. A wounded crane is very dangerous and will attack anyone who comes near with his sharp bill.

The Demoiselle Crane lives in South Europe and in Asia. When the crane sits on its nest, the lower part of its leg extends forward rather than backward, as a man's leg bends.

flies south as far as Mexico in the winter. The *Florida crane* is found in southern Georgia and in Florida.

Cranes eat small plants, insects, frogs, worms, reptiles, small fish, and the eggs of water animals. Groups of cranes gather during the mating season to dance. The birds dance crazily and hop into the air with great excitement. At other times, the cranes stand on one leg and doze lazily, with their heads drawn back on their shoulders. They build nests in bushes or in marshes. The female lays only two eggs in a season.

Scientific Classification. Cranes are in the crane family, *Gruidae*. The whooping crane is genus *Grus*, species *G.*

americana. The little brown crane is *G. canadensis*, variety *canadensis*. The sandhill crane is *G. canadensis tabida*. The Florida crane is *G. canadensis pratensis.*   JOSEPH J. HICKEY

See also BIRD (Refuges and Sanctuaries; color picture: Birds of Other Lands); ANIMAL (color picture: Animals of the Polar Regions); HERON.

CRANE. See DERRICKS AND CRANES.

CRANE, HART (1899-1932), an American poet, is best known for his complex work *The Bridge* (1930), a major poem in modern American literature. Its subject is the Brooklyn Bridge in New York City, but its aim is to portray the history of the United States. The bridge becomes a symbol which spans the American migration from the Atlantic to the Pacific.

In *The Bridge*, Crane interweaves legendary figures from American history with modern American inventions. Rip Van Winkle is portrayed as a passenger on a New York City subway. The subway itself is a vehicle that carries the reader backward into the American past and forward to a vision of America's future. Although Crane was optimistic about life in America, his poem shows his awareness of the problems created by an industrial society.

HAROLD HART CRANE was born in Garrettsville, Ohio. He published only one other book of poetry during his lifetime, *White Buildings* (1926).   CLARK GRIFFITH

CRANE, STEPHEN (1871-1900), an American author, pioneered in writing naturalistic fiction and poetry. His first novel, *Maggie: A Girl of the Streets* (1892), deals with a girl driven to suicide by poverty and sweatshop labor. In *The Red Badge of Courage* (1895), Crane stressed the irony of chance making a man weak in the midst of impersonal forces. In this novel, which brought Crane fame, he limited his point of view to a common soldier in the Civil War. He dramatized the soldier's bewilderment and fear as he eventually overcomes his initial cowardice. Crane wrote four volumes of short stories. They include such notable works as "The Open Boat" and "The Monster." His free-verse poems, collected in *The Black Riders* (1895) and *War Is Kind* (1899), show Crane as a pathfinder for present-day poets who are devoted to experimental reform and revolt from sentimentality. Crane's *Collected Works* were published in 1925-1926.

Crane was born in Newark, N.J., the son of a Methodist minister. He studied briefly at Lafayette and Syracuse universities in New York. He then turned to newspaper writing in New York City. He served as a reporter during the Spanish-American and Turkish wars. The last two years of Stephen Crane's life were spent in England. He died of tuberculosis at 28.   HARRY H. CLARK

Stephen Crane

CRANE FLY. See DADDY LONGLEGS.

CRANE'S-BILL. See GERANIUM.

CRANIAL NERVE. See NERVOUS SYSTEM (The Peripheral Nervous System).

CRANIUM. See HEAD.

CRANK. See GASOLINE ENGINE (Crankshaft); STARTER; WHEEL AND AXLE.

CRANKCASE. See GASOLINE ENGINE (Parts).

CRANKSHAFT. See AUTOMOBILE (diagram: How an Automobile Runs); GASOLINE ENGINE (Parts).

CRANMER, THOMAS (1489-1556), was the first Protestant archbishop of Canterbury. He became famous for promoting the English Reformation during the reigns of Henry VIII and Edward VI.

Cranmer was born at Aslacton in Nottinghamshire. He attended Cambridge University, and later was appointed one of the university's public examiners of theology. In 1529, Cranmer came to the attention of Henry VIII, when he met with the king's advisers concerning Henry's divorce proceedings against Catherine of Aragon. Cranmer suggested that the divorce question be submitted to a debate by the English universities, which gave Henry a favorable verdict.

Culver

Thomas Cranmer

In 1533, Cranmer was appointed archbishop of Canterbury. As archbishop, he supported Henry's efforts to check the power of the pope and to become "justly and rightly . . . the Supreme Head of the Church of England." By the will of Henry VIII, Cranmer became one of the regents for young Edward VI. During Edward's reign, Cranmer supported many measures reforming the church and its doctrine.

When the Roman Catholic Queen Mary took the throne in 1553, Cranmer and his Protestant workers were imprisoned in the Tower of London. In 1554, they were moved to a prison at Oxford, on the charge of heresy. Cranmer became so weak that he signed statements repudiating his former acts as archbishop. In one of his recantations, he acknowledged his submission to the pope. Two days before his execution, it was arranged that Cranmer should make a final recantation, declaring his belief in every article of the Roman Catholic faith and repudiating his former writings. But, on the day he was to be burned at the stake, Cranmer declared that his only sins were his previous recantations. He thrust the hand that had signed the recantations into the fire and exclaimed, "This hath offended; oh, this unworthy hand!"   GEORGE L. MOSSE

See also BOLEYN, ANNE; CATHERINE OF ARAGON; HENRY (VIII) of England; MARY (I); REFORMATION (In England); RIDLEY, NICHOLAS.

CRANNOG. See LAKE DWELLING.

CRANSTON, R.I. (pop. 71,913; alt. 85 ft.), is an industrial city on the west side of upper Narragansett Bay, just southwest of Providence, R.I. (see RHODE ISLAND [political map]). It has been an important textile center since 1824, when William Sprague set up a shop for printing patterns with indigo dye. Other Cranston manufactures include textile machinery, brass and copper tubing, fire extinguishers, and plastic products. Cranston was first settled about 1638 by friends of Roger Williams, the founder of Rhode Island. It was incorporated as a town in 1754, and received its city charter in 1910. It has the mayor-council form of government.   CLARKSON A. COLLINS III

CRAPE, a variant of crepe. See CREPE.

Gottscho-Schleisner

Crape Myrtle blooms in early autumn. These flowers have delicate, fringed petals that may be pink, purple, or white.

CRAPE MYRTLE is a handsome shrub or small tree about 10 to 20 feet tall. It is native to southern Asia, but is often planted along streets in the southern United States. It blooms from July to September. The flowers are about an inch wide and grow in clusters. The petals are usually bright pink to red-purple, or sometimes white. The leaves grow from 1 to 3 inches long.

Scientific Classification. The crape myrtle belongs to the loosestrife family, *Lythraceae*. It is genus *Lagerstroemia*, species *L. indica*.   ARTHUR CRONQUIST

CRAPPIE, *KRAP ih*, is a fresh-water fish which is closely related to sunfish and black bass. It is found in sluggish, shallow waters of middle western and southern United States. The crappie is silvery olive with dark-green spots. It is about a foot long when full grown. It has a high fin on its back and a similar one on its belly. Each of these high fins contains five to eight spines, and about 18 soft rays. The tail fin is shaped like the letter *V*.

The Crappie, found in the waters of the midwestern and southern states, is silvery olive in color, with dark-green spots.

Hugh Davis

The crappie has a large mouth. It feeds on insects, small fishes, and other animals. Crappies are good to eat, and they are good game fish. Spinners may be used in trolling or casting for crappies. Crappies are called by many other names, including bridge perch, bachelor perch, chinquapin perch, strawberry bass, calico bass, and sacalait.

Scientific Classification. The crappie belongs to the sunfish family, *Centrarchidae*. The white crappie is classified as genus *Pomoxis*, species *P. annularis*. The black crappie is *P. nigro-maculatus*. CARL L. HUBBS

See also BASS.

CRASSUS, MARCUS LICINIUS (112?-53 B.C.), was a Roman statesman, financier, and military leader. Crassus, Caesar, and Pompey formed the *First Triumvirate* (a three-man ruling body) in 60 B.C. Crassus had previously held the high government posts of praetor, consul, and censor. He was a good businessman, and was called *the Rich* because he made much money through real estate investments. He used his triumvirate position to gain favors for his friends in business.

In 71 B.C., Crassus crushed the revolt of the gladiator Spartacus (see SPARTACUS). Seeking military glory, Crassus launched a war against Parthia, an area in central Asia. In 53 B.C., Parthian archers trapped Crassus' army, and killed Crassus and most of his troops. CHESTER G. STARR

See also CAESAR, GAIUS JULIUS; TRIUMVIRATE.

CRATER is a funnel- or bowl-shaped depression in the earth. It may be formed on plains, or on the sides of mountains, but most craters lie at the tops of volcanic cones. A few are blasted out by explosions. But the majority are formed simply by the volcanic cone building up around them as showers of rock fragments, thrown into the air by explosions, fall back around the vent. Ordinary craters range from a few feet to a mile across, and may be as much as 2,000 feet deep. Other craters are formed by the sinking of the ground surface as supporting liquid lava is withdrawn from beneath. The great depression occupied by Crater Lake in Oregon and the crater of Kilauea in Hawaii were formed in this way. Geologists call small sunken craters *pit craters*. The larger ones, called *calderas*, may be as much as 20 miles across. GORDON A. MACDONALD

See also METEOR (Meteorites; picture).

CRATER LAKE is the deepest lake in the United States and one of the scenic wonders of the world. It is located in the crater of Mount Mazama, an inactive volcano in the Cascade Mountains of southwestern Oregon. The lake is round and 6 miles across at its widest point. It covers a 20-square-mile area. Its surface is a little over 6,000 feet above sea level and its dark blue water is about 2,000 feet deep. There are no known outlets and no streams flowing into this lake.

Geologists believe the lake was formed thousands of years ago, after the last glacial period, when the top of Mount Mazama, then about 14,000 feet high, collapsed and was swallowed up inside the mountain. This left a huge "bowl" which gradually filled with water. A small volcano called Wizard Island formed in the lake when lava erupted later from the interior of Mount Mazama.

At first there were no fish in Crater Lake but trout were placed there in 1888 and fish have been added

each year. The Klamath Indians had legends about this mysterious lake. They believed its waters had healing qualities. John Hillman, a mining prospector, discovered Crater Lake in June, 1853. He named it Deep Blue Lake. The lake area was made a national park in 1902. RICHARD M. HIGHSMITH, JR.

See also OREGON (color picture).

CRATER LAKE NATIONAL PARK was created in southwestern Oregon to preserve Crater Lake and the forests around it. The walls of an ancient volcano, Mount Mazama, rise from several hundred to 2,000 feet above the surface of the lake. They have been changed by the weather into fantastic forms and to various shades of brown and bright yellow. Several peaks of the Cascade Mountains, including Mount Scott, Cloud Cap, and Llao Rock, rise near Crater Lake. Coniferous trees cling to broken rocks around the lake and are reflected by the waters. There are more than 500 kinds of flowering plants, ferns, and flowers in the meadows and on the slope of the volcano. Wild animals and birds are also plentiful. Each year more than 300,000 tourists visit the park. President Theodore Roosevelt set 10 Oregon townships aside in 1902 to create the park. William Gladstone Steel of Oregon was partly responsible for the creation of the park, and was appointed second superintendent. The park covers an area of 160,290.33 acres. RICHARD M. HIGHSMITH, JR.

CRATERS OF THE MOON NATIONAL MONUMENT is in south-central Idaho. For location, see IDAHO (physical map). This weird region has a number of volcanic cones, craters, lava flows, caves, natural bridges, and other unusual sights. Each year many tourists visit the 53,545.05-acre monument. It was established as a national monument in 1924.

CRAVAT. See NECKTIE.

CRAWFISH. See CRAYFISH.

CRAWFORD, FRANCIS MARION (1854-1909), became the most productive and versatile American novelist of his time. His most ambitious novels are *Saracinesca* (1887) and its three successors, about an Italian family. But *Marzio's Crucifix* (1887) and *A Cigarette-Maker's Romance* (1890) have also won praise.

Crawford was born in Lucca, Italy, the son of the sculptor Thomas Crawford (see CRAWFORD, THOMAS). He received his education in England, Germany, and Italy, and became the master of nearly twenty languages. In his youth, he edited a newspaper in India, but he lived most of his life in Italy. EDWARD WAGENKNECHT

CRAWFORD, ISABELLA VALANCY. See CANADIAN LITERATURE (After Confederation).

CRAWFORD, THOMAS (1813?-1857), an American sculptor, designed the *Statue of Freedom* on the dome of the Capitol in Washington, D.C. He also designed the bronze doors for the main eastern entrances of the Senate and House wings. Crawford created a monument to George Washington in Richmond, Va. His other works include statues of the composer Ludwig van Beethoven and the statesman Henry Clay, *Mercury and Psyche*, and *The Indian*. He also sculptured several biblical subjects.

Crawford was born in New York City. He went to Rome at the age of 20 to study under the Danish sculptor Bertel Thorvaldsen. His statue *Orpheus Entering Hades* brought him his first fame. He became blind the year before he died. JEAN LIPMAN

CRAWFORD, WILLIAM HARRIS (1772-1834), an American politician and statesman, became a Southern leader in national politics. His Democratic-Republican party followers believed in an extreme form of states' rights. Crawford served as a United States senator from Georgia from 1807 to 1813 and as secretary of the treasury under Presidents Madison and Monroe from 1816 to 1825. He had a chance to be elected President of the United States in 1824 (see ADAMS, JOHN QUINCY [Election of 1824]). He was born in Amherst County, Virginia.   RICHARD N. CURRENT

CRAYFISH, or CRAWFISH, is a fresh-water crustacean that is closely related to the lobster. It lives in and along lakes and rivers of every continent except Africa. The crayfish seldom grows over six inches long. It varies in color from white through pink, orange, and brown, to

Hugh Spencer   Cornelia Clarke

The Crayfish escapes from danger by using snapping motions of its abdomen to swim backward rapidly. It paddles with the leaf-like growths on the end of its tail. The female crayfish, *right*, carries its eggs on the underside of its abdomen until they hatch.

greenish black and dark blue. The clear white crayfish is a blind animal that lives in underground rivers.

A hard structure called the *exoskeleton* covers the body of the crayfish. This serves as a suit of armor to protect

The Fresh-Water Crayfish sheds its protective outer skin, or *exoskeleton*, when its body has outgrown the hard shell.

John H. Gerard, NAS

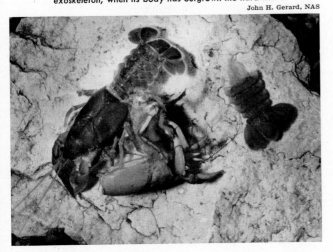

the soft tissues of the body from injury. The body is divided into sections, or segments. The front part of the body is rigid, but the back part, or abdomen, has movable segments. The crayfish has five legs on each side of the body. The two front legs are shaped into large, sharp claws, or pincers. They are similar to those of the lobster, and are used to capture and hold the prey. The four other pairs of legs are used for walking. There are also structures used in swimming, called *swimmerets*, under the abdomen of the crayfish. The crayfish also has two long feelers, or antennae, and two shorter ones.

The crayfish feeds on snails, small fish, tadpoles, or the young of insects. It is more active at nightfall and at daybreak, when it comes out of its burrow or from under a stone. It has burrowing habits which may destroy cropland or weaken levees and mill dams. One kind digs down to water in damp meadows and throws up clay "chimneys" in the process. The crayfish is a fighter. If it loses an eye, or one of its walking legs, or one of its claws in battle, a new member soon grows in its place.

The crayfish is considered good food in Europe. In America it is eaten chiefly in cities or districts where there are many people who came from Europe.

Scientific Classification. Crayfish belong to the family *Astacidae*. The American crayfish are genus *Cambarus*, species *C. virilis*, and *C. bartoni*. European crayfish are *Astacus fluviatilis*.   JERRY LAURENS BARNARD

See also CRUSTACEAN; LOBSTER.

CRAYON is a piece of charcoal, colored chalk, waxy substance, or other material, shaped like a pencil. It is used for drawing. School children use waxy crayons to color pictures on paper. They write on blackboards with chalk crayons. *Pastel crayons* are made of a fine chalk paste. Artists use them to draw pictures called *pastels*, which have soft colors and a dry, dusty look. Charcoal crayons are used chiefly for quick sketches. Crayons used in lithographic printing are smooth, greasy, and usually made of a mixture of wax, soap, resin, and lampblack. See also CHALK; PASTEL.   ERIC Q. BOHLIN

CRAZY BONE. See FUNNY BONE.

CRAZY HORSE (1844?-1877) was a great chief of the Minneconjou band of the Oglala Sioux Indians. The U.S. Cavalry destroyed his village because he disregarded the government's order to enter a reservation. Seeking revenge, he became one of the main leaders in the Sioux War of 1876. Crazy Horse led the Sioux and Cheyenne who defeated General George Crook in the battle of the Rosebud in Montana. Eight days later, he led the Indians in the battle of the Little Bighorn, where General George A. Custer and his command were wiped out (see CUSTER, GEORGE ARMSTRONG).

As a boy, Crazy Horse was named Curly. After his first great war deed, his father, who was himself a chief named Crazy Horse, gave his name to the boy. Crazy Horse had light skin and hair. He had a quiet manner, and did not boast of his great war deeds as was the tribal custom. He had unusual spiritual powers. The Sioux called him their "Strange One." In 1877, he voluntarily surrendered to American troops. The jealousy of Sioux who were friendly to the whites led to his arrest (see RED CLOUD). Crazy Horse was killed in 1877 at Fort Robinson, Nebr., by a soldier while the chief

Photo by Don Muller and Dan Grigg © Korczak

A Huge Memorial to Crazy Horse is being sculptured out of a mountain in the Black Hills by Korczak Ziolkowski. This photo of a model of the sculpture shows how the completed work will look.

was being forced into a jail cell. A gigantic figure of Crazy Horse is being sculptured out of a mountain in the Black Hills of South Dakota by Korczak Ziolkowski.   E. ADAMSON HOEBEL

CRAZY HORSE MEMORIAL. See SOUTH DAKOTA (Places to Visit; color picture); CRAZY HORSE.

CREAM. See MILK (Fats); SEPARATOR; BUTTER.

CREAM NUT. See BRAZIL NUT.

CREAM OF TARTAR, also called POTASSIUM BITARTRATE, or POTASSIUM HYDROGEN TARTRATE, is a white, crystalline substance with a slightly acid taste. It is found in grapes and other fruits. It is used in baking recipes, and in the manufacture of baking powder. It is also used in tin-plating metals and as a laxative·in medicine. Cream of tartar comes from *argol*, the crude tartar sediment that settles in wine barrels. Cream of tartar has the chemical formula $KHC_4H_4O_6$. See also BAKING POWDER.   OTTO THEODOR BENFEY

CREAM SEPARATOR. See SEPARATOR.

CREAMERY. See BUTTER (How a Creamery Makes Butter).

CREASY, SIR EDWARD SHEPHERD. See BATTLES, FIFTEEN DECISIVE.

CREATION. See GENESIS.

CRÈCHE. See TABLEAU.

CRÉCY, *KRAY SEE*, **BATTLE OF,** was the first important battle of the Hundred Years' War. It took place in 1346 at the site of the present town of Crécy, in the French department of Somme. English troops under Edward III defeated a much larger French army under Philip VI. Almost half the French force was wiped out, including more than a thousand knights. English archers on foot proved more effective than armor-clad French knights astride their chargers. The Battle of Crécy was one of the first times English soldiers used gunpowder. The hero of the battle was Edward, the Black Prince, son of Edward III of England.   ROBERT S. HOYT

See also EDWARD (III); EDWARD (The Black Prince); HUNDRED YEARS' WAR.

CREDIT, in education. See UNIVERSITIES AND COLLEGES (Curriculum).

CREDIT in business permits a business or individual to purchase goods or services and pay for them at a later date. By using credit, a government borrows money to provide vital services for its citizens. Businesses borrow money to buy raw materials and build factories. Individuals borrow money to buy expensive items such as homes and automobiles.

Types of Credit. There are many types of credit. They can be called by different names. Most economists agree that the most important types are commercial credit, consumer credit, and investment credit.

Commercial credit is used by businessmen to obtain money to carry on their business. For example, suppose a toy manufacturer wants to increase his production before Christmas by hiring more workers and buying more materials. But he does not have enough money on hand. To solve his problems, he uses his credit to borrow the money and repay it from the money he receives from the Christmas sales. These loans usually run from 60 days to 6 months and are called *short-term credit*.

Consumer credit permits individuals to purchase goods they could not afford if they had to pay immediately. A person may use the *installment plan* or the *deferred-payment* plan to buy a new car. He may buy a refrigerator from a department store through a *charge account* with that store. Or, he may buy a house with a *mortgage* from a bank. Normally, the person who buys on credit agrees to repay a certain part of his debt each month. But in all cases, he obtains the goods immediately and pays for them over a period of time.

Investment credit allows a business to obtain credit for capital goods. For example, suppose the toy manufacturer wants to expand his business by building another factory, but lacks the money. He borrows the money and repays it over several years because the loan is very large. This is called *long-term credit*.

Sources of Credit. Credit comes from many places. Some credit is available for any purpose, while other credit is available only for specific uses. In the United States, commercial banks provide the largest share of credit of all types. Insurance companies provide investment and consumer credit. Credit unions and finance companies provide consumer credit.

Government agencies offer credit, usually for a specific purpose. Several government agencies offer credit only to farmers and farmer organizations. Others offer credit for housing or to assist small businesses.

Dangers of Credit. Consumers, businesses, and governments must be careful they do not use too much credit. A consumer who uses too much credit creates financial hardship for himself and may lose the goods he has purchased. A business that cannot pay its debts can go bankrupt. Governments that borrow too much can destroy the public's confidence in the national currency. In modern times, inflations and depressions have resulted from the misuse of credit by a government and its citizens.   JAMES B. LUDTKE

Related Articles in WORLD BOOK include:

Banks and	Finance	Loan Company
Banking	Company	Mortgage
Credit Card	Inflation and	Pawnbroker
Credit Union	Deflation	Savings and
Farm Credit	Installment	Loan Associa-
Administration	Plan	tion

CREDIT, LETTER OF. See LETTER OF CREDIT.

CREDIT CARD permits its holder to buy goods or obtain services without paying for them immediately. The buyer pays later. In the mid-1960's, millions of persons were using credit cards to make telephone calls, rent automobiles, and to buy all types of merchandise. Credit cards are generally issued by business firms only to persons who have established a good record for paying their bills.

Credit cards usually are made of plastic or stiff cardboard. Each card has a number that helps the business identify the credit card holder. Sometimes these cards are called *charge plates*.

Several companies issue credit cards that can be used in thousands of stores or businesses. These cards are used by many businessmen who want to keep a full record of the expenses of a trip. Hotel and oil company credit cards are among the most common types.

In most cases, a person who uses a credit card gets a bill for the amount of money he spent for credit purchases during the previous month. Unless some other form of credit has been agreed upon, he is expected to pay the bill promptly.

CREDIT INSURANCE. See INSURANCE (Casualty, Surety, and Fidelity Insurance).

CREDIT MOBILIER OF AMERICA, *moh BEEL yer*, was a joint-stock company responsible for a major political scandal in the history of the United States. It was first chartered in 1859 as the Pennsylvania Fiscal Agency. In 1864 it came under the control of the Union Pacific Railroad Company, which renamed it and turned it into a construction company for the Union Pacific. That railroad had been chartered by the government on the following terms: for each mile of track built, the government was to give the road 10 sections of public land and from $16,000 to $48,000 in United States bonds, depending on how difficult the country was to build through and how much work needed to be done.

Actually, this was far more than was needed to build the road. But since the same men owned the Union Pacific and the Credit Mobilier, the railroad gave the contracts to the construction company on such terms as to make sure that all the government funds should be spent, with enormous profits for the owners. The result was that shares in Credit Mobilier rose with suspicious rapidity. To keep the government in line, Oakes Ames, manager of Credit Mobilier, who was also a congressman from Massachusetts, distributed stock at far below market price to members of Congress and government officials, and even loaned them money to pay for it. These transactions were exposed in 1872. Vice-President Schuyler Colfax and other high government officials were accused of accepting bribes. Congress strongly reprimanded one of the government directors of the railroad and two Congressmen, Ames and James Brooks of New York. The builders of the Union Pacific kept their profits, and the government funds intended as a permanent endowment for the road passed into private hands.

The name *Credit Mobilier* was taken from a French banking firm which was likewise involved in a public scandal. Established at Paris in 1852, the firm became powerful, and, at the expense of small investors, the promoters acquired huge fortunes. Extravagant speculation ruined the firm in 1869. The small investors lost their investments, but the promoters kept the great sums they had built up.   JOHN D. HICKS

CREDIT UNION is a cooperative savings and loan association operated by the members exclusively for their own mutual benefit. The members pool their savings. When one of them needs to borrow money for some useful or necessary purpose, he may do so at a low rate, commonly one per cent a month on the unpaid balance. Credit unions are often organized among the employees of companies or members of farm groups, labor unions, and educational, religious, and social institutions. In the early 1960's, there were about 21,500 credit unions in the United States with a total membership of over 14,600,000. The unions had savings of about $7,-200,000,000 and assets of over $3,300,000,000.

Cooperative credit societies originated in Germany when Hermann Schulze, mayor of Delitzsch, organized one in 1848. Alphonse Desjardins organized the first credit union in North America in 1900 at Levis, Quebec, in Canada. Desjardins came to Boston early in 1909 and helped Edward A. Filene, a Boston department store executive, draft a bill in the Massachusetts legislature to make credit unions legal in that state. About half of all credit unions operate under federal charters under the supervision of the United States Bureau of Federal Credit Unions. The others are chartered by individual states.   G. L. BACH

See also COOPERATIVE; FEDERAL CREDIT UNIONS, BUREAU OF.

CREDITOR. See DEBT.

CREE INDIANS once occupied a large part of Canada, from southwestern Quebec to Saskatchewan. They were related by language to the Algonkian family.

In the middle 1700's a small group of Cree moved west into Alberta and south into the United States. These *Plains Cree* became buffalo hunters, and lived like the other Plains tribes (see INDIAN, AMERICAN [Plains Indians]).

Woodland, or *Woods*, *Cree* lived mainly by hunting and fishing. They hunted moose on the southern borders of their forest country, but caribou provided the chief game farther north. These Cree also hunted bear, beaver, wild fowl, and fish, wandering far and wide in search of their food. The Woodland Cree wore clothing and moccasins of moosehide, caribou skins, and other furs. These Indians usually traveled by birchbark canoe in summer, bypassing the tangled forests and swamps. They used snowshoes and sleds for winter hunting in the deep, soft snow of the forest. Cree society was organized around the family. Dream visions were important to the Cree hunter, because he believed that they brought him a protective guardian spirit.

About 1,000 Plains Cree live on reservations in Manitoba and Montana. The 32,000 Woodland Cree live on reserves in Quebec, Ontario, Manitoba, Saskatchewan, and Alberta. Many of the Cree live much as their ancestors did.   ELMER HARP, JR.

CREED is one's belief, or set of beliefs, about a definite subject. If a man says "I believe honesty is the best policy," and means it, that is his business creed in dealing with other people. Creeds are usually associated with religion. But they can just as well be connected with any other kinds of beliefs. One may have a political creed or an educational creed as well as a religious creed.

The creed of any church contains the statements, or

articles, of faith which the members of that church accept. There are as many creeds as there are religious sects. In the Christian church, most of the creeds have come down from a few that were established by the early church. The first of these is the *Apostles' Creed*. It is so named because it is supposed to have been set down by the 12 Apostles. The next creed of importance was called the *Nicene Creed*. It was adopted by the Council of Nicaea, in A.D. 325. See NICENE COUNCILS.

Later, the Council of Trent and Vatican Council I added several articles to the Nicene Creed. It then included all the articles of faith of the Roman Catholic Church.

Protestant creeds were adopted during the Reformation in the 1500's. The Lutheran Church has as its creed the *Symbolic Book of the Evangelical Church*. The Church of England has the *Thirty-Nine Articles*, and the Presbyterian Church has the *Westminster Confession of Faith*. The creeds of other Protestant denominations were formed by modifying one or more of these creeds. They are all similar in their main ideas.   A. EUSTACE HAYDON

See also APOSTLES' CREED; REFORMATION; THIRTY-NINE ARTICLES; TRENT, COUNCIL OF; VATICAN COUNCIL.

CREED, AMERICAN'S. See AMERICAN'S CREED.

CREEK INDIANS formed a confederation that included a group of tribes originally located in present-day Alabama and Georgia. The Creek were also called the MUSKOGEE (*mus KOH gee*). They later moved to Oklahoma as one of the Five Civilized Tribes (see FIVE CIVILIZED TRIBES).

Creek farming settlements lay along the Coosa, Tallapoosa, and Chattahoochee rivers. There were almost 50 towns in the Creek confederacy, which was created mainly as protection against enemy attack. The Creek enjoyed music and played the ball game now called lacrosse. Every summer they held a four- or eight-day festival called the *puskita*, or *busk*, to celebrate the ripening of new corn. During this period of peace, the people threw away their old clothes and household utensils. They kindled new fires as symbols of the new year. The Creek were noted for their diplomatic skill and for their wisdom in council.

During colonial days, the Creek were friendly with the British colonists but not with the Spaniards. The Creek fought against the United States in the Creek War (1813-1814), which ended in the surrender of Creek lands (see INDIAN WARS [In the South]). The Creek then moved to Indian Territory (now Oklahoma), where they established their own government, schools, and other institutions. The Creek and other tribes in Indian Territory helped separate the white settlers who were moving westward from the hostile Southern Plains tribes.

Today, most Creek live in Oklahoma. A few live in Alabama, Louisiana, and Texas. Only a few of the old customs remain. The Old Creek Indian Council House still stands in Okmulgee, Okla., as a memorial to the tribe.   WILLIAM H. GILBERT

CREEL, GEORGE (1876-1953), a newspaperman and author, served as chairman of the Committee on Public Information, the United States information agency in World War I. His committee promoted voluntary newspaper censorship of confidential war information. Creel served as chairman of the advisory committee of the Works Progress Administration in 1935 and as U.S. Commissioner to the Golden Gate International Exposition in 1939.

Born in Lafayette County, Missouri, Creel edited the Kansas City *Independent* from 1899 to 1909. His crusade for clean government in Kansas City won him acclaim. Later he worked in Denver with the *Post* and the *Rocky Mountain News* from 1909 to 1913. His many books include *How We Advertised America* (1920) and *War Criminals and Punishment* (1944).   JOHN E. DREWRY

CREEPER. See VIRGINIA CREEPER.

CREEPER is the name of a family of small, busy birds much like the woodpeckers in their habit of climbing trees. Most creepers are found in Europe, but the common *brown creeper* lives in North America. It is widespread in southern Canada but is frequently observed in the southern part of the United States in winter. The creeper is smaller than the sparrow. Its brown plumage, streaked with white, looks almost like the rough bark of the trees it climbs. It is grayish-white on its underparts. The bird moves around a tree from the base upward. It uses its curved bill and sharp tongue to pick out every insect and spider egg it can find in the bark. Insects and seeds make up its only food.

The creeper has a "wild, sweet song," heard only when the bird makes its nest behind loose bark. The female lays five to eight white eggs with brown spots.

The Brown Creeper uses its strong feet and 12 stiff tail feathers to cling to the bark where it feeds.

Scientific Classification. The creeper belongs to the creeper family, *Certhiidae*. The brown creeper is genus *Certhia*, species *C. familiaris*.

See also BIRD (color pictures: Birds of Other Lands [Blue Honey Creeper; Wall Creeper], Types of Beaks).

CREEPING BENT. See BENT.

CREEPING CHARLIE. See LOOSESTRIFE.

CREIGHTON UNIVERSITY is a coeducational liberal arts school conducted by the Jesuits at Omaha, Nebr. It has a graduate school; schools of medicine, law, dentistry, pharmacy, and commerce; and grants degrees in the physical sciences, nursing, and journalism. Creighton was founded in 1878. For enrollment, see UNIVERSITIES AND COLLEGES (table).   HARRY A. DOLPHIN

CREMASTER. See BUTTERFLY (Pupa).

CREMATION. See FUNERAL CUSTOMS.

CRÉMAZIE, OCTAVE. See CANADIAN LITERATURE (The Rise of French-Canadian Literature).

CREOLE, *KRE ohl*, is a term used loosely to indicate descendants of French or Spanish settlers of an area. It comes from the Spanish word *criollo*, meaning *native to the place*. It is also used in speaking of Creole peoples' languages or local products, as in the terms *Creole pralines* or *Creole cooking*. In the United States, *Creole* now refers only to white descendants of French or Spanish settlers of the Gulf States. In colonial Latin and South America, white persons born in the Western Hemisphere were called *Criollos* (Creoles). See NEW ORLEANS (The People); LATIN AMERICA (Struggle for Independence).   WILTON MARION KROGMAN

CREOSOTE, *KRE oh soht,* is a heavy, oily liquid made by distilling wood or coal tar. It has a penetrating, smoky smell and is nearly colorless when pure. Creosote as marketed is commonly a brownish color, and is a mixture of a number of substances such as cresol. Creosote oil taken from beechwood tar has been used in medicine. This oil is chiefly made up of creosote and guaiacol.

Creosote obtained from coal tar is one of the most effective wood preservatives. It has been used for this purpose for more than 100 years. Creosote is also used as pitch for roofing. Creosote is also sometimes used to neutralize disagreeable odors. It is a dangerous poison.   AUSTIN EDWARD SMITH

See also CRESOL; TAR.

CREOSOTE BUSH, or GREASEWOOD, is a desert shrub that grows in southwestern United States and Mexico. It is an evergreen, and smells like balsam. The creosote bush grows about 5 to 8 feet high. It has many branches, and produces a resin. The leaves are made up of two tiny leaflets about one third of an inch long, and shaped slightly like an egg. They have no stalk. The creosote bush has tiny yellow flowers. The fruit is round

Willis Peterson

Creosote Bushes require a great amount of sunlight and grow only in desert regions in southwestern United States and Mexico.

and white, and feels like felt. Creosote bushes grow in sandy, light soil, and need much sunlight.

Scientific Classification. The creosote bush belongs to the caltrop family, *Zygophyllaceae.* It is genus *Larrea,* species *L. tridentata.*   J. J. LEVISON

CREPE, *krayp,* is the term for fabrics woven so that the cloth has a crinkled, or rippled, surface. Crepe fabrics are woven from tightly twisted yarns, some of which may be twisted to the right and some to the left, causing the yarns to spring back into *kinks,* or curls, after the weaving. Crepe fabrics may also be made by weaving, chemical treatment, or embossing (see EMBOSSING). Crepe fabrics may be woven from silk, wool, rayon, or synthetics. *Mourning crepe* is a black, dull silk with deep grooves pressed into the surface. It is used for mourning bands to be worn on the arm, or as part of funeral wreaths. *Crepe paper,* used in decorating, is colored paper which is crinkled to look like crepe cloth. The word *crepe* comes from the Latin verb form *crispare,* which means *to curl.*   KENNETH R. FOX

CRERAR, *KREE rahr,* **HENRY DUNCAN GRAHAM** (1888-1965), distinguished himself as commander of the First Canadian Army in the invasion of the Rhineland and western Netherlands in World War II. He served as Chief of the Canadian General Staff in 1940 and 1941, and commanded the First Canadian Corps in Great Britain and Italy from 1942 to 1944. He was noted for his skill and determination.

Born in Hamilton, Ont., Crerar studied at Upper Canada College, at Lausanne, Switzerland, and at the Royal Military College in Kingston, Ont. He joined the Canadian Expeditionary Force in 1914 as an artillery captain and served throughout World War I. Crerar retired from the army in 1945.   JEAN BRUCHÉSI

CRESCENDO. See MUSIC (Terms).

CRESCENT, *KREHS uhnt,* is a symbol that resembles the moon in its first quarter. In heraldry, the crescent is usually shown with its *horns* (ends) pointing up. If the horns are shown pointing left, the crescent is called *decrescent.* If the horns point right, it is called *increscent.* If the horns are shown pointing down, it is called a *crescent reversed.*

The people of Constantinople used the crescent as their symbol. When the Turks conquered the city, they adopted it as their symbol. It appears in the flag of Turkey. In Moslem countries, a flag with a red crescent on it means the same thing as a red cross on a flag in other countries.   ARTHUR E. DuBOIS

CRESOL, *KREE sohl,* is the common name for a group of chemicals that scientists call *hydroxytoluenes.* Creosote oil contains cresols, and is used to preserve railroad ties, fence posts, and other wood used outdoors (see CREOSOTE). Antiseptic soaps and emulsions are made from a purified mixture of the known cresols: orthocresol, metacresol, and paracresol. These soaps and emulsions find medical use as antiseptics for minor cuts and wounds, and as disinfectants for hands, instruments, and hospital facilities.   JAMES S. FRITZ

CRESS is any one of three green plants in the mustard family. They are used in salads and to garnish meats. The best-known cress plant is called *water cress* because it grows in water in sandy creek bottoms. It has smooth, bright-green leaves on long slender stems. *Garden cress,* or *peppergrass,* has a sharper taste than water cress. It grows in the Middle West. *Swedish cress,* sometimes called *upland cress* or *winter cress,* grows in Sweden. It is served as a vegetable there.

Water cress may be raised as a winter crop in greenhouses. It grows best in running water. Garden cress is usually planted in the early spring and harvested about six or seven weeks later. The cresses are rich in minerals, but are usually eaten in too small amounts to provide much food value.

Scientific Classification. Cresses belong to the mustard family, *Cruciferae.* Water cress is genus *Nasturtium,* species *N. officinale.* Garden cress is *Lepidium sativum.* Swedish cress is *Barbarea vulgaris.*   S. H. WITTWER

See also MUSTARD.

CRETACEOUS PERIOD, *kree TAY shus,* is a period in the geologic time scale of the earth's history. Scientists believe that the Cretaceous Period began 130 million years ago. See also EARTH (table: Outline of Earth History).

A Medieval Fort in Iráklion harbor stands as a reminder of the numerous tyrants who have invaded Crete.

CRETE, *kreet,* is a Greek island in the Mediterranean Sea. It lies about 81 miles from the Greek mainland, and nearly twice as far from Turkey. For location, see GREECE (color map). Crete is the fifth largest island in the Mediterranean Sea. It is about 186 miles long and from 7 to 35 miles wide. Its coastline is 360 miles long. Crete covers 3,217 square miles. Crete and several nearby islands make up four *nomoi* (departments).

Mountain ranges run from one end of Crete to the other. Mt. Ida, the highest peak on the island, reaches 8,058 feet above sea level. Fertile valleys lie between the mountains. Crete has a mild climate, with a dry season during the summer, and rain in winter. The chief industries are farming, sheep and goat raising, and light manufacturing. Its principal exports include almonds, cheese, citrus fruits, olive oil, and wines.

Homer told of more than 100 cities in ancient Crete. But today, there are only three major urban areas, all of which lie along the northern coast. These are Khaniá, the capital; Iráklion; and Réthimnon. There are no good natural harbors along the island's southern coast, and little commerce enters or leaves this area. Historians estimate that about 1,000,000 persons lived in ancient Crete. But only 483,258 persons live on the island today.

Crete and the Aegean islands were one of the three areas in which ancient Mediterranean civilization reached advanced stages. They share with ancient Egypt and the valleys of the Tigris and Euphrates rivers the honor of being the scene of man's earliest struggles to rise out of barbarism. But the island played relatively little part in ancient Greek history. Archaeologists have found remains of a Neolithic culture that flourished in Crete from about 10,000 B.C. to 3300 B.C. A Minoan, or Aegean, civilization followed the Neolithic culture, and lasted to about 1400 B.C. Crete achieved great advances in art, architecture, and engineering during this era (see AEGEAN CIVILIZATION).

In 67 B.C., Crete was conquered by Roman legions commanded by Pompey. In the following centuries, the island came under the rule of successive invaders, including the Byzantines, the Venetians, the Ottoman Turks, and the Egyptians. In A.D. 823, for example, Crete passed from the control of the Eastern Roman emperors to that of the Saracens. The Saracens built the capital of Candia (present-day Iráklion). The Byzantines expelled the Saracens in 861, and retained control for almost 400 years. In 1204, the Byzantine Emperor sold Crete to the Venetians. They held the island against both Genoese and Ottoman assaults until the Ottoman conquest of 1669.

Crete remained under Ottoman administration until the late 1800's. But most of the people of the island were Christian in faith, Greek in speech, and pro-Greek in sentiment. Difficulties constantly arose between the Cretans and the Turkish Moslem minority. These troubles intensified in the early 1800's, when Greek nationalism increased on the island. The Ottoman Empire gave up control of Crete after the Greco-Turkish War (1897-1898). After the Ottomans left, Great Britain, France, Italy, and Russia agreed to allow Prince George of Greece to serve as governor of Crete.

The strong movement for union with Greece con-

Crete Lies Southeast of Greece.

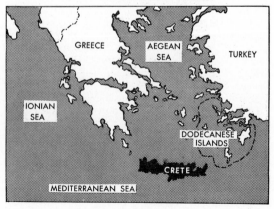

tinued in the early 1900's. Crete became part of Greece soon after the Balkan Wars of 1912-1913. A Cretan leader, Eleutherios Venizelos, played a dominant role in Greek politics from that time until 1935. The Greek government fled to Crete after the German attack on Greece on Apr. 6, 1941. The Greeks had to evacuate their government to Cyprus on May 31, when German airborne troops attacked Crete. Axis forces retained control of Crete until the surrender of May, 1945. After the war, Cretan recovery depended chiefly on the revival of exports and the gradual restoration of prosperity in Greece as a whole.   HARRY N. HOWARD

Related Articles in WORLD BOOK include:

Architecture (Greek)	Clothing (Ancient Times; color picture, Costumes of Ancient Peoples)	Daedalus
Ariadne		Knossos
		Venizelos, Eleutherios

CRETINISM, *KREE tin iz'm*, is a condition, present at birth, that results when none or not enough of the thyroid hormone, *thyroxin*, is produced. Children suffering from this condition are called *cretins*. In these children, the thyroid gland may be absent or abnormally small. Or the gland may even be greatly enlarged but not functioning. The thyroid hormone influences growth. Therefore, a cretin does not show proper physical or mental growth. He has a large head, but short arms and legs. His face is broad and the bridge of his nose is flattened. His eyelids are puffed and his tongue protrudes between his lips. His pale, dry skin is cold and sometimes yellowish. Tooth and bone formation are delayed.

Doctors treat cretinism with thyroid extract, and begin treatment as soon as possible. When treatment is started early, the child's body often develops normally and brain development improves.   BENJAMIN F. MILLER

See also THYROID GLAND; PARACELSUS, PHILIPPUS.

CRETONNE, *kree TAHN*, is a printed drapery fabric made of cotton, linen, rayon, or synthetics. It has a variety of weaves and finishes but is not glazed. Chintz is sometimes called cretonne, but cretonne is heavier and has bolder designs. Cretonne is made in widths of either 36 or 50 inches. See also CHINTZ.   KENNETH R. FOX

CREUSA. See MEDEA.

CREVASSE, *kreh VAS*, is a deep crack, or fissure, in an earth embankment or a glacier. Levees which are built to stop rivers from flooding sometimes leak water through crevasses. Huge crevasses, common on all glaciers, make it dangerous or even impossible to cross glaciers. See also GLACIER.   WALTER H. BUCHER

CRÈVECOEUR, ST. JOHN DE. See AMERICAN LITERATURE (Histories).

CRIBBAGE is a card game for two, three, or four persons. It requires a full pack of cards. Each player keeps his score on a *cribbage board*, using two *pegs*. The object of the game is to *peg* (score) 121 points. But the game may also be set at 61 points.

When two persons play, they *cut* (divide) the pack to decide who will deal. The one who gets the lower card deals six cards to his opponent and six to himself. Each player then places two cards face down. These four cards form the *crib*, which is used at the end of the hand. The nondealer cuts the rest of the cards and turns up the top card of the lower part of the pack. This card is the *turnup* or *starter*. If it is a jack, the dealer pegs 2 for *his heels*.

The nondealer begins by laying down a card and call-

ing its value. The dealer then lays down a card and adds its value to the first card. They continue until the value of the cards totals 31. The player who reaches 31 pegs 2 points. If a player cannot lay down a card without going beyond 31, he must say "go." His opponent then pegs 1 for *go* after playing as many cards as he can without passing 31. Whenever a *go* occurs, the opponent of the one who last played begins a new count. When each player has used all his cards, he pegs the total points for his hand.

In scoring, face cards count 10, the ace counts 1, and the others count according to their spots. Points are

Brown and Bigelow

In a Cribbage Game, each of the players keeps his own score by moving two pegs on the special cribbage board.

scored both during the play and at the end of the hand. Each combination of 15 points and each pair counts 2 points. A *run* of three or more cards in sequence scores 1 for each card. Three cards of a kind count 6 and four of a kind count 12. At the end of the hand, the nondealer counts his score first. Each player includes the turnup in the count of his hand. A player holding a jack of the same suit as the turnup pegs 1 for *his nobs*. The crib belongs to the dealer, and he adds its value to his score.   LILLIAN FRANKEL

CRICK, FRANCIS H. C. (1916-   ), is a British biologist. He shared the 1962 Nobel prize in physiology and medicine with biologist James D. Watson and biophysicist Maurice H. F. Wilkins. Crick and Watson built a model of the molecular structure of *deoxyribonucleic acid* (DNA), the substance that transmits genetic information from one generation to the next. The model, resembling a twisted ladder, is called the *Watson-Crick model*. See NUCLEIC ACID.

Originally a physicist, Crick helped develop radar during World War II. In 1949, he began research work in molecular biology at Cambridge University. Born in Northampton, England, he studied at London and Cambridge universities.   IRWIN H. HERSKOWITZ

See also BIOLOGY (picture, Highlights).

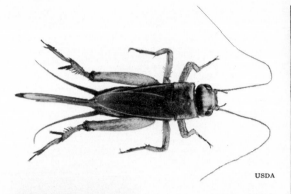

USDA

European House Crickets, *above,* grow about 1 inch long.

Tree Crickets chirp louder than most other crickets.

Cornelia Clarke

Wingless Camel Crickets belong to the katydid family.

Cornelia Clarke

Foldes, Black Star

The Common North American Field Cricket, *above,* is known for its song. It usually grows about an inch long.

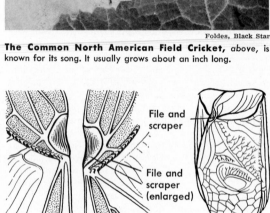

File and scraper

File and scraper (enlarged)

The Organs with Which the Cricket "Sings." At the right are shown the cricket's upper wings, folded along its back so that the right wing nearly covers the left. At the left, portions of the wings are shown separated, with the sound-producing organs enlarged. Each wing has a "file," or thickened vein with crossridges, and a "scraper," or hard, sharp-edged portion. The scraper of either wing may be rubbed against the file of the other wing to produce the mating call.

CRICKET is a kind of jumping insect related to grasshoppers. Crickets differ from grasshoppers in having prominent feelers at the tip of the abdomen. Crickets' wings lie flat over each other on top of their backs. Some crickets are wingless. The slender antennae are much longer than the body in most kinds of crickets. The *ovipositor,* an organ from which the eggs are laid, is usually slender and cylindrical.

The best-known crickets are the *house cricket* of Europe and the *common, black,* or *field cricket* of America. These blackish or brownish insects are about an inch long. The *tree cricket* is a light yellow-greenish in color. It spends most of its life in trees and in bushes. The tiny *ant-loving crickets* are wingless and as broad as they are long. They live in ants' nests. *Mormon crickets, camel (cave) crickets, mole crickets,* and *Jerusalem crickets* are not considered true crickets (see MOLE CRICKET; MORMON CRICKET).

Only the male cricket produces sound. But both sexes have hearing organs located in their front legs just below the knee. Crickets remain in sheltered places during the day, and go out at night for food. They eat many foods including grain, remains of other insects, woolen articles, and bookbindings. In autumn, most crickets lay their eggs in soil. The eggs hatch the following spring.

In China and Japan, people keep singing crickets in cages as pets.

Scientific Classification. Crickets are in the order *Orthoptera* and the cricket family, *Gryllidae.* URL LANHAM

See also ORTHOPTERA; WEATHER (picture: Weather Facts).

CRICKET is a game played with a bat and a ball by two 11-man teams. It is one of the most popular games in England and in several other Commonwealth countries. Baseball, the "national game" of the United States, was developed from cricket. In both games, one player pitches or bowls a ball and an opposing player tries to hit the ball with a bat and score runs. The team that scores the most runs wins the game.

Cricket players play the game on a level, oval-shaped field of grass. The action centers around two *wickets*. Each wicket consists of three short stumps with two *bails* (sticks) connecting the tops of the stumps. A member of the fielding side called the *bowler* stands behind one of the wickets. He *bowls* (delivers) the ball with a stiff-armed motion at the opposing wicket, trying to knock off one of the bails. The ball usually bounces off the ground before hitting the wicket. The *batsman* or *striker* stands at the far wicket facing the bowler. He tries to hit the ball with a long flat-sided bat. If he misses the ball and it knocks a bail off the wicket, he is out. If he drives the ball into the field, he and the *nonstriker* (a teammate standing at the opposite wicket) may try to score a run. If the batsmen run to the opposite wickets before a member of the fielding team knocks off a bail with the ball, they score a run for their team. The batsmen score a run each time they both safely reach the wickets. Sometimes, the two batsmen can run back and forth between the two wickets scoring several runs before the ball is brought close enough to the wicket to put them out. A major cricket match

Sir Donald Bradman, the contributor of this article, is an Australian and one of the greatest batsmen in cricket history.

may last from three to five days, and each team may score hundreds of runs.

Cricket players wear peaked caps, white or cream trousers and open-necked shirts, and white spiked or crepe-soled boots. Batsmen and wicketkeepers wear protective leg pads and gloves.

Cricket Field and Equipment

The Field may vary in size, but most official fields are about 450 feet wide and 500 feet long. The wickets stand 22 yards apart in the center of the field. The area between them is called the *pitch*. The *bowling crease* is a line drawn through the wicket that extends 4 feet 4 inches on either side of the center stump. At each end of the bowling crease, lines called *return creases* are marked to the rear of the wicket. The return creases are marked only a short distance back, but they are considered actually to extend to the end of the field.

The bowler must bowl the ball between the return creases. The *popping crease* is parallel to the bowling crease and 4 feet in front of the wicket. The popping crease is marked 8 feet 8 inches long, but it actually extends to either side of the cricket field. A batsman is required to step inside of the popping crease to score a run.

The Wickets are 9 inches wide, and consist of three stumps 28 inches high. The stumps are close enough together so the ball cannot go between any two of them. The bails are $4\frac{3}{8}$ inches long and rest in grooves on the tops of stumps. They do not extend beyond the outer edges of the stumps, and do not rise more than a half inch above them.

Cricket Players must have quick reflexes. The fielder, center, cannot stop the ball as it bounces past. The batsmen race back and forth between the wickets, trying to score as many runs as possible before the ball is fielded and returned.

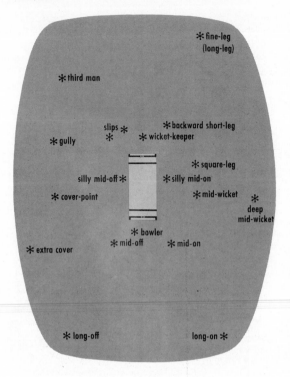

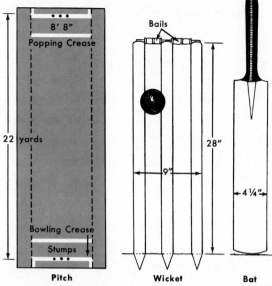

Cricket Field and Equipment. The fielding positions, *left*, are those often used for a right-handed batsman. The positions vary according to the skills of the batsman and the bowler. The pitch is marked with batting and bowling creases. The stumps are close together so the ball cannot go between them. Bats vary in length.

Bat and Ball. The rules of cricket do not specify the material to be used in making a cricket ball. However, a cricket ball usually has a cork core wrapped with twine and a leather cover. The ball must be between $8\frac{13}{16}$ and 9 inches in circumference, and it must weigh between $5\frac{1}{2}$ and $5\frac{3}{4}$ ounces.

The bat cannot be more than 38 inches long nor more than $4\frac{1}{4}$ inches wide at any point. It has a round handle at one end. The rest of the bat is a flat, bladelike hitting surface. Young players should use a small bat so that they can swing it easily.

Cricket Rules

A cricket match may consist of one or two innings. Important matches are played in two innings. A team's innings ends when 10 of its 11 men have been put out. Team captains flip a coin to decide who will bat first. In a match of three days or more, a captain whose team batted first and is ahead by more than 150 runs after the other team has batted may decide that his team has enough runs to win. He may order the other side to *follow-on* (bat its second innings immediately after its first innings). If the other team then scores more runs and takes the lead, his team can take the field to bat in its second innings.

The team that has the most runs wins. But the score is sometimes given in the number of *wickets* (outs). In a two-innings game, a team that scores more runs than the other team after the other team has batted twice wins the game without finishing the last innings. That team wins by a certain number of wickets. For example, if only four men have been put out, the team wins by six wickets because six men have not been put

out. A team may also win by *innings*. For example, if a team batting first and third scores fewer runs than the other team scored in one innings, the second team wins by one innings without batting a second time.

Scoring. Most runs are scored by running from one wicket to the other. Batsmen also score runs when they hit the ball out of bounds. A *boundary, four* (four runs) occurs when the batsman hits the ball and it bounces out of bounds. A *boundary, six* (six runs) occurs when the batsman hits a ball that goes over the boundary before it touches the ground.

Runs called *extras* may also be scored by bowling. Extras are scored on *byes, leg byes, wide balls,* and *no balls.* A bye is a run scored from a ball that passes the batsman and the stumps without touching either of them. A leg bye is a run scored where a ball strikes the batsman anywhere but on the hand. In byes and leg byes, the batsman may score runs until the ball is brought back to the wicket. When a bowler delivers a *wide ball* (one that goes outside the return creases), the opposing team scores a run. If the bowler throws the ball, or if he does not have his front foot behind the bowling crease when he bowls, it is ruled a no ball.

Outs. There are several ways to put out a batsman. The most direct way is to bowl the bail off the wicket. The batsman is also out if (1) he hits a ball that is caught by a fielder or lands in a fielder's clothing without touching the ground; (2) he touches the ball with his hands while it is in play; (3) he hits the ball a second time except to keep it from hitting the wicket; (4) he *breaks the wicket* (knocks off the bail) with his bat, clothing, or any part of his body; (5) he stops the ball with his body to prevent it from hitting the wicket

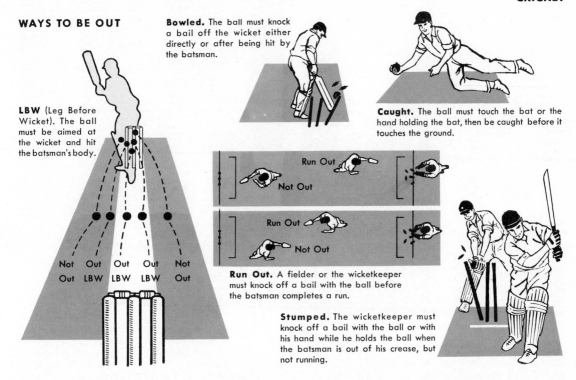

WAYS TO BE OUT

Bowled. The ball must knock a bail off the wicket either directly or after being hit by the batsman.

Caught. The ball must touch the bat or the hand holding the bat, then be caught before it touches the ground.

LBW (Leg Before Wicket). The ball must be aimed at the wicket and hit the batsman's body.

| Not Out | Out LBW | Out LBW | Out LBW | Not Out |

Run Out — Not Out
Run Out — Not Out

Run Out. A fielder or the wicketkeeper must knock off a bail with the ball before the batsman completes a run.

Stumped. The wicketkeeper must knock off a bail with the ball or with his hand while he holds the ball when the batsman is out of his crease, but not running.

(called *Leg Before Wicket*, or *LBW*); (6) he tries to prevent or willfully prevents a player from fielding or catching a ball; (7) he tries to score and the wicket is broken before he crosses the popping crease; or (8) he steps outside the crease when not trying to run, and the wicket is broken by the wicketkeeper with the ball in his hand, without any other fielder having touched the ball (called *stumping*).

Umpires control the game and make all decisions. One umpire stands behind the bowler's wicket to give decisions on whether the striker is out LBW or caught, and to rule on run outs at his end. A second umpire stands at 90 degrees to the striker's wicket to rule on a stumping or a run out at his end. The umpire at the bowler's end must also decide whether the ball is in play. The ball is in play from the moment the bowler begins his run up to the crease. The ball is *dead* (not in play) when the umpire judges that (1) it is finally in the hands of a wicketkeeper or bowler, (2) it has crossed the boundary, (3) it has lodged in the clothing of a batsman or an umpire, or (4) it has been called "lost." The ball is also dead if the umpire calls unfair play or if he suspends play because a player has been hurt or when a player is out for any reason.

Cricket Teams

The Batting Side. The team captain decides the order in which his team's batsmen will bat. When each batsman is out, a teammate replaces him until 10 men are out. One batsman always remains *not out*. At major cricket grounds, members of the batting side who are not at the wickets usually sit in balconies in the grandstand waiting their turn at bat.

The Fielding Side is made up of the bowler, the wicketkeeper, and nine other fielders. The other fielders' positions vary in name and location. The most common positions are shown in the diagram of the field that appears in this article. The players near the pitch move from one side of the field to the other, according to whether the batsman is left or right handed.

After the bowler has delivered six balls (eight in Australia), another bowler bowls at the opposite wicket. The striker then becomes the nonstriker, and his teammate at the other wicket becomes the striker. This is an *over*. The fielders then move to new positions.

Batting

A right-handed batsman should hold the bat with his left hand near the top of the handle with his knuckles facing the same way as the hitting side of the bat. His right hand should be close below the left.

A right-handed batsman should stand with his feet about 6 inches apart, one on each side of the popping crease. The batsman's grip and stance should be easy and relaxed, and his weight should be evenly balanced. His left shoulder should point toward the bowler, and the top of the bat handle should rest against the inside of his left thigh. The bottom of the bat should be behind his right instep. The position is reversed for left-handed batsmen.

The Batting Strokes may be divided roughly into two categories, *forward play* and *back play*. Each may be used defensively or to attack and try to score runs. For both strokes, the batsman swings the bat back in a movement called the *back-lift*, then forward and down past his feet, then up to meet the ball.

CRITICAL

The Bowler looks over his shoulder at the point on which he wants to bounce the ball. He then brings his arm over, keeping it stiff to prevent jerking, and follows through after releasing the ball.

Sport and General

Skillful Bowlers deliver the ball at varying speeds. They try to confuse the batsman by changing speeds and making the ball change direction either before or after it bounces.

On a forward stroke, the batsman pushes his left foot forward as near as he can to the path of the ball. When the ball is bowled slowly, the batsman may take two or three short steps toward the ball, rather than one long step. He should swing the bat forward as close to his left leg as possible. A forward stroke is best for a ball bouncing near enough to the batsman to be hit on the *half-volley* (as it comes off the ground), to protect the wicket and to drive the ball into the field. To protect the wicket, he may start the swing farther back.

The back stroke is basically a defensive stroke. It is better for a ball that bounces far enough from the wicket for the batsman to be able to see which way it will bounce. The batsman brings his back leg into the path of the ball, keeps his left elbow up, and keeps his head over the point where the ball will meet the bat. There should be no space for the ball to pass between the bat and his body. By putting more power into the stroke, the batsman can drive the ball into the field.

Good batsmen usually swing the bat forward in a straight line to meet the ball. However, batsmen can

The Batsman guards the wicket. He uses the forward stroke, *left*, for a ball that has just bounced, trying to hit it into the field. On the back stroke, *right*, the batsman simply tries to keep the ball from hitting the wicket.

score many runs by *cutting* or *hooking* (swinging the bat at an angle to the path of the ball), and driving the ball to their *on-side* (near side of the wicket).

In playing back, the batsman can use a wide variety of strokes, according to the length and direction of the ball. One of the great arts of batsmanship is to be able to hit between two fieldsmen, giving them little chance to play the ball.

In Running, the striker usually calls for a run when he thinks he and the nonstriker can make one or more runs. But when he hits the ball behind his crease, the nonstriker calls for a run. The nonstriker should always be *backing up* (moving away from the wicket and his own crease) and ready to run.

Bowling

A bowler does not jerk or throw the ball. He does not bend or straighten his arm during the delivery. According to the official rules, he must have one foot behind the bowling crease when he releases the ball. Under an experimental rule introduced in 1965, he must have his front foot on or behind the batting crease. The length and direction of the bowl are the two most important points in bowling. A good length bowl bounces only a few feet in front of the batsman so he cannot easily hit it.

Good bowling is based on coordinated body, arm, and shoulder motion. The run-up to the bowling crease is designed to give the bowler enough momentum and balance to bowl the ball at the *pace* (speed) he desires. Then, at the final stride, a right-handed bowler's left shoulder should point toward the batsman. When his left foot has swung forward, the bowler's right shoulder should move forward and point in the direction that the ball will travel. The bowler continues his arm motion after releasing the ball to gain the most power.

His wrist must be loose. His hand is cocked back before he bowls the ball, and the hand pivots on the wrist in the delivery swing. This action makes the ball travel much faster than the arm. Bowlers can make a ball *curve* (change direction in flight) or *break* (change direction as it bounces) by controlling the ball's speed and by gripping and spinning the ball in special ways.

Wide Ball · Boundary, Six

Out · No-Ball · Boundary, Four

The Umpires stand at either end of the pitch. They use arm signals to indicate their decisions to players and spectators.

History

Cricket was probably first played in the 1300's in England, and became a major sport there in the 1700's. By the 1800's, cricket had spread to Australia, India, New Zealand, South Africa, and the West Indies.

The first printed rules appeared in 1744. Since 1788, cricket rules have been made and published in England by the Marylebone Cricket Club (MCC). Modern cricket style and method of play were largely created by W. G. Grace, a great English player of the late 1800's.

International matches called *test matches* began between England and Australia in 1877. Test matches are now played by England, Australia, India, New Zealand, Pakistan, the West Indies, and South Africa.

Since 1882, the test match between England and Australia has been played for *The Ashes*. The term was first used after Australia had beaten England in London. After that defeat, an English newspaper printed a mock death notice of English cricket. The last words were "The body will be cremated [burned] and the ashes taken to Australia." A year later, an English team went to Australia and defeated the Australians. Two Australian women burned a bail, put the ashes in a small urn, and presented it to the English team manager. The urn was later sent to Lord's, a major cricket ground in London. It is still kept there, no matter which country wins *The Ashes*.

Each country holds a nationwide championship series for the first class cricket teams. This series is called the County Championship in England, the Sheffield Shield in Australia, the Plunket Shield in New Zealand, the Currie Cup in South Africa, and the Ranji Trophy in India. Sir Donald Bradman

CRILE, GEORGE WASHINGTON (1864-1943), gained fame as a surgeon. His contributions to the development of surgery included studies on shock, hemorrhage, blood transfusion, surgical treatment of high blood pressure, and a nerve-block system of anesthesia. He had wide interests and wrote such books as *Diseases Peculiar to Civilized Man* (1934); *The Phenomena of Life* (1936); and *Intelligence, Power and Personality* (1941).

Crile was born in Chili, Ohio. He received his medical degree from Western Reserve University (now Case Western Reserve) in 1887 and taught there intermittently from 1893 to 1924. Crile founded the Cleveland Clinic Foundation in 1921. Noah D. Fabricant

CRIME violates the laws of a community, state, province, or nation. It is punishable in accordance with these laws. Crimes vary according to the time and the place where they occur. An act that is completely acceptable in one community may be considered a crime in another. But the laws of most countries consider as crimes such offenses as arson, bigamy, burglary, forgery, murder, and treason. A criminal may be imprisoned or face other punishment, according to the laws of the community in which he lives.

Criminal Law. Not all offenses against the law are crimes. The laws that set down the punishments for crimes form the *criminal law*. The law describes as crimes those offenses considered most harmful to the community. For example, if a person murders another person, he threatens the safety of people in general. For this reason, the community punishes him for his crime. On the other hand, a person may wrong someone else in some other way that offends the *civil law*. Such offenses are settled when a person makes restitution to another. He does this either by voluntary agreement or as the result of a court judgment. Civil offenses are called *torts* (see Tort).

Generally speaking, all crimes were torts in early society. Even murder developed as a private matter between the criminal and the family of the victim. The family might settle the matter either by revenging itself on the murderer or by accepting a payment from him. The act of taking revenge became known as a *vendetta*. Later, the idea of crime as an offense against society led to the development of criminal laws. But punishment of crime remained primarily a matter of revenge. Then people began to consider punishment as a means of preventing crimes. Criminologists today believe that society must protect itself against criminals rather than revenge itself on them. This protection can be achieved either by reforming criminals and teaching them to become useful citizens, or by removing them from society permanently.

The Nature of Crime. Ideas about crime and its punishment depend on the customs and ideas of the community. Blasphemy, heresy, sorcery, and witchcraft were once considered serious crimes punishable by death. Then crimes against religion ceased to be offenses against the community, and freedom of religion and scientific ideas gained wider acceptance.

During the Middle Ages and afterward, many offenses were punishable by death. For example, a man might pay with his life for stealing a loaf of bread. Most countries now use the death penalty only for such serious crimes as murder and treason.

Modern civilization has brought a large increase in the number of acts that are considered crimes. A more complex way of living resulted in a new idea of man's responsibility to his fellows. For example, selling cigarettes to a child may be a crime. A person who drives his automobile is responsible for keeping it in repair. If he fails to do so, he may be criminally negligent.

Causes of Crime. People once considered criminals as sinners who chose to offend against the laws of God and man. But criminologists today regard society itself as in large part responsible for crimes committed against it. Causes of crime include poverty, undesirable living

The Crimean Peninsula juts into the Black Sea, *above*. The main battles of the Crimean War took place there. On Feb. 17, 1855, Turkish forces thoroughly defeated Russia in the Battle of Yevpatoriya, *left*.

Culver

conditions, and inadequate education. Crime results fundamentally from society's failure to provide a decent life for all the people, and to develop a sense of social responsibility in its citizens. Crime may become common in times when values are changing rapidly, as after a war, or in places where people with different values and background are thrown together.

Classes of Crime. The common law recognizes three classes of crime: *treason, felony,* and *misdemeanor.* Death or life imprisonment is the usual penalty for treason. Laws in the United States define a felony as a crime that is punishable by a term of one year or more in a state or federal prison. A person who commits a misdemeanor may be punished by a fine or a jail term of less than one year.

Punishments. Criminal law sets forth the penalties for crimes. Usually it provides both a maximum and minimum penalty for each offense. The defendant receives his sentence after he has been found guilty in a trial. For some crimes, the jury itself decides the penalty. But the judge selects the penalty for most crimes. In either case, the judge or jury takes into consideration all the circumstances of the crime, and the character of the defendant. FRED E. INBAU

See also the articles concerning specific crimes that are listed at the end of the LAW article. See also CRIMINOLOGY.

CRIMEA, *kry ME uh,* is a peninsula which juts from the southern part of Russia into the Black Sea and the Sea of Azov. The Crimea covers an area of about 9,900 square miles and is joined to the mainland by the narrow Isthmus of Perekop. The population of the Crimea is about 1,450,000. For location, see RUSSIA (physical map).

The Crimea rises gradually from coastal plains to the low Crimean Mountains along the southern coast. There are forests of cedar, magnolia, and olive trees, and many flowers grow in the meadows. The grassy plains furnish pasture for herds of sheep and horses. Grapes from the Crimea's vineyards go to make much of the wine of

Russia. Grains flourish in the northern lowlands of the peninsula. Important deposits of iron, marble, and limestone have been found in the Crimea, and salt is dried along the coasts. The chief industries of the peninsula are shipbuilding, mining, and fishing. Resorts and health centers line the coasts.

The Crimea was one of the strongholds of opposition to the Soviet government after the Russian Revolution of 1917. Soviet troops put down the opposition in 1921, and the Crimea became an autonomous republic within the Russian Soviet Federated Socialist Republic. In World War II, German troops occupied the peninsula from 1941 to 1944. The Crimea's autonomous status was removed in 1945, and it became a province of the Russian Soviet Federated Socialist Republic. In 1954, the Crimea was transferred to the Ukrainian Soviet Socialist Republic. The capital of the Crimea is Simferopol.

Other cities of the Crimea include Kerch', Sevastopol, historically important Balaklava, and Yalta, which was the scene of the historic conference in World War II. THEODORE SHABAD

See also BALAKLAVA, BATTLE OF; CRIMEAN WAR; SEVASTOPOL; YALTA.

CRIMEAN WAR (1853-1856) was fought between Russian forces and the allied armies of England, France, Turkey, and Sardinia. The immediate cause was a dispute among France, Russia, and Turkey about the control of the Holy Places in Jerusalem. The real causes of the war were political, commercial, strategic, and dynastic rivalries among the various nations. In the fighting, the allied armies drove the Russian forces out of Turkish territory and pursued them to the Crimean Peninsula. Chief battles took place at the River Alma, at Balaklava, at Inkerman, at Yevpatoriya, and at Sevastopol. The terms of peace were signed in Paris on March 30, 1856. WARREN B. WALSH

See also BALAKLAVA, BATTLE OF; NIGHTINGALE, FLORENCE; PARIS, TREATIES OF (The Treaty of 1856).

CRIMINAL LAW. See CRIME; LAW.

CRIMINOLOGY, KRIHM *uh* NAHL *oh jih*, deals with the scientific study of crime and its treatment. It concerns the nature of crime, factors associated with criminal behavior, case studies of criminals, and the treatment of offenders. Most scientific research in criminology has been done in sociology, psychology, psychiatry, and related areas. In the United States, criminology is chiefly taught in college or university departments of sociology that consider the social and environmental causes of crime. But in European universities, criminology is generally taught in schools of law or medicine that give strong emphasis to the study of the relationship of biological factors to criminal behavior.

Early Criminology

The Classical School of criminology originated in a revolt against the harsh and arbitrary decisions of judges during the 1700's. At that time, judges acted according to the circumstances surrounding a criminal case rather than the offense committed. Punishments varied considerably, and were often severe.

The rise of the Classical School is most closely associated with the Italian Criminologist Cesare Beccaria (1738-1794). Criminologists usually consider his book, *Crimes and Punishments* (1764), as the foundation stone of the Classical School.

Beccaria assumed that the criminal offender had free will, and that pleasure and pain governed his choices. He attempted to make punishment less arbitrary and less severe. He felt that everyone who violated a specific law should receive identical punishment regardless of age, sex, wealth, or position. But he thought that children and the insane should be excused from punishment because they did not have a well-developed free will.

Most of Beccaria's protests and recommendations were related to the administration of courts and of punishments. He urged that laws should be clear, providing a scale of crimes from the least serious to the most dangerous to society. In that way, each person would know just what punishment to expect if he committed a certain act. The purpose of punishment was to make sure that the guilty did not repeat the crime and that others were prevented from committing similar crimes. Beccaria felt that crime is prevented by the certainty and speed of punishment rather than by its severity.

Lawmakers in France worked out Beccaria's ideas in detail, and enacted them in the Code of 1791 and its later revisions. In English and American criminal law, the principles of the Classical School have been modified slightly, but retained.

The Positive School of criminology, also known as the *Italian School*, developed in the late 1800's. Its leaders included Cesare Lombroso, Enrico Ferri, and Raffaele Garofalo. The Classical School had been interested in the crime itself, but the Positive School turned the interest from crime to criminals.

Cesare Lombroso (1836-1909) believed that criminals had certain physical traits that made them different from other persons. He felt these traits resemble those man possessed at a lower stage of biological development. As a prison physician, he studied many criminals and reported that most of them had large jaws, receding foreheads, and other primitive physical traits. He called these characteristics *atavism*, and believed the *atavistic*

Fingerprint Experts use various powders and liquids to get impressions of latent fingerprints.

Criminologists Use Chemicals, *right,* to determine whether poison is present in human organs.

FBI

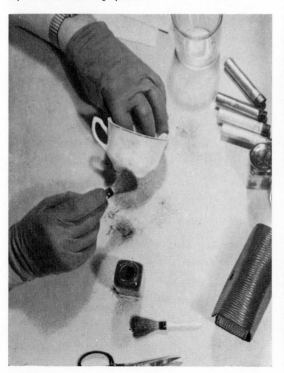

criminal was a man "born" to be a criminal.

Criminologists found it easy to attack Lombroso's theory, because they observed that many criminals did not have these physical traits. Charles Goring in England in 1913 was among the first to deny Lombroso's theory of the born-criminal type. But even though Lombroso's ideas have now largely been proved false, he laid the basis for the science of modern criminology because he approached crime from the scientific viewpoint.

Enrico Ferri (1856-1929), another Italian, believed that society should try to prevent crime rather than to concentrate on punishment. He thought that scientific methods should be used in handling criminals. Ferri emphasized the effects of climate, customs, religion, and education in causing crime. He divided criminals into five classes: (1) born criminals, (2) criminally insane, (3) those who have formed the habit of crime, (4) those who commit crimes because of special circumstances (occasional criminals), and (5) those who are driven to crime by sudden, overwhelming emotion. In his book, *Criminal Sociology*, he described the way crime statistics change as social conditions vary as the "law of criminal saturation."

Raffaele Garofalo (1852-1934) agreed with Lombroso and Ferri that crime can be understood only by the use of scientific methods. He stressed the study of the criminal nature and the circumstances in which the criminal lives. Garofalo felt the criminal is a result of his biology and his own peculiar social environment—that he does not freely choose to commit crimes. He added his own definition of crime and classification of criminals to provide a new refinement to the Positive School of criminology.

In general, the Positive School shifted the emphasis of criminology from the study of the actual crime to the study of criminals and what might have caused their criminal acts.

Modern Criminology

Since the early 1900's, criminology has found leadership in the United States. Today, criminologists believe that crime results from many causes rather than one or two major factors. They do not consider the criminal as a special physical type. They do not believe that a person inherits criminal tendencies. Instead, they believe that crime results from the inability of the individual to deal with the world in which he lives, or from the failure of society to provide a proper environment. In the complex society of today, crime may result from the conflict between material goals and expected forms of behavior. These conflicts include association with criminals or persons with unfavorable attitudes toward the law; poverty, poor housing, and overcrowding; and other social conditions. Modern criminologists are interested in the connection between crime and such biological factors as inherited intelligence, glands, and bodily structure. But the greatest emphasis comes from sociologists who are concerned with environmental conditions that cause individuals to commit crime. Psychology and psychiatry have also thrown light on the motivation and emotions that play important roles in crime causation.

Detailed case studies of delinquents and statistical analyses of the many factors associated with delinquency indicate that offenders usually come from unwholesome backgrounds. For example, they frequently are the victims of broken homes, bad neighborhoods, emotional frustrations, lack of affection from parents, or poor supervision and discipline in the home. With such varied contributing causes, it is obvious that criminology does not assume that any single factor causes a man to commit a crime.

Techniques. Modern criminology uses sociologists, psychologists, psychiatrists, and other specialists working together to seek answers to questions about crime. Case studies and statistical tools are necessary in any important study of these causes. Usually, a group of delinquent boys and girls or of adult criminals is compared with a group of school children or adults in the community who are not delinquent but who are similar in all other important respects to the delinquent group. In this way, criminologists can measure significant differences between the two groups. These differences help to reveal many of the factors responsible for causing the delinquent or criminal group to commit crimes. Descriptions of delinquents or criminals are almost meaningless without a group of nondelinquents or noncriminals (usually called a *control group*) with which to make comparisons.

Rehabilitation. Modern criminology is also interested in the general field of *penology*, or the study of punishment. But it emphasizes treatment, rather than punishment, of the criminal. Prisons and parole systems exist to protect society and to reform the offender. Nearly all persons sent to prison are later released and returned to society. For this reason, the best way to protect society is to discover the major causes of criminal behavior. Then, criminologists and other specialists try to rehabilitate the offender so that on release he will be a well-adjusted citizen.

Capital Punishment. Most criminologists are opposed to the death penalty and to other forms of cruel and revengeful punishments. Modern criminologists favor applying scientific methods to the study of the causes of crime, and the handling of delinquents and criminals in courts, prisons, and upon their release from prisons.

Careers in Criminology

Most criminologists have university training in sociology, psychology, psychiatry, or related areas. Requirements vary for work in criminology, but most professional criminologists have master's or doctor's degrees. Technicians in the field, sometimes called *crimino-technicians* or *criminalists*, are involved in law enforcement, ballistics analysis, and other police investigative work. Other persons who work in the general area of criminology include social workers, such as parole and probation officers or correctional officers in prison; and policy-making administrators, such as prison superintendents, lawyers, and judges.   MARVIN E. WOLFGANG

Related Articles in WORLD BOOK include:

CRINOID. See SEA LILY.

CRINOLINE, *KRIHN oh lin*, is a stiff fabric used for garment interlinings and in the binding of books. Crinoline is made from cotton, rayon, or synthetic fibers. It has a plain weave and a dull finish. It is *sized* (stiffened) with starch, glue, or some other thick substance. Crinoline comes in white, black, or gray, and is made in bolts 27 inches wide. The original crinoline was made from horsehair and linen or cotton yarn. The women of the 1800's used crinoline petticoats to make their huge skirts billow out. That period is often referred to as the "crinoline days." Skirts stiffened by crinoline became popular again in the 1950's.   KENNETH R. FOX

CRIOLLO. See CREOLE.

CRIPPLE. See HANDICAPPED (The Crippled).

CRIPPS, SIR STAFFORD (1889-1952), a noted English statesman and diplomat, held several important governmental posts. He served as ambassador to the Soviet Union from 1940 to 1942, and negotiated a wartime treaty of friendship. In 1942, he worked on a solution to India's demands for independence. India rejected his plan. Also in 1942, he became lord privy seal and leader of the House of Commons, in which he represented East Bristol. Cripps became president of the board of trade in 1945. From 1947 to 1950, he held two important government posts, minister of economic affairs and chancellor of the exchequer. He retired from public life in 1950. Sir Stafford was born RICHARD STAFFORD CRIPPS in London.   C. L. MOWAT

CRISIS, THE. See PAINE, THOMAS (American Revolutionary).

CRISTALLO. See GLASS (The Middle Ages).

CRISTÓBAL, *kris TOH bul* (pop. 817; alt. 10 ft.), is a town in the Panama Canal Zone. It stands at the end of the Canal that opens into the Atlantic Ocean (see PANAMA [map]). Cristóbal has shipping facilities including docks, fueling station, and shipyard. The city serves as the port for the adjoining Panamanian city of Colón.

CRISTOFORI, BARTOLOMMEO. See PIANO (History).

CRITIAS. See THIRTY TYRANTS.

CRITIC is a person who discusses and judges the various arts and types of literature. A true critic strives to analyze and define the art he criticizes, to investigate its principles, and to judge individual works. He tries to maintain high standards of workmanship in the art and to promote appreciation of it.

Critics use various methods for providing useful criticism. Some have stressed basic principles and compared the various arts. For example, Aristotle analyzed Greek drama and Greek epic poetry in his *Poetics* and described the essential differences between them. Others have laid down strict rules and made themselves the dictators of taste in their country. Nicolas Boileau-Despréaux dictated literary taste in France in the 1600's, and Samuel Johnson did the same in England during the 1700's. A number of critics, including Matthew Arnold and John Ruskin, have assumed the role of philosophers, social thinkers, and moralists. Some of the most penetrating and influential criticism has been written by persons who themselves are artists and writers. Outstanding examples include T. S. Eliot, Henry James, George Bernard Shaw, Émile Zola, August Strindberg, Luigi Pirandello, and Allen Tate.   JOHN W. GASSNER

The WORLD BOOK has a separate biography on each critic mentioned in this article. See also CRITICISM.

CRITICAL MASS. See ATOMIC BOMB (Critical Mass); ATOMIC ENERGY (The Birth of the Atomic Age).

CRITICISM is the act, skill, or art of analyzing and judging works of art. The term criticism comes from the Greek *krinein*, which means *to separate* or *to discern*. Creative artists as well as amateur and professional critics have written criticism.

Critical Writings take various forms. They may be prose or verse, short essays or long books, partly biographical works or purely technical ones, or comments by critics and reviewers. The prefaces or introductions authors write for their own works are sometimes critical essays. Victor Hugo's preface to *Cromwell* expressed the ideals of romantic art. Émile Zola outlined the aims of naturalism in literature in his preface to *Thérèse Raquin*. George Bernard Shaw sometimes wrote prefaces nearly as long and almost as important as his plays. His introductions to *Man and Superman* and *Major Barbara* are two famous examples of his critical writing.

Types of Criticism. Criticism may be divided into two main types, impressionistic and objective. *Impressionistic criticism* has been described as "the adventures of the soul among masterpieces." The critic describes his own impressions and feelings about the work he sees. His purpose is to communicate his opinion rather than to analyze the nature of his subject. *Reviewing* is an impressionistic type of criticism that informs the public about a work of art as soon as it is created (see REVIEWING). *Objective criticism* tries to judge a work on the basis of criteria, or standards, that are as free as possible from personal bias. There are many forms of objective criticism. For example, a critic may classify works of art under various categories. He will then compare a particular work with others of the same kind to determine how well it realizes the possibilities of the type of art it represents. A critic may also attempt to explain the character of a particular art and the conditions peculiar to it. For example, he might discuss the differences between plays, which are intended for performance on the stage, and novels, intended for private reading.

Some types of objective criticism are concerned with the basic principles of an art or the arts in general. The philosophy of art makes up a special branch of study known as *aesthetics* (see AESTHETICS). Great philosophers, such as Plato and Aristotle, developed philosophies of art that influenced all later criticism. Historians and sociologists often analyze the history of an art by relating it to the changing conditions of society or to the influence of a particular age. Arnold Hauser's *The Social History of Art* is an example.

The Influence of Criticism on the arts has always been great. From time to time, critics have tried to impose absolute standards on artists. From the 1500's to the 1700's, scholarly critics in France tried to force playwrights to observe strict rules concerning the unity of time, place, and action. The German critic Gotthold Lessing finally helped end this restrictive criticism. Most critics today avoid setting standards for the arts. Much of today's criticism is impressionistic and journalistic. But it has great influence on the public because it indicates the values in works to buy or performances to attend.   JOHN W. GASSNER

See also BOOK REPORT; BOOK REVIEW; CRITIC.

CRITTENDEN COMPROMISE

CRITTENDEN COMPROMISE was a proposal submitted to the United States Senate in 1860 by Senator John Crittenden of Kentucky in an effort to keep the Southern States from leaving the Union. The Compromise proposed six amendments to the Constitution. Among other things it provided that slavery be protected south of 36° 30', and prohibited north of that line. It also denied the right of Congress to abolish slavery "in places under its exclusive jurisdiction." It protected the interstate slave trade, and it provided for compensation by the United States to the owners of slaves who had been helped to escape. Defeat of the Compromise was due partly to President-elect Lincoln's firm stand against any extension of slavery. JOHN D. HICKS

CRO-MAGNON MAN, *kroh MAN yun,* was the first type of modern man. Cro-Magnon people lived in Europe and North Africa between about 25,000 and 8000 B.C. They lived either in caves or in the open, depending on the climate. The name comes from the Cro-Magnon cave near Dordogne, France, where remains were found. These people were splendid physical specimens, averaging about 5 feet 8 inches tall. They had long heads and broad faces. Anthropologists believe that the modern races of Europe are descended from Cro-Magnon Man.

Cro-Magnon people used flint and bone for tools and weapons. Some of their knives and spear points are among the finest stonework ever made. The Cro-Magnons were the first known artists. Archaeologists have found many beautiful cave paintings showing wild cattle, deer, and many other animals. These paintings may have served magic or ceremonial purposes. Cro-Magnon men also carved bone and sculptured clay. They buried their dead in graves, with offerings. Scholars believe they had one of the earliest systems of social organization. WILTON MARION KROGMAN

See also PREHISTORIC MAN (color pictures).

CROATIA AND SLAVONIA, *kroh AY shih uh* and *sluh VOH nih uh,* was a crownland within the Dual Monarchy of Austria-Hungary. With the breakup of Austria-Hungary after World War I, Croatia and Slavonia joined the new Kingdom of the Serbs, Croats, and Slovenes, renamed Yugoslavia in 1929. In 1946, Croatia became one of the people's republics of Yugoslavia. Croatia includes Slavonia, and has a population of 4,160,000, and an area of 21,829 square miles. See also YUGOSLAVIA; ZAGREB. JOSEPH S. ROUCEK

CROATOAN. See LOST COLONY.

CROCE, BENEDETTO (1866-1952), was probably the most distinguished Italian philosopher of the 1900's. He believed that there are two kinds of knowledge: that which comes from understanding and that obtained from the imagination. Croce felt that imagination rules art. He believed that art does not attempt to classify objects as science does, but only feels and presents them. Croce also gained wide attention as the editor of *La Critica,* a journal of literature, philosophy, and history. His works include *Aesthetic* (1902), *Logic* (1905), and *Philosophy of the Practical* (1908).

Croce was appointed a senator in 1910 and served as Italian minister of education from 1920 to 1921. After World War II, he helped form a new government. He was born in Pescasseroli, Italy. EUGENE T. ADAMS

914

Educational Bureau, Coats and Clark, Inc.

A Crocheted Edging adds decoration to guest towels.

CROCHET

Seventeen-at-School

When Learning to Crochet, beginners should use heavy yarn, and follow written directions.

CHAIN STITCH

Make a loop or slipknot in thread and place it on hook.

SINGLE CROCHET

Crochet a chain of 21 stitches. Insert hook in second loop back.

CROCHET, *kroh SHAY,* is a type of lace made by techniques similar to those used in knitting. Crochet lace is heavy and relatively inexpensive. Almost any yarn or thread may be crocheted, but the most common is a hard-twist cotton thread. The lace is made by looping a single yarn or thread into fabric or a chain by means of a needle called a *crochet hook.* It is a narrow piece of metal, bone, wood, or plastic about 6 inches long that ends in a barblike hook. The French word *crochet* (meaning *crook* or *crooked*), applied to this hook, gave the lace its name.

A person can create many more variations of pattern with crochet stitches than with knitting needles. Variety in pattern is achieved by combining the three main stitches: chain, single crochet, and double crochet. The *chain* stitch is used to cast on and create pattern spaces. A loop of thread is placed upon the hook. The thread is wound over the needle, and drawn through this loop. *Single crochet* creates solid-pattern shapes and bars in an openwork pattern. *Double crochet* is used in the same way as single crochet, but is twice as wide. Other crochet stitches include *netting,* the *rose stitch,* and the *shell stitch.*

The Pineapple Design is one of the most popular crochet patterns for doilies.

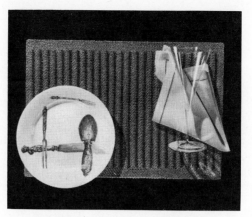

A Luncheon Place Mat, crocheted in the "rippling river" pattern with gold metallic thread, is both decorative and durable.

Courtesy Educational Bureau, Coats and Clark Inc.

Matching Sets of hats and handbags can be made with large hooks and heavy yarn.

Arrange thread from ball around fingers of left hand.

Hold the work with thumb and forefinger of the left hand.

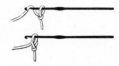

Catch thread and pull it back through loop for first stitch.

Continue making chain stitches. Practice makes even stitches.

Catch the thread and draw it back through the chain.

Catch the thread again and draw it back through both.

Continue to make a single crochet in each chain stitch.

At end of row, make a chain, turn work, and start second row.

Crocheting is done with fine thread and a fine hook for lacy doilies and trimmings. A medium thread and needle are used for crocheting bedspreads, gloves, and potholders. With wool yarn and a needle of medium size, a person can crochet stoles, berets, sweaters, and afghans.

Heavy yarns or fabric strips may be crocheted with a large hook to make rugs or mats.

Crocheting is an ancient craft. Although the lace can be made by machine, craftsmen in Belgium, Italy, France, and China continue to produce it by hand. An excellent type of Italian crochet work is called *Orvieto lace*.

The Irish have made perhaps the most beautiful crochet. Crochet lace was introduced into Ireland about 1820. Using very fine thread, Irish women developed a type of lace using a series of three-leafed shamrocks, roses, and little rings surrounded by a lacy background of chain stitches with small *picots*, or knots. This type of lace can be recognized by the whiteness of the linen thread used. Irish lace is used mainly for such things as collars, trimmings, and doilies.   HELEN MARLEY CALAWAY

CROCKETT, DAVID (1786-1836), was one of the most famous frontiersmen in United States history. A hunter, scout, soldier, and Congressman, he also became a humorist who wrote and told tall tales about himself. An expert shot, he once reported he had killed 105 bears in nine months. A folk tale relates that once when he aimed his rifle at a raccoon in a tree, the animal recognized Crockett and said, "Don't shoot, Colonel. I'll come down. I know when I'm a gone coon."

Early Life. Crockett was born on Aug. 17, 1786, in Greene County, Tennessee. At 13, he ran away from home for three years. He then returned home and worked for a year to pay a $76 debt owed by his father, an innkeeper. When he was 18, Crockett married Polly Finley. When his first wife died, he married a young widow, Elizabeth Patton. The Crocketts moved four times, each time farther into the wilds of western Tennessee.

In 1813, Crockett volunteered as a scout for Andrew Jackson, who was ordered to subdue the warring Creek Indians. He later served in the Tennessee militia and won the rank of colonel.

915

"Davy" Crockett, *right,* was a scout, soldier, and politician. He is credited with many frontier adventures, including fights with such wild animals as the cougar, *above.*

Political Career. Crockett's first political office was as justice of the peace. His sincere manner and funny stories won him a seat in the Tennessee legislature from 1821 to 1823. In 1826, someone, as a joke, nominated him for the U.S. Congress. During the campaign tour, a flock of noisy guinea hens wandered into a meeting and drowned out Crockett's opponent's speech with their "cr-cr-kt" sounds. Crockett rose to say that those hens had been saying "Crockett!" He imitated their sounds to make them resemble his name. The story was repeated everywhere, and he won the election.

In Washington, D.C., Crockett and his stories caused a sensation. He served three terms between 1827 and 1835. He voted independently, and ardently disliked President Andrew Jackson's land and Indian policies.

Crockett's career as an author began when he wrote *A Narrative of the Life of David Crockett.* Although several more books are credited to him, he wrote only two others, *An Account of Colonel Crockett's Tour to the North and Down East,* and *Colonel Crockett's Exploits and Adventures in Texas.*

The Alamo. After leaving Congress, Crockett joined 181 Americans in the Alamo in San Antonio, where 5,000 Mexicans besieged them. The Americans fought to the last man, and Crockett died in the final assault on Mar. 6, 1836, his body riddled with bullets. Bold and brave, Crockett rates with Daniel Boone as a great frontiersman. HOWARD R. LAMAR

See also FOLKLORE (American Folklore); FINK, MIKE.

CROCODILE, *CROCK oh dile,* is one of the largest living reptiles. Crocodiles, alligators, gavials, and caymans look much alike, and are all called *crocodilians.* Both crocodiles and alligators have a long, low, cigar-shaped body, short legs, and long powerful tails with which they swim. They both have tough hides, long snouts, and sharp teeth to grasp their prey. In most crocodiles, however, the snout comes to a point in front, where an alligator's snout is rounded. The American crocodile is only about two-thirds as heavy as an old American alligator of the same length, and can move much more quickly. The lower fourth tooth is extra long in both animals. It fits into a pit in the alligator's upper jaw, but the crocodile's fourth tooth fits into a groove in the side of the upper jaw.

Crocodiles live in tropical countries throughout the world. They prefer large bodies of shallow water, sluggish rivers, open swamps, and marshes. Their webbed feet allow them to walk on the soft ground. Their eyes and nostrils are higher than the rest of the head. This arrangement fits in with the crocodile's life in the water, for it likes to float with only its eyes and nostrils above the surface. Its throat has a slit-like valve just in front of the tube leading to its nostrils. This valve shuts tight when the animal is under water. It keeps the water from entering through the mouth when the reptile seizes its prey.

Crocodiles eat many small animals, such as fishes, birds, and mammals, which they seize and swallow whole. Occasionally they attack large animals and men. A crocodile can twist a large animal into pieces by seizing a part of it and then rapidly turning lengthwise in the water. These reptiles are more aggressive than the

The Nile Crocodile of Africa was considered sacred by the ancient Egyptians. This type of crocodile is a vicious killer which sometimes leaves the water to attack humans. It may grow to be 20 feet long.

The Man-Eating Nile Crocodile, *left,* has a sharper snout than that of the American alligator, *right.*

Zoological Society of Philadelphia

The Jaws of a Crocodile can easily snap a heavy wooden board in two. Yet a man can hold the vicious mouth shut with his hands. The great power centers in closing the jaws.

American or Chinese alligators. Large wild ones should be left strictly alone.

Like most reptiles, crocodiles lay eggs. These look like hens' eggs, but are longer and have a less brittle shell. Crocodiles conceal their eggs in nests of rubbish and vegetation, or bury them in sand beaches. The female of some types guards the nest until the young are hatched. When she can hear them grunting, she digs them out. Not much is known about the breeding habits and general behavior of crocodiles.

Most of the true crocodiles inhabit the Eastern Hemisphere, but four species live in North and South America. The *American crocodile* lives in the extreme south of Florida, on the larger West Indian islands, and in Central America and areas near it. The usual length of adult American crocodiles is about 12 feet. The *Nile crocodile* reigns supreme in Africa. It lives almost everywhere on the continent except in the Sahara desert and on the northern coast. This reptile was known by ancient peoples and described by the Greek historian, Herodotus. The small, long-snouted crocodile of the Congo Basin grows no longer than 8 feet. The two kinds of dwarf crocodilians of Africa, one of which is very rare, are closely related to true crocodiles.

The giant *salt-water crocodile* lives in many places from India to northern Australia, and even in the Solomon Islands. The *mugger* lives in India, and the *Siamese crocodile* inhabits Java, Thailand, and nearby parts of Asia. There is also an *Australian crocodile*. Sumatra and the Malay Peninsula have the false *gavial*. The false gavial has a narrower snout than most other crocodilians.

The crocodilians are remnants of a large and ancient group of reptiles. Marks these reptiles have left on rocks show they once reached a length of 50 feet. This is more than twice as long as any crocodiles living today. There are now 12 species of crocodiles.

Crocodiles are important in commerce. The tough skin makes a high-grade leather that manufacturers frequently use in making such products as traveling bags, handbags, and shoes. Crocodile musk glands are used in the manufacture of perfume.

Scientific Classification. Crocodiles belong to the family *Crocodylidae*. The Nile crocodile is genus *Crocodylus*, species *C. niloticus*. The American crocodile is classified as *C. americanus*.   CLIFFORD H. POPE

See also ALLIGATOR; CROCODILE BIRD; GAVIAL; LIFE (table, Length of Life of Animals); REPTILE.

The Crocodile Bird has earned the name "Zic-zac" because of its noisy cry.

CROCODILE BIRD is an African bird that is a close relative of the plover. The crocodile bird flies down and feeds on insects living on the crocodile. It is said that the crocodile bird will even enter the open mouth of the crocodile and feed on the leeches it finds living there. The birds are especially common along the Nile River.

A. W. Ambler, NAS

Scientific Classification. The crocodile bird belongs to the family *Glareolidae*. It is classified as genus *Pluvianus*, species *P. aegyptius*.   ALFRED M. BAILEY

CROCUS, *KROH kuhs,* is a flowering herblike plant that grows in southern Europe and Asia, and is cultivated in many regions of the world. The crocus plant grows from a thick, bulblike stem called a *corm*. The leaves look like large leaves of grass. Crocus flowers grow at ground level. Each blossom is made up of six nearly equal segments, and has three stamens and a pistil. Some crocuses bloom early in spring, and others bloom in the autumn.

Gardeners plant crocuses about 3 inches deep in rich, well-drained soil. New corms form on top of old ones, so gardeners replant crocuses every few years. Probably the most popular crocuses are the purple and *cloth-of-gold*, a brilliant orange yellow. The autumn crocus is *colchicum*. The *wild crocus*, also called the pasqueflower, is an anemone, not a true crocus (see ANEMONE).

Crocus is the Latin word for *saffron*. Saffron was once used extensively to make a yellow dye and as a spice for food. Commercial saffron is obtained from the dried

Crocus Flowers are funnel-shaped. The most common varieties are colored yellow, purple, lilac, or white.

J. C. Allen and Son

stigma of crocus plants cultivated chiefly in France, Italy, and Spain. The dye has largely been replaced by aniline dyes.

Scientific Classification. Spring crocuses belong to the iris family, *Iridaceae*. They make up the genus *Crocus*. The cloth-of-gold crocus is genus *Crocus*, species *C. susianus*. Autumn crocuses belong to the lily family, *Liliaceae*. They are genus *Colchicum*.   ALFRED C. HOTTES

See also ANILINE; COLCHICUM; FLOWER (color picture: Spring Garden Flowers); SAFFRON.

CROESUS, *KREE sus* (reigned 560-546 B.C.), was the last king of Lydia, a country in what is now western Turkey. His great wealth inspired the phrase *rich as Croesus*. Croesus raised Lydia to the peak of its power, conquering Greek coastal cities and extending his empire to the Halys River in central Asia Minor.

Croesus succeeded his father, Alyattes, as king. In 549 B.C., he formed an alliance with Babylonia, Egypt, and Sparta against Persia. Croesus attacked the Persians in 546 B.C., expecting help from his allies. But help could not reach him, and he withdrew to Sardis, his capital city. Cyrus, the Persian leader, followed him there, and defeated him.

Some historians believe Croesus was burned to death. Others say Cyrus made him governor of Media, a Persian province.   JACOB J. FINKELSTEIN

See also ORACLES.

CROFTING. See BLEACHING.

CROIX DE GUERRE. See DECORATIONS AND MEDALS (France; color picture).

CROLY, HERBERT (1869-1930), was an American political philosopher. He favored the development of large corporations and labor unions. He believed they would result in more goods, lower costs, and higher wages. Croly's most important book was *The Promise of American Life* (1909). It warned against the carelessness and wastefulness of American economic planning in the past, and called for a national program of discipline and economic planning under a strong central government. It also called for a tax on the incomes of corporations, a federal inheritance tax, and support of trade unions.

Croly was born in New York City. He graduated from Harvard University in 1910. In 1914, he founded the *New Republic* magazine.   CHARLES FORCEY and LINDA FORCEY

CROMPTON, SAMUEL (1753-1827), was an English weaver. By 1779, he had developed an improved spinning machine that led to major growth in the cotton industry. The new machine was called *the mule* because it was a cross between two machines, the spinning jenny and the water frame, while a mule is a cross between two animals. The mule made the strong, uniform cotton yarn required for fine muslin and calico.

Crompton did not get a patent on his machine, and he received little of the money that cloth manufacturers promised him. But Parliament gave him a national gift of $25,000 in 1812 when he was able to show that the more than 4½ million mules in use had revolutionized the cotton industry. Crompton was born at Firwood, Lancashire.   MONTE A. CALVERT

CROMWELL, OLIVER (1599-1658), led the forces of Parliament during the English Civil War. He ruled England during the period of the Commonwealth and

Oliver Cromwell

Protectorate (1649-1658). Few men have inspired more love and reverence, and at the same time more fear and hatred. Cromwell was a man of iron will, true to a high moral purpose.

Cromwell was born at Huntingdon. His family had been favored by the English kings. He studied at Sidney Sussex College, Cambridge, and in 1620 married Elizabeth Bourchier. He was elected to Parliament in 1628. In 1640, Cromwell was elected to what became known as the Short Parliament and to the Long Parliament that followed (see LONG PARLIAMENT).

The Civil War. When the Civil War broke out in 1642, Cromwell became the leading force in Parliament. He had had no military experience until he was 40, but he was a born military genius. He trained his cavalry until he had the best-drilled regiments in England. He picked men for their religious enthusiasm as well as for their military forcefulness, and never lost a battle. In 1645, the Self-Denying Ordinance was passed, excluding members of Parliament from military command. But an exception was made in favor of Cromwell, who continued to lead his "Ironsides," as his forces were called.

When the break came between the two factions of the Puritans, the Presbyterians and the Independents, Cromwell sided with the Independents. He strengthened his hold on the army, while the Presbyterians dominated Parliament. Cromwell feared that the Presbyterians would restore the tyrannical king, Charles I, to power. He finally agreed to the execution of the king, and was one of the signers of the king's death warrant.

The Protectorate. The Long Parliament had been in session for 12 years, but its members refused to disband or submit to Cromwell. He disbanded the Long Parliament in 1653 with the aid of his troops, and summoned a new one. But the new Parliament was not able to accomplish anything, and dissolved of its own accord. The officers of the army then took matters into their hands. They drew up the *Instrument of Government*, and made Cromwell Lord Protector. A Parliament was assembled, but the members seemed to have no purpose except to remain in Parliament. Cromwell dissolved it and relied on the army for support. The only other Parliament which he ever called, in 1656, offered him the title of king, which he refused. Although Cromwell was a determined opponent of absolutism, he governed almost as absolutely as had Charles I. The troubled conditions of the times forced him to adopt stern measures.

After Cromwell's death, his son, Richard (1626-1712), tried to continue his father's policy, but he lacked the strength. In May, 1659, he had to resign, and the people of England welcomed the return of King Charles II in 1660.   W. M. SOUTHGATE

Related Articles in WORLD BOOK include:

Cavalier	Ironsides	Restoration
Charles (I; II) of England	Puritan	Roundhead
Furniture (English)		

CROMWELL, RICHARD (1626-1712), ruled England as lord protector from September, 1658, to May, 1659. He succeeded his father, Oliver Cromwell, as lord protector. But he could not govern effectively, and a group of political and army leaders forced him to resign. In 1660, Parliament invited Charles Stuart to return from the Continent and rule as Charles II. Cromwell fled to France. He returned to England about 1680 and lived under a different name in Cheshunt for the rest of his life.

Cromwell was born in Huntingdon. He fought with Parliament's forces against King Charles I during the English Civil War (1642-1648). Cromwell was admitted to the Council of State and was named chancellor of Oxford University in 1657.   VERNON F. SNOW

CROMWELL, THOMAS (1485?-1540), was a trusted adviser to King Henry VIII of England. A talented and ruthless administrator, Cromwell directed England's civil and religious affairs in the 1530's.

Cromwell is often called the architect of the English Reformation for his part in establishing Protestantism in England. Pope Clement VII had refused Henry's request for a divorce from Catherine of Aragon. Cromwell showed Henry that he could get the divorce by breaking with the Roman Catholic Church and by making himself head of an independent Church of England. Cromwell seized property belonging to monasteries for the king and demanded total obedience to the new religion. But later he fell from favor, and was beheaded.

Historians believe Cromwell was born in Putney, England. He became an assistant to Thomas Cardinal Wolsey in 1524. When Wolsey fell from power in 1529, Cromwell became principal secretary, vicar general, and lord privy seal. He was made Earl of Essex and lord chancellor in 1539.   LACEY BALDWIN SMITH

CRONIN, A. J. (1896-   ), a British physician, became the author of several popular novels. He wrote *Hatter's Castle* (1931), his first novel, while recovering from an illness. This story of country life in Scotland brought Cronin literary fame. Cronin developed a pattern of centering his novels on a single problem or profession. *The Stars Look Down* (1935) describes poor working conditions in an English mining community. *The Citadel* (1937) is the story of a young Scottish doctor and also a critical study of the medical profession. *The Keys to the Kingdom* (1942) is a moving story about a Roman Catholic missionary priest in China.

ARCHIBALD JOSEPH CRONIN was born in Cardross, Scotland. He studied at the University of Glasgow and practiced medicine from 1919 to 1930. He moved to the United States in the mid-1940's.   JOHN ESPEY

CRONOS. See SATURN (god).

CROOKES, SIR WILLIAM (1832-1919), made many contributions to physics and chemistry. He invented the Crookes tube; the radiometer, which measures light energy; and the spinthariscope, a device for studying radioactivity. In 1886, he stated that some elements contain isotopes, or atoms which differ in weight. Crookes isolated the element thallium, and believed that all elements originally came from one fundamental substance. Crookes ranked as the foremost authority of his time on the industrial uses of chemistry.

Crookes was born in London and studied at the Royal College of Chemistry.   R. T. ELLICKSON

See also RADIOMETER; SPINTHARISCOPE.

CROOKES TUBE, *krooks*, is an electric vacuum tube with which Sir William Crookes performed experiments that led eventually to the discovery of the electron. The

The Crookes Tube is used to produce cathode rays.

device is a glass tube from which the air has been pumped. Metal wires, serving as electrodes, are sealed into opposite ends of the tube. When the electrodes are connected with a source of high voltage, some interesting effects take place as a result of the discharge of electricity through the small amount of gas that remains in the tube. A greenish fluorescence appears on the walls of the tube, and a piece of metal placed in front of the *cathode* (negative electrode) throws a shadow on the fluorescence at the other end. These effects are caused by cathode rays, which were later proved to be streams of electrons projected from the cathode. The electron is the smallest unit of negative electricity.   MARCEL SCHEIN

See also CATHODE RAYS; CROOKES, SIR WILLIAM.

CROP (of birds). See BIRD (Digestion).

CROP is a large number of plants of any given kind that are grown for man's use. Crops may be grown to feed man and the animals he raises for food. These are called *food crops*. Other crops produce fiber for use in clothing, paper, and other products. These are called *fiber crops*. Others are grown to *ornament* (decorate) man's surroundings.

Food crops include fruits, vegetables, *forage* (animal feed), and grains such as barley, corn, oats, rice, and wheat. Cotton, flax, and hemp provide fiber crops. Ornamental crops include flowers, lawn grasses, shrubs, and decorative trees.   WILLIAM RAYMOND KAYS

For more detailed information, see AGRICULTURE (Growing Crops).

CROP DUSTER. See AIRPLANE (On the Farm; picture: Crop-Dusting Airplanes).

CROP INSURANCE provides partial protection for a farmer's income in case of bad weather or loss of crops. It is usually a government program, because poor crop conditions over a wide area could ruin an insurance company. In the United States, the Federal Crop Insurance Corporation has insured such major crops as corn, cotton, tobacco, and wheat since 1938. The usual plan provides indemnities for insured farmers when their production falls below 50 or 75 per cent of average yield for the farm. The crop insurance program has been experimental, and has covered only a fraction of the total crop grown. Total premiums paid have ranged from $17 million to $51 million.   HAROLD G. HALCROW

See also FEDERAL CROP INSURANCE CORPORATION.

CROPPING SYSTEM is a method of growing crops and producing high yields without weakening the soil. It involves the combination of many cultivation methods to make the best possible use of the land. Farmers must consider the composition of their soil and the slope, drainage, and *erosion* (wearing away) problems of their land in determining the crops and production methods best suited for their land. Two important

CROQUET

cultivation methods are the rotation of crops and the use of proper fertilizers.

One of the oldest and most widely used ways of preserving the soil is through the *rotation of crops* (alternating the crops grown in a field from one year to the next). A single crop will use up vital minerals and organic matter in the soil if it is grown in the same field year after year. But different kinds of crops planted in the field on a regular schedule will replace lost minerals and organic matter. For example, corn takes nitrogen out of the soil, while crops such as alfalfa and clover put nitrogen into the soil. If corn is planted in a field one year, alfalfa or clover may be planted in it the next year to replace the nitrogen used by the corn crop. The nitrogen producing crop can also be plowed into the soil. When it rots, it replaces lost organic matter and enriches the soil.

On sloping land, grasses and deep-rooted crops are often alternated with other crops to hold the soil in place and prevent erosion.

The use of fertilizers is gradually replacing the crop rotation system as a means of producing the most profitable crops year after year while still keeping soil fertile. Nitrogen fertilizers and other fertilizers have been developed that can be used to return lost minerals and organic matter to the soil. When these fertilizers are added, and the proper cultivation methods are used, the same crop can be planted in a field year after year without harming the soil. If nitrogen fertilizer is added to the soil, corn can be planted in the same field for many years.

Other developments which save the soil include chemical insecticides and fungicides that kill harmful insects, weeds, and fungus growths.   WILLIAM R. VAN DERSAL

CROQUET, *kroh KAY,* is a game that appeals to persons of almost all ages. It is popular with families, because it may easily be set up on lawns or in other play areas. Many municipal recreation departments have installed croquet courts, as have some parks and schools. Croquet is played outdoors on smooth grass for informal play, and on clay courts for tournaments. Play can be simple, or involve carefully planned strategy.

A Croquet Set consists of eight wooden balls painted in four colors; mallets with which to hit the balls; two stakes; and nine wide arches called *wickets*. The game requires an oblong, level, reasonably smooth area. Court dimensions may vary according to the space available, but should, if possible, be at least 30 by 60 feet. The stakes should be centered at each end of the court, and the wickets placed in positions according to the accompanying diagram. In informal play, the placement of the wickets may be varied, adding to the challenge of the game.

The Game is usually played by four persons in two teams, each player with a mallet and one ball of matching color. Partners assist each other whenever possible. The game also may be played by two or three teams, or by two, three, or four individuals.

The object of the game is to hit the ball through all the wickets from stake to stake and back again. The ball passes through the first two wickets, then to the near right wicket, the center one, the far right one, and through the far double wickets to hit the stake. It returns to the home stake through the wickets on the other side in the same order. The player or team finishing the course first wins.

A player may hit the ball only once each turn. But he gets two strokes if his ball goes through a wicket, hits a stake, or hits an opponent's ball. If his ball hits that of an opponent, he may do one of several things. He may place his ball beside the other and hit it so that the other ball is sent out of position. This is done by putting his foot firmly on his own ball so that it will not move when he hits it. He then proceeds with his second shot. He also may hit both balls without using his foot, thus driving them both away. Other alternatives are placing his ball (1) two mallet lengths from the opponent's ball and taking one shot, or (2) one mallet's length and taking two shots. He may not hit the ball of an opponent again until he has passed through a wicket. A ball that has been hit once, or touched, is "dead." A "dead" ball may not be played again until the opponent has played.

Roque, which is the word croquet without the *c* and *t,* is the form of croquet used in league play in the United States. It uses 10 wickets, and the court is often

Culver

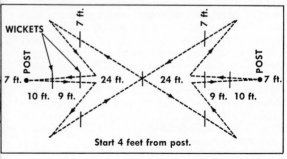

Croquet gained popularity in the 1800's. It won distinction as the first game played in the United States by both men and women, *left.* The informal croquet court, *below,* requires 9 *wickets.*

WICKETS

POST

POST

7 ft. ● - - - - 24 ft. ✳ 24 ft. - - - - ● 7 ft.

7 ft.   7 ft.

10 ft. 9 ft.   9 ft. 10 ft.

Start 4 feet from post.

surrounded by a low wall from which the balls may rebound. The standard size of the court is 50 by 100 feet. Points are scored in roque, one for each wicket passed through and stake hit, with 16 points to win a game. A simplified version of croquet may be played inside on a table.

History. Croquet originated in France, where it was first known as *jeu de le maillet*. Later, it became known as *pall-mall* in England, and gave its name to a famous London street. It came to the United States with the early settlers. DOROTHY DONALDSON

CRORE. See RUPEE.

CROSBY, BING (1904-   ), is one of the most popular singers and motion-picture stars in the United States. During the 1930's he made the "crooning" style of singing famous throughout the world. He won an award in 1944 from the Academy of Motion Picture Arts and Sciences for his performance as a singing priest in the film *Going My Way*.

Wide World

Bing Crosby

He was born HARRY LILLIS CROSBY in Tacoma, Wash., and studied law for a time. He started his career in 1924 with a Los Angeles dance band. By 1931, he was a member of the "Rhythm Boys," a singing trio with Paul Whiteman's orchestra. Radio performances and phonograph records increased Crosby's fame. He had four sons by his first wife, the late Dixie Lee. He and his second wife, actress Kathryn Grant, have two sons and a daughter. HARRIET VAN HORNE

CROSS is a sacred emblem of the Christian faith. It is a symbol of redemption, signifying Christ's death on the cross for man's sins.

Use Through the Ages. Slaves and criminals were punished on the cross, or crucified, long before the time of Jesus. They were tied or nailed to a standing cross until they died of thirst or hunger. Such a cross was made by fastening a piece of wood to a tree or pole. The arms of the condemned man were attached to this wood, or beam. Then he was lifted to an upright position. The prisoners often had to carry these beams to the places where they were to die. The New Testament says Jesus was forced to do this (John 19: 17).

The cross has had an enduring part in the profession of the Christian faith. The use of the cross as a symbol of faith goes back at least as far as the A.D. 100's. Tertullian, an early Christian writer, says that the Christians of his time used it daily. In his writings, St. Augustine speaks of the way the sign of the cross was used in performing *sacraments* (the sacred acts of the Church).

Roman Catholics touch the fingers to the forehead, breast, left shoulder, and right shoulder. The Russian and Greek churches touch the right shoulder first.

Crosses were put up to mark the graves of heroes, kings, and bishops during the Middle Ages. Often, too, crosses were set up in market places. People preached beneath them. Today, churches often have a floor plan in the shape of a cross. Many forms of the cross have come down to us. The *Latin cross* is said to be the kind

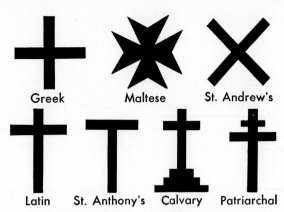

Greek   Maltese   St. Andrew's

Latin   St. Anthony's   Calvary   Patriarchal

Various Forms of Crosses Famous in History

on which Jesus died. It is a long upright pole with a crosspiece near the top. FULTON J. SHEEN

Other Crosses. The *Greek cross* has four arms of the same length. Another name for it is the *Cross of Saint George*. This cross is used with the *Cross of Saint Andrew* and the *Cross of Saint Patrick* to form the British Union Flag. In this British flag, the Cross of Saint George stands for England, the Cross of Saint Andrew for Scotland, and the Cross of Saint Patrick for Ireland (see FLAG [color picture: Historical Flags of the World]). The *Maltese cross* with eight sharp points was used as an emblem by an order of knights of the Middle Ages.

See also CATHEDRAL; IRELAND (picture).

CROSS-COUNTRY is a type of long-distance racing in track and field sports. Runners usually race across fields, through woods, and over hills. Because distances and terrains differ for each race, no national or world records exist for this event. In the United States, the National Federation of High School Athletic Associations has set a minimum distance of $1\frac{1}{2}$ miles and a maximum distance of 3 miles for races. The National Collegiate Athletic Association and the Amateur Athletic Union have set a 3-mile minimum and a 7-mile maximum. Races that exceed 7 miles are not cross-country events. See also TRACK AND FIELD.

CROSS-EYE, or CROSSED EYE, is a general term describing eyes that do not look straight ahead. Doctors call this condition STRABISMUS or SQUINT. In most cross-eyed persons, one eye looks straight ahead while the other eye looks in toward the nose, upward, or out toward the side.

The most common form of cross-eye occurs in farsighted children under the age of 4. To see clearly, farsighted children often force their eyes together. This results in strabismus. This condition can be corrected in part or completely by eyeglasses.

Cross-eye may also be inherited. It may result from eye muscles weakened by scar tissue or partly paralyzed muscular nerves. Cross-eye may also result from being able to use only one eye to see.

A child with one eye always crossed does not see double. But his vision will not develop properly unless this condition is corrected. Blindness may even result. A child with cross-eye should be treated by an eye physician. Surgery may be necessary to correct the eye muscles. WILLIAM F. HUGHES

CROSS OF GOLD. See BRYAN (William Jennings).

CROSS-POLLINATION

CROSS-POLLINATION is a method by which many plants form seeds to grow new plants. Male pollen produced in anthers of stamens and female eggs produced in *ovaries* (seed cases) of pistils form seeds. Plants that make seeds in their own pistils with the pollen of other plants are *cross-pollinating* plants. Some willow trees, for example, have only male stamens, and others have only female pistils. Each new plant thus formed has two parent plants. A plant which makes seeds from its own stamens and pistils is called *self-pollinating*.

Purdy, U.S.D.A.

Self-Pollination of Onion Plants. Sometimes plant breeders wish to have flowers fertilized only by the pollen of the plants on which they grow. The flowers of the plants shown in this picture have been put into separate cellophane bags along with some flies. As they move from flower to flower, the flies deposit pollen on the pistils of the same plant.

Pollen may be carried from one plant to another by wind, water, insects, or birds. The plants are constructed so they can help the pollination. Many flowers, for example, contain nectar to attract birds and insects. The orchid carries its pollen in a sticky bundle which sticks to the insect when it reaches for the nectar. When the insect goes on to the next flower, the pollen is brushed onto the pistil when the insect pushes in for the nectar. The milkweed has its pollen in two little masses which are connected by a kind of strap. The bee gets its feet tangled in the strap and carries away the pollen, leaving it in the next flower. WILLIAM C. BEAVER

See also BREEDING; BURBANK, LUTHER; FLOWER (How Flowers Reproduce); HYBRID; POLLEN AND POLLINATION.

CROSS REFERENCE is a method used in books, indexes, library catalogs, and filing systems to direct attention to additional information about a subject in another part of the book or index. Cross references are widely used in encyclopedias, dictionaries, and textbooks. For instance, this article on CROSS REFERENCE mentions indexes. At the end of the article there is a cross reference reading "See also INDEX." The reader can find more information about indexes in that article. This type of cross reference is sometimes called a *related subject* or *article*. Cross references may also appear within the text of an article or chapter. THE WORLD BOOK ENCYCLOPEDIA article on the famous American author whose pen name was Mark Twain illustrates another kind of cross reference. Because he is best known as Mark Twain, his biography is given under TWAIN, MARK. But because his real name was Samuel Langhorne Clemens, there is an entry CLEMENS, SAMUEL LANGHORNE, which refers the reader to the article on Mark Twain in inverted form: Twain, Mark. This is a direct reference, and will be "See TWAIN, MARK," not "See also." Some books use the symbols *cf.* (from the Latin *confer*, meaning *compare*), or *q.v.* (from the Latin *quod vide*, meaning *which see*). R. B. DOWNS

See also INDEX.

CROSSBILL is a gentle, friendly bird of the finch family. The ends of its bill cross each other.

The male red, or American, crossbill is colored brick red, with wings and tail of brown. It is about the size of an English sparrow. The plumage of the female is a slightly mottled, greenish yellow. This bird breeds from the northern states northward. In the region of the Allegheny Mountains, it breeds as far south as the Carolinas. In winter, crossbills wander in small flocks to the Gulf of Mexico, and west as far as Idaho and Arizona. They build their nests in the upper half of an evergreen, and the female lays 3 or 4 pale-greenish eggs with purple or lilac spots. Crossbills feed chiefly on seeds of cone-bearing trees. They also eat small quantities of buds and a few insects. The bird uses its crossed bill to lift the scales from the cones to get the seeds.

The white-winged crossbill is similar in habits to the red crossbill. It breeds from the northern states northward and wanders in winter as far south as Virginia.

Scientific Classification. The crossbills belong to the finch family, *Fringillidae*. The red crossbill is genus *Loxia*, species *L. curvirostra*, variety *minor*. The white-winged crossbill is *L. leucoptera*. ARTHUR A. ALLEN

See also FINCH.

The Red Crossbill Feeds on Seeds from Cones.

Culver

Powerful Crossbows called arbalests could pierce ordinary plate armor. An archer, *left*, sets a crossbow with a windlass and tackle system used in the 1400's. Archers, *right*, protect soldiers storming a fort.

CROSSBOW was a popular weapon in the Middle Ages. It has a short, stiff bow set across the end of a stock. The bowman draws its string back and hooks it on a *nut* (catch). He places a short *quarrel* (arrow) against the string, aims, and shoots by pulling a trigger that releases the nut. The crossbow was so stiff that the bowman put his foot in a stirrup at one end and pulled the string taut with a hook or cord. It could be cocked and held ready, but was slower and had a much shorter range than the longbow. See also ARCHERY.

CROSSROADS OF AMERICA. See INDIANA; INDIANAPOLIS.

CROSSROADS OF THE PACIFIC. See HONOLULU.

CROSSROADS OF THE SOUTH. See JACKSON (Miss.).

CROSSROADS OF THE WORLD. See PANAMA.

CROTON, *KROH tun,* is a group of popular shrubs belonging to the spurge family. They grow in Florida and California, and in tropical climates throughout the world. The leaves have smooth edges and are often lobed. They may be spotted, streaked, or banded with yellow, white, green, and red. Because of these colors, the leaves are often used in wreaths. The flowers are small and hardly noticeable. The fruits are round and split into two berrylike parts.

J. Horace McFarland

Leaves of the Croton are mottled with bright colors. On some plants no two leaves have the same pattern.

Crotons grow best in good soil with a fair amount of moisture. Croton plants are used in lawns and parks, and in tubs on porches and patios.

Scientific Classification. The common croton belongs to the spurge family, *Euphorbiaceae.* It is genus *Codiaeum,* species *C. variegatum,* variety *pictum.* J. J. LEVISON

CROTON BUG. See COCKROACH.

CROUP, *kroop,* is an inflammation of the air passages that commonly occurs with respiratory infections. Children between the ages of 2 and 6 seem to be most susceptible. The condition is caused by anything that interferes with the passage of air to and from the lungs.

For example, the small muscles that control breathing may not function properly. Sometimes pressure on the windpipe closes it so that air cannot pass through freely. In severe cases, a membrane may form over the airway, allowing no air to pass. This occurs most often in diphtheria (see DIPHTHERIA). Doctors call this condition *membranous croup.* Infections caused by streptococci and the influenza bacilli often result in croup.

Children with croup usually have symptoms common to all infectious diseases, such as a general feeling of discomfort, loss of appetite, and fever. Soon they develop the typical "croup cough," a hollow, barking sound that ends with a peculiar high-pitched whistle as they inhale. They breathe with a loud crowing or wheezing sound. As the condition progresses, they may turn blue because they cannot obtain enough air.

Doctors treat croup as they do other infectious diseases. They use drugs that destroy the germs which cause the condition. They often prescribe vaporizers to aid breathing. If membranous croup develops, it cuts off all passage of air. Then a surgeon often cuts an opening through the child's throat into the windpipe and inserts a metal tube. This life-saving operation allows the child to breathe again. ALBERT P. SELTZER

CROUPIER. See ROULETTE.

CROUSE, RUSSEL (1893-1966), wrote and produced many popular plays with Howard Lindsay. They wrote *Life with Father* (1939), which set a Broadway record for the number of consecutive performances. Crouse and Lindsay won a Pulitzer prize for *State of the Union* (1945). They also produced *Arsenic and Old Lace* (1945) and *Detective Story* (1949). Russel Crouse was born in Findlay, Ohio. See also LINDSAY, HOWARD. GEORGE FREEDLEY

CROW is the name of a group of large black birds. The crow family includes crows, jays, ravens, magpies, rooks, jackdaws, and fish crows. Crows live in all parts of the world except New Zealand. The common crow is a clever, fearless bird often seen in meadows, orchards, and woods throughout much of North America. It usually winters in the United States or farther south.

The common crow is about 18 or 19 inches long. It has glossy black plumage and a strong, sharp-pointed bill. Bristly feathers cover the base of the bill. The crow's feet are strong and well-adapted for walking. Male and female crows look about the same, but the female is

The Common Crow of North America is a very intelligent bird which can easily be tamed for a pet. Some crows have been taught to talk as clearly as parrots do.

Arthur W. Ambler, NAS

slightly smaller. The crow does not have a musical voice, but it can make a variety of noises and can imitate sounds. Crows make good pets if obtained when young. Sometimes their owners can teach them to speak a few words like parrots do. Crows build their bulky nests along hedges or high in treetops. The female lays four to six eggs. The eggs are pale bluish-green, with irregular blotches and spots of brown and gray.

Farmers do not like crows because they pull up sprouting corn and eat it. They also eat young birds and eggs. But crows help farmers by eating insect pests. Scientists estimate that on an average farm, crows will eat 19 bushels of insects in a single season. The crow's diet varies with the time of year and the kinds of food available to him.

Scientific Classification. The crow belongs to the crow family, *Corvidae*. The common crow is genus *Corvus*, species *C. brachyrhynchos*.   ALBERT WOLFSON

Related Articles in WORLD BOOK include:

Blue Jay	Jay	Raven
Jackdaw	Magpie	Rook

CROW, JIM. See JIM CROW.

CROW INDIANS were the wealthiest tribe of the northern plains in the early 1800's. They owned many large herds of horses with elaborately decorated riding gear. Their tall, spacious tepees clustered in camps along the southern branches of the Yellowstone River in Montana and Wyoming. The name is a translation of the Crow Indian word *absaroke*, which means *crow*, *sparrow hawk*, or *bird people*.

Crow men were noted for their handsome profiles. Some leaders allowed their hair to grow several feet long. Crow women, known for their fine craftsmanship, made clothing of antelope and deer skin, and decorated it with dyed porcupine quills and glass beads. The sun dance and tobacco-planting ceremonies were especially sacred to these Indians.

The Crow were originally farmers, and lived on the Missouri River in what is now North Dakota. They moved westward before 1780 and became nomadic buffalo hunters. In 1805, Meriwether Lewis and William Clark, the American explorers, noted that the Crow were middlemen in lively trade between tribes on the Missouri and those west of the Rocky Mountains.

The Crow suffered heavy losses in their wars with the powerful Blackfoot and Sioux. They readily sought the friendship and protection of whites. A number of their young men served as scouts for the U.S. Army in the frontier wars with the Sioux and Cheyenne. The Crow reservation today lies in the tribe's traditional homeland of southeastern Montana.   JOHN C. EWERS

CROWBAR. See FIRE FIGHTING (picture).

CROWFOOT. See BUTTERCUP.

CROWLEY. See LOUISIANA (Manufacturing).

CROWN. See TEETH (picture: The Parts of a Tooth).

CROWN. See TREE (The Parts of a Tree).

CROWN is an English coin worth five shillings, or one-fourth of a pound sterling. This is equal to about 60 cents in U.S. money. Once widely used, crowns are now coined only for special occasions. They are rarely seen in circulation. On one side, the crown bears a likeness of the king or queen who was reigning when the coin was minted. A coat of arms with symbolic designs is on the other. The crown was first issued in gold in the 1500's during the reign of Henry VIII. The crown, as it

This English Crown was minted in 1707 during the reign of Queen Anne of England. Both sides of the old coin are shown.

Chase Manhattan Bank Money Museum

is known today, dates from 1551. Early crowns were made of fine silver, called crown silver. Since 1951, crowns have been struck in copper-nickel alloy instead of silver.   BURTON HOBSON

CROWN is a circular ornament worn on or around the head as a symbol of authority, merit, or distinction. A royal crown is a king's symbol of supreme authority, but is generally worn only on state occasions. Such crowns are usually elaborate affairs of gold, engraved, and ornamented with precious gems.

The British royal crown consists of a gold band studded with diamonds, pearls, and other precious

Historic Crowns of Europe include the crown of the Holy Roman Empire, *left*, and the Imperial Crown of old Austria, *right*.

Art Institute of Chicago

British Information Services

Historic British Crowns include St. Edward's Crown, *left*, copied from a crown worn by Edward the Confessor; and the British Imperial State Crown, worn by the monarch on state occasions.

stones. From the band rise crosses, fleurs-de-lis, and four arches, topped by a jeweled gold cross. The crown of the British ruler has much historic interest, and is considered to be priceless (see GEM [color picture]; ELIZABETH II [color picture]). A few crowns made for princes in India have famous, valuable jewels.

The Crown is a term often used to mean a monarch in his official capacity. The term can also mean a monarch's rule, position, or empire, of which the crown is a symbol.

The History of Crowns. Various jeweled headdresses were worn by rulers of ancient Egypt and Assyria. The Greeks gave a crown or diadem of olive leaves to their athletes as a symbol of victory. Later the Romans adopted this custom. Their crowns were made of metal, usually gold, and were worn by the Roman emperors. From the reign of Constantine (306-337), the diadem was regarded as the symbol of royal power. Later European rulers probably borrowed the practice of wearing a crown from the Romans.

Iron Crown of Lombardy was a crown worn by the Lombard kings and the emperors of the Holy Roman Empire when they became kings of Lombardy. It is made of gold, decorated with jewels and cloisonné enamel. Its name comes from an inner iron circlet which tradition says was beaten from a nail of the cross of Christ. Lombard workmen probably made it in the A.D. 500's. Charlemagne, Charles V, and Napoleon I wore the Iron Crown. It is preserved in the Cathedral of Saint John the Baptist at Monza, Italy.   WILLIAM M. MILLIKEN

CROWN COLONY is a British overseas possession acquired by conquest or cession. It differs from a *protectorate*, where the British exercise control by virtue of treaties with local rulers (see PROTECTORATE). Great Britain's Commonwealth Office rules crown colonies, and a governor and members of the Overseas Service govern them. In some places, especially those of strategic importance, such as Gibraltar, the governor legislates alone. In others, an executive council and a legislative assembly assist the governor in the administration and legislation of the colony. Members of some of the legislative assemblies may be elected, while members of others may be appointed.   ROBERT G. NEUMANN

CROWN POINT is a high spur of land on the southwestern shore of Lake Champlain in New York. It became an early frontier post and fortress. The location was important because Lake Champlain was a water highway between Canada and the northern English colonies. The lake is so narrow at Crown Point that a few cannon could command the passage and shut off an enemy's fleet. The French built Fort St. Frederic at Crown Point in 1731 and destroyed it in 1759 to prevent its capture by an advancing English army. The English built a new and larger fort near the place where Fort St. Frederic had stood. The English fort was intended to protect nearby Fort Ticonderoga from attack by water. At the start of the Revolutionary War, a group of "Green Mountain Boys" under Seth Warner took Crown Point while Colonel Benedict Arnold and Ethan Allen captured Ticonderoga. The ruins of the early French fort and of the English fort are preserved in a New York state park. Crown Point is now the name of a township and a village in Essex County, N.Y. See also GREEN MOUNTAIN BOYS.   JOHN R. ALDEN

CROZER THEOLOGICAL SEMINARY. See UNIVERSITIES AND COLLEGES (table).

CRUCIBLE. See IRON AND STEEL (Methods of Making Steel).

CRUCIFIXION. See JESUS CHRIST (The Crucifixion).

CRUDE OIL. See PETROLEUM.

CRUIKSHANK, *CROOK shank,* **GEORGE** (1792-1878), an English artist, became famous for his caricatures and illustrations. His works include over 5,000 items, ranging from caricatures to historical paintings.

As a caricaturist, he commented on his times for more than 50 years. As an illustrator, he worked closely with Charles Dickens to produce a famous series of etchings for *Oliver Twist*. He also illustrated books by such writers as Oliver Goldsmith, Henry Fielding, and Miguel de Cervantes. He joined a movement to suppress alcoholism, and produced a series of drawings on the evils of drunkenness. Cruikshank was born in London, the son of a political caricaturist.   NORMAN RICE

CRUISER is a smaller warship than a battleship, but faster and with a longer cruising range. It carries no heavy armor, but is armed with hard-hitting attack weapons. A cruiser is used for specialized attack missions, scouting, and screening. It often serves as command staff headquarters afloat. Cruisers are also important in task force organization.

Cruisers were once classified as light, heavy, and battle cruisers. *Light* and *heavy* cruisers differed primarily in the size of the guns in their main batteries. A light cruiser mounted 6-inch guns, while heavy cruisers carried 8-inch guns. *Battle* cruisers were actually fast battleships with light armor.

Like the battleship, the conventional cruiser is becoming obsolete. But the United States Navy has converted several cruisers into guided-missile cruisers. The most modern cruiser is the nuclear-powered guided-missile cruiser U.S.S. *Long Beach*. This ship displaces 15,947 tons when fully loaded.   RAYMOND V. B. BLACKMAN

See also BATTLESHIP; NAVY, UNITED STATES (picture: Warships of the Navy); WARSHIP.

CRUSADES

Comment li Rois loys prinst la croix
pour aller quere mer le seconde fois
J homs Rois loys
qui not pas bn
que ault pelermaiges ot fait
truunoz honte et triunoz te
proce au Roiaume de france
que noustur a Saintr enslise.

Giraudon

Saint Louis Departs from Southern France for North Africa in this illustration from a medieval chronicle in the Hermitage in Leningrad, Russia. The king and his army planned to capture the territory from the Moslems, but he died of plague when he reached Africa. His death ended the Eighth Crusade.

A Crusader's Fortress, the Krak des Chevaliers, was powerfully built to withstand Moslem attacks. This castle, which stands in Syria, was built by the Knights of Saint John (Knights Hospitallers) in the 1100's. Such fortresses could house several thousand fighting men and their servants.

Aerofilms, Ltd.

CRUSADES were Christian military expeditions to recapture the Holy Land, where Jesus had lived. *Moslems* (members of the Islamic faith) held the Holy Land. The crusades began shortly before A.D. 1100 and lasted until almost 1300. The men who fought in them came from western Europe.

Christians were aroused to organize the crusades primarily by religious faith. But the expeditions also were part of the larger effort by Europeans to increase their power, territory, and riches. Even before the crusades, the Christians had begun to reconquer lands in Europe that had been seized by the Moslems. By the time of the First Crusade, the Christians had already retaken southern Italy and Sicily and had put the Moslems on the defensive in Spain.

The word *crusade* comes from the Latin word *crux*, meaning *cross*. Those who joined the great expeditions sewed the symbol of the cross of Christ on their *tunics* (outer clothing). "To take the cross" meant to become a crusader.

How the Crusades Began. Arabs, who were of the Islamic faith, conquered the area around the eastern shore of the Mediterranean Sea in the A.D. 600's. Jerusalem and other places where Jesus had lived remained under Arab rule until the 1000's. To Christians, these places were sacred. Most of the Arab rulers allowed the Christians to visit the sacred places. But during the 1000's, the fierce Seljuk Turks swept in from Turkestan in Asia, took all of Asia Minor (now Turkey) from the Byzantine Empire, and occupied Arab Syria, which included the Holy Land. The Turks captured Jerusalem in 1071. Then they began to interfere with Christian pilgrims who tried to visit the holy places.

In the early 1090's, the Byzantine emperor, Alexius Comnenus, asked Pope Urban II for help in fighting the Turks. Urban viewed the appeal as an opportunity to win glory for the church. He also believed that a military expedition against a common foe would help reduce warfare among European kings and nobles. In the autumn of 1095, Urban called a great assembly of churchmen and nobles at Clermont, France. There, he delivered a stirring sermon. He called on the knights of Europe to stop their feuds and rescue the Holy Land from the Turks. The assembly was aroused, and shouts of "God wills it!" filled the air. Preachers such as Peter the Hermit swiftly spread the enthusiasm throughout Europe. Thousands enrolled in the sacred cause.

But not all the crusaders took the cross for religious reasons. Some, such as the Normans, hoped to win glory, wealth, and new lands. Merchants, such as those in the Italian cities of Genoa and Venice, joined in search of new markets.

The First Crusade (1096-1099). Led by Peter the Hermit, bands of common people started out for the Holy Land before the main armies of knights. These people were poorly trained and poorly equipped for fighting. They marched toward Constantinople (now Istanbul), the capital of the Byzantine Empire. Few reached their goal. Some starved. Eastern Europeans killed others. The

Bryce Lyon, the contributor of this article, is Professor of Medieval History at Brown University and author of Mediaeval History.

First and Third Crusades

This map shows where the First and Third Crusades started and the routes the crusaders followed to the Holy Land. The First Crusade began in 1096 and ended in 1099. The crusaders succeeded in capturing Jerusalem. They also established the Latin States of the Crusaders: *Edessa, Antioch, Tripolis,* and *Jerusalem.* The Third Crusade began in 1189 and ended in 1192. The crusaders failed to recapture Jerusalem, but won an agreement with the Turks to permit Christians to visit the city.

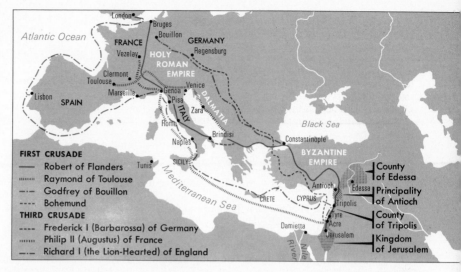

FIRST CRUSADE
—— Robert of Flanders
····· Raymond of Toulouse
–·– Godfrey of Bouillon
---- Bohemund

THIRD CRUSADE
---- Frederick I (Barbarossa) of Germany
····· Philip II (Augustus) of France
–··– Richard I (the Lion-Hearted) of England

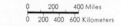

WORLD BOOK map   FGA

Turks slaughtered most of those who crossed into Asia Minor.

The expedition went far better for the knights, who were trained warriors. Most of the knights came from France. Their chief leaders included Count Robert of Flanders, Count Raymond of Toulouse, Godfrey of Bouillon, and Bohemund, a Norman lord from Sicily.

Separate armies of knights left Europe in the autumn of 1096. Some marched overland to Constantinople. Others went there by ship. The crusaders joined and invaded Asia Minor in early 1097. They then began their long march to Jerusalem. On the way, they fought many bloody battles. Antioch, in Syria, was the most important city on their route, and it was the most difficult to capture. Fleets from Italy brought in supplies and more fighters as the crusaders marched south. As the expedition continued, the leaders of the crusade quarreled among themselves. The crusaders finally arrived at Jerusalem in the summer of 1099, and captured the city after six weeks of fighting.

Most of the crusaders then returned home. Those who remained founded a group of four states on the eastern shore of the Mediterranean Sea. These states were called the *Latin States of the Crusaders.* From the north to the south, they were named: the County of Edessa, the Principality of Antioch, the County of Tripolis, and the Kingdom of Jerusalem.

The Second Crusade (1147-1149). Too few crusaders remained to defend the Holy Land. Less than 50 years after the victories of the First Crusade, the Turks conquered the County of Edessa.

The Turkish triumph brought about the Second Crusade. This time the preachings of Saint Bernard stirred Europe. King Louis VII of France and Emperor Conrad III of Germany led armies into Asia Minor, but they did not cooperate with each other. The Turks defeated them before they reached Edessa. This failure encouraged the Turks to renew their attacks on Christian strongholds.

The Third Crusade (1189-1192) followed the Turkish recapture of the city of Jerusalem in 1187. The Turks reconquered much of the Holy Land under their leader, Saladin. Only Tyre, Tripolis, and Antioch remained in Christian hands.

The most important rulers of Europe launched the Third Crusade. One of them, the German Emperor Frederick I (called Barbarossa), died before arriving in the Holy Land. Quarrels among the other rulers kept the crusaders from complete success. King Philip II (called Philip Augustus) of France returned home soon after arriving in the Holy Land. He pretended to be ill. But his real reason for returning was to plot against King Richard I (the Lion-Hearted) of England, who remained to fight in the Holy Land. Richard was a great warrior. He defeated Saladin in several battles and recaptured Acre, which is north of Jerusalem. He could not retake Jerusalem, but he persuaded the Turks to let Christian pilgrims enter the city freely.

The Fourth Crusade (1201-1204) was the last serious expedition against the Moslems. Pope Innocent III persuaded many French nobles to take part in this expedition. The crusaders bargained with the Venetians to take them by ship to the eastern Mediterranean. But when they got to Venice, they could not pay the costs. The Venetians said they would transport the crusaders to the Holy Land if the crusaders helped them attack the Byzantine Empire. The combined forces of the Venetians and crusaders first captured the town of Zara, in Dalmatia. Then they seized Constantinople after a fierce battle. The victors removed the Byzantine Emperor from his throne and replaced him with Count Baldwin of Flanders. The Venetians and crusaders divided Byzantine territory and riches among themselves. They ruled the Byzantine Empire until 1261.

The Fourth Crusade was not a crusade against the Moslems at all. It was an expedition for economic and political gain. The real victors were the Venetians, who expanded their trading area into Byzantine lands. The crusaders never reached the Holy Land, and much of it remained in the hands of the Moslems.

The Children's Crusade (1212) was not important to history. But for hundreds of years, it has interested people as a tragic story.

The crusaders were boys and girls stirred by religious

fervor to go to the Holy Land. Many were less than 12 years old. There were two armies of them, one from France and one from Germany. None of the children reached the Holy Land. Many died of hunger, cold, and other hardships on their long march south to the Mediterranean Sea. Others were drowned in storms at sea, or sold as slaves to the Moslems. Few of the young crusaders ever returned to their homes.

Other Crusades continued in the 1200's, but they had little success.

In the Fifth Crusade (1217-1221), the Christians captured the town of Damietta at the mouth of the Nile River in Egypt. But they soon gave up Damietta in exchange for a truce with the Moslems. The crusade was a failure.

Emperor Frederick II of the Holy Roman Empire led the Sixth Crusade (1228-1229). He was a skillful bargainer. Without fighting a single battle, he got the Moslems to turn over Jerusalem to the Christians. The Holy City remained Christian until the Moslems seized it again in 1244.

The fall of Jerusalem caused King Louis IX of France (Saint Louis) to lead the Seventh Crusade (1248-1254). Louis took Damietta without a fight. But the Turks then surrounded and captured the crusaders. They freed Louis and his noblemen only after the Christians paid a huge ransom. Seeking revenge, Louis led the Eighth Crusade (1270) against the Moslems of northern Africa. He landed his army at Tunis. But, old and ill, he died at Carthage. His army returned to Europe.

In the East, meanwhile, the Moslems continued to make gains against the Christians. They captured Antioch in 1268. In 1291, they seized Acre, the last Christian foothold in Syria.

By this time, Europeans were losing interest in the Holy Land. There were weak attempts to organize crusades in the 1300's and 1400's, but none of them succeeded. Europe was turning its attention westward to the Atlantic Ocean and beyond. In 1492, the Spaniards drove the Moslem Moors out of Europe. In the same year, Columbus sailed to the New World. Europe turned toward America to satisfy its ambition to expand. The Holy Land belonged to the Moslems.

Results of the Crusades. The expeditions to the Holy Land prepared Europe for expansion into America. They acquainted westerners with the way of life of the East. Europeans acquired new tastes in food and clothing. Their desire to travel increased. During the crusades, they learned how to make better ships and better maps. And they learned new ways to make war. The crusades quickened the progress of western Europe by bringing profit and prosperity to Italian trading cities. They enriched European life in many ways.   BRYCE LYON

Related Articles in WORLD BOOK include:

Byzantine Empire	Knights Templars
Feudalism	Louis (IX) of France
Flag (color pictures: His-	Moslems
torical Flags of the World)	Palestine
Frederick (I and II) Holy	Peter the Hermit
Roman Emperors	Philip (II) of France
Godfrey of Bouillon	Richard (I) of England
Innocent (III)	Saladin
Knights and Knighthood	Seljuk
Knights of Saint John	Urban (II)

CRUSOE, ROBINSON. See ROBINSON CRUSOE.

CRUSTACEAN, *crus TAY shun*, is an animal without a backbone. An armorlike shell covers its body. Crustaceans make up a class of joint-footed animals called *arthropods*. There are about 30,000 *species* (kinds) of crustaceans. They include crayfish, crabs, lobsters, and shrimp. Like other animals with shells, crustaceans are often called *shellfish*.

Their Bodies. All crustaceans are covered with a hard coating of *chitin*. This covering is sometimes like bone, sometimes tough and leathery, and sometimes thin and transparent. The hardness of the body covering depends on the amount of lime in the chitin. The covering is a kind of suit of armor which protects the animal.

The body of the crustacean is divided into sections. Each section usually bears a pair of jointed legs. The sections of the body and head are closely jointed. Legs under and in front of the face are used to hold, tear, and taste food. Other legs on the head are used as jaws, toothbrushes, and feelers. Special legs under the body are used for walking. Large legs, or pincers, on the body are used for catching fish, cracking young oysters, digging burrows, and fighting. Slow swimming legs under the tail are sometimes used to hold the eggs. The legs at the end of the tail are flattened to form a fan-shaped fin which is used in swimming backward.

Crustaceans have one, two, or more compound or single eyes. The eyes of larger kinds are usually on stalks that turn and move the eyes. The lobster has two compound eyes that are really clusters of many simple eyes.

Life Story. Crustaceans reproduce by means of eggs which are usually hatched in water. Some crustaceans, such as lobsters, carry their eggs and young on the hairs of the swimming legs. The eggs of different crustaceans hatch at various stages of development. Young lobsters and crayfish look like their parents, while young crabs do not. After the eggs hatch, the young crustaceans grow until their shells become too tight. Then the growing crustacean exchanges its old shell for a larger new one. The process of changing shells is called *molting*, and takes place several times during growth. The new shell forms inside the old one, and is soft and wrinkled like a suit packed in a small box. When the lobster molts, its shell splits along the back. The lobster humps up through the opening in its old shell, draws its pincers back, its legs up, and its tail forward and out. The shell of the crab cracks around the middle, so that the crab can back out, pulling each leg from its sheath.

Before molting begins, most of the blood in the claws flows into the body, and lime in the joints of the claws dissolves. The muscles of the claws shrivel because of loss of blood and are able to pass through the small soft joints of the old shell. Sometimes there are accidents during molting. A leg or a feeler often breaks off. There is little pain and bleeding, however, because the limb usually breaks where there are few nerves and blood vessels. When the animal molts again, it grows a new limb. The new limb may be smaller at first, but usually becomes full sized after several molts. Eyes which are lost are often replaced by an extra feeler.

Scientific Classification. Crustaceans are the class *Crustacea*, phylum *Arthropoda*.   J. LAURENS BARNARD

Related Articles in WORLD BOOK include:

Arthropod	Copepod	Fiddler Crab	Shrimp
Barnacle	Crab	Hermit Crab	Water Flea
Blue Crab	Crayfish	Lobster	

CRUZEIRO is the monetary unit of Brazil. See MONEY (table: Values of Monetary Units).

CRYOBIOLOGY, *KRY oh by AHL oh jee*, is the study of how extremely low temperatures affect living things. Cryobiologists use temperatures that range from 0° C. (32° F.), the freezing point of water, down to just above −273.15° C. (−459.67° F.), which is absolute zero (see ABSOLUTE ZERO). The word *cryobiology* comes from the Greek *kryos* (icy cold) and *biology* (the science of living things).

Cryobiologists are chiefly concerned with freezing living matter to preserve it for future use. The freezing must be done rapidly to keep the cells alive. Cryobiologists use a liquid gas, usually nitrogen, to get temperatures far below normal freezing in a few seconds. Cells bathed in the liquid gas stop working. But they stay alive and unchanged in a state of "suspended animation." They can remain in this state without harm for long periods. After rapid thawing, the cells resume their normal work almost at once.

The rapid freezing of tissues such as skin, eye corneas, and blood makes it possible to store these parts in "banks." Doctors may use skin from such a bank to graft onto a badly burned patient. They use healthy corneas that have been stored to replace diseased or damaged ones. Blood banks previously could keep blood only for three weeks before it spoiled. But frozen whole blood can be stored indefinitely now.

In *cryosurgery*, surgeons use extreme cold to destroy tissue. For example, they can perform a "bloodless" operation by using special instruments equipped with *freezing tips*. When they insert the instrument tip into diseased tissue, the cooled tip kills the unwanted tissue. A shield around the remainder of the instrument protects healthy tissue.

Food industries use the techniques of cryobiology to preserve food. Manufacturers can freeze and store foods indefinitely without harming the flavor, consistency, or nutritional value.   JOSEPH F. SAUNDERS

CRYOGENICS, *CRY oh JEHN icks*, is the study, development, and improvement of extremely low-temperature processes, techniques, and equipment. The temperatures range from −150° C. (−238° F.) to near absolute zero, −273.15° C. (−459,67° F.). The word *cryogenics* comes from the Greek word *kryos*, which means *icy cold*. Extremely low temperatures were first produced by making liquid air in the 1870's (see LIQUID AIR). In 1956, scientists reached the lowest temperatures yet. This was done by magnetizing copper nuclei at very low temperatures. When the magnet was turned off, the copper nuclei became demagnetized and cooled to temperatures within millionths of a degree of absolute zero.

The most common means of producing extremely low temperatures are with liquid hydrogen and liquid helium. Liquid hydrogen gives a temperature of about −253° C.; liquid helium, −269° C. See HELIUM.

Many important advances have resulted from cryogenics, including the discovery of *superconductivity*. This is the ability of some metals to conduct electricity with almost no resistance at temperatures near absolute zero. Superconductivity can be destroyed if the metal or alloy is exposed to a magnetic field. See CRYOTRON.

Cryogenics has helped in the development of rocket fuels and in manufacturing steel. Also being developed in cryogenics are superconductive bearings with greatly reduced friction, electric motors with extraordinary efficiency, and powerful magnetic lenses for electron microscopes. In addition, the study of cryogenics has contributed to producing sensitive electronic amplifiers and the creation of high magnetic fields for thermonuclear reactors.   KLAUS D. TIMMERHAUS

CRYOLITE, *CRY oh lite*, is a soft mineral that often looks like snow ice. It is usually white, but sometimes has a bluish, reddish, or brown color. A cryolite solution is used in the electrolytic process by which aluminum is produced from bauxite ore. Cryolite is also used in making some sodium salts and ceramics, such as porcelain. It is a compound of aluminum, sodium, and fluorine and has the chemical formula Na_3AlF_6. The main cryolite deposits of commercial importance are at Ivigtut, Greenland. Eskimos call cryolite *ice stone*. See also ALUMINUM (Producing Aluminum).   WILLIAM C. LUTH

CRYOSURGERY. See CRYOBIOLOGY; SURGERY (Technique).

CRYOTRON, *CRY oh trahn*, is a tiny electronic device that can be used as a switch or an amplifier. Cryotrons are only about $\frac{1}{10}$ of an inch long. They are so small that 100 of them will fit into an ordinary thimble. This makes it possible to greatly reduce the size of computers and other electronic apparatus.

Cryotrons work on the principle of *superconductivity*. This is the ability of some metals, such as lead, to conduct electric current with no resistance at temperatures below −420° F., or near absolute zero (see ABSOLUTE ZERO). A container of liquid helium surrounds cryotrons and cools them to these temperatures. However, a magnetic field can destroy superconductivity. This causes resistance to return to superconductive material so that little or no current will flow.

In a cryotron, a superconductive coil of fine wire is wound around another superconductive wire. A flow of current through the coil produces a magnetic field (see ELECTRICITY [Electricity and Magnetism]). The other wire will conduct current with no resistance so long as no current flows through the coil. By regulating the flow of current in the coil, the flow in the second wire can be turned on or off. In this way, a cryotron acts as a switch or amplifier. See ELECTRONICS.

Dudley A. Buck, a scientist at the Massachusetts Institute of Technology, began work on the cryotron in 1954, and completed it in 1957.   JOHN ROBINSON PIERCE

CRYOVAC. See SARAN.

CRYPT, *krihpt*, is an underground room or vault. It usually refers to a vault under a church. The word comes from the Greek *kryptein* (to hide). Saints and martyrs were often buried in crypts. Chapels and altars were sometimes built over the spot where their bones were supposed to lie. One famous crypt is that of Saint Helena in Jerusalem. Legend says she found there the cross on which Christ died. Other famous crypts include those of Saint Peter's in Rome, of Saint Nicholas at Bari, of Canterbury Cathedral, and of Glasgow Cathedral.   ALAN GOWANS

See also ALTAR; CATACOMBS.

CRYPTOGAM. See BOTANY (Terms).

CRYPTOGRAPHY. See CODES AND CIPHERS.

CRYSTAL. See GLASSWARE.

Katherine H. Jensen

Crystals of Barite, a common barium sulfate mineral, belong to the orthorhombic system.

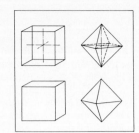

Isometric Crystals have 3 axes, all at right angles, and all of equal length. Gold forms crystals in this system.

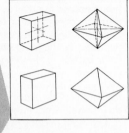

Orthorhombic Crystals have 3 axes, all at right angles and of different lengths. Topaz has such crystals.

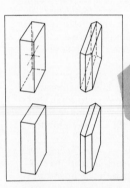

Monoclinic Crystals have 3 axes, 2 making an angle different from 90°, the third perpendicular to the first two. The axes have unequal lengths.

CRYSTAL AND CRYSTALLIZATION

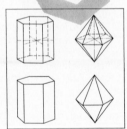

Tetragonal Crystals have 3 axes, all at right angles. Two sides are equal, and the third is longer or shorter.

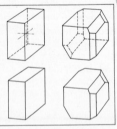

Triclinic Crystals have 3 axes, all inclined and of different lengths. Copper sulfate forms such crystals.

Hexagonal Crystals have 4 axes, 3 at angles of 120°, the fourth at right angles to them and either longer or shorter.

CRYSTAL AND CRYSTALLIZATION. Living things, such as dandelions and dogs, grow from tiny seeds or eggs to a form that distinguishes them from other living things. Most nonliving substances, such as table salt, sugar, or ice, can also grow from a very small beginning into definite shapes. These shapes consist of smooth, flat surfaces that meet in sharp edges and corners. The process by which nonliving substances grow into bodies of such shapes is called *crystallization*, and the bodies themselves are called *crystals*. The study of crystals is called *crystallography*.

How Crystallization Takes Place. Anyone can see how crystals grow by making a simple experiment. Dissolve some ordinary salt in a glass of cold water. Put in more salt until some stays undissolved even after stirring and waiting. Then pour the clear salt solution into another glass. Lay a stick across the top of the second glass and from it let a piece of string hang down into the water. Let the glass stand in a place where it will not be disturbed. After a month or more, small clear cube-shaped salt crystals will have appeared on the string. Alum, which can be bought at a drugstore, produces crystals shaped like two pyramids with one base. This shows that nonliving things grow differently from living things. Living things grow from substances unlike themselves. They take food into their bodies and make it over into their own substance. But crystals merely add on new layers of their own substance.

How Crystals Are Built Up. From the way crystals grow, it is clear that they owe their shapes to the manner in which the atoms of which they consist are put together. The atoms of crystals are arranged in a regular geometric relation to one another. This arrangement is always the same for the same substance at the same temperature. The surfaces of a crystal are smooth and flat because the atoms are arranged in a definite pattern in rows upon rows throughout the entire crystal.

We cannot actually see the atoms arranged this way inside the crystal because they are so very small. But when X rays or electron beams are passed through a crystal, they reveal the pattern of the atoms by the way they come out on the other side. X ray crystallography shows the arrangement of atoms below the crystal's surface. Scientists also use an *ion microscope* to "see" the atoms that form the surface of certain metal crystals. See Ion Microscope; X Rays (Uses).

Some minerals occur as masses of irregular crystal grains, and are not shaped like crystals on the outside. The individual grains do not have flat faces, because they touched other grains as they grew, rather than growing surrounded by a fluid. Such irregular crystal grains are said to be *anhedral*.

Classification of Crystals. Crystals are distinguished and classified by the geometry of the crystal faces, or flat surfaces, that give them their shapes, especially by the angles in which adjoining crystal faces meet. This is a highly technical subject. Many crystals have large numbers of faces. Yet, by looking at only the simplest types of crystal forms we can understand one of the ways that crystals are classified.

The six basic types of crystals, illustrated with this article, make up the six *crystal systems*.

The Isometric System has a cube as its simplest form. In this system, each of the six faces is a square and all of them meet at right angles. In the illustration of the isometric system, the lower drawing shows a cube as it looks in nature. The upper drawing shows the same cube with three imaginary axes drawn on the inside. These axes are parallel to the edges of the cube. Corresponding axes are shown in the illustrations of the simplest forms of the other crystal systems.

Another common form of isometric crystal is the *octahedron*. It consists of a double four-sided pyramid, of which each face is an equilateral triangle. Galena, pyrite, alum, and garnet crystallize in this system.

Orthorhombic System. In a simple orthorhombic crystal the left side, the right side, and the top are all rectangles. Not one of these is a square. But they meet at right angles. All three axes have different lengths. A pyramid-shaped orthorhombic crystal consists of *scalene* triangles, or triangles with three sides of different lengths. About 200 minerals crystallize in the orthorhombic system, including topaz, celestite, and chalcocite.

Tetragonal System. The simplest type of tetragonal crystal is a prism in which the sides are rectangles, and the top and bottom are squares. All faces of this crystal meet at right angles. Generally, the upright axis is

longer or shorter than the other two, which are equal. In the tetragonal pyramid, the sides are identical isosceles triangles. Cassiterite and rutile crystallize in the tetragonal system.

Hexagonal System. In this system, prisms consist of six sides or of three sides, instead of four as in the other systems. The sides meet the top and bottom surfaces at right angles. Three of the four corresponding axes are equal. The fourth is longer or shorter. The hexagonal pyramid has six sides. The hexagonal system includes beryl, tourmaline, hematite, and calcite crystals.

Triclinic System. In triclinic crystals, the faces generally do not meet at right angles. This results in odd-shaped crystals. Only a few minerals crystallize in the triclinic system.

Monoclinic System. In a simple monoclinic crystal, four sides consist of rectangles and two of parallelograms. But only the left and right sides meet the top and bottom surfaces at right angles. The top and bottom surfaces are inclined, instead of being horizontal as they are in the first four systems. The monoclinic system is one of the commonest, and includes the crystals of such well-known minerals as borax, muscovite, hornblende, and azurite.   GEORGE TUNELL

See also Gem; Mineral; Quartz; Snow.

CRYSTAL BALL. See Fortunetelling.

CRYSTAL PALACE. See Fairs and Expositions.

CRYSTAL SET. See Radio (picture, A Simple Radio).

CRYSTALLINE LENS. See Eye (The Eyeball).

CRYSTALLINE ROCKS consist of countless crystals of one or several kinds of minerals grown together solidly. In granite and some other crystalline rocks, the crystals can be seen with the unaided eye. But in other types, the crystals are so small that a viewer must use a magnifying glass or microscope to see them. Crystalline rocks form in various ways. For example, molten rock solidifies into crystals as it cools. Travertine, a type of limestone, forms from calcite (calcium carbonate) crystals precipitated from ground water. Earth pressures and heat turn fine-grained limestone into marble by coarsening the crystal structure. See also Limestone; Rock.   A. J. Eardley

CRYSTALLOGRAPHY. See Crystal and Crystallization.

CRYSTALLOID. See Colloid.

CTENOPHORE, *TEEN uh for*, is a small transparent sea animal that lives in all the oceans of the world. Ctenophores are also called *comb jellies* and *sea walnuts*. The ctenophore body may be shaped like a ball, a thimble, or a belt. It looks a little like a jellyfish. The size of most *species* (kinds) varies from that of a pea to a thimble. One unusual species, called *Venus's-girdle*, is shaped like a belt and may grow more than 3 feet long.

Ctenophore means *a comb bearer*. The animal gets this name from the eight bands of comblike organs on the sides of its body. The combs are made of groups of *cilia* (tiny hairlike structures). Ctenophores move slowly through the water by beating these cilia. In some species, the combs give off flashes of light.

Scientific Classification. Ctenophores make up the phylum *Ctenophora*.   ROBERT D. BARNES

CUB. See Bear; Lion; Tiger.

CUB SCOUT. See Boy Scouts.

CUBA

Bearded Fidel Castro, *center,* rode on a tank during his triumphant parade into Havana in January, 1959. The Cuban dictator quickly turned his country into a tightly controlled Communist state.

CUBA, *KYOO buh,* is an island country in the West Indies. Cuba, a Communist satellite state, became the center of a world crisis in October, 1962. The United States revealed that Russia had installed missile bases there capable of launching atomic attacks on U.S. cities. The U.S. *quarantined* (blockaded) Cuba to stop

Cuba (in black) lies about 90 miles south of Florida and about the same distance north of Jamaica.

------------------ **FACTS IN BRIEF** ------------------

Type of Government: Dictatorship.
Capital: Havana.
Official Language: Spanish.
Divisions: 6 provinces.
Area: 44,218 square miles. *Greatest Distances*—(northwest-southeast) 759 miles; (north-south) 135 miles. *Coastline* —2,100 miles.
Elevation: *Highest*—Turquino Peak, 6,560 feet; *Lowest*— sea level.
Population: *1953 Census*—5,829,029; distribution, 57 per cent urban, 43 per cent rural. *Estimated 1970 Population*—8,676,000; density, 196 persons to the square mile. *Estimated 1975 Population*—9,864,000.
Chief Products: *Agriculture*—sugar cane, cattle, tobacco, bananas, citrus fruits, coffee, vegetables. *Mining*— barium, chromium, copper, gold, iron, manganese, nickel, silica. *Manufacturing*—cigarettes, cigars, refined sugar, rum, textiles.
Flag: Three blue horizontal stripes alternate with two white stripes. A white star appears on a red triangle at the left. The flag was patterned after the United States flag. The blue stripes once stood for military districts. The star and triangle are Masonic emblems. The star also symbolizes independence. See FLAG (color picture: Flags of the Americas).
National Anthem: "Himno Nacional de Cuba."
National Holiday: Independence Day, May 20.
Money: *Basic Unit*—peso. For the value of the peso in dollars, see MONEY (table: Values). See also PESO.

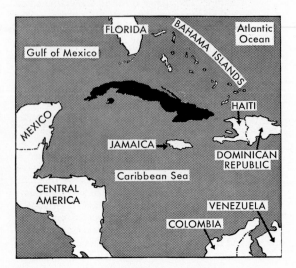

Columbus Cathedral faces on Cathedral Square in Havana. People once thought the church contained the remains of Christopher Columbus. But now it is believed that they were those of Columbus' son, Diego.

arms shipments, and demanded that Russia remove the missiles and bases. Russia finally agreed to this.

Cuba's big sugar crop once made it one of the most prosperous nations in Latin America. But sugar production fell sharply after Fidel Castro established a communist dictatorship. Living standards dropped, and Cuba depended on Russian economic aid to survive.

Christopher Columbus discovered Cuba in 1492. He is said to have called it "the loveliest land that human eyes have beheld." Cuba has been called the *Pearl of the Antilles* because of its beauty. The word *Cuba* comes from the Indian word *Cubanacan*, meaning *center place*. Cuba is slightly smaller than Pennsylvania, and has over half as many people.

The Land and Its Resources

Location, Size, and Surface Features. Cuba lies between the Gulf of Mexico and the Caribbean Sea. Cuba is the largest and westernmost island in the West Indies. It is about 759 miles long and averages about 50 miles in width. It covers 44,218 square miles.

The Land. About half of the island is flat or rolling land. Broad grasslands lie in the central part. But much of Cuba is hilly or mountainous. The Sierra Maestra range lies in the southeast. The Sierra de Trinidad lies in central Cuba, and the Sierra de los Órganos range in the western part.

Inland Waterways. Most Cuban rivers and streams are short and too shallow for navigation in the dry season.

Otis P. Starkey, the contributor of this article, is Professor of Geography, Indiana University, and coauthor of Introductory Economic Geography.

In the wet season, small boats are used on many streams. Parts of the southern coast are swampy.

Coasts and Islands. Most of Cuba's coasts are fringed with coral islands and reefs that form sheltered bays and lagoons. About 200 harbors are located on the coasts. Most of these harbors are bottle-shaped, with the "neck" of the bottle protecting an inner harbor from winds and waves. The most important harbors are Havana, Cárdenas, Matanzas, Nuevitas, and Antilla on the north coast; Cienfuegos on the south coast; and Santiago de Cuba and Guantánamo on the southeast coast. Cuba's coastline is 2,100 miles long. The Isle of Pines, which lies off the southwest coast, has an area of 1,180 square miles.

Natural Resources. Cuba's fertile limestone soil is one of its most important natural resources. The best soil is found in the center of the island, where sugar cane, tobacco, and vegetables are grown. Mineral resources include barium, chromium, copper, gold, iron, nickel, petroleum, and silver. They are found mainly in eastern Cuba.

Forests, found chiefly in the mountains, produce cedar, ebony, logwood, mahogany, and rosewood. The coconut palm, and such fruits as bananas, mangoes, and oranges, are grown widely. Game animals and birds of Cuba include deer, quail, snipe, turkey grouse, and wild pigs.

Climate. Cuba lies within the tropics, and trade winds from the northeast give it a pleasantly warm climate. The average temperature ranges from about 71 degrees in winter to 82 degrees in summer. The rainy season lasts from May to October in Cuba. Rainfall there averages about 50 inches a year. Hurricanes often hit

Cuban Farmers usually live in small houses that have earth floors and thatched roofs. But some farm families in Cuba have moved into new homes provided by the land reform program that began in 1959.

Max W. Hunn

Cuba, particularly in the western half of the country.

The People and Their Work

The People. About three out of four Cubans are white people of Spanish descent. Most of the rest are Negroes or mulattoes. When the Spaniards arrived in the late 1400's, there were two Indian groups in Cuba, the Arawak and the Ciboney. These Indian groups died out during the 1500's. Many of them died from overwork and disease after the Spaniards enslaved them.

Way of Life. Cuban workers once received more pay than workers in most other Latin-American countries. But their present wages do not go far because, under the Communist government, the prices of food and manufactured goods are so high. Some Cubans earn wages for only a few months of the year, during the *zafra* (sugar harvest).

One out of three Cuban workers belongs to a labor union. The largest unions make up the Workers' Federation of Cuba. The Communists organized other groups, such as the Federation of Cuban Women and the Association of Young Rebels, to tighten their control.

Health conditions are good in Cuba, compared with those in many Latin-American countries. But malaria and typhoid fever still are serious problems.

The people prepare many Spanish dishes. *Arroz con pollo,* a rice and chicken dish, and *Moros y Cristianos,* a soup of black beans, rice, and onions, are popular.

Cubans enjoy cockfights and *jai alai,* one of the world's fastest sports (see COCKFIGHTING; JAI ALAI). Other sports include soccer, baseball, polo, horse racing, golf, boating, and swimming. The people hunt deer, wild boar, quail, snipe, and alligators. The country is famous for its tarpon fishing. Cuban waters also contain marlin, barracuda, sharks, dolphins, amber jack, kingfish, and swordfish.

Cities. Havana is the capital and largest city of Cuba. Camagüey is the largest city in the interior of

The Presidential Palace, in Havana, is the official residence of the Cuban president. The impressive stone structure combines several styles of architecture.

Delta Air Lines

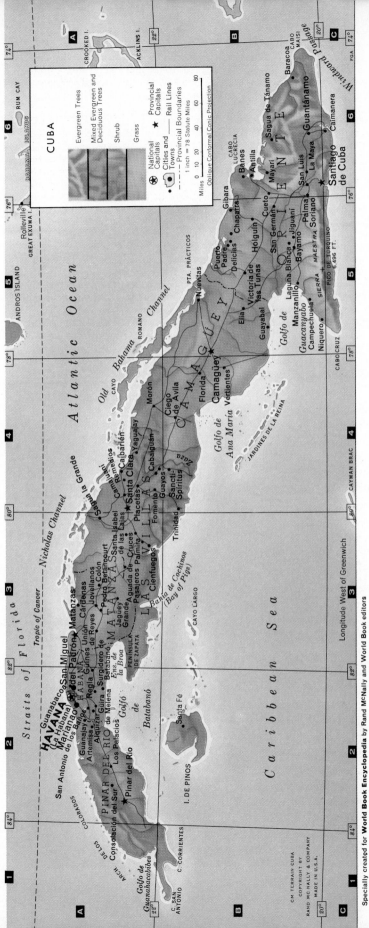

CUBA

| National Capitals |
| Provincial Capitals |
| Cities and Towns |
| National Boundaries ·—·—· |
| Provincial Boundaries ----- |
| Rail Lines |

Evergreen Trees
Mixed Evergreen and Deciduous Trees
Shrub
Grass

1 inch = 78 Statute Miles

Miles 0 10 20 40 60 80

Oblique Conformal Conic Projection

CM TERRAIN CUBA
COPYRIGHT BY
RAND MC NALLY & COMPANY
MADE IN U.S.A.

Specially created for **World Book Encyclopedia** by Rand McNally and World Book editors

Provinces

CAMAGÜEY		B 4
Pop.	785,400	
LA HABANA		A 2
Pop.	2,023,600	
LAS VILLAS		A 3
Pop.	1,178,800	
MATANZAS		A 3
Pop.	447,000	
ORIENTE		B 5
Pop.	2,443,600	
PINAR DEL RIO		A 2
Pop.	555,800	

Cities and Towns

Aguada de		
Pasajeros*	5,112	A 3
Alquízar	7,111	A 2
Antilla	6,481	B 6
Artemisa	25,000	A 2
Banes	24,700	B 6
Baracoa	11,459	A 6
Bauta*	11,518	A 2
Bayamo	35,200	B 5
Belucal*	19,882	A 2
Cabaiguán	15,399	A 4
Caibarién	24,645	C 6
Calabazar*	5,945	A 2
Camagüey	153,100	B 5
Camajuaní	12,574	A 4
Campechuela	5,536	B 5
Cárdenas	57,200	A 3
Chaparra	5,604	B 5
Ciego de		
Ávila	51,000	B 4
Cienfuegos	78,700	A 3
Colón	15,755	A 3
Consolación del		
Sur	6,146	A 2
Cruces	10,704	A 3
Cueto	5,983	B 6
Delicias	5,849	B 5
El Cotorro*	13,251	A 2
Elia	5,447	B 5
Florida	31,400	B 4
Fomento	7,852	A 4
Gibara	8,144	B 5
Guanabacoa	32,490	A 2
Guanajay	12,908	A 2
Guan-		
tánamo	122,400	B 6
Guayabal	5,889	B 5
Guayos	5,509	A 4
Güira de		
Melena	13,715	A 2
Havana (La		
Habana) 940,700		
*1,640,700		A 2
Holguín	77,700	B 5
Jagüey		
Grande	5,244	A 3
Jaruco*	5,291	A 2
Jiguaní	6,940	B 5
Jovellanos	10,444	A 3
Laguna		
Blanca	5,920	B 5
La Maya	5,037	B 6
Los Palacios	5,250	A 2
Manzanillo	78,000	B 5
Marianao	219,278	A 2
Matanzas	75,500	A 3
Mayarí	6,386	B 6
Morón	24,300	A 4
Niquero	7,204	B 5
Nuevitas	12,390	B 5
Palma		
Soriano	30,600	B 6
Palmira	6,261	A 3
Pedro Betan-		
court	6,863	A 3
Perico*	6,041	A 3
Pinar del		
Rio	66,700	A 2
Placetas	34,200	A 4
Puerto Padre 9,705		B 5
Rancho		
Boyeros*	5,765	A 2
Regla	26,755	A 2
Remedios	10,602	A 4
Sagua de		
Tánamo	7,604	B 6
Sagua la		
Grande	32,500	A 3
San Antonio		
de los		
Baños	22,300	A 2
San Germán	5,802	B 5
San José de		
las Lajas	13,011	A 2
San Luis	11,110	B 6
San Miguel		
del		
Padrón	60,631	A 2
San Nicolás		
de Barí*	5,738	A 3
Sancti		
Spíritus	55,400	B 4
Santa Clara	120,600	A 4
Santa Fé	5,372	A 2
Santa Isabel		
de las		
Lajas	5,362	A 3
Santiago de		
Cuba	231,000	B 6
Santiago de		
las Vegas	10,974	A 2
Surgidero		
de Bata-		
banó	5,075	A 2
Trinidad	25,500	B 4
Unión de		
Reyes	5,351	A 3
Vertientes	7,021	B 4
Victoria de		
las Tunas	25,600	B 5
Yaguajay	5,191	A 4

Physical Features

Golfo de		
Guacanayabo	B 5
Golfo de Guana-		
cabibes (Gulf)	A 1
Jardines de la Reina		
(Is.)	B 4
Nicholas Channel	A 3
Old Bahama		
Channel	A 4
Pico de Turquino		
(Mtn.)	B 5
Pinos, Isla de (Isl.)	B 2
Punta Prácticos		
(Pt.)	B 5
Romano (Isl.)	A 5
Sierra Maestra		
(Mts.)	B 5
Windward Passage	C 6
Zapata,		
Península de	A 3
Zaza R.	A 4

*Not on map; key shows general location.

Bahía de Cochinos (Bay
of Pigs) (Bay) ...A 3
Cabo Corrientes
(Cape) ...B 1
Cabo Cruz (Cape) ...C 5
Cabo Lucrecia
(Cape) ...B 6
Cabo Maisi (Cape) ...B 6
Cabo San Antonio
(Cape) ...B 1
Cayo (Isl.) ...A 4
Cayo Largo (Isl.) ...B 3
Colorados, Archipiélago
de los (Archi-
pelago) ...A 1
Ensenada de la Broa
(Bay) ...A 2
Golfo de Ana María
(Gulf) ...B 4
Golfo de Batabanó
(Gulf) ...A 2

*Population of metropolitan area, including suburbs.

Source: Census figures and official estimates.

CUBA

Cuba, and Cienfuegos ranks as the chief sugar-shipping port on the southern coast. Guantánamo, near the southeastern coast, serves as a center of the sugar industry. Santiago de Cuba, a port on the southeastern coast, is the headquarters of Cuba's mining industries. See the separate articles on Cuba's cities listed in the *Related Articles* section of this article.

Agriculture. All farming is strictly controlled by the government. Before the communists took over, farms were privately owned. The country has a year-round growing season because of its mild climate. United States companies once owned much of the farmland. Sugar cane was the most common crop, and the largest sugar factories were owned by Americans. The Castro government limited ownership of rural land to farms of 100 acres. The government seized the large sugar estates. In 1960, Castro took over the sugar factories. American and other investors lost more than a billion dollars.

The National Institute of Agrarian Reform, a government bureau, took over operation of the sugar factories and many of the estates. It set up collectives, or "people's farms," in which the farmers were employees of the state. But by 1962, Cuban agriculture was in bad condition. The sugar output dropped greatly,

and fruits and vegetables were so scarce in the cities that food was rationed. In the mid-1960's, after a strong drive to improve production, Cuba produced about 6,000,000 tons of raw sugar a year, equal to the totals reached before Castro seized power.

Tobacco is the second most important crop. But tobacco production fell under the communists. The best tobacco comes from the Vuelta Abajo region of western Cuba. Other crops include coffee, cacao, vegetables, and such fruits as the banana, date, pomegranate, plantain, papaya, avocado, and mango. Henequen and kenaf are plants grown to provide fiber for making rope.

The Tourist Industry was one of Cuba's largest industries until Fidel Castro became the country's dictator in 1959. Since then, tourism has almost disappeared because of Castro's anti-American policies. Most of Cuba's visitors came from the United States.

Mining. Cuba's mines produce many minerals, including iron, copper, barium, silica, platinum, gold, and silver. The chromium and asphalt deposits are among the purest in the world. Cuba mines more manganese than any other Latin-American country. A rich deposit of nickel was found near Moa Bay in eastern Cuba in 1953. Prospectors discovered oil in 1954. American companies owned many of the Cuban mines until the Castro government seized control in 1960.

Havana, Largest City in the West Indies, stands on Cuba's northern coast. The city's large hotels stand in the Vedado district along Malecon Drive, foreground. Havana was a tourist center until the communists took control in Cuba.

Cuban Tourist Commission

932d

Farmers Harvest Sugar Cane, *above,* in the winter, and carry the stalks to refineries. There, huge vacuum pans, *right,* boil the sirup into a mixture of sugar crystals and thick sirup.

Cuban Cigars, famous throughout the world, are packed into a box by a cigar worker.

Manufacturing. Sugar refining and the manufacture of cigars and cigarettes are the leading Cuban manufacturing industries. Food canning also is important. Other manufactured products include textiles, rum, flour, cement, fertilizer, drugs, soft drinks, shoes, and furniture.

Forest Products. Cuba has forests of mahogany, cedar, ebony, logwood, and rosewood. Much of the wood is used to make cigar boxes and furniture. Charcoal is one of the country's most important forest products, because people use it for cooking fuel. The royal palm furnishes thatch for the homes of the farmers.

Trade. Sugar and its by-products, including molasses and rum, make up most of Cuba's exports. The United States once bought more Cuban sugar than any other country. But in 1961, an anti-American campaign by the communist government finally caused the U.S. to stop Cuban sugar imports. Cuba now exports most of its sugar to communist bloc nations. Tobacco and tobacco products, such as cigars, are the next most important exports. Other exports include fruits, vegetables, coffee,

Workers Load Pineapples in Pinar del Río province. Pineapples are one of the main fruits grown in Cuba.

henequen, and meat. Cuba's main imports include food, textiles, machinery, automobiles, drugs, chemicals, and minerals. About four-fifths of Cuba's trade is with communist countries.

Transportation and Communication. Cuba has more than 3,700 miles of public railroads. The main railroads run from one end of the island to the other, and connect the most important cities. There are also nearly 7,600 miles of local railroads which connect the sugar plantations with the main railroads. The nation has more than 8,300 miles of public highways. The Central Highway, opened in 1931, is 706 miles long. It extends almost the entire length of the island, from Pinar del Río to Santiago de Cuba.

Telephone and telegraph lines connect the larger Cuban cities and towns. There are more than 150 radio stations, and several television stations.

Social and Cultural Achievements

Universities: University of Havana, founded in 1721; Catholic University of St. Thomas of Villanova, Havana, founded in 1946; Oriente University, Santiago de Cuba, founded in 1947.

Museums: National Museum and Martí Museum, Havana; Municipal Museum, Cárdenas; Bacardí Museum, Santiago de Cuba; Agramonte Museum, Camagüey.

Libraries: National Library, Library of the Economic Society, Municipal Library, and Congressional Library, Havana; Bacardí Library, Santiago de Cuba.

Education. The communist government *nationalized* (assumed control of) education in 1961, taking over an estimated 1,000 private schools. At that time, about 24 out of every 100 Cubans could not read and write. Thousands of teachers fled from Cuba after the communists seized power. To replace them, the government recruited young people, taught them communist principles, and sent them into the provinces of Cuba to teach others.

Religion. Most Cubans are Roman Catholics. But Fidel Castro's government persecuted many religious leaders and curtailed religious freedom.

The Arts. Much of the inspiration for Cuban literature, art, and music has come from the Negro population of the country. Many of the leading artists and writers have been Negroes or mulattoes.

The Cuban liberator, José Martí (1853-1895), wrote dozens of books. Cubans consider him their greatest student and thinker. Fernando Ortiz (1881-   ) is a modern scholar who has written much about Cuban Negroes, sugar, and tobacco. Perhaps the greatest Cuban poet was Julian del Casal (1863-1893). Nicolás Guillen (1904-   ) also wrote many poems.

The first Cuban paintings were church frescoes. José Nicolás de Escalera (1734-1804) and Vicente Escobar (1757-1854) were early Cuban painters. Modern painters include Eduardo Abela, and Cundo Bermúdez.

Cuba is one of the leading Latin-American countries in sculpture. José de Villalta Saavedra was an outstanding Cuban sculptor. Cubans enjoy the works of modern sculptors such as Teodoro Ramos Blanco, who models Negroes, and Juan José Sicre, who created many monuments in Cuba.

There are many rhythmic folk dances in Cuba, especially among the Negroes. Cuban dances include the habanera, guaracha, conga, danzón, rumba, and mambo. Music for these gay dances is provided by orchestras which often have ankle bells, bongo drums, gourds, bottles, hard sticks, earthenware jars, and castanets among their instruments. Composers include José Ardévol, Alejandro García Caturla, Amadeo Roldan, Ernesto Lecuona, and Eduardo Sánchez de Fuentes.

Cuban handicraft workers make tiles and pottery. They also make brooms, fireplace fans, baskets, hammocks, and tortoise-shell combs. Iron grillwork decorates many buildings.

History

Early Years. Columbus landed on the north coast of Cuba in 1492 and claimed it for Spain. It soon became Spain's richest colony in the West Indies and was often raided by Dutch, French, and British pirates. The British captured Havana in 1762 during the Seven

The Capitol at Havana was built in 1929 at a cost of $20,-000,000. It resembles the United States Capitol in Washington, D.C.

Years' War. They held the island until 1763, when they returned it to Spain under the Treaty of Paris.

The Spaniards usually treated their colonies poorly. They refused to let Cuba trade with other countries. Spaniards born in Cuba were not allowed to hold office. Taxes were heavy.

Rebellions. The slaves of Cuba, led by Black José Aponte, revolted against their owners in 1812. The slave leaders were seized and hanged. Later revolts were put down by the Spaniards. But in 1868, Carlos Manuel de Céspedes (1819-1874), with 147 followers, began a struggle against the authorities which lasted for ten years. This revolt was known as the Ten Years' War. At the end of this time, Spain promised reform. Slavery was finally abolished in Cuba in 1886.

Revolution Against Spain. Bartolomé Masó, Máximo Gómez, Calixto García, and José Martí were among the leaders of a revolution that broke out against the Spaniards in 1895. Public opinion in the United States favored the rebels. The American battleship *Maine*, which was sent to Havana to protect American citizens, mysteriously exploded on February 15, 1898. The United States then declared war against Spain. The naval battle at Santiago de Cuba, and the land battles at El Caney and San Juan Hill, all fought in July, were the chief events in the war. Spain gave up all claims to Cuba in the Treaty of Paris, signed December 10, 1898. See SPANISH-AMERICAN WAR.

United States Control. The United States established a military government, under which progress was made in education, public works, and health.

For many years, a disease called yellow fever had killed many Cuban residents every year. In 1881, a Cuban doctor, Carlos Finlay, had said he believed that yellow fever was carried by mosquitoes. In 1900, the Walter Reed Commission of the United States Army proved his theory correct. A Cuban doctor, Aristides Agramonte, was on the commission. Mosquito-control programs were started to stamp out yellow fever.

The Cubans adopted a constitution in 1901 which included the Platt Amendment. This amendment gave the United States the right to intervene in Cuban internal affairs. It also gave the U.S. a naval base at Guantánamo. Tomás Estrada Palma was elected the first president of Cuba in 1902, and the American forces left the country. Palma was re-elected in 1906, but the Liberal party revolted against him. American commissioners were sent to negotiate a compromise. They failed, and an American provisional government was set up. American troops returned to Cuba. The provisional government controlled Cuba until 1909. Then the people elected José Gómez, a Liberal, as president.

Independence. American forces left Cuba in 1909. After that, Cuba had a period of fifteen years of democratic government. But a split in the Liberal party in 1924 gave Gerardo Machado, a Liberal party politician, the chance to seize the government. He ruled with an iron hand until 1933, when an army revolt led by Sergeant Fulgencio Batista placed Ramón Grau San Martín, another Liberal party politician, in office.

Batista removed Grau from office in 1934, and ruled Cuba as a dictator until 1944, although several presidents held office. In 1934, Cuba and the United States signed a treaty that nullified the Platt Amendment.

A new constitution was adopted in 1940. In that same year, Batista ran for president and was elected. In 1941, Cuba joined World War II on the Allied side. The United States had naval and air stations in Cuba during the war. Grau was elected president again in 1944, when Batista retired. Carlos Prio Socarras, another Liberal party politician, was elected president in 1948. In 1952, Batista overthrew Prio's government. He became provisional president and dictator of Cuba.

The Castro Revolution. On July 26, 1953, rebel forces, led by Fidel Castro, unsuccessfully attacked the Moncada Army Barracks in Santiago de Cuba. Castro's rebellion became known as the *26th of July Movement*, taking its name from the date of this first attack. Castro's rebel forces staged another unsuccessful revolt in the province of Oriente in 1956. Castro then retreated to the Sierra Maestra mountains at the southern tip of Cuba. From the mountain headquarters, the rebels engaged in guerrilla warfare for two years.

Late in 1958, a large-scale civil war broke out in Cuba. In January, 1959, Batista fled to exile in the Dominican Republic, and Castro's forces gained control of the government. Castro became premier and dictator of Cuba in February, 1959. Raúl Castro, Fidel's brother, and Ernesto "Ché" Guevara also became leaders in the new government. Both men were leaders in the 26th of July Movement, and were known to have communist backgrounds.

Relations with the United States became seriously strained in 1960 when Castro seized almost all American-owned property. Property owned by other foreigners and by wealthy Cubans was also nationalized. Sugar factories and estates, mines, power plants, telephone and transportation companies, banks, hotels, and apartment houses were all taken over by the government.

The United States reacted first by stopping purchases of Cuban sugar, then by cutting off almost all trade. Only needed food and medicine was sent to Cuba. Castro angrily denounced the United States for its actions, and obtained military and economic aid from Communist countries. The United States finally broke off diplomatic relations with Cuba in January, 1961.

Conditions in Cuba worsened steadily. All activities were brought under state control, and a secret police force was formed to control the people. More than 100,000 Cubans left the country. Most of them settled in nearby Florida. In Miami, relief centers were set up to provide clothes, food, and work for the refugees.

In April, 1961, a band of Cuban exiles invaded Cuba at the Bay of Pigs on Cuba's southern coast, less than 100 miles from Havana. The invaders planned to advance into Cuba and overthrow Castro. But Castro's forces completely crushed the invasion. The Bay of Pigs invasion became an important issue in the United States because it had been launched with U.S. support.

A secret Cuban military court later found the 1,179 prisoners captured in the invasion guilty of treason. Castro released them in 1962 in exchange for a ransom paid in food, drugs, and nonmilitary supplies. Cuba's military power, strengthened by other Communist countries, at this time ranked second only to that of the United States in the Western Hemisphere.

A Communist Satellite. In December, 1961, Castro announced that he had been a communist since his

CUBA

student days. He aligned Cuba with the Communist bloc. Communists took over all positions of responsibility in the country. The Organization of American States (OAS) excluded Cuba from active membership because of Cuba's Communist threat to the hemisphere.

Both farm and industrial production soon began to drop in Cuba. Food shortages plagued Cuban households. In March, 1962, the government announced rationing of such commodities as meat, rice, beans, lard, cooking oils, soap, and toothpaste. Castro blamed the U.S. economic pressure for the shortages. But bad management caused most of the difficulty.

Russia promised Castro about $300,000,000 in credits for economic development. Only a part of this actually reached Cuba. But Russia did send some economic aid, such as factories, fertilizer plants, and construction equipment. Cuba's economy grew weaker despite the Soviet help. Cuba's 1962 sugar cane harvest was one of the smallest in the nation's history.

The Cuban Crisis began to build up in August, 1962. Shiploads of Russian technicians and Russian military equipment began arriving in Cuba. On Oct. 22, 1962, President Kennedy announced that Russia had built missile bases in Cuba that could launch atomic attacks against the U.S. and other parts of the Western Hemisphere. United Nations Ambassador Adlai Stevenson showed photographs of the missiles and the bases before a special session of the UN Security Council. U.S. reconnaissance planes took the pictures.

President Kennedy ordered a naval *quarantine* (blockade) of Cuba to halt the flow of weapons to the island. He demanded that Russia remove all missiles and missile bases from Cuba. On October 28, Premier Khrushchev agreed to U.S. demands, and invited the UN to inspect and verify the dismantling of the bases in Cuba.

Acting UN Secretary-General U Thant flew to Cuba on October 30 to set up a UN inspection staff. But Castro refused to cooperate. Castro said Cuba would not allow the inspection. He also demanded that the United States give up its Guantánamo Bay naval base, and denounced the quarantine as "an act of piracy."

Communist China supported Castro. But the crisis lowered Castro's stature before the other nations of the

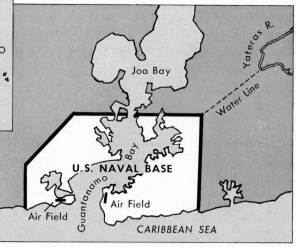

The U.S. Naval Base at Guantánamo was a center of tension during the Cuban crisis of 1962. Maps *above* and *right* show the location of the base. Castro demanded that the United States give up the base, but the U.S. refused, and sent U.S. Marines, *below*, to reinforce the base. A treaty in 1903 gave the United States the right to establish a permanent naval base at Guantánamo. The treaty provided that it can be nullified only by the mutual consent of both countries.

United Press Int.

A Cuban Missile Site is shown in this aerial photograph taken by a high-flying U.S. plane. Aerial photos proved that Russia was putting offensive missiles in Cuba. In October, 1962, the U.S. demanded that all offensive weapons be removed from Cuba. Russia began dismantling the bases.

MISSILE TRANSPORTERS

HEAVY EQUIPMENT

12 PROBABLE GUIDELINE MISSILES

5 MISSILE DOLLIES

20 LONG CYLINDRICAL TANKS

MISSILE TRANSPORTERS

United Press Int.

world. Castro's image had changed from that of a powerful new leader to that of a Russian puppet. The Organization of American States unanimously supported the U.S. in the greatest show of solidarity among Western Hemisphere nations since World War II.

Cuba Today. By 1963, great changes had taken place in the Cuban economy. Cuba had lost its largest sugar and tobacco customer, the United States. The flow of U.S. tourists had stopped. There were shortages of food, machinery, and parts.

Several non-Communist countries, including Canada, France, and Great Britain, began trading with Cuba during the 1960's. But by 1965, the world price of sugar, Cuba's major export, had declined greatly. Cuba, therefore, received less in trade for its sugar. A 1965 trade pact with Russia created a market for some of the crop. In 1966, Russia canceled a $61 million debt owed by Cuba. Also in 1966, Communist China canceled most of the terms of a trade agreement it had made with Cuba in 1964.

Cuban exile groups made several raids on the Cuban coast. After the United States announced in 1963 it would not allow such raids to be launched from its shores, the exile units moved into Central America.

Cuba's relations with the United States continued to be strained. In January, 1964, Castro shut off the water to the U.S. Navy base at Guantánamo Bay. U.S. tankers supplied the base with fresh water. Later that year, the U.S. completed a plant that made fresh water out of salt water and also produced electric power for the base. The plant made the base independent of Cuba. President Lyndon B. Johnson directed the navy to employ fewer Cubans at the base. To stop the flow of U.S. money into Cuba, he also ordered all remaining Cuban employees to spend their salaries on the base.

In May, 1966, Castro charged that U.S. guards at the base shot a Cuban as part of a United States plan to attack Cuba. The United States denied his charges.

Cuba's relations with other Latin American countries were also strained. In July, 1964, most nations in the OAS voted to break diplomatic and economic ties with Cuba. The OAS charged Cuba with aggression for sending military arms to revolutionaries in Venezuela.

In November, 1965, the Castro government agreed to allow Cubans to leave the country. U.S. planes began flying from 3,000 to 4,000 Cubans a month to the U.S. in 1966. But skilled laborers and men eligible for military service were not allowed by Castro to leave Cuba.   OTIS P. STARKEY

Related Articles in WORLD BOOK include:

Outline

I. **The Land and Its Resources**
    A. Location, Size, and   B. Natural Resources
       Surface Features   C. Climate
II. **The People and Their Work**
    A. The People   G. Manufacturing
    B. Way of Life   H. Forest Products
    C. Cities   I. Trade
    D. Agriculture   J. Transportation and
    E. Tourist Industry   Communication
    F. Mining
III. **Social and Cultural Achievements**
IV. **History**

Questions

What is Cuba's most important product?
What mineral was discovered in Cuba in 1954?
Who discovered Cuba?
What is the official language of Cuba?
Who is Fidel Castro?
To what religious faith do most Cubans belong?
What state compares in size to Cuba?
What was the Platt Amendment?
What kind of climate does Cuba have?
Who seized Cuba's government in 1933, 1952, and 1959?

CUBBERLEY, ELLWOOD PATTERSON (1868-1941), an American educator, helped develop the profession of school administration in the United States. He served as professor of education at Stanford University from 1898 to 1917, and as dean of the school of education from 1917 to 1933. Cubberley also wrote many books on education. He was born at Andrews, Ind., and studied at Indiana and Columbia universities. Before going to Stanford, he served as superintendent of schools in San Diego, Calif.   GALEN SAYLOR

CUBE, in geometry, is a solid bounded by six equal squares, such as a child's alphabetical block. All the edges that make up the length, width, and depth of a cube are equal to each other. The *volume* of a cube, or the space it fills, is expressed in cubic inches, cubic feet, cubic centimeters, or some other cubic unit. The volume is found by multiplying the number that represents the length of one of the edges by itself, then multiplying by the length again. For example, if the edge of a cube is 4 inches, the volume of the cube is 4×4×4, or 64 cubic inches. In arithmetic, the *cube* of a number is the product obtained when a number is used as a factor three times. Thus, the cube of 4 is 4×4×4, or 64. This can be indicated by 4^3. See also CUBE ROOT; HEXAHEDRON; ROOT. HOWARD W. EVES

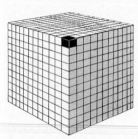

A **Cube** is bounded by six equal squares. Each face of a cube representing one cubic foot is 12 inches long and 12 inches wide. The volume is 12×12×12, or 1,728 cubic inches. The small black cube is $\frac{1}{12}$ of the length, breadth, and depth.

CUBE ROOT is one of three equal factors of a number (see FACTOR). The same number *(m)* taken as a factor three times will be the cube root of another number *(n)*. Thus, $m \times m \times m = n$. For example, 2 is the cube root of 8, because $2 \times 2 \times 2 = 8$, and -5 is the cube root of -125, because $-5 \times -5 \times -5 = -125$. A real number has only one real cube root, which is positive or negative, according to whether the given number is positive or negative. Another symbol is placed in front of a number to indicate that its root is to be *extracted*, or determined. This symbol is written $\sqrt{}$, and is called the *root sign*, or *radical sign*. If the root to be extracted is a cube root, a small figure 3 is placed above the root sign. Thus, $\sqrt[3]{8}$ indicates that the cube root of 8 is to be determined.

Finding Cube Roots by Tables. Perhaps the easiest way of finding cube roots is to use a *table of cube roots*, a *table of cubes*, or a *table of logarithms*. These tables provide correct answers and eliminate tedious calculations. In most cases, the numbers will not have exact cube roots. In these cases, tables are especially helpful.

Calculating Cube Roots. Sometimes tables may not be available. Or, if they are, they will not be accurate enough for a particular purpose. In this case, a person must make his own calculations.

One simple method can be used to calculate the cube root of a number between 1 and 1,000. For example, a person might wish to find the cube root of 200. Since

$5 \times 5 \times 5 = 125$, and $6 \times 6 \times 6 = 216$, it is easy to see that 6 is the closest *integral*, or whole number, cube root of 200. A closer complete approximation can be made by dividing 200 by the square of 6, or 6×6, which equals 36. To the nearest tenth, this gives 5.6. Thus, $6 \times 6 \times 5.6$ is approximately 200.

To get the second approximation of the cube root of 200, average the three factors 6, 6, and 5.6. This will give $\dfrac{6 + 6 + 5.6}{3} = 5.9$. This procedure is repeated to obtain a still better approximation. Thus, $\dfrac{200}{5.9 \times 5.9} = \dfrac{200}{34.81} = 5.74$, and the next approximation is given by $\dfrac{5.9 + 5.9 + 5.74}{3} = 5.85$. Repeating once more gives $\dfrac{200}{5.85 \times 5.85} = \dfrac{200}{34.2225} = 5.8441$, which gives the next approximation $\dfrac{5.85 + 5.85 + 5.8441}{3} = 5.8480$.

This process may be continued indefinitely. In each approximation beyond the second, you can retain a number of digits that is one less than twice the number of digits found in the previous approximation. For example, the second approximation, 5.9, contains two digits. The third approximation may retain three digits. The fourth approximation may retain five digits.

If the number whose cube is desired is not between 1 and 1,000, either multiply or divide it successively by 1,000 to bring it within this range. The cube root of this number will lie between 1 and 10. After finding the cube root, either divide or multiply it successively by 10 as many times as necessary to give the cube root of the original number.   HOWARD W. EVES

See also CUBE; LOGARITHMS; ROOT.

CUBEB, *KYOO beb,* is the dried, unripe berry of a climbing vine belonging to the pepper family. It grows in Penang, Sumatra, New Guinea, and neighboring islands. It resembles black pepper. Cubebs are used as spices in Asia, and as medicine in Europe and America. Drugs prepared from cubebs are used as kidney stimulants, urinary antiseptics, and expectorants. Cubebs, in the form of cigarettes, were formerly used to treat hay fever, asthma, and pharyngitis.

Scientific Classification. The cubeb belongs to the family *Piperaceae.* It is classified as genus *Piper,* species *cubeba.*   HAROLD NORMAN MOLDENKE

CUBIC MEASURE. See WEIGHTS AND MEASURES.

CUBISM was a movement in painting that sought to break down objects into the basic shapes of cubes, spheres, cylinders, and cones. Cubism developed in France in the early 1900's. Its emphasis on the relationships of pure shapes and lines had a great influence on all later art.

Pablo Picasso and Georges Braque led the Cubist movement. The Cubists were influenced by the strength and simplicity of African Negro sculpture and by the structural landscapes of Paul Cézanne (see CÉZANNE, PAUL). They became increasingly concerned with the problem of how to represent form in space. They developed a semigeometric method of analyzing objects into basic shapes. They would begin with a familiar object, such as a table or a guitar. Step by step, they would break it down, flatten it out, change its shapes and colors, and then reassemble it into planes.

Early Cubism grew from Pablo Picasso's *Les Demoiselles d'Avignon*, of 1907, *above*. African Negro sculpture influenced it.

Analytic Cubism divided objects into many fragments and planes, as in Georges Braque's *Man with a Guitar* of 1911, *right*.

The result was a new construction with only a trace of the original subject. The Cubists also introduced the dimension of time into painting by presenting various views of the object at the same time. Their experiments in this area were related to similar ones in the sciences.

Pablo Picasso's *Les Demoiselles d'Avignon*, painted in 1907, is considered the first Cubist painting. His later Cubist work *The Three Musicians* (1921) appears in color in the PAINTING article. In addition to Picasso and Braque, important Cubist painters include Juan Gris (1887-1927) and Fernand Léger.   PETER SELZ

See also BRAQUE, GEORGES; LÉGER, FERNAND; PAINTING (After 1900); PICASSO, PABLO; GRIS, JUAN.

CUBIT, *KYOO bit*, is a measure of length used by several early civilizations. It was based on the length of the forearm from the tip of the middle finger to the elbow.

The Cubit Was Used by Many Early Civilizations.

No one knows when this measure was established. The length of the arm, or cubit, was commonly used by many early peoples, including the Babylonians, Egyptians, and Hebrews. The royal cubit of the ancient Egyptians was about 21 inches long. That of the ancient Romans was 17.5 inches. The Hebrew cubit was 17.58 inches. In the English system the cubit is 18 inches. See also MEASUREMENT (Length and Distance). JOHN W. RENNER

CUCHULAINN, *koo KUHL in*, (25 B.C.?-A.D. 2?), also spelled CUCHULLIN, is the hero of the *Tain Bo Cuailnge* (pronounced *thawn boh KOOL nyih*), or the *Cooley Cattle Raid*. This is Ireland's most famous tale of ancient times, as well as the oldest epic poem of Western Europe. It tells how Cuchulainn defended his country single-handed against invaders from Ulster. The story is based on fact, but the details are mythological. Cuchulainn's father was said to be Lug, the sun-god. The boy was called *Setanta* until he was 7 years old. Then he won the name of Cuchulainn, or *Hound of Culan*, by guarding the house of Culan, whose ferocious watchdog he had killed. After the young warrior had been wounded in battle, he tied himself to a pillar so that he might die on his feet.   KNOX WILSON

CUCKOO, *COOK oo*, is the name of several beautiful closely related birds. The name *cuckoo* comes from the pleasant song of the European cuckoo. The two common kinds of cuckoos in North America are the *black-billed cuckoo* and the *yellow-billed cuckoo*. They are shy birds, but can be recognized by their call. Their song is a series of low, mournful, quivering notes. Both of these cuckoos are slender birds, about a foot long. Their tails are long and rounded. These cuckoos differ from most

A **Black-Billed Cuckoo** seems to like damp and cloudy weather. For this reason it is often called a *rain crow*, and many people believe frequent cuckoo calls mean that it is going to rain.

J. Horace McFarland

Cucumbers grow on long, trailing vines that are similar to melon vines. The vines bear yellow or whitish flowers on short stems. Cucumbers rank among the oldest known vegetables.

birds because two of the toes of their feet point forward and two backward. They have rather long and slightly curved beaks.

Both cuckoos have olive-brown backs and white breasts. The most important difference between the black-billed cuckoo and the yellow-billed cuckoo is the color of the bill. The black-billed cuckoo also has red circles around its eyes, and the yellow-billed cuckoo has larger white marks on its tail.

These cuckoos make their homes in woods, thickets, and orchards. They build untidy nests. There may be two to seven eggs in one nest. The eggs are green-blue with a dull surface. The American cuckoos have often been called *rain crows*. Many people think that frequent cuckoo calls mean that it is going to rain. The birds feed on insect pests such as hairy caterpillars that are shunned by other birds. Because they are insect-eaters, cuckoos migrate to the tropics during the winter months.

The European cuckoo resembles a sharp-shinned hawk in size and color pattern, and has a sweeter song than the American cuckoo. It does not care for its own young. It lays its eggs in other birds' nests or carries them there in its bill, and leaves them to be hatched by the other bird.

Scientific Classification. The cuckoos belong to the cuckoo family, *Cuculidae*. The yellow-billed cuckoo is genus *Coccyzus*, species *C. americanus*. The black-billed is *C. erythrophthalmus*. The European cuckoo is classified as *Cuculus canorus*.   ARTHUR A. ALLEN

See also BIRD (color pictures: Birds That Help Us [Yellow-Billed Cuckoo], Birds of Other Lands [Emerald Cuckoo], Birds' Eggs); ROAD RUNNER.

CUCUMBER is a common garden vegetable native to southern Asia, but cultivated as an annual in many parts of the world. The cucumber plant is a hairy-stemmed vine that bears many tendrils. Its triangular leaves may have three pointed lobes. It bears yellow or whitish flowers on short stems. Its edible fruit, commonly called *cucumber*, may grow from 1 inch to 3 feet long. The pulpy fruit contains many seeds and is covered by a thin, smooth or prickly skin. The flesh is usually white or yellowish.

Small cucumbers used for pickling are often called

gherkins. But the true gherkin is another plant closely related to the cucumber. It bears many little spiny fruits shaped like olives.

People eat the young cucumber fruits raw or pickle them. The raw fruits are eaten in salads and sandwiches. The yellow, mature fruits are tough and contain many hard seeds. Such cucumbers are sometimes pickled or served as a hot vegetable. Cucumbers have little food value.

Cucumbers grow best in warm weather and are easily killed by frost. Gardeners grow the plants from seed. They sow the seed in small hills of loam or light soil as soon as warm weather comes. They build the hills about 4 feet apart to allow room for the vines to grow. When the young plants start to grow, workers thin them so only four or five remain in each hill. The plants grow rapidly in warm weather and if they have enough moisture. Small fruits that are suitable for pickles appear quite soon. Gardeners pick these fruits every two or three days.

Sometimes gardeners grow cucumbers in greenhouses. The plants grow much as they do in fields. But usually, because of the limited space, the gardener trains the vines on cords or wires. A cucumber plant frequently yields 100 or more fruits.

Several kinds of beetles attack young cucumber plants. Gardeners often spray the young plants with rotenone dust to destroy the insects. The *melon aphid* also attacks the cucumber plants and spreads *mosaic*, a virus disease.

Scientific Classification. The cucumber belongs to the gourd family, *Cucurbitaceae*. It is genus *Cucumis*, species *C. sativus*. Gherkins are *C. anguria*.   JOHN H. MacGILLIVRAY

CUD is a small mass of food that animals called *ruminants* bring up from their stomachs for a second chewing. Ruminants include such animals as antelopes, camels, cattle, deer, and goats.

See also RUMINANT; CATTLE (Stomach).

CUDAHY, *KUD uh hih,* **MICHAEL** (1841-1910), an American meat packer, developed and introduced cold-storage facilities in packing plants. This made possible year-round meat curing and livestock marketing. Cudahy went to work for a meat packer in Milwaukee, Wis., at the age of 14. In 1875, he became a partner in

Armour and Company. With P. D. Armour, he formed the Armour-Cudahy Company in 1887. Three years later, he established the Cudahy Packing Company, one of the largest in the United States, in Omaha, Nebr. Cudahy was born in Callan, Ireland, and came to the United States with his parents in 1849. JOHN B. McFERRIN

CUE. See BILLIARDS (The Cue); SHUFFLEBOARD.

CUENCA, *KWAYNG kah* (pop. 65,058; alt. 8,306 ft.), is a commercial center in the mountains of southern Ecuador. For location, see ECUADOR (color map). More than half of Ecuador's output of Panama hats comes from Cuenca. The city also trades in cinchona bark, animal and alligator hides, and gold. Cuenca was founded in 1557. C. LANGDON WHITE

CUERNAVACA, *KWEHR nah BAH kah* (pop. 37,144; alt. 5,058 ft.), is the capital of the state of Morelos in Mexico. It lies about 37 miles south of Mexico City (see MEXICO [political map]). The city's mild climate and beautiful scenery have made it a popular resort. The city has many beautiful estates and ancient buildings. Tourist attractions include the Palace of Cortes and the Borda gardens. The Spaniards founded the city in 1521. JOHN A. CROW

CUERVO DE PRIETO QUINTUPLETS. See QUINTUPLETS.

CUESTA. See HOGBACK.

CUFFE, PAUL (1759-1817), an American seaman and merchant, encouraged the colonizing of Negroes in Sierra Leone, Africa. He financed the voyage of 38 free Negroes in 1815. He also sought to strengthen the legal position of Negroes in America. His efforts led to a law, passed in 1783, which gave Negroes in Massachusetts the right to vote. Cuffe, part Negro and part Indian, was born on Cuttyhunk Island, Mass. He also became a minister among the Quakers. LOUIS FILLER

CUGNOT, NICOLAS JOSEPH. See AUTOMOBILE (The Steam Car; illustration).

CUISENAIRE METHOD, *kwee zuh NEHR*, is a teaching system designed to help students discover basic mathematical principles by themselves. The method uses rods of 10 different colors and lengths that can easily be handled by children. By using the rods, students can prove numerical relationships and understand principles of proportion. They can also learn addition, subtraction, multiplication, division, factors, and fractions.

The rods help the student understand mathematical principles rather than merely memorize them. For example, two white rods placed end to end are the same length as a red rod. The red rod then stands for the number 2 if the white rod represents 1. A red rod and a white rod placed end to end are as long as a light-green rod. The light-green rod then stands for 3, because it is as long as three white rods. The rods can also be used to represent different sets of numbers. For example, if the white rod is assigned a value of 3, the red rod becomes 6. If the red rod is given a value of 1, then the white rod becomes $\frac{1}{2}$.

Students can discover many facts about mathematical relationships by working with the rods. For example, three red rods placed end to end are as long as one dark-green rod. The dark-green rod is two-thirds as long as a blue rod. The student can see that the three red rods equal two-thirds of a blue rod. If the dark-green rod has a value of 12, then the student learns that 3×4 equals 12. He can also conclude that 12 is $\frac{2}{3}$ of 18.

Schoolteachers use the Cuisenaire Method in the United States, Canada, and parts of Europe. Georges Cuisenaire, a school teacher from Thuin, Belgium, developed the method. LOLA J. MAY

CULEBRA CUT. See PANAMA CANAL (Gaillard Cut).

CULEX. See MALARIA (Malaria in Animals).

CULIACÁN. See SINALOA.

CULLINAN STONE. See DIAMOND (Famous Diamonds; picture).

CULLODEN MOOR. See SCOTLAND (Union with England).

CULPEPPER FLAG. See FLAG (picture, Flags in American History [Southern Flags]).

CULTIVATOR. See FARM AND FARMING (Terms).

CULTURAL DEPRIVATION describes a condition in which a person lacks the skills needed to adjust successfully to life in our rapidly changing society. A child's home training may fail to give him the basic intellectual, emotional, and social skills needed to adapt to formal schooling. For example, a child's vocabulary may be so limited that he is unable to understand his teacher. Therefore, he will do poorly in school. His inadequate education will probably reduce his earning ability as an adult.

Most culturally deprived children become culturally deprived, low-income adults. Social scientists conclude that cultural deprivation is responsible for the rise in the number of low-income families.

About one out of every five U.S. families has an annual income of less than $3,000. In more than three-fourths of these families, the wage earner did not complete high school. In large cities, about one child in three comes from a low-income family.

Several local, state, and federal programs were started in the early 1960's to reduce cultural deprivation. The federal government's Economic Opportunity Act of 1964 is designed to aid culturally deprived persons by bettering their educational and financial opportunities. The *Head Start* program prepares preschool children for formal education (see HEAD START).

Other terms used to describe culturally deprived persons include *educationally deprived, lower class,* and *underprivileged.* D. KEITH OSBORN

See also ECONOMIC OPPORTUNITY, OFFICE OF.

CULTURAL LAG is a theory that describes how and why culture changes. According to this theory, social change starts with the invention of new technology, but the ideas of people tend to delay the use of the invention and to interfere with its most efficient application. For example, the invention of the automobile created antagonism on the part of people who understood horses but could not understand this new mechanical device. Their ideas *lagged* behind the invention.

An American sociologist, William F. Ogburn, introduced this theory in the 1920's. He claimed that cultural lag is practically a universal process. Critics of the theory point out that, although this theory might explain some cultural change, not all social change follows this pattern. They maintain that ideas sometimes lead the way to important social changes without involving material inventions, as in many of the cultural changes of the Renaissance. JOHN F. CUBER

See also CULTURE (How Cultures Grow and Change).

CULTURE

CULTURE. We often use the word *cultured* to describe a person who appreciates good paintings, literature, or music. But, in the social sciences, culture has a different meaning. In the broadest sense, it refers to all distinctively human activities, and includes achievements in every field, which man passes on from one generation to the next. Culture means such activities as using a language, getting married, bringing up children, earning a living, running a government, fighting a war, and taking part in religious ceremonies. In a narrower sense, we refer to a culture as the sum total of the ways of life of a group of people. We may speak of Eskimo culture, Hottentot culture, or our own Western culture.

Some cultures belong to large groups of people, and others to small tribes. No two cultures are exactly alike. Simple cultures are usually the product of people who have no written language (see PRIMITIVE MAN). More complex cultures develop into civilizations (see CIVILIZATION).

Scientists who study the cultures of peoples living in the past and present are called *anthropologists*. Social scientists called *sociologists* specialize in the study of our present-day culture. See ANTHROPOLOGY; SOCIOLOGY.

Scientists believe that the ability to develop culture is one of the greatest differences between men and animals. Culture must be learned, and men can learn so much more than animals that they can store up knowledge by means of speech and writing. Through many generations, man has acquired more and more knowledge, and cultures have grown and changed. But animals continue to live as they have always lived, because they cannot pass on their knowledge. Animal life may change gradually over hundreds of thousands of years, but such changes involve heredity more than learning. *Social animals*, such as ants, bees, and other insects, live in highly organized communities. But these societies seem to depend mainly on heredity. Each ant colony or beehive resembles every other colony or hive. For a discussion of the differences between men and animals that make culture possible, see MAN.

We can break down each culture into a number of *traits*. In Western culture, a man is allowed to be married to only one wife at a time. In the Arab culture, he may have four wives. *Monogamy*, or single marriage, is a trait in Western culture. *Polygyny*, or marriage to several women at once, is a trait of Arab culture. Several traits of a culture may be closely related. For example, tribes in eastern Africa keep cattle, live on milk products, use cow dung to plaster their houses, and wear cowhide garments. They consider cattle as wealth, and use them to buy wives. Such a group of related traits is called a *culture complex*. Many cultures that are different in other ways may share the same complex. The area in which this situation occurs is known as a *culture area*. For examples of culture areas, see INDIAN, AMERICAN (Regional Groupings of Indians).

Various cultures stress different traits. Important traits that seem to guide other traits are called *key traits*. Prestige through wealth in cattle, as among the East Africans, is a key trait. It influences the people's food, clothing, shelter, and economic system. A great interest in life after death, which characterized the

Waagenaar, Pix; Underwood & Underwood; Andre de Dienes, Rapho-Guillumette

CULTURE IS LEARNED

People Transmit Their Knowledge from one generation to the next. Cultures without writing pass it on only by word of mouth. Systems of writing enabled men to store records in great libraries. Television and other recent forms of communication represent man's continuing need for efficient ways of accumulating and distributing his knowledge.

CULTURAL TRADITIONS VARY GREATLY

Patterns of Living often depend on the environment. Desert nomads travel in small, independent groups. A village community requires greater cooperation from its members. People who live together in a huge city become extremely dependent on each other.

ancient Egyptians, is another key trait. Throughout their lives, the Egyptians prepared for death. Large numbers of people spent all their time building and decorating tombs, and creating objects to be placed in them. The culture of the North American Plains Indians emphasized accumulating honors for bravery in warfare, while Indians of the northwest coast acquired rank through wealth. A combination of key traits is known as a *system of values*, or a *culture pattern*.

The study of various cultures is important in giving us an understanding of our own behavior. It also helps us understand how to get along with the different groups of people living in the world.

How Cultures Are Alike

All cultures have certain things in common. These may deal with the *material* aspects of life, such as shelter. Or they may involve such *nonmaterial* activities as maintaining a government or creating myths. Elements common to all cultures include (1) technology, (2) institutions, (3) language, and (4) the arts.

Technology, as anthropologists use the term, includes what might be called the basic equipment for everyday living, and the way people use it. Man has no claws or fangs to catch animals for food, so he had to develop tools. All human cultures include the use of tools. Scientists have never found a group of people who lacked tools. Machines, which are complex tools, serve an extremely important function in our lives. But people of almost every culture use simple machines to make their work easier. See TOOL; MACHINE.

Another element found in all cultures is fire. All men use it to cook food and for keeping warm. But not every group knows how to make fire. In a few cultures, people have inherited it from their ancestors. Each family always tries to keep a fire burning. If it goes out, they borrow some live coals from neighbors. See FIRE.

Everyone needs food, and most people prepare it in some way for eating. Most peoples either wear clothing or decorate their bodies with grease, clay, or earth pigments. Nearly everyone makes some kind of shelter, at least during seasons of cold or rain. But different cultures meet these needs in different ways. See FOOD; CLOTHING; SHELTER.

Institutions. An institution is a group of people who either live together or meet regularly for some purpose. The group controls the behavior of its members through a system of organization. Usually, some persons lead and others follow. Who leads and who follows depends on differences in sex, age, and individual qualities. A culture usually has several kinds of institutions. These may include the family; political, economic, and religious institutions; and voluntary associations.

In all cultures, men, women, and children live together in families. The *family* is the one basic institution found everywhere. In simple cultures, the family educates the children. Advanced cultures have special education systems. See FAMILY; EDUCATION, HISTORY OF.

In the simplest cultures, the only institution larger than the family is the band, a group of families that live and collect food together. Many Indian tribes lived in bands. The members of each band form a kind of inde-

Biblioteca Vaticana; Eastman Chemical Products, Inc.; Hedda Morrison, Pix; Werner Wolff, Black Star

EVERYDAY CUSTOMS
ARE PART OF CULTURE

Fashions in Clothing may indicate important cultural differences. The styles shown vary from casualness to great formality. They represent various religious beliefs, standards of beauty, and attitudes toward women.

Dorothy Reed
American Teen-Ager

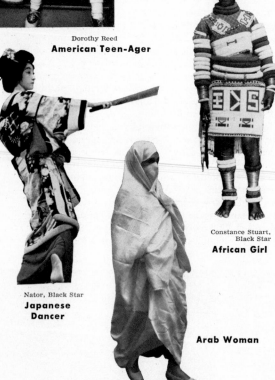

Nator, Black Star
Japanese Dancer

Constance Stuart, Black Star
African Girl

Arab Woman

Emil Brunner, Pix

All cultures have some sort of *religious institutions*. In simple cultures, the band of related families can be its own religious unit. In complex cultures, there are separate religious institutions.

Anthropologists believe that many religious practices, especially in primitive cultures, grow out of the need people feel for comfort and reassurance. In farming regions, for example, the rain may sometimes fail just when it is needed to make the crops grow. This is an anxious time for everyone. A religious ceremony, such as the snake dance of the Hopi Indians of Arizona, may relieve the people's tension. While there is much more to religion than this, the need for relief from disturbance has often brought people together in religious congregations with leaders and followers.

Among most peoples, religion includes special songs, dances, costumes, and rituals. In probably all cultures, people believe that the spirit lives on in some form after death. Many persons in primitive cultures believe that spirits reappear from time to time, often in dreams. They believe that some individuals can communicate with the spirits (see MAGIC). These spirits often become gods. The gods are usually associated with things that disturb people, such as war, thunder, and love. In cultures with a division of labor, members of each trade or occupation may have a special god. Many anthropologists believe that the concept of a single god, governing all nature and all people, arises only in the most complex cultures. See RELIGION.

A fifth kind of institution is the *voluntary association*. It is composed of persons who come together of their own will through some common interest. Voluntary associations include such organizations as the Boy Scouts, college fraternities and sororities, and Indian secret societies. In some of the most complex societies, like our own, there are a great number of voluntary associations. They form a vital part of the web of relationships that holds our culture together.

Language. A third ingredient that all cultures have in common is the use of language. Each language provides a system of communication for the culture of which it is a part. But each language also provides for growth. It may reflect culture changes by adding new words and dropping old ones. Its grammar may become simplified in order to allow for easier change. English, for example, has a large vocabulary but a simple grammar.

Every language has three definite parts: sounds, vocabulary, and grammar. Each language uses only a small number of all the possible *sounds*. Some of these sounds differ from those of other languages. That is why persons who learn English after they grow up may pronounce certain sounds peculiarly. A language also has its own *vocabulary* that serves the needs of the people who speak it. For example, Arabs have more than five hundred words for different kinds of camels, and Eskimos have many words for kinds or conditions of snow. The Arabs use a single word for both snow and ice, and Eskimos have no word at all for camel. Snow creates no problem for the Arabs, and Eskimos have never had anything to do with camels. We know about both snow and camels, but neither is vital to our culture, so we have only one word for each. All languages have rules of *grammar* for the arrangement of sounds into words, phrases, and sentences. Primitive peoples may not be

pendent nation, although it may have only a few dozen citizens. As cultures become more complex, greater numbers of people gather together to live and work. The nation may then have a chief or king, soldiers, tax collectors, messengers, or governors of provinces. Any such system of governing men, simple or complex, is called a *political institution*. There are many different systems of government, but the structures of most are basically the same. See GOVERNMENT; LAW.

Complex cultures, particularly those whose people grow food instead of hunting and collecting, usually have a division of labor. For example, one man may be an expert toolmaker. He makes tools for others, and they give him food in return. The toolmaker needs apprentices to help him and to learn his trade. The toolmaker and his apprentices, with their clients, form an *economic institution*. Economic institutions arise from both manufacturing and trade. In our own culture, a factory represents the former, a department store the latter. See ECONOMICS.

able to state rules of grammar, but they follow them nevertheless. See LANGUAGE.

The Arts. The desire for beauty seems to exist in every culture. The arts include myths and tales of ancient heroes, dancing, acting out legends and rituals, painting, sculpture, singing, instrumental music, and various combinations of these forms of expression. Like language, art serves basically as a means of communication. A clown can express strong emotions of sadness or joy with a single gesture. People tend to spend more time, energy, and skill on art than on any other activity. This is because communication holds together people who share a culture, and the arts are the most efficient form of communication. See ART AND THE ARTS.

Why Cultures Differ

The many cultures of mankind may resemble each other generally, but they differ greatly in details. We need only to glance through the pages of THE WORLD BOOK to find examples of ways of living that differ from

Museum of the American Indian

Cultures Borrow from Each Other. Sometimes people combine the borrowed elements with their own traditions to produce new traits. The peyote ritual of the North American Indians, shown *above* in a drawing by an Indian, mixes Christian customs with Indian rites. In other situations, especially those involving technology, people adopt new ways without much change. Such is the case with the Arab tribesman, *below*, operating a power tool.

Black Star

our own. Some persons eat with knives and forks, some with chopsticks, and others with their fingers. The ancient Spartans punished children severely for misbehaving, but the Eskimos rarely touch a child in anger. Our culture believes in individual competition, but the Pueblo Indians feel it is wrong for one person to outdo his fellow men. Why do these differences exist?

One reason is that men differ greatly from each other physically. There is little difference between one earthworm and another, or between two robins of the same age and sex. But individual men and women differ greatly. The bodies of no two persons are exactly alike. The uniqueness of each human being makes life interesting, and allows cultures to change.

Men also behave differently from each other. Among animals, each animal behaves much the same as every other animal of the same kind. Even when animals of one species live on widely separated continents, they utter the same kinds of cries and calls, and build the same kinds of homes. Much animal behavior seems to be inherited. Animals have little to learn, and learn it quickly and simply. Humans have far more to learn, and learn it much more slowly. Each child must learn from his parents, brothers and sisters, playmates, and teachers, the thousands of details he needs in order to grow up in his own culture.

Men are hardy creatures, and settled long ago on every continent except Antarctica. They have lived for thousands of years in small groups, exposed to many different kinds of climate. Most of these groups have been separated from other groups and their cultures. Each group has worked out a way of living to suit its own particular conditions.

How Cultures Grow and Change

Some cultures appear to have gone on for thousands of years without change. This may be basically true, but details in such cultures have probably changed considerably. For example, hunters cannot usually change their basic culture if they live in an isolated area where food is scarce and there are no animals or plants to raise. Even a new method of hunting might kill off all the game, so there would be no point in using it. But changes would occur in fields unrelated to food-getting or to the social framework. The people might adopt new ways of decorating themselves, or of holding ceremonies, or of singing their songs.

A struggle goes on continually in every culture between the new ideas of some individuals and the forces of *conformity*, or the desire to do things in the same way everyone else does them. The *mores*, or fixed social and moral customs of a society, tend to enforce conformity (see MORES). Cultures need a certain amount of conformity in order to keep groups of people working together. But they also need new ideas to permit progress. A balance of these two forces keeps cultures strong and progressive.

Cultures grow and change in two main ways: (1) by invention and (2) by borrowing.

Invention is the only source of original cultural change. Inventions usually come from gifted persons who have keen powers of observation and the ability to link together in their minds the things they have seen. Inventors also have the ability to imagine the results of their inventions. The man who invented the bow and arrow made hunting easier than it had been when the spear was the best weapon. The inventor of the sail improved navigation, and made it more efficient than when men used paddles and oars to travel in ships. But all inventions do not involve making new tools or machines. Many original ideas occur in the fields of social structure and religion.

People do not accept all inventions. They will reject a new invention, or use it as a toy, if it is not immediately useful. For example, the wheeled cart was invented in or near Mesopotamia around 3000 B.C. People soon used it to haul loads, because they had oxen to hitch to it. The Maya Indians of Central America also invented the wheel. But they used it as a toy, because they had no draft animals. A single device may be invented in several places at the same time or at different periods. Pottery and metalworking, for instance, were probably invented and put to use in both Asia and America. Even with present-day communications, several men may work completely independently of each other and arrive at the same conclusions. In this way, two mathematicians in different countries developed non-Euclidean geometry at almost exactly the same time. See INVENTION.

Borrowing, also known as *diffusion*, occurs more frequently than invention, because it requires less originality. The idea of the wheel probably originated in west-central Asia, and traveled throughout the world. Arabs carried the knowledge of fine steelmaking, developed in India, to Syria and Spain. From these countries, it spread to England and Germany. Diffusion may sometimes take place slowly, and in a roundabout way. For example, tobacco and tobacco-smoking originated in tropical America, and spread throughout the temperate regions of both North and South America. Early colonists carried the custom back to Europe. From there it traveled to Africa and Asia. Russians introduced the practice of smoking into Siberia, where the people developed a special kind of pipe with a flaring bowl. This form of pipe, as well as the knowledge of tobacco, traveled across Bering Strait and was adopted by the Eskimos. In this way, smoking traveled around the world before it reached a people who lived "next door" to its place of origin.

In our own culture, among other things, we have borrowed corn, beans, squash, potatoes, and tobacco from the American Indians. We learned from the Arabs how to use soap and the compass. Our knowledge of papermaking comes from the Chinese. Our seven-day week originated with the Babylonians, and our alphabet with the Phoenicians of western Asia.

When Cultures Meet

The people of one culture meet those of other cultures as groups grow. They usually exchange ideas and products. The impact of one culture on another is called *acculturation* (see ACCULTURATION). Such contact may be friendly or hostile. For example, when a band of New Guinea warriors attacks an enemy village by surprise, the victors may kill the men, and capture the women and children. If the captive women know some special skill, such as making shell beads, they may pass this trait on to the culture of their captors.

When people with a complex culture invade the territory of people with a simple culture, the earlier inhabitants often die out. This happens because the earlier people cannot withstand new diseases, or because they are pushed out of their hunting grounds. Even if they do not die out, their culture may disappear as the conquerors absorb them. Some cultures, such as the Tasmanian, have disappeared in this way. Others, including those of some Indians from eastern North America, survive only in a few tribal ceremonies.

When a strong people with a simple culture conquers a weaker but more civilized people, the victors may absorb much of the older culture. The ancient Romans conquered the Greeks, but the Greeks had a more advanced culture in arts and sciences, and became teachers of the Romans.

Cultures have blended throughout the world as modern transportation and communication bring all kinds of peoples together. For example, the Japanese have adopted such western institutions as steelmaking, deepwater shipping, railroads, newspapers, and parliamentary government. But they have kept many essentials of their own earlier culture, such as a love of ceremony, distinctive ways of eating and dressing, and elements of the samurai code and Shinto religion.

Theories About Culture

The concept of culture held by most anthropologists originated fairly recently. The first definition of culture as a sociological term was that of E. B. Tylor, a British anthropologist, who wrote in 1871: "Culture . . . is that complex whole which includes knowledge, belief, art, morals, custom, and any and all other capabilities and habits acquired by man as a member of society." In this definition, Tylor considered culture as the sum total of human achievements. In 1916, Clark Wissler, an American anthropologist, distinguished between culture in general and the separate cultures of individual groups of people. He also stated that culture has to be learned. During the 1920's, the functional anthropologists, headed by A. R. Radcliffe-Brown and Bronislaw Malinowski of Great Britain, emphasized the fact that each culture is an integrated whole, like a living being. Since that time, American anthropologists, including Alfred L. Kroeber, Ruth Benedict, and Clyde Kluckhohn, have developed two new fields of cultural research. Their studies have investigated (1) culture and the individual personality, and (2) the systems of values developed by various cultures. These two fields treat cultures as living and functioning wholes. Further work in analyzing cultures may perhaps bring culture closer to the biological basis on which it ultimately, though indirectly, depends.   CARLETON S. COON

Outline

I. How Cultures Are Alike
    A. Technology   C. Language
    B. Institutions   D. The Arts

Questions

What basic elements do all cultures have in common?
Why do people sometimes reject a new invention?
What has our culture borrowed from other cultures?
How does a culture trait differ from a culture complex?
How do cultures change?
Why do cultures need both conformity and new ideas?
What is an example of an economic institution in our own culture?
Why do cultures differ so much in details?
Why do animals fail to develop a culture?
In what different ways can acculturation work?

CULTURE consists of microorganisms or tissue cells grown in the laboratory on a *culture medium* (material containing nutrients). Microorganisms grown in cultures include bacteria, yeasts, and viruses. A *pure* culture contains only one *species* (type) of microorganism. A *mixed* or *contaminated* culture contains more than one type. The kinds of nutrients required depend on the organism's needs. Common nutrients include carbohydrates, proteins, and minerals. They are usually dissolved in water. Solid medium may be made by adding agar-agar or gelatin (see AGAR-AGAR; GELATIN).   MARTIN FROBISHER

CULVER-STOCKTON COLLEGE. See UNIVERSITIES AND COLLEGES (table).

CUM LAUDE. See DEGREE, COLLEGE.

CUMBERLAND. See ENGLAND (color map: The 38 Counties of England).

CUMBERLAND, Md. (pop. 33,415; alt. 690 ft.), ranks high among the cities of western Maryland in size and industrial importance. It lies at the picturesque "Narrows" where Wills Creek empties into the Potomac River (see MARYLAND [political map]).

Cumberland industries produce such diversified products as bakery goods, beer, brick, Celanese fibers, dairy products, electronics products, macaroni, microscopic drills, paper, plate glass, and steel shafting.

Cumberland has many historic homes and monuments. Fort Cumberland, built in 1754, served as a base for George Washington's expeditions before and during the French and Indian War. General Edward Braddock's march on Fort Duquesne started there, in 1755. Cumberland was the east end of the National Road. The first Baltimore and Ohio train entered the town in 1842. Cumberland, incorporated as a city in 1856, has a commission government.   FRANCIS C. HABER

CUMBERLAND COLLEGE. See UNIVERSITIES AND COLLEGES (table).

CUMBERLAND GAP is a natural pass through the Appalachians, at the meeting point of Virginia, Kentucky, and Tennessee. The gap was used as a gateway to the West by pioneer settlers. Between 1775 and 1880, about 200,000 persons passed through the gap. The gap is 1,600 feet above sea level, cutting through the 2,000-to 3,000-foot Cumberland Mountains. It is narrow, and has steep sides about 500 feet high. Railroads run through the gap. Laurel and rhododendron cover the area. The Cumberland Gap National Historical Park was established in 1955 (see NATIONAL PARK [Historical Parks]). It covers over 20,000 acres and is the largest historical park in the country.

Thomas Walker's exploring party used the gap in 1750, and in 1775 Daniel Boone blazed his "Wilderness Road" through the pass (see BOONE, DANIEL). Cumberland Gap was the route of Union armies invading Tennessee in 1862 and 1863.   E. WILLARD MILLER

See also UNITED STATES, HISTORY OF (color picture: Americans Explored and Won a Rich New Land); KENTUCKY (color picture).

CUMBERLAND MOUNTAINS, part of the Appalachian Mountain system, extend across part of eastern Tennessee and Kentucky, and form the boundary between Virginia and Kentucky. Some geographers call this mountain region the Cumberland Plateau. Streams have carved a complex pattern of narrow, steep-sided valleys into the mountains. The Cumberlands rise about 2,000 feet above sea level, but some ridges are 500 to 1,000 feet higher than the general level. The Cumberland Mountains contain rich coal fields. See also APPALACHIAN MOUNTAINS.   E. WILLARD MILLER

CUMBERLAND RIVER, an important branch of the Ohio River, rises in the rugged Cumberland Mountains in eastern Kentucky. It empties into the Ohio River at Smithland, in northwestern Kentucky. The winding course of the Cumberland is 720 miles long, and the river drains an area of about 18,000 square miles. The Cumberland drops 68 feet to make the Great Falls in Cumberland Falls State Park, Kentucky. It is navigable 461 miles upstream to Wolf Creek Dam. The principal cities on the Cumberland are Nashville and Clarksville, Tenn. See also OHIO RIVER.   E. WILLARD MILLER

CUMBERLAND ROAD. See NATIONAL ROAD.

CUMMINGS, E. E. (1894-1962), was an American poet and playwright. Seeking a spontaneous and fresh presentation, he generally disregarded the rules of grammar and punctuation. He frequently coined his own words and compounds, and ran words and sentences together. He often abandoned the use of capital letters and spelled his name e e cummings. Beneath the deceptively complex surface, however, his poems offer a relatively simple point of view.

Cummings was always concerned with preserving individuality in an age he felt was dominated by Communism and American materialism. He denounced Russia's "apotheosis of mediocrity" and called the United States "a pseudocommunity enslaved by perpetual obscenities of mental concupiscence." His verse plays *Him* (1927) and *Santa Claus* (1946), as well as much of his lyric poetry, defend individualism and offer sentimental and romantic justifications of love, feeling, and intuition as opposed to science and systematic knowledge.

e e cummings
Marion Morehouse

EDWARD ESTLIN CUMMINGS was born in Cambridge, Mass., the son of a prominent Boston clergyman. Cummings volunteered as an ambulance driver in World War I, and vividly described his experiences in a detention camp in his first book, *The Enormous Room* (1922). He returned to Paris in 1921, and published the poems that won him a reputation as a radical experimenter. His poems were collected in *Poems 1923-1954*.   ELMER W. BORKLUND

CUMULUS. See CLOUD.

CUNARD, SIR SAMUEL (1787-1865), founded the Cunard line of steamships. In 1838 he and two Englishmen formed a company for mail service between England and America by steam rather than by sailing vessels. The *Britannia* made the company's first voyage in 1840. Cunard was made a baronet for services the Cunard lines rendered to Great Britain in the Crimean War. He was born in Halifax, N.S.   W. H. BAUGHN

CUNAXA, BATTLE OF. See CYRUS THE YOUNGER.

CUNEIFORM, *kyoo NEE uh fawrm*, was a system of writing used long before modern alphabets were invented. The name comes from the Latin *cuneus*, meaning *wedge*. Cuneiform writing was so named because cuneiform strokes, made with a stylus, are broad at one end and pointed at the other, like a wedge.

Cuneiform writing is hard to translate because the characters may represent either a word or a syllable. One character may have several different meanings.

The most common material used for cuneiform writing was clay, molded into a square slab or tablet. Cuneiform characters were scratched on the tablets while the clay was still moist. Then the tablets were dried in the sun or baked in an oven until they hardened.

Its Beginnings. The Sumerian people were probably the inventors of cuneiform writing. They developed it from picture writing. The earliest known inscriptions are from the lower Tigris-Euphrates Valley in Mesopotamia, or Iraq. Tablets found in Uruk (Warka) and nearby sites may have been written as early as 3000 B.C. Many of the characters in these groups retain their picturelike forms, for the wedgelike type of writing did not develop until about 2500 B.C. The latest cuneiform clay tablet that has been discovered was written only a few years before the Christian Era began in A.D. 1.

The cuneiform writings of the Sumerians are not only the oldest, but also the most complicated. The Akkadian-Sumerian system had about 600 characters. The Hittites used about 350 characters, the Elamites about 200, and the Persians only 39. An alphabetic cuneiform script of only 30 symbols was recovered about 1929 from excavations in northern Syria.

Cuneiform Translation was not attempted until shortly before 1800. European travelers in western Iran then noticed the ancient inscriptions carved 300 feet above the ground on the steep side of Behistun Rock. In 1802, a German named Georg Grotefend (1775-1853) began to translate these inscriptions. Several other scholars, notably an Englishman named Rawlinson, became interested, and by the mid-1800's the translation was complete. It turned out to be a record of the accomplishments of the Persian king Darius, written in three languages. This record proved to be the key to cuneiform writing in other languages.

Since 1802 several hundred thousand cuneiform tablets have been recovered and placed in museums. The information gained from them has shed new light on the early history of man.   WILLIAM A. MCDONALD

See also ALPHABET; ARCHAEOLOGY; DARIUS; COMMUNICATION.

CUNNINGHAM, ANN PAMELA (1816-1875), founded the Mount Vernon Ladies' Association of the Union in 1853 to make a national shrine of Mount Vernon, President George Washington's home (see MOUNT VERNON LADIES' ASSOCIATION OF THE UNION). In 1853, she visited Mount Vernon and was distressed to see the home going to ruin. She started her campaign in newspapers. In 1856, the state of Virginia granted a charter to the association. The association raised about $200,000 to buy the mansion and 202 acres of land. On Feb. 22, 1859, the association bought the property. During the Civil War, Mount Vernon was neutral ground. After the war, Miss Cunningham moved in and took over direction of the estate. She was born in Laurens County, S.C.   HELEN E. MARSHALL

CUNNINGHAM, GLENN. See TRACK AND FIELD.

CUNNINGHAM, MERCE (1919-   ), is an American dancer and *choreographer* (dance composer). Cunningham's dances do not have the usual elements of plot and character. He often creates dances without knowledge of the music that will accompany them. He became particularly known for his methods of *chance composition*. Often, in choreographing a dance, he would

Examples of Cuneiform Writing

MEANING	Outline Character about 3000 B.C.	Cuneiform about 2000 B.C.	Assyrian about 700 B.C.	Babylonian about 500 B.C.
The Sun				
God or Heaven				
Mountain				
Man				
Ox				
Fish				

Merce Cunningham performed with Barbara Lloyd in his dance *Rain Forest*. Artist Andy Warhol designed the plastic pillows.

write the name of a movement, the name of a dancer, a length of time, and a space on the stage. He would then toss dice or dip into a grab bag to determine who would do what movement for how long and where.

Cunningham was born in Centralia, Wash. From 1940 to 1945, he was a soloist with the Martha Graham company. In 1953, he formed his own group with experimental composer John Cage as musical director. Cunningham's major works include *Aeon* (1961), *Field Dances* (1963), *Winterbranch* (1964), and *Walkaround Time* (1968).   SELMA JEANNE COHEN

CUPEL. See ASSAYING (Dry Process).

CUPID, *KYOO pid*, in Roman mythology, was the son of the goddess of love, Venus. He is called *Eros* in Greek mythology. A wound from one of his arrows made a person fall in love. Once Cupid was wounded with his own arrow, and fell in love with a mortal princess named Psyche. The gods finally made her immortal so that she could be united with Cupid forever.

Visual Education Service

Cupid Was God of Love in Roman mythology.

Cupid is represented as a chubby, naked little boy with golden wings. His face is dimpled and smiling, and he carries a bow and arrows.   VAN JOHNSON

See also PSYCHE; VENUS.

CUPOLA, *KYOO poh luh*, is a word that comes from the Latin and means a *little bowl* or *cup*. It is used in architecture to mean a roof that resembles a bowl turned upside down. Some authorities use the terms *cupola* and *dome* to mean the same thing. Others apply the word cupola to small domes only. The inner vault of a large dome is often called a cupola. But the word is less accurately used when applied to a small lookout on top of a roof. See also DOME.   KENNETH J. CONANT

CURAÇAO. See NETHERLANDS ANTILLES.

CURARE, *kyoo RAH ree*, is a powerful poison. It is made from various poisonous plants, including several species of the *Strychnos* plant. It is sometimes called oorara, oorari, or urari. Curare is a black, thick syrup that soon turns into a hard, brittle mass. Several alkaloids found in curare, such as curarine, tubocurarine, and protocurarine, make it a strong poison.

South American tribes use curare as an arrow poison for hunting. It is a powerful poison only when injected into the blood stream or outer tissues of the body. It paralyzes many of the muscles of man and other mammals. Some of these muscles are used in breathing. A victim of curare poisoning usually dies of suffocation. Curare has been used in the treatment of tetanus and hydrophobia. It is also used during anesthesia to cause relaxation of the muscles, which permits using smaller amounts of the anesthetic.   A. K. REYNOLDS

CURASSOW, *KYOO ruh soh*, is a large, handsome bird of tropical America. The *crested curassow* of northern South America looks something like a turkey. Its feathers are black, with a purplish-green gloss on the back and on the breast. It is white underneath. The long

United Press Int.

The Crested Curassow is a South American game bird that looks like a barnyard fowl. Its flesh is good to eat.

feathers of its crest can be raised forward or lowered as easily as wings. The curassow's bill is strong, and often has a raised knob on top. Curassows can be tamed, and their flesh is good to eat. They feed on nuts and fruits and range north to southeastern Mexico.

Scientific Classification. Curassows belong to the guan family, *Cracidae*. The crested curassow is genus *Crax*, species *C. alector*.   JOSEPH J. HICKEY

CURB EXCHANGE. See STOCK EXCHANGE (History).

CURCULIO, *kur KYOO lee oh*, is any one of a large group of snout beetles. This group includes some of the most destructive beetles that attack nut and fruit trees.

One of the most important curculios is the *plum curculio*, which feeds on plum, peach, apricot, cherry, and apple trees. It lives east of the Rocky Mountains in the United States. The plum curculio is a brownish beetle with gray and black markings. It is about $\frac{1}{4}$ inch long. It has a thick body and a long snout. The *grubs* (young) feed on fruit near the stone. The plum curculio can be killed by spraying the fruit trees with lead arsenate.

Scientific Classification. The curculios are in the snout beetle family, *Curculionidae*. The plum curculio is genus *Conotrachelus*, species *C. nenuphar*.   R. E. BLACKWELDER

CURD. See CHEESE (How Cheese Is Made).

CURFEW is the time of day which once brought with it evening and the end of work. The word comes from the French expression *couvrefeu* which means *cover the fire*. At curfew time a bell was rung, the lights went out, and the fires were covered. Sometimes the bell itself was called a curfew. William the Conqueror introduced the custom of curfew in England during the Middle Ages. In 1103 Henry I repealed the law, but the bell continued to be rung. It may still be heard in parts of Great Britain.

In the United States, some communities have a curfew hour after which children are not allowed on the streets or in public places. The custom began a long time ago, but in Omaha, Nebr., about 1880, a curfew law was passed. Children under 15 had to be indoors after eight o'clock in the evening unless they were with an adult or could show written permission of their parents or guardians to be away from home. Many cities in the United States passed similar curfew laws.

CURIA REGIS

Sometimes communities find curfew laws for adults necessary during time of war. Persons of an enemy nationality are often required to be in their homes after a certain hour in wartime.   EMORY S. BOGARDUS

CURIA REGIS, *KYOOR ee uh REE jis,* was a group that helped kings govern during the Middle Ages. The group was often called the *King's Council* or *King's Court.* Its members consisted of leading barons, churchmen, and other officials. The court advised the king on important affairs of state, agreed to taxation and legislation, and served as a high court to settle difficult legal cases. The English Parliament and Cabinet, and European systems of administration and law, have developed from the curia regis.

For normal government business, the king depended on his household officials and a few trusted barons and churchmen. This small group, also called *curia regis,* met daily.   BRYCE LYON

CURIE, *KYOO ree,* is a unit used to measure radioactivity. Originally, it was the amount of radioactivity given off by 1 gram of radium. Today, the curie is defined as the quantity of any radioactive material that produces 3.7×10^{10} nuclear disintegrations a second. A *millicurie* is a thousandth of a curie.

CURIE, *kyoo REE,* is the name of a famous family of French physicists. They received three Nobel prizes for their work concerning radioactivity.

Pierre Curie (1859-1906), the son of a Paris physician, studied and taught physics at the Faculté des Sciences in Paris. While still in his 20's, he did important research on the magnetic properties of metals. The temperature at which these magnetic properties suddenly change is

isolated small amounts of two highly radioactive new chemical elements, and named them *radium* and *polonium.* For this work they received, along with Becquerel, the 1903 Nobel prize for physics.

Pierre Curie received a professorship at the Sorbonne in Paris. After his death in 1906, Marie Curie was appointed to succeed him. In 1911, she received the Nobel prize for chemistry for her work on the isolation of radium and polonium, and for her investigations of their chemical properties.

Marie Curie was instrumental in founding the Radium Institute in Paris, and became its first director. During World War I, she took a mobile radiographic unit to the battlefront, where she was accompanied by her eldest daughter, 17-year-old Irène, who acted as a nurse. Marie Curie was born in Warsaw, Poland, on Nov. 7, 1867.

Irène Joliot-Curie (1897-1956), after World War I, came to the Radium Institute to serve as her mother's assistant in the laboratory. Also working in the Institute was Frédéric Joliot (1900-1958), a recent graduate of the Paris Institute for Industrial Physics and Chemistry. In 1926, he and Irène Curie were married. He was interested in fundamental atomic and nuclear processes. In 1933, he and his wife and Marie Curie investigated the formation of electrons and positrons by the passage of high-energy radiation through matter. They determined the conditions under which these formations could occur.

In 1934, the Joliot-Curies worked on the bombardment of various elements by alpha rays. They demonstrated that such a bombardment of boron created a radioactive isotope of nitrogen. This discovery paved the way for the production of artificial radioactive elements. Their work brought them the Nobel prize for chemistry in 1935.

Joliot-Curie was active in the French resistance movement during the German occupation. He also continued his research, which contributed materially toward the achievement of the release of atomic energy. After the liberation of France, he was named head of the French Atomic Energy Commission. Irène became a member of the

Wide World

Marie Curie

United Press Int.

Pierre Curie

Wide World

Irène Joliot-Curie

known today as "the Curie point." In 1880, with his brother Jacques, he discovered and studied the piezoelectric properties of crystals. Pierre Curie was born in Paris on May 15, 1859.

Marie Sklodowska Curie (1867-1934), the daughter of teachers in Poland, came to Paris to study physics and chemistry. She married Pierre Curie in 1895. The next year, Antoine Henri Becquerel discovered natural radioactivity (see BECQUEREL). The Curies became interested in the radiations given off by radioactive substances, and worked together in investigating them.

They discovered that uranium ore contained much more radioactivity than could be accounted for by the uranium itself, and set about searching for its source. From tons of the uranium ore, or pitchblende, they

commission. Under the direction of this group, the French put an atomic pile into operation in 1948. The Joliot-Curies became outspoken Communists during the 1940's. Irène Joliot-Curie died in 1956 of leukemia, the same disease that had taken her mother's life 22 years earlier.

Ève Curie (1904-   ), another daughter of Pierre and Marie Curie, did not inherit the scientific interest of her family. But she became well known as an author and lecturer. Her book *Madame Curie,* a biography of her mother, has been published in more than 20 languages. At the beginning of World War II, she became a coordinator of women's war activities in France.   G. GAMOW

See also PITCHBLENDE; POLONIUM; RADIOACTIVITY; RADIUM; URANIUM.

CURITIBA, *KOO ree TEE buh* (pop. 576,000; alt. 2,949 ft.), is the capital of the state of Paraná in Brazil. It lies on a plateau, near the Iguaçu River in the center of a rich lumbering and coffee-growing area. For location, see BRAZIL (political map).

CURIUM, *KYOO ree uhm* (chemical symbol, Cm), is a man-made radioactive element. It has an atomic number of 96. Its most stable isotope has a mass number of 247. Curium was discovered in 1944 by three American scientists, Glenn T. Seaborg, Ralph A. James, and Albert Ghiorso. They produced curium by bombarding plutonium, element 94, with helium ions in the cyclotron at the University of California in Berkeley (see ION AND IONIZATION). Numerous isotopes of curium are produced by charged-particle bombardment of lighter transuranium elements (see TRANSURANIUM ELEMENTS). A process of neutron capture in these lighter elements produces weighable amounts of isotopes with mass numbers from 242 through 248. Curium is so radioactive that it glows in the dark. GLENN T. SEABORG

See also ELEMENT, CHEMICAL (table); RADIOACTIVITY; SEABORG, GLENN THEODORE.

CURLEW, *KUR lyoo,* is a long-legged bird that is related to sandpipers and snipes. It is found from Patagonia, in the far south of South America, to the Arctic region in North America. Curlews have long, slender bills which curve downward. They are wading birds, but they nest on dry ground, often a long distance from any body of water.

The *long-billed curlew* is one of the most common. It is 2 feet long and has a short, rounded tail. Its back is pale brown and spotted with black and dark-brown marks. The breast of the long-billed curlew is rusty brown and is more or less streaked. It has slender, bare legs. It gets its name from its slender bill, which is about 8 inches long. It uses its bill to catch small crabs, shellfish, snails, worms, grasshoppers, and beetles.

The *whimbrel,* or Hudsonian curlew, is a smaller member of the group. Commonly found on the eastern coast of North America, it migrates to South America in the winter. The rare *Eskimo curlew* is still smaller.

Scientific Classification. The curlew is in the sandpiper family, *Scolopacidae.* The long-billed curlew is genus *Nu-*

The Whimbrel Is a Handsome Curlew.
Cruickshank, National Audubon Society

menius, species *N. americanus.* The whimbrel is *N. phaeopus;* the Eskimo curlew is *N. borealis.* ALFRED M. BAILEY

See also SANDPIPER; SNIPE.

CURLEY, JAMES MICHAEL (1874-1958), a colorful American politician, was best known as mayor of Boston. He also served as a Democratic state legislator, member of the U.S. House of Representatives, and governor of Massachusetts.

Curley served four terms as mayor of Boston (1914-1918, 1922-1926, 1930-1934, and 1946-1950). His methods and honesty were disputed, but he was popular among Boston's poor. When he was fined $30,000 in a fraud case in 1938, thousands of citizens donated money to pay the fine. Later, while serving as mayor in 1947, Curley went to prison after being convicted in a mail fraud case. He served five months. President Harry S. Truman issued him a full pardon in 1950. Curley was born in Boston. CHARLES FORCEY and LINDA FORCEY

CURLING is a game played on a level sheet of ice. Two four-man *rinks* (teams) compete on a sheet of ice that is 146 feet long and 14 feet wide. The players slide heavy stones along the ice toward a circular target. Curling probably originated in Scotland and The Netherlands about 300 years ago. It has become very popular in Canada and parts of the United States. A curling tournament is called a *bonspiel.*

The Game usually consists of 10 or 12 *ends.* Each player slides two stones toward the *house* (target), a 12-foot circle at the opposite end of the ice, alternating with his opponent from the other rink. When all 16 stones have been delivered, an *end* has been played. The stones of one rink that are closer to the center of the house than any stones of the opposing rink score one point each. The opposing rink receives no points in that end. Then the rinks repeat the process, sliding the stones toward the house at the other end of the ice.

Each player delivers the stones from a *hack* (foothold) that is 126 feet from the center of the house at the opposite end of the ice. The $42\frac{1}{2}$-pound stones used in Canada and the United States are flat on the top and bottom. Each stone has a handle on top.

To deliver the stone, the player puts the ball of his right foot in the hack, then crouches with his feet together. The stone rests on the ice to his right and slightly in front of him. Grasping the handle in his right hand, he slides the stone straight back, rising as he does so. The stone comes up off the ice at the top of his backswing. Then, as his arm and the stone swing forward, he turns his arm either in or out. This action causes the stone to turn as he releases it, and it *curls* (curves) either to the right or left as it slides along. The game gets its name from this action.

The Rink is composed of a lead, a No. 2 player, a No. 3 player, and the *skip* or captain. They deliver the stones in that order. The lead is usually the least experienced player. He delivers first, because it is simpler to deliver when there are no stones on the ice.

Before the lead delivers his stones, the skip stations himself in the house at the opposite end. He indicates with his broom the spot at which he wishes the lead to aim his stone. After the lead delivers his stone, the skip judges its speed. If he thinks it will fall short of the target, he shouts a command, "Sweep." The

other two players then run ahead of the sliding stone, sweeping the ice vigorously. Sweeping smooths the ice surface and lessens resistance to the stone. Curling experts believe sweeping can add from 6 to 10 feet to a delivery. When the skip wants the sweepers to stop sweeping, he shouts, "Brooms up." After the lead delivers his stones, he joins another player in sweeping while his rinkmates deliver their stones.

CURLY-COATED RETRIEVER is a dog trained to bring back game that has been shot. It gets its name from its black or liver-colored coat, which is a mass of thick, tight curls. This coat keeps the dog from getting chilled

Curling Players Sweep the Ice so that the large, round stones will be able to slide easily toward the target. A diagram of half of a curling rink is shown below.

72 ft. to opposite **hog line**

Hog Line
Player must release the stone before reaching this line.

14 ft.

21 ft.

Center Line

The Curling Target, called the **house,** consists of three circles. The center is the **tee,** or **button.**

12 ft. dia.

8 ft. dia.

4 ft. dia.

Tee Line

6 ft.

Back Line

6 ft. from **back line** to **hack line** (below, not shown), where player begins delivery

The Curly-Coated Retriever Is a Good Hunting Dog.

while swimming. The curly-coat will work in cold water for a long time. It stands about 24 inches high at the shoulder, and weighs from 60 to 70 pounds. A curly-coat is fairly easy to train, and makes a good guard or watchdog.   MAXWELL RIDDLE

See also RETRIEVER.

CURRANT is a small berry of a plant that belongs to the saxifrage family. It is closely related to the gooseberry. The plant is a low, bushy shrub. Currants are round and smooth, and have a tart flavor.

Both the *red currant* and the *black currant* grow wild in Northern Europe, and are easily grown in cool, moist regions of North America. The red currant is used to make jellies, jams, wines, and pies. The black currant is more popular in Canada and Europe, and has a sharper flavor than the red currant. White and yellowish currants are usually eaten as a fresh dessert. The *golden currant,* or *Missouri flowering currant,* grows wild in North America. It is popular as a garden plant.

The currant plant is hardy, growing best in rich, well-drained soil with some moisture near the surface. Pruning, or cutting, the stems and shoots of the currant bush may be necessary. All shoots over three years old should be cut away in the early spring. There should be about nine shoots on each plant for the best fruiting. These should be three one-year-old shoots, three two-year, and three three-year-old shoots.

The currant worm is a serious enemy of currant bushes and gooseberry plants. It is the young, or *larva,* of a European sawfly. Currant worms can be killed by

J. Horace McFarland
Currant Berries Grow in Clusters Like Grapes.

spraying lead arsenate on the plants. Rotenone should be dusted on the bushes when the fruits begin to ripen.

Currant plants serve as a shelter for the fungus that causes the disease *white pine blister rust*, which is harmful to white-pine trees. It is unlawful to grow currant plants in states which have large white-pine forests.

Scientific Classification. Currants belong to the saxifrage family, *Saxifragaceae*. The red currant is genus *Ribes*, species *R. rubrum*. The black currant is *R. nigrum;* the golden currant, *R. aureum*.   ROY E. MARSHALL

See also GOOSEBERRY; ROTENONE; SAXIFRAGE.

CURRENCY. See MONEY.

CURRENT, ELECTRIC. See ELECTRIC CURRENT.

CURRENTS, OCEAN. See OCEAN (How the Ocean Moves).

CURRICULUM, *kuh RICK yoo luhm*, includes all the school-sponsored activities that influence learning. A curriculum consists mainly of subjects studied in the classroom. It also includes some activities that take place outside the classroom, such as lectures and school plays, because these activities also serve to teach the students.

Even if there were no schools, children would learn. They can and do learn many things from their parents, from reading, television, and movies. But modern educators believe that children learn more efficiently if they are guided by an organized curriculum. The principal advantage of a planned curriculum is that it gives each subject and activity an appropriate place alongside the others. A school counselor often helps students select the curriculum that is best for them in high school.

Curriculum Change takes place when it becomes necessary to teach new understandings, new ideas, and new attitudes. In the United States, the curriculum has changed considerably since the 1600's. The first elementary schools taught only reading and writing, because educators believed that these skills provided students with all the education they needed to become useful citizens. But today, elementary schools also offer instruction in mathematics, geography, history, science, arts, and foreign languages. These and other subjects prepare students for the more advanced work they will do in high school. During the 1960's, new educational theories led to many curriculum changes. In mathematics, for example, *set theory* is an important part of the curriculum (see SET THEORY).

General and Specialized Curriculums. Elementary schools have a *general curriculum* in which all students take the same basic subjects. A *specialized curriculum* usually begins some time between grades 7 and 9. After the student has a background in a subject, he may continue to study that subject if it has a special interest for him. These courses are called *electives*, because the student may *elect* (choose) to take them. The curriculum offers a greater opportunity for specialization as the student advances. In high school, as many as half of his courses may be electives. Most activities outside the classroom are entirely elective.

In college, the curriculum becomes more highly specialized. Even in a general liberal arts curriculum, a student must take a *major* (or a special area of study), such as history. The student must also take a *minor* (a secondary field of specialization), such as literature. The major and the minor are taken in addition to the other more general courses.

Curriculum Planning is done by school personnel and committees. Actually, the final planning is done by the teachers for, and often with, the help of the students. In public education, the city, state, or county boards of education are responsible for the curriculum. The curriculum plan should take into account the research of psychologists and experts in the field of learning. In the United States, the curriculum reflects the demands of educational research and the public.   W. M. ALEXANDER

See also EDUCATION; EDUCATION, HISTORY OF.

CURRIE, SIR ARTHUR WILLIAM (1875-1933), a Canadian soldier, won fame as an able administrator and a courageous officer in the second battle of Ypres during World War I. In 1917, he was appointed commander of all Canadian forces in Europe. After the war, he acted as Inspector-General of the Canadian Army. From 1920 until his death, he was principal and vice-chancellor of McGill University in Montreal. Currie was born in Napperton, Ont. He was educated in the Strathroy Collegiate Institute. He joined the Canadian Militia in 1895.   JEAN BRUCHESI

CURRIER AND IVES was a firm of American lithographers. The company published more than 4,000 color pictures showing the manners, customs, and sports of the times; the California gold rush; railroads and clipper ships; fires; and other historic events. The prints were widely used for decoration and for illustration. Published at low cost, the prints later became rare and costly.

Nathaniel Currier (1813-1888), the senior member of the partnership, issued his first two prints in 1835 in New York City. They were *The Ruins of the Merchants' Exchange* and *View of the Great Conflagration*. Currier was born in Roxbury, Mass. He served as apprentice to William S. and John B. Pendleton, brothers who oper-

Currier and Ives made the engraving, *Home to Thanksgiving.* It became one of the most famous prints of the Currier and Ives series.

ated the first lithographing shop in Boston, before he opened his own shop in New York.

James Merritt Ives (1824-1895) served first as bookkeeper and later as artist and art director of the firm. After 1857, all prints carried the joint name. Currier retired in 1880, and Ives carried on the business with William Currier, the son of Nathaniel. Ives was born in New York City.   S. W. HAYTER

CURRY is a seasoning that is most often used with lamb, veal, chicken, and shrimp dishes. It is used as either a sauce or powder. Curry originated in India. It contains a large amount of turmeric, an aromatic root that gives it a yellow color. Curry also contains garlic, pepper, ginger, cumin, and other spices. See also TURMERIC.

CURRY, JABEZ LAMAR MONROE (1825-1903), an American statesman and educator, worked for 60 years to make education possible for all Negro and white children in the South. He administered the George Peabody Fund for public education in the South after 1888, and served as agent of the Slater Fund for Negro

Schools after 1890. In 1899, he became president of the Southern Educational Board.

Curry served in the U.S. House of Representatives (1857-1861), in the Confederate Congress (1861-1863 and 1864), and in the Confederate Army (1864-1865). He was president of Howard College—now Samford University—(1865-1868), and United States minister to Spain (1885-1888 and 1902). Alabama placed a statue of him in the Statuary Hall collection in Washington, D.C.

Curry was born in Lincoln County, Georgia. He was graduated from the University of Georgia and from Harvard Law School.   RICHARD N. CURRENT

See also PEABODY EDUCATION FUND.

CURRY, JOHN STEUART (1897-1946), an American painter, became famous for his dramatic scenes of Midwestern rural life and for his murals. His paintings hang in many museums throughout the United States. The best known of his works include *Baptism in Kansas* and *Tornado Over Kansas,* which appears in the PAINTING article. Curry painted murals for the U.S. Department of

John Steuart Curry, *above,* is noted as a painter of dramatic scenes from Midwestern farm life. He painted *Baptism in Kansas, left,* in 1928.

Justice and the Department of the Interior buildings in Washington, D.C., and for the Kansas Capitol in Topeka. Curry belonged to the movement among the artists of the 1930's known as regionalism, which was an attempt to recapture the American scene.

Curry was born in Dunavant, Kans. He studied at the Kansas Art Institute, at the Art Institute of Chicago, and then for a year in Paris.   MILTON W. BROWN

CURTIN, JOHN JOSEPH (1885-1945), was prime minister of Australia during World War II. He united the nation behind the war effort, and introduced military draft despite his party's traditional opposition to it. Curtin realized that the United States would play the major role in the war in the Pacific. He allowed U.S. General Douglas MacArthur to use Australia as a base in the fight against Japan.

Curtin was born in Creswick, Victoria. He entered Labour Party politics as a youth and served in Parliament from 1928 to 1931 and from 1934 until his death. In 1935, he became Labour Party leader, and healed a major party split. He served as prime minister from 1941 to 1945.   ROBIN W. WINKS

CURTIS, CHARLES (1860-1936), served as 31st Vice-President of the United States under President Herbert Hoover. He had served in the U.S. House of Representatives from 1893 to 1907, and in the U.S. Senate from 1907 to 1913 and 1915 to 1929. Curtis was an experienced parliamentarian as a member of the Senate Rules Committee. He became majority leader of the Senate during President Calvin Coolidge's administration, and gained fame for his ability to have the Senate complete its work without extra sessions.

Curtis, whose mother was part Kaw Indian, was born in North Topeka, Kans. As a youth, he worked as a jockey. But his interest turned to law, and he was admitted to the bar in 1881. He practiced law successfully, and became Shawnee County attorney. IRVING G. WILLIAMS

See also VICE-PRESIDENT OF THE UNITED STATES (picture).

CURTIS, CHARLES G., an American inventor. See TURBINE (History).

CURTIS, CYRUS HERMANN KOTZSCHMAR (1850-1933), an American publisher, founded the Curtis Publishing Company in 1890. He started his first publication, *Young America*, as a 12-year-old newsboy. Later he moved to Boston and, in 1872, founded a magazine called *The People's Ledger*. Four years later, he took this publication to Philadelphia. There, Curtis started another magazine, *The Tribune and Farmer*, which became the *Ladies' Home Journal* in 1883. Curtis bought *The Saturday Evening Post* in 1897 and *The Country Gentleman* in 1911.

Curtis also owned and published eight large daily newspapers. They included the *Philadelphia Public Ledger*, which he bought in 1913. Curtis purchased the *Philadelphia Press* in 1920, the *New York Post* in 1924, and the *Philadelphia Inquirer* in 1930. He organized the Curtis-Martin Newspapers, Inc., a newspaper chain, in 1925.

Curtis was born in Portland, Me. He engaged in many philanthropic activities.   JOHN E. DREWRY

CURTIS ACT. See INDIAN TERRITORY.

CURTIS INSTITUTE OF MUSIC in Philadelphia prepares gifted students for professional careers. All students are on full-time scholarships. The institute was

founded and endowed in 1924 by Mary Louise Curtis Bok, and named for her father, Cyrus H. K. Curtis. It grants degrees of Mus.B., Mus.M. (in composition), and honorary Mus.D. The institute's faculty has included such distinguished musicians as Leopold Auer, Josef Hofmann, William Kincaid, Moriz Rosenthal, Carlos Salzedo, Rudolf Serkin, Martial Singher, and Efrem Zimbalist. The enrollment of the Curtis Institute of Music is about 140.   J. H. MATTIS

CURTIS PUBLISHING COMPANY. See PHILADELPHIA (Publishing).

CURTISS, GLENN HAMMOND (1878-1930), an American inventor, made important contributions to the development of aircraft. He became a successful manufacturer of airplanes, and made thousands of planes during World War I. His Wasp held a number of records. In 1919, a Navy-Curtiss flying boat, commanded by A. C. Read, made the first flight across the Atlantic Ocean.

Curtiss was born in Hammondsport, N.Y., and educated in the town's elementary schools. An interest in bicycle racing as a boy led to his flying career. From bicycles he turned to building motorcycles, one of which he raced at 137 mph. In 1904, he began building engines for the first dirigibles in the United States, designed by Thomas Scott Baldwin. Curtiss built his first engine for an airplane in 1907, as a member of Alexander Graham Bell's Aerial Experiment Association. The next year, he helped design an airplane called the *June Bug*. It had a box tail and was controlled by *ailerons* (hinged flaps on the wings). Orville and Wilbur Wright had obtained a patent on a method of twisting wings to control flight. They claimed Curtiss' ailerons violated their patent. The Wright brothers won a court suit against Curtiss.

In 1910, Curtiss won $10,000 by flying one of his planes from Albany, N.Y., to New York City in 2 hours, 51 minutes. He built the first planes for the United States Navy in 1911 after demonstrating that planes could land and take off from ships.   PAUL EDWARD GARBER

See also AIRPLANE (picture: Glenn H. Curtiss' June Bug).

CURVE. See PARABOLA; CIRCLE; BASEBALL (picture: Pitching); BOWLING.

CURZON LINE was the eastern boundary of Poland proposed by the Allies in 1919, after World War I. It was named for Lord George Curzon, a British diplomat. Before the war, Poland had been divided among Austria-Hungary, Germany, and Russia. The line was to be the frontier between Russia and a new Poland. Both countries rejected the plan, and fighting broke out in 1920. The Treaty of Riga in 1921 moved the border east of the Curzon Line. At the beginning of World War II in 1939, Germany and Russia divided Poland between them at the Curzon Line. The line is now the boundary between Poland and Russia.   WILLIAM A. JENKS

See also POLAND (The Peace Settlement).

CUSA, NICHOLAS OF (1400-1464), was a German cardinal, theologian, and scholar. As a priest, he favored the reform of the calendar and the unity of Christendom. He was sent to Constantinople to bring about the reunion of the Eastern Church with the church in the West. In 1449, he was made a cardinal. Pope Nicholas V sent him as papal legate to Germany to bring about various reforms within the church. As a scientist, he was perhaps the first to propose the hypothesis of the revolution of the earth around the sun. He was born at Cues, or Cusa, Germany. JAMES A. CORBETT and FULTON J. SHEEN

CUSCO, or CUZCO, *KOOS koh* (pop. 78,857; alt. 11,440 ft.), lies in southern Peru. For location, see PERU (color map). Cusco was the capital of the Inca Empire. Francisco Pizarro, the Spanish soldier, took it in 1533. Cusco has many Inca and Spanish colonial buildings. The city is a trading center for nearby farmers. C. LANGDON WHITE

CUSCUS, or PHALANGER, is a mammal that grows about as big as a house cat. It lives in trees in New Guinea, Indonesia, and the northern tip of Australia. The cuscus moves slowly and is most active at night. It has large eyes, woolly fur, and short ears. The fur varies from black to a honey color. The base of the tail is woolly, but the tip is covered with coarse scales. The cuscus eats both animal and vegetable matter. It is easily caught, and is often used as food.

Scientific Classification. The cuscus belongs to the order *Marsupialia*. It is in the phalanger family, *Phalangeridae*. A common cuscus is classified as genus *Spilocuscus*, species *S. nudicaudatus*. FRANK B. GOLLEY

See also MARSUPIAL; OPOSSUM.

CUSHING, HARVEY (1869-1939), an American physician and surgeon, was one of the world's greatest brain surgeons. He won fame for his achievements in neurosurgery and for experimental work on the brain, nervous system, and pituitary gland.

In 1926, Cushing won a Pulitzer prize in biography for *The Life of Sir William Osler* (1925), the life story of his friend and fellow physician. His other writings include a surgical and physiological classic, *The Pituitary Body and Its Disorders* (1912), and *Tumors of the Nervus Acusticus* (1917) and *From a Surgeon's Journal, 1915-1918* (1938).

Cushing joined Johns Hopkins University in 1896. He was made associate professor of surgery in 1903. He was professionally connected with the university until 1911, when he became professor of surgery at Harvard. He was born in Cleveland, studied medicine at Harvard, and was graduated in 1895. NOAH D. FABRICANT

CUSHING, RICHARD CARDINAL (1895-   ), an American religious leader, was named a cardinal of the Roman Catholic Church in 1958 by Pope John XXIII. He had gained wide recognition as a gifted writer and preacher. Ordained as a priest in 1921, Cushing engaged in parish work in Boston until the late 1930's. He was named auxiliary bishop of Boston in 1939, and became archbishop of the archdiocese in 1944. He was a close family friend of President John F. Kennedy, and celebrated the marriage and funeral Masses of the President. Born in South Boston, Cushing was graduated from Boston College. JAMES A. CORBETT and FULTON J. SHEEN

CUSHMAN, CHARLOTTE (1816-1875), an American actress, won fame for her roles as Lady Macbeth in *Macbeth*, Meg Merrilies in *Guy Mannering*, and Nancy Sykes in *Oliver Twist*. Miss Cushman became the first member of the theatrical profession to win a place in the Hall of Fame. At the time of her last stage appearance, William Cullen Bryant presented her with a laurel crown. Miss Cushman began her career as a singer, but when she strained her voice, she turned to acting. She played Romeo and other male roles opposite her sister Susan early in her stage career. Miss Cushman was born in Boston. WILLIAM VAN LENNEP

CUSPID. See TEETH (Permanent Teeth).

CUSTER, GEORGE ARMSTRONG (1839-1876), an American army officer, won fame as an Indian fighter in the West. On June 25, 1876, Custer and about 225 men under his immediate command were killed by Indians in the Battle of the Little Bighorn. Not a man survived. This massacre, known as "Custer's Last Stand," became famous because of a controversy that began after the battle. The truth of all that happened in the battle will never be known.

Early Career. Custer was born in New Rumley, Ohio. As a boy, he wanted to be a soldier. In 1861, he was graduated at the bottom of his class at the U.S. Military Academy. The Civil War had just begun, and Custer won fame as a fearless cavalry leader. At the age of 23

Custer's Last Battle on the Little Bighorn Was Painted by Edgar S. Paxson.

Brown Bros.
George A. Custer

he became the youngest general in the Union Army.

Many men who served with the "boy general" admired him. Many others hated him. Some of Custer's enemies were jealous of him and called him a "glory hunter."

After the war, the Army dropped Custer to his permanent rank of captain. He joined the Seventh Cavalry Regiment in 1866, and later became a lieutenant colonel in command. He won greater fame and made more enemies as he fought Indians in the Southwest and in the Dakota and Montana territories.

The 1876 Campaign. In 1876, the Army planned to round up the Sioux and Cheyenne Indians and bring them onto reservations. Custer's regiment joined the expedition, commanded by General Alfred H. Terry.

As the troops moved into the Montana Territory, scouts reported that an Indian village lay somewhere ahead. Terry ordered Custer to find it. Four days later, on June 25, Custer saw the village about 15 miles away. It lay in a valley along the Little Bighorn River. Custer believed there would be only about 1,000 Indians, who could be rounded up easily by the 650 men in his regiment. Actually, between 2,500 and 5,000 Indians were in the camp. It was the largest gathering of hostile tribes in Western history.

The Battle. Custer ordered an immediate attack. He divided his regiment into three columns—one under Captain Frederick W. Benteen, one under Major Marcus A. Reno, and one under himself. Benteen was ordered off to the left to search the mountain valleys for Indians. Custer ordered Reno to charge ahead across the river and attack the Indian village. Custer's column advanced into the bluffs to the right, presumably to attack the side or the rear of the village.

After bloody fighting in the valley, Reno retreated across the river and up the bluffs. Benteen's column joined Reno's men. The soldiers held off the Indians until Terry arrived on June 27.

About five miles away, sometime during the fighting in the valley and the first shooting on the bluffs, the Indians wiped out Custer and his entire column.

The Controversy over the battle began almost immediately. Custer's enemies accused him of disobeying Terry and of seeking greater glory by attacking the Indians. However, Terry's written orders had given Custer full discretion. Custer's supporters charged that Reno had been a coward, and could have rescued Custer if he had not retreated.

Many authors have defended Custer, and many have supported Reno. Various books also have theorized about Custer's plans after dividing his regiment, and about the events of the battle in which he was killed. But no one really knows.   JAMES D. SHACTER

See also CRAZY HORSE; INDIAN WARS (The Sioux Wars); SITTING BULL.

CUSTER BATTLEFIELD NATIONAL MONUMENT is in southeastern Montana. It includes part of the site of the Battle of the Little Bighorn. The 765.34-acre area

was a national cemetery from 1876 until it was established as a national monument on March 22, 1946.

See also MONTANA (color picture).

CUSTIS, GEORGE WASHINGTON PARKE (1781-1857), grandson of Martha Washington, became the adopted son of George Washington. He is known for his *Recollections of Washington* (1860) and for his plays. One of them, *Pocahontas*, told the story of the Indian princess and Captain John Smith. In another play, Custis brought a locomotive steam carriage onto the stage. He was born in Mt. Airy, Md. His mansion became the home of his son-in-law, General Robert E. Lee. It stands in Arlington National Cemetery, across the Potomac River from Washington, D.C.   ARVID SHULENBERGER

See also WASHINGTON, GEORGE (picture: Washington's Family).

CUSTIS, MARTHA. See WASHINGTON, MARTHA CUSTIS.

CUSTOM is the practice of preserving ideas and actions from generation to generation. The term also refers to a specific act that follows the traditions of past generations. Customs vary widely from place to place and from group to group. They also vary throughout the history of a particular group.

Not all customs are equally important. *Mores* are customs that people regard as extremely important. Violators of mores may receive severe punishment. In the United States, for example, a man or woman may go to prison for marrying more than one person at a time. Other customs, called *folkways*, are not so important, and persons who do not observe them receive only mild punishment. Folkways include eating habits, ways of dressing, and methods of playing games.

Most persons usually follow the traditions handed down to them. They rarely ask why the customs are what they are, or whether some other way of doing things might not be better. Much training in schools, at home, and elsewhere consists of teaching time-honored customs and making people observe them as completely as possible. People conform to customs because it is easier than not doing so. Most persons have found that they can get into trouble by inventing new ideas or practices. Society often ridicules and punishes persons who do not observe custom.   JOHN F. CUBER

Related Articles. See the various country articles where customs are discussed, such as INDIA (Ways of Life). See also the following articles:

Amusements	Feasts and Festivals	Holiday
Anthropology	Feud	Kiss
Beard	Folklore	Mores
Cannibal	Folkway	Religion
Clothing	Food	Segregation
Culture	Funeral Customs	Shelter
Duel	Hairdressing	Siesta
Etiquette	Hara-Kiri	Sociology
Fashion	Harem	Vendetta

CUSTOMS, BUREAU OF, collects all duties, taxes, and fees due on merchandise imported into the United States. The bureau cooperates with other government agencies in regulating the entrance and exit of goods and persons into or out of the country. It also administers certain navigational laws and treaties.

The bureau enforces laws against smuggling. It examines all export permits and declarations of a product's value. It may inspect merchandise to ensure that the goods entering or leaving the United States do not violate any law. It also registers and licenses U.S. civilian ships, regulates U.S. fishing vessels, and supervises the use of U.S. territorial waters by foreign ships.

The U.S. Customs Service was established in 1789 by the first Congress. Customs provided most of the government's revenue for almost 130 years. Nine Customs regions are divided into 42 districts and 291 ports of entry, including Puerto Rico and the Virgin Islands. The Bureau of Customs collected more than $2⅓ billion a year in the mid-1960's. An agency of the Treasury Department, it is directed by the commissioner of customs. Headquarters are at 2100 K Street NW, Washington, D.C. 20226. Critically reviewed by the BUREAU OF CUSTOMS

CUSTOMS COURT, UNITED STATES, reviews and settles disputes between collectors for the Bureau of Customs and importers and exporters. For example, the court may settle a disagreement between an importer and a customs collector over the value placed on imported merchandise.

The court consists of nine judges appointed by the President of the United States. The President names one of these nine as chief judge. Not more than five judges may be appointed from the same political party. The judges hear cases in three divisions of three judges each. The court was created in 1890 as the Board of United States General Appraisers. It received its present name in 1926. Critically reviewed by the BUREAU OF CUSTOMS

See also COURT (color diagram).

CUSTOMS DUTIES. See TARIFF; EXPORTS AND IMPORTS; FREE TRADE; CUSTOMS, BUREAU OF.

CUSTOMS UNION is an association of two or more countries to encourage trade. The countries making such an arrangement agree to eliminate duties and other restrictive regulations on trade among them. Members of the union apply a single set of tariffs to all countries outside the union. A *free trade area* is like a customs union, except that the members of a free trade area may apply separate tariffs against those who are not members.

The best-known customs unions have included the Zollverein, Benelux, and the European Economic Community (EEC). The Zollverein was formed by German states in the 1830's. These states became the German nation in 1871. Belgium, The Netherlands, and Luxembourg established Benelux in the 1940's. Belgium, France, Italy, Luxembourg, The Netherlands, and West Germany set up the European Economic Community by the Treaty of Rome in 1957. HAROLD J. HECK

See also ZOLLVEREIN; BENELUX; EUROPEAN COMMUNITY.

CUT GLASS. See GLASS (Cutting).

CUTANEOUS SENSE. See TOUCH.

CUTCH. See CATECHU.

CUTICLE. See NAIL (picture: Care of the Nails); SKIN.

CUTLASS FISH is a long, slender salt-water fish. It lives in waters of the West Indies, the western Pacific Ocean, and the Southern United States. The cutlass fish has a long, pointed hairlike tail. Its lower jaw is longer than its upper jaw, and it has long, doglike teeth. It usually grows about 5 feet long. The *dorsal* (back) *fin* extends the length of the body. Cutlass fish living in Japanese waters swim into fairly shallow

water to lay their eggs. The fish are caught for food in some areas.

Scientific Classification. The cutlass fish belongs to the cutlass fish family, *Trichiuridae*. It is classified as genus *Trichiurus*, species *T. lepturus*. LEONARD P. SCHULTZ

CUTTER. See BOATS AND BOATING (The Yacht); COAST GUARD, UNITED STATES (Protecting Life).

CUTTER. See CLOTHING (Ready-to-Wear Clothes; Garmentmakers).

CUTTING. See GRAFTING.

CUTTLEFISH is a *mollusk* (soft boneless animal) in the same class as the squid. It is found in most seas except those surrounding the Americas. It usually occurs in deep water, but sometimes near the shore. It ranges in size from a few inches to about 6 feet long. The body is brown with crossbands and purple spots. It is brilliantly metallic in the sunlight, and often changes color. The oval body is surrounded with a frilled fin. The cuttlefish has eight short arms and two long *tentacles* (feelers) that surround the mouth. Both the arms and the tentacles have four rows of hard and rough suckers. The tentacles can be pulled into pockets behind the eyes. The cuttlefish uses its arms to attach

The Cuttlefish has a broad head with two large eyes. The sepia used by artists is made from the substance in the ink sac of the cuttlefish. The internal shell, or cuttlebone, is often put in bird cages to provide the birds with lime salts.

Schall, Pix

itself to various objects, and to capture fish and other forms of marine life for food.

The cuttlefish has an internal shell called the *cuttlebone*. The broad cuttlebone is spongy and chalky. It is fed to canaries and parrots because of its lime food value. It is also used in making toothpaste.

The cuttlefish moves by forcing water in or out of the space between the cuttlebone and body. To hide from its enemies, the cuttlefish can darken the water as it moves by pouring out an inky substance containing the brown *pigment* (coloring matter) called sepia. Ink made from sepia was widely used in ancient times.

Scientific Classification. The common cuttlefish is in the cuttlefish family, *Sepiidae*. It is classified in the genus *Sepia*, species *S. officinalis*. R. TUCKER ABBOTT

See also NAUTILUS; OCTOPUS; SQUID.

J. C. Allen & Son

The Cutworm gets its name from its habit of cutting down young plants at ground level. It destroys more than it eats.

CUTWORM is the caterpillar of certain dull-colored, night-flying moths. Cutworms have a smooth skin and vary in color from light gray to black. Some are striped or spotted. Cutworms are quite destructive. Groups of cutworms have been known to destroy entire fields of young wheat, corn, or garden vegetables overnight. These destructive caterpillars also may cause a great deal of damage to tomatoes, tobacco, cotton, and various kinds of fruit trees.

From one to four generations of cutworms may grow each year. Some spend the winter as pupae, others as larvae. Solitary cutworms feed beneath the soil. Climbing cutworms crawl up the plants at night to feed. Gardeners kill both kinds of cutworms by using poisoned baits and sprays.

Scientific Classification. Cutworms are in the owlet moth family, *Noctuidae*. One kind, the variegated cutworm, is genus *Lycophotia*, species *L. margaritosa*. Another, the greasy cutworm, is *Euxoa ypsilon*.   E. GORTON LINSLEY

See also MOTH.

CUVIER, *kyoo VYAY,* **BARON** (1769-1832), GEORGES LÉOPOLD CHRÉTIEN FRÉDÉRIC DAGOBERT CUVIER, was a French naturalist. He founded *comparative anatomy,* a branch of zoology that compares the body parts of different animals. Cuvier also began the science of *paleontology* (the study of fossils) when his comparisons led him to the fossil remains of prehistoric animals. He wrote *The Animal Kingdom,* which became a famous authoritative source on zoology.

Cuvier began his work by dissecting animals from the sea. He then dissected many large animals, including the rhinoceros and the elephant. He could usually identify an animal from a single bone or body organ. Cuvier proposed the theory of *geological catastrophe* to explain why many fossil animals were no longer alive. This theory held that great volcanic upheavals and similar catastrophes destroyed many forms of life.

Cuvier was born in Montbéliard, France. At the age of 14, he went to school in Stuttgart, Germany. He

began to study sea animals while tutoring the son of a wealthy family on the Normandy coast. He later taught at the College of France.   A. M. WINCHESTER

See also ZOOLOGY (The Development of Zoology).

CUZCO. See CUSCO.

CYANIDE, *SY uh nide,* is the name given to metal salts containing the CN group (a carbon atom linked to a nitrogen atom). Sodium cyanide (NaCN), and potassium cyanide (KCN) are important industrial chemicals. Potassium cyanide is used in the cyanide process of separating gold from its ores. Strong acids react with metal cyanides to make hydrogen cyanide (HCN), a deadly poison gas. Organic cyanides are *nitriles*. Acrylonitrile, an important plastics ingredient, is made from cyanide. Chemists use cyanide in solutions for electroplating. They also use it in producing drugs and other chemicals.   JAMES S. FRITZ

See also LETHAL CHAMBER; PRUSSIC ACID.

CYANITE. See KYANITE.

CYANOSIS, *SY uh NO sis,* is a bluish color of the skin and mucous membranes. The condition usually results when not enough oxygen is present in the arterial blood. Cyanosis often occurs in persons who live at high altitudes, where the oxygen in the air is reduced. Certain kinds of lung diseases and heart diseases also can cause cyanosis. *Blue babies* have a great degree of cyanosis because the circulation of blood through their hearts is defective (see BLUE BABY). Doctors often give patients with cyanosis oxygen by means of oxygen tents or masks. See also OXYGEN TENT.   WILLIAM DAMESHEK

CYBELE. See RHEA (goddess).

CYBERNETICS, *SY bur NET icks,* is a branch of science that deals with control mechanisms and the transmission of information. Its name comes from a Greek word meaning *steersman.* The word *cybernetics* was adopted by the American mathematician Norbert Wiener, who wrote *Cybernetics* (1948).

Wiener noted that the means for internal control and communication in an animal, such as its nervous system, were similar to those in a machine. He also realized that biologists who studied animals, and engineers who designed automatic control equipment, did not usually know each other's fields of work. He proposed that control and communication in both fields be studied together as the science of cybernetics.

An important part of cybernetics is the study of *feedback.* If the path of a guided missile is not what it is supposed to be, or if the body temperature of a man is too high or too low, information concerning the error is *fed back* to the controlling device, which then acts to correct the error.   STANFORD GOLDMAN

See also AUTOMATION (Feedback); INFORMATION THEORY; WIENER, NORBERT.

CYCAD, *SY cad,* is a large subtropical and tropical seed plant. It is related to cone-bearing trees such as the pine and spruce, but looks like a palm or fern. Some cycads have unbranched, erect stems that may be 60 feet high. Other forms have a partially underground stem, called a tuber, that resembles a potato. Some species reach ages of nearly a thousand years.

The cycad's leathery, fernlike leaves grow in a circle at the end of the stem. New leaves grow every year and live several years. The cycad has a *strobilus* (large cone) that contains seeds. The cone grows erect in the center of the circle of leaves. When the seeds mature, part of the strobilus shrivels, allowing the seeds to drop to the ground.

Scientists have found fossils which show that cycads were common during prehistoric times. The cycads are the most primitive seed plants, but not necessarily the most ancient. They grow in only a few small areas. One kind, called *Zamia*, is common in tropical America.

Huntington Bot. Gardens

The Cycad Plant, like the pine, bears its seeds in cones.

Scientific Classification. Cycads belong to the cycas family, *Cycadaceae*. RICHARD J. PRESTON, JR.

See also CONE-BEARING TREES; GYMNOSPERM; SEED.

CYCLADES, *SIHK luh deez*, are a group of more than 200 Greek isles lying off the southeastern coast of Greece in the Aegean Sea. For location, see GREECE (color map). Their name comes from the Greek word *kyklos*, meaning *circle*. The Cyclades form a protective circle around the sacred isle of Delos, the central and smallest island of the group. In Greek mythology, Delos once floated, but Poseidon anchored it in place to become the birthplace of Apollo.

The chief islands of the Cyclades are Andros, Paros, Tinos, Naxos, and Siros. The Cyclades have a combined area of 993 square miles, and a combined population of about 100,000. Chief products include olives, grapes, fish, tobacco, hides, marble, and limestone. The soil is fertile, but dry. The capital and principal city of the Cyclades is Siros, or Hermoupolis. HARRY N. HOWARD

See also MELOS; PAROS.

CYCLAMEN, *SYKE luh men*, is an attractive plant of the primrose family. Cyclamens grow wild in the Mediterranean region of Europe, and are cultivated in homes and greenhouses in America. The leaves and flowers of the cyclamen spring from a swollen, turniplike root. Most of the leaves are veined in silver. The dainty flowers are white, rose, or purple, and have no fragrance. They measure about 2½ inches long. The petals turn back as though the flowers were inside out. Cyclamens are grown from seed. They need rich soil, abundant water, and temperatures between 50° and 60° F. The cyclamen blooms during the winter months.

Scientific Classification. The cyclamen belongs to the primrose family, *Primulaceae*. It is classified as genus *Cyclamen*. MARCUS MAXON

See also FLOWER (color picture: Enjoying Flowers Indoors); PRIMROSE.

CYCLE. See ELECTRIC CURRENT (Alternating); GASOLINE ENGINE (Cycle); LIFE CYCLE; OCEAN (The Food Cycle in the Sea); WATER (The Water Cycle).

CYCLONE is a low-pressure area in the atmosphere in which winds spiral inward. Cyclones may cover areas larger than the entire United States, or a few hundred miles across. A special, intense kind of cyclone only a few hundred yards to a few miles across is a *tornado*.

All cyclones have two characteristics: (1) the atmospheric pressure is lowest at the center, and (2) the winds spiral in toward the center. In the Northern Hemisphere, the winds blow counterclockwise. In the Southern Hemisphere, they blow inward in a clockwise direction.

The largest cyclones usually move slowly, perhaps a few hundred miles a day. Small cyclones may move slowly or rapidly, depending on atmospheric pressure.

Some parts of the world have so many cyclones that their average atmospheric pressure is below that of the rest of the world. For example, in the *Aleutian Low* in the North Pacific Ocean, the pressure is low most of the winter. Such a region may be called a *semipermanent* low pressure center or a *center of action*.

Storms usually occur with cyclones. The falling atmospheric pressure usually serves as a fairly good indication that bad weather is coming. Sometimes, however, cyclones do not bring bad weather. This is because the kind of air also has much to do with the weather. If a cyclone forms in dry air, for example, there may not be any clouds.

A tropical cyclone is a severe kind of cyclone that occurs over warm ocean waters in the tropics. The cyclones are called *hurricanes* if they form in the West Indies, and *typhoons* if they form in the Pacific Ocean. These storms may bring winds up to 150 or 180 miles an hour, terrific rains, violent thunder, and lightning.

Cyclones may be either warm-core or cold-core types. *Warm-core* cyclones are warmer at the center than near

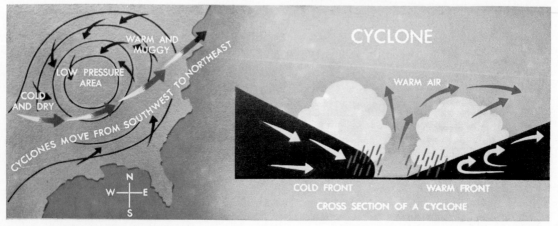

CYCLONE

WARM AND MUGGY

LOW PRESSURE AREA

COLD AND DRY

CYCLONES MOVE FROM SOUTHWEST TO NORTHEAST

N W E S

WARM AIR

COLD FRONT   WARM FRONT

CROSS SECTION OF A CYCLONE

the edges. They are fairly shallow and become weaker in the upper atmosphere. They often occur over especially warm land areas, such as the desert of the southwestern United States. *Cold-core* cyclones are coldest near the center and warmer near the edges. These cyclones may be very deep, and are more intense several thousand feet in the air than they are at the surface of the earth. GEORGE F. TAYLOR

See also HURRICANE; TORNADO; WEATHER; WIND.

CYCLONITE. See RDX.

CYCLOPEDIA. See ENCYCLOPEDIA.

CYCLOPROPANE. See ANESTHESIA.

CYCLOPS, *SY klahps,* was one of a race of giant shepherds in Greek mythology. They lived in Sicily, and each of them had only one eye in the center of his forehead. They made weapons and armor for the gods. Apollo destroyed them because they made the thunderbolt used to kill his son Aesculapius. See also AESCULAPIUS; APOLLO; POLYPHEMUS. PADRAIC COLUM

CYCLORAMA, *SY kloh RAHM uh,* is a painting done on a curved surface. The painting usually pictures a scenic panorama or an historical event. The artist tries to make the painting extremely realistic, and gives much attention to achieving a deep perspective. He plans the cyclorama so that when a person sees it, he feels that he is a part of the scene represented. The cyclorama is usually in a large circular room, with lighting designed to heighten the realistic effect of the work.

Cycloramas on the Civil War include one at Atlanta, Ga., which depicts the Battle of Atlanta, and one at Gettysburg, Pa., picturing the Battle of Gettysburg. A cyclorama at Waterloo, Belgium, shows Napoleon's defeat at Waterloo. *Cyclorama* also refers to the backdrop curtain on a theater stage. WILLIAM M. MILLIKEN

See also CIVIL WAR (picture).

CYCLOTRON is an atom-smashing machine, or *particle accelerator.* The American physicist, Ernest O. Lawrence, invented the cyclotron in 1930. He had the idea that a charged particle such as a proton could be bent into a circular path by the action of an intense magnetic field, instead of accelerating it in a straight line, as is done in a linear accelerator. He put a vacuum chamber containing two D-shaped electrodes, called *dees,* between the poles of a powerful magnet. A high-frequency voltage (rapidly changing electrical charges) was applied to the electrodes. Protons were started out at the center of the chamber. As they moved into the space between the dees, the change of charge acted like a push on a swing and speeded them up. The magnetic field kept them going in a circular path so that they entered the next dee. Each time they crossed the dee separation, they acquired another boost in energy. Their increased speed caused them to spiral farther away toward the outer edge of the chamber. Finally, at their maximum energy, they hit a target near the edge of the chamber. Many cyclotrons have been built in this country and in foreign lands. They are used to accelerate helium nuclei, or *alpha particles,* to as high as 50 million electron volts (Mev); deuterons, or nuclei of heavy hydrogen, to 25 Mev; and protons to 10 Mev. Extremely heavy ions may be accelerated up to 200 Mev. These particles can be made to emerge from the cyclotron as a beam. When they bombard various elements, they produce radioisotopes. RALPH E. LAPP

See also ATOM SMASHER; DEUTERIUM.

The Constellation Cygnus, or The Swan

CYGNET, a young swan. See SWAN.

CYGNUS, *SIHG nuhs,* is a constellation in the Northern Hemisphere. Its most prominent feature is the Northern Cross, which is formed by its five brightest stars. The brightest star, Deneb, marks the upper end of the cross toward the northeast. The double star Albireo marks the foot of the cross toward the southwest. In mythology, Cygnus often stands for the swan into which Jupiter (Zeus) changed himself in order to court Leda. I. M. LEVITT

CYLINDER. See GASOLINE ENGINE.

CYLINDER, *SILL in duhr,* is a solid bounded by a curved *lateral surface,* or side, and two flat surfaces called *bases.* The two bases have the same area and are bounded by circles or other closed curves. Objects with cylindrical shapes, although usually not solids, may be seen every day. A tin can has a cylindrical shape. So do a water pipe and a soda straw. Examples of cylinders that are solids include the handle on a rake or a fence post made from a log. See CIRCLE.

You can easily test whether an object is a cylinder. Place a pencil so that it touches the curved surface in a straight line. Move the pencil so that this straight line moves around the curved surface. On a cylinder, the pencil will always point in the same direction. That is, all its positions will be parallel to each other. In a *right circular cylinder,* such as a tin can, this line is perpendicular to the bases. In other kinds of cylinders, the line may form less than a right angle with the bases.

Parts of a Cylinder. In a right circular cylinder, the radius of each of the bases is the *radius of the cylinder.* The diameter of the bases is the *diameter of the cylinder,* and their circumference is the *circumference of the cylinder.* The perpendicular distance between the bases of a cylinder is its *altitude.*

The Area of the Lateral Surface of a right circular cylinder equals the area of a rectangle whose length equals the circumference of the cylinder, and whose width equals the altitude of the cylinder. Thus, to find the area of the lateral surface, multiply the circumference by the altitude. If L stands for the area of the lateral surface, r for the radius of the cylinder, and h for the altitude, then $L = 2\pi rh$.

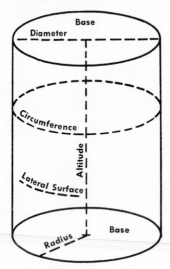

The Volume of a Cylinder equals the product of the area of one base times the altitude. If V stands for the volume, r for the radius of the base, and h for the altitude, then $V = \pi r^2 h$.

The Total Area of a Cylinder equals the area of the lateral surface plus the area of the bases. If A stands for the total area of a cylinder, then $A = L + 2\pi r^2$, or $A = 2\pi r(h + r)$.   MILES C. HARTLEY

CYLINDER BLOCK. See GASOLINE ENGINE (Cylinder Block).

CYMBAL, *SIHM bul*, is a circular brass percussion instrument, shaped like a broad-brimmed hat. It has a small *boss*, like the crown of a hat, in the center. A leather thong attached to the boss serves as a handle. A variety of sound effects can be obtained by striking two cymbals together, or by striking one cymbal with beaters. Cymbals come in all sizes, but most percussionists in symphony orchestras prefer cymbals with a diameter of 14 or 15 inches. All cymbals are hand-made, and no two sound exactly alike.

Objects resembling cymbals were found in the ruins of an Indus civilization of 3000 B.C. They were used in Israel as early as 1100 B.C. The name comes from the Greek, *kymbalon*, meaning *hollow of a cup*. Cymbals made their earliest orchestral appearance in 1680 in the opera *Esther*, in Hamburg, Germany. The finest cymbals are made by an Armenian family, Zildjian, which has held the secret since 1623.   CHARLES B. RIGHTER

CYMBELINE. See SHAKESPEARE, WILLIAM (Types of Plays; table, Fourth Period; Famous Quotations).

CYMBIDIUM ORCHID. See ORCHID (picture).

CYME, *sym*, is a type of flower, each stalk of which has a blossom. They are produced from the top downward, or from the center outward. Common examples of cymes include crab apples, forget-me-nots, phlox, and certain species of dogwood. See also INFLORESCENCE.

CYMRY. See CELT.

CYNEWULF. See ENGLISH LITERATURE (Beginnings).

CYNIC SCHOOL OF PHILOSOPHY was founded in the 300's B.C. by Antisthenes, a disciple of Socrates. He took as his starting point the doctrine of his great teacher that virtue rather than pleasure is the chief end of life, and constitutes true happiness. He argued that the wise man is the one who looks with contempt on all the ordinary pleasures of life, and lives without regard for riches or honors. Continued happiness, he declared, is not possible if man has wants and desires which may not be satisfied. He is bound by no obligations to society, state, or family, because these things give rise to desires that cannot be satisfied.

Among the enthusiastic followers of Antisthenes was Diogenes, who carried the principles of the school to an extreme, living, it is said, on the coarsest bread and sleeping at night in a tub. Zeno, of the later Roman period, was another distinguished Cynic. The Cynics form the link between Socrates and the Stoics.

Some authorities say that the name *cynic* refers to *Cynosarges*, the name of the building in Athens where the Cynics first met. Others say that the name comes from the Greek word for dog, and refers to the rude manners of the Cynics. In ordinary speech, a person who sneers at the idea that goodness exists in human nature is often called a *cynic*.   H. M. KALLEN

See also DIOGENES; STOIC; ZENO.

CYNOSURE. See NORTH STAR.

CYO. See CATHOLIC YOUTH ORGANIZATION.

CYPRESS, *SY pruhs*, is any one of a group of tall evergreen trees that grow in North America, Europe, and Asia. There are about 13 species or kinds, six of which grow naturally in southwestern United States. The *bald cypress* is not a true cypress, but is related to the sequoia. Cypresses adapt readily to warm climates, and gardeners often use them as ornamentals. The trees have small, scalelike leaves that grow in dense fan-shaped sprays. Their globe-shaped cones are covered by woody scales that look like small shields. The wood is light brown, durable, and smells strongly of cedar.

The *Monterey cypress* is one of the most picturesque trees in North America. It is named for the Monterey Peninsula of California, its native region. Its trunk is rather small, rarely more than 20 inches in diameter. It has long, strong, massive limbs that spread and grow in unusual shapes. The whole tree is gnarled and bent by the constant strong ocean winds. This cypress is a favorite subject for artists because of its picturesque beauty.

Scientific Classification. The cypresses belong to the pine family, *Pinaceae*. Monterey cypresses belong to the cypress family, *Cupressaceae*. They are genus *Cupressus*, species *C. macrocarpa*.   RICHARD J. PRESTON, JR.

See also BALD CYPRESS; CONE-BEARING TREES; TREE (table: Famous Trees).

CYPRESS GARDENS, Fla., is a beautiful garden and water playground on Lake Eloise. It lies near Winter Haven in the central part of the state. The site of the gardens was a wild swamp until the 1930's. It has been developed into gardens of rare and exotic plants from all parts of the world. Huge cypress and oak trees shade footpaths and banks of gardenias, azaleas, camellias, and other flowers. Water-skiing shows are held daily. See also FLORIDA (color picture).   KATHRYN ABBEY HANNA

CYPRUS

Capital ★

● Other City or Town

—— Road

▲ MOUNTAIN

～ River

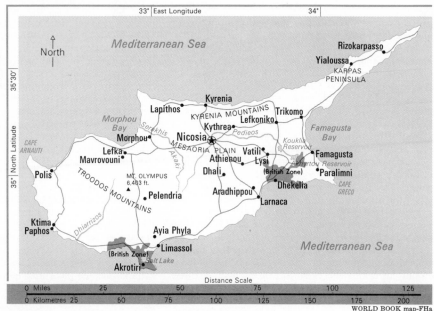

WORLD BOOK map-FHa

CYPRUS is an island republic in the northeast corner of the Mediterranean Sea. It lies about 40 miles south of Turkey and 60 miles west of Syria. Geographically, Cyprus is part of Asia. But its people live much like southern Europeans and have a standard of living second only to Israel's in the eastern Mediterranean area. Cyprus is a leading tourist resort noted for its hilltop castles, old churches, beaches, and rugged mountains.

About four-fifths of the people in Cyprus are of Greek origin, and most of the rest are of Turkish origin. Nearly all of the people regard themselves as Greeks or Turks rather than as *Cypriots* (citizens of Cyprus). This division is reflected in many ways. For example, the 1960 constitution provided that the president of the country must be a Greek Cypriot, elected by Greek Cypriots. The vice-president must be a Turkish Cypriot, elected by the Turkish Cypriots. Seventy per cent of the civil service posts must be filled by Greek Cypriots, the remainder by Turkish Cypriots. But in 1963, President Makarios tried to make changes in the constitution. Civil war erupted. Turkish Cypriots withdrew from the government, and the constitution was suspended.

Cyprus became independent in 1960. Its official name is KYPRIAKI DIMOKRATIA in Greek and KIBRIS CUMHURIYEITI in Turkish (REPUBLIC OF CYPRUS). Nicosia, a city with a metropolitan area population of 103,000, is the capital (see NICOSIA).

Government. A president is the head of state and government. Under the 1960 constitution, the vice-president could veto decisions on defense or foreign affairs. The Council of Ministers had seven Greek and three Turkish members, and the House of Representatives had 35 Greeks and 15 Turks. The vice-president

The contributor of this article, Francis Noel-Baker, is a former member of the British Parliament and author of many articles and publications on Greece and Cyprus.

and other Turkish members withdrew from the government during the civil war. The president continued to govern without the Turks. By 1967, the Turkish Cypriots had set up their own administration to govern all Turks living in Turkish zones of Cyprus.

People. About half of the people of Cyprus make their living by farming. Most of the farmers raise potatoes, citrus fruits, grapes, and other crops on small plots of ground.

Most of the people in the villages live in simple houses built around a courtyard. Most houses in the cities are more modern. Large apartment house units are replacing houses in many cities. Some older Cypriot men in rural areas wear richly decorated vests and baggy black trousers called *vraka*. Some of the women wear long skirts and short blouses called *sarkas*.

About 95 per cent of the people under 40 and 60 per cent of those over 40 can read and write. Cyprus has

---
FACTS IN BRIEF

Capital: Nicosia.

Official Languages: Greek and Turkish.

Form of Government: Republic. *Head of State*—President.

Area: 3,572 square miles. *Greatest Distances*—128 miles (east-west), 75 miles (north-south).

Population: *1960 Census*—577,615. *Estimated 1970 Population*—633,000; density, 177 persons to the square mile. *Estimated 1975 Population*—665,000.

Chief Products: *Agriculture*—barley, carrots, grapefruit, grapes, lemons, oranges, potatoes, wheat. *Mining*—asbestos, copper, gypsum, iron. *Manufacturing*—cement, cigarettes, furniture, olive oil, shoes, textiles, wines.

Flag: The flag is white with a map of Cyprus in copper-yellow (for copper) in the center above two green crossed olive branches (for peace). See FLAG (color picture: Flags of Asia and the Pacific).

Money: *Basic Unit*—Cyprus pound. For its value, see MONEY (table: Values).

CYPRUS

separate schools for students of Greek and Turkish origin. Elementary education is free and compulsory for children from 6 to 12 years of age. Some children between 4 and 6 attend infant schools. The country has technical schools and a teacher training academy.

Most of the Greeks are Christians and belong to the independent Orthodox Church of Cyprus. Most of the Turks are Moslems. The tall steeple of a Christian church standing near the picturesque minaret of a Turkish mosque is a common sight in Cyprus.

Land. Cyprus is an island of great scenic beauty. Its long and varied coastline alternates between rugged rock formations and golden sandy beaches. The broad, fertile Mesaoria Plain separates its two mountain ranges, Troodos and Kyrenia. Troodos, in the western end of the island, is the larger of the two ranges. Parts of it are covered with thick forests. Mt. Olympus, its highest peak, rises 6,403 feet above sea level. The Kyrenia range stretches along the northern coast.

Cyprus has a pleasant climate, with plenty of sunshine throughout the year. Snow falls on the Troodos Mountains during the early part of the year. Winters are mild in the inland plain, but temperatures sometimes go over 100° F. there during the summer. Rainfall averages from 12 to 16 inches a year on the plain. Some parts of the Troodos receive more than 40 inches.

Economy. Farmers grow carrots, grapefruit, grapes, lemons, oranges, and potatoes for export. By irrigating the land, they have greatly increased crop yields.

Mining is the most important industry in Cyprus. The island's chief mineral deposits are asbestos, and copper and iron ores. Cyprus also produces olive oil and wines. Tourism is a major source of income.

Cyprus has no railroads, but good highways cover the island. Famagusta, Larnaca, and Limassol are the principal ports, and Nicosia has an international airport.

History. The earliest known people to live in Cyprus date back to about 6000 B.C. Greek settlers arrived there about 1200 B.C., and started city-states similar to those in ancient Greece (see GREECE, ANCIENT [The City-State]). Before the time of Christ, the Assyrians, Egyptians, Persians, Greeks, and Romans conquered Cyprus. Saint Paul and Saint Barnabas brought Christianity to the island in A.D. 45. In A.D. 330, Cyprus became a part of the Byzantine Empire. Richard the Lion-Hearted of England captured Cyprus in 1191, but he sold it to a French nobleman. The Ottoman Turks invaded Cyprus in the 1570's, and ruled Cyprus until they turned the island over to Great Britain in 1878. Britain declared Cyprus a Crown Colony in 1925.

In the 1950's, Greek Cypriots, under the leadership of Archbishop Makarios, started the campaign for *enosis* (union with Greece). A Greek Cypriot secret organization called *EOKA* started guerrilla attacks on the British. Britain declared a state of emergency on the island in 1955, and in 1956 exiled Makarios to the Seychelles Islands in the Indian Ocean. Greece and Turkey met in Zurich, Switzerland, in 1959, and agreed that Cyprus should become an independent republic. Britain accepted the Zurich agreement. Cyprus became independent on Aug. 16, 1960, under a constitution agreed upon by the leaders of the Greek Cypriots and Turkish Cypriots, and guaranteed by Great Britain, Greece, and Turkey. Great Britain retained control of two military base areas along the southern coast, at Akrotiri and Dhekelia.

Archbishop Makarios became president of the new republic. In 1963, Makarios announced proposals to change the constitution. He claimed that the constitution granted benefits to the Turkish Cypriots that were out of proportion to the size of the Turkish Cypriot community. Turkish Cypriot leaders saw these benefits as protection against Greek Cypriot control. Fighting broke out between the two groups. In 1964, the United

A Street Scene in Nicosia shows some of the small shops that are typical of older sections of the city. Many merchants display their goods on the storefronts. This street is in the Greek section of Nicosia.

Nations sent a peace-keeping force to Cyprus while a solution to the conflict was being worked out.

In November, 1967, another sharp clash between the two groups caused a new crisis. Cyrus Vance, a U.S. special envoy, helped negotiate a settlement, but disagreement continued. In December, 1967, Turkish Cypriots formally set up an administration which had ruled their areas since 1963. Makarios was re-elected in 1968. Greek and Turkish Cypriots began new talks, and relations between the two Cypriot groups improved in 1968.   FRANCIS NOEL-BAKER

See also MAKARIOS, ARCHBISHOP.

CYRANO DE BERGERAC, *see rah NO duh BEHR zhuh RAHK,* **SAVINIEN DE** (1619-1655), was a French author and soldier. He was also known for his skill in sword fighting and for his long nose. Edmond Rostand's famous play *Cyrano de Bergerac* (1897) contains a somewhat fanciful account of Cyrano's colorful life.

Cyrano wrote a comedy *The Ridiculous Pedant* (1653) and a tragedy *The Death of Agrippina* (1654). But his most famous books are two science fiction works: *The Other World, or the States and Empires of the Moon* (1657) and *The States and Empires of the Sun* (1662). A free thinker, he questioned traditional religious beliefs and the church's authority. He also said animals have intelligence and that matter is made up of atoms.

Cyrano was born in Périgord. Twice wounded in battle, he left military life in 1642 to study science and literature in Paris.   JULES BRODY

CYRENAICA. See LIBYA (History).

CYRIL OF ALEXANDRIA, SAINT (A.D. ? -444), presided over the Council of Ephesus which condemned Nestorius in 431. He served as Patriarch of Alexandria from 412, and did much to shape Catholic doctrine on the Trinity and the Person of Christ. He was born in Alexandria.   WALTER J. BURGHARDT

CYRIL OF JERUSALEM, SAINT (A.D. 315?-386), played a prominent part in the struggles regarding the Trinity in the mid-300's (see TRINITY). He was banished from Jerusalem three times for opposing Arianism (see ARIANISM). He was one of 150 orthodox bishops at the Council of Constantinople in 381. He was born near Jerusalem.   WALTER J. BURGHARDT

CYRILLIC ALPHABET. See ALPHABET (Other Systems); RUSSIAN LANGUAGE.

CYRUS THE GREAT (reigned 559-529 B.C.), sometimes called CYRUS THE ELDER, founded the ancient Persian Empire. His ancestors had been vassals of the Median kings, ruling Anshan near the Persian Gulf.

There is a legend that Cyrus' grandfather Astyages tried to have him killed when an infant. Astyages feared that he might be overthrown by his grandson. Cyrus was protected by a shepherd and was eventually restored to his parents. When he grew up, he formed an army of Persians, overthrew his grandfather, and became king of Media and Persia. He made himself master of Lydia by defeating Croesus in 546 B.C. A few years later, he defeated Nabonidus, King of Babylon.

Cyrus was a wise, generous ruler. He permitted the Jews to return to Jerusalem from captivity in Babylonia. He took the title *King of the World*, and tried to organize his lands.   RICHARD N. FRYE

CYRUS THE YOUNGER (424?-401 B.C.), a Persian prince, was a son of King Darius II, ruler of the Achaemenid Empire. Cyrus served as *satrap* (governor) of a province in Asia Minor. Darius died in 404 B.C., and Cyrus' older brother Artaxerxes became king. Cyrus revolted against Artaxerxes, and tried to seize the throne. He led 10,000 Greek *mercenaries* (hired troops) into Babylonia, where he fought his brother in 401 B.C. at the Battle of Cunaxa. Cyrus was killed, and the leaders of his forces imprisoned. The Greek mercenaries fled. The story was told by the Greek historian Xenophon in his *Anabasis* (see XENOPHON).   RICHARD N. FRYE

CYST, *sihst,* is a sac in the body that contains fluid and has no outside opening. Cysts of the skin occur more often than others. These usually form when the opening of an oil gland becomes blocked. Some cysts are formed around a foreign substance which gets into the body, while others form around blood, following an injury. A cyst that forms in the salivary gland under the tongue is called a *ranula*. Cysts of internal organs are usually caused by abnormal development of the organ. Cysts are removed by surgery. See also WEN.   JOHN B. MIALE

CYSTIC DUCT. See GALL BLADDER.

CYSTIC FIBROSIS, *fie BROH siss,* is a hereditary disease in which the body *secretes,* or produces, abnormally thick mucus. The mucus becomes so thick that it forms plugs in many body organs, reducing their ability to work properly. Doctors do not know what causes the mucus to thicken. They treat cystic fibrosis with antibiotics, with enzymes to replace the pancreatic juices, and sometimes with surgery.

CYSTITIS, a bladder inflammation. See BLADDER.

CYTISINE. See LABURNUM.

CYTOCHROME. See IRON (How Our Bodies Use Iron).

CYTOLOGY, *sy TAHL oh jih,* is the study of the internal structure and organization of cells. Microscopic studies of the structure of the cell provided an explanation of cell division, and served as a foundation for genetics (see GENETICS). These studies also showed that each structure in the cell has some function, and that each activity of the cell is related to changes in the chemicals that make up the cell. *Cytochemistry* is the study of the chemical activities that take place inside cells. See also CELL.   NEAL D. BUFFALOE

CYTOPLASM. See CELL (Inside a Living Cell); PROTOPLASM; BLOOD (Platelets).

CZAR, *zahr,* was the title used by the emperors of Russia. *Czar* comes from *Caesar,* the name used by the emperors of Rome. The first Russian ruler to adopt the title was Ivan the Terrible, in 1547. The last czar was Nicholas II (1868-1918). The Russian empress was called the *czarina,* and the crown prince was called the *czarevitch.* See also CAESAR; KAISER.

CZECH, *check,* is a Slavic person, usually found in two Czechoslovak provinces, Bohemia and Moravia. More than half the population of Czechoslovakia is Czech. The rest of the people are chiefly Slovak. The Czechs are descendants of early Slavic immigrants.

At one time, all the Slavic peoples spoke the same language. The Czechs, however, gradually developed a separate language that includes many German, Latin, and English words. Dialects are found in Bohemia, Moravia, Silesia, and Slovakia.   WILTON MARION KROGMAN

See also BOHEMIA; CZECHOSLOVAKIA (The People); MORAVIA.

Prague, the capital of Czecho-slovakia, is a city of many bridges. Government buildings and factories line the banks of the Vltava (Moldau) River.

Rapho-Guillumette

CZECHOSLOVAKIA

CZECHOSLOVAKIA, CHECK oh sloh VAH kee ah, is one of Eastern Europe's leading manufacturing countries. Czech factories produce a wide variety of products, ranging from automobiles to tanks and television sets. Czech products form part of the foreign economic aid sent to less developed countries in Asia and Africa by the Communist bloc nations of Eastern Europe. The fertile soil of Czechoslovakia produces good wheat and barley crops and many other farm products.

Czechoslovakia is a beautiful country with snow-capped mountains, rounded hills, and rolling plains. It is a little smaller than the state of New York. Czechoslovakia is the homeland of the Czechs and Slovaks, two Slavic peoples noted for their love of music and sports. The Czechs live in two western areas called *Bohemia* and *Moravia*. The Slovaks live in an eastern area called *Slovakia*.

The Hungarians ruled the Slovaks for 1,000 years,

S. Harrison Thomson, the contributor of this article, is Professor Emeritus of History at the University of Colorado, and author of Czechoslovakia in European History.

and the Austrian monarchs ruled the Czechs for almost 400 years. In 1918, the Czechs and Slovaks formed Czechoslovakia, which was a free republic until shortly before World War II. In 1945, it became a Communist country. Its official name is ČESKOSLOVENSKÁ SOCIALISTICKÁ REPUBLIKA (CZECHOSLOVAK SOCIALIST REPUBLIC). Prague is the capital and largest city.

The Land

Czechoslovakia is a landlocked country. Its borders touch those of Germany, Poland, Russia, Hungary, and Austria. A long, narrow country, it is made up of three natural regions. These regions are Bohemia, Moravia,

---

FACTS IN BRIEF

Capital: Prague.

Official Languages: Czech and Slovak.

Form of Government: Socialist Republic (Communist dictatorship).

Head of State: President (5-year term).

Area: 49,371 square miles. *Greatest Distances*—(east-west) about 475 miles; (north-south) about 185 miles.

Elevation: *Highest*—Gerlachovka Peak, 8,737 feet above sea level. *Lowest*—380 feet above sea level, near Zemplin on the Hungarian border.

Population: *1961 Census*—13,745,577; distribution, 52 per cent rural, 48 per cent urban. *Estimated 1970 Popula-*

tion—14,564,000; density, 295 persons to the square mile. *Estimated 1975 Population*—15,006,000.

Chief Products: *Agriculture*—barley, hops, oats, potatoes, rye, sugar beets, wheat. *Mining*—coal, kaolin, magnesite. *Manufacturing*—automobiles, boots and shoes, electric motors, machinery, television sets, textiles.

Flag: A blue triangle at the staff represents Slovakia. Two horizontal stripes, white over red, are for Bohemia and Moravia. See FLAG (picture: Flags of Europe).

National Anthem: "Kde domov můj" ("Where Is My Homeland").

Money: *Basic Unit*—koruna, or crown. For the value of the koruna in dollars, see MONEY (table: Values).

and Slovakia. These areas also were once its political divisions. Bohemia, in the western part of the country, is a saucer-shaped plateau with a ring of mountains around the edge. Gaps in the mountain ranges lead into the countries to the north and west. Moravia lies in the middle of the country. It slopes from the mountains in the north and west to the Morava River in the south. Part of Czechoslovakia near Ostrava, drained by the Oder River, often is considered part of Upper Silesia. The low area between the mountains that joins the Oder valley with the Morava valley is called the Moravian Gate. Slovakia, in the east, has the highest mountains, the Tatras. Some are over 8,000 feet high.

Rivers and Lakes. The Vltava (Moldau) River flows into the Labe (Elbe). The Labe then flows northwest through Germany to the North Sea, draining most of Bohemia. The rest of the country is drained by the Danube and its branches, the Morava, Váh, Nitra, and Hron. The Danube flows south and east to the Black Sea. Many lakes nestle in the mountain valleys.

Natural Resources. Western Bohemia, southern Moravia, and Slovakia all have deposits of coal. Northeastern Moravia has iron ore. Czechoslovakia also has deposits of graphite, manganese, lead, zinc, mercury, silver, and gold. Other mineral resources include uranium, clay, and sand used for making glass. Western Bohemia has many mineral springs with world-famous health resorts, such as Karlovy Vary (Karlsbad) and Mariánské Lázně (Marienbad).

The soil is one of the country's most important resources. About half the land can be farmed. Forests cover one-third of the land. Czechoslovakia has large water power resources. The government has built dams and hydroelectric plants on many rivers to provide water for farming and electric power.

Climate. Czechoslovakia lies about as far north as southern Canada. Its climate is much like southern Canada's, with hot summers and cold winters. Temperatures average 20° F. in January and 70° F. in July. The country has about 20 to 40 inches of rain each year.

The People

Czechoslovakia has two major groups, the Czechs and the Slovaks. Both groups are of Slavic origin. The Moravians are related to the Czechs, and speak the same language. There are more than twice as many Czechs and Moravians as there are Slovaks in the country. About 5 out of every 100 persons in Czechoslovakia belong to minority groups, including German-speaking peoples of Bohemia and Magyars of Slovakia.

Czechoslovakia (Shown in Black) Lies South of Poland.

The Slovaks and the Czechs are unlike in many ways. The Czechs have almost always been more like the peoples of northern and western European countries, and have had an international way of life. They have mixed only slightly with the neighboring people.

The Slovaks, Moravians, and Czechs are united by a common love of the arts and of age-old traditions. Singing and folk dancing are popular in all parts of the country. Christmas is an important festival time. The holidays begin early in December, with Saint Barbara's Day and Saint Nicholas' Day, and last until Twelfth Night, in January. The people enjoy sports, including skiing, ice skating, tennis, and swimming.

Cities. Prague, an old city on the Vltava (Moldau) River, is the capital of Czechoslovakia. Bratislava, the principal river port, is a leading commercial city. Brno and Plzeň are major manufacturing centers. Ostrava lies in the heart of Czechoslovakia's largest industrial

Czechoslovakia Is a Little Smaller than New York State.

area. See the separate articles on cities in Czechoslovakia listed in the *Related Articles* section of this article.

Manufacturing. Czechoslovakia is one of the most industrialized countries in East Europe. Industry provides about two-thirds of the national income and employs over one-third of the working people. Since 1945, the government has taken over almost all industry. Handicrafts are the only private industry. The chief manufactured products include automobiles, bicycles, electric motors, glass, machine tools, steel mill and mining equipment, television sets, and textiles. Two of Czechoslovakia's factories are world-famous. They are the Škoda factory at Plzeň, which produces munitions, automobiles, trucks, and tanks, and the Bat'a shoe factory at Gottwaldov. Most of the important industries are located in Bohemia and Moravia.

Agriculture contributes about one-eighth of the national income. The government controls almost all the farmland. About one-fifth of the working people work in agriculture and forestry. Czechoslovakia's chief crops are barley, oats, potatoes, sugar beets, rye, and wheat. Hops are grown to make beer. Dairying and stock raising are also important.

Mining. Czechoslovakia's most important mineral products are coal; kaolin, a pure white clay; and magnesite, a form of magnesium. Others include antimony,

Regions and Historic Provinces

BOHE-
MIA ..6,039,087..B 2
Jiho-
český* 649,637..B 2
Praha
(Prague)*
1,005,379..A 2
Severo-
český*
1,086,392..A 2
Středo-
český*
1,269,195..A 2
Východo-
český*
1,199,808..A 2
Západo-
český* 828,676..B 1
MORA-
VIA ..3,532,444..B 3
Jihomo-
ravský*
1,900,865..B 3
Severomo-
ravský*
1,631,579..B 4
SLO-
VAKIA 4,174,046..B 4
Středoslo-
venský*
1,301,011..B 4
Východoslo-
venský*
1,112,884..B 5
Západoslo-
venský*
1,760,151..B 3

Cities and Towns

Banská
Bystrica .26,234..B 4
Bardejov ..10,460..B 5
Benátky nad
Jizerou* ..4,285..A 2
Benešov ...9,114..B 2
Beroun ....15,752..B 2
Bílina ....11,600..A 1
Blansko ...10,477..B 3
Brandýs nad
Labem-Stará
Boleslav .13,168..A 2
Bratislava 259,508..B 3
Břeclav ...12,396..B 3

Brezno ....10,255..B 4
Brno .....323,741..B 3
Bruntál ....8,020..B 3
Čadca .....12,475..B 4
Čakovice* ..5,655..A 2
Čáslav .....10,337..B 2
Čelákovice* .7,750..A 2
Česká Lípa .14,379..A 2
Česká
Třebová .13,407..B 3
České Bu-
dějovice .67,944..B 2
Český Brod* 5,719..A 2
Český
Krumlov ..9,165..B 2
Český
Těšín ....15,414..B 4
Cheb ......22,778..A 1
Chomutov ..35,202..A 1
Chrudim ...16,318..B 2
Děčín .....40,569..A 2
Dobříš .....4,778..B 2
Dobrovice* ..2,116..A 2
Dolný Kubín 4,620..B 4
Domažlice ..8,167..B 1
Dunajská
Streda ....8,887..C 3
Dvůr Králové
(nad
Labem) ..15,153..A 2
Frýdek-
Místek ...29,031..B 4
Galanta ....7,473..B 3
Gottwaldov
(Zlín) ...56,154..B 3
Handlová ..15,336..B 4
Havířov ...64,870..B 4
Havlíčkův
Brod ....15,706..B 2
Hlohovec ..13,489..B 3
Hlučín .....9,556..B 4
Hodonín ...18,800..B 3
Hradec
Králové .58,565..A 2
Hranice ...11,256..B 3
Hronov .....9,974..A 3
Humenné ..12,572..B 5
Jablonec
(nad
Nisou) ..27,829..A 2
Jaroměř ...11,956..A 2
Jeseník .....8,914..A 3
Jičín .....12,461..A 2
Jihlava ...36,140..B 2
Jindřichův
Hradec ..10,787..B 2
Jirkov .....12,140..A 1

Karlsbad
(Karlovy
Vary) ...43,819..A 1
Karviná ...60,268..B 4
Kbely* .....6,927..A 2
Kladno ....51,952..A 2
Klatovy ...14,816..B 1
Kolárovo ..10,083..C 3
Kolín .....24,132..A 2
Komárno ...24,995..C 4
Košice ....93,864..B 5
Kosmonosy* .3,597..A 2
Kostelec nad
Černými
Lesy* ....3,159..B 2
Kralupy (nad
Vltavou) .12,907..A 2
Krnov .....22,061..A 3
Kroměříž ..21,413..B 3
Kutná
Hora ....16,907..B 2
Levice ....14,596..B 4
Liberec ...68,603..A 2
Lidice ....A 2
Liptovský
Mikuláš .12,834..B 4
Litoměřice .17,423..A 2
Litvínov ..21,314..A 1
Louny .....12,941..A 1
Lučenec ...16,670..B 4
Lysá nad
Labem* ...8,902..A 2
Malacky ...10,111..B 3
Mariánské
Lázně (Ma-
rienbad) .12,876..B 1
Martin ....26,612..B 4
Mělník ....13,974..A 2
Michalovce 17,324..B 5
Mladá
Boleslav .26,576..A 2
Modřany ...10,325..A 2
Most ......53,897..A 1
Náchod ....18,043..A 3
Neratovice* .8,820..A 2
Nitra .....36,931..B 4
Nové Mesto nad
Váhom ..13,127..B 3
Nové
Zámky ...23,006..C 4
Nový
Bohumín 11,935..B 4
Nový Jičín .16,960..B 4
Nymburk ..12,705..A 2
Olomouc ...73,591..B 3
Opava .....44,795..B 3
Orlová ....21,039..B 4
Ostrava ..251,959..B 4
Ostrov ....18,706..A 1
Otrokovice-
Kvitko-
vice .....10,903..B 3

Pardubice .57,483..A 2
Pelhřimov ..7,812..B 2
Pezinok ...11,219..B 3
Piešťany ..19,947..B 3
Písek .....20,641..B 2
Plzeň ....141,736..B 1
Poděbrady .12,075..A 2
Poprad ....15,916..B 5
Považská
Bystrica .12,331..B 4
Prachatice .5,197..B 2
Prague
(Praha)
1,014,254..A 2
Přerov ....32,603..B 3
Prešov ....36,919..B 5
Příbram ...27,712..B 2
Prievidza .20,777..B 4
Prostějov .33,824..B 3
Radotín* ...6,152..B 2
Rakovník ..12,144..A 1
Říčany .....8,394..B 2
Rimavská
Sobota ..11,385..B 5
Rokycany .12,552..B 1
Roudnice .10,825..A 2
Rožňava ..10,753..B 5
Ružomberok 19,227..B 4
Rychnov ...6,337..A 3
Sadská* ...3,011..A 2
Sázava* ...2,285..B 2
Semily ....6,810..A 2
Senica ....7,321..B 3
Slaný .....12,286..A 2
Sokolov ...19,612..A 1
Spišská Nová
Ves .....19,042..B 5
Stará Boleslav
see Brandýs
nad Labem-
Stará
Boleslav
Šternberk .11,424..B 3
Strakonice .15,489..B 1
Suchdol* ...4,297..B 2
Šumperk ..20,417..B 3
Švermov ...6,412..A 2
Svitavy ...13,601..B 3
Tábor .....20,344..B 2
Tachov .....6,544..B 1
Teplice ...50,651..A 1
Topol'čany 11,331..B 4
Třebíč ....19,994..B 2
Trebišov ...9,789..B 5
Trenčín ...23,579..B 4
Třinec ....24,788..B 4
Trnava ....33,770..B 3
Trutnov ...23,614..A 2
Turnov ....11,704..A 2
Týnec .....3,048..B 2

Uherské
Hradiště .13,406..B 3
Uhříněves* .4,833..A 2
Ústí (nad
Labem) .69,555..A 2
Ústí nad
Orlicí ...11,200..B 3
Úvaly* .....4,999..A 2
Valašské
Meziříčí .13,628..B 3
Varnsdorf .13,657..A 2
Veltrusy* ..2,029..A 2
Vlašim .....6,917..B 2
Vrchlabí ..10,404..A 2
Vsetín ....19,480..B 4
Vyškov ....12,972..B 3
Žatec .....15,404..A 1
Zbraslav* ..5,414..B 2
Žďár nad
Sázavou .11,321..B 2
Žiar nad
Hronom ...9,832..B 4
Žilina ....35,366..B 4
Znojmo ....25,047..B 3
Zvolen ....22,013..B 4

Physical Features

Berounka R. ....B 1
Beskids (Mts.) .....B 4
Bohemian-Moravian
Highlands ....B 2
Dukla Pass ....B 5
Dumbier (Mtn.) .....B 4
Duna R. ....C 3
Dyje R. ....B 3
Gerlachovka (Mtn.) .B 5
Hron R. ....B 4
Ipel R. ....B 4
Jablunkov Pass .....B 4
Keilberg (Mtn.) ....A 1
Labe R. ....A 2
Little Carpathians
(Mts.) ....B 3
Low Tatra Mts. .....B 4
Lužnice R. ....B 2
Morava R. ....B 3
Nitra R. ....B 4
Ohře R. ....A 1
Ondava R. ....B 5
Sázava R. ....B 2
Schneekoppe
(Mtn.) ....A 2
Sudetes (Mts.) .....A 2
Tatra Mts. ....B 4
Torysa R. ....B 5
Váh R. ....B 3
Vltava R. ....B 2
White Carpathians
(Mts.) ....B 3

Source: Census figures and official estimates.